PUBLIC PAPERS OF THE PRESIDENTS
OF THE
UNITED STATES

PUBLIC PAPERS OF THE PRESIDENTS
OF THE
<u>UNITED STATES</u>

Barack Obama

2011

(IN TWO BOOKS)

BOOK II—JULY 1 TO DECEMBER 31, 2011

UNITED STATES GOVERNMENT PUBLISHING OFFICE
WASHINGTON : 2015

Published by the
Office of the Federal Register
National Archives and Records Administration

For sale by the Superintendent of Documents, U.S. Government Publishing Office
• Internet: bookstore.gpo.gov • Phone: (202) 512–1800 • Fax: (202) 512–1204
• Mail: Stop IDCC, Washington, DC 20401

Foreword

The second half of 2011 was marked by unrest around the world and hard-won progress here at home.

In August, a long and contentious debate surrounding the Congress's refusal to raise the debt ceiling finally concluded with a compromise to reduce the deficit and avert a default that would have devastated our economy and stifled our recovery. In early September, I addressed a joint session of the Congress and put forward specific proposals designed to put more teachers back in our classrooms, more cops back on the beat, and more construction workers back on the job rebuilding our roads, bridges, and schools—all without adding a dime to the deficit. And when the Congress refused to act, I took action on my own to strengthen the middle class and create jobs.

My Administration also took steps to promote travel and boost tourism, create summer employment opportunities for young people, help families refinance their mortgages at historically low rates, and accelerate the loan process for companies ready to go to work rebuilding America. I also nominated Richard Cordray to be the Director of the Consumer Financial Protection Bureau and serve as America's consumer watchdog to help protect working Americans from the worst abuses of the financial industry.

In the fall, I was honored to commemorate the 10th anniversary of September 11th in New York City, in Shanksville, Pennsylvania, and at the Pentagon. And in December, I traveled to Fort Bragg to welcome the last American troops home from Iraq—marking the end of nearly 9 years of war and the beginning of a new era for the Iraqi people.

Elsewhere in the Middle East, revolutions begun during the Arab Spring continued to gain momentum. We stood with the Libyan people as they rose up and demanded their rights. A coalition that included the United States, NATO, and Arab nations persevered through the summer to protect civilians. And with conviction and resolve, the Libyan people fought for their own future and eventually broke the back of the regime—culminating in the death of Muammar Qadhafi.

Back at home, we granted States long-overdue flexibility to meet higher standards for our schools and our students than the ones set by No Child Left Behind. We helped make college more affordable and put higher education within reach for every American. We announced new fuel efficiency standards that will nearly double the average fuel economy of our vehicles by 2025—including the first-ever fuel efficiency standards for work trucks, buses, and other heavy duty vehicles. We took action to reduce life-threatening prescription drug shortages and prevent price gouging on vital medications. And nearly a half-century after the March on Washington, we dedicated a memorial to Dr. Martin Luther King, Jr., on our National Mall.

As we move into the fourth year of my presidency, we will continue to improve the lives of the American people and stand up for the rights of our brothers and sisters around the world. I remain confident that America is stronger than ever, and I know that together, we are equal to the task at hand.

Preface

This book contains the papers and speeches of the President of the United States that were issued by the Office of the Press Secretary during the period July 1–December 31, 2011. The material has been compiled and published by the Office of the Federal Register, National Archives and Records Administration.

The material is presented in chronological order, and the dates shown in the headings are the dates of the documents or events. In instances when the release date differs from the date of the document itself, that fact is shown in the textnote. Every effort has been made to ensure accuracy: Remarks are checked against an audio recording, and signed documents are checked against the original. Textnotes and cross references have been provided by the editors for purposes of identification or clarity. Speeches were delivered in Washington, DC, unless otherwise indicated. The times noted are local times. All materials that are printed in full text in the book have been indexed in the subject and name indexes and listed in the document categories list.

The Public Papers of the Presidents series was begun in 1957 in response to a recommendation of the National Historical Publications Commission. An extensive compilation of messages and papers of the Presidents covering the period 1789 to 1897 was assembled by James D. Richardson and published under congressional authority between 1896 and 1899. Since then, various private compilations have been issued, but there was no uniform publication comparable to the Congressional Record or the United States Supreme Court Reports. Many Presidential papers could be found only in the form of mimeographed White House releases or as reported in the press. The Commission therefore recommended the establishment of an official series in which Presidential writings, addresses, and remarks of a public nature could be made available.

The Commission's recommendation was incorporated in regulations of the Administrative Committee of the Federal Register, issued under section 6 of the Federal Register Act (44 U.S.C. 1506), which may be found in title 1, part 10, of the Code of Federal Regulations.

A companion publication to the Public Papers series, the Weekly Compilation of Presidential Documents, was begun in 1965 to provide a broader range of Presidential materials on a more timely basis to meet the needs of the contemporary reader. Beginning with the administration of Jimmy Carter, the Public Papers series expanded its coverage to include additional material as printed in the Weekly Compilation. On January 20, 2009, the printed Weekly Compilation of Presidential Documents was superseded by the online Daily Compilation of Presidential Documents. The Daily Compilation provides a listing of the President's daily schedule and meetings, when announced, and other items of general interest issued by the Office of the Press Secretary. In 2012, the Government Printing Office and the Office of the Federal Register released a mobile web application (http://m.gpo.gov/dcpd) that catalogues the daily public activities of the President of the United States and enhances features of the online Daily Compilation with user-friendly search capability, allowing users to access Presidential content by date, category, subject, or location.

Also included in the printed edition are lists of the President's nominations submitted to the Senate, materials released by the Office of the Press Secretary that are not printed in full text in the book, and proclamations, Executive orders, and other Presidential documents released by the Office of the Press Secretary and published in the *Federal Register*. This information appears in the appendixes at the end of the book.

Volumes covering the administrations of Presidents Herbert Hoover, Harry S. Truman, Dwight D. Eisenhower, John F. Kennedy, Lyndon B. Johnson, Richard Nixon, Gerald R. Ford,

Jimmy Carter, Ronald Reagan, George H.W. Bush, William J. Clinton, and George W. Bush are also included in the Public Papers series.

The Public Papers of the Presidents publication program is under the direction of John Hyrum Martinez, Director of the Publications and Services Division, Office of the Federal Register. The series is produced by the Presidential and Legislative Publications Unit, Laurice A. Clark, Supervisor. The Chief Editor of this book was Joseph K. Vetter; the Manging Editor was Joshua H. Liberatore, assisted by Stacey A. Mulligan and Amelia E. Otovo.

The frontispiece and photographs used in the portfolio were supplied by the White House Photo Office. The typography and design of the book were developed by the Government Publishing Office under the direction of Davita E. Vance-Cooks, Director.

Oliver A. Potts
Director of the Federal Register

David S. Ferriero
Archivist of the United States

Contents

Foreword . . . v

Preface . . . vii

Cabinet . . . xi

Public Papers of Barack Obama,
July 1–December 31, 2011 . . . 823

Appendix A
Digest of Other White House Announcements . . . 1577

Appendix B
Nominations Submitted to the Senate . . . 1617

Appendix C
Checklist of White House Press Releases . . . 1629

Appendix D
Presidential Documents Published in the *Federal Register* . . . 1645

Subject Index . . . A–1

Name Index . . . B–1

Document Categories List . . . C–1

Cabinet

Vice President..	Joseph R. Biden, Jr.
Secretary of State..	Hillary Rodham Clinton
Secretary of the Treasury	Timothy F. Geithner
Secretary of Defense...................................	Leon E. Panetta
Attorney General...	Eric H. Holder, Jr.
Secretary of the Interior	Kenneth L. Salazar
Secretary of Agriculture..............................	Thomas J. Vilsack
Secretary of Commerce	Gary F. Locke (resigned August 1) John E. Bryson (confirmed October 20)
Secretary of Labor.......................................	Hilda L. Solis
Secretary of Health and Human Services...	Kathleen Sebelius
Secretary of Housing and Urban Development...	Shaun L.S. Donovan
Secretary of Transportation	Raymond H. LaHood
Secretary of Energy.....................................	Steven Chu
Secretary of Education.................................	Arne Duncan
Secretary of Veterans Affairs.......................	Eric K. Shinseki
Secretary of Homeland Security..................	Janet A. Napolitano
Chief of Staff	William M. Daley
Administrator of the Environmental Protection Agency..	Lisa P. Jackson
United States Trade Representative...........	Ronald Kirk

Director of the Office of Management and
Budget .... Jacob J. "Jack" Lew

Chair of the Council of Economic Advisers   Austan D. Goolsbee
(resigned August 5)
Alan B. Kreuger
(confirmed November 3)

United States Permanent Representative to
the United Nations...................................... Susan E. Rice

Administration of Barack Obama

2011

The President's Weekly Address
July 2, 2011

Right now there are a lot of folks who are still struggling with the effects of the recession. They're wondering how they'd deal with an unexpected expense if their car breaks down. They're worried about layoffs. They're not sure if they can help their kids pay for college. And for many families, these challenges were around long before the recession hit in 2007.

I ran for President because I believed in an America where ordinary folks could get ahead, where if you worked hard, you could have a better life. That's been my focus since I came into office, and that has to be our focus now. It's one of the reasons why we're working to reduce our Nation's deficit. Government has to start living within its means, just like families do. We have to cut the spending we can't afford so we can put the economy on a sounder footing and give our businesses the confidence they need to grow and create jobs.

The good news is, Democrats and Republicans agree on the need to solve the problem. And over the last few weeks, the Vice President and I have gotten both parties to identify more than $1 trillion in spending cuts. That's trillion with a "t." But after a decade in which Washington ran up the country's credit card, we've got to find more savings to get out of the red. That means looking at every program and tax break in the budget—every single one—to find places to cut waste and save money. It means we'll have to start making some tough decisions and scale back worthy programs. And nothing can be off limits, including spending in the Tax Code, particularly the loopholes that benefit very few individuals and corporations.

Now, it would be nice if we could keep every tax break, but we can't afford them. Because if we choose to keep those tax breaks for millionaires and billionaires or for hedge fund managers and corporate jet owners or for oil and gas companies pulling in huge profits without our help, then we'll have to make even deeper cuts somewhere else. We've got to say to a student, you don't get a college scholarship. We have to say to a medical researcher, you can't do that cancer research. We might have to tell seniors, you have to pay more for your Medicare.

That isn't right, and it isn't smart. We've got to cut the deficit, but we can do that while making investments in education and research and technology that actually create jobs. We can live within our means while still investing in our future. That's what we have to do. And I'm confident that the Democrats and Republicans in Congress can find a way to give some ground, make some tough choices, and put their shoulders to the wheel to get this done for the sake of the country.

On Monday, we celebrate Independence Day, the day we declared a new nation, based on a revolutionary idea: that people ought to determine their own destiny, that freedom and self-governance weren't gifts handed to us by kings or emperors, but the rights of every human being. We've learned in the years since that democracy isn't always pretty. We have arguments. We disagree. But time and again we've proven that we could come together to solve problems. We remember that while we may not see eye to eye on everything, we share a love for this country and a faith in its future. That's the spirit we need to harness now. That's how we'll meet this challenge, and that's how we'll reach a brighter day. Thanks for listening, and have a wonderful Fourth of July.

NOTE: The address was recorded at approximately 3:35 p.m. on July 1 in the Blue Room at the White House for broadcast on July 2. The transcript was made available by the Office of the Press Secretary on July 1, but was embargoed for release until 6 a.m. on July 2.

Remarks at an Independence Day Celebration
July 4, 2011

The President. Hello, everybody! Happy Fourth of July! On behalf of the entire Obama family, we want to welcome you here to the White House.

Right now, in small towns and big cities all across America, folks are getting together in their backyards; they're raising flags, firing up grills, and enjoying time with family and with friends. It's a tradition that we try to follow here at the White House, although I've got to say we've got a few more people here than most. And I cannot think of anybody I would rather celebrate with than all of you, the men and women of our military and our extraordinary military families.

So let me just check to see who we've got here. I understand we've got some Army here. How about Navy? Air Force! Marines! And we've got some Coast Guard.

After all that you do for our country every day, we wanted to give you guys a chance to get out of the uniform, relax a little bit, and have some fun.

But of course, it's also a time for us to reflect on the meaning of America. In many ways, I think that that small band of patriots who signed their names to the Declaration of Independence and risked their lives for freedom might be surprised to see their legacy all these years later: a nation that's led revolutions in commerce, that sent a man to the Moon, that lifted up the poor, that cured the sick, a nation that fought for democracy and served as a beacon of hope around the world.

But all this could only happen because of our Founders' central faith that through democracy and individual rights, ordinary people have it within their means to forge a nation that's more just and more equal and more free. And all of you are heirs to that legacy. You represent the latest in a long line of heroes who have served our country with honor and who've made incredible sacrifices to protect the freedoms that we all enjoy.

And I've got some of those heroes here with us today, like Army Sergeant First Class Justin

Gang. Where's Justin? Right here. While on patrol in Iraq, his convoy was struck by an IED and fell under enemy fire. Even after being wounded by shrapnel himself, he helped to secure the scene and evacuate his wounded comrades to safety. And today we honor his extraordinary courage.

Navy Hospitalman First Class Obi Nwagwu. Born in Nigeria, he became an American citizen and volunteered to serve in our Nation's military. And as an orthopedic technician, he helps our wounded warriors regain their strength and resume their lives back home. And today we honor his incredible dedication, Obi.

Air Force Master Sergeant Heather Adkins.

Audience member. Whoo!

The President. Is that Heather's husband up there?

M. Sgt. Heather Adkins, USAF. No, Heather doesn't have a husband.

The First Lady. [*Inaudible*]

The President. I'm not trying to get anybody in trouble here. [*Laughter*] Whether it's partnering with Iraqi Army or making sure our troops have shelter in some of the toughest places on the planet, she knows how to get things done. And today we honor her tireless devotion.

Marine Corps Staff Sergeant Keith Kesterson. He rushed through enemy fire to free a fellow marine trapped inside a burning vehicle. And after untangling the marine's equipment, he extinguished the flames and pulled him to safety. And today we honor his unyielding loyalty.

Coast Guard Chief Petty Officer Marlene Riklon, where's Marlene? Right over here. Come on over here. Less than 24 hours after the devastating earthquake in Haiti she was on the scene helping direct aid and save lives in the midst of chaos. And today we honor her incredible dedication.

These American patriots, all the services that are represented up here today, all of you who are out there today, you're the reason why

America and our Armed Forces remain the greatest force for peace and security that the world has ever known. And together, you're standing with all of those around the world who are reaching for the same freedoms and the same liberties that we celebrate today.

So I just want to close by saying thank you. You've done everything we could have asked of you. Your families have served alongside of you with strength and devotion. America is proud of all of you. And as long as I have the privilege of serving as your Commander in Chief, I'm going to make sure that you have the support that you need in the field; I'm going to make sure that you get the care you deserve when you come home. And with the help of Michelle and Dr. Jill Biden, we will make sure America takes care of your families and recognizes the extraordinary sacrifices that they are making.

This day is possible because of your service. And so I think it's only appropriate that we give you a chance to celebrate it together as well.

God bless you. God bless the United States of America. And happy Fourth of July, everybody. Thank you.

NOTE: The President spoke at approximately 6:30 p.m. on the South Lawn at the White House. In his remarks, he referred to Sgt. Brent A. Larimer, USMC, 1st Battalion, 2d Marine Regiment, Alpha Company; and Jill T. Biden, wife of Vice President Joe Biden.

Remarks Prior to White House Press Secretary James F. "Jay" Carney's Briefing
July 5, 2011

All right. Hello, everybody. I just wanted to give you an update on the deficit negotiations that we've been having for the last several weeks. And I want to wish, again, everybody a happy Fourth of July.

Over the July 4 weekend, my team and I had a series of discussions with congressional leaders in both parties. We've made progress, and I believe that greater progress is within sight, but I don't want to fool anybody, we still have to work through some real differences.

Now, I've heard reports that there may be some in Congress who want to do just enough to make sure that America avoids defaulting on our debt in the short term, but then wants to kick the can down the road when it comes to solving the larger problem of our deficit. I don't share that view. And I don't think the American people here—sent us here to avoid tough problems. That's in fact what drives them nuts about Washington, when both parties simply take the path of least resistance. And I don't want to do that here.

I believe that right now we've got a unique opportunity to do something big: to tackle our deficit in a way that forces our Government to live within its means, that puts our economy on a stronger footing for the future and still allows us to invest in that future.

Most of us already agree that to truly solve our deficit problem, we need to find trillions in savings over the next decade and significantly more in the decades that follow. That's what the bipartisan fiscal commission said, that's the amount that I put forward in the framework I announced a few months ago, and that's around the same amount that Republicans have put forward in their own plans. And that's the kind of substantial progress that we should be aiming for here.

To get there, I believe we need a balanced approach. We need to take on spending in domestic programs, in defense programs, in entitlement programs. And we need to take on spending in the Tax Code, spending on certain tax breaks and deductions for the wealthiest of Americans. This will require both parties to get out of our comfort zones and both parties to agree on real compromise.

I'm ready to do that; I believe there are enough people in each party that are willing to do that. And what I know is that we need to come together over the next 2 weeks to reach a deal that reduces the deficit and upholds the full faith and credit of the United States Government and the credit of the American people.

That's why, even as we continue discussions today and tomorrow, I've asked leaders of both parties and both Houses of Congress to come here to the White House on Thursday so we can build on the work that's already been done and drive towards a final agreement. It's my hope that everybody's going to leave their ultimatums at the door, that we'll all leave our political rhetoric at the door, and that we're going to do what's best for our economy and do what's best for our people.

And I want to emphasize—I said this at my press conference: This should not come down to the last second. I think it's important for us to show the American people and their leaders that we can find common ground and solve our problems in a responsible way. We know that it's going to require tough decisions. I think it's better for us to take those tough decisions sooner rather than later.

That's what the American people expect of us. That's what a healthy economy is going to require. That's the kind of progress that I expect to make. So I promise I will keep you guys updated as time goes on. All right?

NOTE: The President spoke at 4:49 p.m. in the James S. Brady Press Briefing Room at the White House.

Remarks at a Question-and-Answer Session With Twitter Participants
July 6, 2011

Twitter Cofounder and Executive Chairman Jack Dorsey. Good afternoon, and welcome to the White House. I am Jack Dorsey from Twitter.

Through more than 200 million tweets per day, people around the world use Twitter to instantly connect to what's most meaningful to them. In every country—Egypt and Japan, the U.K. and the United States—much of this conversation is made up of everyday people engaging in spirited debate about the future of their countries.

Our partners at Salesforce Radian6 studied more than a million tweets discussing our Nation's politics over the recent weeks, and they found that America's financial security to be one of the most actively talked about topics on Twitter. They further found that President Obama's name comes up in more than half of these conversations.

And so today this vibrant discussion comes here to the White House, and you get to ask the questions. To participate, just open your web browser and go to askobama.twitter.com. Neither the President or I know the questions that will be asked today. That decision is driven entirely by the Twitter users.

And so let's get the conversation started. Ladies and gentlemen, the President of the United States.

The President. Hello, everybody! How you doing, Jack?

Mr. Dorsey, Thank you.

The President. Good to see you.

Mr. Dorsey. Good seeing you.

The President. Thank you.

Well, first of all, everybody can sit down. [*Laughter*] It's much easier to tweet from a seated position. [*Laughter*]

Mr. Dorsey. And I understand you want to start the conversation off with a tweet of yourself.

The President. I am going to make history here as the first President to live tweet. So we've got a computer over here.

[*At this point, the President sent a tweet.*]

Mr. Dorsey. It's only a hundred and forty characters. [*Laughter*]

The President. All right, I think I have done this properly. But here's the test.

Mr. Dorsey. Then you tweeted.

The President. How about that? Not bad. Thank you. So I think my question will be coming up at some point.

Mr. Dorsey. Yes. So what was your question?

[*The President's question appeared on a viewing screen.*]

Mr. Dorsey. Here it is.

The President. Here's the question: "In order to reduce the deficit, what costs would you cut and what investments would you keep?"

And the reason I thought this was an important question is, as all of you know, we are going through a spirited debate here in Washington, but it's important to get the whole country involved in making a determination about what are the programs that can help us grow, can create jobs, improve our education system, maintain our clean air and clean water, and what are those things that are a waste that we shouldn't be investing in because they're not helping us grow or create jobs or creating new businesses. And that debate is going to be heating up over the next couple of weeks, so I'd love to hear from the American people, see what thoughts they have.

National Economy/Housing Market

Mr. Dorsey. Excellent. Well, first question comes from a curator in New Hampshire. And we have eight curators around the country helping us pick tweets from the crowd so that we can read them to the President.

And this one comes from William Smith: "What mistakes have you made in handling this recession, and what would you do differently?"

The President. You know, that's a terrific question. When I first came into office, we were facing the worst recession since the Great Depression. So looking around this room, it's a pretty young room; it's certainly the worst recession that we've faced in our lifetimes. And we had to act quickly and make some bold and sometimes difficult decisions.

It was absolutely the right thing to do to put forward a Recovery Act that cut taxes for middle class folks so they had more money in their pocket to get through the recession. It was the right thing to do to provide assistance to States to make sure that they didn't have to lay off teachers and cops and firefighters as quickly as

they needed to. And it was the right thing to do to try to rebuild our infrastructure and put people back to work building roads and bridges and so forth.

It also was the right thing to do, although a tough decision, to save the auto industry, which is now profitable and gaining market share—the U.S. auto industry—for the first time in a very long time.

I think that—probably two things that I would do differently. One would have been to explain to the American people that it was going to take a while for us to get out of this. I think even I did not realize the magnitude, because most economists didn't realize the magnitude, of the recession until fairly far into it, maybe 2 or 3 months into my Presidency where we started realizing that we had lost 4 million jobs before I was even sworn in.

And so I think people may not have been prepared for how long this was going to take and why we were going to have to make some very difficult decisions and choices. And I take responsibility for that, because setting people's expectations is part of how you end up being able to respond well.

The other area is in the area of housing. I think that the continuing decline in the housing market is something that hasn't bottomed out as quickly as we expected. And so that's continued to be a big drag on the economy.

We've had to revamp our housing program several times to try to help people stay in their homes and try to start lifting home values up. But of all the things we've done, that's probably been the area that's been most stubborn to us trying to solve the problem.

Job Creation/Technology Research and Development/Manufacturing Sector

Mr. Dorsey. Mr. President, 27 percent of our questions are in the jobs category, as you can see from the screen over here. Our next question has to do about jobs and technology. It comes from David: "Tech and knowledge industries are thriving, yet jobs discussion always centers on manufacturing. Why not be realistic about jobs?"

The President. Well, it's not an either-or question, it's a both-and question. We have to be successful at the cutting-edge industries of the future like Twitter. But we also have always been a country that makes stuff. And manufacturing jobs end up having both higher wages typically, and they also have bigger multiplier effects. So one manufacturing job can support a range of other jobs: suppliers and the restaurant near the plant and so forth. So they end up having a substantial impact on the overall economy.

What we want to focus on is advanced manufacturing that combines new technology, so research and development to figure out how are we going to create the next Twitter, how are we going to create the next Google, how are we going to create the next big thing, but make sure that production is here.

So it's great that we have an Apple that's creating iPods, iPads, and designing them and creating the software, but it would be nice if we're also making the iPads and the iPods here in the United States, because that's some more jobs that people can work at.

And there are going to be a series of decisions that we've got to make. Number one, are we investing in research and development in order to emphasize technology? And a lot of that has to come from Government. That's how the Internet got formed. That's how GPS got formed. Companies on their own can't always finance the basic research because they can't be assured that they're going to get a return on it.

Number two, we've got to drastically improve how we train our workforce and our kids around math and science and technology.

Number three, we've got to have a top-notch infrastructure to support advanced manufacturing, and we've got to look at sectors where we know this is going to be the future, something like clean energy, for example. For us not to be the leaders in investing in clean energy manufacturing so that wind turbines and solar panels are not only designed here in the United States, but made here in the United States makes absolutely no sense. We've got to invest in those areas for us to be successful.

So you can combine high tech with manufacturing, and then you get the best of all worlds.

Education Reform

Mr. Dorsey. You mentioned education. There's a lot of questions coming about education and its impact on the economy. This one in particular is from a curator who is pulling from a student in Ohio named Dustin: "Higher ed is necessary for a stronger economy, but for some middle class Americans it's becoming too expensive. What can be done?"

The President. Well, here is some good news. We've already done something that is very significant, and people may not know. As part of a higher education package that we passed last year, what we were able to do was to take away subsidies that were going to banks for serving as middlemen in the student loan program and funnel that to help young people, through Pell grants and lower rates on student loans. And so there are millions of students who are getting more affordable student loans and grants as a consequence of the steps that we've already taken. This is about tens of billions of dollars' worth of additional Federal dollars that were going to banks are now going to students directly.

In addition, what we've said is that starting in 2013, young people who are going to college will not have to pay more than 10 percent of their income in repayment. And that obviously helps to relieve the burden on a lot students. Because, look, I'm a guy who had about $60,000 worth of debt when I graduated from law school, and Michelle had 60,000. And so we were paying a bigger amount every month than our mortgage. And we did that for 8, 10 years. So I know how burdensome this can be.

I do think that the universities still have a role in trying to keep their costs down. And I think that it's important. Even if we've got better student loan programs, more grants, if the costs keep on going up, then we'll never have enough money, you'll never get enough help to avoid taking on these huge debts. And so working with university presidents to try to figure out, where can you cut cost—of course, it may mean that the food in the cafeteria is a little worse and the gym is not as fancy. But I think all of us have to figure out a way to make sure that higher education is accessible for everybody.

One last point. I know, Twitter, I'm supposed to be short, but—[*laughter*]. City—community colleges is a huge, underutilized resource, where what we want to do is set up a lifelong learning system where you may have gotten your 4-year degree, but 5 years out, you decide you want to go into another field or you want to brush up on new technologies that are going to help you advance. We need to create a system where you can conveniently access community colleges that are working with businesses to train for the jobs that actually exist. That's a huge area where I think we can make a lot of progress.

National Debt and Deficit

Mr. Dorsey. You mention debt a lot. That's come up in conversation a lot recently, especially in some of our recent questions, specifically the debt ceiling.

The President. Right.

Mr. Dorsey. And this is formulated in our next question from RenegadeNerd out of Atlanta: "Mr. President, will you issue an Executive order to raise the debt ceiling pursuant to section 4 of the 14th Amendment?"

The President. Can I just say, RenegadeNerd, that picture is—captures it all there. [*Laughter*] Dexter's got his hand over there, he's looking kind of confused. [*Laughter*]

Let me, as quickly as I can, describe what's at stake with respect to the debt ceiling. Historically, the United States, whenever it has a deficit, it finances that deficit through the sale of Treasurys. And this is a very common practice. Over our lifetimes, typically, the Government is always running a modest deficit. And Congress is supposed to vote on the amount of debt that Treasury can essentially issue. It's a pretty esoteric piece of business, typically has not been something that created a lot of controversy.

What's happening now is, is that Congress is suggesting we may not vote to raise the debt ceiling. If we do not, then the Treasury will run out of money. It will not be able to pay the bills that are owing, and potentially, the entire world capital markets could decide, you know what, the full faith and credit of the United States doesn't mean anything. And so our credit could be downgraded, interest rates could go drastically up, and it could cause a whole new spiral into a second recession or worse.

So this is something that we shouldn't be toying with. What Dexter's question referred to was there are some people who say that under the Constitution, it's unconstitutional for Congress not to allow Treasury to pay its bills and are suggesting that this should be challenged under the Constitution.

I don't think we should even get to the constitutional issue. Congress has a responsibility to make sure we pay our bills. We've always paid them in the past. The notion that the U.S. is going to default on its debt is just irresponsible. And my expectation is, is that over the next week to 2 weeks, that Congress, working with the White House, comes up with a deal that solves our deficit, solves our debt problems, and makes sure that our full faith and credit is protected.

Immigration Reform

Mr. Dorsey. So back to jobs. We have a question from New York City about immigrant entrepreneurs: "Immigrant entrepreneurs can build companies and create jobs for U.S. workers. Will you support a startup visa program?"

The President. What I want to do is make sure that talented people who come to this country to study, to get degrees, and are willing and interested in starting up businesses can do so, as opposed to going back home and starting those businesses over there to compete against the United States and take away U.S. jobs.

So we're working with the business community as well as the entrepreneurial community to figure out are there ways that we can streamline the visa system so if you are studying here, you've got a Ph.D. in computer science or you've got a Ph.D. in engineering, and you say, I'm ready to invest in the United States, create jobs in the United States, then we are able to say to you, we want you to stay here.

And I think that it is possible for us to deal with this problem. But it's important for us to look at it more broadly. We've got an immigration system that's broken right now, where too many folks are breaking the law, but also our laws make it too hard for talented people to contribute and be part of our society. And we've always been a nation of laws and a nation of immigrants. And so we need comprehensive immigration reform, part of which would allow entrepreneurs and high-skilled individuals to stay here because we want to be attracting that talent here. We don't want that—we don't want to pay for training them here and then having them benefit other countries.

Alternative and Renewable Energy Sources and Technologies/Advanced Battery Manufacturing

Mr. Dorsey. Our next question was just— was sent just an hour ago and touches on alternative energy and job creation: "Will you focus on promoting alternative energy industries in oil States like Louisiana and Texas?"

The President. I want to promote alternative energy everywhere, including oil States like Louisiana and Texas. This is something that I'm very proud of and doesn't get a lot of attention. We made the largest investment in clean energy in our history through the Recovery Act. And so we put forward a range of programs that provided credits and grants to start-up companies in areas like creating wind turbines, solar panels.

A great example is advanced battery manufacturing. When I came into office, advanced batteries, which are used, for example, in electric cars, we only accounted for 2 percent of the world market in advanced batteries. And we have quintupled our market share or even gone further, just over the last 2 years. And we're projecting that we can get to 30 to 40 percent of that market. That's creating jobs all across the Midwest, all across America.

And whoever wins this race on advanced battery manufacturing is probably going to win the race to produce the cars of the 21st century. China is investing in it. Germany is investing in it. We need to be investing in it as well.

Mr. Dorsey. I wanted to take a moment and point out the map just behind you. These are tweets coming in, in real time, and these are questions being asked right now. And it flips between the various categories that we've determined and also just general #AskObama questions.

Collective Bargaining Rights

So our next question is coming up on the screen now, from Patrick: "Mr. President, in several States we have seen people lose their collective bargaining rights. Do you have a plan to rectify this?"

The President. The first thing I want to emphasize is that collective bargaining is the reason why the vast majority of Americans enjoy a minimum wage, enjoy weekends, enjoy overtime. So many things that we take for granted are because workers came together to bargain with their employers.

Now, we live in a very competitive society in the 21st century. And that means in the private sector, labor has to take management into account. If labor is making demands that make management broke and they can't compete, then that doesn't do anybody any good.

In the public sector, what is true is that some of the pension plans that have been in place and the health benefits that are in place are so out of proportion with what's happening in the private sector that a lot of taxpayers start feeling resentful. They say, well, if I don't have health care where I only have to pay $1 for prescription drugs, why is it that the person whose salary I'm paying has a better deal?

What this means is, is that all of us are going to have to make some adjustments. But the principle of collective bargaining, making sure that people can exercise their rights to be able to join together with other workers and to negotiate and kind of even the bargaining power on either side, that's something that has to be protected. And we can make these adjustments in a way that are equitable but preserve people's collective bargaining rights.

So typically, the challenges against bargaining rights have been taking place at the State level. I don't have direct control over that. But what I can do is to speak out forcefully for the principle that we can make these adjustments that are necessary during these difficult fiscal times, but do it in a way that preserves collective bargaining rights. And certainly at the Federal level, where I do have influence, I can make sure that we make these adjustments without affecting people's collective bargaining rights.

I'll give you just one example. We froze Federal pay for Federal workers for 2 years. Now, that wasn't real popular, as you might imagine, among Federal workers. On the other hand, we were able to do that precisely because we wanted to prevent layoffs and we wanted to make sure that we sent a signal that everybody is going to have to make some sacrifices, including Federal workers.

By the way, people who work in the White House, they've had their pay frozen since I came in, our high-wage folks. So they haven't had a raise in 2½ years, and that's appropriate, because a lot of ordinary folks out there haven't either. In fact, they've seen their pay cut in some cases.

Homeownership/Housing Market

Mr. Dorsey. Mr. President, 6 percent of our questions are coming in about housing, which you can see in the graph behind me. And this one in particular has to do with personal debt and housing: "How will admin work to help underwater homeowners who aren't behind in payments, but are trapped in homes they can't sell?" From Robin.

The President. This is a great question. And remember, I mentioned one of our biggest challenges during the course of the last 2½ years has been dealing with a huge burst of the housing bubble.

What's happened is a lot of folks are underwater, meaning their home values went down so steeply and so rapidly that now their mortgage, the amount they owe, is a lot more than the assessed worth of their home. And that obviously burdens a lot of folks. It means if

they're selling, they've got to sell at a massive loss that they can't afford. It means that they don't feel like they have any assets because the single biggest asset of most Americans is their home.

So what we've been trying to do is to work with the issuers of the mortgages—the banks or the service companies—to convince them to work with homeowners who are paying, trying to do the right thing, trying to stay in their homes, to see if they can modify the loans so that their payments are lower and, in some cases, maybe even modify their principal so that they don't feel burdened by these huge debts and feel tempted to walk away from homes that actually they love and where they're raising their families.

We've made some progress. We have—through the programs that we set up here—have probably seen several million home modifications, either directly because we had control of the loan process or because the private sector followed suit. But it's not enough. And so we're going back to the drawing board, talking to banks, try to put some pressure on them to work with people who have mortgages to see if we can make further adjustments, modify loans more quickly, and also see if there may be circumstances where reducing principal is appropriate.

Job Creation/National Economy/Infrastructure Improvement Efforts

Mr. Dorsey. And our next question comes from someone you may know. This is Speaker Boehner.

The President. Oh, there you go. [*Laughter*]

Mr. Dorsey. "After embarking on a record spending binge that left us deeper in debt, where are the jobs?"

[*Speaker of the House of Representatives John A. Boehner's question, which appeared on a viewing screen, contained several extra computer code characters.*]

Mr. Dorsey. And I want to note that these characters are his fault. [*Laughter*]

The President. Yes, first of all——

Mr. Dorsey. Not his fault, not his fault.

The President. ——John obviously needs to work on his typing skills. [*Laughter*] Well, look, obviously, John is the Speaker of the House, he's a Republican, and so this is a slightly skewed question. [*Laughter*] But what he's right about is that we have not seen fast enough job growth relative to the need. I mean, we lost, as I said, 4 million jobs before I took office, before I was sworn in. About 4 million jobs were lost in the few months right after I took office, before our economic policies had a chance to take any effect.

And over the last 15 months, we've actually seen 2 million jobs created in the private sector. And so we're each month seeing growth in jobs. But when you've got a 8-million-dollar—8-million-job hole and you're only filling it a hundred thousand, 200,000 jobs at a time each month, obviously, that's way too long for a lot of folks who are still out of work.

There are a couple of things that we can continue to do. I actually worked with Speaker Boehner to pass a payroll tax cut in December that put an extra thousand dollars in the pockets of almost every single American. That means they're spending money. That means that businesses have customers. And that has helped improve overall growth.

We have provided at least 16 tax cuts to small businesses, who have needed a lot of help and have been struggling, including, for example, saying zero capital gains taxes on startups, because our attitude is we want to encourage new companies, young entrepreneurs to get out there, start their business, without feeling like if they're successful in the first couple of years, that somehow they have to pay taxes, as opposed to putting that money back into their business.

So we've been able to cooperate with Republicans on a range of these issues. There are some areas where the Republicans have been more resistant in cooperating, even though I think most objective observers think it's the right thing to do. I'll give you a specific example.

It's estimated that we have about $2 trillion worth of infrastructure that needs to be rebuilt: roads, bridges, sewer lines, water mains; our air traffic control system doesn't make sense; we don't have the kind of electric grid that's smart, meaning it doesn't waste a lot of energy in transmission; our broadband system is slower than a lot of other countries.

For us to move forward on a major infrastructure initiative where we're putting people to work right now—including construction workers, who were disproportionately unemployed when the housing bubble went bust—to put them to work rebuilding America at a time when interest rates are very low, contractors are looking for work, and the need is there, that is something that could make a huge, positive impact on the economy overall. And it's an example of making an investment now that ends up having huge payoffs down the road.

We haven't gotten the kind of cooperation that I'd like to see on some of those ideas and initiatives. But I'm just going to keep on trying, and eventually, I'm sure the Speaker will see the light. [*Laughter*]

Help for Small Businesses/Lines of Credit

Mr. Dorsey. Speaking of startups, there's a ton of questions about small businesses and how they affect job creation. This one comes from Neal: "Small biz create jobs. What incentives are you willing to support to improve small business growth?"

The President. Well, I just mentioned some of the tax breaks that we've provided not only to small businesses, but also in some cases we've provided big businesses. For example, if they're making investments in plants and equipment this year, they can fully write down those costs, take—essentially depreciate all those costs this year, and that saves them a pretty big tax bill. So we're already initiating a bunch of steps.

The biggest challenge that I hear from small businesses right now actually has to do with financing, because a lot of small businesses got their financing from community banks. Typically, they're not getting them from the big Wall Street banks, but they're getting them from their various regional banks in their communities. A lot of those banks were pretty overextended in the commercial real estate market, which has been hammered. A lot of them are still digging themselves out of bad loans that they made that were shown to be bad during the recession.

And so what we've tried to do is get the Small Business Administration, the Federal agency that helps small businesses, to step in and to provide more financing: waiving fees, seeing if we can lower interest rates in some cases, making sure that the threshold for companies that qualify for loans are more generous. And that's helped a lot of small businesses all across the country. And this is another example of where, working with Congress, my hope is, is that we can continue to provide these tax incentives and maybe do even a little bit more.

Employment Opportunities for Veterans

Mr. Dorsey. Our next question was tweeted less than 5 minutes ago and comes to us from Craig: "My question is, can you give companies a tax break if they hire an honorable-discharged veteran?"

The President. This is something that I've been talking a lot about internally. We've got all these young people coming back from Iraq and Afghanistan, have made incredible sacrifices, have taken on incredible responsibilities. You see some 23-year-old who's leading a platoon in hugely dangerous circumstances, making decisions, operating complex technologies. These are folks who can perform. But unfortunately, what we're seeing is that a lot of these young veterans have a higher unemployment rate than people who didn't serve. And that makes no sense.

So what we'd like to do is potentially combine a tax credit for a company that hires veterans with a campaign to have private companies step up and do the right thing and hire more veterans. And one of the things that we've done is, internally in the Federal Government, we have made a huge emphasis on ramping up our outreach to veterans and the hiring of veterans, and this has been a top priority of mine. The notion that these folks who are sacrificing for our freedom and our security end up com-

ing home and not being able to find a job I think is unacceptable.

National Debt and Deficit/Budget Debate/Bipartisanship

Mr. Dorsey. Mr. President, this next question comes from someone else you may recognize. And what's interesting about this question, it was heavily retweeted and voted up by our user base. This comes from Nick Kristof: "Was it a mistake to fail to get Republicans to commit to raise the debt ceiling at the same time tax cuts were extended?"

The President. Nicholas is a great columnist. But I have to tell you, the assumption of the question is, is that I was going to be able to get them to commit to raising the debt ceiling.

In December, we were in what was called the lame duck session. The Republicans knew that they were going to be coming in as the majority. We only had a few short weeks to deal with a lot of complicated issues, including repealing "don't ask, don't tell," dealing with a START Treaty to reduce nuclear weapons, and come to terms with a budget. And what we were able to do was negotiate a package where we agreed to do something that we didn't like, but that the Republicans badly wanted, which is to extend the Bush tax cuts on the wealthy for another 2 years.

In exchange, we were able to get this payroll tax that put a thousand dollars—tax cut that put a thousand dollars in the pockets of every American, which would help economic growth and jobs. We were also able to get unemployment insurance extended for the millions of Americans out there who are still out of work and whose benefits were about to run out. And that was a much better deal than I think a lot of people expected.

It would have been great if we were able to also settle this issue of the debt ceiling at that time. That wasn't the deal that was available. But here's the more basic point: Never in our history has the United States defaulted on its debt. The debt ceiling should not be something that is used as a gun against the heads of the American people to extract tax breaks for corporate jet owners or oil and gas companies that are making billions of dollars because the price of gasoline has gone up so high.

I mean, I'm happy to have those debates. I think the American people are on my side on this. What we need to do is to have a balanced approach where everything is on the table. We need to reduce corporate loopholes. We need to reduce discretionary spending on programs that aren't working. We need to reduce defense spending. Everything has—we need to look at entitlements, and we have to say, how do we protect and preserve Medicare and Social Security for not just this generation, but also future generations. And that's going to require some modifications, even as we maintain its basic structure.

So what I'm hoping to see over the next couple of weeks is people put their dogmas aside, their sacred cows aside, they come together, and they say, here's a sensible approach that reduces our deficit, makes sure that Government is spending within its means, but also continues to make investments in education, in clean energy, and basic research that are going to preserve our competitive advantage going forward.

Taxes/Budget Debate/National Debt and Deficit

Mr. Dorsey. So speaking of taxes, our next question is coming from us to—from Alabama, from Lane: "What changes to the tax system do you think are necessary to help solve the deficit problem and for the system to be fair?"

The President. Well, I think that, first of all, it's important for people to realize that since I've been in office, I've cut taxes for middle class families repeatedly. The Recovery Act cut taxes for 95 percent of working families. The payroll tax cut that we passed in December put an extra thousand dollars in the pockets of every family in America.

And so we actually now have the lowest tax rates since the 1950s. Our tax rates are lower now than they were under Ronald Reagan. They're lower than they were under George Bush senior or George Bush junior. They're lower than they were under Bill Clinton.

The question is, how do we pay for the things that we all think are important, and how

do we make sure that the tax system is equitable? And what I've said is that in addition to eliminating a whole bunch of corporate loopholes that are just not fair, the notion that corporate jets should get a better deal than commercial jets or the notion that oil and gas companies that made tens of billions of dollars per quarter need an additional break to give them an incentive to go drill for oil, that doesn't make sense.

But what I've also said is, people like me who have been incredibly fortunate—mainly because a lot of folks bought my book—[*laughter*]—for me to be able to go back to the tax rate that existed under Bill Clinton, to pay a couple of extra percentage points so that I can make sure that seniors still have Medicare or kids still have Head Start, that makes sense to me. And, Jack, we haven't talked about this before, but I'm assuming it makes sense to you, given Twitter has done pretty well. [*Laughter*]

I think that for us to say that millionaires and billionaires can go back to the tax rate that existed when Bill Clinton was President, that doesn't affect middle class families who are having a tough time and haven't seen their incomes go up. It does mean that those who are in the top 1, 2 percent, who have seen their incomes go up much more quickly than anybody else, pays a little bit more in order to make sure that we can make the basic investments that grow this country; that's not an unreasonable position to take. And the vast majority of Americans agree with me on that.

That doesn't mean that we can just continue spending anything we want. We're still going to have to make some tough decisions about defense spending or even some programs that I like but we may not need. But we can't close the deficit and debt just by cutting things like Head Start or Medicare. That can't be an equitable solution to solving the problem. And then we say to millionaires and billionaires, you don't have to do anything. I don't want a $200,000 tax break if it means that some senior is going to have to pay $6,000 more for their Medicare that they don't have or a bunch of kids are going to be kicked off of Head Start and aren't going to get the basics that they need in order to succeed in our society. I don't think that's good for me; I don't think it's good for the country.

Homeownership

Mr. Dorsey. So we have a follow-up question to your answer about homeowners being underwater. And this one came in under 10 minutes ago from Shnaps: "Is free market an option? Obama on homeowners underwater: Have made some progress, but plus needed, looking at options."

The President. Well, when Shnaps—[*laughter*]—when Shnaps talks about free market options, I mean, keep in mind that most of this is going to be a function of the market slowly improving because people start having more confidence in the economy; more people decide, you know what, the housing market has kind of bottomed out, now is the time to buy. They start buying. That starts slowly lifting up prices, and you get a virtuous cycle going on.

So a lot of this is going to be determined by how well the overall economy does: Do people feel more confident about jobs? Do they feel more confident that they're going to be able to make their mortgage? And given the size of the housing market, no Federal program is going to be able to solve the housing problem. Most of this is going to be free market.

The one thing that we can do is make sure that for homeowners who have been responsible, didn't buy more house than they could afford, had some tough luck because they happened to buy at the top of the market, can afford to continue to pay for that house, can afford their current mortgage, but need some relief, given the drop in value—that we try to match them up with bankers so that each side ends up winning. The banker says, you know, I'm going to be better off than if this house is foreclosed upon and I have to sell it at a fire sale. The mortgage owner is able to stay in their home, but still pay what's owed.

And I think that that kind of adjustment and negotiation process is tough. It's difficult partly because a lot of banks these days don't hold mortgages. They were all sold to Wall Street and were sliced and diced in these complex fi-

nancial transactions, so sorting through who owns what can be very complicated. And as you know, some of the banks didn't do a very good job on filing some of their papers on these foreclosure actions, and so there's been litigation around that.

But the bottom line is we should be able to make some progress on helping some people, understanding that some folks just bought more home than they could afford and probably they're going to be better off renting.

Education

Mr. Dorsey. So 10 percent of our questions now are about education, and this one was surfaced from our curator in California by Marcia: "Public education here in California is falling apart. Not graduating enough skilled workers or smart citizens. Privatization looming?"

The President. Look, when America was making a transition from an agricultural society to an industrial society, we as a country made a decision that we were going to have public high schools that would upgrade the skills of young people as they were leaving the farms and start participating in a more complex industrial economy. When my grandfather's generation came back from World War II, we made a decision that we were going to have a GI bill that would send these young people to college because we figured that would help advance our economy.

Every time we've made a public investment in education, it has paid off many times over. For us now to give short shrift to education when the world is more complex than ever and it's a knowledge-based society and companies locate based on whether they've got skilled workforces or not, that makes no sense.

And so we've got to get our priorities straight here. It is important for us to have a healthy business climate, to try to keep taxes low, to make sure that we're not spending on things that don't work. It's important that we get a good bang for the buck in education. And so my administration has pushed more reform more vigorously across the country through things like Race to the Top than most previous administrations have been able to accomplish.

So we don't just need more money, we need more reform.

But we do have to pay for good teachers. Young, talented people aren't going to go into teaching if they're getting paid a poverty wage. We do have to make sure that buildings aren't crumbling. It's pretty hard for kids to concentrate if there are leaks and it's cold and there are rats running around in their schools. And that's true in a lot of schools around the country.

We do have to make sure that there are computers in a computer age inside classrooms and that they work and that there's Internets that are actually—there are Internet connections that actually function.

And I think that those States that are going to do well and those countries that do well are the ones that are going to continue to be committed to making education a priority.

Dependence on Foreign Oil/Fuel Efficiency Standards/Alternative and Renewable Energy Sources and Technologies

Mr. Dorsey. We have another follow-up sent about 10 minutes ago in response to your answer on Vietnam vets. From Brendan: "We definitely need to get more vets into jobs, but when are we going to support the troops by cutting oil dependence?"

The President. Reducing our dependence on oil is good for our economy, it's good for our security, and it's good for our planet. So it's a "threefer." And we have not had a serious energy policy for decades. Every President talks about it; we don't get it done.

Now, I'd like to see robust legislation in Congress that actually took some steps to reduce oil dependency. We're not going to be able to replace oil overnight. Even if we are going full throttle on clean energy solutions like solar and wind and biodiesel, we're going to need oil for some time. But if we had a goal where we're just reducing our dependence on oil each year in a staggered set of steps, it would save consumers in their pocketbook, it would make our businesses more efficient and less subject to the whims of the spot oil market, it would make us less vulnerable to the kinds of

disruptions that have occurred because of what happened in the Middle East this spring, and it would drastically cut down on our carbon resources.

So one—what I—unfortunately, we have not seen a sense of urgency coming out of Congress over the last several months on this issue. Most of the rhetoric has been about, let's produce more. Well, we can produce more, and I'm committed to that, but the fact is, we only have 2 to 3 percent of the world's oil reserves; we use 25 percent of the world's oil. We can't drill our way out of this problem.

What we can do that we've already done administratively is increase fuel efficiency standards on cars, just to take one example. That will save us millions of barrels of oil, just by using existing technologies and saying to car companies, you can do better than 10 miles a gallon or 15 miles a gallon. And you're starting to see Detroit respond. U.S. car companies have figured out, you know what, if we produce high-quality electric vehicles, if we produce high-quality, low-gas—or high-gas-mileage vehicles, those will sell.

And we're actually starting to see market share increase for American cars in subcompact and compact cars for the first time in many years. And that's partly because we increased fuel efficiency standards through an administrative agreement. It's also because, as part of the deal to bail out the auto companies, we said to them, start focusing on the cars of the future instead of looking at big gas guzzlers of the past.

Taxes

Mr. Dorsey. So all of our questions now are coming in real time—this one less than 10 minutes ago—and surfaced from a curator: "So will you raise taxes on the middle class at least to President George W. Bush levels?"

The President. No, the—what we've said is let's make permanent the Bush tax cuts for low- and moderate-income folks, people in— for the 98 percent of people who frankly have not seen their wages go up or their incomes go up over the last decade. They don't have a lot of room; they're already struggling to meet the rising cost of health care and education and gas prices and food prices.

If all we do is just go back to the pre-Bush-tax-cut rates for the top income brackets—for millionaires and billionaires—that would raise hundreds of billions of dollars. And if you combine it with the cuts we've already proposed, we could solve our deficit and our debt problems.

This is not something that requires radical solutions. It requires some smart, common-sense, balanced approaches. I think that's what the American people are looking for, and that's what I've proposed. And that's what I'm going to keep on trying to bring the parties together to agree to, is a balanced approach that has more cuts than revenue, but has some revenue, and that revenue should come from the people who can most afford it.

Space Program

Mr. Dorsey. So a slight deviation from the economy. We have a lot of questions—and this will be our last before we start reading some responses to your question—about the space program. And this one from Ron: "Now that the space shuttle is gone, where does America stand in space exploration?"

The President. We are still a leader in space exploration. But frankly, I have been pushing NASA to revamp its vision. The shuttle did some extraordinary work in low-orbit experiments, the International Space Station, moving cargo. It was an extraordinary accomplishment, and we're very proud of the work that it did. But now what we need is that next technological breakthrough.

We're still using the same models for space travel that we used with the Apollo program 30, 40 years ago. And so what we've said is, rather than keep on doing the same thing, let's invest in basic research around new technologies that can get us places faster, allow human space flight to last longer.

And what you're seeing now is NASA, I think, redefining its mission. And we've set a goal to let's ultimately get to Mars. A good pit stop is an asteroid. I—we haven't identified the actual asteroid yet, in case people are wonder-

ing. [*Laughter*] But the point is, let's start stretching the boundaries so we're not doing the same thing over and over again, but rather, let's start thinking about what's the next horizon, what's the next frontier out there.

And—but in order to do that, we're actually going to need some technological breakthroughs that we don't have yet. And what we can do is, for some of this low-orbit stuff, some of the more routine space travel—obviously, no space travel is routine, but it could become more routine over time—let's allow the private sector to get in so that they can, for example, send these low-Earth-orbit vehicles into space, and we may be able to achieve a point in time where those of you who are just dying to go into space, you can buy a ticket, and a private carrier can potentially take you up there, while the Government focuses on the big breakthroughs that require much larger investments and involve much greater risk.

Defense Contracts/Illegal Drugs/Campaign Finance Reform

Mr. Dorsey. So, Mr. President, we received a lot of responses to your question over the last hour. And we wanted to go through seven of them that we picked out and just spend some time giving feedback on each. This one from Brian: "Cut defense contracting, end war on drugs, eliminate agribiz and big oil subsidies, invest in public campaign financing."

The President. Well, that's not a bad list. [*Laughter*] The defense contracting is something we're already making progress on.

I think with respect to the war on drugs, what we've always said is that investing in prevention, reducing demand, is going to be the most cost-effective thing that we can do. We still have to interdict the big drug kingpins, and we still have to enforce our drug laws. But making sure that we're spending more on prevention and treatment can make a huge difference.

With respect to some of these big agribusiness and big oil subsidies, those are the examples of the kinds of loopholes we can close. And public campaign financing is something that I've supported in the past. There is no doubt that money has an impact on what happens here in Washington. And the more we can reduce money's impact on Washington, the better off we're going to be.

U.S. Foreign Aid/Foreign Policy/Budget Debate

Mr. Dorsey. Our next response from Elizabeth in Chicago: "Stop giving money to countries that waste it—Pakistan. Keep military, share the wealth between branches, and don't cut education."

The President. You know, the one thing I would say is, on the notion of giving money to countries that waste it—and Pakistan is listed there—I think it's important for people to know that foreign aid accounts for less than 2 percent of our budget. And if you defined it just narrowly as the kind of foreign aid to help feed people and what we think of classically as foreign aid, it's probably closer to 1 percent.

So sometimes, people have an exaggerated sense that we spend 25 percent of the Federal budget on foreign aid. It's a tiny amount that has a big impact. And I think America, to be a leader in the world, to have influence, to help stabilize countries and create opportunity for people so that they don't breed terrorists or create huge refugee flows and so forth, it's smart for us to make a very modest investment in foreign aid. It's a force multiplier, and it's something that even in tough fiscal times America needs to continue to do as part of our role as a global leader.

Taxes

Mr. Dorsey. This next one is pretty simple, from Daniel: "We need to raise taxes, period." [*Laughter*]

The President. As I said before, if wealthy individuals are willing to simply go back to the rates that existed back in the 1990s, when rich people were doing very well—it's not like they were poor, and by the way, that's when we saw the highest job growth rates, and that's when we saw the highest—the greatest reduction in poverty, and that's when we saw businesses very profitable—if the wealthiest among us, and I include myself in this category, are willing to give up a little bit more, then we can solve this problem. It does not take a lot.

And I just have to say, when people say, "Job-killing tax increases, that's what Obama is proposing. We're not going to"—you're entitled to your own opinions, but not your own facts. And the facts are that a modest increase for wealthy individuals is not shown to have an adverse impact on job growth.

I mean, we can test the two theories. You had what happened during the nineties, right? Taxes for wealthy individuals were somewhat higher, businesses boomed, the economy boomed, great job growth. And then the 2000s, when taxes were cut on wealthy individuals, jobs didn't grow as fast, businesses didn't grow as fast. I mean, it's not like we haven't tried what these other folks are pitching. It didn't work. And we should go with what works.

Defense Spending/Education

Mr. Dorsey. So our next response—we have about 9 minutes left and four more responses—this one from Tammy: "Cut military spending on oil subsidies, and keep education investments."

The President. I agree with this. The one thing I'll say about military spending: We've ended the war in Iraq, our combat mission there, and our—all our troops are slated to be out by the end of this year. We've already removed 100,000. I announced that we were going to begin drawing down troops in Afghanistan and pivot to a transition process where Afghans are taking more responsibility for their defense.

But we have to do all of this in a fairly gradual way. We can't simply lop off 25 percent off the defense budget overnight. We have to think about all the obligations we have to our current troops who are in the field and making sure they're properly equipped and safe. We've got to make sure that we are meeting our commitments for those veterans who are coming home. We've got to make sure that, in some cases, we've got outdated equipment that needs to be replaced.

And so I'm committed to reducing the defense budget, but as Commander in Chief, one of the things that we have to do is make sure that we do it in a thoughtful way that's guided by our security and our strategic needs. And I think we can accomplish that. And the nice thing about the defense budget is it's so big, it's so huge, that a 1-percent reduction is the equivalent of the education budget. Not—I'm exaggerating, but it's so big that you can make relatively modest changes to defense that end up giving you a lot of head room to fund things like basic research or student loans or things like that.

Alternative and Renewable Energy Sources and Technologies

Mr. Dorsey. Our next response from southwest Ohio, MostlyModerate: "Cut subsidies to industries which are no longer in crisis or are unsuccessful: cotton, oil, corn subsidies from ethanol."

The President. Well, there's been a interesting debate taking place in Congress recently. I'm a big supporter of biofuels. But one of the things that's become clear is, is that we need to accelerate our basic research in ethanol and other biofuels that are made from things like woodchips and algae, as opposed to just focusing on corn, which is probably the least efficient energy producer of these various other approaches.

And so I think that it's important for even those folks in farm States, who traditionally have been strong supporters of ethanol, to examine are we, in fact, going after the cutting-edge biodiesel and ethanol approaches that allow, for example, Brazil to run about a third of its transportation system on biofuels. Now, they get it from sugar cane, and it's a more efficient conversion process than corn-based ethanol. And so us doing more basic research in finding better ways to do the same concept, I think, is the right way to go.

Mr. Dorsey. I believe you addressed this next one, so we're going to skip past it.

The President. I did.

Mr. Dorsey. But from Ryan: "I would cut defense spending."

Welfare Programs

Mr. Dorsey. And James: "I'd cut costs by cutting some welfare programs. People will never try harder when they are handed everything."

The President. Well, here's what I would say. I think we should acknowledge that some welfare programs in the past were not well designed and in some cases did encourage dependency. And as somebody who worked in low-income neighborhoods, I've seen it, where people weren't encouraged to work, weren't encouraged to upgrade their skills, were just getting a check, and over time, their motivation started to diminish. And I think even if you're progressive, you've got to acknowledge that some of these things have not been well designed.

I will say that today, welfare payments are not the big driver of our deficit or our debt. There are work obligations attached to welfare, that the vast majority of folks who are getting welfare want to work, but can't find jobs. And what we should be doing is in all our social programs evaluating what are upgrading people's skills, giving them the tools they need to get into the workforce, nudging them into the workforce, but letting them know that we're there to support you and encourage you as long as you're showing the kind of responsibility for being willing to work that every American should be expected to show.

And I'm somebody who believes that we can constantly improve any program, whether it's a defense program—those who say that we can't cut military at all, they haven't spent a lot of time looking at military budgets. Those who say that we can't make any changes to our social welfare programs or else you're being mean to poor people, that's not true. There are some programs that can always be improved. And some programs, if they don't work, we should have the courage to eliminate them, and then use that money to put it into the programs that do work.

But the bottom line is that our core values of responsibility, opportunity, making sure that the American Dream is alive and well so that anybody who is willing to put in the time and the effort and the energy are able to get a good education in this society, find a job that pays a living wage, that they're able to send their kids to college without going broke, that they've got basic health care, they're going to be able to retire with some dignity and some respect, that that opportunity is open to anybody regardless of race or religion or sexual orientation or—that that basic principle, that's what holds us together. That's what makes us Americans.

We're not all tied together by ethnicity or a single religion. What ties us together is this idea that everybody has got a shot. As long as you carry out your responsibilities, you can make it. You can get into the middle class and beyond. And you can start a company and suddenly help bring the whole world together. That's what makes this country outstanding.

But in order to do that, it requires us to both have a commitment to our individualism and our freedom and our creativity and our idiosyncrasies, but it also requires us to have a commitment to each other and recognize that I would not be President if somebody hadn't helped provide some scholarships for my school and you would not have Twitter if the Department of Defense, at some point, and a bunch of universities hadn't made some invest-

ments in something that ended up being the Internet. And those were public goods that were invested in.

So you and I are sitting here because somebody, somewhere, made an investment in our futures. We've got the same obligation for the folks who are coming up behind us. We've got to make sure that we're looking out for them, just like the previous generations looked out for us. And that's what I think will help us get through what are some difficult times and make sure that America's future is even brighter than the past.

Mr. Dorsey. And on that note, thank you very much, Mr. President.

The President. Thank you. I appreciate it. Thank you.

All right, thank you, guys. Thanks.

NOTE: The President spoke at 2:04 p.m. in the East Room at the White House. In his remarks, he referred to Twitter participant Dexter Smith; and Nicholas D. Kristof, columnist, New York Times.

Statement on a Change to the Presidential Condolence Letter Policy
July 6, 2011

As Commander in Chief, I am deeply grateful for the service of all our men and women in uniform and grieve for the loss of those who suffer from the wounds of war, seen and unseen. Since taking office, I've been committed to removing the stigma associated with the unseen wounds of war, which is why I've worked to expand our mental health budgets and ensure that all our men and women in uniform receive the care they need.

As a next step and in consultation with the Secretary of Defense and the military chain of command, I have also decided to reverse a longstanding policy of not sending condolence letters to the families of servicemembers who

commit suicide while deployed to a combat zone. This decision was made after a difficult and exhaustive review of the former policy, and I did not make it lightly. This issue is emotional, painful, and complicated, but these Americans served our Nation bravely. They didn't die because they were weak. And the fact that they didn't get the help they needed must change. Our men and women in uniform have borne the incredible burden of our wars, and we need to do everything in our power to honor their service and to help them stay strong for themselves, for their families, and for our Nation.

Remarks Prior to White House Press Secretary James F. "Jay" Carney's Briefing
July 7, 2011

Hello, everybody. I'm going to make a very brief statement.

I just completed a meeting with all the congressional leaders from both Chambers, from both parties, and I have to say that I thought it was a very constructive meeting. People were frank. We discussed the various options available to us. Everybody reconfirmed the importance of completing our work and raising the debt limit ceiling so that the full faith and credit of the United States of America is not impaired.

What we decided was that staffs, as well as leadership, will be working during the weekend, and that I will reconvene congressional leaders here on Sunday with the expectation that, at that point, the parties will at least know where each other's bottom lines are and will hopefully be in a position to then start engaging in the hard bargaining that's necessary to get a deal done.

I want to emphasize that nothing is agreed to until everything is agreed to. And the parties are still far apart on a wide range of issues. But again, I thought that all the leaders here came in a spirit of compromise, in a spirit of wanting to solve problems on behalf of the American people. Everybody acknowledged that the issue of our debt and our deficit is something that needs to be tackled now. Everybody acknowledged that in order to do that, Democrats and Republicans are going to be required in each Chamber. Everybody acknowledged that we have to get this done before the hard deadline of August 2 to make sure that America does not default for the first time on its obligations. And everybody acknowledged that there's going to be pain involved politically on all sides. But our biggest obligation is to make sure that we're doing the right thing by the American people, creating an environment in which we can grow the economy and make sure that more and more people are being put back to work.

So I want to thank all the leaders. I thought it was a very constructive meeting. And I will be seeing them back here on Sunday. A lot of work will be done between now and then.

NOTE: The President spoke at 1:02 p.m. in the James S. Brady Press Briefing Room at the White House.

Remarks on the National Economy and an Exchange With Reporters
July 8, 2011

The President. Good morning, everybody. Obviously, over the last couple of days, the debate here in Washington has been dominated by issues of debt limit, but what matters most to Americans, and what matters most to me as President, in the wake of the worst downturn in our lifetimes, is getting our economy on a sounder footing more broadly so the American people can have the security they deserve.

And that means getting back to a place where businesses consistently grow and are hiring, where new jobs and new opportunity are within reach, where middle class families once again know the security and peace of mind they've felt slipping away for years now. And today's job report confirms what most Americans already know: We still have a long way to go and a lot of work to do to give people the security and opportunity that they deserve.

We've added more than 2 million new private sector jobs over the past 16 months, but the recession cost us more than 8 million. And that means that we still have a big hole to fill. Each new job that was created last month is good news for the people who are back at work and for the families that they take care of and for the communities that they're a part of. But our economy as a whole just isn't producing nearly enough jobs for everybody who's looking.

We've always known that we'd have ups and downs on our way back from this recession. And over the past few months, the economy has experienced some tough headwinds, from natural disasters to spikes in gas prices to State and local budget cuts that have cost tens of thousands of cops and firefighters and teachers their jobs. The problems in Greece and in Europe, along with uncertainty over whether the debt limit here in the United States will be raised, have also made businesses hesitant to invest more aggressively.

The economic challenges that we face weren't created overnight, and they're not going to be solved overnight. But the American people expect us to act on every single good idea that's out there. I read letter after letter from folks hit hard by this economy. None of them ask for much. Some of them pour their guts out in these letters. And they want me to know that what they're looking for is that we have done everything we can to make sure that they are rewarded when they're living up to their responsibilities, when they're doing right by their communities, when they're playing by the rules. That's what they're looking for, and they feel like the rules have changed. They feel that leaders on Wall Street and in Washington—and believe me, no party is exempt—have let them down. And they wonder if their efforts will ever be reciprocated by their leaders.

They also make sure to point out how much pride and faith they have in this country, that as hard as things might be today, they are positive that things can get better. And I believe that we can make things better. How we respond is up to us. There are a few things that we can and should do right now to redouble our efforts on behalf of the American people.

Let me give you some examples. Right now there are over a million construction workers out of work after the housing boom went bust, just as a lot of America needs rebuilding. We connect the two by investing in rebuilding our roads and our bridges and our railways and our infrastructure. And we could put back to work right now some of those construction workers that lost their jobs when the housing market went bust. Right now we can give our entrepreneurs the chance to let their job-creating ideas move to market faster by streamlining our patent process. That's pending before Congress right now. That should pass.

Today Congress can advance trade agreements that will help businesses sell more American-made goods and services to Asia and South America, supporting thousands of jobs here at home. That could be done right now. Right now there are a lot of middle class families who sure could use the security of knowing that the tax cut that I signed in December to help boost the economy and put a thousand dollars in the pockets of American families, that that's still going to be around next year. That's a change that we could make right now.

There are bills and trade agreements before Congress right now that could get all these ideas moving. All of them have bipartisan support. All of them could pass immediately. And I urge Congress not to wait. The American people need us to do everything we can to help strengthen this economy and make sure that we are producing more jobs.

Also to put our economy on a stronger and sounder footing for the future, we've got to rein in our deficits and get the Government to live within its means, while still making the investments that help put people to work right now and make us more competitive in the future. As I mentioned, we've had some good meetings. We had a good meeting here yesterday with leaders of both parties in Congress. And while real differences remain, we agreed to work through the weekend and meet back here on Sunday.

The sooner we get this done, the sooner that the markets know that the debt limit ceiling will have been raised and that we have a serious plan to deal with our debt and deficit, the sooner that we give our businesses the certainty that they will need in order to make additional investments to grow and hire and will provide more confidence to the rest of the world as well, so that they are committed to investing in America.

Now, the American people sent us here to do the right thing not for party, but for country. So we're going to work together to get things done on their behalf. That's the least that they should expect of us, not the most that they should expect of us. I'm ready to roll up my sleeves over the next several weeks and next several months. I know that people in both parties are ready to do that as well. And we will keep you updated on the progress that we're making on these debt limit talks over the next several days. Thank you.

Meeting With House Democratic Leader Nancy Pelosi

Q. How was the meeting with Mrs. Pelosi?
The President. It was good.

NOTE: The President spoke at 11:05 a.m. in the Rose Garden at the White House.

Statement on the Launch of the Space Shuttle *Atlantis*
July 8, 2011

Today Americans across the country watched with pride as four of our fellow citizens blasted off from the Kennedy Space Center in the Space Shuttle *Atlantis* and America reached for the heavens once more.

Behind *Atlantis* and her crew of brave astronauts stand thousands of dedicated workers who have poured their hearts and souls into America's space shuttle program over the past three decades. To them and all of NASA's incredible workforce, I want to express my sincere gratitude. You helped our country lead the space age, and you continue to inspire us each day.

Today's launch may mark the final flight of the space shuttle, but it propels us into the next era of our never-ending adventure to push the very frontiers of exploration and discovery in space. We'll drive new advances in science and technology. We'll enhance knowledge, educa-

tion, innovation, and economic growth. And I have tasked the men and women of NASA with an ambitious new mission: to break new boundaries in space exploration, ultimately sending Americans to Mars. I know they are up to the challenge, and I plan to be around to see it.

Congratulations to *Atlantis*, her astronauts, and the people of America's space program on a picture-perfect launch, and good luck on the rest of your mission to the International Space Station and for a safe return home. I know the American people share my pride at what we have accomplished as a nation and my excitement about the next chapter of our preeminence in space.

NOTE: The statement referred to Christopher J. Ferguson, commander, Douglas G. Hurley, pilot, and Sandra H. Magnus and Rex J. Walheim, mission specialists, Space Shuttle *Atlantis*.

Statement on the Death of Elizabeth A. Ford
July 8, 2011

Throughout her long and active life, Elizabeth Anne Ford distinguished herself through her courage and compassion. As our Nation's First Lady, she was a powerful advocate for women's health and women's rights. After leaving the White House, Mrs. Ford helped reduce the social stigma surrounding addiction and inspired thousands to seek much-needed treatment. While her death is a cause for sadness, we know that organizations such as the

Betty Ford Center will honor her legacy by giving countless Americans a new lease on life.

Today we take comfort in the knowledge that Betty and her husband, former President Gerald Ford, are together once more. Michelle and I send our thoughts and prayers to their children Michael, John, Steven, and Susan.

NOTE: The statement referred to Susan Ford Bales, daughter of former First Lady Ford.

The President's Weekly Address
July 9, 2011

Earlier this week, we did something that's never been done here at the White House: We had a Twitter town hall. I even sent my first live tweet as President. The questions at the town hall were sent in from across the country and covered all kinds of topics, from jobs and the economy to education and energy.

Lots of people also submitted different versions of another question. They'd start by saying that our politics has grown so contentious. Then they'd ask, "When will both parties in Congress come together on behalf of the people who elected them?"

That's a really important question, and it goes to the heart of a debate we're having right now in this country, and that's the debate about how to tackle the problem of our deficits and our debt.

Now, there are obviously real differences in approach. I believe we need a balanced approach. That means taking on spending in our domestic programs and our defense programs. It means addressing the challenges in programs like Medicare so we can strengthen those programs and protect them for future generations. And it means taking on spending in the Tax Code, spending on tax breaks and deductions for the wealthiest Americans.

But I also know that Republicans and Democrats don't see eye to eye on a number of issues. And so we're going to continue working over the weekend to bridge those gaps.

The good news is, we agree on some of the big things. We agree that after a decade of racking up deficits and debt, we need to get our fiscal house in order. We agree that to do that, both sides are going to have to step outside of their comfort zones and make some political sacrifices. And we agree that we simply cannot afford to default on our national obligations for the first time in our history, that we need to uphold the full faith and credit of the United States of America.

With a recovery that's still fragile and isn't producing all the jobs we need, the last thing we can afford is the usual partisan game-playing in Washington. By getting our fiscal house in order, Congress will be in a stronger position to focus on some of the job-creating measures I've already proposed, like putting people to work rebuilding America's infrastructure or reforming our patent system so that our innovators and entrepreneurs have a greater incentive to generate new products or making college more affordable for families. And businesses that may be holding back because of the uncertainty surrounding the possibility of a default by the U.S. Government will have greater confidence to invest and create jobs.

I know we can do this. We can meet our fiscal challenge. That's what the American people sent us here to do. They didn't send us to kick our problems down the road. That's exactly what they don't like about Washington. They sent us here to work together. They sent us here to get things done.

Right now we have an extraordinary—and an extraordinarily rare—opportunity to move forward in a way that makes sure our Government lives within its means, that puts our economy on a sounder footing for the future, and that still invests in the things we need to prosper in the years to come. And I'm hopeful that we will rise to the moment and seize this opportunity on behalf of all Americans and the future we hold in common.

Thanks, every body, and have a great weekend.

NOTE: The address was recorded at approximately 5 p.m. on July 8 in the Library at the White House for broadcast on July 9. The transcript was made available by the Office of the Press Secretary on July 8, but was embargoed for release until 6 a.m. on July 9.

Statement Recognizing South Sudan as an Independent and Sovereign State
July 9, 2011

I am proud to declare that the United States formally recognizes the Republic of South Sudan as a sovereign and independent state upon this day, July 9, 2011. After so much struggle by the people of South Sudan, the United States of America welcomes the birth of a new nation.

Today is a reminder that after the darkness of war, the light of a new dawn is possible. A proud flag flies over Juba, and the map of the world has been redrawn. These symbols speak to the blood that has been spilled, the tears that have been shed, the ballots that have been cast, and the hopes that have been realized by so many millions of people. The eyes of the world are on the Republic of South Sudan. And we know that Southern Sudanese have claimed their sovereignty and shown that neither their dignity nor their dream of self-determination can be denied.

This historic achievement is a tribute, above all, to the generations of Southern Sudanese who struggled for this day. It is also a tribute to the support that has been shown for Sudan and South Sudan by so many friends and partners around the world. Sudan's African neighbors and the African Union played an essential part in making this day a reality. And along with our many international and civil society partners, the United States has been proud to play a leadership role across two administrations. Many Americans have been deeply moved by the aspirations of the Sudanese people, and support for South Sudan extends across different races, regions, and political persuasions in the United States. I am confident that the bonds of friendship between South Sudan and the United States will only deepen in the years to come. As Southern Sudanese undertake the hard work of building their new country, the United States pledges our partnership as they seek the security, development, and responsive governance that can fulfill their aspirations and respect their human rights.

As today also marks the creation of two new neighbors, South Sudan and Sudan, both peoples must recognize that they will be more secure and prosperous if they move beyond a bitter past and resolve differences peacefully. Lasting peace will only be realized if all sides fulfill their responsibilities. The Comprehensive Peace Agreement must be fully implemented, the status of Abyei must be resolved through negotiations, and violence and intimidation in Southern Kordofan, especially by the Government of Sudan, must end. The safety of all Sudanese, especially minorities, must be protected. Through courage and hard choices, this can be the beginning of a new chapter of greater peace and justice for all of the Sudanese people.

Decades ago, Martin Luther King reflected on the first moment of independence on the African Continent in Ghana, saying, "I knew about all of the struggles, and all of the pain, and all of the agony that these people had gone through for this moment." Today we are moved by the story of struggle that led to this time of hope in South Sudan, and we think of those who didn't live to see their dream realized. Now, the leaders and people of South Sudan have an opportunity to turn this moment of promise into lasting progress. The United States will continue to support the aspirations of all Sudanese. Together, we can ensure that today marks another step forward in Africa's long journey toward opportunity, democracy, and justice.

The President's News Conference
July 11, 2011

The President. Good morning, everybody. I want to give a quick update on what's happening with the debt negotiations, provide my perspective, and then I'm going to take a few questions.

As all of you know, I met with congressional leaders yesterday. We're going to be meeting again today, and we're going to meet every single day until we get this thing resolved.

The good news is that all the leaders continue to believe, rightly, that it is not acceptable for us not to raise the debt ceiling and to allow the U.S. Government to default. We cannot threaten the United States full faith and credit for the first time in our history. We still have a lot of work to do, though, to get this problem solved. And so let me just make a couple of points.

First of all, all of us agree that we should use this opportunity to do something meaningful on debt and deficits. And the reports that have been out there have been largely accurate that Speaker Boehner and myself had been in a series of conversations about doing the biggest deal possible so that we could actually resolve our debt and our deficit challenge for a long stretch of time. And I want to say I appreciate Speaker Boehner's good faith efforts on that front.

What I emphasized to the broader group of congressional leaders yesterday is, now is the time to deal with these issues. If not now, when? I've been hearing from my Republican friends for quite some time that it is a moral imperative for us to tackle our debt and our deficits in a serious way. I've been hearing from them that this is one of the things that's creating uncertainty and holding back investment on the part of the business community. And so what I've said to them is, let's go. And it is possible for us to construct a package that would be balanced, would share sacrifice, would involve both parties taking on their sacred cows, would involve some meaningful changes to Medicare, Social Security, and Medicaid that would preserve the integrity of

the programs and keep our sacred trust with our seniors, but make sure those programs were there for not just this generation, but for the next generation; that it is possible for us to bring in revenues in a way that does not impede our current recovery, but is fair and balanced.

We have agreed to a series of spending cuts that will make the Government leaner, meaner, more effective, more efficient, and give taxpayers a greater bang for their buck. That includes defense spending. That includes health spending. It includes some programs that I like very much, and we'd—be nice to have, but that we can't afford right now.

And if you look at this overall package, we could achieve a situation in which our deficits were at a manageable level and our debt levels were stabilized, and the economy as a whole, I think, would benefit from that. Moreover, I think it would give the American people enormous confidence that this town can actually do something once in a while, that we can defy the expectations that we're always thinking in terms of short-term politics and the next election and every once in a while we break out of that and we do what's right for the country.

So I continue to push congressional leaders for the largest possible deal. And there's going to be resistance. There is frankly resistance on my side to do anything on entitlements. There is strong resistance on the Republican side to do anything on revenues. But if each side takes a maximalist position, if each side wants 100 percent of what its ideological predispositions are, then we can't get anything done. And I think the American people want to see something done. They feel a sense of urgency, both about the breakdown in our political process and also about the situation in our economy.

So what I've said to the leaders is, bring back to me some ideas that you think can get the necessary number of votes in the House and in the Senate. I'm happy to consider all options, all alternatives that they're looking at. The things that I will not consider are a 30-day or a

60-day or a 90-day or a 180-day temporary stopgap resolution to this problem. This is the United States of America, and we don't manage our affairs in 3-month increments. We don't risk U.S. default on our obligations because we can't put politics aside.

So I've said—I've been very clear to them: We're going to resolve this, and we're going to resolve this for a reasonable period of time, and we're going to resolve it in a serious way. And my hope is, is that as a consequence of negotiations that take place today, tomorrow, the next day, and through next weekend, if necessary, that we're going to come up with a plan that solves our short-term debt and deficit problems, avoids default, stabilizes the economy, and proves to the American people that we can actually get things done in this country and in this town.

All right, with that, I'm going to take some questions, starting with Ben Feller [Associated Press].

National Debt and Deficit/Taxes

Q. Thank you very much, Mr. President. Two quick topics: Given that you're running out of time, can you explain what is your plan for where these talks go if Republicans continue to oppose any tax increases, as they've adamantly said that they will? And secondly, on your point about no short-term stopgap measure, if it came down to that and Congress went that route, I know you're opposed to it, but would you veto it?

The President. I will not sign a 30-day or a 60-day or a 90-day extension. That is just not an acceptable approach. And if we think it's going to be hard—if we think it's hard now, imagine how these guys are going to be thinking 6 months from now in the middle of an election season where they're all up. It's not going to get easier, it's going to get harder. So we might as well do it now: pull off the bandaid; eat our peas. [*Laughter*] Now is the time to do it. If not now, when?

We keep on talking about this stuff, and we have these high-minded pronouncements about how we've got to get control of the deficit and how we owe it to our children and our

grandchildren. Well, let's step up. Let's do it. I'm prepared to do it. I'm prepared to take on significant heat from my party to get something done. And I expect the other side should be willing to do the same thing if they mean what they say that this is important.

And let me just, Ben, comment on this whole issue of tax increases, because there's been a lot of information floating around there. I want to be crystal clear: Nobody has talked about increasing taxes now. Nobody has talked about increases—increasing taxes next year. What we have talked about is that starting in 2013, that we have gotten rid of some of these egregious loopholes that are benefiting corporate jet owners or oil companies at a time where they're making billions of dollars of profits. What we have said is, as part of a broader package, we should have revenues, and the best place to get those revenues are from folks like me who have been extraordinarily fortunate, and that millionaires and billionaires can afford to pay a little bit more, going back to the Bush tax rates.

And what I've also said to Republicans is, if you don't like that formulation, then I'm happy to work with you on tax reform that could potentially lower everybody's rates and broaden the base, as long as that package was sufficiently progressive so that we weren't balancing the budget on the backs of middle class families and working class families and we weren't letting hedge fund managers or authors of bestselling books off the hook.

That is a reasonable proposition. So when you hear folks saying, well, the President shouldn't want massive, job-killing tax increases when the economy is this weak, nobody is looking to raise taxes right now. We're talking about potentially 2013 and the out-years. In fact, the only proposition that's out there about raising taxes next year would be if we don't renew the payroll tax cut that we passed in December, and I'm in favor of renewing it for next year as well. But there have been some Republicans who said we may not renew it.

And if we don't renew that, then the $1,000 that's been going to a typical American family this year as a consequence of the tax cut that I worked with the Republicans and passed in December, that lapses. That could weaken the economy.

So I have bent over backwards to work with the Republicans to try to come up with a formulation that doesn't require them to vote sometime in the next month to increase taxes. What I've said is to identify a revenue package that makes sense, that is commensurate with the sacrifices we're asking other people to make, and then, I'm happy to work with you to figure out how else we might do it.

Q. Do you see any path to a deal if they don't budge on taxes?

The President. I do not see a path to a deal if they don't budge, period. I mean, if the basic proposition is, "It's my way or the highway," then we're probably not going to get something done because we've got divided Government. We've got Democrats controlling the Senate; we probably are going to need Democratic votes in the House for any package that could possibly pass. And so if in fact Mitch McConnell and John Boehner are sincere—and I believe they are—that they don't want to see the U.S. Government default, then they're going to have to compromise just like Democrats are going to have to compromise, just like I have shown myself willing to compromise.

Chip Reid [CBS News].

National Debt and Deficit/Budget Debate

Q. Thank you, Mr. President. You said that everybody in the room is willing to do what they have to do, wants to get something done by August 2. But isn't the problem the people who aren't in the room, and in particular, Republican Presidential candidates and Republican Tea Partiers on the Hill and the American public? The latest CBS News poll showed that only 24 percent of Americans said you should raise the debt limit to avoid an economic catastrophe. There are still 69 percent who oppose raising the debt limit. So isn't the problem that you and others have failed to convince the American people that we have a crisis here, and how are you going to change that?

The President. Well, let me distinguish between professional politicians and the public at large. The public is not paying close attention to the ins and outs of how a Treasury auction goes. They shouldn't. They're worrying about their family; they're worrying about their jobs; they're worrying about their neighborhood. They've got a lot of other things on their plate. We're paid to worry about it.

I think, depending on how you phrase the question, if you said to the American people, is it a good idea for the United States not to pay its bills and potentially create another recession that could throw millions of more people out of work, I feel pretty confident I can get a majority on my side on that one.

And that's the fact. If we don't raise the debt ceiling, and we see a crisis of confidence in the markets, and suddenly, interest rates are going up significantly, and everybody is paying higher interest rates on their car loans, on their mortgages, on their credit cards, and that's sucking up a whole bunch of additional money out of the pockets of the American people, I promise you, they won't like that.

Now, I will say that some of the professional politicians know better. And for them to say that we shouldn't be raising the debt ceiling is irresponsible. They know better.

And this is not something that I am making up. This is not something that Tim Geithner is making up. We're not out here trying to use this as a means of doing all these really tough, political things. I'd rather be talking about stuff that everybody welcomes, like new programs or the NFL season getting resolved or— [*laughter*]. Unfortunately, this is what's on our plate. It's before us right now. And we've got to deal with it.

So what you're right about, I think, is, is that the leaders in the room here at a certain point have to step up and do the right thing, regardless of the voices in our respective parties that are trying to undermine that effort.

I have a stake in John Boehner successfully persuading his caucus that this is the right thing to do, just like he has a stake in seeing me successfully persuading the Democratic Party that we should take on these problems that we've been talking about for too long, but haven't been doing anything about.

Q. Do you think he'll come back to the $4 trillion deal?

The President. I think Speaker Boehner has been very sincere about trying to do something big. I think he'd like to do something big. His politics within his caucus are very difficult, you're right. And this is part of the problem with a political process where folks are rewarded for saying irresponsible things to win elections or obtain short-term political gain, when we actually are in a position to try to do something hard we haven't always laid the groundwork for. And I think that it's going to take some work on his side, but look, it's also going to take some work on our side, in order to get this thing done.

I mean, the vast majority of Democrats on Capitol Hill would prefer not to have to do anything on entitlements, would prefer frankly not to have to do anything on some of these debt and deficit problems. And I'm sympathetic to their concerns, because they're looking after folks who are already hurting and already vulnerable, and there are a lot of families out there and seniors who are dependant on some of these programs.

And what I've tried to explain to them is, number one, if you look at the numbers, then Medicare in particular will run out of money, and we will not be able to sustain that program no matter how much taxes go up. I mean, it's not an option for us to just sit by and do nothing. And if you're a progressive who cares about the integrity of Social Security and Medicare and Medicaid and believes that it is part of what makes our country great that we look after our seniors and we look after the most vulnerable, then we have an obligation to make sure that we make those changes that are required to make it sustainable over the long term.

And if you're a progressive that cares about investments in Head Start and student loan programs and medical research and infrastructure, we're not going to be able to make progress on those areas if we haven't gotten our fiscal house in order.

So the argument I'm making to my party is, the values we care about—making sure that everybody in this country has a shot at the American Dream and everybody is out there with the opportunity to succeed if they work hard and live a responsible life, and that Government has a role to play in providing some of that opportunity through things like student loans and making sure that our roads and highways and airports are functioning, and making sure that we're investing in research and development for the high-tech jobs of the future—if you care about those things, then you've got to be interested in figuring out how do we pay for that in a responsible way.

And so yes, we're going to have a sales job; this is not pleasant. It is hard to persuade people to do hard stuff that entails trimming benefits and increasing revenues. But the reason we've got a problem right now is people keep on avoiding hard things, and I think now is the time for us to go ahead and take it on.

Rich Wolf [USA Today].

Social Security/Budget Debate

Q. Thank you, Mr. President. You keep talking about balance, shared sacrifice, but in the $4 trillion deal that you're talking about roughly, it seems to be now at about 4 to 1 spending to taxes; we're talking about $800 billion in taxes, roughly. That doesn't seem very fair to some Democrats. I'm wondering if you could clarify why we're at that level. And also, if you could clarify your Social Security position: Would any of the money from Social Security, even from just chained CPI, go toward the deficit as opposed to back into the trust fund?

The President. With respect to Social Security, Social Security is not the source of our deficit problems. Social Security, if it is part of a package, would be an issue of how do we make sure Social Security extends its life and is strengthened? So the reason to do Social Security is to strengthen Social Security to make sure that those benefits are there for seniors in the out-years. And the reason to include that potentially in this package is if you're going to take a bunch of tough votes, you might as well do it now, as opposed to trying to muster up the political will to get something done further down in the future.

With respect to a balanced package, is the package that we're talking about exactly what I would want? No. I might want more revenues and fewer cuts to programs that benefit middle class families that are trying to send their kids to college, or benefit all of us because we're investing more in medical research.

So I make no claims that somehow the position that Speaker Boehner and I discussed reflects 100 percent of what I want. But that's the point. My point is, is that I'm willing to move in their direction in order to get something done. And that's what compromise entails. We have a system of government in which everybody has got to give a little bit.

Now, what I will say is, is that the revenue components that we've discussed would be significant and would target folks who can most afford it. And if we don't do any revenue—because you may hear the argument that why not just go ahead and do all the cuts and we can debate the revenue issues in the election, right? You'll hear that from some Republicans. The problem is, is that if you don't do the revenues, then to get the same amount of savings you've got to have more cuts, which means that it's seniors or it's poor kids or it's medical researchers or it's our infrastructure that suffers.

And I do not want, and I will not accept, a deal in which I am asked to do nothing, in fact, I'm able to keep hundreds of thousands of dollars in additional income that I don't need, while a parent out there who is struggling to figure out how to send their kid to college suddenly finds that they've got a couple thousand dollars less in grants or student loans.

That's what the revenue debate is about. It's not because I want to raise revenues for the sake of raising revenues or I've got some grand ambition to create a bigger government. It's because if we're going to actually solve the problem, there are a finite number of ways to do it. And if you don't have revenues, it means you are putting more of a burden on the people who can least afford it. And that's not fair. And I think the American people agree with me on that.

Sam Stein [Huffington Post].

National Economy/Job Growth/Budget Debate

Q. Thank you, Mr. President. With unemployment now at 9.2 percent and a large chunk of those lost jobs coming from the private sector, is now a really good time to cut trillions of dollars in spending? How will we still create jobs? And then to piggyback on the Social Security question, what do you say to members of your own party who say it doesn't contribute to the deficit, let's consider it, but not in the context of this deal?

The President. Our biggest priority as an administration is getting the economy back on track and putting people back to work. Now, without relitigating the past, I'm absolutely convinced, and the vast majority of economists are convinced, that the steps we took in the Recovery Act saved millions of people their jobs or created a whole bunch of jobs.

And part of the evidence of that is as you see what happens with the Recovery Act phasing out. When I came into office and budgets were hemorrhaging at the State level, part of the Recovery Act was giving States help so they wouldn't have to lay off teachers, police officers, firefighters. As we've seen that Federal support for States diminish, you've seen the biggest job losses in the public sector, teachers, police officers, firefighters losing their jobs.

So my strong preference would be for us to figure out ways that we can continue to provide help across the board. But I'm operating within some political constraints here, because whatever I do has to go through the House of Representatives.

What that means then is, is that among the options that are available to us is, for example, the payroll tax cut, which might not be exactly the kind of program that I would design in order to boost employment, but does make a difference because it puts money in the pockets of people who are then spending it at businesses, large and small. That gives them more customers, increases demand, and it gives businesses a greater incentive to hire. And that would be, for example, a component of this overall package.

Unemployment benefits, again, puts money in the pockets of folks who are out there knocking on doors trying to find a job every day. Giving them those resources, that puts more money into the economy and that potentially improves it—improves the climate for businesses to want to hire.

So as part of a component of a deal, I think it's very important for us to look at what are the steps we can take short term in order to put folks back to work. I am not somebody who believes that just because we solve the deficit and debt problems short term, medium term, or long term, that that automatically solves the unemployment problem. I think we're still going to have to do a bunch of stuff, including, for example, trade deals that are before Congress right now that could add tens of thousands of jobs.

Republicans gave me this list at the beginning of this year as a priority, something that they thought they could do. Now I'm ready to do it, and so far we haven't gotten the kind of movement that I would have expected.

We've got the potential to create an infrastructure bank that could put construction workers to work right now, rebuilding our roads and our bridges and our vital infrastructure all across the country. So those are still areas where, I think, we can make enormous progress.

I do think that if the country as a whole sees Washington act responsibly, compromises being made, the deficit and debt being dealt with for 10, 15, 20 years, that that will help with businesses feeling more confident about aggressively investing in this country, foreign investors saying America has got its act together and are willing to invest. And so it can have a positive impact in overall growth and employment.

It's not the only solution. We're still going to have to have a strong jobs agenda. But it is part of a solution. I might add it is the primary solution that the Republicans have offered when it comes to jobs. They keep on going out there and saying, "Mr. President, what are you doing about jobs?" And when you ask them, well, what would you do? "We've got to get Government spending under control, and we've got to get our deficits under control." So I say, okay, let's go. Where are they? I mean, this is what

they claim would be the single biggest boost to business certainty and confidence. So what's the holdup?

With respect to Social Security, as I indicated earlier, making changes to these programs is so difficult that this may be an opportunity for us to go ahead and do something smart that strengthens Social Security and gives not just this generation but future generations the opportunity to say this thing is going to be in there for the long haul.

Now, that may not be possible, and you're absolutely right that, as I said, Social Security is not the primary driver of our long-term deficits and debt. On the other hand, we do want to make sure that Social Security is going to be there for the next generations, and if there is a reasonable deal to be had on it, it is one that I'm willing to pursue.

Q. Are there things with respect to Social Security, like raising the retirement age, means testing—are those too big a chunk for——

The President. I'm probably not going to get into the details, Sam, right now of negotiations. I might enjoy negotiating with you, but I don't know how much juice you've got in the Republican caucus. [*Laughter*] That's what I figured.

All right, Lesley Clark [McClatchy Newspapers].

Budget Debate/National Debt and Deficit

Q. Thank you, Mr. President.
The President. Thank you.
Q. Have you—you've talked with economists, you said that economists have agreed that a deal needs to be made. Have you worked with new U.S. business leaders at all to lobby Congress to raise the debt ceiling? And if so, who are you talking to?

The President. I have spoken extensively to business leaders. And I'll be honest with you: I think that business leaders in the abstract want to see a resolution to this problem. What I've found is that they are somewhat hesitant to weigh in on some of these issues even if they're willing to say something privately to me, partly because they've got a whole bunch of business pending before Congress and they don't want to make anybody mad.

So this is a problem of our politics and our politicians, but it's not exclusively a problem of our politics and our politicians. I mean, the business community is a lot like everybody else, which is we want to cut everybody else's stuff and we want to keep our stuff. We want to cut our taxes, but if you want to raise revenue with somebody else's taxes, that's okay. And that kind of mindset is why we never get the problem solved.

There have been business leaders, like Warren Buffett, who I think have spoken out forcefully on this issue. I think some of the folks who participated in the Bowles-Simpson Commission made very clear that they would agree to a balanced approach even if it meant for them, individually, that they were seeing slightly higher taxes on their income, given that they're—I think the average CEO, if I'm not mistaken, saw a 23-percent raise this past year while the average worker saw a 0- to 1-percent raise last year.

So I think that there are a lot of well-meaning businesspeople out there who recognize the need to make something happen. But I think that they've been hesitant to be as straightforward as I'd like when it says, this is what a balanced package means. It means that we've got some spending cuts, it means that we've got some increased revenue, and it means that we're taking on some of the drivers of our long-term debt and deficits.

Q. And can you say, as the clock ticks down, whether or not the administration is——

The President. I'm sorry.

Q. Can you say, as the clock ticks down, whether or not the administration is working on any sort of contingency plans if things don't happen by August 2?

The President. We are going to get this done by August 2.

George Condon [National Journal].

Bipartisanship

Q. Mr. President, to follow on Chip's question, you said that the Speaker faces tough politics in his caucus. Do you have complete confidence that he can deliver the votes on any-

thing that he agrees to? Is he in control of his caucus?

The President. That's a question for the Speaker, not a question for me. My experience with John Boehner is—has been good. I think he's a good man who wants to do right by the country. I think that it's a—as Chip alluded to, the politics that swept him into the Speakership were good for a midterm election; they're tough for governing. And part of what the Republican caucus generally needs to recognize is that American democracy works when people listen to each other, we're willing to give each other the benefit of the doubt, we assume the patriotism and good intentions of the other side, and we're willing to make some sensible compromises to solve big problems. And I think that there are members of that caucus who haven't fully arrived at that realization yet.

Q. So your confidence in him wasn't shaken by him walking away from the big deal he said he wanted?

The President. These things are a tough process. And look, in fairness, a big deal would require a lot of work on the part of Harry Reid and Nancy Pelosi and myself to bring Democrats along. But the point is, is if everybody gets in the boat at the same time, it doesn't tip over. I think that was Bob Dole's famous comment after striking a deal with the President and Mr. Gingrich back in the nineties. And that is always the case when it comes to difficult but important tasks like this.

Last question. April Ryan [American Urban Radio Networks].

National Economy/Debt and Deficit

Q. Mr. President, hi. I want to revisit the issue of sacrifice. In 2009, you said that—expect the worst to come; we have not seen the worst yet. And now with these budget cuts looming, you have minorities, the poor, the elderly, as well as people who are scared of losing jobs, fearful. And also, what say you about Congressman Chaka Fattah's bill, the "Debt Free America Act"? Do you support that bill? Are you supporting the Republican bill that is similar to his, modeled after Congressman Fattah's bill?

The President. Well, I'm not going to comment on a particular bill right now. Let me speak to the broader point that you're asking about, April.

This recession has been hard on everybody, but obviously, it's harder on folks who've got less. And the thing that I am obsessed with, and have been since I came into office, is all those families out there who are doing the right thing every single day, who are looking after their families, who are just struggling to keep up and just feel like they're falling behind, no matter how hard they work.

I got a letter this past week from a woman who—her husband had lost his job, had pounded the pavement, finally found a job. They felt like things were stabilizing for a few months. Six months later he lost his second job. Now they're back looking again and trying to figure out how they are going to make ends meet. And there are just hundreds of thousands of folks out there who really have seen as tough of an economy as we've seen in our lifetimes.

Now, we took very aggressive steps when I first came into office to yank the economy out of a potential great depression and stabilize it. And we were largely successful in stabilizing it. But we stabilized it at a level where unemployment is still too high, and the economy is not growing fast enough to make up for all the jobs that were lost before I took office and the few months after I took office.

So this unemployment rate has been really stubborn. There are a couple of ways that we can solve that. Number one is to make sure that the overall economy is growing. And so we have continued to take a series of steps to make sure that there's money in people's pockets that they can go out there and spend. That's what these payroll tax cuts were about.

We've taken a number of steps to make sure that businesses are willing to invest, and that's what the small-business tax cuts and some of the tax breaks for companies that are willing to invest in plants and equipment—and zero capital gains for small businesses—that's what that was all about, was giving businesses more incentive to invest.

We have worked to make sure that the training programs that are out there for folks who are having to shift from jobs that may not exist anymore so that they can get the training they need for the jobs that do exist, that those are improved and sharpened.

We have put forward a series of proposals to make sure that regulations that may be unnecessary and are hampering some businesses from investing, that we are examining all of those for their costs and their benefits. And if they are not providing the kind of benefits in terms of the public health and clean air and clean water and worker safety that have been promised, then we should get rid of some of those regulations.

So we've been looking at the whole menu of steps that can be taken. We are now in a situation where because the economy has moved slower than we wanted, because of the deficits and debt that result from the recession and the crisis, that taking a approach that costs trillions of dollars is not an option. We don't have that kind of money right now.

What we can do is to solve this underlying debt and deficit problem for a long period of time so that then we can get back to having a conversation about, all right, since we now have solved this problem, that's not—no longer what's hampering economic growth, that's not feeding business and uncertainty, everybody feels that the ground is stable under our feet, are there some strategies that we could pursue that would really focus on some targeted job growth, infrastructure being a primary example.

I mean, the infrastructure bank that we've proposed is relatively small. But could we imagine a project where we're rebuilding roads and bridges and ports and schools and broadband lines and smart grids, and taking all those construction workers and putting them to work right now? I can imagine a very aggressive program like that that I think the American people would rally around and would be good for the economy not just next year or the year after, but for the next 20 or 30 years.

But we can't even have that conversation if people feel as if we don't have our fiscal house in order. Right? So the idea here is, let's act now. Let's get this problem off the table. And then with some firm footing, with a solid fiscal situation, we will then be in a position to make the kind of investments that, I think, are going to be necessary to win the future.

So this is not a right or left, conservative/liberal situation. This is how do we operate in a smart way, understanding that we've got some short-term challenges and some long-term challenges. If we can solve some of those long-term challenges, that frees up some of our energies to be able to deal with some of these short-term ones as well.

All right? Thank you very much, everybody.

NOTE: The President's news conference began at 11:15 a.m. in the James S. Brady Press Briefing Room at the White House. In his remarks, the President referred to Warren E. Buffett, chief executive officer and chairman, Berkshire Hathaway Inc.; Erskine B. Bowles and Alan K. Simpson, Cochairs, National Commission on Fiscal Responsibility and Reform; former Sen. Robert J. Dole; and former Speaker of the House of Representatives Newton L. Gingrich.

Memorandum on Regulation and Independent Regulatory Agencies
July 11, 2011

Memorandum for the Heads of Independent Regulatory Agencies

Subject: Regulation and Independent Regulatory Agencies

America's free market is the greatest force for prosperity the world has ever known. It is the key to our global leadership and the success of our people. But throughout our history, one of the reasons it has worked is that we have sought a proper balance—a balance that promotes economic growth, innovation, competitiveness, and job creation, while protecting the health, safety, and security of the American people. Over the past two and a half years, the pursuit of that balance has guided my Administration's approach to rules and regulations. And in January of this year, I signed an Executive Order requiring executive agencies to reduce regulations that place unnecessary burdens on American businesses and the American people while ensuring that regulations protect our safety, health, and environment. I initiated a careful, Government-wide review of regulations already on the books in order to reduce outdated, unjustified regulations that stifle job creation and make our economy less competitive. We are taking immediate steps to eliminate millions of hours in annual paperwork burdens for large and small businesses

and save more than $1 billion in annual regulatory costs. And hundreds of reform proposals from 30 agencies, now available for public scrutiny, promise to deliver billions of dollars in additional savings.

The Executive Order also requires executive agencies to consider costs and benefits and to reduce burdens on the American people; to expand opportunities for public participation; to simplify and harmonize rules; and to promote flexibility and freedom of choice.

With full respect for the independence of your agencies, I am asking you today to join in this review and produce your own plans to reassess and streamline regulations. For rules going forward, I am also asking you to follow the key cost-saving, burden-reducing principles outlined in the January Executive Order.

I hope you see this as an opportunity to do something big and lasting—to change the ways of Washington; to focus on what works; and to forge a 21st-century regulatory system that makes our economy stronger and more competitive, while we meet our fundamental responsibilities to one another.

I look forward to working with all of you on this important initiative, and I thank you for your attention and service to our country.

BARACK OBAMA

Remarks on Presenting the Medal of Honor to Sergeant First Class Leroy A. Petry
July 12, 2011

The President. Thank you, Chaplain Rutherford. Please be seated. Good afternoon, everyone, and welcome to the White House as we present our Nation's highest military decoration, the Medal of Honor, to an extraordinary American soldier, Sergeant First Class Leroy Petry.

This is a historic occasion. Last fall, I was privileged to present the Medal of Honor to Staff Sergeant Salvatore Giunta for his heroism in Afghanistan, and Sal joins us this afternoon. Where's Sal? Good to see you.

So today is only the second time during the wars in Afghanistan and Iraq, indeed, only the second time since Vietnam, that a recipient of the Medal of Honor from an ongoing conflict has been able to accept this medal in person. And having just spent some time with Leroy, his lovely wife Ashley, their wonderful children, in the Oval Office, then had a chance to see the entire Petry family here, I have to say this could not be happening to a nicer guy or a more inspiring family.

Leroy, the Medal of Honor reflects the deepest gratitude of our entire Nation. So we're joined by Members of Congress, Vice President Biden, leaders from across my administration, including Deputy Secretary of Defense Bill Lynn, and leaders from across our Armed Forces, including the Vice Chairman of the Joint Chiefs of Staff, General Jim "Hoss" Cartwright, Army Secretary John McHugh, and Army Chief of Staff General Marty Dempsey.

We're honored to welcome more than 100 of Leroy's family and friends, many from his home State of New Mexico, as well as his fellow Rangers from the legendary Delta Company, 2d Battalion, 75th Ranger Regiment. And as always, we are humbled by the presence of members of the Medal of Honor Society.

Today we honor a singular act of gallantry. Yet as we near the 10th anniversary of the attacks that thrust our Nation into war, this is also an occasion to pay tribute to a soldier and a generation that has borne the burden of our security during a hard decade of sacrifice.

I want to take you back to the circumstances that led to this day. It's May 26, 2008, in the remote east of Afghanistan, near the mountainous border of Pakistan. Helicopters carrying dozens of elite Army Rangers race over the rugged landscape. And their target is an insurgent compound. The mission is high risk. It's broad daylight. The insurgents are heavily armed. But it's considered a risk worth taking because intelligence indicates that a top Al Qaida commander is in that compound.

Soon, the helicopters touch down, and our Rangers immediately come under fire. Within minutes, Leroy, then a Staff Sergeant, and another soldier are pushing ahead into a courtyard, surrounded by high mud walls. And that's when the enemy opens up with their AK–47s. Leroy is hit in both legs. He's bleeding badly, but he summons the strength to lead the other Ranger to cover, behind a chicken coop. He radios for support. He hurls a grenade at the enemy, giving cover to a third Ranger who rushes to their aid. An enemy grenade explodes nearby, wounding Leroy's two comrades. And then a second grenade lands, this time, only a few feet away.

Every human impulse would tell someone to turn away. Every soldier is trained to seek cover. That's what Sergeant Leroy Petry could have done. Instead, this wounded Ranger, this 28-year-old man with his whole life ahead of him, this husband and father of four, did something extraordinary. He lunged forward, toward the live grenade. He picked it up. He cocked his arm to throw it back.

What compels such courage? What leads a person to risk everything so that others might live? For answers, we don't need to look far. The roots of Leroy's valor are all around us.

We see it in the sense of duty instilled by his family, who joins us today: his father Larry, his mother Lorella, and his four brothers. Growing up, the walls of their home were hung with pictures of grandfathers and uncles in uniform, leading a young Leroy to believe "that's my calling too."

We see it in the compassion of a high school student who overcame his own struggles to mentor younger kids to give them a chance. We see it in the loyalty of an Army Ranger who lives by a creed: Never shall I fail my comrades. Or as Leroy puts it, "These are my brothers, family just like my wife and kids, and you protect the ones you love." And that's what he did that day when he picked up that grenade and threw it back, just as it exploded.

With that selfless act, Leroy saved his two Ranger brothers, and they are with us today. His valor came with a price. The force of the blast took Leroy's right hand. Shrapnel riddled his body. Said one of his teammates, "I had never seen someone hurt so bad." So even his fellow Rangers were amazed at what Leroy did next. Despite his grievous wounds, he remained calm. He actually put on his own tourniquet. And he continued to lead, directing his team, giving orders, even telling the medics how to treat his wounds.

When the fight was won, as he lay in a stretcher being loaded onto a helicopter, one of his teammates came up to shake the hand that Leroy had left. "That was the first time I shook the hand of someone who I consider to be a true American hero," that Ranger said. Leroy Petry "showed that true heroes still exist and that they're closer than you think."

That Ranger is right. Our heroes are all around us. They're the millions of Americans in uniform who have served these past 10 years, many, like Leroy, deploying tour after tour, year after year. On the morning of 9/11, Leroy was training to be a Ranger, and as his instructor got the terrible news, they told Leroy and his class, "Keep training, you might be going to war." Within months Leroy was in Afghanistan for the first of seven deployments since 9/11.

Leroy speaks proudly of the progress our troops have made: Afghan communities now free from the terror of the Taliban and Afghan forces that are taking more responsibility for their security. And he carries with him the memories of Americans who have made the ultimate sacrifice to make this progress possible.

Earlier in the Oval Office, Leroy gave me the extraordinary privilege of showing me the small plaque that is bolted to his prosthetic arm. On it are the names of the fallen Rangers from the 75th Regiment. They are, quite literally, part of him, just as they will always be part of America.

One of those names is of the Ranger who did not come back from the raid that day, Specialist Christopher Gathercole. Christopher's brother and sister and grandmother are here with us today. I would ask that they stand briefly so that we can show our gratitude for their family's profound sacrifice.

Our heroes are all around us. They're the force behind the force: military spouses like Ashley, who during Leroy's many deployments, during missed birthdays and holidays, has kept this family "Army Strong." So we're grateful to you, Ashley, and for all the military spouses who are here.

They're military children, like Brittany and Austin and Reagan, and 7-year-old Landon, who at the end of a long day is there to gently rub his dad's injured arm. And so I want to make sure that we acknowledge these extraordinary children as well.

Our heroes are all around us. They're our men and women in uniform who through a decade of war have earned their place among the greatest of generations. During World War II, on D-day, it was the Rangers of D Company who famously scaled the cliffs of Pointe du Hoc. After 9/11, we learned again: "Rangers Lead the Way." They were some of the first boots on the ground in Afghanistan. They have been deployed continuously ever since.

Today, we can see our progress in this war and our success against Al Qaida, and we're beginning to bring our troops home from Afghanistan this summer. Understand, there will be more fighting and more sacrifices in the months and years to come. But I am confident that because of the service of men and women like Leroy, we will be able to say of this generation what President Reagan once said of those

Rangers who took the cliffs on D-day: "These are the heroes who helped end a war."

I would ask all of our Rangers, members of the 9/11 generation, to stand and accept the thanks of a grateful nation.

Finally, the service of Leroy Petry speaks to the very essence of America, that spirit that says, no matter how hard the journey, no matter how steep the climb, we don't quit. We don't give up. Leroy lost a hand, and those wounds in his legs sometimes make it hard for him to stand. But he pushes on, and even joined his fellow Rangers for a grueling 20-mile march. He could have focused only on his own recovery, but today he helps care for other wounded warriors, inspiring them with his example. Given his wounds, he could have retired from the Army, with honor, but he chose to reenlist, indefinitely. And this past year he returned to Afghanistan—his eighth deployment—back with his Ranger brothers on another mission to keep our country safe.

This is the stuff of which heroes are made. This is the strength, the devotion that makes our troops the pride of every American. And this is the reason that, like a soldier named Leroy Petry, America doesn't simply endure, we emerge from our trials stronger, more confident, with our eyes fixed on the future.

Our heroes are all around us. And as we prepare for the reading of the citation, please join me in saluting one of those heroes, Leroy Petry.

[*At this point, Maj. Reginald McClam, USMC, Marine Corps Aide to the President, read the citation, and the President presented the medal.*]

The President. Can you give Leroy a big round of applause?

[*Brig. Gen. Donald L. Rutherford, USA, Army Deputy Chief of Chaplains, said a prayer.*]

The President. Thank you all for attending this extraordinary ceremony for this extraordinary hero. I hope that all of you will join the family. There is going to be an outstanding reception. I hear the food is pretty good around here. [*Laughter*] And I know the music is great because we've got my own Marine Band playing.

So thank you so much for your attendance. And once again, congratulations, Leroy, for your extraordinary devotion to our country.

Thank you very much.

NOTE: The President spoke at 2:23 p.m. in the East Room at the White House. In his remarks, he referred to Pfc. Lucas Robinson, USA, and Sgt. Daniel Higgins, USA, D Company, 2d Battalion, 75th Ranger Regiment; Edward F. Gathercole, brother, Jennifer Daly, sister, and Maryann Haines, grandmother, of Spc. Christopher Gathercole, USA; and Brittany Velotta, Austin West, and Reagan West, stepchildren, Lorella Tapia, mother, and Larry, Lloyd, and Lincoln Petry, brothers, of Sfc. Petry.

Statement on the Terrorist Attacks in Mumbai, India
July 13, 2011

I strongly condemn the outrageous attacks in Mumbai, and my thoughts and prayers are with the wounded and those who have lost loved ones. The U.S. Government continues to monitor the situation, including the safety and security of our citizens. India is a close friend and partner of the United States. The American people will stand with the Indian people in times of trial, and we will offer support to India's efforts to bring the perpetrators of these terrible crimes to justice. During my trip to Mumbai, I saw firsthand the strength and resilience of the Indian people, and I have no doubt that India will overcome these deplorable terrorist attacks.

Statement on the Election of Janice K. Hahn to the United States House of Representatives
July 13, 2011

I want to extend my congratulations to Congresswoman-elect Janice Hahn for her victory in California's 36th Congressional District. Janice and I both believe that in order to win the future, we need to create jobs and grow our economy and pursue a balanced approach to deficit reduction. In Congress, Janice will continue to fight for the people of the South Bay and add another chapter to her family's long history of dedicated service to the people of California. I look forward to working with her.

The President's News Conference
July 15, 2011

The President. Hello, everybody. As you know, yesterday we had another meeting with the congressional leaders. We're not having one today, so I thought it would be useful to give you guys an update on where we are.

All the congressional leaders have reiterated the desire to make sure that the United States does not default on our obligations and that the full faith and credit of the United States is preserved. That is a good thing. I think we should not even be this close to a deadline on this issue; this should have been taken care of earlier. But it is encouraging that everybody believes that this is something that has to be addressed.

And for the general public—I've said this before but I just want to reiterate—this is not some abstract issue. These are obligations that the United States has taken on in the past. Congress has run up the credit card, and we now have an obligation to pay our bills. If we do not, it could have a whole set of adverse consequences. We could end up with a situation, for example, where interest rates rise for everybody all throughout the country, effectively a tax increase on everybody, because suddenly, whether you're using your credit card or you're trying to get a loan for a car or a student loan, businesses that are trying to make payroll, all of them could end up being impacted as a consequence of a default.

Now, what is important is that even as we raise the debt ceiling, we also solve the problem of underlying debt and deficits. I'm glad that congressional leaders don't want to default, but I think the American people expect more than that. They expect that we actually try to solve this problem, we get our fiscal house in order.

And so during the course of these discussions with congressional leaders, what I've tried to emphasize is we have a unique opportunity to do something big. We have a chance to stabilize America's finances for a decade, for 15 years or 20 years, if we're willing to seize the moment.

Now, what that would require would be some shared sacrifice and a balanced approach that says we're going to make significant cuts in domestic spending. And I have already said I am willing to take down domestic spending to the lowest percentage of our overall economy since Dwight Eisenhower.

It also requires cuts in defense spending, and I've said that in addition to the $400 billion that we've already cut from defense spending, we're willing to look for hundreds of billions more.

It would require us taking on health care spending. And that includes looking at Medicare and finding ways that we can stabilize the system so that it is available not just for this generation, but for future generations.

And it would require revenues. It would require, even as we're asking the person who needs a student loan or the senior citizen or people—veterans who are trying to get by on a disability check, even as we're trying to make sure that all those programs are affordable, we're also saying to folks like myself that can afford it that we are able and willing to do a little bit more; that millionaires and billionaires can afford to do a little bit more; that we can close corporate loopholes so that oil companies aren't getting unnecessary tax breaks or that corporate jet owners aren't getting unnecessary tax breaks.

If we take that approach, then I am confident that we can not only impress the financial markets, but more importantly, we can actually impress the American people that this town can actually get something done once in a while.

Now, let me acknowledge what everybody understands: It is hard to do a big package. My Republican friends have said that they're not willing to do revenues, and they have repeated that on several occasions.

My hope, though, is that they're listening not just to lobbyists or special interests here in Washington, but they're also listening to the American people. Because it turns out poll after poll, many done by your organizations, show that it's not just Democrats who think we need to take a balanced approach; it's Republicans as well.

The clear majority of Republican voters think that any deficit reduction package should have a balanced approach and should include some revenues. That's not just Democrats, that's the majority of Republicans. You've got a whole slew of Republican officials from previous administrations. You've got a bipartisan commission that has said that we need revenues.

So this is not just a Democratic understanding. This is an understanding that I think the American people hold that we should not be asking sacrifices from middle class folks who are working hard every day, from the most vulnerable in our society, we should not be asking them to make sacrifices if we're not asking the most fortunate in our society to make some sacrifices as well.

So I am still pushing for us to achieve a big deal. But what I also said to the group is if we can't do the biggest deal possible, then let's

still be ambitious, let's still try to at least get a down payment on deficit reduction. And that we can actually accomplish without huge changes in revenue or significant changes in entitlements, but we could still send a signal that we are serious about this problem.

The fallback position, the third option, and I think the least attractive option, is one in which we raise the debt ceiling, but we don't make any progress on deficit and debt. Because if we take that approach, this issue is going to continue to plague us for months and years to come. And I think it's important for the American people that everybody in this town set politics aside, that everybody in this town sets our individual interests aside, and we try to do some tough stuff. And I've already taken some heat from my party for being willing to compromise. My expectation and hope is, is that everybody, in the coming days, is going to be willing to compromise.

Last point I'll make, and then I'll take questions. We are obviously running out of time. And so what I've said to the Members of Congress is that you need, over the next 24 to 36 hours, to give me some sense of what your plan is to get the debt ceiling raised through whatever mechanisms they can think about and show me a plan in terms of what you're doing for deficit and debt reduction.

If they show me a serious plan, I'm ready to move, even if requires some tough decisions on my part. And I'm hopeful that over the next couple of days we'll see this logjam break—this logjam broken, because the American people I think understandably want to see Washington do its job. All right?

So with that, let me see who's on the list. We're going to start with Jake Tapper [ABC News].

Budget Debate/Entitlement Reform

Q. Thank you, Mr. President. You've said that reducing the deficit will require shared sacrifice. We know—we have an idea of the taxes that you would like to see raised on corporations and on Americans in the top two tax brackets, but we don't yet know what you specifically are willing to do when it comes to entitlement spending. In the interest of transparency, leadership, and also showing the American people that you have been negotiating in good faith, can you tell us one structural reform that you are willing to make to one of these entitlement programs that would have a major impact on the deficit? Would you be willing to raise the retirement age? Would you be willing to means test Social Security or Medicare?

The President. We've said that we are willing to look at all those approaches. I've laid out some criteria in terms of what would be acceptable. So, for example, I've said very clearly that we should make sure that current beneficiaries as much as possible are not affected. But we should look at what can we do in the out-years, so that over time some of these programs are more sustainable.

I've said that means testing on Medicare, meaning people like myself, if—I'm going to be turning 50 in a week. So I'm starting to think a little bit more about Medicare eligibility. [*Laughter*] Yes, I'm going to get my AARP card soon and the discounts.

But you can envision a situation where for somebody in my position, me having to pay a little bit more on premiums or copays or things like that would be appropriate. And again, that could make a difference. So we've been very clear about where we're willing to go.

What we're not willing to do is to restructure the program in the ways that we've seen coming out of the House over the last several months where we would voucherize the program and you potentially have senior citizens paying $6,000 more. I view Social Security and Medicare as the most important social safety nets that we have. I think it is important for them to remain as social insurance programs that give people some certainty and reliability in their golden years.

But it turns out that making some modest modifications in those entitlements can save you trillions of dollars. And it's not necessary to completely revamp the program. What is necessary is to say, how do we make some modifications, including, by the way, on the providers' side. I think that it's important for us to keep in mind that drug companies, for example, are still doing very well through the Medicare program. And although we have made drugs more available at a cheaper price to seniors who are in Medicare through the Affordable Care Act, there's more work to potentially be done there.

So if you look at a balanced package even within the entitlement programs, it turns out that you can save trillions of dollars while maintaining the core integrity of the program.

Q. And the retirement age?

The President. I'm not going to get into specifics. As I said, Jake, everything that you mentioned are things that we have discussed. But what I'm not going to do is to ask for even— well, let me put it this way: If you're a senior citizen and a modification potentially costs you a hundred or 200 bucks a year more or—even if it's not affecting current beneficiaries— somebody who's 40 today, 20 years from now is going to end up having to pay a little bit more, the least I can do is to say that people who are making a million dollars or more have to do something as well.

And that's the kind of tradeoff, that's the kind of balanced approach and shared sacrifice that I think most Americans agree needs to happen.

Q. Thank you.

The President. Hans [Hans Nichols, Bloomberg News].

Budget Debate/Spending Cuts/Balanced Budget Amendment

Q. Yes. Thank you, Mr. President. I just thought I heard you kind of open up the door to this middle-of-the-road possibility. I think you said, "Show me a serious plan, and then I'm prepared to move." Just a few minutes before you came here, House Republicans said they'd be voting on this $2.4 trillion package as a balanced budget amendment. Is that a serious plan? Is it dead on arrival, or does it short circuit what you expect to happen in the next 24, 36 hours?

The President. I haven't looked at it yet, and I think—my expectation is that you'll probably see the House vote on a couple of things just to make political statements. But if you're trying to get to $2.4 trillion without any revenue, then you are effectively gutting a whole bunch of domestic spending that is going to be too burdensome and is not going to be something that I would support.

Just to be very specific, we've identified over a trillion dollars in discretionary cuts, both in defense and domestic spending. That's hard to do. I mean, that requires essentially that you freeze spending. And when I say freeze, that means you're not getting inflation so that these are programmatic cuts that, over the course of 10 years, you'd be looking at potentially a 10-percent cut in domestic spending.

Now, if you then double that number, you're then, at that point, really taking a big bite out of programs that are really important to ordinary folks. I mean, you're talking then about students accumulating thousands of dollars more in student loan debt every year; you're talking about Federal workers and veterans and others potentially having to pay more in terms of their health care.

So I have not seen a credible plan, having gone through the numbers, that would allow you to get to $2.4 trillion without really hurting ordinary folks. And the notion that we would be doing that and not asking anything from the wealthiest among us or from closing corporate loopholes, that doesn't seem like a serious plan to me.

I mean, the notion that, for example, oil company tax breaks—where the oil executives themselves say that they probably don't need them to have an incentive to go out and drill oil and make hundreds of billions of dollars—if we haven't seen the other side even budge on that, then I think most Democrats would say that's not a serious plan.

One last point on the balanced budget amendment. I don't know what version they're going to be presenting, but some of the balanced budget amendments that have been floating up there—this cap—or cut, cap, and balance, for example, when you look at the numbers, what you're looking at is cuts of half a trillion dollars below the Ryan budget in any

given year. I mean, it would require cutting Social Security or Medicare substantially.

And I think it's important for everybody to understand that all of us believe that we need to get to a point where eventually we can balance the budget. We don't need a constitutional amendment to do that; what we need to do is to do our jobs.

And we have to do it the same way a family would do it. A family, if they get overextended and their credit card is too high, they don't just stop paying their bills. What they do is they say, how do we start cutting our monthly costs? We keep on making payments, but we start cutting out the things that aren't necessary. And we do it in a way that maintains our credit rating. We do it in a way that's responsible. We don't stop sending our kids to college; we don't stop fixing the boiler or the roof that's leaking. We do things in a sensible, responsible way. We can do the same thing when it comes to the Federal budget.

Economic Strengthening Efforts/Spending Cuts

Q. So within that $2 trillion band, if you end up going for this middle-of-the-road package, which I think you referred to as the second option, would that need to have, for your signature, some sort of stimulative measures, either payroll tax extension or the extension of the unemployment insurance?

The President. I think both would be good for the economy. A payroll tax cut is something that has put a thousand dollars in the pocket of the typical American family over the last 6, 7 months and has helped offset some of the rising costs in gasoline and food. And I think that American consumers and American businesses would benefit from a continuation of that tax cut next year.

Unemployment insurance—obviously, unemployment is still too high. And there are a lot of folks out there who are doing everything they can to find a job, but the market is still tight out there. And for us to make sure that they are able to stay in their homes potentially or they're able to still support their families, I think, is very important and contributes to the overall economy.

So I think there are ways that you can essentially take a little over a trillion dollars in serious discretionary cuts, meaningful discretionary cuts, and then start building on top of that some cuts in non-health-care mandatory payments, ethanol programs, or how we calculate various subsidies to various industries. That could potentially be layered on. And we could still do something like a tax cut for ordinary families that would end up benefiting the economy as a whole.

That is not my preferable option, though. I just want to be clear. I think about this like a layer cake. You can do the bare minimum, and then you can make some progressively harder decisions to solve the problem more and more.

And we're in a position now where if we're serious about this and everybody is willing to compromise, we can, as I said before, fix this thing probably for a decade or more. And that's something that I think would be good for the overall business climate and would encourage the American people that Washington actually is willing to take care of its business.

Q. Good for the business—for the climate, though, but not required for your signature—is that what I heard?

The President. I'm sorry, I lost you on that one.

Q. So you're saying these stimulative measures would be good for the business climate and good for the economy, but you're not saying that they need to be included for you to sign either a $2 trillion or $4 trillion——

The President. I've got to look at an overall package, Hans. I don't know what the Speaker or Mr. McConnell are willing to do at this point.

Okay. Chuck Todd [NBC News].

Debt Ceiling Negotiations/National Debt and Deficit/Budget Debate

Q. Mr. President, this process got kind of ugly in the last week. And it appears from the outside that things even got a little futile at these meetings. Any regrets on your role in how this went? And do you have any regrets that you never took Bowles-Simpson, which was $4 trillion over 10 years, and spent the last 6 months selling that, which was a balanced package, to the American people?

The President. No. First of all, I think this notion that things got ugly is just not true. We've been meeting every single day, and we have had very constructive conversations.

The American people are not interested in the reality TV aspects of who said what and did somebody's feelings get hurt. They're interested in solving the budget problem and the deficit and the debt. And so that may be good for chatter in this town; it's not something that folks out in the country are obsessing about.

I think with respect to Bowles-Simpson, it was important for us to—Bowles-Simpson wouldn't have happened had I not set up the structure for it. As you will recall, this was originally bipartisan legislation that some of the Republican supporters of decided to vote against when I said I supported it; that seems to be a pattern that I'm still puzzled by. And so we set it up. They issued a report. And what I said was this provides us an important framework to begin discussions.

But there were aspects of Bowles-Simpson that I said from very early on were not the approach I would take. I'll give you an example. On defense spending, a huge amount of their savings on the discretionary side came out of defense spending. I think we need to cut defense, but as Commander in Chief, I've got to make sure that we're cutting it in a way that recognizes we're still in the middle of a war, we're winding down another war, and we've got a whole bunch of veterans that we've got to care for as they come home.

And so what we've said is, a lot of the components of Bowles-Simpson we are willing to embrace. For example, the domestic spending cuts that they recommend we've basically taken. Others, like on defense, we have taken some but not all the recommendations because it's important for it to be consistent with our defense needs and our security needs.

The bottom line is that this is not an issue of salesmanship to the American people; the American people are sold. The American people are sold. I just want to repeat this. The whole——

Q. You don't think the whole debate would have been different? You had Republican support on it.

The President. Chuck——

Q. Tom Coburn, the Republican Senator, signed onto it.

The President. Chuck, you have 80 percent of the American people who support a balanced approach. Eighty percent of the American people support an approach that includes revenues and includes cuts. So the notion that somehow the American people aren't sold is not the problem. The problem is Members of Congress are dug in ideologically into various positions because they boxed themselves in with previous statements.

And so this is not a matter of the American people knowing what the right thing to do is. This is a matter of Congress doing the right thing and reflecting the will of the American people. And if we do that, we will have solved this problem.

Lori Montgomery [Washington Post].

Balanced Budget Amendment/National Debt and Deficit/Budget Debate

Q. Thank you, Mr. President. I wanted to ask you about the two trains that seem to be rolling down the tracks on the Hill. Specifically, Leader McConnell has laid out an elaborate plan to raise the debt limit. He said last night that it looks like they're going to pair that with a new committee that would be tasked with coming up with the big solution that you talk about by the end of the year. Your comment on that proposal.

Meanwhile, in the House, they're saying, well, we can be flexible on some of our demands if we could get a balanced budget amendment. And they note that Vice President Biden voted for a BBA in 1997. Is there any way that that could be part of a solution? Is there any version of a BBA that you would support?

The President. First of all, for the consumption of the general public, BBA meaning a balanced budget amendment.

Q. Thank you.

The President. I think I already addressed this question earlier. We don't need a constitutional amendment to do our jobs. The Constitution already tells us to do our jobs and to make sure that the Government is living within its means and making responsible choices.

And so this notion that we're going to go through a multiyear process instead of seizing the moment now and taking care of our problems is a typical Washington response. We don't need more studies. We don't need a balanced budget amendment. We simply need to make these tough choices and be willing to take on our bases. And everybody knows it. I mean, we could have a discussion right here about what the numbers look like, and we know what's necessary.

And here's the good news: It turns out we don't have to do anything radical to solve this problem. Contrary to what some folks say, we're not Greece, we're not Portugal. It turns out that our problem is we cut taxes without paying for them over the last decade; we ended up instituting new programs like a prescription drug program for seniors that was not paid for; we fought two wars, we didn't pay for them; we had a bad recession that required a Recovery Act and stimulus spending and helping States and all that accumulated and there's interest on top of that.

And to unwind that, what's required is that we roll back those tax cuts on the wealthiest individuals, that we clean up our Tax Code so we're not giving out a bunch of tax breaks to companies that don't need them and are not creating jobs, we cut programs that we don't need, and we invest in those things that are going to help us grow.

And every commission that's been out there has said the same thing and basically taken the same approach, within the margin of error.

So my general view is that if the American people looked at this, they'd say, boy, some of these decisions are tough, but they don't require us to gut Medicare or Social Security. They don't require us to stop helping young people go to college. They don't require us to stop helping families who've got a disabled child. They don't require us to violate our obligations to our veterans. And they don't re-quire—quote, unquote—"job-killing tax cuts." They require us to make some modest adjustments to get our house in order, and we should do it now.

With respect to Senator McConnell's plan, as I said, I think it is a—it is constructive to say that if Washington operates as usual and can't get anything done, let's at least avert Armageddon. That's—I'm glad that people are serious about the consequences of default.

But we have two problems here. One is raising the debt ceiling. This is a problem that was manufactured here in Washington, because every single one of the leaders over there have voted for raising the debt ceiling in the past, and has typically been a difficult, but routine process. And we do have a genuine underlying problem that our debt and deficits are too big. So Senator McConnell's approach solves the first problem. It doesn't solve the second problem. I'd like to solve that second problem.

Q. But are you looking at this option as a more likely outcome at this point? Or can you share with us why you have some hope that the talks that have been going on might actually produce an outcome?

The President. I always have hope. Don't you remember my campaign? [*Laughter*] Even after being here for 2½ years, I continue to have hope. You know why I have hope? It's because of the American people. When I talk to them and I meet with them, as frustrated as they are about this town, they still reflect good common sense. And all we have to do is align with that common sense on this problem, it can get solved.

And I'm assuming that at some point Members of Congress are going to listen. I just want to repeat, every Republican—not—I won't say every. A number of Republican former elected officials—they're not in office now—would say a balanced approach that includes some revenue is the right thing to do. The majority of Republican voters say that approach is the right thing to do. The proposal that I was discussing with Speaker Boehner fell squarely in line with what most Republican voters think we should do. So the question is, at what point

do folks over there start listening to the people who put them in office? Now is a good time.

Sam Youngman [The Hill].

Bipartisanship

Q. Good morning, Mr. President. I'd like to go back to something Chuck asked, his first question, about the tone of this debate. I faintly remember your campaign. And I'm guessing that while it hasn't been ugly, as you say, it's not what you had in mind when you said you wanted to change the tone in Washington. When you have Senator McConnell making comments that he views these negotiations through the prism of 2012, how much does that poison the well? And going forward, if—big if—you can get a deal on this, can you get anything done with Congress for the next year and a half?

The President. Well, let me say this. And I'm not trying to poke at you guys. I generally don't watch what is said about me on cable. I generally don't read what's said about me, even in The Hill. And so part of this job is having a thick skin and understanding that a lot of this stuff is not personal.

That's not going to be an impediment to—whatever Senator McConnell says about me on the floor of the Senate is not going to be an impediment to us getting a deal done. The question is going to be whether at any given moment we're willing to set politics aside, at least briefly, in order to get something done.

I don't expect politicians not to think about politics. But every so often there are issues that are urgent, that have to be attended to, and require us to do things we don't like to do that run contrary to our base, that gets some constituency that helped elect us agitated because they're looking at it from a narrow prism. We're supposed to be stepping back and looking at it from the perspective of what's good for the country. And if we are able to remind ourselves of that, then there's no reason why we shouldn't be able to get things done.

Look, we've been obsessing over the last couple of weeks about raising the debt ceiling and reducing the debt and deficit. I'll tell you what the American people are obsessing about right now is that unemployment is still way too high and too many folks' homes are still underwater and prices of things that they need, not just that they want, are going up a lot faster than their paychecks are if they've got a job.

And so even after we solve this problem we still got a lot of work to do. Hans was mentioning we should renew the payroll tax for another year, we should make sure unemployment insurance is there for another year——

Q. Sir, I don't believe that was my point. [*Laughter*]

The President. But you were making the point about whether or not that issue could be wrapped into this deal. My point is that those are a whole other set of issues that we need to be talking about and working on. I've got an infrastructure bank bill that would start putting construction workers back to work rebuilding our roads and bridges. We should be cooperating on that.

Most of the things that I've proposed to help spur on additional job growth are traditionally bipartisan. I've got three trade deals sitting ready to go. And these are all trade deals that the Republicans told me were their top priorities. They said this would be one of the best job creators that we could have. And yet it's still being held up because some folks don't want to provide trade adjustment assistance to people who may be displaced as a consequence of trade. Surely we can come up with a compromise to solve those problems.

So there will be huge differences between now and November 2012 between the parties, and whoever the Republican nominee is, we're going to have a big, serious debate about what we believe is the right way to guide America forward and to win the future. And I'm confident that I will win that debate, because I think that we've got the better approach. But in the meantime, surely we can, every once in a while, sit down and actually do something that helps the American people right here and right now.

Q. It's in the meantime, sir, that I'm curious about. As you just said, raising the debt ceiling is apparently fairly routine, but it's brought us to the point of economic Armageddon, as you

said. If you can get past this one, how can you get any agreement with Congress on those big issues you talked about?

The President. I am going to keep on working, and I'm going to keep on trying. And what I'm going to do is to hope that, in part, this debate has focused the American people's attention a little bit more and will subject Congress to scrutiny. And I think increasingly the American people are going to say to themselves, you know what, if a party or a politician is constantly taking the position "my way or the high way," constantly being locked into ideologically rigid positions, that we're going to remember at the polls.

It's kind of cumulative. The American people aren't paying attention to the details of every aspect of this negotiation, but I think what the American people are paying attention to is who seems to be trying to get something done, and who seems to be just posturing and trying to score political points. And I think it's going to be in the interests of everybody who wants to continue to serve in this town to make sure that they are on the right side of that impression.

And that's, by the way, what I said in the meeting 2 days ago. I was very blunt. I said the American people do not want to see a bunch of posturing; they don't want to hear a bunch of sound bites. What they want is for us to solve problems, and we all have to remember that. That's why we were sent here.

Last question. Scott Horsley [National Public Radio].

National Debt and Deficit/Budget Debate

Q. Thank you, Mr. President. I wonder if you've seen any sign this week of daily meetings that Republicans are being more aligned with that American majority, or if we are in the same place today that we were on Monday.

The President. It's probably better for you to ask them how they're thinking. I do think that—and I've said this before—Speaker Boehner, in good faith, was trying to see if it was possible to get a big deal done. He had some problems in his caucus. My hope is, is that after some reflection, after we walked through all the numbers this week and we looked at all the options, that there may be some movement, some possibility, some interest to still get something more than the bare minimum done.

But we're running out of time. That's the main concern that I have at this point. We have enough time to do a big deal. I've got reams of paper and printouts and spreadsheets on my desk, and so we know how we can create a package that solves the deficits and debt for a significant period of time. But in order to do that, we got to get started now. And that's why I'm expecting some answers from all the congressional leaders sometime in the next couple of days.

And I have to say this is tough on the Democratic side too. Some of the things that I've talked about and said I would be willing to see happen, there are some Democrats who think that's absolutely unacceptable. And so that's where I'd have a selling job, Chuck, is trying to sell some of our party that if you are a progressive, you should be concerned about debt and deficit just as much as if you're a conservative. And the reason is because if the only thing we're talking about over the next year, 2 years, 5 years, is debt and deficits, then it's very hard

to start talking about how do we make investments in community colleges so that our kids are trained, how do we actually rebuild $2 trillion worth of crumbling infrastructure.

If you care about making investments in our kids and making investments in our infrastructure and making investments in basic research, then you should want our fiscal house in order, so that every time we propose a new initiative somebody doesn't just throw up their hands and say, "Ah, more big spending, more Government."

It would be very helpful for us to be able to say to the American people, our fiscal house is in order. And so now the question is: What should we be doing to win the future and make ourselves more competitive and create more jobs, and what aspects of what Government is doing are a waste and we should eliminate. And that's the kind of debate that I'd like to have.

All right? Thank you, guys.

NOTE: The President's news conference began at 10:58 a.m. in the James S. Brady Press Briefing Room at the White House. In his remarks, the President referred to Erskine B. Bowles and Alan K. Simpson, Cochairs, National Commission on Fiscal Responsibility and Reform.

Statement on Representative Dale E. Kildee's Decision Not To Seek Reelection
July 15, 2011

For more than 30 years, Dale Kildee has never forgotten the people he represents or what drives his work in the United States Congress. As a teacher, State legislator, and Congressman, Dale made fighting for the families he represents his top priority and worked to improve education in Michigan and across the Nation. We will miss Dale's voice in Congress. Michelle and I wish him well and join the people of Michigan in thanking him for his many years of service.

Letter to Congressional Leaders on Review of Title III of the Cuban Liberty and Democratic Solidarity (LIBERTAD) Act of 1996
July 15, 2011

Dear _____:

Consistent with section 306(c)(2) of the Cuban Liberty and Democratic Solidarity (LIBERTAD) Act of 1996 (Public Law 104–114) (the "Act"), I hereby determine and report to the Congress that suspension, for 6 months beyond August 1, 2011, of the right to bring an action under title III of the Act is necessary to the national interests of the United States and will expedite a transition to democracy in Cuba.

Sincerely,

BARACK OBAMA

NOTE: Identical letters were sent to Daniel K. Inouye, chairman, and W. Thad Cochran, ranking member, Senate Committee on Appropriations; John F. Kerry, chairman, and Richard G. Lugar, ranking member, Senate Committee on Foreign Relations; Harold D. Rogers, chairman, and Norman D. Dicks, ranking member, House Committee on Appropriations; and Ileana Ros-Lehtinen, chairman, and Howard L. Berman, ranking member, House Committee on Foreign Affairs.

The President's Weekly Address
July 16, 2011

Today, there's a debate going on in Washington over the best way to get America's fiscal house in order and get our economy on a stronger footing going forward.

For a decade, America has been spending more money than we've taken in. And for several decades, our debt has been rising. Let's be honest, neither party in this town is blameless. Both have talked this problem to death without doing enough about it. And that's what drives people nuts about Washington. Too often, it's a place more concerned with playing politics and serving special interests than resolving real problems or focusing on what you're facing in your own lives.

But right now we have a responsibility and an opportunity to reduce our deficit as much as possible and solve this problem in a real and comprehensive way.

Simply put, it will take a balanced approach, shared sacrifice, and a willingness to make unpopular choices on all our parts. That means spending less on domestic programs. It means spending less on defense programs. It means reforming programs like Medicare to reduce costs and strengthen the program for future generations. And it means taking on the Tax Code and cutting out certain tax breaks and deductions for the wealthiest Americans.

Now, some of these things don't make folks in my party too happy. And I wouldn't agree to some of these cuts if we were in a better fiscal situation. But we're not. That's why I'm willing to compromise. I'm willing to do what it takes to solve this problem, even if it's not politically popular. And I expect leaders in Congress to show that same willingness to compromise.

The truth is, you can't solve our deficit without cutting spending. But you also can't solve it without asking the wealthiest Americans to pay their fair share or without taking on loopholes that give special interests and big corporations tax breaks that middle class Americans don't get.

It's pretty simple. I don't think oil companies should keep getting special tax breaks when they're making tens of billions in profits. I don't think hedge fund managers should pay taxes at a lower rate than their secretaries. And I don't think it's fair to ask nothing of someone like me when the average family has seen their income decline over the past decade and when many of you are just trying to stretch every dollar as far it will go.

We shouldn't put the burden of deficit reduction on the backs of folks who've already borne the brunt of the recession. It's not reasonable, and it's not right. If we're going to ask seniors or students or middle class Americans to sacrifice, then we have to ask corporations and the wealthiest Americans to share in that sacrifice. We have to ask everyone to play their part because we are all part of the same country. We're all in this together.

So I've put things on the table that are important to me and to Democrats, and I expect Republican leaders to do the same. After all, we've worked together like that before. Ronald Reagan worked with Tip O'Neill and Democrats to cut spending, raise revenues, and reform Social Security. Bill Clinton worked with Newt Gingrich and Republicans to balance the budget and create surpluses. Nobody ever got everything they wanted. But eventually they worked together, and they moved this country forward.

That kind of cooperation should be the least you expect from us, not the most you expect

867

from us. You work hard, you do what's right, and you expect leaders who do the same. You sent us to Washington to do the tough things, the right things, not just for some of us, but for all of us; not just what's enough to get through the next election, but what's right for the next generation.

You expect us to get this right, to put America back on firm economic ground, to forge a healthy, growing economy, to create new jobs and rebuild the lives of the middle class. And that's what I'm committed to doing.

Thanks.

NOTE: The address was recorded at approximately 2:15 p.m. on July 15 in the Library at the White House for broadcast on July 16. In the address, the President referred to former Speaker of the House of Representatives Newton L. Gingrich. The transcript was made available by the Office of the Press Secretary on July 15, but was embargoed for release until 6 a.m. on July 16.

Statement on Nelson Mandela International Day
July 17, 2011

As the people of the world celebrate Nelson Mandela's 93d birthday on July 18, Madiba continues to be a beacon for the global community and for all who work for democracy, justice, and reconciliation. On behalf of the people of the United States, we congratulate Nelson Mandela and honor his vision for a better world.

Nelson Mandela said, "There is no passion to be found playing small, in settling for a life that is less than the one you are capable of living." A man who devoted 67 years of his life to public service, Madiba sets the standard for service worldwide, whether we are students, shopkeepers, or farmers, Cabinet Ministers or Presidents. He calls on us to serve our fellow human beings and better our communities.

Michelle and my daughters Sasha and Malia recently met Madiba during an official visit to South Africa that focused on service, youth leadership, education, and healthy living. Their time with Madiba was the most moving part of their trip. Mandela's legacy exemplifies wisdom, strength, and grace, and on the anniversary of his birth, we salute the example of his life.

In 2009, the United States was honored to join 192 other United Nations member states in the creation of Nelson Mandela International Day. As the global community honors Madiba on July 18 through individual and collective acts of service, we honor the man who showed his own people and the world the path to justice, reconciliation, and democracy.

Remarks on the Nomination of Richard A. Cordray To Be Director of the Consumer Financial Protection Bureau and an Exchange With Reporters
July 18, 2011

The President. Good afternoon, everybody. It has been almost 3 years since the financial crisis pulled the economy into a deep recession. And millions of families are still hurting because of it. They're trying to get by on one income instead of two, on fewer shifts at the plant or at the hospital. They're cutting expenses, giving up on a family night out so there's money for groceries. And for a lot of families, things were tough even before the recession.

So we've got to get the economy growing faster and make sure that small businesses can hire again, so that an entrepreneur out there can sell a new product, so that the middle class is getting stronger again, and so folks feel confident in their futures and their children's futures.

That's why we can't let politics stand in the way of doing the right thing in Washington. We can't stand in the way when it comes to doing the right thing on deficits. And that's why I want to take steps like making sure payroll taxes for middle class families don't go back up next year. That's why it's so important that we tackle the problems that led us into this recession in the first place.

One of the biggest problems was that the tables were tilted against ordinary people in the financial system. When you get a home loan, it came with pages of fine print. When you got a credit card, it was as if the contract was written in another language. These kinds of things opened the door to unscrupulous practices: loans with hidden fees and terms that meant your rate could double overnight. It led to people getting mortgages they couldn't afford, and it put honest businesses at a disadvantage. And it encouraged dangerously risky behavior on Wall Street, which dragged the economy into the mess that we're still trying to clean up.

That's why we passed financial reform a year ago. It was a commonsense law that did three things. First, it made taxpayer-funded bailouts illegal, so taxpayers don't have to foot the bill if a big bank goes under. Second, it said to Wall Street firms, you can't take the same kind of reckless risks that led to the crisis. And third, it put in place the stronger—the strongest consumer protections in history.

Now, to make sure that these protections worked—so ordinary people were dealt with fairly, so they could make informed decisions about their finances—we didn't just change the law. We changed the way the Government did business. For years, the job of protecting consumers was divided up in a lot of different agencies. So if you had a problem with a mortgage lender, you called one place. If you had a problem with a credit card company, you called somebody else. It meant there were a lot of people who were responsible, but that meant nobody was responsible.

And we changed that. We cut the bureaucracy and put one consumer watchdog in charge, with just one job: looking out for regular people in the financial system. Now, this is an idea that I got from Elizabeth Warren, who I first met years ago. Back then—this is long before the financial crisis—Elizabeth was sounding the alarm on predatory lending and the financial pressures on middle class families. And in the years since, she's become perhaps the leading voice in our country on behalf of consumers. And let's face it, she's done it while facing some very tough opposition and drawing a fair amount of heat. Fortunately, she's very tough.

And that's why I asked Elizabeth Warren to set up this new bureau. Over the past year, she has done an extraordinary job. Already, the agency is starting to do a whole bunch of things that are going to be important for consumers: making sure loan contracts and credit card terms are simpler and written in plain English. Already, thanks to the leadership of the bureau, we're seeing men and women in uniform who are getting more protections against fraud and deception when it comes to financial practices. And as part of her charge, I asked Elizabeth to find the best possible choice for Director of the Bureau.

And that's who we found in Richard Cordray. Richard was one of the first people that Elizabeth recruited, and he's helped stand up the Bureau's enforcement division over the past 6 months. I should also point out that he took this job, which meant being away from his wife and 12-year-old twins back in Ohio, because he believed so deeply in the mission of the Bureau. Prior to this, as Ohio's attorney general, Rich helped recover billions of dollars in things like pension funds on behalf of retirees, and stepped up the State's efforts against unscrupulous lending practices. He's also served as Ohio's treasurer and has successfully worked with people across the ideological spectrum: Democrats and Republicans, banks and consumer advocates.

Now, last but not least, back in the eighties, Richard was also a five-time Jeopardy champion—[*laughter*]—and a semifinalist in the Tournament of Champions. Not too shabby. That's why all his confirmation—all his answers at his confirmation hearings will be in the form of a question. That's a joke. [*Laughter*]

So I am proud to nominate Richard Cordray to this post. And we've been recently reminded why this job is going to be so important. There is an army of lobbyists and lawyers right now working to water down the protections and the reforms that we passed. They've already spent tens of millions of dollars this year to try to weaken the laws that are designed to protect consumers. And they've got allies in Congress who are trying to undo the progress that we've made. We're not going to let that happen.

The fact is the financial crisis and the recession were not the result of normal economic cycles or just a run of bad luck. They were abuses and there was a lack of smart regulations. So we're not just going to shrug our shoulders and hope it doesn't happen again. We're not going to go back to the status quo where consumers couldn't count on getting protections that they deserved. We're not going to go back to a time when our whole economy was vulnerable to a massive financial crisis. That's why reform matters. That's why this Bureau matters. I will fight any efforts to repeal or undermine the important changes that we passed. And we are going to stand up this Bureau and make sure it is doing the right thing for middle class families all across the country.

Middle class families and seniors don't have teams of lawyers from blue chip law firms. They can't afford to hire a lobbyist to look out for their interests. But they deserve to be treated honestly. They deserve a basic measure of protection against abuse. They shouldn't have to be a corporate lawyer in order to be able to read something they're signing to take out a mortgage or to get a credit card. They ought to be free to make informed decisions, to buy a home or open a credit card or take out a student loan, and they should have confidence that they're not being swindled. And that's what this Consumer Bureau will achieve.

I look forward to working with Richard Cordray as this bureau stands up on behalf of consumers all across the country. I want to thank both Elizabeth and Tim Geithner for the extraordinary work that they've done over at Treasury to make sure that, a year after we passed this law, it is already having an impact and it's going to have impact for years to come.

Thank you very much and congratulations, Rich.

National Debt and Deficit/Budget Debate

Q. Mr. President, any progress in your talks with Speaker Boehner yesterday? Any progress?

The President. We're making progress.

NOTE: The President spoke at 1:15 p.m. in the Rose Garden at the White House. In his remarks, he referred to Margaret "Peggy" Cordray, wife, and Danny and Holly Cordray, children, of Director-designate Cordray.

Remarks Prior to White House Press Secretary James F. "Jay" Carney's Briefing and an Exchange With Reporters
July 19, 2011

The President. Hello, everybody. I wanted to give folks a quick update on the progress that we're making on the debt ceiling discussions.

I was in contact with all the leadership over the course of the weekend and continued to urge both Democrats and Republicans to come together around an approach that not only lifts the debt ceiling, but also solves the underlying challenges that we face when it comes to debt and deficits.

Some progress was made in some of the discussions, some narrowing of the issues. Speaker Boehner and the Republican House caucus felt it necessary to put forward the plan that they're going to be voting on today. I think everyone's estimation is, is that that is not an approach that could pass both Chambers, it's not an approach that I would sign, and it's not balanced. But I understand the need for them to test that proposition.

The problem we have now is we're in the 11th hour, and we don't have a lot more time left. The good news is that today a group of Senators, the Gang of Six, Democrats and Republicans—I guess now Gang of Seven, because one additional Republican Senator added on—put forward a proposal that is broadly consistent with the approach that I've urged.

What it says is we've got to be serious about reducing discretionary spending both in domestic spending and defense, we've got to be serious about tackling health care spending and entitlements in a serious way, and we've got to have some additional revenue so that we have an approach in which there is shared sacrifice and everybody is giving up something.

And so for us to see Democratic Senators acknowledge that we've got to deal with our long-term debt problems that arise out of our various entitlement programs and for Republican Senators to acknowledge that revenues will have to be part of a balanced package that makes sure that nobody is disproportionately hurt from us making progress on the debt and deficits, I think, is a very significant step. And as I said, the framework that they put forward is broadly consistent with what we've been working on here in the White House and with the presentations that I've made to the leadership when they've come over here.

So here's where we stand. We have a Democratic President and administration that is prepared to sign a tough package that includes both spending cuts, modifications to Social Security, Medicaid, and Medicare that would strengthen those systems and allow them to move forward and would include a revenue component. We now have a bipartisan group of Senators who agree with that balanced approach. And we've got the American people who agree with that balanced approach.

My hope, and what I will be urging Speaker Boehner, Nancy Pelosi, as well as Leader Reid and Mitch McConnell, is that they, tomorrow, are prepared to start talking turkey and actually getting down to the hard business of crafting a plan that can move this forward in time for the August 2 deadline that we've set forward.

Just a couple of other points I will make. Some of you may ask, what does it mean for the plan that Senator McConnell and Senator Reid had been working on? Our attitude is, is that that continues to be a necessary approach to put forward. In the event that we don't get an agreement, at minimum, we've got to raise the debt ceiling. So that's the bare minimum

that has to be achieved, but we continue to believe that we can achieve more.

And so I want to congratulate the Gang of Six for coming up with a plan that I think is balanced. We just received it, so we haven't reviewed all the details of it. It would not match perfectly with some of the approaches that we've taken, but I think that we're in the same playing field. And my hope is, is that we can start gathering everybody over the next couple of days to choose a clear direction and to get this issue resolved.

So far at least, the markets have shown confidence that leadership here in Washington are not going to send the economy over a cliff. But if we continue to go through a lot of political posturing, if both sides continue to be dug in, if we don't have a basic spirit of cooperation that allows us to rise above immediate election year politics and actually solve problems, then I think markets here, the American people, and the international community are going to start reacting adversely fairly quickly.

So I think it's very important for in these next couple of days to understand we don't have any more time to engage in symbolic gestures, we don't have any more time to posture. It's time to get down to the business of actually solving this problem. And I think we now are seeing the potential for a bipartisan consensus around what that would take.

It will be hard. It will be tough. There are still going to be a lot of difficult negotiations that have to take place in order for us to actually get something done. And as I said, we have to have that fail-safe that Senator McConnell and Senator Reid are working on. But the hope is, is that everybody seizes this opportunity.

All right? Okay, guys, I'm going to let Jay answer questions today. I think I've been pretty good to you guys. [*Laughter*] But after the votes today in the House, I'll call up Speaker Boehner and the other leadership, and we'll arrange for times where we bring folks back here, and hopefully, we'll be able to report on some additional progress over the next few days.

All right? Thank you very much, guys.

National Debt and Deficit

Q. When will you announce whether you will be supporting the Gang of Six plan? Would that be in the next day?

The President. Well, as I said, I think what you're going to be seeing is an evaluation of that plan versus the things that we've been looking at. I think what you're going to see is some significant overlap. But obviously, just because we might agree in principle with a range of issues with six Senators or seven Senators, that doesn't get us out of the House of Representatives; that doesn't get us out of the Senate. There's going to have to be a broader agreement on the part of all the leadership that we're going to get this done in a serious way, and we've got a tight deadline to do it.

All right? Thanks, guys.

NOTE: The President spoke at 1:32 p.m. in the James S. Brady Press Briefing Room at the White House. In his remarks, he referred to Sens. Saxby C. Chambliss, Thomas A. Coburn, G. Kent Conrad, Michael D. Crapo, Richard J. Durbin, and Mark R. Warner.

Message to the Congress on Continuation of the National Emergency With Respect to the Former Liberian Regime of Charles Taylor
July 20, 2011

To the Congress of the United States:

Section 202(d) of the National Emergencies Act (50 U.S.C. 1622(d)) provides for the automatic termination of a national emergency unless, prior to the anniversary date of its declaration, the President publishes in the *Federal Register* and transmits to the Congress a notice stating that the emergency is to continue in effect beyond the anniversary date. In accordance with this provision, I have sent the enclosed notice to the *Federal Register* for publication stating that the national emergency and related measures dealing with the former regime of Charles Taylor are to continue in effect beyond July 22, 2011.

The actions and policies of former Liberian President Charles Taylor and other persons, in particular their unlawful depletion of Liberian resources and their removal from Liberia and secreting of Liberian funds and property, continue to undermine Liberia's transition to democracy and the orderly development of its political, administrative, and economic institutions and resources. These actions and policies continue to pose an unusual and extraordinary threat to the foreign policy of the United States. For this reason, I have determined that it is necessary to continue the national emergency with respect to the former Liberian regime of Charles Taylor.

BARACK OBAMA

The White House,
July 20, 2011.

NOTE: The notice is listed in Appendix D at the end of this volume.

Remarks at a Town Hall Meeting and a Question-and-Answer Session in College Park, Maryland
July 22, 2011

The President. Hello, Maryland! Hello! Nice to see you. Thank you so much. Everybody, please have a seat. I see some smart folks up there wore shorts. [*Laughter*] My team said I should not wear shorts. [*Laughter*] My legs aren't good enough to wear shorts.

Audience member. Yes, they are! [*Laughter*]

The President. Thank you. I'll tell Michelle you said so. [*Laughter*]

It is wonderful to be back in Maryland. I hope everybody is keeping cool, staying hydrated. It is great to be back here in College Park.

I have a few acknowledgments that I want to make, some special guests that we have. First of all, one of the best Governors in the country, Martin O'Malley is in the house. Where's Martin? He was here. There he is over there. By the way, for those of you who have not heard him, outstanding singer and rock-and-roller. So if you ever want to catch his band, it is top notch.

Also, one of the best Senators in the country, Ben Cardin is in the house. We've got College Park Mayor Andrew Fellows is here. Former Congressman Frank Kratovil is here. You wouldn't know it looking at him, but Frank is an outstanding basketball player. [*Laughter*] The Terps might be able to use him even at this age. [*Laughter*] He is a point guard, got all kinds of moves. [*Laughter*]

And I want to thank your still quasi-new president here at Maryland, Wallace Loh, for the outstanding work that he's doing.

So this is a town hall. I want to spend some time answering some of your questions, but just want to say a few things at the top. First of all, I have to say it's nice to get out of Washington. [*Laughter*] Don't get me wrong, there's nothing I enjoy more than sitting, hour after hour, day after day—[*laughter*]—debating the fine points of the Federal budget with Members of Congress. [*Laughter*] But after a while you do start feeling a little cooped up. So I'm happy to be spending my morning with you.

I'm going to spend most of my time answering your questions, but let me do say a few words about the debate that's taking place right now in Washington, about debt and deficits. Obviously, it's dominating the news. Even though it's taking place in Washington, this is actually a debate about you and everybody else in America and the choices that we face.

And most people here, whether you're still a student or you're a graduate or you're a parent, your number-one concern is the economy. That's my number-one concern. It's the first

thing I think about when I wake up in the morning; it's the last thing I think about when I go to bed at night. And I won't be satisfied until every American who wants a job can find one and until workers are getting paychecks that actually pay the bills, until families don't have to choose between buying groceries and buying medicine, between sending their kids to college and being able to retire in some dignity and some respect.

So we have gone through a very difficult 2½ years, the worst financial crisis and the worst recession we've seen since the Great Depression. And although some progress has been made, there's no doubt that this economy has not recovered as fast as it needs to. And the truth is, it's going to take more time, because a lot of the problems that we're facing right now—slow job growth, stagnant wages—those were there even before the recession hit.

For a decade, the average income, the average income of the American worker had flatlined. Those at the very top saw their incomes going up 50 percent, 100 percent. But those in the middle, the vast majority of Americans, they had been struggling to keep up before the recession hit.

And so these challenges weren't caused overnight; they're not going to be solved overnight. But as John F. Kennedy once said, "Our problems are manmade, therefore they can be solved by man."

In the United States, we control our own destiny. The question we have to answer, though, is: Where do we want to go? What's our vision for the future, and how do we get there? Now, in the short term, I've been urging Congress to pass some proposals that would give the economy an immediate boost. And these are proposals, by the way, that traditionally have had support in both parties.

I want to extend the tax relief that we put in place back in December for middle class families so that you have more money in your paychecks next year. If you've got more money in your paychecks next year, you're more likely to spend it, and that means small businesses and medium-sized businesses and large businesses will have more customers. And they'll be in a position to hire.

I want to give more opportunities to all those construction workers out there who lost their jobs when the housing bubble went bust. We could put them to work, giving loans to private companies that want to repair our roads and our bridges and our airports, rebuilding our infrastructure, putting Americans to work doing the work that needs to be done. We have workers in need of a job and a country that's in need of rebuilding, and if we put those two things together we can make real progress.

I want to cut redtape that stops too many inventors and entrepreneurs from turning new ideas into thriving businesses. I want Congress to send me a set of trade deals that would allow our businesses to sell more products in countries in Asia and South America that are stamped with the words "Made in America."

So these are some things that we could be doing right now. There are proposals in Congress, as we speak, and Congress needs to act now. But I also believe that over the long term, the strength of our economy is going to depend on how we deal with the accumulated debt and deficits that have built up over the last decade. And that's what the discussion in Washington is about right now.

Now, I know it's hard to keep up with the different plans and the press conferences and the back and forth between the parties, but here's what it all boils down to; it's not that complicated: For a decade, we have been spending more money than we take in. Last time the budget was balanced was under a Democratic President, Bill Clinton. And a series of decisions were made—whether it was cutting taxes or engaging in two wars or a prescription drug benefit for seniors—that weren't paid for, and then a financial crisis on top of that, Recovery Act to try to pull us out of a Great Depression—all those things contributed to this accumulated debt.

And regardless of what you feel about the particular policies—some of you may have supported the wars or opposed the wars; some of you may have agreed with the Recovery Act, some of you may be opposed—regardless of

your views on these various actions that were taken, the fact is they all cost money. And the result is that there's simply too much debt on America's credit card.

Neither party is blameless for the decisions that led to this problem, but both parties have a responsibility to solve it. If we don't solve it, every American will suffer. Businesses will be less likely to invest and hire in America. Interest rates will rise for people who need money to buy a home or a car or go to college. We won't have enough money to invest in things like education and clean energy or protect important programs like Medicare, because we'll be paying more and more interest on this national debt and that money just flows overseas instead of being spent here on the things that we need.

Now, the one thing we can't do—cannot do—is decide that we are not going to pay the bills the previous Congresses have already racked up. So that's what this whole issue of raising the debt ceiling is all about. Basically, there are some people out there who argue we're not going to raise the debt ceiling any more. And the problem is, effectively what that's saying is, we're not going to pay some of our bills. Well, the United States of America does not run out without paying the tab. We pay our bills. We meet our obligations. We have never defaulted on our debt. We're not going to do it now.

But even if we raise the debt ceiling, this debate shouldn't just be about avoiding some kind of crisis, particularly a crisis manufactured in Washington. This is a rare opportunity for both parties to come together and choose a path where we stop putting so much debt on our credit card. We start paying it down a little bit. And that's what we've been trying to do.

So for my part, I've already said that I'm willing to cut a historic amount of Government spending in order to reduce the deficit. I'm willing to cut spending on domestic programs, taking them to the lowest level since Dwight Eisenhower. I'm willing to cut defense spending at the Pentagon by hundreds of billions of dollars. I'm willing to take on the rising costs of health care programs like Medicare and Medicaid so that these programs will be there for the next generation, for folks—for a population generally that's getting older and living longer. We've got to make sure that these programs, which are the crown jewels of our social safety net, that—sort of mixed metaphors there— [*laughter*]—that those are there for the future.

And some of these cuts would just eliminate wasteful spending: weapons we don't need, fraud and abuse in our health care system. But I want to be honest. I've agreed to also target some programs that I actually think are worthwhile. They're cuts that some people in my own party aren't too happy about. And frankly, I wouldn't make them if money wasn't so tight. But it's just like a family. If you've got to tighten your belts, you make some choices.

Now, here's the thing, though—and this is what the argument is about—we can't just close our deficit with spending cuts alone, because if we take that route, it means that seniors would have to pay a lot more for Medicare or students would have to pay a lot more for student loans. It means that laid-off workers might not be able to count on temporary assistance or training to help them get a new job. It means we'd have to make devastating cuts in education and medical research and clean energy research, just at a time when gas prices are killing people at the pump.

So if we only did it with cuts, if we did not get any revenue to help close this gap between how much money is coming in and how much money is going out, then a lot of ordinary people would be hurt and the country as a whole would be hurt. And that doesn't make any sense. It's not fair.

And that's why I've said if we're going to reduce our deficit, then the wealthiest Americans and the biggest corporations should do their part as well. Before we stop funding clean energy research, let's ask oil companies and corporate jet owners to give up the tax breaks that other companies don't get. I mean, these are special tax breaks. Before we ask college students to pay more for their education, let's ask hedge fund managers to stop paying taxes that are lower on their rates than their secretaries. Before we ask seniors to pay more for

Medicare, let's ask people like me to give up tax breaks that we don't need and we weren't even asking for.

Look, I want everybody in America to do well. I want everybody to have a chance to become a millionaire. I think the free market system is the greatest wealth generator we've ever known. This isn't about punishing wealth, it's about asking people who have benefited the most over the last decade to share in the sacrifice. And I think these patriotic Americans are willing to pitch in—if they're asked—because they know that middle class families shouldn't have to pick up the whole tab for closing the deficit.

So this idea of balance, this idea of shared sacrifice, of a deficit plan that includes tough spending cuts, but also includes tax reform that raises more revenue, this isn't just my position. This isn't just the Democratic position. This isn't some wild-eyed socialist position. [*Laughter*] I mean, this is a position that's being taken by people of both parties and no party. It's a position taken by Warren Buffet, somebody who knows about business and knows a little something about being wealthy. [*Laughter*] It's a position that's been taken by every Democratic and Republican President who've signed major deficit deals in the past, from Ronald Reagan to Bill Clinton. And I was pleased to see this week that it's a position taken by Democrats and Republicans in the Senate.

So we can pass a balanced plan like this. It's not going to make everybody happy. In fact, it will make everybody somewhat unhappy. The easiest thing for a politician to do is to give you more stuff and ask less in return. It's a lot harder to say, we got to cut back on what you're getting and you got to pay a little more. That's never fun. But we can do it in a balanced way that doesn't hurt anybody badly, that doesn't put the burden just on one group.

So we can solve our deficit problem. And I'm willing to sign a plan that includes tough choices I would not normally make, and there are a lot of Democrats and Republicans in Congress who, I believe, are willing to do the same thing. The only people we have left to convince are some folks in the House of

Representatives. We're going to keep working on that. [*Laughter*] Because I still believe we can do what you sent us here to do.

In 2010, Americans chose a divided Government, but they didn't choose a dysfunctional Government. And—[*applause*]. So there will be time for political campaigning, but right now this debate shouldn't be about putting on—scoring political points. It should be about doing what's right for the country, for everybody. You expect us to work together. You expect us to compromise. You've all been working hard. You've been doing whatever you have to do in order to get by and raise your families. You're meeting your responsibilities. So it's time for those of us in Washington to do the same thing. And I intend to make that happen in the coming days.

So thank you, everybody. Let me take some questions.

All right, so the way this works is you put up your hand and I call on you. [*Laughter*] But I am going to go girl, boy, girl, boy to make sure that it's even and fair. All right? So I'm going to start with you right there.

Yes. Hold on, we got a mike here, so—and introduce yourself if you don't mind.

Freedom of Religion

Q. Hello, Mr. President.

The President. Hi.

Q. My name is Amanda Knief—and I'm a big fan. I'm from Iowa, originally.

The President. Nice.

Q. Yes. [*Laughter*] I'm an atheist. And in Zanesville, Ohio, in 2008, you asserted that no organization receiving taxpayer funds would be able to discriminate in hiring or firing based on a person's religion. However, you have not rescinded the Executive order that permits this type of discrimination. In a time of economic hardship, when it is difficult for a person to get a job based on her skills, what would you say to a woman who has been denied employment because of her religion or lack of religious beliefs by a taxpayer-funded organization?

The President. Well, this is a very difficult issue, but a more narrow one than, I think, might be implied. It's very straightforward that

people shouldn't be discriminated against for race, gender, sexual orientation, and—or religious affiliation.

What has happened is, is that there has been a carve-out, dating back to President Clinton's Presidency, for religious organizations in their hiring for particular purposes. And this is always a tricky part of the First Amendment. On the one hand, the First Amendment ensures that there's freedom of religion. On the other hand, we want to make sure that religious bodies are abiding by general laws.

And so where this issue has come up is in fairly narrow circumstances where, for example, you've got a faith-based organization that's providing certain services; they consider part of their mission to be promoting their religious views, but they may have a daycare center associated with the organization, or they may be running a food pantry, and so then the question is, does a Jewish organization have to hire a non-Jewish person as part of that organization?

Now, I think that the balance we've tried to strike is to say that if you are offering—if you have set up a nonprofit that is disassociated from your core religious functions and is out there in the public doing all kinds of work, then you have to abide generally with the nondiscrimination hiring practices. If, on the other hand, it is closer to your core functions as a synagogue or a mosque or a church, then there may be more leeway for you to hire somebody who is a believer of that particular religious faith.

It doesn't satisfy everybody. I will tell you that a lot of faith-based organizations think that we are too restrictive in how we define those issues. There are others like you, obviously, who think that we're not restrictive enough. I think we've struck the right balance so far. But this is something that we continue to be in dialogue with faith-based organizations about to try to make sure that their hiring practices are as open and as inclusive as possible.

Okay? Thank you.

Yes, sir. Back here. Hold on a second; we got a mike.

National Debt and Deficit

Q. Yes. Most of the American people are on your side about a balanced approach.

The President. Right.

Q. What we also know is most of the budget cuts are going to be in the out-years. So the question is, why push so hard for a big settlement now, when if you push hard and let the American people vote in 2012 and get rid of these hooligans in the House, we might actually have a reasonable settlement, maybe more like a 1-to-1 relationship instead of 3 to 1 or worse?

The President. The challenge I have in these negotiations is, whether I like it or not, I've got to get the debt ceiling limit raised.

Q. The 14th Amendment?

The President. Well, I'll answer that question later. But I just want to make sure that everybody understands defaulting is not an option.

There are some on either side that have suggested that somehow we could manage our way through. But I just want everybody to be clear, the United States Government sends out about 70 million checks every month. We have to refinance bonds that we've issued, essentially IOUs to investors. We do that every week. If suddenly, investors—and by the way, a lot of those investors are Americans who have Treasury bills, pension funds, et cetera—if suddenly they started thinking that we might not pay them back on time, at the very least, at the bare minimum, they would higher—charge a much higher interest rate to allow the United States to borrow money.

And if interest rate costs go up for the United States, they're probably going to go up for everybody. So it would be a indirect tax on every single one of you. Your credit card interest rates would go up. Your mortgage interest would go up. Your student loan interest would potentially go up. And ironically, the costs of servicing our deficit would go up, which means it would actually potentially be worse for our deficit if we had default. It could also plunge us back into the kind of recession that we had back in 2008 and '09. So it is not an option for us to default.

My challenge, then, is I've got to get something passed. I've got to get 218 votes in the House of Representatives.

Now, the gentleman asked about the 14th Amendment. There's a provision in our Constitution that speaks to making sure that the United States meets its obligations. And there have been some suggestions that a President could use that language to basically ignore this debt ceiling rule, which is a statutory rule. It's not a constitutional rule. I have talked to my lawyers. They do not—they are not persuaded that that is a winning argument. So the challenge for me is to make sure that we do not default, but to do so in a way that is as balanced as possible and gets us at least a downpayment on solving this problem.

Now, we're not going to solve the entire debt and deficit in the next 10 days. So there's still going to be more work to do after this. And what we're doing is to try to make sure that any deal that we strike protects our core commitments to Medicare and Medicaid recipients, to senior citizens, to veterans. We want to make sure that student loans remain affordable. We want to make sure that poor kids can still get a checkup, that food stamps are still available for folks who are desperately in need. We want to make sure that unemployment insurance continues for those who are out there looking for work.

So there are going to be a certain set of equities that we're not willing to sacrifice. And I've said we have to have some revenue as part of the package.

But I'm sympathetic to your view that this would be easier if I could do this entirely on my own. [*Laughter*] It would mean all these conversations that I've had over the last 3 weeks, I could have been spending time with Malia and Sasha instead. But that's not how our democracy works. And as I said, Americans made a decision about divided Government. I'm going to be making the case as to why I think we've got a better vision for the country. In the meantime, we've got a responsibility to do our job.

But it was an excellent question. Thank you.

All right. Young lady right here, right in the front. Yes, hold on, let's get you a mike so we can hear you. Stand up. What's your name?

The President's Accomplishments

Q. My name is Kasa. I have two questions. One is, is there anything—like, obviously, you've had a successful Presidency, but is there anything——

The President. Well, that's not obvious to everyone. [*Laughter*] But I appreciate you thinking it's obvious.

Q. I think it's successful; that's all that matters. But is there anything you regret or would have done differently? And my second question is, can I shake your hand? [*Laughter*]

The President. Yes, I'll come and shake your hand, I promise. I will. [*Laughter*] Do I have any major regrets? You know, when I think— and I think about this all the time. I mean, I'm constantly rerunning in my head did we make the right move here, could we have done more there. I think, overall, in an extremely difficult situation, we've made good choices, we've made good decisions.

Now, but we've been constrained, even when we had a Democratic Congress, because the way the Senate works these days is you've got to get essentially 60 votes in order to get anything through the Senate. Frank remembers this, because we got a lot of good stuff out of the House that never survived in the Senate. So because of what's—the rules of the filibuster in the Senate, it meant that, on economic policy, I might have done some things more aggressively if I could have convinced more Republicans in the Senate to go along.

I do think that in the first year, right after we found out that 4 million people had lost their jobs before I was sworn in, I think that I could have told the American people more clearly how tough this was going to be, how deep and long lasting this recession was going to be.

That's always a balance for a President. On the one hand, you want to project confidence and optimism. And remember, in that first year, people weren't sure whether the banking system was going to melt down and whether we were going to go into a great depression.

And so it was important for me to let the American people know we're going to be all right, we're going to be able to get through this.

On the other hand, I think maybe people's expectations were that somehow we were going to be able to solve this in a year. And we knew pretty soon after I took office that this was going to last for a while, because, historically, when you have recessions that arise out of financial crises, they last a lot longer than the usual business cycle recessions.

Beyond that, I also think that over the first 2 years I was so focused on policy and getting the policy right, that sometimes I forgot part of my job is explaining to the American people why we're doing this policy and where we're going. And so I think a lot of people started trying to figure out, well, how do all these pieces fit together. The auto industry has been saved, and that was a good thing. Well, that saved a million jobs, but people weren't sure how did that relate to our housing strategy or how did that relate to health care. And so I think that was something that I could have done better.

That's just two items on what I'm sure are a very long list—[*laughter*]—of things that I could do better. But having said that, the basic thrust of my first 2½ years have been entirely consistent with what I said I was going to do during the campaign, because what I promised was that not only were we going to deal with the immediate crisis, I said we are going to start laying the foundation for us to solve some of these long-term problems.

So when we changed, for example, the student loan program to take billions of dollars that were going to the banks, as middlemen in the student loan program, and redirected them so that students—millions more students— would benefit from things like Pell grants, that was in pursuit of this larger goal that we have to once again be the Nation that has the highest percentage of college graduates and that we have the best skilled workforce, because that's what it's going to take to win the future.

When we initiated health care reform, it was based on a long-term assessment that if we don't get control of our health care costs and stop sending people to the emergency room for very expensive care, but instead make sure they've got adequate coverage so that they are getting regular checkups and they are avoiding preventable diseases like diabetes, that unless we do that, we're going to go broke just on health care spending.

When we made the biggest investment in clean energy in our history over the last 2½ years, it's because of my belief that we have to free ourselves from the lock-grip that oil has on our economic well-being and our security.

And so I'm going to keep on pushing for those things that position us to be the most competitive, the most productive nation on Earth in the 21st century. And I think on that front, we have been very successful.

All right. Let me see. This gentleman right here in the blue shirt.

Drug Addiction Treatment and Prevention

Q. Mr. President, good to meet you. My name is Steve. I'm a doctoral student here.

The President. What are you studying?

Q. Political rhetoric.

The President. Uh-oh. [*Laughter*] How am I doing so far?

Q. Pretty good, pretty good.

The President. All right. I feel like I'm getting graded up there. [*Laughter*] Go ahead.

Q. All right. Much sacrifice is being asked of our generation. So when are our economic perspectives going to be addressed? For example, when is the war on drugs and society going to be abandoned and replaced by a more sophisticated and cost-effective program of rehabilitation such as the one in Portugal?

The President. I have stated repeatedly, and it's actually reflected in our most recent statement by our Office of Drug Policy, that we need to have an approach that emphasizes prevention, treatment, a public health model for reducing drug use in our country. We've got to put more resources into that. We can't simply focus on interdiction because, frankly, no matter how good of a job we're doing, when it comes to an interdiction approach, if there is high demand in this country for drugs, we are going to continue to see not only drug use, but

also the violence associated with the drug trade.

This has obviously become extremely severe for Mexico, and we are working now with the Mexican Government, in part to help them deal with these transnational drug dealers, but one of the things that I've said to President Calderon is we understand that we have an obligation here in this country to reduce demand and the only way that you reduce demand is through treatment and prevention.

And there are a lot of communities around the country where if you are—if you have a serious drug problem and you decide, I'm going to kick the habit, and you seek out treatment—assuming you're not wealthy, because it may not be covered even if you have health insurance—but particularly if you're poor, you may have a 90-day wait before you can even get into a program. Well, obviously, if you're trying to kick a habit, waiting 90 days to get help is a problem.

So I agree with you that we have to make sure that our balance in our approach is also focused on treatment, prevention. And part of our challenge is also getting into schools early and making sure that young people recognize the perils of drug use.

Now, am I—just to make sure that I'm actually answering your question—am I willing to pursue a decriminalization strategy as an approach? No. But I am willing to make sure that we're putting more resources on the treatment and prevention side. Okay?

All right. Right here, right in the front.

Compromise in Government/Bipartisanship

Q. Hi. My name is Mary Wagner. I teach government at Blake High School in Montgomery County.

The President. Great.

Q. And one of the things that we teach our students when we're teaching them about this governmental system that we have is how important it is in a two-party system to compromise. And my students watched the Republican leadership after the last election saying things out loud like, we're not going to compromise with the Democrats. And does that mean—are things changing? Do we not use compromise anymore? And what should I teach my students about how our Government works if people are saying out loud, we're not going to compromise with the other party?

The President. I think you should keep on teaching your students to compromise, because that's not just how government works, that's how life works. How many people here are married? [*Laughter*] For those of you who are not, but intend to get married, let me just tell you—[*laughter*]—you'd better get used to compromise.

All of us have particular views, a particular vision, in terms of where we think things should go. But we live in societies, we live in communities. And that means we never get our way a hundred percent of the time. That's what we teach our kids. That's what we teach our students. That's how government has to work.

And there's this notion—I was actually reading an article on the way over here, and the basic notion was that, well, Obama is responsible, but he doesn't fight enough for how he believes, and the Republicans are irresponsible, but are full of conviction. So this was sort of the way the article was posed. And this notion that somehow if you're responsible and you compromise, that somehow you're giving up your convictions, that's absolutely not true.

I mean, look, the—I think it's fair to say that Abraham Lincoln had convictions. But he constantly was making concessions and compromises. I've got the Emancipation Proclamation hanging up in the Oval Office, and if you read that document—for those of you who have not read it—it doesn't emancipate everybody. It actually declares the slaves who are in areas that have rebelled against the Union are free, but it carves out various provinces, various parts of various States that are still in the Union, you can keep your slaves.

Now, think about that. That's—the Great Emancipator was making a compromise in the Emancipation Proclamation because he thought it was necessary in terms of advancing the goals of preserving the Union and winning the war. And then ultimately, after the war was

completed, you then had the 13th and 14th and 15th Amendments.

So you know what, if Abraham Lincoln could make some compromises as part of governance, then surely we can make some compromises when it comes to handling our budget.

Now, but you're absolutely right that the culture is now pushing against compromise, and here are a couple of reasons. I mean, one reason is the nature of congressional districts. They've gotten drawn in such a way where some of these districts are so solidly Republican or so solidly Democrat, that a lot of Republicans in the House of Representatives, they're not worried about losing to a Democrat; they're worried about somebody on the right running against them because they compromised. So even if their instinct is to compromise, their instinct of self-preservation is stronger, and they say to themselves, I don't want a primary challenge. So that leads them to dig in.

You've got a media that has become much more splintered. So those of you who are of a Democratic persuasion are only reading the New York Times and watching MSNBC—[*laughter*]—and if you are on the right, then you're only reading the Wall Street Journal editorial page and watching FOX News. [*Laughter*] And if that's where you get your information, just from one side, if you never even have to hear another argument, then over time, you start getting more dug in into your positions.

They've actually done studies—this is interesting—that if you put people in a room who agree with each other basically—if you just put a group of very liberal folks together and they're only talking to each other for long periods of time, then they start becoming—they kind of gin each other up and they become more and more and more liberal. And the same thing happens on the conservative side; they become more and more and more conservative. And pretty soon, you've got what you have now, which is, everybody is demonizing the other side; everybody considers the other side completely extremist, completely unscrupulous, completely untrustworthy. Well, in that kind of atmosphere, it's pretty hard to compromise.

So we have to wind back from that kind of political culture. But the only way we do it is if the American people insist on a different approach and say to their elected officials, we expect you to act reasonably, and we don't expect you to get your way a hundred percent of the time, and we expect you to have strong convictions, but we also expect you to manage the business of the people. And if you're sending that message, eventually, Congress will get it. But it may take some time. You've got to stay on them.

All right? Gentleman back there, right there. You got a microphone. Oh, I'm sorry, I was pointing to this gentleman right there. Yes.

Persons With Disabilities/Budget Debate

Q. Mr. President, good morning to you.

The President. Good morning.

Q. I have cerebral palsy, as does my brother. And I come to you to implore you to do as much as you can to protect services and supports for people with disabilities in your negotiations with Speaker Boehner and Leader Cantor. I know that's hard because Mr. McConnell has said he wants to make you a one-term President. But the issue is we need the vital therapies that Medicaid provides. We need a generous IDEA budget so people like me with severe disabilities can graduate from high school with a diploma and go to college. So please don't leave us holding the bag. I know that a lot of people at Easter Seals are very worried, but given your experience with your father-in-law, I know you'll do the right thing, sir. It's an honor to speak with you.

The President. Thank you. That's a wonderful comment. And the reference to my father-in-law, he actually had muscular dystrophy, but ended up being pretty severely handicapped by the time he was 30, 35, but still went to work every single day, never missed a day of work, never missed a ballgame of Michelle's brother, never missed a dance recital of Michelle's, raised an incredible family, took care of all his responsibilities, didn't leave a lot of debt to his kids—an extraordinary man.

And you're exactly right that the enormous potential that so many people have, if they just get a little bit of help, that has to be factored in when we're making decisions about our budget, because if we're not providing services to persons with disabilities and they are not able to fulfill their potential—graduate from high school, go to college, get a job—then they will be more reliant on Government over the long term because they'll be less self-sufficient. That doesn't make any sense.

I mean, so we've always got to factor in, are we being penny wise and pound foolish? If we cut services for young people—let's say a lot of States are having to make some tough budget decisions—I know Martin has had to make some tough ones here. But I know one of the things that Martin has tried to do is to preserve as much as possible Maryland's commitment to education, because he knows, look, I may save some money—[*applause*]—he knows, short term, I may save some money if I lay off a whole bunch of teachers and classroom sizes get larger and we're giving less supplemental help to kids in need. But over the long term, it's more likely, then, that those kids end up dropping out of school, not working, not paying taxes, not starting businesses, maybe going to prison. And that's going to be a huge drag on the State's capacity to grow and prosper.

So we've always go to think about how do we trim back on what we need now, but keep our eyes on what are our investments in the future. And this is what you do in your own family. Think about it. Let's say that something happens, somebody in your family loses a job; you've got less income coming in. You're probably going to cut back on eating out. You're probably going to cut back on the kind of vacations you take, if any. But you're not going to cut out the college fund for your kid. You're not going to cut out fixing the roof if it's leaking, because you know that if I don't fix the roof, I'm going to get water damage in my house, and that's going to cost me more money.

Well, the same thing is true here in America when it comes to infrastructure, for example. We've got all these broken-down roads and bridges, and our ports and airports are in terrible shape.

I was talking to the CEO of Southwest Airlines, and we've been doing a lot of work on the need for a next-generation air control system. And he said to me—think about this—that if we fixed, updated an air control system that was basically put in place back in the thirties, if we upgraded that to use GPS and all the new technologies, the average airline would save 15 percent in fuel—15 percent—which, some of that you'd get in terms of lower airfare. That's 15 percent less carbon going into the atmosphere, for those of you who are concerned about climate change. So why wouldn't we do that? Now, it costs some money to do it initially, but if we make the investment, it will pay off.

All right, how much time do I have, Reg? I got time for one more question? Okay. Well, this one—all right, well, she is standing and waving, so—[*laughter*].

Gentrification and Urban Revitalization

Q. Hi, my name is Darla Bunting. I'm a third grade literacy teacher in Southeast DC. And I view gentrification as a catch-22, because on one hand, you're bringing major businesses to underdeveloped areas of different cities, but on the other hand, the very people who live in the neighborhoods, it kind of seems as though they're not reaping the benefits. And I wanted to know how can we create sustainable neighborhoods that allow people who are still trying to achieve the American Dream to be able to afford and live in these brand new neighborhoods and communities?

The President. Well, first of all, I have to say that gentrification has been a problem in some communities. But right now, frankly, that would probably be a problem that a lot of communities would welcome if there was a lot of investment going on. We're probably seeing in a lot of cities around the country the reverse problem, which is no investment, people not building new homes, young people not moving back into some of these communities, and so they're emptying out. So as problems go for cities, this is probably not a bad problem to

have because it means the city is growing and attracting new businesses and new energy.

I think that this is typically an issue for local communities to make determinations about how do you get the right balance. If, in fact, certain areas of a city are growing, how do you make sure that it still has housing for longtime residents who may not be able to afford huge appreciation in property values? How do you make sure that the businesses that have been there before are still able to prosper as an economy changes?

What we have done is try to refocus how the Federal Government assists cities. The Federal Government provides help to cities through the Department of Transportation, through the Department of Housing and Urban Development. Obviously, Health and Human Services does a lot of stuff to manage services for low-income persons. But sometimes the whole is less than the sum of its parts. Sometimes there's not enough coordination between various Federal agencies when they go into a particular community.

So one of the things that we've been trying as part of a new approach to urban revitalization is sending one Federal team to a particular city to gather all the Federal agencies together and say, what's working with the city, what's the plan for this city, and how do we get all these pieces to fit together? And so in a situation like you described, we might say, how do we continue to foster growth, but can we help some of those small businesses who feel like they're getting pushed out so that they can stay and they can upgrade and they can take advantage of these new opportunities? And so far, we're seeing some success in this new approach.

But as I said, for a lot of cities right now, the big problem is not gentrification. The big problem is property values have plummeted, you got a bunch of boarded-up buildings, a bunch of boarded-up stores. And the question is, how do you get economic activity going back in those communities again?

Even though I—Reggie said one more question, I'm actually going to call on Tom McMillen, just because he's a friend of mine and he had his hand up earlier. And he was a pretty good ballplayer. I mean, I'm not sure he was as good as Frank, but I hear he was pretty good. [*Laughter*]

National Debt and Deficit/National Economy/Job Growth/Taxes

Former Rep. C. Thomas McMillen. Well, thank you, Mr. President, for coming out to the University of Maryland. You have an open invitation to Comcast arena. And Frank and I and a couple of us will be glad to set up a pickup game if you want to do that, so——

The President. There you go. [*Laughter*] There you go.

Former Rep. McMillen. But my serious question is the following: You know, we're focused so much on this debt right now and the debt limit, but this country could be sliding into another slowdown. And how do we avoid what happened to President Roosevelt in the thirties? Because we ought to be focusing on getting this economy going again.

The President. Good. For those of you who've studied economic history and the history of the Great Depression, what Tom is referring to is, Roosevelt comes in—FDR comes in, he tries all these things with the New Deal; but FDR, contrary to myth, was pretty fiscally conservative. And so after the initial efforts of the New Deal and it looked like the economy was growing again, FDR then presented a very severe austerity budget. And suddenly, in 1937, the economy started going down again. And ultimately, what really pulled America out of the Great Depression was World War II.

And so some have said, I think rightly, that we've got to be careful that any efforts we have to reduce the deficit don't hamper economic recovery, because the worst thing we can do for the deficit is continue to have really bad growth or another recession.

So what I've tried to emphasize in this balanced package that we've talked about is how do we make a serious downpayment and commitment to deficit reduction, but as much as possible, focus on those structural long-term costs that gradually start coming down, as opposed to trying to lop off everything in the first

year or two, and how do we make sure that as part of this package we include some things that would be good for economic growth right now.

So back in December, we passed a payroll tax cut that has saved the typical family a thousand dollars this year. That's set to expire at the end of this year. And what I've said is, as part of this package, we should renew that payroll tax cut so that consumers still have more in their pockets next year until the economy gets a little bit stronger.

I've said that we have to renew unemployment insurance for another year, because obviously, the economy is still not generating enough jobs and there are a lot of folks out there who are hugely reliant on this. But it's also, unemployment insurance is probably the money that is most likely to be spent. By definition, people need it, and so it recirculates in the economy, and it has an effect of boosting aggregate demand and helping the economy grow.

So as much as possible, what I'm trying to do is to make sure that we have elements in this package that focus on growth now. And then, I think it's going to be important for us to, as soon as we get this debt limit done, to focus on some of the things that I mentioned at the top: patent reform, getting these trade deals done, doing an infrastructure bank that would help to finance the rebuilding of America and putting a lot of workers who've been laid off back to work. We don't have time to wait when it comes to putting folks back to work.

Now, what you'll hear from the other side is the most important thing for putting people back to work is simply cutting taxes or keeping taxes low. And I have to remember—I have to remind them that we actually have sort of a comparison. We have Bill Clinton, who created 22 million jobs during the 8 years of his Presidency, in which the tax rates were significantly higher than they are now and would be higher even if, for example, the tax breaks for the high-income Americans that I've called for taking back, even if those got taken back, taxes would still be lower now than they were under Bill Clinton, but the economy did great, generated huge amounts of jobs. And then we had the 8 years before I was elected, in which taxes were very low, but there was tepid job growth.

Now, I'm not saying there's an automatic correlation. But what I am saying is that this theory that the only thing, the only answer to every economic problem we have, the only answer for job creation is to cut taxes for the wealthiest Americans and for corporations is not borne out by the evidence. And we should be a little more creative in how we think about it.

The last thing I'll say, because we've got a lot of young people here, I know that sometimes, things feel discouraging. We've gone through two wars. We've gone through the worst financial crisis in any of our memories. We've got challenges environmentally. We've got conflicts around the world that seem intractable. We've got politicians who only seem to argue. And so I know that there must be times where you kind of say to yourself, golly, can't anybody get their act together around here? And what's the world that I'm starting off in? And how do I get my career on a sound foundation? And you got debts you've got to worry about.

I just want all of you to remember, America has gone through tougher times before, and we have always come through. We've always

emerged on the other side stronger, more unified. The trajectory of America has been to become more inclusive, more generous, more tolerant.

And so I want all of you to recognize that when I look out at each and every one of you, this diverse crowd that we have, you give me incredible hope. You inspire me. I am absolutely convinced that your generation will help us solve these problems. And I don't want you to ever get discouraged, because we're going to get through these tough times just like we have before, and America is going to be stronger, and it's going to be more prosperous, and it's going to be more unified than ever before, thanks to you.

God bless you all. God bless America.

NOTE: The President spoke at 11:04 a.m. in Ritchie Coliseum at the University of Maryland. In his remarks, he referred to Warren E. Buffett, chief executive officer and chairman, Berkshire Hathaway Inc.; Gary C. Kelly, chief executive officer, Southwest Airlines Co.; and Personal Aide to the President Reginald L. Love. He also referred to his brother-in-law Craig M. Robinson. A participant referred to the Individuals with Disabilities Education Act (IDEA).

Remarks Following a Meeting With Prime Minister John P. Key of New Zealand
July 22, 2011

President Obama. I want to welcome Prime Minister Key to the Oval Office. We have had occasion to work together at various multilateral summits in Asia and have always been struck by the intelligence and thoughtfulness that the Prime Minister brings to his work.

Obviously, we are very pleased that the relationship between New Zealand and the United States is growing stronger by the day. Part of that has to do with the great affection that our peoples have towards each other. Part of it has to do with a great deal of common interests and a set of common values.

So the Prime Minister and I discussed a range of economic issues, including our great interest in promoting a more effective trade regime among the Asia-Pacific nations, and we're working on this Trans-Pacific Partnership; we hope to have a framework agreement by the time that we go to Honolulu for the APEC meeting.

We discussed how countries can cooperate around disaster response. Obviously, we are still heartbroken by the loss of life and property resulting from the earthquakes in Christchurch and are incredibly impressed by the resilience of the people of New Zealand as they rebuild from that tragedy. But both of us, having seen what happened in Japan as well, understand that when these kinds of natural disasters strike, it's important for us to be able to pool our resources to help each other.

We discussed our security cooperation and continue to thank New Zealand for its participation in our efforts in Afghanistan. We're very grateful to the outstanding service men and women whom New Zealand has sent there.

And we discussed a wide range of regional issues. Our respective Foreign Ministers are currently in Bali, or at least—I'm not sure if they've left yet——

Prime Minister Key. Yes. They're close.

President Obama. ——but they're talking about how we can work on a wide range of issues, everything from green growth to trying to standardize regulations to include the flow of trade. And throughout this process, whether it's in APEC settings, now the East Asia Summit, we've always found New Zealand to be an outstanding partner. And Prime Minister Key personally has always been an outstanding partner on these issues.

So, welcome. We know it's hot out there, so this is a warmer welcome than you perhaps had expected. [*Laughter*] But we very much appreciate your visit.

Bombing and Shootings in Norway

I do want to also just make note—we were just discussing the fact that there has been a bombing in Oslo, Norway, as well as a shooting there. We don't have information yet, but I wanted to personally extend my condolences to the people of Norway. And it's a reminder that the entire international community has a stake in preventing this kind of terror from occurring. And so we have to work cooperatively together both on intelligence and in terms of prevention of these kinds of horrible attacks.

I remember fondly my visit to Oslo and how warmly the people of Norway treated me. And so our hearts go out to them, and we'll provide any support we can to them as they investigate these occurrences.

So with that, John, welcome again. Thank you for being here.

Prime Minister Key. Mr. President, firstly, thank you for the invitation to Washington, to the White House.

Similarly, I echo your sympathies and concern for that situation in Norway. If it is an act of global terrorism, I think what it shows is no country, large or small, is immune from that risk. And that's why New Zealand plays its part in Afghanistan as we try and join others like the United States in making the world a safer place.

We've had a very good and tremendous reception the last couple of days. I want to thank you for that personally. We're excited about the opportunities of the Trans-Pacific Partnership. We're excited about the chance to put together a regional trade deal which includes the United States and which will expand over time beyond the nine countries, and I think it can deliver strengthened and continued economic growth, jobs, and higher incomes and better opportunities.

I just want to thank the United States for its response when it came to the Christchurch earthquake. Your urban search and rescue team were fabulous, and your call immediately after the earthquake, and the tremendous outpouring of support from the people of America. So thank you very much, indeed.

We are great friends and strategic partners. The Marines are coming down next year to commemorate their amazing contributions, so we're looking forward to welcoming them to New Zealand.

Thank you for allowing us to have this visit. And we thoroughly enjoyed our time here, and we'll see you very soon.

President Obama. You're welcome, and I look forward to returning the visit sometime.

Prime Minister Key. Great.

President Obama. My understanding is the American team is heading out to New Zealand for the World Rugby Cup——

Prime Minister Key. The Rugby World Cup.

President Obama. ——the Rugby World Cup. And so good luck, guys. Although, I hear the

New Zealanders, the Kiwis are pretty good at rugby so—[*laughter*]—I don't think we're seeded number one in the tournament, but I have confidence that we will acquit ourselves well.

All right. Thank you, everybody.

NOTE: The President spoke at 2:10 p.m. in the Oval Office at the White House. In his remarks, he referred to Secretary of State Hillary Rodham Clinton; and Minister of Foreign Affairs Murray S. McCully of New Zealand.

Statement on Certification of Repeal of the United States Military's "Don't Ask, Don't Tell" Policy
July 22, 2011

Today we have taken the final major step toward ending the discriminatory "don't ask, don't tell" law that undermines our military readiness and violates American principles of fairness and equality. In accordance with the legislation that I signed into law last December, I have certified and notified Congress that the requirements for repeal have been met. "Don't ask, don't tell" will end once and for all in 60 days—on September 20, 2011.

As Commander in Chief, I have always been confident that our dedicated men and women in uniform would transition to a new policy in an orderly manner that preserves unit cohesion, recruitment, retention, and military effectiveness. Today's action follows extensive training of our military personnel and certification by Secretary Panetta and Admiral Mullen that our military is ready for repeal. As of September 20th, servicemembers will no longer be

forced to hide who they are in order to serve our country. Our military will no longer be deprived of the talents and skills of patriotic Americans just because they happen to be gay or lesbian.

I want to commend our civilian and military leadership for moving forward in the careful and deliberate manner that this change requires, especially with our Nation at war. I want to thank all our men and women in uniform, including those who are gay or lesbian, for their professionalism and patriotism during this transition. Every American can be proud that our extraordinary troops and their families, like earlier generations that have adapted to other changes, will only grow stronger and remain the best fighting force in the world and a reflection of the values of justice and equality that the define us as Americans.

Remarks on the Federal Budget and an Exchange With Reporters
July 22, 2011

The President. Good evening, everybody. I wanted to give you an update on the current situation around the debt ceiling. I just got a call about a half hour ago from Speaker Boehner, who indicated that he was going to be walking away from the negotiations that we've been engaged in here at the White House for a big deficit reduction and debt reduction package. And I thought it would be useful for me to just give you some insight into where we were and why I think that we should have moved forward with a big deal.

Essentially what we had offered Speaker Boehner was over a trillion dollars in cuts to

discretionary spending, both domestic and defense. We then offered an additional $650 billion in cuts to entitlement programs: Medicare, Medicaid, Social Security. We believed that it was possible to shape those in a way that preserved the integrity of the system, made them available for the next generation, and did not affect current beneficiaries in an adverse way.

In addition, what we sought was revenues that were actually less than what the Gang of Six signed off on. So you had a bipartisan group of Senators, including Republicans who are in leadership in the Senate, calling for what effectively was about $2 trillion above the Republican baseline that they've been working off of. What we said was give us $1.2 trillion in additional revenues, which could be accomplished without hiking taxes—tax rates, but could simply be accomplished by eliminating loopholes, eliminating some deductions, and engaging in a tax reform process that could have lowered rates generally while broadening the base.

So let me reiterate what we were offering. We were offering a deal that called for as much discretionary savings as the Gang of Six. We were calling for taxes that were less than what the Gang of Six had proposed. And we had— we were calling for modifications to entitlement programs—would have saved just as much over the 10-year window. In other words, this was an extraordinarily fair deal. If it was unbalanced, it was unbalanced in the direction of not enough revenue.

But in the interest of being serious about deficit reduction, I was willing to take a lot of heat from my party. And I spoke to Democratic leaders yesterday, and although they didn't sign off on a plan, they were willing to engage in serious negotiations, despite a lot of heat from a lot of interest groups around the country, in order to make sure that we actually dealt with this problem.

It is hard to understand why Speaker Boehner would walk away from this kind of deal. And frankly, if you look at the commentary out there, there are a lot of Republicans that are puzzled as to why it couldn't get done. In fact, there are a lot of Republican voters out there who are puzzled as to why it couldn't get done. Because the fact of the matter is the vast majority of the American people believe we should have a balanced approach.

Now, if you do not have any revenues, as the most recent Republican plan that's been put forward both in the House and the Senate proposed, if you have no revenues at all, what that means is more of a burden on seniors, more drastic cuts to education, more drastic cuts to research, a bigger burden on services that are going to middle class families all across the country. And it essentially asks nothing of corporate jet owners, it asks nothing of oil and gas companies, it asks nothing from folks like me who've done extremely well and can afford to do a little bit more.

In other words, if you don't have revenues, the entire thing ends up being tilted on the backs of the poor and middle class families. And the majority of Americans don't agree on that approach.

So here's what we're going to do. We have now run out of time. I told Speaker Boehner, I've told Democratic Leader Nancy Pelosi, I've told Harry Reid, and I've told Mitch McConnell I want them here at 11 o'clock tomorrow. We have run out of time. And they are going to have to explain to me how it is that we are going to avoid default. And they can come up with any plans that they want and bring them up here, and we will work on them. The only bottom line that I have is that we have to extend this debt ceiling through the next election, into 2013. And the reason for it is we've now seen how difficult it is to get any kind of deal done. The economy is already weakened. And the notion that 5 or 6 or 8 months from now we'll be in a better position to try to solve this problem makes no sense.

In addition, if we can't come up with a serious plan for actual deficit and debt reduction and all we're doing is extending the debt ceiling for another 6, 7, 8 months, then the probabilities of downgrading U.S. credit are increased, and that will be an additional cloud over the economy and make it more difficult for us and more difficult for businesses to create jobs that the American people so desperately need.

So they will come down here at 11 o'clock tomorrow. I expect them to have an answer in terms of how they intend to get this thing done over the course of the next week. The American people expect action. I continue to believe that a package that is balanced and actually has serious debt and deficit reduction is the right way to go. And the American people, I think, are fed up with political posturing and an inability for politicians to take responsible action as opposed to dodge their responsibilities.

All right, with that, I'm going to take some questions.

Ben [Ben Feller, Associated Press].

The President's Relationship With the Speaker of the House of Representatives/Budget Debate/National Debt and Deficit

Q. Thank you, Mr. President. You said you want the leaders back here at 11 to give you an answer about the path forward. What is your answer about the path forward? What path do you prefer, given what's just happened?

The President. Well——

Q. And also, sir, quickly, what does this say about your relationship with Speaker Boehner?

The President. Well, with respect to my relationship with Speaker Boehner, we've always had a cordial relationship. We had very intense negotiations; I'm going to have my team brief you exactly on how these negotiations proceeded. Up until sometime early today when I couldn't get a phone call returned, my expectation was that Speaker Boehner was going to be willing to go to his caucus and ask them to do the tough thing but the right thing. I think it has proven difficult for Speaker Boehner to do that. I've been left at the altar now a couple of times.

And I think that one of the questions that the Republican Party is going to have to ask itself is can they say yes to anything? Can they say yes to anything? I mean, keep in mind it's the Republican Party that has said that the single most important thing facing our country is deficits and debts. We've now put forward a package that would significantly cut deficits and debt. It would be the biggest debt reduction package that we've seen in a very long time.

And it's accomplished without raising individual tax rates. It's accomplished in a way that's compatible with the "no tax" pledge that a whole bunch of these folks signed on to, because we were mindful that they had boxed themselves in, and we tried to find a way for them to generate revenues in a way that did not put them in a bad spot.

And so the question is, what can you say yes to? Now, if their only answer is what they've presented, which is a package that would effectively require massive cuts to Social Security, to Medicare, to domestic spending, with no revenues whatsoever, not asking anything from the wealthiest in this country or corporations that have been making record profits—if that's their only answer, then it's going to be pretty difficult for us to figure out where to go. Because the fact of the matter is that's what the American people are looking for, is some compromise, some willingness to put partisanship aside, some willingness to ignore talk radio or ignore activists in our respective bases and do the right thing.

And to their credit, Nancy Pelosi, Harry Reid, the Democratic leadership, they sure did not like the plan that we were proposing to Boehner, but they were at least willing to engage in a conversation because they understood how important it is for us to actually solve this problem. And so far I have not seen the capacity of the House Republicans in particular to make those tough decisions.

And so then the question becomes, where's the leadership? Or alternatively, how serious are you actually about debt and deficit reduction? Or do you simply want it as a campaign ploy going into the next election?

Now, in terms of where we go next, here's the one thing that we've got to do. At minimum, we've got to increase the debt ceiling—at minimum. I think we need to do more than that. But as I've said before, Republican Leader McConnell in the Senate put forward a plan that said he's going to go ahead and give me the responsibility to raise the debt ceiling. That way folks in Congress can vote against it, but at least it gets done. I'm willing to take the responsibility. That's my job. So if they want to give me the responsibility to do it, I'm happy to do it.

But what we're not going to do is to continue to play games and string this along for another 8, 9 months, and then have to go through this whole exercise all over again. That we're not going to do.

Jessica Yellin [CNN].

Budget Debate

Q. Standing here tonight, Mr. President, can you assure the American people that they will get their Social Security checks on August 3? And if not, who's to blame?

The President. Well, when it comes to all the checks, not just Social Security—veterans, people with disabilities, about 70 million checks are sent out each month—if we default, then we're going to have to make adjustments. And I'm already consulting with Secretary Geithner in terms of what the consequences would be.

We should not even be in that kind of scenario. And if Congress—and in particular, the House Republicans—are not willing to make sure that we avoid default, then I think it's fair to say that they would have to take responsibility for whatever problems arise in those payments. Because, let me be—let me repeat: I'm not interested in finger-pointing, and I'm not interested in blame, but I just want the facts to speak for themselves. We have put forward a plan that is more generous to Republican concerns than a bipartisan plan that was supported by a number of Republican Senators, including at least one that is in Republican leadership in the Senate. Now, I'll leave it up to the American people to make a determination as to how fair that is. And if the leadership cannot come to an agreement in terms of how we move forward, then I think they will hold all of us accountable.

But that shouldn't even be an option. That should not be an option. I'm getting letters from people who write me and say, "At the end of every month, I have to skip meals"—senior citizens on Social Security who are just hanging on by a thread, folks who have severe disabilities who are desperate every single month to try to figure out how they're going to make ends meet. But it's not just those folks. You've got business contractors who are providing services to the Federal Government, who have to wonder are they going to be able to get paid and what does that do in terms of their payrolls.

You've got just a huge number of people who, in one way or another, interact with the Federal Government. And even if you don't, even if you're not a recipient of Social Security, even if you don't get veterans' benefits or disabilities, imagine what that does to the economy when suddenly, 70 million checks are put

at risk. I mean, if you're a business out there, that is not going to be good for economic growth. And that's the number-one concern of the American people.

So we've got to get it done. It is not an option not to do it.

Q. And your degree of confidence?

The President. I am confident simply because I cannot believe that Congress would end up being that irresponsible that they would not send a package that avoids a self-inflicted wound to the economy at a time when things are so difficult.

Scott Horsley [National Public Radio].

Budget Debate

Q. Mr. President, can you explain why you were offering a deal that was more generous than the Gang of Six, which you seemed to be embracing on Tuesday when you were here?

The President. Because what had become apparent was that Speaker Boehner had some difficulty in his caucus. There are a group of his caucus that actually think default would be okay and have said that they would not vote for increasing the debt ceiling under any circumstances.

And so I understand how they get themselves stirred up and the sharp ideological lines that they've drawn. And ultimately, my responsibility is to make sure that we avoid extraordinary difficulties to American people and American businesses.

And so, unfortunately, when you're in these negotiations, you don't get 100 percent of what you want. You may not even get 60 or 70 percent of what you want. But I was willing to try to persuade Democratic leadership as well as Democratic Members of Congress that even a deal that is not as balanced as I think it should be is better than no deal at all. And I was willing to persuade Democrats that getting a handle on debt and deficit reduction is important to Democrats just as much as it's important to Republicans. And frankly, a lot of Democrats are persuaded by that.

As I said in the last press conference, if you're a progressive, you should want to get our fiscal house in order, because once we do, it allows us to then have a serious conversation about the investments that we need to make, like infrastructure, like rebuilding our roads and our bridges and airports, like investing more in college education, like making sure that we're focused on the kinds of research and technology that's going to help us win the future. It's a lot easier to do that when we've got our fiscal house in order. And that was an argument that I was willing to go out and make to a lot of skeptical Democrats, as you saw yesterday.

But ultimately, that's what we should expect from our leaders. If this was easy, it would have already been done. And I think what a lot of the American people are so disappointed by is this sense that all the talk about responsibility, all the talk about the next generation, all the talk about making sacrifices, that when it comes to actually doing something difficult, folks walk away.

And last point I'll make here. I mean, I've gone out of my way to say that both parties have to make compromises. I think this whole episode has indicated the degree to which at least a Democratic President has been willing to make some tough compromises. So when you guys go out there and write your stories, this is not a situation where somehow this was the usual food fight between Democrats and Republicans. A lot of Democrats stepped up in ways that were not advantageous politically. So we've shown ourselves willing to do the tough stuff on an issue that Republicans ran on.

Norah [Norah O'Donnell, CBS News].

Budget Debate

Q. Mr. President, there seems to be an extraordinary breakdown of trust involved here. And I wonder if you could address what we're hearing from Republicans, which is that there was a framework and a deal that was agreed with your Chief of Staff, with the Treasury Secretary, about a certain number of revenues, that the Republicans had agreed to that. And then after you brought that to your party and the discussion of that, the goal line was moved. Is this an example of where the goal line has moved and that that's what has led to this breakdown in trust?

The President. Norah, what I'll do is we'll do a ticktock; we'll go through all the paper. We'll walk you through this process. What this came down to was that there doesn't seem to be a capacity for them to say yes.

Now, what is absolutely true is we wanted more revenue than they had initially offered. But as you'll see, the spending cuts that we were prepared to engage in were at least as significant as the spending cuts that you've seen in a whole range of bipartisan proposals, and we had basically agreed within $10 billion, $20 billion; we were within that range.

So that wasn't the reason this thing broke down. We were consistent in saying that it was going to be important for us to have at least enough revenue that we could protect current beneficiaries of Social Security, for example, or current beneficiaries of Medicare, that we weren't slashing Medicaid so sharply that States suddenly were going to have to throw people off the health care rolls. And we were consistent in that.

So I want to be clear. I'm not suggesting that we had an agreement that was signed, sealed, and delivered. The parties were still apart as recently as yesterday. But when you look at the overall package, there's no changing of the goalposts here. There has been a consistency on our part in saying we're willing to make the tough cuts and we're willing to take on the heat for those difficult cuts, but that there's got to be some balance in the process. What I've said publicly is the same thing that I've said privately. And I've done that consistently throughout this process.

Now, with respect to this breakdown in trust, I think that we have operated aboveboard consistently. There haven't been any surprises. I think the challenge really has to do with the seeming inability, particularly in the House of Representatives, to arrive at any kind of position that compromises any of their ideological preferences. None.

And you've heard it. I mean, I'm not making this up. I think a number of members of that caucus have been very clear about that. And——

Q. But they were willing to move on some revenues, apparently.

The President. Absolutely. The—but what you saw—and again, you'll see this from the description of the deal—essentially what they had agreed to give on is to get back to a baseline—this starts getting technical, but there were about $800 billion in revenue that were going to be available. And what we said was when you've got a ratio of $4 in cuts for every $1 of revenue, that's pretty hard to stomach. And we think it's important to make sure that whatever additional revenue is in there covers the amount of money that's being taken out of entitlement programs. That's only fair.

If I'm saying to future recipients of Social Security or Medicare that you're going to have to make some adjustments, it's important that we're also willing to make some adjustments when it comes to corporate jet owners or oil and gas producers or people who are making millions or billions of dollars.

Wendell [Wendell Goler, FOX News]. Where's Wendell?

Q. He's not here.

The President. Wendell is not here.

Lesley [Lesley Clark, McClatchy Newspapers]. Is Lesley here?

National Debt and Deficit/Budget Debate

Q. Yes, Mr. President.

The President. There you are.

Q. Thank you. You've said that your bottom line has been the big deal, but that's not going to happen. Are you going to be willing to go back to just raising the debt ceiling still?

The President. Well, I think I've been consistently saying here in this press room and everywhere that it is very important for us to raise the debt ceiling. We don't have an option on that. So if that's the best that Congress can do, then I will sign a extension of the debt ceiling that takes us through 2013.

I don't think that's enough. I think we should do more. That's the bare minimum; that's the floor of what the American people expect us to do. So I'd like to see us do more. And when I meet with the leadership tomorrow, I'm going to say, let's do more. But if they tell me that's

the best they can do, then I will sign an extension that goes to 2013, and I will make the case to the American people that we've got to continue going out there and solving this problem. It's the right thing to do, and it's time to do it. We can't keep on putting it off.

Speaker of the House of Representatives John A. Boehner

Q. You suggested that Speaker Boehner didn't return phone calls this afternoon. Could you elaborate a little bit on that?

The President. You know, I'm less concerned about me having to wait for my phone call returned than I am the message that I received when I actually got the phone call.

I'm going to make this the last question. Go ahead.

Stock Market/National Debt and Deficit/Budget Debate

Q. Yes, the markets are closed right now, obviously. What assurances can you give people on Wall Street? Are you going to be reaching out to some people on Wall Street so that when Monday comes we don't see a reaction to the news that's developing right now?

The President. I think it's very important that the leadership understands that Wall Street will be opening on Monday, and we better have some answers during the course of the next several days.

Q. What can you say to people who are watching who work on Wall Street who might find this news a bit alarming, perhaps?

The President. Well, I think what you should say—well, here's what I'd say: I remain confident that we will get an extension of the debt limit and we will not default. I am confident of that.

I am less confident at this point that people are willing to step up to the plate and actually deal with the underlying problem of debt and deficits. That requires tough choices. That's what we were sent here to do.

I mean, the debt ceiling, that's a formality. Historically, this has not even been an issue. It's an unpleasant vote, but it's been a routine vote that Congress does periodically. It was raised 18 times when Ronald Reagan was President. Ronald Reagan said default is not an option, that it would be hugely damaging to the prestige of the United States and we wouldn't—we shouldn't even consider it. So that's the easy part. We should have done that 6 months ago.

The hard part is actually dealing with the underlying debt and deficits and doing it in a way that's fair. That's all the American people are looking for—some fairness. I can't tell you how many letters and e-mails I get, including from Republican voters, who say, look, we know that neither party is blameless when it comes to how this debt and deficit developed—there's been a lot of blame to spread around—but we sure hope you don't just balance the budget on the backs of seniors. We sure hope that we're not slashing our commitment to make sure kids can go to college. We sure hope that we're not suddenly throwing a bunch of poor kids off the Medicaid rolls so they can't get basic preventative services that keep them out of the emergency room. That's all they're looking for, is some fairness.

Now, what you're going to hear, I suspect, is, well, if you—if the Senate is prepared to pass the "cap, cut, and balance" bill, the Republican plan, then somehow we can solve this problem—that's serious debt reduction. It turns out, actually, that the plan that Speaker Boehner and I were talking about was comparable in terms of deficit reduction. The difference was that we didn't put all the burden on the people who are least able to protect themselves, who don't have lobbyists in this town, who don't have lawyers working on the Tax Code for them, working stiffs out there, ordinary folks who are struggling every day. And they know they're getting a raw deal, and they're mad at everybody about it. They're

mad at Democrats and they're mad at Republicans, because they know somehow, no matter how hard they work, they don't seem to be able to keep up. And what they're looking for is somebody who's willing to look out for them. That's all they're looking for.

And for us not to be keeping those folks in mind every single day when we're up here, for us to be more worried about what some funder says or some talk radio show host says or what some columnist says or what pledge we signed back when we were trying to run or worrying about having a primary fight, for us to be thinking in those terms instead of thinking about those folks is inexcusable.

I mean, the American people are just desperate for folks who are willing to put aside politics just for a minute and try to get some stuff done.

So when Norah asked or somebody else asked why was I willing to go along with a deal that wasn't optimal from my perspective, it was because even if I didn't think the deal was perfect, at least it would show that this place is serious, that we're willing to take on our responsibilities even when it's tough, that we're willing to step up even when the folks who helped get us elected may disagree. And at some point, I think, if you want to be a leader, then you got to lead.

Thank you very much.

NOTE: The President spoke at 6:06 p.m. in the James S. Brady Press Briefing Room at the White House. In his remarks, he referred to Sens. Saxby C. Chambliss, Thomas A. Coburn, G. Kent Conrad, Michael D. Crapo, Richard J. Durbin, and Mark R. Warner.

The President's Weekly Address
July 23, 2011

For years, the Government has spent more money than it takes in. The result is a lot of debt on our Nation's credit card, debt that, unless we act, will weaken our economy, cause higher interest rates for families, and force us

to scale back things like education and Medicare.

Now, folks in Washington like to blame one another for this problem. But the truth is neither party is blameless. And both parties have a responsibility to do something about it. Every day, families are figuring out how stretch their paychecks, struggling to cut what they can't afford so they can pay for what's really important. It's time for Washington to do the same thing. But for that to happen, it means that Democrats and Republicans have to work together. It means we need to put aside our differences to do what's right for the country. Everyone is going to have to be willing to compromise. Otherwise, we'll never get anything done.

That's why we need a balanced approach to cutting the deficit. We need an approach that goes after waste in the budget and gets rid of pet projects that cost billions of dollars. We need an approach that makes some serious cuts to worthy programs, cuts I wouldn't make under normal circumstances. And we need an approach that asks everybody to do their part.

So that means, yes, we have to make serious budget cuts, but it's not right to ask middle class families to pay more for college before we ask the biggest corporations to pay their fair share of taxes. It means that before we stop funding clean energy, we should ask oil companies and corporate jet owners to give up the tax breaks that other companies don't get. Before we cut medical research, we should ask hedge fund managers to stop paying taxes at a lower rate than their secretaries. Before we ask seniors to pay more for Medicare, we should ask the wealthiest taxpayers to give up tax breaks we simply can't afford under these circumstances.

That's the heart of this approach: serious cuts balanced by some new revenues. And it's been the position of every Democratic and Republican leader who has worked to reduce the deficit, from Bill Clinton to Ronald Reagan. In fact, earlier this week, one of the most conservative Members of the Senate, Tom Coburn, announced his support for a balanced, bipartisan plan that shows promise. And then a funny thing happened. He received a round of applause from a group of Republican and Democratic Senators. That's a rare event in Washington.

So there will be plenty of haggling over the details in the days ahead. But this debate boils down to a simple choice. We can come together for the good of the country and reach a compromise. We can strengthen our economy and leave for our children a more secure future, or we can issue insults and demands and ultimatums at each another, withdraw to our partisan corners, and achieve nothing. Well, we know the right thing to do. And we know what the American people expect us to do.

NOTE: The address was recorded at approximately 4 p.m. on July 22 in the Red Room at the White House for broadcast on July 23. The transcript was made available by the Office of the Press Secretary on July 22, but was embargoed for release until 6 a.m. on July 23.

Statement on the Death of John M. Shalikashvili
July 23, 2011

With the passing of General John M. Shalikashvili, the United States has lost a genuine soldier-statesman whose extraordinary life represented the promise of America and the limitless possibilities that are open to those who choose to serve it. From his arrival in the United States as a 16-year-old Polish immigrant after the Second World War, to a young man who learned English from John Wayne movies, to his rise to the highest ranks of our military, Shali's life was an "only in America" story. By any measure, he made our country a safer and better place.

As Chairman of the Joint Chiefs of Staff, he strengthened our alliances in Europe and in Asia, forged closer defense ties with Russia, and championed the Partnership for Peace with the former Soviet states. At the same time, he oversaw successful military operations in Bosnia and Haiti and elsewhere. Most of all, he fought tirelessly to improve the quality of life for our soldiers, sailors, airmen, marines, and coastguardsmen, and their families, who serve to keep us safe.

Michelle and I extend our heartfelt condolences to General Shalikashvili's wife Joan and their son Brant.

Message to the Congress Reporting on the Executive Order Blocking Property of Transnational Criminal Organizations
July 24, 2011

To the Congress of the United States:

Pursuant to the International Emergency Economic Powers Act (50 U.S.C. 1701 *et seq.*) (IEEPA), I hereby report that I have issued an Executive Order (the "order") declaring a national emergency with respect to the unusual and extraordinary threat that significant transnational criminal organizations pose to the national security, foreign policy, and economy of the United States.

Organized crime is no longer a local or regional problem; it has become a danger to international stability. Significant transnational criminal organizations have become increasingly sophisticated and dangerous to the United States, and their activities have reached such scope and gravity that they destabilize the international system. These groups have taken advantage of globalization and other factors to diversify their geographic scope and range of activities. They have increased and deepened their ties to governments and the international financial system, relying not only on bribery and violence, but also more and more on the ability to exploit differences among countries and to create and maintain legal facades to hide illicit activities.

The specific harms that significant transnational criminal organizations threaten today are many. They corrupt—and in some cases coopt—governments, thereby destabilizing them and weakening democratic institutions and the rule of law. They threaten U.S. economic interests by subverting, exploiting, and distorting legitimate markets, and could gain influence in strategic sectors of the world economy.

Significant transnational criminal organizations that engage in cybercrime threaten sensitive public and private computer networks, undermine the integrity of the international financial system, and impose costs on the American consumer. Those that engage in the theft of intellectual property not only erode U.S. competitiveness, but also endanger the public health and safety through the distribution of tainted and counterfeit goods. Many of them also engage in drug trafficking.

Finally, significant transnational criminal organizations increasingly support the activities of other dangerous persons. Some of these organizations are involved in arms smuggling, which can facilitate and aggravate violent civil conflicts. Others are involved in human smuggling, exacerbating the problem of forced labor. There is also evidence of growing ties between significant transnational criminal organizations and terrorists.

The Executive Order I have issued today is one part of a comprehensive strategy to address the growing threat of transnational organized crime. The order targets significant transnational criminal organizations and the networks that support them, striking at the core of those networks—their ability and need to move money. It does this by blocking the property and interests in property of four transnational criminal organizations, listed in the Annex to the order, that currently pose significant threats to U.S. domestic and foreign economic interests, as well as to U.S. promotion of transparency and stability in the international political and financial systems. The order provides criteria for the further blocking of persons determined by the Secretary of the Treasury, in consultation with the Attorney General and the Secretary of State:

- to be a foreign person that constitutes a significant transnational criminal organization;

- to have materially assisted, sponsored, or provided financial, material, or technological support for, or goods or services to or in support of, any person whose property and interests in property are blocked pursuant to the order; or

- to be owned or controlled by, or to have acted or purported to act for or on behalf of, directly or indirectly, any person whose property and interests in property are blocked pursuant to the order.

I have delegated to the Secretary of the Treasury the authority, in consultation with the Attorney General and the Secretary of State, to take such actions, including the promulgation of rules and regulations, and to employ all powers granted to the President by IEEPA as may be necessary to carry out the purposes of the order.

The order is effective at 12:01 a.m. eastern daylight time on July 25, 2011. All executive agencies of the United States Government are directed to take all appropriate measures within their authority to carry out the provisions of the order.

I am enclosing a copy of the Executive Order I have issued.

BARACK OBAMA

The White House,
July 24, 2011.

NOTE: This message was released by the Office of the Press Secretary on July 25. The Executive order is listed in Appendix D at the end of this volume.

Remarks to the National Council of La Raza
July 25, 2011

The President. Thank you so much. What an extraordinary crowd. Thank you. Please have a seat.

It is good to be back with NCLR. It is good to see all of you. Right off the bat, I should thank you because I have poached quite a few of your alumni to work in my administration. [*Laughter*] They're all doing outstanding work. Raul Yzaguirre, my Ambassador to the Dominican Republic; Latinos serving at every level of my administration. We've got young people right out of college in the White House. We've got the first Latina Cabinet Secretary in history, Hilda Solis. So we couldn't be prouder of the work that so many folks who've been engaged with La Raza before, the handiwork that they're doing with our administration. And as Janet mentioned, obviously, we're extraordinarily proud of someone who is doing outstanding work on the Supreme Court, Sonia Sotomayor.

Now, recently, 100 Latino officials from across the Government met with Latino leaders from across the country at the White House. I know some of you were there. And I think all who attended would agree that we weren't just paying lip service to the community. Our work together, not just that day but every day, has been more than just talk.

What I told the gathering at the White House was we need your voice. Your country needs you. Our American family will only be as strong as our growing Latino community. And so we're going to take these conversations on the road and keep working with you, because for more than four decades, NCLR has fought for opportunities for Latinos from city centers to farm fields. And that fight for opportunity—the opportunity to get a decent education, the opportunity to find a good job, the opportunity to make of our lives what we will—has never been more important than it is today.

And we're still climbing out of a vicious recession, and that recession hit Latino families especially hard. I don't need to tell you Latino unemployment is painfully high. And there's no doubt that this economy has not recovered as fast as it needs to. The truth is, it's going to take more time. And a lot of the problems we face right now, like slow job growth and stagnant wages, these were problems that were there even before the recession hit.

These challenges weren't caused overnight; they're not going to be solved overnight. But that only makes our work more urgent, to get this economy going and make sure that opportunity is spreading, to make sure that everyone who wants a job can find one; and to make sure that paychecks can actually cover the bills; to make sure that families don't have to choose between buying groceries or buying medicine, that they don't have to choose between sending their kids to college or being able to retire.

My number-one priority, every single day, is to figure out how we can get businesses to hire and create jobs with decent wages. And in the short term, there are some things we can do right away. I want to extend tax relief that we already put in place for middle class families to make sure that folks have more money in their paychecks. And I want to cut redtape that keeps entrepreneurs from turning new ideas into thriving businesses. I want to sign trade deals so our businesses can sell more goods made in America to the rest of the world, especially to the Americas.

And the hundreds of thousands of construction workers—many of them Latino—who lost their jobs when the housing bubble burst, I want to put them back to work rebuilding our roads and our bridges and new schools and airports all across the country. There is work to be done. These workers are ready to do it.

So bipartisan proposals for all of these jobs measures would already be law if Congress would just send them to my desk, and I'd appreciate if you all would help me convince them to do it. We need to get it done. [*Applause*] We need to get it done.

Now, obviously, the other debate in Washington that we're having is one that's going to have a direct impact on every American. Every day, NCLR and your affiliates hear from families figuring out how to stretch every dollar a little bit further, what sacrifices they've got to make, how they're going to budget only what's truly important. So they should expect the same thing from Washington. Neither party is blameless for the decisions that led to our debt, but both parties have a responsibility to come together and solve the problem and

make sure that the American people aren't hurt on this issue.

Because—I just want to talk about this for a second, because it has a potential impact on everybody here and all the communities you serve—if we don't address the debt that's already on our national credit card, it will leave us unable to invest in things like education, to protect vital programs.

So I've already said I'm willing to cut spending that we don't need by historic amounts to reduce our long-term deficit and make sure that we can invest in our children's future. I'm willing to take on the rising costs of health care programs like Medicare and Medicaid to make sure they're strong and secure for future generations.

But we can't just close our deficits by cutting spending. That's the truth, and Americans understand that. Because if all we all do is cut, then seniors will have to pay a lot more for their health care, and students will have to pay a lot more for college, and workers who get laid off might not have any temporary assistance or job training to get them back on their feet. And with gas prices this high, we'd have to stop much of the clean energy research that will help us free ourselves from dependence on foreign oil.

Not only is it not fair if all of this is done on the backs of middle class families and poor families, it doesn't make sense. It may sound good to save a lot of money over the next 5 years, but not if we sacrifice our future for the next 50.

And that's why people from both parties have said that the best way to take on our deficit is with a balanced approach, one where the wealthiest Americans and big corporations pay their fair share too. Before we stop funding energy research, we should ask oil companies and corporate jet owners to give up special tax breaks that other folks don't get. Before we ask college students to pay more to go to college, we should ask hedge fund managers to stop paying taxes that are lower in their—in terms of rates than their secretaries. Before we ask seniors to pay more for Medicare, we should ask people like me to give up tax breaks that we don't need and weren't even asking for.

So, NCLR, that's at the heart of this debate. Are we a nation that asks only the middle class and the poor to bear the burden? After they've seen their jobs disappear and their incomes decline over a decade? Are we a people who break the promises we've made to seniors or the disabled and leave them to fend for themselves?

That's not who we are. We are better than that. We're a people who look out for one another. We're a people who believe in shared sacrifice, because we know that we rise or fall as one Nation. We're a people who will do whatever it takes to make sure our children have the same chances and the same opportunities that our parents gave us—not just the same chances, better chances, than our parents gave us. That's the American way.

And that's what NCLR is all about. That's what the Latino community is all about. When I spoke to you as a candidate for this office, I said you and I share a belief that opportunity and prosperity aren't just words to be said, they are promises to be kept. Back then, we didn't know the depths of the challenges that were going to lie ahead. But thanks to you, we are keeping our promises.

We're keeping our promise to make sure that America remains a place where opportunity is open to all who work for it. We've cut taxes for middle class workers and small businesses and low-income families. We won credit card reform and financial reform and protections for consumers and folks who use payday lenders or send remittances home from being exploited and being ripped off.

We worked to secure health care for 4 million children, including the children of legal immigrants. And we are implementing health reform for all who've been abused by insurance companies and all who fear about going broke if they get sick. And these were huge victories for the Latino community that suffers from lack of health insurance more than any other group.

We're keeping our promise to give our young people every opportunity to succeed.

NCLR has always organized its work around the principle that the single most important investment we can make is in our children's education and that if we let our Latino students fall behind, we will all fall behind. I believe that.

So we've tied giving more money to reform. And we're working with States to improve teacher recruitment and retraining and retention. We're making sure English language learners are a priority for educators across the country. We're holding schools with high dropout rates accountable so they start delivering for our kids. We're emphasizing math and science and investing in community colleges so that all of our workers get the skills that today's companies want. And we've won new college grants for more than 100,000 Latino students. And as long as I am President, this country will always invest in its young people.

These are victories for NCLR; they are victories for America. And we did it with your help. We're keeping our promises.

Of course, that doesn't mean we don't have unfinished business. I promised you I would work tirelessly to fix our broken immigration system and make the "DREAM Act" a reality. And 2 months ago, I went down to the border of El Paso to reiterate—[*applause*]. El Paso is in the house—[*laughter*]—to reiterate my vision for an immigration system that holds true to our values and our heritage and meets our economic and security needs. And I argued this wasn't just the moral thing to do, it was an economic imperative.

In recent years, one in four high-tech startups in America—companies like Google and Intel—were founded on immigrants. One in six new small-business owners are immigrants. These are job creators who came here to seek opportunity and now seek to share opportunity.

This country has always been made stronger by our immigrants. That's what makes America special. We attract talented, dynamic, optimistic people who are continually refreshing our economy and our spirit. And you can see that in urban areas all across the country where communities that may have been hollowed out when manufacturing left or were having problems because of an aging population, suddenly, you see an influx of immigration, and you see streets that were full of boarded-up buildings, suddenly, they're vibrant with life once again. And it's immigrant populations who are providing that energy and that drive.

We have a system right now that allows the best and the brightest to come study in America and then tells them to leave, set up the next great company someplace else. We have a system that tolerates immigrants and businesses that breaks the rules and punishes those that follow the rules. We have a system that separates families, and punishes innocent young people for their parents' actions by denying them the chance to earn an education or contribute to our economy or serve in our military. These are the laws on the books.

Now, I swore an oath to uphold the laws on the books, but that doesn't mean I don't know very well the real pain and heartbreak that deportations cause. I share your concerns, and I understand them. And I promise you, we are responding to your concerns and working every day to make sure we are enforcing flawed laws in the most humane and best possible way.

Now, I know some people want me to bypass Congress and change the laws on my own. Believe me—[*applause*]—and believe me, right now dealing with Congress, the idea——

Audience members. Yes, you can! Yes, you can! Yes, you can!

The President. But believe me, the idea of doing things on my own is very tempting. [*Laughter*] I promise you. Not just on immigration reform. [*Laughter*] But that's not how our system works.

Audience member. Change it!

The President. That's not how our democracy functions. That's not how our Constitution is written.

So let's be honest. I need a dance partner here, and the floor is empty. [*Laughter*]

Five years ago, 23 Republican Senators supported comprehensive immigration reform because they knew it was the right thing to do for the economy and it was the right thing to do

for America. Today, they've walked away. Republicans helped write the "DREAM Act" because they knew it was the right thing to do for the country. Today, they've walked away. Last year, we passed the "DREAM Act" through the House only to see it blocked by Senate Republicans. It was heartbreaking to get so close and see politics get in the way, particularly because some of the folks who walked away had previously been sponsors of this.

Now, all that has to change. And part of the problem is, is that the political winds have changed. That's left States to come up with patchwork versions of reform that don't solve the problem. You and I know that's not the right way to go. We can't have 50 immigration laws across the country.

So yes, feel free to keep the heat on me and keep the heat on Democrats. But here's the only thing you should know. The Democrats and your President are with you—[*applause*]— are with you. Don't get confused about that. Remember who it is that we need to move in order to actually change the laws.

Now, usually, as soon as I come out in favor of something, about half of Congress is immediately against it even if it was originally their idea. [*Laughter*] You notice how that works? [*Laughter*] So I need you to keep building a movement for change outside of Washington, one they can't stop, one that's greater than this community.

We need a movement that bridges party lines, that unites business and labor and faith communities and law enforcement communities and all who know that America cannot continue operating with a broken immigration system. And I will be there every step of the way. I will keep up this fight, because Washington is way behind where the rest of the country knows we need to go.

And I know that can be frustrating. This is a city where compromise is becoming a dirty word, where there's more political upside in doing what's easier for reelection, what's easier for an attack ad, than what's best for the country. But, NCLR, I want you to know, when you feel frustration or you're feeling cynical, and when you hear people say we can't solve our problems or we can't bring about the change that we've fought so hard for, I do want you to remember everything that we've already accomplished together just in 2½ years. And I want you to remember why we do this in the first place.

Recently, I heard the story of a participant at this gathering that we had at the White House that I was telling you about at the top of my speech. So this participant's name was Marie Lopez Rogers. And Marie was born to migrant farm workers in Avondale, Arizona. As a young girl, she and her brother would help their parents in the cotton fields. And I'm assuming the temperatures were sort of like they've been the last couple days here in DC. And it was in those cotton fields that Marie's father would tell her, "If you don't want to be working in this heat, you better stay in school." And so that's what Marie did.

And because of that, because of the tireless, back-breaking work of her parents, because of their willingness to struggle and sacrifice so that one day their children wouldn't have to, Marie became the first in her family to go to college. And interestingly, she now works at the very site where she used to pick cotton, except now city hall sits there, and Marie is the town's mayor.

So that's the promise of America. That is why we love this country so much. That is why

all of us are here. That's why I am here. Some of us had parents or grandparents who said, maybe I can't go to college, but someday my child will go to college. Maybe I can't start my own business, but I promise you someday my child will start his or her own business. I may have to rent today, but someday my child will have a home of her own. My back may be tired, my hands may be cut, I may be working a field, but someday, someday my daughter will be mayor or Secretary of Labor or a Supreme Court Justice.

Hermanos y hermanas, that promise is in our hands. It's up to us to continue that story. It's up to us to hand it down to all of our children: Latino, Black, White, Asian, Native American, gay, straight, disabled, not disabled. We're one family, and we need each other. And if we remember that and continue to focus on that, if we come together and work together as one people and summon the best in each other, I'm confident that promise will endure.

Thank you very much. God bless you. God bless the United States of America.

NOTE: The President spoke at 12:50 p.m. at the Washington Marriott Wardman Park hotel. In his remarks, he referred to Janet Murguia, president and chief executive officer, National Council of La Raza; and Oralia Lopez, mother of Mayor Marie Lopez Rogers of Avondale, AZ.

Remarks Honoring the 2010 World Series Champion San Francisco Giants
July 25, 2011

The President. Well, hello, everybody. Have a seat, have a seat. This is a party. Welcome to the White House, and congratulations to the Giants on winning your first World Series title in 56 years. Give that a big round.

I want to start by recognizing some very proud Giants fans in the house. We've got Mayor Ed Lee; Lieutenant Governor Gavin Newsom. We have quite a few Members of Congress—I am going to announce one; the Democratic Leader in the House, Nancy Pelosi is here. We've got Senator Dianne Feinstein who is here. And our newest Secretary of De-

fense and a big Giants fan, Leon Panetta is in the house.

I also want to congratulate Bill Neukom and Larry Baer for building such an extraordinary franchise.

I want to welcome obviously our very special guest, the "Say Hey Kid," Mr. Willie Mays is in the house. Now, 2 years ago, I invited Willie to ride with me on Air Force One on the way to the All-Star Game in St. Louis. It was an extraordinary trip. Very rarely when I'm on Air Force One am I the second most important guy on there. [*Laughter*] Everybody was just passing me by—"Can I get you something, Mr. Mays?" [*Laughter*] What's going on?

Willie was also a 23-year-old outfielder the last time the Giants won the World Series, back when the team was in New York. And even though there have been some great Giants teams since then, none of them had brought a championship back to the bay area.

And then this team came along. Manager Bruce Bochy once called them a bunch of "misfits and castoffs." Let me take a look at these guys. Or as GM Brian Sabean put it, "We've got a lot of characters with a lot of character."

One of these characters is Tim Lincecum. Where's Tim? I see him back there. Recognize the hair. [*Laughter*] When Tim entered the draft 5 years ago, nine teams passed him over before the Giants picked him up. Nobody thought somebody that skinny—[*laughter*]—with that violent a delivery could survive without just flying apart. But now, with two Cy Youngs under his belt, everybody understands why he's called "The Freak." [*Laughter*] Before Game 5 last year, Tim was so relaxed he was singing in the clubhouse. That's how his teammates knew they were about to see something special. And after watching him pitch 8 incredible innings, including a stretch of 11 strikes in a row, America learned sometimes it's a good idea to bet on the skinny guy. [*Laughter*] So you and me.

And then there's the guy with the beard. Where's he? [*Laughter*] I do fear it. [*Laughter*] Have you guys seen the SportsCenter ad where it's—ESPN—where it starts doing a dance? [*Laughter*]

Now, underneath Brian's beard and the spandex tuxedo—[*laughter*]—and the sea captain costume and the cleats with his face on them is also one of the most dominant closers in baseball. And I do think, Brian, you should know that Michelle was very relieved that the press was going to be talking about what somebody else wears here in the White House—[*laughter*]—so that it's not just her making a fashion statement.

So even though this team is a little different, even though these players haven't always fol-

lowed the traditional rules, one thing they know is how to win. And maybe some of that wisdom comes from all the old-time greats who never won a Series, but know that being a Giant means being a Giant for life. And that's why greats like Willie McCovey can often be found hanging around the clubhouse, pulling young players aside and offering them hitting tips. And the love goes both ways. Brian said, "What those players went through when they played, to not bring one home like we did, this is for them."

So for this team, winning the World Series means remembering their roots, especially when those roots run deep. Last year, after all the confetti had been cleaned up and the players had gone home, Willie Mays took the trophy back to the site of the old Polo Grounds in New York. And he visited students at P.S. 46, on the spot where the stadium once stood, and told them stories about playing stickball with the neighborhood kids all those years ago.

And the rest of this team has also made a point of giving back, whether it's supporting wounded warriors and their families or becoming the first professional sports team to join the "It Gets Better" campaign against bullying.

So that's what this team is all about: characters with character. And so once again I want to congratulate this team and wish them all the best of luck in the rest of the season, unless the White Sox are in the World Series—[*laughter*]—which right now is not a sure thing.

All right? Congratulations, everybody.

Manager Bruce Bochy. Thank you, Mr. President. We have a few gifts here. But first, we want to thank you very much for having us here. We know you're busy, and on behalf of the Giant family, we're honored and privileged for you to have us here.

The President. Thank you.

Mr. Bochy. So a special day for us after having a special season. Thank you.

[*At this point, a baby in the audience cried.*]

The President. He's really upset that I quit talking. [*Laughter*]

[*The President was presented with a team jersey.*]

The President. Oh, that's terrific. Thank you—44. Thank you. Thank you, guys. Beautiful. Thank you. All right? What else we got?

Pitcher Matt Cain. We just wanted to present you with a team-signed bat.

The President. Thank you so much.

Mr. Cain. Your name, special edition. So it's right there—[*inaudible*].

The President. That is beautiful. Thank you so much. Thank you. Congratulations. Thank you. This is beautiful.

Managing General Partner and Chief Executive Officer William H. Neukom. Mr. President, on behalf of the entire Giants organization, our investors, many of whom are here today, the front office, many of whom are also here today, and of course, this amazing ball club, with the trainers and the coaches and the players and the broadcast folks, on behalf of all of us, we thank you for making time for us and for your kind words. And we wish you well, and

we'd like our general manager to make a presentation to you and the family, if he may.

The President. Oh, thank you.

Senior Vice President and General Manager Brian R. Sabean. A custom glove. Real deal.

The President. Oh, that's what I need right there. [*Laughter*]

Mr. Sabean. In White Sox colors.

The President. I notice that you put the silver and black on there. I appreciate that. That was good. [*Laughter*] Thank you.

I've got—we should do something like this every day. Look at all this loot. [*Laughter*] This is good. All right, let's strike the podium. We'll take a good picture.

NOTE: The President spoke at 4:15 p.m. in the East Room at the White House. In his remarks, he referred to Laurence M. Baer, president, Willie H. Mays, Jr., assistant to the president and former center fielder, Brian Wilson, pitcher, and Willie L. McCovey, senior adviser and former first baseman, San Francisco Giants.

Address to the Nation on the Federal Budget
July 25, 2011

Good evening. Tonight I want to talk about the debate we've been having in Washington over the national debt, a debate that directly affects the lives of all Americans.

For the last decade, we've spent more money than we take in. In the year 2000, the Government had a budget surplus. But instead of using it to pay off our debt, the money was spent on trillions of dollars in new tax cuts, while two wars and an expensive prescription drug program were simply added to our Nation's credit card.

As a result, the deficit was on track to top $1 trillion the year I took office. To make matters worse, the recession meant that there was less money coming in, and it required us to spend even more: on tax cuts for middle class families to spur the economy, on unemployment insurance, on aid to States so we could prevent more teachers and firefighters and police offi-

cers from being laid off. These emergency steps also added to the deficit.

Now, every family knows a little credit card debt is manageable. But if we stay on the current path, our growing debt could cost us jobs and do serious damage to the economy. More of our tax dollars will go toward paying off the interest on our loans. Businesses will be less likely to open up shop and hire workers in a country that can't balance its books. Interest rates could climb for everyone who borrows money: the homeowner with a mortgage, the student with a college loan, the corner store that wants to expand. And we won't have enough money to make job-creating investments in things like education and infrastructure or pay for vital programs like Medicare and Medicaid.

Because neither party is blameless for the decisions that led to this problem, both parties have a responsibility to solve it. And over the last several months, that's what we've been trying to do. I won't bore you with the details of every plan or proposal, but basically, the debate has centered around two different approaches.

The first approach says, let's live within our means by making serious, historic cuts in Government spending. Let's cut domestic spending to the lowest level it's been since Dwight Eisenhower was President. Let's cut defense spending at the Pentagon by hundreds of billions of dollars. Let's cut out waste and fraud in health care programs like Medicare, and at the same time, let's make modest adjustments so that Medicare is still there for future generations. Finally, let's ask the wealthiest Americans and biggest corporations to give up some of their breaks in the Tax Code and special deductions.

This balanced approach asks everyone to give a little without requiring anyone to sacrifice too much. It would reduce the deficit by around $4 trillion and put us on a path to pay down our debt. And the cuts wouldn't happen so abruptly that they'd be a drag on our economy or prevent us from helping small businesses and middle class families get back on their feet right now.

This approach is also bipartisan. While many in my own party aren't happy with the painful cuts it makes, enough will be willing to accept them if the burden is fairly shared. While Republicans might like to see deeper cuts and no revenue at all, there are many in the Senate who have said, "Yes, I'm willing to put politics aside and consider this approach because I care about solving the problem." And to his credit, this is the kind of approach the Republican Speaker of the House, John Boehner, was working on with me over the last several weeks.

The only reason this balanced approach isn't on its way to becoming law right now is because a significant number of Republicans in Congress are insisting on a different approach, a cuts-only approach, an approach that doesn't ask the wealthiest Americans or biggest corporations to contribute anything at all. And because nothing is asked of those at the top of the income scale, such an approach would close the deficit only with more severe cuts to programs we all care about, cuts that place a greater burden on working families.

So the debate right now isn't about whether we need to make tough choices. Democrats and Republicans agree on the amount of deficit reduction we need. The debate is about how it should be done. Most Americans, regardless of political party, don't understand how we can ask a senior citizen to pay more for her Medicare before we ask a corporate jet owner or the oil companies to give up tax breaks that other companies don't get. How can we ask a student to pay more for college before we ask hedge fund managers to stop paying taxes at a lower rate than their secretaries? How can we slash funding for education and clean energy before we ask people like me to give up tax breaks we don't need and didn't ask for?

That's not right. It's not fair. We all want a Government that lives within its means, but there are still things we need to pay for as a country, things like new roads and bridges, weather satellites and food inspection, services to veterans and medical research.

And keep in mind that under a balanced approach, the 98 percent of Americans who make under $250,000 would see no tax increases at all. None. In fact, I want to extend the payroll tax cut for working families. What we're talking about under a balanced approach is asking Americans whose incomes have gone up the most over the last decade—millionaires and billionaires—to share in the sacrifice everyone else has to make. And I think these patriotic Americans are willing to pitch in.

In fact, over the last few decades, they've pitched in every time we passed a bipartisan deal to reduce the deficit. The first time a deal was passed, a predecessor of mine made the case for a balanced approach by saying this: "Would you rather reduce deficits and interest rates by raising revenue from those who are not now paying their fair share, or would you rather accept larger budget deficits, higher interest rates, and higher unemployment? And I think I know your answer."

Those words were spoken by Ronald Reagan. But today, many Republicans in the House refuse to consider this kind of balanced approach, an approach that was pursued not only by President Reagan, but by the first President Bush, by President Clinton, by myself, and by many Democrats and Republicans in the United States Senate. So we're left with a stalemate.

Now, what makes today's stalemate so dangerous is that it has been tied to something known as the debt ceiling, a term that most people outside of Washington have probably never heard of before.

Understand, raising the debt ceiling does not allow Congress to spend more money. It simply gives our country the ability to pay the bills that Congress has already racked up. In the past, raising the debt ceiling was routine. Since the 1950s, Congress has always passed it, and every President has signed it. President Reagan did it 18 times. George W. Bush did it seven times. And we have to do it by next Tuesday, August 2, or else, we won't be able to pay all of our bills.

Unfortunately, for the past several weeks, Republican House Members have essentially said that the only way they'll vote to prevent America's first-ever default is if the rest of us agree to their deep, spending-cuts-only approach.

If that happens and we default, we would not have enough money to pay all of our bills, bills that include monthly Social Security checks, veterans' benefits, and the Government contracts we've signed with thousands of businesses.

For the first time in history, our country's AAA credit rating would be downgraded, leaving investors around the world to wonder whether the United States is still a good bet. Interest rates would skyrocket on credit cards, on mortgages, and on car loans, which amounts to a huge tax hike on the American people. We would risk sparking a deep economic crisis, this one caused almost entirely by Washington.

So defaulting on our obligations is a reckless and irresponsible outcome to this debate. And Republican leaders say that they agree we

must avoid default. But the new approach that Speaker Boehner unveiled today, which would temporarily extend the debt ceiling in exchange for spending cuts, would force us to once again face the threat of default just 6 months from now. In other words, it doesn't solve the problem.

First of all, a 6-month extension of the debt ceiling might not be enough to avoid a credit downgrade and the higher interest rates that all Americans would have to pay as a result. We know what we have to do to reduce our deficits; there's no point in putting the economy at risk by kicking the can further down the road.

But there's an even greater danger to this approach. Based on what we've seen these past few weeks, we know what to expect 6 months from now. The House of Representatives will once again refuse to prevent default unless the rest of us accept their cuts-only approach. Again they will refuse to ask the wealthiest Americans to give up their tax cuts or deductions. Again they will demand harsh cuts to programs like Medicare. And once again the economy will be held captive unless they get their way.

This is no way to run the greatest country on Earth. It's a dangerous game that we've never played before, and we can't afford to play it now. Not when the jobs and livelihoods of so many families are at stake. We can't allow the American people to become collateral damage to Washington's political warfare.

And Congress now has one week left to act, and there are still paths forward. The Senate has introduced a plan to avoid default, which makes a downpayment on deficit reduction and ensures that we don't have to go through this again in 6 months.

I think that's a much better approach, although serious deficit reduction would still require us to tackle the tough challenges of entitlement and tax reform. Either way, I've told leaders of both parties that they must come up with a fair compromise in the next few days that can pass both Houses of Congress and a compromise that I can sign. I'm confident we can reach this compromise. Despite our disagreements, Republican leaders and I have found common ground before. And I believe that enough members of both parties will ultimately put politics aside and help us make progress.

Now, I realize that a lot of the new Members of Congress and I don't see eye to eye on many issues. But we were each elected by some of the same Americans for some of the same reasons. Yes, many want Government to start living within its means. And many are fed up with a system in which the deck seems stacked against middle class Americans in favor of the wealthiest few.

But do you know what people are fed up with most of all? They're fed up with a town where compromise has become a dirty word. They work all day long, many of them scraping by, just to put food on the table. And when these Americans come home at night, bone tired, and turn on the news, all they see is the same partisan three-ring circus here in Washington. They see leaders who can't seem to come together and do what it takes to make life just a little bit better for ordinary Americans. They're offended by that. And they should be.

The American people may have voted for divided Government, but they didn't vote for a dysfunctional Government. So I'm asking you all to make your voice heard. If you want a balanced approach to reducing the deficit, let your Member of Congress know. If you believe we can solve this problem through compromise, send that message.

America, after all, has always been a grand experiment in compromise. As a democracy made up of every race and religion, where every belief and point of view is welcomed, we have put to the test time and again the proposition at the heart of our founding: that out of many, we are one. We've engaged in fierce and passionate debates about the issues of the day, but from slavery to war, from civil liberties to questions of economic justice, we have tried to live by the words that Jefferson once wrote: "Every man cannot have his way in all things. . . . Without this mutual disposition, we are disjointed individuals, but not a society."

History is scattered with the stories of those who held fast to rigid ideologies and refused to listen to those who disagreed. But those are not the Americans we remember. We remember the Americans who put country above self and set personal grievances aside for the greater good. We remember the Americans who held this country together during its most difficult hours, who put aside pride and party to form a more perfect Union.

That's who we remember. That's who we need to be right now. The entire world is watching. So let's seize this moment to show why the United States of America is still the greatest nation on Earth, not just because we can still keep our word and meet our obligations, but because we can still come together as one Nation.

Thank you, God bless you, and may God bless the United States of America.

NOTE: The President spoke at 9:01 p.m. in the East Room at the White House.

Statement on the Death of Richard E. Chavez
July 27, 2011

Michelle and I were saddened to learn of the passing of Richard Estrada Chavez yesterday. Richard spent his life in the service of others alongside his brother Cesar and his wife Dolores Huerta, cofounders of the United Farm Workers. It was Richard who designed the UFW's iconic eagle, a symbol of hope that has helped carry the struggle for the rights of farm workers forward for almost five decades.

Throughout his years of service, Richard fought for basic labor rights, but also worked to improve the quality of life for countless farm workers. And beyond his work, Richard was a family man. I was honored to have Richard visit the Oval Office last year on Cesar Chavez Day with other family members, and will never forget the stories they shared. Richard understood that the struggle for a more perfect

Union and a better life for all America's workers didn't end with any particular victory or defeat, but instead required a commitment to getting up every single day to keep at it.

Our thoughts and prayers are with Richard's family and loved ones. We take comfort in knowing that the work he was passionate about will be continued by all he helped to inspire.

Message to the Congress on Continuation of the National Emergency With Respect to Actions of Certain Persons to Undermine the Sovereignty of Lebanon or Its Democratic Processes and Institutions
July 28, 2011

To the Congress of the United States:

Section 202(d) of the National Emergencies Act (50 U.S.C. 1622(d)) provides for the automatic termination of a national emergency unless, prior to the anniversary date of its declaration, the President publishes in the *Federal Register* and transmits to the Congress a notice stating that the emergency is to continue in effect beyond the anniversary date. In accordance with this provision, I have sent to the *Federal Register* for publication the enclosed notice stating that the national emergency declared with respect to the actions of certain persons to undermine the sovereignty of Lebanon or its democratic processes and institutions is to continue in effect beyond August 1, 2011.

Certain ongoing activities, such as continuing arms transfers to Hizballah that include increasingly sophisticated weapons systems, serve to undermine Lebanese sovereignty, contribute to political and economic instability in the region, and continue to pose an unusual and extraordinary threat to the national security and foreign policy of the United States. For these reasons, I have determined that it is necessary to continue the national emergency declared on August 1, 2007, to deal with that threat and the related measures adopted on that date to respond to the emergency.

BARACK OBAMA

The White House,
July 28, 2011.

NOTE: The notice is listed in Appendix D at the end of this volume.

Remarks on the Federal Budget
July 29, 2011

I want to speak about the ongoing and increasingly urgent efforts to avoid default and reduce our deficit.

Right now the House of Representatives is still trying to pass a bill that a majority of Republicans and Democrats in the Senate have already said they won't vote for. It's a plan that would force us to relive this crisis in just a few short months, holding our economy captive to Washington politics once again. In other words, it does not solve the problem, and it has no chance of becoming law.

What's clear now is that any solution to avoid default must be bipartisan. It must have the support of both parties that were sent here to represent the American people, not just one faction. It will have to have the support of both the House and the Senate. And there are multiple ways to resolve this problem. Senator Reid, a Democrat, has introduced a plan in the Senate that contains cuts agreed upon by both parties. Senator McConnell, a Republican, offered a solution that could get us through this. There are plenty of modifications we can make to either of these plans in order to get them passed through both the House and the Senate and would allow me to sign them into law. And today I urge Democrats and Republicans in the Senate to find common ground on a plan that can get support from both parties in the House, a plan that I can sign by Tuesday.

Now, keep in mind, this is not a situation where the two parties are miles apart. We're in rough agreement about how much spending can be cut responsibly as a first step toward reducing our deficit. We agree on a process where the next step is a debate in the coming months on tax reform and entitlement reform, and I'm ready and willing to have that debate. And if we need to put in place some kind of enforcement mechanism to hold us all accountable for making these reforms, I'll support that too if it's done in a smart and balanced way.

So there are plenty of ways out of this mess. But we are almost out of time. We need to reach a compromise by Tuesday so that our country will have the ability to pay its bills on time, as we always have, bills that include monthly Social Security checks, veterans' benefits, and the Government contracts we've signed with thousands of businesses. Keep in mind, if we don't do that, if we don't come to an agreement, we could lose our country's AAA credit rating, not because we didn't have the capacity to pay our bills—we do—but because we didn't have a AAA political system to match our AAA credit rating.

And make no mistake, for those who say they oppose tax increases on anyone, a lower credit rating would result potentially in a tax increase on everyone in the form of higher interest rates on their mortgages, their car loans, their credit cards. And that's inexcusable.

There are a lot of crises in the world that we can't always predict or avoid: hurricanes, earthquakes, tornadoes, terrorist attacks. This isn't one of those crises. The power to solve this is in our hands. And on a day when we've been reminded how fragile the economy already is, this is one burden we can lift ourselves. We can end it with a simple vote, a vote that Demo-crats and Republicans have been taking for decades, a vote that the leaders in Congress have taken for decades.

It's not a vote that allows Congress to spend more money. Raising the debt ceiling simply gives our country the ability to pay the bills that Congress has already racked up. I want to emphasize that. The debt ceiling does not determine how much more money we can spend, it simply authorizes us to pay the bills we already have racked up. It gives the United States of America the ability to keep its word.

Now, on Monday night, I asked the American people to make their voice heard in this debate, and the response was overwhelming. So please, to all the American people, keep it up. If you want to see a bipartisan compromise—a bill that can pass both Houses of Congress and that I can sign—let your Members of Congress know. Make a phone call. Send an e-mail. Tweet. Keep the pressure on Washington, and we can get past this.

And for my part, our administration will be continuing to work with Democrats and Republicans all weekend long until we find a solution. The time for putting party first is over. The time for compromise on behalf of the American people is now. And I am confident that we can solve this problem. I'm confident that we will solve this problem. For all the intrigue and all the drama that's taking place on Capitol Hill right now, I'm confident that common sense and cooler heads will prevail.

But as I said earlier, we are now running out of time. It's important for everybody to step up and show the leadership that the American people expect.

Thank you.

NOTE: The President spoke at 10:36 a.m. in the Diplomatic Reception Room at the White House.

Remarks on Fuel Efficiency Standards
July 29, 2011

Thank you, everybody. Thank you. Good morning. I have been having a lot of fun this week, but—[*laughter*]—nothing more fun and more important to the future of the American economy than the agreement that we're announcing today.

I am extraordinarily proud to be here today with the leaders of the world's largest auto companies and the folks who represent autoworkers all across America. And—[applause]—I'm glad that I have a chance to see some of the great cars that you are manufacturing. As some of you may know, it's only a matter of time until Malia gets her learner's permit—[laughter]—so I'm hoping to see one of those models that gets a top speed of 15 miles an hour—[laughter]—the ejector seat anytime boys are in the car. [Laughter] So hopefully, you guys have some of those in the pipeline.

Now, for the last few months, gas prices have just been killing folks at the pump. People are filling up their tank, and they're watching the cost rise $50, $60, $70. For some families, it means driving less. But a lot of folks don't have that luxury. They've got to go to work. They've got to pick up the kids. They've got to make deliveries. So it's just another added expense when money is already tight.

And of course, this is not a new problem. For decades, we've left our economy vulnerable to increases in the price of oil. And with the demand for oil going up in countries like China and India, the problem is only getting worse. The demand for oil is inexorably rising far faster than supply. And that means prices will keep going up unless we do something about our own dependence on oil. That's the reality.

At the same time, it's also true that there is no quick fix to the problem. There's no silver bullet here. But there are steps we can take now that will help us become more energy independent. There are steps we can take that will save families money at the pump, that will make our economy more secure, and that will help innovative companies all across America generate new products and new technologies and new jobs.

So I've laid out an energy strategy that would do that. In the short term, we need to increase safe and responsible oil production here at home to meet our current energy needs. And even those who are proponents of shifting away from fossil fuels have to acknowl-

edge that we're not going to suddenly replace oil throughout the economy. We're going to need to produce all the oil we can.

But while we're at it, we need to get rid of, I think, the $4 billion in subsidies we provide to oil and gas companies every year at a time when they're earning near-record profits and put that money toward clean energy research, which would really make a big difference.

Those are all short-term solutions though. In the long run, we're going to have to do more. We're going to have to harness the potential of startups and clean energy companies across America. We're going to need to build on the progress that I've seen in your factories, where workers are producing hybrid cars and more fuel-efficient engines and advanced electric vehicles. We need to tap into this reservoir of innovation and enterprise.

And that's why we're here today. This agreement on fuel standards represents the single most important step we've ever taken as a nation to reduce our dependence on foreign oil. Think about that.

Most of the companies here today were part of an agreement that we reached 2 years ago to raise the fuel efficiency of their cars over the next 5 years. And the vehicles on display here are ones that benefited from that standard. Folks buying cars like these in the next several years will end up saving more than $3,000 over time because they can go further on a gallon of gas.

And today these outstanding companies are committing to doing a lot more. The companies here today have endorsed our plan to continue increasing the mileage on their cars and trucks over the next 15 years. We've set an aggressive target, and the companies here are stepping up to the plate.

By 2025, the average fuel economy of their vehicles will nearly double to almost 55 miles per gallon. So this is an incredible commitment that they've made. And these are some pretty tough business guys. They know their stuff. And they wouldn't be doing it if they didn't think that it was ultimately going to be good business and good for America.

Think about what this means. It means that filling up your car every 2 weeks instead of filling it up every week. It will save a typical family more than $8,000 in fuel costs over time. And consumers in this country as a whole will save almost $2 trillion in fuel costs. That's trillion with a "t."

And just as cars will go further on a gallon of gas, our economy will go further on a barrel of oil. In the next 15 years, we're going to reduce the amount of oil we need by 2.2 million barrels per day. And this will help meet the goal that I've set for America: reducing our dependence on foreign oil by one-third.

Using less oil also means our cars will produce fewer emissions. So when your kids are biking around the neighborhood, they'll be breathing less pollution and fewer toxins. It means we're doing more to protect our air and water. And it means we're reducing the carbon pollution that threatens our climate.

Lastly, these standards aren't just about the bad things we'll prevent; it's about the good things that we'll build. As these companies look for ways to boost efficiency, they'll be conducting research and development on test tracks. They're going to look to startups working on biofuels and new engine technologies. They're going to continue to invest in advanced battery manufacturing. They're going to spur growth in clean energy. And that means new jobs in cutting-edge industries all across America.

I'll give you a couple of examples. There's a company called Celgard in North Carolina that's expanding its production line to meet demand for advanced batteries. And they've hired 200 employees, and they're adding 250 more. There's A123, a clean energy manufacturer in Michigan that just hired its 1,000th worker as demand has soared for its vehicle components. Companies like these are taking root and putting people to work in every corner of the country.

And after a very difficult time for the automotive sector in this country, after a period of painful restructuring, with the Federal Government lending a helping hand to two of the Big Three American automakers, we're seeing growth and a rise in sales, led by vehicles using

new, more fuel-efficient technologies. And that bodes well for the future. That tells us that these standards are going to be a win for consumers, for these companies, for our economy, for our security, and for our planet.

So we are happy to welcome all the auto companies to this effort. But I do want to pay special tribute to the extraordinary progress of General Motors, Ford, and Chrysler. It was little more than 2 years ago that many doubted whether these companies would still be around, much less moving forward and leading the kind of change that we're seeing.

I also want to point out all this progress we're talking about today, the promise of this agreement, it is only possible because we've made investments in technology. It's only possible because we're willing as a nation to make sure that young people could afford to go to college and get engineering degrees, to make sure that we're backing the basic research of our scientists, to make sure innovative small businesses could get the credit to open their doors and ultimately maybe be a supplier for one of these big companies.

So as we look to close the deficit, this agreement is a reminder of why it's so important that we have a balanced approach. We've got to make serious spending cuts while still investing in our future, while still investing in education and research and technology like clean energy, which are so important for our economy.

And finally, this agreement ought to serve as a valuable lesson for leaders in Washington. This agreement was arrived at without legislation. You are all demonstrating what can happen when people put aside differences. These folks are competitors, you've got labor and business, but they decided, we're going to work together to achieve something important and lasting for the country.

So when it comes to tackling the deficit or it comes to growing the economy, when it comes to giving every American an opportunity to achieve their American Dream, the American people are demanding the same kind of resolve, the same kind of spirit of compromise, the same kind of problem solving that all these folks on stage have shown. They're demanding that people come together and find common ground; that we have a sensible, balanced approach that's based on facts and evidence and us reasoning things out and figuring out how to solve problems and asks everybody to do their part.

That's what I'm fighting for. That's what this debate is all about. That's what the American people want.

So I want to once again thank automakers. I want to thank workers. I want to thank the State of California. I want to thank—[*applause*]—which has been—the State of California has consistently been a leader on this issue. I want to thank the environmental leaders and elected officials, including Leader Pelosi, who is here, and the leaders here from the Michigan delegation and—because obviously the State of Michigan has a huge stake and has been on the cutting edge of these issues and have helped to pave the way forward. I want to thank all of you for helping to reduce our dependence on oil, on growing the economy, and leaving for future generations a more secure and prosperous America.

So congratulations, gentlemen. Thank you very much. Good work.

NOTE: The President spoke at 10:57 a.m. at the Walter E. Washington Convention Center. Participating in the event were Daniel F. Akerson, chairman and chief executive officer, General Motors Co.; Alan R. Mulally, president and chief executive officer, Ford Motor Co.; Sergio Marchionne, chief executive officer, Chrysler Group LLC; John Krafcik, president and chief executive officer, Hyundai Motor America; James E. Lentz, president and chief operating officer, Toyota Motors Sales USA, Inc.; Josef Kerscher, president, BMW Manufacturing Co.; Andrew Goss, president, Jaguar Land Rover North America; Doug Speck, president and chief executive office, Volvo Cars North America; John W. Mendel, executive vice president, American Honda Motor Co., Inc.; Scott E. Becker, administration and finance senior vice president, Nissan North America, Inc.; James O'Sullivan, president and chief executive officer, Mazda North American Operations; and Bob King, president, United Auto Workers.

Remarks Following a Meeting With West African Leaders
July 29, 2011

Okay. Well, I just wanted to publicly welcome four very distinguished leaders to the White House: President Yayi of Benin, President Conde of Guinea, President Issoufou of Niger, and President Ouattara of Cote d'Ivoire.

Although, obviously, we've got a lot of things going here in Washington today, it was important for us, I think, to maintain this scheduled appointment with four leaders of nations that represent Africa's democratic progress, which is vital to a stable and prosperous and just Africa, but is also critical to the stability and prosperity of the world.

All these leaders were elected through free and fair elections. They've shown extraordinary persistence in wanting to promote democracy in their countries despite significant risks to their own personal safety and despite enormous challenges, in some cases—most recently in Cote d'Ivoire—in actually implementing the results of these elections.

But because of their fortitude and because of the determination of their people to live in democratic, free societies, they have been able to arrive at a position of power that is supported by the legitimate will of their peoples. And as such, they can serve as effective models for the continent.

These countries all underscore what I emphasized when I visited Ghana and gave a speech about Africa as a whole: This is a moment of great opportunity and significant progress in Africa. Politically, a majority of sub-Saharan African countries are now embracing democracy. Economically, Africa is one of the fastest growing regions in the world.

And we just had a very productive discussion where we discussed how we can build on both the political progress, the economic progress, and address the security challenges that continue to confront Africa. And I emphasized that the United States has been and will continue to be a stalwart partner with them in this process of democratization and development.

Despite the impressive work of all these gentlemen, I've said before and I think they all agree: Africa does not need strongmen, Africa needs strong institutions. So we are working with them as partners to build effective judiciaries, strong civil societies, legislators that are effective and inclusive, making sure that human rights are protected.

With respect to economic development, all of us agree that we can't keep on duplicating a approach that breeds dependence, but rather, we need to embrace an approach that creates sustainability and capacity within each of these countries through trade and investment and the development of human capital and the education of young people throughout these countries.

We discussed as well that not only do we want to encourage trade between the United States and each of these respective countries, but we want to encourage inter-African and regional trade, and that requires investments in infrastructure in those areas.

We are partners in resolving conflicts peacefully and have worked effectively with ECOWAS and the African Union to resolve crisis—crises in the region. And we appreciate very much the assistance that we've received on battling terrorism

that currently is trying to gain a foothold inside of Africa.

And finally, we discussed how we can partner together to avert the looming humanitarian crisis in eastern Africa. And I think it hasn't gotten as much attention here in the United States as it deserves, but we're starting to see famine developing in—along the Horn of Africa, in areas like Somalia in particular. And that's going to require an international response, and Africa will have to be a partner in making sure that tens of thousands of people do not starve to death.

So let me just close by saying that many of the countries here are—either have celebrated or are in the process of celebrating their 50th year of independence. As President Issoufou pointed out, I'm also celebrating my 50th year of at least existence. [*Laughter*]

And when we think about the extraordinary progress that's been made, I think there's much we can be proud of. But of course, when we think about the last 50 years, we also have to recognize there have been a lot of opportunities missed. And so these leaders, I think, are absolutely committed to making sure that 50 years from now they can say that they helped to turn the tide in their countries, to establish strong, democratic practices, to help establish economic prosperity and security. And we just want you to know the United States will stand with you every step of the way.

Thank you very much, everyone.

NOTE: The President spoke at 4:13 p.m. in the Cabinet Room at the White House.

Statement on the First Anniversary of the Tribal Law and Order Act of 2010
July 29, 2011

A year ago today, I was proud to sign the Tribal Law and Order Act into law. American Indians and Alaska Natives have long been victimized by violent crime at far higher rates than the rest of the country, and the Tribal Law and Order Act is already helping us better address the unique public safety challenges that confront tribal communities. Over the past

year, tribes have gained greater sentencing authority. The rights of defendants are stronger. Services for victims are better. We're working together to combat alcohol and drug abuse and to help at-risk youth in more effective ways. We've established new guidelines and training for officers handling domestic violence and sex crimes. And we've expanded recruitment and retention of Bureau of Indian Affairs and tribal officers and given them better access to the criminal databases they need to keep people safe. These are important steps in addressing serious issues. And as long as I am President, we will continue to strengthen and fortify our government-to-government relationship with Indian Country.

The President's Weekly Address
July 30, 2011

Today I'd like to speak with you about the ongoing and urgent efforts to avoid a first-ever default and get our fiscal house in order.

Republicans in the House of Representatives just spent precious days trying to pass a plan that a majority of Republicans and Democrats in the Senate had already said they wouldn't vote for. It's a plan that wouldn't solve our fiscal problems, but would force us to relive this crisis in just a few short months. It would hold our economy captive to Washington politics once again. If anything, the past few weeks have demonstrated that's not acceptable.

Any solution to avoid default must be bipartisan. It must have the support of both parties that were sent here to represent the American people, not just one faction of one party. There are multiple ways to resolve this problem. Congress must find common ground on a plan that can get support from both parties in the House and in the Senate. And it's got to be a plan that I can sign by Tuesday.

The parties are not that far apart here. We're in rough agreement on how much spending we need to cut to reduce our deficit. And we agree on a process to tackle tax reform and entitlement reform. There are plenty of ways out of this mess. But there is very little time.

We need to reach a compromise by Tuesday so that our country will have the ability to pay its bills on time, bills like Social Security checks, veterans' benefits, and contracts we've signed with thousands of American businesses. If we don't, for the first time ever, we could lose our country's AAA credit rating. Not because we didn't have the capacity to pay our bills—we do—but because we didn't have a AAA political system to match it. And make no mistake, for those who reflexively oppose tax increases on anyone, a lower credit rating would be a tax increase on everyone; we'd all pay higher interest rates on mortgages and car loans and credit cards.

That would be inexcusable and entirely self-inflicted by Washington. The power to solve this is in our hands. All that's needed is a simple vote that Democrats and Republicans have taken for decades, including all of the leaders in Congress today. It was done 18 times under President Reagan, 7 times under George W. Bush. And it must be done again now. It's not a vote that allows Congress to spend more money. Raising the debt ceiling simply gives our country the ability to pay the bills that Congress has already racked up, it gives the United States of America the ability to keep its word, and it lets businesses and our economy breathe a sigh of relief.

On Monday night, I asked you to make your voice heard in this debate, and the response was overwhelming. One of the e-mails we received was from a woman named Kelly Smith, who wanted to send this message to Washington. "I keep my home clean," Kelly wrote. "I work hard at a full-time job, give my parents any monies I can so they can afford their medications, I pay my bills, and by all appearances, I am a responsible person. All I'm asking is that you be responsible. I have my house in order, and all I'm asking is that you get yours the same way."

Here in Washington, we need to get our house in order. And I have to say, Democrats in Congress and some Senate Republicans have been listening and have shown themselves willing to make compromises to solve this crisis. Now all of us, including Republicans in the House of Representatives, need to demonstrate the same kind of responsibility that the American people show every day. The time for putting party first is over. The time for compromise on behalf of the American people is now.

Thank you.

NOTE: The address was recorded at approximately 5:05 p.m. on July 29 in the Blue Room at the White House for broadcast on July 30. The transcript was made available by the Office of the Press Secretary on July 29, but was embargoed for release until 6 a.m. on July 30.

Statement on the Situation in Syria
July 31, 2011

I am appalled by the Syrian Government's use of violence and brutality against its own people. The reports out of Hama are horrifying and demonstrate the true character of the Syrian regime. Once again, President Asad has shown that he is completely incapable and unwilling to respond to the legitimate grievances of the Syrian people. His use of torture, corruption, and terror puts him on the wrong side of history and his people. Through his own actions, Bashar al-Asad is ensuring that he and his regime will be left in the past and that the courageous Syrian people who have demonstrated in the streets will determine its future. Syria will be a better place when a democratic transition goes forward. In the days ahead, the United States will continue to increase our pressure on the Syrian regime and work with others around the world to isolate the Asad Government and stand with the Syrian people.

Remarks on the Federal Budget
July 31, 2011

Good evening. There are still some very important votes to be taken by Members of Congress, but I want to announce that the leaders of both parties, in both Chambers, have reached an agreement that will reduce the deficit and avoid default, a default that would have had a devastating effect on our economy.

The first part of this agreement will cut about $1 trillion in spending over the next 10 years, cuts that both parties had agreed to early on in this process. The result would be the lowest level of annual domestic spending since Dwight Eisenhower was President, but at a level that still allows us to make job-creating investments in things like education and research. We also made sure that these cuts wouldn't happen so abruptly that they'd be a drag on a fragile economy.

Now, I've said from the beginning that the ultimate solution to our deficit problem must be balanced. Despite what some Republicans have argued, I believe that we have to ask the wealthiest Americans and biggest corporations to pay their fair share by giving up tax breaks and special deductions. Despite what some in my own party have argued, I believe that we need to make some modest adjustments to programs like Medicare to ensure that they're still around for future generations.

That's why the second part of this agreement is so important. It establishes a bipartisan committee of Congress to report back by November with a proposal to further reduce the deficit, which will then be put before the entire Congress for an up-or-down vote. In this stage, everything will be on the table. To hold us all accountable for making these reforms, tough cuts that both parties would find objectionable would automatically go into effect if we don't act. And over the next few months, I'll continue to make a detailed case to these lawmakers about why I believe a balanced approach is necessary to finish the job.

Now, is this the deal I would have preferred? No. I believe that we could have made the tough choices required on entitlement reform and tax reform right now rather than through a special congressional committee process. But this compromise does make a serious down payment on the deficit reduction we need and gives each party a strong incentive to get a balanced plan done before the end of the year.

Most importantly, it will allow us to avoid default and end the crisis that Washington imposed on the rest of America. It ensures also that we will not face this same kind of crisis again in 6 months or 8 months or 12 months. And it will begin to lift the cloud of debt and the cloud of uncertainty that hangs over our economy.

Now, this process has been messy; it's taken far too long. I've been concerned about the impact that it has had on business confidence and consumer confidence and the economy as a whole over the last month. Nevertheless, ultimately, the leaders of both parties have found their way toward compromise. And I want to thank them for that.

Most of all, I want to thank the American people. It's been your voices—your letters, your e-mails, your tweets, your phone calls— that have compelled Washington to act in the

final days. And the American people's voice is a very, very powerful thing.

We're not done yet. I want to urge members of both parties to do the right thing and support this deal with your votes over the next few days. It will allow us to avoid default. It will allow us to pay our bills. It will allow us to start reducing our deficit in a responsible way. And it will allow us to turn to the very important business of doing everything we can to create jobs, boost wages, and grow this economy faster than it's currently growing.

That's what the American people sent us here to do, and that's what we should be devoting all of our time to accomplishing in the months ahead.

Thank you very much everybody.

NOTE: The President spoke at 8:40 p.m. in the James S. Brady Press Briefing Room at the White House.

Statement on the Observance of Ramadan
August 1, 2011

As Ramadan begins, Michelle and I would like to send our best wishes to Muslim communities in the United States and around the world. Ramadan is a festive time that is anticipated for months by Muslims everywhere. Families and communities share the happiness of gathering together for iftar and prayers. Bazaars light up the night in many cities from Rabat to Jakarta. And here in the United States, Muslim Americans share Ramadan traditions with their neighbors, fellow students, and coworkers.

For so many Muslims around the world, Ramadan is also a time of deep reflection and sacrifice. As in other faiths, fasting is used to increase spirituality, discipline, and consciousness of God's mercy. It is also a reminder of

the importance of reaching out to those less fortunate. The heartbreaking accounts of lost lives and the images of families and children in Somalia and the Horn of Africa struggling to survive remind us of our common humanity and compel us to act. Now is the time for nations and peoples to come together to avert an even worse catastrophe by offering support and assistance to ongoing relief efforts.

Times like this remind us of the lesson of all great faiths, including Islam, that we do unto others as we would have them do unto us. In that spirit, I wish Muslims around the world a blessed month, and I look forward to again hosting an iftar dinner here at the White House. *Ramadan Kareem.*

Remarks on the Federal Budget
August 2, 2011

Good afternoon, everybody. Congress has now approved a compromise to reduce the deficit and avert a default that would have devastated our economy. It was a long and contentious debate. And I want to thank the American people for keeping up the pressure on their elected officials to put politics aside and work together for the good of the country.

This compromise guarantees more than $2 trillion in deficit reduction. It's an important first step to ensuring that as a nation we live within our means. Yet it also allows us to keep making key investments in things like education and research that lead to new jobs and assures that we're not cutting too abruptly while the economy is still fragile.

This is, however, just the first step. This compromise requires that both parties work together on a larger plan to cut the deficit, which is important for the long-term health of our economy. And since you can't close the deficit with just spending cuts, we'll need a balanced approach where everything's on the table. Yes, that means making some adjustments to protect health care programs like Medicare so they're there for future generations. It also means reforming our Tax Code so that the wealthiest Americans and biggest corporations pay their fair share. And it means getting rid of taxpayer subsidies to oil and gas companies and tax loopholes that help billionaires pay a lower tax rate than teachers and nurses.

I've said it before, I will say it again: We can't balance the budget on the backs of the very people who have borne the biggest brunt of this recession. We can't make it tougher for young people to go to college or ask seniors to pay more for health care or ask scientists to give up on promising medical research because we couldn't close a tax shelter for the most fortunate among us. Everyone is going to have to chip in. It's only fair. That's the principle I'll be fighting for during the next phase of this process.

And in the coming months, I'll continue also to fight for what the American people care most about: new jobs, higher wages, and faster economic growth. While Washington has been absorbed in this debate about deficits, people across the country are asking what we can do to help the father looking for work. What are we going to do for the single mom who's seen her hours cut back at the hospital? What are we going to do to make it easier for businesses to put up that "Now Hiring" sign?

That's part of the reason that people are so frustrated with what's been going on in this town. In the last few months, the economy's already had to absorb an earthquake in Japan, the economic headwinds coming from Europe, the Arab Spring, and the rile [rise]° in oil prices, all of which have been very challenging for the recovery. But these are things we couldn't control. Our economy didn't need Washington to come along with a manufactured crisis to make things worse. That was in our hands. It's pretty likely that the uncertainty surrounding the raising of the debt ceiling—for both businesses and consumers—has been unsettling and just one more impediment to the full recovery that we need. And it was something that we could have avoided entirely.

So voters may have chosen divided Government, but they sure didn't vote for dysfunctional Government. They want us to solve problems. They want us to get this economy growing and adding jobs. And while deficit reduction is part of that agenda, it is not the whole agenda. Growing the economy isn't just about cutting spending; it's not about rolling back regulations that protect our air and our water and keep our people safe. That's not how we're going to get past this recession. We're going to have to do more than that.

And that's why, when Congress gets back from recess, I will urge them to immediately take some steps—bipartisan, commonsense steps—that will make a difference, that will

---

° White House correction.

create a climate where businesses can hire, where folks have more money in their pockets to spend, where people who are out of work can find good jobs.

We need to begin by extending tax cuts for middle class families so that you have more money in your paychecks next year. If you've got more money in your paycheck, you're more likely to spend it. And that means small businesses and medium-sized businesses and large businesses will all have more customers. That means they'll be in a better position to hire.

And while we're at it, we need to make sure that millions of workers who are still pounding the pavement looking for jobs to support their families are not denied needed unemployment benefits.

Through patent reform, we can cut the redtape that stops too many inventors and entrepreneurs from quickly turning new ideas into thriving businesses, which holds our whole economy back. And I want Congress to pass a set of trade deals—deals we've already negotiated—that would help displaced workers looking for new jobs and would allow our businesses to sell more products in countries in Asia and South America, products that are stamped with the words "Made in America."

We also need to give more opportunities to all those construction workers out there who lost their jobs when the housing boom went bust. We could put them to work right now by giving loans to private companies that want to repair our roads and our bridges and our airports, rebuilding our infrastructure. We have workers who need jobs and a country that needs rebuilding; an infrastructure bank would help us put them together.

And while we're on the topic of infrastructure, there's another stalemate in Congress right now involving our aviation industry which has stalled airport construction projects all around the country and put the jobs of tens of thousands of construction workers and others

at risk because of politics. It's another Washington-inflicted wound on America, and Congress needs to break that impasse now, hopefully before the Senate adjourns, so these folks can get back to work.

So these are some things that we could be doing right now. There's no reason for Congress not to send me those bills so I can sign them into law right away as soon as they get back from recess. Both parties share power in Washington, and both parties need to take responsibility for improving this economy. It's not a Democratic responsibility or a Republican responsibility, it is our collective responsibility as Americans. And I'll be discussing additional ideas in the weeks ahead to help companies hire, invest, and expand.

So we've seen in the past few days that Washington has the ability to focus when there's a timer ticking down and when there's a looming disaster. It shouldn't take the risk of default, the risk of economic catastrophe, to get folks in this town to work together and do their jobs. Because there's already a quiet crisis going on in the lives of a lot of families, in a lot of communities, all across the country. They're looking for work, and they have been for a while, or they're making do with fewer hours or fewer customers, or they're just trying to make ends meet. That ought to compel Washington to cooperate. That ought to compel Washington to compromise, and it ought to compel Washington to act. That ought to be enough to get all of us in this town to do the jobs we were sent here to do. We've got to do everything in our power to grow this economy and put America back to work. That's what I intend to do, and I'm looking forward to working with Congress to make it happen.

Thanks very much, everybody.

NOTE: The President spoke at 1:06 p.m. in the Rose Garden at the White House.

Message to the Congress Certifying the Public Debt Limit Increase
August 2, 2011

To the Congress of the United States:

Pursuant to section 3101A(a)(1)(A) of title 31, United States Code, I hereby certify that the debt subject to limit is within $100,000,000,000 of the limit in 31 U.S.C. 3101(b) and that fur- ther borrowing is required to meet existing commitments.

BARACK OBAMA

The White House,
August 2, 2011.

Remarks Prior to a Cabinet Meeting and an Exchange With Reporters
August 3, 2011

The President. Well, obviously, this has been an eventful last few days. As I said yesterday, we have now averted what could have been a disastrous blow to the economy. And we have identified on the front end over a trillion dollars in spending reductions that can be done sensibly and safely without affecting core programs. And we now have a committee process in Congress that is charged with finding additional savings. It's going to be challenging work, and I'm encouraging Congress to take it with the utmost seriousness.

In the meantime, the American people have been continuing to worry about the underlying state of the economy, about jobs, about their wages, about reduced hours, about fewer customers. The economy is still weakened, partly because of some things we couldn't control, like the Japanese earthquake and the situation in Europe, as well as the Arab Spring and its effect on oil prices. Unfortunately, the debt ceiling crisis over the last month, I think, has had an unnecessary negative impact on the economy here as well.

So I'm meeting with my Cabinet here to make sure that, even as they have been throughout these last several weeks, they are redoubling their efforts to focus on what matters most to the American people, and that is: how are we going to put people back to work; how are we going to raise their wages, increase their security; how are we going to make sure that they recover fully, as families and as com- munities, from the worst recession we've had since the Great Depression.

A good example of how undone work here in Washington can have an adverse impact on that economy is what's going on with the Federal Aviation Administration. And I'm going to be hearing from Ray LaHood about the situation that is looming as a consequence of Congress not acting. Some of you may be aware of the fact that the FAA routinely gets authorities extended through Congress; it's happened 20 times since 2007. This time, Congress has decided to play some politics with it. And as a consequence, they left town without getting this extension done.

Here is what this means: Thousands of FAA workers being furloughed, including safety inspectors. It also means projects all across the country involving tens of thousands of construction workers being suspended because Congress didn't get its work done. And that means folks who are on construction sites, doing work and bringing home a paycheck, now potentially find themselves going home without one, and important projects all across the country are left undone.

Here's what also happens. It turns out that this extension gives the authority to collect fees from airlines. The airlines are still collecting these fees because it's priced into their tickets, but they're not turning them over to the Federal Government, and the Federal Government stands to lose $200 million a week. That would be a billion dollars at a time when we're worrying about how we pay for everything from education to Head Start. And we don't anticipate it's going to be easy to get that money back. Even though the airlines are collecting it, they're keeping it.

So this is a lose-lose-lose situation that can be easily solved if Congress gets back into town and does its job. And they don't even have to come back into town. The House and the Senate could, through a procedural agreement, basically do this through unanimous consent. And they can have the fights that they want to have when they get back. Don't put the livelihoods of thousands of people at risk. Don't put projects at risk. And don't let a billion dollars, at a time when we're scrambling for every dollar we can, get left on the table because Congress did not act.

So I'm urging the House and the Senate to take care of this. This is an example of a self-inflicted wound that is unnecessary. And my expectation and I think the American people's expectation is, is that this gets resolved before the end of this week.

All right? Thank you very much, everybody.

Federal Aviation Administration's Operating Authority

Q. Mr. President, anything that you can do, sir? Can you intervene? Is there anything you can do?

The President. Well, I am—I have made calls to key leaders, and I am urging them to get this done. But this is, as I said, not the kind of situation that is complicated. All they have to do is do what they've done 20 times since 2007. There's not a big issue in terms of drafting legislation or arguing about the details of policy. Just do what they've done in the past to make sure that these folks are on the job, including looking after the safety of our airlines.

All right? Thank you very much.

The President's Birthday

Q. Are you ready for 5–0, Mr. President?

The President. I'm going to get advice from some around the table—[*laughter*]—about how to handle this milestone. [*Laughter*] All right?

NOTE: The President spoke at 2:05 p.m. in the Cabinet Room at the White House.

Remarks at a Democratic National Committee Fundraiser in Chicago, Illinois
August 3, 2011

The President. Hello, Chicago! Oh, it is good to be with some good friends! This is a warm welcome right here.

Let me first of all say thank you to the extraordinary, extraordinary talent that's on stage. First of all, one of the greatest jazz musicians of our time, Herbie Hancock; OK Go band—give it up; DJ Greg Corner—give it up; the lovely and talented Jennifer Hudson from Chicago; the not as lovely or talented, but— [*laughter*]—very determined, very brilliant, very loyal, very tough mayor of the city of Chicago, Rahm Emanuel.

I don't know—you know, I'm watching from Washington, but it looks to me like Rahm's doing a pretty good job. And as far as I can tell, he hasn't cursed in public yet. [*Laughter*] He's come close, he says. [*Laughter*] But what he has done is provided extraordinary energy and

extraordinary vision to a job that he has wanted for a long time. And I don't know too many people who love the city of Chicago more than your mayor, and I couldn't be more proud of him, so—[*applause*].

Now, we've got a few more dignitaries in the house. We've got the Governor of the great State of Illinois, Patrick Quinn, in the house. We've got one of the finest Senators in the United States of America, Dick Durbin, in the house. We've got one of the greatest Members of Congress in the country in Jan Schakowsky in the house. We've got the ageless Jesse White, the secretary of state, in the house. A great friend of mine, somebody who I wouldn't have been elected to the United States Senate without him, the former senator of the Illinois State Senate, Emil Jones is here. And I know we've got a lot of other important people—like you—in the house.

Now, it's warm, and it's hot, and you just listened to some good music, and you don't want to have a long political speech. But I just wanted to first of all say I could not have a better early birthday present——

Audience member. I love you!

The President. ——than spending tonight with all of you. I love you back.

And it's true that I turn 50 tomorrow, which means that by the time I wake up, I'll have an e-mail from AARP asking me to call President Obama and tell him to protect Medicare. [*Laughter*]

When I look out at this crowd, I think back to that incredible night in November—I'm still trying to figure out how the weather was over 60 degrees in November—in Grant Park back in 2008. And it was the culmination of this incredible journey, this long journey that we took together, a campaign that drew on the hard work and support of all of you and people all across the country, men and women who believed that change was possible. In the face of long odds, in the face of frustrations, in the face of setbacks, you said, we don't have to accept politics as usual, and we can once again have a country that is living up to our finest ideals and our highest aspirations.

And that was a lovely night. But you remember what I told you that night. I said——

Audience member. Yes, we can!

The President. ——I said, "Yes, we can," but I said this would not be easy. I said that wasn't the end of the journey, that was just the beginning. The economy was already hammering families. Decisions that had been deferred for too long in Washington were finally catching up with us. All these problems were gathering all at once. And we knew the road ahead was going to be difficult, that the climb was going to be steep.

I have to admit, I didn't know how steep the climb was going to be. [*Laughter*] Because we didn't realize—we just found out a week ago that the economy that last few months in 2008 was even worse than we had realized. I mean, the economy had contracted by 8 percent. It

was the worst economy we had ever seen. The next quarter, before any of our economic policies had a chance to go into place, same kind of thing. We lost 8 million jobs like that, hadn't seen anything like it in most of our lifetimes.

But here's what I knew. You did not elect me President to duck the tough issues. You elected me President to do the tough things, to do the big things, even if it took time.

You elected me to make sure that the economy was working not just for those at the very top, but that we had a broad-based, shared prosperity, from the machinist on the line to the CEO in the boardroom.

And I ran because I believed that our success is defined not by stock prices or corporate profits alone, but by whether ordinary people can find a good job that supports a family, whether they can send their kids to college, whether they can retire with dignity and respect, maybe have a little left over for a ballgame or a vacation, not be bankrupt when they get sick.

So what we did was we took a series of emergency measures that first year to save the economy from collapse. And I promise you not all of them were popular. But we did what we needed to do to start getting the economy growing again. And it has been growing, not as fast as we want, but we got the economy growing instead of contracting because we wanted to help families get back on their feet.

We went in and we said—I didn't sign up to be a CEO of an auto company, but I said I'm not going to let a million jobs, especially here in the Midwest, go away, so we're going to intervene, and we're going to ask in return that the auto companies restructure themselves. And we've now seen for the first time in a very long time all the Big Three automakers making a profit. And making a profit selling small cars and compact cars and doing stuff that a lot of Americans thought couldn't be done anymore.

And we said, even as we're saving the economy, there's some—still some issues out there that haven't been dealt with in a very long time, so we're going to make sure that we've got equal pay for equal work, because I don't want Malia and Sasha getting paid less than anybody for doing a good job.

And we're going to make sure that in this country that we love, that nobody is discriminated against on the basis of sexual orientation. We're going to make sure they can serve in our military and protect the country that they love.

And we're going to invest in clean energy, because we're tired of being dependent on foreign oil. So we want wind turbines and electric cars made right here in the United States of America. And we're going to increase our investment in basic research to find cures for cancer and Alzheimer's. And we're going to revamp our education system so it starts working for every child and not just some children.

And yes, we are going to go ahead and make sure that every family in America can find affordable health care and that they are not losing their home or going bankrupt because they get sick. And it was hard, but because of you, we kept on driving and we got it done.

So it's been a long, tough journey. But we have made some incredible strides together.

[At this point, a baby in the audience cried.]

The President. Yes, we have. [*Laughter*] But the thing that we all have to remember is, is that as much good as we've done, precisely because the challenges were so daunting, precisely because we were inheriting so many challenges, that we're not even halfway there yet.

When I said, "Change we can believe in," I didn't say, "Change we can believe in tomorrow." [*Laughter*] Not, "Change we can believe in next week." We knew this was going to take time, because we've got this big, messy, tough democracy. And that's a great thing about America is, is that there are all these contentious ideas that are out there, and we've got to make our case. And we knew that these challenges weren't made overnight and they weren't going to be solved overnight.

And so, as we look forward, we know we've still got a lot of work to do on the economy. Now, I hope we can avoid another self-inflicted wound like we just saw over the last couple of weeks, because we don't have time to play these partisan games. We've got too much work to do.

Over the next several months, I hope Congress is focused on what the American people are focused on, making sure that the economy is growing, making sure that businesses are getting financing, making sure that young people are getting trained for the jobs of the future, making sure that we're getting all those construction workers that got laid off after the housing boom went bust and putting them to work rebuilding our roads and our bridges, rebuilding Chicago, rebuilding Detroit, rebuilding rural communities all across the country, putting people back to work.

I want to make sure that America is not just an importer; I want us to export. I want to build electric cars in America, and I want to ship them all around the world, because we've got the best technologies. I want us to focus on how we can revamp old buildings and old facilities so they're energy efficient. And we can start cutting down on our electricity bills, and we can start cutting down on our carbon emissions. And we can stop being so dependent on foreign oil, and you don't have to pay as much at the pump. That's what the American people are looking for. That's what we've got to focus on.

We've got more work to do to make sure that we've got an immigration system in this country that makes some sense. We are a nation of laws, and we are a nation of immigrants. And we want to welcome extraordinary talent to our shores and have a legal immigration system that works for everybody. We've got to make that happen.

We've got to—and a lot of the stuff that we've already done, we've got to make sure it gets implemented effectively. We finally put some commonsense rules so that banks aren't taking the kinds of risks that almost led to an economic meltdown and that consumers are protected when you get credit cards or mortgages.

And frankly, there are some folks in Congress who are trying to block us from making that progress. And that's why your voice has to be heard, where we stand up and we say: We want a financial system that is fair for everybody. There's nothing wrong with that.

And on the foreign policy front, you elected me in part based on a promise that we would end the war in Iraq, and we have ended combat operations there. And by the end of this year, we will have our troops out of Iraq, as I promised and as I committed. And in Afghanistan, we've got Al Qaida on the run, and we are going to begin transitioning to give Afghans more responsibility, but also to start bringing our troops home, because we've got a lot of work to do here at home to rebuild America.

But our foreign policy can't just be about war, it's also got to be about peace. It's also got to be about helping countries feed the hungry. It's got to be about helping countries transition to democracy. It's got to be about respecting human rights all around the world and making sure that America continues to be a beacon of hope. That's part of why you elected me. That's part of the unfinished business of this administration.

And as we think about this world, we understand that it's shrunk and it's going to be more competitive. And if we're going to leave the kind of America behind to our children and our grandchildren, then we've still got some work to do. Yes, we've got to get our fiscal house in order. And all the progressives out there, I want you to understand that we can't just ignore this debt and deficit, we've got to do something about it. But economic growth, making ourselves more competitive isn't just about cutting programs. It's also about making investments in our people.

It's also about making sure we've got the best education system in the world, that we've got the best scientists and engineers and mathematicians in the world, making sure that we prize our diversity, making sure that we've got a social safety net for the aged and the infirm and our children. That's part of what makes us a great nation.

So, Chicago, we've got more work to do. We've got more work to do. And look, let me just say this, it is going to continue to be challenging every single step of the way.

Audience member. But we can do it!

The President. But we can do it. [*Applause*] You know, I'm always amused when the pundits in Washington say, "Boy, you know, Obama hasn't gotten this passed yet," or, "Some of his supporters are disappointed about this," and, "The campaign, it was so smooth." And I'm thinking, what campaign were they watching? [*Laughter*] I mean, there—at least once a month, folks would say, "He can't win." At least once a month, people would say, "Oh, that was a terrible debate for him," or, "Oh, he's lost support in this or that group," or, "Oh, that State is going to go red on him."

What they didn't understand was, is that for all the mistakes I'll make, for all the boneheaded moves I made—might make, for all the frustrations and the challenges and resistance we have to bringing about change, when I've got you guys behind me, when I've got the American people, when I listen to them and I'm reminded of your decency and those core values that say I am my brother's keeper and I am my sister's keeper and what makes us a great nation is not just the height of our skyscrapers or the size of our GDP or the power of our military, but the fact that we look after one another and we take responsibility for ourselves, but also for our neighbors, when we're working together and we're joining hands, Black and White and Hispanic and Asian and Native American and gay and straight—when the American people join together, we cannot be stopped.

We say to ourselves, "Yes, we can." It doesn't matter how tough a week I have in Washington, because I know you've got me— you've got my back. When I come to Chicago, when I travel across the country, I know we can't be stopped. I know America is the greatest nation on Earth. And I know we will bring about the change that all of us believe in.

God bless you all. Thank you, and God bless the United States of America.

NOTE: The President spoke at 7:22 p.m. at the Aragon Entertainment Center.

Remarks During a Democratic National Committee Video Teleconference and a Question-and-Answer Session in Chicago
August 3, 2011

The President. Hey, guys. How are you? I am beaming in from Chicago. We're having a little birthday celebration in my hometown. But I just want to say thank you to all of you. I can't think of a better group of folks to spend my birthday with.

You may hear the 'L' train in the background. It's passing right next to us. You know, when we started this whole journey back in 2008, the one thing that I was clear about was that this was not going to be about me. This was going to be about us. It was going to be about the values we hold dear as Americans. It was going to be about grassroots folks being empowered, talking about how we can create jobs in our community and improve our schools and make sure our kids have opportunities to go to college and how people can retire with dignity and respect. And those bread-and-butter issues were not going to be settled in Washington. They were going to be settled on the ground, in neighborhoods. And as somebody who cut my teeth as a community organizer, I knew that nothing was more powerful than the American people when they make common cause and they decide that they want to bring about change.

And what was true in 2008 is just as true today. We've obviously been through a lot of battles over the last 2½ years dealing with one of the worst recessions in our history and certainly one of the toughest economic situations in my lifetime. But despite all that, what we've been able to do is to work to make sure that the economy has started recovering. We were able to save over a million jobs through our intervention in the auto industry. We were able to finally get health care done so that families were more secure. We were able to make sure that things like "don't ask, don't tell" got ended and that we were going to make sure that ordinary folks were benefiting from tax cuts, small businesses were benefiting. All those things we could not have done had it not been for you.

And so as we gear back up to fight some tough battles—and you saw this week how tough some of these battles are going to be—it is absolutely critical that all of you stay involved.

And so I want to thank everybody at these house parties, but I want to urge all of you to get involved as a team to start going out not only spreading the message, but also listening to people and finding out what's on their minds and figuring out how we can engage them and get them involved. And that's where these neighborhood teams are so important. We're already had contact with 42,000 individuals face to face across the Nation because of the teams that are activated in the States that are represented on this phone call. We have had 2 million calls made to folks all across the country, contacting them, listening to their concerns, and finding out how they want to get involved in this campaign.

But this is always easier to do as a team and as a group than it is for folks to do this individually. Obviously, I want you to talk to your friends and your family and the Republican uncle that you got who isn't persuaded yet, and you corner him at an event, and you talk issues at the workplace, around the water cooler, having conversations with friends of yours about why it's so important for them to be engaged.

All that's important, but what's most important is when you guys as a team think about your neighborhoods and all the people that may have gotten turned off to politics, may be disillusioned, maybe are going through a tough time because of this difficult economy. When they know their neighbors, their friends, folks who are—they see at parent-teacher night, when those folks see you, you're the best ambassador we could have. And when you go out as a team, it's going to strengthen your capacity to move people in a direction that could bring about the change we want.

So I just want to emphasize to you how important you are, and I hope that you use this house party, in addition to having some cake—I don't know if you guys have party hats—but in addition to having a good party, I hope you guys talk about how your neighborhood teams can get together and really do some great work on the ground.

We're in for a long battle. We've got 16 months in which we're just going to have to be knocking on doors, making phone calls, turning out voters. But it starts now. It builds now. And it starts with you.

So thank you, everybody, for being part of this. And I think I'm going to get a chance to answer a couple questions before I sign off.

Organizing for America Deputy Director Jeremy Bird. Excellent. Mr. President, thank you so much for joining us. Our first question we're going to take from North Carolina, in Greensboro, North Carolina. And you'll be able to take the question live.

2012 Presidential Campaign/Tax Code Reform/Military Operations in Iraq and Afghanistan

Q. Hi, Mr. President. Happy birthday!

[At this point, "Happy Birthday" was sung.]

Q. It's such a great honor——
The President. [*Inaudible*]
Q. I'm sorry?
The President. I said you all have great voices.
Q. Oh, thank you. We do our best. It's such a great honor to continue the great work we started in 2008. I want to continue to do great work for you for the next year and a half. While I'm out there canvassing, though, I have difficulty answering some of the detailed questions in regards to taxes and the wars. As one of the best organizers I know, which is you, Mr. President, what type of advice do you have for someone like me?

The President. Well, first of all, I just want to thank all of you guys for the great work you're doing, and I can't wait to see you guys at the convention in North Carolina. It is going to be absolutely outstanding.

But a couple things I'd say. First of all, when you go out and talk to people, I want to make sure that everybody understands you've got to listen as much as you talk. So part of what people want to know is, is that they're being heard. What are their concerns? What are—what's keeping them up at night? What would they like to see happen in Washington?

So making sure we listen, that's really important. The second thing is that we always have to talk about values. People are concerned about issues, but they also want to know what do we stand for. And so if somebody asks about taxes, nobody is really interested in hearing what precise marginal tax rate change would you like to see in the Tax Code. What they want to know is that our campaign stands for a fair, just approach to the Tax Code that says everybody has to chip in and that it's not right if a hedge fund manager is being taxed at a lower rate than his or her secretary. And so that's a values issue: Is the Tax Code fair?

If somebody asks about the war, whether it's Iraq or Afghanistan—if it's Iraq, you have a pretty simple answer, which is all our folks are going to be out of there by the end of the year. If it's Afghanistan, you can talk about, look, we think it's time for us to transition to Afghan lead and rebuild here at home. So again, it's a values issue: Where are we prioritizing our resources?

I think the key is not to get too bogged down in detail, but having said that, the last point I'd make is, it's Jeremy's job to make sure that you guys have good talking points and know the answers to some of these questions. And so when your neighborhood teams start forming, on any given issue, every single week, you should be getting sort of updates in terms of what is going on in Washington. We're going to be rolling out plans to improve our infrastructure and put construction workers back to work. We're going to be rolling out plans to make sure that we continue the payroll tax cut that's put $1,000 in the pockets of every American on average. So we'll have a bunch of issues, and those will change week to week. And you should be able to get the kind of information that you need that at least gives you enough of a sense of what we're doing and what we care about that you can answer these questions intelligently.

And you know, the last point I'd make: Sometimes it's not so bad to say, "I don't know." So if somebody asks you something about, well, where does the President stand on Cyprus—[*laughter*]—there's nothing wrong with you saying, "I'm not sure, but here's what I can promise you: I'll find out an answer, and we'll make sure to call you back and give you an answer." And people appreciate that. They don't expect you to know the ins and outs of every single policy. But they do expect that you're going to treat them with courtesy and that you're going to get back to them if you don't know the answer to something.

All right? Thank you, guys.

Q. Thank you so much!

Mr. Bird. Thank you, North Carolina. Mr. President, we're going to take one more question, and this question comes from Maureen, who's calling in from Shaker Heights in Ohio. And we're going to turn it over to Maureen and her house party right now.

Maureen.

2012 Presidential Campaign

The President. Hey, Maureen!

Q. Hello. Happy birthday.

The President. Thank you.

Q. I have a question for you. All right, in 2008, I went door to door with my father and with you, and we had a great time. In 2012, I'm going to be recruiting others, and I want them to help me knock doors. And if you were asking someone to volunteer, how would you ask them?

The President. You know, first of all, Maureen, thank you to everybody in Shaker Heights, and thanks to everybody in Ohio for the unbelievable work you guys have already done. That's how we won Ohio.

But I think the main thing is to give people a sense that this campaign is about them and not about just electing a President. It's about being part of a community and going out there and talking to your fellow members of your community about what values you care about. So make sure that people feel ownership over the process.

And also, make it fun. I mean, I think that if you say to folks, you know what, we're going to go door to door, but at the end of it, we're all going to get together and have a picnic, or come over to your house and talk about the issues that are important to us, and let's bring some kids along, and make it a community event, that makes it a lot more effective.

So I think that asking people to get engaged because the future is going to be determined by this election. We've already seen over this last week just how different the visions are of the two parties in terms of where we should take this country. I think it's very clear who's going to be looking out for working families, who wants to invest in things like education, who wants to make sure that we've got strong social insurance programs like Medicare and Social Security that are going to look after people, but also how do we maintain those in a responsible way.

So you can make the pitch saying, this is really an important moment in our history; we've got to get involved right now. But you also want to make it fun and make them feel like they're part of something larger. A lot of folks just respond to wanting to be with their friends and doing something interesting.

And if you do that, I guarantee you won't get 100-percent takeup because people are busy and they may not be able to go every time. But as the people at your house party know, it turns out it's actually pretty fun to spend some time with people and work on issues that you care about.

So I couldn't be more appreciative of you guys, and I'm really very grateful.

All right, Maureen? Good luck.

Q. Thank you very much, Mr. President.

The President. Thank you, guys.

Q. Happy birthday!

2012 Presidential Campaign

Mr. Bird. All right. Mr. President, we'll take one last question, and then we can conclude. Our question came from the question-and-answer pile, from Grand Rapids, Michigan. And the question was, what's the most important thing we as volunteers can do to further your campaign?

The President. Well, we've already talked about it. The most important thing you can do is to be engaged and to reach out to your circle of friends and family, not to try to give them just a laundry list of things that we've already done, but to listen to them and give them a sense that they can make a difference if they get involved.

This democracy works when people get involved. This democracy works when people are paying attention. And this democracy works when people are joining together to make their voices heard. And that's what all of you are all about.

The more you guys are out there engaging people, talking to people, listening to them, asking their ideas, the more this is a bottom-up as opposed to a top-down operation.

One of the great things in 2008 was folks were just starting their own organizations. We had folks in Idaho who just decided out of the— we're going to start a Idaho for Obama. And we didn't have any staff there, we didn't have any money. And yet they were able to organize an 18,000-person rally just out of their own energy and input, and they owned this thing.

And that's the thing I want to emphasize to all of you. You own this campaign. You own this country. And if you use that power that you've got, then we're going to be able to continue to get all the things done that we want to get done. I know that over the last 2½ years there have been times where people have been frustrated. This past week was a frustrating week. But think about all we've accomplished together. We've been able to start turning around this economy. We've been able to get health care passed. We've been able to make sure that there's an equal day's pay for an equal

day's work. We've been able to make sure that children were able to get health insurance that didn't have it before. We've been able to end this war in Iraq in a responsible way.

And so that should give us confidence that we can make happen all the things that are still undone, whether it's making sure that the economy is growing faster and creating more jobs to getting immigration reform passed, to making sure that we've got an energy policy that makes sense in this country and making sure that we've got a Tax Code that's fair and that's just and that we're dealing with our deficits and debt in a responsible way, and it's not all on the backs of middle class families.

Those are things that I know we can accomplish, but this election is going to be a seminal election, in some ways maybe more important than the last one. And with your voices, I'm absolutely confident that we not only can win, but more importantly, we can deliver the change that's needed for the American people.

So I've got to go downstairs. I'm going to have to—there's a big crowd wanting to sing me "Happy Birthday." I don't know if there's cake down there. But I know they've been waiting for me. But I want to say to all of you, thank you for your good wishes. Thanks for your courage. Thanks for your determination and tenacity. And I'm going to see you all, hopefully, when I get to the various States and cities and towns where you guys are gathered.

All right? Have fun. See you.

NOTE: The President spoke at 6:59 p.m. at the Aragon Entertainment Center. The transcript was released by the Office of the Press Secretary on August 4. Audio was not available for verification of the content of these remarks.

Remarks at a Democratic National Committee Fundraiser in Chicago
August 3, 2011

The President. Thank you. Everybody have a seat, have a seat, have a seat.

Well, if you guys are taking off your jackets, I'm going to take mine off too. [*Laughter*] It's too hot. It is too hot.

Well, it is wonderful to see all of you.

[*At this point, Mayor Rahm I. Emanuel of Chicago took the President's jacket.*]

The President. Thank you. Now, that's service. [*Laughter*] I still have that pothole in front of my house. [*Laughter*] Golly, I've been working on that. Trees need trimming. [*Laughter*]

It is wonderful to see all of you. I know that most of you had a chance to listen to me speak downstairs, so I'm not going to give another long speech. The main thing I just want to do is to say thank you to all of you. A lot of folks came, traveled from across the country.

And obviously, we've just gone through an extraordinary week in Washington, an extraordinary 2 weeks in Washington. It's not the kind of extraordinary that the American people are looking for. [*Laughter*] Because at a time when so many families are struggling, at a time when we should be singularly focused on how to make ourselves more competitive and make sure our kids have the best educations possible and how are we transforming our energy strategy and how are we building on high-tech industries and the huge competitive advantages that we have, politics continues to get in the way.

And I think this episode was just a severe example of what's been going on for quite some time. And it's part of what led me to run for President. It's part of what led Rahm to get into public service. And it's part of the reason why, hopefully, all of you are here tonight, because you recognize we've still got some more work to do.

The good news is that after this week we have made a legitimate downpayment on deficit reduction in a way that's actually responsible, that is not going to dismantle our social safety net, isn't going to prevent us from making the key investments we need to win the future.

But it also sets the stage for what is going to be a singular debate over the next year and a half, and that is two alternative visions about where the country needs to go.

I give the other side credit. They are single minded in their focus in wanting to cut programs and shrink Government. My argument, Dick Durbin's argument, the argument that I think all of you believe in, is that we need a Government that is smart, that is living within its

means, but also we need a Government that is making the kind of commitment to opportunity for everybody, for every child; that is making investments that the private sector alone can't make; that are setting policies that allow us to be competitive into the future; that is looking after our seniors and poor children and the disabled and empowering them; and that all of us have a role to play in that kind of America and all of us have to make some sacrifices to deliver that kind of America.

And I think most of the American people believe the same thing. But in this kind of environment of 24-hour cable chatter and big money flooding the airwaves and slash-and-burn politics, sometimes I think that core belief in what is possible here in America gets lost. It's our job to constantly restore it and revitalize it and to have confidence in the American people, that if we're making our arguments with the same kind of passion and commitment that the other side is showing, that ultimately our democracy will make a decision, and I think it will be a decision to pursue the kind of vision that all of us believe in.

But we're going to have a lot of work to do, and it's going to be tough. And this week, I think, signifies not only how tough it's going to be, but exactly what's at stake. And for you to make the kind of commitment to be here tonight, to be committed to engaging, the fact that you're in, is going to make all the difference in the world.

So thank you very much, everybody. And I think we're going to just take a bunch of questions. Then, I'm going to have a chance to walk around the room and shake everybody's hands before I head back home and see my kids. Malia is coming home from camp tomorrow just for her daddy's birthday, and I'm very happy about that.

NOTE: The President spoke at 8:21 p.m. at the Aragon Entertainment Center. The transcript was released by the Office of the Press Secretary on August 4. Audio was not available for verification of the content of these remarks.

Statement on Congressional Action on Federal Aviation Administration Reauthorization Legislation
August 4, 2011

I'm pleased that leaders in Congress are working together to break the impasse involving the FAA so that tens of thousands of construction workers and others can go back to work. We can't afford to let politics in Washington hamper our recovery, so this is an important step forward.

Directive on Creation of an Interagency Atrocities Prevention Board and Corresponding Interagency Review
August 4, 2011

Presidential Study Directive/PSD–10

Memorandum for the Vice President; the Secretary of State; the Secretary of the Treasury; the Secretary of Defense; the Attorney General; the Secretary of Homeland Security; Assistant to the President and Chief of Staff; Director of the Office of Management and Budget; United States Trade Representative; Representative of the United States of America to the United Nations; Assistant to the President and National Security Advisor; Director of National Intelligence; Counsel to the President; Assistant to the President for Legislative Affairs; Director of the Central Intelligence Agency; Administrator of the United States Agency for International Development; Chairman of the Joint Chiefs of Staff; Chief Executive Officer, Millennium Challenge Corporation; Director of the Peace Corps; Deputy Assistant to the President and National Security Advisor to the Vice President; Director of the National Security Agency; and Director of the Defense Intelligence Agency

Subject: Creation of an Interagency Atrocities Prevention Board and Corresponding Interagency Review

Preventing mass atrocities and genocide is a core national security interest and a core moral responsibility of the United States.

Our security is affected when masses of civilians are slaughtered, refugees flow across borders, and murderers wreak havoc on regional stability and livelihoods. America's reputation suffers, and our ability to bring about change is constrained, when we are perceived as idle in the face of mass atrocities and genocide. Unfortunately, history has taught us that our pursuit of a world where states do not systematically slaughter civilians will not come to fruition without concerted and coordinated effort.

Governmental engagement on atrocities and genocide too often arrives too late, when opportunities for prevention or low-cost, low-risk action have been missed. By the time these issues have commanded the attention of senior policy makers, the menu of options has shrunk considerably and the costs of action have risen.

In the face of a potential mass atrocity, our options are never limited to either sending in the military or standing by and doing nothing. The actions that can be taken are many—they range from economic to diplomatic interventions, and from non-combat military actions to outright intervention. But ensuring that the full range of options is available requires a level of governmental organization that matches the methodical organization characteristic of mass killings.

Sixty-six years since the Holocaust and 17 years after Rwanda, the United States still lacks a comprehensive policy framework and a corresponding interagency mechanism for preventing and responding to mass atrocities and genocide. This has left us ill-prepared to engage early, proactively, and decisively to prevent threats from evolving into large-scale civilian atrocities.

Accordingly, I hereby direct the establishment of an interagency Atrocities Prevention Board within 120 days from the date of this Presidential Study Directive. The primary purpose of the Atrocities Prevention Board shall be to coordinate a whole-of-government approach to preventing mass atrocities and genocide. By institutionalizing the coordination of atrocity prevention, we can ensure: (1) that our national security apparatus recognizes and is responsive to early indicators of potential atrocities; (2) that departments and agencies develop and implement comprehensive atrocity prevention and response strategies in a manner that allows "red flags" and dissent to be raised to decisionmakers; (3) that we increase the capacity and develop doctrine for our foreign service, armed services, development professionals, and other actors to engage in the full spectrum of smart prevention activities; and (4) that we are optimally positioned to work with our allies in order to ensure that the burdens of atrocity prevention and response are appropriately shared.

To this end, I direct the National Security Advisor to lead a focused interagency study to develop and recommend the membership, mandate, structure, operational protocols, authorities, and support necessary for the Atrocities Prevention Board to coordinate and develop atrocity prevention and response policy. Specifically, the interagency review shall identify:

- operational protocols necessary for the Atrocities Prevention Board to coordinate and institutionalize the Federal Government's efforts to prevent and respond to potential atrocities and genocide, including but not limited to: identifying (standing and *ex officio*) members of the Atrocities Prevention Board; defining the scope of the Atrocity Prevention Board's mandate and the means by which it will ensure that the full range of options and debate is presented to senior-level decisionmakers; identifying triggers for the development of atrocity prevention strategies; identifying any specific authority the Atrocities Prevention Board or its members should have

with respect to alerting the President to a potential genocide or atrocity;

- how the Intelligence Community and other relevant Government agencies can best support the Atrocities Prevention Board's mission, including but not limited to: examining the multiplicity of existing early warning assessments in order to recommend how these efforts can be better coordinated and/or consolidated, support the work of the Atrocities Prevention Board, and drive the development of atrocity prevention strategies and policies; examining options for improving intelligence and open source assessments of the potential for genocide and mass atrocities; and examining protocols for safely declassifying and/or sharing intelligence when needed to galvanize regional actors, allies, or relevant institutions to respond to an atrocity or genocide; and

- steps toward creating a comprehensive policy framework for preventing mass atrocities, including but not limited to: conducting an inventory of existing tools and authorities across the Government that can be drawn upon to prevent atrocities; identifying new tools or capabilities that may be required; identifying how we can better support and train our foreign and armed services, development professionals, and build the capacity of key regional allies and partners, in order to be better prepared to prevent and respond to mass atrocities or genocide.

In answering these questions, the interagency review shall consider the recommendations of relevant bipartisan and expert studies, including the recommendations of the bipartisan Genocide Prevention Task Force, co-chaired by former Secretaries Madeleine K. Albright and William Cohen.

I direct the National Security Advisor, through the National Security Staff's Director for War Crimes and Atrocities, to oversee and direct the interagency review, which shall include representatives from the following:

Office of the Vice President
Department of State
Department of the Treasury
Department of Defense
Department of Justice
Department of Homeland Security
United States Mission to the United Nations
Office of the Director of National Intelligence
Central Intelligence Agency
United States Agency for International Development
Joint Chiefs of Staff
Peace Corps

National Security Agency
Defense Intelligence Agency

Executive departments and agencies shall be responsive to all requests from the National Security Advisor-led interagency review committee for information, analysis, and assistance.

The interagency review shall be completed within 100 days, so that the Atrocities Prevention Board can commence its work within 120 days from the date of this Presidential Study Directive.

BARACK OBAMA

Remarks at Washington Navy Yard
August 5, 2011

Well, thank you very much, everybody. Good morning. I'm glad somebody told me that was the last one because I had lost count. [*Laughter*]

It is great to be here at the Navy Yard. And first of all, I want to thank Admiral Mullen for being here and for his four decades of extraordinary service to this country. And I want to thank him for saying that for an old guy I look okay. [*Laughter*] I appreciate that.

This may be one of the oldest shipyards in the United States, but today it's used to develop some of the most advanced technology in the military. Although I hear your engineers are still working on a solution to the traffic when the Nationals are playing. [*Laughter*] That's not ready yet.

Let me start by saying a few words about our economy. There is no doubt this has been a tumultuous year. We've weathered the Arab Spring's effect on oil and gas prices, the Japanese earthquake and tsunami's effect on supply chains, the extraordinary economic uncertainty in Europe. And recently, markets around the globe have taken a bumpy ride.

My concern right now, my singular focus, is the American people. Getting the unemployed back on the job, lifting their wages. Rebuilding that sense of security the middle class has felt slipping away for years. And helping them re-

cover fully, as families and as communities, from the worst recession that any of us have ever seen.

Today we know that our economy created 154,000 new private sector jobs in July. And that's the strongest pace since April. The unemployment rate went down, not up. But while this marks the 17th month in a row of job growth in the private sector, nearly 2.5 million new private sector jobs in all, we have to create more jobs than that each month to make up for the more than 8 million jobs that the recession claimed. We need to create a self-sustaining cycle where people are spending and companies are hiring and our economy is growing. And we've known that will take some time.

But what I want the American people and our partners around the world to know is this: We are going to get through this. Things will get better, and we're going to get there together.

The bipartisan compromise on deficit reduction was important in terms of putting us on sounder fiscal footing going forward. But let's be honest: The process was divisive. It was delayed. And if we want our businesses to have the confidence they need to get cash off the sidelines and invest and hire, we've got to do better than that. We've got to be able to work together to grow the economy right now and strengthen our long-term finances. That's what the American people expect of us: leaders that can put aside our differences to meet our challenges.

So when Congress gets back in September, I want to move quickly on things that will help the economy create jobs right now: extending the payroll tax credit to put $1,000 in the pocket of the average worker, extending unemployment insurance to help people get back on their feet, putting construction workers back to work rebuilding America. Those are all steps that we can take right now that will make a difference. And there's no contradiction between us taking some steps to put people to work right now and getting our long-term fiscal house in order. In fact, the more we grow, the easier it will be to reduce our deficits.

Now, both parties share power. Both parties share responsibility for our progress. Moving our economy and our country forward is not a Democratic or a Republican responsibility. It's not a public or a private responsibility. It is the responsibility of all Americans. It's in our nature to do the tough things when necessary, to do the right things when called. And that's the spirit that Washington needs right now.

It's also the kind of spirit found in the men and women who proudly serve in our country's uniform, and it's a spirit that endures long after they take those uniforms off. Today's veterans are Americans who have done their duty. They have fought our wars with valor, from the jungles of Vietnam to the deserts of Iraq to the mountains of Afghanistan. And they include the members of today's military, the 9/11 generation, some of whom are here today, who volunteered to serve at a time of war knowing they would be sent into harm's way.

To these men and women, I want to say that all of you have served our country with honor. Over the last decade, you have performed heroically and done everything we have asked of you in some of the most dangerous places on the planet. Your generation has earned a special place in American history.

Today, nearly 3 million extraordinary servicemembers like you have completed their service and made the transition back to civilian life. They've taken their leadership experience, their mastery of cutting-edge technologies, their ability to adapt to changing circumstances, and they've become leaders here at home. Just think about how many veterans have led their comrades on life-and-death missions by the time they were 25 years old. That's the kind of responsibility and experience that any business in America should want to take advantage of.

These veterans are already making an impact, making companies and communities stronger. But for every success story, there are also stories of veterans who come home and struggle to find a job worthy of their experience and worthy of their talent.

Veterans like Nick Colgin. When Nick was in Afghanistan, he served as a combat medic with the 82d Airborne. Over the course of his deployment, Nick saved the life of a French soldier who was shot in the head and helped 42 people escape from a flooding river. He earned a Bronze Star for his actions. But when Nick got back home to Wyoming, he couldn't get a job as a first-responder. So he ended up having to take classes through the post-9/11 GI bill, classes he easily could have taught, just so he could qualify for the same duties at home that he was doing every single day in Afghanistan.

They're veterans like Maria Canales. She was a financial specialist in the Army, helping provide financial support for her unit in Iraq. And when she got home, she finished earning her degree in business management. But even with her education and her experience in the Army, Maria still couldn't find a steady, working job in accounting or finance. That isn't right, and it doesn't make any sense, not for our veterans, not for the strength of our country.

If you can save a life in Afghanistan, you can save a life in an ambulance in Wyoming. If you can oversee millions of dollars in assets in Iraq, you can help a business balance its books here at home. Our incredible service men and women need to know that America values them not simply for what they can do in uniform, but for what they can do when they come home. We need them to keep making America stronger.

Our companies need skilled workers like our veterans to grow, and there's no reason why we can't connect the two. And keeping our commitments to our veterans has been one of my top priorities as Commander in Chief, and that includes helping them make the transition back to civilian life.

That's why we're fully funding the post-9/11 GI bill, which is helping more than 500,000 veterans and their family members pursue a college education. That's why we supported extending the bill to include noncollege degrees and on-the-job and apprenticeship training. That's why I directed the Federal Government to be a model employer and hire more veterans, including more than 100,000 in the past year and a half alone.

So today we're taking it a step further.

First, we need to do more to make the transition from military to civilian life easier for our veterans. That's why I'm directing the Departments of Defense and Veterans Affairs to design what we're calling a reverse boot camp. The problem is that right now, we spend months preparing our men and women for life in the military, but we spend much less time preparing them for life after they get out. So we'll devote more time on the back end to help our veterans learn about everything from benefits to how they can translate their military training into an industry-accepted credential. In addition, we'll make it easier for veterans to go to their local One-Stop Career Center and get help pursuing a career that fits them best.

These steps will help bridge part of the gap between veterans looking for work and companies looking to hire. But that's only part of the equation. The other half is about encouraging companies to do their part. That's why I'm proposing a new returning heroes tax credit for companies that hire unemployed veterans. And I'm proposing an increase in the existing tax credit for companies who hire unemployed veterans with a disability, who still have so much to offer our country.

And finally, we're challenging the private sector to hire or train 100,000 unemployed post-9/11 veterans or their spouses by the end of 2013. This builds on commitments that many companies have already made as part of the Joining Forces campaign championed by my wife Michelle and Dr. Jill Biden. Siemens, for example, recently met their goal of hiring 300 veterans, so they're aiming to hire 150 more by December. Microsoft is helping more than 10,000 veterans get IT-certified over the next 2 years. And today groups from the U.S. Chamber of Commerce to Accenture to Lockheed Martin have all agreed to do their part to help veterans get back in the workforce.

The bottom line is this: We still have a long way to go and a lot of work to do to give folks the economic security and opportunity they deserve. And that begins with connecting Americans looking for work, including our veterans, with employers looking to hire.

Over the last few years, another generation of young veterans has learned that the challenges don't end in Kandahar or Baghdad. They continue right here at home. Today we're saying to our veterans, you fought for us, and now we're fighting for you, for the jobs and opportunities that you need to keep your families strong and to keep America competitive in the 21st century. And at a time when there is so much work to be done in this country, we need everyone's help to do it.

So thank you, God bless you, God bless all our Services, and God bless the United States of America.

NOTE: The President spoke at 11:20 a.m. In his remarks, he referred to Jill T. Biden, wife of Vice President Joe Biden.

Statement on Congressional Passage of Federal Aviation Administration Reauthorization Legislation
August 5, 2011

I'm pleased that Congress has passed an agreement which will allow tens of thousands of people to return to their jobs, rebuilding runways and working on construction projects all over America, while removing the uncertainty hanging over the jobs of thousands of hard-working FAA employees. This impasse was an unnecessary strain on local economies across the country at a time when we can't allow politics to get in the way of our economic recovery. So I'm glad that this stalemate has finally been resolved.

The President's Weekly Address
August 6, 2011

This week, Congress reached an agreement that's going to allow us to make some progress in reducing our Nation's budget deficit. And through this compromise, both parties are going to have to work together on a larger plan to get our Nation's finances in order. That's important. We've got to make sure that Washington lives within its means, just like families do. In the long term, the health of our economy depends on it.

But in the short term, our urgent mission has to be getting this economy growing faster and creating more jobs. That's what's on people's minds; that's what matters to families in this country. And the fact is, this has been a tumultuous year for the economy. We've weathered the Arab Spring's effect on oil and gas prices, the Japanese earthquake and tsunami's effect on supply chains, the economic situation in Europe. And in Washington, there was a contentious debate over our Nation's budget that nearly dragged our country into financial crisis.

So our job right now has to be doing whatever we can to help folks find work, to help create the climate where a business can put up that job listing, where incomes are rising again for people. We've got to rebuild this economy and the sense of security that middle class families have felt slipping away for years. And while deficit reduction has to be part of our economic strategy, it's not the only thing we have to do.

We need Democrats and Republicans to work together to help grow this economy. We've got to put politics aside to get some things done. That's what the American people expect of us. And there are a number of steps that Congress can take right away when they return in September.

We need to extend tax cuts for working and middle class families so you have more money in your paychecks next year. That would help millions of people to make ends meet. And that extra money for expenses means businesses will have more customers and will be in a better position to hire.

Yesterday I proposed a new tax credit for companies that hire veterans who are looking for work after serving their country. We've got a lot of honorable and skilled people returning from Iraq and Afghanistan and companies that could benefit from their abilities. Let's put them together.

We need to make sure that millions of workers who are still pounding the pavement looking for jobs are not denied unemployment benefits to carry them through hard times.

We've got to cut redtape that stops too many inventors and entrepreneurs from quickly turning new ideas into thriving businesses, which holds back our whole economy.

It's time Congress finally passed a set of trade deals that would help displaced workers looking for new jobs and that would allow our businesses to sell more products in countries in Asia and South America, products stamped with three words: Made in America.

And we ought to give more opportunities to all those construction workers who lost their jobs when the housing boom went bust. We could put them to work right now, by giving loans to companies that want to repair our roads and bridges and airports, helping to rebuild America.

Those are a few commonsense steps that would help the economy. And these are ideas that have been supported by both Democrats and Republicans in the past. So I'm going to keep calling on both parties in Congress to put aside their differences and send these bills to

931

my desk so I can sign them right away. After all, both parties share power. Both parties share responsibility for our progress. Moving our economy and our country forward is not a Democratic or a Republican responsibility, it is our responsibility as Americans.

That's the spirit we need in Washington right now. That's how we'll get this economy growing faster and reach a brighter day.

Thanks for listening, and have a great weekend.

NOTE: The address was recorded at approximately 12 p.m. on August 5 in the Diplomatic Reception Room at the White House for broadcast on August 6. The transcript was made available by the Office of the Press Secretary on August 5, but was embargoed for release until 6 a.m. on August 6.

Statement on United States Military Casualties in Afghanistan
August 6, 2011

My thoughts and prayers go out to the families and loved ones of the Americans who were lost earlier today in Afghanistan. Their deaths are a reminder of the extraordinary sacrifices made by the men and women of our military and their families, including all who have served in Afghanistan. We will draw inspiration from their lives and continue the work of se-curing our country and standing up for the values that they embodied. We also mourn the Afghans who died alongside our troops in pursuit of a more peaceful and hopeful future for their country. At this difficult hour, all Americans are united in support of our men and women in uniform, who serve so that we can live in freedom and security.

Statement on the 13th Anniversary of the Terrorist Attacks Against U.S. Embassies in Africa
August 7, 2011

Today marks the 13th anniversary of Al Qaida's terrorist attacks against the U.S. Embassies in Nairobi, Kenya, and Dar es Salaam, Tanzania. The United States joins with the people and Government of Kenya, where 218 people lost their lives and over 5,000 were injured, and Tanzania, where the attack killed 11 people and wounded at least 85 others, to remember and reflect on those who were injured and the families and loved ones of those who lost their lives.

These attacks in East Africa stand as testament to Al Qaida's commitment to use unspeakable violence to kill innocent men, women, and children, regardless of their religion, race, or nationality. The death of Harun Fazul, the architect of these terrible acts, on June 11, 2011, was an important blow to Al Qaida and its ability to threaten so many innocents around the region. Today the remembrance of these tragic attacks spurs us to continue to work closely with our allies in East Africa and around the world to bring terrorists to justice and to redouble our efforts to prevent these attacks in the future. We join with our friends and allies in advancing peace and security for Americans, Kenyans, Tanzanians, and all people in building a world that is worthy of the legacy of the victims of these bombings. And as we extend our hearts and prayers to the families of those killed, we pledge that they will not be forgotten.

Remarks on the National Economy
August 8, 2011

Good afternoon, everybody. On Friday, we learned that the United States received a downgrade by one of the credit rating agencies, not so much because they doubt our ability to pay our debt if we make good decisions, but because after witnessing a month of wrangling over raising the debt ceiling, they doubted our political system's ability to act. The markets, on the other hand, continue to believe our credit status is AAA. In fact, Warren Buffett, who knows a thing or two about good investments, said, "If there were a AAAA rating, I'd give the United States that." I and most of the world's investors agree.

That doesn't mean we don't have a problem. The fact is, we didn't need a rating agency to tell us that we need a balanced, long-term approach to deficit reduction. That was true last week. That was true last year. That was true the day I took office. And we didn't need a rating agency to tell us that the gridlock in Washington over the last several months has not been constructive, to say the least. We knew from the outset that a prolonged debate over the debt ceiling—a debate where the threat of default was used as a bargaining chip—could do enormous damage to our economy and the world's. That threat, coming after a string of economic disruptions in Europe, Japan, and the Middle East, has now roiled the markets and dampened consumer confidence and slowed the pace of recovery.

So all of this is a legitimate source of concern. But here's the good news: Our problems are imminently [eminently]° solvable, and we know what we have to do to solve them. With respect to debt, our problems is not confidence in our credit; the markets continue to reaffirm our credit as among the world's safest. Our challenge is the need to tackle our deficits over the long term.

Last week, we reached an agreement that will make historic cuts to defense and domestic spending. But there's not much further we can cut in either of those categories. What we need to do now is combine those spending cuts with two additional steps: tax reform that will ask those who can afford it to pay their fair share and modest adjustments to health care programs like Medicare.

Making these reforms doesn't require any radical steps. What it does require is common sense and compromise. There are plenty of good ideas about how to achieve long-term deficit reduction that doesn't hamper economic growth right now. Republicans and Democrats on the bipartisan fiscal commission that I set up put forth good proposals. Republicans and Democrats in the Senate's Gang of Six came up with some good proposals. John Boehner and I came up with some good proposals when we came close to agreeing on a grand bargain.

So it's not a lack of plans or policies that's the problem here, it's a lack of political will in Washington. It's the insistence on drawing lines in the sand, a refusal to put what's best for the country ahead of self-interest or party or ideology. And that's what we need to change.

I realize that after what we just went through, there's some skepticism that Republicans and Democrats on the so-called super-committee, this joint committee that's been set up, will be able to reach a compromise, but my hope is that Friday's news will give us a renewed sense of urgency. I intend to present my own recommendations over the coming weeks on how we should proceed. And that committee will have this administration's full cooperation. And I assure you, we will stay on it until we get the job done.

Of course, as worrisome as the issues of debt and deficits may be, the most immediate concern of most Americans, and of concern to the marketplace as well, is the issue of jobs and the slow pace of recovery coming out of the worst recession in our lifetime.

° White House correction.

And the good news here is that by coming together to deal with the long-term debt challenge, we would have more room to implement key proposals that can get the economy to grow faster. Specifically, we should extend the payroll tax cut as soon as possible, so that workers have more money in their paychecks next year and businesses have more customers next year.

We should continue to make sure that if you're one of the millions of Americans who's out there looking for a job, you can get the unemployment insurance that your tax dollars contributed to. That will also put money in people's pockets and more customers in stores.

In fact, if Congress fails to extend the payroll tax cut and the unemployment insurance benefits that I've called for, it could mean 1 million fewer jobs and half a percent less growth. This is something we can do immediately, something we can do as soon as Congress gets back.

We should also help companies that want to repair our roads and bridges and airports so that thousands of construction workers who've been without a job for the last few years can get a paycheck again. That will also help to spur economic growth.

These aren't Democratic proposals. These aren't big government proposals. These are all ideas that traditionally Republicans have agreed to, have agreed to countless times in the past. There's no reason we shouldn't act on them now, none.

I know we're going through a tough time right now. We've been going through a tough time for the last 2½ years. And I know a lot of people are worried about the future. But here's what I also know. There will always be economic factors that we can't control: earthquakes, spikes in oil prices, slowdowns in other parts of the world. But how we respond to those tests, that's entirely up to us.

Markets will rise and fall, but this is the United States of America. No matter what some agency may say, we've always been and always will be a AAA country. For all of the challenges we face, we continue to have the best universities, some of the most productive workers, the most innovative companies, the most adventurous entrepreneurs on Earth. And what sets us apart is that we've always not just had the capacity, but also the will to act, the determination to shape our future, the willingness in our democracy to work out our differences in a sensible way and to move forward, not just for this generation, but for the next generation.

And we're going to need to summon that spirit today. The American people have been through so much over the last few years, dealing with the worst recession, the biggest financial crisis since the 1930s, and they've done it with grace. And they're working so hard to raise their families, and all they ask is that we work just as hard here in this town to make their lives a little bit easier. That's not too much to ask. And ultimately, the reason I am so hopeful about our future—the reason I have faith in these United States of America—is because of the American people. It's because of their perseverance and their courage and their willingness to shoulder the burdens we face together as one Nation.

U.S. Military Casualties in Afghanistan

One last thing. There is no one who embodies the qualities I mentioned more than the men and women of the United States Armed Forces. And this weekend, we lost 30 of them, when their helicopter crashed during a mission in Afghanistan. And their loss is a stark reminder of the risks that our men and women in uniform take every single day on behalf of their county. Day after day, night after night, they carry out missions like this in the face of enemy fire and grave danger. And in this mission, as in so many others, they were also joined by Afghan troops, seven of whom lost their lives as well.

So I've spoken to our generals in the field, as well as President Karzai. And I know that our troops will continue the hard work of transitioning to a stronger Afghan Government and ensuring that Afghanistan is not a safe haven for terrorists. We will press on. And we will succeed.

But now is also a time to reflect on those we lost, and the sacrifices of all who serve, as well as their families. These men and women put their lives on the line for the values that bind us together as a nation. They come from different places, and their backgrounds and beliefs reflect the rich diversity of America.

But no matter what differences they might have as individuals, they serve this Nation as a team. They meet their responsibilities together. And some of them—like the 30 Americans who were lost this weekend—give their lives for their country. Our respon-

sibility is to ensure that their legacy is an America that reflects their courage, their commitment, and their sense of common purpose.

Thank you very much.

NOTE: The President spoke at 1:52 p.m. in the State Room at the White House. In his remarks, he referred to Warren E. Buffett, chief executive officer and chairman, Berkshire Hathaway Inc.

Remarks at a Democratic National Committee Fundraiser
August 8, 2011

The President. Thank you, everybody. Well, first of all, let me just thank Don and Katrina, the entire clan, for welcoming us all here today.

For those of you who helped to organize this, I couldn't be more grateful. I know it's a little warm, by the way, so any gentlemen who want to take off their jackets, I'm going to lead the way. [*Laughter*]

Audience member. It's hot in here.

The President. That's right. You can at least take the tie off too. There you go. [*Laughter*]

I have to tell you that the last time I saw Don and Katrina—or the first time I saw them, rather, was down in Florida, and we had an extraordinary time there, and it was a scary time. It was a moment when we were going—we were just getting a glimmer of the worst recession in our lifetimes, how bad it might be. And we had gotten a sense of how dysfunctional politics in Washington could be.

And there was a sense that for ordinary families, the American Dream, the idea that each successive generation can do a little better than the previous one, and that if people work hard and play by the rules, that they can succeed, that that had been diminished and people had begun to doubt it.

And thanks to the support of folks like you, we were able to win in 2008 and begin a process of transformation. Now, what I think has been clear certainly this week is that this process is not complete. With respect to the economy, we've had a couple of very difficult days in the stock market, but the truth of the matter

is, is that the challenges go beyond the stock market. As Don said, we have been able to reverse what it turns out was an 8-percent contraction in the economy that quarter before I took office.

We've had 17 months now of consecutive private sector job growth. Corporate profits have been up. The credit markets have stabilized. But what's absolutely true even before these last couple days in the stock market is that recovery wasn't happening fast enough, and some of the headwinds that we've been dealing with are ones that are going to take some time to fix.

The truth of the matter is, is that we now live in a global economy where everything is interconnected, and that means that when you have problems in Europe and in Spain and in Italy and in Greece, those problems wash over into our shores.

We have competition from China and India and Brazil, places that most folks didn't think of in economic terms 30 or 40 years ago as competitors of the United States, and now they're competing and they're producing more engineers and they're producing more scientists. And they are ready to steal market share, or at least win market share, from our companies if we're not careful.

We have a health care system that still spends way too much money, considering what it gives in return. We still have a education system that's not educating enough of our kids. And Lord knows we still have a dysfunctional political system in Washington, as we just witnessed over the last couple of weeks.

And so for all the progress that we've made over the last 2½ years—and that progress has been extraordinarily significant, not only health care reform but financial regulatory reform, making sure that we have—are starting to transform our education system with things like Race to the Top, which says we're going to give more money to schools but we expect reform in exchange for more money. Despite the transformations that have taken place in our foreign policy, where we are—we have now ended the war in Iraq and we are transitioning into a posture where in Afghanistan, Afghans can take responsibility for their own security—despite all those changes, we've got a lot of unfinished business.

And some of you have noted that I've now turned 50. [*Laughter*] And these are dog years that Presidents live, so—[*laughter*]—the gray hairs are accelerating much more rapidly than I anticipated. [*Laughter*]

But I was in Chicago for a big birthday bash—birthday celebration, and I made this point to folks. On that cold, wintry day of the Inauguration or that beautiful day in Chicago, the day we won the election, I told people that this was not the end, this was just the beginning. That this was going to be a long, difficult journey. That for us to transform this country so that all these beautiful kids who are here today are getting the kind of America that we want them to have, it means that we're going to have to get serious, and it means that we're going to have to start working together much more effectively than we have in the past.

Now, here's the good news. There are no challenges that we're facing that we don't have the solutions to. We know what to do.

So the most recent discussions obviously have been about debt and deficit. Look, we do have a serious problem in terms of debt and deficit, and much of it I inherited when I showed up. And because of the financial crisis, it got worse. So there's no doubt that we've got to fix our long-term finances.

But there's a way to do this that doesn't require radical changes in our commitment to the poor and our commitment to seniors and our commitment to building infrastructure and our commitment to medical research.

What it requires is that those of us who have the capacity can pay our fair share when it comes to taxes, like we did just as recently as 2000, when Bill Clinton was President, and requires us to make some modest adjustments in programs like Medicare that allow us to get a better bang for our buck on health care.

And if we did those things over the course of 20, 30 years, because this is a 20- or 30-year problem, then the problem would be solved. It's not rocket science. And it doesn't require us to decimate the things that we know are going to help us grow and become competitive.

This is not rocket science in terms of how we can create more jobs in this country. Let me just use an example like infrastructure. I don't know if anybody here recently has been to Asia, and you go to Shanghai or you go to Beijing or you go to Singapore. The notion that these guys have better airports than us is astonishing.

Well, the truth is now would be a great time for us to rebuild America. Interest rates are low. All these folks who worked in the housing bubble, construction workers and contractors, they're ready to work. They're willing to come on a job on time, under budget.

We could transform America right now, rebuilding our roads and our bridges and our airports and also rebuilding a new infrastructure for the 21st century: high-speed rail and a new generation of air traffic control that could actually save 15 percent of fuel costs and, as a consequence, reduce global warming. The problem is not that we can't do it. The problem is, is that we haven't shown the political will to do it.

We can easily imagine ways in which we can finally gain energy independence in this country. And the fact of the matter is, is that we've already cut oil imports since I came into office, and we can keep on going further by transforming our auto fleets and have folks driving electric cars and develop those cars right here in the United States and put those folks back to work.

And we've already shown what we did in the auto industry, that even businesses that are troubled, if you go in there and you start harnessing American know-how and American ingenuity and you give folks some support, that there is no reason why we can't be the single most efficient automakers in the world and significantly cut our dependence on foreign oil. What's missing is not the technical know-how. What's missing is the political will.

So here's the challenge, though. This is a democracy, and that means that we've got an entire other vision that's out there. And the Republican Party has been presenting its vision quite vividly over the last 6 months. And their basic vision is, is that they don't believe in Government as a partner with the private sector in creating the kind of growth that we need.

And they've made a decision that in terms of how to deal with the budget deficit, all they want to do is they just want to cut. And they don't want to cut selectively and surgically. Their basic attitude is, you know what, Medicare, we can voucherize, even if it means $6,000 more in expenses for our seniors. And Pell grants, we can cut some of those, even though it means that young people aren't going to be able to go to college.

And when it comes to medical research and when it comes to the kind of innovation agenda that's always been the hallmark of America, you know what, that's not important. The private sector can do it, even though the private sector will acknowledge that they're not going to be willing to put up the costs that helped to create things like the Internet.

And so they've got a very different vision. And as a consequence of this debt ceiling debacle being behind us now, what we're going to have is 16 months in which we debate this vision for America. And it's going to be as fundamental a debate as 2008. In some ways, it may be even a more profound debate, because the contrast is going to be clearer and it's going to be sharp.

In the meantime, as President of the United States, my job is to work with Congress to try to get as much done as possible. Whether we're going to see any progress out of this Congress right now—because so far we haven't seen much when it comes to innovative ideas that actually put people to work and grow the economy—remains to be seen. And we're going to be working as hard as we can to make progress even in the midst of this sharply divided Government.

But I want everybody to understand, if we are going to get to the vision that we all believed in, in 2008, and we still believe in, it is going to be imperative that we run a clear, forceful campaign. And I can't do that without your support.

I'm not going to be able to mobilize the country around some of the tough, necessary choices that need to be made unless we've got the kind of grassroots support at every level that you guys so vividly displayed back in 2008.

But I believe we can do it. I joke sometimes not only is my hair gray, but I got a little dings here and there—[*laughter*]—from some of the battles we've been fighting. But I remain as fundamentally optimistic now as I was when I started running in 2007. And the reason I'm optimistic is because of you.

When I meet the American people, they believe in commonsense solutions to problems. When I meet the American people, they know that if somebody works hard, they should be able to find a job and get paid a decent wage. And they should have some basic protections when they retire. They shouldn't go bankrupt when they get sick. And every kid should be able to get a great education and be able to go to college.

When I talk to the American people, they understand that we can't just have a foreign policy that's based on our military, but diplomacy matters as well, and that our commitment to help other countries develop their own capacities is something that is good for us.

And they understand, most of all, that what makes America great is not just the height of our skyscrapers or the size of our GDP, but it's also our mutual regard for each other and our ability in this incredible diversity that we have to see that as a strength and not a source of weakness, and to be able to bring people together.

So that's the project, and it is unfinished. And I don't know about you, but I think we have no choice but to finish it. We cannot go backwards at this point, so we're going to have to go forward. We're going to have to go forward. And the only way I'm going to be able to go forward is with you.

So I appreciate you guys coming out on a muggy, Washington-style summer night. And my hope is, is that this is just the beginning of your commitment to what is going to be a tough road ahead over the next 18 months. But then, another 4 years of tough stuff that we're going to have to do in order to deliver the kind of America we want.

So with that, I'm going to take two questions, and then I'm going to move on to the next thing. But I'm sure that somebody here must have a couple of questions.

[At this point, the President took questions from participants, and no transcript was provided.]

NOTE: The President spoke at 6:40 p.m. at the residence of R. Donahue Peebles and Katrina L. Peebles.

Remarks at a Democratic National Committee Fundraiser
August 8, 2011

Thank you. All right, everybody have a seat here. Thank you so much. It is wonderful to be here. And I was doing a quick taping outside, and it sounded like—I don't know if it was Matthew or Barzun who were warming you up pretty good. *[Laughter]* But I appreciate it.

I want to spend most of my time answering questions and then going from table to table, so I'm not going to make a lot of remarks at the top.

Obviously, we've had a tough couple of weeks in the economy. Too much of it was self-inflicted. It had to do with political paralysis here in Washington. And that's not a surprise to a lot of folks, but I think for the American people they recognize that we don't have time for some of the squabbling that's been taking place because there are too many folks who are still out of work, too many businesses who are still trying to grow. And for us to have seen the kind of brinksmanship that we saw on the debt ceiling made absolutely no sense in terms of where we need to take the country.

Having said that, despite the tough couple of weeks that we've had, I think the bigger challenge that we face is to keep our eye focused on the underlying challenges that we're going to have to solve here in the United States of America over the next 4 or 5 years so that we can be competitive and we can pass on the kind of America we want to future generations.

Markets will go up and down, but the underlying challenges have held steady for too long. We have an education system that is failing too many of our kids. And if we don't fix that, then we're not going to be able to compete with China or India or Brazil, who are very hungry and know that whichever country has the best workforce, the most highly skilled workforce, is going to be the country that succeeds economically.

We've had a health care system that, for too long, costs way too much and doesn't produce good enough results. And so we started with health care reform to move that in the right direction, but we've still got more work to do, particularly in Medicare and Medicaid, which is the main driver of our Federal debt.

We're going to have to fix our Tax Code, because for years it has been rife with loopholes and for years it's been inefficient and for years it hasn't been fair. And we're going to have to raise more revenue to close our deficit and deal with our debt over the long term, but we've got to do it in a way that is reflective of who we are as Americans, and that means that everybody pitches in, in order to make sure that the country is successful.

We know that we've got to invest in basic research, and nowhere is that more necessary than in the energy sector, because whatever is happening on any particular day in the spot oil market, we know what the long-term trends are going to be, which is oil consumption is going to be going up, and not only is that going to be a millstone around the neck of the economy, but we also know that if we keep on using fossil fuels at the pace that we're using right now, it's going to have an impact on the environment.

So there are a set of things that we know need to happen, and what I want to emphasize to you—and I'll emphasize it during the Q&A, and as I have a chance to greet you going around the tables—is that the problem is not a technical one. This is not—there are some tough issues, like can we—how fast can we replace our use of fossil fuels given the needs of a modern economy. But when it comes to, for example, dealing with our long-term debt and deficit, the problem is not that we don't know the math. We've had commission after commission after commission looking at this thing. And the challenge is simply that the politics in this town doesn't seem to be equipped to make modestly tough choices.

And by the way, these choices are not radical. When it comes to getting a sustainable debt level, if we went back to the rates that existed when Bill Clinton was President and we made some modest adjustments to Medicare that preserved the integrity of the system, our long-term debt and deficit problems would go away. And most people here wouldn't notice those changes. But we've become so dug in when it comes to sort of ideological purity that we're not willing to make modest adjustments like that.

Now, here's the good news. The good news is that I think there has been enough frustration at Washington—it sort of reached a fever pitch last week—that we're now looking at 16 months in which there's going to be a clear contrast and a clear choice to be made.

I think people understand that—they thought maybe divided Government might make some sense. They didn't think dysfunctional Government was going to make a lot of sense, and that's what they're seeing right now. And I think the American people are not persuaded that an agenda of simply slashing commitments to things like student loan pro-

grams or privatizing or voucherizing Medicare are somehow going to be the solutions. They're not buying that bill of goods.

And what they do need to believe though is, is that the medium- and long-term solutions that we're proposing, if implemented, can actually make a difference in their lives, in their day-to-day lives. And what's also encouraging is, is that as I travel around the country or I read letters from people every single day, what I'm struck by is the core decency and common sense that so many people display.

Folks aren't paying attention to the ins and outs, day to day of every single debate that goes on here in Washington. But they have pretty good instincts and they've got good values. And they know we can do better, and they're willing to chip in. But they want to make sure that everybody else is chipping in as well.

And so I'm hoping that all of you are willing to get involved in what I think is going to be even more consequential an election than 2008 was. I think even more is at stake, partly because the alternative visions that are being presented are even starker now than I think they were before.

And I can tell you that I'm going to be fighting as hard as I can for that vision of an America that is generous and big and bold and aggressive in promoting equal opportunity for all people all across this land. And I think that that's what most of you believe in as well. So I'm looking forward to working with you.

And if you're willing to sign up and get involved, knowing that we're in for a tough fight, I promise you the American people are going to come through for us and I'm going to have 4 more years after this next year and a half, which means that I'm going to be really gray by the time I'm done. [*Laughter*]

But thank you very much, everybody. Thank you.

NOTE: The President spoke at 7:29 p.m. at the St. Regis Hotel. In his remarks, he referred to Matthew W. Barzun, national finance chair of the President's 2012 election campaign. Audio was not available for verification of the content of these remarks.

Remarks at the Iftar Dinner
August 10, 2011

Good evening, everyone, and welcome to the White House. Tonight is part of a rich tradition here at the White House of celebrating the holy days of many faiths and the diversity that define us as a nation. So these are quintessentially American celebrations: people of different faiths coming together, with humility before our Maker, to reaffirm our obligations to one another, because no matter who we are or how we pray, we're all children of a loving God.

Now, this year, Ramadan is entirely in August. That means the days are long, the weather is hot, and you are hungry. [*Laughter*] So I will be brief.

I want to welcome the members of the diplomatic corps who are here; the Members of Congress, including two Muslim American Members of Congress, Keith Ellison and Andre Carson; and leaders and officials from across my administration. Thank you all for being here. Please give them a big round of applause.

To the millions of Muslim Americans across the United States and more—the more than 1 billion Muslims around the world, Ramadan is a time of reflection and a time of devotion. It's an occasion to join with family and friends in celebration of a faith known for its diversity and a commitment to justice and the dignity of all human beings. So to you and your families, *Ramadan Kareem*.

Now, this evening reminds us of both the timeless teachings of a great religion and the enduring strengths of a great nation. Like so many faiths, Islam has always been part of our American family, and Muslim Americans have long contributed to the strength and character of our country, in all walks of life. This has been especially true over the past 10 years.

In 1 month, we will mark the 10th anniversary of those awful attacks that brought so much pain to our hearts. It will be the time to honor all those that we've lost, the families who carry on their legacy, the heroes who rushed to help that day, and all who have served to keep us safe during a difficult decade. And tonight it's worth remembering that these Americans were of many faiths and backgrounds, including proud and patriotic Muslim Americans.

Muslim Americans were innocent passengers on those planes, including a young married couple looking forward to the birth of their first child. They were workers in the Twin Towers, Americans by birth and Americans by choice, immigrants who crossed the oceans to give their children a better life. They were cooks and waiters, but also analysts and executives.

There, in the towers where they worked, they came together for daily prayers and meals at iftar. They were looking to the future: getting married, sending their kids to college, enjoying a well-deserved retirement. And they were taken from us much too soon. Today, they live on in the love of their families and the Nation that will never forget. And tonight we're deeply humbled to be joined by some of these 9/11 families, and I would ask them to stand and be recognized, please.

Muslim Americans were first-responders: the former police cadet who raced to the scene to help and then was lost when the towers collapsed around him, the EMTs who evacuated so many to safety, the nurse who tended to so many victims, the naval officer at the Pentagon who rushed into the flames and pulled the injured to safety. On this 10th anniversary, we honor these men and women for what they are: American heroes.

Nor let us forget that every day for these past 10 years, Muslim Americans have helped to protect our communities as police and firefighters, including some who join us tonight. Across our Federal Government, they keep our homeland secure, they guide our intelligence and counterterrorism efforts, and they uphold the civil rights and civil liberties of all Americans. So make no mistake, Muslim Americans help to keep us safe.

We see this in the brave service of our men and women in uniform, including thousands of Muslim Americans. In a time of war, they volunteered, knowing they could be sent into harm's way. Our troops come from every corner of our country, with different backgrounds and different beliefs, but every day they come together and succeed together, as one American team.

During the 10 hard years of war, our troops have served with excellence and with honor. Some have made the ultimate sacrifice, among them Army Specialist Kareem Khan. Galvanized by 9/11 to serve his country, he gave his life in Iraq and now rests with his fellow heroes at Arlington. And we thank Kareem's mother Elsheba for being here again tonight. Like Kareem, this generation has earned its place in history, and I would ask all of our servicemembers here tonight, members of the 9/11 generation, to stand and accept the thanks of our fellow Americans.

This year and every year, we must ask ourselves: How do we honor these patriots, those who died and those who served? In this season of remembrance, the answer is the same as it was 10 Septembers ago. We must be the America they lived for and the America they died for, the America they sacrificed for. An America that doesn't simply tolerate people of different backgrounds and beliefs, but an America where we are enriched by our diversity. An America where we treat one another with respect and with dignity, remembering that here in the United States there is no "them" or "us," it's just "us." An America where our fundamental freedoms and inalienable rights are not simply preserved, but continually renewed and refreshed, among them the right of every person to worship as they choose. An America that stands up for dignity and the rights of people around the world, whether a young person demanding his or her freedom in the Middle East or North Africa or a hungry child in the Horn of Africa, where we are working to save lives.

Put simply, we must be the America that goes forward as one family, like generations before us, pulling together in times of trial, staying true to our core values, and emerging even stronger. This is who we are, and this is who we must always be.

And tonight, as we near a solemn anniversary, I cannot imagine a more fitting wish for our Nation. So God bless you all, and God bless the United States of America.

Thank you.

NOTE: The President spoke at 8:35 p.m. in the East Room at the White House.

Remarks at Johnson Controls, Inc., in Holland, Michigan
August 11, 2011

The President. Thank you! Thank you, everybody. Please, please have a seat.

Hello, Johnson Controls! It is good to be back in Holland, Michigan. A couple people I want to thank. In particular, your CEO Steve Roell is here. Steve. And sitting next to him, one of my favorite people and one of the finest Senators in the country, Carl Levin is in the house.

So I just had a chance to see what you guys are doing in this plant. It is very impressive. Elizabeth was giving me the tour, and she was very patient with me. And I think I understood about half of what she said. [*Laughter*]

At a time when Americans are rightly focused on our economy, when Americans are asking about what's our path forward, all of you here at Johnson Controls are providing a powerful answer. This is one of the most advanced factories in the world. You're helping America lead in a growing new industry. You're showing us how we can come back from the worst recession that we've had in generations and start making things here in America that are sold all around the world.

And that's why I'm here today. I've said it before, I will say it again: You cannot bet against the American worker. Don't bet against American ingenuity. The reason a plant like this exists is because we are a country of unmatched freedom, where groundbreaking ideas flourish. We've got the finest universities, the finest technical schools, the most creative scientists, the best entrepreneurs, all of which is why we are home to the world's most dynamic and successful businesses, large and small.

And that's why even in these difficult times, there is not a single country on Earth that wouldn't trade places with us. Not one. We've got to remember that.

But we also know that we face some tough challenges right now. You know what they are. You live them every day in your communities, in your families. You know too many people who are out of work or struggling to get by with fewer shifts or fewer customers. Paychecks aren't big enough. Costs are too high. And even though the economy has started growing again since the recession started in 2007, the fact is, it's not growing fast enough.

Now, some of what we're facing today has to do with events beyond our control. As the economy was improving and improving through 2009, 2010, the beginning of this year, suddenly, it was hit with the unrest in the Middle East that helped send gas prices through the roof. Europe is dealing with all sorts of financial turmoil that is lapping up on our shores. Japan's tragic earthquake hurt economies around the globe, including ours, cut off some supply chains that were very important to us. And all of this has further challenged our economy. And as we've seen, it's playing out in the stock market, wild swings, up and down, and it makes folks nervous. And it affects the savings of families all across America.

Now, challenges like these—earthquakes, revolutions—those are things we can't control. But what we can control is our response to these challenges. What we can control is what happens in Washington. Unfortunately, what we've seen in Washington the last few months has been the worst kind of partisanship, the worst kind of gridlock, and that gridlock has undermined public confidence and impeded our efforts to take the steps we need for our economy. It's made things worse instead of better.

So what I want to say to you, Johnson Controls, is, there is nothing wrong with our country. There is something wrong with our politics. There's something wrong with our politics that we need to fix.

We know there are things we can do right now that will help accelerate growth and job creation, that will support the work going on here at Johnson Controls, here in Michigan, and all across America. We can do some things right now that will make a difference. We know there are things we have to do to erase a legacy of debt that hangs over the economy. But time and again, we've seen partisan brinksmanship get in the way, as if winning the next election is more important than fulfilling our responsibilities to you and to our country. This downgrade you've been reading about could have been entirely avoided if there had been a willingness to compromise in Congress. See, it didn't happen because we don't have the capacity to pay our bills, it happened because Washington doesn't have the capacity to come together and get things done. It was a self-inflicted wound.

That's why people are frustrated. Maybe you hear it in my voice; that's why I'm frustrated. Because you deserve better. You guys deserve better.

All of you, from the CEO down, are working hard, taking care of your kids or your parents, maybe both. You're living within your means. You may be trying to save for your child's college education or saving for retirement. You're donating to the church or the food pantry. You're trying to help the community. You're doing your part. You're living up to your responsibilities. It's time for Washington to do the same, to match your resolve and to match your decency and to show the same sense of honor and discipline. That is not too much to ask. That's what the American people are looking for.

And if that can happen, we know what's possible. We know what we can achieve. Look at this factory. Look what's happening in Holland, Michigan. Every day, hundreds of people are going to work on the technologies that are helping us to fight our way out of this recession. Every day, you're building high-tech batteries so that we lead the world in manufacturing, the best cars and the best trucks. And that just doesn't mean jobs in Michigan. You're buying equipment and parts from suppliers in Florida and New Mexico and Ohio and Wisconsin and all across America.

So let's think about it, what made this possible? The most important part is you: your drive, your work ethic, your ingenuity, your management. The grit and optimism that says: "We've got an idea for a new battery technology or a new manufacturing process, and we're going to take that leap, and we're going to make an investment. And we're going to hire some folks, and we're going to see it through." That's what made it possible.

But what also made this possible are the actions that we took together, as a nation, through our government, the fact that we were willing to invest in the research and the technology that holds so much promise for jobs and growth, the fact that we helped create together the conditions where businesses like this can prosper.

That's why we're investing in clean energy. That's why I brought together the world's largest auto companies who agreed, for the first time, to nearly double the distance their cars can go on a gallon of gas. That's going to save customers thousands of dollars at the pump. It's going to cut our dependence on foreign oil. It's going to promote innovation and jobs, and it's going to mean more groundbreakings and more jobs posting for companies like Johnson Controls. And that's how America will lead the world in automotive innovation and production and exports in this country.

Think about it. That's what we got done, and by the way, we didn't go through Congress to do it. [*Laughter*] But we did use the tools of government—us working together—to help make it happen.

Now, there are more steps that we can take to help this economy grow even faster. There are things we can do right now that will put more money in your pockets, will help businesses sell more products around the world, will put people to work in Michigan and across the country. And to get these things done, we do need Congress.

They're commonsense ideas that have been supported in the past by Democrats and Republicans, things that are supported by Carl Levin. The only thing keeping us back is our politics. The only thing preventing these bills from being passed is the refusal of some folks in Congress to put country ahead of party. There are some in Congress right now who would rather see their opponents lose than see America win.

And that has to stop. It's got to stop. We're supposed to all be on the same team, especially when we're going through tough times. We can't afford to play games, not right now, not when the stakes are so high for our economy.

And if you agree with me—it doesn't matter if you're a Democrat or a Republican or an Independent—you've got to let Congress know. You've got to tell them you've had enough of the theatrics. You've had enough of the politics. Stop sending out press releases. Start passing some bills that we all know will help our economy right now. That's what they need to do. They've got to hear from you.

Let me be specific. I'll give you some examples. You've got to tell them to extend the payroll tax cut so middle class families will continue to have more money to spend. We passed this in December. The average family received $1,000 from that tax cut, and you need to get it again, because the economy is still weak. It's going to help you make ends meet, but it's also going to mean more customers for businesses. It'll increase demand. It's right for the economy, and I would sign that bill today if it came to my desk.

Tell Congress to get past their differences and send me a road construction bill so that companies can put tens of thousands of people to work right now building our roads and bridges and airports and seaports. I mean, think about it, we—America used to have the best stuff: best roads, best airports, best seaports. We're slipping behind because we're not investing in it, because of politics and gridlock. Do you want to put people to work right now rebuilding America? You've got to send that message to Congress.

943

Send a message to Congress to come to an agreement on trade deals that will level the playing field and open markets to our businesses so we can sell more goods to countries around the world. We've got a lot of Americans driving Kias and Hyundais. I want folks in Korea driving Fords and Chevys and Chryslers. I'd like to see that. I want to see billions of dollars more products sold around the world stamped with three words: Made in America. [*Applause*] Made in America. Those trade bills are teed up; they're ready to go. Let's get it done.

Tell Congress we need to reform the patent system so entrepreneurs like the ones who developed some of the technology here can turn their ideas into businesses more quickly, so companies like this one can better compete against companies around the world. We shouldn't make it so difficult for somebody with a good idea to translate that into a business.

Tell Congress we've got hundreds of thousands of bright, talented, skilled Americans who are returning home from Iraq and Afghanistan. And I've proposed connecting those veterans looking for work with businesses that need their skills. You've got 24-year-olds and 25-year-olds that are leading platoons and handling equipment that's worth tens or hundreds of billions of dollars, and they come back here and they can't find a job? Let's put them to work. These are things we can do right now.

These are things I've already proposed, we've worked out the glitches, the legislation is drafted, let's get it done.

Now, given the weaknesses of the economy, we need to do even more than that. And over the coming weeks, I'm going to be putting out more proposals, week by week, that will help businesses hire and put people back to work. And I'm going to keep at it until every single American who wants a job can find one.

Now, we do have to pay for these things. And in order to pay for these things, Congress has to finish the job of reducing the Nation's budget deficit in a sensible, responsible way. Not just with more cuts this year or next year. Those cuts would weaken the economy more

than it already is, and we've already cut a trillion dollars in what's called discretionary spending. What we need is a long-term plan to get our Nation's finances in order. That's the only way we can invest in places like this. That's how we can fund the research at the Department of Energy. That's how we can fund the community college that trains folks to be able to work here. That's how we can fund the infrastructure and the technology that will help us win the future, by doing what you do, what families do.

Think about it: When things are tight you cut out those things you cannot afford, even if it's tough, to pay for the things that really matter. You don't cut out the college fund for your kids. You stop maybe going out as often. You don't stop taking care of your parent who needs care. You cut back on some of the things that you don't really need. It's the same principle applies to government. And by the way, in your own families, I'm assuming you don't just keep all the stuff you like and tell your spouse, you got to get rid of all the stuff she likes or he likes. [*Laughter*] That wouldn't work in my household. You don't just cut out the stuff that's important to you and—or keep all the stuff that's important to you and cut out the stuff that's important for your kids. The same is true for us as an American family.

We can't ask the people in this room—working families, middle class families—to bear the entire burden. We're not going to balance our budgets on the back of middle class and working people in this country. Everybody has got to do their part. Everybody has got to do their part. Everybody has got to chip in. That's fair. You learn it in kindergarten. That's what all this fuss was about in Washington: Are we going to deal with our deficit in a way that's fair? And that means closing tax loopholes for billionaires before we cut college loans for young people. That means ending Government subsidies for oil and gas companies that are doing very well before you cut health care for seniors. It means making sure that the biggest corporations pay their fair share in taxes before we gut the investments in technology and clean energy that made this factory a reality.

Now, that's just common sense. It should have bipartisan support. These are things we could be doing right now. And that's how we can jump-start this economy and speed up the recovery and get more folks working, while making sure that we get our fiscal house in order. We can do both.

And I'll be laying out more proposals in the days ahead. And I'm going to keep after every idea and every serious proposal to help us grow this economy, until everybody who wants a job can find one.

But I want everybody to understand here, the problem is not that we don't have answers. The problem is, is that folks are playing political games. And we've got a long way to go. We didn't get into this mess overnight, and it's going to take time to get us out. That's the truth. But that's no excuse for inaction. It's time to put aside ultimatums. It's time to stop drawing lines in the sand.

You know, in the aftermath of this whole debt ceiling debacle, and with the markets going up and down like they are, there's been a lot of talk in Washington right now that I should call Congress back early. The last thing we need is Congress spending more time arguing in DC. What I figure is, they need to spend more time out here listening to you and hearing how fed up you are. That's why I'm here. That's why I'll be traveling to a lot of communities like this one over the next week. That's what Congress should be doing: go back home, listen to people's frustrations with all the gridlock. Listen to how frustrated folks are with the constant bickering and the unwillingness to compromise and the desire to score points, even if it's at the expense of our country. And if

they're listening hard enough, maybe they'll come back to Washington ready to compromise and ready to create jobs and ready to reduce our deficit, ready to do what you sent them there to do.

You know, America voted for divided Government. And that makes it tough. You got one party controlling the House of Representatives, another party controlling the Senate. So they voted for—you voted for divided Government. But you didn't vote for dysfunctional Government. You didn't vote for a do-nothing Government. You didn't vote for a Government that— where folks are just looking out for special interests. You didn't vote for a Government that is beholden to lobbyists.

We've got a lot of work to do, and the only way we will get it done is if everybody, Democrats and Republicans, find a way to put country ahead of party. That's what I'm fighting for. I'm here to enlist you in that fight. You've got to hold everybody accountable, because if we can come together and find common ground, there is no stopping the United States of America. There is no holding us back. We can strengthen this economy, and we can put our Nation back to work. And we can lead the world in growing industries. And we will make it through these economic storms and reach calmer waters stronger than we were before.

Thank you very much, everybody. God bless you. Thank you.

NOTE: The President spoke at 2:47 p.m. In his remarks, he referred to Elizabeth Rolinski, vice president of operations, Johnson Controls Power Solutions.

Remarks at a Democratic National Committee Fundraiser in New York City
August 11, 2011

The President. Well, I must say, first of all, this is a pretty good-looking crowd. [*Laughter*] I want to thank Harvey and Georgina and Anna and Shelby for being such extraordinary hosts. To Governor Cuomo, congratulations on

the great work that you've been doing here in the great State of New York. And to all of you, thanks for being here.

What I'm going to do is, I enjoy having a conversation as opposed to giving a long speech, although I've been known to—[*laughter*]. So I'm just going to make a few brief remarks at the top.

Obviously, this country has gone through as tough of a time as we've seen in my lifetime over the last 2½ years. But even by those standards, this last month and a half have been extraordinary. And I was just in Michigan at a advanced battery plant. We actually have jumpstarted an entire industry here in the United States, building advanced batteries that are going to go into electric vehicles. Not only does it create jobs, manufacturing jobs that pay well, but it also is going to make a huge contribution in terms of our environment and reducing carbon emissions.

And when you couple it with the fact that for the first time in 30 years we've not only raised fuel efficiency standards, but we actually were able to get the entire industry to agree voluntarily to double fuel efficiency standards by the biggest environmental step we've made in the last 30 years on that front.

What was remarkable was to see outside of Washington the enthusiasm, the energy, the hopefulness, the decency of the American people. And what I said to them is you deserve better. You deserve better than you've been getting out of Washington over the last 2½ months, for that matter, for the last 2½ years.

What's striking as I travel around the country is people understand that this country is going through a fundamental change because of globalization, because of technology, and they recognize that we've got to up our game. We're going to have to be more competitive. We're going to have to educate our kids better. We're going to have to design our businesses more effectively. We're going to have to revamp how all sorts of systems work in order for us to meet the challenge of the 21st century.

And they're ready to go, and they're doing it at the local level. Businesses are getting smarter and more productive, and workers are going back to school to retrain, and people are cooperating in their communities to redesign how they live and work and play and educate their kids.

And so they look at what's happening in Washington, and they think, these folks are really from outer space, because they don't seem to understand how critical it is for us all to work together—Republicans, Democrats, Independents—in order to move this country forward.

Now, here's the good news. As frustrating as the last couple of months have been, I think as Washington reached a low-water mark, I think that the country suddenly realized exactly what Harvey just said, which is, we're going to have to get involved, and we're going to have to get engaged, and we're going to have to speak out, and we're going to have to register the fact that we expect more and we expect better.

And if that energy is harnessed and tapped, then I'm absolutely convinced that this country is going to be on the upswing over the next few years. There is not a single problem we're facing that we cannot solve—I won't say easily, but we can't solve—with some determination and some hard work.

We can put people back to work, and we can get this economy growing again, if we're putting in place some sensible policies of the sort that were reflected at this advanced battery plant that I saw. We can educate our kids. We know what works. There are schools in New York City that take kids from the toughest neighborhoods, and those kids excel. And they're going to top colleges and doing great. The problem is we just haven't been able to scale up, partly because of our politics.

We know what it takes to change the energy equation in this country and free ourselves from dependence on foreign oil. And it doesn't require radical changes in our behavior. It requires us taking smart, sensible steps. And the fact that we have been putting this off decade after decade is a tragedy. But it can be fixed.

Our health care system, the most expensive in the world, but doesn't give us the best outcomes. We know what to do in order to fix it, and we've made great strides with health care reform, but we've got more work to do.

And the debt, I don't know if you've noticed, but when the stock market went down, what did everybody buy after the downgrade?

Audience member. Treasurys.

The President. U.S. Treasurys.

Audience members. Yes.

The President. Everybody understands that the United States still has the greatest economic potential and the greatest businesses, the greatest universities on Earth, and the greatest workers on Earth. And so the market voted with its feet in terms of its confidence in the marketplace. And what they also understand is, if we were just willing to make some modest adjustments to our Tax Code and to how entitlement programs like Medicare and Medicaid work, this problem would vanish. We could solve it.

So the upshot is this. When I ran in 2008, I think that a lot of folks believed we elect Obama and suddenly we're going to fix politics in Washington. And Andrew is familiar with this, because everybody figures, well, we're going to fix politics in Albany. And then it turns out that there are a lot of bad habits that have been built up over time and we're also a big, diverse country and not everybody agrees with me, not everybody agrees with the folks who live in Manhattan—[*laughter*]—west of here. [*Laughter*] You guys may not be familiar with it. [*Laughter*]

And so democracy is messy, and it's tough, and our system is broken to a large degree. And that makes this election more important than 2008. Two thousand eight put us in a position to do some extraordinary things, and I can't be prouder of what we did. But in 2008, I also think everybody figured, we get through this one election and then it's all done. And then, after 2½ years, and it's been tough, and there have been setbacks, there are a lot of folks who suddenly feel deflated, this is hard, I'm not sure I believe in change. [*Laughter*] They've still got the Obama poster, but it's all kind of frayed. [*Laughter*] And Obama is grayer. [*Laughter*] He doesn't seem as cool. [*Laughter*]

But in some ways, that's a healthy thing, because what that means is in 2012, as Harvey just said, we realize this is about us. This is not about my election; it's not about one person. It's about competing visions about where we're going to take the country. Are we going to have a country that's inclusive? Are we going to have a country that gives opportunity to everybody? Are we going to have a country where everybody is sharing sacrifices, but also sharing opportunities? Are we going to have a country in which what we project to the world is not just our military might, but it's also our capacity to champion human rights and women's rights and feed folks and help them become self-sufficient?

And those competing visions are going to be determined in this next election as much as they ever have before. And so I hope you guys aren't tired because we've got a lot more work to do. And this is an ongoing project.

I'm going—on the 28th, I'm going to be at the dedication of the new King Memorial, which I've flown over, and it looks spectacular. And now that King has his own memorial on the Mall I think that we forget, when he was alive, there was nobody who was more vilified, nobody who was more controversial, nobody who was more despairing at times. There was a decade that followed the great successes of Birmingham and Selma in which he was just struggling, fighting the good fight, and scorned, and many folks angry. But what he understood, what kept him going, was that the arc of moral universe is long, but it bends towards justice. But it doesn't bend on its own. It bends because all of us are putting our hand on the arc and we are bending it in that direction. And it takes time. And it's hard work. And there are frustrations.

And if everybody here is reminded of that fact, then I'm absolutely confident that America's arc is going to be bending in the direction of justice and prosperity and opportunity.

So I hope you will join me. Thank you.

NOTE: The President spoke at 7:15 p.m. at the residence of Harvey Weinstein and Georgina Chapman. In his remarks, he referred to Anna Wintour, editor in chief, Vogue magazine, and her partner J. Shelby Bryan, chairman of the board of directors and chief executive officer, PingTone Communications, Inc.; and Gov. Andrew M. Cuomo of New York. Audio was not available for verification of the content of these remarks.

Remarks Honoring the 2011 Super Bowl Champion Green Bay Packers
August 12, 2011

The President. Hello, everybody. Everybody, have a seat. On this spectacular day, I want to welcome everybody to the White House. Thank you all for being here.

I'm just going to come out and say it: This hurts a little bit. [*Laughter*] This is a hard thing for a Bears fan to do. It doesn't hurt as much as the NFC Championship Game hurt—[*laughter*]—but it still hurts, you guys coming to my house to rub it in. [*Laughter*] What are you going to do, go to Ditka's house next or—[*laughter*].

But in the interest of good sportsmanship, congratulations to the Green Bay Packers on your 4th Super Bowl championship and record 13th NFL championship.

Oh, you know, the problem you have, though, in your franchise—your fans are not that enthusiastic. [*Laughter*] You guys have got to work on that. I'm surprised they're not wearing cheeseheads. Oh, there they are. [*Laughter*] All right, my mistake. [*Laughter*]

Look, obviously, it's good to have football right around the corner. Like every football fan, I was thrilled to have the lockout ended. Nobody likes long, frustrating negotiations—[*laughter*]—with a rigid opposition, taking it to the brink. [*Laughter*]

I want to recognize Packers President Mark Murphy, GM Ted Thompson, for the outstanding job they've done, as well as Coach Mike McCarthy for guiding them to the next championship.

And I would like to welcome all the players to the White House; some of them I've had a chance to meet before, wonderful guys. I guess I especially have to welcome Charles Woodson. Where's Woodson?

[*At this point, cornerback Charles Woodson approached the podium.*]

The President. See, hold on a second. I wasn't asking for some certificate you're about to give me, aren't you? [*Laughter*] He's really rubbing it in. Look at that.

Now, look, I admit Woodson is a pretty good ballplayer. And for those who don't know, I gave Charles a little bulletin board material, apparently, last year. And so after the Packers beat the Bears, Charles addressed the team—everybody on ESPN saw it; I saw it while I was working out in the morning—and Charles said, "If the President doesn't want to come to watch us at the Super Bowl, then we're going to him."

Then I flew to Green Bay later that week to visit a local company, and Governor Walker and Mayor Schmitt—where's Mayor Schmitt? There he is right there. He gave me a jersey from Charles on which he'd written, "See you at the White House." [*Laughter*] So basically, Charles has been giving me a hard time now for several months.

Charles, you're a man of your word. And I've now learned something that every NFL quarterback already knows too well: Don't mess with Charles Woodson.

Now, in the Super Bowl, the Packers showed just what a championship team is made of and that you deserved those rings Coach McCarthy had you fitted on the night before. The game was a lot like your season. Some key players went down with injuries in the first half, including Donald and Charles. But everybody stepped up. Your offense exploded behind one of the greatest performances by a quarterback in a Super Bowl. Where's Aaron?

Your defense was flying all over the place like Clay Matthews's hair. Where's Clay? There he is. And you brought the Lombardi Trophy back home.

Aaron earned the game's MVP award: 304 yards, three touchdowns, no interceptions. This was a performance that capped off an incredible playoff run that proved he's not just one of the best quarterbacks in the game, he's one of the best quarterbacks perhaps of all time. And I know that he's going to be having an extraordinary career going forward.

We also know that the Packers are made of more than one player or one season. They're made of the people of Green Bay. Back in the twenties, fans passed the hat at the games to support the team. In 1923, after some rough financial years, local businessmen banded together to pay the bills. Two more times—in 1935 and 1950—the community came to the rescue to keep the club afloat, and today, 112,000 people own a piece of this franchise. It is the only publicly owned team in pro sports, so—[*applause*]. And after the Super Bowl, hundreds of those fans woke up the next day, put on their snow boots, and headed over to Lambeau Field to shovel it out for the victory pep rally.

That support goes both ways. The Packers have raised more than $4 million for charities in communities all across Wisconsin and Michigan. More than 300 schools participate in the Packers Fit Kids program to promote childhood health. They've given scholarships to local students, sponsored food and blood drives, found creative ways to support our troops and their families.

So even a Bears fan can admit that the relationship between Green Bay and its team is something special. It reflects those old-school, small-town values of community and hard work that have always defined what it meant to be an American. And Super Bowl spotlight or not, that's something that's alive in towns across this country every single day.

So to all the Green Bay Packers, to all the fans, congratulations. Enjoy it while it lasts. [*Laughter*] Because Bears fans have two dates circled on our calendars: September 25 and Sunday Night Football on Christmas Day. And if you guys are on a roll by then, just keep in mind that there's only one place—one person here who can ground all planes in and out of Green Bay—[*laughter*]—if he has to.

So congratulations.

Charles, what do you got here? You can step up to the mike.

Mr. Woodson. Well, on behalf of the Green Bay Packers organization and all the players, we would like to present you with this. Of course, all the fans own the team, and it hurts

us a little bit to give you this as well—[*laughter*]—but to give you shares of the Green Bay Packers.

[*The President was presented with a framed share of stock.*]

The President. Man, that is outstanding. The—well, if I'm a part owner, I think—[*laughter*].

Coach Mike McCarthy. We figured this is the only way we could get you away from the Bears. [*Laughter*]

The President. No, what I'm thinking is, I think we should initiate a trade to send Rodgers down to the Bears. [*Laughter*]

Audience members. Boo!

The President. What do you think? No? How about——

Mr. Woodson. A minority owner, thank you. [*Laughter*]

Coach McCarthy. Aaron, go ahead.

The President. All right, what else we got?

Quarterback Aaron Rodgers. On behalf of the team, we also want to give you the right colors to wear on those two dates you mentioned. [*Laughter*] We got you this jersey, right here.

[*The President was presented with a team jersey bearing the words "Commander in Chief."*]

The President. All right, man. Thank you. Commander in Chief.

Mr. Rodgers. Why don't you change into that right now?

The President. Thank you. Good to see you, man. Absolutely.

All right. Let's get a good picture. They're going to break this down.

NOTE: The President spoke at 2:57 p.m. on the South Portico at the White House. In his remarks, he referred to Michael K. Ditka, former head coach, National Football League's Chicago Bears; Mayor James J. Schmitt of Green Bay, WI; and Donald Driver, wide receiver, and Clay Matthews, linebacker, Green Bay Packers.

Message to the Congress on Continuation of the National Emergency Regarding Export Control Regulations
August 12, 2011

To the Congress of the United States:

Section 202(d) of the National Emergencies Act (50 U.S.C. 1622(d)) provides for the automatic termination of a national emergency unless, prior to the anniversary date of its declaration, the President publishes in the *Federal Register* and transmits to the Congress a notice stating that the emergency is to continue in effect beyond the anniversary date. In accordance with this provision, I have sent to the *Federal Register* for publication the enclosed notice, stating that the emergen-

cy caused by the lapse of the Export Administration Act of 1979, as amended, is to continue in effect for 1 year beyond August 17, 2011.

BARACK OBAMA

The White House,
August 12, 2011.

NOTE: The notice is listed in Appendix D at the end of this volume.

The President's Weekly Address
August 13, 2011

On Thursday, I visited a new high-tech factory in Michigan where workers are helping America lead the way in a growing clean energy industry.

They were proud of their work, and they should be. They're not just showing us a path out of the worst recession in generations. They're proving that this is still a country where we make things; where new ideas take root and grow; where the best universities, most creative entrepreneurs, and most dynamic businesses in the world call home. They're proving that even in difficult times, there's not a country on Earth that wouldn't trade places with us.

That doesn't mean we don't face some very tough economic challenges. Many Americans are hurting badly right now. Many have been unemployed for too long. Putting these men and women back to work and growing wages for everybody has got to be our top priority.

But lately, the response from Washington has been partisanship and gridlock that's only undermined public confidence and hindered our efforts to grow the economy.

So while there's nothing wrong with our country, there is something wrong with our politics, and that's what we've got to fix. Be-

cause we know there are things Congress can do right now to get more money back in your pockets, get this economy growing faster, and get our friends and neighbors back to work.

That payroll tax cut that put $1,000 back in the average family's pocket this year, let's extend it. Construction workers who've been jobless since the housing boom went bust, let's put them back to work rebuilding America. Let's cut redtape in the patent process so entrepreneurs can get good ideas to market more quickly. Let's finish trade deals so we can sell more American-made goods around the world. Let's connect the hundreds of thousands of brave Americans coming home from Iraq and Afghanistan to businesses that need their incredible skills and talents.

These are all things we can do right now. So let's do them. And over the coming weeks, I'll put forward more proposals to help our businesses hire and create jobs. And I won't stop until every American who wants a job can find one.

But we can't let partisan brinksmanship get in our way, the idea that making it through the next election is more important than making things right. That's what's holding us back, the fact that some in Congress would rather see their opponents lose than see America win.

So you've got a right to be frustrated. I know I am. Because you deserve better. And I don't think it's too much for you to expect that the people you send to this town start delivering for you.

Members of Congress are at home in their districts right now. And if you agree with me, whether you're a Democrat or a Republican, or not much of a fan of either, let them know. If you've had it with gridlock and you want them to pass stalled bills that will help our economy right now, let them know. If you refuse to settle for a politics where scoring points is more important than solving problems, if you believe it's time to put country before party and the interests of our children before our own, then let them know.

And maybe they'll get back to Washington ready to compromise, ready to create jobs, ready to get our fiscal house in order, ready to do what you sent them here to do.

Yes, we've still got a long way to go to get to where we need to be. We didn't get into this mess overnight, and it's going to take some time to get out of it. That's a hard truth, but it's no excuse for inaction. After all, America voted for divided Government, not dysfunctional Government, and we've got work to do. And when we come together and find common ground, there is no stopping this country; there's no stopping our people; there's no holding us back. And there is every reason to believe we'll get through this storm to a brighter day.

Thanks for listening, and have a great weekend.

NOTE: The address was recorded at approximately 5 p.m. on August 12 in the Library at the White House for broadcast on August 13. The transcript was made available by the Office of the Press Secretary on August 12, but was embargoed for release until 6 a.m. on August 13.

Remarks at a Town Hall Meeting and a Question-and-Answer Session in Cannon Falls, Minnesota
August 15, 2011

The President. Hello, Cannon Falls! Hello, Minnesota! Oh, well, what a spectacular setting. Let's get the grill going.

Audience member. Fishing!

The President. And do a little fishing? Yeah? It is wonderful to see all of you here today. Thank you for showing up, and what a incredible setting. Everybody, feel free to have a seat; we're going to be here for a while. [*Laughter*]

A couple introductions I want to make real quick, although these folks don't need any introduction. The outstanding Governor of Minnesota Mark Dayton is in the house. Two of the finest Senators in the country, Amy Klobuchar and Al Franken are here; from your congressional delegation, Tim Walz, Keith Ellison. We've got the Secretary of the Department of Agriculture, Tom Vilsack is here. And I want to thank the mayor of Cannon Falls, Minnesota,

for organizing perfect weather; Robby Robinson is here.

So I am very pleased to be out of Washington, and it is great to be here. What I'm going to do is I'm just going to say a few things at the top, and then what I want to do is just open it up for questions and comments, and I want to hear from you guys. That's the reason that we're on this bus tour.

Obviously, America has gone through extraordinary challenges over the last 2½ years. We've gone through the worst recession since the Great Depression, dating all the way back to 2007, 2008. But here's the interesting thing: If you ask people around the world, people would still tell you America has got the best universities, we've got the best scientists, we've got the best entrepreneurs, we've got so much going for us that folks would gladly trade places with us. Around the world, people still understand the extraordinary power, but also the extraordinary hope that America represents.

So there is nothing wrong with America that can't be fixed; what's broken is our politics. Think about it: Over the last 6 months, we've had a string of bad luck. There have been some things that we could not control. You had an Arab Spring in the Middle East that promises more democracy and more human rights for people, but it also drove up gas prices, tough for the economy, a lot of uncertainty. And then you have the situation in Europe, where they're dealing with all sorts of debt challenges, and that washes up on our shores. And you had a tsunami in Japan, and that broke supply chains and created difficulties for the economy all across the globe.

So there were a bunch of things taking place over the last 6 months that were not within our control. But here's the thing: The question is, how do we handle these challenges? Do we rise to the occasion? Do we pull together? Do we make smart decisions? And what's been happening over the last 6 months, and a little bit longer than that if we're honest with ourselves, is that we have a political culture that doesn't seem willing to make the tough choices to move America forward.

We've got a willingness to play partisan games and engage in brinkmanship that not only costs us in terms of the economy now, but also is going to place a burden on future generations. And the question is, can we break out of that pattern? Can we break out of that pattern? Think about it: We just went through this debacle with the debt ceiling, an entirely self-inflicted wound. It wasn't something that was necessary. We had put forward a plan that would have stabilized our debt and our deficits for years to come. But because we've got a politics in which some folks in Congress—not the folks who are here, but some in Congress— would rather see their opponents lose than America win, we ended up creating more uncertainty and more damage to an economy that was already weak.

Now, we can't have patience with that kind of behavior anymore. I know you're frustrated, and I'm frustrated too. We've got to focus on growing this economy, putting people back to work, and making sure that the American Dream is there not just for this generation, but for the next generation.

Another way of putting this is, we expect our political representatives to show the same level of responsibility that all of you show. I don't know most of you, but I can guess that you're all working hard. You're managing your budgets. You're putting something away for your kids' college education, maybe for your retirement. You're at the local church, working in the food pantry or doing something to help out your community, coaching Little League. You are following through on your responsibilities, and that's true all across the country. People are doing the right thing.

Well, if you can do the right thing, then folks in Washington have to do the right thing. And if we do that, there is not a problem that we face that we cannot solve.

Think about it: Our biggest challenge right now is putting people to work; biggest challenge is getting the economy growing as rapidly as it needs to grow. It's been growing. We've been able to reverse the recession. We've added over 2 million jobs in the private sector over the last 17 months. But we're not growing it as fast as we need to to drive down the unemployment rate in a significant way and to give people confidence.

So here are some things that we could do right now, what I've been talking about now for months. We could renew the payroll tax cut that we gave you in December that put $1,000 in the pocket of a typical family so that you've got more money in your pockets to spend to meet your obligations. It also means businesses have more customers. And it means they might hire a few more folks as a consequence. All we need to do is renew it. It's already in place. If we have certainty next year that that same tax cut is going to be in place, then that's going to help businesses make decisions to hire people and open up and make investments. That's something we could do right now. Congress can do that right now.

Congress right now could start putting folks to work rebuilding America. One of the biggest things that caused this recession was the housing bubble and all those subprime loans that were going out that were getting packaged in Wall Street and folks were making millions and billions of dollars off them and then the whole thing came crashing down. And no one has been hit harder than construction workers.

And so for us to say at a time when interest rates are low, contractors are begging for work, construction workers are lining up to find jobs—let's rebuild America. We could be rebuilding roads and bridges and schools and parks all across America right now, could put hundreds of thousands of folks to work right now.

There's a bill sitting in Congress right now that would set up an infrastructure bank to get that moving, attracting private sector dollars, not just public dollars. Congress needs to move.

Right now we've got our veterans coming home from Iraq and Afghanistan, who've taken their place among the greatest of generations, have made extraordinary sacrifices. These are—I meet these young people—[applause]—I meet young people, 23, 24 years old, they're in charge of platoons, making life or death decisions. They're in charge of millions, tens of millions, a hundred million dollars' worth of equipment, and they're coming home and they can't find work. So we've said, let's give tax credits to companies that are hiring our veterans, and let's put them back to work, and let's let them use their skills to get this country moving again. Congress could do that right now.

Trade deals. You know, trade deals haven't always been good for America. There have been times where we haven't gotten a fair deal out of our trade deals. But we've put together a package that is going to allow us to start selling some Chevys and some Fords to Korea so that—we don't mind having Hyundais and Kias here, but we want some "Made in America" stuff in other countries. That's something that Congress could do right now.

Patent reform is something that a lot of folks don't talk about, but our entrepreneurs, when they come up with a good idea, if we could reform how that system works and cut some of the redtape, we could have entrepreneurs creating businesses like Google and Microsoft right now, all across the country. But we've got to make this investment, and Congress could make that decision to make it happen.

So there is no shortage of ideas to put people to work right now. What is needed is action on the part of Congress, a willingness to put the partisan games aside and say, we're going to do what's right for the country, not what we think is going to score some political points for the next election.

Now, we also need to do this in a way that allows Government to live within its means. Like I said, everybody here, you make responsible choices about what you can afford and what you can't afford. America needs to do and can do the exact same thing. There are some programs that don't work; we should stop funding them. There is some redtape that needs to be cut; we should cut it. But the fact of the matter is that solving our debt and deficit problems simply requires all of us to share in a little bit of sacrifice, all of us to be willing to do a little bit more to get this country back on track. And that's not too much to ask.

Basically, what we need to do is, we need to cut about $4 trillion over the next 10 years. Now, that sounds like a big number; it is a big number. But if we were able to, as I proposed, cut about $2 trillion in spending, if folks who could best afford it—millionaires and billionaires—were willing to eliminate some of the loopholes that they take advantage of in the Tax Code and do a little bit more, and if we were willing to take on some of the long-term costs that we have on health care, if we do those things, we could solve this problem tomorrow. I put a deal before the Speaker of the House, John Boehner, that would have solved this problem. And he walked away because his belief was we can't ask anything of millionaires and billionaires and big corporations in order to close our deficit.

Now, Warren Buffett had an op-ed that he wrote today, where he said, "We've got to stop coddling billionaires like me." That's what Warren Buffett said. He pointed out that he pays a lower tax rate than anybody in his office, including the secretary. He figured out that his tax bill, he paid about 17 percent. And the reason is because most of his wealth comes from capital gains. You don't get those tax breaks. You're paying more than that. And—now, I may be wrong, but I think you're a little less wealthy than Warren Buffett. That's just a guess. [*Laughter*]

The point is, is that if we're willing to do something in a balanced way, making some tough choices in terms of spending cuts, but also raising some revenue from folks who've done very well, even in a tough economy, then we can get control of our debt and deficit and we can start still investing in things like education and basic research and infrastructure that are going to make sure that our future is bright. It's not that complicated, but it does require everybody being willing to make some compromises.

I was in Holland, Michigan, the other day, and I said, I don't know about how things work in your house, but in my house, if I said, "You know, Michelle, honey, we got to cut back, so we're going to have you stop shopping completely. You can't buy shoes, you can't buy dresses, but I'm keeping my golf clubs." [*Laughter*] You know, that wouldn't go over so well.

The point is, something is happening in Washington where we think that kind of compromise that we do every day in our own families, with our neighbors, with our coworkers, with our friends, that somehow that's become a dirty word. And that's got to change. That's got to stop.

So here's the bottom line: Obviously, with the markets going up and down last week and this downgrade, a lot of folks were feeling a little anxious and distressed and feeling like, boy, we've been working so hard over the last 2½ years to get this economy back out of recession, and some folks worry that we might be slipping back. I want all of you to understand:

There is nothing that we're facing that we can't solve with some spirit of America first, a willingness to say, we're going to choose party— we're going to choose country over party, we're going to choose the next generation over the next election. If we are willing to do that, then I have absolutely no doubt that we can get this economy going again, we can put people to work back again, small businesses can start growing again. But I'm going to need your help to make it happen. You've got to send a message to Washington that it's time for the games to stop. It's time to put country first. It is time for the games to stop.

Some folks were asking me, well, why don't you just call Congress back? And I said, you know, I don't think it's going to make people feel real encouraged if we have Congress come back and all they're doing is arguing again. So what they need to do is come to Cannon Falls, they need to come to—they need to go back to their districts, talk to ordinary folks, find out how frustrated they are, and hopefully, when they get back in September, they're going to have a new attitude.

But I want everybody to understand here that I'm not here just to enjoy the nice weather, I'm here to enlist you in a fight. We are fighting for the future of our country. And that is a fight that we are going to win. That is a promise that I make with your help.

Thank you very much, everybody.

Thank you. All right, so everybody have a seat. We're—here's how we're going to do it. I'm just going to call on folks, and we're going to go girl, boy, girl, boy to make sure that— [*laughter*]—make sure it's fair. I've got a couple of daughters, so I know that sometimes, you know—all right.

Right here, go ahead. Yes, yes. Hold on, we got a mike. And introduce yourself for me.

Alternative and Renewable Energy Sources and Technologies

Q. Okay. Hi, I'm Cecilia Findorff, and first off, President Obama, I just—I want to say, as a young voter, thank you for helping me believe that it will be good some day, like——

The President. It's going to be good.

Q. But I have a question, I promise.

The President. You bet.

Q. My question is, how are you going to use renewable energy to create jobs in the future?

The President. Well, this is a great question, especially for rural communities all across America. Tom Vilsack, who was the former Governor of Iowa, knows a little bit about agriculture. And so when I put Tom in as the head of the Department of Agriculture, one of the first things we talked about was, how can we mobilize the incredible resourcefulness and hard work of rural communities all across this country, not just to create jobs, but also to win back energy independence. And as a consequence, we have put billions of dollars into energy research and to help move in a direction of greater reliance on fuels that are homegrown.

So let me give you a couple of examples. One obviously is biofuels. And a lot of folks here are familiar with corn-based ethanol, but the fact of the matter is, the technology is moving where we need to start taking advantage of a whole range of biofuels, using refuse, using stuff that we don't use for food to create energy. And we are seeing incredible progress on that front, but it's key to make sure that we continue to make the research and that we also use the incredible purchasing power of the Federal Government to encourage it.

So one of the things that I know we're doing is we're actually working with the Department of Defense to start saying, let's run some of these—let me just say this: The Department of Defense uses a lot of fuel, so the question is, can we get trucks and jeeps and, in some cases, even fighter jets running on alternative fuels, which is important for our national security, but also could provide an incredible boost to communities all across Minnesota, all across the country?

The other thing that we have to do is look at things like wind power and solar power and the next generation of electric vehicles. You will recall when I came into office they were talking about the liquidation of GM and Chrysler, and a lot of folks said, you can't help them, and it's a waste of the Government's money to try

to help them. But what I said was, we can't afford to lose up to a million jobs in this country, particularly in the Midwest, but we also can't afford to lose leadership in terms of building an auto industry that we used to own.

And so we turned around those auto companies; they are now making a profit for the first time in decades, they're gaining market share for the first time in years. But what we said was, if we're going to help you, then you've also got to change your ways. You can't just make money on SUVs and trucks. There's a place for SUVs and trucks, but as gas prices keep on going up, you've got to understand the market. People are going to be trying to save money.

And so what we've now seen is an investment in electric vehicles, and then what we did was we put investments in something called advanced battery manufacturing, because those electric cars, how well they run depends on how good the batteries are, how long they can run before they get recharged. We only had 2 percent of the advanced battery manufacturing market when I came into office. We're on track now to have 30, 40, 50 percent of that market. We are making batteries here in the United States of America that go into electric cars made here in the United States of America. It creates jobs and it creates energy independence and it also improves our environment.

So that's the kind of approach that we have to take, using the private sector, understanding that ultimately the private sector is going to be creating jobs, but also understanding that the Government can be an effective partner in that process. And nowhere is that more true than in rural America. So, great question.

All right, gentleman right here. You can borrow my mike. Oh, you got it? Okay.

Broadband Technology/Public Confidence in Economic Future/Deficit and National Debt

Q. Mr. President, I'm Gary Evans from Winona, Minnesota. I run a broadband company there, and I've got a couple of messages that I hope you'll take back to your colleagues in DC. The first is, 2 years ago we had 60 employees; tomorrow we will cross a hundred. We are making the investments in this country, so my first message is: Help the job creators; do what it takes. Secondly, it was already apparent as the debt debate went on that the mood in America had shifted again to skepticism, so I'm hoping that you and your colleagues will do everything possible to make certain that confidence is restored to the country and that we have a bright future. I think broadband is a key, and I appreciate what you did for it during the stimulus act. Thank you.

The President. Thank you. We were talking earlier about rural America. Despite all its incredible advantages, especially its people, a disadvantage is that rural America, by definition, is a little more spread out. It's a little more stretched out, right? Population density isn't as great. So as a consequence, when we've seen all these investments in wireless and broadband and all these new technologies that are stitching the world together, a lot of times rural America is left out.

And that's why, when we came into office, one of the big investments we said we were going to make is in broadband technology so that we can connect every single town all across America. We want 98-percent coverage when it comes to broadband, and we want that same kind of coverage when it comes to wireless, because what that means is, is that if there's a small business in Cannon Falls that's got a great idea, you don't have to just confine your market to Cannon Falls; you can start selling in Rochester and then you start selling in Des Moines and then you start selling in New York and maybe you start selling something in Paris. And there are incredible opportunities in terms of business growth, but it requires a connection to all these wider markets.

The days are gone where any business is going to succeed just by selling right where they're located. And that's why we've made such a big investment in this, and I'm pleased to see that it's working.

In terms of boosting folks' confidence, I think people would actually feel pretty confident if they felt like their leaders were working together. I mean, that's my belief. But I also think that they're looking for some practical common sense. I know it's not election season yet, but I just have to mention, the debate the other party candidates were having the other day, when they were asked to reduce our deficit, reduce our debt, would you be willing to take a deal where it was $5 of spending cuts for every $1 of increased revenues, who would take it? Everybody said no. They said, how about 10 to 1? Ten dollars of cuts for every dollar increase in revenue? Are you saying that none of you would take it? And everybody raised their hand. None of them would take it. Think about that. I mean, that's just not common sense.

Ronald Reagan, George H.W. Bush, Bill Clinton—the last time we had a balanced budget—all of them understood that you have to take a balanced approach to solving our deficit and debt problems, the same way a family would. If you knew that you had to cut down your—on your budget, you wouldn't stop funding the college fund for your kid. You wouldn't say, sorry, Johnny, you know, things are tight so we're going to keep on taking our annual vacation and I'm going to buy a new car next year, but you're not going to college. That's not how you balance your budget.

Well, the American people are expecting that same kind of common sense reflected. And if it was there, I guarantee you confidence would go up. I speak to CEOs of companies all across America, and what they tell me is, you know what, we're actually willing to do a little bit more when it comes to our personal taxes, because they know they've done very well. They said, the single most important thing we want is making sure that middle class families and small businesses are successful, because if they're successful we're going to be successful and we'll have more products. That's what we're waiting for. And that can be achieved, but it's going to require all of us working together.

All right, who's next? Yes, this young lady in the green, right there. And then I'll call on this guy back there because you've been—you've had your hand up a bunch of times. [*Laughter*]

Agricultural Sector

Q. Okay, thank you. Welcome, President Obama.

The President. Thank you.

Q. My name is Eunice Biel from Harmony, and my husband and son and his wife were dairy farmers. And so I just wanted—for years, we have—we've never had very much money, but we have been creating wealth for this country. And I would just like to say that I am—with your rural committee, I just wanted you to keep that in mind that we always create wealth for this country. Thank you.

The President. You bet. You bet. You know, one thing that I think is worth noting, because—again, I'm going to brag on Vilsack here, because he's done a great job—through the Department of Agriculture, we've provided $5 billion in assistance, in terms of loans and other forms of assistance, to small and medium-sized farmers all across the country. And that creates a lot of jobs.

One of our great strengths as a country is agriculture. And one of the pledges that I made when I came into office was we're going to double our exports. And a big component of that is agricultural exports. And so far, we've seen agricultural exports rise to over $100 billion. It creates over two—that means over 800,000 jobs all across America. But the fact of the matter is, is that a lot of family farmers are still struggling. And so one of the things that we're going to be talking about during this tour—and we've got a big roundtable discussion tomorrow, drawing on the work that our Rural Council did—is how we can make sure that we can get more capital to small farmers, how can we help young farmers who want to go into farming be able to buy land because land prices have gone up so high, how can we make sure that they're able to market their products effectively, because right now, if you're not a mega-farm, a lot of times you get squeezed.

So there are a lot of things that we can be doing to help the farm economy. And if you help the farm economy in rural communities, you help the economy of entire States. And if you help entire States, then that's good for the country as a whole. So thank you for what you do.

Young man over here.

Deficit and National Debt/Medicare and Medicaid

Q. Well, thank you, President Obama, for coming to the great State of Minnesota, home of Senator Paul Wellstone.

The President. And Franken and Klobuchar.

Q. Yes, for sure. My name is Will Morrison. I actually live in Rochester, Minnesota, home of the Mayo Clinic. Well, I just want to say I don't think we should solve this debt crisis— and it is a crisis—on the backs of the middle class and the poor. They don't have special interests, they don't have lobbyists. And I want to be their lobbyist and special interest. And I just think that if we are serious about this debt, we need to ask the millionaires and billionaires to give up their tax breaks so not all the burden is on us.

The President. Well, we—look, I can completely agree with you.

Q. So with that, I just want to say thank you so much for a great job you are doing. I support you 100 percent. And you got my vote in 2008, and I'm going to vote for you in 2012. Good luck.

The President. Thank you. Thank you. I do want to just say one thing about this debt. When I came into office, we had about a trillion dollars of debt—or deficits already. The debt is the accumulation of the annual deficits, year after year. We had a balanced budget in 2000. We then launched two wars that we didn't pay for. First time we had ever, by the way, not decided to pay for wars that we were going to fight; we just put it on the credit card.

We added a prescription drug plan for seniors, which was important to do, but we didn't pay for it. And we had tax cuts in 2001 and 2003 that were not paid for. So that added a huge amount of debt. And then with the recession coming in, that added more debt, because what happens is you get less tax revenue, businesses have fewer sales, folks may have been laid off. And you're also sending more money out because of things like unemployment insurance, helping farms stay afloat, making sure that we were putting folks to work through things like broadband.

So the debt problem is real and the deficit problem is real, but as I said before, it is actually a manageable problem. And if you don't believe me, think about it: Even after the downgrade, the next day, when the stock markets were going haywire and everybody was thinking, what's the best risk-free investment, what did they invest in? They invested in Treasurys. So the market said this is—America is still one of our best bets. They're betting on us. And that's why you have to recognize this is not a financial crisis although it could turn into one if we don't do anything about it; this is a political crisis. This is manageable.

Now, I don't want to lie to you. That doesn't mean that we can't—and we don't have to make some tough choices. We do. We cut in this debt deal about a trillion dollars' worth of spending over 10 years. We protected programs for student loans through the Pell grant program, for example. We protected programs for hungry kids. We protected health care for seniors. We protected people who are the most vulnerable and need the most help from Government. But we made some cuts in areas, including defense spending, by the way, where we had just gotten kind of carried away. And that was important to do.

Now, that solves about one-fourth of the problem. We've got more work to do. The key—and I want everybody to pay attention to this as the debate unfolds over the next couple of months—the key is not to try to cut more out of programs for poor folks or programs for seniors. The key right now is to get a long-term plan for fiscal stability. And in the short term, we should actually make more investments that would put people to work and get the economy moving. And if you combine those two things, we can actually solve this problem and grow the economy at the same time.

The one area where we are going to have to take a look at how we can improve the system is our health care programs, Medicare and Medicaid. Now, my grandma, even though she worked hard all her life, had a decent income most of her life, she was hugely reliant on

Medicare at the end of her life. So I know what Medicare means to seniors.

What is also true, though, is our health care costs have been skyrocketing and more seniors are joining up Medicare because the population is getting older. So part of what I recommended when we were in these negotiations—although we didn't get a commitment from the other side—is to say, can we manage to reduce the overall cost of Medicare in a way that still preserves the integrity of the system and strengthens it so it's there for future generations?

Now, what some of the folks on the other side are proposing is actually to turn Medicare into a voucher program. So instead of fixing the system, they'd just completely overhaul it. And what would happen would be, is you'd get a voucher that says, you're allowed to get x amount—spend x amount on health care, and if your health care costs keep on going above that, you're out of luck. And it was estimated that under their plan the average senior would pay about $6,000 more per year for their Medicare when it kicked in. I think that's a bad idea. I think there are better ways for us to manage the Medicare problem than to put a burden on seniors.

And one example is, if I were paying my fair share of taxes, then we don't have to put that kind of burden on seniors. We don't have to. I don't want a tax break that requires 33 seniors or 40 seniors to pay thousands of dollars more on their health care. I don't need it. And it's not the right thing to do.

All right. The young lady right here has been waiting for a while. Hold on, one second, get your microphone. We want to all hear you.

Social Security/Role of Government

Q. Welcome to Minnesota.

The President. Thank you.

Q. Mr. President, I've been sleeping in my truck for 2 days to ask you this question. [*Laughter*] I am recovering from lung cancer. I tried to get Social Security disability and they turned me down. My question to you is, we can talk about Social Security a little bit?

The President. Well, Social Security—here's my commitment. I don't know about the other folks, but I'll make a commitment as long as I'm President of the United States: Social Security will not only be there for you, but it's also going to be there for the next generation and the generation after that because it's one of the most important social insurance programs that we have. And by the way, you pay into Social Security. They call it an entitlement, but it's not an entitlement; you're paying for it. It's getting taken out of your paycheck.

So it is true that as the population gets older there's going to be more and more pressure on the Social Security system. But the Social Security system is not the cause of our debt and our deficit. So don't let folks fool you by saying that in order to get a handle on our debt, we've got to slash Social Security. There are some modest adjustments that can be made that will make it solvent for 75 years, and that's about as long as you can think ahead as a country.

And the way to do it is similar to the way that Ronald Reagan and Tip O'Neill fixed Social Security back in 1983. They said, okay, we'll make some modest adjustments that are phased in over a very long period of time; most folks don't notice them. But if we do that and all the money goes back into Social Security—it doesn't go anywhere else—then there's no reason why Social Security won't be there for future generations. But again, this is an example of where everybody gets so dug in on their positions.

And I have to say, in fairness, because I've commented on the other side not always being flexible, there have been times where our side, when Democrats aren't always as flexible as we need to be. I mean, sometimes I do get frustrated when I hear folks say, you can't make any changes to any Government programs. Well, that can't be right. I mean, most companies every year, they're kind of thinking, what can we do better? Are there some changes we could make in order to have the operation go a little smoother? The Government should have to do the same thing. But that doesn't mean we have to make radical changes that dismantle what is the most important social insurance program that we have. But again, the problem is not the program, the problem is our politics.

You'll hear a lot of folks, by the way, say that government is broken. Well, government and politics are two different things. Government is our troops who are fighting on our behalf in Afghanistan and Iraq. That's government. Government are also those FEMA folks when there's a flood or a drought or some emergency who come out and are helping people out. That's government. Government is Social Security. Government are teachers in the classroom. Government are our firefighters and our police officers and the folks who keep our water clean and our air clean to breathe and our agricultural workers. And when you go to a national park, and those folks in the hats, that's government.

So don't be confused: As frustrated as you are about politics, don't buy into this notion that somehow government is what's holding us back. Now, too much government, if it's oppressive and bureaucratic and it's not listening to people and it's not responsive to the needs of people and isn't customer friendly, that's a problem. And if you stand in line at some government office and nobody seems to be paying any attention to you, well, that needs to be fixed. And if somebody is trying to regulate a small business and they're not paying attention to the realities of the small business, that's a problem.

But don't buy into this whole notion that somehow government doesn't do us any good. Government is what protects us. The Government is what built the Interstate Highway System. Government is what sent a man to the Moon. It's what invested in the research and development that created innovations all across this country.

All right. I think it's a gentleman's turn, isn't it? Right back there. Yes, sir. Right there.

Our mike guys are doing a great job, aren't they? Give them a round of applause.

Education Reform

Q. Thank you. Are we on? First of all, welcome to Cannon Falls, President Obama. We're really pleased to have you here.

The President. Thrilled to be here.

Q. You just did a little lead-in to my question a couple of minutes ago when you said that the government is a lot of things. And as we look around us right now and we see that we are ringed by school buses all the way around this way, that's kind of where I'm headed here. It's because we can't improve the economy unless we improve its foundations, and education is at the foundation of this economy. I would like to know what it is that your administration is planning on doing to bolster education in the face of State cuts, Federal cuts, 45 students to a classroom, cutting teachers, and so forth. Thank you.

The President. Well, let me tell you first of all what we did when I came into office. The Recovery Act, about a third of it was support to States to prevent layoffs of teachers and fire-fighters and police officers. And thanks to the work that Amy and Al and Keith and Tim and others did, even after the first round of the Recovery Act, we then gave States some additional assistance to prevent layoffs of teachers.

Now, at a certain point, the money ran out. And States are still going through a tough time. I personally believe that one of the most effective ways that we could help the economy is making sure that we're not seeing more teacher layoffs, and I'm going to be working with Congress and State governments all across the country to prevent that from happening, because you're exactly right: We can't eat our seed corn. We can't shortchange investments in the future, and no investment is more important than education.

Now, the challenge we have in education is not just money though. We've also got to make it work better. And that's why what my administration has done is to say, we're going to put more money into education, but we're also going to look for high standards and reform at the State levels. And what we've tried to do is collaborate with Governors and say, look, instead of a No Child Left Behind law that labels schools failures but doesn't give them help that they need, what we think you should do is we'll work with you to come up with what are the things that work. How do we help train young

teachers more effectively? How do we make sure that there's good data, so instead of just teaching to the test, teachers are able to get results from a test to use to actually improve teaching in the classroom while it's taking place right then?

And the steps we've taken, including something called Race to the Top that creates competition and says, you know what, if you're doing a really great job and you're coming up with innovative new ideas, we'll give you a little extra money to implement those reforms and those good ideas. We're actually starting to see improvement across the country. The problem is, if the improvement is undermined because teachers are getting laid off and kids are ending up having to go to school 4 days a week in some States instead of 5, or if suddenly things like music and art and PE that used to be critical to any school experience, suddenly, that stuff is going away, then that's undermining the reforms that we're making.

So my argument to every Governor and every local school district is, figure out what you can do without, but don't shortchange education. And ultimately, the most important thing in education are our teachers, and we've got to give them support and buck them up. In fact, we should be paying them more than they're getting paid. If we're doing that, then we'll be in pretty good shape.

All right. Gentleman in the yellow—oh, I'm sorry, it's a lady's turn. Right there, in the sunglasses, in the blue blouse, right there. There we go.

Medical Marijuana/Health Care Reform

Q. Hi, Mr. President. My name is Teresa Morrill, and I just want to say that I'm really excited that you're here in Cannon Falls. And my question is, is there something we can do about the rising cost of prescription drugs? And number two, if you can't legalize marijuana, why can't we just legalize medical marijuana to help the people that need it?

The President. Well, a lot of States are making decisions about medical marijuana. As a controlled substance, the issue, then, is, is it being prescribed by a doctor as opposed to—well, I'll leave it at that. [*Laughter*]

With respect to prescription drugs, the prescription drug program that now is part of Medicare obviously has been very helpful, but the costs had been going up and up and up. So part of the Affordable Care Act health care reform, also known as Obamacare—by the way, you know what? Let me tell you, I have no problem with folks saying "Obama cares." I do care. If the other side wants to be the folks who don't care, that's fine with me.

But yes, I do care about families who have been struggling because of crushing health care costs. I met a young man here who—right here—who, as a consequence of health care reform—he's got a blood disorder that, if it weren't for the health care reform act, his family would have been capped out and he wouldn't have the help that he needs. So—and you can tell he's an outstanding young man and he's going to do great things, and his family is not going bankrupt as a consequence of it.

Now, the same thing is true on prescription drugs. What we did as part of the Affordable Care Act was we said, first of all, we're going to give a $250 rebate to every senior out there who's using the prescription drug plan to help lower their costs a little bit, and what we've done is we're starting to close what's called the doughnut hole. And for those of you who aren't familiar with the doughnut hole, the way the original prescription drug plan was structured, you would get some coverage up to a certain point, a couple thousand dollars. Once you spent a few thousand dollars, suddenly, it just went away and you were on your own, out of pocket, until you got on the other side where you'd spent many more thousands of dollars, and then you would get a prescription drug plan again.

Well, we said, that doesn't make any sense; let's close that hole. And as part of the Affordable Care Act, we will be closing that holes, and we're also making it cheaper for generics to get onto the market as well as brand-name drugs. So overall, the health care act should be lowering prices for prescription drugs over the next few years. It's getting phased in, so it didn't all take into effect right away after I signed the bill; it's getting phased in over the next several years. But you should start seeing some relief if your family needs prescription drugs. That was part of the Affordable Care Act. All right?

Gentleman in the yellow shirt right here.

Health Care Reform

Q. Hello, Mr. President. I'm Pat Tullo from Cannon Falls Township. First, I want to echo the sentiments of those who have spoken before me in praising you and thanking you for all of your efforts and all the things that you've tried to do during probably one of the most difficult situations faced by any President in the face of unreasonable obstruction and opposition. So thank you.

The President. Well, thank you.

Q. I'd like to follow up on health care reform. As of 2 days ago, we now have a split in the Eleventh Circuit and Sixth Circuit Courts of Appeals, where, inevitably, this is heading for the U.S. Supreme Court regardless of how the Fourth Circuit rules. I don't have a lot of confidence in the U.S. Supreme Court with its conservative wing. My concern is that they will drive this toward striking down the individual responsibility mandate, which I understand to be so critical to making the system work; if everybody doesn't buy in, it really doesn't work. My question to you, sir, is, what do we do? This is a giant step backward if it happens. And I know I'm counting on—I'm talking about things that haven't happened yet, but just in terms of contingency planning, you must be thinking about this.

The President. Well, first of all, I think it's important for everybody to understand that the Affordable Care Act won't have fully taken effect until 2013. So on a big change like this where we're helping a lot of people, you want to phase it in and do it right.

Now, there are a lot of different component parts to it. I just mentioned prescription drugs, helping seniors be able to afford their prescription drugs. You've got the law that says that folks can stay on their parents' health insurance up until they're 26 years old, so a lot of young people, especially if they don't have a job yet or they don't have a job that gives health insurance, they've got some security as they're getting started off in life.

All the patient—essentially patient rights that were in the bill, all those things are going to be there. So no lifetime caps and no fine print that the insurance company gives you where you think you're covered and then when you're sick you go to try to get insurance and it turns out that they're not covering you for that, all that stuff is going to be in place.

And what we're doing is each State is setting up what's called an exchange where, essentially, you can pool with your friends who also don't—and neighbors who don't have health insurance, and now you've got a big purchasing unit, right, just like a big company does, and that means you can negotiate with the insurance companies and you can get a better deal.

How many people here have tried to buy health insurance on their own without a company? And you know what happens, right? They will charge you an arm and a leg, because their attitude is you're not part of a big enough pool that we can spread the risk across.

So we're setting up these exchanges. Now, where the individual responsibility mandate comes in has to do with the part of the law that says an insurance company can't reject you because you've got a preexisting condition. And—which I think is the right thing to do.

Here's the problem: If an insurance company has to take you, has to insure you, even if you're sick, but you don't have an individual mandate, then what would everybody do? They would wait until they get sick and then you'd buy health insurance, right? No point in you—I mean, it's just like your car insurance. If you could buy—if the car insurance companies had to give you insurance, you'd just wait until you had an accident and then you'd be dialing on the phone from the wreck, and you'd say, "State Farm, I'd like to buy some car insurance please." [*Laughter*]

So that's why the individual mandate is important. Because the basic theory is, look, everybody here at some point or another is going to need medical care, and you can't be a free-

rider on everybody else. You can't not have health insurance, then go to the emergency room and each of us who've done the responsible thing and have health insurance, suddenly, we now have to pay the premiums for you. That's not fair. So if you can afford it, you should get health insurance just like you get car insurance.

This should not be controversial, but it has become controversial partly because of people's view that—well, let me just say this: You've got a Governor who's running for President right now who instituted the exact same thing in Massachusetts. This used to be a Republican idea, by the way, this whole idea of the individual mandate, and suddenly, some—it's like they got amnesia. [*Laughter*] It's like, oh, this is terrible; this is going to take away freedom for Americans all over the world, all over the country. So that's a little puzzling.

One court has said—actually, the majority of courts that have looked at it, the lower courts, have said—individual mandate is fine. Medical care is different from everything else. There's nothing wrong with saying to people who can afford to get health insurance, you need to buy health insurance just like car insurance. You can't wait and then go to the emergency room, because we can't turn you away at the emergency room. And if you're broke, then we'll give you some help, but if you can afford it, you should buy it. That's what the majority of courts have said.

There have been two appeals courts so far. One has said it's fine. The other one has taken sort of the conservative line that this restricts freedom and Congress doesn't have the authority to do it. If the Supreme Court follows existing precedent, existing law, it should be upheld without a problem. If the Supreme Court does not follow existing law and precedent, then we'll have to manage that when it happens.

But I just want to make everybody understand that there are a lot of components to the health care law that are good for you, even if you don't have health insurance or even if you have health insurance. It's true that we helped 30 million people get health insurance. But it was also the strongest patient bill of rights that has ever been passed to make sure that if you do have health insurance, the insurance companies don't jerk you around, that they treat you fairly. And that is going to stay in place. And that's the right thing to do.

All right, I've got time for one more question. And I'm going to ask this young lady right here. I always want to end with the next generation.

Q. I'm Vanessa Peer, and I'm from Cannon Falls. And I'm going to say, happy birthday to Val. [*Laughter*]

The President. Oh, happy birthday, Val. Val looks like she's about 29. [*Laughter*]

Q. And why Cannon Falls?

The President. Why Cannon Falls? Well, I had heard that Cannon Falls has some of the smartest, best looking kids around. And you have confirmed the rumor about the outstanding children of Cannon Falls. [*Laughter*]

So thank you very much, everybody. God bless you.

NOTE: The President spoke at 11:56 a.m. at Hannah's Bend Park. In his remarks, he referred to Warren E. Buffett, chief executive officer and chairman, Berkshire Hathaway Inc.; and former Gov. W. Mitt Romney of Massachusetts, 2012 Republican Presidential candidate.

Remarks at a Town Hall Meeting and a Question-and-Answer Session in Decorah, Iowa
August 15, 2011

The President. Hello, Decorah! Hello, Iowa! It is good to be back. This place is as pretty as I remembered it. It is spectacular.

Everybody, please have a seat. Everybody, have a seat. It is wonderful to see all of you. First of all, I've got a few introductions I just want to make real quick. The attorney general of Iowa, a great friend of mine, one of my earliest supporters, Tom Miller, is in the house. The mayor of Decorah, Donald Arendt, is here. Give him a big round of applause. You may remember this guy; he did a great job in Iowa. He's now one of the finest Secretaries of Agriculture we've ever had. Tom Vilsack's in the house. And I want to thank Diane and everybody at the Seed Saver Exchange for this unbelievable setting. Give them a big round of applause.

And they gave me a pack of seeds for Michelle's garden. [*Laughter*] So I'm going to be in good stead when I get home.

This is a town hall meeting, so I want to spend most of my time answering your questions. But if you don't mind, I just want to make a couple remarks at the top.

We obviously have gone through one of the toughest times in our history economically over these last 2½ years. We've gone through the worst recession since the Great Depression, dating back to 2007, 2008. But what I said earlier today when I was in Cannon Falls is something I believe with every fiber of my being, and that is that there is not a country on Earth that would not be willing to trade places with the United States of America. We've got the best universities. We've got the best entrepreneurs. We've got the best scientists. We've got the best market system, the most dynamic in the world.

And so as tough as things are, all of us are incredibly blessed to have been born in the United States of America. And that's why we continue to attract people from all around the world who see us as a beacon of hope.

But having said that, we have to acknowledge we've got some big challenges. Now, some of the challenges are not of our own making. We had reversed the recession, avoided a depression, got the economy moving again, created 2 million private sector jobs over the last 17 months. But over the last 6 months, we've had a run of bad luck, some things that we could not control. We had an Arab Spring that promises democracy and potentially a growth of human rights throughout the Middle East, but it also caused high gas prices that put a crimp on a lot of families just as they were trying to dig themselves out from the recession. Then we had a tsunami in Japan that disrupted supply chains and affected markets all around the world. And then in Europe, there are all kinds of challenges around the sovereign debt there, and that has made businesses hesitant, and some of the effects of Europe have lapped onto our shores. And all those things have been headwinds for our economy.

Now, those are things that we can't completely control. The question is, how do we manage these challenging times and do the right things when it comes to those things that we can control? See, the problem we have is not with our country. The problem is that our politics is broken. The problem is, is that we've got the kind of partisan brinksmanship that is willing to put party ahead of country, that's more interested in seeing their political opponents lose than seeing the country win.

And nowhere was that more evident than this most recent debt ceiling debacle. The fact of the matter is that our debt and deficits are manageable if we make some intelligent choices and make sure that there are shared sacrifices as well as shared opportunities. And had we made some decent decisions over just the last 2, 3 months, had we been willing to seize the opportunity that was before us, then there is no reason why we had to go through this downgrade. Because that did not have to do with economics, that had to do with politics. It was an assessment that our Congress is not able to come up with the kinds of compromises that move this country forward.

And I don't know about you, but I'm pretty frustrated about that. I am pretty frustrated about that because, given the challenges we face, we don't have time to play games. There are a lot of folks—a lot of our neighbors, a lot of our friends—who've been out of work too long. We've got too many small businesses that are struggling. I see a lot of young people in the audience here today, and they're thinking about what are their prospects for the future, graduating from college knowing they've got a

lot of debt, needing to find a job. They don't have patience for the kind of shenanigans we've been seeing on Capitol Hill. They understand that now is the time for all of us to pull together and do what it takes to grow the economy and put people back to work.

Now, the good news is there are things we could be doing right now that would make a difference for our economy. Back in December, when some of my folks on the other side of the aisle were more willing to compromise, we were able to put a package together that cut taxes for families by an average of a thousand dollars.

And what I've said is, let's continue this payroll tax cut into next year so as the economy is strengthening, ordinary families who are still digging themselves out of credit card debt or seeing their homes underwater, they've got a little more purchasing power. That will be good for small businesses and large businesses, and they will hire.

We could right now say we are going to go ahead and renew that tax cut, and that would be good for the American people and good for the economy. There's no reason to wait.

There's no reason for us to wait putting construction workers back to work all across the country. Nobody took a bigger hit than those who were involved in the housing boom when the boom went bust. So why don't we put them to work right now rebuilding our roads and our bridges and our schools all across America? There's a proposal in Congress right now. Congress should pass it and get it done.

There's no reason why we shouldn't be helping our small businesses and startup businesses. We've passed 16 tax cuts for small businesses. And right now we've got a bill pending that is called the "American Invents" bill. It basically reforms our patent system so if somebody has got a creative idea, they can turn it into a business right away without redtape, without bureaucracy. That's who we are: a nation of inventors. This traditionally has had bipartisan support. What are we waiting for? We should pass it right now to give a spark to industry.

We've got pending trade legislation. Tom Vilsack and I were talking on the way over, on the bus here, and the truth of the matter is, is that the agricultural sector in America, the cornerstone of States like Iowa, is doing very well. But we could be doing more. And my general attitude is, why don't we want to open up markets so that the extraordinary bounty of the heartland of America is making its way there, but also manufacturing is making its way there.

Look, we've got a whole bunch of Kias and Hyundais here in the United States of America on our roads, and that's fine and good. But I want some Chryslers and some GMs and some Fords on the roads of the South Korea as well. We should go ahead and get those trade deals done.

So there are a whole host of ideas that we could be implementing right now that traditionally have had bipartisan support. The only thing that is preventing us from passing them is that there are some folks in Congress who think that doing something in cooperation with me or this White House, that that somehow is bad politics. Well, you know what, you guys didn't send us there to be thinking about our jobs. You sent us there to be thinking about your jobs and your future.

Now, we do have to be thinking about how we invest in education and how we invest in infrastructure and how we invest in basic research, but still do it while the Government is living within its means. And neither party is blameless on this. The truth is we had a balanced budget in 2000—the last time we had a Democratic President—and what we ended up doing was we had two wars that we didn't pay for, a prescription drug plan we didn't pay for. We had two tax cuts that we did not pay for, and the result was a burgeoning debt. And then what ended up happening was, because of the recession and the lack of regulation on Wall Street, this wrenching recession meant less tax revenues coming in and more going out, because we were providing help to States to make sure teachers and police officers and firefighters weren't laid off and to make sure that we could help small businesses and put people back to work.

So we've got a genuine problem with deficits and debt. But here, again, is the good news: If everybody is willing to make some modest sacrifices, this problem we could solve. We could solve it tomorrow. We could solve it next week. If the Speaker of the House had taken the bargain that he and I were talking about, we would have had it solved last month, and we would not have gone through everything that we went through over the last several weeks. But it does require compromise and it requires some balance.

Warren Buffett had an article published today in which he said, "Stop coddling billionaires." He pointed out that—I think he made about 36 million on income; it was, I guess, an off-year for him—[*laughter*]—but he pointed out that he paid an effective rate of 17 percent when it came to taxes, which meant that he paid a lower tax rate than anybody else in his office, including his secretary, because most of his income came in the form of capital gains.

And he made a simple point. He said, look, nobody's income has gone up faster than the top 1 percent. In fact, nobody's gone up faster than the top one-tenth of 1 percent. There's nothing wrong, when it comes to closing our deficit and managing our debt, to say that we should ask a little bit of help from everybody. I don't want a tax cut if it means that senior citizens have to pay an extra $6,000 a year for their Medicare. That's not fair, and that's not right.

I think it makes sense for us to say, you know what, let's close some loopholes that only oil and gas companies are able to take advantage of to make sure that we don't have to cut back on Pell grants for students who are trying to go to college and get a better education.

Now, that doesn't mean that we defend every single Government program. Everybody has got to make sacrifices. There are programs that aren't working well. And sometimes there are those in my party who will defend everything, even if it's not working. Well, we do have to make some cuts on things that we don't need, and that allows us to invest in the things that we do. But there's got to be balance, and there's got to be fairness.

And that's not just my view; the majority of Republicans agree with that view. Although I have to tell you, when I saw the other day—my friends in the Republican Presidential primary, they were asked, "Would you take a deal in which, for every $1 of tax increases, we cut $10 in Government spending?" Ten-to-one ratio, and nobody was willing to take that deal. And what that tells me is, okay, you've gotten to the point where you're just thinking about politics, you're not thinking about common sense. You've got to be willing to compromise in order to move the country forward.

So here's the upshot: We do have real challenges. We're going to have to make some tough decisions. And I know that during the 2½ years that I've been President, we've gone through a lot of ups and downs and a lot of tough times. And our job is not finished until every single American who's looking for a job can find a job and until we have fixed the problems that caused me to run for President in the first place, so that we're growing a middle class and people have basic security and they know if they're following the rules, if they're working hard, if they're looking after their families and meeting their responsibilities, that they've got a chance at the American Dream. You guys are meeting your responsibilities. You're meeting your responsibilities. You're working hard. And if you've gotten laid off and you don't have a job, you're out there looking for a job. You're looking after your family. You're tightening your belt where you need to, but you're still making investments to help your kids with their future. You're operating with common sense, and you're donating time at your church or a food pantry or Little League. Well, if you're meeting your responsibilities, the least you can ask is your elected representatives meeting theirs.

And so I understand that after this last midterm, you voted for divided Government. But you didn't vote for dysfunctional Government. You didn't vote for a broken Government that can't make any decisions, can't move the country forward at all. That's not what you voted for.

And so some people have been saying, well, Mr. President, why don't you call Congress back for a special session? And what I've said is the last thing that people need for confidence right now is to watch folks on Capitol Hill arguing all over again.

What they need to do is come to Decorah or go to Cannon Falls or meet with their constituents back home and hear the frustration and understand that people are sick and tired of the nonsense and the political games. And hopefully, when they come back in September, they're going to have a wakeup call that says we need to move the country forward. You've got to start focusing on doing the people's business. That's what everybody's expecting.

I want you to help hold all of us accountable, me included. I am enlisting you in this fight, because if you are—if you're making your voices heard, if you're letting people know that enough is enough, it is time to move forward, it is time for us to win the future. If your voices are heard, then sooner or later these guys have to start paying attention. And if they don't start paying attention, then they're not going to be in office, and we will have a new Congress in there that will start paying attention to what is going on all across America.

I'm confident in the power of your voice. I'm confident in your values; those are the values that we share. I don't care whether you're a Democrat or Republican or an Independent. All of us here are patriots, and everybody here cares about our country and puts it first. And if we can have that kind of politics, then nothing can stop us.

Thank you very much, everybody. God bless you. Thank you. Thank you, Decorah.

All right. So here's what we're going to—everybody have a seat. We got a bunch of questions coming. What we're going to do is folks who have a question can just raise their hand. We've got people with microphones in the audience. And I'm going to go boy, girl, boy, girl, so it's fair. [*Laughter*] We want to be fair.

All right, let's start with this young lady right here. Right in front. And you got a microphone coming right behind you.

Bipartisanship/President's Governing Style/President's Accomplishments

Q. Okay. I have to say before I ask my question that I'm a very big supporter. So——

The President. Thank you. What's your name?

Q. Emily.

The President. Hey, Emily.

Q. Emily Neal. And this is my daughter Kaia.

The President. Hey, Kaia.

Q. Anyhow, so——

The President. What you eating there? Hold on a second. [*Laughter*]

Q. She broke her arm.

The President. Is that a cookie?

Q. You want to give him a cookie?

The President. How did you get a cookie that early?

Q. Is that allowed?

The President. Before dinner? [*Laughter*] All right, go ahead. Go ahead.

Q. Oh, you don't want to know what I do for a living. That's funny. Okay. So when you ran for office, you built a tremendous amount of trust with the American people, that you seemed like someone who wouldn't move the bar on us. And it seems, especially in the last year, as if your negotiating tactics have sort of cut away at that trust by compromising some key principles that we believed in, like repealing the tax cut, not fighting harder for single payer. Even Social Security and Medicare seemed on the line when we were dealing with the debt ceiling. So I'm just curious, moving forward, what prevents you from taking a harder negotiating stance, being that it seems that the Republicans are taking a really hard stance?

The President. Well, let me—no, this a good question, and I'm glad you asked it, because obviously, I've been getting a lot of this in the press lately. First of all, when it comes to health care, I said during the campaign that we were not going to be able to get a single-payer system and that my priority was making sure that every American who needed health insurance was able to buy it and were going to be treated fairly and it was going to be affordable. We were going to eliminate preexisting conditions—or we were going to eliminate the bar on people getting health insurance if they had preexisting conditions.

And the health care bill that we passed was not perfect, but we covered 30 million people.

We had the strongest patient bill of rights ever. We made sure that folks who were under 26 could stay on their parents' health insurance. We made sure that there were no lifetime limits and that if you got sick, your insurance company—if you'd been paying your premiums, that they better be paying for your medical care and not trying to wiggle out of it.

So this was a landmark piece of legislation. Yes, getting it through Congress was messy, and it didn't have every single provision in there that we wanted, but it was entirely consistent with what I campaigned on.

Now, with respect to the Bush tax cuts, I said very clearly that I thought the high-end tax cuts for folks like Warren Buffett should lapse. After the midterms, though, the economy was still weak. It wasn't clear that we could get—that in Congress we could hold the line. We couldn't get what's called decoupling, which meant Republicans would not go along with just voting for continuing the middle class tax cuts and letting the high-end lapse. And what that meant was, the choice I had to make would have been to let all the Bush tax cuts lapse, including those for the middle class, which would have meant that the average family saw their taxes go up $3,000 on average, at a time when they were still digging themselves out of a debt hole. It would have been very bad for the economy.

We also would not have gotten uninsurance—unemployment insurance continued into this year. We would not have been able to do the payroll tax, and so the economy would have been much weaker. And so I made a decision that it was better for us at that point to strengthen the economy, because we only extended those tax cuts for another 2 years. And we would be able to take our case to the American people as the economy got stronger as to why we've got a different approach than the Republicans do.

Now, on this debt ceiling, it's pretty straightforward. I felt that it was important for us to try to solve the problem rather than play games. And that was particularly important because if we had allowed default—if you think that the stock market gyrations this last couple weeks was bad, if we had had a default, then we might not—genuinely might have gone back into a financial crisis. Because the truth of the matter is, even though we got downgraded, I don't know if you've noticed, but when the market got all crazy, what do you think people bought? Where did they put their money to avoid risk? They bought Treasury bills.

So the market voted to say, we have complete confidence in America right now. But if we had defaulted, that meant that we might not have the legal authority to issue Treasury bills and we would have had problems making our Social Security payments, making our payments to our troops, our veterans, and so forth. And that was not a risk worth taking.

Now, I know that people would like to say, well, just do something to get these guys under control. This was a unique situation in which, frankly, the collateral damage from an actual default would have been so great that I didn't want to risk the livelihoods and the well-being of millions of people even though I thought the other side was very unreasonable. Now, that's a unique circumstance.

Moving forward, my basic attitude is, we know what to do. I'll be putting forward, when they come back in September, a very specific plan to boost the economy, to create jobs, and to control our deficit. And my attitude is, get it done. And if they don't get it done, then we'll be running against a Congress that's not doing anything for the American people, and the choice will be very stark and will be very clear.

But I guess my broader point is this. Look, I think it was Mario Cuomo who once said, "Campaigning is in poetry, and governing is in prose." And my job as President goes beyond just winning the political argument. I've got a whole bunch of responsibilities, which means I have to make choices sometimes that are unattractive and I know will be bad for me politically and I know will get—make supporters of mine disappointed.

But what I want everybody to think about is the trajectory in which we've gone. So yes, maybe you didn't get a public option, but we got the closest thing we've ever had to universal health care. And yes, the economy is not

fully healed, but it's a lot better off than it was when I came into office. And yes, we haven't transformed our energy system yet, but I tell you what, administratively we just doubled fuel efficiency standards on cars, the first time that's happened in 30 years, which will do more for our environment than any piece of legislation that we've seen in a very long time. And we will be getting our troops out of Iraq by the end of this year. We've already got a hundred thousand out, and they're all going to be out by the end of this year. And we're starting to transition out of Afghanistan.

And so look, the bottom line is we're moving in the right direction. But I know it's frustrating, because the other side's unreasonable, and you don't want to reward unreasonableness. I—look, I get that. But sometimes you've got to make choices in order to do what's best for the country at that particular moment, and that's what I've tried to do. All right?

Okay. It's a guy's turn. This gentleman in the back, in the blue shirt.

Health Care Reform

[*At this point, there were technical problems with the questioner's microphone.*]

Q. You are heard.

The President. There you go. [*Laughter*]

Q. We—you talk about universal health care. I guess my question is, if it's so good, why are you allowing so many large companies to opt out?

The President. Well, you know what? Here's what it is, is that any time you're changing big systems like this, there are going to be—there's going to be a transition period. So the overall health care reform does not take fully—does not fully take effect until 2013. That's when we have the exchanges set up, which means that if you don't have health insurance or if you're a small business that only has a few employees and you can't get a good rate, you're going to be able to go into the exchange and essentially be part of a big pool—just like a big company or the Federal workers are—and get a better deal from your insurance companies. But those exchanges are just now being set up. It took about a couple years to get it set up.

So, in the meantime, the question is, how do you manage that transition in a way in which a bunch of companies don't say to themselves, well, we're just going to eliminate health care that's not great, but is better than nothing? And our basic attitude has been, we're willing to give some waivers to some companies that are doing something when it comes to health care, because those employees don't have a better option right now. But as we build up this better option, then they'll be able to take advantage of that better option. All right?

So the whole issue here has to do with, how do we transition to get to the point where all these exchanges all across the country are up and running? Now, there are some things that have already taken effect that make a difference in your life even if you've got health insurance. I mentioned young people who can stay on their health care—parents' health care till they're 26. Senior citizens, right now, have already gotten a $250 rebate on their prescription drugs, and we're closing the so-called doughnut hole so that if you've got high drug expenses, you're going to start saving potentially thousands of dollars over the next several years as we phase that in.

If you've got health insurance right now, you've got a lot more security in your health insurance than you used to. And in the meantime, there are small businesses all across the country who are getting millions of dollars in subsidies already; they're getting big tax breaks to provide health insurance to their employees that they didn't provide—that they didn't get before.

So this thing is already making a big difference in the lives of millions of people all across the country, but it's not fully implemented yet. And that's not unusual. I mean, when Social Security started, it took a bunch of years before it was the program that we understand it to be right now. The same was true with Medicaid, the same was true with Medicare. So when you start doing something big like this, it takes a couple years in order for us to implement it.

All right. It's a young lady's turn. Okay. Right there in the stripes. Yes.

Tax Code Reform

Q. First of all, I'd like to say what an honor it is to be here with you.

The President. Well, it's great to be here, and it's a beautiful night. It's nice.

Q. We know that the tax system is pretty broken. Is there anything going on about a possible Federal sales tax or a flat tax, anything like that, which would be more fair to all people?

The President. Well, this is the task that this so-called supercommittee is supposed to be working on, and that is changing the Tax Code and reforming it: closing loopholes, closing special-interest tax breaks. Potentially, if you closed a bunch of these loopholes and tax breaks, you could lower the overall rate, broaden the base, and it would be a fairer, easier system that would combine simplification with, actually, more revenue.

So my hope is that Congress is willing to take up tax reform. So far they've said that they're willing to do it, but so far we haven't seen a lot of energy on the part of some folks in actually delivering on tax reform.

Now, I have to tell you, I think it's very important for us to maintain what's called progressivity in the Tax Code though. Because, yes, you can reform the Tax Code where you just have a flat tax, for example; the problem is, Warren Buffett would probably pay even less in taxes, and a lot of companies would pay even less in taxes if you set up that system.

So we can simplify the Tax Code; we can make it less distorting to the economy. There is no reason why an oil and gas company should get a tax break when a small business here in Decorah doesn't get a tax break. There's no reason why you should get a tax break if you build a corporate jet, but you don't get that same tax break if you build a commercial jet.

So there are a lot of distortions like that that we need to change. And my hope is, is that Congress takes tax reform seriously. But no matter what tax reform happens, it is very important for those of us who are best able to pay, to pay our fair share. That's a basic principle that I think all of us agree on, all of us understand. And by the way, that's how it was up until 2000. And when you hear this argument that somehow if you just cut taxes for wealthy folks that the economy is going to be better because they're the job generators, et cetera, just remember that we created tens of millions of jobs under the Tax Code that existed before the Bush tax cuts, and we've had much less job growth since that time.

So we've had an experiment in this theory that you hear propagated all the time. It didn't work. And in the meantime, it helped to create these huge deficits, and it means we're underinvesting in the things that are going to be important.

So States all across the country are laying off teachers. This is not the time for us to be laying off teachers. We should be training teachers, putting the best teachers in front of the classroom, because whoever's best educated is going to win the race for the future.

Now is not the time for us to not invest in infrastructure. We used to have the best roads, the best bridges, the best seaports, and these days China has got better airports than us. Europe has better rail systems. Try to get products to market—we should have the best. We should have the best smart grid that transmits energy from solar panels and wind turbines to high-population centers, which could be a income generator for rural America and would improve our environment and reduce our dependence on foreign oil. Those are investments we should be making right now.

So there are two contrasting visions that are going to be presented over the next year and a half in this debate that we still have to finish about how to close the debt and the deficit and how we move this country forward. And I'm on the side of a vision that says we live within our means, but we still make investments in the future, and everybody pays their fair share, and we've got shared sacrifice and shared opportunity.

And on the other side, you've got a vision that says, we are going to make sure that those who have benefited the most pay the least, and

we underinvest in education, and we underinvest in infrastructure, and we underinvest in basic research. That's their vision. And we dismantle Medicare as we know it and make it into a voucher system. Well, that's—I don't think that's the way that America is going to grow; that's not how America is going to prosper. But the only way that we're going to be able to win that argument is if you guys make a decision that you want a country that's big and bold and generous and not one that's cramped and just believes in a winner-take-all economy in which everybody else is left out in the cold. That's not the kind of America that I was raised in, not the kind of America I believe in.

All right. A gentleman's turn. Right there in the green shirt.

Infrastructure

Q. Thank you, sir. Welcome to Decorah. My name is John Franzen, and I'm with the Decorah City Council—[*applause*]—I'm with the Decorah City Council, my name is John Franzen, and we have several large infrastructure construction companies. You touched on infrastructure, and I think that one of the fastest and best stimulus packages would be infrastructure in America. Can you touch base on that, please?

The President. Well, I completely agree with you. And as I said, if you think about what's happened to our economy, we had a huge housing bubble that popped, and a lot of folks who were feeling pretty good about the wealth invested in their homes suddenly felt poor when their mortgages were bigger than the assessment of their homes. And a lot of developers realized, you know what, we can't sell all the homes that we've already built. And a lot of construction workers got laid off. And those construction workers, by the way, a lot of them had been in manufacturing, and when manufacturing got more efficient or moved offshore, they went into the construction trades. And that's been a huge drag on our economy.

Now, there is no better time for us to invest in infrastructure than right now, first of all, because we need it, but second of all, because interest rates are very low, so financing infrastructure is cheap. And you've got contractors and construction workers who are dying for work. So they'll come in on time, under budget, if we just give them the opportunity.

So what we've said is this: Not only do—should the Government be investing more in infrastructure, but we should be investing in it in a smarter way. There's been bipartisan support for something called an infrastructure bank, where the Federal Government would put seed capital in it, but it would basically leverage the private sector that wants to invest in smart infrastructure projects all across the country. And so if you made a $10 billion investment, that might result in $300 billion worth of investment in projects all across the country that could put people to work right now. Because, look, there are a bunch of companies and a bunch of pension funds out there that are looking for ways to invest. They don't know where to put their money. What better way to invest than investing in America? And it would make the entire economy more productive.

Now, we did some of this during the Recovery Act. So, for example, we said—thanks to Tom Vilsack, we said, you know what, rural America needs broadband access. And so what we've done is to help lay broadband lines; our goal is 98-percent coverage—broadband coverage all across rural America. That's a good investment. Not only does it put people to work, but it makes the incredible productivity of rural America connected with the world. And if you get a product here in Decorah that sells, you can not only sell in Decorah, you can start selling it in Los Angeles, in Singapore, and all around the world if you've got that Internet connection. That's a good investment.

I mentioned a smart grid. We need to replace our electricity grid to make it more efficient, and then you can transmit energy from biofuels or wind power to major population centers. That's good for rural America. That's good for those population centers.

So there's a lot of investments that we can make. All that's missing right now is the will to get it done, and we're going to be pushing

Congress hard in September to move forward on that proposal. All right?

Okay. Let's make sure I get this side here. This young lady right here. We got a microphone right by you.

U.S. Political System/Bipartisanship

Q. You already did a good job by calling me a young lady. [*Laughter*]

The President. See? Absolutely.

Q. Thank you very much, Mr. President. Mr. President, you've got some wonderful ideas. And as a result of my work at Luther College at the Diversity Center, I'm privileged to hear a lot of good ideas. And I'm privileged to work with people, with partners, who may have different points of view, but we come to common ground. Unfortunately, Mr. President, I don't see that you have partners. The Congress doesn't seem to be a good partner. You said so yourself, they're more interested in seeing you lose than the country win.

My question, Mr. President, is what actual strategy do you have behind the plan that you say that you're going to be taking back to Washington so that when Congress comes back they'll have all these good ideas in front of them? And then my second question is, what happens, Mr. President, to our democracy? We are in a very divided country right now. What can you say to help us with democracy itself, good old American democracy? Thank you.

The President. You bet. Well, let me say this. First of all, democracy is always a messy business in a big country like this. We're diverse, got a lot of points of view. We kind of romanticize sometimes what democracy used to be like.

But when you listen to what the Federalists said about the Anti-Federalists and the names that Jefferson called Hamilton and back and forth, I mean, those guys were tough. Lincoln, they used to talk about him almost as bad as they talk about me. [*Laughter*]

So democracy has never been for the faint of heart. And you've got to get involved and get engaged. And folks are throwing elbows, and that's always been the way American democracy has functioned. So we don't want to romanticize it.

But what is true is because of the way our system is set up, we got different branches of Government, separation of powers, and in order to do big things, we always have had to compromise. That's just the nature of how our democracies function. And what that means is, is that everybody cannot get a hundred percent of what they want.

Now, for those of you who are married, there is an analogy here. [*Laughter*] I basically let Michelle have 90 percent of what she wants. But at a certain point, I have to draw the line and say, give me my little 10 percent. [*Laughter*] And now, this is mainly—she's right 90 percent of the time, so—[*laughter*].

But you said in your workplace, right, you guys don't all agree on everything. But at a certain point when you want to move the institution forward, you say, all right, let's try to not focus just on our differences, let's try to figure out what we have in common.

That is something that we have not seen lately, partly because the way congressional districts are drawn, everybody is in very safe districts. And so the Republicans, they're worried about a Republican primary, and they're not really thinking about the general election. That kind of pushes them to take more maximalist positions.

Part of it is the way our media has evolved. It used to be everybody was sitting there watching Walter Cronkite. Now everybody's on their own little blog or their own separate news forum. If you're a Democrat, you're reading the New York Times. If you're a Republican, you're watching FOX News, right? People don't listen to each other as much. The only way that gets fixed is if voters insist on a different kind of politics and reward people who do seem to be listening to the other side and do seem to be focusing on trying to get things done.

Now, in terms of how I deal with the current Congress, what I can do is to present my best ideas about how we move the country forward. And by the way, these are ideas that—many of these ideas traditionally have had Republican

support. It's amusing to watch one of the major Republican candidates now trying to wiggle out of the fact that my health care bill is very similar to the health care bill he passed at a time when he needed to compromise because he was living in a Democratic-majority State.

And so some of these folks know better. And what I—all I can do is to say, I'm going to take the best ideas from everybody, Republicans, Independents, and Democrats, present to them, this is what you should do. But I can't force them to do it. You can force them to do it. And I will take my case to the American people that this vision is how we move the country forward, and if they've got an alternative vision and they don't want to sit there and do nothing for the next 16 months, while unemployment is still high and small businesses are still suffering, then ultimately, they're going to be held to account by you, just like I'm going to be held to account by you.

But we've got to reward folks who are more serious about solving problems than scoring political points. And I make no apologies. Sometimes I—people get mad at me: Well, he's too reasonable. [*Laughter*] Now, think about that. Think about that. People, they're not arguing necessarily that what I'm saying wouldn't work. They're just saying, well, you're too reasonable. I make no apologies for being reasonable.

But ultimately, you do have to hold people accountable, because lives are at stake and the economy is at stake and our children's future is at stake. And so we don't have time for games. All right?

Okay. The gentleman right here.

Rights for Former Felons

Q. Hi. Thanks for coming to Decorah. It's really awesome for you to be here. Mr. Vilsack did a great job before he left office as the Governor—[*applause*]—in reinstating voting rights for——

The President. Yay, Tom Vilsack!

Q. ——in reinstating voting rights for convicted felons. I have found, as somebody who made a mistake when I was young, that 10 years later it's still affecting me. And I want to know, like, if there's anything that is going to be done or could be done so that I can move past that past and many of the people who are all around me and have something better than an entry-level job.

The President. Well, there are obviously a bunch of different aspects to the challenges for folks who have some sort of felony record. It affects them economically. It affects them in terms of voting in some States. One of the strengths of America has always been that this is a land of second chances. And as somebody who feels deeply about my faith, one of the things about my Christian faith is that I believe in redemption and second chances.

And so as a consequence, I think it is very important for us—first of all, if somebody has served their time, for them to be able to participate in their democracy. And historically, many of these issues in terms of eligibility to vote have been set at the State level as opposed to the Federal level, but the Justice Department at the Federal level does have the capacity and the obligation to monitor what States are doing to make sure that they are not purposely exclusionary.

And so we're going to be monitoring voting rights all across the country as long as I'm President of the United States, because I think that the burden of proof should be on States to provide a rationale as to why somebody shouldn't be voting, as opposed to the burden of proof on the person not voting as to why they should have a right to vote. That's my general view.

Economically, there are a lot of good programs out there, and to their credit, we've actually had some good bipartisan support for second-chance legislation that helps provide training programs and allows, for example, expungement of more minor offenses so that people can get back on their feet and contribute economically. And we've actually had some good Democratic and Republican support in Congress for some of that legislation. I think the challenge right now is, when the economy is weak, obviously, you're going to have a tougher time when you apply for a job if there are 100 other applicants for the same job and some of them don't have a record.

If the economy is stronger, then it puts us in a stronger position to be able to push companies to give people a second chance. And so I think my biggest job as President is to make sure that we're strengthening the economy, we're growing it, we're putting people back to work generally, because this is a situation where a rising tide does lift all boats. If the economy is going strong and the unemployment rate is going down generally, then that's going to help you as well. All right?

Okay. Right, the woman with the hat. She's been waving that hat around. [*Laughter*] See, you got to have a hat. That's a huge advantage in terms of getting called on.

Workers' Rights/Labor Unions

Q. Hi, my name is Bev Crumb-Gesme, and I actually used to teach school in the district in which Seed Savers is located. And we have a number of students, former students here that I taught.

The President. How was she? Was she a good teacher? You got thumbs up.

Q. What can I say?

The President. What did you teach?

Q. High school social studies.

The President. Well, that's important stuff.

Q. Many unions, especially public sector unions, helped you get elected in 2008. Those public sector unions and their members gained their salaries and benefits through collective bargaining. Recently, those benefits have been under attack. And I realize that this is a State issue mostly, but what can you do to help support collective bargaining in the States and, most of all, support the public sector unions, the middle class, many of whom are union members? Thank you.

The President. Well, first of all, let's make one thing clear. The right of workers to come together and join a union is part of what built America's middle class. It's the reason why we've got a minimum wage. It's the reason why folks have weekends. It's the reason why you have basic protections on the job from an abusive employer.

There are a whole range of things that people take for granted, even if they're not in a union, that they wouldn't have had if it had not been for collective bargaining. So I think it is very important, whether you are in a union or not—and I speak particularly to young people, because you've grown up at a time when in a lot of circles, "union" somehow is a dirty word—to understand all this is, is people joining together so they've got a little more leverage, so they've got better working conditions, better wages, they can better support their family.

And a lot of us entered into the middle class because our parent or a grandparent was in a union. Remember that. When I hear this kind of antiunion rhetoric and antiunion assaults, I'm thinking, these folks have amnesia. They don't remember that that helped build our middle class and strengthen our economy.

Now, you're right, most of this activity right now is being done at the State level, although I will tell you that some of the assaults on collective bargaining are taking place at the Federal level. You remember this FAA situation where they were shutting down the airports for— threatening to shut down the airports, and we were going to be laying off tens of thousands of people? The reason that happened was because folks on the other side in the House of Representatives decided, let's try to slip in a provision that could make it harder for people to collectively bargain in the aviation industry. And Democrats wouldn't go along. And so they said, okay, well, we're not going to renew funding for this.

So we're seeing some of that at the Federal level as well, and we're fighting back, pushing back against these efforts to diminish the capacity to exercise their basic freedoms and their basic rights.

Now, at the State level, in addition to just providing vocal support for public employees, what I also have been trying to do is to help States so that they can meet their obligations to their public employees and to emphasize how important it is to our future collectively that we have, for example, teachers that are getting

paid a good wage. We can't recruit the kinds of teachers that we need in the classroom.

And in most countries that are doing well right now educationally, their teachers are revered. They get paid on par with doctors and engineers, because there is an understanding that this is a critical profession for the future of the nation.

I do say, though, to my friends in the public sector unions that it is important that you are on the side of reform where reform is needed. Because the truth of the matter is, is that at a time when everybody's belt-tightening, there is nothing wrong with a union saying to itself, you know what, we know budgets are hard right now. Let's sit down and say we're willing to negotiate so that we're making some sacrifices to maintain the number of teachers in the classroom and keep class sizes at a reasonable level. We're willing to make some modifications in terms of how our pension systems work so that they're sustainable for the next generation of teachers, as long as it's a conversation, as opposed to it simply being imposed and collective bargaining rights being stripped away.

So I think it's important—remember we talked about shared sacrifice and burden sharing. Well, this is an area where there's got to be burden sharing as well. If a public sector employee is able to retire at 55 with 80 percent of their wages, and the average public [private]° sector employee has got a 401(k) that they've just seen decline by about 20 percent, and they have no idea how they're going to retire, and they're feeling burdened by a lot of taxes, and they don't feel like the public sector employees are making any adjustments whatsoever to reflect the tough economic realities that are facing folks who are not protected, then there's going to be a natural backlash.

If there's a feeling that unions aren't partners in reform processes in things like education, then they're going to end up being an easy target. So there's got to be an understanding of, on the one hand, we've got to revere public employees. I was saying when I was in Cannon Falls that people are tired of politics,

---

° White House correction.

but they're not tired of government. They may not realize it, but government are our troops in Afghanistan and Iraq. Government are our teachers in the classroom. Government are the FEMA folks who help people when there's a flood or a tornado or a natural disaster.

But we also have to acknowledge—and sometimes Democrats aren't good at this—is acknowledging that not every program in government is working perfectly and we've got to make adjustments to become more efficient and more productive, just like the private sector does. And the more we're willing to be open to new ideas and reform and change, the more we're going to be able to rally public opinion behind all the outstanding work that public employees do, as opposed to public opinion being turned against public employees. All right?

Okay, how many more—we've got time for one more? This is always tough, this last one.

Q. I have a question.

The President. Well, I—hold on a second. The—I'm looking over at this—sir——

Q. How will we——

The President. Sir——

Q. ——come together when your Vice President is calling—[*inaudible*]—Tea Party members terrorists?

The President. Sir, hold on a second. The—I know it's not going to work if you just stand up and start——

Q. [*Inaudible*]

The President. No, he's okay. But, sir, I know it's not going to work if you just stand up when I asked everybody to raise their hand. Okay, so I was about to call on somebody. I didn't see you. I wasn't avoiding you. Please.

Q. [*Inaudible*]

The President. The—whose turn—is it a— I'm going to call on this young man right here. And I'll be happy to talk to you afterwards. Go ahead. This young man right here. We always end with the next generation. Go ahead.

U.S. Political System/Consumer Financial Protection Bureau

Q. Thank you, Mr. President. It's a real benefit of living in Iowa that we get to meet a lot of famous Presidential candidates.

The President. Yes, people seem to—for some reason, they just seem to show up in Iowa all the time, don't they? [*Laughter*]

Q. Yes.

The President. It's shocking.

Q. I'm actually in a picture with you somewhere, but—[*laughter*]—but you're talking a lot about how to bring people together and how to get our democracy to work together. That's all about finding common ground. But over the past—we've seen the rise of the Tea Party, and they really like to cite Thomas Jefferson for his opposition to big government and support of small government. What they don't ever mention is his fear of moneyed interests in politics, so—[*applause*].

Well, what we saw in 2010 in Iowa were— and in Wisconsin—were experienced, dedicated, wise centrist Democratic public servants being challenged by relatively unqualified Republican candidates. But—and these candidates were backed by millions of dollars of out-of-State company funding. And we also now have the Republican frontrunner for President calling corporations people. So I'm wondering what kind of hope do we have for our political spectrum now that we're running—we're going into the first Presidential election where we will be facing unlimited corporate contributions in politics?

The President. All right. Well, let me say this. First of all, in fairness to this gentleman, the—who raised a question, I absolutely agree that everybody needs to try to tone down the rhetoric. Now, in fairness, since I've been called a Socialist who wasn't born in this country, who is destroying America and taking away its freedoms because I passed a health care bill, I'm all for lowering the rhetoric.

I do think that whether it's the Tea Party or activists from whatever walk of life, as I said before, democracy has always been rambunctious in this country. And that's part of what makes America great, is everybody can express their opinions. And there is real anger and frustration—understandable—about the economic situation that we're finding ourselves in. I get that.

Think about it. We came in, you've got a bunch of irresponsible actors, both in Washington and on Wall Street, that almost brought this economy to the ground, and suddenly, everybody else is paying for it. And I think the Tea Party is an expression of that anger and frustration, as much as, sort of, the activism on the Democratic side is an expression of anger and frustration. Obviously, I agree more with the view that it wasn't big government per se that caused this crash, it wasn't food stamps or public employee unions that caused this crash, and that we should direct our anger effectively at how do we prevent the most powerful forces in our society from acting irresponsibly.

I do share your concern that money has become such a powerful factor in politics that it has a distorting effect, and it doesn't just have a distorting effect during election time. I mean, this financial regulatory reform bill that we passed, Dodd-Frank, we set up a Consumer Protection Bureau—a Consumer Finance Protection Bureau. Some of you may be familiar with this. The basic idea is pretty straightforward: that we should have somebody in the Federal Government who makes sure that you're not getting cheated when you take out a credit card, you're not getting cheated when you take out a mortgage, that you're not reading a bunch of fine print that you don't understand and that you've got to be a lawyer to decipher, that consumers should have somebody who's looking out for them in these complex financial transactions that are increasingly a part of our lives.

So we got this thing passed, and we've set it up, and now I've got millions of dollars in lobbyists and special interest donations trying to dismantle this thing before it even gets off the ground, and I can't get the Senate to confirm anybody to take the position. It doesn't matter how well qualified they are. So right now we've nominated the former attorney general of Ohio, who was also the treasurer of Ohio, who, when he was in Ohio, Republicans and Democrats said was a great consumer advocate, who, for the last year and a half, at great sacrifice to himself, has helped to set up this agency. And I've got the Republican Senate—44 of them,

which means that they can filibuster any appointment—saying, we're not going to appoint anybody to this thing unless you water down the enforcement capacities of this agency. Well, that's just—that is pure special interest lobbying at work. And that is not how our democracy should work. That is not how our democracy should work.

And as we go into this Presidential election, what you're going to see is unlimited money that's going to be going on the airwaves, and frankly, we're already seeing it. I mean, I think they've already spent about 20 million, 30 million dollars around the country going after me, and nobody even knows where this money is coming from. You got a bunch of front groups. They're usually called something having to do with freedom or—you know. We don't know who they are. They're not accountable to anybody.

Here's the good news though. I mean, right now the Supreme Court's made a ruling; we're not going to be able to change it. But slowly, surely, when the American people put their voice behind something, eventually the system responds. It may not always respond as fast as we want, but eventually it responds. And so if voters all across the country say, we want a different kind of politics, we will get a different kind of politics.

If all of you are enlisted in the fight to make sure that we've got a country that is looking out for middle class families and promoting common sense and thinking about the next generation and not just the next election and is thinking more about country than it is about party and is less interested in vilifying opponents than figuring out how to get something done, then we're going to start electing folks who do that.

And let me tell you, when we have that kind of politics, watch out. Watch out. You will not be able to stop this country. You will not be able to stop America from making sure that the 21st century is the American century just like the 20th century was. But I'm going to need your help, everybody.

God bless you. God bless America.

NOTE: The President spoke at 5:17 p.m. at Seed Savers Exchange. In his remarks, he referred to Diane Ott Whealy, cofounder, Seed Savers Exchange; Warren E. Buffett, chief executive officer and chairman, Berkshire Hathaway Inc.; former Gov. Mario M. Cuomo of New York; former Gov. W. Mitt Romney of Massachusetts, 2012 Republican Presidential candidate; and Richard A. Cordray, Director-designate, Consumer Financial Protection Bureau.

Remarks at the Opening Session of the White House Rural Economic Forum in Peosta, Iowa
August 16, 2011

Thank you so much. Well, it is wonderful to be back in Iowa, and thank you for arranging perfect weather these last couple of days. [*Laughter*] I have just been having a great time.

I want to first of all make just a few acknowledgments. Richard Avenarius, who is the mayor of Peosta, please—where are you, Mr. Mayor? Well, he was here. [*Laughter*] Give him a round of applause anyway.

This person I know is here—and I want to thank Northeast Iowa Community College for hosting us—Dr. Liang Wee is here, interim president.

I've got a number of members of my Cabinet who are here. All of them do outstanding work day in, day out. So I couldn't be prouder of them. First of all, this guy you should be a little familiar with because he used to be the Governor of this great State, Secretary of Agriculture Tom Vilsack; Secretary of the Interior Ken Salazar; Secretary of Transportation Ray LaHood; Secretary of Housing and Urban Development Shaun Donovan; and the Small Business Administrator, Karen Mills.

Well, this is an outstanding crowd, and I don't want to stand in the way of a lot of good work that's going to be done, so I'm going to just make some brief remarks at the top. We've got small-business owners here. We have farmers. We have ranchers, public servants, clean energy entrepreneurs, and community organizations from all across rural America. And I'm here because I want to hear from you and my Cabinet wants to hear from you.

There are two things that I know for sure: America is going to come back from this recession stronger than before. That I'm convinced of; I believe that. And I'm also convinced that comeback isn't going to be driven by Washington. It's going to be driven by folks here in Iowa. It's going to begin in the classrooms of community colleges like this one. It's going to start on the ranchlands and farms of the Midwest, in the workshops of basement inventors, in the storefronts of small-business owners.

And that's why I'm here today. Obviously, we're going through tough times right now. I don't have to tell you that. A lot of folks are looking for work. Even if you have a job or a small business or a farm, you're maybe getting by with fewer customers or making do with fewer shifts or less money in tips. And for a lot of families in rural parts of the country, these challenges aren't new. For a long time—a decade, maybe longer—you've known what it means to face hardship.

But we also know that while times may be tough, our people are tougher. You know how to make it through a hard season. You know how to look out for each other in the face of drought or tornadoes or disasters, looking out for each other until we reach a brighter day.

And that ethic, that kind of honor and self-discipline and integrity, those are the values that we associate with small towns like this one. Those are the values that built America. And while we've taken some hits, this country still has the best workers, the greatest farms, the top scientists and universities, the most successful businesses and entrepreneurs in the world.

So as I've been saying over the last couple days, there's nothing wrong with this country. We'll get through this moment of challenge. The only question is if, as a nation, we're going to do what it takes to grow this economy and put people back to work right now and can we get our politics to match up with the decency of our people.

The question is if we're going to harness the potential to create jobs and opportunities that exist here in Iowa and all across America. We know what's possible if we're willing to fight for our future and to put aside the politics of the short term and try to get something done. Already this administration has helped nearly 10,000 rural businesses and 35,000 small and medium-sized farms and ranches to get the financing that they need. That's already happened. And that means a restaurant owner can bust down a wall and set up some more tables. It means a family farm can buy a new piece of equipment to get more product to market. And that puts people to work today.

Now, just as the interstate highways knitted the country together 50 years ago, we've also got to do some new things to meet the challenges of the 21st century. We need to expand the reach of broadband, high-speed Internet to 7 million more people and hundreds of thousands of businesses in rural communities. And by taking that step, it's making it possible for folks to take classes and train for new jobs online. It's helping people sell goods, not just down the street, but across the country and around the world. We've invested in clean energy, like advanced biofuels, so that we're moving from an economy that runs on foreign oil to one that runs on homegrown America energy. That's a whole new industry that's taking root here in Iowa and across rural America.

But the rural economy is still not as strong as it could be. That's why I created a Rural Council to look for ways to promote jobs and opportunity right now. And this council has come up with a number of proposals. And we're not wasting time in taking up these proposals; we want to put them to work right now.

So today I'm announcing that we're ramping up our efforts to get capital to small businesses in rural areas. We're doubling the commitment we've already made through key small-business lending programs. We're going to make it easier for people in rural areas looking for work to find out about companies that are hiring.

We're going to do more to speed the development of next-generation biofuels, and we're going to promote renewable energy and conservation. We're going to help smaller local hospitals in communities like this one to recruit doctors and the nurses that they need. And those are just some of the things that we're already announcing today. The reason we brought you all together is because I'm looking forward to hearing from you about what else we can do to jump-start the economy here in rural America.

We want to leave no stone unturned when it comes to strengthening this economy. And we're going to be able to do a lot of stuff administratively. All the proposals we're making today didn't require new laws; it just means that we're doing things smarter, we're eliminating duplication, we're allocating resources to places that we know are really making a difference.

But we could do even more if Congress is willing to get in the game. There are bipartisan ideas, commonsense ideas that have traditionally been supported by Democrats and Republicans that will put more money in your pockets, that will put our people to work, that will allow us to deal with the legacy of debt that hangs over our economy.

I want to cut the payroll tax again to help families make ends meet. That's meant an extra thousand dollars in the pockets of typical American families. That means more customers for your business, more buyers of your products. I want to pass a road construction bill to put tens of thousands of people to work all across America.

We've got young people returning from Iraq and Afghanistan with incredible skills: 25-year-olds who have led platoons, 26-year-olds handling equipment that costs hundreds of millions of dollars. Well, let's connect them to businesses that can use their talents right now.

We should pass trade deals that will level the playing field for American companies. And no folks benefit more than rural Americans when it comes to our trade. That's the reason that our agricultural sector is doing incredibly well and that has spillover effects, ripple effects throughout the economy here.

But it also benefits manufacturing. We've got folks in America driving Kias and Hyundais. I want to see folks in Korea driving Fords and Chryslers and Chevys. I want to sell goods all over the world that are stamped with three words: Made in America.

And all of these proposals will make a difference for rural communities. The only thing that is holding us back is our politics. The only thing that's preventing us from passing the bills I just mentioned is the refusal of a faction in Congress to put country ahead of party. And that has to stop. Our economy cannot afford it. Our economy can't afford it.

So I don't care whether you're a Democrat or Republican, Independent, if you're not registered with any party. I want to enlist your help. I need your help sending a message to Congress that it's time to put the politics aside and get something done.

The folks here in Iowa do the right thing. I've been traveling through these small towns and talking to folks, sitting down at diners. And you listen to people, they take such pride doing the right thing: taking care of their families, working hard, saving for the future, living within their means, giving back to their communities.

You do your part. You meet your obligations. Well, it's time Washington acted as responsibly as you do every single day. It's past time.

We've got a lot of work to do, and the only way it will get done is if Democrats and Republicans put country ahead of party and put the next generation ahead of the next election. And that's what I'm fighting for. That's why I'm out here visiting communities like this one and Decorah and small towns in Minnesota and Illinois.

I'm convinced; I've seen it. When we come together, there's no stopping this country. There is no stopping it. We can create opportunities for training and education and good careers in rural America so young people don't feel like they've got to leave their hometowns to find work. We can strengthen the middle class, restore that sense of economic security that's been missing for a lot of people for way too long. We can push through this period of economic hardship, and we can get to a better place. That's why we're here together. That's what this forum is all about.

So I appreciate all of your participation. I expect great ideas coming out of these breakout sessions. I'm going to join a couple of them. Let's get to work. Thank you very much.

NOTE: The President spoke at 12:05 p.m. at Northeast Iowa Community College.

Remarks During a Breakout Session at the White House Rural Economic Forum in Peosta
August 16, 2011

The President. Everybody, please have a seat. So I'm just going to hang out here for about 20 minutes. Karen's the one who's actually in charge.

Small Business Administration Administrator Karen Gordon Mills. Yes, he's my boss. We have no better advocate for small businesses than the President. So I don't know if you want to hear some of the stories or thoughts that people are starting to come out with.

The President. You know, I think all I want to say by way of introduction is, I had the chance to have breakfast with a couple of your

panelists here, and—three of them, actually—and I was just struck by the creativity and the stick-to-it-ness that so many businesses here are exhibiting.

The good news, Karen, is all of them, uniformly, on a bipartisan basis, felt that the SBA—their local SBA office is doing a great job and working really hard.

Administrator Mills. Well I want to point out—[*inaudible*]—you can take credit for it.

The President. So there you go. Just wanted you to know. [*Laughter*] They were talking behind your back, and it was good.

At the same time, I think that there was a sense in the conversation I had at breakfast this morning that issues of credit are still a problem. In particular, smaller businesses and start-up businesses—$100,000, $200,000—that getting that initial startup capital oftentimes was a challenge.

And we also heard that getting help on things like marketing could make a big difference for businesses that want to break out beyond their immediate communities, and particularly if they're competing with larger businesses, even if they think they've got a better product.

So what I said to them is the same thing that I'd say to the entire group: We genuinely believe that small business is the backbone of America. It's going to be the key for us to be able to put a lot of folks back to work. What we're looking for is, how can we do our jobs better? How can the SBA or USDA or any of the other Federal agencies that touch on rural America on a regular basis help you create the jobs and businesses and ideas that I think are so evident in a lot of communities all across the country?

We also heard, by the way, that there are a lot of young people, I think, who want to be more entrepreneurial. And so are there ways that we can connect, for example, the community colleges—but even beneath that, high schools—to help young people think about how they go about organizing, getting a business started?

So that's my initial report from breakfast, and what I want to do is just hear from all of you. And Karen will be taking copious notes, and she is somebody who I know is going to execute on any ideas that make sense. So with that——

[At this point, the discussion continued, but no transcript was provided.]

NOTE: The President spoke at 12:44 p.m. at Northeast Iowa Community College.

Remarks During a Breakout Session at the White House Rural Economic Forum in Peosta
August 16, 2011

The President. John, sorry to interrupt.

Participant. No. No problem.

The President. You were making a good point. Good to see you. Everybody, please have a seat. I just wanted to jump in. I just came out of a small-business breakout session. So I don't want to interrupt. I just want to emphasize, first of all, I think Vilsack is doing a great job.

Second of all, this issue of energy innovation I think is absolutely vital for rural communities, but for the entire country. If we can harness homegrown fuels—whether it's biofuels, wind, solar, geothermal, you name it—then I think it can generate hundreds of thousands of jobs all across the country. It can help free ourselves from dependence on foreign oil. It diversifies sources of income for farmers. I'm not telling you guys anything that you don't already know.

All I want to emphasize is, is that when you look at farm economies, right now obviously prices are good, but given the volatility of the world market, for us to be able to figure out how we can also use energy and conservation as an enhancement to the core business of feeding people, then I think that we can make enormous progress. And Tom has a lot of creative ideas. Our Department of Energy, we've made this one of our highest priorities. And so I'm very interested in figuring out how the Federal Government can be even more helpful than it already is in moving this agenda forward.

So with that, let me just sit back and listen and—unless somebody has a question for me, then I'll try to answer it.

[At this point, the discussion continued, but no transcript was provided.]

NOTE: The President spoke at 1:09 p.m. at Northeast Iowa Community College.

Remarks at the Closing Session of the White House Rural Economic Forum in Peosta
August 16, 2011

Thank you so much. Please, please, everybody, have a seat.

I just want to again thank my extraordinary Secretary of Agriculture, Tom Vilsack, for leading this forum. You don't have a more passionate advocate for farming communities in rural America than Tom Vilsack. And I will tell you, if you are not fully persuaded that this administration has been all over the rural agenda, spend 5 minutes with Tom Vilsack— [*laughter*]—and his enthusiasm for the steps that we've been taking just bubbles over. And it's been under his leadership more than anybody's that we've been able to make such a difference.

I want to thank all the members of my Cabinet who are here today as well. They've done a terrific job participating in some of these breakout sessions.

As I said earlier, despite the hits that we've taken over the last 2½ years, Tom's right: I am absolutely confident about our future. And I'm confident because I know that while we face serious challenges—and there's no sugarcoating that—there's not a nation on Earth that would not want to trade places with us. There's nothing wrong with our country, although there is some problems with our politics. That's what we need to fix. That's how we're going to unlock the promise of America and the incredible dynamism and creativity of our people.

And having a chance to meet with some of the men and women in this room have only made me feel more confident. I'm excited about the future that you're working towards each and every day. And it ought to remind us of a simple lesson: It's always a mistake to bet against America. It's always a mistake to bet against the American worker. [*Applause*] It's always a mistake to bet against the American worker, the American farmer, the American small-business owner, the American people.

And I know there are naysayers out there. We know that there are some who see hard times and think that we've got to accept less, that our best days are past. We know that there are people who think that for America to get ahead, small towns and rural communities have to be left behind. You hear those sentiments. But we also know that, time and again, those kinds of skeptics and that kind of pessimism has been proven wrong.

You look at the people in this room. Look at what you're achieving. I met with a group of small-business owners, including a woman named Jan Heister, who started a small tooling and manufacturing company around 20 years ago. Started off with nine people in a very small plant, and with the help of a SBA loan, she's got a staff of more than 140 in a 160,000-square-foot factory. Jan's not messing around. [*Laughter*]

This morning I had breakfast with somebody who has not only been interested in wind power because their family got involved in it '77, back in 1977, but are now—have figured out a new technology to help locate where farm—wind farms would ideally be located. And have started a whole new business because they see the incredible potential of clean energy throughout this country.

I saw some of these Future Farmers of America, and their young president, right over there. And when you hear the enthusiasm and energy that these young people display, and the fact that if they can just get a little bit of a break when it comes to getting started on the front end, get a little bit of help with capital, that they are ready to take American agriculture to the next level, it gives you confidence. It gives you hope.

I joined a session with a group of entrepreneurs and ranchers and farmers and clean energy companies, and we were talking about all the ways in which folks right here in the heartland are pioneering new methods of raising crops and earning more off the land. And we talked about the ways in which farmlands are helping our Nation develop new forms of energy: ranches where cattle graze next to solar panels, farms supplying crops for biofuels. I've got a former State senator here who's helping farms manage manure in creative ways—[*laughter*]—in creative ways. [*Laughter*]

So our task as a nation has to be to get behind what you're doing. Our task has to be making sure that nothing stands in your way, that we remove any obstacles to your success. That's why we're doing more to connect rural America with broadband and expanding small-business loans and investing in homegrown American energy. That's why forums like this are important, so that we hear directly from you about what you need and what you're facing. And what's interesting is, in these conversations, one thing you notice: In Washington, you'd think that the only two ways of thinking about our problems is either Government is terrible and it has to be basically eliminated, or Government is the answer to every problem. But when you sit in some of these breakout sessions, I had no idea who was Democrat, who was Republican, who was Independent. What everybody understood was, there are times when Government can make a huge difference. There are times where that SBA office or that USDA office can make all the difference in the world. There are some boneheaded things the Government is doing that need to be fixed.

And so it's a very practical way of thinking about these problems. It's not either-or. It's a recognition that the prime driver of economic growth and jobs is going to be our people and the private sector and our businesses. But you know what, Government can help. Government can make a difference.

So I hope that I can count on you in the days ahead to lend your voice to this fight to strengthen our economy. I need you to keep your pressure on your elected representatives for things like the payroll tax cuts or road construction funds or the other steps that will help to put our country back to work.

That's our great challenge. It has been my central mission for the last 2½ years. It has to be all of our central missions going forward. That's what ought to unite us as a country, regardless of party or ideology, because if we can do that, if we can put country ahead of party, I know that our future is bright. I know that our best days are ahead of us.

And Tom is actually—absolutely right. Not only do I continue to have absolute confidence in you, but you're what gives me strength. As I was driving down those little towns in my big bus—[*laughter*]—I'm—we slowed down, and I'm standing in the front, and I'm waving. I'm seeing little kids with American flags and grandparents in their lawn chairs and folks outside a machine shop. And passing churches and cemeteries and corner stores and farms, I'm reminded about why I wanted to get into public service in the first place.

Sometimes there are days in Washington that will drive you crazy. But getting out of Washington and meeting all of you and seeing how hard you're working, how creative you are, how resourceful you are, and how determined you are, that just makes me that much more determined to serve you as best I can as President of the United States.

So thank you very much, everybody. God bless you.

NOTE: The President spoke at 2:46 p.m. at Northeast Iowa Community College. In his remarks, he referred to Janda K. Heister, president, Premier Tooling & Manufacturing, Inc.; and Riley Pagett, president, Future Farmers of America.

Memorandum on Deferred Enforced Departure for Liberians
August 16, 2011

Memorandum for the Secretary of Homeland Security

Subject: Deferred Enforced Departure for Liberians

Since 1991, the United States has provided safe haven for Liberians who were forced to flee their country as a result of armed conflict and widespread civil strife, in part through granting Temporary Protected Status (TPS). The armed conflict ended in 2003 and conditions improved such that TPS ended effective October 1, 2007. President Bush then deferred the enforced departure of the Liberians originally granted TPS. I extended that grant of Deferred Enforced Departure (DED) to September 30, 2011. I have determined that there are compelling foreign policy reasons to again extend DED to those Liberians presently residing in the United States under the existing grant of DED.

Pursuant to my constitutional authority to conduct the foreign relations of the United States, I have determined that it is in the foreign policy interest of the United States to defer for 18 months the removal of any Liberian national, or person without nationality who last habitually resided in Liberia, who is present in the United States and who is under a grant of DED as of September 30, 2011. The grant of DED only applies to an individual who has continuously resided in the United States since October 1, 2002, except for Liberian nationals, or persons without nationality who last habitually resided in Liberia:

(1) who are ineligible for TPS for the reasons provided in section 244(c)(2)(B) of

the Immigration and Nationality Act, 8 U.S.C. 1254a(c)(2)(B);

(2) whose removal you determine is in the interest of the United States;

(3) whose presence or activities in the United States the Secretary of State has reasonable grounds to believe would have potentially serious adverse foreign policy consequences for the United States;

(4) who have voluntarily returned to Liberia or his or her country of last habitual residence outside the United States;

(5) who were deported, excluded, or removed prior to the date of this memorandum; or

(6) who are subject to extradition.

Accordingly, I direct you to take the necessary steps to implement for eligible Liberians:

(1) a deferral of enforced departure from the United States for 18 months from September 30, 2011; and

(2) authorization for employment for 18 months from September 30, 2011.

BARACK OBAMA

Remarks at a Town Hall Meeting and a Question-and-Answer Session in Atkinson, Illinois
August 17, 2011

The President. Hello, Atkinson! Thank you. Thank you, everybody. Thank you so much. Thank you. Everybody have a seat.

It is good to be back, back home. It is good to be back in Atkinson, good to be back in Henry County. I just came from the Whiteside County Fair. Got some Whiteside folks here. Spent some time with some cows. [*Laughter*]

I want to acknowledge a few people who are with us today, wonderful, wonderful folks. First of all, our Secretary of Transportation, Peoria's own Ray LaHood is in the house. Our outstanding Secretary of Agriculture Tom Vilsack is here. Mayor Gus Junior is in the house. I told Gus that I didn't have any gray hair either when I took office. [*Laughter*] So I just

want you to know what you have ahead in store for you right here. [*Laughter*] But everybody tells me he's doing a great job.

I want to thank the Waffles family for—[*laughter*]—Wyffels, rather, excuse me. I haven't had lunch. [*Laughter*] I want to thank the Wyffels family for hosting us here today. Please give them a big round of applause.

I want to thank Lisa of Lisa's Place. Where's Lisa? Is that Lisa? Because Secret Service had to shut down the road and do all this stuff, I know some of you guys have not been able to enjoy her outstanding food. So as a consequence, my staff has been, I think, trying to eat up as much as possible. [*Laughter*] My understanding is I've got a pie coming. Is that correct? What kind of pie?

Audience member. [*Inaudible*]

The President. Coconut cream and a cinnamon roll. I'm very excited about that. [*Laughter*] Coconut cream is one of my favorite pies. So thank you.

And we also have here—Congressman Bobby Schilling is here.

Now, it is absolutely terrific to be back home. And I just want to first of all say to so many of you, I had a chance when I was still running for the United States Senate, and a lot of people did not know my name—this young lady, she's still got—she's got, like, a picture from the——

Audience member. [*Inaudible*]—autograph.

The President. I will sign it, of course I will.

And so as we've been traveling through the back roads of Iowa and now Illinois, it is such a reminder of why I decided to get involved in public service in the first place.

We've obviously been going through a tough time over these last 2½ years. Right? And we went through the worst recession since the Great Depression. We saw 8 million jobs lost, 4 million before I took office, and then another 4 million the first few months of 2009. A lot of small businesses got hit.

And so I think a lot of times there have been folks who said—who wonder whether our best days are still ahead of us or are they behind us. But I will tell you, when I travel through downstate Illinois, when I travel through Iowa, when I travel through the Midwest, I am absolutely confident about this country. And the reason is because of you. The reason is because of the American people, because, as tough of a time as we've had, there is not a country on Earth that would not readily change places with us right now.

We've still got the best workers in the world. We've got the best entrepreneurs in the world. We've got the best scientists, the best universities. We have so much going for us, and you see it at a company like this one. I was talking to the Wyffel brothers, and they were telling me that they're now expanding, they've hired

some new folks, they're starting to go into new markets around this region.

So we've got so much going for us. There's nothing wrong with our country right now. There is something wrong with our politics. There is something wrong with our politics.

When you look at this debacle we had with the debt ceiling and raising it, what you realize is, is that our politics—engaging in partisan brinksmanship and potentially seeing the first default of the United States of America—that that has no place in how we move forward together. When this country is operating off a common ground, nobody can stop us. But when we're divided, then we end up having a whole lot of self-inflicted problems.

Now, the fact of the matter is, is the economy has gotten better than it was when I first took office. I mean, we've seen over the last 17 months, 2 million—over 2 million private sector jobs created. But everybody here knows we've still got a long way to go, and it is urgent for us to make sure that we are joining together and not thinking about party first, not thinking about elections first, but thinking about country first. That's the message that we need to send to Washington.

There are some things that we could be doing right now to put our neighbors and our friends, some family members back to work. And over the last not just 2 days, but over the last several weeks, I've been talking about some additional things we need to do. There is no reason why we should not extend a payroll tax cut that put $1,000 into the pockets of every single family out there. That means they've got more money to spend, that means businesses have more customers, that means the economy grows, and more people get hired. And we could renew it right now to give businesses certainty that they're going to have customers, not just this year, but next year as well.

The only thing holding us back is our politics. It's traditionally a bipartisan idea; there's no reason why we shouldn't pass it. There's no reason why we shouldn't put Americans back to work all across the country rebuilding America. As I was driving in here, I saw that a new fire station is being built, right? Thanks to the

Recovery Act. Well, we need roads and bridges and schools all across the country that could be rebuilt. And all those folks who got laid off from construction because the economy went south or the housing bubble burst, they're dying for work. Contractors are willing to come in under budget and on time.

And interest rates are low, so we could finance right now the rebuilding of infrastructure all across America that drove not only unemployment in the construction industry down, but drove unemployment down across the board. And traditionally, that hasn't been a Democratic or a Republican issue, that's been an American issue. We've taken pride in rebuilding America.

The only thing that's holding us back right now is our politics. We should be passing trade deals right now because, look, the Koreans, they can sell Kias and Hyundais here in the United States; I think that's great. I want to be selling Fords and Chryslers and Chevys in Korea. And I want products all across the world stamped with three words: Made in America. That's something that we could be doing right now.

There's a bill pending in Congress right now that's called the "America Invents" bill. It basically says entrepreneurs who are coming up with good ideas—let's say if the Wyffel brothers came up with a new strain, and they wanted to patent it in some way—make it easier for them so that they can market it and make money off it and hire people for it.

We could do that right now. The only thing that's holding us back is our politics. Look, over the last 6 months, even though the economy has been growing, even though the economy has been recovering, it has not recovered as fast as it could.

And some of those things are not in our control. We couldn't control the tsunami in Japan that disrupted supply chains. We could not control what happened in the Middle East that drove up gas prices. We don't have complete control over what happens in Europe with their problems. And all those things have affected our economy, but there are so many things that we've got control over right now

that we could be doing to put people back to work.

And by the way, there's no reason to think that putting people back to work is somehow in conflict with us getting our fiscal house in order. You know, this downgrade that happened, they didn't downgrade us because America couldn't pay its bills. They downgraded it because they felt that our political system couldn't seem to make good decisions in order to deal with our budget the same way families deal with their budgets.

And so the fact of the matter is, is that we came close to a grand bargain, which would have said, we're going to cut spending we don't need in order to pay for the things we do. We're going to eliminate unnecessary programs so we can pay for student loans, so they can go to the University of Illinois or University of Iowa. We know that we've got to invest in basic research; that's part of what made us the most productive agricultural powerhouse in the world. So we don't want to cut back agricultural research in order to pay for it; we got to get rid of some things.

But what we've also said is we've got to do it in a balanced way. We've got to do it in a balanced way. A couple days ago, Warren Buffett wrote a op-ed piece in which he said, "It's time to stop coddling billionaires." And he pointed out that he pays a lower tax rate than anybody in his office, including his secretary. That doesn't make any sense.

If everybody took an attitude of shared sacrifice, that we're not going to put the burden on any single person, we can solve our deficit and debt problem next week. And it wouldn't require radical changes, but it does have to be balanced. I don't want a tax break, as lucky as I've been, if that tax break means that a senior citizen is going to have to pay an extra $6,000 for their Medicare. That's not fair.

I think it makes sense before we ask that student to pay a little more for their student loan, we should ask those oil and gas companies to get rid of some corporate tax loophole that they don't need because they've been making record profits.

A lot of this is common sense. I was saying—I was at a town hall in a Minnesota—I pointed out, you know, when there have been times in my life, Michelle and I, things were a little tight, when we were just starting a family and had all these new expenses, and we had to make some choices. We didn't say to ourselves, well, we're not going to put any money into the college fund so we can keep on eating fancy dinners anytime we want. We didn't say to ourselves—I didn't say to Michelle, honey, you got to stop buying clothes, but I'm going to keep my golf clubs. [*Laughter*] What we said was, well, let's figure out what are the things that are going to be important to our family to make sure it succeeds not just now, but in the long term; let's invest in those things and let's stop investing in the things that don't work. And the same approach has to be taken for the American family.

Now, what's been striking as I've been traveling through over the last few days—you guys, you're all fulfilling your responsibilities. You're working hard, you're looking after your families, you're volunteering at church, you're coaching Little League—you're doing everything right. And all you're asking for, if I'm not mistaken, is that your political representatives take their responsibilities just as seriously.

And part of that means that you have to put politics aside sometimes to do what's right for the country. People have been asking me, "Well, why didn't you call Congress back after this whole debt ceiling thing? Why'd you let them leave town?" I say, well, I don't think it would be good for business confidence and certainty just to see Members of Congress arguing all over again. I figured it was time for them to spend a little time back in their districts, hear your frustrations, hear your expectations.

As I've been driving on this bus, just seeing all those flags on the way in, seeing folks waving, little kids ready to go back to school, and grandparents in their lawn chairs, and folks out in front of the machine shop and out in front of the fire stations, you go through small towns all throughout America, and it reminds you how strong we are and how resilient we are and how decent we are. And that should be reflected in our politics; that should be reflected in our Government.

And that's why I'm enlisting you—that's why I've got to enlist you in this fight we have for our future. I need you to send a message. I need you to send a message to folks in Washington: Stop drawing lines in the sand; stop engaging in rhetoric instead of actually getting things done. It's time to put country ahead of party; it's time to worry more about the next generation than the next election. If we do that, I guarantee you, nobody can stop us, Atkinson. Nobody can stop the United States of America.

God bless you. Thank you.

So what I want to do is—now, I just want to take some questions. And it's not very formal, you just raise your hand. We got folks with microphones. I'm going to go boy, girl, boy, girl, so it's fair. [*Laughter*] And I'm going to try to get in as many questions as I can. So do stand up and introduce yourself, though. I want to know who I'm talking to.

All right? I'll start with this gentleman right here since he's right next to the mike.

Agriculture

Q. Is it on?

The President. Yes, there you go.

Q. Rod Catchdig. Welcome to Atkinson, Mr. President.

The President. Thank you, sir.

Q. I farm north of here. We enjoy growing corn and soybeans, and we feel we do it as safely and efficiently as we possibly can. And Mother Nature has really challenged us this growing season—moisture, drought, whatever. Please don't challenge us with more rules and regulations from Washington, DC, that hinder us from doing that. We would prefer to start our day in a tractor cab or combine cab rather than filling out forms and permits to do what we'd like to do.

The President. Well, we've got the Secretary of Agriculture right now, so is there a particular rule that you're worried about?

Q. We hear what's coming down about noise pollution, dust pollution, water runoff. Sometimes the best approach is just common sense, and we are already using that.

The President. Yes. Here's what I'd suggest is, the—if you hear something is happening, but it hasn't happened, don't always believe what you hear. [*Laughter*] No, and I'm serious about that. Because a lot of times, what will happen is the folks in Washington, there may be some staff person somewhere that wrote some article or said maybe we should look into something. And I'm being perfectly honest, the lobbyists and the associations in Washington, they'll get all ginned up and they'll start sending out notices to everybody saying, look what's coming down the pike. And a lot of times, we are going to be applying common sense. And if somebody has an idea, if we don't think it's a good idea, if we don't think that there's more benefit than cost to it, we're not going to do it.

And so I want to make sure that everybody gets accurate information. If you ever have a question as to whether we're putting something in place that's going to make it harder for you to farm, contact USDA. Talk to them directly. Find out what it is that you're concerned about. My suspicion is a lot of times they're going to be able to answer your questions, and it will turn out that some of your fears are unfounded.

But nobody is more interested in seeing our agricultural sector successful than I am, partly because I come from a farm State. And I spent a lot of time thinking about downstate issues as a United States Senator. And I'm very proud of the track record that we've developed. If you look at what's been happening in terms of agricultural exports, what's been happening in terms of agricultural income during the time that I've been President of the United States, I think we've got a great story to tell. And I want to continue to work with you and other farmers to make sure that we're doing it in the right way that's not inhibiting you from being successful.

Q. Thank you. We appreciate that.

The President. Appreciate you, sir. Young lady right back there with the glasses on. There she is.

Housing Market/Lines of Credit

Q. Welcome, Mr. President, to Henry County. My name is LuAnn Levine, and I own a local real estate company here in Henry County, over in Geneseo. So you know we're I'm headed: housing. Every week, I sit around the kitchen table of families that are here today and I listen to the stories of a lost job, upside down in their house. And they ask, "LuAnn, how can you help? What programs are out there?"

I have to say, I saw a turnaround come May and June. My phone was ringing. I was busier than all get-out. I could see that the country—yes, we are in rehab. People have made adjustments, and I saw progress.

Since the debt ceiling fiasco in Washington, the phones have stopped. We have no consumer confidence after what has just happened. Interest rates are a record low. I should be out working 14 hours a day, and I am not. What are your future plans in helping middle class America? Generation X and Y and middle class America will get the country out of where we are. And I want to know what are your continued plans.

The President. Well, first of all, you're absolutely right that housing has been at the key—at the core of a lot of the hardships we've been going through over the last 2½ years. And that's why we've made it such a priority to try to help families stay in their homes the last 2½ years. And that's why we've made it such a priority to try to help families stay in their homes if they can still afford the home. There were some folks who couldn't—who bought homes they couldn't afford, but there were a lot of folks who just had a run of bad luck because somebody lost a job or lost a shift. And so what we've been trying to do is push the banks, push the servicers to do loan modifications that will allow people to stay in their homes and will try to buck up housing prices generally.

Q. Can I please say——

The President. Sure, go ahead.

Q. ——the loan modification system has been a nightmare. Short sales are a nightmare. And the lenders are so tight, and you have to be so perfect, and it's not a perfect world.

The President. Well, what we've been trying to do is make sure that—we've probably had a couple of million loan modifications that have been taking place. The problem is, is that the housing market is so big. And so a lot of families have just had to work down their debts, and they've been successful. And as you said, we were starting to see things bottom out and confidence start picking up.

Now, I can't excuse the self-inflicted wound that was that whole debt debate. It shouldn't have happened the way it did. We shouldn't have gotten that close to the brink. It was inexcusable. But moving forward, I think a lot of this has to do with confidence, as you said.

Q. A hundred percent.

The President. Companies have never been more profitable. They're seeing record profits; it's just they're hoarding their cash, they're not investing it. A lot of banks have now recovered, but they're not lending the way they used to. Now, they need to have slightly tighter lending criteria than they used to have, obviously, because that was part of the reason that we had that housing bubble. But one of the things we've talked about is, can we encourage banks now to take a look at customers who are good credit risks, but are being unfairly punished as a consequence of what happened overall?

There are some other ideas that we're looking at on the housing front. But I'll be honest with you, when you've got many trillions of dollars' worth of housing stock out there, the Federal Government is not going to be able to do this all by itself. It's going to require consumers and banks and the private sector working alongside Government to make sure that we can actually get the housing moving back again. And it will probably take this year and next year for us to see a slow appreciation again in the housing market.

What we can do is make sure we don't do any damage. And that's what happened in this last month. That's why I was so frustrated by it, and I suspect that's why you were so frustrated by it as well.

Q. Very much.

The President. The last thing I'll say, though, is if we get the overall economy moving, if we pass this payroll tax cut, if we get some of these tax credits for businesses that we passed back in December extended into next year so that we're giving incentives for folks to invest in plants and equipment now, if the overall economy is doing well, that means consumers are doing better. It also means that housing will start doing better as well.

All right? Thank you so much for your great question.

Q. Thank you.

The President. Gentleman in the glasses, right there. Yes, sir.

Deficit and National Debt/Budget Debate

Q. Hi, Mr. President. My name is Larry Floriani and I work at the Rock Island Arsenal. And thanks a lot for coming to our town. We're really happy to have you here so we can talk to you.

The President. You bet.

Q. Okay, my question is, what do you think the Simpson-Bowles commission contributed to the deficit and debt discussion, and what do you expect will be accomplished by the new super congressional committee?

The President. Well, first of all, let me thank everybody who does work at the arsenal, because you guys are out there and you've been saving lives and making sure our troops are well equipped for generations now. So thank you.

The Bowles-Simpson committee, this is a committee that I set up to look at our current fiscal situation to see what could be done. And it was a bipartisan committee; it was chaired by a well-known Republican, Alan Simpson, former Senator, and Erskine Bowles, who used to be the Chief of Staff for Bill Clinton. And it had equal numbers of Democrats and Republicans, as well as business sector and private sector leaders.

And basically what they recommended was what I've been talking about, which is a balanced approach in which we're making some modifications to what's called discretionary spending—that's the spending we do every year on everything from farm programs to student loan programs to food stamps to you name it—that we cut defense spending in a sensible way, that we look at how we can make modifications that strengthen Social Security and Medicare for the next generation and how we raise additional revenue so that we bring the overall budget into a sustainable place.

And the truth of the matter is, is that the commission recommendations are ones that not only I, but the so-called Gang of Six, these Senators in the United States Senate, agreed to as well. And that was bipartisan; you had Democrats and Republicans.

It was that kind of balanced package that I proposed to Speaker John Boehner that we move forward on. And frankly, we came pretty close. And I'll tell you, I think Speaker Boehner was prepared to do it. But he got some resistance in his caucus, because they said, we're not going to vote for anything that has revenue in it.

And so instead of doing this big package that got our debt and our deficit sustainable, what we got was this $1 trillion worth of cuts where we needed $4 trillion to close the deficit and the debt, and we got this commission to come up with another 1.5.

Now, I continue to believe that we need a balanced approach. So when this committee comes forward, I'm going to be making a presentation that has more deficit reduction than the 1.5 trillion that they have been assigned to obtain. Because I don't think it's good enough for us to just do it partway. If we're going to do it, let's go ahead and fix it. And if we're going to fix it, the only way, I believe, to do it in a sensible way is you've got to have everything on the table. You can't take things off the table.

And I've been concerned that Speaker Boehner has already said that the folks he assigned, none of them can vote to increase revenues. That's a concern of mine. I was concerned when I saw the Republican Presidential candidates, somebody asked them, "Well, if you got $10 of spending cuts for every $1 in additional revenue, would you be willing to accept it?" And all of them said no.

Now, that's just not common sense. That's—I can't imagine that's how Atkinson runs its operations, right? I mean, if the mayor had to

deal with a situation in which we're not going to pay for anything—we're not going to pay for roads, we're not going to pay for schools, we're not going to pay for garbage pickup, you name it, we're not going to pay for it—but we still expect you to provide those services, the mayor would be in a pretty tough spot. There's no reason why we would expect the Federal Government to do the same—to operate in the same way.

So the bottom line is this: I will be presenting, as I've already presented—I did back earlier this year—a plan that says we're going to have spending cuts and we're going to have revenue. We'll have more spending cuts than we have revenue, but we're going to have to take a balanced approach and everything is going to be on the table, including our long-term obligations, because the thing that is driving the deficit, if you look at—we had a balanced budget back in 2000. Here's what happened. Number one is we decided that we would cut taxes without paying for it. So we had huge tax cuts in 2001, 2003. Then we had two wars. And for the first time in our history, we didn't pay for our wars. When our grandparents fought in World War II, the entire country paid for the wars that it fought. They didn't pass it onto the next generation, didn't put it on a credit card. We were the first generation not to pay for the wars that we fought.

And then we had a big prescription drug plan that was added to Medicare, and that wasn't paid for. Then the recession hits, which means less money is coming in, but more money is going out in terms of helping the unemployed or helping States and local governments not lay off teachers and firefighters and so on.

And you combine all those things, we've got a big debt and a big deficit. The good news is this is not—it doesn't require radical surgery for us to fix it. It just requires us all taking an approach that says we're a family and all of us are going to share a little bit in the burden. And those of us who are most fortunate, that we can do a little bit more.

And corporations, they can afford to close some loopholes and simplify the Tax Code to get it done. All right? Thank you.

All right, it's a—this young lady in the pink right here. Yes.

Employment Opportunities for Veterans/Job Creation

Q. Hello. I'm Jan Lowhouse. I'm from Tiskilwa, Illinois.

The President. Good to see you, Jan.

Q. Thanks. It's about 30 miles east of here. It's a rural community based on farming. My question is about jobs. I think you have done some improvement in jobs, but what can you do without Congress today to make a change in jobs and so we can see a growth in job opportunities?

The President. Well, there are some things that we can do without Congress, and we're trying to do them. So, for example, I set up a jobs council made up of a lot of employers, both small businesses, but also some of the biggest companies in the world, and asked them what can we be doing to encourage job growth. And they've come up with a series of recommendations, some of which don't involve Congress at all, and we're trying to implement them.

So a while back, I announced we've got a lot of vets coming back from Afghanistan and Iraq who have incredible experience: 25-year-olds who were leading platoons into battle; 26-year-olds who were handling $100 million pieces of equipment. But the problem is, is that we're not doing as good of a job helping them market the skills and experience and leadership that they have to employers, and we're not linking them to employers who may be able to use their talents.

And so we just announced a couple weeks ago a whole new initiative where the Department of Defense is going to have a reverse boot camp. Just like you train folks to come into the military, you train them going out to figure out how they're going to get jobs. And we got commitments from local employers—from employers all across the country to say, we are going to hire veterans.

And in some cases, what we want to do is to change certifications, for example. I'll give you a good example. I had lunch with a group of veterans in Minnesota a couple days ago. One was an emergency medic who had been in theater. And you can imagine what that must be like.

And he had come back; he wanted to be a nurse. He was having to take the whole nursing program from scratch. And here he had been dealing with young men and young women in uniform who had had the worst kinds of medical emergency. He's patching them up under the most extraordinary strain. He's having to go back as if he'd never been in the medical field at all. Well, that's a waste of money. That doesn't make sense.

So those are examples of things that we can do administratively. The other thing, this gentleman here asked me about regulations. Well, one of the things we're doing is we're saying, show us particular regulations that may be getting in the way of you hiring. And there are going to be some that are important. We want clean air; we want clean water. But if there's a bunch of bureaucratic redtape and it's not actually improving the situation, let's figure out how to get rid of some existing rules, and let's review every rule that comes in for its costs and its benefits. Again, that's something that we can do administratively.

So there are some things that we can help on. But frankly, we could do a lot more if we got Congress's cooperation. And every proposal that I talked about previously, those are proposals that historically have had support from Republicans and Democrats. These aren't radical ideas. I mean, building roads, when did that become a partisan issue, putting folks back to work? Eisenhower built the Interstate Highway System—[*applause*]. Dwight Eisenhower built the Interstate Highway System; last time I checked, he was a very popular Republican.

But this is what I mean about politics getting in the way sometimes. You can't bring an attitude that says, I'd rather see my opponent lose than America win. You can't have that attitude.

This gentleman right here with the goatee there. There you go, mike is right there.

Taxes

Q. Thank you Mr. President. My name is Justin Hubbs. My question was just about revenue. I see a lot of the Republican Presidential nominees signing pledges not to raise taxes. I was wondering if you could make a pledge that any deal will have a revenue increase.

The President. Well, here's—it's just math. If you have a deal that does not have revenue in it and you still want to close the deficit by, say, $4 trillion, which is what the experts say is required in order to stabilize our debt and our deficit—and this is over a 10-year period—if you have no revenue, then the only way to do that is you've got to drastically cut things like Medicare. You have to—there's no two ways about it. You've got to drastically cut Medicare; you've got to drastically cut Medicaid; you've got to cut back on education support in significant ways that affect school kids right here in Atkinson and all across the country.

So since I'm in Wyffels Hybrids, it's like eating your seed corn. You are cutting back on the things that are going to help you grow and help this country succeed over the long term. It's just not a smart thing to do. It's not how you would run your own family business. And so I think it's also important to understand that we can raise the kind of revenues we're talking about without having an impact on middle class families who already struggling and haven't seen their wages and their incomes go up in over a decade now. That—it can be done. The Tax Code is full of loopholes. Close those loopholes.

When it comes to the corporate tax rate, we could actually lower the overall corporate tax rate, which would make us more competitive, if we closed up a whole bunch of these loopholes that special interests and lobbyists have been able to get into the Tax Code. It might put some lawyers out of business, but it would be the right thing to do.

And when it comes to upper-income folks— I talked about Warren Buffett—but the truth is—I'll just give you one example. The reason Warren Buffett's taxes are so low is because he typically gets his income from capital gains. Capital gains are taxed at 15 percent. Now,

your income taxes, you're not being taxed at 15 percent, most of you. And as a consequence, these days the richer you are, the lower your tax rate. Now, that can't be something that is defensible, regardless of party. I don't care whether you're a Democrat or Republican, an Independent. That can't be the way it is.

One last point I want to make, though, about these pledges: I take an oath. My pledge is to make sure that every day I'm waking up looking out for you, for the American people. And so I don't go around signing pledges because I want to make sure that every single day, whatever it is that's going to be best for the American people, that's what I'm focused on, that's what I'm committed to. And that's how I think every representative in Congress should be thinking, not about some pledge that they signed for some special interest group or some lobbyist or some association somewhere. They should be waking up thinking what's best for the country.

All right. This young lady has been very patient right here. Yes, you.

Education

Q. Hi, I'm Kelly Wyffels—relation to Bob and Bill—and I'm a student at Western Illinois University.

The President. What are you studying?

Q. I'm a supply chain management major and a French major. And I'm wondering what you think is one of the best majors to major in in order to get a job. Our professor seems to think that supply chain you get—there's a lot of job opportunities out there, but I wonder what other majors you think that are good for students to study.

The President. Well, first of all, I can tell you're going to be good, whatever you do. [*Laughter*] So when you finish, you let me know. We'll talk to LaHood or Vilsack, and we may hire you, because you seem very impressive.

Look, the—you're already ahead of the curve because what you understand is that the economy is changing, and the days when just because you're willing to work hard, you could automatically find a job, those days are over.

The truth of the matter is, is that everything requires an education. I don't have to tell the farmers here. You guys are looking at GPS and have all kinds of equipment; you're studying markets around the world. And it is a complicated piece of business that you're engaged in. It's not just a matter of going out with a plow in a field.

And that's happened to every industry. When I go into factories these days, what's amazing is how clean and how quiet they are, because what used to take 1,000 folks to do now only takes 100 folks to do. And one of the challenges in terms of rebuilding our economy is businesses have gotten so efficient that—when was the last time somebody went to a bank teller instead of using the ATM or used a travel agent instead of just going online? A lot of jobs that used to be out there requiring people now have become automated. And that means us investing in our kids' education—nothing's more important. Nothing is more important.

Now, but you're also asking a good question, which is, don't just go to college without having some idea about what interests you. Now, this supply chain management I think is a great field, because the world is shrinking and products from Atkinson end up on a dinner table in China somewhere, and that means that people who understand how to move products and services and people in efficient ways, there's going to be high demand for them. So I don't think your professor is just trying to keep you in class; I think he actually is onto something here.

One of the things I'm worried about and we're trying to put a lot of emphasis on in the Department of Education is, can we do more to encourage math, science, engineering, technology learning. Because I can guarantee you, if you are a skilled engineer, if you are a skilled computer scientist, if you've got strong math skills and technical skills, you are going to be very employable in today's economy. And that has to start even before young people get to college. So we're trying to institute a whole—what's called a STEM program—science, technology, engineering, and math—in the lower schools so that kids start getting oriented towards those fields. That's where we traditionally have had a comparative advantage, but we're losing ground to China and India and places like that where those kids are just focused on those subjects. And we need more of those, so you keep on studying the supply chain management.

I will tell you, though, just in case there are any French teachers here or foreign language teachers, having a foreign language, that's important too. That makes you so much more employable, because if you go to a company and they're doing business in France or Belgium or Switzerland or Europe somewhere, and they find out you've got that language skill, that's going to be important as well. And we don't do that as much as we should; we don't emphasize that as much as we should here in the United States. So congratulations; proud of you.

Q. Thanks.

The President. All right. A couple more? It's a guy's turn, isn't it? Well, I'm going to—I've got to call on this guy right here. What's your name, young man?

Alternative Fuel Sources

Q. My name is Alex McAvoy.

The President. Alex, how old are you?

Q. I'm 10—I'm 11, sorry. [*Laughter*]

The President. Eleven—you just—did you just have a birthday?

Q. Yes, yesterday.

The President. Yesterday was your birthday?

Q. Yes.

The President. Happy birthday.

Q. Thank you, Mr. President.

The President. Give Alex a big round of applause. He made 11.

Q. My grandpa is a farmer, and he owns part—well, yes, he owns part of the local ethanol plant. I was wondering, what are you going to do to keep the ethanol plant running?

The President. Well, that is a great question. Where is your grandpa? Is he close by?

Q. He lives in Geneseo.

The President. Oh, okay. He lives up there. Well, you're an excellent representative for your grandfather, I must say. [*Laughter*] We might have to hire you too. [*Laughter*] I think those of you know that when I was a State senator, when I was a United States Senator, I was a strong supporter of biofuels. I continue to be a strong supporter of biofuels. Tom Vilsack, as our Agricultural Secretary, continues to be a strong supporter of ethanol and biofuels.

I will say that the more we see the science, the more we want to find ways to diversify our biofuels so that we're not just reliant on corn-based ethanol. Now, we can do more to make corn-based ethanol more efficient than it is, and that's where the research comes in. And there are some wonderful research facilities in our own University of Illinois system that have done a lot to advance the science on this.

But the key going forward is going to be, can we create biofuels out of switchgrass and wood chips and other materials that right now are considered waste materials? And part of the reason that's important is because, as I think most farmers here know, particularly if you're in livestock farming, right now the costs of feed keep on going up, and the costs of food as a consequence are also going up. Only about 4 percent of that is accounted for by corn being diverted into ethanol, but as you see more and more demand placed on our food supplies around the world, as folks in China and folks in India start wanting to eat more meat and commodity prices start going up, it's going to be important for us to figure out how can we make biofuels out of things that don't involve our food chain.

And so, hopefully, your grandfather, with his ethanol plant, is starting to work with our Department of Agriculture to find new approaches to the biofuel industry. But this is a huge area of support. This is another example of where we've got to make sure that our budget continues to invest in basic research, and that costs money. And if all we're doing is cutting and we're not thinking about investments, then over time, we're going to fall behind to countries like Brazil, where they've already got a third, I think, of their auto fleet operates on biofuels. Well, that's—there's no reason why we should fall behind a country like Brazil

when it comes to developing alternative energy. I want to be number one in alternative energy, and that's good for the farm economy.

Yes, sir. Hold on right here.

Social Security/Medicare and Medicaid

Q. Thank you, Mr. President, for being the President, and I also——

The President. Thanks.

Q. And I want to go home and maybe ask my mother to cook me a good meal so I could tell her that I lobbied you. She's a senior citizen. What's the likelihood of her Social Security getting the cost of living next year?

The President. Well, let me talk to you about Social Security. It is very likely that she will see a COLA, a cost-of-living increase, next year, because inflation actually rose this year. The reason that there were a couple of years where she did not get a cost-of-living increase was because even though she probably felt like the cost of food and gas and groceries were going up, the overall inflation index actually did not go up. There was a period there where we actually had what's called deflation, where the costs were a little bit lower than they had been comparable the previous year.

So all that is done automatically; it's not something that I make a decision about each year. And I promise you when folks don't get their COLA, they all write to me and say, why—"Mr. President, you didn't give us a cost of living, and don't you care about senior citizens?" And I have to write back and explain to them, no, that's not something I did. These things just happen automatically based on estimates of what inflation is going to be.

While we're on the topic of Social Security, though, I want to make sure everybody understands, Social Security is not in crisis. We have a problem with Medicare and Medicaid because health care costs are going up so fast. Part of the reason we passed health care reform was to make sure that we could start changing how the health care system operates and try to reduce health care inflation.

But we have a genuine problem on Medicare and Medicaid: Health care costs are going up, but at the same time, there's a lot more folks who are entering into the system. And if we don't do anything about Medicare or Medicaid, it will gobble up our entire budget.

Social Security is in a better position. And so when I hear folks say, "Is Social Security going to be there for me 20 years from now?" Yes, it will be there for you 20 years from now. It should be there for you 30 or 40 years from now. And the adjustments that we have to make on Social Security are relatively modest. They're the kind of changes that Ronald Reagan and Tip O'Neill agreed to back in 1983 that created long-term solvency of the system. We can have Social Security solvent for another 75 years with just a few modest changes.

So when your grandmother—tell her it wasn't me who didn't give her her COLA the last couple years. In fact, we tried to pass through Congress a $250 supplement because we knew seniors were having a tough time. We couldn't get it passed through Congress. But they should get some modest increase next year. Okay?

All right. I think I've got time for a couple more questions. One more? Oh, this is always a tough one, this last one. I'm going to call on— I'll just call on you. You're right there in front of me, and the mikes are already there. What's your name?

Government Assistance Programs/Budget Debate

Q. Hi, my name is Pam Dennis. I actually work for the Community Action Agency that serves Henry County. I also serve on the Henry County FEMA board. And I understand that drastic cuts need to be made in order to balance our budget. But with the last couple years being so difficult for jobs, why are budget cuts to programs that are helping these people keep their heads above water? I'm referring to the LIHEAP program, Community Services, and Experience Works, those type of programs that are helping people keep their heads above water. Why couldn't we cut somewhere else and leave those alone for now or at least fewer—a lessened cut?

The President. Yes, well, first of all, I think it's important to understand if we take a bal-

anced approach we don't need drastic cuts. The Low Income Housing Assistance Program, just to take one example, what we've done is we've said—we have modestly reduced it, but partly because we had increased it significantly right when the recession hit, and it turned out that we didn't need as much budgeted as was actually used. And obviously, it varies depending on the weather any given winter. But what we've tried to do is actually keep the bulk of that program in place, and folks will get help in the winter if they can't afford to buy home heating oil. That's not going away.

The general principle you're talking about is right though. We should not cut those things that help the folks who are most vulnerable if we can find other places to cut for folks that would be nice to have, but we don't need. I agree with that general principle.

When Congress gets back in September, my basic argument to them is this: We should not have to choose between getting our fiscal house in order and jobs and growth. We can't afford to do just one or the other. We got to do both. And by the way, the best thing we can do for our deficit and debt is grow the economy, because when the economy is growing, more money in people's pockets, they pay more in taxes, and there's more revenue, and fewer people are on unemployment. And that helps to reduce the strains on our budget.

So we've got to do both. And essentially, the best way for us to do this is to look at some of our long-term obligations and costs, figure out long-term savings that are gradually phased in so they don't hit too hard right now. In the short term, there should be some things that we do that are paid for by some of these long-term savings in order to get the economy rolling and to get the economy moving.

And some of the programs you mentioned, I think, are ones that in a wealthy and decent society like ours we should be able to help people make sure that they're not freezing during the winter. I mean, that's just, I think, a basic obligation we have to our fellow Americans.

Unemployment Insurance Benefits

Q. Some of those programs are dependent upon the unemployment rate. My question is, with the unemployment rate, you're only counting the people who are actually on unemployment. It's not counting the people who worked a temporary job that was not eligible for unemployment or the people who were on unemployment and now that unemployment has ran out. So those people are not being counted.

So that affects specifically the FEMA funding that our Henry County gets. Henry County is not eligible for the FEMA money. They get the set-aside. And this year, because of the unemployment rate, we were not even able to get those set-aside funds. So I think that's kind of a skewed number by using the unemployment rate.

The President. Well, here's a basic principle: With the economy not growing as fast as we want it to, the need is going to outstrip our resources. I mean, we're—there's always going to be more need out there relative to the amount of money that the Federal Government can spend.

But I guess the main argument I'm making to you is that don't think that our choice is we've either got to stop our obligations to the most vulnerable or to our seniors or to our kids, or otherwise, the budget is just going to go sky high—or the deficit and debt are going to go sky high. We can do both in a sensible way.

And I will be presenting before this joint committee a very detailed, specific approach to this problem that allows us to grow jobs right now, provide folks who need help the help they need, and still gets our deficit and debt under control.

We do also have to look at some programs, because they may not be well designed, as well designed as they could be. I'll give you an example. Unemployment insurance, the way it's designed—it was designed back at a time when you'd have layoffs and then people would hire you back when the business cycle went back.

The economy is changing so fast right now, people are having to retrain; companies move to an entirely different State. We've got to rethink how we do unemployment insurance. There is a smart program in Georgia. What they do is they say, all right, instead of you just getting unemployment insurance, just a check, what we're going to do is we will give a subsidy to any company that hires you with your unemployment insurance so that you're essentially earning a salary and getting your foot in the door into that company. And if they hire you full time, then the unemployment insurance is used to subsidize you getting trained and getting a job. And so those kinds of adjustments to programs. We've got to be more creative in terms of not doing things the way we've always done them.

But let me just close by saying this, Atkinson. First of all, it is good to be back. I'm grateful to all of you for your extraordinary welcome and hospitality. Don't bet against America. Don't bet against our workers. Don't bet against our businesses.

We have gone through tougher times than this before, and we've always come out on top. As long as we pull together and as long as American know-how and ingenuity is promoted, there's no reason why we're not going to get this tough time just like we have before. And America is going to emerge stronger, more unified, more successful than it was in the past.

In order for that to happen, though, I'm going to need your help. I need your voices out there, talking to folks from both parties and telling them we expect you to show some cooperation, stop thinking about politics for a little bit, try to make sure that we're moving our country forward.

And if you're delivering that message, it's a lot stronger than me delivering that message, because you're the folks ultimately that put those Members of Congress into office.

All right? Thank you, everybody. God bless you. God bless America.

NOTE: The President spoke at 12:02 p.m. at the Wyffels Hybrids, Inc., production facility. In his remarks, he referred to August "Gus" Junior, village president, Atkinson, IL; Lisa L.

Brants, owner, Lisa's Place restaurant; Robert Wyffels and William Wyffels, Jr., owners, Wyffels Hybrids, Inc.; Warren E. Buffett, chief executive officer and chairman, Berkshire Hathaway Inc.; Erskine B. Bowles and Alan K. Simpson, Cochairs, National Commission on Fiscal Responsibility and Reform; and Sens. Saxby C. Chambliss, Thomas A. Coburn, G. Kent Conrad, Michael D. Crapo, Richard J. Durbin, and Mark R. Warner. A questioner referred to the Low Income Home Energy Assistance Program (LIHEAP).

Remarks at a Town Hall Meeting and a Question-and-Answer Session in Alpha, Illinois
August 17, 2011

The President. Hello, everybody! Oh, it is good to be back home. Everybody have a seat, relax, take a load off there.

We've got some special guests here I want to just acknowledge. First of all, an outstanding public servant, a great Governor, Pat Quinn is in the house. Your former Congressman, now my Secretary of Transportation, great friend of mine, Ray LaHood is here.

We've got another Member of Congress who obviously took a wrong turn somewhere. [*Laughter*] Thought he was heading back to the West Side of Chicago, turned out he's in Alpha. [*Laughter*] Danny Davis is here.

We've got the mayor of Alpha, Marvin Watters is here. Where's Mr. Mayor? There he is back there. Good to see you, sir.

Two great friends of mine, Senators John Sullivan—where's John? There he is. [*Laughter*] And Dave Koehler is here. Good to see you, Dave.

And finally, I want to thank the owners of this great facility, Bruce and Charlie Curry, owners of Country Corner.

I need to confess something to Bruce and Charlie. One of my speechwriters, it's his birthday today, so we let him ride on the little cow pull over there. [*Laughter*] It said birthday parties available, so we had him sit in there. He's still only 29, and he still fit. So he had a great time there.

This is a town hall meeting. Some of you remember I used to do these when I was your Senator instead of your President. I don't want to do a lot of talking at the front, but I just want to talk to you a little bit about what I've been seeing over the last couple of days and what's been going on in Washington.

Obviously, we've been going through as tough of a time as we've seen in my lifetime and in most people's lifetimes these last 2½ years. We went through the worst financial crisis since the Great Depression. When I took office, we had already lost 4 million jobs, and we lost another 4 million just in the few months right after I took office. And we've been fighting our way back over the last 2½ months—or last 2½ years.

We were on the verge of going into a great depression, and we were able to yank ourselves out. The economy is now growing again. Over the last 17 months, we've created over 2 million jobs in the private sector. We saved an auto industry that was on the brink. We have—we've made investments in clean energy, in rebuilding our roads and our bridges.

And thanks to the great work of Secretary LaHood, we've been getting started on the process of making sure we've got the best infrastructure around. Thanks to the great work of our Secretary of Agriculture, Tom Vilsack, we've tried to strengthen rural communities and farming communities all across the country and all across the Midwest.

And so despite the fact that we've gone through tough times, I want everybody to remember we still have the best universities on Earth, the best workers on Earth, the best entrepreneurs on Earth, the best system on Earth. There's not a country in the world that wouldn't trade places with the United States of America.

Now, the fact is, though, times are still tough. And some of the reasons times are still tough we don't have complete control over. The economy was predicted to be growing at about 3.5 percent at the beginning of this year, partly because we had worked a bipartisan package of tax cuts and investment credits to encourage businesses to invest. But then you had the Arab Spring, and that shot gas prices and fuel prices up. And I know a lot of farmers here experienced that spike. And then we had the tsunami in Japan, and that disrupted supply lines and that affected American manufacturing. And then we had the situation in Europe and the debt crisis there, and that started lapping up onto our shores.

And so there are some things we don't have control over, and the question is, how do we meet these challenges? But there are things that we do have control over. And the biggest challenge we have is in Washington. There's nothing wrong with our country, but there's a lot wrong with our politics right now. And that's what I aim to fix. That's what we have to fix.

When you look at this recent debt ceiling debacle and the downgrade, that was a self-inflicted wound, completely unnecessary. The truth of the matter is we've got a real challenge with debt and deficit. We had a balanced budget in 2000, then we fought two wars without paying for them. We ended up creating a prescription drug plan for seniors, which is the right thing to do, but we didn't pay for it. Tax cuts we didn't pay for.

And then the recession hit, and so a lot of money was going out to help local communities keep their firefighters and police officers and teachers on staff. And Pat Quinn knows how important that was to prevent massive layoffs at the State level. Unemployment insurance to help folks get back on their feet, but that all meant a lot of money was going out, less tax revenue was going in because businesses weren't doing as well. So combined, we've got a big debt and deficit challenge that we've got to meet.

But what's frustrating is that 2 months ago, 3 months ago, 6 months ago we could have met that challenge. We could have decided we're going to come together with a balanced package where we're closing corporate loopholes and we're closing tax breaks for the very wealthy and we're cutting spending on things we don't need.

And if we had come together on a bipartisan basis, we could have avoided all this drama over the last 2½ months. But that's not what we did, because what's happened in Washington these days is there is a group of folks who think that, I'd rather see my opponent lose than see America win. There are folks who are willing to engage in political brinksmanship even if it costs the country.

And I know you're frustrated, and I want you to know I'm frustrated. And you should be frustrated. The last 2, 2½ days I've been traveling all across the Midwest, through Iowa and Minnesota and now back home in Illinois. And everywhere I go, what I see are people who are working hard. They're looking after their families. They're farming and feeding people not just here in America, but all around the world. They're going to church. They're helping out at the food pantry. They're coaching Little League.

We just came to visit the football team over at Galesburg. They've got their new coach. And I think to myself, you know what, if folks in Washington were carrying out their responsibilities the way you're carrying out your responsibilities, we'd be just fine. We would be just fine.

So the question is, what do we do going forward? Look, even though private sector job growth is good, we've still got a long way to go before we put everybody back to work. We need to go ahead and act right now on some proposals that are before Congress, ready to be voted on. We should extend the payroll tax cut that we passed in December, put $1,000 in the typical family's pocket. We need to extend that into next year. Because if you've got more money in your pockets, that means businesses have more customers, they're more likely to hire. There's no reason why we can't do that right now.

There's no reason why, as Ray LaHood knows, we've got over $2 trillion worth of repairs that need to be made around the country, and I know there are some right here in this county and right here in this State. And we've got a lot of construction workers that are out of work when the housing bubble went bust and interest rates are low and contractors are ready to come in on time, under budget. This is a great time for us to rebuild our roads and our bridges and locks in the Mississippi and our seaports and our airports. We could be doing that right now if Congress was willing to act.

Right now we could pass trade deals that we negotiated that not only have the support of business, but have the support of the UAW. That doesn't happen very often. And the reason is, is because folks know that not only is that good for agricultural America—opening up markets, because we've got the best farmers in the world—but it's also good for manufacturing. There are a whole bunch of Kias and Hyundais being driven around here. That's great. But I want some Fords and Chevys being driven in Korea. We should pass that bill right now.

We've got legislation right now that we call the "American Invents Act," basically, make patents easier so when people come up with a new product or a new service or a new invention, they're able to turn it around without a lot of redtape and bureaucracy and start businesses that could be hiring. There's no reason to wait. It should be passed right now.

The fact is this: All these things I just mentioned, historically, they've had bipartisan support. I mean, if Ray LaHood was still in there—Ray was a Republican—he'd vote for every single one of these; he'd be sponsoring them all. [*Laughter*] You've got a Democratic President who supports these things. There's no reason for us not to act right now.

And over the course of the next few weeks, I'm going to be putting out more proposals to put people to work right now. And some of them—yes, some of them cost money. And the way we pay for it is by doing more on deficit reduction than the plan that we had to come up with right at the last minute in order to avoid default. We didn't do as much as we could have.

When folks tell you that we've got a choice between jobs now or dealing with our debt crisis, they're wrong. They're wrong. We can't afford to just do one or the other. We've got to do both. And the way to do it is to make some—reform the Tax Code, close loopholes, make some modest modifications in programs like Medicare and Social Security so they're there for the next generation. Stabilize those systems, and you could actually save so much money that you could actually pay for some of the things like additional infrastructure right now.

We can close the deficit and put people to work, but what's required is that folks work together. That's the big challenge. That's the big challenge.

So the main thing is I'm here to enlist you in this fight for America's future. I need you to send a message to your Members of Congress, to your representatives that we're tired of the games. We're tired of the posturing. We don't want more press releases. We want action. We want everybody to work together and stop drawing lines in the sand and saying, we're so rigid, we're not going to do this or we're not going to do that, no matter what. Think about country ahead of party. Think about the next generation instead of the next election.

I had some interviews with some reporters, and they said, why don't you call Congress back right now? And I said, you know what, I hope Congress goes back to their districts. And I want them to listen to how frustrated people are, how angry they are with our politics at a time when we've got so much work to do.

Because the last thing we need is Congress to show up back in Congress and do the exact same thing they've been doing. They've got to think differently about how we're approaching problems. So I want them to be doing the same thing I'm doing, just talking to ordinary folks, and try to remember why they got into public service in the first place. It's not supposed to be to get attention. It's not supposed to be so you get interviewed on cable TV. It's not supposed to be so you have a fancy title.

You're supposed to be in public service to serve the public. And that means that, yes, you don't get your way 100 percent of the time. It means that you compromise. It means you apply common sense. And that's what I'm hoping that everybody takes from visiting their district again and getting out of Washington for a while.

I can tell you nothing is more inspiring to me than the kind of trip that I've been taking over the last few days. We're driving on this big bus, and it's all—you can't see out except when you're standing in front, so I'm out in front. And you know, having breakfast in a diner and going to a football practice, and you're passing rows of kids with flags and grandparents in their lawn chairs and mechanics out in front of their shops and farmers waving from their fields. And it inspires you, because it reminds you about what makes this country so great, why I love this country so much, and why we've got to be doing every single thing we can every minute of every day to make sure that you can continue to achieve your American Dream and pass it on to your kids and your grandchildren.

That's why I ran for President. That's why a whole bunch of you voted for me to be a U.S. Senator and then to be President.

So I need your help, everybody. Thank you. Thank you.

All right, let's see if this mike is working. It is. All right, what I'm going to do is I'm just going to call on folks as they raise their hands. The only rule is we're going to go girl, boy, girl, boy—[*laughter*]—so everybody gets a chance. And there are folks in the audience with microphones. So please stand up and introduce yourself before you ask your question. And I'll start with this young lady right here in the front.

Here we go. You've got a gentleman coming up with a mike.

Tax Reform

Q. Thank you, Mr. President, for being here today in Henry County. My name is Karen Urick. I'm a multigenerational farmer, member of the Henry County Board and Henry County Farm Bureau. My question that I have today is, I have a concern over estate taxes.

In 2013, if the Senate and the Congress fails to act, we will have our estate taxes go back to the 2001 level. We have family farms that are experiencing having to sell their land in order to pay the property taxes. And I was wondering what you see for the future of the estate tax. Thank you.

The President. Well, there's no reason why we have to go all the way back to the 2001 level. There is a compromise that has been discussed where you'd essentially have a $7 million exemption per family. There are some folks who just want to eliminate the estate tax all together. There are others who want to hike it up back to 2001.

There's a mid-level proposal that would exempt most—almost all family farms and, nevertheless, would still hit folks like Warren Buffett and make sure that he is able to pay what he wants to pay in terms of passing on something not only to his family, but also to the country that has blessed him so much.

So this is going to be part of the larger debate we have about the Tax Code. And the one thing I want to emphasize: A lot of folks don't realize this, but there are only 3 percent of the population that has an annual income of more than $200,000 a year. Think about that: 97 percent of folks, their annual income is less than $200,000. And there are only less than 1 percent who are making millions of dollars. And then there's less than one one-hundredth of 1 percent who are in the Warren Buffett category. That top 1 percent—in fact, that top one-tenth of 1 percent—those are the main folks who have seen their incomes skyrocket over the last 10, 15 years. Ordinary families, including family farmers, basically, your incomes and your wages have flatlined over the last decade.

And so when we think about tax reform, we should be thinking about fairness. What's fair? Nobody likes paying taxes. I promise you, I don't like paying taxes. But I do believe in paying what I use—paying for what I use. And if I want good roads and if I want good schools for kids and if I want the best universities in the world and I want to make sure that we're continuing to invest in agricultural research at places like University of Illinois that have helped to make us the most productive farmers in the world, then I think I should have to pay for it. And if I'm better able to pay for it than a waitress who is making $25,000 a year, I don't mind paying a slightly higher rate. There's nothing socialist about that. That's just basic fairness.

And by the way, when you hear folks saying, "Well, you know what, that's job killing," that's not job killing. When Bill Clinton was President we created 22 million jobs with a tax rate that was much higher across the board than it is now. We don't have to go all the way back up there on the estate tax or any other taxes for us to close our deficit and our debt, but we should ask oil and gas companies that are making record profits that they don't benefit from a special tax loophole that the mom-and-pop store in Alpha doesn't get. And I don't think there's anything wrong with asking me to pay a little more so our senior citizens don't have to pay an extra $5,000, $6,000 a year for their Medicare. That's what we're looking for, is balance, in terms of our tax policy.

All right. Who's next? This is an old friend of mine right here. Introduce yourself for everybody.

Environmental Regulations/Agriculture

Q. Phillip Nelson. Welcome back to Illinois, Mr. President.

The President. Good to see you, Phil.

Q. And I just want to say on behalf of Illinois agriculture, we're glad that you're in the heartland. And as you know, Illinois agriculture is the major economic driver in this State that employs close to a million people. And my concern is this: As a fourth-generation farmer, we're very concerned with some of the regulatory challenges that are coming our way as it relates to the Clean Air Act, the Clean Water Act. We're concerned with what's going in the Chesapeake Bay, and the fears that that might come to the Mississippi River Basin. And I guess my challenge, Mr. President, is that you work with the EPA Administrator to put some common sense back into some of these regulatory discussions so we don't regulate farmers out of business.

The President. Well, let me say this about—because I got this question when I was in Atkinson. Some of these regulatory concerns that people have, frankly, are unfounded in the sense that if somebody even has an idea or a thought about some regulation, then right away the message is sent out: They're coming, and they're going to make it impossible for you to farm and this and that and the other. And this thing may still be completely in a theoretical stage, where folks are trying to figure out how do we make sure that our streams and our rivers aren't messed up. And there may not even be a regulation in place before people are already getting worried about what's coming down the pipe.

There is not a rule or regulation that we don't do a complete cost-benefit analysis at this point and that we don't have intensive discussions with those who would potentially be affected. Now, what I do think is true is that in the past—I'll say not under my administration, but, I think, in the past, historically—there have been times where the EPA or other regulatory agencies don't listen to farmers and figure out how can we provide them flexibility in meeting some of their goals.

So I was talking to Tom Vilsack yesterday, and he was using as an example that in the State of Washington—maybe it was Oregon; it was in the Pacific Northwest—there was concern about some of the runoff was making it harder for salmon in those regions, which is also a big industry in Washington. And the problem was—it wasn't pollution, it was actually heating. Some of the runoff from some of the plants in the area were getting too hot, and that was inhibiting salmon. So instead of just coming up with a regulation that prohibited these industries, what they came up with was working with farmers and conservationists, planting trees along the rivers that cooled the waters so that the salmon were unaffected.

Well, that's the kind of creative approach where, if you're listening to folks on the ground and you say, here, we've got a problem that we do need to solve, but is there a smarter way to doing it that ends up being a win-win instead of end up being a lose-lose? Let's work together. And that's the kind of approach that we need to take.

Don't be fooled. I think if somebody goes out and says, we can't afford clean air and clean water, that's wrong. I don't believe that. And I don't think most farmers would agree with that, because, ultimately, nobody is better stewards of the land. And the reason we've got these incredible farms all around us is because we've got incredibly rich soil. We've got to make sure that we're conserving that soil. We've got to make sure that our air and water is—continues to be healthy for our kids. And I think farmers care about that more than anybody.

So we've got the same goal. The question is, are we able to work together to figure out a smart way to achieve these goals? And that's what my administration is going to be committed to doing, all right?

Right there. Yes.

Tourism/U.S. Health

Q. Thank you, President Obama, and welcome to this area. My name is Judy Guenseth, and I'm director of tourism for Galesburg and Knox County. So thank you for coming for——

The President. This is a great tourist location right here, County Corner.

Q. Exactly. Well, and I——

The President. Bring your families.

Q. I also want to congratulate you on recently turning 50. I passed that milestone recently, and it's not as bad as what people think.

The President. How come you look so much better than me? [*Laughter*]

Q. I live in Galesburg. [*Laughter*]

The President. That's why. Okay. All right. That makes sense; that makes sense.

Q. I also want to commend your wife, our First Lady, on her efforts to encourage healthy eating.

The President. Yes.

Q. I believe that people who eat healthy are healthy, and a healthy nation is a productive nation. And I think a lot about our children, our school children, and people who are on food stamps, and just the entire Nation needs to live healthy. But it also, in the long term, it reduces health care costs, and we're thinking about short-term health care costs, but we're also thinking in long-term health care costs.

The President. Right.

Q. So what I'd like to hear is maybe just your philosophy from your administration—ways to expound upon what your wife is doing and encouraging—and positive incentives to encourage people to eat healthy, to live healthy, especially for our schoolchildren.

The President. Well, it's a great question. And first of all, thank you for what you're doing to promote tourism here in Galesburg. I want to point out that America as a whole needs to do a better job of promoting tourism, because—it used to be we just took for granted everybody wanting to come here. Now countries all around the world are promoting their countries, and we want tourism dollars to come here. And so I've set up a tourism council to make sure that they visit not just San Francisco and Manhattan, but they also understand what an incredible travel opportunity there is here in the Midwest and in small towns all across America.

Michelle has done a great job with a combination of nutrition facts, but also exercise. And you're right, the reason she thought it was so important is because she's a mom with two kids. And she knows that Malia and Sasha, if they start off with healthy habits now, they're going to be healthier when they get older. And it turns out—we were just talking about the budget—about a third of our increase in health care cost is directly attributable to obesity and illnesses like diabetes that are entirely preventable and curable if folks got back into the same habits that our parents and our grandparents had.

Now, a lot of it is just movement and exercise and getting kids off the couch. And that's why you see Michelle, she goes to these events, and I will tell you, she is in very good shape. And she was running routes with the—running routes with NFL players and throwing in first pitches and doing double-dutch and—I can't keep up with her.

But food is an important component of it, and this is something that actually can benefit farmers, particularly family farmers. We want more produce, more vegetables and more fruit, consumed all across the country. And a lot of times, farmers are not making all the money from their products because it goes through this chain of shipping and processing and distribution, and there are a lot of middlemen between the farmer and the end user. And so there's an economic component as well as a health component, where if we can get farmers more directly linked to consumers, they're selling their products more directly, they're getting more fresh vegetables, more fresh fruit, then everybody can benefit.

And the way we're trying to do it—Michelle is doing it not by regulation, not by telling folks they have to do something, but by just information. And they've been able to get a lot of agreements with companies. You had Wal-Mart, for example, realizing that more and more people were asking for healthier products in their stores. Voluntarily, they and a whole bunch of other big retailers have said, "We're going to start linking up with family farmers; we're going to start setting up better grocery stores in underserved communities"—like in Danny's district where you can go for miles without seeing a fresh vegetable—"and linking up—setting up farmers markets in urban areas where people can sell produce." And a lot of this stuff we've been able to do voluntarily without legislation.

Now, there are still some legislative elements to this thing. So, for example, we passed the Child Nutrition Act just to make sure that our meals in schools are a little bit healthier so that kids are getting not just processed food, but they're also getting fresh produce as well. And some of the time that's a little bit more expensive in the schools. So the question is, are there some things we can cut out in order to pay to make sure that our kids are healthier? But they'll learn more, they'll be healthier in the long term, and in the long term we will save money, and it's good for farmers as well.

Thanks for the great question. All right. The gentleman right here. You just stood up. There you go.

Entitlement Programs

Q. Thank you, Mr. President. My name is Alfred Ramirez. I'm president of the Hispanic Chamber in the Quad Cities area and an employee of Group O in Milan. I'm going to—this is one of the most painful places I think our country has been in decades or centuries, where we have those in power and influence who are literally tearing our country apart between the haves and the have-nots. We are willing to dismantle programs that they call entitlement programs, and those recipients or beneficiaries of those programs don't have a mind of their own and are merely asking for a handout. And as we look for our adjustments to the budget and our cuts, could you please speak to some of those very programs that are not necessarily sacred, but must stay in place to even have a ripple effect for those who benefit from them?

The President. Well, first of all, let me separate out some of these programs. And I'm going to start with Social Security. People pay into Social Security. It's a social insurance program. They're not getting it for free. It's not a handout. It's taken out of your check. It's been taken out of your check for a lifetime. And it provides you a floor when you retire.

Now, hopefully, people have other savings that help supplement their incomes in their golden years. But we've got to make sure Social Security is there not just for this generation, but for the next generation. Now, Social Security is not posing a huge problem with respect to our debt and our deficit. There is a problem that if we don't make any modifications at all, then in a few years what will start happening is, is that the amount of money going out is more than the amount coming—amount of money going in. And people debate how soon, but in a couple of decades, you'd start having a situation where you'd only get 75 cents on the dollar that you expected on Social Security.

If we make some modest changes now, the kind of changes that Ronald Reagan and Tip O'Neill agreed to back in 1983, we can preserve Social Security, make sure it's there for the future 75 years out. So Social Security is something that we can solve relatively easily. It doesn't mean that we don't make any changes at all, because there may be some tweaks that we can make to the program, but we can assure that Social Security is there for future generations.

The bigger problem is Medicare and Medicaid. And the reason that's a problem is because health care costs keep on going up faster than inflation, people's wages, people's incomes at the same time as folks are getting older, so we've got more people into the system. And if we didn't do anything, then Medicare and Medicaid would gobble up basically the entire Federal budget, and we couldn't pay for our schools, we couldn't pay for fixing our airports, we couldn't pay for basic research. All the things that we expect out of our Federal Government, we couldn't do. All we'd be doing is just paying doctors and hospitals and nursing home facilities. That would take up the whole budget. That's no way to run a country.

The health care bill that I passed begins the process of trying to reduce the cost of health care, reforming the cost of health care by, for example, telling providers instead of having five tests that you charge for each one, have one test and e-mail to the five specialists who may need the test. Start using electronic medical records. Instead of reimbursing you for how many procedures you do, we're going to reimburse you for how well you help the patient get well overall. We're going to say to hospitals, how good are you at reducing infection rates in your hospital so that people aren't being readmitted, getting sick all the time?

So there are a whole bunch of things we can do to make the health care system more efficient. But even if we do all those things, we're still going to have a problem with Medicare and Medicaid. And my basic principle is, let's make sure that we keep this program intact, both programs—Medicare and Medicaid—for people in need: for our seniors, for disabled kids, for folks who've got a parent who's severely ill and they've only got a certain capacity to support them and help them. But let's also make sure that we're making some common-sense changes that allows the program to be there in the future. This is in contrast to the approach that's been taken, I've got to admit, by the House of Representatives when they passed their budget.

They passed a budget that basically called for voucherizing the Medicare system. This is the Republicans in the House of Representatives. And basically, what they say is, here's a flat rate that you get for Medicare, and you know what, if it turns out that it doesn't buy you enough insurance, that's your problem; that's not our problem.

Now, this will cut the deficit. It will save the Government money, but it does so by shifting the costs from the Government to individual seniors. It doesn't solve the problem by actually reducing health care costs. So I think that's the wrong approach to take. I think that's the wrong approach to take.

But I want to be honest with folks: We are going to have to make some modifications to Medicare and Medicaid. They don't have to be radical, but we're going to have to make some modifications to them in order for them to be there for the next generation. That's part of our obligation, because we can't just be not thinking about our kids and our grandkids as we move forward.

But we can do it in a way where the average senior is still protected, is still getting all the help that they need. It's not a voucher program. It is guaranteed health care, because I think that's a core principle that we've got to preserve. All right?

All right. It's getting a little warm out here, huh? You guys doing all right? You guys hanging in there? All right. It's a young woman's turn. Right over there in the striped shirt. You. Yes.

County Fairs/Tourism/Agriculture

Q. Our family does a lot of——
The President. What's your name?
Q. Allie Hand.

The President. Hey, Allie.

Q. Our family does a lot of farming and stuff. And we've noticed the county fairs are shrinking. Is there anything you're going to do about that?

The President. Well, one thing I'm going to do is I went to a county fair today, and they were showing some cows. And I didn't judge them. [*Laughter*] They all looked pretty good to me. [*Laughter*]

But I think the county fair tradition is so important, not only because it's an economic attraction for the community, but also because it brings the community together. It's a focal point for a county, and it reminds people of what holds America together and the heartland together.

And so, working with the State of Illinois, working with tourism bureaus, we want to continue to promote county fairs all across Illinois. One of the things I'd like to see is—and Danny may agree with this, coming from Chicago. There are kids in Danny's district—in fact, the overwhelming majority of kids in Danny's district—they've never seen a cornfield like this. They've never seen a cow. If you asked them what does a tomato plant look like, they'd have no idea.

So part of what I'd like to see is actually more tourism maybe organized through school trips and others for people from outside of rural areas to appreciate what's happening in rural areas. Where are they getting their food from? It doesn't just show up in cellophane in a supermarket. Somebody is growing that. And part of the challenge is America has become so productive agriculturally that you now only have a couple percent of the people who are actively involved in farming. Ninety-eight percent of people, they just eat. [*Laughter*] And I think a county fair can be a powerful education tool, and I'd like to see more kids just coming out here and be able to appreciate all the hard work that goes into the food on their table. And so maybe that's something that your outstanding Governor might want to work on. All right?

I got time for two more questions. Two more questions. Young man in the green, right there. Well, there are two young men in green, but I was calling on this guy right here. Yes.

Social Security

Q. Hello. My name is Eric Palmer, and I go to Augustana College.

The President. Great school.

Q. Yes, it is. First of all, I just want to let you know of one thing: I am not disappointed in you like Michele Bachmann wants everyone to believe.

The President. Thank you. I appreciate that.

Q. My question is about Social Security. I know that one of your ideas to fix the solvency of it is to reevaluate the equation that determines the COLA, the cost-of-living adjustment. But as the law stands right now, we are only taxed on the first $107,000 that we make.

The President. Right.

Q. That means every dime that I make is taxed for Social Security.

The President. Right.

Q. I don't make $107,000. [*Laughter*] But that means that——

The President. Somebody said you will——

Q. Someday, I hope.

The President. Yes, you sound pretty smart. It sounds like you're going to do just great.

Q. Thanks. But that means that people like Mitt Romney only pay into Social Security on the first one-tenth of 1 percent of what they make.

The President. Right.

Q. Can we look forward to you telling the Republicans that it's time that the wealthy pay their fair share?

The President. Well, the—first, this is a very well informed young man here. [*Laughter*] You're exactly right that the way the Social Security system works, there's what's called— there's basically a cap on your Social Security, which there isn't, by the way, on Medicare. But Social Security, it only goes up to the first $107,000. And you're right, somebody who makes—who has net assets of $250 million and are making maybe $5 million a year just on interest or capital gains or something, just a fraction of it's going to Social Security. I think there's a way for us to make adjustments on the

Social Security tax that would be fairer than the system that we use right now.

I do think, in terms of how we calculate inflation, that's important as well. By the way, seniors—a bunch of them were upset over the last couple years because some of—because seniors didn't get a cost-of-living adjustment. I got a lot of letters: "Mr. President, how come I didn't get a COLA this year for my Social Security?" And I answered this question at the previous town hall; I figured I'd clear something up now. The way the system works is you automatically get a cost-of-living adjustment based on the inflation rate. The President doesn't make that decision; it's based on a formula.

And when the economy was really in the drink in 2009 and 2010, there was basically no inflation; prices were actually going down. That's why seniors did not get the cost-of-living adjustment. That doesn't mean that they weren't still having a hard time because food prices or gas prices or what have you might have been going up, or the cost of medicine. So as a consequence, we actually proposed—and I'm sure Danny was one of the cosponsors of this—legislation that would have given an extra $250 to seniors just to help make ends meet. We couldn't get Republican support for it. But seniors who are still upset about not getting your COLA—or if they're not here, but when you go back and you're talking to your grandma and they're still mad at me about it, I just want you guys to set the record straight, okay?

All right, I've got one last question, and I'm going—I've got to ask this young lady right here, the next generation. She gets the last word.

Equipping Law Enforcement Officers

Q. Mr. President, my name is Jordan Vinolcavak, and my stepdad is the sheriff of Henry County. This year could set a record on the number of law enforcement officers killed in the line of duty. Does your administration have any plans that would include better equipping, training, or anything else that would help keep all officers safe?

The President. Well, it's a great question. How old are you, Jordan?

Q. Thirteen.

The President. Thirteen. You're Malia's age. So you're going into eighth grade?

Q. Yes.

The President. Did you already start?

Q. Yes.

The President. Yes? How's school going so far?

Q. Good. Today was my first day. [*Laughter*]

The President. Yes? No wonder you look so cheerful. [*Laughter*] Well, thank you for the question, Jordan, and tell your stepdad we're proud of him for his service. This is an example of what we have to pay for. You're right, we've seen—even though the crime rate overall and the violent crime rate has been going down, fatalities among law enforcement have actually been going up. And part of it is because criminals are getting more powerful weapons than they ever have before.

And so we've got to help our law enforcement, provide them with better protection, provide them with better crime-fighting strategies. That's true in big cities; it's also true in rural communities. We've got to do a better job of tracing weapons that are going to criminals.

I'm a big believer in the Second Amendment. And I'm a big believer in hunting and sportsmen. But I also think that making sure that we're keeping guns out of the hands of criminals is something all of us should be able to agree on.

So—but, Jordan, let me tell you something. We actually have been doing a lot. We've been giving a lot of money to local law enforcement, partly to prevent layoffs, partly to ensure they've got better equipment, things like interoperable radios so that when something happens—let's say you've got all power out, one of these tornadoes hit like hit in Joplin—that they're able to come together and still communicate effectively.

We've got things called burn grants that are very important to local law enforcement in dealing with, for example, methamphetamine production here in the Midwest. But all that costs money. And that's why I want everybody to remember you're going to hear a lot of stuff over the next year and a half, just like you have for the last 2½ years, people attacking government and saying government is the problem.

And I think Jordan just reminded us, government are our police officers and our firefighters. Government is all those young men and women who have been serving, protecting us in Afghanistan and Iraq. Government are the folks who work for FEMA, who when there's a flood come in and help communities get back on their feet. Government is our astronauts. Government are the folks who are helping make sure that our food is properly inspected.

So don't buy into this notion that somehow all our problems would be solved if we eliminate government. Part of the reason we had this financial crisis was because we didn't have government doing a good enough job looking over the shoulders of the banks to make sure that they weren't taking crazy risks.

And part of what happens is that people get so frustrated with politics that they just get fed up and they kind of lump government together with politics. Well, no, government needs to improve. It needs to get more efficient. We've got to be smarter about how we regulate issues. We've got to make sure that we're not wasting taxpayer money.

But there's a difference between politics and government. And what's really broken is a politics that doesn't reflect the core values and the decency and the neighborliness of the American people.

And that's what I'm fighting for, and that's what I need you fighting for. Thank you very much, Alpha. Love you. Appreciate you.

NOTE: The President spoke at 4:51 p.m. at the Country Corner Farm. In his remarks, he referred to State Sens. John M. Sullivan and David Koehler of Illinois; Tim Dougherty, coach, Galesburg High School football team in Galesburg, IL; and Warren E. Buffett, chief executive officer and chairman, Berkshire Hathaway Inc. A participant referred to 2012 Republican Presidential candidate W. Mitt Romney.

Message to the Congress Reporting on Blocking Property of the Government of Syria and Prohibiting Certain Transactions With Respect to Syria
August 17, 2011

To the Congress of the United States:

Pursuant to the International Emergency Economic Powers Act (50 U.S.C. 1701 *et seq.*) (IEEPA) and in light of the Syria Accountability and Lebanese Sovereignty Restoration Act of 2003 (Public Law 108–175) (SAA), I hereby report that I have issued an Executive Order (the "order") that takes additional steps with respect to the Government of Syria's continuing escalation of violence against the people of Syria and with respect to the national emergency declared in Executive Order 13338 of May 11, 2004, as modified in scope and relied upon for additional steps taken in Executive Order 13399 of April 25, 2006, Executive Order 13460 of February 13, 2008, Executive Order 13572 of April 29, 2011, and Executive Order 13573 of May 18, 2011.

In Executive Order 13338, the President found that the actions of the Government of Syria constitute an unusual and extraordinary threat to the national security, foreign policy, and economy of the United States and declared a national emergency to deal with that threat. To address that threat and to implement the SAA, the President in Executive Order 13338 blocked the property of certain persons and imposed additional prohibitions on certain transactions with respect to Syria. In Executive Order 13572, I expanded the scope of that national emergency and imposed additional sanctions.

The order blocks the property and interests in property of the Government of Syria. The order also provides criteria for designations of persons determined by the Secretary of the

Treasury, in consultation with the Secretary of State:

- to have materially assisted, sponsored, or provided financial, material, or technological support for, or goods or services in support of, any person whose property and interests in property are blocked pursuant to the order; or

- to be owned or controlled by, or to have acted or purported to act for or on behalf of, directly or indirectly, any person whose property and interests in property are blocked pursuant to the order.

The order also prohibits the following:

- new investment in Syria by a United States person, wherever located;

- the exportation, reexportation, sale, or supply, directly or indirectly, from the United States, or by a United States person, wherever located, of any services to Syria;

- the importation into the United States of petroleum or petroleum products of Syrian origin;

- any transaction or dealing by a United States person, wherever located, including purchasing, selling, transporting, swapping, brokering, approving, financing, facilitating, or guaranteeing, in or related to petroleum or petroleum products of Syrian origin; and

- any approval, financing, facilitation, or guarantee by a United States person, wherever located, of a transaction by a foreign person where the transaction by that foreign person would be prohibited by section 2 of the order if performed by a United States person or within the United States.

I have delegated to the Secretary of the Treasury the authority, in consultation with the Secretary of State, to take such actions, including the promulgation of rules and regulations, and to employ all powers granted to the President by IEEPA, as may be necessary to carry out the purposes of the order.

All agencies of the United States Government are directed to take all appropriate measures within their authority to carry out the provisions of the order.

I am enclosing a copy of the Executive Order I have issued.

BARACK OBAMA

The White House,
August 17, 2011.

NOTE: This message was released by the Office of the Press Secretary on August 18. The Executive order is listed in Appendix D at the end of this volume.

Statement on the Situation in Syria
August 18, 2011

The United States has been inspired by the Syrian people's pursuit of a peaceful transition to democracy. They have braved ferocious brutality at the hands of their Government. They have spoken with their peaceful marches, their silent shaming of the Syrian regime, and their courageous persistence in the face of brutality, day after day, week after week. The Syrian Government has responded with a sustained onslaught. I strongly condemn this brutality, including the disgraceful attacks on Syrian civilians in cities like Hama and Deir al-Zour, and the arrests of opposition figures who have been denied justice and subjected to torture at the hands of the regime. These violations of the universal rights of the Syrian people have revealed to Syria, the region, and the world the Asad Government's flagrant disrespect for the dignity of the Syrian people.

The United States opposes the use of violence against peaceful protesters in Syria, and we support the universal rights of the Syrian people. We have imposed sanctions on President Asad and his Government. The European Union has imposed sanctions as well. We helped lead an effort at the U.N. Security Council to condemn Syria's actions. We have coordinated closely with allies and partners from the region and around the world. The Asad Government has now been condemned by countries in all parts of the globe and can look only to Iran for support for its brutal and unjust crackdown.

The future of Syria must be determined by its people, but President Bashar al-Asad is standing in their way. His calls for dialogue and reform have rung hollow while he is imprisoning, torturing, and slaughtering his own people. We have consistently said that President Asad must lead a democratic transition or get out of the way. He has not led. For the sake of the Syrian people, the time has come for President Asad to step aside.

The United States cannot and will not impose this transition upon Syria. It is up to the Syrian people to choose their own leaders, and we have heard their strong desire that there not be foreign intervention in their movement. What the United States will support is an effort to bring about a Syria that is democratic, just, and inclusive for all Syrians. We will support this outcome by pressuring President Asad to get out of the way of this transition and standing up for the universal rights of the Syrian people along with others in the international community.

As a part of that effort, my administration is announcing unprecedented sanctions to deepen the financial isolation of the Asad regime and further disrupt its ability to finance a campaign of violence against the Syrian people. I have signed a new Executive order requiring the immediate freeze of all assets of the Government of Syria subject to U.S. jurisdiction and prohibiting U.S. persons from engaging in any transaction involving the Government of Syria. This E.O. also bans U.S. imports of Syrian-origin petroleum or petroleum products, prohibits U.S. persons from having any dealings in or related to Syria's petroleum or petroleum products, and prohibits U.S. persons from operating or investing in Syria. We expect today's actions to be amplified by others.

We recognize that it will take time for the Syrian people to achieve the justice they deserve. There will be more struggle and sacrifice. It is clear that President Asad believes that he can silence the voices of his people by resorting to the repressive tactics of the past. But he is wrong. As we have learned these last several months, sometimes, the way things have been is not the way that they will be. It is time for the Syrian people to determine their own destiny, and we will continue to stand firmly on their side.

NOTE: The statement referred to Executive Order 13582, which is listed in Appendix D at the end of this volume.

The President's Weekly Address
August 20, 2011

Hello from the Country Corner Farm in Alpha, Illinois. For the past few days, I've been traveling to small towns and farm towns here in the heartland of this country. I sat down with small-business owners in Gutenberg, Iowa, and ranchers and farmers in Peosta. I had lunch with veterans in Cannon Falls, Minnesota, and talked to plant workers at a seed distributor in Atkinson, Illinois. And to the girls volleyball team in Maquoketa High School, let me just say one thing: Go Cardinals!

Now, I'm out here for one reason: I think Washington, DC, can learn something from the folks in Atkinson and Peosta and Cannon Falls. I think our country would be a whole lot better off if our elected leaders showed the same kind of discipline and integrity and responsibility that most Americans demonstrate in their lives every single day.

Because the fact is, we're going through a tough time right now. We're coming through a terrible recession. A lot of folks are still looking for work. A lot of people are getting by with smaller paychecks or less money in the cash register. So we need folks in Washington—the people whose job it is to deal with the country's problems, the people who you elected to serve—we need them to put aside their differences to get things done.

There are things we can do right now that will mean more customers for businesses and more jobs across the country. We can cut payroll taxes again so families have an extra $1,000 to spend. We can pass a road construction bill so construction crews who are now sitting idle can head back to the worksite, rebuilding roads, bridges, and airports. We've got brave, skilled Americans returning from Iraq and Afghanistan. Let's connect them with businesses that could use their skills. And let's pass trade deals to level the playing field for our businesses. We have Americans driving Hyundais and Kias. Well, I want to see folks in Korea driving Fords, Chevys, and Chryslers. I want more products sold around the globe stamped with three words: Made in America.

These are commonsense ideas, ideas that have been supported by both Democrats and Republicans. The only thing holding them back is politics. The only thing preventing us from passing these bills is the refusal by some in Congress to put country ahead of party. That's the problem we have right now. That's what's holding this country back. That's what we have to change.

Because, for all the knocks we've taken, despite all the challenges we face, this is still the greatest country on Earth. We still have the best workers and farmers, entrepreneurs and businesses, students and scientists. And you can see that here in Alpha. You can see it along the country roads that connect these small towns and farmlands.

These past few days, I've been seeing little kids with American flags and grandparents in lawn chairs. I've shaken hands with folks outside machine shops and churches, corner stores and farms. It reminds me of why I got into public service in the first place. Getting out of Washington and spending time with the people of this country, seeing how hard you're working, how creative you are, how resourceful you are, how determined you are, that only makes me more determined to serve you as best I can as President. And it only makes me more confident in our future.

That's why it's so important that folks in Washington put country before party. That's why it's so important that our elected leaders get past their differences to help grow the economy and put this Nation back to work. Because here in Alpha, it couldn't be more clear: If we can come together, there is no stopping the United States of America. There's no doubt that our future is bright.

Thanks, and have a great weekend.

NOTE: The address was recorded at approximately 5:35 p.m. on August 17 at the Country Corner Farm Market in Alpha, IL, for broadcast on August 20. The transcript was made available by the Office of the Press Secretary on August 19, but was embargoed for release until 6 a.m. on August 20.

Statement on the Situation in Libya
August 21, 2011

Tonight the momentum against the Qadhafi regime has reached a tipping point. Tripoli is slipping from the grasp of a tyrant. The Qadhafi regime is showing signs of collapsing. The people of Libya are showing that the universal pursuit of dignity and freedom is far stronger than the iron fist of a dictator.

The surest way for the bloodshed to end is simple: Muammar Qadhafi and his regime need to recognize that their rule has come to an end. Qadhafi needs to acknowledge the reality that he no longer controls Libya. He needs to relinquish power once and for all. Meanwhile, the United States has recognized the Transitional National Council as the legitimate governing authority in Libya. At this pivotal and historic time, the TNC should continue to demonstrate the leadership that is necessary to steer the country through a transition by respecting the rights of the people of Libya, avoiding civilian casualties, protecting the institutions of the Libyan state, and pursuing a transition to democracy that is just and inclusive for all of the people of Libya. A season of conflict must lead to one of peace.

The future of Libya is now in the hands of the Libyan people. Going forward, the United States will continue to stay in close coordination with the TNC. We will continue to insist that the basic rights of the Libyan people are respected. And we will continue to work with our allies and partners in the international community to protect the people of Libya and to support a peaceful transition to democracy.

Remarks on the Situation in Libya From Martha's Vineyard, Massachusetts
August 22, 2011

Good afternoon, everybody. I just completed a call with my National Security Council on the situation in Libya. And earlier today I spoke to Prime Minister Cameron about the extraordinary events taking place there.

The situation is still very fluid. There remains a degree of uncertainty, and there are still regime elements who pose a threat. But this much is clear: The Qadhafi regime is coming to an end, and the future of Libya is in the hands of its people.

In just 6 months, the 42-year reign of Muammar Qadhafi has unraveled. Earlier this year, we were inspired by the peaceful protests that broke out across Libya. This basic and joyful longing for human freedom echoed the voices that we had heard all across the region from Tunis to Cairo. In the face of these protests, the Qadhafi regime responded with brutal crackdowns. Civilians were murdered in the streets. A campaign of violence was launched against the Libyan people. Qadhafi threatened to hunt peaceful protestors down like rats. As his forces advanced across the country, there existed the potential for wholesale massacres of innocent civilians.

In the face of this aggression, the international community took action. The United States helped shape a U.N. Security Council resolution that mandated the protection of Libyan civilians. An unprecedented coalition was formed that included the United States, our NATO partners, and Arab nations. And in March, the international community launched a military operation to save lives and stop Qadhafi's forces in their tracks.

In the early days of this intervention, the United States provided the bulk of the firepower, and then our friends and allies stepped forward. The Transitional National Council has established itself as a credible representative of the Libyan people. And the United States, together with our European allies and friends across the region, recognize the TNC as the legitimate governing authority in Libya.

Qadhafi was cut off from arms and cash, and his forces were steadily degraded. From Benghazi to Misurata to the western mountains, the Libyan opposition courageously confronted the regime and the tide turned in their favor.

Over the last several days, the situation in Libya has reached a tipping point as the opposition increased its coordination from east to west, took town after town, and the people of Tripoli rose up to claim their freedom.

For over four decades, the Libyan people have lived under the rule of a tyrant who denied them their most basic human rights. Now the celebrations that we've seen in the streets of Libya shows that the pursuit of human dignity is far stronger than any dictator. I want to emphasize that this is not over yet. As the regime collapses, there is still fierce fighting in some areas, and we have reports of regime elements threatening to continue fighting.

Although it's clear that Qadhafi's rule is over, he still has the opportunity to reduce further bloodshed by explicitly relinquishing power to the people of Libya and calling for those forces that continue to fight to lay down their arms for the sake of Libya.

As we move forward from this pivotal phase, the opposition should continue to take important steps to bring about a transition that is peaceful, inclusive, and just. As the leadership of the TNC has made clear, the rights of all Libyans must be respected. True justice will not come from reprisals and violence; it will come from reconciliation and a Libya that allows its citizens to determine their own destiny.

In that effort, the United States will be a friend and a partner. We will join with allies and partners to continue the work of safeguarding the people of Libya. As remaining regime elements menace parts of the country, I've directed my team to be in close contact with NATO, as well as the United Nations, to determine other steps that we can take. To deal with the humanitarian impact, we're working to ensure that critical supplies reach those in need, particularly those who've been wounded.

Secretary Clinton spoke today with her counterparts from leading nations of the coalition on all these matters. And I've directed Ambassador Susan Rice to request that the U.N. Secretary-General use next month's General Assembly to support this important transition.

For many months, the TNC has been working with the international community to prepare for a post-Qadhafi Libya. As those efforts proceed, our diplomats will work with the TNC as they ensure that the institutions of the Libyan state are protected, and we will support them with the assets of the Qadhafi regime that were frozen earlier this year. Above all, we will call for an inclusive transition that leads to a democratic Libya.

As we move forward, we should also recognize the extraordinary work that has already been done. To the American people, these events have particular resonance. Qadhafi's regime has murdered scores of American citizens in acts of terror in the past. Today we remember the lives of those who were taken in those acts of terror and stand in solidarity with their families. We also pay tribute to Admiral Sam Locklear and all of the men and women in uniform who have saved so many lives over the last several months, including our brave pilots that have executed their mission with skill and extraordinary bravery. And all of this was done without putting a single U.S. troop on the ground.

To our friends and allies, the Libyan intervention demonstrates what the international community can achieve when we stand together as one. Although the efforts in Libya are not yet over, NATO has once more proven that it is the most capable alliance in the world and that its strength comes from both its firepower and the power of our democratic ideals. And the Arab members of our coalition have stepped up and shown what can be achieved when we act together as equal partners. Their actions sent a powerful message about the unity of our effort and our support for the future of Libya.

Finally, the Libyan people: Your courage and character have been unbreakable in the face of a tyrant. An ocean divides us, but we are joined in the basic human longing for freedom, for justice, and for dignity. Your revolution is your own, and your sacrifices have been extraordinary. Now the Libya that you deserve is within your reach. Going forward, we will stay in close coordination with the TNC to support that outcome. And though there will be huge challenges ahead, the extraordinary events in Libya remind us that fear can give way to hope and that the power of people striving for freedom can bring about a brighter day.

Thank you very much.

NOTE: The President spoke at 2:20 p.m. at the Blue Heron Farm. In his remarks, he referred to Prime Minister David Cameron of the United Kingdom; Secretary-General Ban Ki-moon of the United Nations; and Adm. Samuel J. Locklear, USN, commander, Joint Task Force Odyssey Dawn.

Remarks on Hurricane Irene From Martha's Vineyard
August 26, 2011

Good morning, everybody. I want to say a few words about Hurricane Irene, urge Americans to take it seriously, and provide an overview of our ongoing Federal preparations for what's likely to be an extremely dangerous and costly storm.

I've just convened a conference call with senior members of my emergency response team and directed them to make sure that we are bringing all Federal resources to bear and deploying them properly to cope not only with the storm, but also its aftermath. I've also spoken this morning with Governors and mayors of major metropolitan areas along the eastern seaboard to let them know that this administration is in full support of their efforts to prepare for this storm and stands ready to fully support their response efforts. And we will continue to stay in close contact with them.

I cannot stress this highly enough: If you are in the projected path of this hurricane, you have to take precautions now. Don't wait. Don't delay. We all hope for the best, but we have to be prepared for the worst. All of us have to take this storm seriously. You need to listen to your State and local officials, and if you are given an evacuation order, please follow it. Just to underscore this point: We ordered an aircraft carrier group out to sea to avoid this storm yesterday. So if you're in the way of this hurricane, you should be preparing now.

If you aren't sure how to prepare your families or your home or your business for a hurricane or any other emergency, then you can visit ready.gov—that's ready.gov—or listo.gov—that's L–I–S–T–O.gov.

Now, since last weekend, FEMA has been deploying its Incident Management Assistance Teams to staging areas in communities up and down the coast. FEMA has millions of liters of water, millions of meals, and tens of thousands of cots and blankets, along with other supplies, prepositioned along the eastern seaboard. And the American Red Cross has already begun preparing shelters in North Carolina and other States.

These resources are all being coordinated with our State and local partners, and they stand ready to be deployed as necessary. But again, if you are instructed to evacuate, please do so. It's going to take time for first-responders to begin rescue operations and to get the resources we've pre-positioned to people in need. So the more you can do to be prepared now—making a plan, make a supply kit, know your evacuation route, follow instructions of your local officials—the quicker we can focus our resources after the storm on those who need help the most.

To sum up, all indications point to this being a historic hurricane. Although we can't predict with perfect certainty the impact of Irene over the next few days, the Federal Government has spent the better part of last week working closely with officials in communities that could be affected by this storm to see to it that we are prepared. So now is the time for residents of these communities—in the hours that remain—to do the same. And FEMA and Craig Fugate, the director of FEMA, will be keeping people closely posted in the next 24, 48 hours.

Thank you very much.

NOTE: The President spoke at 11:28 a.m. in the Fisher House at Blue Heron Farm.

Statement on the Firebombing of the Royale San Jeronimo Casino in Monterrey, Mexico
August 26, 2011

I strongly condemn the barbaric and reprehensible attack in Monterrey, Mexico, yesterday. On behalf of the American people, our thoughts and prayers are with the victims and their families at this difficult time.

The people of Mexico and their Government are engaged in a brave fight to disrupt violent transnational criminal organizations that threaten both Mexico and the United States. The United States is and will remain a partner in this fight. We share with Mexico responsibility for meeting this challenge, and we are committed to continuing our unprecedented cooperation in confronting these criminal organizations.

Statement on the Terrorist Attack on the United Nations Headquarters in Abuja, Nigeria
August 26, 2011

I strongly condemn today's horrific and cowardly attack on the United Nations headquarters building in Abuja, Nigeria, which killed and wounded many innocent civilians from Nigeria and around the world. I extend the deepest sympathies of the American people to the victims and their families, colleagues, and friends, whom we will keep in our thoughts and prayers.

The people who serve the United Nations do so with a simple purpose: to try to improve the lives of their neighbors and promote the values on which the U.N. was founded—dignity, freedom, security, and peace. The U.N. has been working in partnership with the people of Nigeria for more than five decades. An attack on Nigerian and international public servants demonstrates the bankruptcy of the ideology that led to this heinous action.

The United States strongly supports the work of the United Nations and its lasting bond with the people of Nigeria, a bond that will only emerge stronger in the wake of this murderous act.

The President's Weekly Address
August 27, 2011

In just 2 weeks, we'll come together as a nation to mark the 10th anniversary of the September 11 attacks. We'll remember the innocent lives we lost. We'll stand with the families who loved them. We'll honor the heroic first-responders who rushed to the scene and saved so many. And we'll pay tribute to our troops and military families and all those who have served over the past 10 years to keep us safe and strong.

We'll also recall how the worst terrorist attack in American history brought out the best in the American people: how Americans lined up to give blood, how volunteers drove across the country to lend a hand, how schoolchildren donated their savings, how communities, faith groups, and businesses collected food and clothing. We were united, and the outpouring of generosity and compassion reminded us that in times of challenge, we Americans move forward together, as one people.

This September 11, Michelle and I will join the commemorations at Ground Zero, in Shanksville, and at the Pentagon. But even if you can't be in New York, Pennsylvania, or Virginia, every American can be part of this anniversary. Once again, 9/11 will be a National Day of Service and Remembrance. And in the days and weeks ahead, folks across the country, in all 50 States, will come together in their communities and neighborhoods to honor the victims of 9/11 and to reaffirm the strength of our Nation with acts of service and charity.

In Minneapolis, volunteers will help restore a community center. In Winston-Salem, North Carolina, they'll hammer shingles and lay floors to give a family a new home. In Tallahassee, Florida, they'll assemble care packages for our troops overseas and their families here at home. In Orange County, California, they'll renovate homes for our veterans. And once again, Michelle and I look forward to joining a local service project as well.

There are so many ways to get involved, and every American can do something. To learn more about the opportunities where you live, just go online and visit serve.gov. Even the smallest act of service, the simplest act of kindness, is a way to honor those we lost, a way to reclaim that spirit of unity that followed 9/11.

On this 10th anniversary, we still face great challenges as a nation. We're emerging from the worst economic crisis in our lifetimes. We're taking the fight to Al Qaida and ending the war in Iraq and starting to bring our troops home from Afghanistan. And we're working to rebuild the foundation of our national strength here at home.

None of this will be easy, and it can't be the work of government alone. As we saw after 9/11, the strength of America has always been the character and compassion of our people. So as we mark this solemn anniversary, let's summon that spirit once more. And let's show that the sense of common purpose that we need in America doesn't have to be a fleeting moment. It can be a lasting virtue, not just on one day, but every day.

NOTE: The address was recorded at approximately 1:30 p.m. on August 18 in the Roosevelt Room at the White House for broadcast on August 27. The transcript was made available by the Office of the Press Secretary on August 26, but was embargoed for release until 6 a.m. on August 27.

Remarks on Relief Efforts for Hurricane Irene
August 28, 2011

Good afternoon, everybody. I'm joined today by my Secretary of Homeland Security, Janet Napolitano, and Administrator of FEMA, Craig Fugate, to provide a brief update on our ongoing response efforts to Hurricane Irene.

First, let me say that this is a storm that has claimed lives. Our thoughts and prayers are with those who've lost loved ones and those whose lives have been affected by the storm. You need to know that America will be with you in your hour of need.

While the storm has weakened as it moves north, it remains a dangerous storm that continues to produce heavy rains. One of our chief concerns before Irene made landfall was the possibility of significant flooding and widespread power outages. And we've been getting reports of just that from our State and local partners. Many Americans are still at serious risk of power outages and flooding, which could get worse in the coming days as rivers swell past their banks.

So I want people to understand that this is not over. Response and recovery efforts will be an ongoing operation, and I urge Americans in affected areas to continue to listen for the guidance and direction of their State and local officials.

Before the storm made landfall, the Department of Homeland Security and FEMA worked very closely with our State and local partners, as well as volunteer organizations, to preposition supplies and teams of first-responders along the hurricane's projected track. And the American Red Cross opened shelters in communities across the region. I want to thank those Americans for their work over the past several days, which has saved lives and property up and down the East Coast.

We continue to have search and rescue personnel on alert, as well as water, food, and other needed resources. And moving forward, FEMA is working with State and local responders to assess damage and assist in the recovery.

I do want to underscore that the impacts of this storm will be felt for some time, and the recovery effort will last for weeks or longer. Power may be out for days in some areas, and we will support our State and local partners in every way that we can as they work to restore power in those areas.

So I'm going to make sure that DHS and FEMA and other Federal agencies are doing everything in their power to help folks on the ground. I continue to meet regularly with Secretary Napolitano and Administrator Fugate and the other members of my team to assess our response and ensure that we have what we need in place.

As I've told Governors and mayors from across the affected area, if they need something, I want to know about it. We're going to make sure that we respond as quickly and effectively as possible. And we're going to keep it up as long as hurricane season continues.

Finally, while we're not out of the woods yet, I want to thank everybody at the Federal, State, and local levels who have worked so hard to respond to this storm. This has been an exemplary effort of how good government at every level should be responsive to people's needs, work to keep them safe, and protect and promote the Nation's prosperity.

I want to thank scientists who provide the information necessary for Governors and mayors to make sound decisions, disaster response experts who made sure we were as prepared as possible, to National Guard members and first-responders who risked their lives to ensure their fellow citizens' safety—all ordinary Americans who love their country and volunteered to do their part.

Above all, the past few days have been a shining example of how Americans open our homes and our hearts to those in need and pull together in tough times to help our fellow citizens prepare for and respond to, as well as recover from, extraordinary challenges, whether natural disasters or economic difficulties.

That's what makes the United States of America a strong and resilient nation, a strong and resilient people. And I want to thank all who have been involved very much.

Now I'd like to ask Secretary Napolitano and Administrator Fugate to say a few words. Janet.

[*At this point, Secretary of Homeland Security Janet A. Napolitano and Federal Emergency Management Agency Administrator W. Craig Fugate made brief remarks. The President then continued his remarks as follows.*]

Okay. Thank you very much, everybody. Craig and Janet will continue to keep everybody posted throughout the week. As we have already said, there are a lot of communities that are still being affected. We are particularly concerned about flooding because the continuing rains can end up having an impact well beyond the immediate center of the storm.

And so we're going to continue to monitor that carefully. Assessments are already being done in North Carolina and Virginia. There are still search and rescue teams that are operating throughout the region. And we will continue to keep the American people posted throughout our efforts not only with respect to response, but also with respect to recovery.

So thanks very much, everybody.

NOTE: The President spoke at 5:02 p.m. in the Rose Garden at the White House.

Remarks on the Nomination of Alan B. Krueger To Be Chairman of the Council of Economic Advisers
August 29, 2011

Hurricane Irene

The President. Good morning, everybody. This morning we're continuing to deal with the impact and the aftermath of Hurricane Irene. As I said yesterday, we're going to make sure folks have all the support they need as they begin to assess and repair the damage left by the storm. And that's going to continue in the days ahead.

It's going to take time to recover from a storm of this magnitude. The effects are still being felt across much of the country, including in New England and States like Vermont where there's been an enormous amount of flooding. So our response continues. But I'm going to make sure that FEMA and other agencies are doing everything in their power to help people on the ground.

Nomination for Council of Economic Advisers Chairman

Now, even as we deal with this crisis of the moment, our great ongoing challenge as a nation remains how to get this economy growing faster. Our challenge is to create a climate where more businesses can post job listings, where folks can find good work that relieves the financial burden they're feeling, where families can regain a sense of economic security in their lives.

That's our urgent mission. And that's what I'm fighting for every single day. That's why today I'm very pleased to nominate Alan Krueger to chair the Council of Economic Advisers. Come on down here, Al.

Alan brings a wealth of experience to the job. He's one of the Nation's leading economists. For more than two decades, he's studied and developed economic policy, both inside and outside of government. In the first 2 years of this administration, as we were dealing with the effects of a complex and fast-moving financial crisis—a crisis that threatened a second Great Depression—Alan's counsel as Chief Economist at the Treasury Department proved invaluable.

So I am very pleased to appoint Alan, and I look forward to working with him. As I told him, it's going to be tough to fill the shoes of Austan Goolsbee, who's been a great friend and adviser who I've relied on for years. But I have nothing but confidence in Alan as he takes on this important role as one of the leaders of my economic team.

I rely on the Council of Economic Advisers to provide unvarnished analysis and recommendations, not based on politics, not based on narrow interests, but based on the best evidence, based on what's going to do the most good for the most people in this country. And that's more important than ever right now. We need folks in Washington to make decisions based on what's best for the country, not what's best for any political party or special interest. That's how we'll get through this period of economic uncertainty, and that's the only way that we'll be able to do what's necessary to grow the economy.

So it's that spirit that I'm going to be calling upon in the coming days. Next week, I will be laying out a series of steps that Congress can take immediately to put more money in the pockets of working families and middle class families, to make it easier for small businesses to hire people, to put construction crews to work rebuilding our Nation's roads and railways and airports, and all the other measures that can help to grow this economy.

These are bipartisan ideas that ought to be the kind of proposals that everybody can get behind, no matter what your political affiliation might be. So my hope and expectation is that we can put country before party and get something done for the American people.

That's what I'll be fighting for. And we've got to have a good team to do it. So, Alan, I appreciate your willingness to take on this assignment, and I'm looking forward to working with you once again.

Mr. Krueger. Thank you very much.

The President. Thank you so much.

Thank you, everybody.

NOTE: The President spoke at 11:01 a.m. in the Rose Garden at the White House.

Statement on the Sixth Anniversary of Hurricane Katrina
August 29, 2011

Six years ago today, Hurricane Katrina struck the Gulf Coast, upending families and ravaging communities, and no one will forget the tragic events of those days. But what's required of us is more than remembrance. What's required of us is our continued efforts to make sure that New Orleans and the Gulf Coast fully recover and to make sure that our response to such disasters is the best it can possibly be.

Over the past several years, we've seen what Americans are capable of when tested. We've seen the grit and determination of people on the Gulf Coast coming together to rebuild their communities, brick by brick, block by block. At the same time, we've made sure the Federal Government is doing its part to help. We've cut through redtape to free up funding for recovery efforts in Louisiana and Mississippi. We've taken steps to help school systems get children the tools and resources they need for a proper education. We've broken through gridlock on behalf of tens of thousands of displaced families, making sure they have long-term housing solutions. And we'll keep at it until these communities have come back stronger than before.

When it comes to disaster response, we've worked very seriously to enhance our preparedness efforts so that Americans are ready before disaster strikes and to strengthen our recovery capabilities so that we're more resilient after disaster strikes. Over the last week, we have experienced the power of another storm, Hurricane Irene. Before the storm made landfall, the Department of Homeland Security and FEMA worked closely with our State and local partners to pre-position supplies and teams of first-responders and support their response efforts. Those response efforts are ongoing, and we will continue that partnership, responding as quickly and effectively as possible, for as long as necessary, until the affected communities are back on their feet.

Today is a reminder of not just the immediate devastation that can be caused by these storms, but the long-term needs of communities impacted by disasters, whether in Mississippi or Alabama, Tennessee or Missouri, North Dakota or the East Coast States impacted by Hurricane Irene. This administration will stand by those communities until the work is done.

Remarks at the American Legion National Convention in Minneapolis, Minnesota
August 30, 2011

The President. Hello, Legionnaires! It is wonderful to see all of you. Let me first of all thank Commander Foster for your introduction and for your lifetime of service to your fellow marines, soldiers, and veterans. On behalf of us all, I want to thank Jimmie and I want to thank your entire leadership team for welcoming me here today. Thank you very much.

Your national adjutant, Dan Wheeler; your executive director, your voice in Washington, Peter Gaytan, who does just an extraordinary job; and the president of the American Legion Auxiliary, Carlene Ashworth, thank you for your extraordinary service. To Rehta Foster and all the spouses, daughters, and sisters of the Auxiliary and the Sons of the American Legion, as military families, you also serve, and we salute all of you as well.

There are some special guests here I want to acknowledge. They may have already been acknowledged, but they're great friends so I want to make sure that I point them out. First of all, the wonderful Governor of Minnesota, Mark Dayton, is here. Two Senators who are working on behalf of veterans every single day, Amy Klobuchar and Al Franken; Congressman Keith Ellison—this is his district; Minneapolis Mayor R.T. Rybak, a great friend; to all the other Members of Congress and Minnesota elected officials who are here, welcome.

It is wonderful to be back with the American Legion. Back in Illinois, my home State—[*applause*]. Hey! Illinois is in the house. [*Laughter*] We worked together to make sure veterans across the State were getting the benefits they had earned. When I was in the U.S. Senate, we worked together to spotlight the tragedy of homelessness among veterans and the need to end it.

As President, I've welcomed Jimmie and your leadership to the Oval Office to hear directly from you. And I have been—[*applause*]—I've been honored to have you by my side when I signed advance appropriations to protect veterans' health care from the budget battles in Washington, when I signed legislation to give new support to veterans and their caregivers, and most recently, when I proposed new initiatives to make sure the private sector is hiring our talented veterans.

So, American Legion, I thank you for your partnership. I appreciate the opportunity to talk with you today about what we need to do to make sure America is taking care of our veterans as well as you've taken care of us.

And I'm grateful to be with you for another reason. A lot of our fellow citizens are still reeling from Hurricane Irene and its aftermath. Folks are surveying the damage. Some are dealing with tremendous flooding. As a Government, we're going to make sure that States and communities have the support they need so their folks can recover.

And across the Nation, we're still digging out from the worst economic crisis since the Great Depression. It's taken longer and it's been more difficult than any of us had imagined. And even though we've taken some steps in the right direction, we've got a lot more to do. Our economy has to grow faster. We have to create more jobs, and we have to do it faster. And most of all, we've got to break the gridlock in Washington that's been preventing us from taking the action we need to get this country moving. That's why next week, I'll be speaking to the Nation about a plan to create jobs and reduce our deficit, a plan that I want to see passed by Congress. We've got to get this done.

And here's what else I know. We Americans have been through tough times before, much tougher than these. And we didn't just get through them, we emerged stronger than before. Not by luck, not by chance, but because in hard times, Americans don't quit. We don't give up. We summon that spirit that says, when we come together, when we choose to move forward together, as one people, there's nothing we can't achieve.

And, Legionnaires, you know this story because it's the story of your lives. And in times like these, all Americans can draw strength from your example. When Hitler controlled a continent and fascism appeared unstoppable, when our harbor was bombed and our Pacific Fleet crippled, there were those that declared that the United States had been reduced to a third-class power. But you, our veterans of World War II, crossed the oceans and stormed the beaches and freed the millions, liberated the camps, and showed the United States of America is the greatest force for freedom that the world has ever known.

When North Korea invaded the South, pushing the allied forces into a tiny sliver of territory, the Pusan Perimeter, it seemed like the war could be lost. But you, our Korean veterans, pushed back, fought on, year after bloody year. And this past Veterans Day, I went to Seoul and joined our Korean war veterans for the 60th anniversary of that war, and we marked that milestone in a free and prosperous Republic of Korea, one of our greatest allies.

When communist forces in Vietnam unleashed the Tet Offensive, it fueled the debate here at home that raged over that war. You, our Vietnam veterans, did not always receive the respect that you deserved, which was a national shame. But let it be remembered that you won every major battle of that war—every single one. As President, I've been honored to welcome our Vietnam veterans to the White House and finally present them with the medals and recognition that they had earned. It's been a chance to convey, on behalf of the American people, those simple words with which our Vietnam veterans greet each other: Welcome home.

Legionnaires, it—in the decades that followed, the spirit of your service was carried forth by our troops in the sands of Desert Storm and the rugged hills of the Balkans. And now, it's carried on by a new generation. Next weekend will mark the 10th anniversary of those awful attacks on our Nation. In the days ahead, we will honor the lives we lost and the families that loved them, the first-responders who rushed to save others, and we will honor all those who have served to keep us safe these 10 difficult years, especially the men and women of our Armed Forces.

Today, as we near this solemn anniversary, it's fitting that we salute the extraordinary decade of service rendered by the 9/11 generation, the more than 5 million Americans who've worn the uniform over the past 10 years. They were there, on duty, that September morning, having enlisted in a time of peace, but they instantly transitioned to a war footing. They're the millions of recruits who have stepped forward since, seeing their Nation at war and saying, "Send me." They're every single soldier, sailor, airman, marine, and coastguardsman serving today who has volunteered to serve in a time of war, knowing that they could be sent into harm's way.

They come from every corner of our country, big cities, small towns. They come from every background and every creed. They're sons and daughters who carry on the family's tradition of service, and they're new immigrants who've become our newest citizens. They're our national guardsmen and reservists, who've served in unprecedented deployments. They're the record number of women in our military, proving themselves in combat like never before. And every day for the past 10 years, these men and women have succeeded together, as one American team.

They're a generation of innovators, and they've changed the way America fights and wins its wars. Raised in the age of the Internet, they've harnessed new technologies on the battlefield. They've learned the cultures and traditions and languages of the places where they served. Trained to fight, they've also taken on the role of diplomats and mayors and development experts, negotiating with tribal sheikhs, working with village *shuras*, partnering with communities. Young captains, sergeants, lieutenants, they've assumed responsibilities once reserved for more senior commanders and remind us that in an era when so many other institutions have shirked their obligations, the men and women of the United States military welcome responsibility.

In a decade of war, they've borne an extraordinary burden, with more than 2 million of our servicemembers deploying to the war zones. Hundreds of thousands have deployed again and again, year after year. Never before has our Nation asked so much of our All-Volunteer Force, that 1 percent of Americans who wears the uniform.

We see the scope of their sacrifice in the tens of thousands who now carry the scars of war, both seen and unseen, our remarkable wounded warriors. We see it in our extraordinary military families who serve here at home, the military spouses who hold their families together, the millions of military children, many of whom have lived most of their young lives with our Nation at war and mom or dad deployed.

Most profoundly, we see the wages of war in those patriots who never came home. They gave their all, their last full measure of devotion, in Kandahar, in the Korengal, in Helmand, in the battles for Baghdad and Fallujah and Ramadi. Now they lay at rest in quiet corners of America, but they live on in the families who loved them and in a nation that is safer because of their service. And today we pay humble tribute to the more than 6,200 Americans in uniform who have given their lives in this hard decade of war. We honor them all. We are grateful for them.

Through their service, through their sacrifice, through their astonishing record of achievement, our forces have earned their place among the greatest of generations: toppling the Taliban in just weeks, driving Al Qaida from the training camps where they plotted 9/11, giving the Afghan people the opportunity to live free from terror. When the decision was made to go into Iraq, our troops raced across deserts and removed a dictator in less than a month. When insurgents, militias and terrorists plunged Iraq into chaos, our troops adapted, they endured ferocious urban combat, they reduced the violence and gave Iraqis a chance to forge their own future.

When a resurgent Taliban threatened to give Al Qaida more space to plot against us, the additional forces I ordered to Afghanistan went on the offensive, taking the fight to the Taliban and pushing them out of their safe havens, allowing Afghans to reclaim their communities and training Afghan forces. And a few months ago, our troops achieved our greatest victory yet in the fight against those who attacked us on 9/11, delivering justice to Usama bin Laden in one of the greatest intelligence and military operations in American history.

Credit for these successes, credit for this progress, belongs to all who have worn the uniform in these wars. Today we're honored to be joined by some of them. And I would ask all those who served this past decade, the members of the 9/11 generation, to stand and accept the thanks of a grateful nation.

Thanks to these Americans, we're moving forward from a position of strength. Having ended our combat mission in Iraq and removed more than 100,000 troops so far, we'll remove the rest of our troops by the end of this year and we will end that war.

Having put Al Qaida on the path to defeat, we won't relent until the job is done. Having started to draw down our forces in Afghanistan, we'll bring home 33,000 troops by next summer and bring home more troops in the coming years. As our mission transitions from combat to support, Afghans will take responsibility for their own security and the longest war in American history will come to a responsible end.

For our troops and military families who've sacrificed so much, this means relief from an unrelenting decade of operations. Today, fewer of our sons and daughters are serving in harm's way. For so many troops who've already done their duty, we've put an end to the stop-loss. And our soldiers can now look forward to shorter deployments. That means more time at home between deployments and more time training for the full range of missions that they will face.

Indeed, despite 10 years of continuous war, it must be said: America's military is the best that it's ever been. We saw that most recently in the skill and precision of our brave forces who helped the Libyan people finally break free from the grip of Muammar Qadhafi. And as we meet the test that the future will surely bring, including hard fiscal choices here at home, there should be no doubt: The United States of America will keep our military the best trained, the best led, the best equipped fighting force in history. It will continue to be the best.

Now, as today's wars end, as our troops come home, we're reminded once more of our responsibilities to all who have served. The bond between our forces and our citizens must be a sacred trust. And for me and my administration, upholding that trust is not just a matter of policy, it is not about politics; it is a moral obligation. That's why my very first budget included the largest percentage increase to the VA budget in the past 30 years. So far, we're on track to have increased funding for Veterans Affairs by 30 percent. And because we passed advanced appropriations, when Washington politics threatens to shut down the Government, as it did last spring, the veterans' medical care that you count on was safe.

And let me say something else about VA funding that you depend on. As a nation, we're facing some tough choices as we put our fiscal house in order. But I want to be absolutely clear: We cannot, we must not, we will not balance the budget on the backs of our veterans. As Commander in Chief, I won't allow it.

With these historic investments, we're making dramatic improvements to veterans' health care. We're improving VA facilities to better serve our women veterans. We're expanding outreach and care for our rural veterans, like those that I met during my recent visit to Cannon Falls, including two proud Legionnaires, Tom Newman of Legion Post 620 in Hugo and Joseph Kidd, Post 164 in Stewartville. Are they here right now? They're out there somewhere. That was a good lunch, by the way. [*Laughter*]

For our Vietnam veterans, because we declared that three diseases are now presumed to be related to your exposure to agent orange, we've begun paying the disability benefits that you need. For our veterans of the Gulf war, we're moving forward to address the nine infectious diseases that we declared are now presumed to be related to your service in Desert Storm.

At the same time, our outstanding VA Secretary, Ric Shinseki, is working every day to build a 21st-century VA. Many of our Vietnam vets are already submitting their agent orange claims electronically. Hundreds of you, from all wars, are requesting your benefits online. Thanks to the new Blue Button on the VA website, you can now share your personal health information with your doctors outside of the VA. And we're making progress in sharing medical records between DOD and VA. We're not there yet. I've been pounding on this thing since I came into office. We are going to stay on it, we're going to keep at it until our troops and our veterans have a lifetime electronic medical record that you can keep for your life.

Of course, we've still got some work to do. We got to break the backlog of disability claims. I know that over the past year, the backlog has actually grown due to new claims from agent orange. But let me say this, and I know Secretary Shinseki agrees: When our veterans who fought for our country have to fight just to get the benefits that you've already earned, that's unacceptable. So this is going to remain a key priority for us.

We're going to keep hiring new claims processors, and we're going to keep investing in new paperless systems and keep moving ahead with our innovation competition, in which our dedicated VA employees are developing new ways to process your claims faster. We want your claims to be processed not in months, but in days. So the bottom line is this: Your claims need to be processed quickly and accurately the first time. We're not going to rest until we get that done. We will not rest.

The same is true for our mission to end homelessness among our veterans. Already, we've helped to bring tens of thousands of veterans off the streets. For the first time ever, we've made veterans and military families a priority not just at the VA, not just at DOD, but across the Federal Government. And that includes making sure that Federal agencies are working together so that every veteran who fought for America has a home in America.

We're working to fulfill our obligations to our 9/11 generation veterans, especially our wounded warriors. The constant threat of IEDs has meant a new generation of servicemembers with multiple traumatic injuries, including traumatic brain injury. And thanks to advanced armor and medical technologies, our troops are surviving injuries that would have been fatal in previous wars. So we're saving more lives, but more American veterans live

with severe wounds for a lifetime. That's why we need to be for them for a lifetime.

We're giving unprecedented support to our wounded warriors, especially those with traumatic brain injury. And thanks to the veterans and caregivers legislation I signed into law, we've started training caregivers so that they can receive the skills and the stipends that they need to care for their loved ones.

We're working aggressively to address another signature wound of this war, which has led to too many fine troops and veterans to take their own lives, and that's posttraumatic stress disorder. We're continuing to make major investments: improving outreach and suicide prevention, hiring and training more mental health counselors, and treating more veterans than ever before.

The days when depression and PTSD were stigmatized, those days must end. That's why I made the decision to start sending condolence letters to the families of servicemembers who take their lives while deployed in a combat zone. These Americans did not die because they were weak. They were warriors. They deserve our respect. Every man and woman in uniform, every veteran, needs to know that your Nation will be there to help you stay strong. It's the right thing to do.

In recent months, we've heard new reports of some of our veterans not getting the prompt mental health care that they desperately need, and that too is unacceptable. If a veteran has the courage to seek help, then we need to be doing everything in our power to deliver the lifesaving mental care that they need. So Secretary Shinseki and the VA are going to stay on this. And we'll continue to make it easier for veterans with posttraumatic stress to qualify for VA benefits, regardless of the war that you served in. If you served in a combat theater and a VA doctor confirms a diagnosis of PTSD, that's enough.

Which brings me to the final area where America must meet its obligations to our veterans, and this is a place where we need each other, and that's the task of renewing our Nation's economic strength. After a decade of war, it's time to focus on nation-building here at home. And our veterans, especially our 9/11 veterans, have the skills and the dedication to help lead the way.

That's why we're funding the post-9/11 GI bill, which is now helping more than 500,000 veterans and family members go to college, get their degrees, and play their part in moving America forward. It's why this fall, we'll start including vocational training and apprenticeships as well, so veterans can develop the skills to succeed in today's economy. And that's why I've directed the Federal Government to hire more veterans, including more than 100,000 veterans in the past year and a half alone.

But in this tough economy, far too many of our veterans are still unemployed. That's why I've proposed a comprehensive initiative to make sure we're tapping the incredible talents of our veterans. And it's got two main parts.

First, we're going to do more to help our newest veterans find and get that private sector job. We're going to offer more help with career development and job searches. I've directed DOD and the VA to create what we're calling a reverse boot camp to help our newest veterans prepare for civilian jobs and translate their exceptional military skills into industry—into industry-accepted licenses and credentials. And today I'm calling on every State to pass legislation that makes it easier for our veterans to get the credentials and the jobs for which they are so clearly qualified. This needs to happen, and it needs to happen now.

Second, we're encouraging the private sector to do its part. So I've challenged companies across America to hire or train 100,000 unemployed veterans or their spouses. And this builds on the commitments that many companies have already made as part of the Joining Forces campaign championed by the First Lady and the Vice President's spouse, Dr. Jill Biden: 100,000 jobs for veterans and spouses. And to get this done, I've proposed a returning heroes tax credit for companies that hire unemployed veterans and a wounded warrior tax credit for companies that hire unemployed veterans with a disability.

When Congress returns from recess, this needs to be at the top of their agenda. For the sake of our veterans, for the sake of our economy, we need these veterans working and contributing and creating the new jobs and industries that will keep America competitive in the 21st century.

These are the obligations we have to each other: our forces, our veterans, our citizens. These are the responsibilities we must fulfill. Not just when it's easy, not just when we're flush with cash, not just when it's convenient, but always.

That's a lesson we learned again this year in the life and in the passing of Frank Buckles, our last veteran from the First World War. He passed away at the age of 110. Think about it. Frank lived the American century. An ambulance driver on the western front, he bore witness to the carnage of the trenches in Europe. Then during the Second World War, he survived more than 3 years in Japanese prisoner-of-war camps. Then, like so many veterans, he came home, went to school, pursued a career, started a family, lived a good life on his farm in West Virginia.

Even in his later years, after turning 100, Frank Buckles still gave back to his country. He'd go speak to schoolchildren about his extraordinary life. He'd meet and inspire other veterans. And for 80 years, he served as a proud member of the American Legion.

The day he was laid to rest, I ordered the flags be flown at halfstaff at the White House, at the Government buildings across the Nation, at our Embassies around the world. As Frank Buckles lay in honor at Arlington's Memorial Chapel, hundreds passed by his flag-draped casket in quiet procession. Most were strangers who never knew him, but they knew the story of his service, and they felt compelled to offer their thanks to this American soldier.

And that afternoon, I had the privilege of going over to Arlington and spending a few moments with Frank's daughter Susannah, who cared for her father to the very end. And it was a chance for me to convey the gratitude of an entire nation and to pay my respects to an American who reflected the best of who we are as a people.

And, Legionnaires, it was a reminder, not just to the family and friends of Corporal Frank Buckles, but to the veterans and families of every generation: No matter when you serve, no matter how many years ago that you took off the uniform, no matter how long you live as a proud veteran of this country we love, America will never leave your side. America will never forget. We will always be grateful to you.

God bless you, God bless all our veterans, and God bless the United States of America.

NOTE: The President spoke at 10:52 a.m. at the Minneapolis Convention Center. In his remarks, he referred to Jimmie L. Foster, national commander, American Legion, and his wife Rehta; and Susannah Flanagan, daughter of Frank W. Buckles.

Statement on the Observance of Eid al-Fitr
August 30, 2011

Michelle and I would like to send Eid greetings to Muslim communities in the United States and around the world. Ramadan has been a time for families and communities to share the happiness of coming together in intense devotion, reflection, and service. Millions all over the world have been inspired to honor their faith by reaching out to those less fortunate. This year, many have observed the month while courageously persevering in their efforts to secure basic necessities and fundamental freedoms. The United States will continue to stand with them and for the dignity and rights of all people, whether a hungry child in the Horn of Africa or a young person demanding freedom in the Middle East and North Africa.

As Ramadan comes to an end, we send our best wishes for a blessed holiday to Muslim communities around the world. *Eid Mubarak*.

Statement on the Selection of Yoshihiko Noda as Prime Minister of Japan
August 30, 2011

I offer my personal congratulations to Yoshihiko Noda on his election as Japan's next Prime Minister. The United States will work with him and the Japanese people on initiatives that benefit our two countries, the region, and the world. For the last half century the U.S.-Japan alliance has served as the linchpin of peace and security in the Asia-Pacific region, and together, we can ensure that the next half-century enjoys the same stability and prosperity. The relationship between the United States and Japan is based on common interests and common values, and I look forward to working with Prime Minister Noda to tackle the broad range of economic and security issues that require our attention.

Letter to the Speaker of the House of Representatives Regarding the Minimization of Regulatory Burdens
August 30, 2011

Dear Mr. Speaker:

Thank you for your letter of August 26, 2011. I agree that it is extremely important to minimize regulatory burdens and to avoid unjustified regulatory costs, particularly in this difficult economic period. I have taken a number of steps to achieve those goals.

Executive Order 13563, issued early this year, imposes a series of new requirements designed to reduce regulatory burdens and costs. As you are undoubtedly aware, this Executive Order also called for an ambitious Government-wide review of rules now on the books. The review was recently completed, producing reform plans from 26 agencies. A mere fraction of the initiatives described in the plans will save more than $10 billion over the next 5 years; as progress continues, we expect to be able to deliver savings far in excess of that figure.

I would add that the costs of final, economically significant rules reviewed by the Office of Information and Regulatory Affairs were actually higher in 2007 and 2008 than in the first 2 years of my Administration. And in 2009 and 2010, the benefits of such rules—including not only monetary savings but also lives saved and illnesses prevented—exceeded the costs by tens of billions of dollars.

Your letter draws attention to the rules listed on this year's regulatory agenda. Under both Republican and Democratic administrations, the agenda is merely a list of rules that are under general contemplation, provided to the public in order to promote transparency. Before any such rules can be issued, they must be subject to a long series of internal and external constraints, including the rulemaking requirements of the Administrative Procedure Act and the new burden-reducing, cost-saving requirements of Executive Order 13563. Many rules listed on an agenda, in any given year, are not issued.

You also ask for a list of pending rules that would cost over $1 billion. As noted, the regulatory agenda includes a large number of rules that are in a highly preliminary state, with no reliable cost estimate. I can assure you that all rules that the Administration promulgates, including and especially the expensive rules, are very carefully scrutinized for conformity to the law and Executive Order 13563.

At the present time, seven rules have been proposed to the public with an estimated annual cost in excess of $1 billion; they are listed as an appendix to this letter. Of course, these rules are merely proposed, and before finalizing any of them, we will take account of public comments and concerns and give careful consideration to cost-saving possibilities and alternatives.

I look forward to working closely with you to produce a regulatory system that will, in the words of Executive Order 13563, "protect public health, welfare, safety, and our environment while promoting economic growth, innovation, competitiveness, and job creation."

Sincerely,

BARACK OBAMA

NOTE: The Office of the Press Secretary also released an annex to this letter.

Remarks on Surface Transportation and Federal Aviation Administration Reauthorization Legislation
August 31, 2011

Good morning, everybody. Please have a seat. I want to say a few words about an issue that affects thousands of American workers, as well as millions of Americans who drive on our Nation's roads and bridges every single day.

At the end of September, if Congress doesn't act, the transportation bill will expire. This bill provides funding for highway construction, bridge repair, mass transit systems, and other essential projects that keep our people and our commerce moving quickly and safely. And for construction workers and their families across the coun-

try, it represents the difference between making ends meet or not making ends meet.

If we allow the transportation bill to expire, over 4,000 workers will be immediately furloughed without pay. If it's delayed for just 10 days, it will lose nearly $1 billion in highway funding. That's money we can never get back. And if it's delayed even longer, almost 1 million workers could lose their jobs over the course of the next year.

That includes some of the folks behind me today. We've got Adam Vencill and Chris Negley, who are with the Federal Highway Administration [KCI Technologies].° We've got Hector Sealey and Austin Anderson, who work for the Fort Myers Construction Company [Fort Myer Construction Corporation].° If we don't extend this bill by the end of September, all of them will be out of a job, just because of politics in Washington.

And that's just not acceptable; that's inexcusable. It's inexcusable to put more jobs at risk in an industry that's already been one of the hardest hit over the last decade. It's inexcusable to cut off necessary investments at a time when so many of our highways are choked with congestion, when so many of our bridges are in need of repair, when so many commuters depend on reliable public transit, and when travel and shipping delays cost businesses billions of dollars every single year.

Now, if this story sounds familiar, that's because we've heard it before. Just a few weeks ago, Congress refused to act on another bill, typically a routine bill, that would have ended up pulling thousands of aviation workers off the job and delaying necessary airport improvement projects across the country. And when Congress finally got their act together, they only funded the FAA until September 16. That's why, when they come back next month, not only do they need to pass the transportation bill, but they've also got to pass a clean extension of that FAA bill—for longer this time—and address back pay for the workers who were laid off during the last shutdown.

At a time when a lot of people in Washington are talking about creating jobs, it's time to stop the political gamesmanship that can actually cost us hundreds of thousands of jobs. This should not be a Democratic issue or a Republican issue. This transportation bill has been renewed seven times in the last 2 years alone. That's why my Secretary of Transportation, Ray LaHood, a Republican, is with me today, along with David Chavern from the Chamber of Commerce and Rich Trumka of the AFL–CIO—two organizations who don't always see eye to eye on things—because they

agree on how important it is for our economy that Congress act now.

So I'm calling on Congress, as soon as they come back, to pass a clean extension of the surface transportation bill, along with a clean extension of the FAA bill, to give workers and communities across America the confidence that vital construction projects won't come to a halt.

After that's done, I'm also proposing that we reform the way transportation money is invested to eliminate waste, to give States more control over the projects that are right for them, and to make sure that we're getting better results for the money that we spend. We need to stop funding projects based on whose districts they're in and start funding them based on how much good they're going to be doing for the American people. No more bridges to nowhere. No more projects that are simply funded because of somebody pulling strings. And we need to do this all in a way that gets the private sector more involved. That's how we're going to put construction workers back to work right now doing the work that America needs done, not just to boost our economy this year, but for the next 20 years.

Finally, in keeping with a recommendation from my jobs council, today I'm directing certain Federal agencies to identify high-priority infrastructure projects that can put people back to work. And these projects—these are projects that are already funded, and with some focused attention, we could expedite the permitting decisions and reviews necessary to get construction underway more quickly while still protecting safety, public health, and the environment.

Tomorrow in Dallas, my jobs council will meet with local jobs—local business owners and other folks about what we've done so far to rebuild our infrastructure and what we can do to make sure that America is moving even faster in getting people back to work.

That's what we're going to need to do in the short term: keep people on the job, keep vital projects moving forward, fund projects that are

---

° White House correction.

already underway in a smarter way. Of course, if we're honest, we also know that when it comes to our Nation's infrastructure—our roads, our railways, mass transit, airports—we shouldn't just be playing patch-up or catch-up, we should be leading the world. Ten years ago, our Nation's infrastructure was ranked 6th globally; today, it's 23d. We invest half as much in our infrastructure as we did 50 years ago, with more than one and a half the number of people. Everybody can see the consequences.

And that's unacceptable for a nation that's always dreamed big and built big, from transcontinental railroads to the Interstate Highway System. And it's unacceptable when countries like China are building high-speed rail networks and gleaming new airports while more than a million construction workers who could be doing the same thing are unemployed right here in America.

And so when Congress is back next week, in addition to passing these clean extensions to prevent any halt on existing work, we're going to have to have a serious conversation in this country about making real, lasting investments in our infrastructure, from better ports to a smarter electric grid, from high-speed Internet to high-speed rail. And at a time when interest rates are low and workers are unemployed, the best time to make those investments is right now, not once another levee fails or another bridge falls. Right now is when we need to be making these decisions.

Now is the time for Congress to extend the transportation bill, keep our workers on the job. Now is the time to put our country before party and to give certainty to the people who are just trying to get by. There is work to be done. There are workers ready to do it. And that's why I expect Congress to act immediately.

And to all the folks who are here on the stage, thank you for the outstanding work you're doing in helping to maintain our Nation's infrastructure.

Thank you very much, everybody.

NOTE: The President spoke at 10:45 a.m. in the Rose Garden at the White House. In his remarks, he referred to David C. Chavern, executive vice president and chief operating officer, U.S. Chamber of Commerce; and Richard L. Trumka, president, AFL–CIO.

Memorandum on Speeding Infrastructure Development Through More Efficient and Effective Permitting and Environmental Review
August 31, 2011

Memorandum for the Heads of Executive Departments and Agencies

Subject: Speeding Infrastructure Development through More Efficient and Effective Permitting and Environmental Review

To maintain our Nation's competitive edge, we must ensure that the United States has fast, reliable ways to move people, goods, energy, and information. In a global economy, where businesses are making investment choices between countries, we will compete for the world's investments based in part on the quality of our infrastructure.

Investing in the Nation's infrastructure brings both immediate and long-term economic benefits—benefits that can accrue not only where the infrastructure is located, but also to communities all across the country. And at a time when job growth must be a top priority, well-targeted investment in infrastructure can be an engine of job creation and economic growth.

In partnership with State, local, and tribal agencies, the Federal Government has a central role to play in ensuring that smart infrastructure projects move as quickly as possible from the drawing board to completion. Through permitting processes, Federal executive departments and agencies (agencies) ensure that projects are designed and constructed consistent with core protections for public health, safety, and the environment. Additionally, the environmental review process requires agencies to consider alternatives and public input, which helps agencies identify project designs that are safe and cost-effective, and that enjoy public support.

In the current economic climate it is critical that agencies take steps to expedite permitting and review, through such strategies as integrating planning and environmental reviews; coordinating multi-agency or multi-governmental reviews and approvals to run concurrently; setting clear schedules for completing steps in the environmental review and permitting process; and utilizing information technologies to inform the public about the progress of environmental reviews as well as the progress of Federal permitting and review processes. Of course, the Federal Government is only one actor in the multifaceted permitting and review processes. Infrastructure projects can be delayed due to project design or uncertain funding, or while awaiting reviews or approvals required by State, local, tribal, or other jurisdictions beyond the control or authority of the Federal Government. Nevertheless, agencies must do everything in their control to ensure that their processes for reviewing infrastructure proposals work efficiently to protect our environment, provide for public participation and certainty of process, ensure safety, and support vital economic growth.

As an immediate step to improve the effectiveness and efficiency of Federal permitting and review processes, this memorandum instructs agencies to (1) identify and work to expedite permitting and environmental reviews for high-priority infrastructure projects with significant potential for job creation; and (2) implement new measures designed to improve accountability, transparency, and efficiency through the use of modern information technology. Relevant agencies should monitor the progress of priority projects; coordinate and resolve issues arising during permitting and environmental review; and develop best practices for expediting these decisions that may be in-

stituted on a wider scale, consistent with applicable law.

Section 1. Expedited Review of High-Priority Infrastructure Projects. (a) Within 30 days of the date of this memorandum, the Secretaries of Agriculture, Commerce, Housing and Urban Development, the Interior, and Transportation shall each select up to three high-priority infrastructure projects subject to review by their respective departments for expedited review based on the criteria outlined in subsection (b) of this section, and shall submit their selections to the Chief Performance Officer, who also serves as the Deputy Director for Management of the Office of Management and Budget.

(b) The secretaries identified in subsection (a) of this section shall select high-priority projects, in consultation with heads of other relevant agencies, based on the following criteria:

    (i) the project will create jobs, with consideration given to the magnitude and timing of the direct and indirect employment impacts;

    (ii) all necessary funding to implement the project has been identified and is reasonably expected to be secured within 6 months of completion of the Federal permitting and review processes; and

    (iii) the significant remaining permit decisions, environmental reviews, consultations, or other actions required before construction can commence on the project are within the control and jurisdiction of the executive branch of the Federal Government and can be efficiently and effectively completed within 18 months of the date of this memorandum, with priority given to projects for which required Federal actions can be completed within 12 months of the date of this memorandum.

(c) All agencies rendering permitting decisions, conducting environmental reviews, completing consultations, or taking other actions related to the high-priority projects selected pursuant to this memorandum shall, consistent with applicable law and to the maximum extent practicable, expedite and coordinate their reviews, decisions, consultations, or other actions, and take related actions as necessary, consistent with available resources, including those actions relating to safety, public health, environmental protection, and public participation.

(d) Agencies, consistent with applicable law, shall use the experience gained from expediting the high-priority projects selected under this memorandum, and from reviewing other projects throughout the permitting process, to identify and implement administrative, policy, technological, and procedural best practices that will improve the efficiency and effectiveness of Federal permitting and environmental review for infrastructure projects, while providing for public participation and protecting public health, safety, and the environment.

Sec. 2. Improving Accountability, Transparency, and Efficiency through Information Technology. To improve the accountability, transparency, and efficiency of Federal permitting and review processes, each agency rendering permitting decisions, conducting environmental reviews, completing consultations, or taking other actions related to any of the projects selected under section 1 of this memorandum shall, consistent with applicable law, make relevant information readily available to the public. To this end:

(a) For each selected high-priority project, within 60 days of the date of this memorandum and on a regular basis thereafter, agencies shall track, and make available to the public on agency websites, information related to the actions required to complete Federal permitting, reviews, and other actions required to proceed with the priority project, including:

(i) a list of all the actions required by each applicable agency to complete Federal permitting, reviews, and other actions necessary to proceed with the project;
(ii) the expected completion date for each such action;
(iii) a point of contact at the agency accountable for each such action; and
(iv) in the event that an action is still pending as of the expected date of completion, a brief explanation of the reasons for the delay.

(b) Within 90 days of the date of this memorandum, the Chief Information Officer (CIO) and the Chief Technology Officer (CTO) shall work with appropriate counterparts at agencies to launch the pilot phase of a centralized, online tool that aggregates the information for each of the priority projects described under section 1 of this memorandum, in a manner that facilitates easy access, enables the public to assess the status of permits required for infrastructure projects, and engages the public in new and creative ways of using the information.

(c) Within 120 days of the date of this memorandum, the Chair of the Council on Environmental Quality, in coordination with the CIO and the CTO, shall work with appropriate counterparts at agencies to deploy in one or more agencies information technology tools with significant potential to reduce the time and cost required to complete permitting and environmental reviews, such as by enabling online submission and processing of public comments, or by allowing personnel from different agencies or jurisdictions to coordinate review timelines, share data, and review documents through a common, internet-based platform.

Agencies shall provide all support, documentation, and assistance necessary to implement these directives.

Sec. 3. General Provisions. (a) This memorandum shall be implemented consistent with applicable law and subject to the availability of appropriations.

(b) Nothing in this memorandum shall be construed to impair or otherwise affect the functions of the Director of the Office of Management and Budget relating to budgetary, administrative, and legislative proposals.

(c) Independent agencies are strongly encouraged to comply with this memorandum.

(d) This memorandum is not intended to, and does not, create any right or benefit, substantive or procedural, enforceable at law or in equity by any party against the United States, its departments, agencies, or entities, its officers, employees, or agents, or any other person.

BARACK OBAMA

Statement on the Ozone National Ambient Air Quality Standards
September 2, 2011

Over the last 2½ years, my administration, under the leadership of EPA Administrator Lisa Jackson, has taken some of the strongest actions since the enactment of the Clean Air Act four decades ago to protect our environment and the health of our families from air pollution. From reducing mercury and other toxic air pollution from outdated power plants to doubling the fuel efficiency of our cars and trucks, the historic steps we've taken will save tens of thousands of lives each year, remove over a billion tons of pollution from our air, and produce hundreds of billions of dollars in benefits for the American people.

At the same time, I have continued to underscore the importance of reducing regulatory burdens and regulatory uncertainty, particularly as our economy continues to recover. With that in mind, and after careful consideration, I have requested that Administrator Jackson withdraw the draft ozone national ambient air quality standards at this time. Work is already underway to update a 2006 review of the science that will result in the reconsideration of the ozone standard in 2013. Ultimately, I did not support asking State and local governments to begin implementing a new standard that will soon be reconsidered.

I want to be clear: My commitment, and the commitment of my administration, to protecting public health and the environment is unwavering. I will continue to stand with the hard-working men and women at the EPA as they strive every day to hold polluters accountable and protect our families from harmful pollution. And my administration will continue to vigorously oppose efforts to weaken EPA's authority under the Clean Air Act or dismantle the progress we have made.

The President's Weekly Address
September 3, 2011

At the end of September, if Congress doesn't act, funding for our roads and bridges will expire. This would put a stop to highway construction, bridge repair, mass transit systems, and other important projects that keep our country moving quickly and safely. And it would affect thousands of construction workers and their families who depend on the jobs created by these projects to make ends meet.

Now, usually, renewing this transportation bill is a no-brainer. In fact, Congress has renewed it seven times over the last 2 years. But thanks to political posturing in Washington, they haven't been able to extend it this time, and the clock's running out.

Allowing this bill to expire would be a disaster for our infrastructure and our economy. Right away, over 4,000 workers would be furloughed without pay. If it's delayed for just 10 days, we will lose nearly $1 billion in highway funding that we can never get back. And if we wait even longer, almost 1 million workers could be in danger of losing their jobs over the next year.

These are serious consequences, and the pain will be felt all across the country. In Virginia, 19,000 jobs are at risk; in Minnesota, more than 12,000; and in Florida, over 35,000 people could be out of work if Congress doesn't act.

That makes no sense, and it's completely avoidable. There's no reason to put more jobs at risk in an industry that has been one of the hardest hit in this recession. There's no reason to cut off funding for transportation projects at a time when so many of our roads are congested, so many of our bridges are in need of repair, and so many businesses are feeling the cost of delays.

This isn't a Democratic or a Republican issue, it's an American issue. That's why last week, I was joined at the White House by representatives from the AFL–CIO and the Chamber of Commerce, two groups who don't see eye to eye on much, but who agree that it's critically important for our economy that Congress act now.

That's also why 128 mayors from both parties wrote to Congress asking them to come together and pass a clean extension. These are local leaders who are on the ground every day and who know what would happen to their communities if Congress fails to act.

So I'm calling on Congress, as soon as they come back, to pass a clean extension of the transportation bill to keep workers on the job, keep critical projects moving forward, and to give folks a sense of security.

There's a lot of talk in Washington these days about creating jobs. But it doesn't help when those same folks turn around and risk losing hundreds of thousands of jobs just because of political gamesmanship. We need to pass this transportation bill and put people to work rebuilding America. We need to put our differences aside and do the right thing for our economy. And now is the time to act.

NOTE: The address was recorded at approximately 5:30 p.m. on September 1 in the Blue Room at the White House, for broadcast on September 3. In the address, the President referred to Richard L. Trumka, president, AFL–CIO; and David C. Chavern, executive vice president and chief operating officer, U.S. Chamber of Commerce. The transcript was made available by the Office of the Press Secretary on September 2, but was embargoed for release until 6 a.m. on September 3.

Remarks Following a Tour of Hurricane Damage and an Exchange With Reporters in Paterson, New Jersey
September 4, 2011

The President. Well, obviously, visiting Wayne, visiting Paterson, many of these surrounding communities, gives you a sense of the devastation that's taken place not only here in New Jersey, but in upstate New York and Vermont and a whole range of States that were affected by Hurricane Irene.

I want to thank Governor Christie, Mayor Jones, the entire congressional delegation that has coordinated in an unprecedented way to try to deal with this crisis. And part of what I think has helped to avert even worse tragedies and greater loss of life is because of the extraordinary responsiveness and farsighted thinking of State, local, and Federal officials. I'm very proud of the work that FEMA has done not only from our central Agency, but more importantly, the folks locally here on the ground who have been coordinating with the emergency management teams here in New Jersey.

I want to thank the Red Cross for their extraordinary responsiveness. We've seen a huge outpouring of volunteers, private sector getting involved in trying to do what they can to help communities that have been hard hit.

The main message that I have for all the residents not only of New Jersey, but all those communities that have been affected by flooding, by the destruction that occurred as a consequence of Hurricane Irene, is that the entire country is behind you and we are going to make sure that we provide all the resources that are necessary in order to help these communities rebuild.

And I know that there's been some talk about whether there's going to be a slowdown in getting funding out here, emergency relief. As President of the United States, I want to make it very clear that we are going to meet our Federal obligations, because we're one country, and when one part of the country gets affected, whether it's a tornado in Joplin, Missouri, or a hurricane that affects the Eastern Seaboard, then we come together as one country and we make sure that everybody gets the help that they need. And the last thing that the residents here of Paterson or the residents of

Vermont or the residents of upstate New York need is Washington politics getting in the way of us making sure that we are doing what we can to help communities that have been badly affected.

So again, I want to thank Federal, State, local officials who've been working round the clock to respond to this crisis. We know it could have been worse, but we should not underestimate the heartache that's going through a lot of these communities and affecting a lot of these families. And we want to make sure that we're there to help, and I'm going to make sure that even after the cameras are gone and attention is somewhere else that FEMA and Federal offi-

cials continue to work with our local officials to make sure we're doing the right thing.

All right? Thank you very much, everybody.

Hurricane Irene Damage and Recovery Efforts

Q. Mr. President, Congressman Cantor——

The President. Thank you, guys.

Q.——has talked about offsetting budget cuts——

The President. We're going to make sure that the resources are here. All right?

NOTE: The President spoke at 1:44 p.m. at the Temple Street Bridge. In his remarks, he referred to Mayor Jeffery Jones of Paterson, NJ.

Remarks on Labor Day in Detroit, Michigan
September 5, 2011

The President. Thank you, Detroit. Thank you, Michigan. Oh, this is a——

Audience members. Four more years!

The President. Thank you. Thank you, everybody. It is good to——

Audience members. Four more years! Four more years! Four more years!

The President. Thank you, everybody. Thank you.

Audience members. Four more years! Four more years! Four more years!

The President. Thank you. Thank you, everybody. I can tell Ghana got you fired up. Thank you, Ghana, for that introduction. Thank you all for having me. It is good to be back in Detroit. I'm glad I was able to bring a friend, a proud daughter of the Teamsters, your Secretary of Labor, Hilda Solis, in the house.

We're thrilled to be joined by so many other friends. I want to acknowledge, first of all, two of the finest Senators in the country: Carl Levin and Debbie Stabenow in the house. Outstanding members of the congressional delegation: John Dingell, John Conyers, Sandy Levin, Gary Peters, and Hansen Clarke.

The president of the Metropolitan Detroit Central Labor Council, our host, Saundra Williams; AFL–CIO president, Rich Trumka; president of the Michigan AFL–CIO, Mark

Gaffney; and some proud sons and daughters of Michigan representing working people here and across the country: SEIU President Mary Kay Henry, Teamsters President Jimmy Hoffa, UAW President Bob King, Utility Workers President Mike Langford. We are proud of them, and we're proud of your congressional delegation, who are working every single day with your State and local elected officials to create jobs and economic growth and prosperity here in Michigan and all across the country.

I am honored, we are honored, to spend this day with you and your families, the working men and women of America. This day belongs to you. You deserve a little R&R, a little barbecue—*[laughter]*—little grilling, because you've been working hard. You've been working hard to make ends meet. You've been working hard to build a better life for your kids. You've been working hard to build a better Detroit. But that's not all I'm going to talk to you about.

I also want to talk about the work you've been doing for decades: work to make sure that folks get an honest day's pay for an honest day's work, work to make sure that families get a fair shake. The work you've done that helped build the greatest middle class the world has ever known. I'm talking about the work that got us a 40-hour workweek and weekends, and paid leave and pensions, and the minimum wage and health insurance, and Social Security and Medicare, the cornerstones of middle class security. That's because of your work.

If you want to know who helped lay these cornerstones of an American middle class you just have to look for the union label.

That's the bedrock this country is built on: hard work, responsibility, sacrifice, looking out for one another, giving everybody a shot, everybody a chance to share in America's prosperity, from the factory floor to the boardroom. That's what unions are all about.

And that's something that's worth keeping in mind today. We've come through a difficult decade in which those values were all too often given short shrift. We've gone through a decade where wealth was valued over work and greed was valued over responsibility. And the decks were too often stacked against ordinary folks in favor of the special interests. And everywhere I went while I was running for this office, I met folks who felt their economic security slipping away, men and women who were fighting harder and harder just to stay afloat. And that was even before the economic crisis hit, and that just made things even harder.

So these are tough times for working Americans. They're even tougher for Americans who are looking for work, and a lot of them have been looking for work for a long time. A lot of folks have been looking for work for a long time here in Detroit and all across Michigan and all across the Midwest and all across the country. So we've got a lot more work to do to recover fully from this recession.

But I'm not satisfied just to get back to where we were before the recession; we've got to fully restore the middle class in America. And America cannot have a strong, growing economy without a strong, growing middle class and without a strong labor movement.

That's the central challenge that we face in our country today. That's at the core of why I ran for President. That's what I've been fighting for since I've been President. Everything we've done, it's been thinking about you. We said working folks deserved a break. So within 1 month of me taking office, we signed into law

the biggest middle class tax cut in history, putting more money into your pockets.

We said working folks shouldn't be taken advantage of, so we passed tough financial reform that ended the days of taxpayer bailouts and stopped credit card companies from gouging you with hidden fees and unfair rate hikes and set up a new consumer protection agency with one responsibility: sticking up for you.

We said that if you're going to work hard all day to provide a better life for your kids, then we're going to make sure that those kids get the best education possible. So we helped keep teachers on the job. We're reforming our public schools, and we're investing in community colleges and job training programs. And we ended wasteful giveaways that went to the big banks and used the savings to make college more affordable for millions of your kids.

We said that every family in America should have affordable, accessible health care. We said you shouldn't be discriminated against because you've got a preexisting condition. We said young adults without insurance should be able to stay on their parent's plan. We got that done for you.

And here's what else we said, Detroit. We said that American autoworkers could once again build the best cars in the world. So we stood by the auto industry. And we made some tough choices that were necessary to make it succeed. And now the Big Three are turning a profit and hiring new workers and building the best cars in the world right here in Detroit, right here in the Midwest, right here in the United States of America.

I know it. I've seen it. I've been to GM's Hamtramck plant. I've been to Chrysler's Jefferson North plant. I've seen Detroit prove the cynics and the naysayers wrong.

We didn't just stop there. We said American workers could manufacture the best products in the world. So we invested in high-tech manufacturing, and we invested in clean energy. And right now, there's an advanced battery industry taking root here in Michigan that barely existed before. Half of the workers at one plant in Detroit were unemployed before a new battery company came to town. And we're growing our exports so that more of the world buys products that are stamped with three simple words: Made in America.

So that's what we're fighting for, Michigan. We're fighting for good jobs with good wages. We're fighting for health care when you get sick. We're fighting for a secure retirement even if you're not rich. We're fighting for the chance to give our kids a better life than we had. That's what we're doing to restore middle class security and rebuild this economy the American way, based on balance and fairness and the same set of rules for everybody from Wall Street to Main Street, an economy where hard work pays off, and gaming the system doesn't pay off, and everybody has got a shot at the American Dream. That's what we're fighting for.

On Thursday, we're going to lay out a new way forward on jobs to grow the economy and put more Americans back to work right now. I don't want to give everything away right here, because I want you all to tune in on Thursday, but I'll give you just a little bit.

We've got roads and bridges across this country that need rebuilding. We've got private companies with the equipment and the manpower to do the building. We've got more than 1 million unemployed construction workers ready to get dirty right now. There is work to be done, and there are workers ready to do it. Labor is on board. Business is on board. We just need Congress to get on board. Let's put America back to work.

Last year, we worked together, Republicans and Democrats, to pass a payroll tax cut. And because of that, this year the average family has an extra $1,000 in their pocket because of it. But that's going to expire in a few months if we don't come together to extend it. And I think putting money back in the pockets of working families is the best way to get demand rising, because that then means business is hiring, and that means the Government—that means that the economy is growing.

So I'm going to propose ways to put America back to work that both parties can agree to, because I still believe both parties can work together to solve our problems. And given the urgency of this moment, given the hardship that many people are facing, folks have got to get together.

But we're not going to wait for them. We're going to see if we've got some straight shooters in Congress. We're going to see if congressional Republicans will put country before party. We'll give them a plan, and then we'll say, do you want to create jobs? Then put our construction workers back to work rebuilding America. Do you want to help our companies succeed? Open up new markets for them to sell their products. You want—you say you're the party of tax cuts? Well then, prove you'll fight just as hard for tax cuts for middle class families as you do for oil companies and the most affluent Americans. Show us what you got.

The time for Washington games is over; the time for action is now. No more manufactured crises. No more games. Now is not the time for the people you sent to Washington to worry about their jobs, now is the time for them to worry about your jobs.

Now, let me say a word about labor in particular. Now, I know this is not going to be an easy time. I know it's not easy when there's some folks who have their sights trained on you. After all that unions have done to build and protect the middle class, you've got people trying to claim that you're responsible for the problems middle class folks are facing. You've got some Republicans saying you're the ones exploiting working families. Imagine that.

Now, the fact is, our economy is stronger when workers are getting paid good wages and good benefits. Our economy is stronger when we've got broad-based growth and broad-based prosperity. That's what unions have always been about: shared prosperity.

You know, I was on the plane flying over here, and Carl Levin was with me, and he showed me a speech that Harry Truman had given on Labor Day 63 years ago, right here in Detroit—63 years ago. And just to show that things haven't changed much, he talked about how Americans had voted in some folks into Congress who weren't very friendly to labor. And he pointed out that some working folks and even some union members voted these folks in. And now they were learning their lesson. And he pointed out that—and I'm quoting here—"the gains of labor were not accomplished at the expense of the rest of the Nation. Labor's gains contributed to the Nation's general prosperity."

What was true in—back in 1948 is true in 2011. When working families are doing well, when they're getting a decent wage and they're getting decent benefits, that means they're good customers for businesses. That means they can buy the cars that you build. That means that you can buy the food from the farmers. That means you can buy from Silicon Valley, that you are creating prosperity when you share in prosperity.

So when I hear some of these folks trying to take collective bargaining rights away, trying to pass so-called "right to work" laws for private sector workers, that really means the right to work for less and less and less. When I hear some of this talk, I know this is not about economics, this is about politics.

And I want everybody here to know, as long as I'm in the White House I'm going to stand up for collective bargaining.

Audience members. Four more years! Four more years! Four more years!

The President. That's why we've reversed harmful decisions that were designed to undermine those rights. That's why we passed the Fair Pay Act to stop pay discrimination. That's why we appointed people who are actually fulfilling their responsibilities to make sure that the offices and factories and mine workers that clock in each day, that they're actually safe on the job.

And we're going to keep at it. Because having a voice on the job and a chance to organize and a chance to negotiate for a fair day's pay after a hard day's work, that is the right of every man and woman in America, not just the CEO in the corner office, but also the janitor who cleans that office after the CEO goes home. Everybody has got the same right.

And that's true for public employees as well. Look, the recession had a terrible effect on State and local budgets; we all understand that.

Unions have recognized that; they've already made tough concessions. In the private sector, we live in a more competitive global economy. So unions like the UAW understand that workers have to work with management to revamp business models, to innovate so we can sell our products around the world. We understand that the world is changing; unions understand that the world is changing. Unions understand they need to help drive the change, whether it's on the factory floor or in the classroom or in the Government office.

But what unions also know is that the values at the core of the union movement, those don't change. Those are the values that have made this country great. That's what the folks trying to undermine your rights don't understand. When union workers agree to pay freezes and pay cuts, they're not doing it just to keep their jobs. They're doing it so that their fellow workers—their fellow Americans—can keep their jobs.

When teachers agree to reforms in how schools are run at the same time as they're digging into their pockets to buy school supplies for those kids, they do so because they believe every child can learn. They do it because they know something that those who seek to divide us don't understand: We are all in this together. That's why those crowds came out to support you in Madison and in Columbus. We are one Nation. We are one people. We will rise and we will fall together.

Anyone who doesn't believe it should come here to Detroit. It's like the commercial says: This is a city that's been to heck and back. And while there are a lot of challenges here, I see a city that's coming back.

You ask somebody here if times are tough, they'll say, yes, it's tough, but we're tougher. Look at what we're doing to overcome. Look at what we're doing to rebuild and reinvent and redefine what it means to live in this great city. Look at our parents who catch the first bus to work and our students who stay up late to earn a degree. Look at our workers on the line at Hamtramck and Jefferson North who are building the best cars in the world. Look at our artists who are revamping our city and our young people who are thinking up new ways to make a difference that we never dreamed of. Look how we look out for one another.

That's why we chose Detroit as one of the cities that we're helping revitalize in our Strong Cities, Strong Communities initiative. We're teaming up with everybody—mayors, local officials, you name it—boosting economic development, rebuilding your communities the best way, which is a way that involves you. Because despite all that's changed here, and all the work that lies ahead, this is still a city where men clocked into factories. This is the city that built the greatest middle class the world has ever known. This is the city where women rolled up their sleeves and helped build an arsenal for democracy to free the world. This is a city where the great American industry has come back to life and the industries of tomorrow are taking root. This is a city where people, brave and bold, courageous and clever, are dreaming up ways to prove the skeptics wrong and write the next proud chapter in our history.

That's why I wanted to be here with you today. Because for every cynic and every naysayer running around talking about how our best days are behind us, for everybody who keeps going around saying, "No, we can't"——

Audience members. Yes, we can!

The President. ——for everybody who can always find a reason why we can't rebuild America, I meet Americans every day who, in the face of impossible odds, they've got a different belief. They believe we can. You believe we can.

Yes, times are tough. But we've been through tough times before. I don't know about you, but I'm not scared of tough times. I'm not scared of tough times because I know we're going to be all marching together and walking together and working together and rebuilding together. And I know we don't quit. I know we don't give up our dreams and settle for something less. We roll up our sleeves, and we remember a fundamental truth of our history: We are strong when we are united. We're firing all cylinders.

The union movement is going to be at the center of it. And if all of you are committed to making sure that the person standing next to you, and their kids and their grandkids, that everybody in this city and everybody in this country can unleash his or her potential, if you work hard and play by the rules, you will get a fair shake and get a fair shot. That's the country I want for my kids. That's the country you want for your kids. That's the country we're going to build together.

Thank you very much, Detroit. God bless you, and God bless the United States of America.

NOTE: The President spoke at 1:30 p.m. in a parking lot at the General Motors Plant. In his remarks, he referred to UAW member Ghana Goodwin-Dye.

Statement on Former Secretary of Defense Robert M. Gates
September 6, 2011

I congratulate Robert Gates on his selection as the 24th chancellor of the College of William & Mary. In Bob, one of our Nation's oldest colleges has found one of our Nation's finest public servants. I'm confident that Bob will bring to this new role the same sense of duty and personal integrity that I and other Presidents valued during his distinguished career in Government. As he did at Texas A&M and the Department of Defense, Bob will again help lead an institution devoted to our Nation's most precious resource: our young men and women. I wish Bob the very best as he begins this new chapter at his alma mater, which helped to inspire his commitment to public service five decades ago.

Remarks Honoring the 2010 NASCAR Sprint Cup Series Champion
September 7, 2011

The President. Thank you, everybody. Please, have a seat. Have a seat. Welcome to the White House, and congratulations to Jimmie Johnson on winning his fifth straight Sprint Cup Championship.

Before we start, I do want to acknowledge some people who are here today. First of all, an outstanding American, somebody who's been a great friend and adviser to me, General Ray Odierno, the incoming Army Chief of Staff, is here. So please give him a big round of applause. We've got a host of Members of Congress. I'm not going to name them all, but they're all big NASCAR fans. They're right here in the front row.

Brian France, the CEO of NASCAR, and his wife Amy couldn't make it here because of the storm. But I want to thank them for everything that they do.

It's great to welcome NASCAR back to Washington. It's great to have Number 48 parked outside. [*Laughter*] I was just telling these guys I'm not allowed to drive much these days—[*laughter*]—basically just my golf cart at Camp David, which is called Golf Cart One. [*Laughter*] True. [*Laughter*] But I will say that it's pretty tough to look at Number 48 and not want to jump in and take a few laps, although I'm sure Jimmie would not be happy if I was doing that.

The last time many of these drivers were here, Jimmie was celebrating his third straight championship. He's got a couple more titles under his belt now. But another big change in the Johnson house: He and Chandra are now parents of Genevieve Marie, who was born late July. So congratulations on that.

I told Jimmie you cannot beat daughters. And I know Jimmie is pretty excited to be a daddy. He whipped out, like, the iPhone with the pictures on it the minute I asked about it. [*Laughter*] I hear that he is in charge of taking Genevieve Marie to music class. And because of his unique work schedule, Jimmie is usually the only dad there, so—[*laughter*]. But that's a good sign of being a good dad.

So Jimmie's got a lot to be proud of. And that's especially true when you think of what it means to win five championships in a row. NASCAR is a sport where anything that can go wrong will go wrong at some point during the season—similar to being President. [*Laughter*] That's true even for the best drivers. And with so much extraordinary talent that is going bumper to bumper in every race, just making the Chase is hard enough, let alone winning the whole thing.

And that's why Jimmie is not just one of the best drivers of all time, he's up there with some of the great sports dynasties. If you think about it, the—only the Boston Celtics, the Yankees, and the Canadiens have ever won more than four titles in a row. And now Jimmie's breathing down the necks of Dale Earnhardt and Richard Petty for the most NASCAR titles ever, which is not bad for the son of a machine operator and a school bus driver who still has plenty of seasons ahead of him.

Jimmie's talent has been to make a very difficult, demanding sport look easy. But this year, the Number 48 team also showed its toughness. They entered the last race of the Chase trailing and ended up pulling off an extraordinary comeback.

And if you ask Jimmie, he'll give credit to that team, led by owner Rick Hendrick and crew chief Chad Knaus, who couldn't be here today. We also need to give credit, though, to the other Chase drivers up here who want Jimmie to know that the second he makes a mistake, they will be ready to knock him out of the victory lane. [*Laughter*]

I did observe that lately there's been some trash-talking in NASCAR. [*Laughter*] I was—I thought I was watching WWF. [*Laughter*] But that's good. You got to have a little feistiness, and these guys are extraordinary competitors. And that's what makes this sport so exciting to watch, because everything can come down to just one race, one pit stop, one split-second decision.

Now, what also makes NASCAR special is the difference that it makes in the lives of so many people, especially our troops and their families. And I personally thanked all these guys for what they've been doing on behalf of military families, who are obviously huge fans of NASCAR.

Last month, the drivers and staff toured Walter Reed hospital, served dinner to 400 wounded warriors and their loved ones. NASCAR has been a huge supporter of the Joining Forces program that Michelle and Dr. Jill Biden have set up to support military families. This morning Jimmie made a special visit to the Pentagon to spend time with folks over there. And later this week, NASCAR will be honoring our military and first-responders again in Richmond the night before the anniversary of 9/11.

So I want to congratulate Jimmie. I want to congratulate all the drivers who are on the stage for their extraordinary success, for the success of NASCAR, and for everything that they do for our country.

Good luck heading into this year's Chase, everybody. We will all be watching.

So thank you very much. And I think—Jimmie, do you want to——

Jimmie Johnson. Yes.

The President. ——tell me what you got here?

Mr. Johnson. Absolutely. Well, first of all, thank you for having us here. We all greatly appreciate it. And on behalf of myself and our race team, the Lowe's Hendrick Motorsports team, we have some gloves here that were worn in Las Vegas when I won. I wanted to present them to go——

The President. That's pretty sharp.

Mr. Johnson. ——with the helmet we gave to you last time we were here.

The President. I will wear the helmet and the gloves—[*laughter*]—when I'm——

Mr. Johnson. Halloween?

The President. ——driving—no, "Golf Cart One." [*Laughter*]

Mr. Johnson. Fantastic.

The President. Absolutely.

Mr. Johnson. Be safe.

NOTE: The President spoke at 4:45 p.m. in the East Room at the White House. In his remarks, he referred to Gary and Cathy Johnson, parents of Jimmie Johnson; and Jill T. Biden, wife of Vice President Joe Biden. He also referred to the WWF, the World Wrestling Federation, the former name of the professional wrestling company WWE, Inc.

Address Before a Joint Session of the Congress on Job Growth
September 8, 2011

Mr. Speaker, Mr. Vice President, Members of Congress, and fellow Americans: Tonight we meet at an urgent time for our country. We continue to face an economic crisis that has left millions of our neighbors jobless and a political crisis that's made things worse.

This past week, reporters have been asking: "What will this speech mean for the President? What will it mean for Congress? How will it affect their polls and the next election?"

But the millions of Americans who are watching right now, they don't care about politics. They have real-life concerns. Many have spent months looking for work. Others are doing their best just to scrape by: giving up nights out with the family to save on gas or make the

mortgage, postponing retirement to send a kid to college.

These men and women grew up with faith in an America where hard work and responsibility paid off. They believed in a country where everyone gets a fair shake and does their fair share, where if you stepped up, did your job, and were loyal to your company, that loyalty would be rewarded with a decent salary and good benefits, maybe a raise once in a while. If you did the right thing, you could make it. Anybody could make it in America.

For decades now, Americans have watched that compact erode. They have seen the decks too often stacked against them. And they know that Washington has not always put their interests first.

The people of this country work hard to meet their responsibilities. The question tonight is whether we'll meet ours. The question is whether, in the face of an ongoing national crisis, we can stop the political circus and actually do something to help the economy. The question is whether we can restore some of the fairness and security that has defined this Nation since our beginning.

Those of us here tonight can't solve all our Nation's woes. Ultimately, our recovery will be driven not by Washington, but by our businesses and our workers. But we can help. We can make a difference. There are steps we can take right now to improve people's lives.

I am sending this Congress a plan that you should pass right away. It's called the "American Jobs Act." There should be nothing controversial about this piece of legislation. Everything in here is the kind of proposal that's been supported by both Democrats and Republicans, including many who sit here tonight. And everything in this bill will be paid for—everything.

The purpose of the "American Jobs Act" is simple: to put more people back to work and more money in the pockets of those who are working. It will create more jobs for construction workers, more jobs for teachers, more jobs for veterans, and more jobs for long-term unemployed. It will provide a tax break for companies who hire new workers, and it will cut payroll taxes in half for every working American and every small business. It will provide a jolt to an economy that has stalled and give companies confidence that if they invest and if they hire, there will be customers for their products and services. You should pass this jobs plan right away.

Everyone here knows that small businesses are where most new jobs begin. And you know that while corporate profits have come roaring back, smaller companies haven't. So for everyone who speaks so passionately about making life easier for "job creators," this plan is for you.

Pass this jobs bill—[*applause*]—pass this jobs bill, and starting tomorrow, small businesses will get a tax cut if they hire new workers or if they raise workers' wages. Pass this jobs bill, and all small-business owners will also see their payroll taxes cut in half next year. If you have 50 employees making an average salary, that's an $80,000 tax cut. And all businesses will be able to continue writing off the investments they make in 2012.

It's not just Democrats who have supported this kind of proposal. Fifty House Republicans have proposed the same payroll tax cut that's in this plan. You should pass it right away.

Pass this jobs bill, and we can put people to work rebuilding America. Everyone here knows we have badly decaying roads and bridges all over the country. Our highways are clogged with traffic. Our skies are the most congested in the world. It's an outrage.

Building a world-class transportation system is part of what made us a economic superpower. And now we're going to sit back and watch China build newer airports and faster railroads, at a time when millions of unemployed construction workers could build them right here in America?

There are private construction companies all across America just waiting to get to work. There's a bridge that needs repair between Ohio and Kentucky that's on one of the busiest trucking routes in North America. A public transit project in Houston that will help clear up one of the worst areas of traffic in the country. And there are schools throughout this country that desperately need renovating. How can we expect our kids to do their best in places that are literally falling apart? This is America. Every child deserves a great school. And we can give it to them if we act now.

The "American Jobs Act" will repair and modernize at least 35,000 schools. It will put people to work right now fixing roofs and windows, installing science labs and high-speed Internet in classrooms all across this country. It will rehabilitate homes and businesses in communities hit hardest by foreclosures. It will jump-start thousands of transportation projects all across the country. And to make sure the money is properly spent, we're building on reforms we've already put in place. No more earmarks. No more boondoggles. No more bridges to nowhere. We're cutting the redtape that prevents some of these projects from getting started as quickly as possible. And we'll set up an independent fund to attract private dollars and issue loans based on two criteria: how badly a construction project is needed and how much good it will do for the economy.

This idea came from a bill written by a Texas Republican and a Massachusetts Democrat. The idea for a big boost in construction is supported by America's largest business organization and America's largest labor organization. It's the kind of proposal that's been supported in the past by Democrats and Republicans alike. You should pass it right away.

Pass this jobs bill, and thousands of teachers in every State will go back to work. These are the men and women charged with preparing our children for a world where the competition has never been tougher. But while they're adding teachers in places like South Korea, we're laying them off in droves. It's unfair to our kids. It undermines their future and ours. And it has to stop. Pass this bill, and put our teachers back in the classroom where they belong.

Pass this jobs bill, and companies will get extra tax credits if they hire America's veterans. We ask these men and women to leave their careers, leave their families, risk their lives to fight for our country. The last thing they should have to do is fight for a job when they come home.

Pass this bill, and hundreds of thousands of disadvantaged young people will have the hope and the dignity of a summer job next year. And their parents, low-income Americans who desperately want to work, will have more ladders out of poverty.

Pass this jobs bill, and companies will get a $4,000 tax credit if they hire anyone who has spent more than 6 months looking for a job. We have to do more to help the long-term unemployed in their search for work. This jobs plan builds on a program in Georgia that several Republican leaders have highlighted, where people who collect unemployment insurance participate in temporary work as a way to build their skills while they look for a permanent job. The plan also extends unemployment insurance for another year. If the millions of unemployed Americans stopped getting this insurance and stopped using that money for basic necessities, it would be a devastating blow to this economy. Democrats and Republicans in this Chamber have supported unemployment insurance plenty of times in the past. And in this time of prolonged hardship, you should pass it again right away.

Pass this jobs bill, and the typical working family will get a $1,500 tax cut next year. Fifteen hundred dollars that would have been taken out of your pocket will go into your pocket. This expands on the tax cut that Democrats and Republicans already passed for this year. If we allow that tax cut to expire—if we refuse to act—middle class families will get hit with a tax increase at the worst possible time. We can't let that happen. I know that some of you have sworn oaths to never raise any taxes on anyone for as long as you live. Now is not the time to carve out an exception and raise middle class taxes, which is why you should pass this bill right away.

This is the "American Jobs Act." It will lead to new jobs for construction workers, for teachers, for veterans, for first-responders, young people and the long-term unemployed. It will provide tax credits to companies that hire new workers, tax relief to small-business owners, and tax cuts for the middle class.

And here's the other thing I want the American people to know: The "American Jobs Act" will not add to the deficit. It will be paid for. And here's how: The agreement we passed in July will cut Government spending by about $1 trillion over the next 10 years. It also charges this Congress to come up with an additional $1.5 trillion in savings by Christmas. Tonight I am asking you to increase that amount so that it covers the full cost of the "American Jobs Act." And a week from Monday, I'll be releasing a more ambitious deficit plan, a plan that will not only cover the cost of this jobs bill, but stabilize our debt in the long run.

1039

This approach is basically the one I've been advocating for months. In addition to the trillion dollars of spending cuts I've already signed into law, it's a balanced plan that would reduce the deficit by making additional spending cuts, by making modest adjustments to health care programs like Medicare and Medicaid, and by reforming our Tax Code in a way that asks the wealthiest Americans and biggest corporations to pay their fair share. What's more, the spending cuts wouldn't happen so abruptly that they'd be a drag on our economy or prevent us from helping small businesses and middle class families get back on their feet right away.

Now, I realize there are some in my party who don't think we should make any changes at all to Medicare and Medicaid, and I understand their concerns. But here's the truth: Millions of Americans rely on Medicare in their retirement, and millions more will do so in the future. They pay for this benefit during their working years. They earn it. But with an aging population and rising health care costs, we are spending too fast to sustain the program. And if we don't gradually reform the system while protecting current beneficiaries, it won't be there when future retirees need it. We have to reform Medicare to strengthen it.

I am also well aware that there are many Republicans who don't believe we should raise taxes on those who are most fortunate and can best afford it. But here is what every American knows: While most people in this country struggle to make ends meet, a few of the most affluent citizens and most profitable corporations enjoy tax breaks and loopholes that nobody else gets. Right now Warren Buffett pays a lower tax rate than his secretary, an outrage he has asked us to fix. [*Laughter*] We need a Tax Code where everyone gets a fair shake and where everybody pays their fair share. And by the way, I believe the vast majority of wealthy Americans and CEOs are willing to do just that if it helps the economy grow and gets our fiscal house in order.

I'll also offer ideas to reform a corporate Tax Code that stands as a monument to special interest influence in Washington. By eliminating pages of loopholes and deductions, we can lower one of the highest corporate tax rates in the world. Our Tax Code should not give an advantage to companies that can afford the best connected lobbyists. It should give an advantage to companies that invest and create jobs right here in the United States of America.

So we can reduce this deficit, pay down our debt, and pay for this jobs plan in the process. But in order to do this, we have to decide what our priorities are. We have to ask ourselves, "What's the best way to grow the economy and create jobs?"

Should we keep tax loopholes for oil companies, or should we use that money to give small-business owners a tax credit when they hire new workers? Because we can't afford to do both. Should we keep tax breaks for millionaires and billionaires, or should we put teachers back to work so our kids can graduate ready for college and good jobs? Right now we can't afford to do both.

This isn't political grandstanding. This isn't class warfare. This is simple math. [*Laughter*] This is simple math. These are real choices. These are real choices that we've got to make. And I'm pretty sure I know what most Americans would choose. It's not even close. And it's time for us to do what's right for our future.

Now, the "American Jobs Act" answers the urgent need to create jobs right away. But we can't stop there. As I've argued since I ran for this office, we have to look beyond the immediate crisis and start building an economy that lasts into the future, an economy that creates good, middle class jobs that pay well and offer security. We now live in a world where technology has made it possible for companies to take their business anywhere. If we want them to start here and stay here and hire here, we have to be able to outbuild and outeducate and outinnovate every other country on Earth.

And this task of making America more competitive for the long haul, that's a job for all of us, for Government and for private companies, for States and for local communities, and for every American citizen. All of us will have to up our game. All of us will have to change the way we do business.

My administration can and will take some steps to improve our competitiveness on our own. For example, if you're a small-business owner who has a contract with the Federal Government, we're going to make sure you get paid a lot faster than you do right now. We're also planning to cut away the redtape that prevents too many rapidly growing startup companies from raising capital and going public. And to help responsible homeowners, we're going to work with Federal housing agencies to help more people refinance their mortgages at interest rates that are now near 4 percent. That's a step—[*applause*]—I know you guys must be for this, because that's a step that can put more than $2,000 a year in a family's pocket and give a lift to an economy still burdened by the drop in housing prices.

So some things we can do on our own. Other steps will require congressional action. Today you passed reform that will speed up the outdated patent process, so that entrepreneurs can turn a new idea into a new business as quickly as possible. That's the kind of action we need. Now it's time to clear the way for a series of trade agreements that would make it easier for American companies to sell their products in Panama and Colombia and South Korea, while also helping the workers whose jobs have been affected by global competition. If Americans can buy Kias and Hyundais, I want to see folks in South Korea driving Fords and Chevys and Chryslers. I want to see more products sold around the world stamped with the three proud words: Made in America. That's what we need to get done.

And on all of our efforts to strengthen competitiveness, we need to look for ways to work side by side with America's businesses. That's why I've brought together a jobs council of leaders from different industries who are developing a wide range of new ideas to help companies grow and create jobs.

Already, we've mobilized business leaders to train 10,000 American engineers a year, by providing company internships and training. Other businesses are covering tuition for workers who learn new skills at community colleges. And we're going to make sure the next genera-

tion of manufacturing takes root not in China or Europe, but right here in the United States of America. If we provide the right incentives, the right support—and if we make sure our trading partners play by the rules—we can be the ones to build everything from fuel-efficient cars to advanced biofuels to semiconductors that we sell all around the world. That's how America can be number one again. And that's how America will be number one again.

Now, I realize that some of you have a different theory on how to grow the economy. Some of you sincerely believe that the only solution to our economic challenges is to simply cut most Government spending and eliminate most Government regulations.

Well, I agree that we can't afford wasteful spending, and I'll work with you, with Congress, to root it out. And I agree that there are some rules and regulations that do put an unnecessary burden on businesses at a time when they can least afford it. That's why I ordered a review of all Government regulations. So far, we've identified over 500 reforms, which will save billions of dollars over the next few years. We should have no more regulation than the health, safety, and security of the American people require. Every rule should meet that commonsense test.

But what we can't do—what I will not do—is let this economic crisis be used as an excuse to wipe out the basic protections that Americans have counted on for decades. I reject the idea that we need to ask people to choose between their jobs and their safety. I reject the argument that says for the economy to grow, we have to roll back protections that ban hidden fees by credit card companies, or rules that keep our kids from being exposed to mercury, or laws that prevent the health insurance industry from shortchanging patients. I reject the idea that we have to strip away collective bargaining rights to compete in a global economy. We shouldn't be in a race to the bottom, where we try to offer the cheapest labor and the worst pollution standards. America should be in a race to the top. And I believe we can win that race.

In fact, this larger notion that the only thing we can do to restore prosperity is just dismantle Government, refund everybody's money, and let everyone write their own rules, and tell everyone they're on their own, that's not who we are. That's not the story of America.

Yes, we are rugged individualists. Yes, we are strong and self-reliant. And it has been the drive and initiative of our workers and entrepreneurs that has made this economy the engine and the envy of the world. But there's always been another thread running throughout our history, a belief that we're all connected and that there are some things we can only do together as a nation.

We all remember Abraham Lincoln as the leader who saved our Union, founder of the Republican Party. But in the middle of a Civil War, he was also a leader who looked to the future; a Republican President who mobilized Government to build the transcontinental railroad, launch the National Academy of Sciences, set up the first land-grant colleges. And leaders of both parties have followed the example he set.

Ask yourselves: Where would we be right now if the people who sat here before us decided not to build our highways, not to build our bridges, our dams, our airports? What would this country be like if we had chosen not to spend money on public high schools or research universities or community colleges? Millions of returning heroes, including my grandfather, had the opportunity to go to school because of the GI bill. Where would we be if they hadn't had that chance?

How many jobs would it have cost us if past Congresses decided not to support the basic research that led to the Internet and the computer chip? What kind of country would this be if this Chamber had voted down Social Security or Medicare just because it violated some rigid idea about what government could or could not do? How many Americans would have suffered as a result?

No single individual built America on their own. We built it together. We have been and always will be "one Nation under God, indivisi-

ble, with liberty and justice for all," a nation with responsibilities to ourselves and with responsibilities to one another. And Members of Congress, it is time for us to meet our responsibilities.

Every proposal I've laid out tonight is the kind that's been supported by Democrats and Republicans in the past. Every proposal I've laid out tonight will be paid for. And every proposal is designed to meet the urgent needs of our people and our communities.

Now, I know there's been a lot of skepticism about whether the politics of the moment will allow us to pass this jobs plan or any jobs plan. Already, we're seeing the same old press releases and tweets flying back and forth. Already, the media has proclaimed that it's impossible to bridge our differences. And maybe some of you have decided that those differences are so great that we can only resolve them at the ballot box.

But know this: The next election is 14 months away. And the people who sent us here—the people who hired us to work for them—they don't have the luxury of waiting 14 months. Some of them are living week to week, paycheck to paycheck, even day to day. They need help, and they need it now.

I don't pretend that this plan will solve all our problems. It should not be, nor will it be, the last plan of action we propose. What's guided us from the start of this crisis hasn't been the search for a silver bullet. It's been a commitment to stay at it, to be persistent, to keep trying every new idea that works and listen to every good proposal, no matter which party comes up with it.

Regardless of the arguments we've had in the past, regardless of the arguments we will have in the future, this plan is the right thing to do right now. You should pass it. And I intend to take that message to every corner of this country. And I ask every American who agrees to lift your voice: Tell the people who are gathered here tonight that you want action now. Tell Washington that doing nothing is not an option. Remind us that if we act as one Nation and one people, we have it within our power to meet this challenge.

President Kennedy once said: "Our problems are manmade, therefore they can be solved by man. And man can be as big as he wants."

These are difficult years for our country. But we are Americans. We are tougher than the times we live in, and we are bigger than our politics have been. So let's meet the moment. Let's get to work, and let's show the world once again why the United States of America remains the greatest nation on Earth.

Thank you very much. God bless you, and God bless the United States of America.

NOTE: The President spoke at 7:09 p.m. in the House Chamber of the U.S. Capitol. In his remarks, he referred to Sens. Kathryn A. "Kay" Bailey Hutchison and John F. Kerry; and Warren E. Buffett, chief executive officer and chairman, Berkshire Hathaway Inc.

Remarks at the University of Richmond in Richmond, Virginia
September 9, 2011

The President. Hello, Richmond! Thank you. Thank you, Richmond. Well, it is good to be in Richmond, Virginia. Thank you, Nigel, for that outstanding introduction. Give Nigel a big round of applause.

Everybody is a special guest, but there are a few people I want to acknowledge: First of all, the outstanding president of the University of Richmond, Ed Ayers; the mayor of Richmond, Dwight Jones, is in the house; former Governor of Virginia, and one of my greatest friends, the first person to endorse me outside of Illinois, my home State—right here in Richmond, Virginia—Tim Kaine; and his lovely wife Anne, who I love more. And another history maker and outstanding former Governor, Doug Wilder is in the house.

Now—you guys can sit down, by the way, if you want. [*Laughter*] But you don't have seats—don't—you guys don't sit down. [*Laughter*]

It is good to be here in Virginia, first of all, because the sun is out. I have not seen sun in about 5 days. So it was nice to remember what that's like. It is always nice to get out of Washington once in a while, be with the American people. And I have great memories of Richmond, and I have wonderful feelings about the Commonwealth of Virginia. The people here, I just think, have an innate optimism and a can-do spirit that is typical of this country.

Audience member. We love you!

The President. Well, I love you too. [*Applause*] I love you too.

So it's good to get some fresh air. It's good to get some fresh perspective. I'm grateful to spend some time with you. Because, obviously, we're going through a difficult time in this country, and I know you folks are as frustrated as I am about the economy. I know you're also frustrated not just about our economic conditions, but also what's happening in Washington.

Audience members. Amen!

The President. Tim, I got an "amen" there. [*Laughter*]

You have every right to be frustrated. Here in Virginia, here in Richmond, people don't have time for political concerns. You've got real-life concerns. You may be looking for a job, or you know somebody who's looking for a job.

Audience member. We still love you, Barack!

The President. I love you back. [*Laughter*]

You make sacrifices to make ends meet. You work hard to meet your responsibilities. You expect the people you send to Washington to do the same thing, to meet their responsibilities. You expect, in a time of crisis, that everybody stops the political circus and actually do something to help people, to help the economy, to restore some security and opportunity, restore the American Dream, restore those things that made America the envy of the world. In other words, you expect action. And you deserve it right now.

And that's why, after a few scheduling issues, I went to Congress last night—[*laughter*]—to suggest new ways that we can grow the economy, help businesses, and put more of our fellow Americans back to work. It's called the "American Jobs Act." Next week, I will send it to Congress. They should pass it right away.

Now, everything in the "American Jobs Act"—everything in there—is the kind of proposal that's been supported in the past by both Democrats and Republicans. Nothing radical in this bill. Everything in it will put more people back to work and more money back into the pockets of those who are working. Everything in it will be paid for.

But the reason I'm here in Richmond is because, to make it happen, every one of your voices can make a difference. Every one of your voices will have an impact.

Now, I'm going to talk about the politics in a second, but let me right now just talk about what's in the "American Jobs Act." It will create more jobs for construction workers, more jobs for teachers, more jobs for veterans, more jobs for young people, more jobs for the long-term unemployed. It will provide a tax break to companies if they hire new workers. It will cut payroll taxes in half for every small-business owner and every working American. It will jump-start an economy that has stalled, and it will give companies the confidence that, if they hire new workers and they invest in their businesses, then there are going to be customers there who can afford to actually buy the things they're selling.

Passing this jobs bill will put people to work rebuilding our crumbling roads and our crumbling bridges. And it will also help us rebuild our schools. I just—in the back, I was taking some photos with folks who had helped out to organize this event, and there was a young lady who is a teacher. And she said: "I heard your speech last night. I really appreciate it. I'm teaching eighth grade English, and I teach in a trailer." We shouldn't have people teaching in trailers. We shouldn't have kids learning in trailers. They should have classrooms with Internet and science labs.

So you've got aging bridges on I–95, need to replace them. You've got schools like Nigel's that need to be upgraded. There are millions of unemployed construction workers across America ready to put on their tool belt and get dirty. I don't know about you, I don't want the newest airports, the fastest railroads, to be built in China, I want them to build—I want them to be built right here in the Unites States of America.

Audience members. U.S.A.! U.S.A.! U.S.A.!

The President. I don't want any of our kids to study in subpar schools. I want all our kids to study in great schools. So there's work to be done; there are workers ready to do it. Let's pass this jobs bill right away.

Passing this jobs bill will put thousands of teachers in Virginia and across America back to work when we need them most. This is a new age. Everybody here knows that. You—if you want a good job, a good career, if we want America to succeed, then we've got to have the best trained, most highly skilled workers in the world. You've got places like South Korea that are adding teachers to prepare their kids for a global economy. We're laying off our teachers in droves. It's unfair to our kids. It undermines their future; it undermines our future. It has to stop. Let's pass this bill and put our teachers back in the classroom where they belong.

Passing this bill gives companies new tax credits to hire America's veterans. There are a lot of veterans here in Richmond and all across Virginia. We ask these men and women to leave their careers or interrupt their careers, leave their families, risk their lives to fight for us. They come home, and they can't find a job? The last thing they should have to do is fight for a job when they come home. Pass this bill now and put these folks to work.

Pass this jobs bill, and we'll give small-business owners here in Richmond and here in Virginia a tax cut for hiring new workers, but also for raising workers' wages. Cut their payroll taxes in half, that will give small businesses money they can use to hire more workers.

Pass this bill, and we give hundreds of thousands of disadvantaged youth the hope and the dignity of a summer job next year. And that instills in them good habits that will last a lifetime. It will make it easier for them to find a job in the future and to continue their education.

Passing this bill will give companies a tax credit for hiring anybody who has spent more than 6 months looking for work. And there are a lot of folks like that. This has been a terrible recession. And I get letters from folks, and they write to me about what it's like, month after month, writing letters, sending out résumés, knocking on doors. And folks get discouraged. And when they get discouraged, at some point they drop out of the labor force, and it's very hard for them then to get reattached. And you've got some employers now, if you've been out of work a long time, even if they're looking for a job—or even if they're looking to hire, a lot of times, they'll say, "Well, you've been out of work too long, I'm not sure we want to hire you," which is not fair. It's not right.

So this bill will help people on unemployment insurance to do temporary work to build skills while looking for a full-time job. And we should extend unemployment insurance for another year. Not only is it the right thing to do for those families, but if we cut off unemployment insurance right now, that's money that millions of unemployed folks can't spend on their basic needs. So that money comes out of the economy. That means businesses have fewer customers, and the economy, for everybody, including those who have work, will shrink. That would be a big, unnecessary blow to this economy.

Passing this bill will give a typical working family a $1,500 tax cut next year. So this boosts the thousand-dollar tax cut that Democrats and Republicans already passed for this year. We can't allow that tax cut to expire. It would hit middle class families with a tax increase at the worst possible time. And some of you may have heard, I said to folks yesterday, especially my good Republican friends, I said, you guys have made pledges never to raise taxes on everybody ever again; you can't make an exception when the tax break is going to middle class people.

So this is the "American Jobs Act." It will lead to new jobs for construction workers, teachers, veterans, young people, the long-term unemployed, provide tax credits for businesses and workers. And it will not add to the deficit; it will be paid for.

Look, we spent a whole summer fussing about the deficit. And it is legitimate for us to get a Government that is living within its means, just like families do. Now, Democrats and Republicans have already agreed to cut spending by about a trillion dollars over the next decade. They've agreed to identify another 1.5 trillion in savings by the end of the year. What I said last night is, let's go further. Let's be a little more ambitious.

I believe we need to do more to make sure that we can do—to boost jobs and growth in the short term and still bring down our debt in the long run. So 10 days from now, I'll release a more ambitious deficit reduction plan, and it will follow the balanced approach that I've been talking about for months. Yes, we need to cut wasteful spending. We're going to need to strengthen our retirement programs. And yes, we've got to ask the wealthiest Americans and biggest corporations to pay their fair share.

Look, Virginia, I want to make very clear: I understand nobody likes paying taxes. I understand. I don't like—I pay a lot of taxes. [*Laughter*] I mean, you can look, it's public, the amount of taxes I pay. It's serious. [*Laughter*] And I'm not taking advantage of a bunch of loopholes. So I understand that. But we've always lived based on the principle that everybody has got to do their fair share. And we've got to make some choices. We've got to decide what are our priorities. We've got to ask ourselves what's not just best for me, but what's best for us. What's the best way to grow the economy and create jobs?

Should we keep tax loopholes for oil companies?

Audience members. No!

The President. Or should we use that money to give small-business owners a tax credit when they hire new workers?

Audience members. Yes!

The President. We can't afford to do both.

Should we keep tax breaks for millionaires and billionaires, or should we put teachers back to work so our kids are ready to graduate from college and get a good job? We can't afford to do both.

We've got to make real choices about the kind of country that we want to be. That's not class warfare. That's—I'm not attacking anybody. I'm just—it's simple math. We can't afford for folks who are the most fortunate to do the least and put the largest burden on the folks who are struggling the most. That doesn't make sense.

Now, I put forward this plan, the "American Jobs Act," but we can't stop there. We can't stop there. As I've said since I ran for this office, we've got to look beyond the immediate crisis and start building an economy that lasts, an economy that's not built on housing bubbles, not built on easy credit, not built on Wall Street shenanigans, but an economy that creates good middle class jobs that pay well and restore some sense of security.

And we need—so let me tell you what this means. I mean, we live in a world where technology has made it possible for companies to take their business anywhere. If we want them to start here and stay here and hire here, we have to be able to outbuild, outeducate, and outinnovate every other country on Earth. That's what we've got to fight for.

And that means everybody has got to up their game. All the college students here, I know you guys are having fun in college. That's—I'm glad you're having fun, but you need to hit the books. You're competing now against kids in Bangalore and kids in Beijing, and you've got to—and you can't avoid those math classes and the engineering classes and the science classes. We've got to focus. Everybody has got to up their game. Businesses have to get more efficient and more productive. Employees have to constantly upgrade their skills. Even if you have a good job, you've got to keep on staying on top of it. Government has to become more efficient. We've got to be smarter in terms of how we help people to succeed.

But to do all those things, I'm going to need your help.

Audience member. You got it.

The President. Now, look, I know that we—this has been a long slog, dealing with this economy. And I know that when I came into office, everybody was thinking, well, 6 months, we'll get this all solved and—[*laughter*]—but I told you at the time, I told you at the time, we were—this was going to be a tough, long journey. And I also told you I couldn't do it on my own.

Every kind of proposal in the "American Jobs Act," every proposal to put more workers on the job, more money in their pockets, every single one of these proposals has been supported by Democrats and Republicans before. And so they should be supporting them now. And that will only happen, though, if they set politics aside for a moment to deal with America's problems. And the only way they're going to do that is if they hear from you.

To their credit, I was glad to hear some Republicans, including your Congressman, say that they've got—they see room for us to work together. They said that they're open to some of the proposals to create American jobs.

Look, I know that folks sometime think they've used up benefit of the doubt, but I'm an eternal optimist. I'm an optimistic person. I'm an optimistic person. I believe in America. I believe in our democracy. I believe that if you just stay at it long enough, eventually, after they've exhausted all the options, folks do the right thing.

But we've got to give them a little help to do the right thing. So I'm asking all of you to lift up your voices, not just here in Richmond—anybody watching, listening, following online—I want you to call, I want you to e-mail, I want you to tweet—[*laughter*]—I want you to fax, I want you to visit, I want you to Facebook, send a carrier pigeon. [*Laughter*] I want you to tell your Congressperson, the time for gridlock and games is over. The time for action is now. The time to create jobs is now.

Pass this bill. If you want construction workers on the worksite, pass this bill. If you want teachers in the classroom, pass this bill. You want small-business owners to hire new people, pass this bill. If you want veterans to get their fair share of opportunity that they helped create, pass this bill. If you want a tax break, pass this bill.

Prove you will fight as hard for tax cuts for workers and middle class people as you do for oil companies and rich folks. Pass this bill. Let's get something done.

The next election is 14 months away. We cannot wait. The American people do not have the luxury of waiting another 14 months for some action. Some of you are living paycheck to paycheck, week to week, day by day. Now is not the time for people in Washington to be worrying about their jobs, it's time for them to be worrying about your jobs. Now is the time to put Americans back to work. Now is the time to act.

We are not a people that just look and watch and wait to see what happens. We're Americans. We make things happen. We're tougher than these times. We are bigger than the smallness of our politics. We are patriots, and we are pioneers and innovators and entrepreneurs, who, through individual effort and through a common commitment to one another, will build an economy that is once again the engine and the envy of the world. And we will write our own destiny.

It's within our power. But we've got to seize the moment. So let's just shake off all the naysaying and the anxiety and the hand-wringing. Enough of that. Let's get to work. Let's show the world once again why America is the greatest nation on Earth.

Thank you, everybody. God bless you. God bless America.

NOTE: The President spoke at 11:36 a.m. in Robins Center Arena. In his remarks, he referred to Nigel Richardson, student, Richmond Community High School; Anne Holton, wife of former Gov. Timothy M. Kaine of Virginia; and Rep. Eric I. Cantor.

Letter to the Speaker of the House of Representatives Requesting Disaster Relief Funds
September 9, 2011

Dear Mr. Speaker:

I ask the Congress to consider the enclosed budget request for disaster response needs through Fiscal Year (FY) 2012. It includes a supplemental appropriations request for FY 2011 of $500 million and a budget amendment for FY 2012 of $4.6 billion for the Department of Homeland Security.

The proposed totals for FY 2011 and FY 2012 would increase by $5.1 billion as a result of this request. The additional funding would fund disaster response needs in the Disaster Relief Fund, including approximately $1.5 billion for the Federal share of costs to respond to Hurricane Irene.

This request responds to urgent and essential needs. The supplemental appropriations request would be designated as an emergency requirement. The request for FY 2012 in the budget amendment would constitute disaster relief within the meaning of section 251 of the Balanced Budget and Emergency Deficit Control Act of 1985, as amended by the Budget Control Act of 2011, and would therefore adjust the discretionary spending levels for FY 2012 pursuant to section 251. The details of this request are set forth in the enclosed letter from the Director of the Office of Management and Budget.

Sincerely,

BARACK OBAMA

Message to the Congress on Continuation of the National Emergency With Respect to Certain Terrorist Attacks
September 9, 2011

To the Congress of the United States:

Section 202(d) of the National Emergencies Act, 50 U.S.C. 1622(d), provides for the automatic termination of a national emergency unless, prior to the anniversary date of its declaration, the President publishes in the *Federal*

Register and transmits to the Congress a notice stating that the emergency is to continue in effect beyond the anniversary date. Consistent with this provision, I have sent to the *Federal Register* the enclosed notice, stating that the emergency declared with respect to the terrorist attacks on the United States of September 11, 2001, is to continue in effect for an additional year.

The terrorist threat that led to the declaration on September 14, 2001, of a national emergency continues. For this reason, I have determined that it is necessary to continue in effect after September 14, 2011, the national emergency with respect to the terrorist threat.

BARACK OBAMA

The White House,
September 9, 2011.

NOTE: The notice is listed in Appendix D at the end of this volume.

The President's Weekly Address
September 10, 2011

This weekend, we're coming together as one Nation to mark the 10th anniversary of the September 11 attacks. We're remembering the lives we lost: nearly 3,000 innocent men, women, and children. We're reaffirming our commitment to always keep faith with their families. We're honoring the heroism of first-responders who risked their lives—and gave their lives—to save others. And we're giving thanks to all who serve on our behalf, especially our troops and military families, our extraordinary 9/11 generation.

At the same time, even as we reflect on a difficult decade, we must look forward to the future we will build together. That includes staying strong and confident in the face of any threat. And thanks to the tireless efforts of our military personnel and our intelligence, law enforcement, and homeland security professionals, there should be no doubt: Today America is stronger, and Al Qaida is on the path to defeat.

We've taken the fight to Al Qaida like never before. Over the past 2½ years, more senior Al Qaida leaders have been eliminated than at any time since 9/11. And thanks to the remarkable courage and precision of our forces, we finally delivered justice to Usama bin Laden.

We've strengthened the partnerships and tools we need to prevail in this war against Al Qaida, working closer with allies and partners, reforming intelligence to better detect and disrupt plots, investing in our special forces so terrorists have no safe haven.

We're constantly working to improve the security of our homeland as well, at our airports, ports, and borders; enhancing aviation security and screening; increasing support for our first-responders; and working closer than ever with States, cities, and communities.

A decade after 9/11, it's clear for all the world to see, the terrorists who attacked us that September morning are no match for the character of our people, the resilience of our Nation, or the endurance of our values.

They wanted to terrorize us, but as Americans, we refuse to live in fear. Yes, we face a determined foe, and make no mistake: They will keep trying to hit us again. But as we're showing again this weekend, we remain vigilant. We're doing everything in our power to protect our people. And no matter what comes our way, as a resilient nation, we will carry on.

They wanted to draw us into endless wars, sapping our strength and confidence as a nation. But even as we put relentless pressure on Al Qaida, we're ending the war in Iraq and beginning to bring our troops home from Afghanistan. Because after a hard decade of war, it is time for nation-building here at home.

They wanted to deprive us of the unity that defines us as a people. But we will not succumb to division or suspicion. We are Americans, and we are stronger and safer when we stay true to the values, freedoms, and diversity that makes us unique among nations.

And they wanted to undermine our place in the world. But a decade later, we've shown that America doesn't hunker down and hide behind walls of mistrust. We've forged new partnerships with nations around the world to meet the global challenges that no nation can face alone. And across the Middle East and North Africa, a new generation of citizens is showing that the future belongs to those that want to build, not destroy.

Ten years ago, ordinary Americans showed us the true meaning of courage when they rushed up those stairwells, into those flames, into that cockpit. In the decade since, a new generation has stepped forward to serve and keep us safe. In their memory, in their name, we will never waver. We will protect the country we love and pass it safer, stronger, and more prosperous to the next generation.

NOTE: The address was recorded at approximately 2 p.m. on September 9 in the Library at the White House for broadcast on September 10. The transcript was made available by the Office of the Press Secretary on September 9, but was embargoed for release until 6 a.m. on September 10.

Reading at the National September 11 Memorial in New York City
September 11, 2011

God is our refuge and strength, a very present help in trouble.

Therefore, we will not fear, even though the earth be removed, and though the mountains be carried into the midst of the sea.

Though its waters roar and be troubled, though the mountains shake with its swelling,

There is a river whose streams shall make glad the City of God, the holy place of the Tabernacle of the Most High.

God is in the midst of her. She shall not be moved. God shall help her just at the break of dawn.

The nations raged, the kingdoms were moved. He uttered his voice. The Earth melted.

The Lord of Hosts is with us. The God of Jacob is our refuge.

Come behold the works of the Lord who has made desolations in the Earth.

He makes wars cease to the ends of the Earth. He breaks the bough and cuts the spear in two. He burns the chariot in fire.

Be still and know that I am God. I will be exalted among the nations. I will be exalted in the Earths.

The Lord of Hosts is with us. The God of Jacob is our refuge.

—Psalm 46

NOTE: The President spoke at 8:47 a.m.

Remarks at "A Concert for Hope" Commemorating the 10th Anniversary of the September 11 Terrorist Attacks
September 11, 2011

The Bible tells us, "Weeping may endure for a night, but joy cometh in the morning."

Ten years ago, America confronted one of our darkest nights. Mighty towers crumbled. Black smoke billowed up from the Pentagon. Airplane wreckage smoldered on a Pennsylvania field. Friends and neighbors, sisters and brothers, mothers and fathers, sons and daughters, they were taken from us with a heartbreaking swiftness and cruelty. And on September 12, 2001, we awoke to a world in which evil was closer at hand and uncertainty clouded our future.

In the decade since, much has changed for Americans. We've known war and recession, passionate debates and political divides. We can never get back the lives that were lost on that day or the Americans who made the ultimate sacrifice in the wars that followed.

And yet today it is worth remembering what has not changed. Our character as a nation has

1049

not changed. Our faith in God and in each other, that has not changed. Our belief in America, born of a timeless ideal that men and women should govern themselves, that all people are created equal and deserve the same freedom to determine their own destiny, that belief, through tests and trials, has only been strengthened.

These past 10 years have shown that America does not give in to fear. The rescue workers who rushed to the scene, the firefighters who charged up the stairs, the passengers who stormed the cockpit, these patriots defined the very nature of courage. Over the years, we've also seen a more quiet form of heroism: in the ladder company that lost so many men and still suits up and saves lives every day, the businesses that have been rebuilt from nothing, the burn victim who has bounced back, the families who press on.

Last spring, I received a letter from a woman named Suzanne Swaine. She had lost her husband and brother in the Twin Towers and said that she had been robbed of "so many would-be proud moments where a father watches their child graduate, or tend a goal in a lacrosse game, or succeed academically." But her daughters are in college, the other doing well in high school. "It has been 10 years of raising these girls on my own," Suzanne wrote. "I could not be prouder of their strength and resilience." That spirit typifies our American family. And the hopeful future for those girls is the ultimate rebuke to the hateful killers who took the life of their father.

These past 10 years have shown America's resolve to defend its citizens and our way of life. Diplomats serve in far-off posts, and intelligence professionals work tirelessly without recognition. Two million Americans have gone to war since 9/11. They've demonstrated that those who do us harm cannot hide from the reach of justice anywhere in the world. America has been defended not by conscripts, but by citizens who choose to serve: young people who signed up straight out of high school, guardsmen and reservists, workers and businesspeople, immigrants and fourth-generation soldiers. They are men and women who left behind lives of comfort for two, three, four, five tours of duty. Too many will never come home; those that do carry dark memories from distant places and the legacy of fallen friends.

The sacrifices of these men and women and of our military families reminds us that the wages of war are great, that while service to our Nation is full of glory, war itself is never glorious. Our troops have been to lands unknown to many Americans a decade ago, to Kandahar and Kabul, to Mosul and Basra. But our strength is not measured in our ability to stay in these places, it comes from our commitment to leave those lands to free people and sovereign states and our desire to move from a decade of war to a future of peace.

These 10 years have shown that we hold fast to our freedoms. Yes, we're more vigilant against those who threaten us, and there are inconveniences that come with our common defense. Debates about war and peace, about security and civil liberties, have often been fierce these last 10 years. But it is precisely the rigor of these debates, and our ability to resolve them in a way that honors our values and our democracy, that is the measure of our strength. Meanwhile, our open markets still provide innovators the chance to create and succeed, our citizens are still free to speak their minds, and our souls are enriched in churches and temples, our synagogues and our mosques.

These past 10 years underscores the bonds between all Americans. We have not succumbed to suspicion, nor have we succumbed to mistrust. After 9/11, to his great credit, President Bush made clear what we reaffirm today: The United States will never wage war against Islam or any other religion. Immigrants come here from all parts of the globe. And in the biggest cities and the smallest towns, in schools and workplaces, you still see people of every conceivable race and religion and ethnicity, all of them pledging allegiance to the flag, all of them reaching for the same American Dream. *E pluribus unum*—out of many, we are one.

These past 10 years tell a story of our resilience. The Pentagon is repaired and filled with patriots working in common purpose. Shanksville is the scene of friendships forged between residents of that town and families who lost loved ones there. New York—New York remains the most vibrant of capitals of arts and industry and fashion and commerce. Where the World Trade Center once stood, the sun glistens off a new tower that reaches towards the sky.

Our people still work in skyscrapers. Our stadiums are still filled with fans, and our parks full of children playing ball. Our airports hum with travel, and our buses and subways take millions where they need to go. And families sit down to Sunday dinner, and students prepare for school. This land pulses with the optimism of those who set out for distant shores and the courage of those who died for human freedom.

Decades from now, Americans will visit the memorials to those who were lost on 9/11. They'll run their fingers over the places where the names of those we loved are carved into marble and stone, and they may wonder at the lives that they led. And standing before the white headstones in Arlington and in peaceful cemeteries and small-town squares in every corner of the country, they will pay respects to those lost in Iraq and Afghanistan. They'll see the names of the fallen on bridges and statues, at gardens and schools.

And they will know that nothing can break the will of a truly United States of America. They will remember that we've overcome slavery and civil war, we've overcome breadlines and fascism and recession and riots and communism and, yes, terrorism. They will be reminded that we are not perfect, but our democracy is durable, and that democracy—reflecting, as it does, the imperfections of man—also give us the opportunity to perfect our Union. That is what we honor on days of national commemoration, those aspects of the American experience that are enduring and the determination to move forward as one people.

More than monuments, that will be the legacy of 9/11: a legacy of firefighters who walked into fire and soldiers who signed up to serve; of workers who raised new towers and citizens who faced down their private fears; most of all, of children who realized the dreams of their parents. It will be said that we kept the faith, that we took a painful blow and we emerged stronger than before.

"Weeping may endure for a night, but joy cometh in the morning."

With a just God as our guide, let us honor those who have been lost, let us rededicate ourselves to the ideals that define our Nation, and let us look to the future with hearts full of hope.

May God bless the memory of those we lost, and may God bless the United States of America.

NOTE: The President spoke at 8:12 p.m. at the John F. Kennedy Center for the Performing Arts. In his remarks, he referred to Hannah, Emily, and Sarah Swaine, daughters of John F. Swaine, who was killed in the terrorist attacks of September 11, 2001; and former President George W. Bush.

Remarks on Job Growth Legislation
September 12, 2011

The President. Please, everybody, have a seat on this beautiful morning. It's wonderful to see all of you here.

On Thursday, I told Congress that I'll be sending them a bill called the "American Jobs Act." Well, here it is. This is a bill that will put people back to work all across the country. This is the bill that will help our economy in a moment of national crisis. This is a bill that is based on ideas from both Democrats and Republicans. And this is the bill that Congress needs to pass. No games. No politics. No delays. I'm sending this bill to Congress today, and they ought to pass it immediately.

Standing with me this morning are men and women who will be helped by the "American Jobs Act." I'm standing with teachers. All across America, teachers are being laid off in droves, which is unfair to our kids. It undermines our future, and it is exactly what we shouldn't be doing if we want our kids to be college-ready and then prepared for the jobs of the 21st century. We've got to get our teachers back to work. Let's pass this bill and put them in the classroom where they belong.

I'm standing here with veterans. We've got hundreds of thousands of brave, skilled Americans who fought for this country. The last thing they should have to do is to fight for a job when they come home. So let's pass this bill and put the men and women who served this Nation back to work.

We're standing here with cops and firefighters whose jobs are threatened because States and communities are cutting back. This bill will keep cops on the beat and firefighters on call. So let's pass this bill so that these men and women can continue protecting our neighborhoods, like they do every single day.

I'm standing with construction workers. We've got roads that need work all over the country. Our highways are backed up with traffic. Our airports are clogged. And there are millions of unemployed construction workers who can rebuild them. So let's pass this bill so road crews and diggers and pavers and workers, they can all head back to the jobsite. There's plenty of work to do. This job—this jobs bill will help them do it. Let's put them back to work, and let's pass this bill rebuilding America.

And there are schools throughout the country that desperately need renovating. We cannot—got an "amen" over there. [*Laughter*] We can't expect our kids to do their best in places that are literally falling apart. This is America. Every kid deserves a great school, and we can give it to them. Pass this bill, and we put construction crews back to work across the country repairing and modernizing at least 35,000 schools.

I'm standing here with small-business owners. They know that while corporate profits have come roaring back, a lot of small businesses haven't. They're still struggling getting the capital they need, getting the support they need in order to grow. So this bill cuts taxes for small businesses that hire new employees and

for small businesses that raise salaries for current employees. It cuts your payroll tax in half. And all businesses can write off investments they make this year and next year. Instead of just talking about America's job creators, let's actually do something for America's jobs creators. We can do that by passing this bill.

Now, there are a lot of other ways that this jobs bill, the "American Jobs Act," will help this economy. It's got a $4,000 tax credit for companies that hire anybody who spent more than 6 months looking for a job. We've got to do more for folks who've been hitting the pavement every single day looking for work, but haven't found employment yet. That's why we need to extend unemployment insurance and connect people to temporary work to help upgrade their skills.

This bill will help hundreds of thousands of disadvantaged young people find summer jobs next year, jobs that will help set the direction for their entire lives. And the "American Jobs Act" would prevent taxes from going up for middle class families. If Congress does not act, just about every family in America will pay more taxes next year. And that would be a self-inflicted wound that our economy just can't afford right now. So let's pass this bill and give the typical working family a $1,500 tax cut instead.

And the "American Jobs Act" is not going to add to the debt. It's pully paid for—I want to repeat that: It is fully paid for. [*Laughter*] It's not going to add a dime to the deficit. Next week, I'm laying out my plan not only to pay for this jobs bill, but also to bring down the deficit further. It's a plan that lives by the same rules that families do. We've got to cut out things that we can't afford to do in order to afford the things that we really need. It's a plan that says everybody, including the wealthiest Americans and biggest corporations, have to pay their fair share.

The bottom line is, when it comes to strengthening the economy and balancing our books, we've got to decide what our priorities are. Do we keep tax loopholes for oil companies, or do we put teachers back to work? Should we keep tax breaks for millionaires and billionaires, or should we invest in education and technology and infrastructure, all the things that are going to help us outinnovate and outeducate and out-build other countries in the future?

We know what's right. We know what will help businesses start right here and stay here and hire here. We know that if we take the steps outlined in this jobs plan, that there's no reason why we can't be selling more goods all around the world that are stamped with those three words: Made in America. That's what we need to do to create jobs right now.

I have to repeat something I said in my speech yesterday—on Thursday. There are some in Washington who'd rather settle our differences through politics and the elections than try to resolve them now. In fact, Joe and I, as we were walking out here, we were looking at one of the Washington newspapers and it was quoting a Republican aide saying, "I don't know why we'd want to cooperate with Obama right now. It's not good for our politics." That was very explicit.

Vice President Joe Biden. It was.

The President. I mean, that's the attitude in this town: "Yes, we've been through these things before, but I don't know why we'd be for them right now." The fact of the matter is the next election is 14 months away, and the American people don't have the luxury of waiting 14 months for Congress to take action. Folks are living week to week, paycheck to paycheck. They need action. And the notion that there are folks who would say, "We're not going to try to do what's right for the American people because we don't think it's convenient for our politics," we've been seeing that too much around here. And that's exactly what folks are tired of.

And that's okay, when things are going well, you play politics. It's not okay at a time of great urgency and need all across the country. These aren't games we're playing out here. Folks are out of work. Businesses are having trouble staying open. You've got a world economy that is full of uncertainty right now, in Europe, in the Middle East. Some events may be beyond our control, but this is something we can control. Whether we not—whether or not we pass this bill, whether or not we get this done, that's something that we can control. That's in our hands.

You hear a lot of folks talking about uncertainty in the economy. This is a bit of uncertainty that we could avoid by going ahead and taking action to make sure that we're helping the American people.

So if you agree with me, if you want Congress to take action, then I'm going to need everybody here and everybody watching. You've got to make sure that your voices are heard. Help make the case. There's no reason not to pass this bill. Its ideas are bipartisan. Its ideas are common sense. It will make a difference. That's not just my opinion. Independent economists and validators have said this could add a significant amount to our gross domestic product and could put people back to work all across the country. So the only thing that's stopping it is politics. And we can't afford these same political games. Not now.

So I want you to pick up the phone. I want you to send an e-mail. Use one of those airplane skywriters. Dust off the fax machine. Or you can just, like, write a letter. [*Laughter*] So long as you get the message to Congress: Send me the "American Jobs Act" so I can sign it into law. Let's get something done. Let's put this country back to work.

Thank you very much, everybody. God bless you.

NOTE: The President spoke at 10:58 a.m. in the Rose Garden at the White House.

Memorandum on Revisions to the Unified Command Plan 2011
September 12, 2011

Memorandum for the Secretary of Defense

Subject: Revisions to the Unified Command Plan 2011

Pursuant to my authority as Commander in Chief, I hereby approve and direct the implementation of the revised Unified Command Plan.

Consistent with title 10, United States Code, section 161(b)(2) and title 3, United States Code, section 301, you are directed to notify the Congress of these revisions on my behalf.

You are authorized and directed to publish this memorandum in the *Federal Register*.

Barack Obama

NOTE: This memorandum was not received for publication in the *Federal Register*.

Message to the Congress Transmitting the "American Jobs Act of 2011"
September 12, 2011

To the Congress of the United States:

Today, I am pleased to submit to the Congress the enclosed legislative proposal, the "American Jobs Act of 2011," together with a section-by-section analysis of the legislation.

The American people understand that the economic crisis and the deep recession were not created overnight and will not be solved overnight. The economic security of the middle class has been under attack for decades. That is why I believe we need to do more than just recover from this economic crisis—we need to rebuild the economy the American way, based on balance, fairness, and the same set of rules for everyone from Wall Street to Main Street. We can work together to create the jobs of the future by helping small business entrepreneurs, by investing in education, and by making things the world buys.

To create jobs, I am submitting the American Jobs Act of 2011—nearly all of which is made up of the kinds of proposals supported by both Republicans and Democrats, and that the Congress should pass right away to get the economy moving now. The purpose of the American Jobs Act of 2011 is simple: put more people back to work and put more money in the pockets of working Americans. And it will do so without adding a dime to the deficit.

First, the American Jobs Act of 2011 provides a tax cut for small businesses, to help them hire and expand now, and an additional tax cut to any business that hires or increases wages. In addition, the American Jobs Act of 2011 puts more money in the pockets of working and middle class Americans by cutting in half the payroll tax that comes out of the pay-check of every worker, saving typical families an average of $1,500 a year.

Second, the American Jobs Act of 2011 puts more people back to work, including teachers laid off by State budget cuts, first responders and veterans coming back from Iraq and Afghanistan, and construction workers repairing crumbling bridges, roads and more than 35,000 schools, with projects chosen by need and impact, not earmarks and politics. It will repair and refurbish hundreds of thousands of foreclosed homes and businesses in communities across the country.

Third, the American Jobs Act of 2011 helps out-of-work Americans by extending unemployment benefits to help them support their families while looking for work, and by reforming the system with training programs that build real skills, connect to real jobs, and help the long-term unemployed. It bans employers from discriminating against the unemployed when hiring, and provides a new tax credit to employers hiring workers who have been out of a job for over 6 months. And, it expands job opportunities for hundreds of thousands of low-income youth and adults through a new Pathways Back to Work Fund that supports summer and year round jobs for youth; innovative new job training programs to connect low-income workers to jobs quickly; and successful programs to encourage employers to bring on disadvantaged workers.

Lastly, this legislation is fully paid for. The legislation includes specific offsets to close corporate tax loopholes and asks the wealthiest Americans to pay their fair share that more than cover the cost of the jobs measures. The legislation also increases the deficit reduction target for the Joint Committee by the amount of the cost of the jobs package and specifies that, if the Committee reaches that higher target, then their measures would replace and turn off the specific offsets in this legislation.

I urge the prompt and favorable consideration of this proposal.

BARACK OBAMA

The White House,
September 12, 2011.

Remarks at Fort Hayes Arts and Academic High School in Columbus, Ohio
September 13, 2011

The President. Hello, Columbus! Oh, it is good to be back in the State of Ohio. Just a couple of people I want to make sure you know are here. First of all, my outstanding Secretary of Education, Arne Duncan, is in the house. Superintendant of Columbus City Schools, Dr. Gene T. Harris, is here. The principal of Fort Hayes Metropolitan Education Center, Milton Ruffin, is here. And the mayor of the great city of Columbus, Michael Coleman, is in the house.

It is a great honor to be here at Fort Hayes, one of the best high schools in Ohio.

I want to thank Tom for that introduction. He just gave me a quick tour, and let me just say, these buildings look great. He did a good job. I wouldn't mind taking a few classes here. You've got computers in every classroom, got state-of-the-art graphic design and science labs, new media center, music rooms. And when you combine that with outstanding teachers and a challenging curriculum, you've got the foundation for what you need to learn and graduate and compete in this 21st-century economy.

So, Fort Hayes, I'm here to talk about exactly that, about the economy. I came to talk about how we can get to a place where we're creating good, middle class jobs again: jobs that pay well, jobs that offer economic security. And the renovation of Fort Hayes is a great example of where those jobs can come from if we can finally get our act together in Washington, if we can get folks in that city to stop worrying so much about their jobs and start worrying about your jobs.

Now, yesterday I sent Congress the "American Jobs Act." This is it right here. It's pretty thick. This is a plan that does two things: It puts people back to work, and it puts more money in the pockets of working Americans. Everything in the "American Jobs Act" is the kind of proposal that in the past has been supported by both Republicans and Democrats. Everything in it will be paid for. And every one of you can make it happen by sending a message to Congress that says: Pass this bill.

Ohio, if you pass this bill, then right here in this State, tens of thousands of construction workers will have a job again. This is one of the most commonsense ideas out there. All over the country, there are roads and bridges and schools just like Fort Hayes in need of repair. Some of the buildings here at Fort Hayes were originally built during the Civil War. That's old. And when buildings are that old, they start falling apart. They start leaking, and ceiling tiles start to cave in, and there's no heat in the winter or air conditioning in the summer. Some of the schools the ventilation is so poor it can make students sick.

How do we expect our kids to do their very best in a situation like that? The answer is we can't. Every child deserves a great school, and we can give it to them, but we got to pass this bill.

Your outstanding Senator, Sherrod Brown, has been fighting to make this happen. And those of you here at Fort Hayes have been making it happen. See, a few years back, you decided to renovate this school. And you didn't just repair what was broken, you rebuilt this school for the 21st century, with faster Internet and cutting-edge technology. And that hasn't just created a better, safer learning environment for the students, it also created good jobs for construction workers.

You just heard Tom say it's created over 250 jobs for masons and concrete workers and carpenters and plumbers and electricians, and many of those jobs are filled by the good people of Columbus, Ohio.

But here's the thing. There are schools all throughout Ohio that need this kind of renovation. There's a bridge in Cincinnati that connects Ohio to Kentucky that needs this kind of renovation. There are construction projects like these all across the country just waiting to get started. And there are millions of unemployed construction workers who are looking for a job. So my question to Congress is: What on Earth are we waiting for?

I don't know about you, but I don't want any student to study in broken-down schools. I want our kids to study in great schools. I don't want the newest airports and the fastest railroads being built in China. I want them being built right here in the United States of America. There is work to be done. There are workers ready to do it. So let's tell Congress, pass this bill right away.

Audience members. Pass this bill! Pass this bill! Pass this bill!

The President. Pass this jobs bill, and there will be funding to save the jobs of up to 14,000 Ohio teachers and cops and firefighters. Think about it. There are places like South Korea that are adding teachers to prepare their kids for the global economy, at the same time as we're laying off our teachers left and right; where we've got school districts that have eliminated all extracurriculars: art, sports, you name it.

You've got situations where—I just heard a story from Arne Duncan driving over here. I met this young man yesterday. He's a music teacher in Philly, and his budget—total budget is $100 for teaching music in a whole bunch of schools. So they're using buckets to do drums because they can't afford actual musical instruments.

You've seen it here in Ohio. Budget cuts are forcing superintendents here in Columbus and all over the State to make layoffs they don't want to make. It is unfair to our kids, it undermines our future, and it has to stop. Tell Congress to pass the "American Jobs Act" so we can put our teachers back in the classroom where they belong.

Tell them to pass this bill so we can help the people that create most of the new—we can help the people who create most of the new jobs in this country. That's America's small-business owners. It's all well and good that big corporations have seen their profits roaring back; that's good. We want them to be able to hire people as well. But smaller companies haven't come back.

So this bill cuts taxes for small businesses that hire new employees. It cuts taxes for small businesses that raise salaries for current employees. It cuts small-business payroll taxes in half. So let's tell Congress, instead of just talking about helping America's job creators, let's actually do something to help America's job creators. Let's pass this bill right away.

Audience members. Pass this bill! Pass this bill! Pass this bill!

The President. If Congress passes this jobs bill, companies will get new tax credits for hiring America's veterans. We ask these men and women to leave their careers, leave their families, risk their lives to make sure that we're protected. The last thing they should have to do is fight for a job when they come home. That's why Congress needs to pass this bill. It will help hundreds of thousands of veterans all across the country.

It will help hundreds of thousands of young people find summer jobs next year. It's also got a $4,000 tax credit for companies that hire anybody who's spent more than 6 months looking for a job. The "American Jobs Act" extends unemployment insurance, but it also says if you're collecting benefits, you'll get connected to temporary work as a way to build your skills and enhance your résumé while you're looking for a permanent job.

And finally, if we get Congress to pass this bill, the typical working family will get $1,500 in tax cuts next year—$1,500 that would have been taken out of your paycheck will go right back into your pocket. But if Congress doesn't act, if Congress refuses to pass this bill, then middle class families will get hit with a tax increase at the worst possible time. Now, we can't let that happen.

Audience members. No!

The President. Some folks have been working pretty hard to keep tax breaks for the wealthiest Americans. Tell them they need to fight just as hard—they need to fight harder—for middle class families. Tell them to pass this jobs bill.

So the "American Jobs Act" will lead to new jobs for construction workers, jobs for teachers, jobs for veterans, jobs for young people, jobs for the unemployed. It will provide tax relief for every worker and small business in America. And it will not add to the deficit. It will be paid for.

We will pay for this plan, we'll pay down our debt, and we'll do it by following the same principle that every family follows: We'll make sure that Government lives within its means. We'll cut what we can't afford, to pay for what we really need, including some cuts we wouldn't make if we hadn't racked up so much debt over the last decade.

And here's the other thing, Columbus. We got to make sure that everybody pays their fair share, including the wealthiest Americans and biggest corporations. After all, we've got to decide what our priorities are. Do you want to keep tax loopholes for oil companies?

Audience members. No!

The President. Or do you want to renovate more schools like Fort Hayes so that construction workers have jobs again? Do you want to keep tax breaks for multimillionaires and billionaires?

Audience members. No!

The President. Or do you want to put teachers back to work and help small businesses and cut taxes for middle class families?

So, Columbus, we know what's right. We know what to do to create jobs now and in the future. We know that if we want businesses to start here and stay here and hire here, we've got to outbuild and outeducate and outinnovate every country on Earth. We've got to start manufacturing. We've got to sell more goods around the world that are stamped with three proud words: Made in America.

We need to build an economy that lasts. And, Columbus, that starts now. That starts with your help. Democrats and Republicans have supported every kind of proposal that's in the "American Jobs Act," and we need to tell them to support those proposals now.

Already, yesterday there were some Republicans quoted in Washington saying that even if they agree with the proposals in the "American Jobs Act," they shouldn't pass it because it would give me a win.

Audience members. Boo!

The President. That's the kind of games-playing we've gotten used to in Washington. Think about that. They supported this stuff in the past, but they're thinking maybe they don't do it this time because Obama is promoting it. Give me a win? This isn't about giving me a win. This isn't about giving Democrats or Republicans a win. It's about giving the American people a win. It's about giving Ohio a win. It's about your jobs and your lives and your futures and giving our kids a win.

Maybe there's some people in Congress who'd rather settle our differences at the ballot box than work together right now. But I've got news for them: The next election is 14 months away, and the American people don't have the luxury of waiting that long. You've got folks who are living week to week, paycheck to paycheck. They need action, and they need it now.

So I'm asking all of you to lift your voice, not just here in Columbus, but anybody who is watching, anybody who is listening, anybody who is following online. I need you to call and e-mail and tweet and fax and visit and tell your Congressperson that the time for gridlock and the time for games is over. The time for action is now.

Tell them that if you want to create jobs right now, pass this bill. If you want construction workers renovating schools like this one, pass this bill. If you want to put teachers back in the classroom, pass this bill. If you want tax cuts for middle class families and small-business owners, then what to do you do? Pass this bill.

Audience members. Pass this bill!

The President. If you want to help our veterans share in the opportunity that they defend, pass this bill.

Now is the time to act. We're not a people who just watch things happen. We're Americans; we make things happen. We are tougher than the times we live in. We are bigger than the politics that we've been putting up with. We are patriots and pioneers and innovators and entrepreneurs, who, through individual effort, but also through a commitment to one another, built an economy that's the engine and the envy of the world.

We write our own destiny. It's within our power to write it once more. So let's meet this moment. Let's get to work. Let's show the world once again why the United States of America is the greatest country on Earth.

Thank you very much, Ohio. Thank you, Columbus. God bless you. And God bless the United States of America.

NOTE: The President spoke at 2:33 p.m. In his remarks, he referred to Tom Sisterhen, construction manager, Smoot Alfred Resources; and Jason Chuong, music teacher, Philadelphia, PA, public school system.

Remarks at North Carolina State University in Raleigh, North Carolina
September 14, 2011

The President. Hello, North Carolina! Thank you! Thank you so much. How's it going, Raleigh? It is good to be back at NC State! Good to have all these wolves in my wolfpack. I just hope none of the students here are skipping class on account of me. [*Laughter*] Your professors can see you on TV, you know.

I want to thank so many people who helped to set this up, but a couple of folks in particular I want to acknowledge. First of all, the outstanding Governor of the great State of North Carolina, Bev Perdue is in the house. Bev has been working tirelessly on behalf of the State and obviously helped to guide so much of the emergency efforts that were taking place after the hurricane. So we're grateful to her. And we also have one of the finest public servants I know: The former Governor of the great State of North Carolina, Jim Hunt is in the house.

I want to thank Chancellor William Woodson, chancellor of North Carolina State University, as well as Thomas Ross, president of North Carolina State University [the University of North Carolina].° And I want to thank the Power Sound of the South for their outstanding performance. Thank you.

Now, everybody can sit down if you want. You all have seats—[*laughter*]—that's fine. I got a few—except folks in the front. See, this is the hard core right here. I want to thank Erv for the introduction. Now, as he mentioned, I just visited his small business, which is called WestStar Precision. It's down the road in Apex. And like Erv said, what they do is what a lot of companies here in the Research Triangle do so well. They hire smart people. They give them the best technology. They create something of lasting value. And that's how this country built a strong and growing economy and a strong, expanding middle class. That's our history, and that's what we've got to get back to. And that's why I came to Raleigh here today.

I came to talk about how America can get back to a place where we're creating good middle class jobs again: jobs that pay well, jobs that offer some security, jobs that are available for all the young people who are going to be graduating from NC State. Because I know that's what the students are thinking about. And we can do that if we can finally get Washington to act, if we can get folks to stop worrying so much about their jobs and start worrying a little more about your jobs.

Now, on Monday, I sent Congress this piece of legislation. It's called the "American Jobs Act." It's a plan that does two things: It puts

---

° White House correction.

more people back to work, and it puts more money back into the pockets of working Americans. Everything in this proposal, everything in this legislation, everything in the "American Jobs Act," is the kind of proposal that in the past, at least, has been supported by Democrats and Republicans. Everything in it will be paid for. Anybody who wants to know more about it, you can read it on whitehouse.gov. [*Laughter*] I know you guys don't have enough to read. And every single one of you can help make this bill a reality by telling Congress to pass this bill. Pass this jobs bill.

Now, let me tell you why you need to pass this bill. Tell them to pass this bill so we can help the people who create most of the new jobs in this country, and that's small-business owners like Erv. Because while corporate profits have come roaring back, smaller companies haven't. So what this jobs bill does is it cuts taxes for small businesses that hire new employees. It cuts taxes for small businesses that raise the salaries of their current employees. It cuts small businesses' payroll taxes in half, and that would help 170,000 small-business owners in North Carolina alone. And if they choose to make new investments next year, it lets them write off those investments.

And for small-business owners who have contracts with the Federal Government, we're going to do more than that. Today I'm ordering all Federal agencies to make sure those small-business owners get paid a lot faster than they do now. In many cases, it will be twice as fast. So that puts more money in their pockets quicker, which means they can hire folks quicker.

Now, we've got to tell Congress to do their part. You've got some Republicans in Congress, they like to talk about how, "We're in favor of America's job creators." Well, you know what, if you're in favor of America's jobs creators, this is your bill. This will actually help America's job creators. So we need to pass this jobs bill right away.

But that's not all this bill does. Pass this jobs bill, and companies will get new tax credits for hiring America's veterans. Now, we ask these men and women to leave their careers, leave

their families, risk their lives to fight for us, to fight for our freedoms. The last thing they should have to do is fight for a job when they come home. That's why Congress needs to pass this bill.

Pass this bill because it will help hundreds of thousands of young people find summer jobs next year. It's also got a $4,000 tax credit for companies that hire anybody who's spent more than 6 months looking for a job. It extends unemployment insurance, which means it's providing help and support for folks who are out there, want to work, but haven't found a job yet. And that also puts more money into the economy, because they spend that money in small businesses and in large businesses, and that means they have more customers and they'll hire more people. But we're also saying that if you're collecting unemployment insurance, you're going to get connected to temporary work as a way to keep your skills sharp while you're looking for a permanent job.

Pass this bill, and right here in North Carolina, about 19,000 construction workers will have a job again. This is a commonsense idea. Governor Perdue can tell you, there are a lot of roads and a lot of bridges that need fixing. There is a lot of work that needs to be done in schools and airports. All these things are in need of repair. In North Carolina alone, there are 153 structurally deficient bridges that need to be repaired. Four of them are near here, on or around the Beltline. Why would we wait to act until another bridge falls? All across North Carolina, all across the country, there are schools with leaking ceilings and lousy heating, ventilation so poor, it can make students sick. How can we expect our kids to do their best in places like that?

And the answer is, we can't. This is America. I don't know about you, but I don't want any of our young people studying in broken-down schools. I want our kids to study in the best schools. I don't want the newest airports or the fastest railroads being built in China. I want them being built right here in the United States of America. There are construction projects like these all across the country just waiting to get started. There are millions of unemployed construction workers looking for work. My question is, what's Congress waiting for? There's work to be done; there are workers ready to do it. Let's pass this jobs bill right away, and let's get it done. Let's go!

Pass this jobs bill, and there will be funding to save the jobs of up to 13,000 North Carolina teachers, cops, and firefighters. I hope some of the young people here plan to go into teaching, plan to go into education. But here's the challenge: We've got incredibly talented young people who want to teach, but while places like South Korea are adding teachers to prepare their kids for the global economy, we're laying off teachers left and right. You've seen it here in North Carolina. Budget cuts are forcing superintendents all over the State to make layoffs they don't want to make. It's unfair to our kids. It undermines their future; it undermines our future. It has to stop. If we want our kids ready for college, ready for careers in the 21st century, tell Congress to pass the "American Jobs Act" and put teachers back into the classroom where they belong.

Audience member. [Inaudible]

The President. Yes, we can. We could pass this thing, but we need Congress to help us do it.

Now, if we pass this bill, the typical working family in North Carolina will get a $1,300 tax cut next year. Thirteen hundred dollars that would have been taken from your paycheck will now go into your pocket. That will help local businesses know that they've got customers. But if Congress doesn't act, if Congress refuses to pass this bill, middle class families will get hit with a tax increase at the worst possible time. We can't let that happen.

As I pointed out last Thursday, there are folks in Congress who have been fighting pretty hard to keep tax breaks for the wealthiest Americans. You need to tell them they need to fight just as hard to help middle class families. Tell them to pass this jobs bill.

So that's the "American Jobs Act." It will lead to new jobs for young people, for construction workers, for teachers, for veterans, for the unemployed. It will provide tax relief for every worker and every small business in America. It will not add to the deficit. It will be paid for.

We will pay for this plan. We will pay down our debt. We'll do it following the same principles that every family follows. We'll make sure the Government lives within its means. We'll cut what we can't afford to pay for what we really need. And that means we're going to have to make—we're going to have to cut some things we wouldn't make if we hadn't racked up so much debt over the last decade.

But it does mean that we're going to keep on doing the things that matter, like making sure that you guys who are here at NC State aren't coming up with all that debt. That's why we've made sure to increase Pell grants. That's why we've made sure to increase student loan affordability, to make sure you guys can get the education you deserve. But in order to do that, we've got to make sure everybody pays their fair share, including the wealthiest Americans and the biggest corporations.

Ultimately, North Carolina, this comes down to what our priorities are. Do you want to keep tax loopholes for oil companies?

Audience members. No!

The President. Or do you want to renovate more schools and rebuild more roads and bridges so construction workers have jobs again? Do you want to keep tax breaks for multimillionaires and billionaires?

Audience members. No!

The President. Or do you want to cut taxes for small-business owners and middle class families?

Audience members. Yes!

The President. It would be nice if we could do it all, but we can't. We've got to make choices. That's what governing is about. And we know what's right. We know what we have to do to create jobs right now and create jobs in the future. We know that if we want businesses to start here and stay here and hire here, we've got to be able to outbuild and outeducate and outinnovate every country on Earth. We've got to give workers new skills for new jobs. We've got to give our young people a chance to earn a college education. And we've got to follow Erv's example. We've got to start manufacturing and selling more goods around the world stamped with three proud words: Made in America. Made in North Carolina. Made in Raleigh.

We need to build an economy that lasts. And, Raleigh, that starts now.

Audience member. I love you, Barack!

The President. I love you back. That starts— [*applause*]—but if you love me, if you love me, you got to help me pass this bill. [*Applause*] If you love me, you got to help me pass this bill. It starts with your help. Democrats and Republicans have supported every kind of proposal that's in the "American Jobs Act" in the past. But we got to tell them, support it now. That's where you come in.

Already, you've got some Republicans in Washington who've said that some of this stuff may have to wait until the next election——

Audience members. Boo!

The President. ——and said maybe we can just kick our problems down the road and stretch this thing out rather than work together right now. Some of them were even quoted as saying, even if they agreed with some of the things in this bill, that they don't want to pass it because it would give me a win.

Audience members. Boo!

The President. Give me a win? Give me a break! [*Laughter*] That's exactly why folks are fed up with Washington. This isn't about me. This isn't about giving me a win. This isn't about giving Democrats or Republicans a win. It's not about positioning for the election. It's about giving the American people a win. That's what it's about. It's about giving small-business owners and entrepreneurs a win. It's about giving students a win. It's about giving working families a win. It's about giving all of us a win. I get fed up with that kind of game-playing. And we've been seeing it for too long—too long. We're in a national emergency. We've had— we've been grappling with a crisis for 3 years. And instead of getting folks to rise up above partisanship in a spirit that says we're all in this together, you got folks who are purposely dividing—purposely; thinking just in terms of how does this play out in terms of this election.

Now, that's not all Republicans. There are some Republicans who get it. I was in Ohio yesterday, and their Republican Governor, who—he doesn't agree with me on a lot of stuff, but he agreed that it's a good idea to cut taxes for the middle class. He said: "This is not a time for partisanship. This is a time to figure out a way in which we can get things moving in this country." He's absolutely right. A faction in Washington may be content to wait until the next election to do anything, but I've got news for them. The next election is 14 months away, and the American people don't have the luxury to wait that long. There are a whole bunch of students here who will graduate by then and will be looking for a job. They can't wait that long. There are a lot of folks living to paycheck to paycheck, day to day. They can't wait that long. They need action; they need action now. So, Raleigh, you need to put leaders—you need leaders who will put country before party and your jobs and your lives and your well-being and your futures above everything else.

So for those of you who did skip class today—[*applause*]—I've got a homework assignment for you. [*Laughter*] That's right. I am asking all of you, not just here at NC State, but—not just you who are in Raleigh, but anyone watching, anyone listening, anybody following online: I need you to lift your voice. Make it heard. You can call. You can e-mail. You can tweet. You can fax. You can Facebook. You can visit. You can write a letter. When was the last time you did that? [*Laughter*] Tell your Congressperson that the time for partisanship and politics is over. It's not—now is not the time for it. The time for gridlock and games is over. The time for action is now.

So I just want to say—I just want to make sure everybody understands their homework assignment. Tell them, tell them that if you want to create jobs, pass this bill. If you want construction workers back on the worksite, pass this bill. If you want teachers back in the classroom, pass this jobs bill. If you want tax cuts for middle class families and small-business owners, pass this jobs bill. If you want to help our veterans share in the opportunity that they have defended, pass this bill.

Now is the time to act. We are not people who just watch things happening. We make things happen. We're Americans. We are tougher than the hand that we've been dealt. We're bigger than the politics we've been putting up with. We're patriots and pioneers and innovators and entrepreneurs. Through individual effort, but also through a commitment to one another, we have built an economy that is the engine and the envy of the world. We're not going to stop now. The time for hand-wringing is over. The time for moping around—we've got to kick off our bedroom slippers and put on our marching shoes. We've got to get it to work.

There are people who—there may be people whose refrain is, no, we can't. But I believe, yes, we can. We are a people who write our own destiny. And we will write our destiny once more. So let's seize this moment. Let's get to work. Let's show the world once again why the United States of America is the greatest country on Earth.

Thank you, North Carolina. Thank you, Raleigh. God bless you. God bless the United States of America.

NOTE: The President spoke at 12:51 p.m. In his remarks, he referred to Ervin F. Portman, founder and president, WestStar Precision; and Gov. John R. Kasich of Ohio.

Remarks at the Congressional Hispanic Caucus Institute Annual Awards Gala
September 14, 2011

Hello, everybody. *Buenas noches*. Thank you so much. Thank you, everybody. Please, please, have a seat.

I want to thank Congressman Gonzalez, Senator Menendez for your outstanding leadership. I want to thank the Congressional Hispanic Caucus Institute for inviting us here this evening. It is wonderful to be back with all of you to help kick off Hispanic Heritage Month.

Now, before I begin, I want to acknowledge a few people who are with us here tonight. We are honored to be joined by Her Royal Highness Princess Cristina of Spain. We are honored to be joined by our first Latina Supreme Court Justice, Sonia Sotomayor. I want to recognize House Minority Leader Nancy Pelosi, our great friend and champion, as well as congratulate Secretary Ken Salazar and Secretary Hilda Solis for their awards tonight and for their outstanding work.

I also want to give a special shout-out to my friend Rey Decerega, the program director here at CHCI. Not many people can give the President of the United States stitches in his lip and get away with it. [*Laughter*] Rey is in unique company. [*Laughter*] I sent him a photograph of the moment, as he was throwing his elbow at me, and said, he's the only person who ever did that and the Secret Service did

not arrest. [*Laughter*] And I hear he's pretty tough off the basketball court too.

Finally, I want to thank all the members of the Congressional Hispanic Caucus here tonight. And I also want to apologize for them because they spent last week listening to me talk. So you probably thought you could escape this by coming to this dinner.

But I'm here because we're at a critical time for our country. The fight we're having right now—the fight to put more Americans back to work, to make our country stronger in the long run, to prove that we can get something done here in Washington—this fight could not be more important for the people in this room, for the Latino community, and for millions of Americans who need help.

I don't have to tell you these are tough times. You know how hard this recession has hit families, especially Latino families. You know the sacrifices that folks are making every single day just to pay the mortgage or fill up the car or to keep the lights on, keep kids in school.

These are families in Los Angeles and San Antonio and Miami. But they're also families in Decatur and Des Moines. As I said when I spoke here last year, problems in the Latino community are problems for the entire American community. Our future is tied to how well the Latino community does. The reverse is also true. When our country is hurting, everyone feels the pain.

Right now most Americans—whether they are Black, White, Latino, Asian, Native American—they're working hard to meet their responsibilities. All they want in return is for that hard work to pay off. And they want those of us in Washington to meet our responsibilities and do our part to make their lives just a little bit easier, to create those ladders of opportunity.

And that's why last week, I asked Congress a simple question: In the face of a national emergency, can we finally put a stop to the political circus and actually do something to help the economy? Can we restore some of the fairness and the security that has defined this nation since our founding?

I believe we can, and I believe we must. And that's why, on Monday, I sent the "American Jobs Act" to Congress and asked them to pass it right away. The proposals in this legislation have, in the past, been supported by Democrats and Republicans. And all of it will be paid for.

And the idea behind this bill is simple: to put more people back to work and put more money into the pockets of those who are working. It will create more jobs for construction workers and teachers and veterans and the long-term unemployed. It will give tax breaks to companies who hire new workers, and to small-business owners, and to the middle class. And it will help restore confidence in our economy so businesses will invest and hire.

Passing this jobs bill will put people to work rebuilding our decaying roads and our bridges and will repair and modernize 35,000 schools by fixing roofs, insulating windows, and installing science labs and high-speed Internet, and getting our kids out of trailers—[*applause*]— all throughout the community, especially in the Latino community, where our children—the population is growing fastest.

At a time when countries like China are building high-speed rail lines and gleaming new airports, we've got over a million unemployed construction workers—many of them Latino—who could be doing the same thing right here in the United States. That's not right. It's time for us to fix it. And that's why Congress should pass this bill right away.

Passing this jobs bill will put thousands of teachers in every state back to work helping our kids compete with their peers around the world. Because at a time when teachers are being hired in countries like South Korea, we can't be laying them off in San Diego or Philadelphia, not when our children's future is at stake. Let's put teachers back in the classroom where they belong.

Passing this jobs bill will cut taxes for small business—including 250,000 Latino-owned businesses. And it will give companies a tax credit if they hire American veterans, because if you risk your life serving this country, you shouldn't have to worry about finding a job when you get home. This is our chance to help make it right.

Passing this jobs bill will give hundreds of thousands of disadvantaged young people a summer job next year. And their parents, who desperately want to work, will have more ladders out of poverty. That's why Congress needs to pass this bill right now.

Passing this jobs bill will give companies up to a $4,000 tax credit if they hire someone who's been looking for a job for more than 6 months. It will build on a program in Georgia that takes the people who collect unemployment insurance and gives them temporary work as a way to build up their skills while they look for a permanent job. And this plan will also extend unemployment insurance for another year, and that benefits over 1 million Latinos and their families. They need help, and it would be a huge blow to our economy if these families stopped spending money on necessities. Let's pass this bill and keep that from happening.

And finally, passing this jobs bill will give the typical working family a $1,500 tax cut next year. Money that would have been taken out of your paycheck will now go into your pocket. Twenty-five million Latino workers will benefit. Some folks have been working pretty hard in Congress to keep tax breaks for wealthy

Americans. The least they can do is fight just as hard for the middle class and people at the bottom. Let's get this done. Let's make sure that ordinary folks get some relief as well.

So this is what the "American Jobs Act" is all about: New jobs for construction workers and teachers, veterans, young people, long-term unemployed; tax credits for middle class families and for small businesses. And we'll pay for it—all of it—in a way that not only covers the cost of the plan, but helps to bring down our debt and our deficits over the long term.

I'll be talking more about how we're going to pay for this plan on Monday, but the bottom line is it has to be done in a balanced way where everyone shares the sacrifice and nobody is asked to bear the whole burden.

We need to make more spending cuts on top of the trillion dollars of cuts I've already signed into law, and that's going to be tough. We need to make modest adjustments to programs like Medicare and Medicaid that will help preserve them for the next generation while protecting current retirees. But we also need to make some real choices when it comes to our Tax Code, choices about what kind of country do we want to be.

Instead of asking middle class families to bear even more of a burden, let's ask big corporations to give up tax loopholes that small businesses don't get. Instead of telling seniors "you're on your own," let's make sure our wealthiest citizens aren't paying taxes at a lower rate than their secretaries. That's not right. In this country, everybody should be getting a fair shake, and everybody should be paying their fair share. That's who we are as Americans. That's who we have to be now.

A jobs bill that puts Americans back to work, a balanced approach to pay for it that will lower our deficit in the long run, these are the steps Congress needs to take right now to put our country on a stronger footing. But we also know we've got to do more. If we're going to continue to grow our economy at a time when companies can set up shop anywhere in the world, we've got to do more; we've got to look a little further down the road.

And that starts with giving our children the best opportunity to succeed, something I know Latino families are focused on every single day. Because if we're going to outbuild and outinnovate every other country on Earth, the most important thing we can do is make sure that every single young person in this country has an opportunity to thrive. The most important investment we can make is in education.

That's why we launched the Race to the Top initiative, which now reaches almost one-quarter of our country's Latino students, to help encourage schools to do the very best with our kids: identify and support students before they drop out, implement effective bilingual education programs, make English language learners a priority.

We have strengthened Pell grants, and we're investing in community colleges that help teach the skills that companies need. And that's part of the reason why the number of young Latinos enrolled in college rose by 24 percent in the last year. They can actually afford to go to school because of the help that Members of Congress who are here tonight helped deliver. We've got more Latinos attending college than ever before. And even though we're not there yet, we are going to do everything in our power—I will do everything in my power—to make the "DREAM Act" a reality.

This has been a long and frustrating road for all of us. Republicans helped write the "DREAM Act" because they knew it was the right thing to do for our country. That was a while back. But then last year, we passed the "DREAM Act" through the House only to see it blocked by Senate Republicans. And now, for the first time in a decade, the bill doesn't have a single Republican cosponsor, not one. Nothing about the need for the legislation changed. Nothing about the language in the legislation changed. The only thing that changed was politics in Washington.

That's heartbreaking. It's heartbreaking to see innocent young people denied the right to earn an education or serve in our military because of their parents' action and because of the actions of a few politicians in Washington.

It's heartbreaking to see these incredibly bright, gifted people barred from contributing to our country and to our economy.

Because the truth is, reforming our immigration system is crucial for our economic future. This country was built and sustained by people who risked everything because they believed in the idea of America, the idea that anybody with a dream and a willingness to work can make a life for themselves here. That is part of the American Dream. That's the essence of the American Dream.

That's why it doesn't make sense that we educate more foreign-born workers than any country in the world, but our broken, outdated immigration system often sends them home to invent and build and grow their companies someplace else. It doesn't make any sense that immigrant workers are forced into the shadows, earning unfair wages, at the same time that businesses are breaking the rules and getting away with it, while those that follow the rules get punished.

We need an immigration policy that works, one that meets the needs of our families and our businesses while honoring our tradition as a nation of immigrants and a nation of laws. Because no matter what you may hear, in this country, there is no "us" or "them," there is only "us": one Nation under God, indivisible. And immigrants are part of that American family and a source of our strength.

Now, as I mentioned when I was at La Raza a few weeks back, I wish I had a magic wand and could make this all happen on my own. There are times when—until Nancy Pelosi is Speaker again—I'd like to work my way around Congress. But the fact is, even as we work towards a day when I can sign an immigration bill, we've got laws on the books that have to be upheld. But as you know as well as anyone that—anybody else, how we enforce those laws is also important. That's why the Department of Homeland Security is applying common-sense standards for immigration enforcement. And we've made progress so that our enforcement policies prioritize criminals who endanger our communities, not students trying to achieve the American Dream.

But we live in a democracy, and at the end of the day, I can't do this all by myself under our democratic system. If we're going to do big things—whether it's passing this jobs bill or the "DREAM Act" or comprehensive immigration reform—we're going to have to get Congress to act. I know Nancy Pelosi is ready to act. I know the CHC is ready to act. But we got to get more folks in Congress to act. It's time to stop playing politics and start listening to the people who sent us to Washington in the first place, because the rest of America is way ahead of us on this.

So everybody here tonight, keep the heat on me, keep the heat on Nancy, the rest of the Democrats. We feel good about where we're at. But if we're being honest, we know the real problem isn't the Members of Congress in this room. It's the Members of Congress who put party before country because they believe the only way to resolve our differences is to wait 14 months till the next election.

And I've got news for them. The American people don't have the luxury of waiting 14 months. Some of them are living paycheck to paycheck, month to month, day to day. Others want to go to college right now. They want to defend their country right now. And that's why I'm asking everybody in the Latino community—not just here, but all across the country—lift up your voice. Make yourself heard. If you think it's time to pass a jobs bill that will put millions of Americans back to work, call on Congress to do the right thing.

If you think it's time to give businesses the incentive to hire and put more money into your pockets, make yourself heard. Tell Congress to do the right thing. And if your Congress man or woman is already on the right page, talk to somebody else's Congressman. [*Laughter*]

If you think it's time to stop the political games and finally pass the "DREAM Act" and reform our immigration system, pick up the phone, get on the computer, tell your representatives in Washington the time for action is now. We can't wait. Not when so much is at stake.

These are difficult times. But remember, we've been through worse. And think about everybody here—your parents, your grandparents, your great-grandparents—they struggled in ways we can't even imagine to deliver that American Dream to you. We've always been a nation full of vision, a bold and optimistic America that does big things. We don't have a cramped vision. We don't try to exclude. We try to embrace and bring people in to this idea of America.

It's a vision where we live within our means, but we invest in our future; where everybody makes sacrifices, but nobody has to bear the burden alone, and everybody shares in our success; where we live up to the idea that no mat-ter what you look like, no matter where you come from, no matter what your surname—whether your ancestors landed at Ellis Island or came over on a slave ship or crossed the Rio Grande—we are all connected, and we all rise and fall together.

That's the America I believe in. That's the America that you believe in. That's the America we can once more have, as long as all of us are working together.

Thank you. God bless you, and God bless the United States of America.

NOTE: The President spoke at 8:24 p.m. at the Walter E. Washington Convention Center.

Remarks on Presenting the Medal of Honor to Sergeant Dakota L. Meyer
September 15, 2011

Thank you, everybody. Please be seated. Thank you, Chaplain Kibben. Good afternoon, everyone. And on behalf of Michelle and myself, welcome to the White House.

It's been said that "where there is a brave man, in the thickest of the fight, there is the post of honor." Today we pay tribute to an American who placed himself in the thick of the fight, again and again and again. In so doing, he has earned our Nation's highest military decoration, the Medal of Honor. And we are extraordinarily proud of Sergeant Dakota Meyer.

Today is only the third time during the wars in Afghanistan and Iraq that a recipient of the Medal of Honor has been able to accept it in person. And we are honored to be joined by one of the two other recipients, Sergeant First Class Leroy Petry, who is here.

I would point out something else. Of all the Medal of Honor recipients in recent decades, Dakota is also one of the youngest. He's 23 years old. And he performed the extraordinary actions for which he is being recognized today when he was just 21 years old.

Despite all this, I have to say Dakota is one of the most down-to-earth guys that you will ever meet. In fact, when my staff first tried to arrange the phone call so I could tell him that I'd approved this medal, Dakota was at work, at his new civilian job, on a construction site. He felt he couldn't take the call right then because, he said, "If I don't work, I don't get paid." [*Laughter*] So we arranged to make sure he got the call during his lunch break. [*Laughter*] I told him the news, and then he went right back to work. [*Laughter*] That's the kind of guy he is. He also asked to have a beer with me, which we were able to execute yesterday.

Dakota is the kind of guy who gets the job done. And I do appreciate, Dakota, you taking my call. [*Laughter*] The Medal of Honor reflects the gratitude of the entire Nation. So we're joined here by Members of Congress, including somebody from your home State, the Republican leader of the Senate, Mitch McConnell. We are joined here by leaders from across my administration, including Secretary of Veterans Affairs Ric Shinseki and Navy Secretary Ray Mabus, and leaders from across our Armed Forces, including the Commandant of the Marine Corps, General James Amos.

We're honored to welcome Dakota's father Mike, who's here; his extraordinary grandparents; and more than 120 of Dakota's family and friends, many from his home State of Kentucky. I want to welcome Dakota's comrades from the Marine Embedded Training Team

2–8, and we are humbled by the presence of the members of the Medal of Honor Society.

Dakota, I realize the past 2 years have not been easy for you, retelling the story of that day and standing here today. You're a very modest young man. But as you've said, you do it for a simple reason—retelling the story—because it helps you to honor those who didn't come home and to remind your fellow Americans that our men and women in uniform are over there fighting every single day.

So that's how we'll do this today. It's fitting that we do so this week, having just marked the 10th anniversary of the attacks that took our Nation to war, because in Sergeant Dakota Meyer, we see the best of a generation that has served with distinction through a decade of war.

Let me tell the story. I want you to imagine it's September 8, 2009, just before dawn. A patrol of Afghan forces and their American trainers is on foot, making their way up a narrow valley, heading into a village to meet with elders. And suddenly, all over the village, the lights go out. And that's when it happens. About a mile away, Dakota, who was then a corporal, and Staff Sergeant Juan Rodriguez-Chavez could hear the ambush over the radio. It was as if the whole valley was exploding. Taliban fighters were unleashing a firestorm from the hills, from the stone houses, even from the local school.

And soon, the patrol was pinned down, taking ferocious fire from three sides. Men were being wounded and killed, and four Americans—Dakota's friends—were surrounded. Four times, Dakota and Juan asked permission to go in; four times they were denied. It was, they were told, too dangerous. But one of the teachers in his high school once said, "When you tell Dakota he can't do something, he's going to do it." [*Laughter*] And as Dakota said of his trapped teammates, "Those were my brothers, and I couldn't just sit back and watch."

The story of what Dakota did next will be told for generations. He told Juan they were going in. Juan jumped into a Humvee and took the wheel; Dakota climbed into the turret and manned the gun. They were defying orders,

but they were doing what they thought was right. So they drove straight into a killing zone, Dakota's upper body and head exposed to a blizzard of fire from AK–47s and machine guns, from mortars and rocket-propelled grenades.

Coming upon wounded Afghan soldiers, Dakota jumped out and loaded each of the wounded into the Humvee, each time exposing himself to all that enemy fire. They turned around and drove those wounded back to safety. Those who were there called it the most intense combat they'd ever seen. Dakota and Juan would have been forgiven for not going back in. But as Dakota says, you don't leave anyone behind.

For a second time, they went back, back into the inferno; Juan at the wheel, swerving to avoid the explosions all around them; Dakota up in the turret, when one gun jammed, grabbing another, going through gun after gun. Again they came across wounded Afghans. Again, Dakota jumped out, loaded them up, and brought them back to safety.

For a third time, they went back, insurgents running right up to the Humvee, Dakota fighting them off. Up ahead, a group of Americans, some wounded, were desperately trying to escape the bullets raining down. Juan wedged the Humvee right into the line of fire, using the vehicle as a shield. With Dakota on the guns, they helped those Americans back to safety as well.

For a fourth time, they went back. Dakota was now wounded in the arm. Their vehicle was riddled with bullets and shrapnel. Dakota later confessed: "I didn't think I was going to die. I knew I was." But still they pushed on, finding the wounded, delivering them to safety.

And then, for a fifth time, they went back, into the fury of that village, under fire that seemed to come from every window, every doorway, every alley. And when they finally got to those trapped Americans, Dakota jumped out. And he ran toward them, drawing all those enemy guns on himself, bullets kicking up the dirt all around him. He kept going until he came upon those four Americans, laying where they fell, together as one team.

Dakota and the others who had joined him knelt down, picked up their comrades and—through all those bullets, all the smoke, all the chaos—carried them out, one by one. Because, as Dakota says, "That's what you do for a brother."

Dakota says he'll accept this medal in their name. So today we remember the husband who loved the outdoors, Lieutenant Michael Johnson; the husband and father they called "Gunny J," Gunnery Sergeant Edwin Johnson; the determined marine who fought to get on that team, Staff Sergeant Aaron Kenefick; the medic who gave his life tending to his teammates, Hospitalman Third Class James Layton; and a soldier wounded in that battle who never recovered, Sergeant First Class Kenneth Westbrook.

Dakota, I know that you've grappled with the grief of that day, that you've said your efforts were somehow a "failure" because your teammates didn't come home. But as your Commander in Chief, and on behalf of everyone here today and all Americans, I want you to know, it's quite the opposite. You did your duty, above and beyond, and you kept the faith with the highest traditions of the Marine Corps that you love.

Because of your honor, 36 men are alive today. Because of your courage, four fallen American heroes came home, and—in the words of James Layton's mom—they could lay their sons to rest with dignity. Because of your commitment—in the thick of the fight, hour after hour—a former marine who read about your story said that you showed how "in the most desperate, final hours . . . our brothers and God will not forsake us." And because of your humble example, our kids—especially back in Columbia, Kentucky, in small towns all across America—they'll know that no matter who you are or where you come from, you can do great things as a citizen and as a member of the American family.

Therein lies the greatest lesson of that day in the valley and the truth that our men and

women in uniform live out every day. "I was part of something bigger," Dakota has said, part of a team "that worked together, lifting each other up and working toward a common goal. Every member of our team was as important as the other." So in keeping with Dakota's wishes for this day, I want to conclude by asking now-Gunnery Sergeant Rodriguez-Chavez and all those who served with Dakota—the Marines, Army, Navy—to stand and accept thanks of a grateful nation.

Every member of our team is as important as the other. That's a lesson that we all have to remember—as citizens and as a nation—as we meet the tests of our time, here at home and around the world.

To our Marines, to all our men and women in uniform, to our fellow Americans, let us always be faithful. And as we prepare for the reading of the citation, let me say, God bless you, Dakota. God bless our Marines and all who serve. And God bless the United States of America. Semper Fi.

[*At this point, Lt. Cmdr. Matthew R. Maasdam, USN, Navy Aide to the President, read the citation, the President presented the medal, and Rear Admiral Margaret G. Kibben, USN, Chaplain of the U.S. Marine Corps, said a prayer.*]

Thank you all for joining us here today. We are grateful for Dakota. We are grateful for all our men and women in uniform. And I hope that all of you have not only been inspired by this ceremony, but also will enjoy the hospitality of the White House. I hear the food is pretty good. [*Laughter*]

Thank you very much, everybody. God bless you.

NOTE: The President spoke at 2:50 p.m. in the East Room at the White House. In his remarks, he referred to Dwight and Jean Meyer, grandparents of Sgt. Meyer; and Carlat Freitas, mother of PO3 James Layton, USN, who was killed in Afghanistan on September 8, 2009.

Statement on New Hampshire Governor John H. Lynch's Decision Not To Seek Reelection
September 15, 2011

John Lynch, for nearly four terms as Governor, has worked across party lines time and time again to grow the New Hampshire economy, improve high school graduation rates, and make it easier for businesses to invest in research and development. Through some tough economic times, John maintained key services for Granite State residents, all while keeping faith with New Hampshire's independent spirit. Michelle and I wish John and his family well and join the people of New Hampshire in thanking him for his many years of service.

Memorandum on Pelly Certification and Icelandic Whaling
September 15, 2011

Memorandum for the Vice President, the Secretary of State, the Secretary of the Treasury, the Secretary of Defense, the Attorney General, the Secretary of the Interior, the Secretary of Agriculture, the Secretary of Commerce, the Secretary of Labor, the Secretary of Health and Human Services, the Secretary of Housing and Urban Development, the Secretary of Transportation, the Secretary of Energy, the Secretary of Education, the Secretary of Veterans Affairs, the Secretary of Homeland Security, the Assistant to the President and Chief of Staff, the Administrator of the Environmental Protection Agency, the Director of the Office of Management and Budget, the United States Trade Representative, the Representative of the United States of America to the United Nations, and the Chair of the Council of Economic Advisers

Subject: Pelly Certification and Icelandic Whaling

On July 19, 2011, Secretary of Commerce Gary Locke certified under section 8 of the Fisherman's Protective Act of 1967, as amended (the "Pelly Amendment")(22 U.S.C. 1978), that nationals of Iceland are conducting whaling activities that diminish the effectiveness of the International Whaling Commission (IWC) conservation program. In his letter of July 19, 2011, Secretary Locke expressed his concern for these actions, and I share these concerns.

To ensure that this issue continues to receive the highest level of attention, and in accordance with Secretary Locke's recommendations, I direct: (1) relevant U.S. delegations attending meetings with Icelandic officials and senior Administration officials visiting Iceland to raise U.S. concerns regarding commercial whaling by Icelandic companies and seek ways to halt such action; (2) Cabinet secretaries to evaluate the appropriateness of visits to Iceland depending on continuation of the current suspension of fin whaling; (3) the Department of State to examine Arctic cooperation projects, and where appropriate, link U.S. cooperation to the Icelandic government changing its whaling policy and abiding by the IWC moratorium on commercial whaling; (4) the Departments of Commerce and State to consult with other international actors on efforts to end Icelandic commercial whaling and have Iceland abide by the IWC moratorium on commercial whaling; (5) the Department of State to inform the Government of Iceland that the United States will continue to monitor the activities of Icelandic companies that engage in commercial whaling; and (6) relevant U.S. agencies to continue to examine other options for responding to continued whaling by Iceland.

I direct the Secretaries of State and Commerce to continue to keep the situation under review and to continue to urge Iceland to cease its commercial whaling activities. It is my expectation that departments and agencies make substantive progress towards their implementation. To this end, within 6 months, or immediately upon the resumption of fin whaling by Icelandic nationals, I direct departments and agencies to report to me on their actions through the Departments of State and Commerce.

I believe that these actions hold the most promise of effecting a reduction in Iceland's commercial whaling activities, and support our broader conservation efforts.

BARACK OBAMA

Message to the Congress Reporting on Pelly Certification and Icelandic Whaling
September 15, 2011

To the Congress of the United States:

On July 19, 2011, Secretary of Commerce Gary Locke certified under section 8 of the Fisherman's Protective Act of 1967, as amended (the "Pelly Amendment")(22 U.S.C. 1978), that nationals of Iceland are conducting whaling activities that diminish the effectiveness of the International Whaling Commission (IWC) conservation program. This message constitutes my report to the Congress consistent with subsection (b) of the Pelly Amendment.

In 1982, the IWC set catch limits for all commercial whaling at zero. This decision, known as the commercial whaling moratorium, is in effect today. Iceland abided by the moratorium until 1992, when it withdrew from the IWC. In 2002, Iceland rejoined the IWC with a reservation to the moratorium on commercial whaling. In 2003, Iceland began a lethal scientific research whaling program. In 2004, Secretary of Commerce Donald L. Evans certified Iceland under the Pelly Amendment for lethal scientific research whaling. When Iceland resumed commercial whaling in 2006, Secretary Carlos M. Gutierrez retained Iceland's certification, which remains in effect today.

Iceland's commercial harvest of fin whales escalated dramatically over the past few years. In addition, Iceland recently resumed exporting whale products. Of particular concern to the United States, Iceland harvested 125 endangered fin whales in 2009 and 148 in 2010, a significant increase from the total of 7 fin whales it commercially harvested between 1987 and 2007.

Iceland's sole fin whaling company, Hvalur hf, suspended its fin whaling due to the earthquake and tsunami in Japan, where it exports its whale meat. Despite this suspension, Iceland continues to permit whaling and has a government issued fin whale quota in effect for the 2011 season that continues to exceed catch levels that the IWC's scientific body advised would be sustainable if the moratorium was removed. This continues to present a threat to the conservation of fin whales. Further, Icelandic nationals continue to hunt minke whales commercially and Iceland's exports of whale meat to Japan reportedly increased significantly in both March and April 2011.

Iceland's actions threaten the conservation status of an endangered species and undermine multilateral efforts to ensure greater worldwide protection for whales. Iceland's increased commercial whaling and recent trade in whale products diminish the effectiveness of the IWC's conservation program because: (1) Iceland's commercial harvest of whales undermines the moratorium on commercial whaling put in place by the IWC to protect plummeting whale stocks; (2) the fin whale harvest greatly exceeds catch levels that the IWC's scientific body advised would be sustainable if the moratorium were removed; and (3) Iceland's harvests are not likely to be brought under IWC management and control at sustainable levels through multilateral efforts at the IWC.

In his letter of July 19, 2011, Secretary Locke expressed his concern for these actions, and I share these concerns. To ensure that this issue continues to receive the highest level of attention, I direct: (1) relevant U.S. delegations attending meetings with Icelandic officials and senior Administration officials visiting Iceland to raise U.S. concerns regarding commercial whaling by Icelandic companies and seek ways to halt such action; (2) Cabinet secretaries to evaluate the appropriateness of visits to Iceland depending on continuation of the current suspension of fin whaling; (3) the Department of State to examine Arctic cooperation projects, and where appropriate, link U.S. cooperation to the Icelandic government changing its whaling policy and abiding by the IWC moratorium on commercial whaling; (4) the Departments of Commerce and State to consult with other international actors on efforts to end Icelandic commercial whaling and have Iceland abide by the IWC moratorium on commercial whaling; (5) the Department of State to inform the Government of Iceland that the United States will continue to monitor the activities of Icelandic companies that engage in commercial whaling; and (6) relevant U.S. agencies to continue to examine other options for responding to continued whaling by Iceland.

I concur with the Secretary of Commerce's recommendation to pursue the use of non-trade measures and that the actions outlined above are the appropriate course of action to address this issue. Accordingly, I am not directing the Secretary of the Treasury to impose trade measures on Icelandic products for the whaling activities that led to the certification by the Secretary of Commerce. However, to ensure that this issue continues to receive the highest level of attention, I am directing the Departments of State and Commerce to continue to keep the situation under review and continue to urge Iceland to cease its commercial whaling activities. Further, within 6 months, or immediately upon the resumption of fin whaling by Icelandic nationals, I have directed relevant departments and agencies to report to me through the Departments of State and Commerce on their actions. I believe these actions hold the most promise of effecting a reduction in Iceland's commercial whaling activities.

BARACK OBAMA

The White House,
September 15, 2011.

Remarks at a Democratic National Committee Fundraiser
September 15, 2011

Thank you, Sylvia. I'm going to be quick because I want to make this more of a dialogue than a monologue. And a lot of you guys are old friends, been supporting us for a long time. And we're going to be seeing each other a lot out on the campaign trail as you guys are bringing in folks from various cities, getting them involved.

So let me just say this. Last week, obviously, I presented to Congress the "American Jobs Act." And what I tried to underscore in that speech is the urgency for action in Washington. Now, over the last 2½ years, we've been busy trying to make sure that we did not spill into a depression, trying to make sure that we stabilized the financial system, trying to make sure that we saved the auto industry. And we were successful in stabilizing the economy, but what we have not been able to do is get the kind of recovery that puts people back to work the way we need to. And there are a number of things that we can do administratively, but ultimately, we have to make sure that Washington is working on behalf of folks who are hurting out there, as opposed to working contrary to the interests of people all across the country.

And in the "American Jobs Act," what we've said was, look, if Congress is able to take some action now—not 14 months from now, not 6 months from now, but now—we can put teachers back in the classroom, we can put construction workers back to work, we can put our veterans back to work, we can make sure that young people have opportunities for summer jobs, we can start dealing with the unemployed, and we can pay for it in a way that's responsible and that involves everybody sharing in the burdens of what are a difficult time.

Now, right away, the commentary was, well, this Congress, they are accustomed to doing nothing, and they're comfortable with doing nothing, and they keep on doing nothing. But I will tell you, we intend to keep the pressure on. And I, just this week, have traveled to North Carolina, and we've been to Ohio. Before that, right after I made the speech, we were in Virginia. In Virginia, we had probably about 12,000 people, in North Carolina, about 10,000. And folks are ready for action.

And for those of you who have been supporters for a long time, as you know, there's a time for governance, and there's a time for making a political case. My hope is, is that we're going to keep on seeing some governance out of Washington over the next several months, because the American people can't afford to wait for an election to actually see us start doing something serious about our jobs. But we are going to run this like a campaign, in the sense that we've got to take it to the American people and make the case as to why it is possible for Washington to make a difference right now.

And so far, people have been responding with extraordinary enthusiasm. But it's going to take hard work to get a Congress that, I think, their natural instinct is right now—the Republicans in the House, their natural instinct right now is not to engage in the kind of cooperation that we'd like to see. So ultimately, I think, if we are doing what the American people are looking for on jobs and on the economy, then we will be able to start seeing the recovery take off once again and get to the point where we're starting to bring down unemployment in a significant way.

It's estimated that the "American Jobs Act" would add 2 percentage points to the GDP and add as many as 1.9 million jobs and bring the unemployment rate down by a full percentage point. But even if we get that done, there's still going to be some long-term challenges that we have to deal with in the economy that precede a recession. The fact of the matter is, for a decade now, incomes and wages have flatlined for the American people: for ordinary Americans, for working families. They are working harder, making less, with higher expenses. And that's been going on for a long, long time.

And 2012 is going to be one of those elections that, in some ways, may be more impor-

tant than 2008, because, having worked our way through this recession, having still—having us still needing to make sure that we're taking action to drive the unemployment rate down, there is going to be a sharp divide in terms of where the Republican candidate is and my position in terms of where we need to take the country. We're going to have to make decisions about do we make investments in infrastructure? Do we actually have an energy policy? Do we have an education policy that makes sure that everybody has a chance at the American Dream? Are we going to make sure that we implement our health care plan so that 30 million people have health insurance and we start driving down costs? How are we going to approach foreign policy?

Those issues are still going to be looming, and I encourage all of you to watch—if you need some inspiration, watch the Republican Presidential debates. [*Laughter*] Because you will have a sense that there is going to be a clear choice presented. There's not going to be a lot of ambiguity in terms of alternative visions about where we want to take the country. I believe in a country that is big and generous and bold and is investing in the future and in which there's fairness and everybody shares in the success and shares in the burdens of moving our country forward. And they've got a different philosophy. And that's going to be tested before the American people like never before.

So bottom line is, I appreciate all of you guys being here. We're going to have a lot of hard work, but this group is no stranger to hard work, because, as many of you can attest, it's always hard at a time when our politics are divided and at a time when the economy is struggling. So it's going to require that everybody here bring every ounce of effort that they've got into making sure that the campaign is successful, but also that we're able to get a clear mandate for the kinds of changes that we want to make to ensure that America is—continues to be a land where everybody has opportunity.

All right. Thanks very much, everyone.

NOTE: The President spoke at 6:44 p.m. at the residence of Frank White, Jr., and Sylvia D. Davis.

Remarks at a Democratic National Committee Fundraiser
September 15, 2011

Thank you. I am going to keep my opening remarks very brief, because I want to have a conversation with you more than anything else. And so my first task is just to thank Elizabeth, her wonderful children, for hosting us here. It is true that I have been here before. I think the first time I was here, I had just been elected to the Senate, and I still remember Smith and you being incredibly gracious to me and opening up your home at a time when I was still the new kid on the block. [*Laughter*] So I appreciate that, and I thank you for your extraordinary public service as well.

I want to thank all of you for being here. Many of you are old friends and have been supporters for a long time. Some of you are new, and I'm very grateful for you taking the time to be here.

As Elizabeth described aptly, we are going through extraordinary times. These are no ordinary times. We are going through the worst economic crisis since the Great Depression. And historically, after financial recessions, it is a challenge and a struggle. And over the last 2½ years, what we've been able to do is stabilize an economy, but at a level where unemployment remains way too high.

And so last week, I went before Congress, and I explained to them why they need to act—to put construction workers back to work and teachers back in the classroom and veterans back to work and dealing with the long-term unemployed—and tried to communicate a sense of urgency. The country does not have patience for the traditional political games here in Washington. Those games are okay when unemployment is at 5 percent and basically people can choose to ignore it. But right now they need action. And certainly what they don't need is to make sure that Washington is an impediment to economic growth and putting people back to work.

As Elizabeth said, this particular Congress has not shown itself particularly eager to work with me to solve problems. I think that's—[*laughter*]—that's a fair assessment. [*Laugh-*

ter] But the American people, that's what they're demanding, that's what they're insisting on. And so we are going to be, over the next several weeks and next several months, out there talking very specifically about how Washington could make a difference right now.

Of course, I didn't run for the Presidency just to deal with immediate concerns. There are a wide range of problems that existed long before this particular recession hit. We still have an education system that is not training our kids for the 21st century and the demands of a global economy. We still are suffering from a lack of an energy policy that can deal both with our environmental challenges, but also our economic challenges.

Our health care bill, I think, is going to make a huge difference, providing 30 million people affordable coverage for the first time. But it's got to be implemented, and it's only part of the way there. We still have enormous inequality in our society and providing the ladders of opportunity for people who want to live out that American Dream, but are finding too many roadblocks along the way.

We still have a fiscal situation that arises not only from this most recent crisis, but also some long-term trends, where those of us in this room do very well, while folks who are struggling don't do quite as well. And there's, I think, an innate sense among the American people that things aren't fair, that the deck is stacked against them, that no matter how hard they work, their costs keep on going up, their hours are longer, they're struggling to make their mortgage, and somehow nobody's paying attention.

And all those long-term trends—our structural deficit, energy policy, education—2012 is going to offer a clearer contrast than I think we've ever seen before; 2008 was a big election—obviously, I thought so, because—[*laughter*]. But in some ways 2012, I think, is going to be more clarifying, because if you see the direction that the Republican Party is now going in, you have a party that offers a fundamentally different vision of where America should be and what we should be aspiring to and what our core values are. And that contest is going to, I think, help shape America for not just the next 5 years, but for decades to come. And that's why your involvement and your engagement is going to be absolutely critical.

Now, I know that over the last couple of months there have been Democrats who voiced concerns and nervousness about, well, in this kind of economy, isn't this just—aren't these just huge headwinds in terms of your re-election? And I just have to remind people that—here's one thing I know for certain: The odds of me being reelected are much higher than the odds of me being elected in the first place. [*Laughter*] And in that spirit, I just want to point out, it was somebody during the photo line who—I think right here—made what I think is a very important wish. And that is that my next Inauguration is warmer than the last one. [*Laughter*]

But we remain very confident about our ability to win a contest of ideas in 2012, as long as we can get the message out. Now, the campaign has not begun. My job—I've got a day job, and I'm going to have to spend a lot of time continuing to govern over the next several months. And that's why your voices, you being

out there talking about the "American Jobs Act," talking about our track record in terms of what we've done over the last 3 years, talking to people about what's at stake, is going to be so important.

Elizabeth has done an extraordinary job in the past representing the United States. Well, this is one of those times where all of you are going to have to be my ambassadors over the next several months to make sure that people who I think continue to believe in change and continue to believe in hope are mobilized effectively in 2012. And if you're there with me, then I'm confident that we'll have an Inauguration, although I can't promise good weather. [*Laughter*]

All right. Thank you very much, everybody. And then, I think we're going to move the press out, and then, we'll have a conversation.

NOTE: The President spoke at 7:54 p.m. at the residence of former U.S. Ambassador to Portugal Elizabeth Frawley Bagley. In his remarks, he referred to Vaughan E. Bagley, daughter, and Conor R. Bagley, son, of former Ambassador Bagley. Audio was not available for verification of the content of these remarks.

Remarks on Signing the Leahy-Smith America Invents Act in Alexandria, Virginia
September 16, 2011

Thank you so much, everybody. Please, please have a seat. I am thrilled to be here at Thomas Jefferson High School for Science and Technology. And thank you so much for the wonderful welcome.

I want to thank Rebecca for the unbelievable introduction. Give Rebecca a big hand. In addition to Rebecca, on stage we've got some very important people. First of all, before we do, I want to thank your wonderful principal, Dr. Evan Glazer, who's right here. Stand up, Evan. [*Applause*] Yay! The people who are responsible for making some great progress on reforming our patent laws here today: Senator

Patrick Leahy of Vermont and Lamar Smith, Republican from Texas.

And in addition, we've got Representative Bob Goodlatte, Representative Jim Moran, Representative Melvin Watt are all here; Becky Blank, who's our Acting Secretary of Commerce; David Kappos, who's the Director of U.S. Patent and Trademark Office. And we've got some extraordinary business leaders here: Louis Foreman, CEO of Enventys; Jessica Matthews, CEO of Uncharted Play; Ellen Kullman, CEO of DuPont; John Lechleiter, CEO of Eli Lilly. And we've got another outstanding student, Karishma Popli, your classmate.

This is one of the best high schools in the country. And as you can see, it's filled with some pretty impressive students. I have to say, when I was a freshman in high school, none of my work was patentworthy. [*Laughter*] I was—we had an exhibit of some of the projects that you guys are doing, and the first high school student satellite, a wheelchair controlled by brain waves, robots. There's one thing—I don't know exactly how to describe it—[*laughter*]—but it's measuring toxicity in the oceans. It's unbelievable stuff.

So to the students here, I could not be more impressed by what you guys are doing. I'm hoping that I will learn something just by being close to you—[*laughter*]—that through osmosis—[*laughter*]—I will soak in some knowledge. I already feel smarter just standing here. [*Laughter*]

One President who would have loved this school is the person that it's named after, Thomas Jefferson. He was a pretty good inventor himself, and he also happened to be the first American to oversee our country's patent process.

And that's why we're here today. When Thomas Edison filed his patent for the phonograph, his application was approved in just 7 weeks. And these days, that process is taking an average of 3 years. Over the last decade, patent applications have nearly tripled. And because the Patent Office doesn't have the resources to deal with all of them, right now there are about 700,000 applications that haven't even been opened yet.

These are jobs and businesses of the future just waiting to be created. The CEOs who are represented here today, all of them are running companies that were based on creativity and invention and the ability to commercialize good ideas. And somewhere in that stack of applications could be the next technological breakthrough, the next miracle drug, the next idea that will launch the next Fortune 500 company. And somewhere in this country—maybe in this room—is the next Thomas Edison or Steve Jobs, just waiting for a chance to turn their idea into a new, thriving business.

So we can't afford to drag our feet any longer, not at a time when we should be doing everything we can to create good, middle class jobs that put Americans back to work. And we have always succeeded because we have been the most dynamic, innovative economy in the world. That has to be encouraged. That has to be continued.

We have to do everything we can to encourage the entrepreneurial spirit, wherever we find it. We should be helping American companies compete and sell their products all over the world. We should be making it easier and faster to turn new ideas into new jobs and new businesses. And we should knock down any barriers that stand in the way. Because if we're going to create jobs now and in the future, we're going to have to outbuild and outeducate and outinnovate every other country on Earth.

We've got a lot of competition out there. And if we make it too hard for people with good ideas to attract investment and get them to market, then countries like China are going to beat us at it and beat us to it.

So that's why I asked Congress to send me a bill that reforms the outdated patent process, a bill that cuts away the redtape that slows down our inventors and entrepreneurs. And today I'm happy to have the opportunity to finally sign that bill. It's a bill that will put a dent in the huge stack of patent applications waiting for review. It will help startups and small-business owners turn their ideas into products three times faster than they can today. And it will improve patent quality and help give entrepreneurs the protection and the confidence they need to attract investment, to grow their businesses, and to hire more workers.

So I want to thank all the Members of Congress for helping to get this done. I especially want to thank Patrick Leahy and Lamar Smith, who led the process in a bipartisan way in the House and in the Senate.

I have to take this opportunity, while I've got some Members of Congress here, to say I've got another bill that—[*laughter*]—I want them to get passed to help the economy right away. It's called the "American Jobs Act." And these things are connected. This change in our patent laws is part of our agenda for making us competitive over the long term. But we've also got a short-term economic crisis, a set of challenges that we have to deal with right now.

And what the "American Jobs Act" does is it puts more people back to work and it puts more money into the pockets of working Americans. And everything in the proposal, everything in the "American Jobs Act," is the kind of proposal that's been supported by Democrats and Republicans in the past. Everything in it will be paid for. And you can read the plan for yourselves during all the free time that you guys have here at Thomas Jefferson—[*laughter*]—on whitehouse.gov. I want Congress to pass this jobs bill right away.

Let me give you an example of why this is relevant. We're surrounded today by outstanding teachers, men and women who prepare our young people to compete in a global economy. If Congress passes this jobs bill, then we can get thousands of teachers all across the country who've been laid off because of difficulties at the State and local level with their budgets, we can get them back to work, back in the classroom.

This jobs bill will put unemployed construction workers back to work rebuilding our schools and our roads and our bridges. And it will give tax credits to companies that hire our veterans, because if you serve our country, you shouldn't have to worry about finding a job when you get home.

It connects the long-term unemployed to temporary work to keep their skills sharp while they're looking for a job, and it gives thousands of young people the hope of a job next summer. And it will cut taxes for every middle class family and small-business owner in America. And if you're a small-business owner that hires more workers and raises salaries, you get an extra tax credit.

It won't add to the deficit. And we'll pay for it by following the same rules that every family follows: Spend money on things you need, cut back on things you don't. And we'll make sure that everybody pays their fair share, including those of us who've been incredibly fortunate and blessed in this country.

So this bill answers the urgent need to create jobs right away. But, as I said, we can't stop there. We have to look further down the road and build an economy that lasts into the future, and that's going to depend on the talents of young people like you; an economy that creates good, middle class jobs that pay well and offer families a sense of security.

We live in a world that is changing so rapidly, companies like the ones represented here today, they can set up shop anywhere where there's an Internet connection. And if we want startups here and if we want established companies like a DuPont or a Eli Lilly to continue to make products here and hire here, then we're going to have to be able to compete with any other country around the world.

So this patent bill will encourage that innovation. But there are other steps that we can take. Today, for example, my administration is announcing a new center that will help companies reduce the time and cost of developing lifesaving drugs. When scientists and researchers at the National Institutes of Health discover a new cure or breakthrough, we're going to make it easier for startup companies to sell those products to the people who need them. We got more than 100 universities and companies to agree that they'll work together to bring more inventions to market as fast as possible. And we're also developing a strategy to create jobs in biotechnology, which has tremendous promise for health, clean energy, and the environment.

Now, to help this country compete for new jobs and businesses, we also need to invest in basic research and technology, so the great ideas of the future will be born in our labs and in classrooms like these. You guys have such an unbelievable head start already, but as you go to MIT and Caltech and UVA and wherever else you guys are going to go, what you're going to find is, is that the further you get along in your pursuits, the more you're going to be relying on research grants. And Government's are—always played a critical role in financing the basic research that then leads to all sorts of inventions.

So we're going to have to make sure that we're continuing to invest in basic research so you can do the work that you're capable of and still pay the rent, which is important, you will find out. [*Laughter*]

We need to continue to provide incentives and support to make sure that the next generation of manufacturing takes root not in China or in Europe, but right here in the United States. Because it's not enough to invent things here, our workers should also be building the products that are stamped with three proud words: Made in America.

And if we want companies to hire our workers, we need to make sure we give every American the skills and education that they need to compete. We've got to have more schools like Thomas Jefferson. And it's got to start even before kindergarten and preschool and before high school. The reason that you guys are doing so well is you had a foundation very early on in math and science and language arts that allowed you to succeed even at a very young age. We've got to make sure that opportunity is available for all kids. All kids, including this little guy right here—[*laughter*]—with the hair. Right.

That's why we're boosting science and technology and engineering and math education all across the country. And that's why we're also working with businesses to train more engineers and revitalize our community colleges so they can provide our workers with new skills and training. And finally, that's why we're making sure that all of our children can afford to fulfill their dream of a college education, that they can afford to go to school and that Pell grants and student loan programs ensure that they don't come out of college with mountains of debt.

So this is the economy we need to build, one where innovation is encouraged, education is a national mission, and new jobs and businesses take root right here in America.

So that's the long-term project. We still have a short-term agenda, and that is putting people to work right now. We've got to do everything we can to get this economy growing faster in the short term. That's why I'm asking Members of Congress to meet their responsibilities, send me the "American Jobs Act" right away.

There are folks in Washington who may be fine waiting until the next election to settle our differences and move forward. But the next election is 14 months away. The American people can't wait that long. There are a lot of people out there who are living paycheck to paycheck, even day to day. They're working hard. They're making tough choices. They're meeting their responsibilities. But they need us to do the same.

So I need everybody who's listening, here and across the country, tell Congress: Pass the "American Jobs Act." We came together to pass patent reform. We should be able to come together to also put people back to work.

And to all the students at Thomas Jefferson, I could not be prouder of you. I expect that among you are going to be incredible scientists and engineers and business leaders. You guys are going to transform the world. And I'm just looking forward to taking advantage of the incredible science and technology that you develop in the years to come.

You guys are our future. And whenever I see what young people like you are doing, I know that America's future is going to be bright.

Thank you so much, everybody. God bless you. God bless the United States of America.

NOTE: The President spoke at 11:17 a.m. at Thomas Jefferson High School for Science and Technology. In his remarks, he referred to Rebecca Hyndman, student, Thomas Jefferson High School for Science and Technology; and Steven P. Jobs, chairman of the board, Apple Inc. H.R. 1249, approved September 16, was assigned Public Law No. 112–29.

The President's Weekly Address
September 17, 2011

I've spent some time lately traveling the country and talking with folks outside of Washington. And the number-one issue for the people I meet is, how can we get back to a place where we're creating good, middle class jobs that pay well and offer some security?

That's the idea behind the "American Jobs Act." It's a jobs bill that does two simple things: put more people back to work, and more money back in the pockets of people who are working.

This jobs bill puts construction workers back to work rebuilding our roads and bridges and modernizing our schools. This jobs bill puts teachers back in the classroom and keeps cops and firefighters on our streets. This jobs bill gives tax credits to companies that hire our veterans, because if you sign up to fight for our country, the last thing you should have to do is fight for a job when you come home. This jobs bill connects the long-term unemployed to temporary work to keep their skills sharp while they look for a job, and it gives hundreds of thousands of young people the hope of a job next summer.

This jobs bill cuts taxes for every small-business owner in America. It cuts them even more for small-business owners that hire new workers and raise workers' salaries. And it cuts taxes for every working family in America so you'll have more money in your pockets and businesses know they'll have more customers to buy what they sell.

That's the "American Jobs Act," and you can check it out for yourself on whitehouse.gov.

It will create new jobs. It will cut taxes for every worker and small business in the country. And it will not add to the deficit; it will be paid for.

On Monday, I'll lay out my plan for how we'll do that, how we'll pay for this plan and pay down our debt, by following some basic principles: making sure we live within our means and asking everyone to pay their fair share.

But right now we've got to get Congress to pass this jobs bill. Everything in the "American Jobs Act" is the kind of idea that's been supported by Democrats and Republicans before. And if they're ideas you agree with, then every one of you can help make it happen by telling your Congressperson to pass this jobs bill right away.

I know some of them would rather wait another year to wage another election than work together right now. But most Americans don't have the luxury of waiting. It was 3 years ago this week that a financial crisis on Wall Street made things much more difficult for working folks on Main Street. And too many are still hurting as a result.

So the time for action is now. No more games, no more gridlock, no more division or delay. It's time for the people you sent to Washington to put country before party, to stop worrying so much about their jobs and start worrying more about yours.

It's time to get to work and show the world once again why the United States of America remains the greatest nation on Earth.

Thanks.

NOTE: The address was recorded at approximately 5:10 p.m. on September 16 in the Diplomatic Reception Room at the White House for broadcast on September 17. The transcript was made available by the Office of the Press Secretary on September 16, but was embargoed for release until 6 a.m. on September 17.

Remarks on the Federal Budget and Job Growth Legislation
September 19, 2011

Good morning, everybody. Please have a seat.

A week ago today, I sent Congress the "American Jobs Act." It's a plan that will lead to new jobs for teachers, for construction workers, for veterans, and for the unemployed. It will cut taxes for every small-business owner and virtually every working man and woman in America. And the proposals in this jobs bill are the kinds that have been supported by Democrats and Republicans in the past. So there shouldn't be any reason for Congress to drag its feet. They should pass it right away. I'm ready to sign a bill. I've got the pens all ready.

Now, as I said before, Congress should pass this bill knowing that every proposal is fully paid for. The "American Jobs Act" will not add to our Nation's debt. And today I'm releasing a plan that details how to pay for the jobs bill while also paying down our debt over time.

And this is important, because the health of our economy depends in part on what we do right now to create the conditions where businesses can hire and middle class families can feel a basic measure of economic security. But in the long run, our prosperity also depends on our ability to pay down the massive debt we've accumulated over the past decade in a way that allows us to meet our responsibilities to each other and to the future.

Now, during this past decade, profligate spending in Washington, tax cuts for multimillionaires and billionaires, the costs of two wars, and the recession turned a record surplus into a yawning deficit, and that left us with a big pile of IOUs. If we don't act, that burden will ultimately fall on our children's shoulders. If we don't act, the growing debt will eventually crowd out everything else, preventing us from investing in things like education or sustaining programs like Medicare.

So Washington has to live within its means. The Government has to do what families across this country have been doing for years. We have to cut what we can't afford to pay for what really matters. We need to invest in what will promote hiring and economic growth now, while still providing the confidence that will come with a plan that reduces our deficits over the long term.

These principles were at the heart of the deficit framework that I put forward in April. It was an approach to shrink the deficit as a share of the economy, but not to do so so abruptly with spending cuts that would hamper growth or prevent us from helping small businesses

and middle class families get back on their feet.

It was an approach that said we need to go through the budget line by line looking for waste, without shortchanging education and basic scientific research and road construction because those things are essential to our future. And it was an approach that said we shouldn't balance the budget on the backs of the poor and the middle class, that for us to solve this problem, everybody, including the wealthiest Americans and biggest corporations, have to pay their fair share.

Now, during the debt ceiling debate, I had hoped to negotiate a compromise with the Speaker of the House that fulfilled these principles and achieved the $4 trillion in deficit reduction that leaders in both parties have agreed we need, a grand bargain that would have strengthened our economy instead of weakened it. Unfortunately, the Speaker walked away from a balanced package. What we agreed to instead wasn't all that grand. But it was a start: roughly $1 trillion in cuts to domestic spending and defense spending.

Everyone knows we have to do more, and a special joint committee of Congress is assigned to find more deficit reduction. So today I'm laying out a set of specific proposals to finish what we started this summer, proposals that live up to the principles I've talked about from the beginning. It's a plan that reduces our debt by more than $4 trillion and achieves these savings in a way that is fair, by asking everybody to do their part so that no one has to bear too much of the burden on their own.

All told, this plan cuts $2 in spending for every dollar in new revenues. In addition to the $1 trillion in spending that we've already cut from the budget, our plan makes additional spending cuts that need to happen if we're to solve this problem. We reform agricultural subsidies, subsidies that a lot of times pay large farms for crops that they don't grow. We make modest adjustments to Federal retirement programs. We reduce by tens of billions of dollars the tax money that goes to Fannie Mae and Freddie Mac. We also ask the largest financial firms—companies saved by tax dollars during the financial crisis—to repay the American people for every dime that we spent. And we save an additional $1 trillion as we end the wars in Iraq and Afghanistan.

These savings are not only counted as part of our plan, but as part of the budget plan that nearly every Republican on the House voted for.

Finally, this plan includes structural reforms to reduce the cost of health care in programs like Medicare and Medicaid. Keep in mind, we've already included a number of reforms in the health care law, which will go a long way towards controlling these costs. But we're going to have to do a little more. This plan reduces wasteful subsidies and erroneous payments while changing some incentives that often lead to excessive health care costs. It makes prescriptions more affordable through faster approval of generic drugs. We'll work with Governors to make Medicaid more efficient and more accountable. And we'll change the way we pay for health care. Instead of just paying for procedures, providers will be paid more when they improve results, and such steps will save money and improve care.

These changes are phased in slowly to strengthen Medicare and Medicaid over time. Because while we do need to reduce health care costs, I'm not going to allow that to be an excuse for turning Medicare into a voucher program that leaves seniors at the mercy of the insurance industry. I'm not going to stand for balancing the budget by denying or reducing health care for poor children or those with disabilities. So we will reform Medicare and Medicaid, but we will not abandon the fundamental commitment that this country has kept for generations.

And by the way, that includes our commitment to Social Security. I've said before, Social Security is not the primary cause of our deficits, but it does face long-term challenges as our country grows older. And both parties are going to need to work together on a separate track to strengthen Social Security for our children and our grandchildren.

So this is how we can reduce spending: by scouring the budget for every dime of waste and inefficiency, by reforming Government spending, and by making modest adjustments to Medicare and Medicaid. But all these reductions in spending, by themselves, will not solve our fiscal problems. We can't just cut our way out of this hole. It's going to take a balanced approach. If we're going to make spending cuts, many of which we wouldn't make if we weren't facing such large budget deficits, then it's only right that we ask everyone to pay their fair share.

You know, last week, Speaker of the House John Boehner gave a speech about the economy. And to his credit, he made the point that we can't afford the kind of politics that says it's "my way or the highway." I was encouraged by that. Here's the problem: In the same speech, he also came out against any plan to cut the deficit that includes any additional revenues whatsoever. He said—I'm quoting him—there is "only one option." And that option—and only option—relies entirely on cuts. That means slashing education, surrendering the research necessary to keep America's technological edge in the 21st century, and allowing our critical public assets like highways and bridges and airports to get worse. It would cripple our competiveness and our ability to win the jobs of the future. And it would also mean asking sacrifice of seniors and the middle class and the poor, while asking nothing of the wealthiest Americans and biggest corporations.

So the Speaker says we can't have it "my way or the highway" and then basically says, "My way or the highway." [*Laughter*] That's not smart. It's not right. If we're going to meet our responsibilities, we have to do it together.

Now, I'm proposing real, serious cuts in spending. When you include the $1 trillion in cuts I've already signed into law, these would be among the biggest cuts in spending in our history. But they've got to be part of a larger plan that's balanced, a plan that asks the most fortunate among us to pay their fair share, just like everybody else.

And that's why this plan eliminates tax loopholes that primarily go to the wealthiest taxpayers and biggest corporations, tax breaks that small businesses and middle class families don't get. And if tax reform doesn't get done, this plan asks the wealthiest Americans to go back to paying the same rates that they paid during the 1990s, before the Bush tax cuts.

I promise that it's not because anybody looks forward to the prospects of raising taxes or paying more taxes. I don't. In fact, I've cut taxes for the middle class and for small businesses, and through the "American Jobs Act," we'd cut taxes again to promote hiring and put more money into the pockets of people. But we can't afford these special lower rates for the wealthy, rates, by the way, that were meant to be temporary. Back when these first—these tax cuts, back in 2001, 2003, were being talked about, they were talked about as temporary measures. We can't afford them when we're running these big deficits.

Now, I am also ready to work with Democrats and Republicans to reform our entire Tax Code, to get rid of the decades of accumulated loopholes, special interest carve-outs, and other tax expenditures that stack the deck against small-business owners and ordinary families who can't afford Washington lobbyists or fancy accountants. Our Tax Code is more than 10,000 pages long. If you stack up all the volumes, they're almost 5 feet tall. And that means that how much you pay often depends less on what you make and more on how well you can game the system, and that's especially true of the corporate Tax Code.

We've got one of the highest corporate tax rates in the world, but it's riddled with exceptions and special interest loopholes. So some companies get out paying a lot of taxes, while the rest of them end up having to foot the bill. And this makes our entire economy less competitive and our country a less desirable place to do business.

That has to change. Our Tax Code shouldn't give an advantage to companies with the best connected lobbyists. It should give an advantage to companies that invest in the United States of America and create jobs in the United States of America. And we can lower the corporate rate if we get rid of all these special deals.

So I am ready, I am eager to work with Democrats and Republicans to reform the Tax

Code to make it simpler, make it fairer, and make America more competitive. But any reform plan will have to raise revenue to help close our deficit. That has to be part of the formula. And any reform should follow another simple principle: Middle class families shouldn't pay higher taxes than millionaires and billionaires. That's pretty straightforward. It's hard to argue against that. Warren Buffett's secretary shouldn't pay a higher tax rate than Warren Buffett. There's no justification for it.

It is wrong that in the United States of America, a teacher or a nurse or a construction worker who earns $50,000 should pay higher tax rates than somebody pulling in $50 million. Anybody who says we can't change the Tax Code to correct that, anyone who has signed some pledge to protect every single tax loophole so long as they live, they should be called out. They should have to defend that unfairness, explain why somebody who's making $50 million a year in the financial markets should be paying 15 percent on their taxes, when a teacher making $50,000 a year is paying more than that, paying a higher rate. They ought to have to answer for that. And if they're pledged to keep that kind of unfairness in place, they should remember: The last time I checked, the only pledge that really matters is the pledge we take to uphold the Constitution.

Now, we're already hearing the usual defenders of these kinds of loopholes saying this is just "class warfare." I reject the idea that asking a hedge fund manager to pay the same tax rate as a plumber or a teacher is class warfare. I think it's just the right the thing to do. I believe the American middle class, who have been pressured relentlessly for decades, believe it's time that they were fought for as hard as the lobbyists and some lawmakers have fought to protect special treatment for billionaires and big corporations.

Nobody wants to punish success in America. What's great about this country is our belief that anyone can make it and everybody should be able to try, the idea that any one of us can open a business or have an idea and make us millionaires or billionaires. This is the land of opportunity. That's great. All I'm saying is that those who have done well, including me, should pay our fair share in taxes to contribute to the Nation that made our success possible. We shouldn't get a better deal than ordinary families get. And I think most wealthy Americans would agree if they knew this would help us grow the economy and deal with the debt that threatens our future.

It comes down to this: We have to prioritize. Both parties agree that we need to reduce the deficit by the same amount, by $4 trillion. So what choices are we going to make to reach that goal? Either we ask the wealthiest Americans to pay their fair share in taxes, or we're going to have to ask seniors to pay more for Medicare. We can't afford to do both. Either we gut education and medical research, or we've got to reform the Tax Code so that the most profitable corporations have to give up tax loopholes that other companies don't get. We can't afford to do both.

This is not class warfare. It's math. [*Laughter*] The money is going to have to come from someplace. And if we're not willing to ask those who've done extraordinarily well to help America close the deficit and we are trying to reach that same target of $4 trillion, then the logic, the math says everybody else has to do a whole lot more. We've got to put the entire burden on the middle class and the poor. We've got to scale back on the investments that have always helped our economy grow. We've got to settle for second-rate roads and second-rate bridges and second-rate airports and schools that are crumbling.

That's unacceptable to me. That's unacceptable to the American people. And it will not happen on my watch. I will not support—I will not support—any plan that puts all the burden for closing our deficit on ordinary Americans. And I will veto any bill that changes benefits for those who rely on Medicare, but does not raise serious

revenues by asking the wealthiest Americans or biggest corporations to pay their fair share. We are not going to have a one-sided deal that hurts the folks who are most vulnerable.

Look, none of the changes I'm proposing are easy or politically convenient. It's always more popular to promise the Moon and leave the bill for after the next election or the election after that. That's been true since our founding. George Washington grappled with this problem. He said: "Towards the payment of debts, there must be revenue; that to have revenue there must be taxes; and no taxes can be devised which are not more or less inconvenient and unpleasant." He understood that dealing with the debt is—these are his words—"always a choice of difficulties." But he also knew that public servants weren't elected to do what was easy; they weren't elected to do what was politically advantageous. It's our responsibility to put country before party. It's our responsibility to do what's right for the future.

And that's what this debate is about. It's not about numbers on a ledger; it's not about figures on a spreadsheet. It's about the economic future of this country, and it's about whether we will do what it takes to create jobs and growth and opportunity while facing up to the legacy of debt that threatens everything we've built over generations.

And it's also about fairness. It's about whether we are, in fact, in this together and we're looking out for one another. We know what's right. It's time to do what's right.

Thank you very much.

NOTE: The President spoke at 10:56 a.m. in the Rose Garden at the White House. In his remarks, he referred to Warren E. Buffett, chief executive officer and chairman, Berkshire Hathaway Inc.

Message to the Congress Transmitting a Plan for Economic Growth and Deficit Reduction
September 19, 2011

To the Congress of the United States:

This continues to be a time of challenge for our country. We face an economic crisis that has left millions of our neighbors jobless, and a political crisis that has made things worse. Millions of Americans are looking for work. Across our country, families are doing their best just to scrape by—giving up nights out with the family to save on gas or make the mortgage, or postponing retirement to send a child to college.

These men and women grew up with faith in an America where hard work and responsibility paid off. They believed in a country where everyone gets a fair shake and does their fair share; they believed that if you worked hard and played by the rules, you would be rewarded with a decent salary and good benefits. If you did the right thing, you could make it in America.

For decades now, Americans have watched that compact erode. They have seen the decks too often stacked against them. And they know that Washington has not always put their interests first. Too often, our Nation's capital has been consumed by partisanship. Too often, the needs of special interests or politics have been put ahead of what is best for the country.

That is what must change. The American people work hard to meet their responsibilities. Now, as the Nation faces an economy that is not growing and creating jobs as it should, so must its leaders. While the continued recovery of our economy will be driven by the businesses and workers across our land, policymakers in Washington can take steps to help Americans right now and set the most favorable conditions we can for growth and job creation for years to come. We can live within our means and invest for the future.

That is why last week I presented to the Congress and the American people the American Jobs Act, to provide a jolt to the economy and give companies confidence that if they invest and hire, there will be customers for their products and services. This jobs bill will put more people back to work and more money in the pockets of those who are working. It will create more jobs for construction workers, more jobs for teachers, more jobs for veterans, and more jobs for the long-term unemployed. It will provide a tax break for companies that hire new workers, and it will cut payroll taxes in half for every working American and every small business. It will create jobs for people to rebuild our aging infrastructure and repair and modernize at least 35,000 schools. Moreover, the proposals in the American Jobs Act are the kind of proposals that have been supported by Democrats and Republicans in the past.

I am committed to paying for this jobs bill. The Budget Control Act that I signed into law last month will cut annual Government spending by about $1 trillion over the next 10 years. It also charges the Joint Select Committee on Deficit Reduction with finding an additional $1.5 trillion in savings. As part of this jobs bill, I am asking the Congress to increase that amount so that it covers the full cost of the American Jobs Act. In addition, I believe that the Congress should seize the opportunity that this new Committee presents and do much more so that we can put the country on a sustainable fiscal path, which is critical for our long-term economic growth and competitiveness.

For this reason, I am sending to the Congress this detailed plan to pay for this jobs bill and realize more than $3 trillion in net deficit reduction over the next 10 years. Combined with the approximately $1 trillion in savings from the first part of the Budget Control Act, this would generate more than $4 trillion in deficit reduction over the next decade. This would bring the Nation to the point where current spending is no longer adding to our debt and where our debt is no longer increasing as a share of our economy—an important milestone on the way to restoring fiscal discipline and moving us toward balance.

This plan is a balanced one that asks everyone to do their part. It includes nearly $580 billion in cuts and reforms to mandatory programs of which $320 billion is savings from Federal health programs such as Medicare and Medicaid. These changes are necessary to maintain the promise of Medicare as we know it.

The plan also realizes more than $1 trillion in savings over the next 10 years from our drawdowns in Afghanistan and Iraq. And the plan calls for the Congress to undertake comprehensive tax reform that lowers tax rates, closes loopholes, boosts job creation here at home, cuts the deficit by $1.5 trillion, and observes the Buffett Rule—that people making more than $1 million a year should not pay a smaller share of their income in taxes than middle-class families pay.

To assist the Committee in its work, I also included specific tax loophole closers and measures to broaden the tax base. Together with the expiration of the high-income tax cuts from 2001 and 2003, these measures would be more than enough to reach this $1.5 trillion target. They include cutting tax preferences for high-income households, eliminating tax breaks for oil and gas companies, closing the carried interest loophole for investment fund managers, and eliminating benefits for those who use corporate jets.

In sum, the plan I am sending to the Congress today is a blueprint for how we can reduce this deficit, pay down our debt, and pay for the American Jobs Act in the process. I have little doubt that some of these proposals will not be popular with those who benefit from these affected programs. And some of these changes are ones that we would not make if it were not for our fiscal situation. But we are all in this together, and all of us must contribute to getting our economy moving again and on a firm fiscal footing.

After all, we are all connected. No single individual built America on his or her own. We built it together. We have been, and always will be, "one Nation under God, indivisible, with liberty and justice for all." We have always been a people with responsibilities to ourselves and with responsibilities to one another. This means that as Americans work hard to find a job, keep their businesses afloat and grow, and provide for their kids, their representatives in Washington must meet their responsibilities and make the tough choices needed to get our economy back on track.

This plan lives up to a simple idea: as a Nation, we can live within our means while still making the investments we need to prosper. It follows a balanced approach: asking everyone to do their part, so no one has to bear all the burden. And it says that everyone—including millionaires and billionaires—has to pay their fair share.

These may be tough times for our country, but I have a deep faith in the American spirit, and we are tougher than the times we live in and bigger than the politics we have recently seen. If we all put partisanship aside and roll up our sleeves, I have no doubt that we can meet the challenges of the moment and show the world once again why the United States of America remains the greatest country on Earth.

BARACK OBAMA

The White House,
September 19, 2011.

Remarks at a Democratic National Committee Fundraiser in New York City
September 19, 2011

Hello. It is wonderful to see all of you. Let me thank Jane and Ralph for the extraordinary hospitality, the host committee who helped put this together, and all of you for being here.

We have had an interesting day. [*Laughter*] And I think this is going to be an extraordinary fall. And the reason is, is because at this point, there are enormous stakes, and we're in a battle for the hearts and minds of America. You know, over the last 2½ years, obviously, we've gone through extraordinary times. And a lot of people in this room have seen directly the damage that's been done as a consequence of this recession.

And over those last 2½ years, we've had to make a bunch of tough choices. And I could not be prouder of the choices we made, because as a consequence of those choices, we were able to pull this economy out of a great depression, we've been able to stabilize the financial system, we've been able to make sure that 30 million people get health care and that we provide millions of kids the opportunity to go to college that otherwise wouldn't have had it.

But what's also been clear is that during this entire time, ordinary folks have been hurting very badly. And although we stabilized the economy, we've stabilized it at a level that's just too high, in terms of unemployment and in terms of hardship all across America.

And my hope has been for the last 2½ years that in the midst of a crisis like this, that we could pull America together to move forcefully on behalf of the American Dream and on behalf of all those who aspire for something better for their kids. And what has been clear over the last 2½ years is that we have not had a willing partner.

Now, we've been able to get some stuff done despite that and despite a filibuster in the Senate. But at least over the last 9 months, what we've seen is some irreconcilable differences, let's put it that way; a fundamentally different vision about where America needs to go. And the speech that I gave at the joint session described a vision that is fundamentally different from the one that's offered by the other side and that was then amplified today by our discussion about how we're going to lower our deficit even as we're creating growth and creating jobs all across the economy.

This is going to be a tough fight over the next 16 months. But we don't have 16 months or 14 months to wait. People need action now. Everywhere I travel, folks are hurting now. And so we are going to keep pushing as hard as

we can this week, next week, and all the weeks that follow to try to get as much done as we can now to put people back to work, to put teachers back to work, to put construction workers on the job rebuilding our roads and our bridges and our schools, to make sure that small businesses can thrive, to make sure that we're paying for it in a balanced and responsible way.

And you're already hearing the moans and groans from the other side about how we are engaging in class warfare and we're being too populist and this and that and the other—all the usual scripts. I mean, it's predictable, the news releases that come out from the other side. But the truth of the matter is, is that if we don't succeed, then I think that this country is going to go down a very perilous path. And it's not going to be good for those of us who have done incredibly well in this society and it's certainly not going to be good for the single mom who's working two shifts right now trying to support her family. It's not going to be good for anybody.

So the bottom line is this: As proud as I am of what we've accomplished over the last 2½ years, a lot of work remains undone. And back in 2008, when I got elected, I was very clear on that very beautiful November night in Grant Park in Chicago, and then very clear on that cold January day in DC, that this was going to be a long-term project. This was not going to be easy, and there were going to be a lot of bumps along the way.

But what I am absolutely confident about is that if we stay on it and if we understand that our core job, our core mission is to make sure that we have a strong, thriving middle class in this country and that we've got opportunity for everybody and not just some and that those ladders of opportunity are for every child, regardless of where they live and where they come from, if we have a big, generous vision of what America has been and can be, then I'm confident the American people will follow us. That's where they want to be. That's what they believe in.

They've felt some doubts. They've been discouraged, because a lot of these problems predate the financial crisis. And they've now been going through 15 years in which they've seen hardship.

But I remain confident that despite all the naysaying, that's still where they want to go. And we're going to have to fight for that vision over the next several months and over the next year.

I can't do it alone. I can only do it with the help of all of you. And so the fact that you are present here tonight is something that is hugely encouraging to me, and I want to make sure that we spend most of our time in a conversa-tion as opposed to a speech, because I've already given a long speech today. [*Laughter*]

So with that, I think we're going to clear out the crew. Enjoy New York, guys. [*Laughter*] Although—but don't try to take a cab anywhere during UNGA.

NOTE: The President spoke at 7:24 p.m. at the residence of Jane D. Hartley and Ralph L. Schlosstein. Audio was not available for verification of the content of these remarks.

Remarks at a United Nations Meeting on Libya in New York City
September 20, 2011

Good morning. Mr. Secretary-General, on behalf of us all, thank you for convening this meeting to address a task that must be the work of all of us: supporting the people of Libya as they build a future that is free and democratic and prosperous. And I want to thank President Jalil for his remarks and for all that he and Prime Minister Jibril have done to help Libya reach this moment.

To all the heads of state, to all the countries represented here who have done so much over the past several months to ensure this day could come, I want to say thank you as well.

Today, the Libyan people are writing a new chapter in the life of their nation. After four decades of darkness, they can walk the streets, free from a tyrant. They are making their voices heard in new newspapers and on radio and television, in public squares and on personal blogs. They're launching political parties and civil groups to shape their own destiny and secure their universal rights. And here at the United Nations, the new flag of a free Libya now flies among the community of nations.

Make no mistake: Credit for the liberation of Libya belongs to the people of Libya. It was Libyan men and women and children who took to the streets in peaceful protest, who faced down the tanks and endured the snipers' bullets. It was Libyan fighters, often outgunned and outnumbered, who fought pitched battles, town by town, block by block. It was Libyan activists, in the underground, in chat rooms, in mosques, who kept a revolution alive, even after some of the world had given up hope.

It was Libyan women and girls who hung flags and smuggled weapons to the front. It was Libyans from countries around the world, including my own, who rushed home to help, even though they too risked brutality and death. It was Libyan blood that was spilled and Libya's sons and daughters who gave their lives. And on that August day, after all that sacrifice, after 42 long years, it was Libyans who pushed their dictator from power.

At the same time, Libya is a lesson in what the international community can achieve when we stand together as one. I said at the beginning of this process, we cannot and should not intervene every time there is an injustice in the world. Yet it's also true that there are times where the world could have and should have summoned the will to prevent the killing of innocents on a horrific scale. And we are forever haunted by the atrocities that we did not prevent and the lives that we did not save. But this time was different. This time, we, through the United Nations, found the courage and the collective will to act.

When the old regime unleashed a campaign of terror, threatening to roll back the democratic tide sweeping the region, we acted as united nations, and we acted swiftly, broadening sanctions, imposing an arms embargo. The United States led the effort to pass a historic resolution at the Security Council authorizing all necessary measures to protect the Libyan people. And when the civilians of Benghazi were threatened with a massacre, we exercised that authority. Our international coalition stopped the regime in its tracks and saved countless lives and gave the Libyan people the time and the space to prevail.

Important too is how this effort succeeded, thanks to the leadership and contributions of many countries. The United States was proud to play a decisive role, especially in the early days, and then in a supporting capacity. But let's remember that it was the Arab League that appealed for action. It was the world's most effective alliance, NATO, that's led a military coalition of nearly 20 nations. It's our European allies, especially the United Kingdom and France and Denmark and Norway, that conducted the vast majority of air strikes protecting rebels on the ground. It was Arab States who joined the coalition as equal partners. And it's been the United Nations and neighboring countries, including Tunisia and Egypt, that have cared for the Libyans in the urgent humanitarian effort that continues today.

This is how the international community should work in the 21st century: more nations bearing the responsibility and the costs of meeting global challenges. In fact, this is the very purpose of this United Nations. So every nation represented here today can take pride in the innocent lives we saved and in helping Libyans reclaim their country. It was the right thing to do.

Now, even as we speak, remnants of the old regime continue to fight. Difficult days are still ahead. But one thing is clear: The future of Libya is now in the hands of the Libyan people. For just as it was Libyans who tore down the old order, it will be Libyans who build their new nation. And we've come here today to say to the people of Libya: Just as the world stood by you in your struggle to be free, we will now stand with you in your struggle to realize the peace and prosperity that freedom can bring.

In this effort, you will have a friend and partner in the United States of America. Today I can announce that our Ambassador is on his way back to Tripoli. And this week, the Ameri-

can flag that was lowered before our Embassy was attacked will be raised again over a reopened American Embassy. We will work closely with the new U.N. Support Mission in Libya and with the nations here today to assist the Libyan people in the hard work ahead.

First and most immediately, security. So long as the Libyan people are being threatened, the NATO-led mission to protect them will continue. And those still holding out must understand, the old regime is over, and it is time to lay down your arms and join the new Libya. As this happens, the world must also support efforts to secure dangerous weapons, conventional and otherwise, and bring fighters under central, civilian control. For without security, democracy and trade and investment cannot flourish.

Second, the humanitarian effort. The Transitional National Council has been working quickly to restore water and electricity and food supplies to Tripoli. But for many Libyans, each day is still a struggle to recover from their wounds, reunite with their families, and return to their homes. And even after the guns of war fall silent, the ravages of war will continue. So our efforts to assist its victims must continue. In this, the United States—the United Nations will play a key role. And along with our partners, the United States will do our part to help the hungry and the wounded.

Third, a democratic transition that is peaceful, inclusive, and just. President Jalil has just reaffirmed the Transitional National Council's commitment to these principles, and the United Nations will play a central role in coordinating international support for this effort. We all know what is needed: a transition that is timely; new laws and a constitution that uphold the rule of law; political parties and a strong civil society; and for the first time in Libyan history, free and fair elections.

True democracy, however, must flow from its citizens. So as Libyans rightly seek justice for past crimes, let it be done in a spirit of reconciliation and not reprisals and violence. As Libyans draw strength from their faith, a religion rooted in peace and tolerance, let there be a rejection of violent extremism, which offers nothing but death and destruction. As Libyans rebuild, let those efforts tap the experience of all those with the skills to contribute, including the many Africans in Libya. And as Libyans forge a society that is truly just, let it enshrine the rights and role of women at all levels of society. For we know that the nations that uphold the human rights of all people, especially their women, are ultimately more successful and more prosperous.

Which brings me to the final area where the world must stand with Libya, and that is restoring prosperity. For too long, Libya's vast riches were stolen and squandered. Now that wealth must serve its rightful owners, the Libyan people. As sanctions are lifted, as the United States and the international community unfreeze more Libyan assets, and as the country's oil production is restored, the Libyan people deserve a government that is transparent and accountable. And bound by the Libyan students and entrepreneurs who have forged friendships in the United States, we intend to build new partnerships to help unleash Libya's extraordinary potential.

Now, none of this will be easy. After decades of iron rule by one man, it will take time to build the institutions needed for a democratic Libya. I'm sure there will be days of frustration, there will be days when progress is slow, there will be days when some begin to wish for the old order and its illusion of stability. And some in the world may ask, can Libya succeed? But if we have learned anything these many months, it is this: Don't underestimate the aspirations and the will of the Libyan people.

So I want to conclude by speaking directly to the people of Libya. Your task may be new,

the journey ahead may be fraught with difficulty, but everything you need to build your future already beats in the heart of your nation. It's the same courage you summoned on that first February day, the same resilience that brought you back out the next day and the next, even as you lost family and friends, and the same unshakeable determination with which you liberated Benghazi, broke the siege of Misurata, and have fought through the coastal plains and the western mountains.

It's the same unwavering conviction that said there's no turning back, our sons and daughters deserve to be free.

In the days after Tripoli fell, people rejoiced in the streets and pondered the role ahead, and one of those Libyans said, "We have this chance now to do something good for our country, a chance we have dreamed of for so long." So to the Libyan people, this is your chance. And today the world is saying with one unmistakable voice, we will stand with you as you seize this moment of promise, as you reach for the freedom, the dignity, and the opportunity that you deserve.

So congratulations. And thank you very much.

NOTE: The President spoke at 11:12 a.m. at United Nations Headquarters. In his remarks, he referred to Secretary-General Ban Ki-moon of the United Nations; Chairman Mustafa Mohammed Abdul Jalil of the National Transitional Council of Libya; Chairman Mahmoud Jibril of the Executive Board of the National Transitional Council of Libya; and Col. Muammar Abu Minyar al-Qadhafi, former leader of Libya.

Remarks Prior to a Meeting With President Hamid Karzai of Afghanistan in New York City
September 20, 2011

President Obama. Well, I want to welcome President Karzai and his delegation. We have a lot of important business to do. And I very much appreciate the efforts that he's been tak-

ing in rebuilding Afghanistan and proceeding on the transition path that will ensure that Afghans are ultimately responsible for their security and their prosperity.

We received some tragic news today that President Rabbani, who had been heading up the reconciliation process, was killed in a suicide attack. He was a man who cared deeply about Afghanistan and had been a valued adviser to President Karzai, had made enormous contributions to rebuilding the country. So it is a tragic loss. We want to extend our heartfelt condolences to you, his family, and the people of Afghanistan.

But, Mr. President, I think we both believe that despite this incident, we will not be deterred from creating a path whereby Afghans can live in freedom and safety and security and prosperity and that it is going to be important to continue the efforts to bring all elements of Afghan society together to end what has been a senseless cycle of violence.

So we very much appreciate your presence here today. I know that you're going to have to leave after our meeting. But we want to give you an opportunity to speak to the press as well.

President Karzai. Thank you very much, Mr. President, for your message of condolence and support to myself and to Afghan people on the very tragic loss and martyrdom of Professor Burhanuddin Rabbani, the chairman of the Afghan Peace Council, the former Afghan President, and Afghan patriot, who, as we see, has sacrificed his life for the sake of Afghanistan and for the peace of our country.

The mission that he had undertaken was vital, Mr. President, for the Afghan people and for the security of our country and for peace in our country. We will miss him very, very much. I don't think, Mr. President, that we can fill his place easily. He was one of the few people in Afghanistan with the distinction that we cannot easily find in societies, a terrible loss. But as you rightly say, this will not deter us from continuing on the path that we have, and we'll definitely succeed.

Thank you, Mr. President, for condemning this act of brutality and cowardice against President Rabbani. I will take that message from you to the Afghan people. This is a sad day for us in Afghanistan, but a day of unity and a day of continuity of our efforts.

Thank you.

President Obama. Thank you very much.

NOTE: The President spoke at 12:06 p.m. at the Waldorf-Astoria Hotel.

Remarks at the Opening of an Open Government Partnership Event in New York City
September 20, 2011

Good afternoon, everyone. And welcome to this inaugural event of a partnership that's already transforming how governments serve their citizens in the 21st century.

One year ago, at the U.N. General Assembly, I stated a simple truth: that the strongest foundation for human progress lies in open economies, open societies, and in open governments. And I challenged our countries to come back this year with specific commitments to promote transparency, to fight corruption, to energize civic engagement, and to leverage new technologies so we can strengthen the foundations of freedom in our own countries.

Today we're joined by nations and organizations from around the world that are answering this challenge. In this Open Government Partnership, I'm pleased to be joined by leaders from the seven other founding nations of this initiative. I especially want to commend my friend, President Rousseff of Brazil, for her leadership in open government and for joining the United States as the first cochairs of this effort.

We're joined by nearly 40 other nations who've also embraced this challenge, with the goal of joining this partnership next year. And we're joined by civil society organizations from around the world, groups that not only help hold governments accountable, but who partnered with us and who offer new ideas and help us to make better decisions. Put simply, our countries are stronger when we engage citizens beyond the halls of government. So I welcome our civil society representatives, not as spectators, but as equal partners in this initiative.

This, I believe, is how progress will be achieved in the 21st century: meeting global challenges through global cooperation, across all levels of society. And this is exactly the kind of partnership that we need now, as emerging democracies from Latin America to Africa to Asia are all showing how innovations in open government can help make countries more prosperous and more just, as new generations across the Middle East and North Africa assert the old truth that government exists for the benefit of their people, and as young people everywhere, from teeming cities to remote villages, are logging on and texting and tweeting and demanding government that is just as fast, just as smart, just as accountable.

This is the moment that we must meet. These are the expectations that we must fulfill. And now we see governments around the world meeting this challenge, including many represented here today. Countries from Mexico to Turkey to Liberia have passed laws guaranteeing citizens the right to information. From Chile to Kenya to the Philippines, civil society groups are giving citizens new tools to report corruption. From Tanzania to Indonesia, and as I saw firsthand during my visit to India, rural villages are organizing and making their voices heard and getting the public services that they need. Governments from Brazil to South Africa are putting more information online, helping people hold public officials accountable for how they spend taxpayer dollars.

Here in the United States, we've worked to make government more open and responsive than ever before. We've been promoting greater disclosure of government information, empowering citizens with new ways to participate in their democracy. We are releasing more data in usable forms on health and safety and the environment, because information is power, and helping people make informed decisions and entrepreneurs turn data into new products that create new jobs. We're also soliciting the best ideas from our people in how to make government work better. And around the world, we're standing up for freedom to access information, including a free and open Internet.

Today the eight founding nations of our partnership are going even further, agreeing to an open government declaration rooted in several core principles. We pledge to be more transparent at every level, because more information on government activity should be open, timely, and freely available to the people. We pledge to engage more of our citizens in decisionmaking, because it makes government more effective and responsive. We pledge to implement the highest standards of integrity, because those in power must serve the people, not themselves. And we pledge to increase access to technology, because in this digital century, access to information is a right that is universal.

Next, to put these principles into practice, every country that seeks to join this partnership will work with civil society groups to develop an action plan of specific commitments. Today the United States is releasing our plan, which we are posting on the White House website and at opengovpartnership.org.

Among our commitments, we're launching a new online tool called "We the People" to allow Americans to directly petition the White House, and we'll share that technology so that any government in the world can enable its citizens to do the same. We've developed new tools called "smart disclosures" so that the data we make public can help people make health care choices, help small businesses innovate, and help scientists achieve new breakthroughs.

We'll work to reform and expand protections for whistleblowers who expose government waste, fraud, and abuse. And we're continuing our leadership of the global effort against corruption by building on legislation that now requires oil, gas, and mining companies to disclose the payments that foreign governments demand of them.

Today I can announce that the United States will join the global initiative in which these industries, governments, and civil society all work together for greater transparency so that taxpayers receive every dollar they're due from the extraction of natural resources.

So these are just some of the steps that we're taking. And today is just the beginning of a partnership that will only grow, as Secretary Clinton leads our effort on behalf of the United States, as these nearly 40 nations develop their own commitments, as we share and learn from each other and build the next generation of tools to empower our citizens and serve them better.

So that's the purpose of open government. And I believe that's the essence of democracy. That's the commitment to which we're committing ourselves here today. And I thank all of you for joining us as we meet this challenge together.

I want to thank you very much for your participation. And with that, I would like to turn over the chair to my cochair, President Rousseff.

NOTE: The President spoke at 2:35 p.m. at the Waldorf-Astoria Hotel.

Remarks at the Closing of an Open Government Partnership Event in New York City
September 20, 2011

Well, thank you, Rakesh, for that wonderful testimony. Thank you all to the leaders who shared their action plans and the steps that they're taking and your willingness to participate in this initiative. We are extraordinarily grateful.

As I said earlier, today is just the beginning of this partnership. Those who are the founding members have to go back home and work to meet the commitments that we've made and to be held accountable. The 38 nations joining us today will be working on their own action plans. And we look forward to our next meeting in Brazil next year, when our partnership welcomes more countries who share our commitment to open government.

I want to thank all the participants. I particularly want to thank the civil society organizations that are doing extraordinary work.

I very much appreciated the statement by the representative from the United Kingdom that this is not always comfortable, if done right, because governments are human institutions, which means that even with the best of

intentions we are flawed and we make mistakes, and it's a natural human impulse to try to cover up mistakes and to resist the kind of openness that's been discussed here today.

But as Rakesh, I think, said so well, the more open we are, the more willing we are to hear constructive criticism, the more effective we can be. And ultimately, governments are here to serve the people, not to serve those in power.

And so I'm very grateful for all of you for participating. Thank you for embracing this challenge to make sure our governments are as open and accountable and as effective as they can be so that we can meet the aspirations of all our citizens.

Thank you very much.

NOTE: The President spoke at 3:30 p.m. at the Waldorf-Astoria Hotel. In his remarks, he referred to Rakesh Rajani, head, Twaweza; and Francis Maude, chairman, Open Government Partnership.

Remarks Prior to a Meeting With Prime Minister Recep Tayyip Erdogan of Turkey and an Exchange With Reporters in New York City
September 20, 2011

President Obama. Well, I want to welcome Prime Minister Erdogan and his delegation to New York City and to the United States. Turkey is a NATO ally, a great friend and partner on a whole host of issues. I want to thank him for all the work that we've done together: the cooperation in Afghanistan; the work that we most recently did in trying to provide freedom for Libya; and in addition, the NATO obligations that both of us carry out together, most recently symbolized by the agreement of Turkey to host a missile defense radar.

Prime Minister Erdogan has shown great leadership on a range of issues and promoting democracy. And we are very grateful to him for the work that we've done together.

I do want to stress my deepest condolences for the loss of life through the explosion that took place in Ankara. And I understand that the investigation is ongoing, but I think that this reminds us that terrorism exists in many parts of the world and that Turkey and the United States are going to be strong partners in preventing terrorism. And we look forward to working with you on these issues.

So, Mr. Prime Minister, thank you for your service, and thank you for your friendship.

Prime Minister Erdogan. Thank you very much, Mr. President. I'm very pleased that we have this occasion to meet during this week as we meet here for the 66th General Assembly of the United Nations.

And as you have described the relationship between Turkey and the United States, we have a model partnership. And this is a process which is ongoing in which we have taken some very important steps and we will continue to take some important steps. One of those issues that is very common to both of us is fighting against terrorism and fighting against terrorism based on a common platform. We have, unfortunately, lost three citizens today as a result of the blast in Ankara, but in the later hours there was another attack in Siirt, in a city in the eastern part of Turkey, where four young girls

were killed as a result of an attack in a car, and these were civilian citizens. And so these are events which give us great sadness. And this is an area which we have to work on.

As for whether or not we can completely eradicate terrorism, I'm not very optimistic in thinking that perhaps we can completely eradicate it. But I think that we have a lot of room to work together to make sure that we minimize terrorism to the lowest possible extent. And to do that we have to keep working together on many areas of this effort, work together in planning, use technology so that we can continue to take joint steps in trying to fight against terrorism. And those are some of the issues that we all will talk about.

I have also recently visited Egypt, Tunisia, and Libya, and we have also worked together in those countries, and Afghanistan as well, and also in Iraq. So these are many of the areas where we will continue to talk to each other so that Turkey and the United States continue with this model partnership to move into a better future.

And let me take this opportunity to—also to thank you for your hospitality today.

President Obama. Thank you very much, everybody.

Middle East

Q. [*Inaudible*]

Q. Was there any discussion of the Palestinian—[*inaudible*]?

President Obama. We're starting the meeting now.

NOTE: The President spoke at 4:46 p.m. at the Waldorf-Astoria Hotel. Prime Minister Erdogan spoke in Turkish, and his remarks were translated by an interpreter.

Statement on the Repeal of the United States Military's "Don't Ask, Don't Tell" Policy
September 20, 2011

Today the discriminatory law known as "don't ask, don't tell" is finally and formally re-

pealed. As of today, patriotic Americans in uniform will no longer have to lie about who they are in order to serve the country they love. As of today, our Armed Forces will no longer lose the extraordinary skills and combat experience of so many gay and lesbian servicemembers. And today, as Commander in Chief, I want those who were discharged under this law to know that your country deeply values your service.

I was proud to sign the Repeal Act into law last December because I knew that it would enhance our national security, increase our military readiness, and bring us closer to the principles of equality and fairness that define us as Americans. Today's achievement is a tribute to all the patriots who fought and marched for change: to Members of Congress from both parties who voted for repeal, to our civilian and military leaders who ensured a smooth transition, and to the professionalism of our men and women in uniform who showed that they were ready to move forward together, as one team, to meet the missions we ask of them.

For more than two centuries, we have worked to extend America's promise to all our citizens. Our Armed Forces have been both a mirror and a catalyst of that progress, and our troops, including gays and lesbians, have given their lives to defend the freedoms and liberties that we cherish as Americans. Today every American can be proud that we have taken another great step toward keeping our military the finest in the world and toward fulfilling our Nation's founding ideals.

Remarks at a Democratic National Committee Fundraiser in New York City
September 20, 2011

The President. Hello, everybody! Hello, New York! I'm in a New York state of mind. Thank you. Thank you. What do you think about Michelle Obama? She's not bad.

Everybody, please have a seat. Have a seat. Did you notice how she's getting cuter? [*Laughter*] She is remarkable, and it is the reason that I've got remarkable kids. I have improved my gene pool. [*Laughter*] And it is true, this is the closest we get to a date—which I'm going to have to fix in about 14 months. [*Laughter*]

It is wonderful to see all of you. Thank you so much for being here tonight in this spectacular setting. There are a couple of people I want to make sure to acknowledge: First of all, the remarkable Alicia Keys—thank you so much, Alicia, for your performance; one of the finest public servants in the country, Mayor Cory Booker; the outstanding former mayor of New York City, David Dinkins; the New York City public advocate, Bill de Blasio; and my dear friend, the DNC Treasurer, Andy Tobias. We love Andy.

Now, the truth is, this is not my idea of a date night. Normally, our dates don't end with me being before 400 of our closest friends. But it is wonderful to be here. And I'm here because I need your help. I need your help, just like I needed your help in 2008. In fact, I need your help to finish what we started in 2008.

Back then, we started this campaign not because we thought it was a sure thing; I just want to remind everybody of that. The odds were not good. This was not going to be a cakewalk. My name was Barack Hussein Obama. [*Laughter*] You didn't need a poll to know that might be an issue. [*Laughter*] But we forged ahead because we had an idea about what this country is, what it has been, and what it can be.

Most of the people in this room—many of our parents, our grandparents—we grew up with a faith in an America where hard work and responsibility paid off, and if you stepped up, and if you did your job, and if you were loyal to your company, that loyalty would be rewarded with a decent salary and good benefits; you might get a raise. And you had an assurance that life would be better for your kids and your grandkids.

Over the last decade—over the last couple of decades, that faith was shaken. Seemed as if the rules changed. The deck kept getting stacked against middle class Americans, and nobody in Washington seemed willing or able to do anything about it. And in 2007, all of this culminated in a once-in-a-lifetime economic crisis, a crisis that's been much worse and much longer than your average recession, something that most of us have never seen in our lifetimes. And from the time I took office, we knew that because this crisis had been building for years, it was going to take us years to fully recover.

So the question now is not whether people are still hurting; of course, people are still hurting. As Michelle was saying, I read letters and e-mails every night. I talk to people when I'm out on the road. Their stories are heartbreaking: men and women who've poured their lives into a small business, perhaps a business that's been in their family for generations, suddenly closed; folks who have to cross off items from the grocery list so that they can pay for gas to get to the job—if they've got a job; parents who postpone retirement so that their children don't have to drop out of college; fathers who write to me and say, "Do you know what it's like to have to come home and explain to your family that you've lost your job, and then spend months after months looking for a job, and those résumés go unanswered, and how you start losing confidence in yourself and you don't want to look your kids in the eye?"

The question is not whether this country is going through hard times. The question is, where does this country go next? We can go back to the ideas we tried in the last decade, where corporations got to write their own rules and the most fortunate among us got all of our tax breaks, and jobs got shipped overseas, and incomes and wages flatlined as the cost of everything went up, and this society became less equal, and opportunity was diminished for too many. Or we can build the America we talked about in 2008, an America where everybody gets a fair shake and everybody does their fair share.

And that is what this election is about. That's what we've spent the last 2½ years fighting for. Every decision I've made, all the work that we've done, has been based on a simple idea. And that is that everybody should have a shot and burdens should be shared and opportunities should be shared. And even in the midst of crisis, those were the values that guided us.

So when we wanted to save the auto industry from bankruptcy, there were a lot of Republicans in Congress who fought us tooth and nail, said it was a waste of time and a waste of money. But we did it anyway, and we saved thousands of American jobs. And we made sure taxpayers got their money back. And today, the American auto industry is stronger than ever, and they're making fuel-efficient cars stamped with three proud words: Made in America.

When we wanted to pass Wall Street reform to make sure a crisis like this never happens again, lobbyists and special interests spent millions to make sure we didn't succeed. And we did it anyway. And we passed the toughest reform in history that prevents consumers from getting ripped off by mortgage lenders or credit card companies, which is why, today, there are no more hidden credit card fees, no more unfair rate hikes, and no more deception from banks.

And most of the Republicans voted against it. But we made it happen. And we were able to cut $60 billion in taxpayer subsidies to big banks and use those savings to make college more affordable for millions of kids all across this country who want to go to college. And instead of giving more tax breaks to the biggest corporations, we cut taxes for small businesses and middle class families.

The first law I signed was a bill to make sure that women earn equal pay for equal work, because I've got daughters, and I want to make sure they've got the same chance as our sons. And yes, we passed health care reform so that no one in America will go bankrupt because they get sick, because this is the United States of America and we're better than that.

One other thing we did that is worth mentioning tonight, in particular—I just met backstage with young Americans who were discharged from the military because of "don't ask, don't tell." As of today, that will never happen again. As of today, no one needs to hide who they are to serve the country that they love—as of today.

All of these were tough fights. But they're making a difference all across the country. And we've got more fights that we've got to win. We've got a long way to go to make sure that everybody in this country gets a fair shake, that the vision that mobilized us in 2008 is realized: making sure that every American has a chance to get ahead. And that's where I need your help.

We've got a lot of work to do. About a week ago, I sent to Congress a bill called the "American Jobs Act." Some of you might have heard about this. As I said before a joint session of Congress, every proposal in there has been supported by Democrats and Republicans in the past. Everything in it will be paid for. It will put people back to work. It will put more money back in the pockets of working people. And Congress should pass that jobs bill right away.

We've got millions of constructions workers who don't have jobs right now. This bill says, let's put those men and women to work rebuilding our roads and our bridges and our highways and our schools. I don't want the best airports and the fastest railroads being built in China. I want them here in the United States of America. There's work to be done, workers ready to do it. We've got to tell Congress to pass this jobs bill now.

Now, in places like South Korea, they can't hire teachers fast enough, call teachers, nationbuilders. They know that educating their children is the key to competing in a global economy. Here, we're laying off teachers in droves. It's unfair to our kids. It undermines their future. And if we pass this jobs bill, thousands of teachers in every State will be back in the classroom where they belong. That's why we've got to tell Congress to pass this jobs bill.

If we pass this bill, companies will get tax credits for hiring American veterans. We ask these men and women to suspend their careers, leave their families, risk their lives to protect this country. They should not have to beg for a job when they come home.

The jobs act will cut taxes for virtually every worker in America, cut taxes for every small-business owner, give an extra tax cut to every small business who hires more workers or gives their workers an increase in wages.

So don't just talk about America's job creators, do something for America's job creators. Don't make a pledge that you'll never raise taxes, except when it comes to middle class taxes or when Obama proposes a tax cut. Be consistent. Pass this jobs bill.

Now, a lot of folks in Congress have said we're not going to support any new spending that's not paid for. I agree. I think that's important. So yesterday I laid out a plan to pay for the "American Jobs Act" and that brings down ourdebt over time. It adds to the $1 trillion in spending cuts that I already signed this summer, makes it one of the biggest spending cuts in history. But it's phased in so that it doesn't hurt our recovery now. It's a plan that says if we want to close this deficit and we want to pay for this jobs plan, then we've got to ask the wealthiest Americans and the biggest corporations to pay their fair share.

Now, the Republicans say they're in favor of tax reform. Let's go. Let's reform this Tax Code. And let's reform it based on a very simple principle: Warren Buffett's secretary should not be paying a higher tax rate than Warren Buffett. It's a simple principle.

In the United States of America a teacher or a nurse or a construction worker who makes $50,000 a year, they shouldn't pay a higher tax rate than somebody pulling in 50 million. It is not fair. It is not right. It has to change. And the vast majority of Americans agree that it has to change.

Nobody wants to punish success; that's what you hear when they try to respond to what should be some pretty obvious logic. Nobody wants to punish success in America. That's what's great about America, our belief that anybody can make if you try. Anybody can open a business, have a great idea, go out there and make millions, make billions. This is the land of opportunity. It's why people came to New York. All I'm saying is that those who have done well, including the majority of people here tonight, we should pay our fair share in taxes, contribute to the Nation that made our success possible, pass it on, pass on opportunity.

And I think most wealthy Americans would agree if they knew that this would help us grow the economy and deal with the debt that threatens our future and put people back to work.

See, I got some amens right here.

Audience members. Amen!

The President. This is a completely unbiased sampling. [*Laughter*]

Now, you're already hearing the Republicans in Congress dusting off the old talking points. You can write their press releases. "Class warfare," they say. You know what, if asking a billionaire to pay the same rate as a plumber or a teacher makes me a warrior for the middle class, I wear that charge as a badge of honor. I wear it as a badge of honor. Because the only class warfare I've seen is the battle that's been waged against middle class folks in this country for a decade now.

Look, this is what it comes down to, this is about priorities. It's always been about priorities. It's always been about choices. If we want to pay for this jobs plan and close the deficit and invest in our future, the money has to come from somewhere. Don't tell me that you want good schools, don't tell me that you want safe roads, don't tell me that you believe in medical research, and then refuse to pay for it.

We've got to make choices. Would you rather keep tax loopholes for oil companies, or do you want to put construction workers and teachers back on the job? Would you rather keep tax breaks for millionaires and billionaires, or do you want to invest in new schools, in medical research, in training more engineers? Should we ask seniors to pay thousands of dollars more for Medicare, or should we ask the biggest corporations to pay their fair share? That's what this debate is about. It's what's at stake right now.

This notion that the only thing that we can do to restore prosperity is to let corporations write their own rules and give tax breaks to the wealthiest few and tell everybody else that you're on your own, this idea that the only way we compete in a global economy in the 21st century is to make sure that we've got cheap labor and dirty air, that's not who we are. We're better than that. That's not the story of America. We are rugged individualists. We are self-reliant. It's been the drive and initiative of our workers and our entrepreneurs that has made this economy the engine and the envy of the world. But there has always been another thread that says we're in this together, we are connected.

There are some things we can only do together as a nation. And that is not a Democratic idea or a Republican idea; that's been an American idea. Lincoln believed in that idea, and Eisenhower believed in that idea, and FDR believed in that idea.

That's why this country gave millions of returning heroes, including my grandfather, the chance to go to college on the GI bill. That's why a place like New York City has enjoyed the incredible vibrancy, because people thought 20, 30, 40 years ahead. Let's build a park in the middle of this metropolis. It costs money, but it will make this city special. Let's invest in great universities. It might cost a little bit, but think about all those young minds that are going to be shaped, what wonders they're going to create.

It's the reason Michelle and I had the chance to succeed beyond our wildest dreams. Look at where we came from: a little Black girl on the South Side of Chicago, a little mixed kid in Honolulu. [*Laughter*] A single mom—[*applause*]. We're only here because somebody passed on this incredible notion, this exceptional American idea that it doesn't matter where you come from; it doesn't matter who you're born to. If you're willing to put in the effort, if you're willing to make sacrifices, you got a shot. You got a chance.

I was on a bus tour through Iowa and Minnesota and my home State of Illinois, rural country—corn everywhere, beans—[*laughter*]—small towns. And we'd roll through on that bus, through these little towns, and everybody would be lining up along the road. And these were rural communities, conservative—many of them I probably didn't get a lot of votes. But everybody was lined up: little kids with the American flags, grandparents out in their lawn chairs, people waving, guys standing out in front of the auto shop, wiping their hands off, waving in their overalls. And we stopped by a high school football game, talked to the coach, went by a public school, met with some of the kids. And for all the venom and all the shouting in Washington, you've got this incredible sense, sort of, you've got a sense of what the core of America is all about, this incredible decency and optimism, and the belief that, no matter how tough things are sometimes, somehow, if we pull together, we're going to get through it.

And in these little towns, by the way, all across the Midwest, suddenly, you'll see Black faces and Brown faces. And in the country, you can see new waves of immigrants, sort of filling in pockets of towns that previously had been aging, and whole new generations are starting all over again, building this incredible country. And what's amazing is you come here to Manhattan, and as you're driving by and you look at the faces, you sense that same spirit, that same striving, hopeful energy. Everybody just thinking, you know what, we're going to make this happen. We've got big dreams. We're not going to think small.

Those things are connected. This country, as divided as it seems sometimes, that core idea is there. And that's what we tapped into in 2008. It wasn't me; it was all of you. It was the country insisting that we can do better than this. And all that "hopey, changey stuff," as they say—[*laughter*]—that was real. That wasn't something worth being cynical about. That was real. You could feel it. You knew it.

It's still there, even in the midst of this hardship. But it's hard. When I was in Grant Park that night, I warned everybody, this is going to be hard. This is not the end; this is the beginning. And over the last 2½ years, we've had some tough times. And understandably, over time, people sometimes, they get discouraged, and they lose sight of what launched us on this thing in the first place. They start feeling dis-

couraged, and the whole "Hope" poster starts kind of fading. [*Laughter*]

But I tell you what. You travel around the country, you talk to the America people, that spirit is still there. It gets knocked around. I get knocked around. But it's there, and it's worth fighting for. It's worth fighting for. And that's why I need your help, because I need everybody out here to be willing to fight for it. I need everybody here to understand that America was not built by any single individual. We built it together. And we always have been "one Nation under God, indivisible, with liberty and justice for all." And we have been a nation of responsibilities to ourselves, but also responsibilities to one another. And we've got to meet those responsibilities right now.

So maybe some people in Congress would rather settle these differences at the ballot box. I'm ready to settle them at the ballot box. I intend to win this next election because we've got better ideas. We've got better ideas. But in the meantime, that's 14 months away, and the American people don't have the luxury of waiting that long.

So let's get to work right now. Let's act right now. Let's pass that jobs bill. Let's reform the Tax Code. Let's fix some schools. Let's rebuild our roads. Let's put teachers back to work. Let's invest in our basic research. Let's invest in America. Let's rebuild America. Let's think big. Let's dream big. Let's shake off the discouragement and the depression. Let's get to work. Let's get busy.

I'm ready to fight. I hope you are too. God bless you. God bless the United States of America. Thank you.

NOTE: The President spoke at 8:40 p.m. at Gotham Hall. In his remarks, he referred to musician Alicia Keys. The transcript released by the Office of the Press Secretary also included the remarks of the First Lady. The transcript was released by the Office of the Press Secretary on September 21.

Remarks to the United Nations General Assembly in New York City
September 21, 2011

Mr. President, Mr. Secretary-General, fellow delegates, ladies and gentlemen: It is a great honor for me to be here today. I would like to talk to you about a subject that is at the heart of the United Nations: the pursuit of peace in an imperfect world.

War and conflict have been with us since the beginning of civilizations. But in the first part of the 20th century, the advance of modern weaponry led to death on a staggering scale. It was this killing that compelled the founders of this body to build an institution that was focused not just on ending one war, but on averting others; a union of sovereign states that would seek to prevent conflict, while also addressing its causes.

No American did more to pursue this objective than President Franklin Roosevelt. He knew that a victory in war was not enough. As he said at one of the very first meetings on the founding of the United Nations, "We have got to make not merely peace, but a peace that will last."

The men and women who built this institution understood that peace is more than just the absence of war. A lasting peace—for nations and for individuals—depends on a sense of justice and opportunity, of dignity and freedom. It depends on struggle and sacrifice, on compromise, and on a sense of common humanity.

One delegate to the San Francisco Conference that led to the creation of the United Nations put it well. "Many people," she said, "have talked as if all that has to be done to get peace was to say loudly and frequently that we loved peace and we hated war. Now we have learned that no matter how much we love peace and hate war, we cannot avoid having war brought upon us if there are convulsions in other parts of the world."

The fact is, peace is hard. But our people demand it. Over nearly seven decades, even as the United Nations helped avert a third world war, we still live in a world scarred by conflict and plagued by poverty. Even as we proclaim our love for peace and our hatred of war, there are still convulsions in our world that endanger us all.

I took office at a time of two wars for the United States. Moreover, the violent extremists who drew us into war in the first place, Usama bin Laden and his Al Qaida organization, remained at large. Today, we've set a new direction.

At the end of this year, America's military operation in Iraq will be over. We will have a normal relationship with a sovereign nation that is a member of the community of nations. That equal partnership will be strengthened by our support for Iraq: for its Government, for its security forces, for its people, and for their aspirations.

As we end the war in Iraq, the United States and our coalition partners have begun a transition in Afghanistan. Between now and 2014, an increasingly capable Afghan Government and security forces will step forward to take responsibility for the future of their country. As they do, we are drawing down our own forces while building an enduring partnership with the Afghan people.

So let there be no doubt: The tide of war is receding. When I took office, roughly 180,000 Americans were serving in Iraq and Afghanistan. By the end of this year, that number will be cut in half, and it will continue to decline. This is critical for the sovereignty of Iraq and Afghanistan. It's also critical to the strength of the United States as we build our Nation at home.

Moreover, we are poised to end these wars from a position of strength. Ten years ago, there was an open wound and twisted steel, a broken heart in the center of this city. Today, as a new tower is rising at Ground Zero, it symbolizes New York's renewal, even as Al Qaida is under more pressure than ever before. Its leadership has been degraded. And Usama bin Laden, a man who murdered thousands of people from dozens of countries, will never endanger the peace of the world again.

So yes, this has been a difficult decade. But today, we stand at a crossroads of history with the chance to move decisively in the direction of peace. To do so, we must return to the wisdom of those who created this institution. The United Nations founding charter calls upon us "to unite our strength to maintain international peace and security." And Article 1 of this General Assembly's Universal Declaration of Human Rights reminds us that "All human beings are born free and equal in dignity and in rights." Those bedrock beliefs—in the responsibility of states and the rights of men and women—must be our guide.

And in that effort, we have reason to hope. This year has been a time of extraordinary transformation. More nations have stepped forward to maintain international peace and security. And more individuals are claiming their universal right to live in freedom and dignity.

Think about it. One year ago, when we met here in New York, the prospect of a successful referendum in South Sudan was in doubt. But the international community overcame old divisions to support the agreement that had been negotiated to give South Sudan self-determination. And last summer, as a new flag went up in Juba, former soldiers laid down their arms, men and women wept with joy, and children finally knew the promise of looking to a future that they will shape.

One year ago, the people of Cote d'Ivoire approached a landmark election. And when the incumbent lost and refused to respect the results, the world refused to look the other way. U.N. peacekeepers were harassed, but they did not leave their posts. The Security Council, led by the United States and Nigeria and France, came together to support the will of the people. And Cote d'Ivoire is now governed by the man who was elected to lead.

One year ago, the hopes of the people of Tunisia were suppressed. But they chose the dignity of peaceful protest over the rule of an iron fist. A vendor lit a spark that took his own life, but he ignited a movement. In the face of a crackdown, students spelled out the word "freedom." The balance of fear shifted from the ruler to those that he ruled. And now the people of Tunisia are preparing for elections that will move them one step closer to the democracy that they deserve.

One year ago, Egypt had known one President for nearly 30 years. But for 18 days, the eyes of the world were glued to Tahrir Square, where Egyptians from all walks of life—men and women, young and old, Muslim and Christian—demanded their universal rights. We saw in those protesters the moral force of nonviolence that has lit the world from Delhi to Warsaw, from Selma to South Africa, and we knew that change had come to Egypt and to the Arab world.

One year ago, the people of Libya were ruled by the world's longest serving dictator. But faced with bullets and bombs and a dictator who threatened to hunt them down like rats, they showed relentless bravery. We will never forget the words of the Libyan who stood up in those early days of the revolution and said: "Our words are free now. It's a feeling you can't explain." Day after day, in the face of bullets and bombs, the Libyan people refused to give back that freedom. And when they were threatened by the kind of mass atrocity that often went unchallenged in the last century, the United Nations lived up to its charter. The Security Council authorized all necessary measures to prevent a massacre. The Arab League called for this effort. Arab nations joined a NATO-led coalition that halted Qadhafi's forces in their tracks.

In the months that followed, the will of the coalition proved unbreakable, and the will of the Libyan people could not be denied. Forty-two years of tyranny was ended in 6 months. From Tripoli to Misurata to Benghazi, today, Libya is free. Yesterday the leaders of a new Libya took their rightful place beside us, and this week, the United States is reopening our Embassy in Tripoli.

This is how the international community is supposed to work: nations standing together for the sake of peace and security and individuals claiming their rights. Now all of us have a responsibility to support the new Libya, the new Libyan Government as they confront the challenge of turning this moment of promise into a just and lasting peace for all Libyans.

So this has been a remarkable year. The Qadhafi regime is over. Gbagbo, Ben Ali, Mubarak are no longer in power. Usama bin Laden is gone, and the idea that change could only come through violence has been buried with him. Something's happening in our world. The way things have been is not the way that they will be. The humiliating grip of corruption and tyranny is being pried open. Dictators are on notice. Technology is putting power into the hands of the people. The youth are delivering a powerful rebuke to dictatorship and rejecting the lie that some races, some peoples, some religions, some ethnicities do not desire democracy. The promise written down on paper, "All human beings are born free and equal in dignity and rights," is closer at hand.

But let us remember: Peace is hard. Peace is hard. Progress can be reversed. Prosperity comes slowly. Societies can split apart. The measure of our success must be whether people can live in sustained freedom, dignity, and security. And the United Nations and its member states must do their part to support those basic aspirations. And we have more work to do.

In Iran, we've seen a Government that refuses to recognize the rights of its own people. As we meet here today, men and women and children are being tortured, detained, and murdered by the Syrian regime. Thousands have been killed, many during the holy time of Ramadan. Thousands more have poured across Syria's borders. The Syrian people have shown dignity and courage in their pursuit of justice, protesting peacefully, standing silently in the streets, dying for the same values that this institution is supposed to stand for. And the question for us is clear: Will we stand with the Syrian people or with their oppressors?

Already, the United States has imposed strong sanctions on Syria's leaders. We supported a transfer of power that is responsive to the Syrian people. And many of our allies have joined in this effort. But for the sake of Syria and the peace and security of the world, we must speak with one voice. There's no excuse for inaction. Now is the time for the United Nations Security Council to sanction the Syrian regime and to stand with the Syrian people.

Throughout the region, we will have to respond to the calls for change. In Yemen, men, women, and children gather by the thousands in towns and city squares every day with the hope that their determination and spilled blood will prevail over a corrupt system. America supports those aspirations. We must work with Yemen's neighbors and our partners around the world to seek a path that allows for a peaceful transition of power from President Salih and a movement to free and fair elections as soon as possible.

In Bahrain, steps have been taken toward reform and accountability. We're pleased with that, but more is required. America is a close friend of Bahrain, and we will continue to call on the Government and the main opposition bloc, the Wifaq, to pursue a meaningful dialogue that brings peaceful change that is responsive to the people. We believe the patriotism that binds Bahrainis together must be more powerful than the sectarian forces that would tear them apart. It will be hard, but it is possible.

We believe that each nation must chart its own course to fulfill the aspirations of its people, and America does not expect to agree with every party or person who expresses themselves politically. But we will always stand up for the universal rights that were embraced by this Assembly. Those rights depend on elections that are free and fair, on governance that is transparent and accountable, respect for the rights of women and minorities, justice that is equal and fair. That is what our people deserve. Those are the elements of peace that can last.

Moreover, the United States will continue to support those nations that transition to democracy with greater trade and investment so that freedom is followed by opportunity. We will pursue a deeper engagement with governments, but also with civil society: students and entrepreneurs, political parties and the press. We have banned those who abuse human rights from traveling to our country, and we've sanctioned those who trample on human rights abroad. And we will always serve as a voice for those who've been silenced.

Now, I know, particularly this week, that for many in this hall, there's one issue that stands as a test for these principles and a test for American foreign policy, and that is the conflict between the Israelis and the Palestinians.

One year ago, I stood at this podium, and I called for an independent Palestine. I believed then and I believe now that the Palestinian people deserve a state of their own. But what I also said is that a genuine peace can only be realized between the Israelis and the Palestinians themselves. One year later, despite extensive efforts by America and others, the parties have not bridged their differences. Faced with this stalemate, I put forward a new basis for negotiations in May of this year. That basis is clear. It's well known to all of us here. Israelis must know that any agreement provides assurances for their security. Palestinians deserve to know the territorial basis of their state.

Now, I know that many are frustrated by the lack of progress. I assure you, so am I. But the question isn't the goal that we seek, the question is how do we reach that goal. And I am convinced that there is no shortcut to the end of a conflict that has endured for decades. Peace is hard work. Peace will not come through statements and resolutions at the United Nations. If it were that easy, it would have been accomplished by now. Ultimately, it is the Israelis and the Palestinians who must live side by side. Ultimately, it is the Israelis and the Palestinians, not us, who must reach agreement on the issues that divide them: on borders and on security, on refugees and Jerusalem.

Ultimately, peace depends upon compromise among people who must live together long after our speeches are over, long after our votes have been tallied. That's the lesson of Northern Ireland, where ancient antagonists bridged their differences. That's the lesson of Sudan, where a negotiated settlement led to an independent state. And that is and will be the path to a Palestinian state: negotiations between the parties.

We seek a future where Palestinians live in a sovereign state of their own, with no limit to what they can achieve. There's no question that the Palestinians have seen that vision delayed for too long. It is precisely because we believe so strongly in the aspirations of the Palestinian people that America has invested so much time and so much effort in the building of a Palestinian state and the negotiations that can deliver a Palestinian state.

But understand this as well: America's commitment to Israel's security is unshakeable. Our friendship with Israel is deep and enduring. And so we believe that any lasting peace must acknowledge the very real security concerns that Israel faces every single day.

Let us be honest with ourselves: Israel is surrounded by neighbors that have waged repeated wars against it. Israel's citizens have been killed by rockets fired at their houses and suicide bombs on their buses. Israel's children come of age knowing that throughout the region, other children are taught to hate them. Israel, a small country of less than 8 million people, look out at a world where leaders of much larger nations threaten to wipe it off of the map. The Jewish people carry the burden of centuries of exile and persecution and fresh memories of knowing that 6 million people were killed simply because of who they are. Those are facts. They cannot be denied.

The Jewish people have forged a successful state in their historic homeland. Israel deserves recognition. It deserves normal relations with its neighbors. And friends of the Palestinians do them no favors by ignoring this truth, just as friends of Israel must recognize the need to pursue a two-state solution with a secure Israel next to an independent Palestine.

That is the truth. Each side has legitimate aspirations, and that's part of what makes peace so hard. And the deadlock will only be broken when each side learns to stand in the other's shoes, each side can see the world through the other's eyes. That's what we should be encouraging. That's what we should be promoting.

This body—founded, as it was, out of the ashes of war and genocide, dedicated, as it is, to the dignity of every single person—must recognize the reality that is lived by both the Palestinians and the Israelis. The measure of our actions must always be whether they advance the right of Israeli and Palestinian children to live lives of peace and security and dignity and opportunity. And we will only succeed in that effort if we can encourage the parties to sit down, to listen to each other, and to understand each other's hopes and each other's fears. That is the project to which America is committed. There are no shortcuts. And that is what the United Nations should be focused on in the weeks and months to come.

Now, even as we confront these challenges of conflict and revolution, we must also recognize—we must also remind ourselves—that peace is not just the absence of war. True peace depends on creating the opportunity that makes life worth living. And to do that, we must confront the common enemies of humanity: nuclear weapons and poverty, ignorance and disease. These forces corrode the possibility of lasting peace, and together, we're called upon to confront them.

To lift the specter of mass destruction, we must come together to pursue the peace and security of a world without nuclear weapons. Over the last 2 years, we've begun to walk down that path. Since our Nuclear Security Summit in Washington, nearly 50 nations have taken steps to secure nuclear materials from terrorists and smugglers. Next March, a summit in Seoul will advance our efforts to lock down all of them. The New START Treaty between the United States and Russia will cut our deployed arsenals to the lowest level in half a century, and our nations are pursuing talks on how to achieve even deeper reductions. America will continue to work for a ban on the testing of nuclear weapons and the production of fissile material needed to make them.

And so we have begun to move in the right direction, and the United States is committed to meeting our obligations. But even as we meet our obligations, we've strengthened the treaties and institutions that help stop the spread of these weapons. And to do so, we must continue to hold accountable those nations that flout them.

The Iranian Government cannot demonstrate that its program is peaceful. It has not met its obligations, and it rejects offers that would provide it with peaceful nuclear power. North Korea has yet to take concrete steps towards abandoning its weapons and continues belligerent action against the South. There's a future of greater opportunity for the people of these nations if their Governments meet their international obligations. But if they continue down a path that is outside international law, they must be met with greater pressure and isolation. That is what our commitment to peace and security demands.

To bring prosperity to our people, we must promote the growth that creates opportunity. In this effort, let us not forget that we've made enormous progress over the last several decades. Closed societies gave way to open markets. Innovation and entrepreneurship has transformed the way we live and the things that we do. Emerging economies from Asia to the Americas have lifted hundreds of millions of people from poverty. It's an extraordinary achievement. And yet 3 years ago, we were confronted with the worst financial crisis in eight decades. And that crisis proved a fact that has become clearer with each passing year: Our fates are interconnected. In a global economy, nations will rise or fall together.

And today, we confront the challenges that have followed on the heels of that crisis. Around the world, recovery is still fragile. Markets remain volatile. Too many people are out of work. Too many others are struggling just to get by. We acted together to avert a depression in 2009. We must take urgent and coordinated action once more. Here in the United States, I've announced a plan to put Americans back to work and jump-start our economy at the same time as I'm committed to substantially reducing our deficits over time.

We stand with our European allies as they reshape their institutions and address their own fiscal challenges. For other countries, leaders face a different challenge as they shift their economy towards more self-reliance, boosting domestic demand while slowing inflation. So we will work with emerging economies that have rebounded strongly so that rising standards of living create new markets that promote global growth. That's what our commitment to prosperity demands.

To combat the poverty that punishes our children, we must act on the belief that freedom from want is a basic human right. The United States has made it a focus of our engagement abroad to help people to feed themselves. And today, as drought and conflict have brought famine to the Horn of Africa, our conscience calls on us to act. Together, we must continue to provide assistance and support organizations that can reach those in need. And together, we must insist on unrestricted humanitarian access so that we can save the lives of thousands of men and women and children. Our common humanity is at stake. Let us show that the life of a child in Somalia is as precious as any other. That is what our commitment to our fellow human beings demand.

To stop disease that spreads across borders, we must strengthen our system of public health. We will continue the fight against HIV/AIDS, tuberculosis, and malaria. We will focus on the health of mothers and of children. And we must come together to prevent and detect and fight every kind of biological danger, whether it's a pandemic like H1N1 or a terrorist threat or a treatable disease.

This week, America signed an agreement with the World Health Organization to affirm our commitment to meet this challenge. And today I urge all nations to join us in meeting the HWO's goal of making sure all nations have core capacities to address public health emergencies in place by 2012. That is what our commitment to the health of our people demands.

To preserve our planet, we must not put off action that climate change demands. We have to tap the power of science to save those resources that are scarce. And together, we must continue our work to build on the progress made in Copenhagen and Cancun, so that all the major economies here today follow through on the commitments that were made.

Together, we must work to transform the energy that powers our economies and support others as they move down that path. That is what our commitment to the next generation demands.

And to make sure our societies reach their potential, we must allow our citizens to reach theirs. No country can afford the corruption that plagues the world like a cancer. Together, we must harness the power of open societies and open economies. That's why we've partnered with countries from across the globe to launch a new partnership on open government that helps ensure accountability and helps to empower citizens. No country should deny people their rights to freedom of speech and freedom of religion, but also no country should deny people their rights because of who they love, which is why we must stand up for the rights of gays and lesbians everywhere.

And no country can realize its potential if half its population cannot reach theirs. This week, the United States signed a new Declaration on Women's Participation. Next year, we should each announce the steps we are taking to break down the economic and political barriers that stand in the way of women and girls. This is what our commitment to human progress demands.

I know there's no straight line to that progress, no single path to success. We come from different cultures and carry with us different histories. But let us never forget that even as we gather here as heads of different governments, we represent citizens who share the same basic aspirations: to live with dignity and freedom, to get an education and pursue opportunity, to love our families and love and worship our God, to live in the kind of peace that makes life worth living.

It is the nature of our imperfect world that we are first—forced to learn these lessons over and over again. Conflict and repression will endure so long as some people refuse to do unto others as we would have them do unto us. Yet that is precisely why we have built institutions like this: to bind our fates together, to help us recognize ourselves in each other. Because those who came before us believed that peace

1103

is preferable to war and freedom is preferable to suppression and prosperity is preferable to poverty. That's the message that comes not from capitals, but from citizens, from our people.

And when the cornerstone of this very building was put in place, President Truman came here to New York and said, "The United Nations is essentially an expression of the moral nature of man's aspirations." The moral nature of man's aspirations. As we live in a world that is changing at a breathtaking pace, that's a lesson that we must never forget.

Peace is hard, but we know that it is possible. So, together, let us be resolved to see that it is defined by our hopes and not by our fears.

Together, let us make peace, but a peace, most importantly, that will last.

Thank you very much.

NOTE: The President spoke at 10:12 a.m. at United Nations Headquarters. In his remarks, he referred to Nassir Abdulaziz Al-Nasser, President, 66th Session of the U.N. General Assembly; Secretary-General Ban Ki-moon of the United Nations; former President Laurent Gbagbo and President Alassane Dramane Ouattara of Cote d'Ivoire; former President Zine El Abidine Ben Ali of Tunisia; former President Mohamed Hosni Mubarak of Egypt; and Col. Muammar Abu Minyar al-Qadhafi, former leader of Libya.

Remarks Prior to a Meeting With Prime Minister Benjamin Netanyahu of Israel in New York City
September 21, 2011

President Obama. Well, I want to welcome Prime Minister Netanyahu both to the United States and to New York. As I just said in the speech that I gave before the U.N. General Assembly, the bonds between the United States and Israel are unbreakable. And the United States commitment to Israel's security is unbreakable. Indeed, I think it's fair to say that, today, our security cooperation is stronger than it has ever been.

I'm looking forward to a good discussion with Prime Minister Netanyahu about the events not only here in the United Nations, but also developments that have been taking place in the region.

As I just indicated, peace cannot be imposed on the parties. It's going to have to be negotiated. One side's actions in the United Nations will achieve neither statehood nor self-determination for the Palestinians. But Israelis and Palestinians sitting down together and working through these very difficult issues that have kept the parties apart for decades now, that is what can achieve what is, I know, the ultimate goal of all of us, which is two states, side by side, living in peace and security.

Recent events in the region remind us of how fragile peace can be and why the pursuit of Middle East peace is more urgent than ever. But as we pursue that peace, I know that the Prime Minister recognizes that America's commitment to Israel will never waver and that our pursuit of a just and lasting peace is one that is not only compatible, but we think puts Israel's security at the forefront.

So it is a great pleasure to have the Prime Minister here. I want to thank him for his efforts and his cooperation, and I'm looking forward to an excellent discussion.

Prime Minister Netanyahu. Thank you, Mr. President. Well, I want to thank you, Mr. President, for standing with Israel and supporting peace through direct negotiations. We both agree that this is the only way to achieve peace. We both agree that Palestinians and Israelis should sit down and negotiate an agreement of mutual recognition and security. I think this is the only way to get to a stable and durable peace.

But you've also made it clear that the Palestinians deserve a state, but it's a state that has to make that peace with Israel. And therefore, their attempt to shortcut this process, not negotiate a peace—that attempt to get membership—state membership in the United Nations will not succeed.

I think the Palestinians want to achieve a state through the international community, but they're not prepared yet to give peace to Israel in return. And my hope is that there will be other leaders in the world, responsible leaders, who will heed your call, Mr. President, and oppose this effort to shortcut peace negotiations, in fact, to avoid them. Because I think that avoiding these negotiations is bad for Israel, bad for the Palestinians, and bad for peace.

Now, I know that these leaders are under enormous pressure, and I know that they're al-so—and this—from personal experience, I can tell you the automatic majority is against Israel. But I think that standing your ground, taking this position of principle—which is also, I think, the right position to achieve peace—I think this is a badge of honor. And I want to thank you for wearing that badge of honor, and also, I would express my hope that others will follow your example, Mr. President. So I want to thank you for that.

President Obama. Thank you.

NOTE: The President spoke at 11:01 a.m. at United Nations Headquarters.

Remarks Prior to a Meeting With Prime Minister Yoshihiko Noda of Japan in New York City
September 21, 2011

President Obama. I want to welcome Prime Minister Noda and his delegation to New York City and to the United States. As all of you are aware, we have an extraordinary alliance with Japan. They are one of our closest friends, our closest allies. We have worked cooperatively on a range of issues related to security, related to economics. And the bonds of friendship between our peoples is equally strong.

Prime Minister Noda and I have had the opportunity to speak by phone, although this is the first time that we've had a meeting face to face. I know that he, like all of us, has some extraordinary challenges that we have to address. And I know that at the top of his list is rebuilding Japan in the aftermath of the horrific tsunami that occurred. I've repeatedly pledged that America will do everything that we can to make sure that that rebuilding is a success.

At the same time, obviously, we have other important work to do together. As the two largest economies in the world, we have to continue to promote growth that can help put our people to work and to improve standards of living. We have to modernize our alliance to meet the needs of the 21st century. And so I'm looking forward to a very productive discussion and what I'm sure will be an excellent working relationship with the Prime Minister as well as his team.

Prime Minister Noda. The biggest priority and the immediate challenge for the Noda Government is the recovery from the Great East Japan Earthquake disaster and the degrading situation with the nuclear power plant. But at the same time, even from before the earthquake took place, we had a lot of challenges, both in domestically and in foreign policy areas. And those cohorts must be dealt with one by one and thereby creating a stable policy. That's the challenge and—for my Government.

My—our top priority is the reconstruction from the disaster of the earthquake in Japan, the great Japan—Great East Japan Earthquake. The United States has provided enormous amount of support, including Operation Tomodachi and a lot of efforts made by Ambassador Roos. And on behalf of the all Japanese nationals, I thank you. And thank you for your support.

I had a firm belief that the Japan-U.S. alliance is the key pillar of our foreign policy. And through the assistance that we received after the earthquake, this bridge has become an even more unwavering one. And the Japanese public also were assured, and we recognize the significance and importance of our alliance.

I was reported that the meeting between our Foreign Minister Gemba and Secretary of State Clinton was a very fruitful one, and we would like to further deepen and enhance the bilateral alliance between our two countries in the three major fields of security, economy, and also the cultural and people-to-people exchange.

One worry that I've had is that there is an emerging concern that once recovering the economy we might be drawn back into another recession, and Japan and the United States must work on the economic growth and the fiscal situation at the same time. And you have the presence of Secretary Geithner here, and we have to work together at the forum centers—the G–20 and other multilateral forum—and to coordinate with each other. And I'm looking forward to having such discussions with you.

NOTE: The President spoke at 12:20 p.m. at United Nations Headquarters. Prime Minister Noda referred to Minister of Foreign Affairs Koichiro Gemba of Japan. Prime Minister Noda spoke in Japanese, and his remarks were translated by an interpreter. A portion of these remarks could not be verified because the audio was incomplete.

Remarks at a Luncheon Hosted by Secretary-General Ban Ki-moon of the United Nations in New York City
September 21, 2011

Secretary-General Ban. President Obama, Excellencies, distinguished heads of state and government, Your Highnesses, Your Majesties, distinguished ministers, ladies and gentlemen: Welcome to the United Nations. Welcome to our common house.

We are off to a flying start today, I must say. Thank you, President Obama, for your inspiring oratory, and more, for its vital importance.

As ever, we thank the United States and its generous people for hosting United Nations during last 66 years. This is the 66th session. Let me offer a special word of thanks to New Yorkers. In the last month, they have faced an earthquake, then a hurricane, now a perfect storm of the world's leaders, creating lot of traffic jams. [*Laughter*] And we are very much grateful for their patience.

Let me say straight off, this is my fifth lunch with the distinguished leaders of the world, and I'm very much grateful for your strong support. In that regard, I am very glad that it is not my last lunch, and we will have five more lunches in the coming 5 years. [*Applause*] Thank you very much. Taking this opportunity, I would like to really sincerely express my appreciation and thanks to all of the heads of state and government for your strong support. You can count on me. And it's a great and extraordinary honor to serve this great organization.

Mr. President, 50 years ago this week, your predecessor, President John F. Kennedy, addressed the General Assembly. He came, he said, to join with other world leaders, and I quote, "to look across this world of threats to a world of peace," unquote. Looking out upon the world, we see no shortages of threats. And closer to home, wherever we might live, we see the familiar struggles of political life: left versus right, rich versus poor, and up versus down. Seldom, however, has the debate been more emotional or strident; yet seldom has the need for unity been greater.

We know the challenges. I won't reprise my speech, except to say that we do indeed have a rare and generational opportunity to make a lasting difference in people's lives. If there is a theme in all that has been said today by the leaders, it would be the imperative of unity, solidarity in realizing that opportunity. We must act together. There is no opt-out clause for global problem-solving. Every country has something to give in and to gain.

Excellencies, let me close with a question. By any chance, do you ever feel that you have become a slave, you have become a slave of— to this machine? [*Laughter*]

[*At this point, Secretary-General Ban held up his mobile phone.*]

Somehow, I sense that I'm not alone. I have seen so many leaders having and speaking over the phone, even while at the summit meetings. Thanks to device like this, the world has been more connected. But let us not mistake—misunderstand that with being united. Being connected depends on technology. Being united depends on us: on leaders, on institutions, and on the decisions you make.

We have come a long way since last year. Outside this building, the new flags of Southern Sudan and Libya proudly wave in the September breeze. And today I am very pleased to recognize the presence of Southern Sudan President, His Excellency Salva Kiir, who came to New York for the first time after their independence, and President of National Transitional Council of Libya, His Excellency Abdul Jalil, who received very strong support yesterday. And they will continue to receive such support. Let us give them a big applause.

We can be proud of the firm stand we took for freedom and democracy in Cote d'Ivoire, North Africa, and elsewhere. We can be proud of the many lives we saved, the hungry people we fed, the children we helped to grow up healthy and strong. And we can do more to make the Arab Spring a season of hope for all, to put the sustainable back into development, to prevent the crises before they explode.

And so, distinguished heads of state and government, Excellencies, Your Majesties, let us raise a glass to clarity of vision, to unity of purpose, to a common resolve for action, to the United Nations, and to continued success of each and every heads of state and government present here.

Thank you very much. Cheers.

President Obama. Cheers.

[*Secretary-General Ban offered a toast.*]

Secretary-General Ban. Cheers.
President Obama. Cheers.
Secretary-General Ban. Cheers. Thank you. Cheers.
President Obama. Good afternoon, everyone. These lunches come right after my remarks to the General Assembly, so I've already spoken too long. [*Laughter*] I just—as the host of the United Nations, I want to welcome all of you. In particular, though, I want to cite Secretary-General Ban for his extraordinary leadership. As you begin your second term, I want to take this opportunity to thank you, not just for your leadership, but also for your lessons in life.

As we all know, the Secretary-General is a very modest man, but he's led a remarkable life. Born into World War II, as a young boy in the middle of the Korean war having to flee the fighting with his family, just as his home country has risen, so he has risen to leadership on the world stage.

A lot of us are envious of him because, in running for a second term, he ran unopposed—[*laughter*]—and he won unanimously. [*Laughter*] I'm still trying to learn what his trick is. [*Laughter*]

But, Secretary-General, that fact reflects the high esteem with which all of us hold you and your leadership. And I want to quote something that you said when you began your new term: "We live in a new era where no country can solve all challenges and where every country could be part of the solution." I could not agree more. Today, we see the difference you've made in Cote d'Ivoire, in Sudan, in Libya, in confronting climate change and nuclear safety, in peacekeeping missions that save lives every single day.

So we want to salute you. We want to salute those who serve in U.N. missions around the world, at times, at great risk to themselves. We give them their mandate, but it is they who risk their lives—and give their lives—so people can live in peace and dignity.

So I want to propose a toast: To the leader who, every day, has to work hard to try to unite nations, and to all the men and women who sustain it, especially those brave humanitarians in blue helmets. In an era of great tumult and great change, let all of us be part of the solution.

[*President Obama offered a toast.*]

Secretary-General Ban. Thank you very much.
President Obama. Cheers.

NOTE: The President spoke at 1:54 p.m. at United Nations Headquarters.

Remarks at the Clinton Global Initiative Annual Meeting in New York City
September 21, 2011

Thank you very much. Thank you. It is wonderful to be here today. It is wonderful to see so many do-gooders all in one room. [*Laughter*] And our do-gooder-in-chief, Bill Clinton, thank you for not only the gracious introduction, but the extraordinary work that he has been doing each and every day. You are tireless, and we are proud of what you've been doing.

I want to thank the outstanding team here at CGI: the CEO Bob Harrison, Deputy Director Ed Hughes, all the dedicated staff. And although she is not part of CGI, she's certainly part of what makes Bill so successful—someone who he does not get to see enough because of me—[*laughter*]—but I'm grateful that he's not bitter about it. [*Laughter*] She's one of the best Secretaries of State that we've ever had, Hillary Clinton.

Now, this is the third time that I've been here. Last year, I was the warmup act for Michelle. [*Laughter*] I just gave a big speech at the U.N. this morning, and so I will not subject you to another one. I wanted to stop by for two reasons.

First, I want to express my appreciation for the extraordinary work that has been done by CGI. It's been said that "no power on Earth can stop an idea whose time has come." And as you know, when Bill Clinton sees an idea out there, he—there's no stopping him. CGI was an idea whose time had come. And thanks to his relentless determination—but also, I think he'd agree, thanks to, most importantly, your commitments—you've created new hope and opportunity for hundreds of millions of people in nearly 200 countries. Think about that, hundreds of millions of people have been touched by what you've done. That doesn't happen very often.

That's the other thing I want to talk about. Around the world, people are still reeling from the financial crisis that unfolded 3 years ago and the economic pain that followed. And this morning at the United Nations, I talked about the concerted action that the world needs to take right now to right our economic ship.

But we have to remember, America is still the biggest economy in the world. So the single most important thing we could do for the global economy is to get our own economy moving again. When America is growing, the world is more likely to grow. And obviously, that's the number-one issue on the minds of every American that I meet. If they haven't been out of work since the recession began, odds are they know somebody who has. They feel as if the decks have been stacked against them. They don't feel as if hard work and responsibility pay off anymore, and they don't see that hard work and responsibility reflected either in Washington or, all too often, on Wall Street. They just want to know that their leaders are willing to step up and do something about it.

So as President Clinton mentioned, that's why I put forward the "American Jobs Act," not as a silver bullet that will solve all our problems, but it will put more people back to work. It will put more money into the pockets of working people. And that's what our economy needs right now.

It hires teachers and puts them back in the classroom. It hires construction workers, puts them out rebuilding an infrastructure that has deteriorated, and we know that that's part of our economic success historically. It puts our veterans back to work, after having served overseas, then coming home and not being able to find a job, when they sacrificed immeasurably on behalf of our security.

That's what we need right now, we need more good teachers in front of our kids. I was just having lunch over at the General Assembly with the President of South Korea. And I still remember the first time I met him, in South Korea, and I asked him, "Well, what are your biggest challenges right now?" He says, "Education, it's a big challenge." I said: "Well, I understand. We've got a big challenge in the United States as well." He said, "No, you have to understand, my big challenge is, the parents are too demanding." [*Laughter*] "They're coming into my office, they're saying, our children have to learn English in first grade. So we're having to import teachers from other countries and pay them a premium to meet the educational demands that parents are placing on us, because they know that if their children are to succeed in the 21st-century economy, they'd better know some foreign languages." Well, think about that. That's what's happening in South Korea. Here we're laying off teachers in droves.

Now is the time to upgrade our roads and our bridges and our schools. We used to have the best airports, the best roads, the best bridges, the best ports. I've been asking people recently—I've taken a poll in New York—how do you find LaGuardia compared to the Beijing airport? [*Laughter*] We laugh, but that says something. That's not inevitable; that's a choice that we're making.

We talk about climate change, something that obviously people here are deeply concerned about. Talking to the CEO of Southwest Airlines, they estimate that if we put in the new generation of GPS air traffic control, we would save 15 percent in fuel costs: "Reduce fuel consumption by 15 percent, Mr. President." And think about what that would do, not only to potentially lower the cost of a ticket—maybe they could start giving out peanuts again. [*Laughter*] But think what it would do in terms of taking those pollutants out of our air.

So we know what to do. We know that an American should—who puts his life on the line, her life on the line, should never have to fight for a job when they come home. We know that. We know what our values are.

So this jobs bill addresses the terrible toll that unemployment inflicts on people. It helps long-term unemployed keep their skills sharp. It says to young people who are underprivileged, we're going to give you a chance at a summer job that helps to establish the kind of work habits that carry on for generations. Because part of what happens in this kind of recession environment, the disadvantage of this generation coming in and not being able to get fully employed, that lingers for a lifetime. It affects their lifetime earnings. That's contrary to our values.

This jobs bill cuts taxes for every working family and every small-business owner in America to boost demand and to boost hiring. And if you're a small-business owner who hires a new worker or raises workers' wages, you get an extra tax cut.

So this bill answers the urgent need to create jobs right away. And I appreciate President Clinton's strong support of this plan over the weekend. And the reason that that's important is because he knows a good jobs plan when he sees it. He created more jobs in his tenure than just about anybody. And I'm fighting hard to make sure that we get this bill passed through Congress.

As President Clinton said, every idea in there has been supported in the past by both parties, and everything is paid for. There's no reason why we shouldn't pass it right away. And for those of you who are concerned about the international economy and development, keep this in mind: If the economy is not growing, if Americans aren't getting back to work, it becomes that much harder for us to sustain the critical development assistance and the partnerships that help to undergird development strategies that you care dearly about all across the world.

So this is important, again, not just to the United States; this is important to the world. It will help determine how well we can support what you are doing in the non-for-profit sector. I'm going to be doing everything I can, everything in my power, to get this economy moving again that requires congressional support, but also those things that don't require congressional support.

Consider one of the ideas that we're working on together. Earlier this year, I announced a Better Buildings Initiative to rehire construction workers to make our buildings more energy efficient. And I asked President Clinton and my jobs council to challenge private companies to join us. In June, at CGI America, we announced a commitment to upgrade 300 million square feet of space, from military housing to college campuses. And some of these projects are breaking ground this month, putting people to work right now. Later this year, we'll announce more commitments that will create jobs, while saving billions for businesses on energy bills and cutting down on our pollution.

And it's a good example of what CGI is all about: Everybody working together—Government, business, the non-for-profit sector—to create opportunities today, while ensuring those opportunities for the future. We just need that kind of cooperation in Washington.

I have to say that I do envy President Clinton because when you're out of Washington, it turns out that you're just dealing with people who are reasonable all the time, and—[laughter]. Nobody is looking to score points. Nobody is looking at the polls on any particular issue. You're just trying to solve problems. And that's the ethic that people are looking for in Washington.

We've got enough challenges. It is technically difficult to figure out how we are going to deal with climate change, not impossible, but difficult. There are technical challenges to making sure that we're providing enough safe drinking water around the world or making sure that preventable diseases are eradicated in countries that don't yet have a public health infrastructure. These things are all tough stuff, but they're solvable if everybody's attitude is that we're working together, as opposed to trying to work at odds with each other.

And our future depends on fighting this downturn with everything that we've got right now. And it demands that we invest in ourselves, even as we're making commitments in investments around the world. It demands we invest in research and technology, so the great ideas of tomorrow are born in our labs and our classrooms. It demands we invest in faster transportation and communications networks, so that our businesses can compete. It demands that we give every child the skills and education they need to succeed.

And I thank you for the commitment that you've made to recruit and train tens of thousands of new science, technology, engineering, and math teachers. Nothing could be more important.

We can do all this. We can create jobs now and invest in our future and still tackle our long-term debt problems. Don't tell Bill Clinton it can't be done. He did it. When he was President, he did not cut our way out of prosperity; he grew our way to prosperity. We didn't shortchange essential investments or balance the budget on the backs of the middle class or the poor. We were able to live within our means, invest in our future, and ask everybody to pay their fair share.

And what happened? The private sector thrived. The rich got richer. The middle class grew. Millions rose out of poverty. America ran a surplus that was on track to be debt free by next year. We were a nation firing on all cylinders.

That's the kind of nation that we've got to work to build again. It will take time, after the kind of crisis that we've endured. And this is a once-in-a-generation crisis. But we can get through it. But our politics right now is not doing us any favors.

Nevertheless, I believe we can and we will get there, by remembering what made us great, by building an economy where innovation is encouraged, education is a national mission, new jobs and businesses choose to take right—root right here in the United States. And that's what CGI reflects. It reflects the American spirit, which is big and bold and generous and doesn't shy away from challenges and says that we're all in it together.

And when I think about the contributions that all of you have made, then I'm—that makes me confident. Those of us who have been most blessed by this Nation, we are ready to give back. But we've got to be asked. And that's what I'm hoping Members of Congress recognize. I don't want a small, cramped vision of what America can be. We want a big and generous vision of what America can be. And the world is inspired when we have that vision.

And by the way, that vision is not a Democratic vision or a Republican idea. These are not ideas that belong to one political party or another. They are the things a rising nation does and the thing that retreating nations don't do. And we are not a retreating nation.

So despite the many challenges we face right now, I believe America must continue to be a rising nation, with rising fortunes. And that makes—that means making sure that everybody is participating and everybody is getting a shot, because when all of our people do well, America does well. And when America does

well, that's good for the rest of the world. That's what President Clinton has always understood.

So, Mr. President, thank you for all the opportunities that you help to create every day. Thank you to all of you who are participating in CGI. You are doing the Lord's work. And I can assure you that you will continue to have a partner in the Obama administration for what I expect to be years to come.

Thank you very much.

NOTE: The President spoke at 2:43 p.m. at the Sheraton New York Hotel & Towers. In his remarks, he referred to President Lee Myung-bak of South Korea; and Gary C. Kelly, president and chief executive officer, Southwest Airlines Co. The transcript released by the Office of the Press Secretary also included the remarks of former President William J. Clinton.

Remarks During a Meeting With Prime Minister David Cameron of the United Kingdom and an Exchange With Reporters in New York City
September 21, 2011

President Obama. Let me welcome Prime Minister Cameron to the United States and New York. Obviously, there is an extraordinarily special relationship between the United States and the United Kingdom, and I am very fortunate that over the last year or two, David and I have been able to, I think, establish an excellent friendship as well.

And that's part of what makes the alliance between the United States and the United Kingdom so important, is that it's grounded not only in shared values and broad-based agreement on policy, but it's also based on the individual relationships that we have and the friendships and joint traditions that we have.

We've got a lot to talk about. We have worked closely together to help bring about freedom and peace in Libya. We are coordinating closely in managing a very difficult time for the global economy. We are keenly interested in finding a resolution to the Israeli-Palestinian conflict. On all these issues, I've

always found Prime Minister Cameron to be an outstanding partner.

And so I'm very grateful for his friendship, his hard work, and his dedication and his leadership on the global stage, and I look forward to a very productive discussion today.

David, welcome.

Prime Minister Cameron. Thank you. If I may say, thank you, Barack, for that warm welcome. It's great to be back in America, great to be back in New York, and particularly on this 10th anniversary of 9/11, a reminder of how our countries always work together in defeating terror and trying to make our world a safer place.

As you say, we worked very closely together on Libya, and I think we're getting to a good conclusion there, with a real chance of freedom and democracy for those people. We're working closely together on Afghanistan; also the Middle East peace process, where we're desperate to get that moving again. And I'm looking forward to discussions on the world economy, which we will follow up in Cannes at the G–20, where we've got to get the world economy moving.

So these are very important times. I think the relationship is as strong as it's ever been, and it's been a pleasure working with you these last 16 months.

President Obama. Excellent. Thank you very much, everybody.

Iranian Government's Release of Detained U.S. Citizens Shane Bauer and Joshua Fattal

Q. Can you give us your reaction to the hikers being released?

President Obama. We are thrilled that the hikers were released, and we are thrilled for the families. It was the right thing to do. They shouldn't have been held in the first place, but we're glad they're now home.

NOTE: The President spoke at 3:55 p.m. at the Waldorf-Astoria Hotel. A portion of these remarks could not be verified because the audio was incomplete.

Remarks Prior to a Meeting With President Nicolas Sarkozy of France in New York City
September 21, 2011

President Obama. Well, I want to welcome President Sarkozy to New York City and to the United States. On the anniversary of September 11, President Sarkozy gave a speech at our Embassy in Paris, and he reminded the people of France, but also the world, of the extraordinary friendship that had developed, in part, because of the great sacrifices that our men and women in uniform have made over the decades to preserve freedom and democracy. And so not only am I grateful for the expression of deep friendship that President Sarkozy expressed, but I want to affirm the mutuality of feeling that we have towards the French people.

Do we have an interpreter?

[At this point, an interpreter translated President Obama's previous remarks into French and began a running translation.]

That partnership's been evidenced by the extraordinary work that we've done together in Libya. And I want to thank President Sarkozy for his leadership, as a coalition helped the Libyan people achieve the kind of freedom and opportunity that they're looking for. That partnership is evidenced in the work we did together in Cote d'Ivoire to ensure that the rightfully elected leader of that country was put in place. And our partnership and our mutual leadership will be required to deal with a range of international issues that have been discussed here at the United Nations and are going to be critical in the months and years to come, including trying to find a resolution to the Israeli-Palestinian conflict, but also trying to find a coordinated world strategy, global strategy, to deal with a economy that is still far too fragile.

And of course, we still have the joint project to bring stability and transition to Afghan governance. And we are extraordinarily grateful for the sacrifices that the men and women in uniform from France have made in that effort.

On a personal note, I consider Nicolas a friend as well as a colleague. Thank you for your leadership. Welcome. And I look forward to a very productive discussion.

[President Sarkozy spoke in French, and his remarks were translated by an interpreter.]

President Sarkozy. I should like to say just how delighted we are to be here in the United States, in New York, alongside Barack Obama.

Now, for we, the people of France, I must say, it's actually easy to work with Barack Obama. Whatever the crises we've had to face together, whatever the initiatives we have taken jointly, on every single occasion we have found a listening, openminded attitude on the part of our friend, Barack Obama. In particular, when tackling the crisis, which is still upon us today, the leadership that President Obama has shown, and showed at the time, have been of a special value to us all.

There is still much to do, in particular in paving the way to the G–20 summit in Cannes. This is our priority; our number-one priority— let me make this very clear—is to find the path to growth worldwide.

Lastly, I wish to say to what extent I am sensitive to the boldness, the courage, the intelligence, and the sensitivity of President Obama, my friend. I liked him before his election, I liked him once he was elected, and I especially appreciate him now, when the tough times are upon us.

And there's one thing I want to say, perhaps on a more personal note, and that I really mean from the bottom of my heart. When things are as tough as they are right now, when the going

gets as tough as it is right now, it is especially precious and important to be able to speak to what is the world's number-one power, but to someone who listens, someone who is sensitive to others, someone who is respectful and aware of other people's red lines and prepared to take them into account, especially at a time when, as I said, we are facing fresh difficulties, and we really need, together, to go forward.

[Following the translation of his remarks, President Sarkozy spoke in English.]

President Sarkozy. She speaks like me. *[Laughter]*
President Obama. Thank you very much.

NOTE: The President spoke at 4:53 p.m. at the Waldorf-Astoria Hotel.

Statement on Armenian National Day
September 21, 2011

On behalf of the American people, I want to extend my best wishes to all those who are celebrating Armenian National Day in Armenia, in the United States, and around the world. This 20th anniversary of independence and Armenia's achievements during this time show the

progress that is possible when people are free to determine their own destiny. Here in the United States, we are grateful for the Armenian Americans who enrich our national life every day and who help sustain the strong and growing relationship between our two countries.

Statement on the Iranian Government's Release of Shane Bauer and Joshua Fattal
September 21, 2011

I welcome the release of Shane Bauer and Josh Fattal from detention in Iran and am very pleased that they are being reunited with their loved ones. The tireless advocacy of their families over these 2 years has won my admiration and is now coming to an end with Josh and Shane back in their arms. All Americans join their families and friends

in celebrating their long-awaited return home.

We are deeply grateful to His Majesty Sultan Qaboos bin Said of Oman, Iraqi President Jalal Talabani, the Swiss Government, and to all our partners and allies around the world who have worked steadfastly over the past 2 years to secure the release of Shane and Josh.

Message to the Congress on Continuation of the National Emergency With Respect to Persons Who Commit, Threaten To Commit, or Support Terrorism
September 21, 2011

To the Congress of the United States:

Section 202(d) of the National Emergencies Act (50 U.S.C. 1622(d)) provides for the automatic termination of a national emergency unless, prior to the anniversary date of its declaration, the President publishes in the *Federal Register* and transmits to the Congress a notice stating that the emergency is to continue in effect beyond the anniversary date. In accordance with this provision, I have sent to the *Federal Register* for publication the enclosed notice, stating that the national emergency with respect to persons who commit, threaten to commit, or support terrorism is to continue in effect beyond September 23, 2011.

The crisis constituted by the grave acts of terrorism and threats of terrorism committed by foreign terrorists, including the terrorist attacks on September 11, 2001, in New York and Pennsylvania and against the Pentagon, and the continuing and immediate threat of further attacks on United States nationals or the United States that led to the declaration of a national emergency on September 23, 2001, has not been resolved. These actions pose a continuing unusual and extraordinary threat to the national security, foreign policy, and economy of the United States. For these reasons, I have determined that it is necessary to continue the national emergency declared with respect to persons who commit, threaten to commit, or support terrorism, and maintain in force the comprehensive sanctions to respond to this threat.

BARACK OBAMA

The White House,
September 21, 2011.

NOTE: The notice is listed in Appendix D at the end of this volume.

Remarks at the Hilltop Basic Resources, Inc., River Terminal in Cincinnati, Ohio
September 22, 2011

The President. Hello, Cincinnati! Well, it is good to see all of you. It is good—it's good to be back in Cincinnati. I have to say, I drove by the Bengals' practice, and I was scouting out some plays in case they play the Bears. [*Laughter*] Did I hear somebody boo the Bears?

Audience members. Boo! [*Laughter*]

The President. We've got some folks I just want to make sure are acknowledged here today. First of all, the Secretary of Transportation, Ray LaHood's in the house. Give him a round of applause. We've got the mayor of the great city of Cincinnati, Mark Mallory is here. We've got the mayor of Covington, Mayor Denny Bowman. Senator Rand Paul is here.

Audience members. Boo!

The President. We—Rand is going to be supporting bridges, so we got to—[*applause*].

And we've got Congressman John Yarmuth in the house.

Now, it is good to be back. I was just in Columbus a little while ago, and I figured I couldn't get away with not giving Cincinnati a little bit of love.

I want to thank the good folks at Hilltop Concrete for having us here today. I especially want to thank Ron for his introduction.

Companies like Hilltop, construction companies, have been hit harder by this economic crisis than almost any other industry in America. And there are millions of construction workers who are still out there looking for a job. They're ready to work, but things have been a little tough. Now, that doesn't mean that there is not plenty of construction waiting to get done in this country.

Behind us stands the Brent Spence Bridge. It's located on one of the busiest trucking routes in North America. It sees about a hundred and fifty thousand vehicles every single day. And it's in such poor condition that it's been labeled "functionally obsolete." Think about that: functionally obsolete. That doesn't sound good, does it?

Audience members. No!

Audience member. That's kind of like John Boehner.

The President. It's safe to—[*laughter*]—it's safe to drive on, but it was not designed to accommodate today's traffic, which can stretch out for a mile. Shipping companies try to have their trucks avoid the bridge. Of course, that only ends up costing them more money as well.

The thing is there are bridges and roads and highways like that throughout the region. A major bridge that connects Kentucky and Indiana just closed down for safety reasons. Another aging bridge that crosses over the Ohio River in Ironton could be replaced right now. There are rail stations in Cleveland and Toledo in desperate need of repair. And the same is true in cities all across America. It makes your commute longer. It costs our billions—our businesses billions of dollars. They could be moving products faster if they had better transportation routes. And in some cases, it's not safe.

Now, we used to have the best infrastructure in the world here in America. We're the country that built the intercontinental railroad, the Interstate Highway System. We built the Hoover Dam. We built the Grand Central station. So how can we now sit back and let China build the best railroads and let Europe build the best highways and have Singapore build a nicer airport at a time when we've got millions of unemployed construction workers out there just ready to get on the job, ready to do the work to rebuilding America?

So, Cincinnati, we are better than that. We're smarter than that. And that's why I sent Congress the "American Jobs Act" 10 days ago. This bill is not that complicated. It's a bill that would put people back to work rebuilding America: repairing our roads, repairing our bridges, repairing our schools. It would lead to jobs for concrete workers like the ones here at Hilltop, jobs for construction workers and masons, carpenters, plumbers, electricians, architects, engineers, ironworkers—put folks back to work.

There is work to be done, and there are workers ready to do it. So let's tell Congress to pass this jobs bill right away.

Audience members. Pass this bill! Pass this bill! Pass this bill!

The President. Pass this bill! [*Laughter*] Pass the bill!

Tell them to pass the jobs bill, and not only will we start rebuilding America, but we can also put thousands of teachers back to work.

I was with the President of South Korea—I was up at the United Nations. We were doing a bunch of stuff. And he's told me in the past—I've asked him, I said, what's your biggest challenge? He says, oh, education. I said, well, what are you dealing with? He said, well, you know what, we're hiring so many teachers we can barely keep up, because we know that if we're going to compete in the future, we've got to have the best teachers. And we've got to have our kids in school longer. And we've got to make sure that they're learning math and science.

Well, while they're hiring teachers in droves, what are we doing? We're laying off teachers. It makes no sense in this new global economy where our young people's success is going to depend on the kind of education that they can get. So for us to be laying off teachers doesn't make sense for our kids, it doesn't make sense for us, it doesn't make sense for our economy.

Pass this jobs bill and put teachers back in the classroom where they belong.

Audience members. Pass this bill! Pass this bill! Pass this bill!

The President. They need to go and pass it.

Tell Congress to pass this jobs bill, and companies will get tax credit for hiring America's veterans. We've been through a decade of war now. Almost 2 million people have served. And think about it. They're suspending their careers, they're leaving their families, they're putting themselves in harm way, all to protect us. The last thing they should have to do is fight for a job when they come home. And if we pass this jobs bill, it makes it easier for employers to hire those veterans. That's why we need to tell Congress to do what? To pass the bill.

Audience members. Pass this bill! Pass this bill! Pass this bill!

The President. The "American Jobs Act" will cut taxes for the typical working family by $1,500 next year. It will cut taxes for every small business in America. It will give an extra tax cut to every small-business owner who either hires more workers or raises those workers' wages. How many people here would like a raise?

And we know that most small businesses are the creators of new jobs. We've got a lot of folks in Congress who love to say how they're behind America's jobs creators. Well, if that's the case, then you should be passing this bill, because that's what this bill is all about, is helping small businesses all across America.

Everything in this jobs bill has been supported in the past by Republicans and Democrats. Everything in this jobs bill is paid for. The idea for a big boost in construction is supported by the AFL–CIO, but it's also supported by the Chamber of Commerce. Those two don't get along on much, but they agree we should rebuild America.

And by the way, thanks to the reforms that we've put into place, when we start rebuilding America, we're going to change how business is done. No more earmarks. No more boondoggles. No more bridges to nowhere. We're going to cut the redtape that prevents some of these construction projects from getting started as quickly as possible. And we'll set up an independent fund to attract private dollars and issue loans based on two criteria: how badly is a construction project needed and how much good will it do for the community. Those are the only things we should be thinking about. Not politics. And by the way, that's an idea that's supported by a Massachusetts Democrat and a Texas Republican. It's a good idea.

So my question is, what's Congress waiting for? Why is it taking so long? Now, the bridge

behind us just happens to connect the State that's home to the Speaker of the House——

Audience members. Boo!

The President. ——with the home State of the Republican leader in the Senate.

Audience members. Boo!

The President. Now, that's just a coincidence. [*Laughter*] It's purely accidental that that happened. [*Laughter*] But part of the reason I came here is because Mr. Boehner and Mr. McConnell, those are the two most powerful Republicans in Government. They can either kill this jobs bill or they can help pass this jobs bill. And I know these men care about their States. They care about businesses, they care about workers here. I can't imagine that the Speaker wants to represent a State where nearly one in four bridges are classified as substandard—one in four. I know that when Senator McConnell visited the closed bridge in Kentucky, he said that "roads and bridges are not partisan in Washington." That's great. I know that Paul Ryan, the Republican in charge of the budget process, recently said that "you can't deny that infrastructure does create jobs." That's what he said.

Well, if that's the case, there's no reason for Republicans in Congress to stand in the way of more construction projects. There's no reason to stand in the way of more jobs.

Mr. Boehner, Mr. McConnell, help us rebuild this bridge. Help us rebuild America. Help us put construction workers back to work. Pass this bill.

Audience members. Pass this bill! Pass this bill! Pass this bill!

The President. Let's pass the bill.

Audience members. Pass this bill! Pass this bill! Pass this bill!

The President. Now, some folks in Congress, they say, well, we don't like how it's paid for. Well, it's paid for as part of my larger plan to pay down our debt. And that plan makes some additional cuts in spending. We already cut a trillion dollars in spending. This makes an additional hundreds of billions of dollars in cuts in spending, but it also asks the wealthiest Americans and the biggest corporations to pay their fair share of taxes.

Now, that should not be too much to ask. And by the way, it wouldn't kick in until 2013. So when you hear folks saying, "Oh, we shouldn't be raising taxes right now," nobody's talking about raising taxes right now. We're talking about cutting taxes right now. But it does mean that there's a long-term plan, and part of it involves everybody doing their fair share.

Now, this isn't to punish success. What's great about this country is our belief that anybody can make it. If you're willing to put in the sweat, if you're willing to roll up your sleeves, if you're willing to work hard, you've got a good idea, you're out there taking a risk, God bless you. You can make millions, you can make billions of dollars in America. This is the land of opportunity. That's great. All I'm saying is if you've done well—I've done well—then you should do a little something to give something back. You should want to see the country that provided you with this opportunity to be successful and be able to provide opportunity for the young people who are going to be up—coming up behind you.

And all I'm saying is that everything should be fair. You know, the—you learn the idea of fairness when you're 2, 3 years old, right? You're in the sandbox, and you don't want to let somebody play with your truck, and—[*laughter*]—your mama or your daddy go up, and they say, "No, hon, it's not fair, you've got to share." Isn't that what they say? Things have to be fair. So all I'm saying is that Warren Buffett's secretary should not be paying a lower tax rate on her income than Warren Buffett. That doesn't make any sense. A construction worker who's making 50 or 60 grand a year shouldn't be paying higher tax rates than the guy who's making $50 million a year. And that's how it's working right now. Because they get all these loopholes and tax breaks that you don't get.

So for me to say let's close those loopholes, let's eliminate those tax breaks, and let's make sure that everybody's paying their fair share, there's nothing wrong with that.

Now, this is about priorities. It's about making choices. If we just had all kinds of money and everybody was working and we hadn't

gone through the worst financial crisis since the Great Depression, then maybe we wouldn't have to make choices. But right now we've got to make some choices. We've got to decide what our priorities are. If we want to pay for this jobs plan and close the deficit and invest in our infrastructure and make sure we've got the best education system in the world, the money's got to come from some place. Would you rather that the oil companies get to keep their tax loopholes?

Audience members. No!

The President. Or would you rather make sure that we're hiring thousands of construction workers to rebuild America?

Audience members. Yes!

The President. Would you rather keep in place special tax breaks for millionaires and billionaires?

Audience members. No!

The President. Or would you say, let's get teachers back in the classroom so our children can learn?

Audience members. Yes!

The President. Now, the Republicans, when I talked about this earlier in the week, they said, well, this is class warfare. You know what, if asking a billionaire to pay their fair share of taxes, to pay the same tax rate as a plumber or a teacher, is class warfare, then you know what, I'm a warrior for the middle class. I'm happy to fight for the middle class. I'm happy to fight for working people. Because the only warfare I've seen is the battle against the middle class over the last 10, 15 years.

It's time to build an economy that creates good, middle class jobs in this country. It's time to build an economy that honors the values of hard work and responsibility. It's time to build an economy that lasts. And, Cincinnati, that starts right now. That starts with your help. Maybe some of the people in Congress would rather settle their differences at the ballot box than work together right now. In fact, a while back, Senator McConnell said that his top priority—number-one priority—was to defeat the President. That was his top priority.

Audience members. Boo!

The President. Not jobs, not putting people back to work, not rebuilding America—beating me. Well, I've got news for him and every other Member of Congress who feels the same way. The next election is 14 months away, and I'll be happy to tangle sometime down the road. But the American people right now don't have the luxury of waiting to solve our problems for another 14 months. A lot of folks are living paycheck to paycheck. A lot of folks are just barely getting by. They need us to get to work right now. They need us to pass this bill.

So I'm asking all of you, I need everybody here to lift your voices, not just in Cincinnati, but anybody who's watching TV or anybody who's within the range of my voice, I want everybody to lift up their voices. I want you to call. I want you to e-mail. I want you to tweet. I want you to fax. I want you to visit. If you want, write a letter. It's been a while. [*Laughter*] I want you to tell your Congressperson that the time for gridlock and games-playing is over. Tell them you want to create jobs, so pass this bill.

If you want construction workers rebuilding America, pass this bill. If you want teachers back in the classrooms, pass this bill. If you want to cut taxes for middle class families, pass this bill. If you want to help small businesses, what do you do?

Audience members. Pass this bill!

The President. If you want veterans to share in the opportunities of this country, what should you do?

Audience members. Pass this bill!

The President. Now is the time to act. Because we are not a people that just sit back and wait for things to happen. We go ahead and make things happen. We're tougher than the times we live in. We are bigger than the politics that we've been seeing these last few months. Let's meet this moment. Let's get back to work. Let's show the world once again why America is the greatest nation on Earth.

God bless you, and God bless the United States of America.

NOTE: The President spoke at 2:55 p.m. In his remarks, he referred to West Harrison, IN, resident Ron King; President Lee Myung-bak of South Korea; Sens. John F. Kerry and Kathryn A. "Kay" Bailey Hutchison; and Warren E. Buffett, chief executive officer and chairman, Berkshire Hathaway Inc.

Remarks on the No Child Left Behind Act
September 23, 2011

Thank you so much. Everybody, please have a seat. Well, welcome to the White House, everybody. I see a whole bunch of people who are interested in education, and we are grateful for all the work that you do each and every day.

I want to recognize the person to my right, somebody who I think will end up being considered one of the finest Secretaries of Education we've ever had, Arne Duncan. In addition to his passion, probably the finest basketball player ever in the Cabinet. [*Laughter*]

I also want to thank Governor Bill Haslam of Tennessee for taking the time to be here today and the great work that he's doing in Tennessee. I'm especially appreciative because I found that his daughter is getting married, and he is doing the ceremony tomorrow, so we've got to get him back on time. [*Laughter*] But we really appreciate his presence. Thank you.

And a good friend, somebody who I had the pleasure of serving with during the time that I was in the United States Senate, he is now the Governor of Rhode Island, Lincoln Chafee. It's wonderful to see Lincoln. Thank you all for coming.

And I do want to acknowledge two guys who've just worked tirelessly on behalf of education issues, who happen to be in the front row here: from the House, outstanding Congressman, George Miller, and from the Senate, the pride of Iowa, Tom Harkin.

Now, it is an undeniable fact that countries who outeducate us today are going to outcompete us tomorrow. But today, students are sliding against their peers around the globe. Today, our kids trail too many other countries in math, in science, in reading. And that's true, by the way, not just in inner-city schools, not just among poor kids, even among what are considered our better off suburban schools, we're lagging behind where we need to be. Today, as many as a quarter of our students aren't finishing high school. We have fallen to 16th in the proportion of young people with a college degree, even though we know that 60 percent of new jobs in the coming decade will require more than a high school diploma.

And what this means is if we're serious about building an economy that lasts, an economy in which hard work pays off with the opportunity for solid middle class jobs, we've got to get serious about education. We are going to have to pick up our games and raise our standards.

We're in the midst of an ongoing enormous economic challenge. And I spend a lot of my time thinking immediately about how we can put folks back to work and how we can stabilize the world financial markets. And those things are all important. But the economic challenges we face now are economic challenges that have been building for decades now, and the most important thing we can do is to make sure that our kids are prepared for this new economy. That's the single most important thing we can do. So even as we focus on the near term and what we've got to do to put folks back to work, we've got to be thinking a little bit ahead and start making the tough decisions now to make sure that our schools are working the way that they need to work.

Now, we all know that schools can't do it alone. As parents, the task begins at home. It begins by turning off the TV and helping with homework and encouraging a love of learning from the very start of our children's lives. And I'm speaking from experience now. [*Laughter*] Malia and Sasha would often rather be watching "American Idol" or "SpongeBob," but Michelle and I know that our first job, our first responsibility, is instilling a sense of learning—a sense of a love of learning in our kids. And so there are no shortcuts there; we have to do that job. And we can't just blame teachers and

schools if we're not instilling that commitment, that dedication to learning, in our kids.

But as a nation, we also have an obligation to make sure that all of our children have the resources they need to learn, because they're spending a lot of time outside of the household. They're spending the bulk of their waking hours in school. And that means that we've got to make sure we've got quality schools, good teachers, the latest textbooks, the right technology. And that, by the way, is something we can do something about right away. That's why I sent the jobs bill to Congress that would put thousands of teachers back to work all across the country and modernize at least 35,000 schools.

Congress should pass that bill right now. We've got too many schools that are underresourced, too many teachers who want to be in the classroom who aren't because of budget constraints, not because they can't do the job.

So parents have a role, and schools need more resources. But money alone won't solve our education problems. I've said this before, I will repeat it: Money alone is not enough. We also need reform. We've got to make sure that every classroom is a place of high expectations and high performance. And that's been our vision since taking office. That's why instead of just pouring money into the system that's not working, we launched a competition called Race to the Top. And to all 50 States, to Governors, to school districts, we said, show us the most innovative plans to improve teacher quality and student achievement, we'll show you the money. We want to provide you more resources, but there's also got to be a commitment on your part to make the changes that are necessary so that we can see actual results.

And for less than 1 percent of what we spend on education each year, Race to the Top, under Arne's leadership, has led States across the country to raise their standards for teaching and learning. And by the way, these standards that we're talking about—these high standards that we're talking about—were not developed here in Washington. They were developed by Republican and Democratic Governors throughout the country. Essentially, you had a peer group, a peer review system, where everybody traded best practices and said, here's what seems to work, and let's hold all of our schools to these high standards. And since that's—Race to the Top has been launched, we've seen what's possible when reform isn't just a top-down mandate, but the work of local teachers and principals and school boards and communities working together to develop better standards.

And this is why, in my State of the Union Address this year, I said that Congress should reform the No Child Left Behind law based on the principles that have guided Race to the Top.

And I want to say that the goals behind No Child Left Behind were admirable, and President Bush deserves credit for that. Higher standards are the right goal. Accountability is the right goal. Closing the achievement gap is the right goal. And we've got to stay focused on those goals. But experience has taught us that in its implementation No Child Left Behind had some serious flaws that are hurting our children instead of helping them. Teachers too often are being forced to teach to the test. Subjects like history and science have been squeezed out. And in order to avoid having their schools labeled as failures, some States, perversely, have actually had to lower their standards in a race to the bottom instead of a race to the top. They don't want to get penalized? Let's make sure that the standards are so low that we're not going to be seen failing to meet them. That makes no sense.

And these problems have been obvious to parents and educators all over the country for years now. Despite the good intentions of some—two of them are sitting right here, Tom and George—Congress has not been able to fix these flaws so far. I've urged Congress for a while now, let's get a bipartisan effort, let's fix this. Congress hasn't been able to do it. So I will. Our kids only get one shot at a decent education. They cannot afford to wait any longer. So given that Congress cannot act, I am acting.

So starting today, we'll be giving States more flexibility to meet high standards. Keep in mind, the change we're making is not lowering standards, we're saying we're going to give you more flexibility to meet high standards. We're going to let States, schools, and teachers come up with innovative ways to give our children the skills they need to compete for the jobs of the future. Because what works in Rhode Island may not be the same thing that works in Tennessee, but every student should have the same opportunity to learn and grow, no matter what State they live in.

Let me repeat: This does not mean that States will be able to lower their standards or escape accountability. In fact, the way we've structured this, if States want more flexibility, they're going to have to set higher standards, more honest standards, that prove they're serious about meeting them.

And already, 44 States, led by some of the people on this stage, have set higher standards and proposed new ways to get there, because that's what's critical. They know what's at stake here.

Ricci Hall is a principal of a charter school in Worcester, Massachusetts. Where's Ricci? Oh, Ricci's not here. [*Laughter*] He was—there he is. Ricci—I wasn't sure if he was behind me. Good. Thank you. Every single student who graduated from Ricci's school in the last 3 years went on to college. Every single one. His school ranks in the top quarter of all schools in Massachusetts, and as you know, Massachusetts's schools rank very high among the 50 States. But because Ricci's school did not meet all the technical standards of No Child Left Behind, his school was labeled a failure last year. That's not right. That needs to change. What we're doing today will encourage the progress at schools like Ricci's.

Is John Becker here? He is? All right, here's John. [*Laughter*] I didn't think you were John. [*Laughter*] John teaches at one of the highest performing middle schools in DC, and now with these changes we're making, he's going to be able to focus on teaching his fourth graders math in a way that improves their performance instead of just teaching to a test.

We have superintendents like David Estrop from Springfield, Ohio. Right here. Dave will be able to focus on improving teaching and learning in his district instead of spending all his time on bureaucratic mandates from Washington that don't actually produce results.

So this isn't just the right thing to do for our kids, it's the right thing to do for our country. We can't afford to wait for an education system that is not doing everything it needs to do for our kids. We can't let another generation of young people fall behind because we didn't have the courage to recognize what doesn't work, admit it, and replace it with something that does. We've got to act now. We've got to act now and harness all the good ideas coming out of our States, out of our schools. We can't be tied up with ideology. We can't be worrying about partisanship. We just have to make sure that we figure out what works and we hold ourselves to those high standards. Because now is the time to give our children the skills that they need to compete in this global economy.

We've got a couple of students up on stage who are doing outstanding work because somebody in their schools is dedicated and committed every single day to making sure that they've got a chance to succeed. But I don't want them to be the exception. I want them to be the rule. Now is the time to make our education system the best in the world, the envy of the world. It used to be. It is going to be again, thanks to the people in this room.

God bless you. God bless the United States of America.

Thank you.

NOTE: The President spoke at 10:24 a.m. in the East Room at the White House. In his remarks, he referred to Annie Haslam, daughter of Gov. William E. Haslam of Tennessee; former President George W. Bush; Ricci W. Hall, principal, University Park Campus School; John Becker, teacher, DC Prep Public Charter School; and David C. Estrop, superintendent, Springfield City School District.

Statement on Elections in Zambia
September 23, 2011

On behalf of the American people, I congratulate the people of Zambia on the historic September 20 Presidential, parliamentary, and local elections, and I commend you for building on your commitment to multiparty democracy. Zambia's Electoral Commission, political leaders, civil society, and above all its citizens all contributed to this important accomplishment. The United States looks forward to working with President Michael Sata, Members of Parliament, and representatives of all of Zambia's political parties to build on the longstanding partnership between our two nations.

I also acknowledge former President Rupiah Banda's contributions to Zambia's democratic development, including his 3 years of distinguished leadership and his admirable acceptance of the will of the Zambian people. The hard work of a living democracy does not end when the votes are tallied and the winners announced. Instead, it offers the chance to reconcile and to advance greater security and prosperity for its people. Today is a day for Zambia to celebrate their democratic achievement. I hope that all Zambians will find common ground as you address the challenges and seize the opportunities facing your country and our world.

The President's Weekly Address
September 24, 2011

Over the last few weeks, I've been making the case that we need to act now on the "American Jobs Act," so we can put folks back to work and start building an economy that lasts into the future.

Education is an essential part of this economic agenda. It is an undeniable fact that countries who outeducate us today, will outcompete us tomorrow. Businesses will hire wherever the highly skilled and highly trained workers are located.

But today, our students are sliding against their peers around the globe. Today, our kids trail too many other countries in math and science and reading. As many as a quarter of our students aren't even finishing high school. And we've fallen to 16th in the proportion of our young people with a college degree, even though we know that 60 percent of new jobs in the coming decade will require more than a high school diploma.

What this means is that if we're serious about building an economy that lasts—an economy in which hard work pays off with the opportunity for solid middle class jobs—we had better be serious about education. We have to pick up our game and raise our standards.

As a nation, we have an obligation to make sure that all children have the resources they need to learn: quality schools, good teachers, the latest textbooks, and the right technology. That's why the jobs bill I sent to Congress would put tens of thousands of teachers back to work across the country and modernize at least 35,000 schools. That's why Congress should pass that bill right now.

But money alone won't solve our education problems. We also need reform. We need to make sure that every classroom is a place of high expectations and high performance.

That's been our vision since taking office. And that's why instead of just pouring money into the system that wasn't working, we launched a competition called Race to the Top. To all 50 States, we said, "If you show us the most innovative plans to improve teacher quality and student achievement, we'll show you the money."

For less than 1 percent of what we spend on education each year, Race to the Top has led States across the country to raise their standards for teaching and learning. These standards were developed not by Washington, but by Republican and Democratic Governors throughout the country. And since then, we have seen what's possible when reform isn't just a top-down mandate, but the work of local teachers and principals, school boards and communities.

That's why in my State of the Union Address this year, I said to Congress, you need to reform the No Child Left Behind law based on the same principles that have guided Race to the Top.

While the goals behind No Child Left Behind were admirable, experience has taught us that the law has some serious flaws that are hurting our children instead of helping them. Teachers are being forced to teach to the test, while subjects like history and science are being squeezed out. And in order to avoid having their schools labeled as failures, some States lowered their standards in a race to the bottom.

These problems have been obvious to parents and educators all over this country for years. But for years, Congress has failed to fix them. So now I will. Our kids only get one shot at a decent education. And they can't afford to wait any longer.

So yesterday I announced that we'll be giving States more flexibility to meet high standards for teaching and learning. It's time for us to let States and schools and teachers come up with innovative ways to give our children the skills they need to compete for the jobs of the future.

This will make a huge difference in the lives of students all across the country. For example, yesterday, I was with Ricci Hall, the principal of a school in Worcester, Massachusetts. Every single student who graduated from Ricci's school in the last 3 years went on to college.

But because they didn't meet the standards of No Child Left Behind, Ricci's school was labeled as failing last year.

That will change because of what we did yesterday. From now on, we'll be able to encourage the progress at schools like Ricci's. From now on, people like John Becker, who teaches at one of the highest performing middle schools in DC, will be able to focus on teaching his fourth graders math in ways that improves their performance instead of just teaching to a test. Superintendents like David Estrop from Ohio will be able to focus on improving teaching and learning in his district instead of spending all his time on bureaucratic mandates from Washington that don't get results.

This isn't just the right thing to do for our kids; it's the right thing to do for our country and our future. It's time to put our teachers back on the job. It's time to rebuild and modernize our schools. And it's time to raise our standards, up our game, and do everything it takes to prepare our children to succeed in the global economy. Now is the time to once again make our education system the envy of the world.

Thanks for listening.

NOTE: The address was recorded at approximately 4:35 p.m. on September 23 in the Map Room at the White House for broadcast on September 24. The transcript was made available by the Office of the Press Secretary on September 23, but was embargoed for release until 6 a.m. on September 24.

Remarks at the Congressional Black Caucus Foundation Phoenix Awards Dinner
September 24, 2011

Hello, CBC! Thank you so much. Thank you. Please, everybody have a seat. It is wonderful to be with all of you tonight. It's good to be with "the conscience of the Congress." Thank you, Chairman Cleaver and brother Payne, for all that you do each and every day. Thank you, Dr. Elsie Scott, president and CEO of the CBC Foundation, and all of you for your outstanding work with your internship program, which has done so much for so many young people. And I had a chance to meet some of the young people backstage, an incredible, unbelievably impressive group.

You know, being here with all of you, with all the outstanding members of the Congressional Black Caucus, reminds me of a story that one of our friends, a giant of the civil rights movement, Reverend Dr. Joseph Lowery, told one day. Dr. Lowery, I don't think he minds me telling that he turns 90 in a couple weeks. He's been causing a ruckus for about 89 of those years. [*Laughter*]

A few years back, Dr. Lowery and I were together at Brown Chapel AME Church in Selma. [*Applause*] We've got some Selma folks in the house. And Dr. Lowery stood up in the pulpit and told the congregation the story of Shadrach and Meshach and Abed-nego in the fiery furnace. You know the story: It's about three young men bold enough to stand up for God, even if it meant being thrown in a furnace. And they survived because of their faith and because God showed up in that furnace with them.

Now, Dr. Lowery said that those three young men were a little bit crazy. But there's a difference, he said, between good crazy and bad crazy. Those boys, he said, were good crazy. At the time, I was running for President; it was early in the campaign. Nobody gave me much of a chance. He turned to me from the pulpit and indicated that someone like me running for President, well, that was crazy. [*Laughter*] But he supposed it was good crazy.

He was talking about faith, the belief in things not seen, the belief that if you persevere, a better day lies ahead. And I suppose the reason I enjoy coming to the CBC—what this weekend is all about—is you and me, we're all a little bit crazy, but hopefully, a good kind of crazy. We're a good kind of crazy because no matter how hard things get, we keep the faith, we keep fighting, we keep moving forward.

And we've needed faith over these last couple years. Times have been hard. It's been 3 years since we faced down a crisis that began on Wall Street and then spread to Main Street and hammered working families and hammered an already hard-hit Black community. The unemployment rate for Black folks went up to nearly 17 percent, the highest it's been in almost three decades. Forty percent, almost, of African American children living in poverty, fewer than half convinced that they can achieve Dr. King's dream. You've got to be a little crazy to have faith during such hard times.

It's heartbreaking, and it's frustrating. And I ran for President and the members of the CBC ran for Congress to help more Americans reach that dream. We ran to give every child a chance, whether he's born in Chicago or she comes from a rural town in the Delta. This crisis has made that job of giving everybody opportunity a little bit harder.

We knew at the outset of my Presidency that the economic calamity we faced wasn't caused overnight and wasn't going to be solved overnight. We knew that long before the recession hit, the middle class in this country had been falling behind: wages and incomes had been stagnant; a sense of financial security had been slipping away. And since these problems were not caused overnight, we knew we were going to have to climb a steep hill.

But we got to work. With your help, we started fighting our way back from the brink. And at every step of the way, we've faced fierce opposition based on an old idea, the idea that the only way to restore prosperity can't just be to let every corporation write its own rules or give out tax breaks to the wealthiest and the most fortunate and to tell everybody that they're on their own. There has to be a different concept of what America's all about. It has to be based on the idea that I am my brother's keeper and I am my sister's keeper and we're in this together. [*Applause*] We are in this thing together.

We had a different vision, and so we did what was right, and we fought to extend unemployment insurance, and we fought to expand the earned-income tax credit, and we fought to expand the child tax credit, which benefited nearly half of all African American children in this country. And millions of Americans are better off because of that fight.

Ask the family struggling to make ends meet if that extra few hundred dollars in their mother's paycheck from the payroll tax cut we passed made a difference. They'll tell you. Ask them how much that earned-income tax credit or that child tax credit makes a difference in paying the bills at the end of the month.

When an army of lobbyists and special interests spent millions to crush Wall Street reform, we stood up for what was right. We said the time has come to protect homeowners from predatory mortgage lenders. The time has come to protect consumers from credit card companies that jacked up rates without warning. We signed the strongest consumer financial protection in history. That's what we did together.

Remember how many years we tried to stop big banks from collecting taxpayer subsidies for student loans, while the cost of college kept slipping out of reach? Together, we put a stop to that once and for all. We used those savings to make college more affordable. We invested in early childhood education and community college and HBCUs. Ask the engineering student at an HBCU who thought he might have to leave school if that extra Pell grant assistance mattered.

We're attacking the cycle of poverty that steals the future from too many children, not just by pouring money into a broken system, but by building on what works: with Promise Neighborhoods modeled after the good work up in Harlem; Choice Neighborhoods rebuilding crumbling public housing into communities of hope and opportunity; Strong Cities, Strong Communities, our partnership with local leaders in hard-hit cities like Cleveland and Detroit. And we overcame years of inaction to win justice for Black farmers because of the leadership of the CBC and because we had an administration that was committed to doing the right thing.

And against all sorts of setbacks, when the opposition fought us with everything they had, we finally made clear that in the United States of America nobody should go broke because they get sick. We are better than that. And today, insurance companies can no longer drop or deny your coverage for no good reason. In just a year and a half, about 1 million more young adults have health insurance because of this law—1 million young people. That is an incredible achievement, and we did it with your help, with the CBC's help.

So in these hard years, we've won a lot of fights that needed fighting, and we've done a lot of good. But we've got more work to do. So many people are still hurting. So many people are still barely hanging on. And too many people in this city are still fighting us every step of the way.

So I need your help. We have to do more to put people to work right now. We've got to make that everyone in this country gets a fair shake and a fair shot and a chance to get ahead. And I know we won't get where we need to go if we don't travel down this road together. I need you with me.

That starts with getting this Congress to pass the "American Jobs Act." You heard me talk about this plan when I visited Congress a few weeks ago and sent the bill to Congress a few days later. Now I want that bill back, passed. I've got the pens all ready, I am ready to sign it, and I need your help to make it happen.

Right now we've got millions of construction workers out of a job. So this bill says, let's put those men and women back to work in their own communities rebuilding our roads and our bridges. Let's give these folks a job rebuilding our schools. Let's put these folks to work rehabilitating foreclosed homes in the hardest hit neighborhoods of Detroit and Atlanta and Washington. This is a no-brainer.

Why should we let China build the newest airports, the fastest railroads? Tell me why our children should be allowed to study in a school that's falling apart? I don't want that for my kids or your kids. I don't want that for any kid.

You tell me how it makes sense when we know that education is the most important thing for success in the 21st century. Let's put our people back to work doing the work America needs done. Let's pass this jobs bill.

We've got millions of unemployed Americans and young people looking for work, but running out of options. So this jobs bill says, let's give them a pathway, a new pathway back to work. Let's extend unemployment insurance so that more than 6 million Americans don't lose that lifeline. But let's also encourage reforms that help the long-term unemployed keep their skills sharp and get a foot in the door. Let's give summer jobs for low-income youth that don't just give them their first paycheck, but arm them with the skills they need for life.

Tell me why we don't want the unemployed back in the workforce as soon as possible. Let's pass this jobs bill, put these folks back to work.

Why are we shortchanging our children when we could be putting teachers back in the classroom right now, where they belong; laying off teachers, laying off police officer, laying off firefighters all across the country because State and local budgets are tough? Why aren't we helping? We did in the first 2 years. And then this other crowd came into Congress, and now suddenly, they want to stop. Tell me why we shouldn't give companies tax credits for hiring the men and women who've risked their lives for this country, our veterans. There is no good answer for that. They shouldn't be fighting to find a job when they come home.

These Republicans in Congress like to talk about job creators. How about doing something real for job creators? Pass this jobs bill, and every small-business owner in America, including 100,000 Black-owned businesses, will get a tax cut. You say you're the party of tax cuts. Pass this jobs bill, and every worker in America, including nearly 20 million African American workers, will get a tax cut. Pass this jobs bill and prove you'll fight just as hard for a tax cut for ordinary folks as you do for all your contributors.

These are questions that opponents of this jobs plan will have to answer, because the kinds of ideas in this plan in the past have been supported by both parties. Suddenly, Obama is proposing it, what happened? [*Laughter*] What happened? You all used to like to build roads. [*Laughter*] Right? What happened? Reverend, you know what happened? I don't know. They used to love to build some roads. [*Laughter*]

Now, I know some of our friends across the aisle won't support any new spending that's not paid for. I agree that's important. So last week, I laid out a plan to pay for the "American Jobs Act" and to bring out—down our debt over time. You say the deficit is important? Here we go. I'm ready to go. It's a plan that says if we want to create jobs and close this deficit, then we've got to ask the folks who have benefited most—the wealthiest Americans, the biggest, most profitable corporations—to pay their fair share.

We are not asking them to do anything extraordinary. The reform we're proposing is based on a simple principle: Middle class folks should not pay higher tax rates than millionaires and billionaires. That's not crazy, or it's good crazy. [*Laughter*] Warren Buffett's secretary shouldn't pay a higher tax rate than Warren Buffett. A teacher or a nurse or a construction worker making $50,000 a year shouldn't pay higher tax rates than somebody making $50 million. That's just common sense.

We're not doing this to punish success. This is the land of opportunity. I want you to go out, start a business, get rich, build something. Our country is based on the belief that anybody can make it if they put in enough sweat and enough effort. That is wonderful. God bless you. But part of the American idea is also that once we've done well we should pay our fair share, to make sure that those schools that we were learning in can teach the next generation, that those roads that we benefited from, that they're not crumbling for the next bunch of folks who are coming behind us, to keep up the Nation that made our success possible.

And most wealthy Americans would agree with that. But you know the Republicans are already dusting off their old talking points. That's class warfare, they say. In fact, in the next breath, they'll complain that people living in poverty—people who suffered the most over the past decade—don't pay enough in taxes. That's bad crazy. [*Laughter*] When you start saying, at a time when the top one-tenth of 1 percent has seen their incomes go up four or five times over the last 20 years and folks at the bottom have seen their incomes decline, and your response is that you want poor folks to pay more? Give me a break. If asking a billionaire to pay the same tax rate as a janitor makes me a warrior for the working class, I wear that with a badge of honor. I have no problem with that. It's about time.

They say it kills jobs: "Oh, that's going to kill jobs." We're not proposing anything other than returning to the tax rates for the wealthiest Americans that existed under Bill Clinton. I played golf with Bill Clinton today. I was asking him, "How did that go?" [*Laughter*] Well, it turns out, we had a lot of jobs. The well-to-do, they did even better. So did the middle class. We lifted millions out of poverty. And then we cut taxes for folks like me, and we went through a decade of zero job growth.

So this isn't speculation. We've tested this out. We tried their theory. Didn't work. Tried our theory. It worked. We shouldn't be confused about this.

This debate is about priorities. If we want to create new jobs and close the deficit and invest in our future, the money has got to come from somewhere. And so should we keep tax loopholes for big oil companies, or should we put construction workers and teachers back on the job? Should we keep tax breaks for millionaires and billionaires, or should we invest in our children's education and college aid? Should we ask seniors to be paying thousands of dollars more for Medicare, as the House Republicans proposed, or take young folks' health care away, or should we ask that everybody pay their fair share? This is about fairness. And this is about who we are as a country. This is about our commitment to future generations.

When Michelle and I think about where we came from—a little girl on the South Side of Chicago, son of a single mom in Hawaii, mother had to go to school on scholarships, sometimes got food stamps. Michelle's parents never owned their own home until she had already graduated, living upstairs above the aunt who actually owned the house. We are here today only because our parents and our grandparents, they broke their backs to support us. But they also understood that they would get a little bit of help from their country. Because they met their responsibilities, this country would also be responsible, would also provide good public schools, would also provide recreation parks that were safe, making sure that they could take the bus without getting beat over the head, making sure that their kids would be able to go to college even if they weren't rich.

We're only here because past generations struggled and sacrificed for this incredible, exceptional idea that it does not matter where you come from, it does not matter where you're born, doesn't matter what you look like; if you're willing to put in an effort, you should get a shot. You should get a shot at the American Dream.

And each night, when we tuck in our girls at the White House, I think about keeping that dream alive for them and for all of our children. And that's now up to us. And that's hard. This is harder than it's been in a long, long time. We're going through something we haven't seen in our lifetimes.

And I know at times that gets folks discouraged. I know. I listen to some of you all. [*Laughter*] I understand that. And nobody feels that burden more than I do. Because I know how much we have invested in making sure that we're able to move this country forward. But you know, more than a lot of other folks in this country, we know about hard. The people in this room know about hard. And we don't give in to discouragement.

Throughout our history, change has often come slowly. Progress often takes time. We take a step forward; sometimes we take two steps back. Sometimes we get two steps forward and one step back. But it's never a straight line. It's never easy. And I never promised easy. Easy has never been promised to us. But we've had faith. We have had faith. We've had that good kind of crazy that says, you can't stop marching.

Even when folks are hitting you over the head, you can't stop marching. Even when they're turning the hoses on you, you can't stop. Even when somebody fires you for speaking out, you can't stop. Even when it looks like there's no way, you find a way; you can't stop. Through the mud and the muck and the driving rain, we don't stop. Because we know the rightness of our cause, widening the circle of opportunity, standing up for everybody's opportunities, increasing each other's prosperity. We know our cause is just. It's a righteous cause.

So in the face of troopers and tear gas, folks stood unafraid. Led somebody like John Lewis to wake up after getting beaten within an inch of his life on Sunday, he wakes up on Monday: "We're going to go march."

Dr. King once said: "Before we reach the majestic shores of the promised land, there is a frustrating and bewildering wilderness ahead. We must still face prodigious hilltops of opposition and gigantic mountains of resistance. But with patient and firm determination we will press on."

So I don't know about you, CBC, but the future rewards those who press on. With patient and firm determination, I am going to press on for jobs. I'm going to press on for equality. I'm going to press on for the sake of our children. I'm going to press on for the sake of all those families who are struggling right now. I don't have time to feel sorry for myself. I don't have time to complain. I am going to press on.

I expect all of you to march with me and press on. Take off your bedroom slippers, put on your marching shoes. Shake it off. Stop complaining, stop grumbling, stop crying. We are going to press on. We've got work to do, CBC.

God bless you, and God bless the United States of America.

NOTE: The President spoke at 8:30 p.m. at the Walter E. Washington Convention Center. In his remarks, he referred to Rep. Emanuel Cleaver II, chairman, and Rep. Donald M. Payne, former chairman, Congressional Black Caucus; and Warren E. Buffett, chief executive officer and chairman, Berkshire Hathaway Inc. He also referred to his mother-in-law Marian Robinson.

Remarks at a Democratic National Committee Fundraiser in Medina, Washington
September 25, 2011

Thank you, everybody. Thank you very much. Everybody, please have a seat. Have a seat. What a spectacular setting. I was saying to Mark that I wish I had time to just roam around, because this is as beautiful a collection as I've ever seen. And I want to thank you, Mark, for the extraordinary—Jon—I want to thank Jon and Mary for the extraordinary hospitality. The Shirleys have been strong supporters for a very long time, and I'm very grateful to them for all of it.

I want to spend most of my time answering questions, so my remarks on the front end are going to be very brief. We are going through as tough a time as we have gone through in my lifetime and, looking around, in most of your lifetimes. It is not just a national crisis, it is an international crisis that we've been managing for the last 3 years. And over the last 2½, what we've been able to do is stabilize the economy, but stabilize it at a level that still leaves way too many people hurting.

I get letters from folks all across the country every single day, and the stories you get are just heartbreaking: people who are losing their homes, people who have lost their jobs, people who are wondering whether they can still send their kids to college and whether they're going to be able to retire—if they do.

And the steps that we've taken—whether it's to yank this economy out from a potential depression or expand opportunity for kids to go to college by extending more Pell grants and student loans to young people; whether it's investing in clean energy, investing in bioresearch; whether it's making sure that we've got health care for ever single American that's affordable and accessible—for all those steps that we've taken, we've still got a lot more work to do.

Now, when I was in Grant Park on that beautiful day—beautiful evening, and everybody was feeling good and everybody was feeling full of hope and change, I warned everyone this was going to be hard, that that wasn't the end of a journey, but rather we were just beginning this journey. And that, in fact, has proven to be the case.

Domestically, we still have a lot more to do to heal this economy and to deal with some of the structural problems that existed even before the financial crisis hit. We still don't have an energy policy in this country that will free ourselves from dependence on foreign oil and can also generate new jobs in a new clean energy space.

We still don't have the kinds of trade strategies that will open ourselves up to new markets, but make sure that we've got trade that's fair, between ourselves and particularly the growing markets in the Pacific and the Asia region. We still have enormous challenges because middle class families have not seen their wages and their incomes rise for the last 20 years, even as those of us at the very top have seen an extraordinary explosion in our wealth and our incomes.

And as a consequence, part of the big problem that we have on the fiscal side—making sure that we close our deficits and we're responsible—demands us not only cutting out things that we don't need so that we can invest in things that we do, but it also requires that we have a system that is fair and just and make sure that everybody is carrying their fair burden and paying their fair share.

So what makes this tougher is our politics. I mean, Washington—you guys have been witnesses to what has been going on lately. My hope when I came into office was, because we were in crisis, that the other side would respond by saying now is the time for all of us to pull together. There will be times for partisan argument later, but now is not the time. That was not the decision they made. And so from the moment that I took office, what we've seen is a constant ideological pushback against any kid of sensible reforms that would make our economy work better and give people more opportunity.

We're seeing it even now. I mean, as we speak, there is a debate going on in Congress about whether disaster relief funding should be granted as part of the overall budget to keep the Government open. Now, keep in mind we've never had this argument before. And what makes it worse is that some of the Republicans who are opposing this disaster relief, it's their constituents who have been hit harder than anyone by these natural disasters.

So what I did over the last 2 weeks was say to Members of Congress—Democrat and Republican, but particularly to the Republicans—I'm prepared to work with you, but these games have to stop. And given how high unemployment is right now, we've got to act. We can't just be engaged in the usual partisan bickering here in Washington. We put forward a jobs act that would—it's estimated to grow the economy by an additional 2 percent and put as many as 1.9 million back to work. And we're paying for all of it by continuing to make cuts in programs that we don't need and making adjustments to entitlement programs like Medicare and Medicaid, but also making sure that we've got a Tax Code that is fair.

So we are just going to keep on pounding away at this issue. How they will respond, we don't yet know. And part of it is going to depend on how much pressure they're feeling from people all across the country, here in the Pacific Northwest, but everywhere else. And yet we are going to just keep on drawing a clear contrast between a vision that we have for where we want to take this country, one in which we're living within our means, but also investing in infrastructure and investing in schools and investing in education and investing in basic research and innovation.

I'm happy to contrast that with a vision that says somehow we've got to shrink our vision about what America is, that we can't afford a safety net, we can't afford environmental laws, we can't afford a fair Tax Code. I reject that vision, and I think most of the American people do as well.

Now, let me just close by saying this: 2012 is going to be tough. This is going to be a tough—this is not going to be all good feeling, although I do have to remind people 2008 wasn't all good feeling either. [*Laughter*] I mean, sometimes, people—those of you who are involved in the campaign, there is a lot of revisionist history that says our campaign was perfect and we never had any problems and it was all just the big "Hope" posters and everybody was feeling good—Bruce Springsteen singing. [*Laughter*] That wasn't how it felt when I was in the middle of it. [*Laughter*]

So this stuff is always hard. But this is going to be especially hard, because a lot of people are discouraged and a lot of people are disillusioned about the capacity of their leadership and of Government to make significant changes in their—that impact them in a positive way. But I'm determined, because there is too much at stake. The alternative, I think, is an approach to government that will fundamentally cripple America in meeting the challenges of the 21st century. And that's not the kind of society that I want to bequeath to Malia and Sasha and your children and your grandchildren.

So we've got a lot of work to do. You being here today is evidence that you are ready to do the work. But understand, we're just starting off here. We've got 14 months, and I'm going to need all of you to help mobilize people and push back against arguments that say that somehow if we're only—if we've only gotten 80 percent of what we wanted to get done, that that's a failure. No, that's a success. That should be an inspiration for us getting reelected so I can do the other 20 percent.

And so I'm grateful to all of you, and I hope that all of you end up, despite the ups and down inevitable in a campaign, that you guys will be just as excited on Inauguration Day of 2013 as you were Inauguration Day 2009.

All right? Thank you very much.

NOTE: The President spoke at 12:52 p.m. at the residence of Jon A. and Mary Shirley. Audio was not available for verification of the content of these remarks.

Remarks at a Democratic National Committee Fundraiser in Seattle, Washington
September 25, 2011

Thank you, everybody. Everybody, please have a seat. Have a seat. Now, first of all, it is wonderful to see all of you. It is wonderful to be introduced by two Hall of Famers, Lenny Wilkens and Bill Russell. I don't know if you guys noticed that Bill needs a higher mike. [*Laughter*] It was a little low for him. But it was incredible to get to know those two gentlemen during the course of the campaign, and they have just been great, great friends.

In addition, obviously, I want to acknowledge your outstanding Governor, Christine Gregoire. I want to thank the—Robert Cray and the Robert Cray Band. I want to thank—you have some of the best elected officials in the country, and you've got some of the best congressional—I think one of the best congressional delegations in the country. Stand up, congressional delegation—[*inaudible*].

It is great to be back in this gorgeous city, and it's good to be outside of Washington. I'm thrilled to be here with all of you. I've even come here during a Bears-Packers game. [*Laughter*] And that tells you how much I need your help. I've come because I need you to help finish what we started in 2008.

Now, back then, we started this campaign not because we thought it would be a cakewalk. After all, you supported a candidate named Barack Hussein Obama. [*Laughter*] You didn't need a poll to know that that was not going to be easy. Lately, there's been some revisionist history: People talk about, oh, what an incredible, smooth campaign that was. And I'm thinking, that's not how it felt to me. [*Laughter*] But as daunting as it was, as many setbacks as we had, we forged ahead because we had an idea about what this country is. We had an idea about what this country can be.

Many of you, many of our parents, our grandparents, we grew up with faith in an America where, if you work hard, if you're responsible, then it pays off. If you stepped up and you did your job and were loyal to your company, that loyalty would be rewarded with a decent salary and decent benefits and a raise once in a while and some security. And you had some belief that the American Dream could be yours and that your kids could dream even bigger.

And over the last decade, that faith has been profoundly shaken. The rules changed. The deck kept on getting stacked against middle class Americans and those aspiring to be in the middle class. Nobody in Washington seemed willing or able to do anything about it.

So in 2007, all of this culminated in a once-in-a-lifetime economic crisis, a crisis that's been much worse and much longer than your average recession. You know they—historians have looked, and typically a recession that comes about because of a financial crisis is much deeper and much longer. It takes a long time to work its way through. And so, from the time I took office, we knew, because this crisis had been building for years, it was going to take us years to get back to where we wanted to be.

The question now is not whether people are still hurting. They are. Every night, I read letters from constituents all across the country, and the stories are heartbreaking. I talk to people out on the road and men and women who've had to close a business that's been in their family for generations or folks who've had to cross items off the grocery store list to save money so they can fill up the gas tank to get to work, parents having to postpone retirement because they're committed to sending their kids to college. A lot of folks out there are hurting.

And the question is not whether this country has been going through tough times. The question is, where are we going next? We can either go back to the same ideas that the other side is peddling, old worn-out ideas that were tried throughout the last decade, where corporations get to write their own rules and those of us who've been more—most fortunate get to keep all our tax breaks and we abandon our commitment to caring for the vulnerable and we abandon our commitment to investing in the future and investing in infrastructure and investing in education and basic research. Or we can build an America that we talked about in 2008, an America where everybody gets a fair shake and everybody does their fair share. And that's what this election is about. And that's what we've been fighting for, for the last 2½ years.

Think about it. When we wanted to save the auto industry from not just bankruptcy, but liquidation, there were a whole bunch of folks on the other side who fought us tooth and nail. And that was not easy. They said it was going to be a waste of time and a waste of money. You know what? We did it anyway. And we saved thousands of American jobs as a consequence, and we made sure that America is still making cars that we're selling around the world.

And by the way, contrary to the naysayers, the taxpayers are getting their money back. And today, the American auto industry is stronger than ever, and they're making fuel-efficient cars that are stamped with three proud words: Made in America.

When we wanted to pass Wall Street reform to make sure that a crisis like this never happens again, we had lobbyists and special interests spend millions of dollars to make sure we didn't succeed. And you know what? With the help of some of these folks sitting at this table, we did it anyway and passed the toughest reforms in our history and reforms that prevent consumers from getting ripped off by mortgage lenders or credit companies. Today, there are no more hidden credit card fees. There are no more unfair rate hikes, no more deception from banks. That is not an accident. That is because we fought for it, and we got it done.

Most Republicans voted against it, but we were able to cut $60 billion—that's with a "b"—$60 billion in taxpayer subsidies that were going to big banks through the student loan program. We took that money, and now that's going to millions of kids all across the country in increased Pell grants and cheaper student loans so they've got access to college.

Instead of giving more tax breaks to the largest corporations, we cut taxes for small businesses and for middle class families. The first law I signed into law—the first bill I signed into law made sure that women earn equal pay for an equal day's work because I want our daughters to have the same opportunities as our sons.

We repealed "don't ask, don't tell" so that never again will gay and lesbian Americans need to hide in order to serve the country they love. And while we're at it, we passed health care reform to make sure that nobody goes bankrupt because they get sick.

And every one of these issues were tough. Every one of them, we had to fight for. And yet, despite all the good that we've done over the last 2½ years, we've still got so much more work to do. We've got so much more work to do to make sure that everyone in this country gets a fair shake, to make sure that every American has a chance to get ahead. And that's where I need your help.

About 2 weeks ago, I sent to Congress a bill called the "American Jobs Act." Some of you might have heard about this. Everything in it is the kind of proposal that's been supported by Democrats and Republicans in the past. Everything in it will be paid for. It will put people back to work. It will put more money into the pockets of working people. Congress should pass this bill right away.

We've got millions of construction workers who don't have jobs right now. This bill says, let's put these men and women to work rebuilding our roads and our bridges and our highways. I don't want the newest airports in Singapore and the fastest railroads in China. I want them built right here in the United States of America. There's work to be done. There are workers to do it. Let's tell Congress to pass this jobs bill and make it happen right now.

It shouldn't be a partisan issue. What happened? Republicans used to like roads. [*Laughter*] Do you remember that? Mr. Mayor, you remember, don't you? Suddenly, they don't like roads because Democrats are proposing it? That doesn't make any sense.

In places like South Korea, they can't hire teachers fast enough. I had lunch with the President of Korea. I asked him, "What's your biggest problem?" He said: "Oh, the parents. They're too demanding. They're telling me I've got to hire all these teachers, and so we can barely keep pace. We're hiring—we're importing them from abroad. They think that their kids should learn English when they're in kindergarten." Because they know that educating their children is the key to success in this 21st-century economy.

Now, that shouldn't be a partisan idea. But here we are, we're laying off teachers in droves, here in America. There are schools around the country where they've eliminated music, art. They've got one science teacher running around 15 different classrooms because they don't have enough staff; kids learning in trailers. That's unfair to our kids. It undermines our future.

But if we pass this jobs bill, we will put thousands of teachers in every State back in the classroom where they belong. Tell Congress to pass this jobs bill and put our teachers back to work.

Tell Congress to pass this jobs bill, we'll put—we'll give companies tax credits for hiring American veterans. These folks serve us, to keep us free and to keep us safe. They interrupt their careers. They leave their families. They put themselves in harm's way. They shouldn't have to fight for a job when they come home. That's not who we are as Americans. Pass this jobs bill and give veterans more opportunity.

The "American Jobs Act" will cut taxes for virtually every worker in America, cut taxes for every small-business owner in America, gives an extra tax cut to every small business that hires more workers or raises their wages. So don't just talk about helping America's job creators. How about actually helping them? Get this bill passed right away.

A lot of folks in Congress have said, "Well, maybe in the past we might have supported these things, but we're not going to support any new spending that's not paid for." Well, I think that's important. So I also laid out a plan to pay for the "American Jobs Act" that—and not only pays for the jobs act, but brings our debt down to manageable levels over time. It adds to the $1 trillion in spending cuts I already signed this summer, which, when you add it all together, will be one of the biggest spending cuts in history. But it's not all done right now. It's spread out over time so it doesn't endanger a recovery.

Now, it's also a plan that says, if we want to close the deficit and pay for this jobs plan, we can't just cut our way out of the problem. We've got to also ask those of us who are most fortunate, the wealthiest Americans, the biggest, most profitable corporations, to pay their fair share. It's time to reform the Tax Code based on a very simple principle: Warren Buffett's secretary shouldn't be paying a higher tax rate than Warren Buffett. A teacher or a nurse or a construction worker making $50,000 a year shouldn't pay a higher tax rate than somebody pulling in $50 million. It's not fair. It's not right. It has to change.

Now, you're already hearing the other side saying, "Well, hold on, that's class warfare." Let me say this. In America, we believe in success. That's what's great about this country. You have a good idea, you start a new business, you're 6'10'' and a perennial all-star—[*laughter*]—and you're willing to put in the work and the effort and the drive, and you've got an idea that creates a new product or service, we want you to be successful. That's what America is about, the idea that any one of us can make it if we try. Anybody can open a business. Anybody can have an idea that makes us a million—into a millionaire or billionaire. That's great. This is the land of opportunity.

But you know what, if we want to make sure that this is the land of opportunity not just for ourselves, but for our kids and our grandkids, then we've got to make sure that those of us who are doing well should pay our fair share in taxes, to contribute to the Nation's success, the Nation that made our own success possible. And that means investing back in schools, and that means making sure we're building decent roads.

You know, I was just with a group of folks that included some Microsoft executives. The fact is, if we hadn't invested in DARPA and the infrastructure for the Internet, there would be no Microsoft. And most wealthy Americans would agree that we've got to make sure that we are reinvesting to make this a land of opportunity for everybody, to make investments that will help us grow our economy and deal with the debt that threatens our future.

So yes, the Republicans are dusting off their old talking points and calling this tax—this class warfare. But you know what, if asking a billionaire to pay the same tax rate as a plumber makes me a warrior for the middle class, I'll wear that charge. I'll wear that as a badge of honor. [*Applause*] I'll wear that as a badge of honor. Because the only class warfare I've seen is the battle being waged against the middle class in this country for decades.

Look, this is about priorities. It's about choices. If we want to pay for this jobs plan, if we want to close this deficit, if we want to invest in our future, if we want to put teachers back in the classroom, if we want to make sure that we've got the best roads and bridges and airports, if we want to lay broadband lines and wireless service for everybody, the money has got to come from somewhere.

So would you rather keep tax loopholes for oil companies, or would you rather put construction workers and teachers back on the job? Would you rather keep tax breaks for millionaires and billionaires, or do you want to invest in medical research and new technology? Should we ask our seniors to pay thousands of dollars more for their Medicare, or should we ask the most profitable corporations to pay their fair share?

That's what this debate is about. That's what's at stake right now. This notion that the only thing to do to restore our prosperity is to eliminate environmental rules, bust unions, and make sure that we're giving tax breaks to the folks who are most fortunate and tell everybody else that they're on their own, that's not who we are. That's not the story of America. Yes, we are rugged individuals. Yes, we are strong and self-reliant. We don't like being told

what to do by the Government or anybody else. But it has always been the drive and initiative of our workers and entrepreneurs combined with our ability to work together as a society that cares for one another and gives everybody a chance—that's what's made this economy the engine and the envy of the world.

It hasn't just been about "me first." There's always been a running thread that says we're all connected, that there are some things that we can only do together as a nation. It's obvious when we think of our collective defense, when we think about the fire service or when we think about the military. But it's also true when it comes to our schools. It's also true when it comes to protecting our natural resources. That's why Presidents like Lincoln and Eisenhower, two Republicans, invested in railroads and highways and science and technology. It's why this country gave millions of returning heroes, including my grandfather, the chance to study through the GI bill. It's the reason that Michelle and I had the chance to succeed beyond our wildest dreams, because not only did we have great parents and grandparents, but we also had the ability to get student loans. We also had this opportunity that the country gave us.

So don't be confused. No single individual built America on their own, and no single individual makes it on their own. We've built it together. We have been and always will be "one Nation under God, indivisible, with liberty and justice for all," but also a nation with responsibilities to ourselves and responsibilities to one another. And it's time for us to meet those responsibilities right now. It's time for us to meet our responsibilities to each other right now.

And maybe some in Congress would rather settle those differences at the ballot box in November, but I've got news for them. The next election is 14 months away, and the American people cannot wait. They do not have the luxury of us squabbling for another 14 months. A lot of folks are living week to week, paycheck to paycheck, day to day. They need action, and they need it now.

Which brings me to you. I'm asking all of you to lift up your voices. You need to help us out. I want you to put pressure on Congress. The folks here, they're already voting for it, so you've got to go find some people who aren't. And I'm asking you to join me in finishing what we started in 2008.

Now, these have been tough, tough times for everybody, these last 2½ years. I know there are times, there are moments, when folks feel discouraged. You may still have the old "Hope" poster in the back somewhere. [*Laughter*] But you're thinking, man, we're struggling, the unemployment rate's still high, and the politics in Washington seem just as polarized as ever. So you feel frustrated. And there's a natural tendency to sink back into cynicism, to say, you know what, this can't be fixed. But I tell you what, if we had that attitude back in 2008, we never would have won. And more importantly, if we had that attitude throughout our history, then America wouldn't be what it is today.

Every bit of progress that's been worth making has been a struggle, whether it was civil rights or women's rights, the movement to expand educational opportunities to all, the institution of our basic safety net like Social Security and Medicare. It's always been a struggle. And there have been points at every juncture where it's been discouraging. And people have felt like, well, maybe change can't happen. Maybe we're stuck. Maybe America's best days are behind us. And what's prevented that from happening has been the American people, that sense not only of innate decency, that sense of fairness that is just in the DNA of America, but also that sense, you know what, we're not

somebody who—we're not a people who sit back and give up. We don't just let things happen to us. We make things happen.

And that spirit, which we captured in 2008, we need this spirit now more than ever. So I need you guys to shake off any doldrums. I need you to decide right here and right now, and I need you to talk to your friends and your neighbors and your coworkers. You need to tell them, you know what, we're not finished yet. We've got more work to do. We are going to build an America that we believe in, a place where everybody has a fair shot, everybody does their fair share, a generous, big, tolerant America, an optimistic America.

We are tougher than the times that we live in. We are bigger than the small politics that we've been witnessing. We are a people who write our own destiny, and it is fully within our power to write it once more. So let's meet this moment. Let's get to work. Let's show once again why the United States of America is the greatest country on Earth.

God bless you. God bless the United States of America.

NOTE: The President spoke at 2:38 p.m. at the Paramount Theatre. In his remarks, he referred to former National Basketball Association guard Leonard R. Wilkens and center William F. Russell; Mayor Michael P. McGinn of Seattle; President Lee Myung-bak of South Korea; and Warren E. Buffett, chief executive officer and chairman, Berkshire Hathaway Inc. The transcript was released by the Office of the Press Secretary on September 26.

Remarks at a Democratic National Committee Fundraiser in San Jose, California
September 25, 2011

The President. Hello, everybody. It is good to be back in Silicon Valley. It is good to be back at the Thompson residence. I try to make this a regular stop. [*Laughter*] Once every year or two, I figure, well, I need a little dose of John and Sandi and their friends. So thank you

all for being here. Thanks for arranging wonderful weather.

A couple of other people I want to acknowledge. First of all, I hope they're still here, because I love them and they do a great job every single day: Congressman Mike Honda in the house; and Congresswoman Anna Eshoo. We've also got Jean Quan, mayor of Oakland, in the house. And I want to thank Bruce Hornsby and Chris Cornell for their outstanding entertainment.

Now, as I was in the photo line, it turned out there are at least three birthdays here. Where are the birthday boys? There's one of them. There's another one. And then—[*laughter*]—four, five, six, seven. [*Laughter*] So this obviously a propitious day, with so many birthdays. Happy birthday to all of you. It is wonderful to help celebrate. But don't—for the kids, don't let your parents say, this is what you're getting for your birthday. [*Laughter*] I mean, I know that trick and—[*laughter*].

As Sandi said, these folks have been great friends for a long time. Many of you were here when I was still running for President.

Audience member. Senate!

The President. For Senate, even better. And I think, at the time, we understood there were enormous challenges that the country was facing, that there were problems that we had been putting off for decades. But I don't think we fully grasped, at least in 2007, the full magnitude of the challenges we were going to be facing. We've now gone through the worst financial crisis and the worst economic crisis since the Great Depression. So for most of our lifetimes, we've never seen anything like what we've seen over the last 2½ years.

And I think you may remember that, on Inauguration Day, when it was already becoming apparent, we could see the clouds on the horizon—Lehman's had already happened—I warned people my election was not the end. It wasn't the end of the journey, it was the beginning of a journey. And it was going to be a tough journey. Because not only did we have to stabilize the financial system and get the banking system working once again, not only did we have to make sure that we yanked ourselves out of the great depression that could have happened had we not intervened, and not only did we have to take emergency measures like save the U.S. auto industry, but even after we did all that, we were going to have to tackle some fundamental structural problems that

were preventing ordinary people, were preventing middle class families from thriving and prospering and achieving the American Dream.

And we talked, when I was running, about what some of those challenges were. We knew that we were going to have to create an energy policy that would not only free ourselves from dependence on foreign oil, but also start changing how we think about the planet and how we think about climate. We knew that we were going to have to make sure that we changed our health care system that was broken, leaving millions of people without health insurance and leaving folks who did have health insurance less secure than they needed to be. We knew that we were going to have to get control of our Federal budget, but do so in a way that ensured that we could still make the core investments in infrastructure and basic research and education that are so vital for us winning the future. We knew that we were going to have to not only put more money into our education system, but we were going to have to revamp it so that not just a few of our kids are prepared for the 21st century, but all of our kids are prepared for the 21st century.

So we knew that we had all these incredible challenges domestically. And then, overseas, we knew that it was unsustainable for us to continue two wars and to think that the only way that we were going to be able to project American power around the world was through our military. And we had to remind ourselves that diplomacy, the power of our example and the power of our values, ultimately was going to make more of a difference in terms of how influential we are around the world.

But I'm back to report to you, my stockholders—[*laughter*]—in the last 2½ years, we've stabilized the economy. We've ended the war in Iraq. We are on a pathway to bringing our troops home from Afghanistan. We have decimated Al Qaida and killed bin Laden. We have made sure that by 2013, as long as I get a second term, that we are implementing a health care reform package that will provide 30 million people with health insurance and make the entire system more efficient and more effective. We have signed into law everything from making sure that every woman and every young girl who is thinking about a career is going to make sure that she gets paid equally for an equal day's work. We ended "don't ask, don't tell" because we don't believe that anybody——

Audience member. Good job, Mr. President!

The President. ——that anybody who wants to serve this country should be prohibited because of who they love. We passed some of the toughest financial regulations in our history, including making sure that consumers are finally getting the protection they deserve. We made sure that, despite constant battles with Congress, that we continue to make progress on the environmental front. And some of it we did administratively. So we made sure, for example, that for the first time in 30 years we are doubling fuel efficiency standards on cars and trucks and heavy trucks, which will reduce carbon in our atmosphere and actually save folks money over the course of their lifetimes.

So we've done a lot. But here is the challenge I have for all of you. We've got so much more work to do. Yes, we stabilized the economy, but at a level where the unemployment rate was way, way too high. And we still have all sorts of international challenges that we're facing, from Europe to Asia. So we're still going to have to do a lot to restructure our economy to meet the competitive challenges of the 21st century. And that means we've got to continue to invest in cutting-edge research that enables the kind of explosion of technology that's taken place here in Silicon Valley. It means that we've continually got to revamp our education system. It means that we've got to make sure that we're rebuilding the best infrastructure in the world.

And we've got to think short term about how do we put people back to work, as well as long term, how do we make sure that a middle class can thrive in this country again.

And that's why I need your help. That's why I need your help. Because the fact of the matter is, is that too many people are hurting out there right now, and we've got to take some steps right now. So before I even talk to you about the campaign, I need your help to make sure that we get this jobs bill passed that puts people back to work.

Every idea that we have in this jobs bill has, in the past, been supported by Democrats and Republicans. Rebuilding our roads and our bridges and our airports and our schools, that's not a partisan idea, that's part of what made America an economic superpower. We've got all kinds of workers out there who are unemployed because of the housing bubble burst. We could put them to work right now rebuilding America. It will be good for the economy now, but it will also be good for our economic future.

We need to put teachers back in the classroom. We have—even in the midst of this economic crisis, we've actually created 2 million jobs over the last couple of years. The problem is we've also lost half a million jobs, mostly in State and local government, and a huge proportion of those are teachers that should be in our classrooms right now. We've got to change that, and the jobs bill would put people back in the classroom where they belong.

At a time when—I had lunch with the President of South Korea, and I asked him, "What's your biggest challenge?" And he says, "Just keeping pace with the huge demand for education." He said, "Our parents are too demanding." [*Laughter*] He says: "They want kindergarteners to learn English. I'm having to ship teachers in from foreign countries to meet the demand, because we understand that whoever wins the education battle, they're going to win the economic battle of the future." And at the same time as that's happening, we're laying off teachers in this country? That makes absolutely no sense. We've got to put them back in the classroom.

This jobs bill provides a tax cut not only to every working family in America, which will put more money in their pockets and allows them to make sure that they can buy all the great products that are created here in Silicon Valley, but it also cuts taxes for small businesses and entrepreneurs. It cuts taxes for companies that are hiring new workers or who are providing their workers raises. And it provides a tax credit for those who are hiring veterans.

So we've got an opportunity to put people back to work right now. And by the way, it is paid for, every dime. Now, this has caused some controversy: Well, how do you pay for it? Keep in mind that it is absolutely true that we've got to have a Government that lives within its means. And we weren't living within our means over the last decade: two wars we didn't pay for, a prescription drug plan we didn't pay for, tax cuts we did not pay for. So we've already made $1 trillion worth of cuts over the course of this summer. We've slated another half million dollars in cuts, including making some modest modifications to entitlements.

So we're doing our part. But what we've said is the only way we actually close the gap if we want to have long-term fiscal sustainability is we've also got to make sure that everybody is doing their fair share—everybody—and that includes the people in this audience. We've got to do our fair share.

Now—and I want to be very clear about this. I mean, there are just some basic principles. Warren Buffett's secretary should not be paying a higher tax rate than Warren Buffett. It's a pretty straightforward principle. A teacher making $50,000 a year shouldn't be paying a higher tax rate than somebody who's pulling in $50 million.

Contrary to what the Republicans claim, that's not class warfare. This is not about leveling down. The people in this audience, some of you have been extraordinarily successful, and that's what America is all about. We want everybody to thrive. We want everybody to succeed. God bless you. If you're starting a business, you've got a good idea, you've got a new product, a new service, put that out onto the market, create jobs, create opportunity for others. That's great. But we have to remind ourselves that the reason we're successful is because somebody else made an investment in us. Somewhere along the line, somebody made an investment in us either directly—people like myself getting college scholarships—indi-

rectly, because somebody invested in DARPA a few years back.

The fact of the matter is we're not—we didn't do all this on our own, and we've got an obligation to make sure that the folks coming behind us are going to have the same opportunities that we did. That's not class warfare. That is common sense. That's what America is all about. That's our values. Those are our ideals.

Now, I need all of you to be vocal about trying to get this jobs bill passed over the next 14 months. That's going to be absolutely critical. But I'll be honest with you, we're not—I don't know if you've noticed, we're not getting a lot of cooperation from Members of Congress. [*Laughter*]

Audience member. Party of no!

The President. I like that. We might have to use that. [*Laughter*] And for those—some of you here may be folks who actually used to be Republican, but are puzzled by what's happened to that party—[*laughter*]—are puzzled by what's happened to that party. I mean, has anybody been watching the debates lately? [*Laughter*]

You've got a Governor whose State is on fire denying climate change. [*Laughter*] No, no, it's true. You've got audiences cheering at the prospect of somebody dying because they don't have health care and booing a servicemember in Iraq because they're gay. That's not reflective of who we are. We've had differences in the past, but at some level we've always believed, you know what, that we're not defined by our differences. We're bound together.

And so the reason I bring this up is we're going to get everything we can out of this Congress over the next 14 months, because the American people can't wait. But let's face it, we're also going to need changes in Washington if we are going to be able to achieve the kind of vision that we talked about back in 2008. We're going to have to fight for this.

And this is a choice about the fundamental direction of our country—2008 was an important election; 2012 is a more important election. Now, in order for us to be successful in this 2012 election, I'm going to need all of you.

Audience member. You got it!

The President. I'm going to need you to be out there talking to your friends, talking to your neighbors, talking to your coworkers. And I'm going to need you to be advocates for what we believe in. It's not enough just to support me. I need you to go out there, and if other folks have been reading the Wall Street Journal editorial page or watching FOX News, and they're full of inadequate information—[*laughter*]—I need you to push back. I need you to push back.

You have to make an argument that, yes, the President wants to close this deficit, but we can't do it just on the backs of the poor and the middle class and our seniors and that we've got to all do our part.

Yes, what's driven our success historically has been a free market, but we've always been successful because we also made sure that that market operated fairly and that there were basic consumer protections, and people who were providing good products and good services were rewarded, not people who were trying to game the system.

I need you to be out there making arguments that the notion the only way we succeed in international competition is by stripping away laws against polluting our planet. That's a shortsighted approach to economic development, and it's not going to work. We're never going to be able to compete on having the dirtiest air or the cheapest labor. We'll never compete that way.

And in some cases, I may need you to have some arguments with our progressive friends. Because, let's face it, the fact of the matter is, is that over the last 2½ years, even as we've gotten a huge amount done, there's a lot of folks on our side who get dispirited because we didn't get it all done in 2½ years.

That's not how America works. This is a big, messy, tough democracy. And we're not going to get a hundred percent. So if we get a health care bill passed that provides health insurance for 80 million—30 million people and has the strongest patient bill of rights in history and young people can now stay on their folks' insurance so we actually know that a million young people have health insurance right now because of the bill that we put in place—your kids and grandkids—the notion that somebody is out of joint because we didn't get a public option—come on!

No, we haven't gotten everything done on the environmental front because we're in the midst of a very tough economic time and people naturally are more hesitant about big changes at a time when they're worried about their jobs. But that doesn't mean all the good work that we have done and are doing can be ignored. And the other thing that everybody has got to keep in mind—my friend Joe Biden, he has a quote he likes to use. He says, "Don't compare me to the Almighty; compare me to the alternative." [*Laughter*]

So the fact of the matter is, we're going to have a stark choice in this election. But I have to make sure that our side is as passionate and as motivated and is working just as hard as the folks on the other side, because this is a contest of values. This is a choice about who we are and what we stand for. And whoever wins this next election is going to set the template for this country for a long time to come.

So I expect all of you, again, not just to be supporting me, you have to be out there, active, engaged, just as engaged as you were in 2008.

Audience member. We're with you!

The President. And if you do that, here and all across the country, if people of like mind, people who believe in a big and generous and a tolerant and ambitious and fact-based America, an America that believes in science and an America that believes in education, an America that believes that investing in our children is an investment in all of us, if you believe in those things, then I need you out there knocking on doors and making phone calls.

If you guys are working like that, then not only am I optimistic about the election, I'll be optimistic about the future.

Thank you so much, everybody. God bless you. God bless America.

NOTE: The President spoke at 6:56 p.m. at the residence of John W. and Sandra Thompson.

In his remarks, he referred to musicians Bruce Hornsby and Chris Cornell; President Lee Myung-bak of South Korea; Warren E. Buffett, chief executive officer and chairman, Berkshire Hathaway Inc.; and Gov. J. Richard Perry of Texas. The transcript was released by the Office of the Press Secretary on September 26. Audio was not available for verification of the content of these remarks.

Remarks at a Democratic National Committee Fundraiser in San Jose
September 25, 2011

Thank you, everybody. Thank you. I'm just letting Zuckerberg know, I'm taking her on the road. [*Laughter*] So somebody else is going to have to manage things while she's gone.

Thank you so much, Sheryl and David and the kids, for opening up this beautiful home. Thank you all for being here tonight.

I don't want to spend too much time just in monologue. I want to—I know that one of the hallmarks of Silicon Valley and the Internet is that it's a two-way thing, it's not just one way. So I want to make sure that we have a good conversation. But let me just say a couple of things off the top.

First of all, many of you have been involved in my campaign dating back to 2008. Some of you I'm meeting for the first time. But all of you have a commitment to a particular vision of what America should be. Everybody here believes that the reason America is so special is because everybody can make it if they try; at least that's the ideal that we cling to. We all believe that education has to be not just the province of a few, but a gift for the many, because that's not only good for our kids, but that's good for our economic future. We're all committed to innovation and science and a belief that if you unleash the skills and the talents of people, that it's possible for us to create an economy that is doing well, but where prosperity is also broadly shared. We all believe in an America where it shouldn't matter where you come from or what you look like or who you love, but rather do you have values and gifts and talents that you're sharing with other Americans as citizens.

And those values are going to be tested in this election: the values of shared prosperity, being good stewards of the environment, making sure that we are investing in our kids, mak-

ing sure that everybody has a shot. Those values are going to be tested. And so if 2008 was an important election, let me tell you, 2012 is an even more important election, because of all the reasons that Sheryl noted.

The American people are going through a very tough time. This is a big transition, and by the way, it's not unique to America. This is a global shift that's taking place. We've got a world that has shrunk and is interconnected and is more competitive than ever. And every country out there is trying to adjust and trying to figure out, how do we make sure we've got the best educated citizens, and how do we make sure we've got the most dynamic, innovative economy, and how are we making sure that we're investing in industries of the future like clean energy, and how do we make certain that in our international affairs we're projecting power not just based on our military, but also based on our diplomacy and the power of our ideas.

And those changes that are taking place are scary. And given that we've just gone through the worst financial crisis in our lifetimes—I'm looking around the room, and I don't think too many folks were around back in the 1930s. Just a guess. [*Laughter*] Given that so many Americans are still out there hurting each and every day, and although we've been able to stabilize the economy from what could have been a worse catastrophe—we've got 9-percent unemployment. And I get letters every single day from folks who are losing their homes and seeing their businesses shut down, not being able to work enough hours to pay the bills at the end of the month, or having to defer their retirement in order to make sure their kids go to college.

Given all the stresses and strains that ordinary folks are feeling and given the fact that some of the challenges we faced had been building up even before this financial crisis hit—and so the imperatives of having an energy policy that actually works for America and frees ourselves from dependence on foreign oil and improves our economy and makes sure that our planet doesn't reach a tipping point in terms of climate change; a health care system that is still hugely inefficient; an education system that's not educating enough of our kids; underinvestment in infrastructure and basic research—those challenges, those existed even before this crisis.

Given all that's happening, if we don't make good decisions now, then we may be making a set of decisions that have dire consequences for not just this generation, but for many generations to come. Most of the people under this tent will be fine, but America won't reflect the same ideals and values and possibilities that we grew up with.

And I don't know about you, but I believe in a big, generous, optimistic, tolerant, vibrant, diverse America, not a cramped vision of what America can be. But we're going to have to fight for that vision. It's not going to be easy. And the only way that we're going to be successful in 2012 is if people feel as much passion and understand what's at stake and are willing to fight for the kind of America they believe in as we did back in 2008.

I still remember—you were mentioning Inauguration Day. What I remember is the night of the election. And we were in Chicago, and it was a really beautiful night. Everybody has fond memories of the "Hope" poster and Oprah crying. [*Laughter*] But I hope people al-

so remember, I said, "This is not the end, this is the beginning. This is just the start. And we didn't get into this fix overnight, and we're not going to get out of it overnight. We've got a steep hill to climb."

And Sheryl is right, we've made enormous progress over the last 2½ years, everything from making sure 30 million people have health care who didn't have it before, to making sure that we doubled fuel efficiency standards on cars, to making sure that we ended "don't ask, don't tell," to making sure that we signed into law the basic notion that there should be equal pay for equal work, to getting 100,000 troops out of Iraq. We've made enormous progress, but we've got a lot more work to do. And I'm ready to do it, but I can only do it if I've got your help.

So I appreciate you being here tonight. But understand, just as we were just starting on election night, I'll tell you what, we're not even halfway through our journey yet. We've got a lot more work to do, and I'm going to need all of you to be willing to join me.

All right, thank you very much.

NOTE: The President spoke at 8:09 p.m. at the residence of Sheryl K. Sandberg, chief operating officer, Facebook, Inc., and David B. Goldberg. In his remarks, he referred to Mark E. Zuckerberg, founder and chief executive officer, Facebook, Inc.; and talk show host Oprah Winfrey. The transcript was released by the Office of the Press Secretary on September 26. Audio was not available for verification of the content of these remarks.

Remarks at a Question-and-Answer Session With LinkedIn Participants in Mountain View, California
September 26, 2011

LinkedIn Corporation Chief Executive Officer Jeff Weiner. Good morning, everyone.

Audience member. Yes!

Mr. Weiner. Oh, very nice. [*Laughter*] Thank you so much for joining us here today for a very special town hall discussion on a subject we all know to be truly important, and

that's putting America back to work. In just a moment, I'm going to be introducing a very special guest, but before I do, just a few brief introductory remarks.

I think today's venue, the Computer History Museum, here in Silicon Valley, is a very fitting one for our discussion. There's a number of folks who've come to Silicon Valley not just for a job, or even a career path, but because they're interested in changing the world. And that's possible here because of the amazing technologies and companies that have been born in this area.

You think back to the semiconductor revolution, the age of computing, and of course, the Internet, and most recently, with regard to the Internet, the rise of social networks connecting hundreds of millions of people around the world in milliseconds. Perhaps more importantly are the behavioral changes taking place as a result: the way in which we go online, represent our identities, stay connected to friends, family and colleagues, and of course, share information, knowledge, ideas, and opinions. It's fundamentally transforming the world: the way we live, the way we play, and the way we work.

And it's that last dynamic, changing the way we work, which is where LinkedIn is focused. We connect hundreds of millions of people, ultimately, around the world by connecting talent with opportunity: today, 120 million members on a global basis, and that's growing north of two members per second, the fastest rate of growth in our history.

When we talk about connecting talent with opportunity we're not just referring to enabling people to find a job or their dream jobs. We're also talking about enabling people to be great at the jobs that they're already in. This is what we do, day in and day out. But our dream is even bigger than that. There are 153 million people in the American workforce; there are 3.3 billion people in the global workforce. Ultimately, our vision is to create economic opportunity for every one of them.

What's somewhat unusual about this vision is it won't simply be manifested by the employees of our company, but by our members as well, because every individual that joins the LinkedIn network is in a position to, in turn, create economic opportunity for others. We're very fortunate today to be joined by several of our members, and we're going to be hearing from them shortly.

Lastly, on the subject of economic opportunity, there seems to be one number on everybody's minds these days: 9.1 percent, the unemployment rate in this country. Over 14 million Americans are unemployed, and that number grows to north of 25 million when you factor in those that are underemployed and marginally attached to the workforce.

There's one number you may be less familiar with, and that's 3.2 million, the number of available jobs in this country—3.2 million. We have everything we need to begin to put this country back to work: the raw materials, the basic building blocks, and perhaps most importantly, the will of a nation. What we need is the way. With the "American Jobs Act," our President is leading the way.

Ladies and gentlemen, it is my great honor and privilege to introduce the President of the United States.

The President. Thank you. Everybody, please have a seat. Thank you. Thank you very much. It's a nice crowd. [*Laughter*] And I have to say, Jeff, you warmed them up very well.

Mr. Weiner. Thank you, Mr. President.

The President. I thank you so much for your hospitality. And let me begin by just saying how excited I am to be here. Every time I come to Silicon Valley, every time that I come to this region, I am excited about America's future. And no part of the country better represents, I think, the essence of America than here, because what you see is entrepreneurship and dynamism, a forward orientation, an optimism, a belief that if you got a good idea and you're willing to put in the sweat and blood and tears to make it happen, that not only can you succeed for yourself, but you can grow the economy for everybody. And it's that driving spirit that has made America an economic superpower.

But obviously, we're in a period of time right now where the economy is struggling and a lot of folks all across the country are struggling. And so part of what I hope to do is to have a conversation with all of you about how can we continue to spark the innovation that is going to ensure our economic success in the 21st century; how can we prepare our workforce to be able to plug in to this new economy; how do we recognize that, in this competitive environment,

1141

there are all kinds of opportunities that LinkedIn presents for interconnectedness and people being able to work together and spread ideas around the world and create value, but at the same time, understanding that there are some perils as well.

If our kids aren't properly educated, if we don't have an infrastructure that is world-class, if we are not investing in basic research in science, if we're not doing all the things that made us great in the past, then we're going to fall behind.

And we've got a short-term challenge, which is how do we put people back to work right now. And so, as you mentioned, I put forward a proposal, the "American Jobs Act," that would put thousands of teachers back into the classrooms who have been laid off due to downturns in State and local budgets; that would make sure that we are rebuilding our infrastructure, taking extraordinary numbers of construction workers who have been laid off when the housing bubbles went bust and putting them to work rebuilding our roads and our airports and our schools, and laying broadband lines—all the things that help us make a success and also make sure that we're providing small businesses the kinds of tax incentives that will allow them to hire and allow them to succeed.

And I have said to Congress, I understand that there's an election 14 months away, and it's tempting to say that we're not going to do anything until November of 2012, but the American people cannot afford to wait. The American people need help right now. And all the proposals we've put forward in the "American Jobs Act" will not only help us now, but will also help us in the future, will lay the foundation for our long-term success.

Last point I'll make—and then I want to get to questions—it's all paid for. And it's paid for in part by building on some very tough cuts in our budget to eliminate waste and things we don't need—that we've already made a trillion dollars over the next 10 years. We've proposed an additional half a trillion dollars over the next 10 years of spending cuts and adjustments on

programs that we want to keep intact, but haven't been reformed in too long.

But what I've also said is, in order to pay for it and bring down the deficit at the same time, we're going to have to reform our Tax Code in a way that's fair and makes sure that everybody is doing their fair share. I've said this before, I'll say it again: Warren Buffett's secretary shouldn't be paying a lower tax rate than Warren Buffett. Somebody who's making $50,000 a year as a teacher shouldn't be paying a higher effective tax rate than somebody like myself or Jeff, who've been incredibly blessed—I don't know what you make Jeff, but I'm just guessing—[*laughter*]—who've been blessed by the incredible opportunities of this country.

And I say that because whenever America has moved forward, it's because we've moved forward together. And we're going to have to make sure that we are laying the foundation for the success of future generations, and that means that each of us are doing our part to make sure we're investing in our future.

So with that, thank you so much for the terrific venue. I look forward to a bunch of great questions, both live and through whatever other linkages that we've got here. [*Laughter*]

Mr. Weiner. You've got it. So we're going to be going back and forth between folks in the audience members and some previously generated questions from the LinkedIn group. So we're going to start.

National Economy/Job Creation

Our first question is from LinkedIn member Chuck Painter. And, Chuck, we're going to get you a mike——

Q. Good morning, Mr. President.

The President. Good morning.

Q. I'm from Austin, Texas. I've been in sales in the plastics industry for 20 years. I lost my job in 2009 and am fortunate enough to have found another position, become reemployed. My question is, what can we do as American citizens to unite ourselves and help the economy?

The President. Well, first of all, are you a native of Austin? Because that's one of my favorite cities in the country.

Q. Actually, I'm a native of Charlotte, North Carolina, but just relocated to Austin, and I love it there.

The President. Austin is great; Charlotte is not bad. [*Laughter*]

Q. Thank you, thank you, thank you.

The President. That's the reason why I'm having my convention in Charlotte, because I love North Carolina as well. But the—how long did it take you to find a new job after you had gotten laid off?

Q. It took 9 months.

The President. It took 9 months?

Q. Yes, sir.

The President. And that's one of the challenges that a lot of folks are seeing out there. You've got skilled people with experience in an industry. That industry changes, and you were fortunate enough to be able to move. Some folks, because of the decline in the housing industry, are having trouble with mobility in finding new jobs and relocating in pursuit of opportunity.

Q. Yes, sir.

The President. The most important thing that we can do right now is to help jump-start the economy, which has stalled, by putting people back to work. And so not surprisingly, I think the most important thing we can do right now is pass this jobs bill.

Think about it. Independent economists have estimated that if we pass the entire package, the "American Jobs Act," we would increase GDP by close to 2 percent; we would increase employment by 1.9 million persons. And that is the kind of big, significant move in the economy that can have ripple effects and help recovery take off.

There's been a lot of dispute about the kind of impact that we had right after the financial crisis hit. But the fact is, the vast majority of economists who looked at it have said that the Recovery Act, by starting infrastructure projects around the country, by making sure that States had help on their budgets so they didn't have to lay off teachers and firefighters and others, by providing tax cuts to small businesses—and by the way, we've cut taxes about 16 times since I've been in office for small busi-

nesses to give them more capital to work with and more incentives to hire—all those things made a big difference.

The "American Jobs Act" is specifically tailored to putting more of those folks back to work. It's not going to solve all our problems. We've still got a housing situation in which too many homes are underwater. And one of the things that we've proposed as part of the "American Jobs Act" is, is that we're going to help reduce the barriers to refinancing so that folks can get record-low rates. That will put more money into people's pockets. It will provide tax cuts to not only small businesses, but almost every middle class family. That means they've got more money in their pockets, and that means that they're going to be able to spend it on products and services, which provide additional incentives for business to hire folks like you.

So it's the right step to take right now. Long term, we're going to have to pull together around making sure our education system is the best in the world, making sure our infrastructure is the best in the world, continuing to invest in science and technology. We've got to stabilize our finances, and we've got to continue to drive down health care costs, which are a drag on our whole economy. And we've got to continue to promote trade, but make sure that that trade is fair and that intellectual property protection, for example, is available when we're doing business in other countries, like China.

So there are a lot of long-term agendas that we've got to pursue. Right now, though, the most important thing I can do for you, even if you already have a job, is to make sure that your neighbors and your friends also have jobs, because those are ultimately the customers for your products.

Q. Yes, sir. Yes, thank you, Mr. President.

Mr. Weiner. All right. Thank you, Chuck.

We'd now like to take a question from the audience. So anyone interested?

The President. This young lady right here.

Mr. Weiner. Okay. Could we get a mike over there, please? Thank you.

Social Security/Medicare/Job Growth Legislation

Q. Hi. I have a question actually from my mother, who is going to be 65 next March. And she lives in Ohio, which has a very high unemployment rate. She has a GED, and she's always worked in food service. She's currently unemployed, just got approved for Section 8 housing, gets Social Security and food stamps. And she wants to know, when can she get a job, and what's going to happen to Social Security and Medicare?

The President. Well, first of all, where does your mom live in Ohio?

Q. Mentor.

The President. Mentor. What part of Ohio is that?

Q. It's the east side of Cleveland.

The President. Okay. Well, tell mom hi. [*Laughter*] You get points for being such a good daughter and using your question to tell me what's on her mind.

Q. Oh, you have no idea. [*Laughter*]

The President. My mother-in-law lives at home, and so I—in the White House—so I've got some idea. [*Laughter*]

First of all, let me talk about Social Security and Medicare, because this has obviously been an issue that has been discussed a lot in the press lately as we think about our long-term finances. You can tell your mom that Medicare and Social Security will be there for her, guaranteed. There are no proposals out there that would affect folks that are about to get Social Security and Medicare, and she'll be qualifying—she already is starting to qualify for Medicare, and she'll be qualifying for Social Security fairly soon.

Social Security and Medicare, together, have lifted entire generations of seniors out of poverty. Our most important social safety net, and they have to be preserved. Now, both of them have some long-term challenges that we've got to deal with, but they're different challenges.

Social Security is actually the easier one; it's just a pure, simple math problem, and that is that right now the population is getting older, so more people are going on Social Security; you've got fewer workers supporting more re-

tirees. And so if we don't do anything, Social Security won't go broke, but in a few years what will happen is that more money will be going out than coming in. And over time, people who are on Social Security would only be getting about 75 cents on every dollar that they thought they'd be getting.

And so the Social Security system is not the big driver of our deficits, but if we don't want—if we want to make sure that Social Security is there for future generations, then we've got to make some modest adjustments. And when I say modest, I mean, for example, right now Social Security contributions are capped at a little over $100,000 of earnings, and that means the vast majority of people pay Social Security taxes on everything they earn. But if you're earning a million dollars, only one-tenth of your income is taxed for Social Security. We could make that modification; that would solve a big chunk of the problem.

Medicare is a bigger issue because not only is the population getting older and more people are using it, but health care costs have been going up way too fast. And that's why part of my health care reform bill 2 years ago was, let's start changing how our health care system works to make it more efficient. For example, if your mom goes in for a test, she shouldn't have to then, if she goes to another specialist, take the same test all over again and have Medicare pay for two tests. That first test should be e-mailed to the doctor who's the specialist. But right now that's not happening. So what we've said is let's incentivize providers to do a more efficient job, and over time, we can start reducing those costs.

I've made some suggestions about how we can reform Medicare, but what I'm not going to do is what, frankly, the House Republicans proposed, which was to voucherize the Medicare system, which would mean your mom might pay an extra $6,000 every year for her Medicare.

Q. Which she doesn't have.

The President. I'm assuming she doesn't have it.

Q. No.

The President. So we are going to be pushing back against that kind of proposal. And that raises the point I made earlier. If people like myself aren't paying a little more in taxes, then the only way you balance the budget is on the backs of folks like your mom, who end up paying a lot more in Medicare, and they can't afford it, whereas I can afford to pay a little more in taxes.

So that's on Medicare and Social Security. In terms of her finding a job, the most important thing we can do right now is to pass the "American Jobs Act," get people back to work. Because, think about it, if she's been in the food service industry, that industry is dependent on people spending money on food, whether it's at a restaurant or a cafeteria or buying more groceries. And if a construction worker and a teacher or a veteran have a job because of the programs that we proposed in the "American Jobs Act," they're going to be spending more money in food services, and that means that those businesses are going to have to hire more, and your mom is going to be more likely to be hired. All right?

Q. Yes. And one of the other issues, though, is just a matter that there's a big age gap between her and the other folks who are willing to come in and work for less money. They've got less experience.

The President. That is a challenge. It is tough being unemployed if you're in your fifties or early sixties, before retirement. That's the toughest period of time to lose your job. Obviously, it's never fun to lose your job, and it's always hard in this kind of really deep recession, but it's scariest for folks who are nearing retirement and may also be worrying about whether they've got enough saved up to ever retire.

So that's part of the reason why one of the things that we're also proposing, separate and apart from the jobs bill, is we've got to do a better job of retraining workers so that they, in their second or third or fourth careers, are able to go back to a community college, maybe take a short 6-month course or a 1-year course that trains them on the kinds of skills that are going to be needed for jobs that are actually hiring— or businesses that are actually hiring right now.

We've done some great work working with community colleges to try to make sure that businesses help design the training programs so that somebody who enrolls—like your mom, if she goes back to school, she knows that after 6 months she will be trained for the particular job that this business is looking for.

All right? Thanks so much.

Q. Great.

The President. Tell her I said hi.

Q. Thank you. Okay.

Support for Small Businesses/Need for Government Regulation

Mr. Weiner. We're going to go to the group, the LinkedIn group. We had thousands of questions submitted, and here's one of them from LinkedIn member Marla Hughes. Marla is from Gainesville, Florida. She is the owner of Meticulously Clean, home and apartment cleaning service, and her question is: "As a small-business owner, regulation and high taxes are my worst enemies when it comes to growing my business. What are you going to do to lessen the onerous regulations and taxation on small businesses?"

The President. Well, it's hard to say exactly what regulations or taxes she may be referring to, because obviously, it differs in different businesses. But as I said, we've actually cut taxes for small business 16 times since I've been in office. So taxes for small businesses are lower now than they were when I came into office.

Small businesses are able to get tax breaks for hiring; they're able to get tax breaks for investment in capital investments; they are able to get tax breaks for hiring veterans. They're able to get tax breaks for a whole host of areas, including, by the way, a proposal we put forward that says that there should be no capital gains tax on a startup, to encourage more small businesses to go out there and create a business.

In terms of regulations, most of the regulations that we have been focused on are ones that affect large businesses, like utilities, for example. In terms of how they deal with safety issues, environmental issues, we have been putting forward some tough regulations with respect to the financial sector, because we can't have a repeat of what happened in 2007.

And the fact of the matter is, is that if what happened on Wall Street ends up having a spillover effect to all of Main Street, it is our responsibility to make sure that we have a dynamic economy, we have a dynamic financial sector, but we don't have a mortgage brokerage operation that ends up providing people loans that can never be repaid and end up having ramifications throughout the system.

So you're going to hear from, I think, Republicans over the next year and a half that somehow if we just eliminated pollution controls or if we just eliminated basic consumer protections, that somehow that in and of itself would be a spur to growth. I disagree with that. What I do agree with is that there's some regulations that have outlived their usefulness. And so what I've done is I've said to all the agencies in the Federal Government, number one, you have to always take cost as well as benefits into account when you're proposing new regulations. Number two, don't just be satisfied with applying that analysis to new regulations, look back at the old regulations to see if there are some that we can start weeding out.

And we initiated the most aggressive—what we call look-back provisions—when it comes to regulations, where we say to every agency, go through all the regulations that you have on your books that flow through your agencies and see if some of them are still necessary. And it turns out that a lot of them are no longer necessary. Well, let's get rid of them if they've outlived their usefulness.

I think that there were some regulations that had to do with the transportation sector, for example, that didn't take into account that everybody operates on GPS now. Well, you've got to adjust and adapt to how the economy is changing and how technology has changed. And we've already identified about $10 billion worth of savings just in the initial review, and we anticipate that that's only going to be a fraction of some of the paperwork and bureaucracy and redtape that we're going to be able to eliminate.

But I will never apologize for making sure that we have regulations in place to ensure that your water is clean, that your food is safe to eat, that the peanut butter you feed your kids is not going to be contaminated; making sure that if you take out a credit card, there's some clarity about what it exactly is going to do and you're not seeing a whole bunch of hidden fees and hidden charges that you didn't anticipate. That's always been part of what makes the marketplace work, is if you have smart regulations in place, that means the people who are providing good value, good products, good services, those businesses are going to succeed. We don't want to be rewarding folks who are gaming the system or cheating consumers.

And I think that's how most Americans feel about regulations as well. They don't want more than is necessary, but they know that there's some things that we've got to do to protect ourselves and our environment and our children.

Mr. Weiner. Thank you for your question, Marla.

Job Growth Legislation/Student Loan Program

Now we're going to take a question from LinkedIn member Ester Abeja. Ester is an IT analyst from Chicago, Illinois.

The President. There you go.

Mr. Weiner. Ester——

The President. Chicago is all right too. [*Laughter*]

Mr. Weiner. ——what is your question for the President?

Q. Good morning, Mr. President.

The President. Good morning.

Q. As Jeff said, I'm from Chicago, recently unemployed, and my fear is that the longer I'm unemployed, the harder it is going to be for me to get employed. It seems that nowadays employers are hiring people who are currently employed because they're in touch with their skill set. What programs do you think should be in place for individuals such as myself to keep in touch with our skills, be in demand, marketable, and eventually get hired?

The President. Well, first of all, you obviously are thinking ahead about how to keep your skills up. And the most important thing you can do is to make sure that, whether it's through classes or online training, or what have you, that you're keeping your skill sets sharp.

We, as part of the "American Jobs Act," are actually supporting legislation in Congress that says employers can't discriminate against somebody just because they're currently unemployed, because that doesn't seem fair. That doesn't make any sense. But the most important thing probably we can do for you is just make sure that the unemployment rate generally goes down, the labor market gets a little tighter so that employers start looking beyond just the people who are currently employed to folks who have terrific skills and just have been out of the market for a while.

So passing the "American Jobs Act" is going to be important. There's legislation in there that says you can't be discriminated against just because you don't have a job. The one other thing that we can do is, during this interim, as you're looking for a job, making it easier for you to be able to go back to school if you think there's some skill sets that you need, making it economical for you to do it.

One of the things that we did during the last 2½ years, it used to be the student loan program was run through the banks. And even though the Federal Government guaranteed all these loans, so the banks weren't taking any risks, they were taking about $60 billion out of the entire program, which meant that there was less money to actually go directly to students. We ended that. We cut out the middleman, and we said let's use that money to expand the availability of Pell grants, to increase the amount that Pell grants—each Pell grant a student could get. And through that process, you've got millions of people all across the country who are able to actually go back to school without incurring the huge debt loads that they had in the past; although obviously, the cost of a college education is still really high.

But if we can do more to make it easier for you to keep your skills up even when you're not already hired, hopefully, that will enhance your marketability to employers in the future. All right? Just looking at you I can tell you're going to do great.

Q. Thank you.

The President. Thank you.

Mr. Weiner. Thanks, Ester.

Employment Opportunities for Veterans

Our next question is from LinkedIn member Wayne Kulick. Wayne is from Phoenix, Arizona. He spent 25 years flying aircraft for the U.S. Navy and is now program director for American Express. Wayne.

Q. Good morning, Mr. President.

The President. Good morning, sir.

Q. I'm originally from Phoenix, Arizona, where I'm a program director, as Jeff had said. I retired in 2007. When I retired, networking was essentially how I got all my jobs after retirement. How do you envision the Government's role in integrating networking tools that aid veterans that are leaving the service and getting jobs?

The President. It's a great question. And first of all, let me thank you for your service to this country.

Q. My honor.

The President. We are very grateful to you for that. Thank you. But you were extraordinarily skilled, and even then it sounds like you had to rely on informal networks rather than a formal set of processes for veterans in order for you to find a job that used all your skills. We have not done as good of a job in the past in helping veterans transition out of the Armed Services as we should have.

I'll give you an example. I actually had lunch with a group of veterans from the Iraq and Afghan wars up in Minnesota. And a young man I was talking to had just gone back to school. He was getting his nursing degree. He had worked in emergency medicine in Iraq, multiple deployments, had probably dealt with the most incredible kinds of medical challenges under the most extreme circumstances, had received years of training to do this. But when he went back to nursing school, he had to start as if he had never been involved in medicine at all.

And so he had to take all the same classes and take the same debt burdens from taking those classes as if I had just walked in and could barely put a bandaid on myself. But he had to go through the same processes.

Well, that's an example of a failure on the part of both DOD and the VA—the Department of Defense and Veterans Administration—to think proactively: How can we help him make the transition?

So what we've started to say is let's have a sort of a reverse boot camp. As folks are thinking about retiring, as folks are thinking about being discharged, let's work with them while they're still in the military to say is there a way to credential them so that they can go directly into the job and work with State and local governments and employers, so that if they've got a skill set that we know is applicable to the private sector, let's give them a certification, let's give them a credential that helps them do that right away.

We've also then started to put together a network of business, and I actually asked for a pledge from the private sector, and we've got a commitment now that 100,000 veterans will be hired over the next several years. And that creates a network—and maybe they'll end up using LinkedIn, I don't know. But what we want to do is to make sure that, whether it's the certification process, whether it's the job search process, whether it's résumé preparation, whether it's using electronic networking, that we're using the huge capacity of the Veterans Administration and the Department of Defense, and all the Federal agencies, to link up together more effectively.

Because not only is the Federal Government obviously a big employer itself—and we've significantly increased the hiring of veterans within the Federal Government, including, by the way, disabled veterans and wounded warriors—but the Federal Government is also a big customer of a lot of businesses. And there's nothing wrong with a big customer saying to a business, you know what, we're not going to tell you who to hire, but here's a list of extremely skilled veterans who are prepared to do a great job and have shown incredible lead-

ership skills. Now, you think of these—you have 23-, 24-, 25-year-olds who are leading men into battle, who are handling multimillion-dollar pieces of equipment, and they do so flawlessly. Those leadership skills, those technical skills should be able to translate directly into jobs.

The last thing I'll say is obviously the "American Jobs Act" also would be helpful because it provides additional tax incentives for companies to hire our veterans.

Q. Thank you.

The President. Thank you.

Mr. Weiner. Thank you, Wayne. And thank you again for your service.

Let's turn to the audience now. A lot of hands going up. Mr. President, want to pick someone?

The President. Well—[*laughter*]—you kind of put me on the spot here. That guy, the guy in the glasses right back in the—right in the back there. Why not?

Taxes/Education

Q. Thank you, Mr. President. I don't have a job, but that's because I've been lucky enough to live in Silicon Valley for a while and work for a small startup down the street here that did quite well. So I'm unemployed by choice. My question is, would you please raise my taxes? [*Laughter*] I would like very much to have the country to continue to invest in things like Pell grants and infrastructure and job training programs that made it possible for me to get to where I am. And it kills me to see Congress not supporting the expiration of the tax cuts that have been benefiting so many of us for so long. I think that needs to change, and I hope that you will stay strong in doing that.

The President. Well, I appreciate it. What was the startup, by the way? You want to give me a little hint?

Q. It's a search engine. [*Laughter*]

The President. Worked out pretty well, huh?

Q. Yes. [*Laughter*]

The President. Well, look, let me just talk about taxes for a second. I've made this point before, but I want to reiterate this. So often the tax debate gets framed as "class warfare." And look, as I said at the outset, America's success is premised on individuals, entrepreneurs having a great idea, going out there and pursuing their dreams and making a whole lot of money in the process. And that's great. That's part of what makes America so successful.

But as you just pointed out, we're successful because somebody invested in our education, somebody built schools, somebody created incredible universities. I went to school on scholarship. Michelle—her dad was a—what's called a stationary engineer at the water reclamation district; never owned his own home, but he always paid his bills; had multiple sclerosis, struggled to get to work every day, but never missed a day on the job; never went to college, but he was able to send his daughter to Princeton and on to Harvard Law School. We benefited from somebody, somewhere making an investment in us. And I don't care who you are, that's true of all of us.

Look at this room. I mean, look at the diversity of the people here. A lot of us are—parents came from someplace else or grandparents came from someplace else. They benefited from a public school system, or an incredible university network, or the infrastructure that allows us to move products and services around the globe, or the scientific research that—Silicon Valley is built on research that no individual company would have made on their own because you couldn't necessarily capture the value of the nascent Internet.

So the question becomes: If we're going to make those investments, how do we pay for it? Now, the income of folks at the top has gone up exponentially over the last couple of decades, whereas the incomes and wages of the middle class have flatlined over the last 15 years. So this young lady's mom, who's been working in food services, she doesn't have a lot of room to spare. Those of us who have been fortunate, we do. And we're not talking about going to punitive rates that would somehow inhibit you from wanting to be part of a startup or work hard to be successful. We're talking about going back to the rates that existed as recently as in the nineties, when, as I recall, Silicon Valley was doing pretty good and well-to-

do people were doing pretty well. And it turns out, in fact, during that period, the rich got richer. The middle class expanded. People rose out of poverty, because everybody was doing well.

So this is not an issue of do we somehow try to punish those who have done well. That's the last thing we want to do. It's a question of how can we afford to continue to make the investments that are going to propel American forward.

If we don't improve our education system, for example, we will all fall behind. We will all fall behind. That's just—that's a fact. And the truth is, is that on every indicator—from college graduation rates to math and science scores—we are slipping behind other developed countries. And that's going to have an impact in terms of, if you're a startup, are you going to be able to find enough engineers? It's going to have an impact in terms of, is the infrastructure here good enough that you can move products to market? It's going to have an impact on your ability to recruit top talent from around the world. And so we all have an investment in improving our education system.

Now, money is not going to solve the entire problem. That's why we've initiated reforms like Race to the Top that says we're going to have higher standards for everybody. We're going to not just have kids taught to the test, but we're going to make sure that we empower teachers, but we're also going to hold them accountable and improve how we train our principals and our teachers. So we're willing to make a whole bunch of reforms, but at some point, money makes a difference. If we don't have enough science teachers in the classroom, we're going to have problems. Somebody has got to pay for it.

And right now we've got the lowest tax rates we've had since the 1950s. And some of the Republican proposals would take it back—as a percentage of GDP—back to where we were back in the 1920s. You can't have a modern industrial economy like that.

So I appreciate your sentiment. I appreciate the fact that you recognize we're in this thing together. We're not on our own. And those of us who've been successful, we've always got to remember that.

Q. I know a lot of people in that same situation, and every one of them has said to me that they would support an increase in their taxes, so please.

The President. Well, we're going to get to work. Thank you.

Mr. Weiner. Thank you. Thank you for your question.

Global Competitiveness/Education

Next question was submitted to the LinkedIn group; it actually comes from a LinkedIn employee named Theresa Sullivan. It's a two-part question:

"First, do you think our public education system and our unemployment rates are related? And second, what, if any, overhaul in education is necessary to get Americans ready for the jobs of tomorrow, rather than the jobs of 20 years ago?"

The President. There is no doubt that there is a connection, long term, between our economic success, our productivity, and our education system. That's indisputable. When we were at our peak in terms of growth, back in the sixties and the seventies, in large part it was because we were doing a better job of training our workforce than anybody else in the world.

Now the rest of the world has caught up or is catching up. They're hungry. And as I said before, we are slipping behind a lot of developed countries. So our proportion of college graduates has not gone up, while everybody else's has gone up. Our proportion of high school graduates has not gone up, while everybody else's has gone up. And if you've got a billion Chinese and Indians and Eastern Europeans, all who are entering into a labor force and are becoming more skilled, and we are just sitting on the status quo, we're going to have problems.

Now, what can we do? This is a decade-long project; it's not a 1-year project. And we've been pushing since we came into office to look at the evidence, to base reforms on what actually works. The single most important ingredient in improving our schools is making sure we've got great teachers in front of the—in front of every classroom.

And so what we've said is, let's make sure that we've hired enough teachers, let's train them effectively, let's pay them a good wage, let's make sure that we're putting a special emphasis on recruiting more math and science teachers—where STEM education is an area where we've fallen significantly behind. Let's make sure they're accountable, but lets also give them flexibility in the classroom so that they don't have to do a cookie-cutter, teach-to-the-test approach that squashes their creativity and prevents them from engaging students. But at the end of the year, let's make sure that they're doing a good job. And if there are teachers out there who are not doing a good job, let's work to retrain them. And if they're not able to be retrained, then we should probably find them a different line of work. We've got to have top-flight principals and leadership inside the schools. That makes a big difference.

We've also got to focus on—there are some schools that are just dropout factories where less than half of the kids end up graduating. A lot of them, the students are Black and Brown, but that's also the demographic that's growing the fastest in this country. So if we don't fix those schools, we're going to have problems. So we've said to every State, you know what, focus on the lowest performing schools and tell us what your game plan is to improve those schools' performance.

And it may be that we've got to also, in some cases, rethink how we get students interested in learning. IBM is engaged in a really interesting experience in New York where they're essentially setting up schools—similar to the concept I was talking about with community colleges—where they're saying to kids pretty early on—I think as early as eighth grade—we're going to design a program—IBM worked with the New York public schools to design a program—and this is not for the kids who are in the top 1 percent, this is for ordinary public school kids. You follow this program, you work hard, IBM will hire you at the end of this process. And it suddenly gives kids an incentive. They say, oh, the reason I'm studying math and science is there's a practical outcome here. I will have a job. And there are practical applications to what I'm doing in the classroom.

And that's true at high-end jobs, but it's also true—we want to do more to train skilled workers even if they don't have a 4-year degree. It may be that the more the concept of apprenticeship and the concept of a rigorous vocational approach is incorporated in the high schools so the kids can actually see a direct connection to what they're learning and a potential career, they're less likely to drop out, and we're going to see more success.

So one last point I'll make about this is George Bush actually was sincere, I think, in trying to improve the education system across the country through something called No Child Left Behind, that said we're going to impose standards, there's going to be accountability; if schools don't meet those standards we're going to label them as failures, and they're going to have to make significant changes. The intent was good. It wasn't designed as well as it could have been. In some cases, States actually lowered their own standards to make sure that they weren't labeled as failures. There wasn't enough assistance given to these schools to meet the ambitious goals that had been set.

So what we've said is, look, we'll provide States some waivers to get out from under No Child Left Behind if you can provide us with a plan to make sure that children are going to be college and career ready. And we'll give you more flexibility, but we're still going to hold you accountable, and we will provide you the tools and best practices that allow you to succeed.

So last point I'll make on this, there is also a cultural component to this, though. We, as a country, have to recognize that all of us are going to have to up our game and we, as parents, have to instill in our kids a sense of educational excellence. We've got to turn off the TV set. I know it's dangerous to say in Silicon Valley, but put away the video games sometimes and all the electronics unless it's school related. And we've just got to get our kids more motivated

and internalizing that sense of the importance of learning.

And if we don't do that, we're going to continue to slip behind, even if some of these school reform approaches that we're taking are successful.

Mr. Weiner. Thank you, Theresa.

National Economy/Unemployment Insurance Benefits

Our next question comes from LinkedIn member Robert Holly who is joining us from Charlotte, North Carolina. After a promising career in financial services, Robert was, unfortunately, recently laid off. Robert, what is your question?

Q. Good morning, Mr. President.

The President. Good morning.

Q. As Jeff mentioned, I have a 22-year, very successful career in IT management, but I find myself displaced. And not only that, I look at the statistics for unemployment: 16.7 percent for African Americans. My question would be—and not just for the African Americans, but also for other groups that are also suffering—what would be your statement of encouragement for those who are looking for work today?

The President. What I would say is just that given your track record, given your history, seeing you stand here before this group, you're going to be successful. You've got a leg up on a lot of folks. You've got skills, you've got experience, you've got a track record of success. Right now your challenge is not you, it's the economy as a whole. And by the way, this is not just an American challenge, this is happening worldwide.

I hope everybody understands our biggest problem right now—part of the reason that this year, where at the beginning of the year, economists had estimated, and financial analysts had estimated, that the economy was going to be growing at about 3.5 percent, and that has not happened—in part has to do with what happened in the Middle East and the Arab Spring, which disrupted energy prices and caused consumers to have to pull back because gas was getting so high; what's happening in

Europe, which they have not fully healed from the crisis back in 2007 and never fully dealt with all the challenges their banking system faced. It's now being compounded by what's happening in Greece. So they're going through a financial crisis that is scaring the world. And they're trying to take responsible actions, but those actions haven't been quite as quick as they need to be.

So the point is, is that economies all around the world are not growing as fast as they need to. And since the world is really interconnected, that affects us as well. The encouraging thing for you is that when the economy gets back on track in the ways that it should, you are going to be prepared to be successful. The challenge is making sure that you hang in between now and then.

That's why things like unemployment insurance, for example, are important. And part of our jobs act is to maintain unemployment insurance. It's not a end all, be all, but it helps folks meet their basic challenges. And by the way, it also means that they're spending that money and they're recirculating that into the economy, so it's good for businesses generally.

Some of the emergency measures that we've been taking and we've proposed to take help to bridge the gap to where the economy is more fully healed. And historically, after financial crises, recessions are deeper, and they last longer than after the usual business cycle recessions.

So I guess the main message I have for you is the problem is not you, the problem is the economy as a whole. You are going to be well equipped to succeed and compete in this global economy once it's growing again. My job is to work with everybody I can—from the business community to Congress to not-for-profits, you name it—to see if we can speed up this process of healing and this process of recovery.

And in the meantime, we will make sure that things like unemployment insurance that are there to help people during tough times like this are going to continue to be available. And if there are—since you're in IT, if there are areas where you need to be sharpening your skills, as the young lady here mentioned,

we are going to make sure that the resource is available for you to be able to go back to school and do that.

Thank you.

Mr. Weiner. Thank you. That was our last question. We're going to begin to wrap it up, and before I turn it over to you for some concluding remarks, I just wanted to say thank you and let you know how much we appreciate the work that you're doing. I know I speak for a lot of people when I say I can't think of anything more important than creating economic opportunity when it comes to profoundly and sustainably improving the quality of an individual's life, the lives of their family members, the lives of the people that they in turn can create jobs for.

And in hard-hit American cities and developing countries around the world, these folks are creating role models for the next generation of entrepreneurs and professionals that didn't even know it was possible.

So on behalf of myself, on behalf of our visionary founder, Reid Hoffman, without whom none of this would have been possible, on behalf of our employees, of course, our members, on behalf of our country, thank you, Mr. President.

The President. Well, the—thank you so much. Thank you. Well, let me just say these have been terrific questions, and I so appreciate all of you taking the time to do this. I appreciate LinkedIn helping to host this. And for those of you who are viewing, not in this circle, but around the country, maybe around the world, I appreciate the chance to share these ideas with you.

Look, we're going through a very tough time. But the one thing I want to remind everybody is that we've gone through tougher times before. And the trajectory, the trend of not just this country, but also the world economy, is one that's more open, one that's more linked, one that offers greater opportunity, but also one that has some hazards. If we don't prepare our people with the skills that they need to compete, we're going to have problems. If we don't make sure that we continue to have the best infrastructure in the world, we're going to have problems. If we're not continuing to invest in basic research, we're going to have challenges. If we don't get our fiscal house in order in a way that is fair and equitable so that everybody feels like they have responsibilities to not only themselves and their family, but also to the country that's given them so much opportunity, we're going to have problems.

And so I am extraordinarily confident about America's long-term future. But we are going to have to make some decisions about how we move forward. And what's striking to me is, when we're out of Washington and I'm just talking to ordinary folks, I don't care whether they're Republicans or Democrats, people are just looking for common sense. The majority of people agree with the prescriptions I just offered. The majority of people by a wide margin think we should be rebuilding our infrastructure. The majority of folks by a wide margin think that we should be investing in education. The majority of people by a wide margin think we should be investing in science and technology. And the majority of people think by a wide margin that we should be maintaining programs like Social Security and Medicare to provide a basic safety net.

The majority of people by a significant margin think that the way we should close our deficit is a balance of cutting out those things that we don't need, but also making sure that we've got a Tax Code that's fair and everybody is paying their fair share.

So the problem is not outside of Washington. The problem is, is that things have gotten so ideologically driven and everybody is so focused on the next election and putting party ahead of country that we're not able to solve our problems. And that's got to change. And that's why your voices are going to be so important.

The reason I do these kinds of events is I want you to hear from me directly. I want to hear from you directly, but I also want your voices heard in the Halls of Congress. I need everybody here to be speaking out on behalf of the things that you care about and the values that made this country great and to say to folks who you've elected, say to them, we expect you to act responsibly and not act in terms of short-term political interest. Act in terms of what's going to be good for all of us over the long term.

If that spirit, which all of you represent, starts asserting itself all across the country, then I'm absolutely confident the 21st century is going to be the American century just like the 20th century was.

So thank you very much everybody. God bless you.

Mr. Weiner. Thank you, everybody.

The President. Thank you.

NOTE: The President spoke at 10:58 a.m. at the Computer History Museum. In his remarks, he referred to Warren E. Buffett, chief executive officer and chairman, Berkshire Hathaway Inc.; and his mother-in-law Marian Robinson.

Remarks at a Democratic National Committee Fundraiser in La Jolla, California
September 26, 2011

The President. It's wonderful to see you all. Please have a seat. To Liz and Mason, thank you so much for the wonderful introduction. Along with the Phelps, I have to acknowledge my dear, dear friend Christine Forester, who has just been—I was just reminded by our staff this was actually the first fundraiser that I did in this home after I announced in Springfield, Illinois.

So these are some early, early supporters, back when a lot of folks still could not pronounce my name. [*Laughter*] And they have been there ever since, and I could not be more grateful to them. And I could not be more grateful to you. In fact, some of you were in that first fundraiser, weren't you?

Audience member. Yes!

The President. You will recall that I had no gray hair then. [*Laughter*] Do you remember that? Michelle says otherwise I've held up pretty well. [*Laughter*]

In addition to Liz and Mason and Christine, I just want to acknowledge we've got a couple of wonderful Members of Congress here. First of all, Jared Polis is here. Where is Jared? And I'm not sure if he's made it yet from the airport.

Audience member. Yes!

The President. Has he? Bob Filner is in the house. Where is Bob? There he is. Thank you.

Well, I want this mostly to be a conversation rather than a monologue, so I'm going to make some very brief remarks at the top, and then I just want to open it up for questions and conversation.

The last 2½ years have honestly been as tough for America as any 2½ years that we've seen in our lifetimes: the worst financial crisis since the Great Depression, a withering recession that followed. And a lot of folks here in San Diego, here in California, and all across the country, are still struggling, still having a very tough time. And I see it every day. I get letters from people all across the country. I meet people at events, and they've lost their homes, or they've lost their jobs, or they are trying to figure out whether they have to defer retirement in order to make sure that their kids can go to college. And some of these stories are heartbreaking.

But what we've said from the start, what you committed to back in 2008, was a belief that there's nothing that can stop America when we are working together, when we're willing to share opportunity and share sacrifice, when we're willing to think beyond the short term to the kind of America that we're passing on to the next generation. We cannot be stopped. We've been through tougher times before, and we always emerged stronger and more unified.

And I believe that we are in one of those moments that are testing out character, that are testing our unity, but if we make good decisions, there is no reason why we won't emerge stronger from this moment as well.

Now, during the past 2½ years, obviously, we've had a lot to do. We had to yank the country out of a potential depression. We had to stabilize a world financial system. And along the way, what we've tried to do is to keep the commitments and the promises that we made back in 2007, 2008: so whether it was the first bill that I signed, the Lilly Ledbetter bill to make sure that women are getting paid the same for the same day's work; or making sure that we're expanding college opportunities by cutting out the middleman and putting an extra $60 billion into the student loan and the Pell grant programs; or making sure that in a country as wealthy as ours nobody should go bankrupt because they get sick and passing health care reform so that 30 million Americans are going to be able to get health care and everybody is going to be treated properly by their insurance companies; or passing tough financial regulations to make sure we don't have the kind of meltdown we saw on Wall Street again and that consumers are protected; ending "don't ask, don't tell" so that anybody can serve your country regardless of who they love; bringing 100,000 troops back from Iraq and ending that war.

Over the last 2½ years, even as we've been grappling with this economy, even as we've been saving the auto industry and making sure that we've got an energy policy that makes sense, we've still have been trying to make sure that we're also dealing with some of the long-term problems that have been building up for decades. And we've got more work to do. We're not yet finished.

Obviously, the economy is first and foremost in everybody's minds. And a couple of weeks back, I put forward what we call the "American Jobs Act," that says at a time when because of all sorts of headwinds—Europe and high gas prices because of what happened in the Arab Spring—we've got to redouble our efforts to people back to work.

And so this "American Jobs Act" says, at a time when we have to rebuild our infrastructure to be competitive in the 21st century and we've got all these construction workers who are out of work, let's put them to work rebuilding our roads and our bridges and our schools and laying our broadband lines and making sure that—[*applause*]. Let's put teachers back in the classroom at a time when we know that nothing is more important for lasting employment than an education. Let's give businesses more incentives to hire our veterans and long-term unemployed. And let's keep taxes low for small businesses, and let's make sure that taxes don't go up for middle class families at a time when they're still very strained and very stressed.

And we pay for it, because——

[*At this point, a phone rang.*]

The President. Who's that calling? [*Laughter*] That may be Boehner calling. [*Laughter*]

Audience member. Hang up! [*Laughter*]

The President. Because even as we have to restart our economic engines—and the most important thing we can do for our deficit is growing the economy and putting folks back to work. But what is also true is for decades Washington was not living within its means. We were making a series of irresponsible decisions about how we spend money and how we raise revenue.

And so what I said was, not only will we put a jobs act that puts a couple million people back to work, and it's estimated it will raise our GDP by a couple of percent, but we can also pay for it in a responsible way, building off the work we did this summer, which is, we made some judicious cuts spread out over 10 years so it doesn't impact our recovery, but we've cut a trillion dollars from the budget. We're proposing that we can actually find an additional half a billion dollars in savings, making some modest modifications to Medicare and Medicaid to bend the cost curve, but not in a way that hurts beneficiaries. And once we've done that, we've also got to make sure that we've got a Tax Code that is fair and in which everybody does their fair share.

Now, the other side has already taken out the playbook and said, oh, that's class warfare.

What I've said is this is a very simple principle that everybody should understand: Warren Buffett's secretary shouldn't pay a lower [higher]° tax rate than Warren Buffett. A teacher making $50,000 a year or a firefighter making $50,000 a year or $60,000 shouldn't be paying a higher tax rate than somebody making $50 million a year. And that basic principle of fairness, if applied to our Tax Code, could raise enough money that not only do we pay for our jobs bill, but we also stabilize our debt and deficits for the next decade. And as I said when I made the announcement, this is not politics, this is math. [*Laughter*]

Now, the challenge we face in the short term is trying to get Congress to act. So when you leave here today I want you out there advocating for us putting people back to work and paying for it in a responsible way. But more is at stake in 2012 than just the short term. What's also at stake is the long term. For all the good work that we've done over the last 2½ years, we still have a lot of work to do to make sure that this is an economy in which middle class folks, if they are working, they can make it and that people who aspire to be in the middle class are going to be able to succeed.

That means we have to build on the education reforms that we've already initiated to make college more affordable. We still have not done enough to have an energy policy that frees ourselves from dependence on foreign oil. We've done a lot. We've doubled fuel efficiency standards on cars, probably the biggest impact in environmental action over the last 30 years. But we're still wasting too much energy that we can't afford to waste in this new environment.

We still have to implement health care reform, and we've got a whole bunch of folks who would like to see it reversed, because it has been an ideological litmus test, not because it's not working. Already we've got a couple million young people who have health insurance who didn't have it before, and we haven't even fully implemented it yet, because part of our health care reform was allowing the young

---

° White House correction.

people to stay on their parents' health insurance. And it has made a huge difference.

Internationally, we have to continue to bring our troops home from Afghanistan. We've got to make sure that we are leading not just with our military, but with diplomacy and with the power of our example. We still have to reform our immigration system in a sensible way so that young people who are studying here and want to start a business here, we're not training them and then just sending them back home to their home countries. We want them to stay here and start those businesses. We still have to make investments in basic research and science.

And so a lot is at stake in this election, even more than in 2008. Now, this is going to be a tough election because the economy is tough and people are frustrated. And so we've got to understand what's at stake. There are two contrasting visions of where America needs to go. And one vision says that we've got to pull and abandon our commitments to the aging and the vulnerable, and we can't afford to invest in education the way we historically have, and we can't afford to rebuild our infrastructure. We're destined to having a smaller vision of what we can do together. And the other is a big, ambitious, bold, optimistic vision of an America in which we are investing in the future, we're investing in our people. We're mak-

ing certain that we're making the tough decisions to be competitive in the 21st century, and we're doing it in a way that is fair, that everybody shares in opportunity and everybody shares in responsibility. That's what's at stake.

Now, I'm absolutely confident that we're going to win because I think that's—I think the vision that we're putting forward is the one that ultimately America believes in. But they've got to be convinced. They've got to be persuaded. And I can't do it alone. You guys are my ambassadors. You guys are my advocates and my shock troops out there. [*Laughter*] And so I hope you are ready. If you show the same enthusiasm that you showed a little over three years ago, then I'm absolutely confident that America's future is bright.

Thank you very much, everybody.

NOTE: The President spoke at 2:42 p.m. at the residence of Elizabeth and Mason Phelps. In his remarks, he referred to Christine Forester, private member, President's Committee on the Arts and the Humanities; Speaker of the House of Representatives John A. Boehner; and Warren E. Buffett, chief executive officer and chairman, Berkshire Hathaway Inc. Audio was not available for verification of the content of these remarks.

Statement on the Death of Wangari Muta Maathai
September 26, 2011

It is with great sadness that I learned of the passing of Professor Wangari Maathai. On behalf of all Americans, Michelle and I send our deepest condolences to Professor Maathai's family and the people of Kenya at this difficult time. The world mourns with you and celebrates the extraordinary life of this remarkable woman who devoted her life to peacefully protecting what she called "our common home and future."

The work of the Green Belt Movement stands as a testament to the power of grassroots organizing, proof that one person's simple idea—that a community should come together to plant trees—can make a difference, first in one village, then in one nation, and now

across Africa. Professor Maathai's tireless efforts earned her not only a Nobel Peace Prize and numerous prestigious awards, but the respect of millions who were inspired by her commitment to conservation, democracy, women's empowerment, the eradication of poverty, and civic engagement. Professor Maathai further advanced these objectives through her service in the Kenyan Government, the African Union, and the United Nations. As she told the world, "We must not tire, we must not give up, we must persist." Her legacy will stand as an example to all of us to persist in our pursuit of progress.

Remarks at a Democratic National Committee Fundraiser in West Hollywood, California
September 26, 2011

The President. Hello, L.A.! Thank you. Thank you, everybody.

Audience members. Four more years! Four more years! Four more years!

The President. Thank you. It's good to be back in sunny California. It is wonderful to be with all of you.

I've got a few people I just want to introduce real quick. First of all, thank you, Jesse, for the wonderful introduction. I was telling him Michelle and the girls love them some "Modern Family." They love that show. In addition, we've got the outstanding Lieutenant Governor of California, Gavin Newsom, in the house. West Hollywood Mayor John Duran is here. We've got—we must have some Members of Congress here.

Audience members. [*Inaudible*]

*The President.*Well, there you go: Dennis—where? Hey, how are you? [*Laughter*] I want to thank——

Audience member. The Christian God is the one and only true and living God, the Creator of heaven and the universe. Jesus Christ is God. Jesus Christ is God. Jesus Christ is the Son of God. Jesus Christ is the Son of God. You are an antichrist——

Audience members. Boo! Four more years! Four more years! Four more years!

[*At this point, the disruptive audience member was escorted from the room.*]

The President. Is that his jacket? Is that his jacket? Is that his jacket?

First of all, I agree Jesus Christ is the Lord. I believe in that. I do have a question though. I think the young man may have left his jacket. [*Laughter*] So make sure, make sure that he gets his jacket.

Audience member. That's mine.

The President. Oh, that's yours? Hold on, hold on, hold on. It's hers. [*Laughter*] And I think somebody's car keys are in there too. See, we're having all kinds of confusion here. Oh, goodness gracious. There you go. All right,

I wasn't sure. Don't leave your jacket around like that. [*Laughter*]

Audience member. We were waiting for you.

The President. Well, listen, all right, where was I? It is good to be back in L.A. Now, here's the reason I'm here——

Audience member. We love you!

The President. I love you back. That's one good reason. [*Laughter*] But the other reason is I think back to 2008, and that night in Grant Park, it—you would have thought it was L.A. I mean, it was November, but it was warm and it was gorgeous. And people were full of hope.

And I said to you then something I want to remind you of. I said, this is not the end, this is just the beginning. I said that we were going to have some steep hills to climb. We had a lot of work to do, because the challenges that we are facing are ones that had been building up for decades and culminated in 2007 and 2008 in the worst financial crisis that we've seen in our lifetimes.

Now, we didn't know how deep that recession was going to be. But we understood then that there was something different going on here: that for ordinary people all across America, for working families all across America, for the middle class all across America, we had grown up with the belief that if you worked hard, if you met your responsibilities, if you looked after your family, if you did a good job, if you were a responsible member of your community, then you could get ahead. That America was a place—that the idea of America was captured by this notion that if you tried hard here, you could always make it; that you were only bound by the size of your dreams, and that if you did the right thing, there was no reason why you couldn't afford to have a home and have health care that protected you in case you got sick; that you could send your kids to college so they can do even better than you did; that you would be able to retire with some dignity and some respect, maybe take a vacation once in a while.

And you know, for the last decade, it felt like that compact, that bond, that contract that we made with each other had been broken and that too many people were not being treated fairly, that the rules had changed, that the deck kept being stacked against ordinary Americans. And what made it worse was nobody in Washington seemed to care. Nobody in Washington seemed to be doing anything about it.

And this all culminated in the crisis of 2007 and 2008. And we knew that because this crisis had taken years to build up, it was going to take some years to fix. So the question we have to face now is not whether people are hurting. Everybody knows that America has gone through a very difficult time and there are folks all across California and all across the country that are still struggling: our friends, our neighbors, maybe some people in this audience.

I get letters every day from people all across the country who have lost their job, lost their homes, maybe they're having to defer retirement so they can keep their kid in college. And they're worried about the future. It's not just the short term they're worried about. They're worried about whether we can come together and make tough decisions to solve our problems so that we are setting a foundation for years to come, for the next generation, so that we can return to that notion that anybody here, no matter where you come from, no matter what you look like, you can make it if you try. That is what we've been fighting for.

So yes, we're going through tough times. But the question is, where are we going to go next? We can go back to the old, worn-out ideas that the other side has been talking about——

Audience members. No! Boo!

The President. ——where you basically let corporations write their own rules and we dismantle environmental regulations and we dismantle labor regulations and we cut taxes for folks who don't need it and weren't even asking for it, and then we say to you, you know what, you're on your own, good luck, because you're not going to get any help. Nobody is going to give you a hand up. Nobody is going to help kids who have the talent and the will and the

drive to do well, but maybe just haven't had the opportunity yet.

That's one vision of America. But that's not the vision that we fought for in 2008. That's not the vision you believe in. It's not the vision I believe in. And I am confident that is not the vision that America believes in. And that's what this campaign is going to be all about.

What this election is about is whether everybody gets a fair shake and everybody does their fair share. And that's what I've been fighting for since I got to Washington.

Audience member. Thank you!

The President. When—and by the way, we have not been getting any help from the other side. When we wanted to save the U.S. auto industry from collapse—and a million jobs might have been lost, iconic companies gone, our manufacturing base eroded—you had a whole bunch of other folks who said that it was going to be a waste of time and a waste of money.

Well, you know what we did? We did it anyway. We fixed it anyway, and we saved those jobs. And we made sure taxpayers got their money back. And today, the American auto industry is stronger than ever and turning a profit, and they're making fuel-efficient cars that can help save our environment. That's a fight that is worth—[*applause*]—that is a fight that is worth it.

When we wanted to pass Wall Street reform to make sure that we didn't go through the same kind of crisis that we went through in 2007, 2008, and make sure that consumers finally get some protection so you're not cheated when you apply for a mortgage and you're not having hidden fees in your credit cards, the lobbyists and the special interests, they rounded up millions of dollars to fight us. But you know what? We did it anyway because it was the right thing to do. And today, you don't have to suffer from hidden fees and unfair rate hikes, because we knew that we were on the right side of that fight.

Most Republicans voted against it, but we were able to cut $60 billion—$60 billion—that previously was going to banks as middlemen for the student loan program. And we said, why do we need a middleman? Let's take that

$60 billion and let's give that to young people in the form of Pell grants and scholarships and student loans that are cheaper, so that they're not loaded up with debt and they've got opportunity. And as a consequence, right now, all across the country, there are millions of young people that are benefiting. And we could not have done it if you guys hadn't helped to put me into office. That's a fact.

First bill I signed, very simple principle. First bill I signed, it says, you know what, an equal day's pay for an equal day's work. Because I don't want my daughters treated any different than somebody else's sons. I want them to be treated equally in this country. And while we were at it, we appointed two brilliant Supreme Court Justices, who happen to be women, because we thought they'd do a pretty good job, and they have. [*Laughter*]

See, not only did we fight for a vision of an economy that was fair, but also a society that was fair. And that's the reason we fought so hard and finally were able to repeal "don't ask, don't tell." Because we don't think that you should not be able to serve the country you love just because of the person that you love.

And along the way, we happened to also pass health care reform so that nobody in America goes broke because they get sick. So insurance companies can't drop your coverage for no good reason, and going forward, they won't be able to deny you coverage because of a preexisting condition. Think about what that means for women: breast cancer, cervical cancer, no longer a prohibition on you getting insurance because of a preexisting condition. No longer can they charge you higher rates just because you're the one who has to go through childbirth.

And while it will take a couple of years for us to fully reform the health care system, right now almost 1 million young adults across the country have health insurance because they're able to stay on their parent's plan because of the health care reform bill that we passed. The Affordable Care Act is working, and it's working because you guys helped it to pass Congress.

Now, L.A., all of these were tough fights.

Audience member. Don't forget medical marijuana!

The President. Thank you for that. [*Laughter*]

Now, listen, we've still got a long way to go. We've got a lot of work to do to make sure that every American has a shot at success. And that's where I need your help. I've got some short-term stuff we've got to do, and we've got some longer term stuff we've got to do.

In the short term, a couple of weeks ago, I introduced the "American Jobs Act." Now, we all know that even though we may have averted a depression, for a lot of folks out there who have been looking for work for 3 months, for 6 months, for 9 months, it feels like a depression, and they need help.

And so what we said was, look, let us right now focus on putting Americans to work doing the work that America needs done. Let's make sure that construction workers who have been laid off, let's put them back to work rebuilding our roads and our bridges and our schools. America used to have the best infrastructure. That's what made us an economic superpower. And right now we've got millions of folks who are out of work and ready to get on the job, let's put them back to work right now rebuilding America. Pass the jobs bill. I need your help to tell Congress to pass this jobs bill right now.

Audience members. Pass the bill! Pass the bill! Pass the bill!

The President. And by the way, by the way, these are ideas that are traditionally Republican and Democratic ideas. Republicans used to love to build stuff. [*Laughter*] I don't know where suddenly they decide that's a Democratic idea. [*Laughter*]

I don't want the newest airports, the newest high-speed rail lines built in China and Singapore and Europe. Let's build them right here in America. [*Applause*] Let's build them right here in America.

But the jobs bill doesn't just talk about building stuff. Look, in South Korea right now they are hiring teachers in droves because they understand that if we're going to be successful in a 21st-century economy, then we've got to make sure our kids are trained. And yet here in

America, we're laying off teachers in droves right here in California. It doesn't make any sense. It's unfair to our kids. It is unfair to our future. And if we pass this jobs bill, we can put teachers back in the classroom where they belong. Pass this jobs bill!

Tell Congress to pass this bill so companies are getting tax credits for hiring our veterans. The idea that they suspend their careers, leave their families, are over there putting themselves in harm's way for our safety and security, and they've got to come back here and fight to get a job, it's wrong. It's got to change. And passing this bill will help change it. Pass this bill!

The "American Jobs Act" cuts taxes for virtually every worker in America. It cuts taxes for small businesses all across America. It gives an extra tax credit if small businesses hire a new worker or give a worker a raise. Congress and the Republicans are always talking about how much they love job creators. Do something for job creators. Pass this bill and give them the tax breaks that will help them grow their business and hire more workers.

Now, when you—as I said, these are ideas that in the past have been supported by Democrats and Republicans. So when you ask Republicans, well, why not pass it, they say, well, we think it's got to be paid for. Well, I agree. It's true. We've got a deficit. We've got debt. We've got to pay for it, which is why I put forward a very clear plan to pay for it. I said, look, we have already made cuts of a trillion dollars this summer, spread out over 10 years. We can get rid of programs that don't work. There is some waste in Government that we have identified and eliminated. We're proposing an additional half billion—half a trillion dollars in cuts, but we can't just cut our way out of this problem. We've got to have some revenue. And the question is, how do we do that?

Now, I've got a very simple principle, if we reform our Tax Code, we can make sure everybody pays their fair share. And the principle that we should be putting forward is Warren Buffett's secretary shouldn't pay a higher tax rate than Warren Buffett. And by the way, Warren Buffett agrees with me.

I've been incredibly blessed. I shouldn't be paying a lower effective rate than a teacher or a firefighter or a construction worker. And they sure shouldn't be paying a higher tax rate than somebody pulling in $50 million a year. It's not fair, and it's not right. And it's got to change.

Now, let me be clear, nobody wants to punish success. Part of what makes America great is you have a great idea, you have this extraordinary talent, you start a business, you provide a service, and it works out, and you do well. That is good. That is exactly what America is all about. We want to promote that all across the country.

But remember, your success didn't come on your own. There was a teacher somewhere out there who helped to provide you the knowledge you needed to learn. We're in this together. And the question is, how do we make sure that we're going to be creating the same kind of America that allows the next generation to succeed. And so we've got to make some choices, and we've got to decide what are we willing to pay for and make sure that those of us who have benefited the most, that we're giving something back: a fair share for everybody.

That's not class warfare. Republicans are going around talking about, well, that's class warfare. You know what, if asking a billionaire to pay the same tax rate as a plumber is class warfare, then sign me up. [*Applause*] Sign me up. I'll wear that charge as a badge of honor.

The only warfare I've seen waged is against the middle class in this family and ordinary families. So this is about priorities. It's about choices. Are we going to keep tax breaks and loopholes for oil companies that are making record profits?

Audience members. No!

The President. Or are we going to put teachers back in the classroom?

Audience members. Yes!

The President. Are we going to ask millionaires and billionaires to pay a little bit more of their fair share in order to make sure that we're rebuilding America, which by the way, they benefit from and businesses benefit from and makes us more competitive? Are we going to ask seniors who are barely getting by to pay thousands of dollars more in Medicare?

Audience members. No!

The President. Or are we going to ask a corporation that's made record profits and is getting tax breaks that some small business isn't getting, do your fair share?

So this is about who we are as a nation. This is about our values. This is about our priorities. And that's what this debate is about right now. That's what's at stake right now. This notion that the only way that we can restore prosperity is if we strip away all these regulations, and have dirtier air, and eliminate consumer safety laws, and let the banks do whatever they want, and somehow that's going to create jobs. We tried that, you remember? We tried that for 10 years. It didn't work.

So we've got a different vision about how we go forward, and it's a vision that's grounded in the history and the story of America. Yes, we're rugged individualists. Yes, we are self-reliant. We're not looking for a handout. We know we've got to work hard. We know we've got to instill in our kids a sense of responsibility and hard work and achievement. That's how the American Dream is built. But we also know that we've always been a nation that looks out for one another, a belief that we're all connected, that there are some things we can only do as a nation. That is not a Democratic or a Republican idea. It's the idea of Abraham Lincoln when he built the interstate—or the intercontinental railroad. It was the idea of Dwight Eisenhower when he helped to build the Interstate Highway System. When those two Republican Presidents invested in land-grant colleges or the space program, there are some things we can't do on our own. There are some things we do together.

And that's why this country gave millions of returning heroes, including my grandfather, the opportunity to study on the GI bill. Because they understood, you know what, if they succeed, then everybody succeeds. If ordinary folks have an education, if they've got a shot, then everybody has got a shot. Businesses will do well. The wealthy will do well. People will

rise out of poverty. That's the story of America. That's what we're fighting for.

Los Angeles, we built this Nation together, this Nation, indivisible, with liberty and justice for all and responsibilities to each other. And we've got to meet our responsibilities now.

Some people in Congress may think that the only way to settle our differences is wait till the next election. I've got news for them. The next election is 14 months away, and a lot of folks out there can't wait. A lot of people out there can't wait. They're living paycheck to paycheck, day to day. They need help now. And that's why we need to pass this jobs bill now. And I'm going to need your help. [*Applause*] I'm going to need your help.

We need to work short term, and we're going to need to work long term. Because after we pass this jobs bill, we're still going to have work to do. We're still going to have to reform our education system. We're still going to have to make sure that we've got an immigration system in this country that is fair and, yes, secures our borders, but also makes sure that folks who are here aren't living in the shadows. We've still got to make sure that we have an energy policy that is smart for our pocketbooks and frees ourselves from dependence on foreign oil and make sure that we're doing something about climate change.

So we've got a lot more work to do, and I can't do it without you. I know that, over the last 2½ years, sometimes you've gotten tired. I know sometimes you've gotten discouraged. I know that. I know it's been tough. But——

Audience member. Thank you for my Social Security check!

The President. You're welcome. [*Laughter*] But look, here's the thing: I never promised you easy. If you wanted easy, you wouldn't have campaigned for Barack Hussein Obama. [*Laughter*] What I promised was that there was a vision of America out there that we believed in. What I promised was that if we worked hard, we could achieve that vision. What I promised was that I would wake up every single day fighting for you and thinking about you and thinking about how we can expand opportunity and make America more competitive. And there were going to be set-backs, and there were going to be challenges. And there were going to be some folks who are fighting us every inch of the way. And trying to change how Washington works, given the bad habits it's gotten into, was going to be more than a notion. But what I said was if you're willing to stick with me, if you're willing to hang in there, then I was positive that we could achieve our dreams.

Because America has been through tougher times. We have been through tougher times, and we have always been able to get through them when we work together; when we remind ourselves that America and its idea is not a giv-en, it's something that we have to fight for, we have to work for, we have to strive for. When we remember that, and when we turn to the person next to us and we say, you know what, that too is something that's not out of reach,

that if you and I are willing to work together, we can make it happen—that's what our campaign in 2008 was about. That's what the campaign in 2012 will be about.

And so if all of you are in, if all of you are in, if all of you are in, if all of you are in, if all of you are in, if all of you are willing to press on with me, I promise you, I promise you, we will remind the world why America is the greatest nation on Earth.

God bless you, and God bless the United States of America. Thank you. Thank you.

NOTE: The President spoke at 6:19 p.m. at the House of Blues. In his remarks, he referred to actors Jesse Tyler Ferguson and Dennis D. Haysbert. The transcript was released by the Office of the President Secretary on September 27.

Remarks at a Democratic National Committee Fundraiser in West Hollywood
September 26, 2011

The President. Thank you, everybody. Thank you. Everybody, please have a seat. So let me begin by thanking Jeffrey and the entire host committee for helping to organize this. It is a remarkable group. There are a lot of friends here who have been with us since the beginning. Jon remembers me when I had no gray hair.

Audience member. You don't have gray hair. [*Laughter*]

The President. Well, come on. A lot of people here have just been dear, dear friends. And so I'm grateful for everything that you've done. And Jeffrey has been remarkable over the last couple of years, helping us consistently move an agenda forward that creates a more just and fair and more competitive America. So I really appreciate that.

I want to spend most of my time actually in dialogue as opposed to monologue. So I'm just going to make some brief comments at the top, and then I just want to open it up for questions, comments, suggestions, complaints, whatever the case may be. But before I do, I just want to acknowledge that you've got an

outstanding public servant who is working every single day on behalf of Californians, to make sure that this State continues to be a hallmark of the future for America, and that's Governor Jerry Brown. And I'm noticing Jerry is smart because he's sitting next to Eva. [*Laughter*] Nice going. How did you get that seat? [*Laughter*]

We've gone through an unprecedented time in our history. We have not seen anything like this in our lifetimes: a financial crisis that is as bad as anything since the Great Depression, followed by a recession that is deep and lasting and has hurt a lot of people. And my first job when I came to office was to make sure that we didn't tip into a depression, to save the auto industry, to make sure that we stabilized a financial system that was teetering on the brink of meltdown.

But what got me involved in this Presidential business, the reason that all of you supported me back in 2008, wasn't just to solve the crisis. It was a recognition that for decades the American people felt as if the rules had somehow changed on them; that there was an idea that if you worked hard, if you did the right thing—if you looked after your family, if you dedicated yourself to your business or your job, if you were a contributing member of your community—then you could achieve some measure of success. Not necessarily the kind of success that's reflected in this room. I think all of us would acknowledge that some of that has to do with luck and being in the right place at the right time. But you knew that you could have a home and secure a family and send your kids to college. There was this compact that said anybody in America could make it if they tried. You'd struggle sometimes, but you could make it.

And somewhere along the line people felt as if that compact got broken. And that happened long before this financial crisis hit. There are a lot of people all across the country who have done the right thing; they're having an incredibly difficult time. And the crisis compounded. In some ways, the crisis—the financial crisis, the recession—laid bare problems that had been building up for decades, whether it was an education system that wasn't teaching our children what they need to learn to be competitive in the 21st century; whether it was a health care system that was inefficient and left too many people exposed to potential bankruptcy if they got sick; whether it was an energy policy that made us dependent on the most unstable parts of the world and left our economy vulnerable to the spot oil market and was helping to destroy our environment in the process; whether it was a crumbling infrastructure, a system in Washington for keeping the books that involved a lot of money going out oftentimes to the best connected, folks with the lobbyists, the special interests, but also meant that those folks who were most powerful and best able to do it weren't having to pay their fair share of taxes.

People understood across the board that something wasn't right. And so what we did in 2008 was capture a moment in time where people said, we can do better than this. Now, for the last 2 years, we've done an awful lot. Sometimes—I've still got a list in my pocket of campaign promises I made. [*Laughter*] And I

keep on checking things off the list. Equal pay for equal work, first bill I signed. Ending "don't ask, don't tell," done. Health care that's affordable and accessible for every single American, made it happen. And already you've got—even though it's not fully implemented yet, we already have—there was just a report last week over a million young people could now have health insurance that didn't have it before, in part because they can stay on their parent's health care policy. They can actually afford it.

Ending the war in Iraq—100,000 out, there will be all out by the end of this year. A sense of respect around the world that we don't just project our power through our military, but also through our diplomacy, also through our values, through the power of our example.

So an awful lot of stuff we got done. But here's the challenge, is restoring that compact, restoring that sense that we're all in it together and everybody is doing their fair share, where we've got shared sacrifice and shared opportunity, that project is not yet complete. It's not finished.

And that's why we've got to work just as hard in the coming years as we did back in 2007, 2008. If anything, we've got to work harder. If anything, we've got to work harder, in part because it's not going to be as sexy. It's not going to be as new. I'm grayer, I'm all dinged up. [*Laughter*] And those old posters everybody has got in their closet—[*laughter*]—they're all dog eared and faded. [*Laughter*]

But mainly it's going to be hard because people are just tired. They're worn out. Jeffrey used the analogy of the ship. We've been driving through a storm. We had to try to keep this boat afloat through something that we haven't seen in our lifetimes. And people are weary and hurt. And so the energy of 2008 is going to have to be generated in a different way.

It has to be a clear contrast of where we want to take the country and where the other folks want to take the country. Because right now obviously a lot of folks are hurting. But if we can give them a sense of possibility that, as hard as it is, we can still get there, to a place where every kid in this country has a decent education and is equipped for the 21st-century economy, a global economy; if we can try to move forward and say we're going to have an immigration system that makes sense so that we're not sending incredibly talented kids back instead of having them invest in creating new businesses here in America, which has been always part of the American Dream, part of our history; if we can say, down the road, we're not going to wean ourselves completely off of fossil fuels, but if we're smart and we pursue energy efficiency and we put people back to work on clean-energy projects, we can do a lot better than we're doing right now, and over time, if we're investing in technology and we have faith in science, there's no reason why we can't help lead the world to a more sustainable place.

If we stay with it, there's no reason why we can't continue to help usher in democracy around the world in a way that is good for America, but also good for all those millions of young people out there who have finally said: "Enough, we don't want to live under the yoke of dictatorship, and we want opportunity. We want to have a life of possibility."

So there's a vision out there to be had, and we're going to have to drive towards it. Now, short term, what we need to do is just put people back to work. And that's why a couple of weeks ago, I said, pass this jobs bill now. We can put people to work rebuilding America, rebuilding our schools and our roads and our bridges. Construction workers are out of work. Contractors are begging for work; they're able to come on and finish a project on time and under budget. The interest rates are low. Now is the time to do it.

Let's put teachers back in the classroom. We've created over 2 million jobs over the last 18 months in the private sector. But in the public sector, because of budgets that Jerry knows a lot about, we're seeing layoffs of teachers and firefighters. Let's put those folks back to work doing those services that are vital to America's long-term success.

And we pay for it. And the way we pay for it is swallowing some very tough cuts that are necessary, but aren't endangering our economy right now because they're spread out over

10 years—that's what we agreed to this summer—but also saying that we've got to have some revenue and that revenue is going to have to come from us.

The fact of the matter is that Warren Buffett's secretary should not pay a higher tax rate than Warren Buffett. The fact is, is that we made it in part because somebody was paying for decent schools and somebody was paying for—somebody was paying for the research that went into DARPA that created the Internet that created the opportunity for Jeffrey to make a deal with Netflix. [*Laughter*] Somebody made those investments. And now it's our turn. We should be doing the same thing. And that's not class warfare, that's common sense.

Now, the other side has a very different idea about where to take this country. I urge all of you to watch some of these Republican debates. There's a different vision about who we are and what we stand for. And I think the American people want a big, optimistic, bold, generous vision of America, not a cramped vision that says, you're on your own.

But as hard as things have been over these last 2½ years, we're going to have to fight for it. We're going to have to fight for our vision. And I'm going to need your help, so don't get tired on me now. [*Laughter*]

This is when we're tested. We're in Hollywood right now, so think about the movies, the arc of the story. If things were just smooth the whole way through, not only is it a pretty dull movie, but it doesn't reflect our experience. It doesn't reflect life. Character is tested when things are hard. This country is being tested, but I have complete faith in its character. That's what this election is about. It's about values. It's about character. It's about who we are.

And if you're willing to fight with me for that, then I'm confident we're going to come out on the other side doing just fine.

Thank you.

NOTE: The President spoke at 8:16 p.m. at the Fig & Olive restaurant. In his remarks, he referred to Jeffrey Katzenberg, chief executive officer, DreamWorks Animation SKG; Jon

Landau, chief operating officer, Lightstorm Entertainment; actor Eva Longoria; and Warren E. Buffett, chief executive officer and chairman, Berkshire Hathaway Inc. The transcript was released by the Office of the President Secretary on September 27. Audio was not available for verification of the content of these remarks.

Remarks at Abraham Lincoln High School in Denver, Colorado
September 27, 2011

The President. Hello, Denver! What a beautiful day. Thank you so much. How's it going, Lancers? I hear the Lancers have a pretty good ball team. That's the story I've heard.

Well, listen, there are a couple of people here I want to acknowledge who are just outstanding public servants: First of all, a hometown hero who is now one of the best Secretaries of the Interior that we've ever had, Ken Salazar; one of the best Governors in the country, John Hickenlooper; two outstanding Senators, Mark Udall and Michael Bennet; Congresswoman Diana DeGette; Congressman Ed Perlmutter; your own hometown mayor, Michael Hancock; and former friend and—or current friend, former mayor—[*laughter*]— and one of the finest public servants in Colorado history, Federico Pena.

So it is good to be back in Colorado, especially on a gorgeous day like this. It's always like this in late September, isn't it? Absolutely.

It's an honor to be here at Lincoln High School. And I want to give a special thank you to Amelia for that wonderful introduction. I was just talking to Amelia. I said—she's a senior this year. And she's planning to go to college and planning to be a doctor, and I am absolutely certain she is going to succeed in everything that she does. And she's an example, a great example, of how smarter courses and better technology can help guarantee our kids the foundation that they need to graduate and compete in this new global economy. So we couldn't be prouder of Amelia. And we couldn't be prouder of all the students here at Lincoln.

Now, I came here today to talk about the economy. I came to talk about how we can get to a place where we're creating good middle class jobs again, jobs that pay well and jobs that offer security.

We've got a lot to do to make sure that everyone in this country gets a fair shake and a fair shot and a chance to get ahead. And that's the number-one thing that I think about each and every day: your lives, your opportunities. That should be the number-one thing that every public servant in Washington is thinking about.

There's so much that we could accomplish together if Washington can finally start acting on behalf of the people. We've got to get that city to stop worrying so much about their jobs and their careers and start worrying about your jobs and your careers.

And that's why I sent Congress the "American Jobs Act." Now, I know it's kind of thick, but it boils down to two things: putting people back to work and putting more money in the pockets of working Americans. Every single thing in the "American Jobs Act" is the kind of proposal that's been supported by Democrats and Republicans in the past. Everything in it will be paid for.

It's been 2 weeks since I sent it to Congress; now I want it back. I want it back passed so I can sign this bill and start putting people back to work. I've already got the pens all ready, all lined up on my desk, ready to sign the bill. And every one of you can help make it happen by sending a message to Congress, a simple message: Pass this jobs bill.

Look, pass this jobs bill, and right here in Colorado, thousands of construction workers will have a job again. This is one of the most commonsense ideas out there. All over the country there are roads and bridges and schools just like Lincoln that are in need of repair. One of the reasons we came here was this is the fastest growing school in one of the fastest growing school districts in Colorado.

So Lincoln has been adding new AP courses and new language courses, and the wonderful principal and administrators here have been making sure and the teachers here have been making sure that kids have upgraded computers and learning software that's necessary to prepare all of you students for the jobs and the economy of the future. But you know what, things like science labs take money to upgrade. The science labs here at Lincoln High were built decades ago, back in the sixties. I don't know if you've noticed, but science and technology has changed a little bit since the 1960s. The world has changed a little bit since the 1960s. So we need to do everything we can to prepare our kids to compete. We need to do everything we can to make sure our students can compete with any students, anywhere in the world. And every child deserves a great school, and we can give it to them.

We can rebuild our schools for the 21st century with faster Internet and smarter labs and cutting-edge technology. And that won't just create a better learning environment for students, it will create good jobs for local construction workers right here in Denver and all across Colorado and all across the country. There are schools all throughout Colorado in need of renovation.

But it's not just in this State. Last week, I visited a bridge in Cincinnati that connected Ohio to Kentucky. Bridges need renovations. Roads need renovations. We need to lay broadband lines in rural areas. There are construction projects like these all across this country just waiting to get started, and there are millions of unemployed construction workers ready to do the job.

So my question to Congress is: What on Earth are you waiting for? Let's get to work. Let's get to work. Let's get to work.

Why should our children be allowed to study in crumbling, outdated schools? How does that give them a sense that education's important? We should build them the best schools. That's what I want for my kids. That's what you want for your kids. That's what I want for every kid in America.

Why should we let China build the newest airports, the fastest railroads? We should build them right here in America, right here in Denver, right here in Colorado. There is work to be done. There are workers ready to do it. So tell Congress: Pass this jobs bill right away.

Let's pass this jobs bill and put teachers back in the classroom where they belong. Places like South Korea, they're adding teachers in droves to prepare their kids for the global economy. We're laying off our teachers left and right. All across the country, budget cuts are forcing superintendents to make choices they don't want to make.

I can tell you the last thing a Governor like John Hickenlooper wants to do is to lose teachers. It's unfair to our kids. It undermines our future. It has to stop. You tell Congress: Pass the "American Jobs Act," and there will be funding to save jobs of thousands of Colorado teachers and cops and firefighters. It's the right thing to do. Pass the bill.

If Congress passes this jobs bill, companies will get new tax credits for hiring America's veterans. Think about it. These men and women, they leave their careers, they leave their families, they are protecting us and our freedom, and the last thing they should have to do is fight for a job when they come home. That's why Congress needs to pass this bill to make it easier for businesses to hire our veterans and use the skills that they've developed protecting us.

Pass this bill, and it will help hundreds of thousands of young people find summer jobs next year to help them build skills. It provides a $4,000 tax credit for companies that hire anybody who's spent more than 6 months looking for a job. It extends unemployment insurance, but it also says if you're collecting benefits, you'll get connected to temporary work as a way to build your skills while you're looking for a permanent job. Congress needs to pass this bill.

Congress needs to pass this bill so we can help the people who create most of the new jobs in this country: America's small-business owners. It's all terrific that corporate profits have come roaring back, but small companies haven't come roaring back. Let's give them a boost. Pass this bill, and every small-business owner in America gets a tax cut. If they hire new employees or they raise their employees' salaries, they get another tax cut.

There are some Republicans in Congress who like to talk about being the friends of America's job creators. Well, you know what, if you actually care about America's jobs creators, then you should actually help America's jobs creators with a tax cut by passing this bill right away.

Now, finally, if we get Congress to pass this bill, the typical working family in Colorado will get more than $1,700 in tax cuts next year, $1,700 that would have been taken out of your paycheck now goes right back in your pocket.

If Congress doesn't act, if Congress fails to pass this bill, middle class families will get hit with a tax increase at the worst possible time. We can't let that happen. Republicans say they're the party of tax cuts. Well, let them prove it. Tell them to fight just as hard for tax cuts for working Americans as they fight for the wealthiest Americans. Tell them to pass this jobs bill right now.

So let me summarize here. The "American Jobs Act" will lead to new jobs for construction workers, jobs for teachers, jobs for veterans, jobs for young people, jobs for the unemployed. It will provide tax relief for every worker and small business in America. And by the way, it will not add to the deficit. It will be paid for.

Last week, I laid out a plan that would not only pay for the jobs bill, but would begin to actually reduce our debt over time. It's a plan that says if we want to close—create jobs and close the deficit, then we've got to not only make some of the cuts that we've made—tough cuts that, with the help of Mark and Michael, we were able to get done—but we've also got to ask the wealthiest Americans and biggest corporations to pay their fair share.

Look, we need to reform our Tax Code based on a simple principle: Middle class families shouldn't pay higher tax rates than millionaires and billionaires. Warren Buffett's secretary shouldn't pay a higher tax rate than War-

ren Buffett. A teacher or a nurse or a construction worker making $50,000 a year shouldn't pay higher tax rates than somebody making 50 million. That's just common sense.

And keep in mind, I'm not saying this because we should be punishing success. This is the land of opportunity. What's great about this country is that any of these young people here, if they've got a good idea, if they go out there and they're willing to work hard, they can start a business, they can create value, great products, great services. They can make millions, make billions. That's great. That's what America is all about. Anybody can make it if they try.

But what's also a quintessentially American idea is that those of us who've done well should pay our fair share to contribute to the upkeep of the Nation that made our success possible, because nobody did well on their own. A teacher somewhere helped to give you the skills to succeed. Firefighters and police officers are protecting your property. You're moving your goods and products and services on roads that somebody built. That's how we all do well together. We got here because somebody else invested in us, and we've got to make sure this generation of students can go to college on student aid or scholarships like I did. We've got to make sure that we keep investing in the kind of Government research that helped to create the Internet, which countless private sector companies then used to create tens of millions of jobs.

And you know what? I'm positive—I've talked to them—most wealthy Americans agree with this. Of course, the Republicans in Congress, they call this class warfare. You know what, if asking a millionaire to pay the same tax rate as a plumber makes me a class warrior, a warrior for the working class, I will accept that. I will wear that charge as a badge of honor.

The only warfare I've seen is the battle that's been waged against middle class families in this country for a decade now.

Ultimately, Colorado, this comes down to choices and it comes down to priorities. If we want to pay for this jobs plan, put people back to work, close this deficit, invest in our future, then the money has got to come from somewhere. And so my question is: Would you rather keep tax loopholes for oil companies, or do you want construction workers to have a job rebuilding our schools and our roads and our bridges? Would you rather keep tax breaks for billionaires that they don't need, or would you rather put teachers back to work and help small businesses and cut taxes and reduce our deficit?

It's time to build an economy that creates good middle class jobs in this country. It's time to build an economy that honors the values of hard work and responsibility. It's time to build an economy that lasts.

And, Denver, that starts now. And I need your help to make it happen. I just want you to—just remember, Republicans and Democrats in the past have supported every kind of proposal that's in here. There's no reason not to pass it just because I proposed it. We need to tell them it's time to support these proposals right now.

There are some Republicans in Washington who have said that some of this might have to wait until the next election.

Audience members. No!

The President. Maybe we should just stretch this out rather than work together right now. Some even said that if they agree with the proposals in the "American Jobs Act," they still shouldn't pass it because it might give me a win. Think about that. Give me a win? Give me a break! That's why folks in Washington—that's why folks are fed up with Washington.

There are some folks in Washington who don't get it. This isn't about giving me a win. This is about giving Democrats and Republicans a chance to do something for the American people. It's about giving people who are hurting a win. That's what this is about.

It's about giving small-business owners a win and entrepreneurs a win and students a win and working families a win, giving all of us a win.

The next election is nearly 14 months away. The American people don't have the luxury of waiting that long. There are folks here in Colorado who are living paycheck to paycheck, week to week. They need action, they need it now.

So I'm asking all of you, I need you to lift up your voices. Not just here in Denver, but anyone watching, anybody listening, anybody following online, I need you to call, e-mail, tweet, fax, visit, tell your Congressperson—unless it's the Congresspersons here, because they're already on board—tell them you are tired of gridlock, you are tired of the games. Tell them the time for action is now. Tell them you want to create jobs now. Tell them to pass the bill.

If you want construction workers on the job, pass the bill. If you want teachers back in the classroom, pass the bill. If you want a tax cut for small-business owners, pass the bill. If you want to help our veterans share in the opportunity that they defended, pass the bill.

It is time to act. We are not a people who sit back and wait for things to happen. We make things happen. We're Americans. We are tougher than the times that we live in, and we are bigger than the politics we've been seeing out of Washington. We write our own destiny. It is in our power to do so once more. So let's meet this moment, let's get to work, and let's show the world once again why the United States of America is the greatest nation on Earth.

Thank you. God bless you. God bless the United States of America. Go Lancers!

NOTE: The President spoke at 2:20 p.m. In his remarks, he referred to Josefina Petit Higa, principal, Abraham Lincoln High School; and Warren E. Buffett, chief executive officer and chairman, Berkshire Hathaway Inc.

Videotaped Remarks on the Observance of Rosh Hashanah
September 27, 2011

Hello, everybody. *Shana Tova.*

The days between Rosh Hashanah and Yom Kippur are a time for repentance and reflection, an opportunity to reaffirm our friendships, renew our commitments, and reflect on the values we cherish.

As the High Holidays begin, we look back on all the moments during the past year that give us reason to hope. Around the world, a new generation is reaching for their universal rights. Here in the United States, we've responded to our challenges by focusing on the things that really matter: friendship, family, and community.

But this last year was also one of hardship for people around the world. Too many of our friends and neighbors continue to struggle in the wake of a terrible economic recession. And beyond our borders, many of our closest allies, including the State of Israel, face the uncertainties of an unpredictable age.

That is why my administration is doing everything we can to promote prosperity here at home and security and peace throughout the world, and that includes reaffirming our commitment to the State of Israel. While we cannot know all that the new year will bring, we do know this: The United States will continue to stand with Israel, because the bond between our two nations is unshakable.

As Jewish tradition teaches us, we may not complete the work, but that must never keep us from trying. In that spirit, Michelle and I wish you and your families and all who celebrate Rosh Hashanah a sweet year full of health, happiness, and peace.

Thank you.

NOTE: The President's remarks were videotaped at approximately 4:35 p.m. on September 23 in the Map Room at the White House for later broadcast.

Remarks at an "Open for Questions" Roundtable Question-and-Answer Session
September 28, 2011

Yahoo! Inc. Editor-in-Chief for U.S. Hispanic and Latin America Jose Siade. Ladies and gentlemen, *señoras y señores*, welcome to "Open for Questions" with President Obama. I'm Jose Siade from Yahoo! en Español, your host today, coming to you from the White House. I'm honored to be joined today by industry colleagues Karine Medina from MSN Latino and Gabriel Lerner from AOL Latino and HuffPost LatinoVoices.

And sitting next to me, a man that needs no introduction, President Barack Obama.

The President. Thank you so much, Jose. Thank you for having me.

Mr. Siade. Thank you very much, sir, for sitting down with us today. We received hundreds of questions from our audience—from our U.S. Hispanic audience across the country. And we've brought some of those questions in today so you can address them.

The President. Excellent. Look forward to it.

Immigration Reform

Mr. Siade. Very well. Let's jump into the first question, from Claudia in California: "President Obama, there are many illegal aliens currently in the U.S. that can contribute much to the country and cannot do so because of their status. What are you currently doing and what still needs to be done in order to reform immigration laws and solve this issue?"

The President. Well, I appreciate this, Jose. Obviously, this is an issue that I've been working on for years. When I was in the U.S. Senate, I was a cosponsor of comprehensive immigration reform. I have voted for comprehensive immigration reform. And our administration consistently has supported the basic concept that we are a nation of laws, but we're also a nation of immigrants, and that immigrants continually have strengthened America's economy, America's culture, and that we have to create a system that works for all of us.

The way to do that is to be serious about border security, and we have been. We've put more resources in border security than anything that's been done in previous administrations. But what we've also said is, is that for those persons who are here, we have to make sure that we provide a pathway to earning a legal status in this country. They have broken the immigration laws, so they may have to pay a fine, learn English, take other steps. But to create a pathway so that they can get out of the shadows and contribute to society in a more effective way is something that I consider to be a top priority. And we can do it in a way that is compatible with our tradition of everybody being responsible and following the law.

Now, to do that, we've got to get legislation through Congress. And in the past we've seen bipartisan support for comprehensive immigration reform. Unfortunately, over the last several years what you've seen is the Republican Party move away from support of comprehensive immigration reform.

It used to be that we had a lot of Republican sponsors for the "DREAM Act," which would allow young people who have grown up here as Americans and did not break laws themselves, but rather, were brought here by their parents—they should be studying, serving our military, contributing to our society, starting businesses. We used to have Republican co-sponsors for the "DREAM Act." Now we don't.

So our biggest challenge right now: The vast majority of Democrats are supportive of comprehensive immigration reform, but given that the Republicans control the House of Representatives and that we need 60 votes in the Senate, our key approach is trying to push Republicans to get back to where they were only a few years ago. The—in the meantime, what we're trying to do is to manage the enforcement of our inadequate immigration laws in a way that is humane and just.

So we've tried to emphasize making sure that we're focusing on violent criminals, people who are a threat to society and a threat to our communities, for deportation and sending a clear signal that our enforcement priority is not to chase down young people who are going to school and who are following all the other laws and are trying to make a contribution to society. But until we get an actual comprehensive immigration law passed through Congress, we're going to continue to have some of the problems that we've been seeing.

Immigration Policy Enforcement/Immigration Reform

Gabriel Lerner of AOL Latino and HuffPost LatinoVoices. Just to follow up, Mr. President, you just mentioned enforcement of immigration laws in the subject of deportations, and you said that many of those—or it's aimed at criminals. But until now, and until recently, it hadn't been just criminals, or a majority of criminals, those that have been deported. And also, you have been deporting much more immigrants than the previous administration did in 8 years. So laws didn't change; enforcement was done even then. Why that emphasis on deportation during your administration?

The President. Actually, what happened—if you look at the statistics, two things happened. Number one is, is that there was a much greater emphasis on criminals rather than noncriminals. And there's been a huge shift in terms of enforcement, and that began as soon as I came into office. That change has taken place.

Secondly, the statistics are actually a little deceptive, because what we've been doing is with the stronger border enforcement, we've been apprehending folks at the borders and sending them back. That is counted as a deportation, even though they may have only been held for a day or 48 hours, sent back—that's counted as a deportation. So we've been much more effective on the borders. But we have not been more aggressive when it comes to dealing, for example, with "DREAM Act" kids. That's just not the case.

So what we've tried to do is within the constraints of the laws on the books, we've tried to be as fair, humane, just as we can, recognizing, though, that the laws themselves need to be changed. And I've been unwavering in my support of changing the laws so that we're strong on border security, we're going after companies that are taking advantage of undocumented workers—paying them subminimum wages and not respecting workplace safety laws—but also saying that we've got to have a pathway to citizenship and for legal status for those who are already here and have put roots down here and are part of the fabric of our community, because we actually believe that they can contribute to our economy in an effective way.

The other thing that we want to emphasize is, for those who have an ambition to start a business—entrepreneurs, young people who have gotten college degrees or advanced degrees—for us to train them here in the United States and then send them back to start businesses elsewhere makes absolutely no sense. The history of many of our biggest businesses is they were started by immigrants who came here seeking opportunity. And we want to make sure that, both in terms of people who are here doing jobs that other folks may not want to do, but also people who have extraordinary training and can create jobs for all Americans, that we are giving both of those folks opportunities.

National Economy/Job Creation/Education/Infrastructure and Technology Investment

Karine Medina of MSN Latino. So my first question comes from Esther Polanco, and it was submitted on MSN Latino: "Mr. President, your proposed jobs bill addresses tax breaks for small businesses and the repair of infrastructure like roads and bridges. But that seems like a short-term solution to a much larger problem. With the unemployment rate among Latinos at 11.3 percent across the Nation, what do you plan to do for the remainder of your term, and if reelected, to ensure that large factories and Fortune 1000 companies begin hiring again?"

The President. Well, obviously, we're going through the worst financial crisis and recession since the Great Depression. It has been a worldwide phenomenon; it's not just here in the United States. And some of the challenges that we've had over the last several months actually have to do with the fact that in Europe we haven't seen them deal with their banking system and their financial system as effectively as they needed to. The changes that have taken place in the Middle East sent oil prices up, and that gave a shock to the world economy. So there are a lot of forces at work here that we have to address.

But my main goal has consistently been to get the economy growing again and putting people back to work. Now, we've created more than 2 million jobs over the last 18 months in the private sector. The problem is we lost so many during the recession back in 2007, 2008 that we still haven't gotten back to where we need to be, and unemployment is still far too high.

What the jobs act does is a couple of things. Number one, it, yes, puts people back to work rebuilding roads, bridges, schools. Those infrastructure projects could employ a lot of construction workers—including a lot of Latino construction workers—who were laid off after the housing bubble burst. And so that could significantly reduce unemployment in that sector.

It says that we're going to rehire teachers. And the Latino community obviously is deeply concerned about education. A lot of schools are understaffed in Latino communities where the young population, the youth population, is growing rapidly. Putting teachers back to work is not only good for employment, but it's also good for training our young people.

The tax breaks that we give—there are 250,000 Latino small businesses. They hire a lot of people. And if they are getting significant tax breaks, that gives them more capital; it allows them to expand their businesses, grow, and potentially hire more workers. And the bill also addresses summer jobs for disadvantaged youth. It also provides unemployment insurance for those who are still looking for work.

So this is not a small piece of business. It's estimated that if we pass the jobs bill, we would expand the gross domestic product by about 2 percent, and you would see 1.9 million people, potentially, find jobs as a consequence of this bill. So it would significantly reduce the unemployment rate.

You're right, though, that the long-term challenge is how do we create an economy that is more competitive, more productive, and is employing more people. And to do that, we've got to improve our education system, which is why we place such a big emphasis on reform, particularly targeting those schools that are underperforming. And disproportionately Latino and African American youth are dropping out of high school at a time when it's very hard to find a job if you don't have not only a high school degree, but also some advanced training. So that's been a big emphasis.

Because of the work that we did to change how the student loan program worked—instead of going through banks, it's now going directly to students—we've freed up about $60 billion that we're going to be able to provide for Pell grants and scholarships. And as a consequence, we've actually seen the Latino college enrollment rate go up significantly over the last couple of years.

We're still going to have to rebuild our infrastructure. Even though what we've slated is just what we can do over the next year, year and a half, we probably have a 10-year project of rebuilding our roads, bridges, airports, schools. And a sustained effort at investing in our infrastructure could put a lot of people back to work and make us more competitive over the long term.

And then we have to continue to emphasize exports. The United States historically was a manufacturing base: We made things here, and we sold them elsewhere. Over the last 15 years, we have been consuming, importing from China and other places, but the manufacturing has been done there. And what we need to do is start moving manufacturing back here to the United States, particularly in cutting-edge areas like, for example, advanced vehicles, more efficient cars that are built here based on electric technology, for example. That's going to be a growth industry; we need to develop those.

So there's not going to be one single silver bullet. We're going to have to keep on investing in research and development, making sure technology is developed here. We've got to emphasize exports, infrastructure. The most important thing we can do, though, is make sure that our young people are trained, because companies today are going to be locating where there's the most skilled workforce. And making sure that Latino students, who are going to be the largest growing group in the United States—they're the ones who are going to

be the workforce of the future, along with African Americans and Asian Americans, as well as White Americans—all—making sure that every single one of those young people is trained and equipped for this economy of the future, that's the most important thing we can do to get companies to locate here and hire here.

Immigration Policy Enforcement/Immigration Reform

Mr. Lerner. Mr. President, this is a great opportunity for Latinos to ask you questions directly, and this type of question have come repeatedly. So just to complete the subject—and you mentioned border security as tough. Mr. Hugo Sanchez—and I'm sure that's his name—he says: "Mr. President, I'm a naturalized American citizen, and as such, an immigrant. What happened to the investigation of the many violations and challenges to the Federal Government by Sheriff Joe Arpaio in Maricopa, Arizona?" Let me just add that this investigation started March 2009. It is high time to have maybe a resolution on that.

The President. Well, I have to be careful about commenting on individual cases. That's handled typically by the Department of Justice or these other agencies. What I will say is this, that the approach that's been taken to immigration in Arizona, I think, has not always been as productive as it's been.

As you know, we challenged the Arizona law that was supported by the sheriff because we thought that there was a great danger that naturalized citizens, individuals with Latino surnames, potentially could be vulnerable to questioning; the laws could be potentially abused in ways that were not fair to Latino citizens in Arizona.

So rather than comment on the individual case, what I would say is this: that we can't have a patchwork of 50 States with 50 different immigration laws. We can't have a situation in which individual counties are trying to enforce their own immigration laws rather than having a national approach. We think it is very important for the Federal Government to be serious about border security, to go after companies that are taking advantage of undocumented workers, and to provide a pathway for legal status for immigrants. That is a comprehensive approach that needs to be taken. We are going to push hard for it. I have been pushing hard for it, and I'm going to keep pushing hard for it.

The most important thing for your viewers and listeners and readers to understand is that in order to change our laws, we've got to get it through the House of Representatives, which is currently controlled by Republicans, and we've got to get 60 votes in the Senate. And right now we have not gotten that kind of support—sadly, because only a few years ago, as I said, you had some Republicans who were willing to recognize that we needed to fix our immigration system. George Bush, to his credit, recognized that we needed to fix our immigration system. Ronald Reagan understood that immigration was an important part of the American experience. Right now you have not that kind of leadership coming from the Republican Party. We want to partner in a bipartisan way to get this problem solved, and I'm going to keep on pushing to get it done.

Bullying and Harassment Prevention Efforts

Mr. Siade. This question comes from—[*inaudible*]—in Florida: "Since bullying is increasing in an alarming way in the U.S., what can be done to avoid further discrimination or bullying within various racial groups, particularly for Hispanic kids in school?"

The President. I think it's a really important question. We actually had the first-ever conference on bullying here in the White House, because for young people it's hard enough growing up without also then being subject to constant harassment. And the kind of bullying that we're seeing now, including using the Internet and new media, can be very oppressive on young people.

So what we've tried to do is to provide information and tools to parents, to schools, to communities to push back and fight against these kinds of trends. And a lot of the best work has actually been done by young people themselves who start antibullying campaigns in their schools, showing how you have to respect everyone, regardless of race, regardless of religion, regardless of sexual orientation. And when you get a school environment in which that's not accepted by young people themselves, where they say, we're not going to tolerate that kind of bullying, that usually ends up making the biggest difference, because kids react to their peer group more than sometimes they do adults.

And what we need to do is make sure that we're providing tools to schools and to young people to help to combat against bullying, and it's something that we'll continue to work on with local communities and local school districts as well.

Mr. Lerner. So you're going to have a conference on bullying in the White House?

The President. We already did. We had it; it was probably 4 or 5 months ago. And we brought in nonprofit groups, religious leadership, schools, students themselves. And they have now organized conferences regionally, around the country, so that we can prevent this kind of bullying from taking place.

Mexico

Ms. Medina. So the next question comes from Yreka, California, and was asked by Mike: "Is there anything the United States can do to strengthen the Mexican economy? Could we form a stronger partnership with Mexico that would result in less illegal immigration and lowered expense of Border Patrol?"

The President. Well, I think it's very important to recognize, as the question recognizes, that if we can strengthen the Mexican economy, then people have less incentive to look for work in the United States. We welcome immigration, but obviously, a lot of people in Mexico would love to stay home and create businesses and find jobs that allowed them to support their family if they could, but the Mexican economy has not always been able to generate all the jobs that it needs.

This is a long-term challenge. The Mexican economy is very integrated to the world economy and the U.S. economy, so they were affected by the recession very badly themselves. I have a great relationship with President Calderon, and we have looked for a whole range of ways that we can improve cross-border trade. For example, we've been focused on how we can change the border's infrastructure so that goods are flowing more easily back and forth.

Ultimately, though, the Mexican economy is going to depend also on changing some of the structures internally to increase productivity, to train the workforce there, so education in Mexico is going to be also very important. Part of what's happened is—in Mexico is, is that a lot of people have been displaced from the agricultural sector and they've moved to the cities. They don't have the skills, necessarily, for the higher skilled jobs that exist in urban areas. And so an education agenda in Mexico is also important, just as it is here in the United States.

But we very much want to work with Mexico around their development agenda, because the more they are able to generate industry and businesses in Mexico, to some extent that's probably going to be one of the best solutions for the immigration pressures that we've been seeing over the last decade or so.

Defense of Marriage Act

Mr. Lerner. Mr. President, on the Defense of Marriage Act, also called DOMA, this comes from Kevin in North Carolina. He says: "I'm a gay American who fell in love with a foreigner. As you know, due to DOMA, I'm not permitted to sponsor my foreign-born partner for residency. And as a result, we are stuck between a rock and an impossible situation. How do you intend to fix this? Waiting for DOMA to be repealed or struck down in the courts will potentially take years. What do binational couples do in the meantime?"

The President. Well, we made a decision that was a very significant decision, based on my assessment of the Constitution, that this administration would not defend DOMA in the Federal courts. It's not going to be years before this issue is settled. This is going to be settled fairly soon, because right now we have cases pending in the Federal courts.

Administratively, we can't ignore the law. DOMA is still on the books. But we have said—is even as we enforce it, we don't support it, we think it's unconstitutional. The position that my administration has taken I think will have a significant influence on the court as it examines the constitutionality of this law. And once that law is struck down—and I don't know what the ruling will be—then addressing these binational issues could flow from that decision potentially.

I can't comment on where the case is going to go. I can only say what I believe, and that is, is that DOMA doesn't make sense. It's unfair. I don't think that it meets the demands of our Constitution. And in the meantime, if—I've already said that I'm also supportive of Congress repealing DOMA on it's own and not waiting for the courts. The likelihood of us being able to get the votes in the House of Representatives for DOMA repeal are very low at this point so, truthfully, the recourse to the courts is probably going to be the best approach.

Development, Relief, and Education for Alien Minors (DREAM) Act

Mr. Lerner. Me again. On the "DREAM Act" that you mentioned before, and this is, like, a statement from Cesar in New York City. He says: "Mr. President, I am an undocumented law graduate from New York City. I'm just writing to say that your message that you do not have a dance partner is not a message of hope. A real dancer goes out on the dance floor and takes out his or her dance partner. You're just waiting. You have the facts, numbers, dollars, and votes on the side of granting administrative relief for DREAMers. We are doing our part. It is time to do yours, Mr. President."

The President. I just have to continue to say this notion that somehow I can just change the laws unilaterally is just not true. We've—we are doing everything we can administratively. But the fact of the matter is there are laws on the books that I have to enforce. And I think there's been a great disservice done to the cause of getting the "DREAM Act" passed and getting comprehensive immigration passed by perpetrating the notion that somehow, by myself, I can go and do these things. It's just not true.

Now, what we can do is to prioritize enforcement, since there are limited enforcement resources, and say, we're not going to go chasing after this young man or anybody else who's been acting responsibly and would otherwise qualify for legal status if the "DREAM Act" passed.

But we live in a democracy. You have to pass bills through the Legislature, and then I can sign it. And if all the attention is focused away from the legislative process, then that is going to lead to a constant dead end. We have to recognize how the system works and then apply pressure to those places where votes can be gotten, and ultimately, we can get this thing solved. And nobody will be a stronger advocate for making that happen than me.

Cuba

Ms. Medina. This next question is about Cuba, and it comes from—[*inaudible*]—in Florida: "What is your position regarding Cuba and the embargo? What should the Cuban people expect from you and your Government during the remainder of your term and in the future if you're reelected?"

The President. Well, what we did with respect to Cuba was recognize that the Cuban people now have not enjoyed freedom for 50 years, and everywhere else in the world you've been seeing a democratization movement that has been pressing forward. Throughout Latin America, democracies have emerged from previously authoritarian regimes. The time has come for the same thing to happen in Cuba.

Now, what we've tried to do is to send a signal that we are open to a new relationship with Cuba if the Cuban Government starts taking the proper steps to open up its own country and its own—and provide the space and the respect for human rights that would allow the Cuban people to determine their own destiny.

I changed the remittance laws so that family members could more easily send money back to Cuba, because that would give them more power and it would create a economic space for them to prosper. Within Cuba we have changed the family travel laws so that they can travel more frequently, as well as laws that relate to educational travel.

And so we've made these modifications that send a signal that we're prepared to show flexibility and not be stuck in a cold war mentality dating back to when I was born. On the other hand, we have to see a signal back from the Cuban Government that it is following through on releasing political prisoners, on providing people their basic human rights, in order for us to be fully engaged with them. And so far, at least, what we haven't seen is the kind of genuine spirit of transformation inside of Cuba that would justify us eliminating the embargo.

I don't know what will happen over the next year, but we are prepared to see what happens in Cuba. If we see positive movement, we will respond in a positive way. Hopefully, over the next 5 years, we'll see Cuba looking around the world and saying, we need to catch up with history. And as long as I'm President, I will always be prepared to change our Cuba policy if and when we start seeing a serious intention on the part of the Cuban Government to provide liberty for its people. But that's always my watchword, is—are we seeing freedom for the Cuban people to live lives of opportunity and prosperity. If we are, then we'll be supportive of them.

Mr. Lerner. Those conditions will suffice: human rights, free political prisoners? No demand for a change in the economic structure, for example?

The President. Well, it's very hard to separate liberty from some economic reforms. If people have no way to eat other than through the government, then the government ends up having very strict control over them, and they can be punished in all sorts of ways for expressing their own opinions. That's not to say that a condition for us releasing the embargo would be that they have a perfect market system, because obviously, we have trade and exchanges with a number of countries that fall short of a liberal democracy.

But there is a basic, I think, recognition of people's human rights that includes their right to work, to change jobs, to get an education, to start a business. So some elements of freedom are included in how an economic system works. And right now we haven't seen any of that.

But let me just say this. Obviously, if we saw a release of political prisoners, the ability for people to express their opinions and to petition their Government, if we saw even those steps, those would be very significant, and we would pay attention, and we would undoubtedly reexamine our overall approach to Cuba if we saw a serious movement in that direction.

Border Security

Mr. Siade. Mr. President, this question comes from Karina in Ohio: "Mr. President, what is your strategy to stop the flow of weapons bought with drug money in the U.S. and then sent to Mexico, especially after what happened in Operation Fast and Furious?"

The President. Well, this is a great challenge, and I've been the first one to admit—I've said this publicly in bilateral meetings with President Calderon—that there's a two-way street in terms of the problems of transnational drug operations. The Mexican Government I think has been very courageous in taking on these cartels, at great cost, obviously, with respect to violence in Mexico. That's the right thing to do.

We have to be a more effective partner in both reducing demand for drugs here in the United States and for stemming the flow of weapons and cash that help to finance and facilitate these cartels. So we're working very hard to have a much more effective interdiction effort of south to north—or north to south traffic than we have in the past, so we are checking southbound transit to try to capture illegal guns, illegal cash transfers to drug cartels. It is something that we have been building over the last couple of years. It's not yet finished.

And there's going to be more work to do.

Part of the issue here obviously is budgetary. At a time when the Federal Government is looking for ways to save money, we're going to have to figure out ways to operate smarter and more effective in our investigations without a huge expansion of resources because those resources aren't there.

Combating Drugs and Narcotics

Mr. Siade. And in terms of the demand here in the U.S.——

The President. Well, with respect to——

Mr. Siade. ——what kind of efforts?

The President. With respect to the demand in the U.S., our drug czar here in the United States I think has done a very good job working with schools and local communities, working with local law enforcement to try to continue to reduce drug demand. One of the things that I've always believed is that—and this is reflective of my administration's policy—is, is that we can't just think about this as a law enforcement issue, we also have to think of it as a public health issue.

If you think about the enormous changes that have been made in terms of people's use of tobacco, for example, that wasn't because of—they were arrested, it was also because young people were taught that smoking was bad for your health, it didn't make you cool. There were public service announcements. Right? So I think taking a comprehensive approach that includes interdiction and law enforcement, but also takes into account public health strategies, treatment.

A lot of cities around the country, if you decide that you want to rid yourself of drugs, you may have to wait 3 months, 6 months to get into a local treatment program. Well, that's not going to be particularly effective. So what we've been trying to see is can we get more resources into treatment, more resources into a public health approach, even as we continue to target the cartels, the drug kingpins, those who are really responsible for perpetuating the drug trade in communities across the country.

Education Reform

Ms. Medina. From Jose Joga, from here, Washington, DC: "President Obama, what do you believe is the greatest challenge that the Hispanic community faces in this country, and what can we do better to prepare our children to take full advantage of the great opportunities this country offers?"

The President. I think the biggest challenge for all of us, but this is especially true in the

Latino community, is improving our education system. And part of that is the effort we're making in schools. So, for example, we have a program called Race to the Top, where we've been saying we'll give extra money to States and school districts that are improving teacher training and making schools more accountable. It's resulted in over 40 States changing their laws to adopt to best practices in education.

We put forward an additional $4 billion that is being used to target those schools that have a severe dropout problem or the worst performing schools. A lot of them are Latino or African American. And, for example, I was in a school in Miami where they completely—they changed their principal, they changed a third of their staff, they changed their curriculum. They had a complete makeover, extreme makeover. And now graduation rates have gone way up. More kids are taking AP classes and college prep classes.

So a lot of the work has to be done in terms of reforming how education is delivered. We need to improve the construction of schools. My jobs bill includes building and repairing schools. And there—especially in the Latino community, where there's a large youth population, you're seeing overcrowded schools, kids learning in trailers. That's not sending a good signal to people about the importance of education. So passing this jobs bill can be very important in terms of improving the school, the physical plant, but also putting teachers back in the classroom.

But finally, so much of school performance also has to do with attitudes at home with parents and in the community. And a strong message that I send to all students, but especially Latino and African American students, who tend to drop out at higher rates or fall behind faster, is the day is gone when without an education you can somehow get a job that supports you. Even if you're not going to a 4-year college, needing to get some advanced training at a community college, even if you want to work in a factory today, you now have to know computers, you have to have math skills, you have to be able to communicate effectively.

So telling our children, you have to turn off the TV, stop playing the video games, do your homework, aspiring to excellence in education, that's the issue that probably we have to work on. And there's no quick fix there. I mean, that's a 10-year, 20-year project. It's not a 6-month project. But if we can make significant changes there, then I think that the future prospects for our kids are going to be very strong.

Political Involvement of Hispanic Americans

Mr. Lerner. Mr. President, on the—your opinion on the state of integration of Latinos in our political life, this question comes anonymous. I'm sure it's not from the person we are talking about: "With the prospect now of a Romney-Rubio ticket or a Rick Perry-Rubio ticket or a Bachmann-Rubio ticket, do you think it's time for an Hispanic Vice President and maybe President after that?"

The President. I am absolutely certain that within my lifetime we will have a Latino candidate for President who is very competitive and may win. You just look at the demographics, right? I mean, the Latino population is growing faster than any other population. You look at a State like Texas, where it will, within my lifetime, be majority Latino. With numbers comes political power.

Now, the challenge, I think, politically for Latinos across the country is, are folks registering? Are they voting? And we still have not seen the kinds of participation levels that are necessary to match up the numbers with actual political power. And my hope is, is that in 2012, in 2016, in 2020 you continually see participation rates increase more and more for Latinos, and that will inevitably lead to both parties, I think, being more responsive to Latino issues.

If you're voting at a low rate, then you are giving up some of your power. If you're voting at a high rate, then you're going to have more influence. And that's true of every single group. The political system tends to be more responsive to the needs of seniors than it is to the needs of youth. And there's just one reason for that: because seniors vote at much higher rates than young people do. And the same is going to be true with respect to Latino voters. If they are voting at high rates, then not only will you elect more Latino officials, but non-Latino officials will also be more responsive.

Health Care

Mr. Siade. Mr. President, this question is from—[*inaudible*]—in Florida: "How do you propose to improve health care in the U.S. and ensure that all Hispanics have affordable access to it?"

The President. Well, the—I don't just propose, we've actually done. I mean, my—the Affordable Care Act, the health care reform that we passed in 2010, is going to provide 30 million people who didn't have health insurance access to health insurance. A disproportionate number of those people will be Latinos, who are the most likely to not have health insurance. So this is hugely important to the Latino community.

Even now, already, even though the law will not be fully implemented until 2013, you already have evidence that over a million young people are now having health insurance through their parents' coverage, and so their insurance levels have increased. People with preexisting conditions in various States are able to access health care for the first time.

But ultimately, what we're going to be doing is setting up by 2013—so in the next year and a half, 2 years—we are going to be having exchanges where everybody who doesn't have health insurance will be able to buy the same kind of health insurance that Members of Congress get. And if they can't afford it—the premiums—then they will get subsidies, they will get help from the Government in order to be able to purchase that insurance. And that will make a huge difference in the Latino community.

And if you have insurance, then you are less likely to develop preventable diseases. The rates of diabetes and heart disease and other preventable diseases in the Latino community are way too high, so having regular checkups, preventive care, all that can actually, over the long term, reduce our costs of care because people don't show up at the emergency room; they've actually been able to treat their potential illnesses much earlier.

Puerto Rico

Ms. Medina. So this is probably the last question because we are running out of time. So it comes from Jose Serrano, and it's about Puerto Rico: "Mr. President, during your visit to Puerto Rico, you mentioned that the Congress will consider action on the island's status as soon as there is a clear winner from the voters. What percentage of votes or what other requirements are needed in order to establish a clear winner from a referendum?"

The President. Well, I don't have a particular number in mind. The—I think that the key here is that the status of Puerto Rico should be decided by the residents of Puerto Rico. And so the issue for us is if the plebiscite, if the referendum that takes place in Puerto Rico indicates that there's a strong preference from a majority of the Puerto Rican people, I think that will influence how Congress approaches any actions that might be taken to address status issues.

If it's split down the middle, 50–50 or 51–49, then I think Congress's inclination is going to be not to change, but to maintain the status quo until there's a greater indication that there is support for change. But what the task force that I put forward did, I think, was to examine all the arguments on every side, to do so in a fair way, unbiased way, not trying to put the thumb on the scale, and say that a well-structured plebiscite, a well-structured referendum in Puerto Rico could help determine this.

And I think what we've also recommended, although this has not yet been adopted, is that if it's inconclusive, then we can set up a process here in Congress that would lead to further examination of what our options would be. But for now, the most important thing, I think, is to see if there's a clear sense of direction from the Puerto Rican people themselves. If they continue to be divided, it's hard to imagine that Congress is going to be wanting to impose a single solution on the island.

Social Security

Mr. Lerner. Mr. President, this question came pretty repeatedly. On Social Security—[*inaudible*]—from New York. He asks: "I would ask *mi Presidente*, because he's my *Presidente*, when are you going to give us a stimulus on our retired person's check?" And Teresita from Piney Creek, North Carolina, adds: "We have not received anything additional in 2 years, but everything we buy or need keeps increasing really fast."

The President. Well, this is a question that I always get from Social Security recipients as well. The way Social Security is set up is each year there's a cost-of-living adjustment. But over the last 2 years, because of the recession, inflation didn't really exist in the aggregate. So even though one particular good or gas prices might have gone up a little bit, when you looked at the basket of goods, there wasn't a lot of inflation over the last 2 years. That's why the cost-of-living adjustment did not kick in.

And I think people think that this was a decision somehow that was made by us. It's actually something that just happens automatically. We expect that people will be getting a cost-of-living adjustment this year because there has been some significant inflation, particularly in food and fuel prices. So the expectation is that this year you'll get it. You didn't get it in the last 2 years, not because I didn't want to give it to you, but because the law said that if there's no inflation, then you don't get it.

We had actually proposed in Congress to provide a $250 one-time check to seniors to help accommodate the difficult times that they were having, but we couldn't get it passed through Congress.

Mr. Siade. Mr. President, that's all the time that we have with you here today.

For everyone watching at home, if you missed part of the conversation, you can go online later on today and watch the on-demand version of the conversation.

From everyone here at the table and on behalf of everyone who sent in their questions online, I'd like to thank you, Mr. President, for spending the last hour with us.

And, everyone watching online, *muchas gracias y hasta pronto.*

The President. Thank you so much, everybody. I enjoyed it.

NOTE: The President spoke at 11:40 a.m. in the Map Room at the White House. In his remarks, he referred to former President George W. Bush.

Remarks at Benjamin Banneker Academic High School
September 28, 2011

Hey! Thank you. Thank you very much. Everybody, please have a seat. Well, Madam President, that was an outstanding introduction. [*Laughter*] We are so proud of Donae for representing this school so well.

And in addition, I also want to acknowledge your outstanding principal, who has been here for 20 years—first as a teacher, now as an outstanding principal—Anita Berger. Please give her a big round of applause. I want to acknowledge, as well, Mayor Gray is here, the mayor of Washington, DC, is here. Please give him a big round of applause. And I also want to thank somebody who is going to go down in history as one of the finest Secretaries of Education that we've ever had, Arne Duncan is here.

Now, it is great to be here at Benjamin Banneker High School, one of the best high schools not only in Washington, DC, but one of the best high schools in the country. And—but we've also got students tuning in from all across America. And so I want to welcome you all to the new school year, although I know that many of you already have been in school for a while. I know that here at Banneker, you've been back at school for a few weeks now. So everything is just starting to settle in, just like for all your peers all across the country. The fall sports season is underway. Musicals and marching band routines are starting to shape up, I believe. And your first big tests and projects are probably just around the corner.

I know that you've also got a great deal going on outside of school. Your circle of friends might be changing a little bit. Issues that used to stay confined to hallways or locker rooms are now finding their way onto Facebook and Twitter. [*Laughter*] Some of your families might also be feeling the strain of the economy. As many of you know, we're going through one of the toughest economic times that we've gone through in our lifetime—in my lifetime. Your lifetime hasn't been that long. And so, as a consequence, you might have to pick up an afterschool job to help out your family, or maybe you're babysitting for a younger sibling because mom or dad is working an extra shift.

So all of you have a lot on your plates. You guys are growing up faster and interacting with a wider world in a way that old folks like me, frankly, just didn't have to. So today I don't want to be just another adult who stands up and lectures you like you're just kids, because you're not just kids. You're this country's future. You're young leaders. And whether we fall behind or race ahead as a nation is going to depend in large part on you. So I want to talk to you a little bit about meeting that responsibility.

It starts obviously with being the best student that you can be. Now, that doesn't always mean that you have to have a perfect score on every assignment. It doesn't mean that you've got to get straight As all the time, although that's not a bad goal to have. It means that you have to stay at it. You have to be determined, and you have to persevere. It means you've got to work as hard as you know how to work. And it means that you've got to take some risks once in a while. You can't avoid the class that you think might be hard because you're worried about getting the best grade if that's a subject that you think you need to prepare you for your future. You've got to wonder, you've got to question, you've got to explore, and every once in a while, you need to color outside of the lines.

That's what school is for: discovering new passions, acquiring new skills, making use of this incredible time that you have to prepare yourself and give yourself the skills that you're going to need to pursue the kind of careers that you want. And that's why when you're still a student you can explore a wide range of possibilities. One hour you can be an artist; the next, an author; the next, a scientist or a historian or a carpenter. This is the time where you can try out new interests and test new ideas. And the more you do, the sooner you'll figure out what makes you come alive, what stirs you, what makes you excited, the career that you want to pursue.

Now, if you promise not to tell anybody, I will let you in on a little secret: I was not always the very best student that I could be when I was in high school and certainly not when I was in middle school. I did not love every class I took. I wasn't always paying attention the way I should have. I remember when I was in eighth grade I had to take a class called ethics. Now, ethics is about right and wrong, but if you'd asked me what my favorite subject was back in eighth grade, it was basketball. I don't think ethics would have made it on the list.

But here's the interesting thing. I still remember that ethics class, all these years later. I remember the way it made me think. I remember being asked questions like: What matters in life? Or what does it mean to treat other people with dignity and respect? What does it mean to live in a diverse nation, where not everybody looks like you do or thinks like you do or comes from the same neighborhood as you do? How do we figure out how to get along?

Each of these questions led to new questions. And I didn't always know the right answers, but those discussions and those—that process of discovery, those things have lasted. Those things are still with me today. Every day, I'm thinking about those same issues as I try to lead this Nation. I'm asking the same kinds of questions about, how do we as a diverse nation come together to achieve what we need to achieve? How do we make sure that every single person is treated with dignity and respect? What responsibilities do we have to people who are less fortunate than we are? How do we make sure that everybody is included in this family of Americans?

Those are all questions that date back to this class that I took back in eighth grade. And here's the thing: I still don't always know the answers to all these questions. But if I'd have just tuned out because the class sounded boring, I might have missed out on something that not only did I turn out enjoying, but has ended up serving me in good stead for the rest of my life.

So that's a big part of your responsibility, is to test things out. Take risks. Try new things. Work hard. Don't be embarrassed if you're not good at something right away. You're not supposed to be good at everything right away. That's why you're in school. The idea, though, is, is that you keep on expanding your horizons and your sense of possibility. Now is the time for you to do that. And those are also, by the way, the things that will make school more fun.

Down the road, those will be the traits that will help you succeed, as well, the traits that will lead you to invent a device that makes an iPad look like a stone tablet, or what will help you figure out a way to use the sun and the wind to power a city and give us new energy sources that are less polluting, or maybe you'll write the next great American novel.

Now, to do any of those things, you have to not only graduate from high school—and I know I'm just—I'm in the amen corner with Principal Berger here—not only do you have to graduate from high school, but you're going to have to continue education after you leave. You have to not only graduate, but you've got to keep going after you graduate.

That might mean, for many of you, a 4-year university. I was just talking to Donae, and she wants to be an architect, and she's interning with a architectural firm, and she's already got her sights set on what school she wants to go to. But it might, for some other folks, be a community college or professional credentialing or training. But the fact of the matter is, is that more than 60 percent of the jobs in the next decade will require more than a high school diploma—more than 60 percent. That's the world you're walking into.

So I want all of you to set a goal to continue your education after you graduate. And if that means college for you, just getting into college is not enough. You also have to graduate. One of the biggest challenges we have right now is that too many of our young people enroll in college, but don't actually end up getting their degree, and as a consequence—our country used to have the world's highest proportion of young people with a college degree; we now rank 16th. I don't like being 16th. I like being number one. That's not good enough. So we've got to use—we've got to make sure your generation gets us back to the top of having the most college graduates relative to the population of any country on Earth.

If we do that, you guys will have a brighter future and so will America. We'll be able to make sure the newest inventions and the latest breakthroughs happen right here in the United States of America. It will mean better jobs and more fulfilling lives and greater opportunities not only for you, but also for your kids.

So I don't want anybody who's listening here today to think that you're done once you finish high school. You are not done learning. In fact, what's happening in today's economy is—it's all about lifelong learning. You have to constantly upgrade your skills and find new ways of doing things. Even if college isn't for you, even if a 4-year college isn't for you, you're still going to have to get more education after you get out of high school. You've got to start expecting big things from yourself right now.

I know that may sound a little intimidating. And some of you may be wondering how you can pay for college, or you might not know what you want to do with your life yet. And that's okay. Nobody expects you to have your entire future mapped out at this point. And we don't expect you to have to make it on your own. First of all, you've got wonderful parents who love you to death and want you to have a lot more opportunity than they ever had, which, by the way, means don't give them a hard time when they ask you to turn off the video games, turn off the TV, and do some homework. You need to be listening to them. I speak from experience because that's what I've been telling Malia and Sasha. Don't be mad about it, because we're thinking about your future.

You've also got people all across this country—including myself and Arne and people at every level of government—who are working on your behalf. We're taking every step we can to ensure that you're getting an educational system that is worthy of your potential. We're working to make sure that you have the most up-to-date schools with the latest tools of learning. We're making sure that this country's colleges and universities are affordable and accessible to you. We're working to get the best class—teachers into the classroom as well, so they can help you prepare for college and a future career.

Let me say something about teachers, by the way. Teachers are the men and women who might be working harder than just about anybody these days. Whether you go to a big school or a small one, whether you attend a public or a private or a charter school, your teachers are giving up their weekends. They're waking up at dawn. They're cramming their days full of classes and extracurricular activities. And then they're going home, eating some dinner, and then they've got to stay up sometimes past midnight, grading your papers and correcting your grammar and making sure you got that algebra formula properly.

And they don't do it for a fancy office. They don't—they sure don't do it for the big salary. They do it for you. They do it because nothing gives them more satisfaction than seeing you learn. They live for those moments when something clicks, when you amaze them with your intellect or your vocabulary, or they see what kind of person you're becoming. And they're proud of you. And they say, I had something to do with that, that wonderful young person who is going to succeed. They have confidence in you that you will be citizens and leaders who take us into tomorrow. They know you're our future. So your teachers are pouring everything they got into you, and they're not alone.

But I also want to emphasize this: With all the challenges that our country is facing right now, we don't just need you for the future; we actually need you now. America needs young people's passion and their ideas. We need your energy right now. I know you're up to it because I've seen it. Nothing inspires me more than knowing that young people all across the country are already making their marks. They're not waiting; they're making a difference now.

There are students like Will Kim from Fremont, California, who launched a nonprofit that gives loans to students from low-income schools who want to start their own business. Think about that. So he's giving loans to other students. He set up a not-for-profit. He's raising the money doing what he loves, through dodgeball tournaments and capture-the-flag games. But he's creative. He took initiative. And now he's helping other young people be able to afford the schooling that they need.

There is a young man, Jake Bernstein, 17 years old, from a military family in St. Louis, worked with his sister to launch a website devoted to community service for young people. And they've held volunteer fairs, and put up an online database, and helped thousands of families to find volunteer opportunities ranging from maintaining nature trails to serving at local hospitals.

And then last year, I met a young woman named Amy Chyao from Richardson, Texas. She's 16 years old, so she's the age of some of you here. During the summer, I think because somebody in her family had an illness, she decided that she was interested in cancer research. She hadn't taken chemistry yet, so she taught herself chemistry during the summer. And then she applied what she had learned and discovered a breakthrough process that uses light to kill cancer cells. Sixteen years old, it's incredible. And she's been approached by some doctors and researchers who want to work with her to help her with her discovery.

The point is you don't have to wait to make a difference. Your first obligation is to do well in school. Your first obligation is to make sure that you're preparing yourself for college and career. But you can also start making your mark right now. A lot of times young people may have better ideas than us old people do anyway. We just need those ideas out in the open, in and out of the classroom.

When I meet young people like yourselves, when I sat and talked to Donae, I have no doubt that America's best days are still ahead of us, because I know the potential that lies in each of you. Soon enough, you will be the ones leading our businesses and leading our Government. You will be the one who are making sure that the next generation gets what they need to succeed. You will be the ones that are charting the course of our unwritten history. And all that starts right now, starts this year.

So I want all of you who are listening, as well as everybody here at Banneker, I want you to make the most of the year that's ahead of you. I want you to think of this time as one in which you are just loading up with information and skills, and you're trying new things, and you're practicing, and you're honing—all those things that you're going to need to do great things when you get out of school.

Your country is depending on you. So set your sights high. Have a great school year. Let's get to work.

Thank you very much, everybody. God bless you. God bless the United States of America.

NOTE: The President spoke at 1:48 p.m. In his remarks, he referred to Donae Owens, student body president, Benjamin Banneker Academic High School.

Remarks at the Change of Command Ceremony for the Chairman of the Joint Chiefs of Staff at Fort Myer, Virginia
September 30, 2011

Thank you very much. Secretary Panetta, thank you for your introduction and for your extraordinary leadership. To Members of Congress, Vice President Biden, members of the Joint Chiefs, service Secretaries, distinguished guests, and men and women of the finest military in the world.

Most of all, Admiral Mullen, Deborah, Michael, and I also want to also acknowledge your son Jack, who's deployed today. All of you have performed extraordinary service to our country.

Before I begin, I want to say a few words about some important news. Earlier this morning, Anwar al-Awlaki, a leader of Al Qaida in the Arabian Peninsula, was killed in Yemen. The death of Awlaki is a major blow to Al Qaida's most active operational affiliate. Awlaki was the leader of external operations for Al Qaida in the Arabian Peninsula. In that role, he took the lead in planning and directing efforts to murder innocent Americans. He directed the failed attempt to blow up an airplane on Christmas Day in 2009. He directed the failed attempt to blow up U.S. cargo planes in 2010. And he repeatedly called on individuals in the United States and around the globe to kill innocent men, women, and children to advance a murderous agenda.

The death of Awlaki marks another significant milestone in the broader effort to defeat Al Qaida and its affiliates. Furthermore, this success is a tribute to our intelligence community and to the efforts of Yemen and its security forces, who have worked closely with the United States over the course of several years.

Awlaki and his organization have been directly responsible for the deaths of many Yemeni citizens. His hateful ideology and targeting of innocent civilians has been rejected by the vast majority of Muslims and people of all faiths. And he has met his demise because the Government and the people of Yemen have joined the international community in a common effort against Al Qaida.

Al Qaida in the Arabian Peninsula remains a dangerous, though weakened, terrorist organization. And going forward, we will remain vigilant against any threats to the United States or our allies and partners. But make no mistake: This is further proof that Al Qaida and its affiliates will find no safe haven anywhere in the world.

Working with Yemen and our other allies and partners, we will be determined, we will be deliberate, we will be relentless, we will be resolute in our commitment to destroy terrorist networks that aim to kill Americans and to build a world in which people everywhere can live in greater peace, prosperity, and security.

Now, advancing that security has been the life's work of the man that we honor today. But as Mike will admit to you, he got off to a somewhat shaky start. He was a young ensign, just 23 years old, commanding a small tanker, when he collided with a buoy. [*Laughter*] As Mike later explained, in his understated way, when you're on a ship, "colliding with anything is not a good thing." [*Laughter*]

I tell this story because Mike has told it himself to men and women across our military. He has always understood that the true measure of our success is not whether we stumble, it's whether we pick ourselves up and dust ourselves off and get on with the job. It's whether, no matter the storms or shoals that come our way, we chart our course, we keep our eye fixed on the horizon and take care of those around us, because we all we rise and fall together.

That's the story of Mike Mullen. It's the story of America. And it's the spirit that we celebrate today.

Indeed, if there's a thread that runs through his illustrious career, it's Mike's sense of stewardship: the understanding that, as leaders, our time at the helm is but a moment in the life of our Nation; the humility which says the institutions and people entrusted to our care look to us, yet they do not belong to us; and the sense of responsibility we have to pass them safer and stronger to those who follow.

Mike, as you look back as your 4 consequential years as Chairman and your four decades in uniform, be assured our military is stronger and our Nation is more secure because of the service that you have rendered.

Today, we have renewed American leadership in the world. We've strengthened our alliances, including NATO. We're leading again in Asia, and we forged a new treaty with Russia to reduce our nuclear arsenals. And every American can be grateful to Admiral Mullen, as am I, for his critical role in each of these achievements, which will enhance our national security for decades to come.

Today, we see the remarkable achievements of our 9/11 generation of servicemembers. They've given Iraqis a chance to determine their own future. They've pushed the Taliban out of their Afghan strongholds and finally put Al Qaida on the path to defeat. Meanwhile, our forces have responded to sudden crises with compassion, as in Haiti, and with precision, as in Libya. And it will be long remembered that our troops met these tests on Admiral Mullen's watch and under his leadership.

Today, we're moving forward from a position of strength. Fewer of our sons and daughters are in harm's way and more will come home. Our soldiers can look forward to shorter deployments, more time with their families, and more time training for future missions. Put simply, despite the stresses and strains of a hard decade of war, the military that Admiral Mullen passes to General Dempsey today is the best that it has ever been.

And today, thanks to Mike's principled leadership, our military draws its strength from more members of our American family. Soon, women will report for duty on our submarines and patriotic servicemembers who are gay and lesbian no longer have to lie about who they are to serve the country that they love. History will record that the tipping point toward this progress came when the 17th Chairman of the Joint Chiefs of Staff went before Congress and told the Nation that it was the right thing to do.

Mike, your legacy will endure in a military that is stronger, but also in a nation that is more just.

Finally, I would add that in every discussion I've ever had with Mike, in every recommendation he's ever made, one thing has always been foremost in his mind: the lives and well-being of our men and women in uniform. I've seen it in the quiet moments with our wounded warriors and our veterans. I saw it that day in the Situation Room, as we held our breath for the safe return of our forces who delivered justice to Usama bin Laden. I saw it at Dover, as we honored our fallen heroes in their final journey home.

Mike, you have fulfilled the pledge you made at the beginning to represent our troops with "unwavering dedication." And so has Deborah, who we thank for her four decades of extraordinary service, her extraordinary support to our military families, her kindness, her gentleness, her grace under pressure. She is an extraordinary woman, Mike. And we're both lucky to have married up.

Now the mantle of leadership passes to General Marty Dempsey, one of our Nation's most respected and combat-tested generals. Marty, after a lifetime of service, I thank you, Deanie, Chris, Megan, and Caitlin for answering the call to serve once more.

In this sense, today begins to complete the transition to our new leadership team. In Secretary Panetta, we have one of our Nation's finest public servants. In the new Deputy Secretary, Ash Carter, we will have an experienced leader to carry on the work of Bill Lynn, who we thank for his outstanding service. And the new Vice Chairman, Admiral Sandy Winnefeld, will round out a team where, for the first time, both the Chairman and Vice Chairman will have the experience of leading combat operations in the years since 9/11.

Leon, Marty, Ash, Sandy, men and women of this Department, both uniformed and civilian, we still have much to do: from bringing the rest of our troops home from Iraq this year to transitioning to Afghan lead for their own security; from defeating Al Qaida to our most solemn of obligations, taking care of our forces and their families when they go to war and when they come home.

None of this will be easy, especially as our Nation makes hard fiscal choices. But as Commander in Chief, let me say it as clearly as I can: As we go forward we will be guided by the mission we ask of our troops and the capabilities they need to succeed. We will maintain our military superiority. We will never waver in defense of our country, our citizens, or our national security interests. And the United States of America and our Armed Forces will remain the greatest force for freedom and security that the world has ever known.

This is who we are as Americans. And this is who we must always be: as we salute Mike Mullen as an exemplar of this spirit, we salute him for a life of patriotic service; as we continue his legacy to keep the country that we love safe; and as we renew the sources of American strength here at home and around the world.

Mike, thank you, from a grateful nation.

NOTE: The President spoke at 11:41 a.m. In his remarks, he referred to Deborah Mullen, wife, and Michael and John Mullen, sons, of Adm. Michael G. Mullen, USN; and Deanie Dempsey, wife, and Christopher Dempsey, Megan Dempsey Bailey, and Caitlin Dempsey, children, of Gen. Martin E. Dempsey, USA.

Letter to Congressional Leaders Transmitting a Report Related to Afghanistan and Pakistan
September 30, 2011

Dear _____:

In response to section 1117 of the Supplemental Appropriations Act, 2009 (Public Law 111–32) (the "Act"), and in order to keep the Congress fully informed, I am providing the attached report related to Afghanistan and Pakistan. This is the fourth report submitted under section 1117 of the Act and follows the April 2011 submission.

This report covers the period from January 1, 2011, through June 30, 2011. To the extent possible, the report also provides an assessment through August 31, 2011. Events continue to evolve since that time, for example in our relationship with Pakistan, but these developments fall outside the scope of this report. As I noted in my remarks on the way forward in Afghanistan on June 22, we have seen great progress in our fight against al-Qa'ida; we have reversed the Taliban's momentum in Afghanistan; and we continue to see progress in training the Afghan National Security Forces. This will allow us in the coming year to fully recover the 33,000 U.S. troop surge I announced at West Point in December 2009. Beyond that change, we continue to implement the strategy and do not believe further modifications or adjustments to the metrics, resources, or authorities are required at this time. Huge challenges remain, and this is the beginning—but not the end—of our effort to wind down this war.

As the Congress continues its deliberations on the way ahead in Afghanistan and Pakistan, I want to continue to underscore our Nation's interests in the successful implementation of this policy.

Sincerely,

BARACK OBAMA

NOTE: Identical letters were sent to Vice President Joseph R. Biden, Jr., President of the Senate; Senate Majority Leader Harry M. Reid; Senate Minority Leader A. Mitchell McConnell; Daniel K. Inouye, chairman, and W. Thad Cochran, vice chairman, Senate Committee on Appropriations; Carl M. Levin, chairman, and John S. McCain III, ranking member, Senate Committee on Armed Services; John F. Kerry, chairman, and Richard G. Lugar, ranking member, Senate Committee on Foreign Relations; Joseph I. Lieberman, chairman, and Susan M. Collins, ranking member, Senate Committee on Homeland Security and Governmental Affairs; Patrick J. Leahy, chairman, and Charles E. Grassley, ranking member, Senate Committee on the Judiciary; Dianne Feinstein, chair, and Saxby C. Chambliss, vice chairman, Senate Select Committee on Intelligence; Speaker of the House of Representatives John A. Boehner; House Majority Leader Eric I. Cantor; House Democratic Leader Nancy Pelosi; Harold D. Rogers, chairman, and Norman D. Dicks, ranking member, House Committee on Appropriations; Howard P. "Buck" McKeon, chairman, and Adam Smith, ranking member, House Committee on Armed Services; Ileana Ros-Lehtinen, chair, and Howard L. Berman, ranking member, House Committee on Foreign Affairs; Peter T. King, chairman, and Bennie G. Thompson, ranking member, House Committee on Homeland Security; Lamar S. Smith, chairman, and John J. Conyers, Jr., ranking member, House Committee on the Judiciary; and Michael J. Rogers, chairman, and C.A. "Dutch" Ruppersberger, ranking member, House Permanent Select Committee on Intelligence.

Remarks at a Democratic National Committee Fundraiser
September 30, 2011

Well, to Jim and Jeff, thank you so much for the hospitality; to all of you, for being here. I have to say that the good doctor could run for office. [*Laughter*] He's quite an orator. So that was an extraordinarily gracious introduction, and thank you for opening up your home. To all of you who are here, some of you who've been longtime supporters, some of you who I'm seeing for the first time, it's wonderful to be here.

And what I want to do is have more of a conversation than a monologue, so I'm just going to say a few words at the top very briefly, and then we'll open it up for questions.

I was just on the West Coast, traveling across the country, talking to people about the jobs act and why we need to put people back to work, talking to them about a wide range of issues like energy and health care. And I made the argument to them that I'll make to you, which is that this election is in some ways even more consequential than 2008.

I think in 2008 we understood that for decades there had been a host of problems that had been building up over time. That the dream of middle class folks or folks who were aspiring to the middle class—being able to work hard, get a good education, get a good job, act responsibly, buy a home, make sure that their kids are doing even better than they are, retire with some dignity and respect—that dream felt like it was slipping away. And for a whole host of reasons: because we had underinvested in our human capital and our education system and in our infrastructure; because, frankly, we had seen the rules tilted against ordinary folks in favor of those who were well connected in Washington or powerful on Wall Street.

And we argued in 2008, and we captured, I think, the imaginations of a lot of people, that we could bring about some fundamental change if we got past some of the partisan rancor and the constant politicking that had come to characterize Washington.

Now, we've done a lot over these 2½ years. Obviously, in the midst of the worst financial crisis since the Great Depression, we've been able to avoid a great depression, stabilize the financial system. We've been able to move forward on a lot of the campaign pledges that we had talked about from making sure that health care is affordable and accessible to every American, to reforming our education system at the K-through-12 level so that our kids can compete in this global economy, to ending "don't ask, don't tell," to making sure that we signed into law equal pay for equal work.

Extraordinarily proud of the accomplishments and the progress that we've made over the last 2 years. But what we haven't done is change Washington. And we still have work to do to make sure that this town is working on behalf of ordinary folks so that they can start once again believing in the American Dream, because people have lost confidence in the capacity of folks to look out for them as opposed to look out for themselves or their most powerful patrons. And that's part of what 2012 is all about.

We've got the other party that is laying out for all to see what their agenda is, and that is to roll back environmental regulations, to try to shrink the capacity of Government to act in a proactive way to make sure that we can outeducate and outinnovate and outbuild the rest of the world, to basically allow the most powerful forces in our society to write their own rules

and everybody else is going to be on their own. And the argument I made in 2008 applies to 2012: That's not the story of America.

What Jim was just talking about in terms of the history of this home is a story of people making it in part because somebody was investing in public schools, somebody was making sure that we were investing in basic research and development that could ensure that America had the technological edge. The story of America is all of us joining together and everybody sharing in sacrifice, but also sharing in opportunity. And that's what we need to sustain and that's what's at stake in this 2012 election.

Now, it's going to be hard. The economy is coming out of this enormous world recession and people, understandably, are hurting. All around the country where I travel, folks are having a very difficult time. They don't believe in the other side's vision, but they're frustrated.

And so we've got to be able to make the argument—an argument, I believe, that if we stay the course, if we stay on track, if we keep on the task of reforming our education system and making college more affordable, if we stay on track in terms of implementing health care to start making it more efficient, if we stay on track in rebuilding our roads and our bridges and our schools, and if we stay on track in terms of bringing manufacturing back to the United States and making it effective, then I have no doubt that America can compete. Because we still have the universities, we still have the best entrepreneurs, we still have the best scientists, and I believe we've got the best system of government, when it's working.

And the only way it works is if everybody is involved and everybody is paying attention and everybody is engaged. We got people engaged and excited in 2008. We've got to reengage them and reexcite them in 2012. And I can't do that by myself. I'm going to need all of you to be a part of that.

So let me just close by saying this. I could not be prouder to have friends and supporters like the people in this room. I hope you are signed up for a year of hard work. This is not going to be easy. But if we have that same

1187

sense of urgency, what I called in 2008 the "fierce urgency of now," if we still possess that, then not only are we going to be able to succeed in the election, but more importantly, we're going to be able to give the American Dream back to the American people.

Thank you so much, everybody.

NOTE: The President spoke at 7:31 p.m. at the residence of James D'Orta. Audio was not available for verification of the content of these remarks.

The President's Weekly Address
October 1, 2011

Hello, everyone. It's been almost 3 weeks since I sent the "American Jobs Act" to Congress, 3 weeks since I sent them a bill that would put people back to work and put money in people's pockets. This jobs bill is fully paid for. This jobs bill contains the kinds of proposals that Democrats and Republicans have supported in the past. And now I want it back. It's time for Congress to get its act together and to pass this jobs bill so I can sign it into law.

Some Republicans in Congress have said that they agree with certain parts of this jobs bill. If so, it's time for them to tell me what those proposals are. And if they're opposed to this jobs bill, I'd like to know what exactly they're against. Are they against putting teachers and police officers and firefighters back on the job? Are they against hiring construction workers to rebuild our roads and bridges and schools? Are they against giving tax cuts to virtually every worker and small business in America?

Economists from across the political spectrum have said that this jobs bill would boost the economy and spur hiring. Why would you be against that, especially at a time when so many Americans are struggling and out of work?

This isn't just about what I think is right. It's not just about what a group of economists think is right. This is about what the American people want. Everywhere I go, they tell me they want action on jobs. Every day, I get letters from Americans who expect Washington to do something about the problems we face.

Destiny Wheeler is a 16-year-old from Georgia who wants to go to college. She wrote to me saying: "Nowadays it is hard to see myself pushing forward and putting my family in a better position, especially since the economy is rough and my starting situation is so poor. Yet the 'American Jobs Act' gives me hope that I might start to receive a better education, that one day job opportunities will open for me to grasp, and that one day my personal American Dream will be reached." Destiny needs us to pass this jobs bill.

Alice Johnson is an Oregon native who, along with her husband, has been looking for a job for about 2 years. She writes: "I have faithfully applied for work every week. . . . Of the hundreds of applications I have put in, I received interview requests for about 10. . . . I too am sick of all the fighting in Washington, DC. Please tell the Republicans that people are hurting and are hungry and need help. Pass the jobs bill." Alice Johnson needs our help.

Cathleen Dixon sent me pictures of the aging bridge she drives under when she takes her kids to school in Chicago every day. She worries about their safety and writes: "I am angry that in this country of vast resources, we claim that we cannot maintain basic infrastructure. How can we ever hope to preserve or regain our stature in this world, if we cannot find the will to protect our people and take care of our basic needs?"

I also heard from Kim Faber, who told me about the small carpet business her husband owns in New Jersey. "We hang on by a shoestring," she writes. "My husband worries every day about if checks might bounce. He uses our home loan to put money in the business so they will be covered. Please pass this jobs bill! This is the job creating we need right now! It breaks my husband's heart when he has to let people go! Pass the bill!"

Kim said it best: "Pass the bill!" I know one Republican was quoted as saying that their party shouldn't pass this jobs bill because it would give me a win. This isn't about giving me a win, and it's not about them. This is about Destiny Wheeler and Alice Johnson. It's about Cathleen Dixon's children and the Fabers' family business. These are the people who need a win, and I will be fighting for this jobs bill every day on their behalf. If anyone watching feels the same way, don't be shy about letting your Congressman know. It is time for the politics to end. Let's pass this jobs bill.

NOTE: The address was recorded at approximately 4:55 p.m. on September 30 in the Map Room at the White House for broadcast on October 1. In the address, the President referred to Steven G. Faber, former owner and current manager, Faber Brothers Broadloom. The transcript was made available by the Office of the Press Secretary on September 30, but was embargoed for release until 6 a.m. on October 1.

Remarks at the Human Rights Campaign's Annual National Dinner
October 1, 2011

The President. Thank you so much. It is great to be back. I see a lot of friends in the house. I appreciate the chance to join you tonight. I also took a trip out to California last week, where I held some productive bilateral talks with your leader, Lady Gaga. [*Laughter*] She was wearing 16-inch heels. [*Laughter*] She was 8 feet tall. [*Laughter*] It was a little intimidating.

Now, I don't want to give a long speech. Cyndi Lauper is in the house. I can't compete with that. But I wanted to come here tonight, first of all, to personally thank Joe for his outstanding years of leadership at HRC. What he has accomplished at the helm of this organization has been remarkable, and I want to thank all of you for the support that you've shown this organization and for your commitment to a simple idea: Every single American—gay, straight, lesbian, bisexual, transgender—every single American deserves to be treated equally in the eyes of the law and in the eyes of our society. It's a pretty simple proposition.

Now, I don't have to tell you that we have a ways to go in that struggle. I don't have to tell you how many are still denied their basic rights, Americans who are still made to feel like second class citizens, who have to live a lie to keep their jobs or who are afraid to walk the street or down the hall at school. Many of you have devoted your lives to the cause of equality. So you know what we have to do. We've got more work ahead of us.

But we can also be proud of the progress we've made these past 2½ years. Think about it. Two years ago, I stood at this podium, in this room, before many of you, and I made a pledge. I said I would never counsel patience, that it wasn't right to tell you to be patient any more than it was right for others to tell African Americans to be patient in the fight for equal rights a half century ago. But what I also said, that while it might take time, more time than anyone would like, we are going to make progress, we are going to succeed, we are going to build a more perfect Union.

And so let's see what happened. I met with Judy Shepard. I promised her we would pass a hate crimes bill named for her son Matthew. And with the help of my dear friend Ted Kennedy we got it done. Because it should never be dangerous—[*applause*]—you should never have to look over your shoulder to be gay in the United States of America. That's why we got it done.

I met with Janice Langbehn, who was barred from the bedside of the woman she loved as she lay dying. And I told her that we were going to put a stop to this discrimination. And you know what? We got it done. I issued an order so that any hospital in America that accepts Medicare or Medicaid—and that means just about every hospital—has to treat gay partners just as they do straight partners. Because nobody should have to produce a legal contract to hold the hand of the person that they love. We got that done.

I said that we would lift that HIV travel ban. We got that done. We put in place the first comprehensive national strategy to fight HIV/AIDS.

Many questioned whether we'd succeed in repealing "don't ask, don't tell." And yes, it took 2 years to get the repeal through Congress. We had to hold a coalition together. We had to keep up the pressure. We took some flak along the way. But with the help of HRC, we got it done, and "don't ask, don't tell" is history. And all over the world, there are men and women serving this country just as they always have with honor and courage and discipline and valor. We got it done. We got that done. All around the world, you've got gays and lesbians who are serving, and the only difference is now they can put up a family photo. [*Laughter*] No one has to live a lie to serve the country they love.

I vowed to keep up the fight against the so-called Defense of Marriage Act. There's a bill to repeal this discriminatory law in Congress, and I want to see that passed. But until we reach that day, my administration is no longer defending DOMA in the courts. I believe the law runs counter to the Constitution, and it's time for it to end once and for all. It should join "don't ask, don't tell" in the history books.

So yes, we have more work to do. And after so many years, even decades, of inaction you've got every right to push against the slow pace of change. But make no mistake: I want people to feel encouraged here. We are making change. We're making real and lasting change. We can be proud of the progress we've already made.

And I'm going to continue to fight alongside you. And I don't just mean in your role, by the way, as advocates for equality. You're also moms and dads who care about the schools your children go to. You're also students figuring out how to pay for college. You're also folks who are worried about the economy and whether or not your partner or husband or wife will be able to find a job. And you're Americans who want this country to succeed and prosper and who are tired of the gridlock and

the vicious partisanship and are sick of the Washington games. Those are your fights too, HRC.

So I'm going to need your help. I need your help to fight for equality, to pass a repeal of DOMA, to pass an inclusive employment non-discrimination bill so that being gay is never again a fireable offense in America. And I don't have to tell you, there are those who don't want to just stand in our way, but want to turn the clock back, who want to return to the days when gay people couldn't serve their country openly, who reject the progress that we've made, who, as we speak, are looking to enshrine discrimination into State laws and constitutions, efforts that we've got to work hard to oppose, because that's not what America should be about.

We're not about restricting rights and restricting opportunity. We're about opening up rights and opening up opportunity and treating each other generously and with love and respect.

And together, we also have to keep sending a message to every young person in this country who might feel alone or afraid because they're gay or transgender, who may be getting picked on or pushed around because they're different. We've got to make sure they know that there are adults they can talk to, that they are never alone, that there is a whole world waiting for them filled with possibility. That's why we held a summit at the White House on bullying. That's why we're going to continue to focus on this issue. This isn't just kids being kids. It's wrong. It's destructive. It's never acceptable. And I want all those kids to know that the President and the First Lady is standing right by them every inch of the way. I want them to know that we love them and care about them and they're not by themselves. That's what I want them to know.

Now, I also need your help in the broader fight to get this economy back on track. You may have heard, I introduced a bill called the "American Jobs Act." It's been almost 3 weeks since I sent it up to Congress. That's 3 weeks longer than it should have taken to pass this commonsense bill. This is a bill filled with ideas that both parties have supported: tax breaks for companies that hire veterans, road projects, school renovations, putting construction crews back to work rebuilding America, tax cuts for middle class families so they can make ends meet and spend a little more at local stores and restaurants that need the business.

Now, you may have heard me say this a few times before, I'll say it again: Pass the bill. Enough gridlock, enough delay, enough politics. Pass this bill. Put this country back to work. HRC, you know how Congress works. I'm counting on you to have my back. Go out there and get them to pass this bill. Let's put America back to work.

Now, ultimately, these debates we're having are about more than just politics. They're more about—they're about more than the polls and the pundits and who's up and who's down. This is a contest of values. That's what's at stake here. This is a fundamental debate about who we are as a nation.

I don't believe—we don't believe in a small America where we let our roads crumble, we let our schools fall apart, where we stand by while teachers are laid off and science labs are shut down and kids are dropping out.

We believe in a big America, an America that invests in the future, that invests in schools and highways and research and technology, the things that have helped make our economy the envy of the world.

We don't believe in a small America where we meet our fiscal responsibilities by abdicating every other responsibility we have and where we just divvy up the Government as tax breaks for those who need them the least and where we abandon the commitment we've made to seniors though Medicare and Social Security and we say to somebody looking for work or a student who needs a college loan or a middle class family with a child who's disabled that you're on your own. That's not who we are.

We believe in a big America, an America where everybody has got a fair shot and everyone pays their fair share. An America where we value success and the idea that anyone can make it in this country. But also an America that does—in which everyone does their part, including the wealthiest Americans, including

the biggest corporations, to deal with the deficits that threaten our future.

We don't believe in a small America. We don't believe in the kind of smallness that says it's okay for a stage full of political leaders, one of whom could end up being the President of the United States, being silent when an American soldier is booed. We don't believe in that. We don't believe in standing silent when that happens. We don't believe in them being silent since. You want to be Commander in Chief? You can start by standing up for the men and women who wear the uniform of the United States, even when it's not politically convenient.

We don't believe in a small America. We believe in a big America, a tolerant America, a just America, an equal America that values the service of every patriot. We believe in an America where we're all in it together and we see the good in one another and we live up to a creed that is as old as our founding: *E pluribus unum*. Out of many, one. And that includes everybody. That's what we believe. That's what we're going to be fighting for.

I am confident that's what the American people believe in. I'm confident because of the changes we've achieved these past 2½ years, the progress that some folks said was impossible. And I'm hopeful—I am hopeful——

Audience member. Fired up!

The President. I'm fired up too. [*Laughter*] I am hopeful—[*applause*]—I am hopeful—I am still hopeful because of a deeper shift that we're seeing, a transformation not only written into our laws, but woven into the fabric of our society.

It's progress led not by Washington, but by ordinary citizens who are propelled not just by politics, but by love and friendship and a sense of mutual regard. It's playing out in legislatures like New York and courtrooms and in the ballot box. But it's also happening around water coolers and at the Thanksgiving table and on Facebook and Twitter and at PTA meetings and potluck dinners and church socials and VFW halls.

It happens when a father realizes he doesn't just love his daughter, but also her wife. It happens when a soldier tells his unit that he's gay, and they tell him they knew it all along and

1191

they didn't care, because he was the toughest guy in the unit. It happens when a video sparks a movement to let every single young person know they're not alone and things will get better. It happens when people look past their ultimately minor differences to see themselves in the hopes and struggles of their fellow human beings. That's where change is happening.

And that's not just the story of the gay rights movement. That's the story of America, the slow, inexorable march towards a more perfect Union. You are contributing to that story, and I'm confident we can continue to write another chapter together.

Thank you very much, everybody. God bless you.

NOTE: The President spoke at 7:26 p.m. at the Walter E. Washington Convention Center. In his remarks, he referred to musicians Stefani J.A. "Lady Gaga" Germanotta and Cyndi Lauper; and Joe Solmonese, president, Human Rights Campaign.

Remarks Prior to a Cabinet Meeting and an Exchange With Reporters
October 3, 2011

The President. All right, good morning, everybody. I am pulling my Cabinet together to talk about the one topic that's on everybody's minds, and that is how do we put America back to work.

Each of the Secretaries and heads of agencies have been assigned to look at what we can do administratively to accelerate job growth over the next several months. And working with the Jobs Council that we've set up, working with the private sector, we have been looking for a wide range of ideas of administrative action we can take. A good example would be, for example, accelerating the payments to small businesses so that they've got better cash flow, trying to figure out ways that we can be working in the housing market without congressional action to provide some relief for homeowners.

But ultimately, we still have to have congressional action. It's been several weeks now since I sent up the "American Jobs Act." And as I've been saying on the road, I want it back. I'm ready to sign it. And so my expectation is, is that now that we're in the month of October that we will schedule a vote before the end of this month. I'll be talking to Senator Reid, McConnell, as well as Speaker Boehner and Nancy Pelosi, and insisting that we have a vote on this bill.

We've been hearing from Republicans that there are some proposals that they're interested in. That is not surprising, since the contents to the "American Jobs Act" includes proposals that, in the past, have been supported by Republicans and Democratic—Democrats alike. And if there are aspects of the bill that they don't like, they should tell us what it is that they're not willing to go for. They should tell us what it is that they're prepared to see move forward.

I have to tell you that I can't imagine any American that I've been talking to that's not interested in seeing construction workers back on the job rebuilding roads and bridges, schools, airports, putting teachers back in the classroom to make sure that our kids are getting the very best education, making sure our vets get help when they come home and that small businesses have further incentive to hire them.

So I'm very much looking forward to seeing Congress debate this bill, pass it, get it to my desk, so we can start putting hundreds of thousands and millions of Americans back to work. And I will be continuing to put as much pressure as I can bring to bear on my administration and our agencies to do everything we can without Congress's help. But ultimately, they've got to do the right thing for the American people.

All right? Thank you very much, everybody.

Trade Agreements

Q. Are you sending those trade agreements up, sir?

The President. We'll have an announcement on that in the next day or so.

NOTE: The President spoke at 11:17 a.m. in the Cabinet Room at the White House.

Statement on Submitting Trade Agreements With Colombia, Panama, and South Korea to Congress
October 3, 2011

The series of trade agreements I am submitting to Congress today will make it easier for American companies to sell their products in South Korea, Colombia, and Panama and provide a major boost to our exports. These agreements will support tens of thousands of jobs across the country for workers making products stamped with three proud words: Made in America. We've worked hard to strengthen these agreements to get the best possible deal for American workers and businesses, and I call on Congress to pass them without delay, along with the bipartisan agreement on trade adjustment assistance that will help workers whose jobs have been affected by global competition.

Message to the Congress Transmitting Legislation To Implement the United States-Colombia Trade Promotion Agreement
October 3, 2011

To the Congress of the United States:

I am pleased to transmit legislation and supporting documents to implement the United States-Colombia Trade Promotion Agreement (Agreement). The Agreement is an important part of my Administration's efforts to spur economic growth, increase exports, and create jobs in the United States, while promoting our core values. The Agreement will create significant new opportunities for American workers, farmers, ranchers, businesses, and consumers by opening the Colombian market and eliminating barriers to U.S. goods, services, and investment.

The Agreement also represents a historic development in our relations with Colombia. Colombia is a steadfast strategic partner of the United States and a leader in the region. The Agreement reflects the commitment of the United States to supporting democracy and economic growth in Colombia. It will also help Colombia battle production of illegal crops by creating alternative economic opportunities.

Under the Agreement, tariffs on over 80 percent of U.S. consumer and industrial exports will be eliminated immediately. United States agricultural exports in particular will enjoy substantial new improvements in access to Colombia's market. Currently, no U.S. agricultural exports enjoy duty-free access to Colombia. Once the Agreement enters into force, almost 70 percent, by value, of current U.S. agricultural exports will be able to enter Colombia duty-free immediately. In addition, the Agreement will give American service providers greater access to Colombia's $134 billion services market. This will help to level the playing field, since 91 percent of our imports from Colombia have enjoyed duty-free access to our market under U.S. trade preference programs.

The Agreement contains state of the art provisions to help protect and enforce intellectual property rights, reduce regulatory red tape, and eliminate regulatory barriers to U.S. exports. The Agreement also contains the highest standards for protecting labor rights, carrying out covered environmental agreements, and ensuring that key domestic labor and environmental laws are enforced, combined with strong remedies for noncompliance. Colombia has already made significant reforms related to the obligations it will have under the labor chapter. A number of these steps have been taken in fulfillment of the commitments Colombia made in the agreed Action Plan Related to Labor Rights that President Santos and I announced on April 7. Colombia must successfully implement key elements of the Action Plan before I will bring the Agreement into force.

This Agreement forms an integral part of my Administration's larger strategy of doubling exports by the end of 2014 through opening markets around the world. In addition, the Agreement

1193

provides an opportunity to strengthen our economic and political ties with the Andean region, and underpins U.S. support for democracy while contributing to further hemispheric integration and economic growth in the United States. This Agreement is vital to ensuring Colombia continues on its trajectory of positive change.

As a part of an ambitious trade agenda, it is important that the Congress renew a strong and robust Trade Adjustment Assistance Program consistent with reforms enacted in 2009. Renewal of that program is necessary to support Americans who need training and other services when their jobs are adversely affected by trade. As we expand access to other markets abroad, we need to ensure that American workers are provided the tools needed to take advantage of these opportunities and are not left behind in the global economy.

Approval of the Agreement is therefore in our national interest. I urge the Congress to enact this legislation promptly.

BARACK OBAMA

The White House,
October 3, 2011.

Message to the Congress Transmitting Legislation To Implement the United States-Panama Trade Promotion Agreement
October 3, 2011

To the Congress of the United States:

I am pleased to transmit legislation and supporting documents to implement the United States-Panama Trade Promotion Agreement (Agreement). The Agreement is an important part of my Administration's efforts to spur economic growth, increase exports, and create jobs here in the United States, while promoting our core values. The Agreement will create significant new opportunities for American workers, farmers, ranchers, manufacturers, investors, and businesses by opening Panama's market and eliminating barriers to U.S. goods, services, and investment.

The Agreement also represents an important development in our relations with Panama, and accords with the goal, as expressed by the Congress in the Caribbean Basin Trade Partnership Act, to conclude comprehensive, mutually advantageous trade agreements with beneficiary countries of the Caribbean Basin Initiative trade preference program. The Agreement further reflects a commitment on the part of the United States to sustained engagement in support of democracy, economic growth, and opportunity in Panama and the region.

Panama is one of the fastest growing economies in Latin America. Upon entry into force of the Agreement, Panama will immediately eliminate its tariffs on over 87 percent of U.S. exports of consumer and industrial goods and on more than half of U.S. exports of agricultural goods. Panama will eliminate most other duties on U.S. exports within a 15-year transition period. Eighty-five percent of U.S. businesses exporting to Panama are small and medium-sized enterprises. The elimination of duties provided for in the Agreement will help to level the playing field for them and for all U.S. exporters, based on 2010 trade flows, as approximately 98 percent of our imports from Panama already enjoy duty-free access to the U.S. market. In addition, the Agreement will give American service providers greater access to Panama's $20.6 billion services market.

The Agreement contains state of the art provisions to help protect and enforce intellectual property rights, reduce regulatory red tape, and eliminate regulatory barriers to U.S. exports. The Agreement also contains the highest standards for protecting labor rights, carrying out covered environmental agreements, and ensuring that key domestic labor and environmental laws are enforced, combined with strong remedies for noncompliance. Panama has already made significant reforms related to the obligations it will have under the labor chapter.

As a part of an ambitious trade agenda, it is important that the Congress renew a strong and robust Trade Adjustment Assistance Program consistent with reforms enacted in 2009. Renewal of that program is necessary to support Americans who need training and other services when their jobs are adversely affected by trade. As we expand access to other markets abroad, we need to ensure that American workers are provided the tools needed to take advantage of these opportunities and are not left behind in the global economy.

Approval of the Agreement is in our national interest. The Agreement will strengthen our economic and political ties with Panama, support democracy, and contribute to further economic integration in our hemisphere and economic growth in the United States. I urge the Congress to enact this legislation promptly.

BARACK OBAMA

The White House,
October 3, 2011.

Message to the Congress Transmitting Legislation To Implement the United States-South Korea Free Trade Agreement
October 3, 2011

To the Congress of the United States:

I am pleased to transmit legislation and supporting documents to implement the United States-Korea Free Trade Agreement (Agreement), a landmark agreement that supports American jobs, advances U.S. interests, and reflects America's fundamental values.

The Agreement levels the playing field for U.S. businesses, workers, farmers, ranchers, manufacturers, investors, and service providers by offering them unprecedented access to Korea's nearly $1 trillion economy. The Agreement eliminates tariffs on over 95 percent of U.S. exports of industrial and consumer goods to Korea within the first 5 years and, together with the agreement entered into through an exchange of letters in February 2011, addresses key outstanding concerns of American automakers and workers regarding the lack of a level playing field in Korea's auto market. The Agreement also ensures that almost two-thirds of current U.S. agricultural exports will enter Korea duty-free immediately. In addition, the Agreement will give American service providers much greater access to Korea's $580 billion services market.

The Agreement contains state of the art provisions to help protect and enforce intellectual property rights, reduce regulatory red tape, and eliminate regulatory barriers to U.S. exports. The Agreement also contains the highest standards for protecting labor rights, carrying out covered environmental agreements, and ensuring that key domestic labor and environmental laws are enforced, combined with strong remedies for noncompliance.

Increased U.S. exports expected under the Agreement will support more than 70,000 American jobs. The Agreement will bolster our economic competitiveness in the Asia-Pacific region and our regional security interests. The United States once was the top supplier of goods exported to Korea. Over the past decade, our share of Korea's import market for goods has fallen from 21 percent to just 10 percent—behind China and Japan, and barely ahead of the European Union (EU). The EU and several other trading partners are negotiating or have recently concluded trade agreements with Korea. If the United States-Korea trade agreement is not approved, the United States could lose further market share, export-supported jobs, and economic growth opportunities, with damage to our leadership position in the region.

As a part of an ambitious trade agenda, it is important that the Congress renew a strong and robust Trade Adjustment Assistance Program consistent with reforms enacted in 2009. Renewal of that program is necessary to support Americans who need training and other services when their jobs are adversely affected by trade. As we expand access to other markets abroad, we need to ensure that American workers are provided the tools needed to take advantage of these opportunities and are not left behind in the global economy.

Approving and implementing the Agreement is an opportunity to shape history. We must seize the moment together to support jobs for the American people today and to sustain U.S. leadership well into the 21st century. I urge the Congress to enact this legislation promptly.

BARACK OBAMA

The White House,
October 3, 2011.

Message to the Congress Transmitting Legislation To Implement the United States-South Korea Free Trade Agreement
October 3, 2011

To the Congress of the United States:

By separate message, I have transmitted to the Congress a bill to approve and implement the United States-Korea Free Trade Agreement. In that message, I highlighted new commitments that my Administration, in close coordination with the Congress, successfully negotiated to provide additional market access and a level playing field for American auto manufacturers and workers exporting to Korea.

Herewith I am transmitting the letters exchanged between the United States and Korea that contain those commitments, which further enhance the most commercially significant trade agreement the United States has concluded in more than 17 years. The documents I have transmitted in these two messages constitute the entire United States-Korea trade agreement package.

BARACK OBAMA

The White House,
October 3, 2011.

Message to the Congress Transmitting the District of Columbia's Fiscal Year 2012 Budget Request
October 3, 2011

To the Congress of the United States:

Pursuant to my constitutional authority and as contemplated by section 446 of the District of Columbia Self-Government and Governmental Reorganization Act as amended in 1989, I am transmitting the District of Columbia's 2012 Budget Request Act. This transmittal does not represent an endorsement of the contents of the D.C. government's requests.

The proposed 2012 Budget Request Act reflects the major programmatic objectives of the Mayor and the Council of the District of Columbia. For 2012, the District estimates total revenues and expenditures of $10.9 billion.

BARACK OBAMA

The White House,
October 3, 2011.

Remarks at a Democratic National Committee Fundraiser in Dallas, Texas
October 4, 2011

Thank you so much, everybody. Thank you. Everybody please have a seat. Oh, it's good to be back in Texas.

First of all, I just want to say thank you to Emmitt Smith, who, the first time we had a big rally here in Dallas—some of you may remember, it was a big auditorium, and he had just won "Dancing With the Stars"—[*laughter*]—and he gets up there, and he starts preaching. And the crowd is roaring, and he is—and I'm thinking, is there something this guy cannot do? [*Laughter*] But he was a great friend then, at a time when the campaign was still very much in doubt. He is a great friend now and obviously one of not only the greatest athletes of all time, but also just a great citizen to Dallas. So give Emmitt Smith a big round of applause. We are grateful to him.

It is great to be here. We made sure to schedule this game before the Rangers game. [*Laughter*] I will try to wrap up before the first pitch. In addition, Emmitt, I want to thank you for sending me Ron Kirk. You guys trained him well, because he is doing a great job on behalf of all the American people, making sure that we've got free trade and fair trade. And he could not be a better negotiator and a better advocate.

I want to acknowledge your outstanding new mayor here in Dallas. Mike Rawlings is here. Give him a big round of applause. I did not say anything about the Cowboys when we landed. [*Laughter*] And I also want to acknowledge Texas Democratic State chair, Boyd Richie is here. So give Boyd a big round of applause.

So I've come here today because I need your help. I've come here today because we have to finish what we started in 2008.

Back then—we began this campaign not because we thought it would be a cakewalk. Ron and I were remembering—reminiscing a little bit about when I was still a Senator, traveling with Ron, and most of the time I was flying Southwest or American. And Ron got this private plane for us to fly down to Houston. And it was about 100 degrees in July, and it turned out to be a prop plane, and we were bouncing all over the place. [*Laughter*] And Ron was sweating all—as he is prone to do sometimes. [*Laughter*]

We knew that running for President was not going to be easy. You knew it. You knew it wasn't going to be a cakewalk. After all, you supported a candidate named Barack Hussein Obama. [*Laughter*] That requires a leap of faith. You didn't need a poll to know that that might be challenging. [*Laughter*] But we forged ahead because we had an idea about what this country is and what it can be.

Many of you, many of our parents, many of our grandparents, we grew up with a faith in an America where hard work and responsibility paid off, where if you stepped up, you did your job, you were loyal to your company, that loyalty would be rewarded with a decent salary and good benefits, a vacation once in a while, a raise, a secure retirement.

But over the last decade, that faith has been shaken. The rules changed. The deck kept being stacked up against middle class Americans. And the truth is, nobody in Washington seemed to be willing or able to do anything about it.

And so in 2007, all this culminated in a once-in-a-lifetime economic crisis, crisis that's been much worse and much longer than your average recession. This is something we have not seen in our lifetimes before.

And from the moment I took office, we knew that because this crisis had been building for years, it would take years for us to fully recover. And the question is not today whether people are still hurting. Of course, they're still hurting. Every night I get letters and e-mails from families who are struggling. Every time I travel on the road I hear from folks who are worried. And some of the stories are heartbreaking: men and women who have had to close down a small business that's been in a family for generations; folks who are crossing items off their grocery list so that they can fill up their gas tank and get to work; parents who are postponing their retirement so their children can go to college; and obviously, folks who are looking for work, sending out résumé after résumé for month after month and not getting a response back. And that's scary. And it's hard. And a lot of folks are worn down out there.

So the question is not whether this country is going through tough times. You don't need economists, you don't need pundits, you don't need politicians to tell you that. The question is, where are we going next? What does our future look like? Because we're going to have a choice: We have a choice now; we're going to have a choice next year. We can either go back to the same tired, worn-out ideas that held sway over the last decade, ideas that got us into this mess in the first place, ideas that corporations can write their own rules, wealthy folks, like a lot of us, get to keep all our tax breaks, and everybody else is on their own. That's one philosophy.

Or we can decide to build the America we talked about in 2008. An America where everybody gets a fair shake and everybody does their fair share. An America where we're thinking about how we can get ahead and how we can move forward, but also how the guy next to us or the gal over here can also succeed. Because we have confidence that if all of us are pulling in the same direction, then all of us are going to do better.

That's what this election is about. That's what we've been fighting for in Washington. And it has been a contest of ideas in Washington. Because the other side, even in the midst of this crisis, their primary answer has been no. When we wanted to save the auto industry from bankruptcy, there were a whole lot of Republicans in Congress who fought us tooth and nail, said it was a waste of time, waste of money: "Let them liquidate."

Well, you know what? We did it anyway. And we saved hundreds of thousands of American jobs and the taxpayers paid us back—the taxpayers got their money back. And today, the American auto industry is stronger than it's been in years. Today, they're making fuel-efficient cars stamped with three proud words: Made in America. Because we didn't say no, we said yes. We can move forward together.

When we wanted to pass Wall Street reform to make sure a crisis like this never happens again, lobbyists and special interests spent millions to make sure we didn't succeed. A whole bunch of Republicans said no, despite the fact that we had just gone through the worst financial crisis in our history, despite the obvious irresponsibility that had led to a near meltdown. You know what? They said no, but we did it anyway. We passed the toughest reform in generations, reform that prevents consumers from getting ripped off by mortgage lenders and credit card companies. And today, there are no more hidden credit card fees, no more unfair rate hikes, no more deceptions from banks.

We decided if we're going to be successful, we've got to make sure we got the best educated workforce in the world. We said, we've got to figure out how young people can get more access to college. Most Republicans said no. But we were able to cut $60 billion in taxpayer subsidies that were going to the big banks and use those savings to make college more affordable for millions of kids who want to go. Instead of more tax breaks for some of the biggest corporations, we've cut taxes for small businesses and for middle class families.

The first law I signed was a bill to make sure that women got equal pay for equal work because I want our daughters to have the same opportunities as our sons do. We appointed two brilliant women to the Supreme Court. We repealed "don't ask, don't tell" so that we are not preventing people from serving this country because of who they love.

And yes, we passed health care reform because nobody in this country should go broke because they get sick. Millions of working folks in Texas who don't have health insurance are going to have the opportunity to get affordable options because of what we did. And for folks who do have health insurance, your care will be stronger. Insurance companies can't drop your coverage for no good reason. Going forward, they won't be able to deny you coverage because of a preexisting condition.

Think about what that means. Think about what that means for a low-wage worker, who right now is worried: "You know what? If my kid gets sick, if my spouse gets sick, I may go bankrupt. I may lose my—everything I've worked for." Now they've got some protection. Think about what that means for women: breast cancer, cervical cancer, no longer preexisting conditions that can prevent you from getting insurance. They can't discriminate you and charge higher rates just because you women are the ones who go through childbirth. They now have to cover things like mammograms and contraceptions as preventive care. No more out-of-pocket costs.

Insurance companies all across the country, they now have to spend 80 percent of your premium on your care, not just on profits and bonuses and advertising. And if they don't do it, you'll get a rebate. And while it will take a couple years for this reform to fully take effect, nearly 1 million young adults already have health insurance because of this bill—1 million more young people. That's already happening right now. The Affordable Care Act is working.

And so when you hear—when folks go around saying, "Oh, Obamacare," that's right, I care. I don't know about you, but I care. This is the right thing to do.

I don't know how the other side goes around running against helping 30 million people have health insurance who didn't have it. Why is that a—[*laughter*]—that's your main agenda? [*Laughter*] That's your plank, is making sure 30 million people don't have health insurance?

Now, all of these were tough fights in Congress. And there are a lot more that we still have to win. We have a long way to go to make sure that everyone in this country gets a fair shake, that every American has the chance to get ahead. And that's where I need your help. We've still got to have a smarter energy policy in this country, free ourselves from dependence on foreign oil. We still have to have comprehensive immigration reform in this country. We've got to make sure that we are protecting our borders, but we're also providing a means for people to get out of the shadows.

And most importantly, we've still got to put America back to work. We've got to put America back to work. Three weeks ago, I sent Congress a bill called the "American Jobs Act." Some of you might have heard of it. [*Laughter*] Everything in it is the kind of proposal that's been supported by Democrats and Republicans in the past—everything in it. Everything in it will be paid for, so it won't add to our deficit, ideas that have traditionally been bipartisan. It will put people back to work. It will put money back in the pockets of working people. And Congress should pass this bill right away.

Emmitt is a small-businessman working construction. We've got millions of construction workers who don't have jobs right now. This bill says, let's put these men and women to work rebuilding our roads, our bridges, modernizing our schools. I don't want the newest airports, the fastest railroads being built in China. I want them built right here in the United States of America. I want them built here in Dallas, Texas. I don't want our kids studying in crumbling schools. I want our kids studying in the best schools.

So there is work to be done. There are workers ready to do it. There are companies lined up, ready to go. Let's tell Congress, pass this jobs bill right away. Pass this jobs bill, and we can start doing more for the education of our kids. In places like South Korea, they can't hire teachers fast enough. I had lunch with the President of South Korea; I asked him what's his biggest challenge. He says: "Man, these parents are so demanding. They want all our kids to be learning English when they're in first grade, so I'm hiring teachers—I'm importing teachers from overseas, that's how important this is to us. Because we know if we're investing in the future, our kids will win the race of the 21st century."

They know that we are now competing in a global economy. So that's what South Korea is doing. Here, we're laying teachers off in droves. It's unfair to our kids; it undermines our future. But if we pass this jobs bill, thousands of teachers in every State will go back to the classroom where they belong. We need them teaching our children. Let's put them back to work.

If Congress passes this jobs bill, companies will get tax credits for hiring America's veterans. We ask these men and women to leave their careers, their families, to risk their lives for our country. The last thing they should have to do is fight to get a job when they come home.

And the "American Jobs Act" will cut taxes for almost every worker and every small-business owner in America. It will give an extra tax cut to small businesses that are hiring additional workers or raising their wages. We've got a whole bunch of folks in Congress—a bunch of Republicans—who say, well, we're all about helping America's job creators. Well don't just talk about it, you should actually do something. Pass this jobs bill and give those job creators a break.

Now, some folks in Congress have said they're not going to support it. They can't support a bill unless it's paid for. And I think that is important. We've got a serious challenge in terms of dialing down the debt and deficits that have accumulated, not just because of this recession, but because of two wars and because a prescription drug plan and tax cuts that weren't paid for.

So I recently laid out a plan that says not only can we pay for the jobs act, we can also bring down our debt over time. This plan adds to the $1 trillion in spending cuts that I signed this summer. So this will make it one of the biggest spending cuts in history, but we do it gradually over a 10-year period, and we say, alongside it, let's put people to work right now.

And what we say is, in addition to spending cuts, if we want to actually close this deficit instead of just playing politics, then we've got to ask the wealthiest Americans, the biggest corporations to pay their fair share. Now, this is a pretty straightforward proposition.

The principle we put forward is very simple: Middle class families shouldn't pay higher tax rates than a billionaire. Warren Buffett's secretary shouldn't be paying a higher tax rate than Warren Buffett. In the United States of America, a nurse or a teacher or a construction work-

er making 50,000 shouldn't pay higher tax rates than somebody pulling in 50 million. That's not fair. It's not right. It's got to change. We've got a chance to change it.

Nobody wants to punish success in America. What's great about our country, what's great about Dallas, what's great about Texas is our belief that anybody can make it if they're working hard, if they're trying hard, the idea that any one of us can open up a business and have a new product, a new service that can make us millions, maybe billions. That's great. This is the land of opportunity. But we have to remember, none of us succeed on our own. If we have that great idea, maybe it was planted there by that public schoolteacher. So we've got to make sure that that teacher is there for the next child.

We've got to make sure that we've got infrastructure that allows us to move our products and services all across the country. And in order to make sure that that opportunity is there for the next generation, those of us who have done well—and that includes most of the people in this room—we should pay our fair share in taxes to contribute to the Nation that made our success possible. And you know what? I think most wealthy Americans would agree with that if it helps us grow the economy and it helps to bring down our deficits.

Now, this notion that folks are inherently selfish, that's just not true. But you've got to ask them, right? [*Laughter*] People don't voluntarily pay taxes. But if you ask, most wealthy folks here in Dallas or around the country, they'll tell you, you know what, I want to make sure that I'm doing my share for America to succeed. But somebody has got to ask.

Now, some Republicans in Congress, they're already dusting off the old—their old records: "That's class warfare." Let me tell you something, 26 years ago—some of you may have seen this on television, clips have been circulating—26 years ago, another President said that some of these tax loopholes, and I quote, "made it possible for millionaires to pay nothing, while a bus driver was paying 10 percent of his salary, and that's crazy. It's time we stopped it." That was 26 years ago. You know the name of that President? Ronald Reagan. [*Laughter*]

So was that class warfare? By the way, taxes are much lower now than they ever were when Ronald Reagan was President. I know a lot of folks have short memories, but I don't remember Republicans accusing Ronald Reagan of being a Socialist—[*laughter*]—or engaging in class warfare, because he thought that everybody should do their fair share.

I mean, things have just gotten out of whack. [*Laughter*] I'll tell you what, if asking a billionaire to pay the same tax rate as a plumber or a teacher or a bus driver makes me a warrior for the middle class, I will wear that charge with honor. Because the only warfare I've seen is the battle waged against middle class Americans for a decade now. And they're hurting, and they need some help.

This is about priorities. It's about choices. If we want to put people back to work and close this deficit and invest in our future, then the money has got to come from somewhere. So you've got a choice. Would you rather keep tax loopholes for oil companies that are doing just fine? I know I'm in Texas. I know there's a lot of oil here. [*Laughter*] But they're doing fine. They don't need a loophole that nobody else gets. Or do you want to put our construction workers and teachers back to work?

Would you rather keep tax rates for millionaires and billionaires, or do you want to invest in education and medical research and new technologies that can help create a whole new set of businesses out there for the future? Should we be asking seniors to pay thousands of dollars more in Medicare, or should we ask the biggest corporations to pay their fair share? That's what this debate is about. That's what's at stake right now.

This notion that the only thing we should be doing to restore prosperity is to strip away antipollution laws and strip away regulations on Wall Street and give tax breaks to the wealthiest few and tell everybody else, you're on your own, good luck, that's not who we are. That's not how America got built. Yes, we are rugged individualists. We are self-reliant. We value our liberty, and we won't sacrifice it merely for

security. I understand that. That's part of our DNA, and it's been the drive and initiative of our workers and our entrepreneurs that made this economy the engine and the envy of the world.

But there's always been another thread running throughout our history, a belief that we're all connected, that I am my brother's keeper and my sister's keeper, that there are some things that we can only do together as a nation. We understand that when it comes to our defense. We understand that when it comes to fire and police protection. But it's also true when it comes to building an economy that works. It's why Republican Presidents like Lincoln and Eisenhower, they invested in railways and highways and science and technology. It's why this country gave millions of returning heroes, including my grandfather, the chance to go to college on the GI bill. It's why Michelle and I had a chance to succeed beyond our wildest dreams, because our parents, who weren't wealthy, who weren't famous, they lived in a country where we, together, said, you know what, every child should have opportunity.

It's why Michelle and I succeeded. A lot of other countries, that wouldn't have happened. I mean, we worked hard, but—and we were lucky—but a lot of it had to do with the fact that the country made an investment in us. And there are a whole bunch of kids out there who are just as talented as we are, maybe more talented, have just as much drive, just as much ambition. Are we going to be there for them?

No single individual built America on their own. We built it together. Don't believe the hype. Don't believe some of the chatter that you hear, that somehow Government had no role to play. We built this thing together. We are "one Nation under God, indivisible, with liberty and justice for all." But we are also a nation that has responsibilities to ourselves and to one another. And it's time for us to meet those responsibilities right now.

And maybe some people in Congress would rather wait until the election to settle our differences, and I promise you, I will be ready for that election. I will be ready for that debate. I am happy to have a debate before the American people because I believe that the American people understand that we're in this together.

So I'm eager to have that debate. But the next election is 13 months away. The American people don't have the luxury of waiting that long. A lot of folks are living week to week, paycheck to paycheck, day to day. They need action, and they need it now.

So I appreciate all of you coming here in support of the campaign, but I need you to speak out now. I need you to lift up your voices and help us out. I'm asking you to put some pressure on Congress and let them know that we've got work to do. And join me in finishing what we started in 2008. Let's keep building an America that we believe in, a place where everybody has a fair shake and everybody does their fair share.

Dallas, we are not a nation that just sits back and waits for things to happen to us. We make things happen. We're Americans. We are tough and we are resilient, and I am absolutely confident about our future because I believe we are tougher than the times we live in and we are bigger than the politics that we've been seeing.

But we've got to get out there and work. We've got to shape our own destiny. It is fully within our power, but I'm going to need your help. So let's seize this moment. Let's get to work. Let's show them why the United States of America is the greatest country on Earth.

Thank you, everybody. God bless you. Thank you.

NOTE: The President spoke at 12:28 p.m. at the Sheraton Dallas Hotel. In his remarks, he referred to Emmitt J. Smith, former running back, National Football League's Dallas Cowboys; President Lee Myung-bak of South Korea; and Warren E. Buffett, chief executive officer and chairman, Berkshire Hathaway Inc.

Remarks at a Democratic National Committee Fundraiser in Dallas
October 4, 2011

Thank you, everybody. Well, it is wonderful to see all of you. I'm not going to be long. I want to make a few brief remarks and then just have a conversation with all of you.

A lot of folks in this room I know. A lot of you have been there for me in the past. Some of you supported me when I was running for the United States Senate. Downstairs, I was telling the story about Ron Kirk and I—and I think you were with us Lisa, right? Flying down from Dallas to Houston, and it was about 100 degrees, and Ron had a thick wool suit. [*Laughter*] And we got out on that tarmac, and he was—[*laughter*]—dripping from head to toe. And I think on that same trip we went to Austin, and we were in somebody's backyard, and it wasn't that big a yard, and there were about 400 people; they had expected 50. [*Laughter*] And they had to put the sprinklers on to make sure that people didn't pass out. [*Laughter*]

So I've got a lot of fond memories and a lot of great friends here in Texas. I want to thank Naomi and everybody who helped put this together on short notice. But I think that—I suspect the reason we were able to do it on short notice is not only do we have relationships and friendships and common experiences to draw upon, but I think everybody here understands that the stakes are enormous in this upcoming election. They were big in 2008. I actually think they're bigger now.

Because in 2008, we recognized that there were a series of issues that had been building up over decades and that nobody had taken on. We hadn't gotten a smart energy policy. We hadn't been dealing with an education system that was inadequate. Our health care system was broken. Most importantly, middle class families were seeing their wages and their incomes flatline even though the costs of everything were going up. And the society was becoming more unequal, and the paths for middle class families to either stay in the middle class or get into the middle class were becoming blocked.

And what we've done over the last 2½ years has been to lay the foundation to take on those issues, first and foremost by making sure that we didn't plunge into a second Great Depression, making sure that the auto industry didn't collapse, making certain that the financial system didn't melt down. We passed health care reform, something I'm incredibly proud of, to lay the foundation for starting to reduce costs and increase affordability for families all across the country. We put in place financial reform. But all that work that we did, we now have to implement it. We have to make sure that it's done right.

And in the midst of this recession, you've got the other side that's presenting a very different vision about where America should be. I mean, rather than acknowledge that their theories didn't work, they doubled down. So we thought the problem with the financial system was there wasn't enough regulation of these practices. They think we should roll back regulations and let Wall Street do whatever it wants. We thought that one of the problems that we were facing in health care was that we have 30 million people uninsured. They're now running on the idea of making sure that 30 million people don't have health insurance.

And because people are scared and anxious about the future, how this election shakes out is going to help determine the course of this country for a very long time. So we've got a lot at stake, and not just for us, but for our children and our grandchildren, in terms of this election. And I'm confident that we can win, despite all the strong headwinds that are coming at us. But we're only going to win if everybody here, your friends, your coworkers, your neighbors, folks who are living across the country, all of you feel the same sense of urgency that we had in 2008.

In 2008, we were running against something in part, and that got a lot of people excited. It was easier to mobilize, in some ways. Now we're running for something. We're running for a vision of America in which middle class families can find good jobs, in which industries are locating here and not just overseas, that we're not just importing goods to consume, but we're producing goods to sell all across the country.

We're fighting for an education system that works for every child. I know the mayor is fighting for making sure that we've got the best infrastructure in the world, that the airports and the roads and the bridges and the broadband lines and the wireless and whatever it takes for us to compete in the 21st century, that that's happening here in Dallas and that's happening all across the country.

We're fighting to make sure that we've got a Tax Code that is fair and just. And we want to make sure that we are closing this deficit and this debt in a responsible way, and that means everybody is chipping in. You've got the other side saying the big problem with the Tax Code right now is that poor people aren't paying enough. That's their argument. They're doubling down.

And so we've got to make sure that we feel the same urgency in this election as we did back in 2008. Now, it won't be as sexy as in 2008. Back then, I didn't have any gray hair—[*laughter*]—and was all kind of fresh and new. And now I'm dinged up—[*laughter*]—gone through some battles.

But I tell you, the vision that propelled me to get into this campaign in the first place, that vision is still strong. And my enthusiasm and faith in America, that's unabated. I am absolutely confident that we can get through this difficult time, make the changes that are necessary, and deliver to our kids an America that is stronger and more unified and more just and more equal, where opportunity is available for everybody, where we are competitive with any country on Earth. I'm confident we can do it, but we've got to get this election right.

So I thank you for your support. But understand this is just the beginning. This is not the end. We'll be coming back here. And even when I'm not here, I'm going to need you guys working. Somebody—I think Ron was introducing Emmitt Smith and reminding everybody he holds the record for most rushing yards in the history of the NFL. And I don't see that record being broken anytime soon.

Now, Emmitt had some spectacular runs. But I think Emmitt will be the first one to acknowledge that a whole lot of those yards, he was just grinding it out. A whole bunch of those yards, you were just—there wasn't anything fancy about it. You were going between tackle and guard, and there was a block, and you got 4. Sometimes, you got 3. And sometimes it hurt going through that line. Sometimes you got 1. [*Laughter*] You took your knocks. But it was his persistence and his strength that allowed him to achieve that record.

Well, that's what this campaign is going to be like. We may not be throwing the long bomb each and every time. We're just going to have to plug away and stay at it. But if in our hearts we believe what we say we believe about a country that gives everybody a fair shake and asks for a fair share from everybody, if that's really who we are, then we won't be tired, we won't be deterred, we won't be weary. We'll stick at it, and we'll stick with it.

So I know you guys are going to be there with me. I'm grateful for you. And with that, let me just open it up for some questions and conversation. All right?

NOTE: The President spoke at 1:08 p.m. at the Sheraton Dallas Hotel. In his remarks, he referred to Mayor Michael Rawlings of Dallas, TX. Audio was not available for verification of the content of these remarks.

Remarks at Eastfield College in Mesquite, Texas
October 4, 2011

The President. Hello, Dallas! Thank you so much. Thank you, everybody. Please have a seat. Have a seat. It——

Audience member. We love you, Obama!

The President. Thank you. Well, it's good to be back in Texas. [*Applause*] It is good to be back in Texas. I am thrilled to have the opportunity to be with all of you.

I want to thank a couple of people. First of all, the mayor of Mesquite, John Monaco, is here. And the mayor of Dallas, Mike Rawlings, is in the house. And I want to thank the former mayor of Dallas, who I stole from you to be one of the best Trade Representatives this country's ever had, my dear friend Ron Kirk's in the house.

I also want to thank the folks over at the Children's Lab School, who gave me a tour, and I want to especially thank Kim Russell for sharing her story. Thank you, Kim.

Now, teachers like Kim are why I came here today, teachers like Kim and her former students. That's why I've been traveling all across this country for the last few weeks. These are the toughest times we've been through since the Great Depression. And because the problems that led to the recession weren't caused overnight, they won't be solved overnight. That's the hard truth. It took us a decade to see the culmination of some of the bad ideas that had been put into place: the lack of regulation on Wall Street, middle class folks struggling.

So we're not going to solve all those problems overnight. But that doesn't mean we have to sit back and do nothing about this economy. There are steps we can take right now to put people back to work. There are steps we can take right now to put money in the pockets of working Americans. There are things we can do right now to restore some of the security and fairness that has always defined this great country of ours. And that's what will happen if Congress will finally get its act together and pass the "American Jobs Act."

It has now been 3 weeks since I sent this bill to Congress. It's a detailed plan to get this economy moving. It's the kind of proposals that, in the past, Democrats and Republicans have supported. There's nothing radical in these proposals. These are the kinds of things that in the past we've had bipartisan support for. It's fully paid for. And that's why I need you to help me convince the people you sent to Washington that it's time to pass this jobs bill and get America working again.

Now, you just heard Kim's story. There are teachers and educators like Kim all over the country. I met a first grade teacher from Minnesota at the White House who was laid off after having been named the Teacher of the Year in her school district. Her peers, students, determined she was the best teacher in her school district; she got laid off. There's a teacher over in Grand Prairie, Texas, who actually chose to resign in order to protect the job of a single mom who also taught at the school. Think about that. Here in Dallas, all across the State of Texas, you've seen too many teachers lose their jobs because of budget cuts. And thousands more could be at risk in the coming year.

Now, understand, this doesn't just hurt these teachers. It doesn't just hurt them and their families. It hurts our children. It undermines our future as a nation. If you've got Kim, an AP teacher, not in the classroom, those kids aren't going to have the same opportunities. And I want everybody to understand that what is at stake is nothing less than our ability to compete in this 21st-century economy.

Now, I've—I told the story: A while back, I was visiting South Korea and had lunch with the President there. And I asked the President, I said, "What's your biggest challenge right now?" He said, "Well, my biggest challenge is our parents are way too demanding." He said: "They want their kid to learn English when they're in first grade. So in addition to all the science and all the math classes, I'm now having to ship in teachers from outside the country just to teach our kids English, starting in elementary school." This is what the President of South Korea said.

They can't hire teachers fast enough. They call them nation builders. That's what they call teachers in Korea, nation builders, because they know that educating their children is the best way to make sure their economy is growing, make sure that good jobs are locating there, making sure they've got the scientists and the engineers and the technicians who can build things and ship them all around the world. That's what he understands. And the whole country supports him. Here in America, we're laying off teachers in droves. It makes no sense. It has to stop. [*Applause*] It has to stop.

Now, this bill will prevent up to 280,000 teachers from losing their jobs. This bill will support almost 40,000 jobs right here in the great State of Texas. So here's what I need you to do: Tell Congress to pass this bill and put teachers back in the classroom where they belong.

It's not just teachers. Tell Congress to pass the "American Jobs Act," and there also will be funding to save the jobs of firefighters and police officers and first-responders who risk their lives to keep us safe. That's what happens if they pass this bill.

Pass this jobs bill, and hundreds of thousands of unemployed construction workers will get back on the job rebuilding our schools, rebuilding our roads, rebuilding our bridges, rebuilding our ports, rebuilding our airports. The other day I visited a busy bridge in Ohio; actually, it's between Ohio and Kentucky. Speaker Boehner, he's from Ohio; Republican Leader McConnell is from Kentucky. I thought it would be a good place to have an event. [*Laughter*] This bridge is classified as functionally obsolete. That's a fancy way of saying it's old and needs to be fixed. [*Laughter*]

There's a public transit project in Houston that would help clear up one of the worst areas of traffic in the country. There are schools all over this country that are literally falling apart: roof crumbling, rain dripping in, too hot in the summer, too cold in the winter, science labs all worn out, got a couple of beakers and that's it—[*laughter*]—built back in the fifties before the Internet was invented. [*Laughter*]

That's an outrage. Understand, America became an economic superpower in part because we had the best infrastructure. We built the transcontinental railroad, the Interstate Highway System, the Hoover Dam, Grand Central station. How can we sit back, and now we're seeing China build better airports than us, Europe build better railroads than us, Korea more broadband access than us, at a time when millions of unemployed construction workers could be building all that stuff right here in the United States of America?

My question to Congress is, what are you waiting for? The work's there to be done.

There are workers ready to do it. Contractors, they're begging for work. They'll come in on time, under budget. Interest rates have never been lower. It is time for us to put those folks back to work. It's time for them to pass the "American Jobs Act." Pass this bill.

If Congress passes this jobs bill, new companies will get new tax credits for hiring America's veterans. Think about it. We ask these men and women to leave their families, disrupt their careers, risk their lives for our Nation. The last thing they should have to do is to fight for a job when they come home.

Tell Congress, pass this bill so we can help the people who create most of the new jobs in this country: America's small businesses. Folks in the other party, they like to talk a good game about helping America's job creators: "Let's help America's jobs creators." Okay, let's do that. This jobs bill provides tax cuts for nearly every small business in America. If you hire new employees or raise your workers' wages, you get an extra tax cut. So my message to Congress is, don't just talk about helping job creators, actually help some job creators by passing this bill.

Here's another reason why they need to pass this bill. On January 1, if nothing's done, everybody here is going to get a tax hike.

Audience members. Boo! [*Laughter*]

The President. That's right. See, back in December, I got an agreement with the Republicans to lower the payroll tax so that there would be more money in folks' pockets and we could protect ourselves against recession. Now, since that time, we've had a tsunami in Japan; we've had the Arab Spring, which shot up gas prices; we've had problems in Europe. And so the economy has gotten weaker.

That tax cut is scheduled to expire by the end of this year. But if the "American Jobs Act" passes, the typical working family in Texas will have an extra $1,400 in their pockets. Now, if the bill doesn't pass, virtually every worker in America will see their taxes go up at the worst possible time.

So I'm not about to let that happen, Texas. Look, Republicans say they're the party of tax cuts. Tell them to prove it. Tell them to fight just as hard for tax cuts for working Americans as they do for the wealthiest Americans. Pass this bill.

Now, what you'll hear from some of these folks is, well, we're not going to support any new spending that's not paid for. All right, I agree with that. I think that's important. So I laid out a plan to pay for the "American Jobs Act" and then some, a plan that not only pays for the bill to put folks back to work, to raise our growth rate, but to also pay down more of our debt over time. It builds on the $1 trillion in spending cuts that I already signed this summer, making it one of the biggest spending cuts in history.

So look, I believe we've got to make cuts in programs that don't work and things that aren't helping the economy grow so we can pay for the things that are, right? We all believe that Government needs to live within its means. We all agree with that. But we also believe that how you bring down the deficit is important. If we want to actually close the deficit—not just talk about closing the deficit, not just using it for a campaign slogan, not just playing politics—if we want to actually close the deficit, then you've got to combine the tough cuts with a strategy to ask the wealthiest Americans and the biggest corporations to do their part, to pay their fair share.

Look, I'm not telling you anything you don't know. Do you really think the Tax Code is written for you?

Audience members. No!

The President. You think the Tax Code—maybe you've got a bunch of lobbyists in Washington. Maybe you've got a bunch of special interests in there in the back rooms trying to carve something out, I don't know. But most folks don't. So the Tax Code, the way it's structured, is not fair. And so what we've said is, let's reform our Tax Code based on a very simple principle, and it will raise more money without hurting working families. Here's the principle: Middle class families, working families, should not pay higher tax rates than millionaires or billionaires. Right? I don't know how you argue against that; seems pretty straightforward to me. Warren Buffett's secretary shouldn't pay a higher tax rate than Warren Buffett.

Now, when I point this out—it seems very logical to me, but when I point this out, some of the Republicans in Congress, they say, "Oh, you're engaging in class warfare." Class warfare? Let me tell you something. Years ago, a great American had a different view. All right? I'm going to get the quote just so you know I'm not making this up. [*Laughter*] Here's—great American, said that he thought it was "crazy" that certain tax loopholes "made it possible for millionaires to pay nothing, while a bus driver was paying 10 percent of his salary." All right?

You know who this guy was? Wasn't a Democrat. Wasn't some crazy socialist. It was Ronald Reagan. It was Ronald Reagan. Last time I checked, Republicans all thought Reagan made some sense. [*Laughter*] So the next time you hear one of those Republicans in Congress accusing you of class warfare, you just tell them, I'm with Ronald Reagan. [*Laughter*] I agree with Ronald Reagan that it's crazy that a bus driver pays a higher tax rate than a millionaire because of some loophole in the Tax Code.

And by the way, I don't mind being called a warrior for the working class. You guys need somebody fighting for you. The only warfare I've been seeing is the war against middle class families and their ability to get ahead in this economy.

And let me make one last point, because you'll hear this argument made. This is not about trying to punish success. This is the land of opportunity. And what's great about our country is our belief that anybody can succeed. You've got a good idea? Go out there and start a new business. You've got a great product? You invented something? I hope you make millions of dollars. We want to see more Steve Jobs and more Bill Gates. Creating value, creating jobs, that's great.

Your current mayor did great work in the private sector creating jobs, creating value. That's important. But remember, nobody got there on their own. I'm standing here today, Michelle's standing here today—or Michelle's not standing here today, but—[*laughter*]—I know you wish she was. I'm standing here to-day, Michelle—we always remind ourselves, the reason we've had this extraordinary opportunity is because somewhere along the line, some teacher helped us. Somewhere along the line, we got a student loan. We lived in a country that could move products and services everywhere. We lived in a country where if there's a fire, somebody comes and puts out the fire. If you're burglarized, somebody is coming to try to solve the crime. I'm sure the mayor of Dallas feels the same way. We're here because somebody laid the foundation for success. So the question is, are we going to maintain that foundation and strengthen that foundation for the next generation?

And this is all about priorities. This is about choices. If we want to actually lower the deficit and put people back to work, if we want to invest in our future, if we want to have the best science, the best technology, the best research, if we want to continue to be inventing new drugs to solve cancer and making sure that the new cars of the future that are running on electricity are made here in America, if we want to do all those things, then the money has got to come from somewhere. I wish I could do it all for free. I wish I could say to all of you, you don't have to pay any taxes and companies can keep all their stuff and rich people don't have to do anything, and somehow it all worked out.

But you know what, we tried it, and it didn't work. So now you've got a choice. Would you rather keep tax loopholes for big corporations that don't need it? Or would you rather put construction workers back to work rebuilding our schools and our roads and our bridges? Would you rather I keep a tax break that I don't need and wasn't looking for, didn't ask for, and if I don't have it, I won't miss it? Or do you want to put teachers like Kim back to work and help small businesses and cut taxes for middle class families? This is a choice that we've got to make.

And I believe, and I think you believe, it's time we build an economy that creates good, solid, middle class jobs in this country. It's time to build an economy that values the—that honors the values of hard work and responsibility. It's time for us to build an economy that lasts, that's not just based on speculation and financial shenanigans, but rather is based on us making stuff and selling things to other people around the world instead of just importing from all around the world. That's the America I believe in. That's the America you believe in.

And, Dallas, that starts now. That starts with your help. Yesterday the Republican majority leader in Congress, Eric Cantor, said that right now he won't even let this jobs bill have a vote in the House of Representatives.

Audience members. Boo!

The President. This is what he said. Won't even let it be debated. Won't even give it a chance to be debated on the floor of the House of Representatives. Think about that. I mean, what's the problem? Do they not have the time? [*Laughter*] They just had a week off. [*Laughter*] I—is it inconvenient?

Look, I'd like Mr. Cantor to come down here to Dallas and explain what exactly in this jobs bill does he not believe in. What exactly is he opposed to? Does he not believe in rebuilding America's roads and bridges? Does he not believe in tax breaks for small businesses or efforts to help our veterans?

Mr. Cantor should come down to Dallas and look Kim Russell in the eye and tell her why she doesn't deserve to be back in the classroom doing what she loves, helping our kids. Come tell her students why they don't deserve to have their teacher back.

Come tell Dallas construction workers why they should be sitting idle instead of out there on the job. Tell small-business owners and workers in this community why you'd rather defend tax breaks for folks who don't need them—for millionaires—rather than tax cuts for middle class families.

And if you won't do that, at least put this jobs bill up for a vote so that the entire country knows exactly where Members of Congress stand.

Put your cards on the table. I realize that some Republicans in Washington are resistant, partly because I proposed it. [*Laughter*] I mean, they—if I took their party platform and proposed it, they'd suddenly be against it. [*Laughter*]

We've had folks in Congress who've said they shouldn't pass this bill because it would give me a win. So they're thinking about the next election. They're not thinking about folks who are hurting right now. They're thinking, well, how's that going to play in the next election?

Give me a win? Give me a break! [*Laughter*] That's why folks are fed up with Washington. This isn't about giving me a win. This isn't about giving Democrats or Republicans a win. This is about giving people who are hurting a win. It's is about giving small-business owners a win and entrepreneurs a win and students a win and working families a win. It's is about giving America a win.

Dallas, the next election is 13 months away. The American people don't have the luxury of waiting 13 months. A lot of folks are living week to week; some are living paycheck to paycheck; some folks are living day to day. They need action on jobs, and they need it now. They want Congress to do what they were elected to do. They want Congress to do their job. Do your job, Congress!

I need you all to lift your voice, not just here in Dallas, but anyone watching, anyone listening, everybody following online. I need you to call and tweet and fax and visit and e-mail your Congressperson and tell them the time for gridlock and games is over. The time for action is now.

Tell them that if you want to create jobs, pass this bill. If you want to put teachers back in the classroom, pass this bill. If you want construction workers back on the job, pass this bill. If you want tax cuts for the middle class and small-business owners, pass this bill. You want to help some veterans? Pass this bill.

Now is the time to act. We are not people who sit back in tough times. We step up in tough times. We make things happen in tough times. We've been through tougher times before, and we got through them. We're going to get through these to a brighter day, but we're going to have to act. God helps those who help themselves. We need to help ourselves right now.

Let's get together. Let's get to work. Let's get busy. Let's pass this bill. Let's make sure that we are shaping a destiny for our children that we are proud of, and let's remind the entire world why the United States of America is the greatest nation on the planet.

God bless you. God bless the United States of America.

NOTE: The President spoke at 2:47 p.m. In his remarks, he referred to Dallas, TX, teacher Kimberly Russell, who introduced the President; President Lee Myung-bak of South Korea; Warren E. Buffett, chief executive officer and chairman, Berkshire Hathaway Inc.; Steven P. Jobs, chairman of the board, Apple Inc.; and William H. Gates III, chairman, Microsoft Corp.

Statement on Representative Jerry F. Costello's Decision Not To Seek Re-election
October 4, 2011

For over two decades, Jerry Costello has proudly represented the people of southwestern and southern Illinois. Born and raised in the State he now serves, Jerry has distinguished himself as a fierce advocate for improving our Nation's transportation infrastructure to ensure Illinois and the entire country are prepared to lead the way in a 21st-century economy. Michelle and I want to join the people of Illinois in thanking Congressman Costello for his service, and we wish him and his family well in the future.

Remarks at a Democratic National Committee Fundraiser in St. Louis, Missouri
October 4, 2011

The President. Hello, hello, hello! It's good to be back in St. Louis. It's close to home. This is close to home. It's good to be back in the Midwest. Good to be——

Audience member. We love you!

The President. I love you too. It's good to be back in Missouri. I know that the Cardinals game is going on right now. I see some of you checking your phones for the score. [*Laughter*] So I'm going to try to be brief, see if I can get you out of here by——

Audience member. [*Inaudible*]

The President. No, no, no. You've got the ninth inning coming up. A couple of people I just want to acknowledge. First of all, you have one of the finest Governors in the country, somebody who is thinking about the families of Missouri every single day, Jay Nixon. Please give him a big round of applause. I want to acknowledge the outstanding mayor of St. Louis, Francis Slay; Congressman Russ Carnahan in the house; St. Louis County Executive Charlie Dooley; Missouri Attorney General Chris Koster. Two people who are not here, but who are great friends, great supporters, I just want to acknowledge them: First of all, somebody who's been a outstanding friend since I started this incredible journey, Claire McCaskill, your great Senator, as well as Congressman William Lacy Clay, who are both in DC but doing great work. We are proud of them.

Now, I've come here today because I need your help.

Audience member. Okay. [*Laughter*]

The President. I need your help. I need your help to finish what we started in 2008. Back then, we started this campaign not because we thought it was going to be a cakewalk. I mean, after all, your candidate's name was Barack Obama. [*Laughter*] So we knew that was going to be hard. We didn't need a poll for that. But we forged ahead, because we believed that the essence of this country is that no matter where you come from, no matter what you look like, that if you're willing to work hard, if you're willing to make an effort, you can make it here. You can make it if you try.

Most of us come from families—parents, grandparents—who had this inherent faith in America, that if you did the right thing, worked hard, showed up at work, put your all into it, that you could end up living a good, comfortable life. You could be in the middle class. You could make sure that your kids went to college. You could have a retirement that was comfortable and secure. You could go on a vacation once in a while. Decent salary, good benefits, that was the essence of the American Dream.

And over the last decade, that faith that we've had has been shaken for a lot of people. It felt like the rules changed. The deck got stacked against middle class Americans. The divide between haves and have-nots grew wider. Folks in the middle got squeezed. No one in Washington seemed willing or able to do anything about it, and that's why we launched this campaign. Because we had seen a failed philosophy that just let problems pile up, put more and more burden on ordinary folks, and in 19—in 2007, all of this culminated in a once-in-a-lifetime crisis: the biggest financial crisis we've had since the Great Depression, followed by the worst recession we've had since the Great Depression. And that crisis has been much worse and much longer than your average recession.

And from the time I took office, we knew that because we didn't get into this crisis overnight, we weren't going to get out of it overnight, and we were going to have to work hard and plug away slow and steady to make sure that all those piled-up problems, that we started just dealing with them. It was going to take a few years for us to fully recover, but we never lost faith that we could.

So the question now that we face in 2011 is not whether people are still hurting. Of course they are. I get e-mails, I get letters every night from people all across the country who are struggling, and their stories are heartbreaking. Families that—where somebody has lost a job and they're having trouble making the mortgage; maybe they lost their home. Small businesses who had to close, even though they've been in families for generations. Folks having to cross off items off the grocery list so that they can fill up the gas tank and get to work. Parents who are postponing retirement so they can still send their kids to college. I mean, this is tough stuff. And the question is not whether this country is going through tough times. We are. The question is, where are we going next? What's the direction that we're charting for not just ourselves, but for our kids and our grandkids?

Audience member. Will you stop the pipeline?

The President. And we can——

Audience member. President Obama, will you stop the Keystone——

Audience member. Shhh!

The President. We'll be happy to—we can either go back to the ideas that we tried in the last decade, where corporations get to write their own rules and wealthy folks get to keep all their tax breaks, or we can build the kind of America that we talked about——

Audience member. God bless you.

The President. ——an America where everybody gets a fair shake and everybody does their fair share.

And that's what this election is about. That's what we've been fighting for in Washington. When I wanted to save the auto industry from bankruptcy, there were a whole bunch of Republicans in Congress who fought us tooth and nail. Said it was a waste of time, waste of money. You know what? We did it anyway. We saved hundreds of thousands of American jobs. Taxpayers got their money back. Taxpayers got their money back, and today, the American auto industry is stronger than it's been in years. In fact, Ford just announced its plans to add 12,000 new jobs in its U.S. manufacturing plants over the next few years. A lot of those jobs are right here in Missouri. Jobs making cars stamped with three proud words: Made in America.

And we've got a couple people here who are concerned about the environment? In the process, by the way, we doubled fuel efficiency standards on cars, on trucks, on heavy trucks, getting carbon out of the environment. That's the choice we face. Because we got resistance every step of the way.

When we wanted to pass Wall Street reform to make sure a crisis like this never happens again, we had lobbyists and special interests spend millions to make sure we didn't succeed. And you know what? We did it anyway. We passed the toughest reforms in a generation. And those reforms ensure that consumers won't get ripped off by mortgage lenders or credit card companies. And no more hidden fees. No more unfair rate hikes. No more deception.

When we looked and said, you know what, we have to make sure that college is accessible because we want to, once again, be number one when it comes to college graduation rates, we were able to cut $60 billion in taxpayer subsidies to big banks, use those savings to make college more affordable for millions of kids around the country.

Audience member. Hear, hear, Mr. President.

The President. By the way, most Republicans voted against that.

Instead of giving more tax breaks to the biggest corporations, we cut taxes for small businesses and middle class families. First law I signed—first bill I signed into law made sure that women earn equal pay for equal work. I want to make sure my daughters have the same chances as our sons.

And to make sure that those laws are upheld, we appointed two brilliant women to the Supreme Court. We repealed "don't ask, don't tell" so that every single American can serve their country, regardless of who they love. And yes, we passed health care reform because no one in America should go bankrupt because somebody in their family gets sick.

Insurance companies can't drop your coverage for no good reason. They won't be able to deny your coverage because of preexisting conditions. Think about what that means for families all across America. Think about what it means for women.

Audience member. Birth control——

The President. Absolutely. You're stealing my line. Breast cancer, cervical cancer are no longer preexisting conditions. No longer can insurance companies discriminate against women just because you guys are the ones who have to give birth. [*Laughter*]

Audience member. Darn right!

The President. Darn tootin'. [*Laughter*] They have to cover things like mammograms and contraception as preventive care, no more out-of-pocket costs. And while it will take a couple of years for all the reforms to fully take place, already we've got seniors all across the country who have gotten $250 to help them pay for their prescription drug benefit. And nearly 1 million young adults already have health insurance because of it—1 million more young people. That's an incredible achievement. The Affordable Care Act is working.

They call it "Obamacare." I do care, that's right. That's right. The question is, why don't you care? The question is, why don't you care? You should care too. Some of these folks making central to their campaign pledge to make sure that 30 million people don't have health insurance. What kind of inspiring message is that? [*Laughter*]

Now, all these were tough fights in Congress. There are a lot more we still have to win. We've got a long way to go to make sure that everyone in this country gets a fair shake, that everybody has a chance to get ahead. And that's where I need your help.

Now, 3 weeks ago, I sent to Congress a bill called the "American Jobs Act." Everything in this bill has been supported by Democrats and Republicans in the past; nothing radical about this. Everything in it will be paid for. It will put people back to work. It will put money back into the pockets of working families. And Congress should pass this bill right away.

Think about it. Think about—right now we've got millions of construction workers out of work: folks in Missouri, folks in St. Louis, who are desperate to get back to work. This bill says, why don't we put those men and women back to work rebuilding our roads and our bridges and our airports and our schools? I don't want the newest airports built in China. I don't want the best railroads built in Europe. I want them built right here in the United States of America. I want them built in Missouri, with American labor.

I don't want our kids studying in crumbling schools. I want the best schools for our kids. There is work to be done. There are workers to do it. Tell Congress: Pass this bill right away. We don't have the luxury of sitting back.

This bill puts teachers back in the classroom. We know that the most important thing, in order for us to compete as a country, is going to be the quality of education. In places like South Korea, they are hiring teachers in droves. Here in the United States, we're laying them off. It makes no sense. We've got to be able to compete in a global economy. And it's unfair to our kids for us to be shortchanging them because we're not putting teachers in the classroom. It undermines our kids. It undermines our future. If we pass this bill, we will see tens of thousands of teachers back in the classroom where they belong. That's why I need your help. Push them to pass this bill.

This bill gives tax credits to hire veterans, men and women who served our country with incredible honor, put their lives on hold, left their careers, left their families, risked their lives. They shouldn't have to fight to get a job when they come home. This jobs bill helps veterans. This jobs bill helps every single small-business owner in America. Almost every worker in America, they get an extra tax cut if they hire more workers, if they raise workers' wages. Republicans like to talk about job creators; they should actually help job creators. Let's get this jobs bill passed, and they'll actually get some relief.

Now, the excuse that a lot of folks have been using for why they haven't passed this thing yet—you know I'm ready to sign it, I've got the pens all ready—[laughter]—"Well, we can't support any new spending that's not paid for." Well, I think the deficit is important. We worked hard on that. So recently, I laid out a plan that says, not only will this pay for the jobs act, but it will also reduce our deficit and debt even more. Building on the trillion dollars in cuts that we've already made, it makes some tough choices. It says we can't spend on every single thing that we want to. We've got to make some decisions; we've got to make some choices. Cut back on things we don't need to invest

in the things that we do. It's one of the biggest spending cuts in history, but that alone doesn't do the job. That alone doesn't put people back to work. It's not enough.

So what we've said is if you are serious about putting people back to work and also closing this deficit, then we've got to make sure that the wealthiest among us—people like me, the biggest, most profitable corporations—they've got to pay their fair share of taxes. We should be reforming our Tax Code based on a very simple principle: Middle class families shouldn't pay higher tax rates than millionaires or billionaires. Warren Buffett's secretary shouldn't pay a higher tax rate than Warren Buffett. A nurse or a construction worker, a plumber making $50,000 a year, they shouldn't pay higher tax rates than somebody pulling down $50 million. That's not fair. It's not right.

And it needs to change. Not because we want to punish success in America; America is the land of opportunity. You know what? Go out there with a business idea, with a new product, a new service. Make millions of dollars, make billions of dollars—that's great. But understand you didn't do it on your own. You did it because somebody invested in your school. Maybe somebody gave you a scholarship to go to college. You're using roads we all built.

You know, everybody can make it if they try, but we don't do it by ourselves. We don't do it by ourselves. Nobody makes it on their own. The reason Michelle and I have been able to be successful is because a previous generation made that investment. We've got to be willing to make that same investment for the next generation. And those of us who have benefited the most from this great country of ours, we can afford to do our fair share. We can afford it.

Some Republicans lately have been saying, well, that's "class warfare." [Laughter] But it's interesting, some of you may have caught—there's been a clip floating around lately on television talking about this radical guy who made the simple point that a bus driver shouldn't be paying lower tax rates than a millionaire. And this rabble-rouser was named Ronald Reagan.

So you know what? The next time you're talking to somebody that says that's class warfare, you say, I'm just with Ronald Reagan here. [*Laughter*] That's all I'm saying.

People forget these issues did not used to be partisan issues. They don't have to be. The truth of the matter is, is that our first Republican President—pretty good President—a guy named Lincoln, in the middle of the Civil War built the transcontinental railroad, invested in land grant colleges, started the National Academy of Sciences. Did all these things with an eye towards the future saying, you know what, we can't afford not to invest.

Eisenhower built the Interstate Highway System. Previous generations built the Hoover Dam. Our researchers developed the Internet. These people didn't make it on their own, who are now in Silicon Valley. The reason they're successful is not only because of their extraordinary work, but it's because they're building on the collective effort of America.

Nobody makes it on their own. That's what this country is about. We have always been a land of opportunity and self-reliance and rugged individualism, but we've also looked after each other. We've also said we're in it together. And that's the choice that we face right now. We've got a choice. And so I would love to be able to say, we can do everything we need to make ourselves competitive and sharp and successful in this 21st-century economy and nobody has to do anything. It will just happen. [*Laughter*]

But that's not how the world works. We've got to make choices. So the question is, do we want to maintain special tax breaks for oil companies, or do we make a decision that we'd rather use some of that money to make sure that we're rebuilding America? Do we want to make sure that I keep a tax break that I don't need and wasn't even asking for, or do we want to put teachers back in the classroom?

Those are choices we have to make, and they reflect our values. They reflect who we are as a people.

And I so deeply believe in the American people. We make tough choices when times are tough. We pull together and help each other. It's not always easy. And this is a democracy and there are going to be fierce debates going on. But I'm absolutely positive that we will make the right decisions for our children and our grandchildren.

But in order to do that, I need your help. All right? So I'm going to need you to go out there and I want you to e-mail and fax and tweet and visit and write an old-fashioned letter. [*Laughter*] Tell your Members of Congress: Pass this bill. Let's put people back to work. Let's put construction workers on the job. Let's put teachers in the classroom. Let's give small businesses a tax break. Let's help our veterans. Pass this bill. Let's meet our responsibilities. Do your job. Do your job.

We had a couple of Republicans quoted in DC saying, "Well, even if we agreed with this stuff we probably don't want to do it, because it might give Obama a win." [*Laughter*] Now, let me tell you something. There's going to be an election, and I'm looking forward to that election. I'm looking forward to the debate. I think we've got better ideas.

But the election is 13 months away, and people are hurting right now. There are folks living paycheck to paycheck, day to day. They can't afford to wait 13 months. So we need to pass this bill now. And if the American people see Washington putting their needs first, putting country before party, thinking about their constituencies, that's going to give people confidence. That's going to restore a sense of hope. People will remember that we've been through tougher times before and we've come through it.

But they need to see their leaders thinking about them for a change, not thinking about how will this affect their polls, how will this affect the next election. They need to feel a sense of urgency about this.

Which brings me back to what we did in 2008. We surprised a lot of people. And yes, I had less gray hair. [*Laughter*] And I know it was exciting to be for the underdog and——

Audience member. You still look good.

The President. Oh, I appreciate it. Thank you. That's what Michelle says. But this election wasn't about me, it wasn't about one person. It was about us. It was about what we could do together. We've got to have that same sense of urgency this time. And if we do have that same sense of urgency, then, for all the things we've done, we can finish what we started. We can put people back to work. We can have an energy policy in this country that actually makes sense and protects our environment. We can make sure that we're dealing with issues like immigration in a serious way, not just to try to demagogue it. We can make sure that we are moving manufacturing back here to the United States of America, putting people back to work making things; not just importing things from other countries, but selling them to other countries.

We can do all those things. But we've got to have a sense of urgency about it. This is going to be harder than it was last time, and it wasn't easy last time. But I have confidence in you. And I have confidence in the commitments you've made to each other. And if all of you are willing to keep on going and knock on doors and make phone calls, and don't get weary, I'm going to be with you every step of the way. And I promise you, we will get through these difficult times. We will fix our politics. And we will remind everybody just why the United States of America is the greatest country on Earth.

Thank you very much, everybody. God bless you.

NOTE: The President spoke at 6:39 p.m. at the Renaissance Grand Hotel. In his remarks, he referred to Warren E. Buffett, chief executive officer and chairman, Berkshire Hathaway Inc.

Remarks at a Democratic National Committee Fundraiser in St. Louis
October 4, 2011

It is good to be back in the Midwest. There is a lot of foolishness going on on the East Coast. [*Laughter*] So I had to get back to my roots.

It is wonderful to be with all of you. Bob, thanks for everything that you've done, including, by the way, fixing some of the lighting in the White House—[*laughter*]—which we very much appreciate.

To the Carnahans, thank you for the incredible hospitality. What a wonderful greeting. I have a soft spot for anybody who's got daughters. [*Laughter*] So—and you guys have your hands full. [*Laughter*] But they are gorgeous. To all of you who helped to pull this evening together, I'm extraordinarily grateful.

I'm going to be very brief at the top, because I want to spend most of the time just in conversation. We've got a lot of friends here, people who I've known for a long time who have been great supporters for a long time.

We're obviously at a critical junction in our country's history. You guys helped to propel me into office in 2008. We didn't fully understand at that point how deep this crisis was going to be. And we now know that in that final quarter of 2008, when we were still campaigning, that the economy actually shrank by 9 percent. It was the deepest, toughest economic crisis that we've had since the Great Depression.

So we had to go in and move quickly. And we did. And because we moved quickly, by the end of 2010, the economy was growing again. Because we moved quickly, the auto industry was safe. Because we moved quickly and effectively, we were able to stem some of the job loss. And in the meantime, we were able to keep a bunch of promises that we'd talked about during the campaign, whether it was getting our troops from Iraq and making sure that we ended "don't ask, don't tell," to being able to finally pass health care reform and make sure that not only were we bringing down costs over the long term, but also making sure that people who didn't have health insurance could actually have access to coverage.

So I am extraordinarily proud of the track record that we've established over the last 2½ years. But people are still hurting out there, and times are still tough. And it's not just here in the United States, it's global.

The United States, for all our challenges, is still looked upon around the world as somebody who has to help guide this incredible rapid change that's taking place in this 21st-century global economy. But we're not going to be able to lead as effectively as we need to unless we make sure that we get things here at home fixed.

So our immediate task, the thing that's most urgent, in my mind and I'm sure in a lot of other people's minds, is putting people back to work, putting America back to work.

And we've spent the last month talking about this "American Jobs Act," principles, by the way, and proposals that had historically been supported by Democrats and Republicans. I don't know when Republicans decided they don't believe in building roads and bridges. [*Laughter*] I don't know when they decided they don't like tax cuts for small businesses. I don't know when they decided that it didn't make sense for us to put teachers back in the classroom. And I'm hoping that when they reflect upon it a little bit, they'll realize that these are all proposals they've supported in the past.

And we've also put forward a way to pay for it that not only puts Americans back to work, helps avert a potential—another dip in our—[*inaudible*]—but also brings down our deficit and debt in a sustainable way. And it's paid for by combining tough cuts—some of which I wouldn't be making if we weren't in such a tough fiscal situation—with making sure that people like us in this room, who have been incredibly blessed, pay a little bit more and do our fair share, which is basically the formula for deficit reduction that every single expert out there who's looked at it says is the right way to go.

So that's our immediate task. The election is 13 months away; the American people can't wait for the next 13 months. They need help right now. And I'm going to urge everybody who's here to help us in mounting this campaign to make sure Congress acts. And I know you guys have a little pull, at least with one Congressman. [*Laughter*]

But beyond that, this election is actually going to be even more fundamental, because it represents a stark, contrasting vision of where we want to take the country. Do we want a country that has the best education system in the world? Then we're going to have to reform it, but we're also going to have to invest in it. Do we want to make sure that we have the best infrastructure in the world that helped to make us an economic superpower? That means roads and bridges, ports and dams and locks. But it also means making sure that we've got the best broadband and wireless in the world. It also means high-speed rail. It also means having a new-generation aviation system that can help airlines save on fuel and help move products and services more quickly around the country. Or do we just say we're going to try to live off the investments that were made a generation ago or two generations ago or three generations ago, that we've stopped thinking big about what we can do as a country?

Are we going to continue to make investments in science and technology and basic medical research? Or are we going to starve that thing that's been most vital to our technological ascendancy? Are we going to continue to have a safety net that is real for the poor and the vulnerable, but also for middle class families all across the country: a retirement system that works, Social Security that's solvent, a Medicare system that provides care for our seniors?

Internationally, are we going to lead not just with our military, but are we also going to lead with our diplomacy and our vision and the power of our example? Are we—do we think that the only way to compete is to strip away regulations that keep our air and water clean, that make sure that our workers have safe work environments? Or do we think that those are things that we owe to our children and our grandchildren?

So these are fundamental choices that we're going to be making, and they'll be shaped by who gets appointed to the Supreme Court. They'll be shaped by what kind of legislation emerges from Congress. It's going to be shaped by how our national conversation goes about the way forward.

Now, I'm confident that we are going to be able to win that debate, but I can only win it with all of you. Two thousand eight was sort of this weird convergence of everything happening in a way that was exciting and hopeful. This one, this election, is going to be much more just grinding it out. We're going to have to work really hard. I'm a little grayer. We've been around the block a few times. And the American people are tired, and they just want things to go ahead and get better.

So in that kind of environment, we're going to have to provide even more effort than we did in 2008. I hope you guys are ready for it, because if you are, then we're going to win.

And I don't think we have a choice. I think it's that important that we make sure that America is on a trajectory where middle class families in this country can continue to believe in the American Dream and they can continue to believe that if they work hard they are rewarded and that being responsible is rewarded and that regardless of their circumstances, they can see a path to a better life.

That's been the essence of America. I don't want that to go away. We've got to fight for it. And I hope you're willing to join me.

Thank you very much, everybody.

NOTE: The President spoke at 7:35 p.m. at the residence of Thomas S. and Lisa Carnahan. In his remarks, he referred to Robert G. Clark, chairman and chief executive officer, Clayco Inc.; and Rep. J. Russell Carnahan.

Remarks Prior to a Meeting With President Porfirio Lobo Sosa of Honduras
October 5, 2011

President Obama. Well, it's a pleasure to welcome President Lobo to the White House, and this gives us an opportunity to reaffirm the friendship between the American and the Honduran people. Not only has Honduras been a traditionally close partner with the United States, but the people-to-people relationship is profound, particularly given the Honduran-American population that has contributed so much to the growth of our country.

Today also begins a new chapter in the relationship between our two countries. Two years ago, we saw a coup in Honduras that threatened to move the country away from democracy, and in part because of pressure from the international community, but also because of the strong commitment to democracy and leadership by President Lobo, what we've been seeing is a restoration of democratic practices and a commitment to reconciliation that gives us great hope.

And President Lobo's leadership is responsible not only for helping to restore constitutional order and democracy and a commitment to fair and free elections, but it's also allowed

Honduras once again to rejoin the Organization of American States, and for Hondurans—the Honduran relationship with its neighbors to be restored to a normal place.

Of course, much work remains to be done. And I'm looking forward to a excellent conversation with President Lobo about how we can be helpful in ensuring that human rights are observed in Honduras. We will discuss ways in which our two countries can work effectively together to deal with the security situation that exists not only in Honduras, but throughout Central America, and how we can cooperate effectively in preventing the countries of Central America from being corrupted and overrun by the transnational drug trade. And we also will have discussions about how we can continue to strengthen development in Honduras and the region so that people have opportunity, we will see economic growth, see economic development, and expand trade and further interactions between our two countries.

So, Mr. President, I welcome you. I'm looking forward to a good conversation that will help to strengthen the relationship between our two countries. And, again, we are very appreciative of the leadership you've shown during what's been a very difficult time.

President Lobo. Thank you so much, Mr. President. It is indeed a very high honor for me to be here in the White House today. I want to state very emphatically that this is a great opportunity to celebrate the friendship between our peoples. It's also an occasion in which we are reaffirming the permanent gratitude that we have for your friendship, for the permanent assistance we have received from the United States, and very especially because at a time of great crisis you were there to help, and you were there to help us restore the family that is our Nation.

I began my administration bringing together all the forces that make up Honduran society. And what I have tried to establish is unity and reconciliation in my country.

We are on the road, as you said, Mr. President, to a number of things. We have returned to the Organization of American States, and in fact, I was able to visit that organization yesterday. It was a very warm visit. It was a wonderful occasion.

We have reaffirmed our democratic vocation. We have reaffirmed the road to democracy that we are on and that we will continue on. We will be opening even more spaces for our people to be able to express themselves. We have already created spaces within our representative democracy, but we will continue to do that so that there is evermore direct participation from our people in all levels of society.

That is a road we've started on, and we will continue down that path.

The enormous challenge we face is that of crime and drug trafficking. But we have good friends, like you, who have helped us in the past, who continue to help us. And your words today, Mr. President, are a reaffirmation of that good friendship and that good support that we receive from you, and we hope we will have that in the future.

I also want to say to you again today that we will continue to respect human rights and do everything we can to build on what we have already done in that area. We know that there are some areas in which we have weaknesses we need to work on: The investigation of such crimes is one of those. But we hope to be able to get help from the United States on that so that we can overcome the hurdles we have in this respect, and we are able to find those people who are guilty of violations of human rights.

So we are on the road to reconciliation. Next year, our political parties will be holding their primaries. And in 2013, we will be holding our general election, and so we will be complying with our Constitution for a man or woman to be elected President every 4 years.

President Obama. All right. Thank you, everybody.

NOTE: The President spoke at 3:55 p.m. in the Oval Office at the White House. President Lobo spoke in Spanish, and his remarks were translated by an interpreter.

Statement on the Death of Fred L. Shuttlesworth
October 5, 2011

Michelle and I were saddened to hear about the passing of Reverend Fred Shuttlesworth today. As one of the founders of the Southern Christian Leadership Conference, Reverend Shuttlesworth dedicated his life to advancing the cause of justice for all Americans. He was a testament to the strength of the human spirit. And today, we stand on his shoulders and the shoulders of all those who marched and sat and lifted their voices to help perfect our Union.

I will never forget having the opportunity several years ago to push Reverend Shuttlesworth in his wheelchair across the Edmund Pettus Bridge, a symbol of the sacrifices that he and so many others made in the name of equality. America owes Reverend Shuttlesworth a debt of gratitude, and our thoughts and prayers are with his wife Sephira and their family, friends, and loved ones.

Statement on the Death of Steven P. Jobs
October 5, 2011

Michelle and I are saddened to learn of the passing of Steve Jobs. Steve was among the greatest of American innovators: brave enough to think differently, bold enough to believe he could change the world, and talented enough to do it.

By building one of the planet's most successful companies from his garage, he exemplified the spirit of American ingenuity. By making computers personal and putting the Internet in our pockets, he made the information revolution not only accessible, but intuitive and fun. And by turning his talents to storytelling, he has brought joy to millions of children and grownups alike. Steve was fond of saying that he lived every day like it was his last. Because he did, he transformed our lives, redefined entire industries, and achieved one of the rarest feats in human history: He changed the way each of us sees the world.

The world has lost a visionary. And there may be no greater tribute to Steve's success than the fact that much of the world learned of his passing on a device he invented. Michelle and I send our thoughts and prayers to Steve's wife Laurene, his family, and all those who loved him.

The President's News Conference
October 6, 2011

The President. Good morning, everybody. I will take your questions in a second. But first, I just want to say a few words about the economy.

Next week, the Senate will vote on the "American Jobs Act." And I think by now I've made my views pretty well known. Some of you are even keeping a tally of how many times I've talked about the "American Jobs Act." And the reason I keep going around the country talking about this jobs bill is because people really need help right now. Our economy really needs a jolt right now.

This is not a game; this is not the time for the usual political gridlock. The problems Europe is having today could have a very real effect on our economy at a time when it's already fragile. But this jobs bill can help guard against another downturn if the situation in Europe gets any worse. It will boost economic growth; it will put people back to work.

And by the way, this is not just my belief. This is what independent economists have said, not politicians, not just people in my administration. Independent experts who do this for a living have said this jobs bill will have a significant effect for our economy and for middle class families all across America. And what these independent experts have also said is that if we don't act, the opposite will be true. There will be fewer jobs; there will be weaker growth.

So as we look towards next week, any Senator out there who's thinking about voting against this jobs bill when it comes up for a vote, needs to explain exactly why they would oppose something that we know would improve our economic situation at such an urgent time for our families and for our businesses.

Congressional Republicans say one of the most important things we can do is cut taxes. Then they should love this plan. This jobs bill would cut taxes for virtually every worker and small business in America. If you're a small-business owner that hires someone or raises wages, you would get another tax cut. If you hire a veteran, you get a tax cut. Right now there's a small business in Ohio that does high-tech manufacturing, and they've been expanding for the past 2 years. They're considering hiring more, and this tax break would encourage them to do it.

Hundreds of thousands of teachers and firefighters and police officers have been laid off because of State budget cuts. This jobs bill has funding to put a lot of those men and women back to work. It has funding to prevent a lot more from losing their job. I had a chance to meet a young man named Robert Baroz. He's an English teacher in Boston who came to the White House a few weeks ago. He's got two decades of teaching experience; he's got a master's degree; he's got an outstanding track record of helping his students make huge gains in reading and writing. In the last few years, he's received three pink slips because of budget cuts. Why wouldn't we want to pass a bill that puts somebody like Robert back in the classroom teaching our kids?

Some of you were with me when we visited a bridge between Ohio and Kentucky that's been classified as functionally obsolete. That's a fancy way of saying it's old and breaking down. We've heard about bridges in both States that are falling apart, and that's true all across the country.

In Maine, there is a bridge that is in such bad shape that pieces of it were literally falling off the other day. And meanwhile, we've got millions of laid-off construction workers who could right now be busy rebuilding roads, rebuilding bridges, rebuilding schools. This jobs bill gives them a chance to get back to work rebuilding America. Why wouldn't we want that to happen? Why would you vote against that?

The proposals in this bill are not just random investments to create make-work jobs, they are steps we have to take if we want to build an economy that lasts, if we want to be able to compete with other countries for jobs that restore a sense of security to middle class families. And to do that, we've got to have the most educated workers. We have to have the best transportation and communications networks. We have to support innovative small businesses. We've got to support innovative manufacturers.

Now, what's true is we've also got to rein in our deficits and live within our means, which is why this jobs bill is fully paid for by asking millionaires and billionaires to pay their fair share. And some see this as class warfare. I see it as a simple choice: We can either keep taxes exactly as they are for millionaires and billionaires,

with loopholes that lead them to have lower tax rates in some cases than plumbers and teachers, or we can put teachers and construction workers and veterans back on the job.

We can fight to protect tax cuts for folks who don't need them and weren't asking for them, or we can cut taxes for virtually every worker and small business in America. But we can't afford to do both. That's the choice that's going to be before the Senate.

There are too many people hurting in this country for us to do nothing and the economy is just too fragile for us to let politics get in the way of action. We've got a responsibility to the people who sent us here. So I hope every Senator thinks long and hard about what's at stake when they cast their vote next week.

All right. With that, I will take your questions, and I will start with Ben Feller of Associated Press.

National Economy/Bipartisanship/Job Growth Legislation

Q. Thank you very much, Mr. President. I'd like to ask you about two economic matters. Federal Reserve Chairman Bernanke warned Congress this week that the economic recovery is close to faltering. Do you agree?

And secondly, on your jobs bill, the American people are sick of games, and you mentioned games in your comments. They want results. Wouldn't it be more productive to work with Republicans on a plan that you know could pass Congress as opposed to going around the country talking about your bill and singling out—calling out Republicans by name?

The President. Well, first of all, with respect to the state of the economy, there is no doubt that growth has slowed. I think people were much more optimistic at the beginning of this year. But the combination of a Japanese tsunami, the Arab Spring, which drove up gas prices, and most prominently, Europe, I think, has gotten businesses and consumers very nervous. And we did not help here in Washington with the debt ceiling debacle that took place, a bit of game-playing that was completely unnecessary, completely unprecedented in terms of how we dealt with our responsibilities here in Washington.

You combine all that, there is no doubt that the economy is weaker now than it was at the beginning of the year. And every independent economist who has looked at this question carefully believes that for us to make sure that we are taking out an insurance policy against a possible double-dip recession, it is important for us to make sure that we are boosting consumer confidence, putting money into their pockets, cutting taxes where we can for small businesses, and that it makes sense for us to put people back to work doing the work that needs to be done. That's exactly what this jobs bill does.

Now, with respect to working with Congress, I think it's fair to say that I have gone out of my way in every instance, sometimes at my own political peril and to the frustration of Democrats, to work with Republicans to find common ground to move this country forward, in every instance, whether it was during the lame duck session, when we were able to get an agreement on making sure that the payroll tax was cut in the first place and making sure that unemployment insurance was extended, to my constant efforts during the debt ceiling to try to get what's been called a grand bargain in which we had a balanced approach to actually bringing down our deficit and debt in a way that wouldn't hurt our recovery.

Each time, what we've seen is games-playing, a preference to try to score political points rather than actually get something done on the part of the other side. And that has been true not just over the last 6 months; that's been true over the last 2½ years.

Now, the bottom line is this: Our doors are open. And what I've done over the last several weeks is to take the case to the American people so that they understand what's at stake. It is now up to all the Senators and, hopefully, all the Members of the House to explain to their constituencies why they would be opposed to commonsense ideas that historically have been supported by Democrats and Republicans in the past. Why would you be opposed to tax cuts for small businesses and tax cuts for American workers?

My understanding is that for the last decade, they've been saying we need to lower taxes for folks. Well, why wouldn't we want to do that through this jobs bill? We know that we've got roads and bridges and schools that need to be rebuilt. And historically, Republicans haven't been opposed to rebuilding roads and bridges. Why would you be opposed now?

We know that the biggest problem that we've had in terms of unemployment over the last several months has not been in the private sector, it's actually been layoffs of teachers and cops and firefighters. We've created over 2 million jobs in the private sector—a million jobs this year alone in the private sector—but in the public sector, we keep on seeing these layoffs having an adverse effect on economies in States all across the country. Why wouldn't we want to make sure that those teachers are in the classroom teaching our kids?

So here's the bottom line: My expectation and hope is that everybody will vote for this jobs bill because it reflects those ideas that traditionally have been supported by both Democrats and Republicans. If it turns out that there are Republicans who are opposed to this bill, they need to explain to me, but more importantly, to their constituencies and the American people, why they're opposed and what would they do.

We know that this jobs bill, based on independent analysis, could grow the economy almost an additional 2 percent. That could mean an additional 1.9 million jobs. Do they have a plan that would have a similar impact? Because if they do, I'm happy to hear it. But I haven't heard them offer alternatives that would have that same kind of impact, and that's what we need right now.

A lot of the problems that this economy is facing are problems that predate the financial crisis: middle class families seeing their wages and their incomes flat despite rising costs for everything from health care to a college education. And so folks have been struggling not just for the last 3 years, they've been struggling for over a decade now. And at a time when so many people are having such a hard time, we have to have an approach, we have to take action, that is big enough to meet the moment. And what I've heard from Republicans is, well, we're agreeing to do these trade bills. That's great. I'm in favor of those trade bills, and I'm glad they're passing, but that's not going to do enough to deal with the huge problems we have right now with respect to unemployment.

We passed patent legislation. That was bipartisan work. I'm thrilled that I was—we were able to get Republicans and Democrats to work together on that. But that is a long-term issue for our economic competitiveness. It's not putting Americans to work right now.

So the bottom line is this, Ben: If next week Senators have additional ideas that will put people back to work right now and meet the challenges of the current economy, we are happy to consider them. But every idea that we put forward are ones that traditionally have been supported by Democrats and Republicans alike. And I think it's important for us to have a vote on those ideas, because I believe that it's very hard to argue against them.

And if Mr. McConnell chooses to vote against it or if members of his caucus choose to vote against it, I promise you we're going to keep on going and we will put forward maybe piece by piece each component of the bill. And each time they're going to have to explain why it is that they'd be opposed to putting teachers back in the classroom or rebuilding our schools or giving tax cuts to middle class folks and giving tax cuts to small businesses.

National Economy

Q. Do you think the recovery is close to faltering?

The President. I think that if we don't take action, then we could end up having more significant problems than we have right now. And some of it is just simple math. The payroll tax cut that we passed is set to expire. The jobs plan includes an extension of the payroll tax cut.

Now, if that is not extended, then that is over $1,000 out of the pockets of the average American family at a time when they're already feeling a severe pinch. That means they're going to be spending less. That means businesses are going to have less customers. And that's going to have an adverse effect on an economy that is already weaker than it should be.

Okay. Chuck Todd [NBC News].

Job Growth Legislation/Tax Reform

Q. Thank you, Mr. President. Before I get to my question, do we assume by how you're talking about the bill in the Senate that you are okay with the change in how to pay for it, the surtax—the 5.6-percent surtax on millionaires?

The President. We've always said that we would be open to a variety of ways to pay for it. We put forward what we thought was a solid approach to paying for the jobs bill itself. Keep in mind, though, that what I've always said is that not only do we have to pay for the jobs bill, but we also still have to do more in order to reduce the debt and deficit.

So the approach that the Senate is taking I'm comfortable with in order to deal with the jobs bill. We're still going to need to reform this Tax Code to make sure that we're closing loopholes, closing special interest tax breaks, making sure that the very simple principle, what we call the Buffett rule, which is that millionaires and billionaires aren't paying lower tax rates than ordinary families, that that's in place. So there's going to be more work to do with respect to making our tax system fair and just and promoting growth. But in terms of the immediate action of getting this jobs bill passed, I'm fine with the approach that they're taking.

Public Discontent With Political Process/Job Growth Legislation

Q. My question has to do with your powers of persuasion. During the debt ceiling debate, you asked for the American public to call Members of Congress, and switchboards got jammed. You have done a similar thing while going around the country doing this. Talking to Members of Congress, there's not the same reaction; you're not seeing—hearing about phones being jammed. Talking to one Member of Congress, he told me there's a disillusionment he's concerned about with the public that maybe they just don't believe anything can get done anyway. Are you worried about your own powers of persuasion and maybe that the American public is not listening to you anymore?

The President. Well, no. What we've seen is the American people respond very enthusiastically to the specific provisions of the jobs bill. They are very skeptical about Congress's ability to act right now, and that's understandable. The American people are very frustrated. They've been frustrated for a long time. They don't get a sense that folks in this town are looking out for their interests. They get a sense that folks in this town are thinking about their own jobs, their own careers, their own advancement, their party interests. And so if the question is, Chuck, are people feeling cynical and frustrated about the prospects of positive action in this city? Absolutely. And I can go out there and make speeches, but until they actually see action, some of that cynicism is going to be there.

As you said, during the debt ceiling debate, a very solid majority, I think maybe even higher than 70 percent, agreed with the approach that I talked about, which was we should have a balanced approach to deficit reduction.

And what the American people saw is that Congress didn't care, not just what I thought, they didn't care about what the American people thought. They had their own agenda. And so if they see that over and over again, that cynicism is not going to be reduced until Congress actually proves their cynicism wrong by doing something that would actually help the American people. This is a great opportunity to do it. This is a great opportunity to do it.

And keep in mind, if the American jobs bill passes, we're still going to have challenges. We're still going to have to make sure that we've got the best education system in the world because that is going to be critical for our long-term competitiveness and creating good, solid middle class jobs. We're still going to have to keep investing in basic research and science. We're still going to have to make sure that we do even more on infrastructure. I mean, what's contained in the American jobs

bill doesn't cover all the roads and bridges and infrastructure that needs to be improved around the country.

So there—so it's not as if that's going to solve all our problems, but it is an important start that we know would end up growing the economy and putting hundreds of thousands, millions of people back to work at a time when they need it the most. And it's paid for.

The one persuasive argument that the Republicans previously had made against a bill like this is the deficit is growing, we can't afford it. Well, we can afford it if we're willing to ask people like me to do a little bit more in taxes. We can afford it without affecting our deficit. Our proposal is paid for. So that can't be the excuse.

And so yes, until they see Congress actually putting country ahead of party politics and partisanship, they're going to be skeptical. And it doesn't matter how many times I preach to them, this is not a reflection of their lack of faith in the American jobs bill. They haven't seen Congress able to come together and act.

This is a good opportunity, though.

Q. [*Inaudible*]—disillusionment?

The President. What we've seen is, is that they agree with what we've put forward. Now, here's what I'll also say, is that based on the debt ceiling vote, what they've seen is that the Republicans in Congress, even when the American people agree with me, oftentimes will vote against something I'm proposing.

So there may be some skepticism that I personally can persuade Republicans to take actions in the interest of the American people. But that's exactly why I need the American people to try to put some pressure on them. Because I think, justifiably, what they've seen is that oftentimes, even ideas that used to be supported by Republicans, if I'm proposing them, suddenly, Republicans forget it, and they decide they're against it.

Jackie [Jackie Calmes, New York Times].

U.S. Financial System/Consumer Financial Protection Bureau

Q. Thank you, Mr. President. As you travel the country, you also take credit for tightening regulations on Wall Street through the Dodd-Frank law and about your efforts to combat income inequality. There's this movement—Occupy Wall Street—which has spread from Wall Street to other cities. They clearly don't think that you or Republicans have done enough, that you're, in fact, part of the problem.

Are you following this movement, and what would you say to its—people that are attracted to it?

The President. Obviously, I've heard of it. I've seen it on television. I think it expresses the frustrations that the American people feel, that we had the biggest financial crisis since the Great Depression, huge collateral damage all throughout the country, all across Main Street, and yet you're still seeing some of the same folks who acted irresponsibly trying to fight efforts to crack down on abusive practices that got us into this problem in the first place.

So yes, I think people are frustrated and the protestors are giving voice to a more broad-based frustration about how our financial system works. Now, keep in mind, I have said before and I will continue to repeat, we have to have a strong, effective financial sector in order for us to grow. And I used up a lot of political capital, and I've got the dings and bruises to prove it, in order to make sure that we prevented a financial meltdown and that banks stayed afloat. And that was the right thing to do, because had we seen a financial collapse then the damage to the American economy would have been even worse.

But what I've also said is that for us to have a healthy financial system, that requires that banks and other financial institutions compete on the basis of the best service and the best products and the best price, and it can't be competing on the basis of hidden fees, deceptive practices, or derivative cocktails that nobody understands and that expose the entire economy to enormous risks. And that's what Dodd-Frank was designed to do. It was designed to make sure that we didn't have the necessity of taxpayer bailouts. That we said, you know what? We're going to be able to control these situations so that if these guys get into trouble, we can isolate them, quarantine them,

and let them fail. It says that we're going to have a consumer watchdog on the job all the time who's going to make sure that they are dealing with customers in a fair way and we're eliminating hidden fees on credit cards and mortgage brokers are going to have to—actually have to be straight with people about what they're purchasing.

And what we've seen over the last year is not only did the financial sector, with the Republican Party in Congress, fight us every inch of the way, but now you've got these same folks suggesting that we should roll back all those reforms and go back to the way it was before the crisis. Today, my understanding is, we're going to have a hearing on Richard Cordray, who is my nominee to head up the Consumer Financial Protection Bureau. He would be America's chief consumer watchdog when it comes to financial products. Now, this is a guy who is well regarded in his home State of Ohio, has been the treasurer of Ohio, the attorney general of Ohio. Republicans and Democrats in Ohio all say that he is a serious person who looks out for consumers. He has a good reputation. And Republicans have threatened not to confirm him not because of anything he's done, but because they want to roll back the whole notion of having a consumer watchdog.

You've got Republican Presidential candidates whose main economic policy proposals is, we'll get rid of the financial reforms that are designed to prevent the abuses that got us into this mess in the first place. That does not make sense to the American people. They are frustrated by it. And they will continue to be frustrated by it until they get a sense that everybody is playing by the same set of rules and that you're rewarded for responsibility and doing the right thing as opposed to gaming the system.

So I'm going to be fighting every inch of the way here in Washington to make sure that we have a consumer watchdog that is preventing abusive practices by the financial sector.

I will be hugely supportive of banks and financial institutions that are doing the right thing by their customers. We need them to be lending. We need them to be lending more to small businesses. We need them to help do what traditionally banks and financial services are supposed to be doing, which is providing business and families resources to make productive investments that will actually build the economy. But until the American people see that happening, yes, they are going to continue to express frustrations about what they see as two sets of rules.

Discontent With U.S. Financial System

Q. Do you think Occupy Wall Street has the potential to be a Tea Party movement in 2012?

The President. What I think is that the American people understand that not everybody has been following the rules, that Wall Street is an example of that, that folks who are working hard every single day, getting up, going to the job, loyal to their companies, that that used to be the essence of the American Dream. That's how you got ahead—the old-fashioned way. And these days, a lot of folks who are doing the right thing aren't rewarded, and a lot of folks who aren't doing the right thing are rewarded.

And that's going to express itself politically in 2012 and beyond until people feel like once again we're getting back to some old-fashioned American values in which, if you're a banker, then you are making your money by making prudent loans to businesses and individuals to build plants and equipment and hire workers that are creating goods and products that are building the economy and benefiting everybody.

Jake Tapper [ABC News].

U.S. Financial System/Department of Energy Loan Guarantee Program/Bureau of Alcohol, Tobacco, Firearms, and Explosives "Fast and Furious" Program

Q. Thank you, Mr. President. Just to follow up on Jackie's question. One of the reasons why so many of the people of the Occupy Wall Street protests are so angry is because, as you say, so many people on Wall Street did not follow the rules, but your administration hasn't really been very aggressive in prosecuting. In fact, I don't think any Wall Street executives have gone to jail despite the rampant corrup-

tion and malfeasance that did take place. So I was wondering if you'd comment on that.

And then just as a separate question, as you're watching the Solyndra and "Fast and Furious" controversies play out, I'm wondering if it gives you any pause about any of the decisionmaking going on in your administration: some of the e-mails that Democrats put out indicating that people at the Office of Management and Budget were concerned about the Department of Energy; some of the e-mails going on with the Attorney General saying he didn't know about the details of "Fast and Furious." Are you worried at all about how this is—how your administration is running?

The President. Well, first on the issue of prosecutions on Wall Street, one of the biggest problems about the collapse of Lehmans and the subsequent financial crisis and the whole subprime lending fiasco is that a lot of that stuff wasn't necessarily illegal, it was just immoral or inappropriate or reckless. That's exactly why we needed to pass Dodd-Frank, to prohibit some of these practices.

The financial sector is very creative, and they are always looking for ways to make money. That's their job. And if there are loopholes and rules that can be bent and arbitrage to be had, they will take advantage of it. So without commenting on particular prosecutions—obviously, that's not my job, that's the Attorney General's job—I think part of people's frustrations, part of my frustration, was a lot of practices that should not have been allowed weren't necessarily against the law, but they had a huge destructive impact. And that's why it was important for us to put in place financial rules that protect the American people from reckless decisionmaking and irresponsible behavior.

Now, with respect to Solyndra and "Fast and Furious," I think I've been very clear that I have complete confidence in Attorney General Holder in how he handles his office. He has been very aggressive in going after gun running and cash transactions that are going to these transnational drug cartels in Mexico. There has been a lot of cooperation between the United States and Mexico on this front.

He's indicated that he was not aware of what was happening in "Fast and Furious." Certainly, I was not. And I think both he and I would have been very unhappy if somebody had suggested that guns were allowed to pass through that could have been prevented by the United States of America.

He has assigned an Inspector General to look into how exactly this happened, and I have complete confidence in him and I've got complete confidence in the process to figure out who, in fact, was responsible for that decision and how it got made.

Solyndra, this is a loan guarantee program that predates me that historically has had support from Democrats and Republicans as well. And the idea is pretty straightforward: If we are going to be able to compete in the 21st century, then we've got to dominate cutting-edge technologies, we've got to dominate cutting-edge manufacturing. Clean energy is part of that package of technologies of the future that have to be based here in the United States if we're going to be able to succeed.

Now, the loan guarantee program is designed to meet a particular need in the marketplace, which is, a lot of these small startups, they can get angel investors, they can get several million dollars to get a company going, but it's very hard for them to then scale up, particularly if these are new cutting-edge technologies. It's hard for them to find private investors. And part of what's happening is China and Europe, other countries, are putting enormous subsidies into these companies and giving them incentives to move offshore. Even if the technology was developed in the United States, they end up going to China because the Chinese Government will say, we're going to help you get started. We'll help you scale up. We'll give you low-interest loans or no-interest loans. We will give siting. We will do whatever it takes for you to get started here.

And that's part of the reason why a lot of technologies that developed here, we've now lost the lead in: solar energy, wind energy. And so what the loan guarantee program was designed to do was to close that gap and say, let's

see if we can help some of those folks locate here and create jobs here in the United States.

Now, we knew from the start that the loan guarantee program was going to entail some risk, by definition. If it was a risk-free proposition, then we wouldn't have to worry about it. But the overall portfolio has been successful. It has allowed us to help companies, for example, start advanced battery manufacturing here in the United States. It's helped to create jobs. There were going to be some companies that did not work out; Solyndra was one of them. But the process by which the decision was made was on the merits. It was straightforward. And of course, there were going to be debates internally when you're dealing with something as complicated as this.

But I have confidence that the decisions were made based on what would be good for the American economy and the American people and putting people back to work.

And by the way, let me make one last point about this. I heard there was a Republican Member of Congress who's engaging in oversight on this, and despite the fact that all of them in the past have been supportive of this loan guarantee program, he concluded, you know what, we can't compete against China when it comes to solar energy. Well, you know what, I don't buy that. I'm not going to surrender to other countries' technological leads that could end up determining whether or not we're building a strong middle class in this country. And so we're going to have to keep on pushing hard to make sure that manufacturing is located here, new businesses are located here, and new technologies are developed here. And there are going to be times where it doesn't work out, but I'm not going to cave to the competition when they are heavily subsidizing all these industries.

U.S. Financial System

Q. Just a follow-up on Wall Street. Are you satisfied with how aggressive your administration has been when it comes to prosecuting? Because I know a lot of it was legal, but a lot of was not. There was fraud that took place.

The President. Right. Well, let me say this: The President can't go around saying, prosecute somebody. But as a general principle, if somebody is engaged in fraudulent actions, they need to be prosecuted. If they violated laws on the books, they need to be prosecuted. And that's the Attorney General's job, and I know that Attorney General Holder, U.S. attorneys all across the country, they take that job very seriously. Okay?

Hans [Hans Nichols, Bloomberg News].

Consumer Financial Protection Bureau

Q. Thank you, Mr. President. You just spoke of the need for banks to start lending, you talked earlier about how creative they can be in chasing profit, and yet earlier in the week, you said that banks don't have some inherent right to just, you know, get a certain amount of profit. You also said in that interview that you can stop them. How do you plan on stopping them from charging this $5 fee or whatever the fee is? And do you think that your Government has a right to dictate how much profits American companies make?

The President. I absolutely do not think that. I was trying to make a broader point, which is that people have been using financial regulation as an excuse to charge consumers more. Right? I mean, basically the argument they've made is, well, you know what, this hidden fee was prohibited, and so we'll find another fee to make up for it. Now, they have that right, but it's not a good practice. It's not necessarily fair to consumers. And my main goal is to make sure that we've got a consumer watchdog in place who is letting consumers know what fair practices are, making sure that transactions are transparent, and making sure that banks have to compete for customers based on the quality of their service and good prices.

Now, the frustrating thing that we have right now is that you've got folks over in Congress, Republicans, who have said that they see their role as eliminating any prohibitions on any practices for financial companies. And I think that's part of the frustration that the American people feel, because they've just gone through a period in which they were seeing a bunch of

hidden fees, rate hikes that they didn't know about, fine print that they could not understand. That's true for credit cards. That's true for mortgages. It contributed to overall weakness in the economy.

And yes, I think it is entirely appropriate for the Government to have some oversight role to make sure that consumers are protected. So banks—and any business in America—can price their products any way they want. That's how the free market works. As long as there's transparency and accountability and consumers understand what they're getting. And there are going to be instances where a policy judgment is made that, you know what, there are certain practices that just aren't fair. And that's how the market has always operated.

Q. So is it your understanding the Consumer Financial Protection Bureau can't actually prevent the debit card fees from going in place, like the ones that are being discussed——

The President. I think that what the Consumer Finance Protection Bureau could do is to make sure that consumers understood exactly what they were getting, exactly what was happening. And I think that Congress could make determinations with respect to whether or not a certain practice was fair or not. Okay?

David Nakamura [Washington Post].

Alternative and Renewable Energy Sources and Technologies

Q. Thank you, Mr. President. Just following up on Jake's question about Solyndra. The loan program—guaranteed loan program that you talked about was giving out $38 billion in guaranteed loans and promised to save or create 65,000 jobs, green jobs, in clean energy, and there's been reports that actually only 3,500 new jobs have been created in that industry. Why has that industry been so slow to respond to the investment that your administration has provided? And what do you see going forward as to how it will respond?

The President. Well, I think that what has been true historically is that businesses that rely on new technologies, often—a lot of times it's going to take a while before they get take-off. And there are a lot of upfront investments that have to be made in research and capital and so forth, a lot of barriers for companies that are trying to break in. Keep in mind that clean energy companies are competing against traditional energy companies. And traditional energy is still cheaper in a lot of ways.

The problem is, is it's running out, it's polluting, and we know that demand is going to keep on increasing so that if we don't prepare now, if we don't invest now, if we don't get on top of technologies now, we're going to be facing 20 years from now China and India having a billion new drivers on the road, the trendlines in terms of oil prices, coal, et cetera, going up, the impact on the planet increasing. And we're not just going to be able to start when all heck is breaking loose and say, boy, we better find some new energy sources.

So in the meantime, we've got to make these investments, but that makes it more difficult for a lot of these companies to succeed. What's also a problem, as I said, is that other countries are subsidizing these industries much more aggressively than we are. Hundreds of billions of dollars the Chinese Government is pouring into the clean energy sector, partly because they're projecting what's going to happen 10 or 20 years from now.

So look, I have confidence in American businesses and American technology and American scientists and entrepreneurs being able to win that competition. We are not going to be duplicating the kind of system that they have in China where they are basically state-run banks giving money to state-run companies and ignoring losses and ignoring bad management. But there is a role to play for us to make sure that these companies can at least have a fighting shot. And it does mean that there are going to be some that aren't successful, and it's going to be an uphill climb for some. And obviously, it's very difficult for all companies right now to succeed when the economy is as soft and as weak as it.

Department of Energy Loan Guarantee Program

Q. There have been reports with Solyndra in particular that investors warned your administration that the Government—that loan of $500 million in that company might not be a wise use of taxpayers' money. In retrospect, do you think your administration was so eager for Solyndra to succeed that it missed some of the critical warnings?

The President. I will tell you that even for those projects under this loan guarantee program that have ended up being successful, there are those in the marketplace who have been doubtful. So, I mean, there's always going to be a debate about whether this particular approach to this particular technology is going to be successful or not.

And all I can say is that the Department of Energy made these decisions based on their best judgment about what would make sense. And the nature of these programs are going to be ones in which for every success there may be one that does not work out as well. But that's exactly what the loan guarantee program was designed by Congress to do, was to take bets on these areas where we need to make sure that we're maintaining our lead. Okay?

Bill Plante [CBS News].

Bipartisanship/Job Growth Legislation

Q. Thank you, Mr. President. Anybody on Capitol Hill will say that there's no chance that the "American Jobs Act," in its current state, passes either House. And you've been out on the campaign trail banging away at them saying, pass this bill. And it begins, sir, to look like you're campaigning and like you're following the Harry Truman model against the do-nothing Congress instead of negotiating. Are you negotiating? Will you?

The President. I am always open to negotiations. What is also true is they need to do something. I'm not—look, the—Bill, I think it is very clear that if Members of Congress come in and say, "All right, we want to build infrastructure, here's the way we think we can do it; we want to put construction workers back to work, we've got some ideas," I am ready, eager to work with them. They say, "We've got this great idea for putting teachers back in the classroom; it's a little different than what you've proposed in the jobs bill." I'm ready, eager to work with them. But that's not what we're hearing right now. I mean, what we're hearing is that their big ideas, the ones that make sense, are ones we're already doing.

They've given me a list of, well, here's the Republican job creation ideas: Let's pass free trade agreements. It's great that we're passing these free trade agreements. We put them forward; I expect bipartisan support. I think it's going to be good for the American economy. But it's not going to meet the challenge of 9-percent unemployment or an economy that is currently weakening. It's not enough.

Patent reform, very important for our long-term competitiveness. There's nobody out there who actually thinks that that's going to immediately fill the needs of people who are out of work or strengthen the economy right now.

So what I've tried to do is say, here are the best ideas I've heard. Not just from partisans, but from independent economists. These are the ideas most likely to create jobs now and strengthen the economy right now. And that's what the American people are looking for. And the response from Republicans has been, no, although they haven't given a good reason why they're opposed to putting construction workers back on the job or teachers back in the classroom.

If you ask them, well, okay, if you're not for that, what are you for? Trade has already been done; patent reform has been done. What else? The answer we're getting right now is, well, we're going to roll back all these Obama regulations. So their big economic plan to put people back to work right now is to roll back financial protections and allow banks to charge hidden fees on credit cards again or weaken consumer watchdogs. Or alternatively, they've said we'll roll back regulations that make sure we've got clean air and clean water, eliminate the EPA. Does anybody really think that that is going to create jobs right now and meet the challenges of a global economy that are—that is weakening with all these forces coming into play?

I mean, here is a good question, here's a little homework assignment for folks: Go ask the Republicans what their jobs plan is, if they're opposed to the "American Jobs Act," and have it scored, have it assessed by the same independent economists that have assessed our jobs plan. These independent economists say that we could grow the economy as much as 2 percent and as many as 1.9 million workers would be back on the job. I think it would be interesting to have them do a similar assessment—same people. Some of these folks, by the way, traditionally have worked for Republicans, not just Democrats. Have those economists evaluate what, over the next 2 years, the Republican jobs plan would do. I'll be interested in the answer. I think everybody here—I see some smirks in the audience because you know that it's not going to be real robust.

And so, Bill, the question, then, is, will Congress do something? If Congress does something, then I can't run against a do-nothing Congress. If Congress does nothing, then it's not a matter of me running against them; I think the American people will run them out of town because they are frustrated, and they know we need to do something big and something bold.

Now, the American people are also concerned about making sure that we have a Government that lives within its means, which is why I put forward a plan that would also reduce our deficit and our debt in a more aggressive way than what the special committee has been charged with.

Folks want to talk about corporate tax reform. I've already said I'm happy to engage with them on corporate tax reform. I'm happy to engage with them, working to see what we can do to streamline and simplify our Tax Code, eliminate all the loopholes, eliminate these special interest carve-outs and potentially lower rates in the process while raising more revenue.

I am happy to negotiate with them on a whole host of issues, but right now we've got an emergency. And the American people are living that emergency out every single day, and they have been for a long time. They are working really hard. And if they're not on the job, then they're working really hard to find a job. And they're losing their homes, and their kids are having to drop out of school because they can't afford student loans. And they're putting off visiting a doctor because when they lost their job they lost their health insurance. They are struggling.

And as a consequence, by the way, all of us are struggling, even those who are well off. The irony is the same folks that the Republicans claim to be protecting, the well off—the millionaires and the billionaires—they'd be doing better, they'd be making more money if ordinary Americans had some money in their pockets and were out there feeling more confident about the economy. That's been the lesson of our history: When folks in the middle and at the bottom are doing well, the folks at the top do even better.

U.S. Political System/Bipartisanship

Q. Is this kind of public pressure the only leverage you have, sir?

The President. Look, we have a democracy. And right now John Boehner is the Speaker of the House and Mitch McConnell is the Republican leader. And all I can do is make the best arguments and mobilize the American people so that they're responsive.

So far they haven't been responsive to not just me, but public opinion. We saw that during the debt ceiling vote. But we're just going to keep on making the case. But I guess what I'm saying, though, here, Bill, is—and I said this when I made my speech at the joint session—the election is 13, 14 months away. I would love nothing more than to not have to be out there campaigning because we were seeing constructive action here in Congress. That's my goal. That's what I'm looking for.

But I'm also dealing with a Republican majority leader who said that his number-one goal was to beat me, not put Americans back to work, not grow the economy, not help small businesses expand, but to defeat me. And he's been saying that now for a couple of years. So yes, I've got to go out and enlist the American people to see if maybe he'll listen to them if he's not listening to me.

Matt Spetalnick [Reuters]. Where's Matt? There we are.

China/Trade

Q. Thank you, Mr. President. One question on the economy and one on foreign policy. First of all, the Senate has taken up today a bill aimed at pressuring China to let its currency rise. What's your position on that bill? Would you veto or sign it, should it hit your desk?

On the foreign policy front, do you agree with Admiral Mullen's accusation that Pakistan's intelligence agency has used the Haqqani network as a virtual arm? And what, if any, consequences, up to and including a cutoff of aid, would you be willing to consider?

The President. Obviously, we've been seeing a remarkable transformation of China over the last two decades, and it's helped to lift millions of people out of poverty in China. We have stabilized our relationship with China in a healthy way. But what is also true is that China has been very aggressive in gaming the trading system to its advantage and to the disadvantage of other countries, particularly the United States. And I have said that publicly, but I've also said it privately to Chinese leaders. And currency manipulation is one example of it, or at least intervening in the currency markets in ways that have led their currency to be valued lower than the market would normally dictate. And that makes their exports cheaper, and that makes our exports to them more expensive. So we've seen some improvement, some slight appreciation over the last year, but it's not enough.

It's not just currency, though. We've also seen, for example, intellectual property, technologies that were created by U.S. companies with a lot of investment, a lot of upfront capital taken, not protected properly by Chinese firms. And we've pushed China on that issue as well.

Ultimately, I think that you can have a win-win trading relationship with China. I'm very pleased that we're going to be able to potentially get a trade deal with South Korea. But I believe what, I think, most Americans believe, which is trade is great as long as everybody is playing by the same rules.

Now, the legislation that is being presented in Congress is an effort to get at that. My main concern—and I've expressed this to Senator

Schumer—is whatever tools we put in place, let's make sure that these are tools that can actually work, that they're consistent with our international treaties and obligations. I don't want a situation where we're just passing laws that are symbolic knowing that they're probably not going to be upheld by the World Trade Organization, for example, and then suddenly, U.S. companies are subject to a whole bunch of sanctions. We've got a—I think we've got a strong case to make, but we've just got to make sure that we do it in a way that's going to be effective.

Last point is, my administration has actually been more aggressive than any in recent years in going after some of these practices. We've brought very aggressive enforcement actions against China for violations in the tire case, for example, where it's been upheld by the World Trade Organization that they were engaging in unfair trading practices. And that's given companies here in the United States a lot of relief.

So my overall goal is, I believe U.S. companies, U.S. workers, we can compete with anybody in the world. I think we can make the best products. And a huge part of us winning the future, a huge part of rebuilding this economy on a firm basis that's not just reliant on maxed-out credit cards and a housing bubble and financial speculation, but is dependent on us making things and selling things. I am absolutely confident that we can win that competition. But in order to do it, we've got to make sure that we're aggressive in looking out for the interests of American workers and American businesses and that everybody is playing by the same rules and that we're not getting cheated in the process.

China/Pakistan/Afghanistan

Q. Is China—[*inaudible*]?

The President. That is a—that is a term of art, so the Treasury Secretary, I've got to be careful here—it's his job to make those decisions. But it's indisputable that they intervene heavily in the currency markets and that the RMB, their currency, is lower than it probably would be if they weren't making all those purchases in the currency markets to keep the RMB lower.

With respect to Pakistan, I have said that my number-one goal is to make sure that Al Qaida cannot attack the U.S. homeland and cannot affect U.S. interests around the world. And we have done an outstanding job, I think, in going after, directly, Al Qaida in this border region between Pakistan and Afghanistan. We could not have been as successful as we have been without the cooperation of the Pakistan Government. And so, on a whole range of issues, they have been an effective partner with us.

What is also true is that our goal of being able to transition out of Afghanistan and leave a stable Government behind—one that is independent, one that is respectful of human rights, one that is democratic—that Pakistan, I think, has been more ambivalent about some of our goals there. And I think that they have hedged their bets in terms of what Afghanistan would look like. And part of hedging their bets is having interactions with some of the unsavory characters who, they think, might end up regaining power in Afghanistan after coalition forces have left.

What we've tried to persuade Pakistan of is that it is in their interest to have a stable Afghanistan, that they should not be feeling threatened by a stable, independent Afghanistan. We've tried to get conversations between Afghans and Pakistans going more effectively than they have been in the past, but we've still got more work to do. And there is no doubt that there is some connections that the Pakistani military and intelligence services have with certain individuals that we find troubling. And I've said that publicly, and I've said it privately to Pakistani officials as well.

They see their security interests threatened by an independent Afghanistan in part because they think it will ally itself to India and Pakistan still considers India their mortal enemy. Part of what we want to do is actually get Pakistan to realize that a peaceful approach towards India would be in everybody's interests and would help Pakistan actually develop, because one of the biggest problems we have in Pakistan right now is poverty, illiteracy, a lack of development, civil institutions that aren't strong enough to deliver for the Pakistani people. And in that environment you've seen extremism grow. You've seen militancy grow that doesn't just threaten our efforts in Afghanistan, but also threatens the Pakistani Government and the Pakistani people as well. So trying to get that reorientation is something that we're continuing to work on; it's not easy.

Pakistan

Q. I'm sorry, sir—consequences of being—[*inaudible*]?

The President. We will constantly evaluate our relationship with Pakistan based on, is, overall, this helping to protect Americans and our interests? We have a great desire to help the Pakistani people strengthen their own society and their own Government. And so I'd be hesitant to punish aid for flood victims in Pakistan because of poor decisions by their intelligence services. But there is no doubt that we're not going to feel comfortable with a long-term strategic relationship with Pakistan if we don't think that they're mindful of our interest as well.

I'll make this the last question. Aamer Madhani [USA Today].

National Economy/Global Economic Stabilization

Q. Thank you, Mr. President.

The President. Caught you by surprise, huh? [*Laughter*]

Q. You did. What should European leaders do to resolve the sovereign debt crisis going forward? And second, how risky is this continued situation to the U.S. economy? And finally, do you feel that the European leaders have been negligent in pushing austerity too soon?

The President. Those are good questions. The biggest headwind the American economy is facing right now is uncertainty about Europe because it's affecting global markets. The slowdown that we're seeing is not just happening here in the United States, it's happening everywhere. Even in some of the emerging markets like China, you're seeing greater caution, less investment, deep concern.

In some ways, as frustrating as the financial sector has been here in the United States after

the Lehmans collapse, the aggressive actions that were taken right after Lehmans did help us to strengthen the financial sector and the banking sector in ways that the—Europe did not fully go through. And uncertainty around Greece and their ability to pay their debts, runs on—in the capital markets, on the debt that many of these southern European countries have been facing, as well as Ireland and Portugal, all that has put severe strain on the world financial system.

I speak frequently with Chancellor Merkel and President Sarkozy; they are mindful of these challenges. I think they want to act to prevent a sovereign debt crisis from spinning out of control or seeing the potential breakup of the euro. I think they're very committed to the European project.

But their politics is tough because, essentially, they've got to get agreement with not only their own parliaments; they've got to get agreement with 20 Parliaments or 24 Parliaments or 27 Parliaments. And engineering that kind of coordinated action is very difficult.

But what I've been seeing over the last month is a recognition by European leaders of the urgency of the situation. And nobody is obviously going to be affected more than they will be if the situation there spins out of control.

So I'm confident that they want to get this done. I think there are some technical issues that they're working on in terms of how they get a big enough—how do they get enough firepower to let the markets know that they're going to be standing behind euro members whose—who may be in a weaker position.

But they've got to act fast. And we've got a G–20 meeting coming up in November. My strong hope is that by the time of that G–20 meeting, that they have a very clear, concrete plan of action that is sufficient to the task. It will have an effect—it's already having an effect here in the United States; it will continue to have an effect on our economy because the world is now interconnected in ways that it's never been before.

And that's one of the biggest challenges that we have post-2008, after this financial crisis, is that America has always been—well, over the last 20 years—has been the engine for world economic growth. We were the purchasers of last resort, we were the importers of last resort, we would stimulate our economies, and our American consumers would buy stuff around the world. And so if they got into trouble, they could always say, well we're going to sell to the U.S.

Well, we're now going through a situation where families are cutting back and trying to reduce their debts, businesses are more cautious. And the U.S. Government obviously has its own fiscal challenges. I mean, we've got to make sure that we're living within our means, although we've got to do it gradually and not in ways that immediately affect a fragile economy.

So what that means is, Europe is not going to be able to export its way out of this problem. They're going to have to fix that problem. And part of the goal that I've been trying to promote for the last 2 years and I'll repeat at the G–20 is more balanced economic growth worldwide. We've got to get into a posture where the U.S. is always going to be a big market and we're going to welcome goods from all around the world, but we've also got to be selling goods around the world. We can't just be running up our debt in order to help other folks' economies. We've got to have—as not only families, our businesses, and our Government—we've got to make sure that we're being prudent and we're producing here in the United States. And by the way, that's what's going to create strong middle class jobs here in the United States.

I think part of what's going on for the country generally is this sense of, you know what, a lot of that debt that had been built up prior to 2008, that we were living on borrowed time because the underlying fundamentals of the economy weren't as strong as they needed to be.

And that's why not only do we have to put Americans back to work now, but we've also got to keep on reforming our education system

so it's producing the highest skilled graduates in the world. It's why we've got to keep on investing in basic research and science. It's why we've got to make sure that we're rebuilding our infrastructure. It's why we've got to have a smarter energy policy, because that's a huge source of us having to import from other countries instead of being able to export to other countries.

All those things are going to be important, and all those things are going to be challenging. They're going to be hard. But right now we've got the problem of putting people back to work. That's why Congress needs to pass this jobs bill.

And last point I'll make: If Bill is right and everybody on Capitol Hill is cynical and saying there's no way that the overall jobs bill passes in its current form, we're just going to keep on going at it. I want everybody to be clear. My intention is to insist that each part of this, I want an explanation as to why we shouldn't be doing it, each component part: putting people back to work rebuilding our roads, putting teachers back in the classroom, tax cuts for small businesses and middle class families, tax breaks for our veterans. We will just keep on going at it and hammering away until something gets done. And I would love nothing more than to see Congress act so aggressively that I can't campaign against them as a do-nothing Congress.

All right? Thank you very much, everybody.

NOTE: The President's news conference began at 11 a.m. in the East Room at the White House. In his remarks, he referred to Warren E. Buffett, chief executive officer and chairman, Berkshire Hathaway Inc.; Cynthia A. Schnedar, Acting Inspector General, Department of Justice; Rep. Clifford B. Stearns; Adm. Michael G. Mullen, USN (Ret.), former Chairman, Joint Chiefs of Staff; Chancellor Angela Merkel of Germany; and President Nicolas Sarkozy of France.

Remarks Honoring the 2011 NCAA Women's Basketball Champion Texas A&M University Aggies
October 6, 2011

The President. Everybody have a seat. Howdy!

Audience members. Howdy!

The President. Welcome to the White House. Congratulations to Texas A&M Aggies on your first national championship. Now, winning a national title is a pretty big deal for anybody. And it's an even bigger deal when you think about just how far this team has come.

Fifty years ago, Texas A&M didn't have any women, much less a women's basketball team. When they did finally put a team together, the story goes that players had to share uniforms. At one point, they had to use the men's locker room, which probably wasn't perfectly designed for your needs. Coach Blair here would be going door to door just to ask people to watch the games.

This is a team that used to be known as a bunch of lovable losers. But Coach Blair wasn't going to settle for that. As he said, he came to College Station to build champions.

And that's exactly what he's done. Today, this team has thousands of fans cheering them in every game, including some very proud Members of Congress who are here today. They've defied expectations, they've won close games and played with a whole lot of heart. And now the Aggies are the best team in women's basketball.

I think the players would agree that a lot of credit goes to Coach Blair. He's led his team to six consecutive tournament appearances, which is pretty impressive by itself. But he also tries to respond personally to every piece of fan mail he gets during the season. He throws candy to the crowd before each game. I'm sure that adds to the popularity.

Head Coach Gary Blair. That's right, and cavities.

The President. I'm going to try that. [*Laughter*] What do you think, Barton? Do you think that's going to work if I go to the House of Representatives and just throw candy around? [*Laughter*]

During the championship celebration, he was even telling people to buy tickets for next year. So he is a great salesperson as well as a great coach. I don't know where he gets that kind of energy, but that attitude is reflected by the players on this stage.

We've got Danielle Adams, who dropped 30 points in the title game—the second most in history. [*Applause*] That's what I'm talking about. She's now in the pros, tearing it up. As she said, "My teammates are doing everything for me, so I decided to take them on my back and just let them ride." And that's what she did.

Then there's Tyra White, the Silent Assassin. Where did she go? There she is over there. Hit a clutch 3-pointer in the final minutes of the game to seal it for the Aggies.

You have the Sydneys: Colson making it happen on offense, Carter applying pressure on defense.

These ladies are also serious students. I hear that Danielle and Tyra both took their math exams during spring break. The team has mandatory study halls on the road. They visit schools to tell kids about the importance of hard work, because they understand that a good jump shot doesn't mean much if you can't get it done in the classroom.

And that's the kind of focus and the kind of discipline that makes these players such good role models for so many young women, including my daughters Malia and Sasha.

That's also why they're holding a clinic for some local students to teach them a few moves. Have you guys been out there practicing a little bit? Yeah? [*Laughter*] Yeah, man, shoot. So I know that they are thrilled that you guys are willing to work with them. I fully expect them to be draining some 3-pointers after they've gotten some tips from you guys.

So congratulations again. Thank you for the example that you set on and off the court. We are so proud of you. Hopefully, we'll get a chance to see you back soon. And as they say at A&M, Gig 'em!

Mr. Blair. We have a jersey here. The 12th man at A&M means so much in the history of our school and our program. There's always somebody in the stands in case somebody gets injured. But we're the original 12th man, and I want you to wear it. And we also brought one for your wife. On your wife's it says "Number One."

[*At this point, the President was presented with a team jersey.*]

The President. Well, yes, that's—[*laughter*]—I think that's about right. I am 12th.

Mr. Blair. But we'd just like to thank you. And it's an honor for us at Texas A&M to be here, and it's also an honor for us to work with young people like we have a chance in the clinic.

But thank you for your service to the country, and thank you for keeping Bob Gates on

here for quite a while, because he meant a lot to our program.

The President. That is a big Aggies fan right there. [*Laughter*]

Mr. Blair. But thank you, sir, for everything you've done.

The President. Coach, thank you so much. Thank you.

All right, you guys are going to strike the podium, we are going to get a good picture here.

NOTE: The President spoke at 1:52 p.m. in the Rose Garden at the White House. In his remarks, he referred to Rep. Joseph L. Barton; and Danielle Adams, forward/center, Tyra White, guard, Sydney Colson, guard, and Sydney Carter, guard, Texas A&M University women's basketball team. Coach Blair referred to former Secretary of Defense Robert M. Gates.

Remarks Honoring the 1986 Super Bowl Champion Chicago Bears
October 7, 2011

The President. This—oh, everybody have a seat. This is as much fun as I will have as President of the United States, right here. This is one of the perks of the job, right here. Ladies and gentlemen, the greatest team in NFL history, the 1985 Chicago Bears. Now, I know that may get me into some trouble in some cities that I visit. [*Laughter*] But I believe it is the truth.

Cynics might say that I'm only hosting the '85 Bears today because the Green Bay Packers were here a couple months ago and I was not going to be outdone. [*Laughter*] But as it turns out, after this team won the Super Bowl, it never had a chance to celebrate here in the White House. The day after Super Bowl XX, half a million Chicagoans turned out in 25-below wind-chill weather to welcome the champs back from New Orleans. But sadly, the day after that, we endured a national tragedy as the Space Shuttle *Challenger* exploded shortly after lift-off.

So the moment for the Bears to visit the White House was postponed, and the years went by. But shortly after I took office, someone at the NFL realized, hey, there's a Bears

fan living in the White House. [*Laughter*] And they called my staff and asked if we could make this happen. And so today I am proud to say to the players, to the coaches, to the staff of the 1985 Bears: Welcome to the White House for this well-deserved and long-overdue recognition.

Now, I was mentioning as I was visiting with the players and coaches out back that in 1985, I had just moved to Chicago. So, unlike most Chicagoans, I didn't really know what it was like to be a suffering sports fan. [*Laughter*] There are a few Members of Congress and big Bears fans here from Illinois who knew what that was like. But none of us had ever seen what happened that fall. Nobody had ever seen anything like it. This city was invigorated and brought together by this team. This team ruled the city. It riveted the country. They were everywhere. They were like the Beatles. [*Laughter*] And this was before "SportsCenter" and before 24/7 sports news had really taken off. But they just captured the country's imagination.

We loved this team. Everybody in Chicago knew all these guys' names. We even knew the names of the offensive linemen. [*Laughter*] Now, you know offensive linemen, they don't get enough love.

But these guys had their own poster: "The Black 'N' Blues Brothers." When was the last time you saw a poster of an offensive line? [*Laughter*]

But what made this team so captivating wasn't just that they won, wasn't just that they dominated, it was the way they did it. Yes, they were punishing. Yes, they were dominant. But they also had a lot of fun. And you could tell they enjoyed playing together. They were, of course, led by the coach who set the tone, Hall of Famer Mike Ditka. In training camp, he said, "Put a chip on your shoulder in July and keep it there till January."

Some of you may remember that back in 2004, when I was running for the Senate, some people were trying to draft Ditka to run against me. [*Laughter*] I will admit I was a little worried—[*laughter*]—because he doesn't lose. Coach, I'm glad you didn't run, because I have to say, I probably would have been terrible on ESPN. [*Laughter*]

And in a sign that anything is possible, even in Washington, Coach Ditka and Buddy Ryan are here together. [*Laughter*] Now, Coach Ryan's 46 defense changed football forever. Nobody had ever seen anything like it. Nobody knew what to do with it. And with the talent he had on the defensive side of the ball, there wasn't anything other teams could do about it.

I mean, there are guys who hit, and there are guys who hit. And these guys hit. Mike Singletary, Steve McMichael, Otis Wilson, Wilber Marshall, Dan Hampton, Gary Fencik, and Richard Dent, the Super Bowl MVP, a guy I used to actually work out with in the gym and made me feel weak. [*Laughter*]

This was the defense that set the standard, and it is still the standard. And I was just complaining to Coach Ryan, he gave all these tips to his sons who are now coaching, and he should have passed on additional wisdom on to us. But more than 25 years later, the standard

against which all other teams are compared is Coach Ryan's defense.

These guys lived to wreak havoc. It was like they were competing with each other to see who could get to the quarterback or the running back first. There was one game that season in which the other team's offense had the ball in Bears territory a total of 21 seconds. [*Laughter*]

Now, of course, this was also the second-ranked offense in the league that season. Jim McMahon—where's Jim?

James R. McMahon, Jr. Just right here. Do you need me to speak? [*Laughter*]

The President. No, we're not going to let Jim have the mike. [*Laughter*] I'm just going to say nice things about you. [*Laughter*]

Jim played quarterback with no fear and lived life with very few rules—[*laughter*]—a rock-and-roll quarterback who was on the cover of Rolling Stone. And he had kids wearing headbands and shades to school because of Jim. And he gave me a headband, and I'm not wearing it—[*laughter*]—but I wanted you to know that I do have it. [*Laughter*]

Willie Gault might have been the fastest man in football, probably had the highest high fives.

And then there was somebody we all revered, and that was Walter Payton. Even 12 years after we lost him to cancer at the too young age of 45, Chicago still loves "Sweetness." He was without question one of the greatest to ever play the game. And after he high-stepped and leapt his way past Jim Brown's alltime rushing record, he held that record for 18 years. He was also one of the best blocking backs ever, sometimes hitting other guys so hard he'd knock them out of the game. And we are so grateful that his wife Connie is here today with us, so—[*applause*].

We also tragically lost Dave Duerson this year. And Dave was one of the team's hardest hitters. Hopefully, lessons from his brave struggle with the kind of brain injuries those hits might have caused will help today's players down the road. And we're grateful that his former wife Alicia is here today as well.

This team had nine Pro-Bowlers, four future Hall of Famers—five counting Coach Ditka. They won one 3-game stretch by a combined score of 104–3. And even though they were the youngest team in the NFL at that time, these guys were so confident that Kevin Butler, who was the kicker and still the Bears alltime leading scorer, called his then-fiancée Cathy from training camp in July to say that they had to change their wedding date because that was the Super Bowl day. [*Laughter*] They were so confident that the day after they lost their only game of the season, they recorded "The Super Bowl Shuffle." [*Laughter*] They were suggesting that I should dance "The Super Bowl Shuffle." Can't do it. But I do remember it. And in Chicago, you could not get away from this song even if you wanted to. [*Laughter*] I think it's safe to say that this is the only team in NFL history with a gold record and a Grammy nomination.

So this team changed everything for every team that came on after, on and off the field. They changed the laws of football. They were gritty, they were gutsy, they were hard-working, they were fun-loving, sort of how Chicagoans like to think of themselves. And Chicago has always been a diehard football town, but this team did something to our city that we've never gotten over. We love the Bears. And as much fun as it is to finally have these guys here, we want today's Bears to come home to the White House with a championship as well.

But in the meantime, congratulations to all of you. Thank you for helping to bring our city together. Thank you for the incredible fun that you gave to all of us. Stick around, guys, and enjoy yourselves. But as I mentioned back there, don't break anything, and keep your eyes on McMahon. [*Laughter*] All right, Coach?

Former Head Coach Michael K. Ditka. Wait, wait. One second, one second. We want to give the President——

[*At this point, the President was presented with a team jersey.*]

The President. Hey!

Mr. Ditka. On behalf of the 1985 Chicago Bears, we consider him one of us. It was a great group of guys. We're very proud that you honored us by bringing us here. It's only 26 years after the fact, and five administrations, but thank you. [*Laughter*]

The President. Appreciate it, Coach. Thank you so much.

NOTE: The President spoke at 3:08 p.m. on the South Lawn at the White House. In his remarks, he referred to New York Jets Head Coach Rex Ryan and Dallas Cowboys Defensive Coordinator Rob Ryan, sons of former Chicago Bears Defensive Coordinator James D. "Buddy" Ryan; and James L. Brown, former fullback, Cleveland Browns.

Remarks Following a Meeting With Prime Minister Beji Caid Essebsi of Tunisia and an Exchange With Reporters
October 7, 2011

President Obama. Well, it is my great pleasure to welcome Prime Minister Caid Essebsi here to the Oval Office.

As I think all of you know, Tunisia was the first country in the North African-Middle East region to begin this incredible transformation that we now call the Arab Spring. The movement that began with one street vendor protesting and taking his life in response to a government that had not been responsive to human rights set off a transformation in Tunisia that has now spread to countries throughout the region. As a result, Tunisia has been an inspiration to all of us who believe that each individual, man and woman, has certain inalienable rights, and that those rights must be recognized in a government that is responsive, is democratic, in which free and fair elections can take place, and in which the rights of minorities are protected.

We are deeply encouraged by the progress that's already been made in this short period of time. In part because of the extraordinary leadership of the Prime Minister, what we've seen is a orderly process that includes constituent assembly elections this month, that will include the writing of a Constitution and fair and free elections both for a new Parliament and a new President.

So given that Tunisia was the first country to undergo the transformation we know as the Arab Spring, and given it is now the first to have elections, we thought it was appropriate that Tunisia would be the first to visit the White House.

The Prime Minister and I had an excellent discussion about both the opportunities and the challenges that Tunisia face going forward and how the United States can be a helpful partner in that process. In particular, we discussed the importance of having a economic transformation that has taken place alongside the political transformation.

The United States has an enormous stake in seeing the success in Tunisia and the creation of greater opportunity and more business investment in Tunisia. And so in addition to the $39 million that we have already provided in assistance to Tunisia as they make this transformation, we discussed a package that includes loan guarantees, assistance in encouraging trade and foreign investment, a whole range of support programs that will allow Tunisia to create a greater business investment, offer more opportunities for employment to its young people, and further integrate it into the world marketplace.

We also discussed issues regarding the transformation that has taken place in the region as a whole. And I expressed my great admiration and appreciation for the Libyan—for the Tunisian people in the hospitality and kindness that they showed to Libyan refugees during the tumultuous period that has taken place in Libya over the last several months.

Let me just close by pointing out that Tunisia is one of our oldest friends in the world. Tunisia was one of the first countries to recognize the United States of America over 200 years

ago. One of the first trade agreements that we had as a country was with Tunisia. And so I told the Prime Minister that thanks to his leadership, thanks to the extraordinary transformation that's taking place in Tunisia and the courage of its people, I'm confident that we will have at least another two centuries of friendship between our two countries. And the American people will stand by the people of Tunisia in any way that we can during this remarkable period in Tunisian history.

Prime Minister Caid Essebsi. What could I add? I entirely agree with everything that the President said. But first and foremost, I'm very grateful, first of all, for having been invited by President Obama.

I came here to convey the great satisfaction, the great gratitude of the Tunisian people for the constant support that he provided to the change in the revolution that took place in Tunisia. And in fact, he was the very first person to applaud, to congratulate the change that took place in our country on the 14th of January. And this change, this support, I believe is irreversible. I came here to express to him my personal esteem for him, because he was the first to truly understand the depth, the importance of the changes that were occurring in Tunisia, and also the importance for the entire region.

You spoke about the Arab Spring, but up until now the Arab Spring is only really the "Tunisian Spring." So what I do hope is that this—our spring will not limit itself exclusively to Tunisia, and that it will spread throughout the region, and that, of course, it depends for large part on the economic and political success of Tunisia.

And I'm confident in the success of this process, thanks to the support expressed by President Obama today. And I told him that the longstanding and privileged relations that exist between the United States and Tunisia will not last merely for 200 years, but hopefully, until eternity.

The President mentioned the fact that Tunisia was one of the very first countries to recognize the independence of the United States. I also reminded him of the fact that the United

States was also one of the very first countries to recognize the independence of Tunisia.

At any rate, at the end of this visit I would like to reiterate my thanks to President Obama and assure him that in Tunisia he will always find a credible and sincere friend.

President Obama. Thank you, everybody.

2011 Nobel Peace Prize Recipients

Q. Mr. President, the women who won the Nobel today, any reaction?

President Obama. The three women who won the Nobel Prize today are all remarkable examples of not only their own determination and spirit, but also a reminder that when we empower women around the world, then ev-

eryone is better off, that the countries and cultures that respect the contributions of women inevitably end up being more successful that those that don't. All right?

Thank you very much.

NOTE: The President spoke at 4:32 p.m. in the Oval Office at the White House. In his remarks, he referred to President Ellen Johnson Sirleaf of Liberia, Liberian peace activist Leymah Gbowee, and Yemeni human rights activist Tawakkul Karman, recipients of the 2011 Nobel Peace Prize. Prime Minister Caid Essebsi spoke in French, and his remarks were translated by an interpreter.

Statement on the 10th Anniversary of the Commencement of United States Military Operations in Afghanistan
October 7, 2011

Ten years ago today, in response to the 9/11 terrorist attacks, our Nation went to war against Al Qaida and its Taliban protectors in Afghanistan. As we mark a decade of sacrifice, Michelle and I join all Americans in saluting the more than half a million men and women who have served bravely in Afghanistan to keep our country safe, including our resilient wounded warriors who carry the scars of war, seen and unseen. We honor the memory of the nearly 1,800 American patriots and many coalition and Afghan partners who have made the ultimate sacrifice in Afghanistan for our shared security and freedom. We pay tribute to our inspiring military families who have persevered at home with a loved one at war. And we are grateful to our tireless diplomats and intelligence, homeland security, and law enforcement professionals who have worked these 10 years to protect our country and save American lives.

Thanks to the extraordinary service of these Americans, our citizens are safer and our Nation is more secure. In delivering justice to Usama bin Laden and many other Al Qaida leaders, we are closer than ever to defeating Al Qaida and its murderous network. Despite the enormous challenges that remain in Afghani-

stan, we've pushed the Taliban out of its key strongholds, Afghan security forces are growing stronger, and the Afghan people have a new chance to forge their own future. We've fought alongside Afghans and close friends and allies from dozens of nations who have joined us in common purpose. In Afghanistan and beyond, we have shown that the United States is not and never will be at war with Islam and that we are a partner with those who seek justice, dignity, and opportunity.

After a difficult decade, we are responsibly ending today's wars from a position of strength. As the rest of our troops come home from Iraq this year, we have begun to draw down our forces in Afghanistan and transition security to the Afghan people, with whom we will forge an enduring partnership. As our sons and daughters come home to their families, we will uphold our sacred trust with our 9/11 generation veterans and work to provide the care, benefits, and opportunities they deserve. And as we reflect on 10 years of war and look ahead to a future of peace, Michelle and I call upon all Americans to show our gratitude and support for our fellow citizens who risk their lives so that we can enjoy the blessings of freedom and security.

Statement Congratulating the 2011 Nobel Peace Prize Recipients
October 7, 2011

On behalf of the American people, I congratulate the recipients of this year's Nobel Peace Prize: Liberian President Ellen Johnson Sirleaf, Leymah Gbowee of Liberia, and Tawakkul Karman of Yemen. Today's award honors three extraordinary individuals and sends a powerful message that the struggle for universal rights and human dignity can only be fulfilled with the full participation of women around the globe.

President Sirleaf has inspired the world through her journey from a prisoner to the first female President of her country. She has helped Liberia emerge from years of civil war and make great strides toward reconstruction and a democracy that values the contributions of all Liberians, including its women. As a warrior for peace, Leymah Gbowee led her fellow Liberian women as they bravely stood their ground against a brutal dictator in a nonviolent struggle to bring peace to their country and realize a full voice for Liberian women. In Yemen, Tawakkul Karman and her fellow women activists were among the first to take to the streets this year to demand their universal rights, and despite the threats and violence waged against peaceful protestors, she has remained a powerful voice for nonviolence in a country where guns outnumber people.

Each of this year's Nobel recipients have their own story, but their lives reveal a fundamental truth. Nations are ultimately more successful when all of their citizens can reach their full potential, including women. When women and girls have access to proper health care, families are healthier and communities are less subject to the ravages of disease and hunger. When women and girls have the opportunity to pursue their education and careers of their own choosing, economies are more likely to prosper. And when women assume their rightful place as equals—in the halls of government, at the negotiating table, and across civil society—governments are more effective, peaceful resolution of disputes are more lasting, and societies are more likely to meet the aspirations of all their citizens.

I commend President Sirleaf, Leymah Gbowee, and Tawakkul Karman for showing the world that the rights and voices of half of humanity cannot and will not be denied. And I reaffirm the commitment of the United States to advance the rights and role of women everywhere, in our own country and around the world.

NOTE: The statement referred to former President Charles Taylor of Liberia.

The President's Weekly Address
October 8, 2011

Next week, the Senate will vote on the "American Jobs Act." It's a bill that will put more people to work and put more money in the pockets of working Americans. And it will provide our economy with the jolt that it really needs right now.

This is not the time for the usual games or political gridlock in Washington. The challenges facing financial markets around the world could have very real effects on our own economy at a time when it's already fragile. But this jobs bill can help guard against another downturn here in America.

This isn't just my belief. This is what independent economists have said. Not just politicians, not just people in my administration, independent experts who do this for a living have said that this jobs bill will have a significant effect for our economy and middle class families all across America. But if we don't act, the opposite will be true: There will be fewer jobs and weaker growth.

So any Senator out there who's thinking about voting against this jobs bill needs to explain why they would oppose something that we know would improve our economic situation. If the Republicans in Congress think they have a better plan for creating jobs right now, they should prove it. Because one of the same independent economists who looked at our plan just said that their ideas, quote, "wouldn't mean much for the economy in the near term."

If their plan doesn't measure up, the American people deserve to know what it is that Republicans in Congress don't like about this jobs plan. You hear a lot of our Republican friends say that one of the most important things we can do is cut taxes. Well, they should love this plan. The "American Jobs Act" would cut taxes for virtually every worker and small business in America. And if you're a small-business owner that hires new workers, raises wages, or hires a veteran, you get an additional tax cut.

Right now hundreds of thousands of teachers and firefighters and police officers have been laid off because of State budget cuts. This jobs bill will put a lot of these men and women back to work. Right now there are millions of laid-off construction workers who could be repairing our bridges and roads and modernizing our schools. Why wouldn't we want to put these men and women to work rebuilding America?

The proposals in this bill are steps we have to take if we want to build an economy that lasts, if we want to be able to compete with other countries for jobs that restore a sense of security for the middle class. But we also have to rein in our deficit and start living within our means, which is why this jobs bill is paid for by asking millionaires and billionaires to pay their fair share.

Some see this as class warfare. I see it as a simple choice. We can either keep taxes exactly as they are for millionaires and billionaires, or we can ask them to pay at least the same rate as a plumber or a bus driver. And in the process, we can put teachers and construction workers and veterans back on the job. We can either fight to protect their tax cuts, or we can cut taxes for virtually every worker and small business in America. But we can't afford to do both. It's that simple.

There are too many people hurting in this country for us to simply do nothing. The economy is too fragile for us to let politics get in the way of action. The people who represent you in Washington have a responsibility to do what's best for you, not what's best for their party or what's going to help them win an election that's more than a year away. So I need you to keep making your voices heard in Washington. I need you to remind these folks who they work for. And I need you to tell your Senators to do the right thing by passing this jobs bill right away.

Thanks so much.

NOTE: The address was recorded at approximately 1:35 p.m. on October 7 in the Roosevelt Room at the White House for broadcast on October 8. The transcript was made available by the Office of the Press Secretary on October 7, but was embargoed for release until 6 a.m. on October 8.

Remarks During a Meeting With the President's Council on Jobs and Competitiveness in Pittsburgh, Pennsylvania
October 11, 2011

The President. Well, let me just make a few remarks up front, and then, really what I want to do is hear from all of you.

First of all, I had a chance to read the full report last night, and I think it's outstanding. I think you guys did extraordinary work. Jeff, I want to thank you for your leadership on guiding this whole process. I think you have been steady and focused on how can we make sure that we're creating an economy that not only deals with the immediate problem of putting people back to work, but also how do we create a foundation for long-term opportunity for all people, and a growth agenda that is going to make sure that businesses are created here, that businesses stay here, and that they prosper here.

As I look at the introduction of the report, the quote that stands out, "We need a sense of urgency and a bias for action," is something that I think we all feel acutely. And the fact that you've been able to organize around five key steps that, I think, you'd be the first to acknowledge isn't all that needs to be done, but are key areas where we should be able to generate some strong bipartisan agreement and get action going quickly, I think makes it really extraordinary.

A couple of things I'll just remark on in terms of the general context. As you pointed out, I think at the beginning of this year, when we started the Jobs Council, I think all of us felt fairly confident that the economy could grow quickly enough that we could start bringing the unemployment rate down, even if it wasn't moving as quickly as we might like, but generally, the blue chip projections were somewhere between 3- and 4-percent growth.

We have had a very tough string of events over the course of the last 10 months. You had the Arab Spring, which shot up oil prices far higher than any of us anticipated. You've got the tsunami in Japan, which affected supply lines globally. You had, most prominently, the situation in Europe, which has created great uncertainty for businesses across the board. And then, unfortunately, Washington got involved in a self-inflicted wound with the debt ceiling fiasco. And all those things, I think, led to both consumers and businesses taking a big step backwards and saying, we are just not sure where this thing is going.

As a consequence, projections now in terms of growth are significantly lower than they were. And the situation in Europe, in particular, is one in which we're spending a lot of energy talking to our counterparts across the Atlantic, trying to make sure that they handle this in a way that stabilizes the economic situation in the coming months.

So we've had a string of events that have darkened the outlook, and that makes the action that—the actions that are being recommended by the Jobs Council that much more important, because these are areas where we actually have control of the situation. We could do these things, and there's no doubt about the fact that it would have a significant, marked impact on job growth right now.

A couple of comments, and then what I want to do is, I think, hear directly from—I think we've got some people who want to remark on each of various categories.

First of all, with respect to infrastructure, the Council here is quoted as saying, "If there is one thing that Washington should be able to agree on, rebuilding our infrastructure should be one." I mean, when you've got the AFL and the Chamber of Commerce agreeing on anything, that's a sign that it's a good idea.

I think you document as well as anybody has the incredible opportunities at a time when contractors are begging for work, which means they're willing to come in on time, under budget. You've got millions of construction workers who've been laid off as a consequence of the housing bubble going bust who are ready to get on the job. You've got interest rates, never been lower. And you've got this crying need, and as you point out in the report, this is a twofer; this is one where we can not only get immediate job growth, but it also lays the foundation for long-term productivity and efficiencies that will make a difference for every company represented around this table.

So the "American Jobs Act," the jobs plan that I've put forward before Congress obviously has a very significant infrastructure component. It incorporates a lot of the ideas that were contained in this bill, because—in the Job Council report, because one of the things that you mentioned was not only do we need infrastructure, we have to streamline the approval process so that we can actually get these projects moving more quickly than they have in the past. And so we've already identified, Gene, is it 11 or 14?

National Economic Council Director Eugene B. Sperling. Fourteen.

The President. We've already identified 14 high-priority projects in which the permitting process has been significantly expedited, and we're doing that through administrative action. Our goal is, if this serves as an effective model for us being able to move those 14 quickly, that we can then replicate that across the board and the significant investment that was made could have a much more rapid impact than what we've seen before.

With respect to the next area, which is support for small business and emphasizing high-growth firms, many of the recommendations that you gave we've already been trying to implement. We have a task force that, along with SelectUSA, has been looking at, for example, how can we move forward on easing the burdens and allowing IPOs to move more quickly. Are there regulatory constraints on small businesses as they move forward that we can start eliminating?

So where we can act administratively, we've tried to do so. In some areas we might require some additional legislation. For example, on the high-skill immigration area, that's not something that we can necessarily do on our own. We can expedite some of the visas that are already in place and try to streamline that process to make it move faster. We may need some legislative help on that area.

With respect to the National Investment Initiative, I know that we've—if I'm not mistaken, some of the Job Council already had a chance to meet with the Secretary of State to figure out how we can deal with visas and travel promotion. There are other areas where we think that bringing together an interagency approach and making sure that we are knocking down any barriers that are out there for direct investment here in the United States and job creation, that we're going to prioritize those. And I welcome the ideas that have already been put in place.

With respect to regulatory review, as you know, we are already in the process of a look-back that has identified billions of dollars in potential savings, eliminating paperwork. But we want to pursue some of the additional ideas that have been put forward. And obviously,

with respect to skills and improving the capacity of our workforce to get the jobs of the future, that's something that spans both our Education Department as well as our Department of Labor. And I know that Hilda, Arne Duncan, and others are working aggressively on trying to implement many of the ideas that you've put forward.

So I guess the bottom line is this. Jeff, as you pointed out, some of the recommendations contained in the Job Council require legislative action. And these days, things don't move as quickly through Congress as we would like. But there are certain ideas that are contained in this Jobs Council report that historically have received bipartisan support. And the election is 14 months away or 13 months away. We can't wait until another election before we start acting on some of the ideas.

The "American Jobs Act" that I'm putting forward obviously contains many ideas like infrastructure investment that should be pretty straightforward. And our hope is that we are able to get those passed in the next couple of months. But we're not going to wait for Congress. So my instruction to Jeff and Gene and Valerie and all the advisers who are sitting around the table is scour this report, identify all those areas in which we can act administratively without additional congressional authorization, and just get it done.

And we've already been able to get a significant number of your recommendations implemented, but we want to do more. And we will have a very big risk follow-up process to make sure that anything that's within our authority to do as an administration we start doing immediately and we don't wait for Congress, because the American people can't afford to wait. They need help right now. All right?

[*At this point, members of the President's Council on Jobs and Competitiveness continued the discussion.*]

The President. Well, just a couple of comments. I think that, after reading your report, the financial reforms that took place in Sarbanes-Oxley and the Spitzer declaration, I think, need to be examined. This is always a little bit tricky. This is one of the challenges of a decentralized system of our Founders and then the fact that the SEC, for example, is a independent agency.

So one of the questions I've had, John, Steve, Sheryl, is have we begun to engage with both the relevant congressional committees, but also, in this case, the SEC, the relevant agency, to see how we can get those carve-outs that you've described. But because this makes sense to me, if you've got smaller companies, they are not going to have the legal and accounting help at the costs—at the magnitude that a GE is going to have if it decides it wants to go into the capital markets, and trying to figure out how to balance, making sure that they don't get themselves into trouble, but that they're also not priced out of the market is critical.

Do we have a set of concrete proposals in terms of how a carve-out like that might look like?

[The discussion continued.]

The President. Well, Gene, I would say, having not only the NEC, but also Treasury engaged with you guys immediately in trying to get a sense of what tweaks to Sarbanes-Oxley, for example, might be required, starting to speak to the relevant committee chairmen, seeing how this might be structured. The more granular and specific we can get, the more quickly we might be able to get something done on this.

[The discussion continued.]

The President. I mean, I think the only comment I'd make right now is that the proposal we have in the "American Jobs Act" would pull forward $50 billion in infrastructure investment. This is investment we're going to have to make anyway. So we can do it now, or we can do it later; now is the time to do it.

I don't know how Congress will respond to the overall package, but our expectation is, is if they don't pass the whole package we're going to break it up into constituent parts. And having the relevant businesses get behind a effort

to move this infrastructure agenda forward is a priority.

Now, the one thing I want to emphasize is that we took very seriously this notion that citing and delay is a problem. And again, we've already identified 14 high-profile, high-impact projects where we are streamlining our ability to get this thing done. I think the last time we were here, Matt, you mentioned this specifically, and, I think, we've been trying to pursue it.

So my instructions to my agencies are, within the constraints of making sure that people are safe and we're not wasting taxpayer money on these projects, let's do them as quick as we can. But we're going to need a push, I think, from the business community in particular in order to get this across the finish line.

And I would just make one last point. The Recovery Act had a infrastructure component, and at the time, a lot of folks said that, well, it's going to be very hard to spend out this money in an efficient, effective way. Eighty percent of the Recovery Act funds targeted for surface transportation was spent out; the projection was it was—we would have only spent out 55 percent at this point. We spent out 80 percent of it. And the—if I'm not mistaken, and, Gene, you may have the figures on the tip of your fingers here, but less than 1 percent of the overall funding indicated that there were any problems in terms of fraud or misallocation of resources, et cetera; I mean, an extraordinarily low number. We were able to maintain high-quality control while spending this out in a very quick and effective way, partly because there's so much need out there that it's not like we're having to hunt for a lot of projects that could be ready to go. So anybody want to comment?

[The discussion continued.]

The President. Robert, just to pick up on the structure of the infrastructure bank, and I'll try to illustrate my understanding of it. You have this financing authority. It says to a region that wants to build a new bridge, here's a loan; we understand that there is going to be a funding stream as a consequence of the loan we're providing. The regional authority is able to leverage additional private-sector dollars. They're also—they've also identified an ongoing funding stream, whether it's a user fee or something. And as a consequence, what do you anticipate the—for every dollar that's lent by the Federal authority, what kind of private-sector money could you potentially——

Councilmember Robert Wolf. So we looked at the AIFA, which is I think about 10 billion they set aside. And we believe it's scored that that 10 billion would equate to about 100 billion in subordinated debt; the debt would be subordinated at the project level.

The President. So you're looking at 10 to 1.

[Mr. Wolf made further remarks.]

The President. So for each sector you'd have some different models.

[The discussion continued.]

The President. In fact, we're somewhat unique in not allowing as much private participation in the financing of infrastructure projects. Is that correct?

[The discussion continued.]

The President. Gene, do you feel that this point, that in terms of design, there is starting to—we're starting to get some consensus on how this thing would be designed?

[The discussion continued.]

The President. Just a quick comment on this area. What we've seen, as I've been pushing our agencies and administration to take a hard look at this, is exactly what Mark just said, that in any area there's a whole bunch of underbrush that can be cleared out and made much more efficient while still achieving the objectives of public health, welfare, environmental, and so forth.

And where I think the low-hanging fruit will be is those regulations that are just there on the books because nobody has really thought through, over the course of 10, 20, 30 years, is this still the smartest way for us to achieve our objective? And I think that you will get a very

engaged and aggressive partner in this administration in identifying those areas where there's no dispute with respect to the goal, but: something is being done through paper as opposed to e-mail, or we haven't adapted to new technologies, or the rule was written for an obsolete business model that doesn't really apply to today. On those areas, I think we're going to be able to move very rapidly.

What's tougher, and I suspect Matt is—when you refer to sort of the systemic stuff—is where there may be a genuine judgment call with respect to what are our objectives. So I can assure you that there are going to be certain industries where any costs imposed in order to prevent significant environmental degradation is viewed as a job killer. And we're going to have to make a decision as a society, well, how much pollution exactly are you willing to tolerate for those jobs?

Because as I said in my speech before Congress, I don't think we're going to compete effectively internationally in terms of who's willing to have the dirtiest air, because we'll always lose that fight. I mean, there are going to be countries out there that don't have any environmental standards, right? And so if how we're gauging where a particular regulation is smart or not, part of what we're trying to do is at least apply rigorous cost-benefit analysis. But there are going to be some cases where there is a genuine cost, and businesses will say, you know what, we wish we didn't have these costs; on the other hand, the benefits in terms of a lot fewer people in the emergency rooms or with asthma or what have you may be sufficiently significant that, as a society, we say those are costs that we still have to bear.

So I just want to distinguish between those two aspects of regulation: one, I think, which will be easier to move forward rapidly on; the other, which—where there's going to be just some real judgment calls and there's a legitimate values debate that we're going to have to be having.

[The discussion continued.]

The President. At least with respect to the executive agencies, every agency understands

Photographic
Portfolio

Overleaf: Visiting the Martin Luther King, Jr. Memorial on the National Mall, October 14.

Left: Visiting the Flight 93 National Memorial in Shanksville, PA, September 11.

Below left: Viewing the north reflecting pool at the National September 11 Memorial with First Lady Michelle Obama, former President George W. Bush, and former First Lady Laura Bush in New York City, September 11.

Right: Greeting a young girl while touring a neighborhood struck by Hurricane Irene in Wayne, NJ, September 4.

Below: Offering a salute during the dignified transfer of the deceased with Secretary of Defense Leon E. Panetta, left, at Dover Air Force Base, DE, August 6.

Left: Strolling with children from the Valley-land Kids summer program outside a school in Chatfield, MN, August 15.

Below: Comforting a visitor at Section 60 of Arlington National Cemetery in Arlington, VA, September 10.

Right: Receiving a briefing on the situation in Libya from Homeland Security and Counterterrorism Adviser John O. Brennan in Chilmark, MA, August 26.

Below right: Speaking with Libya's Ambassador to the U.S. Ali Suleiman Aujali and his family during an Ambassador credentialing ceremony in the Oval Office at the White House, September 9.

Above left: Toasting Prime Minister Julia E. Gillard of Australia during a dinner at Parliament House in Canberra, Australia, November 16.

Left: Meeting with congressional leaders to discuss deficit reduction and the debt limit in the Cabinet Room at the White House, July 13.

Above: Meeting with Medal of Honor recipient Sgt. Dakota L. Meyer, USMC, on the patio outside the Oval Office at the White House, September 14.

Right: Greeting marines from the Walter Reed National Military Medical Center in Bethesda, MD, during a wounded warriors basketball game on the White House Basketball Court, July 26.

Overleaf: Sitting for a formal portrait with the First Family in the Oval Office at the White House, December 11.

that—because they've been in a lot of Cabinet meetings with me and I think that they will all echo it, those who are here—that they have to be thinking about the economy and job creation as part of the lens through which they've evaluating the actions that they're taking.

As you just pointed out, Brian, there are things that are nice to do, and then there are things that are urgent to do. And part of OIRA's task has been to evaluate any new regulatory proposals under a very rigorous lens. I mean, the one thing that we've been able to— we can document that the hard benefits of regulations we've proposed relative to the costs are greater than we've seen in any recent administration by a factor of two or three. So the job is to evaluate this stuff very rigorously, make sure that we distinguish between what's urgent and what would just be nice if the economy was humming along at 5-percent growth, keep jobs in mind and, as a consequence, I think we can make some significant progress on areas where, regardless of where you land across the political spectrum, you say to yourself, you know, this isn't a smart regulation. And if it's not smart, it shouldn't be done.

Having said that, I just—the only reason I raise this is because I don't want to paper over the fact that once we make all the regulations smarter, eliminate the dumb ones and so forth, there is still going to be some tensions that exist around, well, how much do we value these extra 10,000 jobs versus these extra 100,000 asthma cases. And those are tough decisions that have to be made and have to be discussed both in Congress as well as within the administration.

[The discussion continued.]

The President. Before we turn to Darlene, can I—as you guys were researching this, did you get a sense of why, given three jobs for every engineering graduate, that supply wasn't filling demand here? Is it just a function of kids not being suffiently prepared for the rigors of the engineering program, or are there other— are they not getting the signal that, you know what, if you got an attitude for math, it turns out that your chances of being successful

through an engineering degree may be higher than getting a business administration degree? What's going on there?

[The discussion continued.]

The President. Well, listen, I know we're running out of time. Jeff, I just wanted—again, thank you for your leadership. I want to thank everybody who's participated. The quality of the product is outstanding. It's focused, it's specific. It's not the usual white paper stuff that gets put in a drawer, as somebody mentioned earlier. And we are acting on it.

And to tie what you guys are doing with what Roger just said about the economy, there is no doubt that we still have some tough sledding before us. This was the worst crisis we've had in our lifetimes. I'm looking around the room, I don't see too many folks who were around or active, at least, back in the thirties. And it is true that, historically at least, after financial crises the recessions are deeper, longer, more prolonged.

We still have some big challenges internationally. Europe is the most prominent and immediate challenge, but we've got some structural issues internationally in terms of imbalances. And part of it has to do with the fact that we had become the growth engine for the world based on accumulating debt and consumption. And that was not a sustainable path for us.

The good news is—and it's reflected in your Jobs Council report—there's just a bunch of stuff that we can do right now that not only helps the economy immediately, but puts us on a more stable path over the long term. And most of it should not be controversial. The good news is, is that our problems are imminently solvable and does not necessarily fall into the classic ideological divisions between left and right, conservative, liberal, but are just smart things to do to respond to a historic challenge that we face as a country.

The bad news is that there is a big gap between sensible solutions and what either the political process seems to be willing to act on and also, I think, people's perceptions, which are clouded by news reports that would make it seem as if there is nothing we can do and that we're automatically on a downward decline.

And so I think what the Job Council has been invaluable in providing is a roadmap for the American people; not comprehensive, this is just a piece of the puzzle, but pointing to examples of where, if we do some smart things now, we can have a lot better outcomes in the future. And that can help to build back a sense of confidence, or a sense of confidence about our ability to meet these challenges.

So I just want to thank everybody for their leadership. And I'm looking forward to our next meeting. All right?

NOTE: The President spoke at 12:03 p.m. at the International Brotherhood of Electrical Workers Local Union No. 5 training center. In his remarks, he referred to Secretary of Labor Hilda L. Solis. Participating in the discussion were Jeffrey R. Immelt, chairman and chief executive officer, General Electric Co., in his capacity as Chair of the President's Council on Jobs and Competitiveness; White House Senior Adviser Valerie B. Jarrett; and John Doerr, partner, Kleimer Perkins Caufield & Byers; Stephen M. Case, chairman, Startup America Partnership; Sheryl K. Sandberg, chief operating officer, Facebook, Inc.; Matthew Rose, chairman and chief executive officer, BNSF Railway; Robert Wolf, chairman, UBS Americas; Mark T. Gallogly, founder and managing partner, Centerbridge Partners, L.P.; Brian Roberts, chairman and chief executive officer, Comcast Corporation; Darlene Miller, chief executive officer, Permac Industries; and Roger W. Ferguson, president and chief executive officer, TIAA–CREF, in their capacity as members of the President's Council on Jobs and Competitiveness.

Remarks to the International Brotherhood of Electrical Workers Local Union No. 5 in Pittsburgh
October 11, 2011

Thank you, everybody. Please have a seat. Have a seat.

It is great to be back in Pittsburgh! And it is wonderful to be here at IBEW Local 5. I had a chance to take a tour of your facilities, where you're training workers with the skills they need to compete for good jobs. And I see some of the guys that I met on the tour, both the instructors and the students who are here, and it's an example of how, if we get a good collaboration between business and labor and academia, that there is no reason why we cannot continue to have the best trained workers in the world. And that's got to be one of our best priorities.

So I'm here to talk about how we can create new jobs, particularly jobs doing what you do best, and that's rebuilding America. I brought some folks along with me as well. We got members of my Cabinet and my administration. We've got your mayor, Luke Ravenstahl is here. Where's Luke? Right here. Your county executive, Dan Onorato, is here. And one of my dearest friends, who I stole from the Steelers to serve as the United States Ambassador to Ireland, Dan Rooney's in the house. And congratulations, Steelers. You guys did a little better than my Bears last night. [*Laughter*]

I've also brought a group of leaders with a wide range of new ideas about how we can help companies hire and grow, and we call them our White House Jobs Council. They come from some of the most successful businesses in the country: GE, Southwest, Intel. They come from labor; we got Rich Trumka on here from the AFL–CIO. We've got universities and people across the board who are intimately involved in growing companies, venture capitalists. Most importantly, they come from outside of Washington.

And I told them when we formed this council, I want to hear smart, forward-thinking ideas that will help our economy and our workers adapt to changing times. And together, they've done some extraordinary work to make those ideas happen. So I just want to personally thank every single one of the Job Council members for the great work that they're doing. And they issued a jobs report today. We're implementing a bunch of their ideas; it's going to make a difference all across the country. So thank you very much.

One of our focuses today was on entrepreneurship. And we did this because the story of America's success is written by America's entrepreneurs, men and women who took a chance on a dream and they turned that dream into a business and somehow changed the world. We just lost one of our greatest entrepreneurs and a friend, Steve Jobs, last week. And to see the outpouring of support for him and his legacy tells a story about what America's all about. We like to make things, create things, new products, new services that change people's lives.

And that's what people strive to do every day in this country. Now, most of the time people's dreams are simple: startups and storefronts on Main Street that let folks earn enough to support their family and make a contribution to their community. And sometimes their dreams take off and those startups become companies like Apple or FedEx or Ford, companies that end up hiring and employing hundreds of thousands of Americans and giving rise to entire new industries. And that spirit of entrepreneurship and innovation is how we became the world's leading economic power, and it's what constantly rejuvenates our economy.

So entrepreneurship's how we're going to create new jobs in the future. And I'm proud to say that just last month Pittsburgh won a Federal grant to promote entrepreneurship and job creation by expanding your already successful energy and health care industries in underserved parts of this city. So we're very excited about what Pittsburgh's doing here.

Today my jobs council laid out new actions we can take together—the private sector and Government—to help unleash a new era of entrepreneurship in America that will grow the economy and create jobs and strengthen our ability to compete with the rest of the world. But even as we help to fuel the next big American industry, we also understand that people

are out of work right now. They need help right now. So everything that we talked about with respect to the Job Council is going to help America become more competitive, help entrepreneurs create more jobs, lay the foundation for long-term, sustainable growth.

But right now our economy needs a jolt. Right now. And today the Senate of the United States has a chance to do something about jobs right now by voting for the "American Jobs Act." Now, this is a moment of truth for the U.S. Senate.

In front of them is a bill, a jobs bill, that independent economists have said would grow this economy and put people back to work. This is not my opinion, it's not my administration's opinion. This is people whose job it is for a living to analyze and evaluate what kind of impact certain policies would have. They've said this could grow the economy significantly and put significant numbers of Americans back to work. And no other jobs plan has that kind of support from economists, no plan from Congress, no plan from anybody.

It's a jobs bill with the kind of proposals that Democrats and Republicans have traditionally supported. It's a jobs bill that is entirely paid for by asking those of us who've been most fortunate, who've been incredibly blessed here in America, to contribute a little more to the country that contributed so much to our success.

Today is the day when every American will find out exactly where their Senator stands on this jobs bill. Republicans say that one of the most important things we can do is cut taxes. Then they should be for this plan. This jobs bill would cut taxes for virtually every worker and small business in America, every single one.

If you're a small-business owner that hires new workers or raises wages, you will get another tax cut. If you hire a veteran, you get a tax cut. People who have served overseas should not have to fight for a job when they come home. This jobs bill encourages small-business owners and entrepreneurs to expand and to hire. The Senate should pass it today.

Hundreds of thousands of teachers and firefighters and police officers have been laid off because of State budget cuts. I'm sure, Luke, you're seeing it here in Pittsburgh. You're having to figure out how do we make sure that we keep our teachers in the classroom. The jobs council is uniform in believing that the most important thing for our competitiveness long term is making sure our education system is producing outstanding young people who are ready to go to work.

So this jobs bill that the Senate's debating today would put a lot of these men and women back to work right now, and it will prevent a lot more from losing their jobs.

So folks should ask their Senators, why would you consider voting against putting teachers and police officers back to work? Ask them what's wrong with having folks who have made millions or billions of dollars to pay a little more. Nothing punitive, just going back to the kinds of tax rates that used to exist under President Clinton, so that our kids can get the education they deserve.

There are more than a million laid-off construction workers who could be repairing our roads and bridges and modernizing our schools right now. Right now. That's no surprise to you. Pittsburgh has a lot of bridges—[*laughter*]—has about 300 of them. Did you know that more than a quarter of the bridges in this State are rated structurally deficient? Structurally deficient, that's a fancy way of saying, they need to be fixed. There are nearly 6,000 bridges in Pennsylvania alone that local construction workers could be rebuilding right now. The average age of bridges around Pittsburgh is 54 years old. So we're still benefiting from the investments, the work that was done by our grandparents to make this a more successful, more competitive economy.

Here in Pittsburgh, 54 years old, the average age of these bridges, 13 years older than the national average. The Hulton Bridge over in Oakmont was built more than a hundred years ago. There are pieces of it that are flaking off. How much longer are we going to wait to put people back to work rebuilding bridges like that? This jobs bill will give local contractors and local construction workers the chance to get back to work rebuilding America. Why would any Senator say no to that?

In line with the recommendations of my jobs council, my administration is cutting redtape; we're expediting several major construction projects all across the country to launch them faster and more efficiently. We want to streamline the process, the permitting process, just get those things moving. So we're doing our job, trying to expedite the process. Now it's time for Congress to do their job. The Senate should vote for this jobs bill today. It should not wait. It should get it done.

Now, a lot of folks in Congress have said they won't support any new spending that's not paid for. And I think that's important. We've got to make sure we're living within our means so that we can make the vital investments in our future. That's why I signed into law $1 trillion in spending cuts over the summer. And we'll find more places to cut those things that we don't need. We can't afford everything. We got to make choices; we got to prioritize. Programs that aren't working, that aren't giving us a good bang for the buck, that aren't helping to grow the economy, that aren't putting people back to work, we're going to have to trim those back. So we're willing to make tough choices. The American people, they're already tightening their belts. They understand what it's all about to make tough choices.

But if we want to create jobs and close the deficit, then we can't just cut our way out of the problem. We're also going to have to ask the wealthiest Americans to pay their fair share. If they don't, we only have three other choices: We can either increase the deficit, or we can ask the middle class to pay more at a time when they're just barely getting by—haven't seen their wages or incomes go up at all, in fact, have gone down over the last decade—or we can just sit back and do nothing. And I'm not willing to accept any of those three options.

In a—[*applause*]—whenever I talk about revenue, people start complaining about, "Well, is he engaging in class warfare?" or "Why is he going after the wealthiest?" Look, because I've been fortunate and people bought a bunch of my books, I'm in that category now. [*Laughter*]

And in a perfect world with unlimited resources, nobody would have to pay any taxes. But that's not the world we live in. We live in a world where we've got to make choices.

So the question we have to ask ourselves as a society, as a country, is, would you rather keep taxes exactly as they are for those of us who've benefited most from this country, tax breaks that we don't need and weren't even asking for, or do we want construction workers and electrical workers to have jobs rebuilding our roads and our bridges and our schools? Would we rather maintain these tax breaks for the wealthiest few, or should we give tax cuts to the entrepreneurs who might need it to start that business, launch that new idea that they've got? Or tax breaks to middle class families who are likely to spend this money now and get the economy moving again?

This is a matter of priorities. And it's a matter of shared sacrifice. And by the way, if you ask most wealthy Americans, they'll tell you they're willing to do more. They're willing to do their fair share to help this country that they love.

So it's time to build an economy that creates good, middle class jobs in this country. It's time to build an economy that honors the values of hard work and responsibility. It's time to build an economy that lasts. And that's what this jobs bill will help us do. The proposals in the "American Jobs Act" aren't just a bunch of random investments to create make-work jobs. They're things we have to do if we want to compete with other countries for the best jobs and the newest industries. We have to have the most educated workers.

This week, I'm going to be hosting the President of South Korea. I had lunch with him in Seoul, South Korea. He told me—I said, "What's your biggest problem?" He says: "The parents are too demanding. I'm having to import teachers because all our kids want to learn English when they're in first grade." So they're hiring teachers in droves at a time when we're laying them off. That doesn't make any sense.

We've got to have the best transportation and communications networks in the world. We used to have the best stuff. We used to be the envy of the world. People would come to our countries, and they would say: "Look at the Hoover Dam. Look at the Golden Gate Bridge." Now people go to Beijing Airport, and they say, "I wish we had an airport like that." We can't compete that way, playing for 2d or 3d or 4th or 8th or 15th place.

We've got to support new research and new technology, innovative entrepreneurs, the next generation of manufacturing. Any one of the business leaders here today will tell you that's true. If we want to compete and win in this global economy, if we want this century to be another American century, we can't just go back to an economic model that's based on how much we can borrow, how much debt we can rack up, and how much we can consume. Our prosperity has to be built on what we make and what we sell around the world and on the skills of our workers and the ingenuity of our businesspeople.

We have to restore the values that have always made this a great country: idea of hard work and responsibility that's rewarded; everybody, from Main Street to Wall Street, doing their fair share, playing by the same set of rules.

And so, Pittsburgh, that starts now, and in— I'm going to need your help. Your Senators are voting today on this jobs bill, so this is gut-check time. Any Senator who votes no should have to look you in the eye and tell you what exactly they're opposed to. These are proposals that have traditionally been bipartisan. Republicans used to want to build roads and bridges. That wasn't just a Democratic idea. We've all believed that education was important. You've got to come—if you're voting no against this bill, look a Pittsburgh teacher in the eye and tell them just why they don't deserve to get a paycheck again and, more importantly, be able to transmit all those—all that knowledge to their kids. Come tell the students why they don't deserve their teacher back, so that now they've got under—overcrowded classrooms, or arts classes or musics classes or science classes have been cut back.

Come and look at a construction worker here in Pittsburgh or an electrical worker in the eye, and tell them why they shouldn't be out there fixing our bridges or rebuilding our schools and equipping them with the latest science labs or the latest Internet connection. Explain why people should have to keep driving their kids across bridges with pieces falling off.

Or explain to a small-business owner or workers in this community why you'd rather defend tax breaks for the wealthiest few than fight for tax cuts for the middle class. I think they'd have a hard time explaining why they voted no on this bill other than the fact that I proposed it. And so—[*applause*].

I realize some Republicans in Washington have said that even if they agreed with the ideas in the "American Jobs Act," they're wary of passing it because it would give me a win. Give me a win? This is not about giving me a win. It's why folks are fed up with Washington. This is not about giving anybody a win. It's not about giving Democrats or Republicans a win. It's about giving the American people who are hurting out there a win. It's about giving small businesses, entrepreneurs, and construction workers a win. It's about giving the American people—all of us, together—a win.

I was talking to the Jobs Council—by the way, not everybody here has necessarily voted for me. [*Laughter*] But they're patriots, and they care about their country. And we were talking about how, in normal times, these are all commonsense ideas. These aren't radical ideas. These are things that traditionally everybody would be for, particularly at a time of emergency like we're in, where so many people are out of work and businesses want to see more customers. So for folks outside of Washington, being against something for the sake of politics makes absolutely no sense. It makes absolutely no sense.

And the next election is 13 months away. The American people don't have the luxury of waiting 13 months. They don't have the luxury of watching Washington go back and forth in the usual fashion when this economy needs to be strengthened dramatically. A lot of folks are living week to week, paycheck to paycheck, even day to day. They need action, and they need action now. They want Congress to do what they were elected to do: put country ahead of party, do what's right for our economy, do what's right for our people. In other words, they want Congress to do your job.

So—and I've said this to some folks in the other party. I've said, I promise you, we'll still have a lot of stuff to argue about, even if we get this thing done, about the general direction of the country and how we're going to build it and how we're going to outeducate and outinnovate and outbuild other countries around the world. There will be a lot of time for political debating. But right now we need to act on behalf of the American people.

So for those of you who are in the audience or those of you who are watching, I need you to call, e-mail, tweet, fax, or you can write an old-fashioned letter—I don't know if people still do that—[*laughter*]. Let Congress know who they work for. Remind them what's at stake when they cast their vote. Tell them that the time for gridlock and games is over. The time for action is now. And tell them to pass this bill.

If you want construction workers on the job, pass the bill. If you want teachers back in the classroom, pass the bill. If you want tax cuts for your family and small-business owners, pass this bill. If you want our veterans to share in the opportunity that they upheld and they defended, do the right thing, pass this bill. All right? Now's the time to act.

I know that this is a moment where a lot of folks are wondering whether America can move forward together the way it used to. And I'm confident we can. We're not a people who just sit by and watch things happen to us. We shape our own destiny. That's what's always set us apart. We are Americans, and we are tougher than the times we're in right now. We've been through tougher times before. We're bigger than the politics that has been constraining us. We can write our own story. We can do it again. So let's meet this moment. Let's get to work and show the rest of the world just why it is that America is the greatest country on Earth.

Thank you very much, everybody. God bless you. God bless America.

NOTE: The President spoke at 2:15 p.m. at the IBEW Local Union No. 5 Apprenticeship Training Center. In his remarks, he referred to President Lee Myung-bak of South Korea; and Sens. Robert P. Casey and Patrick J. Toomey.

Statement on Job Growth Legislation
October 11, 2011

Tonight a majority of United States Senators voted to advance the "American Jobs Act." But even though this bill contains the kind of proposals Republicans have supported in the past, their party obstructed the Senate from moving forward on this jobs bill.

Tonight's vote is by no means the end of this fight. Independent economists have said that the "American Jobs Act" would grow the economy and lead to nearly 2 million jobs, which is why the majority of the American people support these bipartisan, commonsense proposals. And we will now work with Senator Reid to make sure that the individual proposals in this jobs bill get a vote as soon as possible.

In the coming days, Members of Congress will have to take a stand on whether they believe we should put teachers, construction workers, police officers, and firefighters back on the job. They'll get a vote on whether they believe we should cut taxes for small-business owners and middle class Americans, or whether we should protect tax breaks for millionaires and billionaires.

With each vote, Members of Congress can either explain to their constituents why they're against commonsense, bipartisan proposals to create jobs, or they can listen to the overwhelming majority of American people who are crying out for action. Because with so many Americans out of work and so many families struggling, we can't take no for an answer. Ultimately, the American people won't take no for an answer. It's time for Congress to meet their responsibility, put their party politics aside, and take action on jobs right now.

Remarks at a Democratic National Committee Fundraiser in Orlando, Florida
October 11, 2011

The President. Thank you very much. Well, thank you. It is good to be in Orlando! It's good to be back in Florida. Some perfect Florida weather out there. To everybody who's watching, come on down to Florida. It's gorgeous.

We've got a couple of special people I want to acknowledge. First of all, your outstanding mayor, Buddy Dyer, is in the house; wonderful Congresswoman Corrine Brown. I want to thank CeCe Teneal for the outstanding performance. And I want to thank Alan Ginsberg and Mark NeJame for their wonderful hard work to make this thing happen. Thank you very much, everybody.

Audience member. We love you!

The President. I love you back. I do. Although I have to say that backstage I had the chance to see Dwight Howard—[*applause*]—and Dwight is a great friend, and I told him I'm a little heartbroken that the NBA season is getting delayed here. [*Laughter*] So I'm hoping those guys are back on the court soon. In the meantime, I'm here because I need all of your help. I need your help.

I've come here because we've got to finish what we started in 2008. A lot of you got involved in that campaign back in 2008, and let's just remember, because sometimes there's revisionist history and everybody says, well, that was such a smooth campaign, and I say, that's not exactly how I remembered it. [*Laughter*]

We campaigned in 2008 not because we thought it was going to be a cakewalk. I mean, after all, you had a candidate named Barack Hussein Obama, so you knew that wasn't going to be easy. You didn't need a poll to tell you

1251

that that was going to be an uphill battle. [*Laughter*] But we forged ahead because we had an idea about what the country was, what it is, what it can be.

Many of you—your parents, your grandparents—grew up with a faith in an America where hard work and responsibility paid off, where if you stepped up and you did your job and you were loyal to your company and looked after your community, that loyalty, that responsibility would be rewarded with a decent salary and good benefits, maybe a raise once in a while, and you could raise your family and send your child to college and retire with some dignity and some respect.

But over the last decade, that faith was shaken. Rules changed. The deck kept being stacked against middle class Americans. And nobody in Washington seemed to be listening, seemed to be willing or able to do anything about it. And in 2007, all of this culminated in the worst economic crisis in our lifetimes, a crisis that's been much worse than your average recession. And it's been especially tough here in Florida.

And from the time I took office, we knew that because this crisis had been building up for years, it wasn't going to be solved overnight. It would take years for us to fully recover. But we understood that if we took some steps to start rebuilding the economy from the bottom up, that there was no doubt that America could be stronger, could be more fair, and could be more just.

So the question now, in 2011, is not whether people are still hurting. Of course they are. Every night I get e-mails and letters from folks from all across the country, and some of the stories are heartbreaking. And I meet folks in VFW halls and diners and men and women who tell me about having to close down a business that's been in their family for generations, or people who are having to cross items off the grocery list just so they can fill up the gas tank, or parents who have to put off retirement to make sure their kids can stay in college. So the question is not whether this country has been going through tough times. The question is,

where are we going next? What does the future hold?

We can either go back to the ideas that tried and failed in the last decade, where corporations write their own rules and the well-connected get tax breaks slipped into the Tax Code and ordinary folks are struggling. Or we can build the America that we talked about in 2008, and that we've been fighting for ever since: an America where everybody gets a fair shake and everybody does their fair share, an America where we're all in it together. An America where we're all in it together and we're looking out for one another, that's what this election is about. And that's what we've been fighting for since I got to Washington.

Think about what we've been through over the last 3 years. When we wanted to save the auto industry from bankruptcy, there were a whole lot of Republicans in Congress who said that's a waste of time, waste of money. They fought us tooth and nail. But you know what, we did it anyway. And we saved hundreds of thousands of American jobs. We made sure taxpayers got their money back.

And because we acted, the American auto industry is stronger. Ford recently announced its plants—its plans to add 12,000 new jobs in its U.S. manufacturing plant over the next few years, jobs making cars stamped with those three proud words: Made in America. So we're working to get manufacturing back here in the United States. We don't want to just import from other places; we want to sell to other places and make it right here with American workers.

When we wanted to pass Wall Street reform to make sure that a crisis like this never happens again and irresponsibility is not rewarded, we had lobbyists and special interests spend millions to make sure that we didn't succeed. But you know what, Orlando? We did it anyway. And we passed the toughest reforms in generations, reforms that prevent consumers from getting ripped off by mortgage bankers or credit card companies. And today, there are no more hidden credit card fees and no more unfair rate hikes and no more deception from banks. I tell you, they fought us every inch of the way, but we got it done.

We were able to cut $60 billion in taxpayer subsidies to big banks and use the savings to make college more affordable for millions of young people out there. Most Republicans voted against it, but it was the right thing to do, and we did it anyway to make sure that our young people have an opportunity.

And because of the efforts of so many of you, we did what we've been trying to do for a century, and we finally got it done; we said that health care should no longer be a privilege in this country, it should be affordable and available to every single American. And we're in the process of implementing it right now.

So no longer can insurance companies drop your coverage for no good reason or deny you coverage because of a preexisting condition, and think about what that means for men, especially for women. Breast cancer, cervical cancer, no longer preexisting conditions. They now have—insurance companies now have to cover things like mammograms and contraception as preventive care. No more out-of-pocket costs.

And while it's going to take a couple of years for the reforms to fully take effect—I see some young people here. We already have nearly 1 million more young adults with health insurance because of the Affordable Care Act. One million young people have the security that's needed.

That's an incredible achievement. Because of you, the Affordable Care Act is working. It is working to make the American Dream a little more secure. Because of you, I signed into law my first bill making sure women earn equal pay for equal work. I want all our daughters to have the same chances that our sons. And while we're at it, we appointed two brilliant women to the Supreme Court. We repealed "don't ask, don't tell," because anybody should be able to serve their country that they love.

In the last few years, as promised, we removed 100,000 troops from Iraq, ended our combat mission there, just like we said we would do. We're now transitioning our forces out of Afghanistan. We're taking the fight directly to Al Qaida. And because of the bravery of the men and women in uniform, Usama bin Laden will never again threaten the United States of America.

So we've made progress. We've made progress making our country safer. We've made progress making our people more secure. But we've got a lot more work to do. We've got so much more work to do to restore that sense of security that has always defined America. Making sure that everybody has got opportunity. Making sure anybody can get in the middle class if they're willing to work. And that's where I need your help.

Today the United States Senate is about to vote on the "American Jobs Act." Some of you might have heard about this. Everything in this bill is the kind of proposal that in the past has been supported by Democrats and Republicans. Everything in this bill will be paid for. It will put people back to work. It will put more money in your pockets. The Senate should pass that bill today.

Think about it. We've got a million construction workers, millions of construction workers, right now who are out of work. When the housing bubble burst they got laid off. This jobs bill says let's put those men and women back to work rebuilding our roads and our bridges and modernizing our schools. I don't want the newest airports, the fastest railroads built in China. I don't want the best schools built in Europe. I want them built right here in the United States of America. I don't want our kids studying in crumbling schools. I want our kids studying in the best schools.

There's work to be done right here in Orlando. There are workers ready to do it right here in Orlando. Let's tell Congress, pass this jobs bill today.

Pass this jobs bill and we put teachers back in the classroom. Now, this week I'm going to have a state visit with one of our closest allies, the President of South Korea. I had lunch with him a while back, and I asked him, "What's your biggest policy challenge?" He said, "You know, my biggest problem is, is that our parents are so demanding." [*Laughter*] He says, "They know education is the key to our future, so I'm having to import teachers to teach kids English in the first grade because they know that they want to succeed education." So they're hiring teachers as fast as they can, and what are we doing? We're laying them off in droves. It's unfair to our kids. It undermines our future. If we pass this jobs bill, thousands of teachers in every State will be back in the classroom where they belong.

If Congress passes this jobs bill, companies will get tax credits for hiring America's veterans. We ask those men and women, our family, our friends, to leave their careers, leave their families, risk their lives to fight for our country. The last thing they should have to do is fight for a job when they come home.

The "American Jobs Act" will cut taxes for almost every worker and small business in America, give an extra tax cut to every small business that hires workers or gives workers a raise. You've got Republicans in Congress who keep on talking about, "We've got to help job creators." Don't just talk about it, actually do something. Pass thisjobs bill, and every single one of those job creators will have more money to hire.

Now, a lot of folks in Congress, they'll tell you, "Well, we may support some of those ideas, but it's got to be paid for." Well, I agree. It does have to be paid for. We have a deficit, and we've got to tackle it in a serious way. So recently, I laid out exactly how we should pay for it—pay this debt down over time and pay for the jobs bill. It's a plan that adds to the $1 trillion in cuts that we already made during the summer, one of the biggest spending cuts in history.

When people talk about we need to shrink the deficit, we just made some tough cuts. And we're willing to do more. But we can't just spend—we can't just cut our way out of the problem; we've also got to grow our way out of the problem. We've got to invest in those things that help us grow and put people back to work.

And our plan says if we want to close our deficit and put people back to work, then we've got to do it in a balanced way and a fair way. It means that, yes, we've got to make some tough

choices, make some tough priorities, get rid of programs that don't work so we can fund the ones that do. But we've also got to ask those who've been most blessed by America—the wealthiest, biggest corporations—we've got to ask them to also do their fair share.

We've got a Tax Code that's all messed up, and we need to reform it. Now, Republicans say they want to reform it too. That's great. We're happy to work with them, but it's got to be based on a very simple principle: Middle class families shouldn't pay higher rates than millionaires or billionaires. Warren Buffett's secretary shouldn't pay a higher rate than Warren Buffett. A teacher or a nurse or a construction worker making $50,000 a year shouldn't be paying a higher rate than somebody making $50 million a year. It's not right, and it's got to change.

Now, I want to be very clear here: Nobody wants to punish success in America. The Republicans talk about "class warfare." That's— our goal is to make success available for everybody. What's great about this country is you've got a good idea, you've got a service that nobody else has thought of, you know what, go out there, start a business, make money. I want everybody out there to be rich. That's great. Anybody in America should be able to make it if they try.

But none of us make it on our own. Somebody—an outstanding entrepreneur like a Steve Jobs, somewhere along the line he had a teacher who helped inspire him. All those great Internet businesses wouldn't have succeeded unless somebody had invested in the Government research that helped to create the Internet. We don't succeed on our own. We succeed because this country has, in previous generations, made investments that allow all of us to succeed.

So this is the land of opportunity. But we have to remember, those of us who have done well, we should all pay our fair share in taxes to contribute to the Nation that makes our success possible. That's not class warfare. That's not an attack on anybody. That's just common sense. That's just fairness.

So when you hear Congress dusting off those old talking points and talking—calling this class warfare, I just have to remind people, 26 years ago, another President said that closing tax loopholes that benefited special interests, the most affluent, he said these Tax Codes that made it possible for millionaires to pay nothing while a bus driver was paying 10 percent of his salary, that's just crazy. It's time we stopped it. You know who said that? That was Ronald Reagan. That was Ronald Reagan.

So I don't understand what these other folks are arguing about. They all say that Ronald Reagan is their guy. [*Laughter*] I'm agreeing with him. I know they've got short memories, but I don't remember Republicans accusing him of engaging in class warfare. He was expressing common sense.

So, you know what, if asking somebody like me, who's done very well, to pay the same tax rate as a plumber or a teacher or a bus driver makes me a warrior for the middle class, I'll wear that as a badge of honor. I'll wear that as a badge of honor. I don't mind, because ultimately, this is about priorities. This is about choices.

It would be great if we didn't have to pay any taxes, nobody, and we could still have great roads and great bridges and great schools and high-speed rail. But you know what, if we want to put people back to work, if we're not willing to just settle for the status quo, if we want to invest in the future, that money has got to come from somewhere.

So would you rather keep tax loopholes for oil companies, or would you rather put construction workers and teachers back on the job? Would you rather keep tax breaks for folks who don't need them and weren't really even asking for them, or do you want to invest in education and medical research and new technology? Should we ask seniors to pay thousands of dollars more for Medicare, which is what some of the Republicans in the House have been proposing, or should we ask everybody to pay their fair share?

That's what this debate is about, and that's what's at stake right now. This notion that the only thing we can do to restore prosperity is to eliminate Government, keep tax breaks for the few, and tell the many that you're on your own, that's not how America got built. That's not how America got great. That's not the story of this country.

We are rugged individualists, and we're strong, and we're self-reliant. And we believe in the principle that everybody who is able and willing should work—everybody who is able should be working out there. There's no free lunch out here. And it's been the drive and the initiative of our workers and entrepreneurs that's made this economy the engine and envy of the world. And we believe in the free market, and we believe in people going out there and pursuing their dreams.

But there's always been this other thread in our history that says we're all connected, we're in this together. There are some things we can only do together as a nation. We don't have a system where we all rely on our own private services to put out fires. We realize, you know what, it works better if we've got a single fire department. We don't decide that somehow each of us are going to have our own private army. We decide, you know what, we should kind of pool our resources and make sure that this Nation can defend itself.

Republican Presidents like Lincoln and Eisenhower, even during difficult times, they invested in railroads and highways and science and technology. And after the war—after World War II, when there were millions of returning heroes, including my grandfather, this country, together, said we're going to help these young people go back to college under the GI bill, and that's going to help lift everybody up. Everybody will benefit from a better educated workforce. Everybody—rich, poor, everybody in the middle—will be lifted up if the country is doing better.

That's why Michelle and I had the chance to succeed, because our parents instilled in us a sense of what it meant to work hard, but also because the country gave us opportunities, scholarships so we could go to college.

So no single individual built America on their own; we built it together. We're "one Nation under God, indivisible, with liberty and justice for all," and with responsibilities to each other as well as to ourselves. And right now we've got to meet those responsibilities in this time of great challenge.

There's some folks in Congress who may think, well, you know what, we'll just settle this all in next year's election. I've got news for them, the next election is 13 months away. The American people don't want to sit and wait. They need help now. There are folks living paycheck to paycheck. There are folks living week to week. They need action. They need action now.

So I need you to lift up your voices, help us out. Tell Congress: Pass this bill. And once we get this bill passed—and we're just going to stay on it. And if they don't vote for it today, we're going to stay on it until they vote for something. We're going to keep pushing.

And I'm going to need you to help us finish what we started in 2008. Let's keep building an America that we can be assured gives everybody opportunity. Everybody gets a fair shake. Everybody gets their fair share.

Audience member. Si, se puede!

The President. Si, se puede! We're not people who just sit there and watch things happen; we make things happen. We're Americans. We are tougher than the times we live in, and we're sure a lot better than the politics we've been seeing.

We're a people who can write our own destiny. And we can do it again, as long as all of you have that same sense of urgency we had in 2008. Let's meet this moment. Let's get to work. Let's remind everybody all around the world just why it is that the United States of America is the greatest country on Earth.

God bless you. God bless the United States of America. Thank you.

NOTE: The President spoke at 6:03 p.m. at the Sheraton Orlando Downtown Hotel. In his remarks, he referred to Alan H. Ginsberg, chief executive officer, the CED Companies; Mark NeJame, founder and senior partner, NeJame, LaFay, Jancha, Ahmed, Barker, Joshi and Moreno, P.A.; Dwight D. Howard, Jr., center, National Basketball Association's Orlando Magic; President Lee Myung-bak of South Korea; and Warren E. Buffett, chief executive officer and chairman, Berkshire Hathaway Inc.

Remarks at a Democratic National Committee Fundraiser in Orlando
October 11, 2011

The President. Hello, everybody! Oh, it is good to see all of you, although I can't see much with that light. First of all, I am just so grateful to John and Ultima for opening up their extraordinary home. Give them a big round of applause.

I want to thank your outstanding mayor, Buddy Dyer, who's in the house. I want to thank all the cohosts of this extraordinary event. We also have Congresswoman Corrine Brown who is here. Thank you, Corrine.

Now, the reason I came here is because I'm trying to resolve the NBA lockout. [*Laughter*] So I don't know who I need to talk to. [*Inaudible*]—I don't know if you've got some clout or who it is, but we need our basketball. [*Laughter*]

The last time that John and Ultima hosted me, I was actually still in the United States Senate. And they could not have been more gracious at that time, and I've been in love with Orlando ever since. But obviously, this area, like the rest of the country, is going through some very challenging times right now. We have just gone through the worst recession since the Great Depression, the worst financial crisis since the 1930s. And as a result, there are a whole bunch of folks who are hurting out there. Before I came here, I was actually at a little pub downtown——

Audience member. Amen.

The President. ——right across—[*laughter*]—I saw you in there too. [*Laughter*] And I was with a group of plumbers and pipefitters, construction workers. They had worked on the Amway Center. They had worked on the new veterans hospital that's going up. But a lot of them now were out of work, and one of them had lost their home. A couple of them were in the process of losing their health care, because it turns out if you don't work enough hours, even if you're in a union, that you end up losing your health care benefits, and you—or at least you have to pay for them yourself, and a lot of these guys couldn't afford it.

And it was a good reminder: As blessed as so many of us are, that there's a big chunk of the country right now that's hurting. And I hear from them every day, and I see folks all across the country who have had to close down a business that had been in their family for years or somebody has lost their home and they're trying to figure out how long they can stay with their brother or their sister, with their whole family. And people who send out résumé after résumé for months now, and they're still not able to find a job.

And so for those of us who, I think, in 2008, decided that we needed to bring about change, I want everybody here to understand that 2008 was just the beginning and we now have to finish what we started in 2008. We have to finish what we started. We knew then that the challenges were immense, that we had gone through a decade in which ordinary people's wages and incomes hadn't gone up while the cost of everything from college to health care had risen. We knew then that the health care system was broken and we had millions of people without health care. We knew then that we didn't have an energy policy in this country. We knew then that too many jobs were being shipped overseas and not enough were taking root here in the United States of America. We knew then that our education system wasn't where it needed to be. We knew then that we were in a war in Iraq that we probably shouldn't have been in in the first place.

And so we, over the last 3 years, have tried to address some of those challenges that we understood existed back in 2008. And we knew that just as those problems weren't created overnight, we weren't going to solve them overnight. But we've made extraordinary progress. The war in Iraq has come to a close, and we've already brought 100,000 troops back.

Audience member. Awesome!

The President. We have finally gotten a health care law in place that promises not only to provide 30 million more people insurance across this country, but also makes sure that the insurance you have is more secure.

We ended a practice where huge Government subsidies were going to the banks for student loans, took $60 billion out of that subsidy to apply to make sure that college was more affordable for young people all across the country.

We have appointed judges all across the country who understand the importance of keeping the doors of justice open to everybody who is—[*applause*]—and by the way, the most diverse Federal appointees that we've ever seen. That includes, by the way, two outstanding women on the Supreme Court.

Audience member. [*Inaudible*]

The President. He would have to take a really big pay cut. [*Laughter*]

We've been able to pass Wall Street reform to make sure that we don't get caught in the same kind of crisis that occurred back in 2008 when Lehman went under, and we aren't going to see taxpayer-funded bailouts of the sort that we've seen in the past.

And so we've made enormous progress, but we've got a lot more work to do. And the only way we're going to be able to make that progress is if I've got your support.

Audience member. Four more years!

The President. If I've got your support. Now, keep in mind, the election is 13 months away. And in the meantime, the American people can't wait for action. And that's why for the last month what I've been spending most of my time on is trying to nudge, cajole, push, shove Congress to do its job and to pass a jobs bill that can start putting construction workers back to work and put teachers back in the classroom and rebuild our infrastructure—our roads, our bridges, our water mains, our sewer systems—rebuild our schools so that we've got the best education possible for us kids.

This is a bill that is paid for. I won't lie to you. It asks some of you to do a little bit more than you've done in the past. But here is the extraordinary thing. When you talk to people who have been incredibly blessed by this country, and there are a lot of people here who started out with not much—and I'm in that category—except good parents and folks who push you, and somehow, we've ended up achieving the American Dream. I think every one of us is willing to do a little bit more to make sure that America is the kind of place where the next generation is going to enjoy the same opportunities we did.

And so what we've said is, look, we can bring down the deficit. We can put people back to work. We're going to make some cuts in programs that don't work so that we can fund the things that do. We can rebuild this country. We can invest in basic research and science that will lead to the kind of innovations that have always made this country great. And we can maintain a social safety net so that our seniors are secure and their Medicare is still in place and Social Security is still available. We can do all those things, but what we need is not a "no, we can't" attitude. We need a "yes, we can" attitude.

And there are some folks in Congress right now who seem to believe that their job is to figure out how to keep their job, instead of spending time thinking about how more Americans can get a job. And that attitude that sees everything through the lens of the next election, that puts party ahead of country, that attitude has to end. And that's people are so frustrated about when they think about Washington.

So the challenge we have now is to maintain the same kind of energy, the same kind of enthusiasm, the same hopefulness that we had in 2008. And that's not always going to be easy because, let's face it, back in 2008, it was sort of lightning in a bottle. There was huge excitement, and I wasn't as gray. Everybody had those "Hope" posters and all that stuff. And it was cool to be an Obama supporter, because it was new and fresh. And now everybody looks and says: "We see him on TV all the time. He is looking old and worn out." Everybody still loves Michelle, though, the First Lady of the United States.

Audience member. And the girls.

The President. And the girls, and Bo—and Bo.

Audience member. And you.

Audience member. And you!

The President. But the point is that in 2008, I hope you got involved not just because it was trendy, but because you shared with me a vision of an America in which everybody has a fair shot and everybody does their fair share, an America in which the middle class was not out of reach or people weren't worried about falling out of it, but it was the glue that held this country together. The idea that if you worked hard and you were responsible, that you showed up at your job every day and you looked after your family and you looked after your community, that that meant that you could pay your bills and send your kids to college and take a vacation once in a while and have a home and retire with some dignity and respect. That if you played by the rules, that you were rewarded. And those values are what we've been fighting for. That's what this whole process has been about.

And we're not there yet. Too many folks are doing the right thing and still falling behind. And that's what they're frustrated by. And that's what they're worried about. That's what they're scared about and anxious about. And so I just want everybody here to understand that that goal, my belief in those values is unwavering. I am absolutely confident that there is no problem we have in this country that cannot be solved if we are working together, if we stick to it, if we are determined, if we don't lose hope.

And I'm going to need all of you to spread that message as you go to your workplaces and you talk to your friends and your neighbors and your churches, your synagogues. I need all of you to insist that that vision we have, an America that is fair and just, where everybody is included, that that vision is still possible. It's not that far away, but we're going to have to work hard to achieve it.

Now, I was mentioning to some of the basketball players who were here that this is like the second quarter, maybe the third, and we've still got a lot of work to do. But I want everybody to know I'm a fourth-quarter player. So I don't miss my shots in the fourth quarter. So as long as we've got a strong team and everybody is committed and engaged and involved, we're not just going to win this election, we are going to win this election, and then we are also going to make sure that we rebuild this country.

We're also going to make sure that our infrastructure is the best in the world once again. We are once again going to have the most—the highest rate of college graduates in the world. We're also going to make sure that we are the most competitive nation in the world. We are also going to make sure that we fix a broken immigration system. We are also going to make sure that we deal with neighborhoods all across

the country that are impoverished and where too many kids are giving up hope. We are also going to make sure that we are respected around the world not just for our military might, but for our values and for the things that we stand for.

We have a lot of work to do, but if you're with me, I guarantee you we're going to make it happen. So God bless you. God bless the United States of America, everybody. Thank you. Thank you very much.

NOTE: The President spoke at 8:31 p.m. at the residence of John and Ultima Morgan. Audio was not available for verification of the content of these remarks.

Remarks at the White House Forum on American Latino Heritage
October 12, 2011

Hello, everybody! Thank you so much. Thank you, everybody. Everybody, please have a seat. Well, welcome to Washington. It is an honor to be here with so many leaders and thinkers who've come together for one reason: to celebrate Latino culture and honor the contributions that so many Latinos have made—and continue to make—to our Nation.

I want to begin by thanking Sergeant First Class Petry for that introduction. Three months ago, I was honored to present Sergeant Petry with our Nation's highest military decoration, the Medal of Honor. And we are so proud of him. He is an inspiration to all of us. And he is the latest in a long line of Latino heroes to wear America's uniform. So I was mentioning to him that I went to Walter Reed this week and—to visit some of our wounded warriors, and a number of them remarked on how they had had a chance to meet Sergeant Petry. He had gone by to talk to some of those guys. And seeing him in uniform, proud, doing what he does, inspired them and made them certain that they were going to pull through. And so that's the kind of effect he's having on people each and every day. And we're really proud of him. So thank you very much. Thank you.

I also want to recognize the Members of Congress who are here. I want to thank my

dear friend and outstanding Secretary of the Interior, Ken Salazar, for organizing this forum. Whenever Ken is asked how long his ancestors have been in this country, he says, "Oh, about 400 years." [*Laughter*] So his roots go way back, just like I know many of yours do.

And that's what today is all about. Diversity has always been America's strength. We are richer because of the men and women and children who've come to our shores and joined our Union. And we are better off because of the ideas that they've brought and the difference that they've made and the impact they've had on our lives.

And nowhere is that more true than with the Latino community. Right now there are 54 million Americans of Latino descent, one-sixth of our population: our neighbors, our coworkers, our family, our friends. You've helped us build our cities, grow our economy, defend our country. And today, for the first time in history, there is a Latina in my Cabinet and a Latina on the bench of the highest court in the land. Hilda Solis is doing an outstanding job.

Now, this forum is about celebrating that heritage, because too often the achievements of Latinos go unrecognized. And there are achievements that have been hard won. We know life hasn't always been easy for Latinos in

1259

this country and still isn't. The land of opportunity hasn't always been the land of acceptance. But the fact that Latinos have done so much and come so far is a testament to the vision that has sustained you. It's a vision that says, maybe I never had a chance to get a good education, but I want my daughter to go to college, maybe get a second degree. Maybe I started out working in the fields, but some day I'll own my own business. Maybe I wasn't born in this country, but I'll sign up to fight for it. Maybe I have to make sacrifices, but those sacrifices are worth it if it means a better life for my family.

That's the story of parents, grandparents, great-grandparents, great-great-grandparents, that determination, that perseverance, that sense of what is possible that has kept the American Dream alive and well in the Latino community. And more than any one person or any one story, those are the values that we have to remember today.

We need to remember those values because times are especially tough right now, and they've been tough for a while. For the better part of a decade, we've seen the rich get richer, the poor get poorer, the middle class get squeezed. That was before the crisis that began in Wall Street and made its way to Main Streets all across America, making it harder for people to find jobs, harder for families to keep their heads above water.

And the Latino community knows this better than most. The unemployment rate among Latinos is one of the highest in the country. And right now too many families are struggling just to get by. That's not right. I ran for President for the same reason many people came to this country in the first place: Because I believe America should be a place where you can always make it if you try; a place where every child, no matter what they look like, where they come from, should have a chance to succeed.

I still believe in that America. I believe we can be that America again. The truth is, the problems we face today were a long time coming and solving them will take time. In a global economy, it will require us to have the best educated workforce, the strongest commitment to research and innovation, the most reliable communications and transportation networks.

But with so many people hurting today, there are things we can do right now to make a difference. There are things we should do right now to put more people back to work and to restore a sense of security and fairness that's been missing for too long.

So that's why I put forward the "American Jobs Act." That's why I sent Congress a jobs bill made up of the kinds of proposals that, traditionally, Democrats and Republicans have supported. Independent economists who do this for a living have said the "American Jobs Act" would lead to more growth and nearly 2 million jobs next year. No other jobs plan has that kind of support from actual economists, no plan from Congress, no plan from anybody.

But apparently, none of this matters to Republicans in the Senate. Because last night, even though a majority of Senators voted in favor of the "American Jobs Act," a Republican minority got together as a group and blocked this jobs bill from passing the Senate. They said no to more jobs for teachers, no to more jobs for cops and firefighters, no to more jobs for construction workers and veterans, no to tax cuts for small-business owners and middle class Americans.

Now, a lot of folks in Washington and the media will look at last night's vote and say, well, that's it. Let's move on to the next fight. But I've got news for them: not this time, not with so many Americans out of work, not with so many folks in your communities hurting. We will not take no for an answer.

We will keep organizing, and we will keep pressuring, and we will keep voting until this Congress finally meets its responsibilities and actually does something to put people back to work and improve the economy.

We'll give Members of Congress a chance to vote on whether they think that we should keep teachers out of work or put them back in the classroom where they belong, teaching our kids.

They'll get a chance to vote on whether they think that construction workers should stay idle while our roads and bridges are falling apart or whether we should put these men and women back to work rebuilding America.

Republicans say that one of the most important things we can do is cut taxes. Well, they get a chance to vote on whether we should cut taxes for middle class families or let them go up. This job would cut taxes for virtually every worker and small business in America; 25 million Latinos would benefit. If you're a small-business owner who hires a new worker or raises wages, you'd get another tax cut. If you hire a veteran, like Sergeant Petry, you'd get another tax cut. Anybody who fights for our country should not have to fight for a job when they come home.

Now, I know some folks in Congress blocked this jobs bill because of how it's paid for. Well, we already agreed to cut nearly $1 trillion in Government spending. We've offered to cut even more in order to bring down the deficit. But we can't just cut without asking those of us who've been most fortunate in our society to pay our fair share. And that's not about punishing success, it's about making choices. If we want to create jobs and close the deficit and invest in our future, the money has got to come from somewhere.

And so we've got to ask ourselves a question: Would we rather keep the Tax Code with its loopholes exactly as they are for millionaires and billionaires, or do you want construction workers to have a job rebuilding roads and bridges and schools? Because you know a lot of our kids in the community are learning in trailers right now. Why wouldn't we want to put people back to work rebuilding those schools? Would you rather fight for special interest tax breaks, or do you want to fight for tax cuts for small businesses and middle class families in your neighborhood? I think I know the answer.

In the end, this is a debate about fairness and who we are as a country. It's a debate about what we believe in. What kind of country do we want to be? When Michelle and I tuck our daughters into bed at night, we think about the fact that we are only where we are because somebody who came before us met their responsibilities. They put the America Dream within our reach. They made sure that there

were student loan programs out there, and they made sure that there were decent schools out there, that there were opportunities for everybody. That's the reason all of you are here today, because somebody made an investment 10 years ago, 20 years ago, 30 years ago, 40 years ago, to ensure that you had a chance at success.

Those aren't White or Black or Latino or Asian or Native American values. Those are American values. Now it's up to us—this generation—to do our part to invest now so that the next generation has a shot.

These are tough times, and a lot of people are living week to week, paycheck to paycheck, even day to day. They need action, and they need it now. They want Congress to work for the people who elected them in the first place. They want Congress to do their job.

So I need your help. I'm going to need—you are opinion leaders all across the country. I need you to e-mail and tweet and fax and write letters and get on the phone, meet face to face. Remind Members of Congress who they work for. Remind them what's at stake here. The time for games and politics is over. Too many in this country are hurting for us to stand by and do nothing.

This jobs bill will help the Latino community right now, and it will help the larger American community right now. We all have a stake in this recovery, and it's up to every single one of us to fight for a better future.

In 1966, Cesar Chavez was struggling to bring attention to the treatment of farm workers in California, and he received a telegram from a friend who knew a little something about standing up for justice. Dr. Martin Luther King wrote: "As brothers in the fight for equality, I extend the hand of fellowship and goodwill. We are with you in spirit and in determination that our dreams for a better tomorrow will be realized."

And here in America, we are united by more than the color of our skin or the language that we speak. We are joined together by a shared creed, a shared set of values. We're connected by the future we want for ourselves and our children. And we determine our own destiny here. Whether your ancestors came from a— came over on a slave ship or crossed the Rio Grande or were here long before the country was founded, we're in this together. And we have the opportunity to right now—to determine our own destiny.

So I hope you will join me in helping us meet this moment. Let's get to work putting the American people back to work. And let's show once again why the United States of America remains the greatest nation on Earth.

Thank you very much, everybody. God bless you, and God bless the United States of America.

NOTE: The President spoke at 11:37 a.m. in the Yates Auditorium at the Department of the Interior. In his remarks, he referred to Sfc. Leroy A. Petry, USA.

Statement on Congressional Passage of Trade Agreements With Colombia, Panama, and South Korea
October 12, 2011

The landmark trade agreements and assistance for American workers that passed tonight are a major win for American workers and businesses. I've fought to make sure that these trade agreements with South Korea, Colombia, and Panama deliver the best possible deal for our country, and I've insisted that we do more to help American workers who have been affected by global competition. Tonight's vote, with bipartisan support, will significantly boost exports that bear the proud label "Made in America," support tens of thousands of good-paying American jobs, and protect labor rights, the environment, and intellectual property. American automakers, farmers, ranchers, and manufacturers, including many small businesses, will be able to compete and win in new markets. I look forward to signing these agreements, which will help achieve my goal of doubling American exports and keeping America competitive in the 21st century.

NOTE: The statement referred to H.R. 3078, H.R. 3079, and H.R. 3080.

Remarks at a Welcoming Ceremony for President Lee Myung-bak of South Korea
October 13, 2011

President Obama. Good morning, everybody. I hope everybody is enjoying the weather.

I am told there is a Korean proverb, which says, "Words have no wings, but they can fly a thousand miles." President Lee, First Lady Kim, I hope my words today will be felt in the hearts of all South Koreans when I say to our allies, our partners, our dear friends, please accept our warmest welcome. *Hwan yong hamnida.*

Today we welcome a leader whose remarkable life embodies the rise of his nation, from an impoverished child who drank water to fill his hungry stomach, to the student who cleaned the streets to pay his tuition, to the activist sent to jail for protesting dictatorship, to the leader guiding his country to new heights, my good friend and partner, President Lee.

Today we celebrate an alliance rooted in the shared values of our people: our servicemembers who have fought and bled and died together for our freedom, our students and workers and entrepreneurs who work together to create opportunity and prosperity, and our families, bound by the generations, including many who are here today, proud and patriotic Korean Americans.

President Lee, our two nations have stood together for more than 60 years. Over the past 2 years we've deepened our cooperation. Today I'm proud to say that the alliance between the United States and the Republic of Korea is stronger than it has ever been.

Our alliance reflects a broader truth. The United States is a Pacific nation, and America is leading once more in the Asia-Pacific. And with our landmark trade agreement, we will bring our nations even closer, creating new jobs for both our people and preserving our edge as two of the most dynamic economies in the world.

Mr. President, your visit thus marks a new chapter in our alliance, because in South Korea the United States has a global partner that is embracing the responsibilities of leadership in the 21st century. As we go forward, let us draw strength from the same sense of solidarity that I've seen during my visit to Korea, in our brave—our very brave armed forces. *Katchi kapshida*—we go together.

We will go together, investing in our societies and the education and skills of our people. We will go together, reaffirming that alliance between the United States and the Republic of Korea is unbreakable. And we will go together, as we partner to meet our global responsibilities, so that our citizens and people around the world may live in security and prosperity.

President Lee, First Lady Kim, members of the Korean delegation, on behalf of Michelle and myself, on behalf of the American people, welcome to the United States.

President Lee. Good morning, everybody.

Audience members. Good morning.

President Lee. Mr. President, whom I consider one of my closest friends, Madam First Lady, ladies and gentlemen, first of all, thank you for your warm welcome extended to me, my wife, and my delegation. It is always a great pleasure visiting this great country. I would also like to convey the warm greetings from your friends back in Korea, Mr. President and Madam First Lady.

The journey of our alliance began 60 years ago, a journey that brought together two peoples from different sides of the Pacific. What brought us together more than anything was the value that all of us here hold so dear: freedom.

Yesterday I paid tribute at the Korean War Memorial just a short distance away from here. There, I was able to pay my respect to the 37,000 American soldiers who fought and died

defending this value. It is written on a wall at that memorial that these American soldiers, quote, "answer the call to defend a country they never knew and a people they never met," unquote. The simple yet poignant words describe how brave and good they were.

Mr. President, Madam First Lady, ladies and gentlemen, the Korean people have never forgotten what these fallen soldiers and their families gave up. We will always remain grateful to all of them.

Our alliance is the bedrock of stability, peace, and progress, and our relationship is evolving. Our two countries are working together to fight disease and poverty, climate change and natural disasters. We are addressing the issues of energy security and eradicating terrorism and extremism and stopping the proliferation of weapons of mass destruction.

We are also working together to promote universal values, such as democracy and human rights. We face these challenges both as a nation and as a partner. We will prevail until we overcome these challenges. We will come out stronger. Our two countries will ensure peace and stability of the peninsula and beyond.

Last night the United States Congress ratified the Korea-U.S. Free Trade Agreement. This historic achievement will open up a new chapter in our relationship. And I would like to take this opportunity to thank President Obama for his steadfast leadership. This agreement will create more jobs. It will expand mutual investments into both of our countries. It will become a new engine of growth that will propel our economies forward. Ladies and gentlemen, it will be a win for both of our countries.

Our two peoples walked alongside together, armed with common values, pursuing the same ideals and achieving common goals, and this is making our security and economic alliance stronger. It is bringing our people closer together. We are true partners and close friends, and we will remain as such in the 21st century. Our alliance that was born of out of the trenches of war will continue to blossom; it will become stronger.

Mr. President, Madam First Lady, ladies and gentlemen, Korea and the United States are global partners now. We are a force for good. I look forward to a constructive as well as an enjoyable time here in Washington, DC, with President Obama and the First Lady. My aim is to further strengthen our common values and our partnership.

Once again, thank you, Mr. President, Madam First Lady, people of America, for this warm reception.

NOTE: The President spoke at 9:25 a.m. on the South Lawn at the White House, where President Lee was accorded a formal welcome with full military honors. In his remarks, President Obama referred to Kim Yoon-ok, wife of President Lee. President Lee spoke in Korean, and his remarks were translated by an interpreter.

The President's News Conference With President Lee Myung-bak of South Korea
October 13, 2011

President Obama. Please, everybody have a seat. Good afternoon. Once again, it is a great honor to welcome my good friend and partner, President Lee, back to the White House. We had a wonderful dinner last night at one of our outstanding local Korean restaurants. Michelle and I are looking forward to hosting the President and First Lady Kim at tonight's state dinner. And today President Lee will address Congress, a high honor reserved for America's closest friends.

This state visit reflects the fact that the Republic of Korea is one of our strongest allies. Because we've stood together, the people of South Korea, from the ruins of war, were able to build an economic miracle and become one of our largest trading partners, creating jobs and opportunity for both our peoples. Because we stood together, South Koreans were able to build a strong and thriving democracy and become a steady partner in preserving security and freedom not only on the Korean Peninsula, but beyond.

As I said this morning, this visit also recognizes South Korea's emergence as one of our key global partners. South Koreans have served bravely with us in Afghanistan and Iraq. South Korean forces have partnered with us to prevent piracy off the shores of Africa and stem the spread of weapons of mass destruction. Once a recipient of aid, South Korea has become a donor nation, supporting development from Asia to Africa. And under President's personal leadership, Seoul served as host to the G–20 summit last year and will host the next Nuclear Security Summit next year.

South Korea's success is a tribute to the sacrifices and tenacity of the Korean people. It's also a tribute to the vision and commitment of President Lee.

Mr. President, you have shown how the international community should work in the 21st century: more nations bearing the responsibility of meeting global challenges. In the face of unprovoked attacks on your citizens, you and the South Korean people have shown extraordinary strength, restraint, and resolve.

And I'd add that in all of our dealings, President Lee has shared my focus on what matters most: the security and prosperity of our citizens. And that, again, has been our focus today.

We agreed to move ahead quickly with the landmark trade agreement that Congress passed last night and which I'll sign in the coming days. It's a win for both our countries. For our farmers and ranchers here in the United States, it will increase exports of agricultural products. From aerospace to electronics, it will increase American manufacturing exports, including those produced by our small businesses. It will open Korea's lucrative services market, and I'm very pleased that it will help level the playing field for American automakers.

As a former executive, President Lee will understand when I say that just as Americans buy Hyundais and Kias, I hope that South Koreans will buy more Fords, Chryslers, and Chevys. And tomorrow President Lee and I will be visiting with autoworkers in Michigan, some of the many Americans who are going to benefit from this agreement.

In short, this agreement will boost American exports by up to $11 billion and support some 70,000 American jobs. It has groundbreaking protections for labor rights, the environment, and intellectual property so that trade is free and fair. It will promote green jobs and clean energy, another area where we're deepening our cooperation. And it keeps us on track to achieve my goals of doubling American exports.

So, President Lee, I thank you for your partnership in getting this deal done, a deal that will also be good for Korean businesses and Korean jobs. I look forward to working with you to bring it into force as quickly as possible.

As we expand our economic cooperation, we're also deepening our security cooperation. Guided by our joint vision for the alliance, we agreed to continue strengthening our capabilities to deter any threat. I can never say it enough: The commitment of the United States to the defense and security of the Republic of Korea will never waver. And as we have for decades, the United States will maintain our strong presence in the Asia-Pacific, which is a foundation for security and prosperity in Asia in the 21st century.

In this regard, we discussed North Korea, which continues to pose a direct threat to the security of both our nations. On this, President Lee [and I]° are entirely united. Together, we've succeeded in changing the equation with the North, by showing that its provocations will be met, not with rewards, but with even stronger sanctions and isolation. So the choice is clear for North Korea. If Pyongyang continues to ignore its international obligations, it will invite even more pressure and isolation. If the North abandons its quest for nuclear weapons and moves toward denuclearization, it will enjoy greater security and opportunity for its people. That's the choice that North Korea faces.

Given the global nature of alliances, President Lee and I discussed the full range of challenges to our security and prosperity. I thanked

the President for South Korea's continued support for reconstruction in Afghanistan, and I updated him on the transition that is underway towards full Afghan responsibility for security. We agreed to continue our support for democratic transitions in the Middle East and North Africa, including Libya.

We've agreed to coordinate more closely on the development that lifts—that can lift people and nations out of poverty. I appreciated hearing the President's plans for next year's Nuclear Security Summit, which I look forward to attending. And as we approach the G–20 and APEC summits next month, we agreed on the need for coordinated global action that focuses on growth and creates jobs for our workers.

Finally, we're strengthening the ties between our people. South Korea is one of the sources of international students studying in the United States. And the number of American students who are studying in Korea has been soaring. So we've directed our teams to sustain this momentum and expand educational exchanges between our people, not unlike the one that once brought a visiting scholar named Lee Myung-bak to an American university just blocks from here.

So again, Mr. President, I thank you for your partnership and your friendship. And because of the progress we've made today, I'm confident that your visit will mark a turning point in the enduring alliance between our two nations.

Thank you very much.

President Lee. Thank you, Mr. President. First of all, I thank President Obama again for inviting me to make a state visit to the United States. My thanks goes out to the Madam First Lady as well. I am pleased to have had the chance to reaffirm once again the strong partnership and friendship between our two countries.

I met with President Obama six times over the last 3 years. Our meetings were always constructive, allowing us to reaffirm the strength of our alliance, an alliance that is firmly based upon shared values and mutual trust. This alliance guarantees peace, stability, and prosperity

---

° White House correction.

on the Korean Peninsula, the Asia-Pacific region, and beyond. We will continue to strengthen what is already a powerful and far-reaching alliance.

I was privileged to have spent many hours with President Obama during my visit to Washington, DC, this time, discussing and sharing views on a wide array of issues, such as security on the Korean Peninsula and the Northeast Asia region, trade and economic cooperation between our two countries, situation in the Middle East, including what is unfolding in Libya, various international security issues, and of course, the global economy and the challenges that we face today.

In particular, we welcome the ratification of the Korea-U.S. Free Trade Agreement by the United States Congress. I am confident that the Korean National Assembly will soon ratify this very important agreement in the near future.

I take this opportunity to sincerely thank President Obama, the congressional leadership, and the Members of Congress for their support and commitment. The Korea-U.S. Free Trade Agreement is a historic achievement that will become a significant milestone in our 130-year relationship. It is a win-win agreement that will benefit both of our countries in countless ways. This agreement will create more jobs, generate more trade, and stimulate our economies.

This free trade agreement will bring numerous benefits to our workers, our companies, our small businesses, and our consumers alike. Furthermore, mutual investments will increase and our economic partnership will become stronger. And the KORUS FTA will bring benefits beyond Korea and the United States. It will be a gateway to enhancing ties between North America and Asia. It will allow us to get ahead and stay ahead in the global markets.

As we all know, the global economy is undergoing many challenges. The Korea-U.S. Free Trade Agreement will demonstrate to the world that we can create good-quality jobs and stimulate growth through open and fair trade. This is a good example. The passage of the KORUS FTA has opened up a new chapter in our partnership, in our alliance.

For the last 60 years we have maintained a strong political, military alliance. Now the KORUS FTA signals the beginning of an economic alliance. This alliance will strengthen and elevate our military and political alliance to a whole new level. Our alliance is evolving into a future-oriented partnership, and it will become stronger.

When President Obama and I adopted a joint vision for the future of the alliance in 2009, we agreed to expand the depth and scope of our strategic alliance. Today we reaffirmed our common commitment to a common future, a future of ensuring peace and stability on the Korean Peninsula and beyond, including the Northeast Asian region. Our alliance will continue to play a pivotal role in overcoming the many global challenges that we face today.

Recently, we were deeply shocked when we read the reports on the attempt to harm the Saudi envoy here in Washington, DC. I and the Korean people strongly condemned all forms of terrorism. And as you can see already, our two countries are working to bring peace and ensure stability around the world. We are partners in Iraq and Afghanistan. We are safeguarding our vital sea lanes off the coast of Somalia.

Today we also talked about the rebuilding of Libya and bringing democracy and economic prosperity to a region wracked by violence and instability. We also agreed to continue our work towards promoting universal values such as human rights, democracy, and freedom across the world.

In particular, we agreed that Korea and the United States will contribute to the economic development and administrative capacity-building in Libya, provide vocational training for its young people, provide medical care, and rebuild and reinvest in its infrastructure. We will coordinate our joint efforts with the United Nations support mission in Libya and the Friends of Libya meetings and our international partners.

We also talked about the worrying state of the global economy and how to overcome the perils that emanated from the euro zone. The situation in Europe is a source of grave concern. We agreed to strengthen international cooperation through the G–20 so that the fiscal situation does not endanger the recovery of our real economies. In particular, our two countries agreed to work together to bring back stability to our financial markets similar to what we did back in 2008.

As we have done for the past 3 years, President Obama and I will remain in complete agreement when dealing with North Korea. Our principled approach will remain steadfast. We agreed that North Korea's continued pursuit of nuclear weapons poses a serious threat to peace and stability of the Korean Peninsula and the world. We will continue to work towards denuclearization of the peninsula.

The second Nuclear Security Summit will be held next March in Seoul. During the summit, we will review the progress made since the first summit in 2010, which was convened under the initiative of President Obama. The leaders will have one goal, and that is to achieve our collective vision of a world free of nuclear weapons.

I thank President Obama and his able team for giving us their full support in the preparations of the summit, and of course, we'll continue to work with them. And I look forward to welcoming President Obama and Mrs. Obama in Seoul next year.

Thank you very much.

President Obama. All right. We're going to start off with Ed Henry [FOX News]. Where's Ed?

Iran/North Korea

Q. Thank you, Mr. President. I appreciate it. President Lee, I wanted to start with you, one question each. First, when you mentioned North Korea, what concrete steps do you think the Obama administration has helped to contain Kim Jong Il?

And, President Obama, I wanted to get your first reaction to the Iranian terror plot. Your Secretary of State called it a dangerous escala-

tion. What specific steps will you take to hold Iran accountable, especially when Mitt Romney charged last week: "If you do not want America to be the strongest nation on Earth, I am not your President. You have that President today"?

President Obama. Well, I didn't know that you were the spokesperson for Mitt Romney. [*Laughter*] But let me just talk about the plot in particular. We have a situation here where the Attorney General has laid out a very specific set of facts. What we know is that an individual of Iranian American descent was involved in a plot to assassinate the Ambassador to the United States from Saudi Arabia. And we also know that he had direct links, was paid by and directed by individuals in the Iranian Government.

Now, those facts are there for all to see. And we would not be bringing forward a case unless we knew exactly how to support all the allegations that are contained in the indictment.

So we have contacted all our allies, the international community; we've laid the facts before them. And we believe that after people have analyzed them, there will not be a dispute that this is, in fact, what happened.

This is a—not just a dangerous escalation, this is part of a pattern of dangerous and reckless behavior by the Iranian Government. One of the principles of international behavior is that our diplomats—we send them around the world—that they are going to be protected, they are not targets for threats or physical violence. And for Iran to have been involved in a plot like this indicates the degree to which it has been outside of accepted norms of international behavior for far too long. This is just one example of a series of steps that they've taken to create violence and to behave in a way that you don't see other countries doing.

So with respect to how we respond, our first step is to make sure that we prosecute those individuals that have been named in the indictment. And I will leave to the Attorney General the task of describing how that will proceed.

The second thing that we're going to continue to do is to apply the toughest sanctions and continue to mobilize the international community to make sure that Iran is further and further isolated and that it pays a price for this kind of behavior.

Keep in mind that when I came into office I think Iran saw itself as being able to play various countries against each other and avoid the kind of isolation that it deserved. Since that time, what we've seen, whether it relates to its nuclear program or its state-sponsored terrorism, that more and more countries have been willing to speak out in forceful ways, whether through the United Nations or through other avenues, to say this is not acceptable behavior. And it is having an impact. I mean, what we've seen is Iran's economy is in a much more difficult state now than it was several years ago, in part because we've been able to unify the international community in naming Iran's misbehavior and saying that it's got to stop and there are going to be consequences to its actions.

Now, we don't take any options off the table in terms of how we operate with Iran. But what you can expect is that we will continue to apply the sorts of pressure that will have a direct impact on the Iranian Government until it makes a better choice in terms of how it's going to interact with the rest of the international community.

There is great similarity between how Iran operates and how North Korea operates: a willingness on their part to break international rules, to flout international norms, to not live up to their own commitments. And each time they do that the United States will join with its partners and allies in making sure that they pay a price.

And I think that—I have to emphasize that this plot was not simply directed at the United States of America. This is a plot that was directed against the Saudi Ambassador. And I think that what you're going to see is folks throughout the Middle East region questioning their ability to work effectively with Iran. This builds on the recognition within the region that Iran in fact has been hypocritical when it comes to dealing with the Arab Spring, given their own repressive activities inside their country, their willingness to prop up the

Syrian regime at a time when they're killing their own citizens.

This is a pattern of behavior that I think increasingly the international community is going to consider out of bounds and is going to continue to punish Iran for. Unfortunately, the Iranian people are the ones that probably suffer the most from this regime's behavior. And we will continue to work to see how we can bring about a Iranian Government that is actually responsive to its people, but also following the rules of the road that other countries in the international community follow.

President Lee. Thank you. To answer your question about North Korea, first of all, President Obama and I, for the last 3 years, we have maintained very close cooperation and coordination when it comes to North Korea policy. We have consistently applied our principled approach towards North Korea.

For North Korea, the only way to ensure happiness for its people and to embark on that path to development is to abandon its nuclear ambitions. And so we have tried through peaceful means, through diplomatic means, to strongly urge North Korea to abandon its nuclear ambitions.

And in this day and age, we realize that no single country can be effective in achieving its diplomatic or economic aims on its own. We know that cooperation is vital in order for a country to become a responsible member of the international community, which is something that we want for North Korea. And so we would of course want North Korea to abandon its nuclear ambitions. And of course, Korea and the United States will continue to consistently apply a principled approach so that we can achieve our strategic objective.

And when it comes to cooperation between our two governments, we speak with one voice, and we will continue to speak with one voice. And it was a chance for me to reaffirm this today.

Q. My name is—[*inaudible*]—from the Dong-a Daily News. I know that President Lee is talking about a South Korea-North Korea-Russia trilateral gas pipeline project. But North Korea is also under a lot of sanctions from the international community and the United States and other countries. But having said that, if this gas line project proceeds as planned, then we would have to provide or compensate North Korea with a substantial amount of money or other forms of compensation. So in your opinion, President Lee, do you think that the gas line—pipeline project will be able to proceed without resolving the North Korean nuclear issue?

President Lee. Yes, thank you. And I don't know if that's a question that I should be answering here in the United States, but since you asked a question I will try to answer that.

In the Far East, we have been discussing this issue for quite some time in trying to import Russian gas into the Republic of Korea. Now, we're discussing right now with the North Koreans whether the Russian gas, which is quite affordable, can travel through North Korea and be imported and be used in South Korea.

This is beneficial, first of all, for Russia because they can sell their natural resource. For North Korea it is beneficial because they could use this natural resource, and also beneficial for South Korea as well. But let me just remind you that South Korea, North Korea, and Russia haven't yet come together to discuss this issue in any detail. But from an economic standpoint of view, it is beneficial for all parties involved. But I understand that this issue is not just economics alone. This issue inevitably involves security matters, which we will consider very closely.

And also, let me remind you that this project will not be implemented anytime soon. Of course, we are mindful of the progress that we are making with regards to the North Korean nuclear issue as well.

President Obama. Jessica Yellin [CNN].

Iran/Job Growth Legislation/Trade

Q. Thank you, Mr. President. First, briefly, to follow on Ed, if I may. On the Iran alleged terror plot, do you have knowledge or do you believe that the nation's Supreme Leader and President had knowledge of the plot? And if so, do you not see that as an act of war?

And if I could turn to the economy, yesterday in a campaign video you said that you will force Congress to take up individual pieces of the "American Jobs Act." Which pieces would you like to see them take up first? And given that so far you've been unable to force Congress to do an up-or-down vote on entire bill and that new unemployment filings are not falling, why not, now, sit down with Members of Congress to see if you can't reach compromise on something that could pass now and create jobs quickly?

President Obama. Okay. First of all, on the Iranian issue, the Attorney General has put forward the facts with respect to the case, and I'm going to let him comment on the details of those facts. What we can say is that there are individuals in the Iranian Government who are aware of this plot. And had it not been for the outstanding intelligence work of our intelligence officials, this plot could have gone forward and resulted not only in the death of the Saudi Ambassador, but also innocent civilians here in the United States.

We believe that if—even if at the highest levels there was not detailed operational knowledge, there has to be accountability with respect to anybody in the Iranian Government engaging in this kind of activity.

And so we will continue the investigation. We will continue to put forward all the facts that we have available to us. But the important thing is for Iran to answer the international community why anybody in their Government is engaging in these kinds of activities, which, as I indicated before, are I think out of bounds for not just a country like Iran that historically has been engaging in these kinds of activities, but violates basic principles of how diplomats are dealt with for centuries.

Now, with respect to the jobs bill, I have said repeatedly that the single most important thing we can do for the economy right now is put people back to work right now. And we have put forward a jobs bill that independent economists—not my team, not my administration—have said would grow the economy substantially and put up to 1.9 million people back to work. These are proposals that historically have been supported not just by Democrats, but also by Republicans. As I've said as I've traveled around the country, I don't know when rebuilding our roads and bridges that are decaying suddenly became a partisan issue.

And I was at a jobs council meeting up in Pittsburgh with CEOs from companies across the board, many of whom have been traditional supporters of the Chamber of Commerce and the Business Roundtable and other organizations that the Republican Party has claimed a lot of support for. And they said, for example, when it came to infrastructure, this is something that anybody in Washington should agree to.

The Republicans haven't given a good answer as to why they have not agreed to wanting to rebuild our roads and our bridges and our schools. They have not given us a good reason as to why they don't want to put teachers back in the classroom. And so what we're going to do is we're going to break each of these bills apart. We're going to say, let's have a vote on putting teachers back in the classroom. Let's have a vote on rebuilding our infrastructure. Let's have a vote on making sure that we are keeping taxes low for small businesses and businesses that are willing to hire veterans, provide tax breaks for further investment that can create jobs. And each time we're going to ask Republicans to support the bill. And if they don't want to support the bill, they've got to answer not just to us, but also the American people as to why they wouldn't.

Now, I think this trade deal that we just passed, the Korea Free Trade Act, shows that we are happy to work with Republicans where they are willing to put politics behind the interest of the American people and come up with proposals that are actually going to create jobs. The Korea Free Trade Act, we believe, will create up to 70,000 jobs. It's a good deal. We got good, strong bipartisan support.

Frankly, we have not seen a lot of ideas coming forward from Republicans that would indicate that same kind of commitment to job creation. If they do—if Senator McConnell or Speaker Boehner say to me, "You know what, we want to get some infrastructure built in this

country; we think that putting construction workers back to work is important," I'll be right there. We'll be ready to go. If they are willing to renew the payroll tax as we worked on together in December, I'll be ready to go.

I don't think the problem here, Jessica, is that I have not been unwilling to negotiate with Republicans. I've shown repeatedly my willingness to work overtime to try to get them to do something to deal with this high unemployment rate. What we haven't seen is a similar willingness on their part to try to get something done. And we're not going to wait around and play the usual political games here in Washington, because the American people are desperate for some relief right now.

Q. Will you invite them to the White House to negotiate on the jobs bill?

President Obama. I think that anytime and anyplace that they are serious about working on putting people back to work, we'll be prepared to work with them. But we're not going to create a lot of theater that then results in them engaging in the usual political talking points, but don't result in action.

People want action. And I'm prepared to work with them. But again, the last time I was here at a press conference I said—I asked you guys to show us the Republican jobs plan that independent economists would indicate would actually put people back to work. I haven't yet seen it. And so eventually, I'm hoping that they actually put forward some proposals that indicate that they feel that sense of urgency about people—needing to put people back to work right now.

All right, Jessica, you can't have four follow-ups. One is good. All right.

South Korea-U.S. Free Trade Agreement/North Korea

Q. My name is—[*inaudible*]. I am a reporter of Korean Broadcasting System, KBS. I have two questions to President Obama. Yesterday U.S. Congress ratified the Korea-U.S. FTA. But Korean National Assembly didn't pass it yet. And Korean opposition party is requesting re-renegotiation on the FTA. What is your opinion and prospect on the future of the Korea-U.S. FTA?

And my second question is about Libya and North Korea. In Libya, there was a people's uprising, and they changed their Government. And do you think such an event will be possible in North Korea in the near future? Thank you.

President Obama. Well, first of all, President Lee assures me that the KORUS FTA will pass through the National Assembly. I have great confidence in his leadership, and my expectation is that it will get done, because it's good for both countries. And businesses will be able to prosper here in the United States as a consequence of lowering many of these trade barriers; the same will be true in Korea. Our workers will benefit, and we can learn from each other. And I think this is one more sign of the close cooperation and friendship between our two peoples.

You're absolutely right that what we've seen in the Arab Spring—in Libya, in Tunisia, in Egypt—is this deep longing on the part of people for freedom and opportunity. And although the path from dictatorship to democracy is always uncertain and fraught with danger, what we've seen also is that human spirit eventually will defeat repressive governments.

So I don't want to predict when that might happen. I think that obviously the people of North Korea have been suffering under repressive policies for a very long time, and none of us can look at a crystal ball and know when suddenly, that type of government collapses on itself.

What we know though is, is that what people everywhere—whether it's in Korea or the United States or Libya or Africa, what people everywhere are looking for is the ability to determine their own destiny, to know that if they work hard that they will be able to be rewarded, that they can speak their mind, they can practice their religion in freedom, that they can enjoy the free flow of information that increasingly characterizes the 21st century. And I don't think that the people of North Korea are any exception.

And I think when they see the extraordinary success and progress that's been made in South Korea, I think inevitably that leads them to recognize that a system of markets and democracy and freedom is going to give their children and their grandchildren more opportunity than the system that they're currently under.

All right, thank you very much, everybody.

NOTE: The President's news conference began at 12:22 p.m. in the East Room at the White House. In his remarks, President Obama referred to Kim Yoon-ok, wife of President Lee; Republican Presidential candidate W. Mitt Romney; and Mansoor Arbarian, a U.S. citizen charged with participating in an alleged Iranian-backed plot to assassinate Saudi Arabia's Ambassador to the U.S. Adil al-Ahmad al-Jubayr. Reporters referred to Chairman Kim Jong Il of North Korea; and Supreme Leader Ayatollah Ali Hoseini-Khamenei and President Mahmud Ahmadinejad of Iran. President Lee and a reporter spoke in Korean, and their remarks were translated by an interpreter.

Remarks at a State Dinner Honoring President Lee Myung-bak of South Korea
October 13, 2011

[*President Obama's remarks were joined in progress.*]

President Obama. ——representing one of America's strongest allies and global partners, the Republic of Korea.

I also want to acknowledge two guests in particular: another son of Korea dedicated to peace and security, the Secretary-General, Ban Ki-moon, is here; and our first Korean American Ambassador to the Republic of Korea, confirmed by the Senate today, Ambassador Sung Kim.

Now, I'm going to be very brief tonight because President Lee has had a very full day and a very wet day—[*laughter*]—as well as extended meetings and press conferences, a State Department banquet, and an address to the Congress, which I understand went extraordinarily well. There is a reason why people call him the Bulldozer. He is unstoppable. [*Laughter*]

Mr. President, today you have spoken with great eloquence about what America and our alliance has meant in your life and the life of your country. This evening I want you and your countrymen to know what Korea and its people have meant to America.

The essence of our alliance, I think, is embodied in a concept that is uniquely Korean. It doesn't translate that easily, but it reflects the deep affection, the bonds of the heart that cannot be broken and that grow stronger with time. Our Korean friends know it well: *jeong*.

In our country, we've felt this *jeong* in our vibrant Korean American communities, including in Hawaii, where I grew up, a melting pot of cultures that made me who I am and that taught me we can all live together in mutual trust and respect.

I felt this *jeong* during my visit to Korea on Veterans Day, the 60th anniversary of the Korean war, when our proud veterans of that war, both Korean and American, came together to celebrate a shared legacy: a free, democratic, and prosperous Republic of Korea.

And I felt this *jeong* in my friendship with President Lee. Mr. President, your life story—from crushing poverty to the Presidency—is an inspiration. Your success, Korea's success, speaks to the truth that with education and hard work, anything is possible. It's a spirit our countries share. You've described it in Korean, and in English it translates as: "Yes, we can." [*Laughter*] It sounds good in Korean too. [*Laughter*]

Finally, I would note that in our lives President Lee and I have both been blessed to find our better halves, leaders in their own right, advocates for women and young people, who we are proud to call our First Ladies. Mr. President, as we say in America, we both married up. [*Laughter*]

And so I want to propose a toast. I believe this is mine.

[*At this point, President Obama was handed a glass.*]

To our friends President Lee and First Lady Kim, and to their delegation, most of all to the enduring alliance between our nations, a partnership of the heart that will never be broken. Cheers. *Gun bae.*

[*President Obama offered a toast. President Lee then made remarks in Korean, which were translated by an interpreter as follows.*]

President Lee. First of all, Mr. President, Madam First Lady, distinguished guests, please allow me to thank you from the bottom of my heart for this warm reception extended to me, my wife, and my delegation. Thank you very much.

And Mr. President and Madam First Lady, my visit to Washington, DC, this time is especially special because before you are the President of the United States of America, you are a very close friend of mine. And this is how I consider you as well as the Madam First Lady. So this visit is very, very special for all of us.

Ladies and gentlemen, the President just spoke about the Korean emotion that we call *jeong* in Korean. I think indeed President Obama knows that deep inside his heart, he understands the essence of what we call *jeong*. *Jeong* can be explained in many different aspects, but one aspect of that is an individual that is humble, yet very strong inside. And I think President Obama exemplifies this trait of what we call *jeong*, and that is why we have a very special tie that we feel whenever I think about President Obama. Ladies and gentlemen, I'm a very, very honest guy—[*laughter*]—so what I say, I really mean it.

And also, Mr. President, I must thank you for one thing, because you have spoken so highly of the outstanding educational system of Korea and the dedication of its teachers and the determination of our Korean parents when it comes to educating their children. You have so many new teacher fans in Korea. [*Laughter*] And I have to be very honest with you. I think you have quite a number of them who like you more than they like me. [*Laughter*]

But, Mr. President, seriously, you do have a lot of teacher fans in Korea. But the real reason, when we look deep down inside, the reason why you are so popular among many Koreans is because everyone, including myself, are deeply impressed by your endless passion for learning and that this is very much a—very much reflected in your life story.

Mr. President, Madam First Lady, ladies and gentlemen, whenever I think about the United States and the people of America, I also have a very personal story of mine, which I would like to share with you briefly tonight. As you know, 60 years ago Korea used to be one of the poorest countries in the world. My family was exceptionally poor, and we really had nothing to eat, nothing to wear. We had to rely on foreign aid for many, many years. And I remember—I think I was about 9 or 10 years old—in my village there came an American missionary lady with boxes and containers full of used clothes that she would come to my village and hand out.

So being a boy whose only wish at that time was to own and wear a pair of blue jeans, I decided to stand in line, along with many people. But I was a very small and shy boy—hard to imagine—[*laughter*]—so a lot of people were pushing, and they were jostling about. So I ended up way at the end of the line. When my turn came, I went up to the American missionary lady, and I asked for a pair of blue jeans, to which she said—she just looked at me and said, "Well, I'm sorry, I'm all out of blue jeans." And of course, I was devastated. I was heartbroken. And this kind American missionary lady takes one look at me, and out of sympathy she hands me something out of the box. She handed me a small rubber ball. Now, this did little to console the boy who was crushed, and because, after all, what was I going to do with a rubber ball?

And so to this day—and I shared this story with President Obama, and I—when I finished the story I remember the President laughing a bit nervously though. But—[*laughter*]—I told him, I said, "Mr. President, as you can see, I do not owe the United States anything, except"—

[*laughter*]—"except maybe for a rubber ball." [*Laughter*]

So, ladies and gentlemen, Mr. President, Madam First Lady, although half-jokingly I say that I do not owe the United States anything, but in reality, my country and my people owe you tremendously. Which other country—no country came to aid the Republic of Korea 60 years ago when my country was being attacked by Communists. No country sacrificed more than 37,000 lives defending freedom for the people of my country. So for that, for many, many years onwards, we will always, always be grateful to the American people.

Mr. President, ladies and gentlemen, just last night, the United States Congress passed and ratified the Korea-U.S. Free Trade Agreement. I've said this before, but please allow me to say it again: I am deeply appreciative and grateful to the leadership of Congress, to all the Members of the United States Congress who supported this measure, and especially to the steadfast leadership of President Obama for pushing this through.

And also, Mr. President, ladies and gentlemen, I know that there are those in the United States Congress who did not vote "yea" for this very important agreement. I think I see a few faces here, maybe—[*laughter*]—but I'm very, very confident, ladies and gentlemen, that in 1 year or even less, that these people who may be a little bit critical of this important agreement will say that they made a mistake, because they will see the visible results of this very important agreement.

And the thing that I want to prove the most, ladies and gentlemen, with the KORUS FTA is that many of those critics were saying that the KORUS FTA was somehow going to make people lose their jobs, but really the KORUS FTA is going to create a lot of good, decent jobs for the people of America. And this is a point that I want to prove by implementing this agreement.

And, ladies and gentlemen, you see Mr. King seated at the head table here. As I was receiving guests, and when he came up to me and I was shaking hands, I thought to myself, this is my chance to explain to Mr. King that the KORUS FTA is going to create a lot of good jobs for his people and the members of his union.

Well, the fact that Mr. King accepted the invitation to be here tonight just goes to show that he believes in the essence and the core values of the KORUS FTA, so I have no worries. [*Laughter*]

Mr. President, Madam First Lady, ladies and gentlemen, our relationship between our two countries began 130 years ago. Sixty years ago, our mutual defense treaty began what is considered to be one of the strongest military and political alliance that the world has ever known. Of course, we are here today to celebrate our journey of the last 60 years, one that has been—always been marked by triumphs, sometimes heartache, but always full of hope. And we are gathered here to reaffirm our friendship and to renew our common commitment towards our shared goals. I know that our relationship will go strong; it will become more mature and complete.

Mr. President, as we talked about over the last few days, we have many, many challenges that are facing us as a nation and as a member of the international community. We do not know when, what type of form, or how it is going to strike us. There is a lot of uncertainty out there. But I believe in our friendship, because when during—if we are faced with challenges, I know that we will overcome them and even come out stronger.

And I just want to emphasize once again, our alliance between the Republic of Korea and the United States ensures us that we are not alone. Neither is Korea alone or the United States. So we can have confidence that we will be able to overcome any challenges that may face us.

Well, ladies and gentlemen, I see the guests today, and I think a lot of you are people who are very much liked by the President and the Madam First Lady. I also see a few of you who I always wanted to see, and so I'm very happy that I have a chance to see and meet with you tonight.

And so once again, Mr. President, Madam First Lady, thank you so much for this honor, and thank you for your invitation.

[*President Lee spoke in English.*]

Okay. I'm going to propose toast for us. [*Laughter*]

[*President Lee continued in Korean, and his remarks were translated by an interpreter as follows.*]

Ladies and gentlemen, please join me now in a toast: First of all, for the health and well-being of President Obama and Madam First Lady, and of course, for our everlasting friendship between our two countries. Cheers.

[*President Lee offered a toast.*]

NOTE: The President spoke at approximately 8:30 p.m. in the East Room at the White House. In his remarks, he referred to Secretary-General Ban Ki-moon of the United Nations; and Kim Yoon-ok, wife of President Lee. President Lee referred to Bob King, president, United Automobile Workers.

Remarks at the General Motors Orion Assembly Plant in Lake Orion, Michigan
October 14, 2011

President Obama. Hello, Detroit! Hello! Everybody, please have a seat. Have a seat. It is great to be back in the Motor City. I notice the mood's a little brighter on this particular visit. [*Laughter*] I'd like to think it's because everybody is excited about the Korea Free Trade Agreement, but I suspect it might just have a

little bit to do with your Lions beating up on my Bears. All right, all right, all right. [*Laughter*] Don't get carried away now. [*Laughter*] Not to mention your Tigers hanging in there last night.

As you can see, President Lee is a pretty good politician. [*Laughter*] He knows how to get on your good side. Today I brought a good friend and one of our closest allies, President Lee of South Korea. Some of you may know, President Lee has got a remarkable story. He grew up a little ways from Detroit, but he embodies that same spirit that Detroit's all about. Through sheer grit and determination, he worked his way from the humblest beginnings. The South Korea of his childhood was an extraordinarily poor country. But he worked his way up, worked his way up, went to school while cleaning streets, and eventually went on to run a Hyundai machinery plant—so he knows a little bit about cars—then the whole company, and ultimately was elected the President of the Republic of Korea. And this is a country that's staged one of the world's greatest economic comebacks that we've ever seen.

So President Lee knows what it's like to go through tough times. He knows what it's like when folks have counted you out. And he knows what it's like to make a big comeback.

So with that, I want to welcome President Lee to Detroit and have him say just a few words.

President Lee Myung-bak of South Korea. Thank you. Folks, I'm a little bit shorter than President Obama, so I'm going to adjust the microphone. [*Laughter*] I hope you'll understand.

Well, first of all, ladies and gentlemen, it's a great pleasure visiting your factory here in Detroit along with one of my closest friends, President Obama.

Well, folks, as you know, the global economy is going through some tough times, and so there's one thing on the minds of both President Obama and I, and that is jobs. It is about creating good, decent jobs, and it is about keeping those jobs. And this is what keeps us awake.

Ladies and gentlemen, before I came here to see you, I just had a brief tour given to me by the members of this factory and I heard about the history, and I also heard about the danger of how this factory was on the brink of being closed. But now, as you can see, we have so many people here, like all of you here working here and earning a good living. And I think

more than anyone else here in this factory, I think it's President Obama who's the happiest man to see this factory being so energetic and enthusiastic.

Ladies and gentlemen, it was 3 years ago when I first met with President Obama, and back then I still remember how we talked about a lot of things. And one of the things that was on President Obama's mind was how to revive the U.S. automotive industry. Because we all know that the U.S. automotive industry was, and is, the leader in the world, and President Obama was concerned what he can do to revive Motor City and the United States automotive industry. And we talked a lot about that. And, folks, I know one or—a few things about automobiles because back when I was in the private sector, I used to build cars myself. So I know a thing or two about automobiles, and I think perhaps this was the reason why President Obama raised this subject. But we talked a lot about how to revive the U.S. automobile industry.

Ladies and gentlemen, President Obama just briefly talked about my past, how I really worked hard throughout my life. And I was once just like you. I was—I did work in factories, and I was also in the boardroom as well, as a CEO of one of the largest companies in Korea. But one thing I learned throughout my experience in my life is this: During times of challenges, when you're faced with difficulties and if you want to create good jobs and maintain these good jobs, there's only one thing and the surest way to do that is for the workers and for the managers to work together. It is about cooperating together, and that is the surest way to ensure good jobs and for you to keep your jobs.

And, ladies and gentlemen, we are here with President Obama because when I was a worker I knew that, more than anything, for all of us to enjoy good life is for all of us to have a good, decent job. And I know how important it is for anyone to have a good, decent job. And the factory here—as I was looking around, I felt once again how important it is for all of us to work together, because I know that 3 years ago, GM Korea and GM Orion, you guys worked together to set up this factory. And today, you are building models here and you're manufacturing cars that 3 years ago—GM Korea and your company has been working together, and that is the reason why I came here, so I can see with my own eyes the good work that all of you are doing here.

Folks, when I was President, as soon as I became President of Korea, I visited GM Korea factory not once, but twice, which was quite unusual for the President of Korea to do so. But I came here today, and as I watch the factory and I took on a tour, I was very, very—and deeply impressed by the way you're operating this factory. I was impressed by the fact that this factory is very proenvironment. You take care of the environment. Also you've adopted the latest IT technology so that efficiency is up. You have the highest standards, and you're building excellent cars here in this factory. And I am confident that this factory is going to continue, and it's going to make good cars, and your lives are going to be good. And I'm sure—and I'm confident in the future.

Lastly, folks, I just want to say one thing before I go. As you know, the KORUS FTA will soon be implemented. I know, folks, that some of you here may think that with the implementation of the KORUS FTA, that somehow your jobs may be exported or go somewhere else. But let me tell you one thing: That is not true. I am here with President Obama today because I want to give this promise to you, and that is that the KORUS FTA will not take away any of your jobs. Rather it will create more jobs for you and your family, and it is going to protect your jobs. And this is the pledge that I give you today.

Soon, folks, Motor City is going to come back again, and it's going to revive its past glory. And I have all the confidence in the world that you are going to do that.

Thank you.

President Obama. Thank you. Give President Lee a big round of applause.

All right. Well, thank you, President Lee.

Thank you, to everybody who has joined us here today. A couple of people I just want to mention. First of all, the CEO of General Motors, Dan Akerson, is here. Where's Dan? There he is. The UAW president, one of the key people who helped make this agreement possible, that is my dear friend Bob King. And my U.S. Trade Representative, who spent a lot of long nights with his Korean counterpart, Ron Kirk is in the house.

I just want to follow up President Lee's remarks with a few words about what the Korea Free Trade Agreement will mean for American jobs and for the American economy. In the last decade, we became a country that was known for what we bought and what we consumed. And a whole bunch of goods poured in here from all around the world, and we spent a lot of money and took on a lot of debt, in a lot of cases, to buy those goods. But it didn't necessarily produce a lot of jobs here in the United States.

So when I took office, I was determined to rebuild this economy based on what this country has always done best, not just buying and consuming, but building, making things, selling those goods all around the world, stamped with three proud words: Made in America. And that's why one of the first decisions that I made as President was to save the U.S. auto industry from collapse. Now—[*applause*].

There were a lot of politicians who said it wasn't worth the time and wasn't worth the money. In fact, there are some politicians who still say that. Well, they should come tell that to the workers here at Orion.

Because 2 years ago, it looked like this plant was going to have to shut its doors. All these jobs would have been lost. The entire community would have been devastated. And the same was true for communities all across the Midwest. And I refused to let that happen.

So we made a deal with the auto companies. We said if you're willing to retool and restructure, get more efficient, get better, get smarter, then we're going to invest in your future, because we believe in American ingenuity. Most importantly, we believe in American workers.

And today I can stand here and say that the investment paid off. The hundreds of thousands of jobs that have been saved made it worth it. An American auto industry that's more profitable and competitive than it's been in years made it worth it. The taxpayers are being repaid. Plants like this are churning out groundbreaking fuel-efficient cars like the Chevy Sonic, the only one of its kind that's made and sold in the United States of America.

And for folks who haven't tried it, you've got to sit in that car. There's a lot of room in there. [*Laughter*] Felt—even for a pretty tall guy like me, I felt pretty good. They took away the keys, though. Secret Service wouldn't let me—[*laughter*]—I checked in the dash. It wasn't there.

Now, here's the thing. We live in a global economy, and that means most of the potential customers for American companies like GM won't just be here in the United States, they'll be all around the world. And the more goods and services we sell abroad, the more jobs we create here at home.

In fact, every $1 billion in exports supports thousands of American jobs. And that's why I've set a goal of doubling our exports, and that's a goal that we're on track to meet. That's why we worked with Panama and Colombia, as well as South Korea, to resolve outstanding issues with these trade agreements, and that's why I pushed Congress to pass them as soon as possible.

Now, Korea is one that is critically important, because understand, Korea has 50 million people; it's one of the fastest growing countries in the world. It's one of our closest allies and our closest friends. And—President Lee and I talked about this when we had dinner the other night—our trade is basically balanced between the United States and Korea. They buy as much stuff from us as they sell to us. And that's how fair and free trade is supposed to be. It's not a one-sided proposition. That's how trade is supposed to be. And I know President Lee doesn't mind me saying this, even though he's a Hyundai guy. [*Laughter*] If Americans can buy Kias and Hyundais from Korea, then I know Koreans should be able to buy some Fords and Chryslers and Chevys that are made right here in the United States of America.

The other thing that happened was—this took a little longer than some people expected because I wasn't going to sign just any trade deal. President Lee wasn't either. We had to work hard to reach an understanding. It was like a scene from a GM dealership, where folks are negotiating about the heated seats and the extended warranty, and you're going back and forth and trying to figure how does it fit together so that it works for everybody. But when all was said and done, President Lee and I walked away with a trade agreement that is a win-win for both countries.

Here in the United States, this trade agreement will support at least 70,000 American jobs. It will increase exports. It will boost our economy by more than our last nine trade agreements combined. And as I said, the good thing is we've got a balanced situation. It's not just a matter of folks sending a bunch of stuff here. Koreans are also buying American products. That's what makes it a win-win.

And by the way, I also held out on sending this agreement to Congress until they promised to renew a law called the TAA—Trade Adjustment Assistance—that helps American workers who've been affected by global competition so that they are able to help transition.

Now, it's because of all these benefits that this trade agreement won the support of business and labor, from automakers and auto workers, from Democrats and Republicans. That doesn't happen very often. And it was good to finally see both parties in Congress come together and pass legislation that is good for the American people, an agreement that will not only build on our strong economic relationship that's been existing for years to come, but also promises, as we've seen at this plant, the capacity for us to exchange ideas and technologies and systems, which will improve productivity on both sides.

Nearly a decade ago, when a Korean business named Daewoo Motors went bankrupt, it was General Motors that stepped in and saved that company, which is now known as GM Korea. And years later, it was the engineers from GM Korea who helped make the Chevy Sonic possible and the collaboration with that company that's helped save this plant and these 17,050 jobs—1,750 jobs.

So on a larger scale, the closer economic ties between the United States and Korea are going to lead to more jobs, more opportunity for both nations. Already, Korean investment—and by the way, it's not just in the auto industry. Already, Korean investment is creating jobs here in Michigan, with LG Chem planning to make lithium and ion batteries in Holland, Michigan, and Hyundai manufacturing suspension modules in Detroit, and Mando opening a new research and development center for brakes and steering in Novi. In Korea, American businesses are going to be pursuing those same investments and opportunities. So it's truly a win-win for everybody involved.

So I just want to say thank you to President Lee for his cooperation and for his leadership. I want to thank the Members of Congress who fought so hard to get this done, especially the delegation from this State. I want to especially thank the people of Detroit for proving that despite all the work that lies ahead, this is a city where a great American industry is coming back to life and the industries of tomorrow are taking root, and a city where people are dreaming up ways to prove all the skeptics wrong and write the next proud chapter in the Motor City's history.

And that's why I came here today. Because for every cynic that's out there running around saying it can't be done, there are a whole bunch of folks that are saying, "Yes, we can."

Yes, times are tough. Times are tough, and they've been tougher in Detroit than just about anyplace else. But we've made it through tough times before. We do not quit. We've rolled up our sleeves. We remembered our history. And we said to ourselves there's nothing that we cannot do when we're willing to do it together. You are all a testimony to the American spirit. These cars are a testimony to the American spirit. And if we can take that same spirit and apply it across the board to all the challenges we face, there is nothing that we cannot do.

God bless you, and God bless the United States of America. Thank you.

NOTE: The President spoke at 2:10 p.m. In his remarks, he referred to Minister of Foreign Affairs and Trade Kim Sung-hwan of South Korea. President Lee spoke in Korean, and his remarks were translated by an interpreter.

Letter to Congressional Leaders on Deployment of United States Armed Forces to Central Africa
October 14, 2011

Dear Mr. Speaker: (Dear Mr. President:)

For more than two decades, the Lord's Resistance Army (LRA) has murdered, raped, and kidnapped tens of thousands of men, women, and children in central Africa. The LRA continues to commit atrocities across the Central African Republic, the Democratic Republic of the Congo, and South Sudan that have a disproportionate impact on regional security. Since 2008, the United States has supported regional military efforts to pursue the LRA and protect local communities. Even with some limited U.S. assistance, however, regional military efforts have thus far been unsuccessful in removing LRA leader Joseph Kony or his top commanders from the battlefield. In the Lord's Resistance Army Disarmament and Northern Uganda Recovery Act of 2009, Public Law 111–172, enacted May 24, 2010, the Congress also expressed support for increased, comprehensive U.S. efforts to help mitigate and eliminate the threat posed by the LRA to civilians and regional stability.

In furtherance of the Congress's stated policy, I have authorized a small number of combat-equipped U.S. forces to deploy to central Africa to provide assistance to regional forces that are working toward the removal of Joseph Kony from the battlefield. I believe that deploying these U.S. Armed Forces furthers U.S. national security interests and foreign policy and will be a significant contribution toward counter-LRA efforts in central Africa.

On October 12, the initial team of U.S. military personnel with appropriate combat equipment deployed to Uganda. During the next month, additional forces will deploy, including a second combat-equipped team and associated headquarters, communications, and logistics personnel. The total number of U.S. military personnel deploying for this mission is approximately 100. These forces will act as advisors to partner forces that have the goal of removing from the battlefield Joseph Kony and other senior leadership of the LRA. Our forces will provide information, advice, and assistance to select partner nation forces. Subject to the approval of each respective host nation, elements of these U.S. forces will deploy into Uganda, South Sudan, the Central African Republic, and the Democratic Republic of the Congo. The support provided by U.S. forces will enhance regional efforts against the LRA. However, although the U.S. forces are combat-equipped, they will only be providing information, advice, and assistance to partner nation forces, and they will not themselves engage LRA forces unless necessary for self-defense. All appropriate precautions have been taken to ensure the safety of U.S. military personnel during their deployment.

I have directed this deployment, which is in the national security and foreign policy interests of the United States, pursuant to my constitutional authority to conduct U.S. foreign relations and as Commander in Chief and Chief Executive. I am making this report as part of my efforts to keep the Congress fully informed, consistent with the War Powers Resolution (Public Law 93–148). I appreciate the support of the Congress in this action.

Sincerely,

BARACK OBAMA

NOTE: Identical letters were sent to John A. Boehner, Speaker of the House of Representatives, and Daniel K. Inouye, President pro tempore of the Senate.

The President's Weekly Address
October 15, 2011

I'm here in Detroit visiting workers at a GM plant in the heart of a resurgent American auto industry, and I brought a guest with me, President Lee of South Korea.

We're here because this week Congress passed landmark trade agreements with countries like Korea and assistance for American workers that will be a big win for our economy. These trade agreements will support tens of thousands of American jobs. And we'll sell more Fords, Chevys, and Chryslers abroad, stamped with three proud words: Made in America.

So it was good to see Congress act in a bipartisan way on something that will help create jobs at a time when millions of Americans are still out of work and need them now. But that's also why it was so disappointing to see Senate Republicans obstruct the "American Jobs Act," even though a majority of Senators voted yes to advance this jobs bill.

We can't afford this lack of action, and there is no reason for it. Independent economists say that this jobs bill would give the economy a jumpstart and lead to nearly 2 million new jobs. Every idea in the jobs bill is the kind of idea both parties have supported in the past.

The majority of the American people support the proposals in this jobs bill. And they want action from their elected leaders to create jobs and restore some security for the middle class right now. You deserve to see your hard work and responsibility rewarded, and you certainly deserve to see it reflected in the folks you send to Washington.

But rather than listen to you and put folks back to work, Republicans in the House spent the past couple of days picking partisan ideological fights. They're seeing if they can roll back clean air and water protections. They're stirring up fights over a woman's right to make her own health care choices. They're not focused on the concrete actions that will put people back to work right now.

Well, we're going to give them another chance. We're going to give them another chance to spend more time worrying about your jobs than keeping theirs.

Next week, I'm urging Members of Congress to vote on putting hundreds of thousands of teachers back in the classroom, cops back on the streets, and firefighters back on the job. And if they vote no on that, they'll have to tell you why. They'll have to tell you why teachers in your community don't deserve a paycheck again. They'll have to tell your kids why they don't deserve to have their teacher back. They'll have to tell you why they're against commonsense proposals that would help families and strengthen our communities right now and in the long term.

In the coming weeks, we'll have them vote on the other parts of the jobs bill: putting construction workers back on the job rebuilding our roads and bridges, providing tax cuts for small businesses that hire our veterans, making sure that middle class families don't see a tax hike next year and that the unemployed and our out-of-work youth have a chance to get back in the workforce and earn their piece of the American Dream.

That's what's at stake: putting people back to work, restoring economic security for the middle class, rebuilding an economy where hard work is valued and responsibility is rewarded, an economy that's built to last. And I'm going to travel all over the country over the next few weeks so that we can remind Congress that that's the most important thing. Because there's still time to create jobs and grow our economy right now. There's still time for Congress to do the right thing. We just need to act.

Thanks.

NOTE: The address was recorded at approximately 2:40 p.m. on October 14 in the assembly line area at the General Motors Orion Assembly Plant in Lake Orion, MI, for broadcast on October 15. The transcript was made available by the Office of the Press Secretary on October 14, but was embargoed for release until 6 a.m. on October 15.

Remarks at a Dedication Ceremony for the Martin Luther King, Jr. Memorial
October 16, 2011

Thank you very much. Thank you. Please be seated.

An earthquake and a hurricane may have delayed this day, but this is a day that would not be denied.

For this day, we celebrate Dr. Martin Luther King, Jr.'s return to the National Mall. In this place, he will stand for all time among monuments to those who fathered this Nation and those who defended it, a Black preacher with no official rank or title who somehow gave voice to our deepest dreams and our most lasting ideals, a man who stirred our conscience and thereby helped make our Union more perfect.

Now, Dr. King would be the first to remind us that this memorial is not for him alone. The movement of which he was a part depended on an entire generation of leaders. Many are here today, and for their service and their sacrifice, we owe them our everlasting gratitude. This is a monument to your collective achievement.

Some giants of the civil rights movement—like Rosa Parks and Dorothy Height, Benjamin Hooks, Reverend Fred Shuttlesworth—they've been taken from us these past few years. This monument attests to their strength and their courage, and while we miss them dearly, we know they rest in a better place.

And finally, there are the multitudes of men and women whose names never appear in the history books: those who marched and those who sang, those who sat in and those who stood firm, those who organized and those who mobilized, all those men and women who through countless acts of quiet heroism helped bring about changes few thought were even possible. "By the thousands," said Dr. King, "faceless, anonymous, relentless young people, Black and White . . . have taken our whole Nation back to those great wells of democracy which were dug deep by the Founding Fathers in the formulation of the Constitution and the Declaration of Independence." To those men and women, to those foot soldiers for justice, know that this monument is yours as well.

Nearly half a century has passed since that historic March on Washington, a day when thousands upon thousands gathered for jobs and for freedom. That is what our schoolchildren remember best when they think of Dr. King, his booming voice across this Mall, calling on America to make freedom a reality for all of God's children, prophesizing of a day when the "jangling discord of our Nation" would be transformed into "a beautiful symphony of brotherhood."

It is right that we honor that march, that we lift up Dr. King's "I Have a Dream" speech, for without that shining moment, without Dr. King's glorious words, we might not have had the courage to come as far as we have. Because of that hopeful vision, because of Dr. King's moral imagination, barricades began to fall and bigotry began to fade. New doors of opportunity swung open for an entire generation. Yes, laws changed, but hearts and minds changed as well.

Look at the faces here around you, and you see an America that is more fair and more free and more just than the one Dr. King addressed that day. We are right to savor that slow but certain progress, progress that's expressed itself in a million ways, large and small, across this Nation every single day, as people of all colors and creeds live together, and work together, and fight alongside one another, and learn together, and build together, and love one another.

So it is right for us to celebrate today Dr. King's dream and his vision of unity. And yet it is also important on this day to remind ourselves that such progress did not come easily, that Dr. King's faith was hard won, that it sprung out of a harsh reality and some bitter disappointments.

It is right for us to celebrate Dr. King's marvelous oratory, but it is worth remembering that progress did not come from words alone. Progress was hard. Progress was purchased through enduring the smack of billy clubs and the blast of firehoses. It was bought with days in jail cells and nights of bomb threats. For every victory during the height of the civil rights movement, there were setbacks, and there were defeats.

We forget now, but during his life, Dr. King wasn't always considered a unifying figure. Even after rising to prominence, even after winning the Nobel Peace Prize, Dr. King was vilified by many, denounced as a rabble-rouser and an agitator, a Communist and a radical. He was even attacked by his own people, by those who felt he was going too fast or those who felt he was going too slow, by those who felt he shouldn't meddle in issues like the Vietnam war or the rights of union workers. We know from his own testimony the doubts and the pain this caused him and that the controversy that would swirl around his actions would last until the fateful day he died.

I raise all this because nearly 50 years after the March on Washington, our work, Dr. King's work, is not yet complete. We gather here at a moment of great challenge and great change. In the first decade of this new century, we have been tested by war and by tragedy, by an economic crisis and its aftermath that has left millions out of work and poverty on the rise and millions more just struggling to get by. Indeed, even before this crisis struck, we had endured a decade of rising inequality and stagnant wages. In too many troubled neighborhoods across the country, the conditions of our poorest citizens appear little changed from what existed 50 years ago: neighborhoods with underfunded schools and broken-down slums, inadequate health care, constant violence, neighborhoods in which too many young people grow up with little hope and few prospects for the future.

Our work is not done. And so on this day, in which we celebrate a man and a movement that did so much for this country, let us draw strength from those earlier struggles. First and foremost, let us remember that change has never been quick. Change has never been simple or without controversy. Change depends on persistence. Change requires determination. It took a full decade before the moral guidance of *Brown* v. *Board of Education* was translated into the enforcement measures of the Civil Rights Act and the Voting Rights Act, but those 10 long years did not lead Dr. King to give up. He kept on pushing, he kept on speaking, he kept on marching until change finally came.

And then when, even after the Civil Rights Act and the Voting Rights Act passed, African Americans still found themselves trapped in pockets of poverty across the country, Dr. King didn't say those laws were a failure, he didn't say this is too hard, he didn't say let's settle for what we got and go home. Instead, he said, let's take those victories and broaden our mission to achieve not just civil and political equality, but also economic justice; let's fight for a living wage and better schools and jobs for all who are willing to work. In other words, when met with hardship, when confronting disappointment, Dr. King refused to accept what he called the "isness" of today. He kept pushing towards the "oughtness" of tomorrow.

And so as we think about all the work that we must do: rebuilding an economy that can compete on a global stage; and fixing our schools so that every child—not just some, but every child—gets a world-class education; and making sure that our health care system is affordable and accessible to all and that our economic system is one in which everybody gets a fair shake and everybody does their fair share. Let us not be trapped by what is. We can't be discouraged by what is. We've got to keep pushing for what ought to be, the America we ought to leave to our children, mindful that the hardships we face are nothing compared to those Dr. King and his fellow marchers faced 50 years ago and that if we maintain our faith, in ourselves and in the possibilities of this Nation, there is no challenge we cannot surmount.

And just as we draw strength from Dr. King's struggles, so must we draw inspiration from his constant insistence on the oneness of man, the belief in his words that "we are caught in an inescapable network of mutuality, tied in a single garment of destiny." It was that insistence, rooted in his Christian faith, that led him to tell a group of angry young protesters, "I love you as I love my own children," even as one threw a rock that glanced off his neck.

It was that insistence, that belief that God resides in each of us, from the high to the low, in the oppressor and the oppressed, that convinced him that people and systems could change. It fortified his belief in nonviolence. It permitted him to place his faith in a government that had fallen short of its ideals. It led him to see his charge not only as freeing Black America from the shackles of discrimination, but also freeing many Americans from their own prejudices and freeing Americans of every color from the depredations of poverty.

And so at this moment, when our politics appear so sharply polarized and faith in our institutions so greatly diminished, we need more than ever to take heed of Dr. King's teachings. He calls on us to stand in the other person's shoes, to see through their eyes, to understand their pain. He tells us that we have a duty to fight against poverty even if we are well off, to care about the child in the decrepit school even if our own children are doing fine, to show compassion toward the immigrant family with the knowledge that most of us are only a few generations removed from similar hardships.

To say that we are bound together as one people and must constantly strive to see ourselves in one another is not to argue for a false unity that papers over our differences and ratifies an unjust status quo. As was true 50 years ago, as has been true throughout human history, those with power and privilege will often decry any call for change as divisive. They'll say any challenge to the existing arrangements are unwise and destabilizing. Dr. King understood that peace without justice was no peace at all, that aligning our reality with our ideals often requires the speaking of uncomfortable truths and the creative tension of nonviolent protest.

But he also understood that to bring about true and lasting change, there must be the possibility of reconciliation, that any social movement has to channel this tension through the spirit of love and mutuality.

If he were alive today, I believe he would remind us that the unemployed worker can rightly challenge the excesses of Wall Street without demonizing all who work there, that the businessman can enter tough negotiations with his company's union without vilifying the right to collectively bargain. He would want us to know we can argue fiercely about the proper size and role of government without questioning each other's love for this country, with the knowledge that in this democracy, government is no distant object, but is rather an expression of our common commitments to one another. He would call on us to assume the best in each other rather than the worst and challenge one another in ways that ultimately heal rather than wound.

In the end, that's what I hope my daughters take away from this monument. I want them to come away from here with a faith in what they can accomplish when they are determined and working for a righteous cause. I want them to come away from here with a faith in other people and a faith in a benevolent God. This sculpture, massive and iconic as it is, will remind them of Dr. King's strength, but to see him only as larger than life would do a disservice to what he taught us about ourselves. He would want them to know that he had setbacks, because they will have setbacks. He would want them to know that he had doubts, because they will have doubts. He would want them to know that he was flawed, because all of us have flaws.

It is precisely because Dr. King was a man of flesh and blood and not a figure of stone that he inspires us so. His life, his story, tells us that change can come if you don't give up. He would not give up, no matter how long it took,

because in the smallest hamlets and the darkest slums, he had witnessed the highest reaches of the human spirit; because in those moments when the struggle seemed most hopeless, he had seen men and women and children conquer their fear; because he had seen hills and mountains made low and rough places made plain, and the crooked places made straight and God make a way out of no way.

And that is why we honor this man, because he had faith in us. And that is why he belongs on this Mall, because he saw what we might become. That is why Dr. King was so quintessentially American, because for all the hardships we've endured, for all our sometimes tragic history, ours is a story of optimism and achievement and constant striving that is unique upon this Earth. And that is why the rest of the world still looks to us to lead. This is a country where ordinary people find in their hearts the courage to do extraordinary things, the courage to stand up in the face of the fiercest resistance and despair and say this is wrong, and this is right; we will not settle for what the cynics tell us we have to accept and we will reach again and again, no matter the odds, for what we know is possible.

That is the conviction we must carry now in our hearts. As tough as times may be, I know we will overcome. I know there are better days ahead. I know this because of the man towering over us. I know this because all he and his generation endured, we are here today in a country that dedicated a monument to that legacy.

And so with our eyes on the horizon and our faith squarely placed in one another, let us keep striving, let us keep struggling, let us keep climbing toward that promised land of a nation and a world that is more fair and more just and more equal for every single child of God.

Thank you. God bless you, and God bless the United States of America.

NOTE: The President spoke at 11:51 a.m. on the National Mall.

Remarks at Asheville Regional Airport in Fletcher, North Carolina
October 17, 2011

The President. Hello, Asheville! It is good to be back in Asheville, North Carolina! I love Asheville. In fact, I think I should be on the tourism promotion bureau of Asheville. Every time I meet somebody, I say, have you guys gone down to Asheville? That's a nice place to be. So it is wonderful to be back in one of my favorite parts of the country. Our family has great memories of staying here, and it's always nice to get out of Washington—*[laughter]*—and breathe some of that mountain air.

I want to recognize a couple of people who are here. First of all, one of the outstanding Senators in the United States Senate, your Senator, Kay Hagan, is in the house. Kay's daughter just got married this weekend, so congratulations to Kay's daughter. We are so thrilled by that.

And we also have your lovely and intelligent mayor of Asheville, Terry Bellamy is in the house. The last time I was here, Terry said she could play basketball. And so we went out—it turned out she was a cheerleader and not a basketball player. *[Laughter]* But she's doing an outstanding job overall. Thank you both for coming.

Now, as you may have noticed, I came here on a plane. It's a pretty nice plane. But I'm leaving on a bus. The bus is pretty hard to miss. And over the next few days, we are going to take this bus through North Carolina and Virginia, and I'm going to get a chance to hear from folks about how they're doing, what direction they want to take the country in.

And I'll be doing a little bit of talking, but mostly I'm going to do a whole lot of listening, because there doesn't seem to be much listening going on in Washington these days. People don't seem to be paying much attention to the folks who sent them there in the first place, and that's a shame. Because once you escape the partisanship and the political point-scoring in Washington, once you start really listening to the American people, it's pretty clear what our country and your leaders should be spending their time on.

Audience members. Jobs!

The President. We should be talking about jobs. When you hear what's going on out in the country, when you take the time to listen, you understand that a lot of folks are hurting out there. Too many people are looking for work. Too many families are looking for that sense of security that's been slipping away for the past decade now.

Here in North Carolina, you've got thousands of construction workers who lost their jobs when the housing bubble went burst. Some of those construction workers are here today. They've got experience. They've got skills. All they want is to be back on the jobsite doing what they do best.

And there is plenty of work to go around. In this airport, right here in Asheville, you've got a runway that needs to be widened and repaired. You've got a taxiway that's in the wrong spot, which means that planes sometimes get too close together. So we could be doing some work right here at the Asheville airport that would help boost tourism, help to boost the economy here, put people to work right now.

But it's not just here in Asheville. All across the State, you've got highways that need to be built. You've got bridges that need to be fixed. You've got schools that need to be modernized. And that's what America used to do best. We used to build things: built the transcontinental railroad, built the Golden Gate Bridge, the Hoover Dam, the Grand Central station. There's no reason why we should sit here and watch the best highways and the newest airports being built in China. We should be building them right here in the United States of America, right here in North Carolina.

Now, our problems were a long time in the making. We're not going to solve them overnight. But there are things we can do right now to put people back to work right now. There are things we should do right now to give the economy the jolt that it needs. So that's why I sent to Congress the "American Jobs Act."

Keep in mind, Asheville, this is the kind of bill containing the kinds of proposals that in the past have received support from Democrats and Republicans. It's completely paid for by asking our wealthiest citizens, folks making more than a million dollars a year, to pay their fair share.

Independent economists—not my economists, but independent economists—have said this jobs bill would create nearly 2 million jobs. That's not my opinion. It's not the opinion of folks who work for me. It's the opinion of people who evaluate these kinds of things for a living. It says this bill will help put people back to work and give our economy a boost right away.

But apparently none of this matters to the Republicans in the Senate, because last week they got together to block this bill. They said no to putting teachers and construction workers back on the job. They said no to rebuilding our roads and our bridges and our airports. They said no to cutting taxes for middle class families and small businesses, when all they've been doing is cutting taxes for the wealthiest Americans. They said no to helping veterans find jobs.

Essentially, they said no to you, because it turns out one poll found that 63 percent of Americans support the ideas in this jobs bill. So 63 percent of Americans support the jobs bill that I put forward; a hundred percent of Republicans in the Senate voted against it. That doesn't make any sense, does it?

Audience members. No!

The President. No, it does not.

Now, it turns out that the Republicans have a plan too. I want to be fair. They call—they put forward this plan last week. They called it the "Real American Jobs Act." The "real one," that's what they called it, just in case you were wondering. [*Laughter*] So let's take a look at what the Republican American jobs act looks like. It turns out the Republican plan boils down to a few basic ideas: they want to gut regulations, they want to let Wall Street do whatever it wants, they want to drill more, and they want to repeal health care reform. That's their jobs plan.

So let's do a little comparison here. The Republican plan says that what's been standing in the way between us and full employment are laws that keep companies from polluting as much as they want. On the other hand, our plan puts teachers, construction workers, firefighters, and police officers back on the job.

Their plan says the big problem we have is that we helped to get 30 million Americans health insurance. They figure we should throw those folks off the health insurance rolls; somehow that's going to help people find jobs. Our plan says we're better off if every small business and worker in America gets a tax cut, and that's what's in my jobs bill.

Their plan says we should go back to the good old days before the financial crisis when Wall Street was writing its own rules. They want to roll back all the reforms that we've put into place. Our plan says we need to make it easier for small businesses to grow and hire and push this economy forward.

All right, so you've gotten a sense—you got their plan, and then we got my plan. My plan says we're going to put teachers back in the classroom, construction workers back to work rebuilding America, rebuilding our schools, tax cuts for small businesses, tax cuts for hiring veterans, tax cuts if you give your worker a raise. That's my plan.

And then you got their plan, which is, let's have dirtier air, dirtier water, less people with health insurance.

All right, so, so far at least, I feel better about my plan. [*Laughter*] But let's admit I'm a little biased. So remember those independent economists who said our plan would create jobs, maybe as many as almost 2 million jobs, grow the economy by as much as 2 percent? So one of the same economists that took a look at our plan took a look at the Republican plan, and they said, well, this won't do much to help the economy in the short term; it could actually cost us jobs. We could actually lose jobs with their plan.

So I'll let you decide which plan is the real "American Jobs Act."

Audience members. Four more years! Four more years! Four more years!

The President. Look, I appreciate the "4 more years," but right now I'm thinking about the next 13 months. Because, yes, we've got an election coming up, but that election is a long ways away, and a lot of folks can't wait. A lot of folks are living paycheck to paycheck. A lot of folks are living week to week. You've got kids right now who've lost their teachers because at the local level you ended up having layoffs. You've got bridges right now that are crumbling and deteriorating. So we don't have time to wait. And we've got a choice right now—right now.

Look, I want to work with Republicans on ways to create jobs right now. And where they've got a decent idea I'm happy to work with them. Just last week, we passed a bipartisan trade agreement with Korea that will allow us to sell more goods overseas and support almost 70,000 jobs here at home. Because my attitude is, if we're buying Hyundais and Kias, I want them buying some Fords and Chryslers and Chevys.

So if they're serious about creating jobs, I'm ready to go. I don't think anybody doubts that I have gone out of my way to try to find areas of cooperation with these Republicans. In fact, some of you have been mad at me for trying too hard to cooperate with them, haven't you? Some of you—I get some of your letters and your e-mails. You're all like, why are you cooperating with them all the time? Because it can't be all about politics; sometimes we've got to try to actually get something done. And so I'm eager to see them stand up with a serious approach to putting people back to work.

It's time to focus less on satisfying some wing of the party and more on commonsense ideas that we can take to put people to work right now and help the middle class and help people get into the middle class, because there are a whole bunch of folks who are hurting out there and have never gotten the opportunity.

So we're going to give Members of Congress another chance to step up to the plate and do the right thing. Kay and I, we've decided, let's go ahead and let them do the right thing one more time. We're going to give them another

chance to do their jobs by looking after your jobs.

So this week, I'm asking Members of Congress to vote—what we're going to do is we're going to break up my jobs bill. Maybe they just couldn't understand the whole thing all at once. [*Laughter*] So we're going to break it up into bite-size pieces so they can take a thoughtful approach to this legislation.

So this week, I'm going to ask Members of Congress to vote on one component of the plan, which is whether we should put hundreds of thousands of teachers back in the classroom and cops back on the street and firefighters back to work. So Members of Congress will have a chance to decide: What kind of future do our kids deserve? Should we stand up for men and women who are often digging into their own pockets to buy school supplies, when we know that the education of our children is going to determine our future as a nation?

They're going to have a chance to decide: Do we want to make sure that we're looking after the men and women who protect our communities every day, our first-responders, our firefighters, our police officers? And then, after they've taken that vote, we're going to give Members of Congress a chance to vote on whether we're going to put construction workers back to work. Should they be just sitting around while roads and bridges and runways fall apart, or should we put them back to work doing the work that America needs done?

After that, we'll give them a chance to decide whether unemployed Americans should continue to struggle, or whether we should give them the experience and support they need to get back in the workforce and build a better life. And we'll ask them to take a stand on whether we should ask people like me to pay a little more so middle class families and small businesses can pay a little less and end up creating the kinds of jobs we need in this economy.

So those are the choices that Members of Congress are going to face in the coming weeks. And if they vote against these proposals again—like I said, maybe they just didn't understand the whole thing, so we're breaking it up into pieces. If they vote against taking steps that we know will put Americans back to work right now——

Audience members. Right now!

The President. ——right now——

Audience members. Right now!

The President. ——then they're not going to have to answer to me. They're going to have to answer to you. They're going to have to come down to North Carolina and tell kids why they can't have their teachers back. They're going to come down to North Carolina and look those construction workers in the eye and tell them why they can't get to work doing the work that America needs done. They're going to have to come down here and explain to working families why their taxes are going up while the richest Americans and largest corporations keep getting sweet deals in the Tax Code. They're going to have to come down and explain to you why they don't have an answer for how we're putting Americans to work right now.

And if they support the Republican plan, they'll have to explain to you why they'd rather deny health care to millions of Americans and let corporations and banks write their own rules instead of supporting proposals that we know will create jobs right now.

So that's where all of you come in. Some of these folks just aren't getting the message, so I need you to send them a message. I need you to make your voices heard. I need you to give Congress a piece of your mind. These Members of Congress work for you. If they're not delivering, it's time to let them know. It's time to get on the phone and write a letter, tweet, pay a visit. Tell your elected leaders to do the right thing. Remind them what's at stake: put-ting people back to work, restoring economic security for middle class families and helping create a ladder for folks who aren't middle class yet to get into the middle class, rebuilding an economy where hard work is valued and re-sponsibility is rewarded, building an economy that lasts for the future and for our children.

If we want to actually lower the deficit and invest in our future, if we want the best roads and best bridges and best airports here in the United States, if we want to continue to invest in our technology and our basic science and re-search so that we can continue to invent new drugs and make sure the new cars of the future that are running on electricity are made right here in North Carolina and made right here in America, if we want to do all those things, then we got to step up. We got to get to work. We got to get busy right now.

We can't do nothing. Too many folks are hurting out there to do nothing. We need to act right now. We are not a people who sit by and do nothing when things aren't right. We're Americans. If something is not working, we go out there and fix it. We stick with it until the problem is fixed. That's the spirit we need to muster right now.

Let's meet this moment. Let's get to work. Let's show the world once again why the Unit-ed States is the greatest country on Earth.

God bless you. God bless the United States. And thank you, Asheville. Thank you, North Carolina.

NOTE: The President spoke at 10:53 a.m. In his remarks, he referred to Carrie C. Hagan, daughter of Sen. Hagan.

Remarks at West Wilkes High School in Millers Creek, North Carolina
October 17, 2011

The President. Hello, Millers Creek! It is good to be here in Millers Creek. It is great to be back in North Carolina. You know, if—I know it's a little warm out here, so if anybody wants to take their jacket off, please feel free. Some of you guys loosen your ties there.

I am thrilled to be here with all of you. I want to thank all the Blackhawks who are here. I want to thank the Blackhawks band. I want to thank the Struttin' Hawks.

I want to especially thank Dr. Stephen Laws for the great introduction, but also for his service. He's about to retire soon, so give him a big round of applause. The Blackhawks principal, Dr. Wayne Shepherd, is here. And I know that there are a few Mountaineers here as well, so—[*applause*]. I also want to thank your Lieutenant Governor, Walter Dalton, and the mayor of North Wilkesboro, Robert Johnson.

Now, I'm down here today because I decided it was time to get out of Washington. I wanted to hit the open road and come visit some of the most beautiful parts of this great country of ours. We just had an unbelievable drive. We came across from Asheville, stopped in Marion for some barbecue, went to the general store in Boone to buy some candy. Halloween is coming up, so I had to stock up a little bit. [*Laughter*] Saw the mountains, saw some lakes, saw all the wonderful people in this part of the country.

And somebody asked me, why do you come back to North Carolina so much? I say, I—there is just something—the people of North Carolina are so nice. They are nice people, they are gracious, and they are kind. And even the folks who don't vote for me are nice. So I love North Carolina. But I also thought it would be good to hear from all of you, because it seems as if your voices aren't being heard in Washington right now.

This is a tough time for a lot of Americans. Here in North Carolina, a lot of folks have spent months looking for work. Others are doing their best just to scrape by. You give up nights with the family to save on gas or make the mortgage, folks postponing their retirement so they can send their kids to college.

Now, I think we all understand most of these problems were not caused overnight. We've been dealing for—some of these problems for a decade now: manufacturing leaving America to go overseas; we've had a health care system that didn't work and put burdens on families and businesses; we haven't had an energy policy in this country that makes sense and frees ourselves from dependence on foreign oil; our schools haven't done everything they need to to make sure our young people

are trained and colleges become more affordable for too many young people.

So there are a lot of challenges that we won't solve overnight because they weren't caused overnight. It's going to take time to rebuild an America where hard work is valued and responsibility is rewarded. It's going to take time to rebuild an America where we restore a sense of security for middle class families and opportunity for folks who are trying to get into the middle class, an America with an economy that's built to last and built to compete, where we are outeducating and outinnovating and outbuilding every other nation on Earth. That's what we've got to build. And we've got to build an economy that works for everybody, not just some people. Not just the folks at the top, but for everybody.

Rebuilding this America will take time. But there are things we can do right now to put people back to work, things we can do right now to help middle class Americans get ahead, things we can do right now to give our economy the jolt that it needs.

So this is why I sent Congress awhile back the "American Jobs Act."

Audience member. Pass this bill!

The President. Now—pass this bill. We need to pass this bill. Let me tell you about this bill. Somebody was just asking me about this bill. I said, look, this is the kind of bill that in the past would have been supported by Democrats and Republicans. It's completely paid for. It asks folks like me, who have been incredibly blessed, to pay a little bit more so that—to pay our fair share, folks making a million dollars or more—so that we can help folks who are struggling to get by.

Independent economists have said this jobs bill would create nearly 2 million jobs, grow the economy by nearly 2 extra percentage points. And that's not—that is not my opinion. That is not the opinion of somebody who works for me. That's the opinion of people whose job it is to analyze these things. Economists have said this would put people back to work.

But there are some folks in Washington who just aren't listening. Last week, all the Republicans in the Senate got together and blocked the jobs bill. They refused to even debate it. Now, keep in mind, one poll showed that about 63 percent of Americans support the ideas in this jobs bill. So why is it that a hundred percent of Republicans in the Senate voted against it? It doesn't make any sense. It doesn't make any sense.

Somebody asked me—we had a wonderful reporter come here, Dave Wagner from Charlotte, and he asked me, well, people tell me this is kind of a Republican area, so why would you come here instead of going to where there are a whole lot of Democrats?

I said, look, this is an American jobs act. It's not the Democratic jobs act. It's not the Republican jobs act. It's the "American Jobs Act." We need to pass it.

Now, I want to be fair here. So to be fair, it turns out the Republicans, they've got their plan too. Ours is called the "American Jobs Act," so they started out calling theirs the "Real American Jobs Act." I said, all right, you don't get points for originality, but let's see what you got. [*Laughter*]

We took a look. It turns out the Republicans' jobs plan boils down to these ideas: they want to gut environmental regulations, they want to roll back Wall Street reform so that we end up with the same financial system we had that got us into this mess in the first place, and they want to repeal health care reform so that 30 million people won't have health insurance. That is what they call their "Real American Jobs Act." It's inspiring stuff. [*Laughter*]

So let's do a comparison. We can do a comparison here. The Republican plan says that what's standing between us and full employment are laws that keep companies from polluting our air and our water. Our plan, on the other hand, says let's put construction workers back to work rebuilding our roads and bridges and schools. Let's put teachers back in the classroom where they belong. Let's make sure that we're not laying off police officers and firefighters, and let's help veterans get a job after they have defended this country.

Their plan says we'll be better off if 30 million Americans don't have health insurance. Our plan says we'll be better off if we give a tax cut to virtually every small business and every worker in America. Their plan says we need to go back to the old days when Wall Street wrote its own rules. Our plan says we need to make it easier for small businesses to grow and to hire and to push this economy forward.

Now, remember I said—here's the kicker. Remember I said that these independent economists had evaluated our plan. We presented it, not folks who work for us. We said, all right, what do you think this will do? They said, this will create up to 2 million jobs; that will grow the economy. One of the same economists took a look at the Republican plan, and you know what they said? They said, well, this isn't going to do much to help the economy in the short term; it could actually lead up to losing jobs, not gaining them. So much for their jobs plan.

So I'll let you decide which is the real American jobs plan. Because the fact is we face a choice in this country right now. I want to work with Republicans in any way possible to create jobs right now. And the fact is—let me say this. Let me say this. I have bent over backwards. I have shown myself to be willing again and again to try to cooperate with Republicans. I've tried so hard to cooperate with Republicans, Democrats have been getting mad at me. [*Laughter*] But the reason I have is because my attitude is, when we're in a time that's difficult, we can't afford to play politics. When we're in a time that's difficult, we should try to find common ground.

Just last week, Congress passed a bipartisan trade agreement with Korea that will allow us to sell more goods into that country. Now, we've got a bunch of Hyundais and Kias here. I think that's fine. But I want to see some Koreans driving Fords and Chryslers and Chevys—open up those markets.

So my attitude is, it's been—it's way overdue for us to stop trying to satisfy some branch of the party and take some commonsense steps to help America and to create jobs and to help the middle class.

And that's why, even though they said no the first time, we're going to give them another chance. I think maybe the first time, because we had it all in one bill, maybe they didn't study it all properly. Maybe they didn't know what they were voting against. So we're going to chop it up into some bite-size pieces and give them another chance to look out for your jobs instead of looking out for their own jobs.

So first thing we're going to do is, this week Congress is scheduled to take a vote on whether we're going to put hundreds of thousands of police officers and firefighters and teachers back on the job. Well, are we going to help State and local governments who are under a severe budget crunch make sure that they are not laying off teachers at a time when we know we've got to excel in education?

All over the country and right here in North Carolina folks are losing their jobs. Nearly 2,000 classroom positions have been eliminated this school year. And here at West Wilkes High, I know some teachers weren't rehired, you've had to increase class sizes, and there's almost no money for things like textbooks. This makes no sense. I can tell you the last thing a superintendent wants to do is to lose good teachers. Your Governor has been fighting against education cuts as well. It's unfair to our kids. It undermines our future.

How are we going to compete when countries like Korea and Germany who are hiring teachers and preparing their kids for the global economy, and we're laying off teachers left and right? One North Carolina teacher said, "We didn't cause the poor economy; if anything, we built the good parts." And he's absolutely right. Our teachers built the good parts of this economy. They give our kids a chance to compete. They give our kids a future. That's why we've got to look out for them. And this jobs bill does it.

My jobs plan would mean more than 13,000 education jobs here in North Carolina. So when the Senate votes this week, you all have to tell them it's time to put our teachers back to work.

We're going to give Members of Congress a chance to vote on the other components of the bill, so we're going to ask them to vote on whether construction workers should sit idly by while China is building the newest roads and bridges and airports or whether we should put our construction workers back to work rebuilding America so that we can compete in the 21st century. That's a choice that Congress is going to have to make.

Congress is going to have to make a decision whether they decide to help unemployed Americans who are struggling or whether we should make sure that we give them the experience and support that they need to get back in the workforce and build a better life.

We'll ask Congress whether we should stand pat and let people like me take advantage of corporate loopholes and pay less in taxes, or should we ask folks like me to pay my fair share so that we give tax cuts to middle class families and small businesses?

These are the choices that Members of Congress are going to have to make in the coming weeks. And if they vote against these proposals, if they vote against taking steps that we know will put Americans back to work, they've got to explain not to me, but to you, why they're doing it. They don't have to answer to me, but they do have to answer to you. You sent them there. They're going to have to come down here to North Carolina and tell kids why they can't have their teachers back. They're going to have to look construction workers in the eye and tell them why they shouldn't be rebuilding roads and bridges and airports. They're going to have to explain to working families why their taxes are going up while the richest Americans and largest corporations are getting a sweet deal.

So that's where you guys come in. Some of these folks are just not getting the message, so I've got to make sure your voices are heard. I need you to give Congress a piece of your mind. Tell these Members of Congress that they don't work for special interests, they don't work for lobbies, they work for you. And if they're not delivering, you need to let them know. And I don't know whether you're going to get on the phone or you're going to tweet them or write them a letter or pay them a visit, but tell them to do the right thing. Tell them what's at stake here.

There are too many of our fellow Americans hurting, and you can't stand by and do nothing. Now is the time to act. And by the way, there's going to be an election, and we're going to have a convention right here in North Carolina. But that convention is 11 months away. The election is 13 months away. And folks can't afford to wait that long.

They can't sit around just listening to a bunch of political arguments. They need action, and they need it now. Because folks are living paycheck to paycheck. There are folks who are living week to week. And I don't accept the idea that in the face of that kind of hardship that we're going to stand by and do nothing. That's not who we are. We are Americans. And you know what, we keep working at things until we get them fixed.

Yes, we had a problem with the financial crisis, and the economy is not where it needs to be, but we can fix it. We just got to stay on it. We got to be persistent. We got to keep on trying things until folks are back to work and the economy is growing again. And we've got to muster that spirit right now: a "can do" spirit. Not a "no, we can't" spirit, but a "yes, we can" spirit. We don't need a "why we can't" attitude, we need a "why we can" attitude.

I know that sometimes everybody watches television, and you see what's going on in Washington, and you get discouraged. But I just want you to remember that we've been through tougher times before. This is a country that's been through a Revolutionary War, a Civil War. We got through slavery. We got through a depression. We got through World War I. We got through World War II. We have been through tougher times before. We are going to get through this, and we're going to get through it together. Because Americans don't quit.

So let's meet this moment. Let's get to work. And let's show the world once again why the United States of America is the greatest nation on Earth.

God bless you. God bless North Carolina. God bless the United States of America.

NOTE: The President spoke at 5:08 p.m. In his remarks, he referred to Stephen C. Laws, superintendent, Wilkes County Schools; and Gov. Beverly E. Perdue of North Carolina.

Statement on the Death of Elouise P. Cobell
October 17, 2011

Michelle and I were saddened to hear about the passing of Elouise Cobell yesterday. Elouise spoke out when she saw that the Interior Department had failed to account for billions of dollars that they were supposed to collect on behalf of more than 300,000 of her fellow Native Americans. Because she did, I was able to sign into law a piece of legislation that finally provided a measure of justice to those who were affected. That law also creates a scholarship fund to give more Native Americans access to higher education and give tribes more control over their own lands. Elouise helped to strengthen the government-to-government relationship with Indian Country, and our thoughts and prayers are with her family and all those who mourn her passing.

NOTE: The statement referred to Public Law No. 111–291, the Claims Resolution Act of 2010, which was approved on December 8, 2010.

Remarks Prior to a Roundtable Discussion With Educators in Jamestown, North Carolina
October 18, 2011

Hope you're enjoying the beautiful North Carolina day. We are here to talk to both teachers and soon-to-be teachers and folks who are training teachers and talking about the importance of education to the economy.

I think all of us are aware at this point that, in this 21st-century global economy, how well we do as a country is going to depend on how well we train our young people. And it starts early. So we're at a terrific early childhood education program here at the community college, where people who are interested in training very young children are getting the skills that they need. But we've also got a couple of teachers: one in fourth grade, one in ninth grade.

And so one of the concerns that I've had over the course of the last several months—in fact, the last couple of years—are the layoffs that we've seen in education and the cutbacks we've seen in education all across the country. States and local governments are under a big crunch. And at precisely the time when we need to be emphasizing education and putting our resources into education, we're seeing cutbacks all across the board. Teachers are losing their jobs. Schools are having to cut back on vital programs that are helping young people.

And the "American Jobs Act," the bill that I put before Congress, would help to curb some of those trends. What we do is to provide $30 billion to make sure that we've got teachers back in the classrooms, to make sure that we're not seeing additional teacher layoffs, that wonderful programs such as the ones that are taking place here are properly and adequately funded, and to make sure that, at the same time, we're also rebuilding some of the schools

around the country that are in a bad state of repair and where young people aren't getting the kind of support that they need in order to achieve.

So I'm going to spend a little time having a conversation here with the teachers and soon-to-be teachers. They're going to talk about their experiences, what's working, what they're excited about, but also the concerns that they've seen in terms of cutbacks in education.

And I hope that Members of Congress are going to be doing a little bit of listening to teachers and educators. We have a tendency to say great things about how important education is in the abstract, but we don't always put our money where our mouth is. And it's absolutely critical right now to make sure that we don't see the kinds of cutbacks that we've been seeing. If that becomes a long-term trend, we're going to fall behind countries like China, Korea, Germany, that are continually making significant investments in teachers.

So I want to thank all of you guys for taking the time to join me. I very much appreciate what you're doing.

NOTE: The President spoke at 10:01 a.m. in the Children's Center at Guilford Technical Community College. Audio was not available for verification of the content of these remarks.

Remarks at Guilford Technical Community College in Jamestown
October 18, 2011

The President. Thank you very much. Everybody, please have a seat. Have a seat. Hello, Jamestown! It is great to be here in North Carolina. Great to be here at the Ragsdale YMCA.

I want to first of all thank Linda for the outstanding introduction. Give her a big round of applause. I want to also acknowledge your Congressman, Mel Watt, in the house. Mel is doing an outstanding job each and every day. I also want to acknowledge your mayor, Keith Volz, for the fine work that he's doing. He invited me back down here. He said there are some pretty good golf courses down here and

some fine restaurants, so I'm going to have to sample both the next time I'm here.

I had a chance to talk to Linda and a group of other teachers before I came out here. And I just want to say thank you to her, not only for the introduction, but also for teaching. I got a chance to learn about the extraordinary work that Guilford Technical Community College is doing to train new teachers and place them in schools where kids need them the most. And one of the best ways to make a difference in the life of our Nation is to make a difference in the life of every child. So I want to thank all the teachers who are in the audience for answering the call, because you are making our Nation stronger.

Now, you may have heard we're taking a little road trip this week. It's a chance to get out of Washington. [*Laughter*] I must admit I'm traveling not in the usual RV. The bus we got parked outside is—Secret Service did a full going over, so it's decked out pretty good. [*Laughter*] But it's a wonderful opportunity to get out of Washington and hit the road. We stopped for a little North Carolina barbecue and sweet tea along the way. We—some hush puppies. Don't tell Michelle exactly what was on the menu. [*Laughter*]

But the main reason we're out here, in addition to seeing the extraordinary views and meeting the wonderful people—there's just something about North Carolina. People are just gracious and kind. Even the folks who don't vote for me are nice to me. [*Laughter*] And I—that's just a—that's a nice thing about this State.

The most important thing I wanted to do was to hear from people like you, because it doesn't seem like your voices are being heard in Washington right now. Times are tough for a lot of Americans. And here in North Carolina, there are a lot of folks who have been spending months looking for work and still haven't found it yet. A lot of people are doing their best just to get by. Maybe they've been able to keep their job, but hours have been cut back or some of their pay and benefits have been rolled back; people who are deciding, you know what, we can't afford taking that night out with the family because we've got to save on gas or we've got to make the mortgage or we've got to postpone our retirement to make sure that our child can go to college.

It's tough. It's hard. And I think most Americans know that our economic problems weren't caused overnight, so they recognize they won't be solved overnight. Even before the most recent economic crisis—[*applause*]— a lot of these challenges took a decade to build up, in some cases longer than a decade. Before the worst financial crisis since the Great Depression, wages and incomes had been flat for the vast majority of Americans for a decade. So

people were struggling even before the crisis hit.

What that means is it's going to take time for us to rebuild an America where hard work and responsibility are rewarded. It will take time to rebuild an America where we restore security and opportunity for folks who are in the middle class or trying to get into the middle class. It's going to take time to rebuild an economy that's built to last and built to compete, an economy that works for everybody, not just for folks at the top.

Rebuilding this America where everybody has got a fair shake and everybody gives their fair share, an economy where you know if you do the right thing and you're looking after your family and you're working hard and you educate yourself and you're educating your kids and you're contributing back to the community, that you know that you will be able to enjoy that piece of the American Dream—restoring that economy will take some time. But we are going to get it done, Jamestown. We are going to keep fighting, and we're going to keep working to put people back to work, to help middle class Americans get ahead and to give our economy the jolt that it needs.

There are things we can do right now to help our economy. And that's why I sent Congress the "American Jobs Act." Now, this is a jobs bill with proposals of the sort that in the past have been supported by Democrats and Republicans. It's paid for by asking our wealthiest citizens, folks who make more than a million dollars a year, to pay their fair share. Independent economists have said this jobs bill would create nearly 2 million jobs. That's not my opinion, that's not the opinion of people who work for me. The people who study the economy for a living are telling us that this jobs bill would put people back to work right away and grow our economy at a time when the recovery has weakened.

But some folks in Washington don't seem to be listening. They don't seem to be listening. Just last week, all the Republicans in the Senate got together and blocked this jobs bill. They refused to even debate it. Now, keep in mind, one poll found that 63 percent of

Americans support the ideas in this jobs bill, but a hundred percent of Republicans in the Senate voted against it. So the majority of the American people think it makes sense for us to put teachers back in the classroom and construction workers back to work and tax breaks for small businesses and tax breaks for folks who are hiring veterans, but we got a hundred percent "no" from Republicans in the Senate.

Now, that doesn't make any sense. Some people asked me yesterday why I was visiting Republican areas of North Carolina. I said, well, first of all, it's because I just like North Carolina. [*Laughter*] Second of all, I'm not the Democratic President or the Republican President, I'm the President. And third of all, I don't care if you're a Republican or a Democrat, because we're all Americans, and we are in this together. We don't need a Republican jobs act or a Democratic jobs act, we need a jobs act. We need to put people back to work right now.

As I said, the ideas we put forward are ideas that in the past have been supported by Democrats and Republicans. So the question is, what makes it different this time, other than that I proposed it?

Now, let me try to be fair. The Republicans did put out their own jobs bill. They called it the "Real American Jobs Act." [*Laughter*] So they don't get points for originality—[*laughter*]—but they put out the plan. And I said, okay, let's see what you got, because I want—nobody has a bigger interest than me in seeing Democrats and Republicans cooperate to get some stuff done. All right? I want that to happen.

So I said, let's see what you got. And here's what the plan boils down to: We're going to gut environmental regulations, we're going to drill more, we're going to roll back Wall Street reform, and we're going to repeal health care reform. Now, that's a plan, but it's not a jobs plan. And if you're wondering, I mean, we can just do a little bit of comparison shopping right now. We'll lift the hood and kick the tires and see our plan and their plan.

The Republican plan says that what's standing between us and full employment is that

we're preventing companies from polluting our air and our water too much. We, on the other hand, have said that—let's put teachers back in the classroom here in North Carolina and all across the country who've been laid off because budgets have been tight at the State or local level. Let's put construction workers back to work rebuilding roads and bridges and schools all across North Carolina and all across the country. And let's put veterans back on the job. All right, so those are two choices.

Their plan says we'll be better off if we deny 30 million Americans affordable health care choices and kick young people off their parents' health insurance plans. Our plan says we're better off if we give virtually every small business and worker in America a tax cut so that they've got more money in their pockets to hire more workers and to spend more at those wonderful restaurants that the mayor talked about.

Their plan says we need to go back to the good old days before the financial crisis when Wall Street wrote its own rules. Our plan says we need to make it easier for small businesses on Main Street to grow and to hire and to push the economy forward.

Now—so there's a contrast in approaches here. But here's the kicker. Remember that group of economists who said our jobs plan would create jobs? Well, one of those same economists took a look at the Republican plan and said that it could actually cost us jobs, that it wouldn't do much to help the economy right now when folks are hurting so bad.

So I—look, we can have an argument about how much regulation we should have. We can have an argument, if you want, about health care. I think we did the right thing. But don't pretend—[*applause*]—but you can't pretend that creating dirtier air and water for our kids and fewer people on health care and less accountability on Wall Street is a jobs plan.

I think more teachers in the classroom is a jobs plan, more construction workers rebuilding our schools is a jobs plan, tax cuts for small-business owners and working families is a jobs plan.

That's the choice we face. And it's up to you to decide which plan is the real "American Jobs Act."

I want to emphasize, I want to work with Republicans on ways to create jobs right now. I'm open to any serious idea. Just last week, Congress passed, on a bipartisan basis, a trade agreement that will allow us to start selling more goods into Korea. Because we buy an awful lot of Hyundais and Kias; I want them to buy some Fords and Chevys and Chryslers. Wherever we have the possibility to work together to move this economy forward, I'm going to seize on that opportunity. That's the kind of progress on the economy we can keep on making. But to do so, we've got to focus less on trying to satisfy one wing of one party. We've got to focus more on doing what it takes to help the American people.

And that's why we're going to give folks in Congress another chance. [*Laughter*] They said no the first time, but we're going to give them another chance to listen to you, to step up to the plate and do the right thing. We are going to give them another chance to do their jobs and look out for your jobs.

And it may be that just the bill was too big the first time; there was just too much stuff, and they weren't clear about what the jobs act would do. It was confusing to them. So what we're going to do is we're going to break it up into separate pieces—[*laughter*]—and we're going to let them vote on each piece, one at a time. That way you can be crystal clear on where you stand on all the elements of the jobs bill.

The first vote that we asked Congress to take is scheduled for later this week. It's a vote that would put hundreds of thousands of police officers back on the beat, firefighters back on the job, and teachers like Linda back in the classroom where they belong. All right? So that's the first part.

All over the country, budget cuts are forcing schools to lay off teachers in startling numbers. Here in North Carolina, nearly 2,000 classroom positions have been eliminated for this school year. I visited a school in Millers Creek yesterday where they've had to increase class sizes. There's almost no money for things like textbooks.

I can tell you, the last thing a superintendent wants to do is lose teachers. Your Governor has been fighting these education cuts. But it is unfair to our kids and it undermines our future not to invest in education.

I had the President of South Korea here, and they are hiring teachers in droves. He's importing teachers from other countries to teach their kids. Their attitude is, we want our kids learning English when they're in first grade. And we're laying off teachers here in North Carolina? We're not going to be able to compete. Our kids will fall behind.

One North Carolina teacher said: "We didn't cause the poor economy. If anything, we built the good parts." And that teacher is absolutely right. Our teachers build the good parts of our economy. It gives our children the skills they need to compete. It gives our children a future that is bright. We've got to invest in our education system. So our plan would mean about 13,000 education jobs right here in North Carolina alone. That's why I need you all to tell the Senate, let's put our teachers back to work.

All right, so that's part number one. Part number two: We're going to give Members of Congress a chance to vote on whether our construction workers should sit around doing nothing while China builds the newest airports and the fastest railroads. That doesn't seem to me like the American way. We used to always have the best stuff. Right? People from all around the world would come to America to see the Golden Gate Bridge and the Hoover Dam and Grand Central station and the interstate highways. We have dropped in terms of infrastructure in this country. We're no longer number one. And that's not how we built ourselves into a great economic superpower.

So Congress will have a chance to say whether unemployed Americans should continue to struggle or whether we are going to put them back to work making our schools state of the art, making sure that our roads and bridges aren't crumbling. They're going to have a chance to vote on whether or not we're going to give people who are long-term unemployed a chance to get back on the job and reform our unemployment insurance system and build a better life. They're going to get a chance to take a stand on whether we should ask people like me to pay our fair share so that middle class families and small businesses can get a tax cut.

I want to—let me just say this. I'm going to make a point here about taxes, because there's been a lot of misinformation out there. I was watching the football game last night, and they had some ad that didn't really make much sense. [*Laughter*] So let me just be crystal clear just in case your friends or neighbors ask about this. What we have said is, in order to pay for the jobs plan and to close our deficit, we should ask the very wealthiest Americans, top 2 percent, to pay a little bit more. I can afford it. Warren Buffett, he can afford it. And the fact of the matter is, is that some of the wealthiest Americans pay a lower tax rate than middle class Americans.

Now—so the question is, are we going to set up a tax system that is fair, that helps us shrink the deficit, helps us to pay off our debts, and helps put people back to work? But I want to be clear: The vast majority of Americans would see a tax cut under this jobs bill. We've been cutting taxes. We haven't been raising taxes, we've been cutting taxes. And we can continue to keep taxes low for middle class and working families if we ask those at the very top to do their fair share. And a lot of them are willing to do it if they feel like it's going to make the country stronger and reduce our deficit and put people back to work.

So don't be bamboozled. [*Laughter*] Don't fall for this notion that somehow the jobs act is proposing to raise your taxes. It's just not true. Under this—here's what will happen. If we don't pass the "American Jobs Act," if we do not pass the provision in there that extends the payroll tax cut that we passed in December, most people here, your taxes will go up by a thousand dollars. So voting no against the jobs bill is voting in favor of middle class families' income taxes going up. And that's a fact. Don't take my word for it; all the reporters here, they can check on the facts on this thing. That's the truth.

And I've got to emphasize this: When you talk to most people who've done well, who've been blessed by this country, they're patriots. They want to do the right thing. They're willing to do more. They want their money well spent; they want to make sure that it's not being wasted. That's why we cut a trillion dollars out of the Federal budget this summer. It's why I'm proposing to cut more to close the deficit. But people are willing to do a little bit more because everybody understands we are in this together. That's how America has always moved forward.

So look, here's the bottom line. Congress has a choice to make in the coming weeks. If they vote against the proposals I'm talking about, if they vote against taking steps that we know will put Americans back to work right now, they don't have to answer to me, they're going to have to answer to you. They're going to have to come down here to North Carolina and tell kids why they can't have their teachers back in the classroom. They're going to have to tell those construction workers, look them in the eye and say, you know what, sorry, we can't afford to rebuild those broken-down roads and those crumbling bridges. They're going to have to explain to working families why their taxes are going up while the richest Americans and the largest corporations keep on getting a sweet deal.

And that's where you come in. You are the ones who are going to be able to persuade them to think differently. We need your voices heard. I need you to give Congress a piece of your mind. Mel Watt's already doing fine, so you don't need to talk to Mel. He's on the program. But these Members of Congress, they work for you. And if they're not delivering, it's time you let them know. You've got to get on the phone or pay them a visit or write them a letter or tweet, whatever you do—[*laughter*]—and remind them to do the right thing.

Remind them of what's at stake here. Remind them that "no, we can't" is no way to face tough times. When a depression hit, we didn't say, "No, we can't." When World War II came, we didn't say, "No, we can't." Our grandparents and great-grandparents, they didn't say: "Nothing we can do about this. Let's just spend all our time arguing in Washington." They didn't say, "It's too hard." They didn't say, "We give up." They said, "Let's roll up our sleeves, let's fight back." And America won. When the space race started, Kennedy didn't say, "We can't go to the Moon; that's too far." He said: "Come on, America. Let's go." America won. We can win the space race. When we confront tough times, we don't give in to what is, we think about what ought to be.

There are too many Americans who are hurting right now for us to just sit by and do nothing. Now is the time to act. Now is the time to say, "Yes, we can." We can create jobs. We can restore the middle class. We can reduce our deficits. We can build an economy that works for everybody. We are not a people who just sit around doing nothing when things

aren't right. We are Americans, and we stand up and we decide that the problem's going to be fixed. And that's the spirit we need to muster right now.

Let's meet this moment. Let's get to work. And let's remind everybody just why the United States of America is the greatest country on Earth.

Thank you. God bless you. God bless North Carolina. God bless the United States of America. Thank you.

NOTE: The President spoke at 11:20 a.m. at the Mary Perry Ragsdale Family YMCA. In his remarks, he referred to Jamestown, NC, teacher Linda Phillips; Gov. Beverly E. Perdue of North Carolina; President Lee Myung-bak of South Korea; and Warren E. Buffett, chief executive officer and chairman, Berkshire Hathaway Inc.

Remarks at Greensville County High School in Emporia, Virginia
October 18, 2011

The President. Hello! Thank you. Hello, Eagles! Well, it is good to be here. Thank you very much. It's great to be back in Virginia. It is great to be here at Greensville County High School.

I want to thank Jami Clements not only for the gracious introduction, but congratulate her on being selected as Greensville County Teacher of the Year. We're proud of everything that Jami has accomplished here at the school, but we also want to thank her for her service in our Armed Forces, and that is an extraordinary combination of service: teaching and serving. And I know that the students feel very lucky to have her in the classroom. And I like that she's teaching biology, because we need some scientists out there.

In addition, I want to acknowledge, first of all, the superintendent of schools, Philip Worrell. Give your superintendent a big round of applause. And I want to acknowledge the principal, Wayne Scott. And finally, I want to thank your mayor, Mr. Sam Adams, for being with us here today.

Now, some of you may have heard we're taking a little road trip at the beginning of this week. The RV is a little bigger than most. [*Laughter*] We've got it parked outside. But I decided it was time to get out of Washington and hit the open road. So we landed in Asheville, North Carolina—and that truly is God's country—and we drove through beautiful mountain roads and stopped for some barbecue and a little sweet tea. And we went to Boone County, North Carolina, and they had a general store there with big barrels of candy, and so we stocked up for Halloween. And don't tell Michelle—[*laughter*]—but we bought a lot of candy. [*Laughter*]

But most importantly, the reason that we have been traveling on the road is because I wanted to hear from folks like you. It doesn't seem like your voices are heard enough in Washington. They don't seem to be listening. So I figured if I brought the press here, then they could hear you.

Because times are tough for a lot of Americans. Here in Virginia, there are a lot of folks who've spent months, maybe some folks spent years, looking for work. Others are doing their best just to get by. Maybe they're giving up going out to a restaurant; they just can't afford it. They've got to save on gas. End of the month they're worried about making the mortgage payment. Some people are postponing retirement to make sure that their children can go to college. Hours have been cut back. Family businesses on the brink of being shut down. So it's hard.

And I think most Americans know that our economic problems weren't caused overnight. Obviously, we're going through the worst financial crisis since the Great Depression, and the aftermath hit Main Streets all across the country. But even before the financial crisis hit, people had seen their wages flat, their incomes flat.

Had a chance to meet some farmers back here today—crops are good this year, but family farms have been going through tough times: health care skyrocketing in terms of cost, college tuition skyrocketing.

We don't have an energy policy in this country, so we're still dependent on foreign oil. When gas shoots up, suddenly, everybody doesn't know what to do. These are problems that built up over a decade or more. They won't be solved overnight. It's going to take time to rebuild an America where hard work is valued and responsibility is rewarded, where people don't feel like they've got the deck stacked against them, where everybody is getting a fair shot and everybody is contributing their fair share.

It is going to take time to rebuild an America where we restore security for the middle class and opportunity for folks trying to get in the middle class, an economy that works for everybody and not just for folks at the top. That's our goal.

And it will take time to rebuild an economy that is competitive in the 21st century, that's built to last—one where we can outbuild and outcompete, outeducate, outinnovate other nations—which means we've got to step up on our education. We've got to invest in basic science. We've got to improve our infrastructure.

We've got to close our deficits. We've got to get our fiscal house in order. We've got a lot of work to do. It's going to take time.

But I'm here to tell you we are going to get it done. We are going to keep fighting. We're going to keep striving. We're going to focus on putting people back to work and helping middle class Americans get ahead, and we will give the economy the jolt that it needs.

And there are things that we can be doing right now to help the American people. That's why I sent Congress the "American Jobs Act." This is a jobs bill that contains the kind of proposals that in the past have been supported by both Democrats and Republicans. It's a bill that's paid for. It will not add to the deficit. It will not be going on the credit card. It will be paid for by asking our wealthiest citizens, our most fortunate, people like me, people who are making more than a million dollars, to pay their fair share.

Independent economists have looked at this jobs bill, and they've said it will create nearly 2 million jobs. That's not my opinion, that's not the opinion of folks who work for me, that's the opinion of people who study the economy for a living. They tell us this will grow the economy and put people back to work right away.

So the question is, if it's paid for, won't add to the deficit, won't result in increasing your taxes, will instead result in lowering your taxes, will put people back to work at a time when the unemployment rate is too high, why wouldn't we do it? Why wouldn't we pass it? It turns out the folks in Washington aren't listening to you.

Last week, all the Republicans in the United States Senate got together and they blocked this jobs bill. They refused to even debate it, even though a majority of Senators wanted it debated. But in the Senate you've got this rule where you got to get these days 60 votes to get something through. Just a majority doesn't seem to be enough.

Meanwhile, one poll found that 63 percent of Americans support the ideas in this jobs bill. And yet a hundred percent of Republicans in the Senate voted against it. Does that make any sense?

Audience members. No!

The President. Now, some people asked me yesterday why I'm visiting some place in North Carolina and Virginia that are mostly Republican. [*Laughter*] What I said was, "I'm not the Democratic President, I'm not the Republican President, I'm the President." I'm everybody's President. I don't care if you're a Republican or a Democrat. This is not the Republican jobs act, this is not called the Democratic jobs act, this is the "American Jobs Act." And everybody would be better off if we passed it.

Now, in fairness, let me say that after I sent Congress the "American Jobs Act," Republicans decided, well, we'd better put out our own jobs act. So they started out calling it the "Real American Jobs Act." That's what they called it, so they don't get points for originality. [*Laughter*] But let's examine what was in this jobs act. I said let's see what you've got.

As it turns out, the Republicans' plan boils down to a few basic ideas. And these are ideas we've heard before. They said, we're going to lower taxes for the wealthiest Americans and corporations. We're going to gut environmental regulations. We're going to drill more. We're going to let Wall Street do what they were doing before we got into this mess. And we're going to repeal health care reform.

All right, now, that is a plan, but it's not a jobs plan. That's a plan, but it's a plan to go back to doing the exact things that we were doing before we had a financial crisis that put so many people out of work. Why would we think that it would work now?

I mean, let's do a little comparison shopping here. Let's kick the tires a little bit on each plan.

The Republican plan says that the only thing that's standing between us and full employment are laws that keep ours companies from polluting our air and our water. My plan says let's put teachers back in the classroom. Let's put police and firefighters back on the job. Let's hire construction workers to rebuild America. Let's put our veterans back on the job.

Their plan says we'd be better off if we kick the 30 million Americans who are slated to get health care off the rolls. So the young people,

for example, who are already getting health insurance by staying on their parent's plan, they'd be out of luck. I don't know how that will contribute to creating jobs.

Our plan says we're better off if we give a tax cut to virtually every small business and every worker in America. That's in the "American Jobs Act."

Their plan says let's go back and let Wall Street do exactly what they were doing before the financial crisis. Let's roll back all the Wall Street reforms that we fought tooth and nail to pass over the objections of lobbyists and special interests in Washington.

Our plan says we need to make it easier for small businesses on Main Street to get financing and to hire and to push this economy forward.

Now—so those are the two plans. Remember those group of economists who said our plan would create jobs? Well, we asked one of them to take a look at the Republican plan. We said, well, maybe we're missing something here. Maybe we don't understand exactly what their strategy is. So we asked independent economists, please evaluate their plan. And the economist says: "Well, you know what, this plan would actually cost jobs. It won't do much to help the economy right now when folks are hurting, and could actually result in fewer jobs, not more jobs."

So I don't know how you present a plan for jobs that results in less jobs—[*laughter*]— right? I mean, they didn't call it the "American No Jobs Act." [*Laughter*] So the question is, Virginia, do you want a plan that results in dirtier air and water for our kids and fewer people on health care and less accountability on Wall Street? Or do we want to keep pushing a plan that puts more teachers in the classroom, more construction workers rebuilding our schools, tax cuts for small-business owners and working families?

That's the choice that we face, and I'll let you decide which plan is the real "American Jobs Act."

I just want to be clear. I want desperately to work with Republicans on ways to create jobs right now. Think about it. Nobody is more interested—other than the folks who are actually out of work—than me in seeing this economy growing strong. I'm open to any serious idea that is presented to create jobs.

Just last week, Congress passed a bipartisan trade deal with Korea that will allow us to sell more American goods overseas, create more jobs here. My attitude is, we're buying a whole lot of Hyundais and Kias; I want to see some Koreans buying some Fords and Chryslers and Chevys. I want them to buy some fine Virginia peanuts. I know they use peanuts over there, but I'll bet they're not as good as Virginia peanuts. [*Laughter*] These are some good peanuts. [*Laughter*]

So that's the kind of progress on our economy that we can keep on making, but to do so we've got to stop playing politics all the time. We can't just try to satisfy one wing of one party. We've got to pull together, focus on creating jobs and helping the middle class right now and helping people get into the middle class.

So what I decided was let's give Congress another chance. We're going to give them another chance to listen to you, to step up to the plate, to do the right thing. We will give them another chance to do their jobs so that you can keep your job or get a job. [*Laughter*]

And so I was thinking about it. I was thinking, well, maybe there was just too much stuff in my bill. Maybe it was confusing to have all these component parts. So what we decided is we're going to break it up into smaller pieces so that we don't confuse anybody, and let them vote on each piece one at a time. That way, you can be crystal clear on where everybody stands on the different components of the "American Jobs Act."

So the first vote we asked Congress to take is scheduled for later this week. And it's a vote that is going to put hundreds of thousands of police back on the beat and firefighters back on the job and teachers back in the classroom where they belong.

And you know why this is so important. I don't have to tell you this. We are competing against Germany and China and Korea and all these countries, and they are hiring teachers in droves. They are focused on making sure their children are top notch in math and science and technology. And yet here, all over the country, including here in Virginia, budget cuts are forcing schools to lay off teachers in disturbing numbers.

Here in Greensville County, you've lost some teachers. You could lose more if we don't pass this jobs bill, and that's not right. It's unfair to our kids. It undermines our future. We can't have other countries adding teachers to prepare their kids for the global economy while we sit by and do nothing.

As one teacher down in North Carolina said: "We didn't cause the poor economy, us teachers. If anything, we built the good parts." He is right. Teachers build the good parts of our economy. They give our children a chance. They create—they give young people the skills that allow them to go out and find a good job or start a business or invent a product. Our plan would mean nearly 11,000 education jobs right here in Virginia.

So I need all of you to tell the Senate: Put those teachers back to work. Put those teachers back to work. Pass the jobs bill, and put those teachers back to work.

But we're not going to stop with that vote. We're going to have a few more votes. We'll give the Senate a chance to vote on putting unemployed construction workers back on the job. Listen, I do not want China and Germany and other countries to build the newest roads and the newest bridges and the newest airports while ours are crumbling. Farmers can't get their products to market if we've got broken-down infrastructure. Businesses can't move their products and their people if we've got infrastructure that isn't state of the art. If we don't have the best airports, if we don't have the best roads, that will hurt our economy over the long term.

Think about it. We are the United States of America. People used to travel from all around the world to look at what we built: the Hoover Dam, Golden Gate Bridge, Grand Central station, Interstate Highway System. Now people aren't coming to see what we built because they're building it over there.

So what we said was, well, the "American Jobs Act," let's put those construction workers back to work. Let's rebuild and make sure our bridges are safe and our roads are safe and our airports are state of the art.

The Senate will have an opportunity to vote on that bill. Then they're going to have a chance to vote on giving unemployed Americans the support they need to get back into the workforce and build a better life. Because in this country, if you're willing to work hard, you should have the chance to get ahead.

And then we're going to ask the Senate to vote on a provision that says veterans—if you are a small business and you hire a veteran, you should get a tax break. Because I don't want folks who have sacrificed halfway around the world for our safety to come back here and not be able to find a job.

And then we're going to ask the Senate to pay for it by making sure that folks like me are paying their fair share. And if I'm paying my fair share, then you get a tax cut or a tax break. Small businesses get a tax cut.

And I have to say there's been a lot of misleading information about this, so let me just be perfectly clear here. Let me be painfully clear, just in case anybody asks you about it. What we are proposing is that the payroll tax cut that we passed in December gets extended, gets expanded, and that will mean an extra $1,500 in your pocket compared to if we do nothing.

If we don't pass this bill your taxes will go up by $1,000 for the average family. I know, everybody says, I don't want that. [*Laughter*]

And to pay for it, people like me can afford to pay a little bit more. Now, understand, we're talking about the top 1, 2 percent of people at the very top of the incomes scales. And we can afford it. We don't need a tax cut. We didn't ask for a tax break. You got corporations who are getting special deals on their Tax Codes. They don't need a special deal. Let's give a good deal to hard-working men and women who are out there struggling to make ends meet.

So if anybody—if you hear anybody saying, "Oh, Obama's plan, he's going to raise your taxes," tell them, no. I'm going to keep your taxes low for 97, 98 percent of the American people.

For the top 1, 2 percent, you'll go up a little bit, but you can afford it. You can afford it. A fair shot for everybody, a fair share from everybody.

So those are the choices that the American people are going to have to face. And those are the choices that the Members of Congress are going to have to face in the coming weeks. And if they vote against taking steps that we know will put people back to work, they're not going to have to answer to me, they're going to have to answer to you. They're going to have to come down to Virginia and tell their kids why they can't have their teachers back. They're going to have to look those construction workers in the eye and say why we shouldn't rebuild America. They're going to have to explain to working families why their taxes are going up, while the taxes of well-to-do people keep on going down.

So that's where you come in. I need your voices heard. I need you to give Congress a piece of your mind.

Tell these Members of Congress they're supposed to be working for you, not working for special interests, not working for campaign contributions. They're working for you, the American people. And they need to deliver, because they're not delivering right now.

You've got to get on the phone—you got to get on the phone and write letters and pay visits and tweet—[*laughter*]—whatever you do, and remind your elected leaders to do the right thing. Tell them what's at stake.

Remind them that "No, we can't" is not a good motto. "No, we can't" is not how we get through tough times. That's not how—this is a country that's gone through a Revolutionary War. This is a country that's gone through a Civil War. This is a country that went through two World Wars, a Great Depression, and we didn't just fold, we didn't just give up. Our grandparents, our great-grandparents, they didn't just say, "No, we can't." They didn't say, "This is too hard." They didn't say, "We give up." They didn't settle on the status quo. They rolled up their sleeves. They went after it. They said, "America can do whatever we put our minds to when we are unified."

President Kennedy didn't look up at the Moon and say: "Oh, that's too far! We can't go there." He said, "We can make it." And we did, because that's the American spirit when it is unleashed.

I know we've been going through tough times. But that's not an excuse for us to just sit back. That should be a motivation for us to try that much harder. There are too many of our fellow Americans who are hurting too bad for us to just sit by and do nothing. Now is the time for us to act. Now is the time for us to say, "Yes, we can." We don't sit back and do nothing when things aren't right. We set our minds to it, and we fix it. We make things work. We stick with it. And that's the spirit we've got to bring right now.

So I just want to say to all of you, Virginia, I hope and I pray that all of us can get together and stay focused on what it takes to continue to make this a great nation. I don't want us to be playing politics all the time. I want us to meet this moment. I want us to get to work. And I want us to show the world once again why the United States of America is the greatest nation on Earth.

Thank you. God bless you. God bless the United States of America.

NOTE: The President spoke at 5:43 p.m.

Remarks at Joint Base Langley-Eustis, Virginia
October 19, 2011

Hello, Joint Base Langley-Eustis! Thank you very much.

I hate following Michelle. [*Laughter*] She's so good. How lucky am I to be married to Michelle Obama? See, for you men out there who are not yet married, let me explain: The whole goal is to marry up, to try to improve your gene pool. [*Laughter*] And we're lucky to have her as First Lady of the United States, I think.

I am thrilled to be here. I want to thank the outstanding leaders who welcomed us here today: Secretary of the Air Force Michael Donley is here; General Mike Hostage is here; Colonels Kory Auch and Kevin Robbins and Reggie Austin are here. I want to give a shout-out to your outstanding senior enlisted leaders, including Chief Master Sergeants Kevin Howell and Marty Klukas. I want you to give a big round of applause to the Air Combat Command Heritage of America Band.

We've got a lot of folks in the house today. We've got Air Combat Command. We've got the 633d Air Base Wing. We've got the 1st Fighter Wing, with our amazing F–22 Raptors. I want to ride in one of those some day. [*Laughter*] We're going to have to set that up.

We've got the 480th Intelligence, Surveillance and Reconnaissance Wing. They can cheer, but they can't talk about what they do. [*Laughter*] They'd have to kill you. And I see we've got some Army too.

I want to salute Melissa Lee. Thank you so much. I want to salute Kathy Hostage. I want to salute Kristen Auch and the extraordinary military spouses who are here as well. We are inspired by them. Michelle is an honorary military spouse because she has to put up with me. [*Laughter*] But she and I both share such incredible admiration for the families of those who are serving in uniform.

We are grateful for our veterans who are here, including some very special airmen who taught the Nation the true meaning of service and honor and equality. We are honored to be joined by several of the legendary Tuskegee Airmen in the house. That's what heroes look like, right there.

Finally, I want to acknowledge your Governor, Bob McDonnell, and his lovely wife Maureen for joining us here today, as well as Congressman Bobby Scott, who's in the house. And I want to thank all the business leaders who have committed to hiring our Nation's heroes.

Those of you here today who have worn the uniform of these United States have done so with honor and have done so with distinction. Some of the most dangerous places on the planet, you have heroically performed and done everything that's been asked of you. Already, your generation has earned a special place in America's history. For that, you've got a grateful nation. As Michelle said, don't forget how everybody understands what you've done for this country.

Over the past decade, nearly 3 million servicemembers, like many of you, our 9/11 generation of veterans, have made the transition back to civilian life. They've taken their leadership experience, their mastery of cutting-edge technologies, their ability to adapt to changing circumstances, and they've become leaders here at home. They've become leaders in businesses all across the country.

Just think about how many veterans have led their comrades on life-and-death missions by the time they were 25. That's the kind of responsibility every business in America should want to take advantage of. Those are the Americans every company should want to hire.

Now, of course, as Michelle mentioned, there are far too many veterans who are coming home and having to struggle to find a job worthy of their talents. There are too many military spouses who have a hard time finding work after moving from base to base and city to city.

That's not right. It doesn't make any sense. It doesn't make sense for our veterans. It doesn't make sense for our businesses. It doesn't make sense for our families. And it doesn't make sense for America.

If you can save a life in Afghanistan, you can save a life in a local hospital or in a local ambulance. If you can oversee millions of dollars of assets in Iraq, you can help a business balance its books here at home. If you can juggle the demands of raising a family while a husband or wife are at war, you can juggle any demands of any job in the United States of America.

We ask our men and women in uniform to leave their families, our guardsmen and reservists to leave their jobs. We ask you to fight, to sacrifice, to risk your lives for our country. The last thing you should have to do is fight for a job when you come home. Not here, not in the United States of America.

So this has been one of my top priorities as your Commander in Chief. That's why we are

fully funding the post-GI—9/11 GI bill, which is helping more than 600,000 veterans and their family members pursue a college education. It's why we fought to make sure the bill included noncollege degrees and on-the-job training. It's why I directed the Federal Government to lead by example and hire more veterans, including 100,000 as of this summer.

And it's also why we're here today. As Michelle mentioned back in August, I challenged American businesses. I challenged them to hire or train 100,000 post-9/11 veterans or their spouses by the end of 2013. And now, just a few months later, thanks to the many extraordinary companies who are here today, we're already a quarter of the way there. Already, they've committed to train or hire 25,000 veterans and spouses in the next 2 years.

And this is incredible. It's a testament to their good business sense. It's a testament to their sense of patriotism. It's a testament to the fact that these veterans and military families are some of the most talented, trained, and experienced citizens that we have. It's a testament to these businesses' commitment to this country.

We're living through an economic crisis that partly came about because too many individuals and institutions were only thinking about their own interests, because they embraced an ethic that said, what's good enough for me is good enough. Well, the men and women of the United States Armed Forces, they've got a different ethic. You believe, your families believe, in something greater than your own ambitions. You've embraced an ethic that says the only thing that's good enough is what's best for the United States of America.

And by making a commitment to these brave men and women, the companies who are represented here today have shown that they've got that same ethic. They share in that belief that we're all in this together. Those companies who are represented here today are showing that they care about this country and those who serve it, not just with words, not just with slogans, not just with TV ads, but with the choices that you're making.

As President and Commander in Chief, I thank you for that. And I also want to thank my extraordinary wife and Dr. Jill Biden, our Second Lady, for leading the effort to support and honor our military families and making today possible. Give them a big round of applause. She does all this, and she looks cute. [*Laughter*] That's right. [*Laughter*]

But considering how many veterans are out there looking for work, we can't stop with today's announcement. We've got more work to do. Some of you probably know that last month I sent Congress a piece of legislation called the "American Jobs Act." Now, this is a bill that's fully paid for, and it's filled with the kind of proposals that traditionally Democrats and Republicans have supported in the past: tax cuts for every small worker—every worker and small business in America, funding to rebuild our schools and put our teachers back in the classroom so our children can get the education they deserve, a tax credit for small businesses that hire America's veterans.

The idea here is even though so many companies who are here today have committed to hiring our Nation's heroes, we want to make it even easier for the businesses that haven't made that commitment yet. It's the right thing to do for our veterans, and it's the right thing to do for America. You give smaller companies who may be interested in hiring, but are having a tough time—give them a tax break if they hire a veteran. Give them an even bigger tax break if they hire a disabled veteran.

Now, so far Congress hasn't acted on this proposal. But I want you to know that I'm pushing them a little bit. I'm going to keep pushing them a little bit. In the coming weeks, we're going to hold a series of votes in the Senate on individual pieces of my jobs bill. And one of the votes I'm going to urge Members of Congress to take is on whether or not they think it's a good idea to give companies an incentive to hire the men and women who have risked their lives for our country. And I'm hopeful we can get both parties on board for this idea.

When I first proposed this idea in a joint session of Congress, people stood up and applauded on both sides of the aisle. So when it comes for a vote in the Senate, I expect to get votes from both sides of the aisle. Don't just applaud about it, vote for it. Vote for it.

Standing up for our veterans is not a Democratic responsibility or a Republican responsibility, it is an American responsibility. It is an obligation for every citizen who enjoys the freedoms that our heroes defend. And it's time for us to meet those obligations here today.

This generation of veterans has learned that the challenges don't end in Kandahar or Baghdad. They continue right here at home. And today, we're saying to those veterans who fought for us, now we are fighting for you—for more jobs, for more security, for the opportunity to keep your families strong, the chance to keep America competitive economically in the 21st century.

These are tough times for America, but we faced tougher times before. And nobody is tougher than the men and women of America's Armed Forces. You all don't quit. Whenever we faced a challenge in this country, whether it was a depression or a Civil War or when our Union was at stake, our harbor was bombed, our country was attacked on that September day, we did not falter. We did not turn back. We picked ourselves up. We pushed ourselves forward. We got on with the task of fulfilling the ideas that so many Americans have struggled for and sacrificed for and given their lives for.

And that's the spirit all of you represent. That's the spirit our whole Nation needs right now. You remind us as a nation that no problem is too hard and no challenge is too great and no destiny is beyond our reach. So let's meet this moment. Let's get together and show the world just why it is that the United States of America is the greatest nation on Earth.

God bless you. God bless our veterans. God bless the men and women in uniform, and God bless the United States of America.

NOTE: The President spoke at 10:41 a.m. In his remarks, he referred to Gen. G. Michael Hostage III, USAF, commander, and CMS Martin S. Klukas, command chief master sergeant, Air Combat Command; Col. Korvin D. Auch, USAF, commander, Col. Reggie L. Austin, USA, vice commander, and CMS Kevin L. Howell, USAF, command chief master sergeant, 633d Air Base Wing; Col. Kevin J. Rob-

bins, USAF, commander, First Fighter Wing; and Col. Melissa R. Lee, USA, 335th Signal Command Theater. The transcript released by the Office of the Press Secretary also included the remarks of the First Lady.

Remarks at Fire Station 9 in North Chesterfield, Virginia
October 19, 2011

The President. Hello, everybody!

Audience members. Hello!

The President. It is good to be in Chesterfield County. Thank you so much for the wonderful welcome.

Audience member. We love you!

The President. Well, I love you back. [*Laughter*]

It is great to be in Virginia. It is great to be here at Fire Station Number 9 with some of Chesterfield's finest.

Audience member. Hooah!

The President. There you go.

First of all, I want to thank Chief Urquhart not only for the introduction, but for the great service that he's been providing for 22 years, is it?

Chesterfield Fire and EMS Battalion Chief Vincent A. Urquhart. Yes, sir.

The President. Twenty-two years. Give him a big round of applause. And I want to say thank you to the chief of Chesterfield County Fire and EMS, Loy Senter. Give him a big round of applause. I appreciate opening up the firehouse here today. But if the bell goes off, just ignore me, do your thing. [*Laughter*]

We've been on a little road trip over the last few days. I've got a pretty nice ride; it's not your normal RV. And it's parked outside. We've been seeing some sights; we've been eating some good food. Most importantly, we've been getting a chance to hear from the American people. And it's always nice to spend a few days outside of Washington, because it doesn't seem like your voices are being heard the way they need to be heard in Washington.

Times are tough all over, and a lot of folks here in Virginia have spent months looking for work. Others are just barely making it, and they're having to make hard choices, and

they're having to make sacrifices. It's hard obviously watching friends or family or neighbors who are struggling. And all of us, I think, are mindful of the fact that the economy is not where it needs to be.

I think most people understand that the economy and its problems didn't happen overnight, so we're not going to solve all these challenges overnight. It's going to take time to rebuild the kind of America in which everybody has a fair shot, everybody is paying their fair share, where responsibility is rewarded, where the deck is not stacked against middle class families—in fact, we have a middle class that is growing again and solid again and secure again, and people who are striving to get in the middle class have ladders of opportunity. That's what we're striving for.

We're going to keep on fighting, we're going to keep on working to make sure that we've got the kind of economy that works for everybody and not just some. And here's the good news: There are things we can do right now that will make a difference. There are things that we can do right now that will put people back to work. There are things we can do right now that will make sure that we are competitive in this global economy.

Some of the challenges we face we're going to have to work on for a while: improving our schools, making sure that we've got the best infrastructure in the world, making sure that we're bringing down our deficit, making sure that we're continuing to invest in science and technology. But there are things we can do right now that will make a difference.

And that's why I sent to Congress the "American Jobs Act." It's a jobs bill—[*applause*]—you can go ahead and clap. Go ahead, nothing wrong with it.

This is a jobs bill that contains the kind of proposals that in the past, at least, have been supported by Democrats and Republicans alike. It's paid for. It will not add to our deficit. And it's paid for by asking the wealthiest of us—people like me—to be able to put in a little bit more so that we can make sure that folks who are struggling get the help they need and that the economy overall is improving.

Independent economists have said it will create nearly 2 million jobs. That's not my opinion. That's not the opinion of people who work for me and have to tell me what I want to hear. [*Laughter*] This is the opinion of independent economists. They say it will help the economy grow. People who study the economy for a living say this would give the economy the jolt that it needs.

Now, a number of people have been asking during the course of this road trip, "Why have you been visiting some of the most Republican parts of North Carolina and Virginia?" And what I've had to remind them is that I'm not the Democratic President, I'm not the Republican President, I'm the President of the United States of America. And I don't care what party you belong to, we're all Americans, and we're all in this together.

And that's why we didn't call this the Democratic jobs plan or the Republican jobs plan, we called it the "American Jobs Act." We need to put people to work right now. I think most Americans understand that. A recent poll showed that 63 percent of the American people support what's in the "American Jobs Act." Unfortunately, we've had a hundred percent of Senate Republicans vote against it. A majority think it's a good idea to keep firefighters on the job.

As tough as the economy may be, I think people may not be aware, for the last 19 months we've had private sector job growth. We've seen more than 2 million jobs created in the private sector. The problem is that State and local governments have been very hard pressed, and so they are cutting back on firefighters, police officers, teachers. And that's one of the biggest challenges we have, not only because these folks sacrifice for us and provide

extraordinary service to us, but also, they go to restaurants, and they go to the hardware store, and they pay a mortgage. And so if folks in the—if we've got firefighters or police officers or teachers who are being laid off, that hurts the small-businessperson down the street. That means that somebody may have their home foreclosed on, and that brings property values down for everybody.

So the provisions that we've got in the bill are ones that most people support: keeping firefighters in the job, keeping cops on the job, putting teachers back in the classroom, giving tax cuts to families, giving tax cuts to small businesses, giving tax cuts to businesses who hire our veterans. I just came from Hampton, and we were down there talking to folks who have served our country—this 9/11 generation—and are coming back after making all those sacrifices and are finding themselves fighting for work. We've got to do something about that.

The question is why Congress isn't willing to move. Now, I just want to be fair. I sent Congress the "American Jobs Act," and then, my Republican friends put out a plan of their own, and they started out calling it the "Real American Jobs Act." So they don't get points for originality. [*Laughter*] But I did say, well, let's see what you've got. What are your ideas? And the primary ideas in their jobs plan was to roll back regulations that keep our air and water clean, to go back to the system we had in Wall Street that caused this crisis in the first place, to end the health care reform that we passed that will provide 30 million people health insurance and make sure that insurance companies can't take advantage of you.

Now, that is a plan, but it's not a jobs plan. We can have an argument about health care, or we can have an argument about environmental regulations, but we can't pretend that that's going to actually put people back to work. And that's the number-one priority that the American people have right now.

Their plan says that somehow if we eliminate regulations that keep our air and water clean for our kids, that that's going to help job growth. My plan says, let's hire construction workers and put them back to work rebuilding roads and bridges and schools and fire stations all across the country.

Their plan says that if we roll back health care reform, that somehow jobs are going to be created. My plan says, let's give a tax cut to small businesses to hire the long-term unemployed and our veterans and make sure that they've got a little more money to keep their doors open, expand their payroll, expand their inventory, get this economy moving.

Their plan says, let's go back to a system on Wall Street where there were the kinds of rules that allowed people to take reckless bets that ended up affecting all of Main Street. My attitude is, to strengthen this economy we've got to make sure that those rules are actually enforced, not watered down, and in the meantime, let's work to make sure that we're keeping taxes low for middle class families who are still struggling to get by.

So I just want to repeat: dirtier air, dirtier water, fewer people on health care, less accountability on Wall Street—that is not a jobs plan.

I understand that some of my Republican friends feel very strongly about these ideas. I'm happy to have a debate. But in the meantime, let's focus on what will actually put people back to work. Keeping first-responders on the job, that's a jobs plan. Putting more teachers in the classroom, that's a jobs plan.

So what we decided to do, since a hundred percent of Republicans in the Senate voted against this plan the first time, is we're going to give them another chance to listen to you. We're going to let them vote on each of these ideas separately, and we'll see if they fight just as hard for your jobs as they fight for their own jobs.

So the first vote we're going to ask is—Congress to take this week would put hundreds of thousands of firefighters back on the job, police officers back on the street, teachers back in the classroom.

Now, Chesterfield's been lucky. It isn't facing layoffs right now. But a lot of these guys have seen their pay frozen. You've got cities in States like Michigan and New Jersey that have

had to lay off big chunks of their forces. That means that firefighters can't always get to fires before they become major fires, and that makes their job more dangerous. It means police officers can't respond to every crime. And when giving our children the best education possible we know is the ingredient for success in this new information- and technology-rich economy, how can we be laying off teachers when other countries are hiring teachers in droves? It's unfair to our kids. It undermines our future.

So this week Congress is going to get to vote on whether or not hundreds of thousands of police officers and teachers and firefighters get back on the job. And I don't know if these Members of Congress—maybe they haven't met some of these firefighters. I don't think they want to tell them that their jobs aren't worth saving. Some of these guys are pretty big. [*Laughter*] Captain Kemp is an ex-marine, which means he's still a marine. And these guys are risking their lives every day on our behalf. These jobs are worth fighting for.

Folks in Congress are also going to get a chance to decide later in the month whether our construction workers should sit around doing nothing while China builds the best railroads, the best schools, the best airports in the world.

We used to have the best stuff. Think about—the world used to say, let's travel to America. Let's see the Golden Gate Bridge. Let's see the Hoover Dam. Let's see these amazing things that America built. Are we going to be the generation where we stop building, where we've got rundown roads and bridges that are deemed obsolete? That's not who America is.

So Congress will have a chance to see if they want to put Americans back to work doing the work that America needs done.

They say that they value our veterans. When I went before the joint Congress to present this "American Jobs Act," I said, let's give tax breaks to companies that are hiring our veterans. And we just got 25,000—a pledge of 25,000 jobs from companies all across the country, aiming for a goal of a hundred thousand veterans being hired by the end of 2013.

So when I talked about this part of the plan before the joint session of Congress, everybody rose up, Democrats and Republicans alike. So the question now is, if you all stood and applauded, how are you going to vote? It's not enough to applaud and go to a Veterans Day parade. People need help. And you've got a chance to help them right now.

These are the choices that Congress will be presented with in the next few weeks. And if they vote against these proposals, if they no—say no to steps we know that will put people back to work right now, they're not going to have to answer to me, they're going to have to answer to you. They're going to have to come down here and tell folks in Virginia and all across the country why people are going to have to cope with fewer first-responders, why your kids can't have teachers back in the classroom. They're going to have to look construction workers in the eye and tell them why they're sitting idle instead of rebuilding infrastructure that we know needs to be rebuilt.

And they're going to have to explain why we couldn't afford to do it when we know that we can pay for all of this, plus keep taxes on middle class families low, prevent them from going up, and all we have to do in order to pay for it is make sure that people like me are paying our fair share of taxes and that companies no longer are getting special tax loopholes. That's it.

So when you hear that, "Well, the reason we're not supporting it, we like the ideas but we don't want to see higher taxes," if we don't pass this bill, taxes for the average family will go up because the payroll tax cut that we passed in December will lapse. If we do pass this bill, for 97, 98 percent of Americans, your taxes will stay low. My taxes will go up a little bit, but I can afford it.

A fair shot for everybody, a fair share from everybody. That's a principle that built America. That's how we created a middle class.

Now, they can do the right thing in Congress and put people back right now—to work right now and reopen firehouses. But I'm going to need your help. I need you, and that's the reason I'm here. It's wonderful to have a chance to see everybody and shake hands and take pictures, but the main reason I'm here is I want you to send a message to Congress that this is important. Let them know. Get on the phone, write a letter, fax, tweet, whatever it is that people do these days—[*laughter*]—and remind Members of Congress what's at stake here.

You know, it takes a special kind of bravery to be a firefighter. When that bell rings, it takes a special kind of courage to answer the call and rush, at great risk to yourself, to help your fellow citizens. And you know what, that's the same kind of spirit that I believe embodies America: looking out for one another, helping each other, being willing to make sacrifices for the greater good. When our friends and neighbors are hurting, we don't cross our arms and just do nothing. We roll up our sleeves, and we say, we're going to help, we'll figure out how to solve this problem. We are not people who sit idly by and ignore our challenges. We step up, and we meet those challenges. And that's the opportunity we have right now.

So I hope everybody is with us. We hope that you are willing to contact your Members of Congress. Tell them to get busy. Tell them to get to work. Tell them to put people back to work. And let's show the world once again why the United States of America is the greatest country on Earth.

Thank you. God bless you, and God bless the United States of America. Thank you very much.

NOTE: The President spoke at 2:29 p.m. In his remarks, he referred to Capt. Brian Kemp of Chesterfield Fire and EMS.

Statement on the Terrorist Attack in Cukurca, Turkey
October 19, 2011

The United States strongly condemns this morning's outrageous terrorist attack against Turkey, one of our closest and strongest allies. On behalf of the American people, I offer my condolences to the families of the victims and to all of the Turkish people.

The United States will continue our strong cooperation with the Turkish Government as it works to defeat the terrorist threat from the PKK and to bring peace, stability, and prosperity to all the people of southeast Turkey. The people of Turkey, like people everywhere, deserve to live in peace, security, and dignity. As they pursue the future they deserve, they will continue to have a friend and ally in the United States.

NOTE: The statement referred to the PKK, the Kurdistan Workers' Party.

Message to the Congress on Continuation of the National Emergency With Respect to Significant Narcotics Traffickers Centered in Colombia
October 19, 2011

To the Congress of the United States:

Section 202(d) of the National Emergencies Act, 50 U.S.C. 1622(d), provides for the automatic termination of a national emergency unless, prior to the anniversary date of its declaration, the President publishes in the *Federal Register* and transmits to the Congress a notice stating that the emergency is to continue in effect beyond the anniversary date. In accordance with this provision, I have sent to the *Federal Register* for publication the enclosed notice stating that the emergency declared with respect to significant narcotics traffickers centered in Colombia is to continue in effect beyond October 21, 2011.

The circumstances that led to the declaration on October 21, 1995, of a national emergency have not been resolved. The actions of significant narcotics traffickers centered in Colombia continue to pose an unusual and extraordinary threat to the national security, foreign policy, and economy of the United States and cause an extreme level of violence, corruption, and harm in the United States and abroad. For these reasons, I have determined that it is necessary to maintain economic pressure on significant narcotics traffickers centered in Colombia by blocking their property and interests in property that are in the United States or within the possession or control of United States persons and by depriving them of access to the U.S. market and financial system.

BARACK OBAMA

The White House,
October 19, 2011.

NOTE: The notice is listed in Appendix D at the end of this volume.

Remarks on the Death of Former Leader Muammar Abu Minyar al-Qadhafi of Libya
October 20, 2011

Good afternoon, everybody. Today the Government of Libya announced the death of Muammar Qadhafi. This marks the end of a long and painful chapter for the people of Libya, who now have the opportunity to determine their own destiny in a new and democratic Libya.

For four decades, the Qadhafi regime ruled the Libyan people with an iron fist. Basic human rights were denied. Innocent civilians were detained, beaten, and killed, and Libya's wealth was squandered. The enormous potential of the Libyan people was held back, and terror was used as a political weapon.

Today we can definitively say that the Qadhafi regime has come to an end. The last major regime strongholds have fallen. The new Government is consolidating the control over the country. And one of the world's longest serving dictators is no more.

One year ago, the notion of a free Libya seemed impossible. But then the Libyan people rose up and demanded their rights, and when Qadhafi and his forces started going city to city, town by town, to brutalize men, women, and children, the world refused to stand idly by.

Faced with the potential of mass atrocities and a call for help from the Libyan people, the United States and our friends and allies stopped Qadhafi's forces in their tracks. A coalition that included the United States, NATO, and Arab nations persevered through the summer to protect Libyan civilians. And meanwhile, the courageous Libyan people fought for their own future and broke the back of the regime.

So this is a momentous day in the history of Libya. The dark shadow of tyranny has been lifted. And with this enormous promise, the Libyan people now have a great responsibility: to build an inclusive and tolerant and democratic Libya that stands as the ultimate rebuke to Qadhafi's dictatorship. We look forward to the announcement of the country's liberation, the quick formation of an interim Government, and a stable transition to Libya's first free and fair elections. And we call on our Libyan friends to continue to work with the international community to secure dangerous materials and to respect the human rights of all Libyans, including those who have been detained.

Now, we're under no illusions. Libya will travel a long and winding road to full democracy. There will be difficult days ahead. But the United States, together with the international community, is committed to the Libyan people. You have won your revolution. And now we will be a partner as you forge a future that provides dignity, freedom, and opportunity.

For the region, today's events prove once more that the rule of an iron fist inevitably comes to an end. Across the Arab world, citizens have stood up to claim their rights. Youth are delivering a powerful rebuke to dictatorship, and those leaders who try to deny their human dignity will not succeed.

For us here in the United States, we are reminded today of all those Americans that we lost at the hands of Qadhafi's terror. Their families and friends are in our thoughts and in our prayers. We recall their bright smiles, their extraordinary lives, and their tragic deaths. We know that nothing can close the wound of their loss, but we stand together as one Nation by their side.

For nearly 8 months, many Americans have provided extraordinary service in support of our efforts to protect the Libyan people and to provide them with a chance to determine their own destiny. Our skilled diplomats have helped to lead an unprecedented global response. Our brave pilots have flown in Libya's skies, our sailors have provided support off Libya's shores, and our leadership at NATO has helped guide our coalition. Without putting a single U.S. servicemember on the ground, we achieved our objectives, and our NATO mission will soon come to an end.

This comes at a time when we see the strength of American leadership across the world. We've taken out Al Qaida leaders, and we've put them on the path to defeat. We're winding down the war in Iraq and have begun a transition in Afghanistan. And now, working in Libya with friends and allies, we've demonstrated what collective action can achieve in the 21st century.

Of course, above all, today's—belongs to the people of Libya. This is a moment for them to remember all those who suffered and were lost under Qadhafi and look forward to the promise of a new day. And I know the American people wish the people of Libya the very best in what will be a challenging but hopeful days, weeks, months, and years ahead.

Thank you very much.

NOTE: The President spoke at 2:07 p.m. in the Rose Garden at the White House.

Remarks on Presenting the Presidential Citizens Medal
October 20, 2011

The President. Thank you very much. Good afternoon, everyone. Welcome to the White House. This is one of my favorite events. We are here to recognize the winners of the Citizens Medal, one of the highest honors a civilian can receive. This is the second year the nominations process has been open to the public, and I notice that once again the women outnumber the men. [*Laughter*] I'm beginning to see a pattern here.

You know, on Sunday, I helped dedicate the National Martin Luther King, Jr. Memorial. And this afternoon, as I'm spending time with these extraordinary people, I'm reminded of the fact that during the last speech that Dr. King ever gave, he retold the story of the Good Samaritan. And most of you know the story. We know it begins with a man lying injured on a road. And Dr. King said that the first people who saw him asked themselves, "If I stop to help this man, what will happen to me?" So they made excuses for not stopping. They said the man was faking his injury, or it wasn't their problem. But according to Dr. King, the Good Samaritan reversed the question: "If I do not stop to help this man, what will happen to him?"

The 13 Americans that we honor today have all faced in their own ways the moment that Dr. King described, that Good Samaritan moment when you see a neighbor in need and you have to ask yourself the question. They come from different backgrounds, and they've devoted their lives to different causes, but they are united by the choice that they've made. They could have made excuses to doing nothing. Instead, they chose to help.

For many of them, a lifelong mission began with a small act of kindness. In 1987, a single mom and her child—her children moved in across the street from Ida Martin. Ida saw their refrigerator was empty except for a bottle of water, so she brought them groceries. And I guess once she got started, she couldn't stop. [*Laughter*] So last year, the organization she founded answered nearly 22,000 requests for aid.

Then there's Milly Bloomquist from Penn Yan, New York. And for decades, she has personified the phrase "above and beyond." At her 90th birthday party, one speaker said that Penn Yan has its own special system for handling emergencies: "If you're out of food, call Milly. If your heat has gone out, call Milly. If you can't pay your electricity bill, call Milly. If you need a winter coat, call Milly."

The right choice is rarely the easy one. And for some of those we honor here today, the choice to help was especially hard because it came in the wake of tragedy. Steve and Liz Alderman lost their son Peter on 9/11. Roger Kemp's daughter Ali was murdered nearly a decade ago. Janice Langbehn was denied the right to visit her partner Lisa as she lay dying in the hospital.

As a father and husband, I can't begin to imagine the grief that they must have felt in that moment, their anger and their sense that the world was not fair. But they refused to let that anger define them. They each became, in Janice's words, an "accidental activist." And thanks to their work, there are parents and partners who will never have to go through what they went through.

Now, I'm happy to say that there was a pretty stiff competition for these medals. Citizens from all walks of life submitted nearly 6,000 nominations online, and it took us 4 months to select the winners. In the end, these 13 individuals were chosen not just for the work they do, but for the example that they set.

Over the past year, we've been reminded time and time again that our lives can be altered by events beyond our control. A tornado or a hurricane can devastate a community. An earthquake halfway around the world can threaten businesses here at home. An economic crisis that begins in one corner of the housing market can spread to leave millions of Americans out of work.

1311

So we don't always get to choose the challenges that we face. But how we respond is entirely up to us. We are each on that Good Samaritan road, the road that Dr. King spoke of more than 40 years ago. We can see that there are people who need our help. And while we come from different backgrounds, we all face the same, simple question: Will we help them, or will we not?

In some ways, in these difficult times, it's easier than ever to walk on by. We can tell ourselves, "I've got enough problems of my own." "I can't make a big enough difference." "If my neighbors are less fortunate, maybe it's their fault." But as Americans, that's not who we are. Because while, yes, we are a nation of individuals, we're also a community; I am my brother's keeper, I am my sister's keeper. That's a creed we all share.

So this afternoon I am proud to share the stage with these extraordinary citizens. I also know that for our Government to truly honor them, we have to do more than hand out medals. We have to follow their example. And that won't always be easy. As individuals, as communities, and as a country, we all face the temptation to find excuses not to help. In these decisive moments, then, we need to choose between doing something and doing nothing. And I hope we will remember the stories of these extraordinary men and women as we make that choice. I hope they inspire us to put ourselves in another person's shoes. And I hope that years from now, when they retell the story of our time, they will say that we too lent a hand to our neighbor in need.

I should just point out that a few people, like Molly, when I said we could not be prouder of what they've accomplished, bristled a little bit and said, "I'm not done yet." [*Laughter*] So these guys are still out there making a difference. And they'll be right there with us if we end up doing the right thing. All right?

So congratulations to all of the winners of the Citizens Medal. I've got some outstanding Military Aides here, and one of them is going to read the citations, one at a time, and then I'll present a medal to each of the honorees.

[*At this point, the Military Aide to the President read the citations, and the President presented the medals.*]

The President. What a remarkable group of Americans.

I want to thank all of you for joining us here today, all the friends and family who are here to celebrate our Citizens Medals winners, because I think that, not to speak for them, but I suspect they'd say that they couldn't have done what they did without the incredible support of all the people who are here. The colleagues and the loved ones who submitted nominations online, I'm sure they're appreciative, and obviously, you made a pretty convincing case.

I think our honorees recognize that our work is not yet done. And so I just want to repeat, I hope that their incredible work ends up setting an example for all of us, both in public service and in our daily lives.

And I know that some folks today who are here also represent the Corporation for National and Community Service. Every day, you help Americans make their country a better place, and I want to thank all of you for your hard work.

So with that, we've got, my understanding is, some pretty good food here—[*laughter*]—maybe even a little music, as we celebrate these extraordinary individuals. Please give them one more big round of applause.

NOTE: The President spoke at 2:25 p.m. in the East Room at the White House. Participating in the ceremony were medal recipients Stephen and Elizabeth Alderman, Clarence L. Alexander, Camilla "Milly" Bloomquist, Judith T. Broder, John Keaveney, Roger Kemp, Janice Langbehn, Ida Martin, Margaret Martin, Michelle McIntyre-Brewer, and Roberto P. Perez; and Sujata and Nirmala Emani, daughters of Vijaya Emani, who was awarded the medal posthumously.

Remarks Following a Meeting With Prime Minister Jens Stoltenberg of Norway and an Exchange With Reporters
October 20, 2011

President Obama. Hello, everybody. I am very happy to welcome Prime Minister Stoltenberg to the Oval Office and his delegation to the United States. Michelle and I have incredibly fond memories of our visits to Oslo, and the extraordinary hospitality that the Norwegian people extended to us and our family.

It is fitting that we meet today, given the events that took place in Libya. Obviously, this was a NATO mission that was executed, I think, very effectively. Part of the reason it was so effective was because of NATO partners like Norway. I've said this before, but I want to repeat: Norway punches above its weight. And their participation in the humanitarian mission, protecting civilians, the capacity of Norwegian pilots, their willingness to engage in some very critical missions there, made an enormous difference.

And so I began the meeting by thanking the people of Norway, the Norwegian military, and the Prime Minister for their leadership in helping to give Libya an opportunity to become a democracy.

The people of Norway and the United States share a lot of bonds. Obviously, we have an enormous Norwegian American population here, but we also share a lot of common values. And so in our discussions we covered a wide range of issues. We discussed our partnership in Afghanistan, where Norway has been a consistent partner, and discussed how we are going to move the transition forward so that Afghans can take full responsibility for their security by 2014, as we agreed to in Lisbon.

We discussed the world economy, and we shared our intentions to work closely with our European partners to stabilize the euro zone area, but also to make sure that we are all participating in creating a system in which free trade, in which coordinated commercial practices, in which our focus on growing the economy, issues like energy security, all involve close coordination between our two countries. And we very much appreciate the partnership there.

We discussed the heartbreaking situation that occurred in Norway on July 22. And as I've said before, I think everybody in the United States was horrified by the events there. But I complimented the Prime Minister and the people of Norway for the grace with which they handled this extraordinarily difficult situation. It underscored the importance of all of us cooperating in preventing terrorism of all kinds. And the United States and Norway have established a very effective intelligence cooperation system, and that is continually being enhanced and improved. And so we both agreed that we're very pleased with the progress that we've made in making sure that we are working closely together to prevent the kind of senseless violence that we saw in Norway so recently and that we've seen around the world over the last several years.

And we also discussed a range of international issues of great importance. We both share the belief that we need a two-state solution in Middle East, and we want to work very closely with both the Israelis and the Palestinians to arrive at a negotiated settlement.

We discussed the situation in Sudan, where—and the conflict between Sudan and South Sudan. And Norway and the United States have been two very important partners in a process to move towards a more peaceful resolution of the conflicts there.

We discussed how we can work together in the United Nations and other multilateral fora around issues like climate change and maternal health.

And so I think that the state of cooperation and respect between the United States and Norway has never been higher. I personally feel a great affinity for the people of Norway and grateful for the friendship and partnership that they've provided. And I hope that this is not the last visit, but one of many that we'll have together here in the United States. And I hope I have a chance to visit Norway again sometime soon.

So welcome, Mr. Prime Minister.

Prime Minister Stoltenberg. Thank you so much.

President Obama. Thank you.

Prime Minister Stoltenberg. Thank you. Thank you so much, Mr. President, for your kind words. And also thank you so much for the hospitality you have shown me and my delegation. And we are very much impressed about your political agenda and also by your global leadership you have shown, and which we appreciate very much in Norway.

We are also very grateful for the sympathy and the condolences you and the people of America conveyed to the people of Norway after the terrible attacks of the 22d of July. And I know that it was of great comfort for those who lost their loved ones. And as you said, it underlines the importance of cooperation in fighting all kinds of terrorism. We will continue to do so, and we will look how—into how we can expand our cooperation in fighting terrorism.

We've worked together—or we work together on many different issues; we cooperate on many different areas. One of them are within—or is within the NATO, the military alliance. And as you mentioned, we have accomplished what we had as our aim for the military operations in Libya. We protected civilians; we were able to stop Qadhafi of killing his own people. And I think it shows that we are able to implement decisions by the U.N. and by the NATO, and that's important in itself.

We appreciate the cooperation we have in Afghanistan. We are looking forward to focusing even more on the transition. Norway went into Afghanistan together with our allies and are going to leave Afghanistan together with our allies.

I appreciate also very much that we had the opportunity to focus on the High North. The High North is a area where we are seeing new possibilities, new challenges, but also new dangers. And the ice is melting. Actually, in the High North, we see the consequences of global warming. But at the same time, that opens up new possibilities for energy developments, but also for sea routes, and it increases the need for cooperation between the countries bordering the Arctic area, and U.S. and Norway are among them.

I appreciate that we can continue our cooperation when it comes to climate change, because we've worked together on halting deforestation, reducing deforestation. And that's the way we can achieve the biggest, the cheapest, and the fastest reductions in emissions. And we worked together in Indonesia in reducing deforestation.

And I appreciate very much that we work together on child mortality, maternal health, and that's an area where we have achieved a lot together during the last years.

So I appreciate very much this opportunity to meet with you, and you are always welcome to Norway and Oslo. Thank you.

President Obama. Thank you very much. Thank you, everybody.

Libya/Death of Former Leader Muammar Abu Minyar al-Qadhafi of Libya

Q. Mr. President, does the Libya—the death of Qadhafi vindicate your policy in Libya?

President Obama. There's no doubt that we did exactly what we said we were going to do in Libya. And I think it underscores the capacity of us to work together as an international community. The United States obviously has unique capacities, and we were proud of the leadership we showed in that process. But increasingly, wherever we have the possibility of working with outstanding partners like Norway, then I think that we're going to be even more effective. And the United States will always preserve its right and duty to protect ourselves, our allies, and our interests.

But I think what this shows is that, on a whole range of international issues, there is enormous capacity and we are able to leverage greater resources, more effectiveness, at lower cost when we're able to work together. So I'm very proud of the work that we did on this operation.

Most importantly, I'm proud of what the Libyan people have achieved. And I think they've got an enormous opportunity ahead of them. They've got a lot of challenges as well, but we have now given them the opportunity to determine their own destiny. And that's something that we've seen across North Africa and the Arab world, that there's nothing unique in aspiring to freedom and human rights and democracy. This is something that all people want to enjoy, and I'm very pleased that the Libyan people are going to have the opportunity to do so. All right?

Thank you very much, everybody.
Q. Thank you.
President Obama. Thank you.

NOTE: The President spoke at 5:16 p.m. in the Oval Office at the White House.

Statement on Azerbaijan's Independence Day
October 20, 2011

On behalf of the American people, I want to extend my best wishes to all those who are celebrating Azerbaijan's Independence Day in Azerbaijan, in the United States, and around the world. This 20th anniversary of independence and Azerbaijan's achievements during this time demonstrate the extraordinary promise and determination of the Azeri people. The United States is committed to developing greater opportunities to work with the Government and people of Azerbaijan.

Statement on Senate Confirmation of John E. Bryson as Secretary of Commerce
October 20, 2011

As Secretary of Commerce, John Bryson will be a key member of my economic team, working with the business community to promote job creation, foster growth, and help open up new markets around the world for American-made goods. At such a critical time for our economy, I nominated John because I believe his decades of experience both in the public and private sector have given him a clear understanding of what it takes to put America on a stronger economic footing and create jobs. I'm confident he will help us do that, and I look forward to working closely with him in the months and years ahead.

Statement on Senate Action on Job Growth Legislation
October 20, 2011

For the second time in 2 weeks, every single Republican in the United States Senate has chosen to obstruct a bill that would create jobs and get our economy going again. That's unacceptable. We must do what's right for the country and pass the commonsense proposals in the "American Jobs Act." Every Senate Republican voted to block a bill that would help middle class families and keep hundreds of thousands of firefighters on the job, police officers on the streets, and teachers in the classroom when our kids need them most.

Those Americans deserve an explanation as to why they don't deserve those jobs, and every American deserves an explanation as to why Republicans refuse to step up to the plate and do what's necessary to create jobs and grow the economy right now.

We must rebuild the economy the American way and restore security for the middle class based on the values of balance and fairness. Independent economists have said the "American Jobs Act" could create up to 2 million jobs next year. So the choice is clear. Our fight isn't over. We will keep working with Congress to bring up the "American Jobs Act" piece by piece and give Republicans another chance to put country before party and help us put the American people back to work.

Remarks on the Withdrawal of United States Military Personnel From Iraq
October 21, 2011

Good afternoon, everybody. As a candidate for President, I pledged to bring the war in Iraq to a responsible end, for the sake of our national security and to strengthen American leadership around the world. After taking office, I announced a new strategy that would end our combat mission in Iraq and remove all of our troops by the end of 2011.

As Commander in Chief, ensuring the success of this strategy has been one of my highest national security priorities. Last year, I announced the end to our combat mission in Iraq. And to date, we've removed more than 100,000 troops. Iraqis have taken full responsibility for their country's security.

A few hours ago, I spoke with Iraqi Prime Minister Maliki. I reaffirmed that the United States keeps its commitments. He spoke of the determination of the Iraqi people to forge their own future. We are in full agreement about how to move forward.

So today I can report that, as promised, the rest of our troops in Iraq will come home by the end of the year. After nearly 9 years, America's war in Iraq will be over.

Over the next 2 months, our troops in Iraq—tens of thousands of them—will pack up their gear and board convoys for the journey home. The last American soldier [soldiers]° will cross the border out of Iraq with their held—heads held high, proud of their success, and knowing that the American people stand united in our support for our troops. That is how America's military efforts in Iraq will end.

But even as we mark this important milestone, we're also moving into a new phase in the relationship between the United States and Iraq. As of January 1 and in keeping with our strategic framework agreement with Iraq, it will be a normal relationship between sovereign nations, an equal partnership based on mutual interests and mutual respect.

In today's conversation, Prime Minister Maliki and I agreed that a meeting of the Higher Coordinating Committee of the strategic framework agreement will convene in the coming weeks. And I invited the Prime Minister to come to the White House in December, as we plan for all the important work that we have to do together. This will be a strong and enduring partnership. With our diplomats and civilian advisers in the lead, we'll help Iraqis strengthen institutions that are just, representative, and accountable. We'll build new ties of trade and of commerce, culture and education that unleash the potential of the Iraqi people. We'll partner with an Iraq that contributes to regional security and peace, just as we insist that other nations respect Iraq's sovereignty.

As I told Prime Minister Maliki, we will continue discussions on how we might help Iraq train and equip its forces, again, just as we offer training and assistance to countries around the world. After all, there will be some difficult days ahead for Iraq, and the United States will continue to have an interest in an Iraq that is stable, secure, and self-reliant. Just as Iraqis have persevered through war, I'm confident that they can build a future worthy of their history as a cradle of civilization.

Here at home, the coming months will be another season of homecomings. Across America, our service men and women will be reunited with their families. Today I can say that our troops in Iraq will definitely be home for the holidays.

This December will be a time to reflect on all that we've been though in this war. I'll join the American people in paying tribute to the more than 1 million Americans who have served in Iraq. We'll honor our many wounded warriors and the nearly 4,500 American patriots—and their Iraqi and coalition partners—who gave their lives to this effort.

And finally, I would note that the end of war in Iraq reflects a larger transition. The tide of war is receding. The drawdown in Iraq allowed us to refocus our fight against Al Qaida and achieve major victories against its leadership,

---

° White House correction.

including Usama bin Laden. Now, even as we remove our last troops from Iraq, we're beginning to bring our troops home from Afghanistan, where we've begun a transition to Afghan security in [and]° leadership. When I took office, roughly 180,000 troops were deployed in both these wars. And by the end of this year that number will be cut in half. And make no mistake: It will continue to go down.

Meanwhile, yesterday marked the definitive end of the Qadhafi regime in Libya. And there too, our military played a critical role in shaping a situation on the ground in which the Libyan people can build their own future. Today, NATO is working to bring this successful mission to a close.

So to sum up, the United States is moving forward from a position of strength. The long war in Iraq will come to an end by the end of this year. The transition in Afghanistan is moving forward, and our troops are finally coming home. As they do, fewer deployments and more time training will help keep our military the very best in the world. And as we welcome home our newest veterans, we'll never stop working to give them and their families the care, the benefits, and the opportunities that they have earned.

This includes enlisting our veterans in the greatest challenge that we now face as a nation: creating opportunity and jobs in this country. Because after a decade of war, the nation that we need to build—and the nation that we will build—is our own, an America that sees its economic strength restored just as we've restored our leadership around the globe.

Thank you very much.

NOTE: The President spoke at 12:49 p.m. in the James S. Brady Press Briefing Room at the White House.

Remarks on Presenting the National Medal of Science and the National Medal of Technology and Innovation
October 21, 2011

Welcome, everybody. Please have a seat. It is a great pleasure to be with so many outstanding innovators and inventors. And I'm glad we could convince them all to take a day off—[*laughter*]—to accept our Nation's highest honor when it comes to inventions and innovation, and that is the National Medals of Science and the National Medals of Technology and Innovation.

It's safe to say that this is a group that makes all of us really embarrassed about our old science projects. [*Laughter*] You know, the volcano with the stuff coming out—[*laughter*]—with the baking soda inside. Apparently, that was not a cutting-edge achievement—[*laughter*]—even though our parents told us it was really terrific.

But thanks to the men and women on the stage, we are one step closer to curing diseases like cancer and Parkinson's. Because of their work, soldiers can see the enemy at night and grandparents can see the pictures of their grandchildren instantly and constantly. Planes are safer, satellites are cheaper, and our energy grid is more efficient, thanks to the breakthroughs that they have made.

And even though these folks have not sought out the kind of celebrity that lands you on the cover of People magazine, the truth is that today's honorees have made a bigger difference in our lives than most of us will ever realize. When we fill up our cars, talk on our cell phones, or take a lifesaving drug, we don't always think about the ideas and the effort that made it all possible. We don't always ask ourselves how many sleepless nights went by and how many family dinners were sacrificed. But the folks behind me, they know. They worked those long nights. They made those sacrifices. They took on those challenges and ran those experiments and devoted their lives to expanding the reach of human understanding.

And that's why we recognize them today. Because America has always been a place

---

° White House correction.

where good ideas can thrive and dreams can become real, where innovation is encouraged and the greatest minds in the world are free to push the very limits of science and technology.

To understand that, you don't have to look any further than the people on this stage. Three-quarters of our honorees were born outside of the United States. From China, Germany, India, Canada, and England, they searched for the best universities and the most advanced labs, and they found them here, because America is the best place in the world to do the work that they do.

And now more than ever, it's critical that we make the investments necessary to keep it that way. We live in a global economy where companies and factories can be located anywhere there's an Internet connection. And to compete in that economy, we can't cut corners by paying workers less or building cheaper products. We won't be able to engage in a race to the bottom; that's not who we are.

The key to our success has always been and always will be our unparalleled ability to think up new ideas, create new industries, and lead the way in discovery and innovation. And that's how the future will be won.

Right now, unfortunately, barely more than 1 in 10 of all undergraduate students are enrolled in what we call the STEM subjects—science, technology, engineering, and math—areas that will be critical if America is going to compete for the jobs of the future. And that's troubling, because no matter how many great minds we attract from around the world, it won't be enough if we can't grow some here at home.

That's why we've worked to make college more affordable, why we've set a goal to train 100,000 new teachers in the next decade, and started a Race to the Top to encourage schools to improve the way they teach these subjects. That's why we're working with businesses to train more engineers and help community colleges provide more workers with the skills that businesses need.

And just as we're working to cultivate the next generation of thinkers, we're also working to fast track the next generation of doers. We've made historic investments in technology and research, made the most meaningful reforms to our patent process in 50 years, and made it easier for entrepreneurs to turn new ideas into new businesses and new jobs. I want to thank someone who helped make that happen. NASA Administrator Charles Bolden is here, and we're very pleased to have him as well.

As the men and the women on this stage will tell you, nobody gets here on their own. Each of them succeeded because they had a great teacher, a great mentor, or a great partner. Some of them don't have to look far for inspiration. In fact, I hear that Jackie Barton's husband won the same award she's getting today in 2006—*[laughter]*—and they plan on displaying their medals next to each other on a mantle at home, which, I would imagine, will intimidate dinner guests. *[Laughter]*

And just as each of today's honorees has had someone in their lives who lit a spark or kept that spark burning, they've paid it back by inspiring somebody else. When Peter Stang won this award, he made sure to thank the 100 postdoctoral and Ph.D. students he's mentored over the years, because, as he said, "this recognizes their work as well." When Jay Baliga first got interested in physics by picking up a book at the local bookstore, he remembered that, and he now tells his students to go beyond the curriculum and come up with ideas of their own. When Richard Tapia remembers what it's like growing up as a son of Mexican immigrants and the first one in his family to go to college, today, he is a world-class mathematician, but he, because of those memories, helps more young people—especially women and minorities—to get involved in math and in science.

And in the end, that's what this today is all about. One of the best ways we can inspire more young people to think big, dream big dreams, is by honoring the people who already do, folks who are smart and aren't afraid to show it, but also folks who have taken that brilliance and gone out and changed the world.

Because that next generation is already coming; they're already knocking on the door. A couple of weeks ago, I got a chance to meet the winners of the Google Science Fair. I want to point out that all three of them were girls. And they had beat out—[*applause*]. Right? They had beat out 10,000 other applicants from over 90 countries. So I had them over to the Oval Office, and they explained their projects to me, and I pretended that I understood. [*Laughter*]

One of the winners, Shree Bose, did her first experiment in second grade by trying to turn spinach blue. [*Laughter*] In fourth grade, she built a remote-controlled garbage can. And for this science fair, at the age of 17, she discovered a promising new way to improve treatment for ovarian cancer—at 17. And she also told me very matter-of-factly that she'll be going to medical school and getting a doctorate, and I suspect she will do so. [*Laughter*] She did not lack confidence.

And it's young people like Shree, but also the people on this stage, who make me incredibly hopeful about the future. Even at a time of great uncertainty, their stories remind us that there are still discoveries waiting to be made and unlimited potential waiting to be tapped. All we have to do is encourage it and support it.

So I want to congratulate today's honorees for their extraordinary and inspiring work. We could not be prouder of all of you.

And now it is my privilege to present the National Medals of Science and the National Medals of Technology and Innovation.

[*At this point, the Military Aide to the President read the citations, and the President presented the medals.*]

The President's Weekly Address
October 22, 2011

This week, we had two powerful reminders of how we've renewed American leadership in the world. I was proud to announce that, as promised, the rest of our troops in Iraq will come home by the end of this year. And in Libya, the death of Muammar Qadhafi showed that our role in protecting the Libyan people and helping them break free from a tyrant was the right thing to do.

In Iraq, we've succeeded in our strategy to end the war. Last year, I announced the end of our combat mission in Iraq. We've already re-

Well, let's, please, give one more big round of applause to the National Medals of Science, the National Medals of Technology and Innovation. We are very proud of them. And I hope all the young people who are either watching or who are here today take inspiration from the extraordinary work that they do.

I will say that the only problem with these wonderful awards is my Military Aides really have to practice reading the citations—[*laughter*]—because they are multisyllabic. [*Laughter*] But you did good. [*Laughter*]

All right, with that, I hope everybody enjoys this wonderful celebration and reception, and again, thank you so much for helping to make the world a better place.

Thank you, everybody.

NOTE: The President spoke at 2:09 p.m. in the East Room at the White House. In his remarks, he referred to Peter P. Dervan, Bren Professor of Chemistry, California Institute of Technology, husband of medal recipient Jacqueline K. Barton; and Shree Bose, Lauren Hodge, and Naomi Shah, winners of the 2011 Google Science Fair. Participating in the ceremony were medal recipients Jacqueline K. Barton, Ralph L. Brinster, Shu Chien, Rudolf Jaenisch, Peter J. Stang, Richard A. Tapia, Srinivasa S.R. Varadhan, Rakesh Agrawal, B. Jayant Baliga, C. Donald Bateman, Yvonne C. Brill, and Michael F. Tompsett.

moved more than 100,000 troops, and Iraqi forces have taken full responsibility for the security of their own country. Thanks to the extraordinary sacrifices of our men and women in uniform, the Iraqi people have the chance to forge their own future. And now the rest of our troops will be home for the holidays.

In Libya, our brave pilots and crews helped prevent a massacre, save countless lives, and give the Libyan people the chance to prevail. Without putting a single U.S. servicemember on the ground, we achieved our objectives.

Soon our NATO mission will come to a successful end, even as we continue to support the Libyan people and people across the Arab world who seek a democratic future.

These successes are part of the larger story. After a decade of war, we're turning the page and moving forward with strength and confidence. The drawdown in Iraq allowed us to refocus on Afghanistan and achieve major victories against Al Qaida and Usama bin Laden. As we remove the last of our troops from Iraq, we're beginning to bring our troops home from Afghanistan.

To put this in perspective, when I took office, roughly 180,000 troops were deployed in these wars. By the end of this year, that number will be cut in half and an increasing number of our troops will continue to come home.

As we end these wars, we're focusing on our greatest challenge as a nation: rebuilding our economy and renewing our strength at home. Over the past decade, we spent a trillion dollars on war, borrowed heavily from overseas, and invested too little in the greatest source of our national strength, our own people. Now, the nation we need to build is our own.

We have to tackle this challenge with the same urgency and the same unity that our troops brought to their fight. That's why we have to do everything in our power to get our economy moving again. That's why I'm calling on Congress to pass the "American Jobs Act," so we can rebuild our country—our schools, our roads, our bridges—and put our veterans, construction workers, teachers, cops, and firefighters back to work. And that's why I hope all of us can draw strength from the example of our men and women in uniform.

They've met their responsibilities to America. Now it's time to meet ours. It's time to come together and show the world why the United States of America remains the greatest source for freedom and opportunity that the world has ever known.

NOTE: The address was recorded at approximately 3:55 p.m. on October 21 in the Diplomatic Reception Room at the White House for broadcast on October 22. In the address, the President referred to Col. Muammar Abu Minyar al-Qadhafi, former leader of Libya, who was killed near Sirte, Libya, on October 20. The transcript was made available by the Office of the Press Secretary on October 21, but was embargoed for release until 6 a.m. on October 22.

Statement on the Death of Crown Prince Sultan bin Abd al-Aziz Al Saud of Saudi Arabia
October 22, 2011

It was with great regret that I learned of the passing of Crown Prince Sultan bin Abd al-Aziz of Saudi Arabia. As Minister of Defense and Aviation for almost 50 years, Crown Prince Sultan dedicated himself to the welfare and security of his people and country and was a valued friend of the United States. He was a strong supporter of the deep and enduring partnership between our two countries forged almost seven decades ago in the historic meeting between President Roosevelt and King Abd al-Aziz Al Saud. On behalf of the American people, I extend my deepest condolences to King Abdallah, the royal family, and the people of Saudi Arabia.

Statement on Libya's Declaration of Liberation
October 23, 2011

On behalf of the American people, I congratulate the people of Libya on today's historic declaration of liberation. After four decades of brutal dictatorship and 8 months of deadly conflict, the Libyan people can now celebrate their freedom and the beginning of a new era of promise.

Now that the fighting in Libya has reached an end, the Transitional National

Council (TNC) must turn its attention to the political transition ahead. We look forward to working with the TNC and an empowered transitional government as they prepare for the country's first free and fair elections. The Libyan authorities should also continue living up to their commitments to respect human rights, begin a national reconciliation process, secure weapons and dangerous materials, and bring together armed groups under a unified civilian leadership. As they take these steps, the United States will continue our close cooperation with our international partners and the U.N. Support Mission in Libya to help advance a stable, democratic transition.

Statement on the Earthquake in Turkey
October 23, 2011

We have been following reports of the earthquake in Turkey's eastern province of Van with great concern. On behalf of the American people, I express my deepest condolences to the families of the victims. Our thoughts and prayers are with the brave men and women who are working to bring assistance to this stricken region. We stand shoulder to shoulder with our Turkish ally in this difficult time and are ready to assist the Turkish authorities.

Statement on Elections in Tunisia
October 23, 2011

Today, less than a year after they inspired the world, the Tunisian people took an important step forward. I congratulate the millions of Tunisians who voted in the first democratic elections to take place in the country that changed the course of history and began the Arab Spring. Just as so many Tunisian citizens protested peacefully in streets and squares to claim their rights, today they stood in lines and cast their votes to determine their own future. Now Tunisia begins the hard work of forming an interim government, drafting a new Constitution, and charting a democratic course that meets the aspirations of all Tunisians. The United States reaffirms its commitment to the Tunisian people as they move toward a democratic future that offers dignity, justice, freedom of expression, and greater economic opportunity for all.

Remarks at a Democratic National Committee Fundraiser in Las Vegas, Nevada
October 24, 2011

The President. Hello, Vegas! Thank you. Thank you so much. It is good to be back in Las Vegas. It is good to be back in Nevada. I love coming to Vegas. The only people who love coming more is my staff. [*Laughter*] I would not be surprised if some of them miss the plane accidentally. [*Laughter*] But is wonderful to be with all of you.

I want to especially thank Stephen for the incredible work that he is doing right now, because as a consequence of his work, we are going to see more tourism dollars in Las Vegas, more tourism dollars in Nevada, more tourism dollars in the United States of America. So please give him a big round of applause for all his efforts.

I see a lot of friends here, folks who have been with me for a long time. And to all of you, I just want to say thank you. But I'm here today not just because I need your help again. I am here because the country needs your help. I'm here because if you thought that the last election was critical to our future, then I can promise you that what happens in the coming year is going to be even more consequential. It's going to matter to our kids; it's going to matter to our grandkids.

For the past 3 years, we've been wrestling with two kind of crises. We've been dealing with an economic crisis that left far too many folks without a job, far too many folks struggling with housing. But we've also been dealing with a political crisis.

All across the country, people are crying out for action. A lot of folks have spent months looking for work. Others are doing their best just to get by, having to make tough decisions every single day. Maybe they don't go out to a restaurant because they can't afford the gas. Maybe they give up their retirement for now so that they can send their child to college. And you know, these Americans are not asking for a lot. They're not looking for handouts. They don't think government can or should solve all their problems. But they do believe what most of you believe: that America should be a place where no matter where you come from, no matter what you look like, you can make it if you try; that this economy works best when it works for everybody, not just for those at the very top; that if opportunity exists for all Americans, then all of us do well—the folks in the middle and the folks at the top, as well as folks at the bottom.

Most Americans believe that hard work should pay off, that responsibility should be rewarded, that everybody in this country deserves a fair shake and everybody has a responsibility to do their fair share. And these beliefs aren't Democratic values. They're not Republican values. They are American values, and they're the bedrock of what this country has always stood for. That's why I ran for President in the first place. That's why so many of you supported me, poured your hearts into this campaign, because you believed that it was time for our politics to reflect our values.

Now, 3 years later, it's clear that a big chunk of Washington has not gotten the message yet. Just look at what's been going on since I introduced my jobs bill in September. Now, this is a bill that is filled with proposals that, tradition-

ally, Democrats and Republicans have supported in the past: tax cuts for workers and small businesses; funding to rebuild our roads and our bridges and our airports, our infrastructure, our transportation system; putting construction workers back on the job; hiring back teachers and cops, firefighters; giving incentives so that veterans are able to find work when they come home, because, I promise you, if you've laid down your life or risked your life for this country, you should not have to fight for a job when you come home.

So those are the proposals contained in this bill. It's a bill that's fully paid for by asking those of us who make more than $1 million to pay a little more in taxes. Independent economists, people who look at this stuff for a living, say that it's the only plan out there right now that would create jobs in the short term as well as lay a foundation for economic growth in the long term. One economist said it would create nearly 2 million jobs next year—2 million. And by the way, that economist did not work for me. And polls show that an overwhelming majority of Americans support the proposals that are in this bill: Democrats, Independents, and Republicans.

So we've got huge challenges in places like Nevada. We've got a jobs bill out there that is paid for and addresses those challenges. The question is why, despite all the support, despite all the experts who say this jobs bill couldn't come at a more important time, when so many people are hurting, why the Republicans in Washington have said no. They keep voting against it. Now, maybe it's just because I am the one sponsoring it. I don't know. But last week, we had a separate vote on a part of the jobs bill that would put 400,000 teachers, firefighters, and police officers back on the job, paid for by asking people who make more than $1 million to pay one-half of 1 percent in additional taxes. For somebody making $1.1 million a year, that's an extra $500—five hundred bucks. And with that, we could have saved 400,000 jobs.

Most people making more than $1 million, if you talk to them, they'll say, I'm willing to pay $500 extra to help the country. They're patriots. They believe we're all in this thing together. But all the Republicans in the Senate said no. Their leader, Mitch McConnell, said that—and I'm going to make sure I quote this properly—saving the jobs of teachers and cops and firefighters was just, I quote, "a bailout"—a bailout. These aren't bad actors who somehow screwed up the economy. They didn't act irresponsibly. These are the men and women who teach our children, who patrol our streets, who run into burning buildings and save people. They deserve our support.

This is the fight that we're going to have right now, and I suspect this is the fight that we're going to have to have over the next year. The Republicans in Congress and the Republican candidates for President have made their agenda very clear. They have two basic economic principles: first, tax cuts for the very wealthiest and the biggest corporations, paid for by gutting investments in education and research and infrastructure and programs like Medicare. That's agenda item number one. Second is just about every regulation that's out there they want to get rid of: clean air, clean water, you name it.

Now, I agree that there are some rules and regulations that put an unnecessary burden on business at a time when we can't afford it. I mean, we've seen this in our travel bureau, where the bureaucracy for getting a visa to come visit Vegas is too long. We want to get them here quicker; they can stay longer and spend more. And that's why, in addition to what we're doing with the travel bureau, we've already identified 500 regulatory reforms that will save billions of dollars over the next few years—billions of dollars over the next few years. But unfortunately, so far at least, we have not gotten any willingness on the other side to say that some regulations we can't give up.

We are not going to win the race in this competitive 21st-century economy by having the cheapest labor or the most polluted air. That's a race to the bottom that we can't win. There's always going to be a country out there that can exploit its workers more or pollute its air more or pollute its water more, have lower worker safety standards. There's always going to be somebody out there to win that competition. The competition we need to win is because we have the best scientists and we've got the best universities and we've got the best workers and we have the best infrastructure and we've got the best resorts and we've got the best ideas and we've got the best system and it's the most transparent and it's the most accountable. That's how we're going to win the competition for the future. And that's what's at stake right now in this race.

And the worst part is that the ideas that the other side are propagating we've tried. I mean, it would be one thing if, you know what, the economy is not doing very well, let's try something new. Let's try a whole radical new agenda. But what they're proposing we tried for 10 years. Remember? Does anybody remember?

Audience members. Yes!

The President. We cut taxes for our wealthiest citizens. We didn't enforce worker safety rules. We didn't enforce antipollution standards. We didn't enforce regulations on Wall Street. And where did we end up? We ended up with a decade in which income and wages for middle class families flatlined and people tried to make up for it by propping up a housing bubble. And when it went bust we had the worst financial crisis and the worst economic crisis since the Great Depression. That's the end of the road if you travel that path.

So we've got a different set of ideas here. We have a different set of values. And I repeat, they are not Democratic values alone. Abraham Lincoln, in the midst of a Civil War, started land-grant colleges and the Homestead Act and built the intercontinental railroad, started the National Academy of Sciences. He understood—the first Republican President—that you've got to invest in the future in order to win it.

Dwight Eisenhower built the Interstate Highway System, invested in math and science in our schools. My grandfather benefited from a GI bill, like millions of others who came home heroes. And somebody said, you know what, if we give them opportunity, if we give them a chance, there is no doubt that everybody will be better off.

I would not be standing here today if somebody had not made an investment and said, you know what, not everybody is going to be born wealthy, not everybody is going to be born well connected; why don't we make sure that we've got college scholarships out there and student loans so that people can go to college and give something back to this country.

So those are the values that we're going to be fighting for. And I have confidence that those are the values of the American people. And I know those are your values. And it's because you were willing to invest so much, not in me, but in an idea that we can have a politics that is different, have a politics that's focused on not just the here and now, not just focused on party, but is focused on country, not just focused on the next election, but focused on the next generation. It's because you made that investment that we've already made some remarkable changes.

I mean, things are tough right now, but I want everybody to remember what we have accomplished because of you. [*Applause*] What we've accomplished because of you. As tough as things are right now, we were able to stabilize this economy and make sure it didn't go into a great depression, because of you. Because of your efforts, we were able to pass health care reform, and 30 million people are going to get health insurance in this country.

I just had somebody who's here tonight—or here this afternoon—mention the fact that their daughter is very sick. And my prayers are with the family. But he said: "She is 23 years old right now. Because of the Affordable Care Act, right now she is able to stay on my insurance." And that is a huge relief for families across the country. A million extra young people have health insurance because of you, and we haven't even finished implementing that plan.

Because of you, as promised, the war in Iraq will end by the end of this year and all our troops will be home—[*applause*]—all of them. And by the way, the country is stronger, and it is safer. And we are making a transition in Af-

ghanistan, and Al Qaida is on the run, and we have decimated their leadership because of you. Because of you, anybody can serve in our military now, regardless of who they love. "Don't ask, don't tell" is history because of you.

Because of you, there are millions of young people who are getting Pell grants and larger scholarships, because we're no longer subsidizing big banks who were basically just a passthrough for student loans. That money is directly going to the students now, and that's making a huge difference all across the country.

So we've made an enormous difference already, but we've got so much more work to do. We've got to pass comprehensive immigration reform. We've got to make sure that we have a system that reflects the fact that we're a nation of laws and a nation of immigrants.

We're going to have to have an energy policy in this country that makes sense, because I am tired of the U.S. economy being held hostage to the spot oil market. We've got to develop clean energy that will not only put money back in the pocket of consumers, but will also save our environment.

We still have to implement health care reform. We still have to implement financial regulatory reform. We have set up a consumer watchdog that is going to make sure no more hidden fees, no more abusive mortgage practices that had such a devastating effect here in Nevada. But we've got to make sure that it's actually implemented. And the other side, one of their main agendas is to roll it back.

And most of all, we've got to grow an economy that is based not on bubbles, not on shifting sands, not on financial maneuvers, but it's based on innovation and based on investment and based on entrepreneurship. We can do those things. We can close the deficit and make the investment in the future that we need. But I'm only going to be able to do it if you're there with me. [*Applause*] I'm only going to be able to do that if you're there with me.

You know, the—I turned 50 this summer. [*Laughter*] My hair is a little grayer now. You noticed that, huh? Yes. My girls say it's distinguished. [*Laughter*] Michelle says it just makes me look old. [*Laughter*] We've gone through some enormous challenges over the last 3 years, and as much good as we have done, I think there's so much left to do that, understandably, a lot of people feel a little disenchanted. A lot of people feel discouraged.

That old "Hope" poster is fading. It's getting dog eared along the edges there. [*Laughter*] But I just want to remind all of you that we never said this was going to be easy. We never said that change was going to happen overnight. The problems that we confront didn't happen overnight; we weren't going to solve them overnight. The challenges we face in terms of rebuilding an economy that works for everybody, making sure that once again we have the best education system in the world, making sure that once again anybody out there who has a good idea can go out there and make it, making sure that we've got a balanced approach to reducing our deficit and getting our fiscal house in order, all those things we knew were going to take some time.

And so the main challenge that I have for all of you here today is to make sure that you remember why we got on this path in the first place, why we took this journey from the start. We didn't do it because it was going to be easy. You supported a candidate named Barack Hussein Obama. Polls didn't need to tell you that that was going to be hard. You didn't do it because you thought that change would happen overnight. You didn't do it because you were easily discouraged.

These days people look back at the campaign, and they say, oh, that campaign was perfect, you know? It's like, well, no it wasn't. [*Laughter*] We had all kinds of setbacks. We defied the odds. So many of you remember. And we'll do it again. [*Applause*] But we will do it again. I still believe in you, and I believe in the American people. And I'm absolutely convinced that as long as we keep our eyes on where we need to go, here in Nevada and all across the country, that indomitable American spirit, that thing that has gotten through—gotten us through every single tough time we've ever been in, from Revolutionary War to Civil War, slavery, the women's rights movement, the union movement, every step of the way—world wars and great depressions—we've always come out stronger on the other side.

There's something about the American people where, when we are tested, when times are tough, it turns out we are tougher. And when our politics isn't working, then the American people rise up and make sure they work.

This is one of those moments. This is one of those times. And if you keep hoping, and you're willing to put your work and your effort behind it, I have no doubt that not only will we win this election, but more importantly, we're going to win the future, and this country is going to be greater than it's ever been.

Thank you very much, everybody. God bless you. God bless the United States of America.

NOTE: The President spoke at 12:57 p.m. at the Bellagio Las Vegas hotel. In his remarks, he referred to Stephen J. Cloobeck, chairman and chief executive officer, Diamond Resorts International, in his capacity as chairman of the board of the Corporation for Travel Promotion, who introduced the President; and Mark Zandi, chief economist, Moody's Analytics.

Remarks in Las Vegas
October 24, 2011

The President. Good afternoon, everybody.
Audience members. Good afternoon!
The President. Thank you for letting me block your driveways. [*Laughter*]
Audience member. You're welcome.

The President. Well, it is wonderful to be with all of you. And I want to thank Jose and Lissette and their wonderful children for letting us set up right in front of their house, and we just had a wonderful visit.

Without a doubt, the most urgent challenge that we face right now is getting our economy to grow faster and to create more jobs. I know it, the people of Nevada know it, and I think most Americans also understand that the problems we face didn't happen overnight, and so we're not going to solve them all overnight either. What people don't understand though is why some elected officials in Washington don't seem to same the—share the same sense of urgency that people all around the country are.

Last week, for the second time this month, Republicans in the Senate blocked a jobs bill from moving forward, a bill that would have meant nearly 400,000 teachers, firefighters, and first-responders being back on the job. It was the kind of proposal that in the past, at least, Republicans and Democrats have supported. It was paid for, and it was supported by an overwhelming majority of the American people. But they still said no.

Your Senator, Majority Leader Harry Reid, he's been fighting nonstop to help get the economy going. But he's not getting some help from some of the members of the Nevada delegation. So we need them to get their act together. Because the truth is, the only way that we can truly attack our economic challenges, the only way we can put hundreds of thousands of people back to work right now, is with bold action from Congress.

That's why I'm going to keep forcing these Senators to vote on commonsense, paid-for jobs proposals. But last month, when I addressed a joint session of Congress about our jobs crisis, I also said that I intend to do everything in my power to act on behalf of the American people, with or without Congress.

So I'm here to say to all of you and to say to the people of Nevada and the people of Las Vegas, we can't wait for an increasingly dysfunctional Congress to do its job. Where they won't act, I will.

In recent weeks, we decided to stop waiting for Congress to fix No Child Left Behind and decided to give States the flexibility they need to help our children meet higher standards. We took steps on our own to reduce the time it takes for small businesses to get paid when

they have a contract with the Federal Government. And without any help from Congress, we eliminated outdated regulations that will save hospitals and patients billions of dollars.

Now, these steps aren't substitutes for the bold action that we need to create jobs and grow the economy, but they will make a difference. So we're not going to wait for Congress.

I've told my administration to keep looking every single day for actions we can take without Congress, steps that can save consumers money, make Government more efficient and responsive, and help heal the economy. And we're going to be announcing these executive actions on a regular basis.

Now, today what I wanted to focus on is housing, which is something obviously on the minds of a lot of folks here in Nevada. Probably the single greatest cause of the financial crisis and this brutal recession has been the housing bubble that burst 4 years ago. Since then, average home prices have fallen by nearly 17 percent. Nationwide, more than 10 million homeowners are underwater. That means that they owe more on their homes than those houses are worth. And here in Las Vegas, the city that's been hit hardest of all, almost the entire housing market is under severe stress.

Now, this is a painful burden for middle class families, and it's also a drag on our economy. When a home loses its value, a family loses a big chunk of their wealth. Paying off mortgage debt means that consumers are spending less and businesses are making less and jobs are harder to come by. And as long as this goes on, our recovery can't take off as quickly as it would after a normal recession.

So the question is not whether or not we do something about it. We have to do something about it. The question is, what do we do, and how fast do we move? One idea that I've proposed is contained in the jobs act that is before Congress right now, and it's called Project Rebuild.

A lot of homeowners in neighborhoods like this one have watched the values of their home decline not just because the housing bubble burst, but also because of the foreclosure sign next door or the vacant home across the street.

Right now there are hundreds of thousands of vacant homes like these and more than a million unemployed construction workers. That doesn't make any sense when there's work to be done and there are workers ready to do it.

So Project Rebuild connects the two by helping the private sector put construction workers to work rehabilitating vacant or abandoned homes and businesses all across the country. That will help stabilize home prices in communities like this one. And it will help families like the Bonillas to buy a new home and build a nest egg.

This is something that Congress can pass right now, because it's in the jobs bill. We will put construction workers back to work, and we will rebuild homes all across Nevada and all across the country.

If Congress passes this jobs bill, we can get Project Rebuild moving right away. If Congress acts, then people in Nevada and all across the country can get significant relief. But remember what I said: We can't just wait for Congress. Until they act, until they do what they need to do, we're going to act on our own, because we can't wait for Congress to help our families and our economy.

Over the past 2 years, we've already taken some steps to help families refinance their mortgages. Nearly 1 million Americans with little equity in their homes have gotten assistance so far. And we've also made it easier for unemployed homeowners to keep their homes while they're looking for a job. And we're working to turn vacant properties into rental housing, which will help reduce the supply of unsold homes and stabilize housing prices here in Las Vegas and all across the country.

But we can do more. There are still millions of Americans who have worked hard and acted responsibly, paying their mortgage payments on time, but now that their homes are worth less than they owe on their mortgage, they're having trouble getting refinancing, even though mortgage rates are at record lows.

So that's going to soon change. Last month, I directed my economic team to work with the Federal Housing Finance Agency, or FHFA, and their partners in the housing industry to identify barriers to refinancing, knock those barriers down, and explore every option available to help many American homeowners to refinance.

And today I am pleased to announce that the agency that is in charge is going to be taking a series of steps to help responsible homeowners refinance and take advantage of low mortgage rates. So let me just name those steps.

Number one, the barrier will be lifted that prohibits responsible homeowners from refinancing if their home values have fallen so low that what they owe on their mortgage is 25-percent higher than the current value of their home. And this is critically important for a place like Las Vegas, where home values have fallen by more than 50 percent over the past 5 years.

So let me just give you an example. If you've got a $250,000 mortgage at 6-percent interest rates, but the value of your home has fallen below $200,000, right now you can't refinance. You're ineligible. But that's going to change. If you meet certain requirements, you will have the chance to refinance at lower rates, which could save you hundreds of dollars a month and thousands of dollars a year on mortgage payments.

Second, there are going to be lower closing costs, and certain refinancing fees will be eliminated, fees that can sometimes cancel out the benefits of refinancing altogether. So people don't bother to refinance because they've got all these fees that they have to pay. Well, we're going to try to knock away some of those fees.

Third, there's going to be more competition so that consumers can shop around for the best rates. Right now some underwater homeowners have no choice but to refinance with their original lender, and some lenders frankly just refuse to refinance. So these changes are going to encourage other lenders to compete for that business by offering better terms and rates, and eligible homeowners are going to be able to shop around for the best rates and the best terms.

So you take these things together, this is going to help a lot more homeowners refinance at lower rates, which means consumers save money, those families save money, and it gets those families spending again. And it also makes it easier for them to make their mortgage payments so that they don't lose their home and bring down home values in the neighborhood.

I'm going to keep on doing everything in my power to help to stabilize the housing market, grow the economy, accelerate job growth, and restore some of the security that middle class families have felt slipping away for more than a decade.

Now, let me just say this in closing. These steps that I've highlighted today, they're not going to solve all the problems in the housing market here in Nevada or across the country. Given the magnitude of the housing bubble and the huge inventory of unsold homes in places like Nevada, it's going to take time to solve these challenges. We still need Congress to pass the jobs bill. We still need them to move forward on Project Rebuild so we can have more homes like this and wonderful families having opportunity to live out the American Dream.

But even if we do all those things, the housing market's not going to be fully healed until the unemployment rate comes down and the inventory of homes on the market also comes down. But that's no excuse for inaction. That's no excuse for just saying no to Americans who need help right now. It's no excuse for all the games and the gridlock that we've been seeing in Washington.

People out here don't have a lot of time or a lot of patience for some of that nonsense that's been going on in Washington. If any Member of Congress thinks there are no unemployed workers or no down-on-their-luck neighborhoods in their district that would benefit from the proposals in the jobs bill, then they better think again. They should come and talk to the families out here in Nevada. These Members of Congress who aren't doing the right thing right now, they still have a chance to take meaningful action to put people back to work and to help middle class families and homeowners like the Bonillas.

But we can't wait for that action. I'm not going to wait for it. So I'm going to keep on taking this message across the country. Where we don't have to wait for Congress, we're just going to go ahead and act on our own. And we're going to keep on putting pressure on Congress to do the right thing for families all across the country. And I am confident that the American people want to see action. We know what to do. The question is whether we're going to have the political will to do it.

All right? So thank you so much, everybody. God bless you. God bless the United States of America. Thanks for welcoming me to your neighborhood. Thank you.

NOTE: The President spoke at 2:15 p.m. at the residence of Jose and Lissette Bonilla. In his remarks, he referred to Margarita, Franco, and Mario Bonilla, children of Mr. and Mrs. Bonilla.

Remarks at a Democratic National Committee Fundraiser in Los Angeles, California
October 24, 2011

Thank you. Thank you so much. Well, it is wonderful to see all of you here tonight, and I want to thank, first of all, J.L. and Mai for hosting us in this beautiful home. And the Smiths and the Browns and the Carters, thank you guys for your friendship and your support. You guys have just been wonderful.

I'm not going to make a long speech. What I'd rather do is have a conversation session with a group this size.

And by the way, I want to excuse if anybody smells chicken on me. [*Laughter*] We stopped at Roscoe's on the way down. [*Laughter*] I think I have a spot on my tie from the hot sauce.

You know, a lot of you were involved in the campaign back in 2008, and it was an extraordinary time, because what we wanted to do was see if we could have a politics that reflected the best of who we are, a politics that was inclusive, a politics that was hopeful, a politics that wasn't just about tearing the other guy down, but was about lifting the whole country up. But also a politics that would focus on challenges that had been weighing down this country for decades: lack of health care for too many people and a system that was way too expensive even if you had health insurance; lack of an energy policy; a foreign policy where we were engaged in wars that weren't making us safer necessarily and costing us huge amounts in terms of lives and treasure; most importantly, an economy that wasn't working for the American people as a whole.

There were a lot of us who were lucky, who were blessed and were doing well. But for middle class families all across the country, you saw a flatlining of wages and incomes, while the costs of everything from college to health care to retirement were going up and up. And a lot of us who had been blessed, we know a lot of family members who still found themselves trapped and struggling in those circumstances.

And what I'm proud of is that over the last 3 years, we didn't know, when I first started running, that we would end up being confronted with the worst financial crisis and the worst economic crisis since the Great Depression. We didn't understand at that time, even after Lehman's went down, how perilous things might be.

But in addition to making sure that we didn't go into a Great Depression and stabilizing the financial system and reversing a contracting economy to one that was growing so that over the last 2 years we've seen private sector job growth just about every month and 2 million jobs created just over the last 2 years— in addition to all that, what we've also been able to do is still make progress on the things that we talked about making progress on.

And sometimes I think people forget how much has gotten done, whether it's passing health care for 30 million Americans who didn't have it and making sure that young people are able to stay on their parents' health insurance and insurance companies aren't dropping you when you've got coverage, to making sure that we were ending "don't ask, don't tell" so that anybody could serve this country that they love regardless of who they love, to ending the war in Iraq, to making sure that college loans and scholarships were accessible to young people all across the country, to saving the auto industry.

A lot of the things that we promised we'd do, we've done. And I carry around a little checklist, and I think we've gotten about 60 percent of it done so far. And that's not bad for 3 years, because I need another 5. [*Laughter*]

So we've made great progress, but we've got so much more work to do. And obviously, in Washington, the politics that I think people are hoping for is not what they're getting. It's still dysfunctional; it's still perversely partisan. You still have folks who seem to be more interested in the short term and the party and elections than they are in the long term and the future and the next generation.

And we are fighting hard to break through and have the decency of the American people reflected in the decisions we make. Right now we've got a big debate about a jobs bill that we're putting forward. Obviously, the biggest problem we have right now is we stabilized the economy, but with an unemployment rate that's way too high. And we're going to have to make a lot of progress if we're going to be able to put people back to work.

And so we put forward ideas that traditionally have been supported by Democrats and Republicans. Let's get construction workers who have been laid off, and let's put them back on the job rebuilding our roads and our bridges and our hospitals and our schools. Let's make sure that teachers are back in the classroom; we're laying them off in droves all across the country at a time when it's critical that our young people are able to succeed. Let's make sure that we're giving tax breaks to small businesses that need financing, but also small businesses who are hiring veterans, for example. These young men and women who have served us—and I get the chance to meet them every day—incredibly talented. And they've gone and fought for us, and then suddenly, they come back here, and they've got to fight for a job? It makes no sense.

And yet we have not gotten a single Republican vote out of this current Senate. And it's primarily because they don't think that politically it's advantageous to do so. And I think that's a mistake, and so we're putting pressure on them.

Today I announced helping homeowners refinance their homes, because a lot of them are underwater now and so they're having trouble refinancing. But that could free up billions of dollars for American consumers who can then shop and go to Will's movies—[*laughter*]—and spend money at whatever business Magic has—[*laughter*]—and could help grow the economy overall.

So the only way that we're going to make progress is, I'm going to keep on making the case, I'm going to keep on pushing, but I'm also going to need to know that we've got a strong base of support behind us that is able to amplify our message, support our message, and get out there and have the same enthusiasm, the same passion as we did the first time.

And I've said this before: This election will not be as sexy as the first one. Back then, I was—it was still fresh and new, and I didn't have any gray hair—[*laughter*]—and everybody loved the "Hope" posters and all that. [*Laughter*] But this time it's—we've got to grind it out a little bit. We've got to grind it out.

But the cause is the same and my passion is the same and my commitment is the same. And so I hope all of you will join me, because I'm confident if you do that we're going to win. And more importantly, we're going to be able to guide the country in a path that helps over the long term.

So all right. Thank you very much, everybody.

NOTE: The President spoke at 6:04 p.m. at the residence of James and Mai Lassiter. In his remarks, he referred to actors Will Smith and Jada Pinkett Smith; Jay Brown, executive vice president for artists and repertoire, Def Jam Recordings, and his wife Kawanna; Troy Carter, founder, chairman, and chief executive officer, Coalition Media Group, and his wife Rebecca; and Earvin "Magic" Johnson, Jr., former guard, National Basketball Association's Los Angeles Lakers. The transcript was released by the Office of the Press Secretary on October 25. Audio was not available for verification of the content of these remarks.

Remarks at a Democratic National Committee Fundraiser in Los Angeles
October 24, 2011

The President. Hello, everybody! Well, it is good to be here tonight. Everybody, please have a seat. Make yourselves comfortable.

Although some of them have already been acknowledged, I just want to say, first of all, thank you to Eva. She is just a powerhouse. I don't know how much—I couldn't say no if she had called me. [*Laughter*] So—and between her and Giselle and all the folks who helped to make this Futuro Fund possible, I am grateful.

To Melanie and Antonio—could not be more gracious hosts—and their beautiful family, thank you so much. We are grateful to you.

We have some great guests. Somebody who—daughter of a Teamster, fighting for

working people every single day, and one of my favorite people, just a great member of my Cabinet, Hilda Solis. We are so proud of her. There are two of my majors—two—there are two of my favorite mayors as well: Mayor Villaraigosa and Mayor Castro. They work hard every single day on behalf of their constituents. So we're proud of them. One of the finest Senators we have in the country, Bob Mendendez of New Jersey is here in the house. And a personal hero of mine, Dolores Huerta is here. Where's Dolores at? Where is she? There she is back there. We love her.

Before I came to Los Angeles today, I was in Las Vegas. And I think as many of you know,

Las Vegas has been hit as hard as any part of the country as a consequence of a housing bubble that burst. Unemployment is higher than it is any place in the country. There are more homes that are underwater than just about any place in the country.

And we went to announce a new program that we have for refinancing of mortgages, because so many people are having difficulty refinancing, taking advantage of these low rates. Their mortgages are now higher than what the homes are being valued for, and as a consequence, the banks won't refinance. And so we took some executive action to try to get this fixed.

But what was interesting was the setting. We went into this subdivision, and we visited the home of the Bonillas, Jose and Lissette. And their story is a classic American story. Jose had come here 26 years ago as an undocumented worker, and he got a job sweeping floors in a supermarket.

He met Lissette, who was also undocumented and was a housekeeper. And when the amnesty program came, they were able to get legal status here in this country. They had three beautiful children, and for 17 years, they lived in a one-bedroom apartment—all three—the three kids in bunk beds in one room and Jose and Lissette slept in the living room. And that's how they raised their family. But they worked incredibly hard, they saved, eventually each of them got U.S. citizenship, and Jose rose up through the ranks until he was finally a manager at this supermarket. But they still didn't have enough money for a home. And then a program that we had set up that we're now trying to replicate all across the country took homes that were vacant, that had been foreclosed on, and converted them. And so they finally got their first home.

And they invited in the President of the United States, after apologizing to their neighbors for blocking the streets—[*laughter*]—to their home, and we sat around the dining room table and talked about their life and their experience and what was happening to their friends and neighbors and those who had lost their homes and those whose families had been sep-

arated. And at one point in the conversation, Jose says: "Understand our dream is not complete. Our dream will not be complete until my children have all gone to college and they have a home of their own and everybody here in this country understands that they are full-fledged Americans."

Now, what struck me in this conversation was not how unique their story is, but how typical their story is of what built this country, that spirit of being willing to take enormous risks, of coming to a new land, of charting a new course, of starting at the bottom and working your way up, of putting your blood, sweat, and tears into this distant vision for the future. That's what built this country. That's the essence of America; that's its foundation. And when I ran for President, I ran not because of the title, not because of a pursuit of power, but because I so deeply believed in those ideals and those values that helped to propel this country forward and made it a beacon for all the world.

That's what America is. That's why all around the world even today people still think about this country differently than they think about other countries, no matter how critical they may be sometimes, no matter how frustrated they may be. The American ideal, the American creed, is one that animates the entire world. And I ran for President because I want to make sure that this country remains that beacon and remains that ideal. And that the hopes of the Joses and the Lissettes, people all across the country, regardless of their station, regardless of what they look like, regardless of where they come from, that they're going to be able to have that piece of the American Dream.

Now, part of the reason that I ran was because too many people felt that dream slipping away. For a decade, we saw that dream neglected. And so even though some of us were extraordinarily fortunate, those of us at the very top were doing very well, the average family saw their wages flatline, their incomes flatline, even as the cost of everything from a college education to their health care to their groceries to their gas was going up. More and more people felt like they were working harder just to stay in the same place or not to fall behind.

We had a health care system that was broken. We have an energy policy that leaves us subject to the whims of the world oil market. We had a Washington that seemed less and less responsive to those values and ideals that we believe in so deeply. And this was all before the worst economic crisis and the worst financial crisis since the Great Depression.

And so we came in knowing that those problems hadn't been created overnight; they weren't going to be solved overnight. But what we were determined to do was to start realigning Washington to our best selves, not our worst, to start pushing to make sure that folks' voices were heard and that we went back to a system in which everybody has a fair shake, everybody gets a shot, that if they're willing to try they can make it in this country, and where we ask a fair share from everybody. And that's what we've been working on over the last 3 years. And it hasn't always been easy; the other side has been fighting us every step of the way.

But despite that, we brought about change. Despite that, we got health care passed, and 30 million Americans are going to have health care in this country. And a million young people already have health care now that didn't have it before. Despite the resistance, we were able to not only prevent this country from going into a great depression and stabilized the financial system, but were also able to pass financial reform so that we never have the same kinds of irresponsibility on Wall Street again. And we have consumers protected, and people, including in places right here in this city, are protected from unscrupulous mortgage brokers and from credit card companies that are charging hidden fees and taking advantage of families.

Despite the resistance, we were able to make sure that anybody can serve this country that they love, put an end to "don't ask, don't tell." Despite their resistance, we were able to bring about an end to a war and start bringing our troops home. Despite that resistance, we were able to stop sending $60 billion to banks

for the student loan program and start sending that $60 billion to students and expand the Pell grant programs and expand access to college.

And all this has made a incredible difference to people all across the country. And that's before you even get into the amazing work that the Cabinet has done, of people like Hilda Solis making sure that workers are treated fairly and not exploited by their employers and, working in concert with people like Bob Menendez, making progress across a whole range of issues.

So we've seen change. We know what it looks like. We know what it takes. But we've got so much more work to do. And I keep a checklist in my desk, and I kind of see, all right, I made a bunch of these promises during the campaign—[laughter]—and let me see, yes, I got that done—[laughter]—and that one, yes. No, that one's not done yet. [Laughter]

So we've got about 60 percent done in 3 years but—so I'm pretty confident we can get the other 40 percent done in the next 5 years. But to do that, I'm going to need your help. To do that, I am going to need your help because this campaign, this Presidency, was never about me. It was about you. It was about the commitments you made to each other. It was about giving voice to the aspirations and the hopes and the dreams of your friends and your neighbors and your family. It's about folks in this room, all of whom have been incredibly successful, remembering that we're successful because somebody allowed us to be successful, because our parents worked hard.

Just meeting Eva's parents, from San Antonio, and I thought how proud they must be, but also the sacrifices they made, remembering that the history of this country is, is that we have always have had to make investments in the future, in our kids, in our grandkids. And those are commitments that you made to each other when you signed on to this campaign those 3 or 4 years ago.

So we've got more work to do, because the economy is still hurting right now. I've been spending the last month trying to get Congress to do something about jobs in this country. We've put together a jobs proposal that contains the best Democratic and Republican ideas. Historically, these are things that both sides support: putting construction workers back to work rebuilding our roads and our bridges and our hospitals so we've got the best infrastructure in the world; rebuilding our schools. We've got kids in trailers all across the country. They've got science labs that were built in the 1960s. What are we doing? We're in the 21st century. Put those folks back to work. Put teachers back in the classroom. We can't be laying off teachers. We've got to be hiring teachers right now so our kids are doing better than any other kids around the world in terms of math and science and technology.

Giving tax breaks to small businesses so they can excel and hire more people, giving them tax breaks for hiring our veterans—we ask these incredible men and women in uniform to put the pause button on their careers, to leave their families, to put themselves at risk. They shouldn't have to fight for a job when they come home. We should be doing everything we can to put them back to work right now. And yet 100 percent of Republican Senators so far have said no. Maybe it's just because I proposed it—[*laughter*]—because the American people support it, it's paid for, economists say it would create almost 2 million jobs.

So that's what we're up against. We're going to have to fight for jobs. We're going to have to fight to have the kind of energy policy that makes sure that we're freeing ourselves from dependence on foreign oil. We are going to have to fight to make sure that we're continuing to improve our schools all across the country. And yes, we are going to have to fight to make sure that immigration reform is a reality in this country.

I want to make a special point about this, because Giselle, she—[*laughter*]—she's opinionated, so she comes up to me and—before we come out—and she's like, "Barack, we got to"—I won't tell exactly what she said, because there's still press here, and it would have to be edited out. [*Laughter*]

Audience member. [*Inaudible*]

The President. She said, "That's true." She said, "Yes, that's true." [*Laughter*]

But I want to be clear. I believe this is a nation of laws, and this is a nation of immigrants. And those two things don't contradict each other. We have a system that is broken, and we are doing everything we can administratively to try to lessen the pain and the hardship that it's causing, yes, to make sure our borders are secure, but also to say that families like the Bonillas, who are here, they are building this country. They are making it better. They are making it stronger. And we've got to give them opportunities.

And it makes no sense—it makes no sense for us, at a time when we're competing with talent all around the world, to have kids here who are excelling in school, who want to go to universities, who want to get an engineering degree or get a business degree and start some enterprise that could end up growing into the next Apple and the next Google, and we want to send them away? These American kids, these kids who grew up alongside our children? It makes no sense.

But again, I'm going to need your help, because we're not going to be able to get this done by ourselves. We're going to have to mobilize and we're going to have to organize and we've got to tap into those best instincts of the American people in order to make it happen. But we're going to get it done. We are going to get it done. Have no doubt that we're going to get it done.

But here's my final point. In order to get it done, we've got to have the same determination, the same focus, the same hard-headedness, the same passion that that family I saw in Las Vegas today has, the same determination that our parents and our grandparents or great-grandparents had. We've been through tougher times before in this country. We've been through slavery and Jim Crow and a Civil War and two World Wars and a Great Depression. And there have been times where most of the folks in this room wouldn't have had opportunity of the sort we have today. We've been through tougher times.

But somewhere along the way, somebody said it doesn't have to be like that. We can imagine something better. We are determined to create a better future. That's what the

Futuro Fund is all about. And that's what this campaign has always been about. This campaign has never been about glitz and glory or just the blind pursuit of power. That's not why we got involved. That's not why you guys signed up back in 2007, 2008. You supported a candidate named Barack Hussein Obama. The odds were not in your favor. The odds were not in your favor.

You knew it wasn't going to be easy. [*Laughter*] If you thought it was going to be easy, you would have signed up for somebody else. You knew it wasn't going to be easy, but you also knew that if we pulled it off, it would be worth it. And so I was joking with some folks—well, not joking really—I'm a lot grayer now than I was then. [*Laughter*] And these President years are dog years. [*Laughter*] And so there's not the same excitement. It's not quite as cool as it was. Nobody—folks, I don't know if you guys still have those "Hope" posters; they're all kind of—all kind of dog eared.

But here's the message I want to deliver to you today—is, don't get weary. [*Laughter*] Don't get tired. Because I'm not tired. I may be gray, but I'm not tired. My passion is still there. My commitment is still there. My vision for this country is still there. And if you're still there, then we're going to win this election and we are going to create the kind of America that our children and our grandchildren deserve.

God bless you. God bless the United States of America.

NOTE: The President spoke at 8:27 p.m. at the residence of Antonio Banderas and Melanie Griffith. In his remarks, he referred to actor Eva Longoria and her parents, Enrique Longoria, Jr., and Ella E. Mireles; Giselle Fernandez, chair, National Latino Gala; Mayor Antonio R. Villaraigosa of Los Angeles, CA; Mayor Julian Castro of San Antonio, TX; and Dolores C. Huerta, cofounder, United Farm Workers of America. The transcript was released by the Office of the Press Secretary on October 25. Audio was not available for verification of the content of these remarks.

Message to the Congress on Continuation of the National Emergency With Respect to the Situation In or In Relation to the Democratic Republic of the Congo
October 25, 2011

To the Congress of the United States:

Section 202(d) of the National Emergencies Act (50 U.S.C. 1622(d)) provides for the automatic termination of a national emergency unless, prior to the anniversary date of its declaration, the President publishes in the *Federal Register* and transmits to the Congress a notice stating that the emergency is to continue in effect beyond the anniversary date. In accordance with this provision, I have sent to the *Federal Register* for publication the enclosed notice stating that the national emergency with respect to the situation in or in relation to the Democratic Republic of the Congo and the related measures blocking the property of certain persons contributing to the conflict in that country are to continue in effect beyond October 27, 2011.

The situation in or in relation to the Democratic Republic of the Congo, which has been marked by widespread violence and atrocities that continue to threaten regional stability, continues to pose an unusual and extraordinary threat to the foreign policy of the United States. For this reason, I have determined that it is necessary to continue the national emergency to deal with that threat and the related measures blocking the property of certain persons contributing to the conflict in that country.

BARACK OBAMA

The White House,
October 25, 2011.

NOTE: The notice is listed in Appendix D at the end of this volume.

Remarks at a Democratic National Committee Fundraiser in Denver, Colorado
October 25, 2011

The President. Hello, hello, hello! Thank you. It's good to see you. You know, I don't know if I'm supposed to do this. I'm going to move this out of here. This looks a little formal here. [*Laughter*] You guys look safe to me. [*Laughter*]

Everybody, please have a seat, have a seat.

Audience member. You too. [*Laughter*]

The President. No, I think I'm just fine right now. I just want to, first of all, say thanks to all of you, everybody who participated, everybody who helped to organize this extraordinary event. It is great to be back in Denver. I've got some fond memories here. If I'm not mistaken, I think it was a little darker that day. [*Laughter*] But right after I gave my convention speech, I think, I came down here to say thank you to a whole bunch of folks, and some of you were there. And it is a thrill to be here.

If I'm not mistaken, we've got a few luminaries that I want to make sure to acknowledge. First of all, I just had a chance to meet your outstanding Lieutenant Governor, Joe Garcia. So he is right here. John Hickenlooper rode over with me. Had to leave, but on the ride over from the airport, he was—all he could talk about was how outstanding Garcia was and how cool he was. [*Laughter*] So I'm making him blush, but that's because he's not a politician, so he's not used to folks talking about him all the time. But we're very proud of the great work that he's done.

Are our Senators here? They were here earlier. Did they have to—is Bennet here? He just went upstairs. Well, you know I'm telling the truth because I'm going to say it behind their backs—[*laughter*]—Mark Udall and Michael Bennet are doing outstanding work on behalf of the people of Colorado. We could not be prouder of all the work that they are doing, and I want to make sure that I'm not—oh, I think I'd better mention the mayor of the city of Denver, Michael Hancock, who is doing outstanding work as well.

So in these kinds of formats what I want to do is not give a long speech, but rather just have a conversation. So I'm just going to make a few remarks at the top.

I just came from Las Vegas and then Los Angeles and San Francisco, but I want to talk about what was going on in Las Vegas. We were in Las Vegas to announce a new approach to housing refinancing. Some of you may have read about it. That's ground zero in terms of what's happening in housing all across the country. And about 50 percent of the homes in Nevada are underwater. Foreclosure rates are sky high. And there are entire subdivisions that are just being emptied out and foreclosed. And we had a chance to make this announcement in front of the home of Jose and Lissette Bonilla.

Jose came here 26 years ago as an undocumented worker, and Lissette he met here, also didn't have legal status. They were able to take advantage of the pathway to citizenship that was created the last time that we had an immigration reform measure out there. He started out sweeping streets in a supermarket and ended up working his way up to become a manager at this supermarket.

They raised three beautiful kids for 17 years in a one-bedroom apartment. And because of a program that we had initiated as part of the Recovery Act, where we took foreclosed homes that had been boarded up and gutted and put folks to work rehabbing them, they finally had their first home 26 years after he had arrived.

And for most of his children—their children's childhood, they had slept in the living room, because they only had a one-bedroom apartment, and the kids all slept in the one bedroom. And now each of them have their own room. And this is a small, modest place. But it was clean and it was—they had pictures of all the kids and their family along the mantle.

And he said to me: "You know, I'm not finished yet. This is part of the American Dream,

1335

but I'm not going to be finished with the American Dream until I know that my kids have gotten through college, and they have a home of their own and they're able to provide a better life for their children the same way that I've been able to provide a better life for mine. And I can't thank America enough for giving me these opportunities."

And so after this conversation we went out and we made the announcement about the refinancing. And I've been thinking about that story ever since, because it captures the essence of who we are. Most people here—that progression maybe happened 50 years ago or 25 years ago or 100 years ago—but all of us benefited from a combination of parents and grandparents who—and great-grandparents—who were willing to defy the odds and take great risks and fight through discrimination and fight through difficulties and challenges and also a society that said, you know what, if you're willing to work hard and take responsibility, then you'll get a fair shake.

And that, of course, required everybody in the society to do their fair share. And somehow, then, the middle class grew, and people at the bottom had ladders into the middle class, but people at the top also did well because the folks at the bottom and the middle were doing well also.

And that idea of America is what has inspired the world. And for about a decade, that's what people felt had been slipping away, even before this financial crisis, even before the recession, that sense that the stack was increasingly—the deck was increasingly stacked against them and that that same progression where each successive generation is doing better and the middle class is growing stronger and if you do your part you can succeed, people have begun to doubt that. And obviously, the financial crisis and the great recession that we've gone through has made it even worse.

So for the last 3 years, what we've been trying to do is to rebuild that compact that we had with each other as Americans from the ground up. And it's hard, because a lot of problems were neglected for years, and we got distracted, and we made some bad decisions.

And when I ran in 2008, what I was committed to was making sure that those ideals and those values that helped me get to where I am, that they live out not just in communities all across America, but they're also reflected in our politics in Washington. And you guys, a lot of you got involved in the campaign because you had those same values and same ideals and same hope and same faith in the possibility that we could have a Government that was responsive to the people. And so 3 years later, we can look back and say, there are a whole bunch of changes that we've made that haven't all paid off yet, but are laying the groundwork for a better America.

We passed health care reform, and that means 30 million people are going to have health insurance that didn't have it before. And we've got a million young people who already have health insurance. And we're going to start making our health care system smarter and more responsive and higher quality at lower cost.

We passed Wall Street reform to make sure that we don't go through the same kinds of nonsense that we went through 3 years ago, and that consumers are protected from unscrupulous dealings and mortgage brokers who are peddling wares that aren't going to be any good and credit card companies who were charging hidden fees and having a consumer watchdog who is going to be looking after ordinary folks in their financial transactions.

We ended "don't ask, don't tell," because we're a country that makes sure that anybody who loves this country are going to be able to serve this country. And we ended the war in Iraq as we promised, because it was time for us to bring our troops home and focus on rebuilding America.

And on student loans and school reform and on a whole host of issues that don't get a lot of attention—on doubling fuel efficiency standards on cars and trucks to not only free ourselves from dependence on foreign oil, but also to start reducing carbon in the atmosphere and making us more competitive, to saving the auto industry—I keep a checklist in my desk of stuff that I promised to do, and we're through about 60 percent of it—[*laughter*]—which isn't bad for 3 years.

So we know change is possible. It's hard and it's messy, and sometimes it's frustrating, but we know it's possible. But here's the thing. There are a lot of people who are still hurting, and there's still a lot more work to do. And so that other 40 percent that is not done, I'm going to need you, because I need 5 more years. I need 5 more years to get it done.

And frankly, this next year the American people are going to have a choice about alternative visions for where they want to take the country. And we're seeing that reflected in the debate we're having about the jobs bill right now. We've put forward a jobs bill that reflects ideas that traditionally have gotten support from Democrats and Republicans. Rebuilding our infrastructure, our roads and our bridges and airports and schools, putting construction workers back to work all across the country, to make sure that we're moving products and services and people faster and more efficiently—a huge boost to the economy—traditionally, hasn't been a Democratic issue. It's been a bipartisan issue. But they've said no.

We've said let's give tax cuts to small businesses; you guys are the party of tax cuts; let's give tax cuts to small businesses and ordinary folks, not just those at the very top. So far, they've said no.

We said let's get teachers back in the classroom. We know that in the 21st century, nothing is going to be more important than our ability to educate our kids and give them the skills they need to compete. They've said no.

And so we're going to keep on putting pressure on them, but in the meantime, we're saying we can't wait for Congress, and we're going to go ahead and do everything we can through executive actions. Whether it's this refinancing program or tomorrow I'm going to be talking about making college more affordable for young people, we're not going to wait for Congress. But we are going to have to mobilize the American people and have them make a choice about the direction of the country that they want to see us go in.

And I'm confident they're going to make the right choice. I believe that—I am confident that they—[*applause*]—I'm confident they want to see a big and bold and generous America, not a cramped vision that says that the only way that we can compete is by gutting regulations and breaking our commitments to the poor and the vulnerable and our seniors, and that all we do is just cut taxes for folks who don't need tax cuts and weren't even asking for them, and that somehow is going to be the path to prosperity.

I don't believe America is going to compete in the 21st century just by having the cheapest labor and the dirtiest air and the dirtiest water and the worst infrastructure, and that somehow that's going to allow us to succeed. And I don't think the American people are going to buy it either.

But because things are tough, because folks are struggling, because the unemployment rate is still way too high, a lot of folks out there have lost confidence in Washington's ability to act. And so we're going to have an uphill battle. This is going to be a different campaign than it was in 2008, because I didn't have gray hair then. [*Laughter*] I was new and fresh. [*Laughter*] And everybody had "Hope" posters. [*Laughter*] You know.

Audience member. We still do. [*Laughter*]

The President. So I guess my main message—and then I'm going to stop—is I'm going to need you to muster up just as much enthusiasm, just as much fire, just as much tenacity as you did in 2008.

This campaign has never been just about me, this Presidency has never been about me, it's been about you and your capacity to bring about change in America. And I believe in you. That's why I'm running. That's why I'm still here. I have confidence in you, and I hope you have confidence in each other.

Thank you very much, everybody.

NOTE: The President spoke at 7:36 p.m. in the Blue Sky Room at the Pepsi Center. In his remarks, he referred to Gov. John W. Hickenlooper of Colorado; and Margarita, Franco, and Mario Bonilla, children of Las Vegas, NV, residents Jose and Lissette Bonilla. Audio was not available for verification of the content of these remarks.

Remarks at a Democratic National Committee Fundraiser in San Francisco, California
October 25, 2011

Hello, San Francisco! Thank you. Thank you so much. Come on, everybody have a seat. It is wonderful to be back in San Francisco, great to be back in California.

I want to thank a couple of people, especially, first of all, I want to thank Jack Johnson for flying from Hawaii to perform here. Terrific. He told me the waves are good right now. [*Laughter*] So this is a big sacrifice. His nephew is going to Berkeley—Kona—and he's trying to surf here too, and it's a little colder, he's discovered. [*Laughter*] But he's going to make a go at it.

I also want to acknowledge the outstanding mayor of Sacramento, who I expect to try to settle the NBA strike, along with the other work he's done—Kevin Johnson's in the house.

And even though she had to be back in DC, I just want to make sure that everybody knows that Nancy Pelosi continues to fight on behalf of you every single day, and she's doing a great job. So we're very proud of her.

Now, as I look around the room, there's some people who've been supporting me since I was running for the United States Senate. And some of you are relatively new to this process. But I'm here to tell you, whether you're an old grizzled veteran—[*laughter*]—or new to the scene, I need your help. I need your help. But I also, more importantly, want to talk to you about how the country needs your help.

I'm here because if you thought the last election was crucial, then I've got to tell you that what happens in the promise—in this year is going to be more consequential, more important to the future of our kids and our grandchildren than just about any election that we've seen in a very long time.

For the past 3 years, we've been wrestling with two kinds of crises: the worst financial crisis and economic crisis since the Great Depression, but we've also been dealing with a profound political crisis.

All across the country, people are crying out for action. A lot of folks have spent months looking for work. They're living paycheck to paycheck; some are living day to day. Others are doing their best just to get by. Maybe they're giving up going out to a restaurant or going to a movie in order to make sure that they can pay the mortgage. There are folks who maybe have delayed retirement so that they can send their child to college. They're feeling enormous pressure and enormous stress.

And they're not looking for that much. They're not asking for that much. They aren't asking for handouts. They don't think that government can or should do everything to solve their problems. But they do believe what most of you believe, which is that America should be a place where you can make it if you try. That no matter who you are, where you come from, what circumstances you're born into, that if you're willing to put in the work and the effort and you do the right thing, that you can make it. A country where everybody has a fair shake and everybody does their fair share, that's what people are looking for.

And those values, which are reflected in how people deal with each other every day in the workplace and at schools and in their communities and their neighborhoods, they'd like to see those values reflected in Washington as well. And they haven't seen enough of that.

Most folks feel as if the economy works best when it works for everybody, not just those at the very top. They believe that hard work should pay off and that responsibility should be rewarded. And these beliefs are not Democratic values; they're not Republican values. They're American values. They're the bedrock of what this country has always stood for.

While I was in line, I met a gentleman who came here from India with 9 bucks in his pocket and is now the president of a community bank. This country continues to attract talent from all across the world precisely because people believe that there's something special about this place, where what you put into it means you can get that piece of the American Dream. And that's why so many of you worked on the campaign in 2008, because you had that same belief, and you didn't see it reflected in our politics.

Now, 3 years later, it's clear that Washington has not gotten the message yet. That's why, over the last month, I've been hammering at Congress to see if they can actually do something for folks who are hurting out here. That's why we introduced a jobs bill that could actually start putting people back to work right now.

And this is a bill that's filled with Democratic and Republican proposals. These are the kinds of proposals that in the past would have gotten bipartisan support: tax cuts for workers and small businesses, funding to rebuild our roads and our bridges and our schools and to put construction workers back to work, funding to hire teachers and our veterans. It's a bill that's fully paid for by asking those of us who've been most blessed in this society to do a little bit more, to pay a little bit more.

So it's all paid for. And independent economists—people who look at this stuff for a living, not the economists who work for me—say it's the only jobs plan out there that would create jobs right now and grow the economy right now. One economist estimated that we could see as many as 2 million jobs created as a consequence of this bill. And polls show that Americans overwhelmingly support the proposals that are in this bill, not just Democrats, but Independents and Republicans as well.

But despite all this support, despite the fact that these are bipartisan ideas, despite all the experts who say this would give the economy the kind of jolt that it needs right now, we've got Republicans in the Senate who keep on voting against it.

Last week, we had a separate vote on a part of the jobs bill that would put 400,000 teachers and firefighters and police officers back on the job. And it was paid for by asking people who make over a million dollars a year to pay one-half of 1 percent more in taxes. So for someone making $1.1 million a year, that's an extra $500—500 bucks—that would save 400,000 jobs all across the country. And not just any

jobs, but jobs that are vital to the well-being of our kids and our communities.

Most people I know who make more than a million dollars a year would make that contribution willingly. They're patriots. They want to see America strong. But all the Republicans in the Senate, a hundred percent, voted no.

And their leader, Mitch McConnell, actually said that saving the jobs of teachers and cops and firefighters would be nothing more than a "bailout." A bailout. Now, these aren't bad actors who acted irresponsibly and recklessly to destroy the economy. They are the men and women who teach our children and protect our communities and risk their lives for us every single day. They're heroes, and they deserve our support. And it would be good for all of us because it would give the entire economy a boost.

So this is the fight that we're having right now. And this is frankly what the next year is probably going to be about. The Republicans in Congress and the folks running for President have made their agenda crystal clear. They have two basic economic priorities, two basic proposals: tax cuts for the wealthiest individuals and biggest corporations, paid for by gutting investments in education and research and our infrastructure, all the things that helped make America an economic superpower; weaken programs like Medicare and our basic social safety net. That's one proposal. And the second proposal is to gut just about every regulation that you can think of.

Now, I agree that there are some rules and some regulations that put an unnecessary burden on businesses at a time when they can least afford it. And that's why we've already identified 500 regulatory reforms that will save billions of dollars over the next year. But what we can't do, and what I won't do, is to let this economic crisis be used as an excuse to wipe out the basic protections that Americans have counted on for decades.

I reject an argument that says we've got to roll back protections that ban hidden fees by credit card companies or rules that keep our kids from being exposed to mercury or laws that prevent the health insurance industry from exploiting people who are sick. And I reject the idea that somehow if we strip away collective bargaining rights that we'll be somehow better off.

We should not be in a race to the bottom, where we take pride in having the cheapest labor and the most polluted air and the least protected consumers. That is not a competition we can win. What we can win is a future in which we have the highest skilled workers and the best technology and the best manufacturing and the best education system and the best infrastructure. That's the race to the future that I want to win, and I know that's the race to the future that you want to win.

And the worst part of it is, is that it's not as if this is a new argument that they're making. They've been making it for decades, and we tried it for an entire decade. For an entire decade, we cut taxes for people who didn't need it and weren't asking for it, we basically suspended environmental regulations, we didn't do anything with respect to consumers, we didn't rein in health care costs and the health care industry, the financial system pretty much could go and do whatever it wanted. And the result was the worst financial crisis since the Great Depression. So it's not as if we haven't tried what they're talking about.

And during that period, for middle class families, wages and incomes actually fell, even as the economy was growing. It's not as if we haven't tried what they're selling. We have. And it didn't work.

More than that, their basic idea that the only thing we can do to restore prosperity is to somehow break up Government and refund everybody their money through tax cuts and let every company write its own rules and tell every American that they're on their own. That's not who we are. That's not the essence of America.

Yes, we are rugged individualists. And we've got entrepreneurs here and folks who work in Silicon Valley; you've been able to take an idea and go out there and make something out of it. It's remarkable, changing the world. And many of you have been rewarded very well for that. So we take pride in our individualism and our

creativity and our self-reliance. We understand that it's the drive and the initiative of our workers and our companies that make this economy prosperous. But there's always been another thread in our history that says we're all connected, that there are some things we can do better as a nation, some things we can do better together.

Because a big chunk of the entrepreneurs who are in this room, you got an education somewhere, and somebody paid for it. You got a college scholarship somewhere along the line, and somebody paid for it. Somewhere along the line, you were able to use platforms and technologies that had been developed because collectively we decided we were going to invest in basic research. There were rules of the road that governed our economic system that allowed you to prosper.

That too is not just a Democratic idea. Our very first Republican President, Abraham Lincoln, in the midst of a Civil War, invested in the Homestead Act and the National Academy of Sciences and built the transnational railroad and land-grant colleges. Because he understood that for America to succeed, everybody had to have a shot, and to do that, all of us had to chip in to make that investment.

Dwight Eisenhower understood it when he built the Interstate Highway System and invested in all the math and science education that ended up helping us send a man to the Moon. My grandfather would not have gone to college had it not been for the GI bill. And there were Republicans in Congress who supported that along with FDR to make that happen. And as a consequence, not only did millions of Americans end up entering the middle class, but we went on the largest economic boom that we'd ever seen in history.

It's not just a Democratic idea, it's an American idea. And that's what we're fighting for. That's what this election is all about. That's the reason I'm standing here, because somebody gave me a shot. Somebody gave me a fair shake. And that required folks before me—not just my mom, not just my grandparents, but an entire society that was committed and invested in every child having opportunity—for me to be able to stand here today. And that is true for most of you.

So the question is, are we going to continue that story, are we going to continue on that journey for our kids and our grandkids? That's what we're going to have to do today. If we want to compete with other countries for good, middle class jobs, then we're going to have to make America the best place on Earth to do business. And yes, that means cutting away unnecessary regulations. It means making government more efficient and more effective. Yes, it means bringing down our deficit and reducing spending that we don't need so we can make investments where we do.

But we can't just cut our way out of prosperity. If we want to win the future, then we've got to invest in education so that every single child has an opportunity not just to graduate from high school, but to get some secondary education and get the skills and the training they need to succeed. If we want businesses to come here, we've got to invest in new roads and bridges and airports and wireless infrastructure and a smart grid. We're not going to be able to succeed otherwise.

We used to have the best stuff. Anybody been to Beijing Airport lately or driven on a— on high-speed rail in Asia or Europe? What's changed? Well, we've lost our ambition, our imagination, and our willingness to do the things that built the Golden Gate Bridge and Hoover Dam and unleashed all the potential in this country.

If we want industries to start here, we're going to have to make sure that all the research and technology that was developed through programs like DARPA or over at NIH, that that continues. That's how the next Apple or the next Google or the next Skype ends up being created. And instead of just buying and consuming things from other countries, we need to go back to what America has always done best, and that is building and manufacturing and selling goods around the world that are stamped with three words: Made in America. That is something that we can do.

So we can't just go back to an economy that's built on debt or built on outsourcing or built on risky financial ventures that jeopardize our economy and threaten the security of the middle class. We need an economy that is built to last and built to compete, an economy where responsibility is rewarded and hard work pays off and everybody has a chance to get ahead. And that's what we're fighting for. That's what's at stake right now.

And that's why I need your help. I know times are tough right now, and this has been a difficult 3 years for a lot of Americans. And when you look at what's going on in Washington, it's easier to become cynical than ever before about the possibilities and prospects of change through our politics. But here's what I want you to remember. The one way to guarantee that change won't happen is for all of us just to give up, to give in, to go home.

The one thing that we absolutely know for sure is that if we don't work even harder than we did in 2008, then we're going to have a government that tells the American people, you are on your own. If you get sick, you're on your own. If you can't afford college, you're on your own. If you don't like that some corporation is polluting your air or the air that your child breathes, then you're on your own.

That's not the America I believe in. It's not the America you believe in. So we're going to have to fight for the America that we believe in. And that's what this campaign's going to be all about.

Change is hard. Change takes time. But change is possible. It took years to overcome the Great Depression and win World War II. But when we did, we emerged as the most prosperous nation on Earth with the largest middle class in history. And from the moment that we emerged from that war, then we had other struggles to fight. It took years for the civil rights movement to culminate not just in *Brown* v. *Board of Education*, but ultimately, the Civil Rights Act and the Voting Rights Act and all the things that we now take for granted.

It took years from the day that JFK told us we were going to the Moon for us actually to get to the Moon. But eventually, because of steady progress, we made that "giant leap for mankind."

And even on this campaign journey that we've been on together—you know, I notice that people now have a revisionist history. They say: "Oh, that campaign was so easy. It was so smooth." [*Laughter*] That's not how I remember it. [*Laughter*] It was hard. And you signed up for hard, because you decided to support a candidate named Barack Hussein Obama. [*Laughter*] Nobody thought that was going to be easy. Nobody thought that was going to be easy, but you did it anyway. You thought it was worth it.

And today, even though we've got a hard road to travel, we can look back on the change that we've made over the past 3 years with enormous pride. Change is the first bill I signed into law that says in this country an equal day's work gets an equal day's pay, because our daughters need to have the same opportunities as all of our sons get.

Change is not just pulling this economy out of the possibilities of a great depression and stabilizing and making sure we didn't have a financial meltdown, but it's also making sure that we restored the American auto industry so that it is more profitable than it's been in a decade. And by the way, it's profitable making cars that are more fuel efficient than ever before. And we've now doubled fuel efficiency standards on cars and trucks, which is going to take carbon out of our atmosphere and make us less dependent on foreign oil. That's change that you produced. That's what change looks like.

Change is the fact that for the first time in our history, you can serve this country that you love regardless of the person that you love. We ended "don't ask, don't tell." That is change.

Change is the reforms that we made in the financial system so that you can't have credit card companies charging you hidden fees and lenders deceiving homeowners into mortgages that they can't afford and Wall Street banks acting so recklessly that you end up having taxpayers bail them out. That's change.

Change is keeping the promise that I made when I started this campaign that this December we will have all of our troops out of Iraq, back home for the holidays. And we're transitioning out of Afghanistan. And we've refocused our efforts on the terrorists who perpetrated 9/11, which is why we've been able to decimate Al Qaida and make sure that Usama bin Laden never again walks on the face of this Earth. That's change.

Change is the thousands of families who are able to pay for college because we took on the banks and the lenders and made tuition more affordable. Change is the 1 million young adults who already have health insurance under the Affordable Care Act and the 30 million more that are finally going to be able to get coverage. When that law is signed, it will mean for families all across the country they won't be bankrupt if somebody in their family gets sick.

So change is possible. We've made change. And we've made it because of you. And so the question is how committed are you going to be to continue this process.

I keep a checklist in my drawer of my campaign promises. About once a week I take it out and make a little check. [*Laughter*] And we've gotten about 60 percent done so far, in 3 years. But I need another 5 to get the other 40 percent done, so we can get comprehensive immigration reform done and we can have a serious energy policy that finally deals with climate change in a serious way and make sure that we continue to grow our economy in a way that's productive and makes our kids' futures bright.

We've got more work to do. We've got more work to do to reform our education system. We've got more work to do to bring our deficit down in a balanced way. And I can only do it with you. You are the ones who produce change.

This campaign has never just been about me. It's always been about you and your commitments to each other, as fellow Americans, as neighbors and coworkers and friends. Who are we? What do we believe in? What do we care about? What are the better angels of our nature that we want to make sure are reflected in our politics day in, day out? That's what you signed up for back in 2007, 2008.

We didn't promise you easy. But we said that, together, we've got this vision for what we want America to look like. So we made a lot of change, but we've got a lot more work to do.

And I know that I'm now a little grayer—[*laughter*]—and it's not as trendy to be an Obama supporter as it was back in 2008. You know, I was, sort of, the new thing, you know, sort of like the new, new thing. [*Laughter*] We've had setbacks. We've had disappointments. I've made mistakes on occasion. Michelle reminds me of those frequently. [*Laughter*] The "Hope" poster is kind of faded and a little dog eared. [*Laughter*]

But that vision is still there. That commitment is still there. That fundamental belief in the American people is still there.

So if you're with me, if you're all in, if we remind ourselves that America was built because each of us decided to believe in a big, generous, bold America, not a cramped, small America, if we remind ourselves that we are tougher than the times that we're in, and if we remind ourselves that we're better than the politics that we've been seeing, then I'm absolutely confident we are not just going to win this election, we're going to remind everybody around the world just why it is that America is the greatest country in the world.

Thank you, so much, everybody. God bless you. Thank you.

NOTE: The President spoke at 2:25 p.m. at the W San Francisco Hotel. In his remarks, he referred to musician Jack Johnson and his nephew Kona Johnson; and Mark Zandi, chief economist, Moody's Analytics. The transcript was released by the Office of the Press Secretary on October 26.

Remarks at a Democratic National Committee Fundraiser in Denver, Colorado
October 25, 2011

The President. Hello, Colorado! Thank you so much. The—let me start off just by saying that there are certain people who I'm not sure that I'd wish politics on them—[*laughter*]—but I sure am glad they are in politics, and Michael Bennet is one of them. He is one of the finest public servants in the country.

You know about what he did here in Denver in helping to lift up the public schools here, and you're seeing some of the foundation that he laid when he was here starting to pay off. Just before we came onstage, he told me a story about a young man who had benefited from the Denver scholarship initiative, the Denver scholarship fund, and he came to a town hall meeting. Nobody in the family had gone to college before, and now suddenly, this kid was a senior at Colorado and—Colorado College and is somebody who is——

[*At this point, an audience member collapsed.*]

The President. ——everybody all right there? Somebody fall down? No, they've been standing too long. [*Laughter*] No, no, the—I'm kidding. Do we have an EMT here? Okay. All right. Make sure she's okay. I think—no, I think she'll be fine. And, Michael, this is no reflection on the length of your introduction. [*Laughter*]

But Michael was telling a story about how this young man now was just running the place in Colorado, excelling, had a bright future, and the satisfaction that you could hear in Michael's voice about this young man's success tells you about the kind of Senator he is.

In Washington, there are workhorses, and there are show horses. And Michael is a workhorse, and he's working hard on behalf of the people of Colorado every single day. We could not be prouder of him, and I couldn't be prouder of calling him a friend.

Now, in addition to Michael, we've got another outstanding public servant here. I think he's still here. Your own mayor, Michael Hancock's in the house. We appreciate the work that he's doing. He is—you know he's tough because he's the youngest of 10 kids. [*Laughter*] And he cares deeply about the people of Denver and the people of Colorado. And I'm confident he's going to do just as outstanding a job as your current Governor, Governor Hick-enlooper, who was here earlier. So we are—you guys are doing a good job electing the right people here in Colorado. That's all I can say.

Now, I am here not just because I need your help; I'm here, more importantly, because America needs your help. I need—I'm here because your country needs your help. I'm here because if you thought the last election was important, then wait till you get a load of this election. [*Laughter*] I can promise——

Audience member. We got your back!

The President. I appreciate that.

I promise you that what we determine over the next 12 months is going to help shape the future of our children and our grandchildren like just about no other election that we've seen. And part of the reason is because the choices are going to be starker and the stakes are going to be higher. And Michael, I think, aptly described what's at stake.

For the past 3 years we've had two kinds of crises. We've had an economic crisis and a financial crisis, but we've also had a political crisis. And those crises are not yet solved. We've got more work to do.

Right now, all across the country, people are crying out for action. Right here in Colorado, there are folks who are hurting: people living paycheck to paycheck, day to day, people losing their homes, people seeing their businesses closed, people who are wondering if anybody is listening. Even the folks who are doing well are having to make decisions that they didn't have to make 10 years ago, that their parents didn't have to make: Maybe we can't eat out tonight because we can't pay the mortgage; maybe we have to delay retirement in order for our child to go to college.

These Americans are not asking for much. They don't expect government to solve all their problems. They don't want a handout. But they do believe what I'm confident everybody here believes, which is that America should be a place where you can make it if you try, where no matter who you are, no matter what you look like, no matter where you come from, if you are willing to put in the work and dream big dreams and make the effort and act respon-

sibly, that you can succeed. That's the essence of what America has always been about.

Americans believe that the economy works best when it works for everybody, not just those at the top. They believe that hard work should pay off and responsibility should be rewarded, that everybody should get a fair shake and everybody should do their fair share. These aren't Democratic values. They are not Republican values. They are American values. They're the bedrock of how this country was built.

And they're the reason I decided to run for office and the reason I ran for President. They're the reason Michael ran for Senator. Because we believe that these values could not just be reflected in our neighborhoods and our workplaces, in our communities and our churches and our synagogues and our mosques, but they also had to be reflected in our government; that there are certain commitments we make to each other as citizens that have to be upheld. And we weren't seeing that reflected in Washington.

As Michael mentioned, for a lot of folks the crisis didn't start with Lehmans. We had a decade in which wages and incomes had flatlined, while the cost of everything from health care to a college education had been shooting up. Folks were working harder and harder just to stay in place. They took out loans, spouse went into the workplace. They just barely were able to keep it together. And that was before the crisis struck.

And so when I decided to run for office, what I said to myself was that if we can harness the energy of the American people, the decency of the American people, if we can direct the common sense of the American people and start operating not based on the next election, but thinking about the next generation, then there's no challenge we can't solve. We've been through tougher times before. But it requires us to think about our politics in a fundamentally different way.

Now, unfortunately, Washington doesn't seem to have gotten the message yet. For the last month, we've been debating a jobs bill. We successfully stabilized an economy that was in free fall. We prevented ourselves from going into a great depression and seeing a financial meltdown. But unemployment is brutally high.

And so even as we're grappling with how do we get our finances together, how do we shrink this deficit in a responsible, balanced way, our challenge also is how do we get Americans to work right now, how do we restore a sense of momentum and confidence in the economy, even as we're solving these long-term problems.

So I put forward a jobs bill that incorporated ideas that traditionally have gotten support from Democrats and Republicans. We said, you know what, all these construction workers that got laid off after the housing bubble burst, how about putting them to work rebuilding our roads and our bridges and our schools all across the country. Not only is it good for our workers, but it's good for our economy. America became an economic superpower because we knew how to build things. We built the Golden Gate Bridge and the Hoover Dam and the Interstate Highway System. And now we're settling for China having the best high-speed rail and Singapore having better airports? When did that happen?

Let's put them to work. And traditionally, building roads hasn't just been a Democratic idea—[*laughter*]—right?

We said, why don't we start putting our teachers back in the classroom? We know that our kids cannot succeed unless they get the best education in the world. And despite some extraordinary reforms that we're doing all across the country, the fact of the matter is, is that State and local governments are broke and they've been laying off teachers in droves. We said, let's give them some help right now, put teachers back to work. That's not just good for the teachers, that's good for our kids. That shouldn't be a Democratic or a Republican idea.

We said, let's give tax cuts to small businesses for hiring new workers or hiring veterans. We send our men and women in uniform overseas. They sacrifice careers, they sacrifice time with their families, they risk their lives. The last thing they should have to do is fight for a job when they come home. Let's give businesses more incentive to hire them. That's not a Democratic or Republican idea, that's an American idea.

And so in—and we said, let's pay for it. It's got to be paid for. We can't afford to add to the deficit. And we put forward a balanced proposal that said those of us who have been blessed by this country, we can afford to do a little bit more to help the many out there who are struggling. Not out of any notion of, what do the Republicans call it, class warfare? [*Laughter*] It's because somebody looked out for me when I was out there struggling. Somebody gave me opportunity.

That's why I'm successful. That's why Michael is successful. That's why most of us are—here have been able to do well in this country. And it's common sense for me to want to give back. That's what I think most of us understood.

So independent economists looked at this jobs plan; they say this is the only jobs plan out there that in the short term and medium term is actually going to produce jobs. Independent economists who don't work for me say we could get as many as 2 million jobs created if this jobs bill plans—passes. All of which—[*applause*]—and by the way, when the polls are taken about the individual components of this, it turns out that the majority of Americans—not just Democrats, but Independents and Republicans—agree with many of these proposals.

Nevertheless, in the United States Senate, we had a hundred percent of Republicans voting no. They said no to putting teachers back in the classroom. They said no to making sure that construction workers can get back on the job. I'm now breaking up the bill into little pieces because they just didn't understand; it was too big. [*Laughter*] And so we're going to do it piece by piece and explain each time.

Last week, we had a separate vote on the teachers bill. It would put 400,000 teachers, firefighters, and police officers back to work. And I want you all to know, for somebody—to pay for it, we would be asking somebody who makes over a million dollars to pay just one-half of 1 percent more in taxes. Now, what this translates into is if you're making $1.1 million a year, that's an extra 500 bucks. For 400,000 jobs all across the country. Isn't that an investment that's worth making, at a time when we're struggling?

Mitch McConnell was asked, why wouldn't you want to do this? He said, saving the jobs of teachers, firefighters, cops, that's just a "bailout." That's what he called it, a "bailout." A bailout? These aren't folks who acted irresponsibly. These aren't folks who were gaming the system. These are folks who teach our kids and patrol our streets and save our homes if there's a fire. They're us. They deserve support.

So this is the—this is a microcosm, this is an example of the challenge that we're going to be having over the next year and the next 2 years. Where do we want to take this country? Who are we? The other side has a very clear idea of where they want to go. Michael talked about the Ryan plan, but it's not just one plan. I mean, you're seeing it in the debates among the Presidential candidates right now. They've got a particular vision, and it basically boils down to two ideas. The first idea is, we're going to cut taxes on the wealthiest individuals, the biggest corporations, and we're going to pay for that by gutting our investments in education, in basic research, in infrastructure, and weakening our social safety net.

Now, that's not my presentation. You can look at the numbers and what they're proposing. And that is pretty much a uniform approach that they're taking. That's idea number one.

The second proposal is, we're going to gut regulations, any regulations pretty much that we can see out there. We have a once-in-a-lifetime financial crisis because of irresponsibility and reckless behavior. What's your solution? Let's roll back all the regulations that might prevent reckless behavior and irresponsible actions on the part of the financial system so they can do it again.

The—we've made enormous strides here in Colorado and all across the country in terms of clean air and clean water. So what's their solution? Let's roll back environmental protec-tions, basic protections. Let's not just roll back regulations. Let's roll back the entire agency responsible for making sure that companies are acting responsibly when it comes to our environment.

Now, we can all agree that there are regulations out there that don't make sense, that are outdated, that need to be updated. We've identified in my administration over 500 regulatory reforms that can save us billions of dollars over the next several years. We've got to— you've got to prune government because it just adds on top of itself, and after a while, nobody's paying attention to some law that was passed back in 1920 that said everybody had to have a compass on a train—[*laughter*]—and didn't know there was GPS. [*Laughter*]

So there are reforms that have to be made. But you know what, this country is not going to compete in the 21st century based on who's got the cheapest labor and the dirtiest air and the dirtiest water. That race to the bottom is not a race we want to be on. I want a race to the top. I want a race to the future. That's what we're fighting for.

I reject the idea that America is going to be more successful if we abandon the 30 million people who don't have health insurance that are going to get health insurance because of the Affordable Care Act or the million young people who right now have health insurance because we passed that law and are now able to stay on their parents' health insurance until they can find a job that provides them health insurance.

And look, here's the other thing. The arguments that the other side's making, they're not new. We tried them. We tried them for a decade, and they didn't work. They didn't help to build the middle class. They didn't alleviate the stress on families out there that are struggling to get by. They added to the burden. They made it tougher, and it made it—they made us less competitive.

So not only will their vision not work, it's also not who we are. We don't have that kind of cramped vision of what America should be. We don't have a vision of America that says you're on your own. Yes, we are rugged individualists.

We are strong and self-reliant. Our economy grows because of extraordinary entrepreneurs and people who are out there pursuing their dreams and pursuing their ideas. That's part of who we are. But we're also a country that understands we're in this together, that we are connected, that I will be more successful if you are successful.

And that is something that was understood by Abraham Lincoln when he invested in the National Academy of Sciences in the midst of the Civil War and started land-grant colleges. It was understood by Dwight Eisenhower when he built the Interstate Highway System and invested in math and science to make sure that we could win the space race. It was understood by JFK when he looked up at the Moon and he said, you know what, I know it's far away, but we can get there if we pull together. And we did.

Audience member. Yes, we did.

The President. Yes, we did.

And it was understood by Republicans in Congress when they worked with FDR to get the GI bill passed, because they said to themselves, young men who were coming back from war, like my grandfather, if we give them an education, that's not just going to be good for them, that's going to be good for the entire country. That will grow a middle class, and business will have more customers, and people will rise out of poverty, and folks at the very top will do even better because of the success of the country as a whole. It's not just a Democratic idea.

And it's because of that idea that I can stand here before you. Because Michelle and I, we didn't grow up in fame and fortune. But we were singularly blessed to grow up in the United States of America. And that's the idea that got me to run for President in 2008. That's the idea that got you to support me in 2008. And that's the idea that we've got to finish. That's the idea that we've got to complete.

And here's the last point I want to make, and that is that as difficult as change may be, change is possible. And if you doubt that change is possible, think about even as we have struggled with an incredibly difficult economy, even as we have struggled with a resistant opposition—[*laughter*]—you like my word choice there? [*Laughter*] Think about what we've done.

Let me tell you what change looks like. Change looks like the Affordable Care Act and 30 million people getting health insurance and patients knowing that when they buy health insurance, they're not going to get cheated.

Change is $60 billion that used to go into banks who were running the student loan program now going directly to students and millions more children out there able to get scholarships and get loans and going to college like never before.

Change is saying that if you love this country and you want to serve it, then it shouldn't matter who you love, you should be able to love this country, and we ended "don't ask, don't tell."

Change is doubling fuel standards, mileage standards, on cars and trucks—unprecedented over the last 30 years—and in the process saving an auto industry that is now competing all around the world and making a profit for the first time in a very long time and building electric cars and the cars of the future.

And change is ending a war and bringing our troops home for the holidays and making sure that—[*applause*]—making sure America is leading once again. Making sure that America's leading once again not only because of our extraordinary military, but also because of the skill of our diplomacy and the power of our ideals and our example.

That's what change is. That is what you accomplished. This election is not going to be about me. Once again, it's going to be about you. It's going to be about your commitments to each other, about our commitments as citizens to the United States of America and all that it can be.

When I decided to run and some of you decided to support me—[*laughter*]—let me just say that you didn't sign up for something easy. You didn't sign up—you know, you were supporting a candidate for President named Barack Hussein Obama. We knew that wouldn't necessarily poll well. [*Laughter*] So there were—there was an easier path to be had. But you understood then, as I hope you understand now, that this was always about your deepest dreams and aspirations for your family and your children and your grandchildren and your country. And nothing's more powerful when—than when the American people make a decision that they want to bring about the sorts of changes that reflect our best ideals. When that happens, you guys can't be stopped.

And so even though my hair is a little grayer now—[*laughter*]—even though I turned 50 and my girls say I look distinguished, but Michelle says I just look old—[*laughter*]—even though there have been setbacks and there have been frustrations and sometimes the pace of change is painfully slow, I want you to understand that we've got more work to do. Our job is not yet done.

We've got—we still have within our grasp the ability to make sure that once again Ameri-ca is a place where anybody can make it if they try. That's what we're fighting for. That's what this campaign will be about. That's why I will need you.

And so I want you all to understand that, yes, it's true I may be older, but let me tell you, my commitment is unwavering. I am as determined as ever. I am as hopeful as ever. And most importantly, I believe in you and the American people as much as I ever have.

So let's get to work, let's get busy, and let's prove once again why the United States of America is the greatest country on Earth.

God bless you. God bless the United States of America. Thank you.

NOTE: The President spoke at 8:41 p.m. at the Ridgeline restaurant at the Pepsi Center. The transcript was released by the Office of the Press Secretary on October 26.

Remarks at the University of Colorado Denver in Denver
October 26, 2011

The President. Thank you! Well, it is great to be back in Colorado. And it is great to be here at CU Denver.

I tend to have some pretty good memories about Denver. We had a little gathering here a few years ago at Mile High. So coming here gets me fired up. Even when it's snowing outside, I'm fired up. I don't know where else you can go sledding in Halloween. [*Laughter*] It's like, what's up with the snow this soon? I mean, is this actually late? This is late for Denver, huh?

I want to start by thanking Mahala for the wonderful introduction and for sharing her story, which I know resonates with a lot of young people here. I want to thank your outstanding Governor, who's here; John Hickenlooper is in the house. There he is. The mayor of Denver, Michael Hancock, is in the house. The Lieutenant Governor, Joe Garcia, is in the house. And one of the finest public servants, somebody you were wise enough to elect and then reelect as United States Senator, Michael Bennet is in the house.

You guys do a good job when it comes to elected officials in Colorado. I just want you to know. You have a good eye for talent. Now—[*applause*].

Audience member. We love you!

The President. I love you back. I do.

Now, I've been doing a lot of traveling lately. And the reason I've been hitting the road so much is because the folks I'm talking to in cities and small towns and communities all across America, they're—let's face it, they're making a little more sense than the folks back in Washington.

Here in Colorado, you've got folks who are spending months—some, years—looking for work. We've got families who are making tough sacrifices just to pay the bills or the mortgage or college tuition. And Americans know we need to do something about it. And I know this is especially hard for a lot of young people.

You guys came of age at a time of profound change. Globalization and technology have all made the world much more competitive. Although this offers unmatched opportunity—I mean, the way that the world is now linked up and synched up means that you can start a business that's global from your laptop—but it also means that we are going to have to adapt to these changes.

And for decades, too many of our institutions—from Washington to Wall Street—failed to adapt, or they adapted in ways that didn't work for ordinary folk, for middle class families, for those aspiring to get into the middle class. We had an economy that was based more on consuming things and piling up debt than making things and creating value. We had a philosophy that said if we cut taxes for the very wealthiest, and we gut environmental regulations, and we don't enforce labor regulations, and somehow if we let Wall Street just write the rules, that somehow that was going to lead to prosperity. And instead what it did was culminate in the worst financial crisis and the deepest recession since the Great Depression.

Now, for the last 3 years, we've worked to stabilize the economy, and we've made some progress. An economy that was shrinking is now growing, but too slowly. We've had private sector job growth, but it's been offset by layoffs of teachers and police and firefighters of the public sector. And we've still got a long way to go.

And now, as you young people are getting ready to head out into the world, I know you're hearing stories from friends and classmates and siblings who are struggling to find work, and you're wondering what's in store for your future. And I know that can be scary. So the——

[*At this point, there was a disruption in the audience.*]

The President. All right. Thank you, guys. We're looking at it right now, all right? No decision has been made. And I know your deep concern about it. So we will address it.

Now, the—so here's what I also know. And I know that's true for folks who are concerned about the environment, folks who are concerned about foreign policy, but also folks who are concerned about the economy.

When I look out at all of you, I feel confident because I know that as long as there are young people like you who still have hope and are still inspired by the possibilities of America, then there are going to be better days for this country. I know that we are going to come through this stronger than before.

And when I wake up every single morning, what I'm thinking about is how do we create an America in which you have opportunity, in which anybody can make it if they try, no matter what they look like, no matter where they come from, no matter what race, what creed, what faith. And the very fact that you are here, investing in your education, the fact that you're going to college, the fact that you're making an investment in your future tells me that you share my faith in America's future. You inspire me: your hopes and your dreams and your opportunities.

And so the truth is, the economic problems we face today didn't happen overnight, and they won't be solved overnight. The challenges we face on the environment or on getting comprehensive immigration reform done, on all these issues we are going to keep on pushing. And it's going to take time to restore a sense of security for middle class Americans. It's going to take time to rebuild an economy that works for everybody, not just those at the top. But there are steps we can take right now to put Americans back to work and give our economy a boost. I know it. You know it. The American people know it.

You've got leaders like Michael Bennet and Mark Udall and Diana DeGette that are looking out for you. But the problem is, there are some in Washington——

[*The disruption continued.*]

The President. ——there are some in Washington who don't seem to share this same sense of urgency. Last week, for the second time this month, Republicans in the Senate blocked a jobs bill from moving forward.

Now, this is a jobs bill that would have meant nearly 400,000 teachers and firefighters and first-responders back on the job. It was the kind of proposal that in the past has gotten Democratic and Republican support.

It was paid for by asking those who have done the best in our society, those who have made the most, to just do a little bit more. And it was supported by an overwhelming majority of the American people. But they still said no. And it doesn't make sense. How can you say no to creating jobs at a time when so many people are looking for work? It doesn't make any sense.

So the truth is, the only way we can attack our economic challenges on the scale that's necessary, the only way we can put hundreds of thousands of people, millions of people, back to work is if Congress is willing to cooperate with the executive branch and we are able to do some bold action like passing the jobs bill. That's what we need.

And that's why I am going to keep forcing these Senators to vote on commonsense, paid-for jobs proposals. And I'm going to need you to help send them the message. You don't need to tell Michael Bennet; he's already on the page. [Laughter] But I'm going to need you guys to be out there calling and tweeting and all the stuff you do. [Laughter]

But, listen, we're not going to wait though. We're not waiting for Congress. Last month, when I addressed a joint session of Congress about our jobs crisis, I said I intend to do everything in my power right now to act on behalf of the American people, with or without Congress. We can't wait for Congress to do its job. So where they won't act, I will.

And that's why, in recent weeks, we've been taking a series of executive actions. We decided we couldn't stop—we couldn't just wait for Congress to fix No Child Left Behind. We went ahead and decided, let's give States the flexibility they need to meet higher standards for our kids and improve our schools.

We said we can't wait for Congress to help small businesses. We're going to go ahead and say to the Federal Government, pay small businesses faster if they're contractors so they've got more money and they can start hiring more people.

We said we're not going to wait for Congress to fix what's going on in our health care system. We eliminated regulations that will save hospitals and patients billions of dollars. And yesterday we announced a new initiative to make it easier for veterans to get jobs, putting their skills to work in hospitals and community centers.

On Monday, we announced a new policy that will help families whose home values have fallen, to refinance their mortgages and to save up to thousands of dollars a year.

All these steps aren't going to take the place of the needed action that Congress has to get going on—they're still going to have to pass this jobs bill, they've got to create jobs, they've got to grow the economy—but these executive actions we're taking can make a difference.

And I've told my administration, we're going to look every single day to figure out what we can do without Congress. What can we do without them? Steps that can save you money and make government more efficient and responsive and help heal this economy. So we're going to be announcing these steps on a regular basis. And that's why I came to Denver today, to do something that will be especially important to all of you here at CU Denver and millions of students—and former students—all across America.

Now, I mentioned that we live in a global economy, where businesses can set up shop anywhere where there's an Internet connection. So we live in a time when, over the next decade, 60 percent of new jobs will require more than a high school diploma. And other countries are hustling to outeducate us today so they can outcompete us tomorrow. They want the jobs of the future. I want you to have those jobs. I want America to have those jobs. I want America to have the most highly skilled workers doing the most advanced work. I want us to win the future.

So that means we should be doing everything we can to put a college education within reach for every American. That has never been more important. It's never been more important, but let's face it, it's also never been more expensive. There was a new report today, tuition gone up again, on average, much faster than inflation, certainly much faster than wages and incomes.

Over the past three decades, the cost of college has nearly tripled. And that is forcing you, forcing students, to take out more loans and rack up more debt. Last year, graduates who took out loans left college owing an average of $24,000. Student loan debt has now surpassed credit card debt for the first time ever.

Now, living with that kind of debt means making some pretty tough choices when you're first starting out. It might mean putting off buying a house. It might mean you can't start a business idea that you've got. It may mean that you've got to wait longer to start a family, or certainly, it means you're putting off saving for retirement because you're still paying off your student loans.

And when a big chunk of every paycheck goes towards student loans instead of being spent on other things, that's not just tough for middle class families, it's painful for the economy, and it's harmful to our recovery because that money is not going to help businesses grow.

And let me say this: This is something Michelle and I know about firsthand. I've been in your shoes. We did not come from a wealthy family. I know—I was raised mostly by a single mom and my grandparents. And Michelle, she had sort of a "Leave It to Beaver" perfect family, but with—[*laughter*]—but she did. They're wonderful. [*Laughter*] But her dad was a blue-collar worker, and her mom stayed at home. But then when she did go to work, she worked as a secretary. So our folks didn't have a lot of money. We didn't even own our own home; we rented most of the time that we were growing up.

So by the time we both graduated from law school, we had between us about $120,000 worth of debt. We combined and got poorer together. [*Laughter*] So we combined our liabilities, not our assets. [*Laughter*] So we were paying more for our student loans than we paid on our mortgage each month.

And look, obviously, we were lucky to have gotten a great education, and we were able to land good jobs with a steady income. But it still took us almost 10 years to finally pay off all our student debt. And that wasn't easy, especially once we had Malia and Sasha, because now we're supposed to be saving for their college, but we're still paying for ours. [*Laughter*]

So the idea is, how do we make college more affordable, and how do we make sure you are burdened with less debt? Now, college—keep in mind, college isn't just one of the best investments you can make in your future. It's one of the best investments America can make in our future. So we want you in school. [*Applause*] We want you in school. But we shouldn't saddle you with debt when you're starting off.

So that's why, since taking office, we've made it a priority to make college more affordable, reduce your student loan debt. Last year, we fought to eliminate these taxpayer subsidies that were going to big banks. They were serving as middlemen in the student loan program. Some of you may have heard about this. So even though the loans were guaranteed by the Federal Government, we were still paying banks billions of dollars to be pass-throughs for the student loan program.

And we said, well, that's not a good idea. [*Laughter*] That's not a good—now, of course, there were some in Washington who opposed me on this. That's surprising. [*Laughter*] I know, shocking. [*Laughter*] So you had some Republicans in Congress who fought us tooth and nail to protect the status quo and to keep these tax dollars flowing to the big banks instead of going to middle class families. One of them said changing it would be "an outrage." The real outrage was letting banks keep these subsidies while students were working three jobs just to try to get by. That was the outrage. And that's why we ended the practice once and for all, to put a college education within reach of more Americans.

Then, in last year's State of the Union Address, I asked Congress to pass a law that tells 1 million students they won't have to pay more than 10 percent of their income towards student loans. And we won that fight too, and that law will take effect by the time—that law is scheduled to take effect by the time freshmen graduate.

But we decided, let's see if we can do a little bit more. So today I'm here to announce that we're going to speed things up. We're going to make these changes work for students who are in college right now. We're going to put them into effect not 3 years from now, not 2 years from now, we're going to put them into effect next year, because our economy needs it right now and your future could use a boost right now.

So here is what this is going to mean. Because of this change, about 1.6 million Americans could see their payments go down by hundreds of dollars a month, and that includes some of the students who are here today. What we're also going to do is we're going to take steps to consolidate student loans so that instead of paying multiple payments to multiple lenders every month, and let me tell you, I remember this. I remember writing like five different checks to five different loan agencies. And if you lost one that month, you couldn't get all the bills together, you missed a payment, and then suddenly, you were paying a penalty. We're going to make it easier for you to have one payment a month at a better interest rate. And this won't cost—it won't cost taxpayers a dime, but it will save you money, and it will save you time.

And we want to start giving students a simple fact sheet. We're going to call it "Know Before You Owe"—Know Before You Owe—so you have all the information you need to make your own decisions about how to pay for college. And I promise you, I wish Michelle and I had had that when we were in your shoes.

So these changes will make a difference for millions of Americans. It will save you money. It will help more young people figure out how to afford college. It can put more money in your pocket once you graduate. And because you'll have some certainty, knowing that it's only a certain percentage of your income that is going to pay off your student loans, we—that means you will be more confident and comfortable to buy a house or save for retirement. And that will give our economy a boost at a

time when it desperately needs it. So this is not just important to our country right now, it's important to our country's future.

When Michelle and I tuck our girls in at night, we think about how we are only where we are because somewhere down the line, somebody decided we're going to give everybody a chance. It doesn't matter if you're not born wealthy, it doesn't matter if your dad is disabled or doesn't own his own home, it doesn't matter if you're a single mom who had to take food stamps, you're still going to get a shot. You're still going to get an education. This country gave us a chance. And because our parents and their generation worked and sacrificed, they passed on opportunity to us. And they didn't do it alone. It was something that we as a country did together.

And now it is our turn, because the dream of opportunity is what I want for you and I want for my daughters and I want them for your children. I want them for all young people, because no matter how tough times are, no matter how many obstacles stand in our way, we are going to make the dream that all Americans share real once again. And that starts right now. It starts with you. [*Applause*] It starts with you.

I am going to keep doing everything in my power to make a difference for the American people. But, Denver, I need your help. Some of these folks in Washington still aren't getting the message. I need your voices heard. I especially need your young—young people, I need you guys involved. I need you active. I need you communicating to Congress. I need you to get the word out. Like I said, tweet them. Tweet them; they're all tweeting all over the place. [*Laughter*] You tweet them back. Whatever works for you.

Tell them, do your job. Tell them, the President has ideas that in the past have been supported by Democrats and Republicans, there's no reason not to support them just to play politics. It's time to put country ahead of party. It's time to put the next generation ahead of the next election. It's time for all of us in Washington to do our job. It's time for them to do their job. Too many people out there are hurting.

Too many people are out there hurting for us to sit around and doing nothing.

And we are not a people who just sit around and wait for things to happen. We're Americans, we make things happen. We fix problems. We meet our challenges. We don't hold back, and we don't quit. And that's the spirit we need right now.

So, Denver, let's go out and meet the moment. Let's do the right thing, and let's go once again show the world just why it is the United States of America is the greatest nation on Earth.

God bless you. God bless the United States of America. Thank you.

NOTE: The President spoke at 10:25 a.m. at the Auraria Event Center. In his remarks, he referred to Mahala Greer, student, University of Colorado Denver; and his mother-in-law Marian Robinson.

Statement on the Observance of Diwali
October 26, 2011

Today, here in America and around the world, Hindus, Jains, Sikhs, and some Buddhists will celebrate the holiday of Diwali, the festival of lights. Many who observe this holiday do so by lighting the *diya*, or lamp, which symbolizes the victory of light over darkness and knowledge over ignorance. I was proud to be the first President to mark Diwali and light the *diya* at the White House, and last year, Michelle and I were honored to join in Diwali celebrations during our visit to India.

Diwali is a time for gathering with family and friends and—as we experienced in India—celebrating with good food and dancing. It is also a time for contemplation and prayer that serves as a reminder of our obligations to our fellow human beings, especially the less fortunate. To all who are observing this sacred holiday here and around the world, happy Diwali and *Saal Mubarak*.

Statement on Representative John W. Olver's Decision Not To Seek Reelection
October 26, 2011

In the Statehouse and Congress, John Olver has proudly served the people of Massachusetts for over 40 years. He has fought tirelessly for a cleaner environment, modern infrastructure, more affordable housing, and more accessible health care. Michelle and I join the people of Massachusetts in thanking Congressman Olver for his service, and we wish John, his wife Rose, and daughter Martha the very best in the future.

Remarks Prior to a Meeting With Prime Minister Petr Necas of the Czech Republic and an Exchange With Reporters
October 27, 2011

President Obama. I want to extend a heartfelt welcome to Prime Minister Necas and his delegation. This gives me a chance to return the hospitality that the Czech people have provided me on the two occasions that I've had an opportunity to visit. I've always been someone who not only wanted to visit, but—wanted to visit the Czech Republic, but also because I come from Chicago. We've got a lot of people who are originally from the Czech Republic, and they've made enormous contributions to our country as well.

Let me say first at the top, the Prime Minister just came from Brussels, where he was part of the negotiations around the euro zone crisis. I'm glad to see that progress was made in the recent meetings. I think it is a important first step. We've seen that, although it's very

1353

complicated, obviously the countries of the euro zone and all of Europe are committed to the European project and are intent on making sure that it continues.

So we've seen that the message that they are going to deal with this in a serious way has calmed markets all around the world. It will help lay the predicate for long-term economic growth not only in Europe, but around the world. The key now is to make sure that it is implemented fully and decisively, and I have great confidence in the European leadership to make that happen.

With respect to the relationship between the United States and the Czech Republic, it continues to be strong. The Czech Republic is one of our greatest allies and has provided the kind of support and cooperation on both security and nonsecurity issues that is a mark of a true ally. As a fellow NATO member, we have consistently reaffirmed our article 5 commitment that says that an attack on any one of us is an attack on all of us and that we have to make sure that we continue to have the kind of strong mutual defense posture that's required. And the Czech Republic has reflected that commitment in the extraordinary efforts it has made in Afghanistan, for which we are deeply appreciative.

I will tell you that when you talk to American commanders in Afghanistan and you ask them who are some of our best and most effective partners, they consistently say the Czech Republic. And so we are very grateful for their contributions, and we are going to be working and collaborating with them as we move into a transition process where we increasingly make sure that Afghans are taking the security lead in their country.

We also are going to have an opportunity to discuss a range of economic and commercial ties and issues. We want to continue to deepen our relationship around research and development, around civil nuclear power, around how we can strengthen trade between our two countries. And so overall, I think it's fair to say that, although the relationship between the United States and the Czech Republic economically is very strong, it can always be stronger. And we're going to look for additional opportunities for collaboration.

Finally, let me just say that the Czechs continue to inspire the world with their own transition from being behind the Iron Curtain to freedom and democracy. And so their strong stance on issues of human rights and democracy and freedom around the world is extraordinarily important. And I know the Prime Minister is committed to making sure that the Czech Republic continues to send a signal around the world, whether it's in the wake of the Arab Spring or other countries where freedom and democracy have not yet been achieved, that they are able to continue to set a great example and provide the kind of leadership and technical assistance that's so important for many of these countries.

So overall, Mr. Prime Minister, I want to thank you for your leadership not only in our bilateral relations, but the Czech Republic's leadership in many multilateral fora. We want to welcome you, and I hope that you enjoy your stay here.

Prime Minister Necas. Thank you. Thank you, Mr. President, for your kind words. Thank you for your hospitality you have shown to me and to my delegation.

We are indeed allies in numerous endeavors in Europe and around the world. We are together in Afghanistan. We are ready to work together on the process of transition in this country.

We are preparing NATO summit in Chicago, in Mr. President's hometown, and also, a city with many Czech connections.

It will be necessary to create a framework for keeping our defense capability in the current economical situation. I would like to discuss the issue of the Czech project to create a special helicopter pilot training center of excellence, as a part of a smart defense initiative within NATO.

We would like to discuss, of course, the economical situation, the situation on both sides of the Atlantic, vis-a-vis the current crisis of euro zone, and last but not least, the promotion of human rights and democracy around the world.

We would like to discuss our participation within Open Government Partnership initiative and, of course, the discussion concerning Center for Civil Nuclear Cooperation, because we do appreciate your strong leadership, your announcement that you'd like to have a vision of a world without nuclear weapons that was announced in Prague.

So thank you for your hospitality.

President Obama. Welcome. Thank you so much. Thank you everybody.

Europe's Economic Stabilization Efforts/U.S. Economy

Q. Mr. President, do you think that the deal in Europe will help prevent another recession?

President Obama. There's no doubt that it's progress. And so the key now is to make sure that there's strong follow-up, strong execution of the plans that have been put forward. But I was very pleased to see that the leaders of Europe recognize that it is both in Europe's interest and the world's interest that the situation is stabilized. And I think they've made significant progress over the last week. And the key now is just to make sure that it drives forward in an effective way.

It will definitely have an impact on us here in the United States. If Europe is weak, if Europe is not growing, as our largest trading partner, that's going to have an impact on our businesses and our ability to create jobs here in the United States.

All right, thanks, guys.

NOTE: The President spoke at 3:21 p.m. in the Oval Office at the White House.

Joint Statement by President Barack Obama and Prime Minister Petr Necas of the Czech Republic
October 27, 2011

Building on the long friendship between our two countries, we met today to discuss how to strengthen and deepen our bilateral relationship and to examine how we can increase our cooperation in promoting common ideals and interests. The United States and the Czech Republic are NATO allies and partners in numerous joint endeavors in Europe and around the world. We agreed to further develop our relations in three main areas: security cooperation; economic and commercial ties, including civil nuclear energy cooperation; and cooperation in the promotion of democracy, open government and human rights around the world. Toward that end, we identified the following goals:

- Negotiate and sign a reciprocal defense procurement agreement

- Establish a center for civil nuclear cooperation

- Cooperate in the implementation of the Open Government Partnership Initiative, which could lead to the establishment of an open government and democracy center in Prague

We discussed other important topics, including the global economic situation and energy security. We confirmed our support for safe and secure nuclear power, and agreed that nuclear power is not only important for ensuring energy security, but also for reaching our goals on reducing carbon emissions. We reviewed our cooperation in eastern Afghanistan, where our troops operate closely together in one of the most challenging areas of the country. We agreed that it will be important to maintain sufficient forces and funding during the transition to ensure that the Afghan National Security Forces are in a position to assume lead security responsibility in 2014.

We also reviewed plans for the upcoming NATO summit in Chicago, where we share the belief that the Atlantic Alliance needs to adapt to meet the security challenges of the 21st century. We agreed that we need to be more efficient in the use of our defense resources.

Finally, we discussed our cooperation in supporting the transition in the Middle East and North Africa and in promoting democracy, open government and human rights around the world. We agreed that the Czech experience offers a powerful and compelling example to others struggling to build new democracies of how to conduct a peaceful and inclusive transition to a free and democratic society.

NOTE: An original was not available for verification of the content of this joint statement.

Statement on Europe's Economic Stabilization Efforts
October 27, 2011

We welcome the important decisions made last night by the European Union, which lay a critical foundation for a comprehensive solution to the euro zone crisis. We look forward to the full development and rapid implementation of their plan. We will continue to support the EU and our European allies in their efforts to address this crisis as we work together to sustain the global recovery and put our people back to work.

Statement on the Selection of Prince Nayif bin Abd al-Aziz Al Saud as Crown Prince and Deputy Prime Minister of Saudi Arabia
October 28, 2011

I congratulate King Abdallah and the Saudi people on the selection of Prince Nayif bin Abd al-Aziz Al Saud as Crown Prince and Deputy Prime Minister of the Kingdom of Saudi Arabia. Crown Prince Nayif has served his nation with dedication and distinction for more than 35 years as Minister of Interior and as Second Deputy Prime Minister since 2009. We in the United States know and respect him for his strong commitment to combating terrorism and supporting regional peace and security. The United States looks forward to continuing our close partnership with Crown Prince Nayif in his new capacity, as we strengthen the deep and longstanding friendship between the United States and Saudi Arabia.

Statement on the United States District Court Approval of the Settlement in the *Pigford II* Class-Action Lawsuit on Discrimination by the Department of Agriculture
October 28, 2011

The U.S. District Court's approval of the settlement between the Department of Agriculture (USDA) and plaintiffs in the *Pigford II* class-action lawsuit is another important step forward in addressing an unfortunate chapter in USDA's civil rights history. This agreement will provide overdue relief and justice to African American farmers and bring us closer to the ideals of freedom and equality that this country was founded on. I especially want to recognize the efforts of Secretary Vilsack and Attorney General Holder, without whom this settlement would not have been reached.

Memorandum on Accelerating Technology Transfer and Commercialization of Federal Research in Support of High-Growth Businesses
October 28, 2011

Memorandum for the Heads of Executive Departments and Agencies

Subject: Accelerating Technology Transfer and Commercialization of Federal Research in Support of High-Growth Businesses

Section 1. Policy. Innovation fuels economic growth, the creation of new industries, companies, jobs, products and services, and the global competitiveness of U.S. industries. One driver of successful innovation is technology transfer, in which the private sector adapts Federal research for use in the marketplace. One of the goals of my Administration's "Startup America" initiative, which supports high-growth entrepreneurship, is to foster innovation by increasing the rate of technology transfer and the economic and societal impact from Federal research and development (R&D) investments. This will be accomplished by committing each executive department and agency (agency) that conducts R&D to improve the results from its technology transfer and commercialization activities. The aim is to increase the successful outcomes of these activities significantly over the next 5 years, while simultaneously achieving excellence in our basic and mission-focused research activities.

I direct that the following actions be taken to establish goals and measure performance, streamline administrative processes, and facilitate local and regional partnerships in order to accelerate technology transfer and support private sector commercialization.

Sec. 2. Establish Goals and Measure Progress. Establishing performance goals, metrics, and evaluation methods, as well as implementing and tracking progress relative to those goals, is critical to improving the returns from Federal R&D investments. Therefore, I direct that:

(a) Agencies with Federal laboratories shall develop plans that establish performance goals to increase the number and pace of effective technology transfer and commercialization activities in partnership with non-federal entities, including private firms, research organizations, and non-profit entities. These plans shall cover the 5-year period from 2013 through 2017 and shall contain goals, metrics, and methods to evaluate progress relative to the performance goals. These goals, metrics, and evaluation methods may vary by agency as appropriate to that agency's mission and types of research activities, and may include the number and quality of, among other things, invention disclosures, licenses issued on existing patents, Cooperative Research and Development Agreements (CRADAs), industry partnerships, new products, and successful self-sustaining spinoff companies created for such products. Within 180 days of the date of this memorandum, these plans shall be submitted to the Office of Management and Budget (OMB) which, in consultation with the Office of Science and Technology Policy (OSTP) and the Department of Commerce, shall review and monitor implementation of the plans.

(b) The Interagency Workgroup on Technology Transfer, established pursuant to Executive Order 12591 of April 10, 1987, shall recommend to the Department of Commerce opportunities for improving technology transfer from Federal laboratories, including: (i) current technology transfer programs and standards for assessing the effectiveness of these programs; (ii) new or creative approaches to technology transfer that might serve as model programs for Federal laboratories; (iii) criteria to assess the effectiveness and impact on the Nation's economy of planned or future technology transfer efforts; and (iv) an assessment of cooperative research and development venture programs.

(c) The Secretary of Commerce, in consultation with other agencies, including the National Center for Science and Engineering Statistics, shall improve and expand, where appropriate, its collection of metrics in the Department of

Commerce's annual technology transfer summary report, submitted pursuant to 15 U.S.C. 3710(g)(2).

(d) The heads of agencies with Federal laboratories are encouraged to include technology transfer efforts in overall laboratory evaluation.

Sec. 3. Streamline the Federal Government's Technology Transfer and Commercialization Process. Streamlining licensing procedures, improving public availability of federally owned inventions from across the Federal Government, and improving the executive branch's Small Business Innovation Research (SBIR) and Small Business Technology Transfer (SBTT) programs based on best practices will accelerate technology transfer from Federal laboratories and other facilities and spur entrepreneurship. Some agencies have already implemented administrative changes to their SBIR and SBTT programs on a pilot basis and achieved significant results, such as reducing award times by 50 percent or more. Over the past year, some agencies have also initiated pilot programs to streamline the SBIR award timeline and licensing process for small businesses. In addition, some agencies have developed new short-term exclusive license agreements for startups to facilitate licensing of inventions to small companies. Therefore:

(a) Agencies with Federal laboratories shall review their licensing procedures and practices for establishing CRADAs with the goal of reducing the time required to license their technologies and establish CRADAs to the maximum practicable extent.

(b) The Federal Chief Information Officer and the Assistant to the President and Chief Technology Officer shall, in coordination with other agencies: (i) list all publicly available federally owned inventions and, when available, licensing agreements on a public Government database; (ii) develop strategies to increase the usefulness and accessibility of this data, such as competitions, awards or prizes; and (iii) report their initial progress to OMB and OSTP within 180 days of the date of this memorandum.

(c) The heads of agencies participating in the SBIR and SBTT programs shall implement administrative practices that reduce the time

from grant application to award by the maximum practicable extent; publish performance timelines to increase transparency and accountability; explore award flexibility to encourage high quality submissions; engage private sector scientists and engineers in reviewing grant proposals; encourage private sector co-investment in SBIR grantees; partner with external organizations such as mentoring programs, university proof of concept centers, and regional innovation clusters; and track scientific and economic outcomes. The OMB, OSTP, and the Small Business Administration shall work with agencies to facilitate, to the extent practicable, a common reporting of these performance measures.

Sec. 4. Facilitate Commercialization through Local and Regional Partnerships. Agencies must take steps to enhance successful technology-innovation networks by fostering increased Federal laboratory engagement with external partners, including universities, industry consortia, economic development entities, and State and local governments. Accordingly:

(a) I encourage agencies with Federal laboratories to collaborate, consistent with their missions and authorities, with external partners to share the expertise of Federal laboratories with businesses and to participate in regional technology innovation clusters that are in place across the country.

(b) I encourage agencies, where appropriate and in accordance with OMB Circular A–11, to use existing authorities, such as Enhanced Use Leasing or Facility Use Agreements, to locate applied research and business support programs, such as incubators and research parks, on or near Federal laboratories and other research facilities to further technology transfer and commercialization.

(c) I encourage agencies with Federal laboratories and other research facilities to engage in public-private partnerships in those technical areas of importance to the agency's mission with external partners to strengthen the commercialization activities in their local region.

Sec. 5. General Provisions. (a) For purposes of this memorandum, the term "Federal laboratories" shall have the meaning set forth for that term in 15 U.S.C. 3703(4).

(b) This memorandum shall be implemented consistent with applicable law and subject to the availability of appropriations.

(c) Nothing in this memorandum shall be construed to impair or otherwise affect the functions of the Director of OMB relating to budgetary, administrative, and legislative proposals.

(d) Independent agencies are strongly encouraged to comply with this memorandum.

(e) This memorandum is not intended to, and does not, create any right or benefit, substantive or procedural, enforceable at law or in equity by any party against the United States, its departments, agencies, or entities, its officers, employees, or agents, or any other person.

BARACK OBAMA

The President's Weekly Address
October 29, 2011

This week, a new economic report confirmed what most Americans already believe to be true: Over the past three decades, the middle class has lost ground while the wealthiest few have become even wealthier. In fact, the average income for the top 1 percent of Americans has risen almost seven times faster than the income of the average middle class family. And this has happened during a period where the cost of everything from health care to college has skyrocketed.

Now, in this country, we don't begrudge anyone wealth or success. We encourage it. We celebrate it. But America is better off when everyone had the chance to get ahead, not just those at the very top of the income scale. The more Americans who prosper, the more America prospers.

Rebuilding an economy where everyone has the chance to succeed will take time. Our economic problems were decades in the making, and they won't be solved overnight. But there are steps we can take right now to put people back to work and restore some of the security that middle class Americans have lost over the last few decades.

Right now Congress can pass a set of commonsense jobs proposals that independent economists tell us will boost the economy right away. Proposals that will put more teachers, veterans, construction workers, and first-responders back on the job. Proposals that will cut taxes for virtually every middle class family and small business in America. These are the same kinds of proposals that both Democrats and Republicans have

supported in the past. And they should stop playing politics and act on them now.

These jobs proposals are also paid for by asking folks who are making more than a million dollars a year to contribute a little more in taxes. These are the same folks who've seen their incomes go up so much, and I believe this is a contribution they're willing to make. One survey found that nearly 7 in 10 millionaires are willing to step up and pay a little more in order to help the economy.

Unfortunately, Republicans in Congress aren't paying attention. They haven't gotten the message. Over and over, they have refused to even debate the same kinds of jobs proposals that Republicans have supported in the past, proposals that today are supported not just by Democrats, but by Independent and Republican voters all across America. Somehow, though, they found time this week to debate things like whether or not we should mint coins to celebrate the Baseball Hall of Fame. And meanwhile, they're only scheduled to work three more weeks between now and the end of the year.

The truth is, we can no longer wait for Congress to do its job. The middle class families who have been struggling for years are tired of waiting. They need help now. So where Congress won't act, I will.

This week, we announced a new policy that will help families whose home values have fallen to refinance their mortgages and save thousands of dollars. We're making it easier for veterans to get jobs putting their skills to work in hospitals and community health centers. We reformed the student loan process so more young people can get out of debt faster. And we're going to keep announcing more changes like these on a regular basis.

These steps will make a difference. But they won't take the place of the bold action we need from Congress to get this economy moving again. And that's why I need all of you to make your voices heard. Tell Congress to stop playing politics and start taking action on jobs. If we want to rebuild an economy where every American has the chance to get ahead,

then we're going to need every American to get involved. That's how real change has always happened, and that's how it'll happen today.

Thanks.

NOTE: The address was recorded at approximately 2:30 p.m. on October 28 in the Library at the White House for broadcast on October 29. The transcript was made available by the Office of the Press Secretary on October 28, but was embargoed for release until 6 a.m. on October 29.

Remarks at the National Italian American Foundation Gala
October 29, 2011

The President. Hello, hello, hello! Thank you so much. *Viva Italia!* Thank you very much, everybody. Thank you. Thank you so much. Thank you, Nancy, for that generous introduction. I am biased, but I think Nancy was one of the best Speakers of the House this country ever had. She was no doubt the best Italian American Speaker of the House we ever had. And I believe that she will be the best Speaker of the House again in 2013.

Now, I was just out passing out Halloween candy—[*laughter*]—for the kids who were coming to the White House, but now that Malia and Sasha are with their friends, they do not notice that I'm gone. [*Laughter*] They're now getting to that age, they don't care. [*Laughter*] They're pleased that I didn't embarrass them too much during the brief time I was with them.

So I am honored to be here to celebrate National Italian American Heritage Month and to commemorate the 150th anniversary of Italian unification. And I want to congratulate the president, the chairman, all of you who are doing so much work to keep that heritage alive for the next generation. And I'm grateful for your generous welcome.

Now, I want to make a confession right off the bat. I do not, in fact, have any Italian ancestry. [*Laughter*] Not all of us are that lucky. [*Laughter*] I can't sing like Frankie Avalon. [*Laughter*] Where's Frankie? I can't—he looks

the same! Unbelievable. [*Laughter*] I can't cook as well as any of your grandmothers. [*Laughter*] Michelle won't let me have seconds or thirds anymore. [*Laughter*] So all I've got to offer is a last name that ends in a vowel. [*Laughter*] This is all I've got.

Nevertheless, it is good to see so many *amici*. [*Laughter*] I see many proud sons and daughters of the old country. I see a couple dozen proud Italian American Members of Congress here tonight. Let me offer a special welcome to the guests who join us from Italy this evening, including Italy's Ambassador to the United States, Ambassador Terzi. Thank you so much for your outstanding work. His counterpart, here as well, and he is doing an outstanding job representing us, our Ambassador to Italy, David Thorne. Italy is one of our strongest allies, a fellow founding member of NATO. We look forward to our work together with them, and we're going to be joining them next week at the G–20 to make a series of decisions that are going to be very important for the world economy.

I've also made sure to keep close the advice of Italian Americans by asking some of them to serve in my Cabinet. And as Nancy mentioned, we could not be prouder of Janet Napolitano, who is keeping us safe every single day, and my outstanding Secretary of Defense, Leon Panetta. And as was mentioned, even though she's not here these evening, Jill Biden is proud to come from a long line of Giacoppas. And so she sends her regards.

Tonight I think it's also important for us to honor the proud service of the countless Italian Americans who have fought for this country since our founding, and who wear the uniform today, from the Chief of Staff of the Army, General Ray Odierno, to a hero whom I was proud to bestow our Nation's highest military decoration, and was the first one in a very long time to personally receive the Medal of Honor, Staff Sergeant Salvatore Giunta.

So in a sense, every American joins us in celebrating this anniversary of Italian unification. What would America be without the contributions of Italy and Italian Americans? What would we be without the daring voyages of Columbus and Verrazano and Vespucci? What would our science and technology be without not just DaVinci and Galileo, but Fermi? What would movies and music be without the magic of Capra, Sinatra, or Sophia Loren, my favorite. [*Laughter*] I'm just saying. [*Laughter*]

What would sports be without the guts and the grit of DiMaggio and Lombardi and La Russa?

Audience member. Piazza!

The President. Piazza! [*Laughter*] The White Sox could still use you. [*Laughter*] What would this city be without the influence of Roman thought and architecture, the Piccirilli brothers who—their work on the Lincoln Memorial—Brumidi's magnificent touch on the Capitol?

Although, I must say, it might be nice to know what our politics would—like without the contribution of Machiavelli. [*Laughter*] We—that's been internalized a little too much here in Washington. [*Laughter*]

America would not be what it is today without the unique contributions and the uncommon pride of Italian Americans. And like so many other groups—as Nancy said, like so many other groups, the Italians came to America in search of opportunity. They came with little. Very few were wealthy. But they came with an unwavering faith in God, an unfailing commitment to family, and an unlikely hope in the possibilities of America, the belief that in

this country, you could be prosperous, you could be free, you could think and talk and worship as you please. It was a place where you could make it if you try.

And it wasn't always easy. Italians weren't always welcome. And when we think about today's immigrants, we have to remind ourselves that those of us who now feel comfortable in our American identity, that that wasn't always the case in the past. The opportunities our forbears hoped for wasn't always within reach right away. But they did not wait for anybody to hand it to them. They built new lives for themselves, and at the same time, they ended up building an entire nation. They enriched our heritage and our culture with their own. They helped forge the very promise of this country: that success is possible if you're willing to work for it. And those efforts built a better America for all of us.

Everybody in this room, just about everybody, has an ancestor or lots of ancestors who fit that story of transplanted roots that somehow grew in American soil, of families that struggled and sacrificed so that our families might know something better. Of parents who said, maybe I can't speak English, but I'll make sure my child can speak English; they might teach English someday. I might not have an education, but I'm going to make sure my child has an education. I might perform backbreaking labor today, but someday my child can be a Senator or a Supreme Court Justice or Speaker of the House or a Secretary in the Cabinet or President of the United States.

So that's what binds us together. That is what has always made our country unique. We've always been and we will always be a nation of immigrants from all over the world. And out of many, somehow we're able to forge ourselves into one people; and this is the place where the highest hopes can be reached and the deepest and most sincere dreams can be made real.

And that's the legacy our forebears left for us, and that's what we now have to leave to our children. These are tough times right now, and millions of Americans are hurting. Millions are without work, and those who have work are still all too often struggling to get by. And for many, the dream that brought so many Italian Americans to these shores feels like it's slipping away.

So we've got work to do. But while these times are hard, we have to remind ourselves they're not as hard as those that earlier generations faced. And the legacy of their courage and their commitment and their determination and their generosity and their willingness to think about the next generation—we have to be just as passionate and just as selfless as they were to keep that dream alive and make sure our children inherit futures that are big and bright and that this country is as generous as it's always been.

And that's what we have to commit to ourselves tonight. So on behalf of all Americans, I want to thank you for everything that the Italian American community has done, everything that you've done to contribute to the chronicles and the character of the greatest nation on Earth.

Thank you, so much. God bless you. God bless the United States of America. Thank you.

NOTE: The President spoke at 8:28 p.m. at the Washington Hilton and Towers hotel. In his remarks, he referred to Joseph V. Del Raso, president, and Jerry Colangelo, chairman, National Italian American Foundation; Italy's Ambassador to the U.S. Giulio Terzi di Sant' Agata; Jill T. Biden, wife of Vice President Joe Biden; Anthony La Russa, Jr., manager, Major League Baseball's St. Louis Cardinals; and former Major League Baseball player Michael J. Piazza.

Remarks on Signing an Executive Order To Reduce Prescription Drug Shortages and an Exchange With Reporters
October 31, 2011

The President. Well, thank you all for being here.

The United States, I think rightly, takes pride on having the most innovative and most successful drug industry in the world, and as a consequence the health of a lot of people, both here in the United States and around the world, is actively promoted. But as we also know, occasionally there are problems in our manufacture and distribution of drugs and how accessible they are to people.

And recently, we have seen how the potential of drug shortages for vital drugs, including some cancers, can really have a adverse impact on patients and those who are caring for patients. Sometimes, we run out of or run low on certain types of drugs, and that drives up prices and it increases patient risk.

And I've got a couple of people here beside me who have had to navigate this problem. Jay Cuetara knows what it's like. In August, the center where he was receiving chemotherapy ran out of the drug being used to treat his cancer. And when that happens, you have pharmacy managers like Bonnie Frawley who have to scramble to make sure that their patients can somehow find the lifesaving medications that are necessary.

So over the last 5 years, the number of these drug shortages has nearly tripled. And even though the FDA has successfully prevented an actual crisis, this is one of those slow-rolling problems that could end up resulting in disaster for patients and health care facilities all across the country.

Congress has been trying since February to do something about this. It has not yet been able to get it done. And it is the belief of this administration, as well as folks like Bonnie and Jay, that we can't wait for action on the Hill, we've got to go ahead and move forward.

So as a consequence, I'm going to be signing an Executive order today that directs the FDA to step up work to reduce the drug shortages and protect consumers. We'll still be calling on Congress to pass a bipartisan bill that will provide additional tools to the FDA and others that can make a difference. But until they act, we will go ahead and move.

As part of this, we're going to require that drug companies let us know earlier about the potential for drug shortages so that we can respond successfully. We're going to make sure that if we find out that prices are being driven up because shortages are being made worse by manipulations of companies or distributors, that we are making sure that we stop those practices. We're going to further empower the FDA and the Department of Justice to investigate any kinds of abuses that would lead to drug shortages.

So there's a combination of tools that are going to be contained in this Executive order that can make sure that lifesaving drugs are available, and if we start seeing shortages, that we're able to catch those ahead of time so that Bonnie doesn't have to try to scramble as a pharmacy manager, and Jay obviously doesn't have to scramble as a patient.

This is something that needs to be done. I want to thank the leadership of both our FDA administrator and our Health and Human Services Secretary for having done outstanding work in preparing this Executive order. And again, I still urge Congress to move forward and build on this Executive order so that we

can provide even more tools for our agencies. And I want to thank Bonnie and Jay for being here and for helping inspire us to get this done.

All right. With that I'm going to sign this bill—or this Executive order—excuse me.

[*At this point, the President signed the Executive order.*]

The President. There you go. Thank you very much, everybody. Appreciate it.

President's Meeting With Quartet Representative to the Middle East Tony Blair

Q. Tony Blair—can you tell us anything about the meeting with Tony Blair this morning?

The President. I enjoyed our meeting with Tony Blair.

Thank you. Thank you, guys.

NOTE: The President spoke at 12:50 p.m. in the Oval Office at the White House. In his remarks, he referred to Margaret A. Hamburg, Commissioner, Food and Drug Administration. The Executive order is listed in Appendix D at the end of this volume.

Statement on the Presidential Election in Kyrgyzstan
October 31, 2011

I congratulate the people and Government of Kyrgyzstan for yesterday's democratic and peaceful Presidential election. In casting their ballots, the Kyrgyz people have taken an important and courageous step on the path of democracy and demonstrated their commitment to an orderly and open transition of power. I commend President Otunbaeva for her leadership and for her dedication to a vision of peace-

ful, democratic change. I also congratulate the many Kyrgyz leaders in Government and civil society who worked to realize this moment of promise. The people of Kyrgyzstan will have a partner in the United States as they undertake the hard work of building upon the democratic gains of the past 18 months and realizing a democratic, prosperous, and just future for all Kyrgyz citizens.

Remarks on Signing a Proclamation Establishing the Fort Monroe National Monument and an Exchange With Reporters
November 1, 2011

The President. Well, one of the great pleasures of this job, but also one of my responsibilities, is making sure that we are preserving

our Nation's treasures so that they can be enjoyed by our children, our grandchildren, our great-grandchildren. And over the years, over a hundred sites have been set aside as national monuments, everything from the Statue of Liberty to the Grand Canyon.

So today I am continuing that proud tradition by adding another monument to the list. Fort Monroe in Hampton, Virginia, has played a remarkable role in the history of our Nation. It was the site of the first slave ships to land in the New World. But during the Civil War, almost 250 years later, Fort Monroe also became a refuge for slaves that were escaping from the South and helped create the environment in which Abraham Lincoln was able to sign that document up there, the Emancipation Proclamation.

In September, Fort Monroe closed its doors as a military base. But thanks to the advocacy of some outstanding citizens and historians and elected officials who are represented here, as well as the great work of our Department of the Interior and Ken Salazar and the—all the people who have been involved in making this day possible, we are going to continue this legacy, making Fort Monroe a national monument.

This is going to give an opportunity for people from all across the country to travel to Fort Monroe and trace the history that has been so important to making America what it is. It's also going to be an incredibly important economic boost to the region. Local officials estimate that this may end up creating as many as 3,000 jobs in the region. It will add millions of dollars to the local economy in and around Hampton. And so this is a win-win. Not only is it good for the people of that region now, but it also allows us to set aside this incredibly important site for the enjoyment and appreciation of generations to come.

So I want to thank everybody who's here for the great work that they've done. I am looking forward to not only visiting myself, but also taking Malia and Sasha down there so they get a little bit a sense of their history. And I thank the Commonwealth of Virginia for giving us this opportunity to appreciate the remarkable history of their State, but also of this country.

So with that, I'm going to sign this bill—or Executive order.

[*At this point, the President signed the proclamation.*]

The President. There you go. Thank you so much.

Just one last point I want to make. As I said, there's a strong economic component to this. We think we can see additional jobs in Virginia as a consequence of this. But for those Members of Congress who are here, I still need some action from Congress—[*laughter*]—on the "American Jobs Act" and other steps. But in the meantime, this is going to make a big difference.

And again, I want to thank everybody here, particularly the private citizens who put their time and money and effort into making this day possible.

All right? Thank you, everybody.

Audience members. Thank you.

Death of Dorothy Howell Rodham

Q. Mr. President, any thoughts on Secretary Clinton's loss?

The President. Ms. Rodham was a remarkable person. Anybody who knows her history knows what a strong, determined, and gifted person she was. For her to have been able to live the life that she did and to see her daughter succeed at the pinnacle of public service in this country, I'm sure was deeply satisfying to her.

My thoughts, Michelle's thoughts, the entire White House's thoughts go out to the entire Clinton family. And I know that she will be remembered as somebody who helped make a difference in this country and this world.

All right?

NOTE: The President spoke at 2 p.m. in the Oval Office at the White House. In his remarks, he referred to Secretary of State Hillary Rodham Clinton. The proclamation is listed in Appendix D at the end of this volume.

Message to the Congress on Continuation of the National Emergency With Respect to Sudan
November 1, 2011

To the Congress of the United States:

Section 202(d) of the National Emergencies Act (50 U.S.C. 1622(d)) provides for the automatic termination of a national emergency unless, prior to the anniversary date of its declaration, the President publishes in the *Federal Register* and transmits to the Congress a notice stating that the emergency is to continue in effect beyond the anniversary date. In accordance with this provision, I have sent to the *Federal Register* for publication the enclosed notice stating that the Sudan emergency is to continue in effect beyond November 3, 2011.

The crisis constituted by the actions and policies of the Government of Sudan that led to the declaration of a national emergency in Executive Order 13067 of November 3, 1997, and the expansion of that emergency in Executive Order 13400 of April 26, 2006, and with respect to which additional steps were taken in Executive Order 13412 of October 13, 2006, has not been resolved. These actions and policies are hostile to U.S. interests and continue to pose an unusual and extraordinary threat to the national security and foreign policy of the United States. Therefore, I have determined that it is necessary to continue the national emergency declared with respect to Sudan and maintain in force the sanctions against Sudan to respond to this threat.

BARACK OBAMA

The White House,
November 1, 2011.

NOTE: The notice is listed in Appendix D at the end of this volume.

Remarks on Transportation Infrastructure Improvement and Job Growth Legislation
November 2, 2011

Hello, everybody. All right. Thank you so much, everybody. Please have a seat on this beautiful day. It is good to see all these construction workers out.

Of all the industries hammered by the economic downturn, construction has been among the hardest hit. Since the housing bubble burst, millions of construction workers have had to look for a job. So today I'm joining many of these workers to say that it makes absolutely no sense, when there's so much work to be done, that they're not doing the work; not when there are so many roads and bridges and runways waiting to be repaired and waiting to be rebuilt.

One of these potential projects is behind me, just a few miles from the Capitol Building. It's the Key Bridge, one of the five major bridges that connect the Commonwealth of Virginia to Washington, DC. Two of these five bridges are rated "structurally deficient," which is a fancy way of saying that you can drive on them, but they need repair. Nearly 120,000 vehicles cross these two bridges every single day, carrying hundreds of thousands of commuters and families and children.

They are deficient roads, and there are deficient bridges like this all across the country. Our highways are clogged with traffic. Our railroads are no longer the fastest and most efficient in the world. Our air traffic congestion is the worst in the world. And we've got to do something about this, because our businesses and our entire economy are already paying for it.

Give you an example. Last month, I visited a bridge in Cincinnati on one of the busiest trucking routes in America. More than 150,000 vehicles cross it every single day. But it is so outdated that it's been labeled "functionally

1365

obsolete." It worked fine when it opened 50 years ago. But today, it handles twice the traffic it was designed for, and it causes mile-long backups. That means that big shipping companies like UPS or FedEx are tempted to change routes, but it turns out that would cost them even more to take the long way. So their trucks, their vans are just sitting there, bleeding money, bleeding time.

Smaller businesses, they don't have a choice. They have to go across these bridges. When a major bridge that connects Kentucky and Indiana was recently closed for safety reasons, one small-business owner whose shop is nearby watched his sales fall 40 percent in just 2 weeks. Farmers, they can lose 5 cents a bushel when a rural bridge closes.

So all told, our aging transportation infrastructure costs American businesses and families about $130 billion a year. That's a tax on our businesses; that's a tax on our consumers. It is coming out of your pocket. It's a drag on our overall economy. And if we don't act now, it could cost America hundreds of billions of dollars and hundreds of thousands of jobs by the end of the decade.

So you're paying already for these substandard bridges. You're paying for these substandard roads. You could be paying to make sure that workers were rebuilding these roads, and you would save money in the long term if you did. And I'm speaking to all the American people right now.

Building a world-class transportation system is one of the reasons that America became an economic superpower in the first place. Today, as a share of our economy, Europe invests more than twice what we do in infrastructure; China, more than four times as much. Think about that. Europe invests, as a percentage of its overall economy, twice as much in roads and bridges and airports and ports; China, four times as much.

How do we sit back and watch China and Europe big—build the best bridges and high-speed railroads and gleaming new airports, and we're doing nothing, at a time when we've got more than a million unemployed construction

workers who could build them right here in America right now?

We're better than that. We are smarter than that. We've just got to get folks in Congress to share the same sense of national urgency that mayors and Governors and the American people do all across the country. I've got to say, we've got some Members of Congress here who get it. Amy Klobuchar from Minnesota, she gets it. She's seen a bridge fall apart in her State. Senator Whitehouse from Rhode Island, he gets it. Congressman Larson from Connecticut gets it. I know the mayor of Washington, DC, gets it. But we've got to have everybody on Capitol Hill get it.

Last month, Republicans in the Senate blocked a jobs bill that would have meant hundreds of thousands of private sector construction jobs repairing bridges like this one. It was the kind of idea that in the past, at least, both parties have voted for, both parties have supported. It was supported by the overwhelming majority of the American people. It was paid for. And yet they said no.

The truth is, the only way we can attack our economic challenges on the scale that's needed is with bold action by Congress. They hold the purse strings. It's the only way we're going to put hundreds of thousands of people back to work right now. Not 5 years from now, not 10 years from now, but right now. It's the only way that we're going to rebuild an economy that's not based on financial bubbles, but on hard work, on building and making things right here in the United States of America.

That's the deal that every American is looking for, that we have an economy where everybody who works hard has the chance to get ahead, where the middle class regains some sense of security that has been slipping away for over a decade now.

So that's why I'm going to keep on pushing these Senators and some Members of the House of Representatives to vote on common-sense, paid-for jobs proposals. In the meantime, while I'm waiting for them to act, we're going to go ahead and do what we can do to help the American people find jobs. We're not going to wait for them and do nothing. I've said that I'll do everything in my power to act on behalf of the American people, with or without Congress.

We can't wait for Congress to do its job. If they won't act, I will. And that's why today I'm announcing that we are actually going to expedite loans and competitive grants for new projects all across the country that will create thousands of new jobs for workers like these. If there's money already in the pipeline, we want to get it out faster. And this comes on the heels of our recent efforts to cut redtape and launch several existing projects faster and more efficiently. See, construction workers, they want to do their jobs. We need Congress to do theirs.

But here's the good news: Congress has another chance. They already voted once against this thing; they've got another chance. This week, they've got another chance to vote for a jobs bill that will help private sector companies put hundreds of thousands of construction workers back on the job rebuilding our roads, our airports, our bridges, and our transit systems.

And this bill, by the way, is one that will begin to reform the way we do projects like this. No more earmarks. No more bridges to nowhere. We're going to stop the picking of projects based on political gain and start picking them based on two criteria: how badly they're needed out there and how much good they'll do for our economy. And by the way, that's an idea that came from the good work of a Texas Republican and a Massachusetts Democrat, because infrastructure shouldn't be a partisan issue.

My Secretary of Transportation, who is here, Ray LaHood, a great man from Peoria—[*applause*]—he's the pride of Peoria—he spent a long time in Congress. He's a Republican, member of my Cabinet. He knows how badly we need to act on this issue. The other Members of Congress here, they understand that this is important to their States. I can't imagine that Speaker Boehner wants to represent a State where nearly one in four bridges is classified as "substandard." I'm sure that the Speaker of the House would want to have bridges and roads in his State that are up to par.

When the Senate Republican leader, Mitch McConnell, visited that closed bridge in Kentucky that I was talking about, he admitted, look, "Roads and bridges are not partisan in Washington." That's a quote from him. Paul Ryan, the Republican in charge of the budget process, recently said, "You can't deny that infrastructure does create jobs." Okay, so if the Speaker of the House, the Republican leader in the Senate, all the Democrats all say that this is important to do, why aren't we doing it? What's holding us back? Let's get moving and put America back to work.

The ideas in this legislation are supported by the leading organizations of Republican mayors, supported by Mayor Gray, who's here. The idea would be a big boost for construction and is therefore supported by America's largest business organization and America's largest labor organization. The Chamber of Commerce and the AFL–CIO think this is a good idea to move forward on. And they don't agree on a lot.

And when 72 percent of the American people support the ideas in this bill—72 percent of Americans agree with this, Republicans, Democrats, and Independents—there's no excuse for a hundred percent of Washington Republicans to say no. That means that the Republicans in Washington are out of touch with Republican voters.

We've got to make this happen. Now, if you don't want to take my word for it, take it from one of my predecessors. It's one of the previous Presidents. He said that, and I'm quoting here, "the bridges and highways we fail to repair today will have to be rebuilt tomorrow at many times the cost." He went on to say that rebuilding our infrastructure is "common sense"—that's a quote—and, quote, "an investment in tomorrow that we must make today." That President was Ronald Reagan. We just put up a statue of him at the airport.

Since when do we have Republicans voting against Ronald Reagan's ideas? [*Laughter*] There's no good reason to oppose this bill, not one. And Members of Congress who do, who vote no, are going to have to explain why to their constituencies.

The American people are with me with this. And it's time for folks running around spending all their time talking about what's wrong with America to spend some time rolling up their sleeves to help us make it right. There's nothing wrong in this country that we can't fix. There are no challenges that we can't meet and especially when it comes to building things in America. It was in the middle of the Civil War that Lincoln built the transcontinental railroad. It was during the Great Depression that we built the Hoover Dam that brought electricity to rural America.

We have built things even in the toughest of times—especially in the toughest of times—because it helps us improve our economy. It gets us going. It taps into that can-do American spirit. It gives us pride about what we can accomplish. Now it's our turn to forge the future.

Everybody here, we are Americans. We're not people who sit back and watch things happening. And if Congress tells you they don't have time, they've got time to do it. We've been—in the House of Representatives, what have you guys been debating? John, you've

been debating a commemorative coin for baseball? [*Laughter*] You had legislation reaffirming that "In God We Trust" is our motto? That's not putting people back to work. I trust in God, but God wants to see us help ourselves by putting people back to work.

There's work to be done. There are workers ready to do it. The American people are behind this. Democrats, Republicans, Independents believe in this. These are ideas that have been supported by all those groups in the past. There's no reason not to do it this time. I want you to make sure your voice is heard in the Halls of Congress. I want us to put people back to work, get this economy growing again, and remind the entire world just why it is that America is the greatest country on Earth.

God bless you, and God bless the United States of America.

NOTE: The President spoke at 11:24 a.m. at the Georgetown Waterfront Park. In his remarks, he referred to Mayor Vincent C. Gray of Washington, DC; and Sens. Kathryn A. "Kay" Bailey Hutchison and John F. Kerry.

Memorandum on Delegation of Authority To Submit the Certification and Reports Specified in the Resolution of Advice and Consent to Ratification of the Treaty Between the United States of America and the Russian Federation on Measures for the Further Reduction and Limitation of Strategic Offensive Arms (the "New START Treaty")
November 2, 2011

Memorandum for the Secretary of State and the Director of National Intelligence

Subject: Delegation of Authority to Submit the Certification and Reports Specified in the Resolution of Advice and Consent to Ratification of the Treaty between the United States of America and the Russian Federation on Measures for the Further Reduction and Limitation of Strategic Offensive Arms (the "New START Treaty")

By the authority vested in me as President by the Constitution and the laws of the United States of America, including section 301 of title 3, United States Code, I hereby authorize and direct the Secretary of State to make the annual certification specified in section (a)(2)(A) of the Resolution of Advice and Consent to Ratification of the New START Treaty, and I hereby authorize and direct the Director of National Intelligence to prepare the report specified in that section. The Secretary of State shall submit the certification along with the report prepared by the Director of National Intelligence to the Senate.

I also hereby authorize and direct the Secretary of State to submit the reports specified in section (a)(10) and section (a)(12)(B) of the

Resolution to the Committees on Foreign Relations and Armed Services of the Senate.

The Secretary of State is authorized and directed to publish this memorandum in the *Federal Register*.

BARACK OBAMA

NOTE: This memorandum was not received for publication in the *Federal Register*.

Remarks Following a Meeting With President Nicolas Sarkozy of France in Cannes, France
November 3, 2011

President Obama. Well, it is wonderful to be back in France. And I want to thank my excellent friend and colleague, Nicolas Sarkozy, for his hospitality. He and I obviously have worked together on a wide range of issues since I've been President, and I always welcome his frank and honest assessment of the situations here.

It's also nice to be back visiting in France. The last time I was in the south of France, or the first time, rather, was as a college student, and I've never forgotten the extraordinary hospitality of the French people and the extraordinary views that are available here.

This morning President Sarkozy and I reaffirmed our strong and enduring ties, and I've said on many occasions that France is not only our oldest ally, but also one of our closest, and I consider Nicolas to be an outstanding and trusted partner on the world stage.

I think it's no surprise that we spent most of our conversation focused on strengthening the global economic recovery so that we are creating jobs for our people and stabilizing the financial markets around the world. The most important aspect of our task over the next 2 days is to resolve the financial crisis here in Europe. President Sarkozy has shown extraordinary leadership on this issue. I agree with him that the EU has made some important steps towards a comprehensive solution, and that would not have happened without Nicolas's leadership. But here at the G–20 we're going to have to flesh out more of the details about how the plan will be fully and decisively implemented.

And we also discussed the situation in Greece and how we can work to help resolve that situation as well. And the United States will continue to be a partner with the Europeans to resolve these challenges.

We had the opportunity also to talk about a range of security issues. One in particular that I want to mention is the continuing threat posed by Iran's nuclear program. The IAEA is scheduled to release a report on Iran's nuclear program next week, and President Sarkozy and I agree on the need to maintain the unprecedented international pressure on Iran to meet its obligations.

And finally, I'm looking forward to joining Nicolas and servicemembers from both of our countries tomorrow to celebrate the alliance between our two countries, which spans more than 200 years, from Yorktown to Libya.

And finally, I want to make mention that this is our first meeting since the arrival of the newest Sarkozy, and so I want to congratulate Nicolas and Carla on the birth of Giulia. And I informed Nicolas on the way in that I am confident that Giulia inherited her mother's looks rather than her father's—[*laughter*]—which I think is an excellent thing. And so now we share one of the greatest challenges and blessings of life, and that is being fathers to our daughters.

So again, Nicolas, thank you for your friendship, thank you for our partnership, and thank you for your gracious hospitality.

President Sarkozy. Well, you see Barack Obama's tremendous influence. For 4 years now, he's been explaining to me that to be a father to daughters is a fantastic experience—he who has two daughters. So I have listened to him. As a matter of fact, I followed his example.

I must tell you that we had a heavy agenda because there is no lack of subjects for concern. And we need the leadership of Barack Obama. We need the solidarity and the support of the United States of America. We need joint common analysis as to the way we can put the world back on the path of growth and stability.

Together, President Obama and myself are trying to build the unity of the G–20. And I wish to pay tribute to the United States for understanding about all the issues we'll be discussing over the next 48 hours, and in particular, the issue of the Greek crisis—the difficulty that the euro is facing, the need to be hand in glove with the United States on the language of the final communique.

Again, I want to thank President Obama for his understanding on all matters, including that of a levy or a tax on financial transactions, where I think we found common ground, at least common analysis, mainly that the world of finance must contribute to solving the crisis that we are all facing today.

I also want to say how delighted I am that President Obama has agreed to stay a few hours after the end of the summit in order to participate in ceremonies to pay tribute to American and French troops who have fought together so many times throughout the course of our joint histories. And I'm delighted to be—to have the opportunity to join President Obama in a—on a television interview, because he is much loved and much liked here in France.

So we have a very heavy agenda ahead of us, and we'll have many opportunities to see you again and explain to you what decisions we've been led to take.

President Obama. Thank you very much.

NOTE: The President spoke at 10:38 a.m. at the Palais de Festivals et des Congres in the Espace Riviera. President Sarkozy spoke in French, and his remarks were translated by an interpreter.

Remarks Prior to a Meeting With Chancellor Angela Merkel of Germany in Cannes
November 3, 2011

President Obama. It's wonderful to be back together with my good friend Angela Merkel. I think that the last time we were in Washington, DC, together, we presented her with the Medal of Freedom, and that indicated the high esteem that not only I, but the United States, hold her and her leadership.

This is going to be a very busy 2 days. Central to our discussions at the G–20 is how do we achieve greater global growth and put people back to work. That means we're going to have to resolve the situation here in Europe. And without Angela's leadership, we would not have already made the progress that we've seen at the EU meeting on October 27.

We are now, having seen some progress, looking forward to working together to figure out how we can implement this in an effective way to make sure that not only is the euro zone stable, but the world financial system is stable

as well. And hopefully, during our bilateral meeting, we'll also have the ability to discuss a wide range of other issues, including security issues that are so important to both our countries.

But I just want to say once again how much I enjoy working with Angela. She exhibits the kind of practical common sense that I think has made her a leader not only in Germany, but around the world.

So thank you very much.

Hold on, hold on, hold on—translation. [*Laughter*] All the Americans reporters speak German, but just in case. [*Laughter*]

[*At this point, an interpreter translated President Obama's remarks into German.*]

Chancellor Merkel. Thank you very much, and let me say that I'm delighted that we have the opportunity for this meeting here. And mainly, the G–20 will afford us an opportunity, during these 2 days of meeting, not only to talk about European matters, but also about global matters that matter to both of us and that are of common interest.

And let me say again that I very fondly remember the evening in the White House and the award.

Thank you.

President Obama. Thank you, everybody.

NOTE: The President spoke at 11:05 a.m. at the InterContinental Carlton Cannes Hotel. Chancellor Merkel spoke in German, and her remarks were translated by an interpreter. A portion of these remarks could not be verified because the audio was incomplete.

Statement on Senate Action on Job Growth Legislation
November 3, 2011

For the third time in recent weeks, every single Republican in the United States Senate has chosen to obstruct a jobs bill that independent economists said would boost our economy and put Americans back to work. At a time when more than a million construction workers are looking for a job, they voted no to putting them back to work doing the work America needs done: rebuilding our roads, bridges, airports, and transit systems. That makes no sense.

It makes no sense when you consider that this bill was made up of the same kinds of commonsense proposals that many of these Senators have fought for in the past. It was fully paid for. And even though it was supported by more than 70 percent of the American people—Republicans, Democrats, and Independents—100 percent of Senate Republicans said no. It's more clear than ever that Republicans in Washington are out of touch with Americans from all ends of the political spectrum.

The American people deserve to know why their Republican representatives in Washington refuse to put some of the workers hit hardest by the economic downturn back on the job rebuilding America. They deserve an explanation as to why Republicans refuse to step up to the plate and do what's necessary to create jobs and grow the economy right now. It's time for Republicans in Congress to put country ahead of party and listen to the people they were elected to serve. It's time for them to do their job and focus on Americans' jobs. And until they do, I will continue to do everything in my power to move this country forward.

Remarks Prior to a Meeting With President Cristina Fernandez de Kirchner of Argentina in Cannes
November 4, 2011

President Obama. Well, it is wonderful to be joined by the President of Argentina, a great friend of not only mine, but the United States. We've spent a lot of time together at the G–20, and I have very much appreciated the engagement and the passion that President Kirchner has brought to the important global issues that we've been discussing.

Obviously, there are a lot of bonds between Argentina and the United States that date back many years, and this is an excellent opportunity for us to build on that history. We have a wide range of areas of common interest and common concern. We'll be discussing the possibilities of deeper cooperation on economics, on trade, on science, on technology, and on security issues. And we'll also have a chance to discuss the upcoming Summit of the Americas in Colombia, and how we can set an agenda that focuses on increasing prosperity and employment and opportunity for people throughout the Americas.

So thank you so much, Madam President, for meeting with me. And I want to congratulate her on her recent election.

President Fernandez de Kirchner. Thank you very much, Mr. President. To me, as President of the Argentine Republic, it is indeed a pleasure to have a chance to meet you, and a great honor as well to have this relationship with you. And of course, the leadership of the United States at the global level cannot be overlooked, not just in the political field, but also in the economic field.

And this meeting is particularly significant to us. I would like to thank you for your kind words. And I would like to say that the G–20 has proved a positive and fruitful meeting. We have had an opportunity to discuss problem candidly and in a straightforward and effective manner. So thank you once again for that too.

Allow me to say as well that the U.S. is a top foreign investor worldwide, needless to say, and it is the second largest foreign investor in Argentina, after Spain. In fact, over 500 American companies have settled down in Argentina, and 60 percent of those companies actually figure among the 100 leading companies of the United States. And they're also flagship companies—I must mention that too.

It is a fact that the bilateral trade and bilateral relations between our two countries are extremely important for us as well. And although it is true that nowadays the United States has a surplus as far as Argentina is concerned, the figures that Argentina has experienced in recent years through its accumulated growth, I dare say, have also been positive for the balance of trade in the United States, since as the industrialization process resumed in Argentina we were obviously in need of products with added value that we were able to purchase from the United States.

Let me mention, by the way, that when President Kirchner took office in 2003, Argentina still had a positive balance, and the differ-

ence was 1 billion at the time. Of course, now the figures have changed, and we're talking about 4.7 billion in favor of the United States this year—the surplus figures being that.

I believe this will be an excellent opportunity for us to discuss, as I was saying, our bilateral and trade relations, and to look at ways to deepen and enhance those relationships. Let me also stress that the bonds between us are not just at an institutional, but also at a personal level. I know that both President Obama and myself are big fans of science and technology and innovation. In fact, I as President created the Minister of Science and Technology in Argentina.

Very recently, we were very pleased to receive a visit from NASA—actually, Mr. Charles Bolden came to see us. And the Argentine Republic has recently launched a satellite in cooperation with NASA. And one of the features of this satellite is that it can be used to measure the salinity levels of the seas and the impact this has on climate change. And we also know this is one issue that has made President Obama lose sleep in recent times—and not just him, but me as well.

There are many other issues and commonalities between us. Of course, international security, drug trafficking, the fight against terrorism, among other many areas of common interest that we both consider important—and trafficking in persons, I should mention as well. So we believe this will be a wonderful opportunity for fruitful and positive discussions between us.

President Obama. Thank you.

NOTE: The President spoke at 2:19 p.m. at the InterContinental Carlton Cannes Hotel. President Fernandez de Kirchner referred to her late husband, former President Nestor C. Kirchner of Argentina. President Fernandez de Kirchner spoke in Spanish, and her remarks were translated by an interpreter.

The President's News Conference in Cannes
November 4, 2011

The President. Good afternoon, everybody. I want to begin by thanking my friend President Sarkozy for his leadership and his hospitality. And I want to thank the people of Cannes for this extraordinary setting.

Over the past 2 years, those of us in the G–20 have worked together to rescue the global economy, to avert another depression, and to put us on the path to recovery. But we came to Cannes with no illusions. The recovery has been fragile. And since our last meeting in Seoul, we've experienced a number of new shocks: disruptions in oil supplies, the tragic tsunami in Japan, and the financial crisis in Europe.

As a result, advanced economies, including the United States, are growing and creating jobs, but not nearly fast enough. Emerging economies have started to slow. Global demand is weakening. Around the world, hundreds of millions of people are unemployed or underemployed. Put simply, the world faces challenges that put our economic recovery at risk.

So the central question coming into Cannes was this: Could the world's largest economies confront this challenge squarely; understanding that these problems will not be solved overnight, could we make progress? After 2 days of very substantive discussions, I can say that we've come together and made important progress to put our economic recoveries on a firmer footing.

With respect to Europe, we came to Cannes to discuss with our European friends how they will move forward and build upon the plan they agreed to last week to resolve this crisis. Events in Greece over the past 24 hours have underscored the importance of implementing the plan, fully and as quickly as possible.

Having heard from our European partners over the past 2 days, I am confidence that Europe has the capacity to meet this challenge. I know it isn't easy, but what is absolutely critical, and what the world looks for in moments such as this, is action.

That's how we confronted our financial crisis in the United States, having our banks submit to stress tests that were rigorous, increasing capital buffers, and passing the strongest financial reforms since the Great Depression. None of that was easy, and it certainly wasn't always popular. But we did what was necessary to address the crisis, put ourselves on a stronger footing, and to help rescue the global economy.

And that's the challenge that Europe now faces. Make no mistake: There's more hard work ahead and more difficult choices to make. But our European partners have laid a foundation on which to build, and it has all the elements needed for success: a credible firewall to prevent the crisis from spreading, strengthening European banks, charting a sustainable path for Greece, and confronting the structural issues that are at the heart of the current crisis.

And here in Cannes we've moved the ball forward. Europe remains on track to implement a sustainable path for Greece. Italy has agreed to a monitoring program with the IMF—in fact, invited it. Tools have been identified that will better enable the world to support European action. And European finance ministers will carry this work forward next week.

All of us have an enormous interest in Europe's success, and all of us will be affected if Europe is not growing, and that certainly includes the United States, which counts Europe as our largest trading partner. If Europe isn't growing, it's harder for us to do what we need to do for the American people: creating jobs, lifting up the middle class, and putting our fiscal house in order. And that's why I've made it clear that the United States will continue to do our part to support our European partners as they work to resolve this crisis.

More broadly, we agreed to stay focused on jobs and growth with an action plan in which each nation does its part. In the United States, we recognize, as the world's largest economy, the most important thing we can do for global growth is to get our own economy growing faster. Back home, we're fighting for the "American Jobs Act," which will put people back to work, even as we meet our responsibilities to reduce our deficit in the coming years.

We also made progress here in Cannes on our rebalancing agenda. In an important step forward, countries with large surpluses and export-oriented countries agreed to take additional steps to support growth and boost demand in their own countries. In addition, we welcome China's determination to increase the flexibility of the RMB. This is something we've been calling for for some time, and it will be a critical step in boosting growth.

Finally, we also made progress across a range of challenges to our shared prosperity. Following our reforms in the United States, the G–20 adopted an unprecedented set of high-level financial reforms to prevent a crisis in the future. We agreed to keep phasing out fossil fuel subsidies, perhaps the single most important step we can take in the near term to fight climate change and create clean energy economies.

And even as our countries work to save lives from the drought and terrible famine in the Horn of Africa, we agreed on the need to mobilize new resources to support the development that lifts nations out of poverty.

So again, I want to thank President Sarkozy and our French hosts for a productive summit. I want to thank my fellow leaders for their partnership and for the progress we've made to create the jobs and prosperity that our people deserve.

So with that, let me take a few questions. I'll start with Jim Kuhnhenn of AP.

Job Growth/U.S. Economy

Q. New jobless numbers today back in the States. You're on a pace to face the voters with the highest unemployment rate of any postwar President. And doesn't that make you significantly vulnerable to a Republican who might run on a message of change? And if I may add, given that you have just witnessed the difficulties of averting economic problems beyond your control, what state do you think the econ-

omy will be in when you face reelection next year?

The President. Jim, I have to tell you the least of my concerns at the moment is the politics of a year from now. I'm worried about putting people back to work right now, because those folks are hurting and the U.S. economy is underperforming. And so everything that we're doing here in the—here at the G–20 mirrors our efforts back home. That is, how do we boost growth, how do we shrink our deficits in a way that doesn't slow the recovery right now, how do we make sure that our workers are getting the skills and the training they need to compete in a global economy? And not only does the "American Jobs Act" answer some of the needs for jobs now, but it will also lay the foundation for future growth through investments in infrastructure, for example.

So my hope is, is that the folks back home, including those in the United States Senate and the House of Representatives, when they look at today's job numbers—which were positive, but indicate once again that the economy is growing way too slow—that they think twice before they vote no again on the only proposal out there right now that independent economists say would actually make a dent in unemployment right now. There's no excuse for inaction. That's true globally; it's certainly true back home as well. And I'm going to keep on pushing it regardless of what the politics are.

Chuck Todd [NBC News].

Global Economic Stabilization Efforts

Q. Thank you, Mr. President. Clearly, there was some sort of dispute between you and the European leaders about how to fund this bailout. And you, in your remarks, emphasized the fact that TARP was done with U.S. funds, that there wasn't any international involvement here. Are you confident now that the European leaders are going to fund this firewall or bailout fund themselves, not looking for handouts from other countries, and that they will do what they have to do?

And the second part of my question is, how hard was it to convince these folks to do stimulus measures when your own stimulus measure—you've mentioned it twice now—is not going anywhere right now on Capitol Hill?

The President. Well, first of all, we didn't have a long conversation about stimulus measures, so that was maybe two or three G–20s ago. We had a discussion about what steps could be taken to continue to spur economic growth. And that may not always involve government spending. For example, the rebalancing agenda that I talked about is one way in which we can make a big difference in spurring on global demand. It requires some adjustments, some changes in behavior on the part of countries. But it doesn't necessarily involve classic fiscal stimulus.

There wasn't a dispute with the Europeans. I think the Europeans agree with us that it is important to send a clear signal that the European project is alive and well, and that they are committed to the euro and that they are committed to resolving this crisis. And I think if you talk to European leaders, they are the first ones to say that that begins with European leaders arriving at a common course of action.

So essentially, what we've seen is all the elements for dealing with the crisis put in place, and we think those are the right elements. The first is having a solution to the specific problem of Greece. And although the actions of Papandreou and the referendum issue over the last couple of days I think got a lot of people nervous, the truth is, is that the general approach, which involved a voluntary reduction on the part of those who hold the Greeks' debt, reducing the obligations of the Greek Government, Greece continuing with reforms and structural change, that's the right recipe. It just has to be carried out. And I was encouraged by the fact that despite all the turmoil in Greece, even the opposition leader in Greece indicated that it's important to move forward on the proposal.

The second component is recapitalization of Europe's banks. And they have identified that need and they are resourcing that need. And that I think is going to be critical to further instill confidence in the markets.

And the third part of it is creating this firewall, essentially sending a signal to the markets that Europe is going to stand behind the euro. And all the details, the structure, how it operates, are still being worked out among the European leaders. What we were able to do was to give them some ideas, some options in terms of how they would put that together.

And what we've said is—and I'm speaking now for the whole of the G–20—what we've said is the international community is going to stand ready to assist and make sure that the overall global economy is cushioned by the gyrations in the market and the shocks that arise as Europe is working these issues through. And so they're going to have a strong partner in us. But European leaders understand that ultimately what the markets are looking for is a strong signal from Europe that they're standing behind the euro.

Q. So you're discouraging them from looking for money—outside money?

The President. No, what we were saying is that—and this is reflected in the communique—that, for example, creating additional tools for the IMF is an important component of providing markets overall confidence in global growth and stability, but that is a supplement to the work that is being done here in Europe.

And based on my conversations with President Sarkozy, Chancellor Merkel, and all the other European leaders, I believe they have that strong commitment to the euro and the European project.

David Muir [ABC News].

U.S. Stock Market/Global Economic Stabilization Efforts

Q. Thank you, Mr. President. I'm curious what you would say to Americans back home who've watched their 401(k)s recover largely when the bailout seemed a certainty, and then this week with the brand new political tumult in Greece, watched themselves lose essentially what they had gained back. You mentioned you're confident in the bailout plan. Are you confident this will actually happen, and if so, that it will work?

The President. Well, first of all, if you're talking about the movements of the U.S. stock market, the stock market was down when I first took office and the first few months I was in office about 3,000 points lower than it is now. So nothing has happened in the last 2 weeks that would suggest that somehow people's 401(k)s have been affected the way you describe.

Am I confident that this will work? I think that there's more work to do. I think there are going to be some ups and downs along the way. But I am confident that the key players in Europe—the European political leadership—understands how much of a stake they have in making sure that this crisis is resolved, that the euro zone remains intact, and I think that they are going to do what's necessary in order to make that happen.

Now, let's recognize how difficult this is. I have sympathy for my European counterparts. We saw how difficult it was for us to save the financial system back in the United States. It did not do wonders for anybody's political standing, because people's general attitude is, you know what, if the financial sector is behaving recklessly or not making good decisions, other folks shouldn't have to suffer for it.

You layer on top of that the fact that you're negotiating with multiple parliaments, a European Parliament, a European Commission—I mean, there are just a lot of institutions here in Europe. And I think several—I'm not sure whether it was Sarkozy or Merkel or Barroso or somebody, they joked with me that I'd gotten a crash course in European politics over the last several days. And there are a lot of meetings here in Europe as well. So trying to coordinate all those different interests is laborious, it's time consuming, but I think they're going to get there.

What is also positive is, if there's a silver lining in this whole process, it's the fact that I think European leaders recognize that there are some structural reforms, institutional modifications they need to make if Europe and the euro zone is to be as effective as they want it to be.

I think that what this has exposed is that if you have a single currency but you haven't worked out all the institutional coordination and relationships between countries on the fiscal side, on the monetary side, that that creates additional vulnerabilities. And there's a commitment on the part of European leaders, I think, to examine those issues. But those are long term. In the short term, what they've got to do is just make sure that they're sending a signal to the markets that they stand behind the euro.

And if that message is sent, then I think this crisis is averted, because some of this crisis is psychological. Italy is a big country with a enormous industrial base, great wealth, great assets, and has had substantial debt for quite some time; it's just the market is feeling skittish right now. And that's why I think Prime Minister Berlusconi's invitation to the IMF to certify that the reform plan that they put in place is one that they will, in fact, follow is an example of the steady, confidence-building measures that need to take place in order for us to get back on track.

Norah O'Donnell [CBS News].

Job Growth/U.S. Economy/Small Businesses

Q. Thank you, Mr. President. The world leaders here have stressed growth, the importance of growth. And yet growth back at home has been anemic, the new jobs report today showing just 88,000 jobs added. The Republicans in Congress have made it clear that they're going to block your jobs bill because they believe the tax hikes in it hurt small businesses. At what point do you feel that you declare stalemate to try and reach common ground? And do you feel like you have been an effective leader when it comes to the economy?

The President. Well, first of all, wherever Republicans indicate an interest in doing things that would actually grow the economy, I'm right there with them. So they've said that passing trade bills with South Korea and Panama and Colombia would help spur growth. Those got done, with significant bipartisan support. They've suggested that we need to reform our patent laws. That's something that was part of my long-term program for economic growth; we've got that done. What I've said is all those things are nice and they're important, but if we want to grow the economy right now then we have to think bigger; we've got to do something bolder and more significant.

So we put forward the "American Jobs Act," which contains ideas that are historically supported by Democrats and Republicans, like rebuilding our infrastructure, our roads, and our bridges, putting teachers back in the classroom, providing tax credits to small businesses.

You say, Norah, that the reason they haven't voted for them is because they don't want to tax small business. Well, actually, that's not—if that's their rationale then it doesn't fly, because the bill that they voted down yesterday, a component of the American jobs bill, essentially said we can create hundreds of thousands of jobs rebuilding our infrastructure, making America more competitive, and the entire program will be paid for by a tax not on millionaires, but people making a million dollars a year or more, which in the United States is about—a little over 300,000 people.

Now, there aren't a lot of small businesses across the country that are making that kind of money. In fact, less than 3 percent of small businesses make more than $250,000 a year. So what they've said is, we prefer to protect 300,000 people rather than put hundreds of thousands of people back to work and benefit 300 million Americans who are hurting because of low growth.

So we're going to keep on pushing. Now, there are steps that we can take absent congressional action. And the refinancing proposal that we put forward in Las Vegas is an example of that—helping students with student loans. We're going to keep on rolling out administra-

tive steps that we can take that strengthen the economy. But if we're going to do something big to jump-start the economy at a time when it's stabilized, but unemployment is way too high, Congress is going to need to act.

And in terms of my track record on the economy, here's just a simple way of thinking about it: When I came into office, the U.S. economy had contracted by 9 percent, the largest contraction since the Great Depression. Little over a year later, the economy was growing by 4 percent, and it's been growing ever since.

Now, is that good enough? Absolutely not. We've got to do more. And as soon as I get some signal from Congress that they're willing to take their responsibilities seriously, I think we can do more. But that's going to require them to break out of the rigid ideological positions that they've been taking. And the same is true, by the way, when it comes to deficit reduction.

We can solve all our problems. We can grow our economy now, put people back to work, reduce our deficit. And you get surprising consensus from economists about how to do it, from both the left and the right. It's just a matter of setting politics aside. And we're constantly remembering that the election is 1 year away. If we do that, there's no reason why can't solve these problems.

All right. Thank you, everybody.

NOTE: The President's news conference began at 3:40 p.m. at the Claude Debussy Theater. In his remarks, the President referred to Prime Minister Georgios Andreas Papandreou of Greece; Chancellor Angela Merkel of Germany; and President Jose Manuel Durao Barroso of the European Commission.

Remarks at Cannes City Hall in Cannes
November 4, 2011

Good afternoon. *Bon apres-midi.* I studied French in school, and that's about as far as I got. [*Laughter*]

But, Mr. President, I understand clearly the affection with which you've once again described our alliance and the friendship be-

tween our peoples. So thank you, Nicolas, my partner, *mon ami.* Thank you.

To Generals Puga and Estrate and members of the French Armed Forces; to Mayor Brochand and the people of Cannes: Thank you for your wonderful hospitality and the beautiful weather—[*laughter*]—that I'm enjoying here today.

We stand here today as free and democratic peoples because of each other. It was the ideas of the enlightenment, centered here in France, that helped inspire a band of colonists across the ocean to seek our freedom. It was the success of our Revolution that helped inspire your own. In our founding documents, we pledge ourselves to the same inalienable rights, and to the truth that all men and women are created equal. We are societies where our diversity is considered a strength, where you can become President even if your name is Obama or Sarkozy. [*Laughter*] We live by a common creed: life, liberty, and the pursuit of happiness—*liberte, egalite, fraternite.*

And for more than two centuries, we haven't simply professed these ideas, we have preserved them, by serving together and by sacrificing together. And not far from here is the hometown of Admiral de Grasse, who helped Americans secure our independence. Here at this memorial, we recall our shared sacrifices in the trenches of the First World War. Just as President Sarkozy and I have honored those who fell at Normandy, let it also be remembered that American and free French forces stormed the beaches of this southern coast. And not far from here, at Rhone, some of them rest in peace in the land that they liberated.

Nor have we simply defended these ideals for ourselves. Together, we have stood up for our ideals around the world. Today we pay special tribute to all those who have served and given their lives—French, American, and forces from our allies and partners—so that Afghanistan will never again become a haven for those who would attack us. They have sacrificed to keep us all safe, and we honor them all.

We saw this same solidarity most recently in the mission to protect the Libyan people. When the old regime threatened to massacre on a horrific scale, the world refused to stand by. The United States was proud to play a decisive role, especially in the early days, taking out Libyan air defenses and conducting precision strikes that stopped the regime in its tracks. But at the same time, this mission showed us

why NATO remains the world's most effective alliance. We acted quickly, in days; the fastest mobilization in NATO history. And whether contributing forces or command staff, every single one of NATO's 28 members played a role. Eighteen nations, including Arab States, provided forces.

And in a historic first, our NATO allies, including France, and especially the extraordinary leadership of President Sarkozy, helped us to conduct 90 percent of our strike missions—90 percent. So that showed more nations bearing the burdens and costs of peace and security. And that's how our alliance must work in the 21st century.

In this mission, French and American soldiers, airmen, naval officers, served shoulder to shoulder: the commanders who planned and executed this complex operation, the pilots who prevented a massacre in Benghazi, the tanker crews from bases here in France who sustained this operation, the airmen who delivered lifesaving aid, the sailors and marines who enforced the arms embargo at sea.

In fact, American pilots even flew French fighter jets off a French aircraft carrier in the Mediterranean. Allies don't get any closer than that. Thanks to their extraordinary service, the last air mission over Libya ended on Monday, and that operation ended in giving the Libyan people the opportunity to live with freedom and democracy. And I might add, we succeeded in bring every single one of our servicemembers back safely, which is a remarkable achievement.

Every man and woman in uniform who participated in this effort can know that you have accomplished every objective. You saved the lives of countless Libyan men, women, and children. And today, the Libyan people have liberated their country and begun to forge their own future, and the world has once again seen that the longing for freedom and dignity is universal.

Thousands of personnel made this operation a success, but we are honored to have some of them join us today. And I would ask you in joining me in saluting Admirals Jim Stavridis and Sam Locklear, as well as General Ralph Jodice, and all our servicemembers who are here for a job well done.

Finally, I would note that this success is part of a larger story. After a difficult decade, the tide of war is receding. The long war in Iraq is finally coming to an end. With our allies and partners, including the extraordinary sacrifices of the French people, we've achieved major victories against Al Qaida, including Usama bin Laden. In Afghanistan, where French and American soldiers fight side by side, we've begun a transition so Afghans can take responsibility for their security and our troops can begin coming home.

Today, America and our allies are moving forward with confidence and with strength. And these men and women in uniform carry on a legacy that I actually can see from the windows of the White House. In one direction, there's the monument to Washington; in the other, a statue of Rochambeau, who served so well at Washington's side. And at the base of that statue are words Washington expressed to his friend after the Revolutionary War in America was won. And I've shared these words with President Sarkozy on one of our visits, so I want to conclude with them this afternoon, because they capture the spirit that we celebrate today.

This is what Washington said to his dear friend from France: "We are fellow laborers in the cause of liberty, and we have lived together as brothers should do—in harmonious friendship."

President Sarkozy, ladies and gentlemen, members of the Armed Forces of France and the United States, for more than two centuries we have stood together in friendship, and because of our unwavering commitment to the cause of liberty, I'm confident that we'll continue to stand together, strong and free, for all the centuries to come. So *vive la France*. God bless America. And long live the alliance between our two great nations.

NOTE: The President spoke at 4:27 p.m. In his remarks, he referred to Gen. Benoit Puga, chief of staff to President Nicolas Sarkozy of France; Brig. Gen. Francois Estrate, head, France's Military Mission to the United Nations; Mayor Bernard Brochand of Cannes, France; Adm. James G. Stavridis, USN, Supreme Allied Commander, Europe; Adm. Samuel J. Locklear III, USN, commander, U.S. Naval Forces Europe and U.S. Naval Forces Africa; and Lt. Gen. Ralph J. Jodice II, USN, commander, Allied Air Component Command Headquarters, Izmir, Turkey.

Statement on the Hajj and Eid al-Adha
November 5, 2011

Michelle and I extend our greetings for a happy Eid al-Adha to Muslims worldwide and congratulate those performing Hajj. Thousands of Muslim Americans are among those who have joined one of the world's largest and most diverse gatherings in making the pilgrimage to Mecca and nearby sites.

As Muslims celebrate this Eid, they will also commemorate Abraham's willingness to sacrifice his son by distributing food to those less fortunate around the world. They join the United States and the international community in relief efforts to assist those struggling to survive in the Horn of Africa and those recovering from the devastating earthquake in Turkey.

The Eid and Hajj rituals are a reminder of the shared roots of the world's Abrahamic faiths and the powerful role that faith plays in motivating communities to serve and stand with those in need. On behalf of the American people, we extend our best wishes during this Hajj season. *Eid Mubarak* and *Hajj Mabrour*.

Remarks on Programs To Aid Veterans Seeking Employment
November 7, 2011

Thank you very much, everybody. Please be seated. This week, we commemorate Veterans Day. We honor the service and the sacrifice of all who have worn the uniform of the United States of America with honor and distinction. And above all, we commit ourselves to serving them, as well as they have served us. That's why we're here today.

Today's 9/11 generation of veterans has already earned a special place in our history. Over a difficult decade, they've performed heroically in some of the world's most dangerous places. They've done everything that we've asked of them. And I'm honored to have some of these extraordinary Americans here at the White House with us this morning.

I'm also proud to be joined by some of America's leading veterans service organizations—the American Legion, Veterans of Foreign Wars, Disabled American Veterans, and Iraq and Afghanistan Veterans of America—as well as Members of Congress who have historically been extraordinarily supportive of our veterans. And we're here today to try to take some steps to better serve today's veterans in a rough economy.

Over the past decade, nearly 3 million servicemembers have transitioned back to civilian life, joining the millions who have served through the decades. And as we end the war in Iraq and we wind down the war in Afghanistan, over a million more will join them over the next 5 years. Just think about the skills these veterans have acquired, often at a very young age. Think about the leadership that they've learned, the cutting-edge technologies that they've mastered, their ability to adapt to changing and unpredictable circumstances you just can't get from a classroom. Think about how many have led others to life-and-death missions by the time they're 25 or 26 years old.

This is exactly the kind of leadership and responsibility that every American business should be competing to attract. This is the kind of talent we need to compete for the jobs and industries of the future. These are the kinds of Americans that every company should want to hire.

And yet, while our economy has added more than 350,000 private sector jobs just over the past 3 months, more than 850,000 veterans remain unemployed. Too many can't find a job worthy of their tremendous talents. Too many military spouses have a hard time finding work after moving from base to base to base. And even though the overall unemployment rate ticked down last month, unemployment among veterans of Iraq and Afghanistan continued to rise. That's not right. It doesn't make sense—not for our veterans, not for our families, not for America—and we're determined to change that.

I've told the story before of a soldier in the 82d Airborne who served as a combat medic in Afghanistan, and he saved lives over there. He earned a Bronze Star for his actions. But when he returned home, he couldn't even get a job as a first-responder. He had to take classes through the post-9/11 GI bill—classes that he probably could have taught—just so he could qualify for the same duties at home that he was doing every single day at war.

You know what? If you can save a life on the battlefield, then you can save a life in an ambulance. If you can oversee a convoy or millions of dollars of assets in Iraq, you can help a business back home manage their supply chain or balance their books. If you can juggle the demands of raising a family while a loved one is at war, you can juggle the demands of almost any job in America.

We ask our men and women in uniform to leave their families and their jobs and risk their lives to fight for our country, and the last thing they should have to do is fight for a job when they come home. And that's why we're here today, to do everything in our power to see to it that America's veterans have the opportunities that they deserve and that they have earned.

Now, I've already directed the Federal Government to lead by example and to hire more veterans. And it has hired more than 120,000 so far. A couple of months ago, I also challenged private companies to hire or train 100,000 post-9/11 veterans or their spouses by the end of 2013. And already companies have hired more than 12,000 and committed to train or hire 25,000 more over the next 2 years.

And I want to thank the extraordinary work of my wife, the First Lady, as well as Dr. Jill Biden for leading this Joining Forces effort to support our military families and our veterans.

Nearly 2 months ago, I sent Congress the "American Jobs Act." It was the only jobs plan independent economists said would boost our economy and put Americans back to work right now, and it was full of the kinds of ideas that have historically been supported by both parties. It was paid for.

And it included two proposals that would have made a big difference for our veterans: the returning heroes tax credit, which would give businesses a tax break for each unemployed veteran that they hire, and the wounded warriors tax credit, which would give businesses a even larger tax break for hiring an unemployed veteran with a disability related to their service in uniform. And these veteran service organizations are here today because they fully support these ideas.

Unfortunately, we have not yet seen progress in Congress. Senate Republicans have so far chosen to block these bills and these proposals. Since then, they've also blocked a jobs bill that would keep teachers in the classroom and first-responders on the street and blocked a jobs bill last week that would have put hundreds of thousands of construction workers back to work rebuilding America. Despite the fact that more than 70 percent of Americans supported the ideas in this bill, not one has yet stepped up on the other side of the aisle to say this is the right thing to do. So they've had three chances to do the right thing. Three times, they've said no.

I believe it's time they said yes to taking action that would boost the economy overall, because the overall economy has an impact on veterans. It's a lot easier for veterans to find jobs if the economy is growing rapidly and unemployment is dropping. And I think it's important for all of us to remember that we're all in this together. It's time we started acting like it. Bold action from Congress ultimately is the only way we're going to put hundreds of thousands of Americans back to work right now and rebuild an economy where everyone who works hard has a chance to get ahead. So I'm going to keep pushing these Senators to vote on commonsense, paid-for ways to create jobs that members of both parties have supported before.

But what I've also said is that I'm going to do everything in my power, as the head of the executive branch, to act on behalf of the American people, with or without Congress. We can't simply wait for Congress to do its job. As Commander in Chief, I won't wait, nor will I let politics get in the way of making sure that veterans share in the opportunity that they defend. If Congress won't act, I will.

And that's why, 2 weeks ago, I announced a new initiative to help trained veterans get jobs in the medical community. And today we're announcing three new initiatives to help America's returning heroes get jobs that meet their talents.

First, we're delivering on the expanded job search services that I promised our post-9/11 veterans 3 months ago. Starting today, post-9/11 veterans looking for work can download what we're calling the veterans Gold Card, which gives you up to 6 months of personalized job search services at career centers across the country.

Second, we're launching an easy-to-use online tool called My Next Move for Veterans that allows veterans to enter information about their experience and skills in the field and match it with civilian careers that put that experience to use.

Third, we're connecting unemployed veterans to job openings. We've partnered with leading job search companies to create a new online service called Veterans Job Bank, where employers can tag jobs postings for veterans using a simple approach designed by major search engines. And already, more than 500,000 job openings have been tagged, thanks to a company called Simply Hired, and companies like Monster and LinkedIn are helping more employers participate.

So all these three initiatives are up and running right now. Just visit whitehouse.gov/vets to find each one. And I'm asking these veterans service organizations to spread the word.

Connecting our veterans to the jobs they deserve isn't just the right thing to do for our veterans, it's the right thing to do for America. But there's still more that we can do to encourage businesses to hire veterans. And this week, Congress will have another chance to do the right thing. They'll get to vote on those tax breaks that I proposed back in September for businesses to hire veterans. Members of Congress will get to say whether or not they think it's a good idea to give companies an incentive—an additional incentive—to hire the men and women who have risked their lives for our country.

And when I first proposed this idea—some of you remember this was a joint session of Congress—people stood and applauded on both sides of the aisle when I announced this bill. That was one of the few times both sides stood up. [*Laughter*] So when these ideas come up for a vote this week, when the TV cameras aren't necessarily on each of them, I expect both sides of the aisle to stand up for our veterans and vote in the affirmative.

There's no good reason to oppose this bill. Not one. Our veterans did their jobs. It's time for Congress to do theirs. It's time for them to put country before party, put our veterans back to work, and pass this element of the jobs package that benefits our veterans and gives businesses an incentive to hire veterans.

Standing up for our veterans is not a Democratic responsibility or a Republican responsibility, it is a American responsibility. It's an obligation of every citizen who enjoys the freedom that these heroes defend. And it is time for us to meet those obligations right now.

As Commander in Chief, I want all our veterans to know that we are forever grateful for your service and for your sacrifice. And just as you fought for us, we're going to keep fighting for you, for more jobs, for more security, for the opportunity to keep your families strong and to keep America competitive in the 21st century. In other words, we're going to keep on fighting, just as you did, to show the world why the United States of America is still the greatest nation on Earth.

Thank you very much, everybody. God bless you. God bless the United States of America.

NOTE: The President spoke at 12:04 p.m. in the Rose Garden at the White House. In his remarks, he referred to Spc. Nicholas Colgin, USA, 82d Airborne Division; and Jill T. Biden, wife of Vice President Joe Biden.

Statement on the Presidential Election in Liberia
November 7, 2011

The Liberian people will go to the polls tomorrow to elect the next President of Liberia. This historic vote is an opportunity for Liberians to strengthen the country's democracy and to deepen its peace, prosperity, and national unity. We encourage all voters of all political preferences to exercise their universal right to participate in the democratic process. All Liberians should have the ability to exercise this right without fear of violence or intimidation.

Liberia has taken important steps to consolidate its democracy since the end of its civil war. Those gains must not be set back by individuals who seek to disrupt the political process. The international community will hold accountable those who choose to obstruct the democratic process. We encourage all security forces in Liberia to exercise maximum restraint and to allow peaceful protest. And we commend all that international election observers, the United Nations Mission in Liberia (UN–MIL), the Economic Community of West African States (ECOWAS), and the Liberian people are doing to ensure a free, fair, and peaceful runoff election.

The United States is deeply committed to its historic relationship with Liberia and its people. We are also deeply committed to the strength of democracy on the African Continent. In that spirit, we will continue to strongly support the success of a peaceful democratic process for the Liberian people and the peace and prosperity of Liberia.

Message to the Congress on Continuation of the National Emergency With Respect to Iran
November 7, 2011

To the Congress of the United States:

Section 202(d) of the National Emergencies Act (50 U.S.C. 1622(d)) provides for the automatic termination of a national emergency unless, prior to the anniversary date of its declaration, the President publishes in the *Federal Register* and transmits to the Congress a notice stating that the emergency is to continue in effect beyond the anniversary date. In accordance with this provision, I have sent to the *Federal Register* for publication the enclosed notice stating that the national emergency with respect to Iran that was declared in Executive Order 12170 of November 14, 1979, is to continue in effect beyond November 14, 2011.

Our relations with Iran have not yet returned to normal, and the process of implementing the agreements with Iran, dated January 19, 1981, is still under way. For these reasons, I have determined that it is necessary to continue the national emergency declared on November 14, 1979, with respect to Iran, beyond November 14, 2011.

BARACK OBAMA

The White House,
November 7, 2011.

NOTE: The notice is listed in Appendix D at the end of this volume.

Remarks at an Obama Victory Fund 2012 Fundraiser
November 7, 2011

Well, first of all, let me just thank Dwight and Toni for your incredible hospitality. I hope you didn't cut down the tree just for this event. [*Laughter*] I'd feel a little guilty about that. It looks like it was a nice, big tree. [*Laughter*]

It's wonderful to see all of you. I've got some friends in the room who I've known a very long time; some people who I'm meeting for the first time. But to all of you, I appreciate yourself extending yourselves in this way.

What I want to do is keep my remarks at the top relatively brief, and then I want to spend some time just in a conversation with you and answering some questions and getting your feedback.

We are at a point in our history, as Dwight indicated, that I think is as important, if not more important, than where we were back in 2008. I'm obviously a little grayer than I was then. I've got some bumps and bruises from some tough political battles in this town. But what we've been able to accomplish over the last 3 years I'm extraordinary proud of.

We were able to prevent America from going into a great depression. We were able to, after a series of quarterly GDP reports that were the worst that we've seen since the Great Depression, reverse it and get the economy to grow again. We've seen 20 straight months of consecutive job growth. We were able to pass health insurance reform, Wall Street reform, end "don't ask, don't tell," end the war in Iraq, the list goes on.

And sometimes when Valerie and I come out of a meeting we have to remind ourselves of some of the stuff we've done because you lose track after 3 years. And so I'm very proud of our track record. But what is absolutely true is that huge swaths of the country are still hurting. A lot of people are still struggling out there. And there's no way in which America right now is fulfilling all of its potential.

We've got entire communities that have been devastated by this recession. We have young people who are struggling to take advantage of the good educations that they've received but are having trouble finding work. And we've got a whole generation of kids out there who aren't getting the kind of education that they need to compete in the 21st century.

And so as proud as I am of what we've already accomplished, I am that much more determined to make sure that over the next 5 years we complete the task that we set out, which was to create a Government that is responsive to not just people who are hurting now, but also responsive to future generations; that we're able to reduce our deficit in a responsible way, in a balanced way; that we're able to make sure our school system is working for every child and not just some children; that we implement health care reform so that we start reducing costs for families and for businesses and for the Federal Government, but also improve quality and make sure that nobody out there is going bankrupt just because somebody in their family is getting sick.

We've got to still implement immigration reform—a big, unfinished piece of business—because we're a nation of laws and a nation of immigrants, and we should be able to reconcile those two imperatives and make sure that we've got a system that works to grow our economy and improve our economy and doesn't leave people in a second-class status in this United States of America.

We still don't have an energy policy that is suitable for the needs of the future. And although we've made enormous progress, I think people forget, for example, that we doubled fuel efficiency standards on cars and trucks just in the last year, which if it had been in legislative form would have probably been the most significant piece of environmental legislation in the last 30 years. A lot of people don't know it. And despite some of those gains, we still are way too dependent on imported oil, and we still haven't done everything we can to transition to a clean energy economy.

In foreign policy, we're ending the war in Iraq and we're transitioning out of Afghanistan. But I didn't run for office only to end a war or only to make sure that we got bin Laden. We also want to make sure that we're creating opportunity all around the world, that we have a positive, proactive agenda that is helping alleviate poverty and helping to provide education and helping to make sure that the Arab Spring is one that turns positive and that gives more people opportunity.

So across the board we've just got a lot more work to do. And the only way we're going to be able to accomplish it is if we've got folks like you as energized, as enthusiastic, as committed as so many of you were in 2008. Because what's holding us back right now are not technical questions. I mean, there are some big technical issues surrounding how do you spur on clean energy, how do we make sure that our manufacturing base is strong here in the United States, and we are at the cutting edge of those technologies that are going to help us win the race for the future.

But those are solvable problems. The challenge we have right now is fixing our politics and making sure that we've got the kind of politics and governance here in Washington which is responsive to the needs of people, not the needs of special interests, that brings out the best in us and not the worst in us.

And that is probably the biggest piece of business that remains unfinished. That's probably the area where we've been most stymied over the last 3 years. My legislative record, our administration record, I'll put up against any President in their first term. But in terms of changing the culture in Washington, the fever has not broken yet. Not everybody has gotten the word yet—[*laughter*]—that this is not how the American people want their Government to operate.

They want common sense. They want responsiveness. They want a focus on the future and the long term. They want compromise where that's appropriate. But they also want to make sure that their leaders stand on principle where needed and are willing to make the tough calls and do the difficult things that will help us ensure that the America that we pass on to our kids and our grandkids is better than the one that we inherited.

And that I think is the biggest challenge. And over the next year we are going to be wrestling with what are two fundamentally different visions of where we need to take the country and where we need to take our politics. And I'm confident that the American people prefer our vision. But we're going to have to communicate that effectively, and to do that, I'm going to need you.

So I just—as I was thinking about riding over here, I was thinking about a group of veterans that I met with today. We made a big announcement about initiatives that are going to help veterans get hired. The unemployment rate for post-9/11 veterans is actually higher than the general population, and that's something that I intend to fix. But it reminded me of something that Michelle and I have both experienced.

The biggest honor of my job is serving as Commander in Chief. And I get the chance to interact a lot with people who are based all around the world; Michelle interacts with military families here, throughout the country. The kind of sacrifices they're making on behalf of their country, the kind of commitment and discipline and putting country ahead of self-interest, is unbelievable.

And for that same spirit to be captured and to be channeled and to be the animating spirit of Washington, that should be our goal. Because if we do that, there's no problem we can't solve. There's no challenge we can't meet. I am absolutely convinced of that.

And so I've said before that this campaign probably won't be as sexy as the first one. It'll be tight. It'll be tough. But I also want to remind people who were on the first campaign, there's been a lot of revisionist history that says how perfect that first one was. [*Laughter*] It didn't feel like that when we were in the middle of it. [*Laughter*] And that's part of our democracy. It's always a little messy, and it's always tough. But it's also worth it when it's done right.

And if you're willing to join me on this journey, I think at the end of the day you'll see that we're actually able to deliver the kind of change that you can believe in.

So thank you very much, everybody. Thank you.

NOTE: The President spoke at 7:15 p.m. at the residence of Dwight and Antoinette Bush. In his remarks, he referred to Senior Adviser to the President Valerie B. Jarrett. Audio was not available for verification of the content of these remarks.

Remarks at the Yeadon Regional Head Start Center in Yeadon, Pennsylvania
November 8, 2011

Thank you, everybody. Please have a seat. It is great to be in Yeadon, great to be in the Philly area. I was told not to mention football at all. [*Laughter*] So I'm not going to say anything about football while I'm here, because I know this is a sensitive subject. [*Laughter*] This is why I have Secret Service along. [*Laughter*]

Now, I want to start by acknowledging some of the folks who are with me here today. First of all, I want to thank one of our finest public servants in this country, and she's just a great friend, but somebody who cares passionately about the health and the welfare of our kids

and our families, Kathleen Sebelius, our Secretary of Health and Human Services. I want to acknowledge the mayor of Yeadon; Dolores Jones-Butler is in the house. Two of my favorite Members of Congress, Chaka Fattah and Bob Brady; and one of my favorite former Members of Congress, who I think is going to be doing big things here in Pennsylvania, is here as well. I guess I can't call you Congressman, huh? [*Laughter*] That's all right? The—Congressman Murphy.

I had a chance to say hello to Mayor Nutter when I landed in Philly. He couldn't be with us this morning. I guess there are a few things going on here today. [*Laughter*] But I wished him well. He's a great partner of ours.

And I also want to say thank you to Miss Pleasantte, Dr. O'Shea, all the staff and the teachers who are here. They are just doing a great job.

I had a chance to visit one of the classrooms here. And I have to say, it got me a little choked up, because—Patrick, you need to remember this. Patrick's got small kids. And they are just so huggable at this age. [*Laughter*] And now—they're still huggable, but they're a little—they're 5'9″ and 5 feet. [*Laughter*] But obviously, you got a lot to handle when you're here.

And the teachers, the staff who are here, they wouldn't be doing this for the money. They're doing it out of love of children. All of you do it because you know that when it comes to learning and when it comes to growing, this is an absolutely critical period in a child's life. We know that 3- and 4-year-olds who go to high-quality preschools, including our best Head Start programs, are less likely to repeat a grade, they're less likely to need special education, they're more likely to graduate from high school than the peers who did not get these services. And so this makes early education one of our best investments in America's future—one of the best.

Right out of the gate, it helps prepare our kids for a competition that's never been tougher, a competition for good, middle class, well-paying jobs. And we're competing now with countries like China and South Korea and Europe, all of which are serious about educating their children. So at a time when a company is able to move anywhere they want in the world and a lot of times will make the decision based on where they can find the most highly skilled workforce, it is absolutely imperative that we make sure that the United States is the place where we've got the best trained, best educated young people. That is a priority.

And this is not, and should not be, a Democratic priority or a Republican priority. This is an American priority. It's an economic imperative. Our future depends on it. And people understand this outside of Washington, which is

why we've been able to work with Democratic and Republican Governors on our efforts to strengthen education from cradle to career, not only with more money—money is important—but also with reforms that challenge schools to develop higher standards and the best practices for teaching and for learning.

Now, unfortunately, in Congress right now, it's a different story. The Republicans in Washington have been trying to gut our investments in education. Earlier this year, nearly every Republican in the House voted for a budget that would have cut hundreds of thousands of children from Head Start. They've tried to cut Pell grants for college students. They just voted against a jobs bill that would have put 400,000 teachers back in the classroom.

Their argument is that we don't have the money. And what I've said is we can make these investments in our children without adding to the deficit simply by asking people who make more than a million dollars a year to pay a little more in taxes, not right now, but starting in 2013. It's the right thing to do for our kids. It's the right thing to do for our country. But so far, they've said no.

It's not just on issues, by the way, that cost money. So far, Congress has failed to move on fixing No Child Left Behind, despite the fact that we've shown them bipartisan reforms that are working in States right now, reforms that are praised not only by Democrats, but also by Republicans. So after trying for months to work with Congress on education, we decided to take matters into our own hands, because our future is at stake, our children deserve action, and we can't wait for Congress any longer.

We can't wait to make sure that our schools give every child the chance to compete with young people from around the world. So in September, I announced that if States exceed the high standards set by No Child Left Behind, then they've got the flexibility to build on the reforms that they've already made. We can't wait to help more young people get to college. So 2 weeks ago, I announced changes that will lower student loan payments by hundreds of dollars a month for around 1.6 million Americans.

We can't wait to give more of our youngest children the same basic opportunities we want all children to have, that we want for our children. And that's why today I'm announcing a new rule that will improve the quality of Head Start programs around the country.

Now, I firmly believe that Head Start is an outstanding program and a critical investment. The children who have the chance to go to the best Head Start programs have an experience that can literally change their lives for years to come. We're making today's announcement because we believe that every child in Head Start deserves that same chance.

Now, under the old rules governing Head Start, there just wasn't enough accountability. If a program wasn't providing kids with quality services, there was no incentive to improve. Under the new rule, programs are going to be regularly evaluated against a set of clear, high standards. If a program meets these standards—and we believe the majority of Head Start programs will—then their grants will be renewed. But if a program isn't giving children the support they need to be ready for school, if classrooms are unsafe, if finances aren't in order, if kids aren't learning what they need to learn, then other organizations will be able compete for that grant. We're not just going to put money into programs that don't work. We will take money and put them into programs that do.

If a group's going to do a better job in the— for the community, then they need that support. If a group would do a better job serving the kids in our communities, then they're going to have that chance.

Now, this is the first time in history that Head Start programs will be truly held accountable for performance in the classroom, and we know that raising the bar isn't always an easy thing to do. But it's the right thing to do. Children in Head Start deserve the best services we have to offer, and we know that Head Start programs can meet this challenge.

So because of this rule and the other executive actions that we've taken to improve our education system, more children will have the chance to study hard, do well in school, graduate on time, go to college without crushing debt. More Americans will grow up to be scientists and innovators and engineers and entrepreneurs. More businesses will be able to find skilled workers.

Of course, there's no substitute for Congress doing its job. And I have to say, these two Congressmen are doing their job. But they need some help. Congress still needs to fix No Child Left Behind. Congress still needs to put teachers back in the classroom where they belong.

So Congress still needs to act. But if Congress continues to stand only for dysfunction and delay, then I'm going to move ahead without them. I have told—[*applause*]—I've told my administration, I want you to keep on looking for actions that we can take without Congress, steps that can save consumers money, make Government more efficient and responsive, help heal the economy, improve our education system, improve our health care system. We want to work with Congress, but we're not going to wait.

I think this is the right thing to do not just as a President, but I think this is the right thing to do as a parent. Because I know there are some things I cannot guarantee my kids. But I can make sure—I can do my best to make certain that they get a chance to succeed or fail on their own merits, just like I did. I can do everything in my power to ensure that their children grow up in a country where anything is possible, as long as you're willing to work for it.

That's what my mom and my grandparents wanted for me. It's what I want for my children. It's the promise that every generation has made to those who came after.

We can't be the first generation of Americans to break that promise. So we've got to prove that we are tougher than the times that we live in and that we're bigger than the politics of the moment. We've got to meet the challenges today by preparing our children for the challenges tomorrow.

That's what's being done at this wonderful facility. We want to replicate these all across the country. We are proud of what you are doing. You've got a President who's got your back.

Thank you very much, everybody. God bless you. God bless the United States of America.

NOTE: The President spoke at 11:43 a.m. In his remarks, he referred to former Rep. Patrick J. Murphy; Mayor Michael A. Nutter of Philadelphia, PA; and Pleasantte Kinsler-Johnson, assistant education coordinator over curriculum, and Lawrence J. O'Shea, executive director, Delaware County Intermediate Unit of Pennsylvania.

Remarks on Signing an Executive Order To Cut Waste and Promote Efficient Spending Across the Federal Government
November 9, 2011

Well, from the day I took office, one of the commitments that I made to the American people was that we would do a better job here in Washington in rooting out wasteful spending. At a time when families have had to cut back, have had to make some tough decisions about getting rid of things that they don't need in order to make the investments that they do, we thought that it was entirely appropriate for our governments and our agencies to try to root out waste, large and small, in a systematic way.

Obviously, this is even more important given the deficits that we've inherited and that have grown as a consequence of this recession. This makes these efforts even more imperative.

Now, this does mean making some tough choices. It means cutting some programs that I think are worthy, but we may not be able to afford right now. A lot of the action is in Congress and legislative and budget. I know the joint committee on trying to reduce our deficits are engaged in a very difficult conversation right now, and we want to encourage them to complete their work. But in the meantime, we don't need to wait for Congress in order to do something about wasteful spending that's out there.

Cutting waste, making Government more efficient, is something that leaders in both parties have worked on, from Senator Tom Coburn, a Republican, to Democrat Claire McCaskill. We haven't seen as much action out of Congress as we'd like, and that's why we launched on our own initiative the campaign to cut waste—not just to cut spending, but to make Government work better for the American people.

For example, we've identified thousands of Government buildings that we don't need. Some have sat empty for years. So we're getting rid of those properties, and that's going to save the American people billions of dollars.

As part of this campaign, I've also asked Federal employees to do their part and share their ideas on making Government more efficient and more effective. And two of them are here today, so I want to introduce them.

Roger Rhoads works at the Department of Commerce. Raise your hand, Roger. There's Roger. He found a way to save the Department almost $2 million a year on its cell phone bills. And I'm sure that there probably is some consumers out there that would like to talk to him and find out what they can save on their cell phone bills.

Celeste Steele is here. Celeste, raise your hand. Celeste works at the Department of Homeland Security, and she's helping save taxpayers tens of millions of dollars by changing the way the Department buys goods and services.

So we've received nearly 20,000 suggestions from Federal employees. I just completed a videoconference with the 4 finalists of our annual SAVE Award, 20,000 submissions of ideas from Federal employees about how we can reduce waste, eliminate duplication, redundancy, paperwork. And these four finalists have some terrific ideas: putting books that have been ordered every year online instead of continuing to incur the shipping costs, to having a tool library over at NASA so that instead of buying very specialized tools over and over again for different projects, we actually keep an inventory of those tools.

In addition to soliciting ideas from Federal employees, I've also tasked Vice President Biden to work with the Secretaries of all our agencies to identify some systemic areas of potential improvement—travel, transportation, IT services—all of which we know can save us potentially billions of dollars. And in September, Joe convened the Cabinet and has really pushed them hard in finding savings across all our agencies.

So today I'm signing an Executive order that builds on their good work. It directs agencies to slash spending in each of these areas—travel, printing, IT—because we believe that we can get better results for less using technology. And overall, spending in the areas covered by this Executive order will shrink by 20 percent. And members of my Cabinet will keep reporting on their progress to Joe Biden and ultimately to me. And we're going to hold them accountable for meeting this 20-percent reduction goal.

These are important steps that can save taxpayers billions of dollars over the next several years. It doesn't replace the importance of the work that Congress needs to do in coming up with a balanced, bold plan to reduce our deficit, but it indicates once again that there are things that we can do right now that will actually deliver better Government more efficiently, more consumer friendly, for less money. And we're going to keep on finding every possible way that we can do that even if Congress is not acting.

So with that, I'm going to sign the bill, but I want to thank all the officials who are behind me here today for taking this project so seriously.

[*At this point, the President signed the Executive order.*]

There you go. Thank you very much, everybody. Thank you.

NOTE: The President spoke at 11:40 a.m. in the Oval Office at the White House. In his remarks, he referred to Securing Americans Value and Efficiency (SAVE) Award finalists Matthew W. Ritsko, Eileen M. Hearty, Kevin Korzeniewski, and Faith Stanfield. The Executive order promoting efficient spending is listed in Appendix D at the end of this volume.

Remarks at the African American Policy in Action Leadership Conference
November 9, 2011

Everybody, please have a seat. It is wonderful to see all of you. I've got some old friends here—[*laughter*]—not old in years, but been knowing you. It is wonderful to see all of you.

I want to, first of all, thank Heather, who is doing outstanding work. Heather has my complete confidence. She has my ear. And so when you're talking to her, you're talking to me, which means she's going to be getting a lot of phone calls, I know. [*Laughter*] But she's up to the task, and we're very proud of her.

I want to thank all of you who are here. We've got some elected officials. Mayor Nutter, congratulations. I know we had a little bit of election work going on yesterday. I was in Philly yesterday, did not say anything about football during my visit. [*Laughter*] Didn't say anything about football games. Mayor Mark Mallory is here. There he is, right there, Cincinnati. We have—I think Congressman [Congresswoman]° Donna Edwards is around here. There she is, right here. And she's been a great partner.

And of course, we've got leaders from all across the country. So many of you have worked so diligently during what has been one of the toughest times in our country's history in order to provide opportunity, to make sure that communities were able to hang on during difficult times, and begin to rebuild again in the

---

° White House correction.

wake of an extraordinary financial crisis and the deepest recession we've seen since the Great Depression.

Obviously, we have enormous challenges. The unemployment rate in the African American community has always historically been higher than the norm. And since the unemployment rate generally is high right now, it is way too high when it comes to the African American community. Many of the challenges that existed before the crisis have been worsened with respect to opportunities for decent housing, with respect to making sure that our schools are equipped to prepare our kids for the 21st century.

So we've got a lot of work to do. But the report that has been prepared that I know our teams are going to be talking about that will be released, I think is a compilation of everything we've done over the last 3 years that has not only lessened the severity of the crisis for millions of people, kept millions of folks out of poverty, made sure that millions of folks still had unemployment benefits, health care, et cetera, but also talks about the foundations that we are laying so that as the economy recovers, the African American community and communities all across the country of every stripe are going to have an opportunity to finally begin to rebuild so that we are seeing good, solid, middle class jobs with good benefits that families who are desperate for their piece of the American Dream, that they're going to be able to achieve it.

Now, some of these strategies are longer term: all the good work that we've done, for example, in education. The payoff is not going to be tomorrow. It's not going to be next year. It's going to be 5 years from now and 10 years from now as we steadily see improvement in the performance of our public schools.

When it comes to health care, we are already seeing enormous improvements in terms of funding for preventive care, for community health clinics. But full implementation is going to be taking place starting in 2013. We'll have those exchanges, and suddenly, families who did not have access to health care will be in a position to get it.

So some of these things are going to be phased in over time, and will not bear full fruit for some years to come. But as all of you know, we've got a sense of urgency right now—the fierce urgency of now—when it comes to putting people back to work. And many of you have been engaged in pushing Congress to pass the "American Jobs Act." This is the only plan that—out there—that independent economists have said would put people to work right now.

It's been estimated that it would grow the economy by as much as an additional 2 percent of GDP; put as many as 1.9 million people back to work; would be targeted at not only getting teachers back in the classroom and construction workers on the job rebuilding America, but also targeting the long-term unemployed; allowing communities that have seen more than their fair share of foreclosures to be able to take those properties and start rebuilding them; improving our infrastructure in vital ways that will spur on economic development; summer youth programs, so that our young people can start getting on track and getting in those habits of work that are so important to instill a sense of responsibility, and a payoff for behaving responsibly.

All those things are contained in the "American Jobs Act." Now, as you know, so far the Senate has just said no, not because these are ideas that are partisan; these are ideas that traditionally have been supported by Democrats and Republicans alike. Their argument for why they're passing it—they haven't passed them so far has been that, well, they don't like how we're paying for it, because we ask, for example, folks who make more than a million dollars a year to pay a little bit more in taxes in order to make sure that our economy is strong.

The American people are behind us on this. Not just Democrats and Independents, but Republicans support many of the ideas in this bill, and so we're going to keep on pushing very hard, and we're going to need your help to continue to mobilize communities to focus on how we can put people to work right now.

In addition, though, we also want to continue to find ways where we don't have to wait for

Congress, where are initiatives that we can take right now administratively that would make a difference in the communities that all of you represent. And so part of the function of this gathering is for all of you to share your best ideas, your best practices. What are things we can get implemented in the next 3 months? Where are areas where you see a potential difference being made?

I'll just give you one example. We, on our own initiative, identified the need for small businesses, who in these difficult economic times have some cash flow problems. We said, you know what, let's speed up payments to them. They've already done the work, or they're in the process of doing the work, and the Federal Government likes to sit on that money until the last day. [*Laughter*] Let's see if we can send them that check a little bit sooner so that they can put that money back to work.

And obviously, African American businesses typically are small businesses, so this is something that can benefit folks right away, and we can start seeing a difference in our communities.

I want to make sure that those are the kinds of ideas that all of you are providing to us, sharing with our Cabinet Secretaries, sharing with our staffs. And what we want to do following up on the report about what we've already done is hopefully 3 months from now, 6 months from now, we'll be able to go back and say, here's some additional steps that we took based on community input.

So I just want to—so use today as an opportunity to share ideas with us. We're going to have breakout sessions. Let's do some brainstorming; we want your input, we want your ideas. At the end of this—the conference, I've asked Valerie Jarrett as well as Gene Sperling, who is my chief economic coordinator, the head of the National Economic Council, to come back and hear what ideas were proposed.

But the last point I want to make is this—and I made this point just recently when we were dedicating the new King Memorial—we have been through tougher times before. Our parents have been through tougher times; our grandparents have been through tougher times. We know tough times. And what we also know, though, is that if we are persistent, if we are unified, and we remain hopeful, then we'll get through these tough times and better days lie ahead.

So I just want everybody to participate here in a spirit of persistence, determination, and unity. And if you maintain that spirit, then I'm confident that not only will the American—the African American community emerge from these difficult economic times stronger than we were before, but this entire Nation is going to come out more unified, better equipped to deal with the challenges of the 21st century than we were before.

So I appreciate all of you. God bless you. God bless America.

NOTE: The President spoke at 11:54 a.m. in the South Court Auditorium of the Dwight D. Eisenhower Executive Office Building. In his remarks, he referred to Heather J. Foster, Director of African American Outreach, White House Office of Public Engagement; and Mayor Michael A. Nutter of Philadelphia, PA.

Joint Statement by President Obama and President Anibal Antonio Cavaco Silva of Portugal
November 9, 2011

Building on the deep friendship and long-standing alliance between the United States and Portugal, we met today to reaffirm the strength of the partnership between our two countries. We acknowledged the very important role played by the Portuguese-American community in bringing our two nations closer together. Determined to further enhance our relationship, we discussed ways of maximizing the work of the U.S.-Portugal Bilateral Commission, which facilitates cooperation in areas as diverse as defense and security, education, science and technology exchanges, economic revitalization, law enforcement, and development in the Azores. We also noted that in recent years, partnerships between Portuguese and American universities are developing state of the art research in areas such as engineering, information technology, and medicine, and we committed to fostering these relationships in the future.

This meeting was an opportunity for exchanging views on the present world economic and financial situation. The United States underscored its full support for Portugal's implementation of its reform program backed by the IMF and the EU.

We also agreed to continue our close cooperation within the U.N. Security Council, where Portugal currently serves as Council President, on issues of mutual concern, such as Syria, Libya, Middle East peace, and Iran. We emphasized the importance that both our countries attach to the role of the United Nations in the promotion of peace, democracy, good governance and human rights.

As two of the original founding members of NATO, we reaffirmed our commitment to the Atlantic Alliance. We discussed ongoing NATO operations, in particular in Afghanistan, where Portugal intends to maintain its contribution. Recalling the success of the 2010 NATO Summit in Lisbon, we reviewed plans for the May 2012 NATO Summit that President Obama will host in Chicago. We agreed that we would work together in the coming months to ensure that the Summit advances our joint goal of ensuring that the Alliance is fully prepared to meet the security challenges of the 21st century.

NOTE: An original was not available for verification of the content of this joint statement.

Message to the Congress on Continuation of the National Emergency With Respect to Weapons of Mass Destruction
November 9, 2011

To the Congress of the United States:

Section 202(d) of the National Emergencies Act (50 U.S.C. 1622(d)) provides for the automatic termination of a national emergency unless, prior to the anniversary date of its declaration, the President publishes in the *Federal Register* and transmits to the Congress a notice stating that the emergency is to continue in effect beyond the anniversary date. In accordance with this provision, I have sent to the *Federal Register* for publication the enclosed notice, stating that the national emergency with respect to the proliferation of weapons of mass destruction that was declared in Executive Order 12938, as amended, is to continue in effect for 1 year beyond November 14, 2011.

BARACK OBAMA

The White House,
November 9, 2011.

NOTE: The notice is listed in Appendix D at the end of this volume.

Remarks at the National Women's Law Center Awards Dinner
November 9, 2011

The President. Well, good evening, everybody.
Audience members. Good evening.
The President. It is great to be back at the National Women's Law Center, surrounded by so many powerful and accomplished women. This is not a new experience for me.

[*Laughter*] Some of you know my household is filled with powerful, accomplished women.

I want to thank Marcia and Duffy for that wonderful, heartfelt introduction and for their extraordinary leadership. Most of all, I want to recognize tonight's honorees, the women and men—there's some men in the group—[*laughter*]—who endured insults and beatings and risked their lives 50 years ago because they believed in a different future for their daughters and for their sons. The Freedom Riders had faith that America could still be perfected. And as has been noted, it is only because they did that I am able to stand here as President of the United States of America. Which is why, when I had a chance to see them backstage, I gave them all a kiss and a hug. [*Laughter*] And I told them that even though I was in diapers at the time, I knew something important was going on. [*Laughter*]

What a remarkable group of people, and how blessed we are to have them here, sharing their stories and continuing to inspire us in so many ways. We are truly grateful to you.

Being here tonight reminds us that history is not always made—in fact, often is not made—by generals or presidents or politicians. Change doesn't always happen quickly or easily. Change happens when a group of students and activists decide to ride a bus down South, knowing full well the dangers that lie ahead. Change happens when a group of legal secretaries decides that the world needs more women attorneys, and they start an organization to fight for people like them. Change happens when one woman decides: "I don't want to be paid less than that man who's doing the exact same job over there. I want to be paid the same." Change depends on persistence, and change depends on determination. That's how change happens.

That's how change happened on August 4, 1961. That's how change will happen today, especially when it comes to securing equal rights and equal opportunities for women.

Now, the last time I spoke here was in 2005. I was brand new to Washington. Some of you still could not pronounce my name. [*Laughter*] And when I was thinking about what to say to this group, I wasn't just thinking about the legal cases you've helped to win or the milestones that you've helped to reach. I was thinking about my daughters and the world I want them to grow up in.

And I think it's fair to say that a few things have changed since then. Michelle helpfully reminds me that I have more gray hair now. [*Laughter*] More people know my name, which I've come to realize is a mixed blessing. [*Laughter*] Malia and Sasha have grown into these strong, smart, remarkable young women. They are growing too fast. Malia has a cell phone now, certainly a mixed blessing. [*Laughter*]

But even after all this time, my wish for my daughters and for yours remains the same. I want them to go out into a world where there is no limit to how big they can dream, how high they can reach. And being here with all of you gives me hope and makes me determined, because although this journey is far from over, today our daughters live in a world that is fairer and more equal than it was 6 years ago, a world where more doors are open to them than ever before.

Today, for the first time in history, our daughters can see not one, not two, but three women sitting on the bench of the highest court in the land. They can come to the White House and see that the top four lawyers on my staff—some of the sharpest legal minds I've ever come across—are women. They can read about the extraordinary leadership of a woman in the House of Representatives who went by the title "Madam Speaker." They can turn on the news and see that one of the most formidable Presidential candidates we've ever seen has become one of the best Secretaries of State that this country has ever known.

Today, women make up almost half of our workforce, the majority of students in our colleges and our graduate schools. Women are breaking barriers in every field, from science to business to sports to the Armed Forces.

And today, thanks to health care reform that many of you helped pass, insurance companies can no longer deny coverage based on preexisting conditions like breast cancer or charge women more because they're more likely to incur costs for things like birth—childbirth. Those same companies must cover the cost of preventive services like mammograms, domestic violence counseling, contraception. We're making sure that women in the military and our veterans get the care that they need.

Today, thanks to the tireless efforts of people like Lilly Ledbetter—one of my favorite people, love that woman—[*laughter*]—we were backstage talking, and she was just saying how grateful she was, how much of a responsibility she now felt with this bill having been passed that was named after her. I said: "Lilly, all that did was just—that was just icing on the cake. It was your work, your courage, your determination that changed things. All we did was ratify what you had already done." And because of her and other courageous women and some of the women in this room tonight, it is easier for women to demand equal pay for equal work.

We passed tax credits that are keeping more women out of poverty and helping them reach the middle class. Companies are being encouraged to make workplaces more flexible so women don't have to choose between being a good employee and a good parent. One of the first things I did after taking office was to create a White House Council on Women and Girls to make sure that every agency in the Federal Government considers the needs of women and girls in every decision they make, not as a sideshow, not as a box to check, but something that is sustained each and every day.

So this is progress. This is progress. This is change. It's laborious. Sometimes it's frustrating. But it's real. And of course, one thing we've learned from the women's movement, from the civil rights movement, from the workers' movement, from every step that we've made to make this country more equal and more just, is that there is always more work to do. There are always more challenges to meet. And that's especially true today, with so many Americans struggling to recover from the worst economic crisis since the Great Depression.

In the early days of this crisis, women weren't hit quite as hard as men. Many of the jobs that we've lost over the last decade have been in construction and manufacturing, industries that traditionally had been dominated by men. And of the 15 job categories projected to grow the most in this country over the next

decade, all but 2 are occupied primarily by women.

But over the last couple of years, women have continued to lose jobs, especially in the public sector. It doesn't help that mothers are the primary or cobreadwinners in 63 percent of households, even as women still earn just 77 cents for every dollar a man does. Some of these women are single moms like my mother was, struggling just to keep up with the bills or pay a mortgage they can't afford. I still remember my mother waking me up—she worked, was going to school, and still took the time to wake me up before she went to work to go over my lessons before she left. And I would complain and grumble, and she would say, "Well, this is no picnic for me either, buster." [*Laughter*]

These are the quiet heroes. Their names don't make the history books. They're never complaining—well, I won't say they're never complaining—[*laughter*]—I was thinking about that for a second—never hesitating to work that extra shift or that extra job if that's what it takes to give their children a better life. And in many ways, that's why we're all here tonight, because we know that it's up to us to keep fighting for them—all those women out there—making sure that they are treated fairly and equally. As hard as they're working, as much as they're sacrificing, as many responsibilities that they shoulder each and every day, we've got to make sure that they are getting the opportunities that they deserve, that somebody is standing up for them. Somebody is fighting for them. Somebody is looking out for them. Somebody is rooting for them.

Of course, let's be clear about one thing: When we talk about these issues that primarily affect women, these are not just women's issues. When women make less than men for the same work, that hurts the entire family who has to get by with less. It hurts businesses who have fewer customers with money to spend. When a health care plan denies women coverage because of a preexisting condition, that puts a strain on emergency rooms, drives up health care costs for everybody. When any of our citizens can't fulfill their potential because of factors that have nothing to do with their talent or their character or their work ethic, that diminishes us. It says something about who we are.

Here's a fact: If you want to look around the world, those countries that are developing fastest, that are doing the best, where their children are succeeding in school, those are societies that respect the rights of women, that are investing in our women.

Lifting women up lifts up our economy and lifts up our country. Now unfortunately, not everybody in Washington seems to feel the same way. In recent weeks, Republicans in the Senate have come together three times to block jobs bills that independent economists say would boost our economy and put millions back to work, including women. Each of these bills was made up of the same kinds of proposals that Democrats and Republicans have historically supported in the past, and they were fully paid for. And even though they were supported by a clear majority of the American people—Republicans, Democrats, Independents—every single Senate Republican said no.

Said no to putting hundreds of thousands of teachers, three-quarters of them women, back in front of the classroom where they belong. No to putting construction workers back on the job and funding a special program that gets more women involved in the construction industry.

Well, I've got news for Congress: We are not done yet. In the weeks ahead, they're going to get a chance to vote on whether we give a tax cut to virtually every small-business owner in America, including 900,000 women. These are folks who run the restaurants and stores and beauty shops and other small businesses that create two-thirds of all new jobs. There's no reason they shouldn't get a break.

The American people are with me with—on this, and Republicans in Congress should be with me too, because it's right for the country. Instead, they're spending time focusing on how to turn back the clock. Instead of figuring out how to put more Americans back to work, they've been trying to figure out how to take away preventive care that is covered under the

Affordable Care Act. Instead of making life easier for women in this country, they want to let insurance companies go back to charging higher prices just because you're a woman. Instead of working to boost our economy, they're out there spending time trying to defund Planned Parenthood and prevent millions of women from getting basic health care that they desperately need: Pap smears and breast exams.

That is not the right direction for this country. These folks know they can't win on the big issues, so they're trying to make the fight about social issues that stir up their base. They're spending their time trying to divide this country against itself rather than coming together to lift up our country.

And we don't have to settle for that. The American people shouldn't have to settle for that. And that's why I need your help. As leaders in your communities, I need you to tell Congress to do their jobs by worrying about the jobs of the millions of Americans they were elected to serve. I need you to make your voices heard. And for my part, I promise to keep doing everything I can to help every single American achieve their own piece of the American Dream.

That's not just a promise I'm making as a President. That's a promise I'm making as a grandson who saw my grandmother hit the glass ceiling at the bank where she worked, passed over for promotions in favor of men that she trained.

It's a promise I'm making as a husband who watched Michelle balance work and family with grace and poise, even when it hasn't been easy.

It's a promise I'm making as a father who wants my daughters to grow up in a world where every door is open to them, where there are no limits on what they can achieve.

It's a promise I'm making as the inheritor of the extraordinary sacrifices that were made by these Freedom Riders, as a friend of people like Lilly Ledbetter, who embody all that's good and decent in this country.

It's a promise I'm making as an American who believes that the future of our country depends on expanding the circle of opportunity for everybody, because that next generation of smart, powerful women, they're already knocking on the door. They're coming, and we need to get ready. [*Laughter*]

Last month, I got a chance to meet the winners of the Google Science Fair. This is an international competition of high school students, the cutting edge of technology and science. All three of the winners turned out to be Americans. All three were girls. They had beat out 10,000 other applicants from more than 90 countries. So I had them in the Oval Office, and they explained their projects to me— [*laughter*]—and I pretended that I understood what they were talking about. [*Laughter*] There's a picture of this conversation hanging up in the West Wing right now, and they're— I've got a puzzled look on my face—[*laughter*]—and they're being very patient.

So one of the winners, Shree Bose, discovered a promising new way to improve treatment for ovarian cancer at the age of 17. Then I asked another winner, Lauren Hodge, if she had skipped a grade in school; she was quite petite. [*Laughter*] And she informed me very politely that she had actually skipped two. [*Laughter*] Okay. [*Laughter*]

It's people like Shree and Lauren, all of you who are here tonight, who make me hopeful about the future. There's a direct line between those women who sat in those jail cells and those young girls explaining their science project in the Oval Office. There's a direct connection. Because that's what America is about, a place where ideas are born and dreams can grow and where a student in a classroom or a passenger on a bus or a legal secretary in an office can stand up and say, "I am going to change the world." We have always been a nation where anything is possible.

That's the kind of nation that we are. That's the kind of opportunity that must exist here in America. That's the kind of opportunity that must exist for every American, no matter what they look like or where they come from. We've come a long way towards making this country more open and more free for our daughters and theirs. We've got a lot more work to do. With the National Women's Law Center, I am confident that the next time I visit, we'll be even closer to guaranteeing every one of our children get the future they deserve.

Thank you very much, everybody. God bless you. God bless the United States of America.

NOTE: The President spoke at 8:36 p.m. at the Washington Hilton hotel. In his remarks, he referred to Marcia D. Greenberger and Nancy Duff Cambell, copresidents, National Women's Law Center; and Naomi Shah, winner of the 2011 Google Science Fair.

Statement on the Anniversary of the Birth of the Founder of Sikhism
November 10, 2011

I send my best wishes to all those observing the anniversary of the birth of Guru Nanak Dev Ji, the first Sikh guru. On this occasion, we are reminded of the fundamental principles of Sikhism, including the equality of all people, the sanctity of living an honest life, and the importance of service to our neighbors. I'm proud that during my Presidency the White House hosted the first celebration of the birth of Guru Nanak, and our country is grateful for the extraordinary contributions that Sikh Americans have made to our Nation. As Sikhs across America and around the world celebrate the life of Guru Nanak, all of us can draw inspiration from his message of equality, honesty, and helping those who are in need.

Statement on the Progress in Russia's World Trade Organization Accession Talks
November 10, 2011

I congratulate PresidentMedvedev and his Government for completing negotiations on the terms and conditions for Russia's accession to the World Trade Organization (WTO), which were adopted today by the WTO working party on Russia's accession. The outcome of today's working party meeting is the last step before WTO Ministers approve these terms and invite Russia to become a WTO member, which we expect to take place at the WTO ministerial conference on December 15–17, 2011. After nearly two decades of negotiations, Russia will now be able to join to the WTO. This is a significant day for U.S.-Russia relations and for our commitment to a growing, rules-based global economy.

Since the beginning of my administration, and with increased intensity after President Medvedev and I met in Washington in June 2010, I have supported Russia's WTO accession. Russia's membership in the WTO will lower tariffs, improve international access to Russia's services markets, hold the Russian Government accountable to a system of rules governing trade behavior, and provide the means to enforce those rules.

Russia's membership in the WTO will generate more exports for American manufacturers and farmers, which in turn will support well-paying jobs in the United States.

Russia also is opening its services market in sectors that are priorities to American companies, including audio-visual, telecommunications, financial services, computer, and retail services.

From day one of its membership in the WTO, Russia will be required to comply with WTO rules on the protection and enforcement of intellectual property rights, including with respect to key rights relied on by U.S. creative and innovative industries.

Russia's membership in the WTO also will benefit American companies and their workers by integrating Russia into a system of rules governing legal transparency and trade behavior and providing the means to enforce those rules.

Upon Russia's accession, the United States will be able to use WTO mechanisms, including dispute settlement, to challenge Russia's actions that are inconsistent with WTO rules.

All of these benefits also apply to Russia's other WTO trading partners, including Georgia, which concluded a far-reaching agreement with Russia yesterday for monitoring trade between their two countries.

I now look forward to working with Congress to end the application of the Jackson-Vanik amendment to Russia in order to ensure that American firms and American exporters will enjoy the same benefits of Russian WTO membership as their international competitors.

Russia's WTO accession would be yet another important step forward in our reset of relations with Russia, which has been based upon the belief that the United States and Russia share many common interests, even as we disagree on some issues. Whether cooperating to supply our forces in Afghanistan, securing nuclear materials, or achieving the New START Treaty, the United States and Russia have demonstrated the ability to produce win-win outcomes on security issues. Russia's dramatic step today towards joining the WTO underscores our ability to cooperate also on economic issues of mutual interest.

Statement on the Department of State's Keystone XL Pipeline Announcement
November 10, 2011

I support the State Department's announcement today regarding the need to seek additional information about the Keystone XL Pipeline proposal. Because this permit decision could affect the health and safety of the American people as well as the environment and because a number of concerns have been raised through a public process, we should take the time to ensure that all questions are properly addressed and all the potential impacts are properly understood. The final decision should be guided by an open, transparent process that is informed by the best available science and the voices of the American people. At the same time, my administration will build on the unprecedented progress we've made towards strengthening our Nation's energy security, from responsibly expanding domestic oil and gas production to nearly doubling the fuel efficiency of our cars and trucks, to continued progress in the development of a clean energy economy.

Statement on Senate Passage of Legislation Providing Tax Credits To Aid Businesses Hiring Veterans
November 10, 2011

Today Republicans and Democrats in the Senate did the right thing and passed tax credits that will encourage businesses to hire America's veterans. Tomorrow our Nation will commemorate Veterans Day and honor the service and the sacrifice of all who have worn the uniform of the United States of America. No veteran who fought for our Nation should have to fight for a job when they come home, and I urge the House to pass these tax credits as well so I can sign them into law. I also urge Congress to pass additional jobs proposals in the weeks ahead to help the millions of other Americans who are still looking for work.

NOTE: The statement referred to H.R. 674.

Remarks at a Veterans Day Ceremony in Arlington, Virginia
November 11, 2011

Thank you, Ric Shinseki, for your extraordinary service to our country and your tireless commitment to our veterans; to Secretary of Defense Leon Panetta; to Chairman Dempsey and Mrs. Dempsey; to our wonderful veterans service organizations for the extraordinary work that you do for our Nation's heroes; to all who tend to and watch over this sacred cemetery; and above all, to every Active Duty member, guardsman, reservist, and veteran of the United States Armed Forces.

There are many honors and responsibilities that come with this job, but none are more humbling than serving as your Commander in Chief. And I'm proud to be with so many of you here today.

Here, where our heroes come to rest, we come to show our gratitude. A few moments ago, I laid a wreath to pay tribute to all who have given their lives to our country. For even though this is a day we rightly honor America's veterans, we gather today in solemn respect, mindful that we are guests here, mindful that we share this hallowed space with a family's moment of quiet grief, mindful that many veterans not far from here are tracing their fingers over black granite for friends who never came home and expect us to do all we can to bring every missing American servicemember home to their families.

To all our Nation's veterans: Whether you fought in Salerno or Samarra, Khe Sanh or the Korengal, you are part of an unbroken chain of men and women who have served this country with honor and distinction. On behalf of a proud and grateful nation, we thank you.

When I spoke here on this day 2 years ago, I said there would be a day before long when this generation of service men and women would begin to step out of uniform. And I made them a promise. I said that when your tour ends, when you see our flag, when you touch our soil, you will be home in an America that is forever here for you, just as you've been there for us.

For many, that day has come. Over the past decade, more than 5 million Americans have worn the uniform of the United States Armed Forces. Of these, 3 million stepped forward after the attacks of September 11, knowing full well that they could be sent into harm's way. And in that time, they have served in some of the world's most dangerous places. Their service has been selfless. Their accomplishments have been extraordinary.

In Iraq, they have battled a brutal insurgency, trained new security forces, and given the Iraqi people the opportunity to forge a better future. In Afghanistan, they have pushed back the Taliban, decimated Al Qaida, and delivered the ultimate justice to Usama bin Laden. In concert with our allies, they have helped end Qadhafi's brutal dictatorship and returned Libya to its people.

Because of their incredible efforts, we can stand here today and say with confidence: The tide of war is receding. In just a few weeks, the long war in Iraq will finally come to an end. Our transition in Afghanistan is moving forward. My fellow Americans, our troops are coming home.

For many military families, this holiday season will be a season of homecomings. And over the next 5 years, more than 1 million Americans in uniform will transition back to civilian life, joining the nearly 3 million who have done so over the past decade and embraced a proud new role, the role of veteran.

This generation of servicemembers, this 9/11 generation, has borne the burden of our security during a hard decade of sacrifice. Our service men and women make up less than 1 percent of Americans, but also more than 1 million military spouses and 2 million children and millions more parents and relatives, all of whom have shared the strains of deployment and sacrificed on behalf of the country that we love.

Only 27 years old on average, these young men and women have shattered the false myth of their generation's apathy, for they came of age in an era when so many institutions failed

to live up to their responsibilities. But they chose to serve a cause greater than their selves. They saw their country threatened. But they signed up to confront that threat. They felt some tug, they answered some call, and they said, let's go. And they've earned their place among the greatest of generations.

That is something for America to be proud of. That is the spirit America needs now, a stronger, newer spirit of service and of sacrifice. That spirit that says, "What can I do to help? What can I do to serve?" That spirit that says, "When my country is challenged, I will do my part to meet that challenge."

So on this Veterans Day, let us commit ourselves to keep making sure that our veterans receive the care and benefits that they have earned, the opportunity they defend and deserve, and above all, let us welcome them home as what they are, an integral, essential part of our American family.

See, when our men and women sign up to become a soldier or a sailor, an airman, marine, or coastguardsman, they don't stop being a citizen. When they take off that uniform, their service to this Nation doesn't stop either. Like so many of their predecessors, today's veterans come home looking to continue serving America however they can. At a time when America needs all hands on deck, they have the skills and the strength to help lead the way.

Our Government needs their patriotism and sense of duty. And that's why I've ordered the hiring of more veterans by the Federal Government. Our economy needs their tremendous talents and specialized skills. So I challenged our business leaders to hire 100,000 post-9/11 veterans and their spouses over the next few years, and yesterday many of these leaders joined Michelle to announce that they will meet that challenge.

Our communities have always drawn strength from our veterans' leadership. Think of all who have come home and settled on in a quiet life of service—as a doctor or a police officer, an engineer or an entrepreneur, as a mom or a dad—and in the process, changed countless lives. Other veterans seek new adventures, from taking on a new business to building a team of globetrotting veterans who use skills learned in combat to help after a natural disaster.

There are also so many in this young generation who still feel that tug to serve, but just don't quite know where to turn. So on this Veterans Day, I ask every American: Recruit our veterans. If you're a business owner, hire them. If you're a community leader—a mayor, a pastor, or a preacher—call on them to join your efforts. Organize your community to make a sustained difference in the life of a veteran, because that veteran can make an incredible difference in the life of your community.

If you're a veteran looking for new ways to serve, check out serve.gov. If you're a civilian looking for new ways to support our veterans and our troops, join Michelle and Jill Biden at joiningforces.gov. Find out what you can do. There is no such thing as too small a difference. That effort you make may have the biggest impact.

I say this because recently, I received a letter from a Vietnam veteran. She wasn't writing to tell me about her own experience. She just wanted to tell me about her son Jeremy. Now, Jeremy isn't deployed, Jeremy's not a veteran or even in the military at all, as badly as he wants to follow in the footsteps of his family and enlist. You see, Jeremy has Down syndrome.

So Jeremy chooses to serve where he can best, with his local Vietnam Veterans of America chapter in Beaver, Pennsylvania. He calls them "the soldiers." And one day last spring, Jeremy spent the day with several of these veterans cleaning up a local highway.

"He worked tirelessly," wrote his mother. "He never asked to take a break. He didn't stop to talk about his beloved Steelers. He didn't even ask for anything to eat or drink. He only asked one thing, several times: 'Mom, will President Obama be proud of me for helping the soldiers?'"

Well, Jeremy, I want you to know, yes, I am proud of you. I could not be prouder of you, and your country is proud of you. Thank you for serving our veterans by helping them to continue their service to America.

And Jeremy's example—one young man's example—is one that we must all now follow. Because after a decade of war, the nation we now need to build is our own. And just as our greatest generation left a country recovering from depression and returned home to build the largest middle class in history, so now will the 9/11 generation play a pivotal role in rebuilding America's opportunity and prosperity in the 21st century.

We know it will be hard. We have to overcome new threats to our security and prosperity, and we've got to overcome the cynical voices warning that America's best days are behind us. But if there is anything our veterans teach us, it's that there is no threat we cannot meet, there is no challenge we cannot overcome. America's best days are still ahead. And the reason for that is because we are a people who defy those voices that insist otherwise. We are a country that does what is necessary for future generations to succeed.

You, our veterans, fight so our children won't have to. We build and we invent and we learn so that we will know greater opportunity. America leads so that the next generation, here and around the world, will know a more hopeful life on this Earth.

So today I thank you all for making that possible. God bless you. God bless our veterans and our troops, and God bless the United States of America.

NOTE: The President spoke at 11:40 a.m. at Arlington National Cemetery. In his remarks, he referred to Gen. Martin E. Dempsey, USA, Chairman, Joint Chiefs of Staff, and his wife Deanie; Jill T. Biden, wife of Vice President Joe Biden; and Beaver, PA, resident Teresa Carr and her son Jeremy.

Remarks at the Quicken Loans Carrier Classic in San Diego, California
November 11, 2011

Hello, everybody! How you feeling tonight? We are so fortunate to be able to witness two of the greatest basketball programs in history: Michigan State Spartans, North Carolina Tar Heels. Two of the best coaches of all time: Coach Izzo, Coach Williams. So we are proud to be here and see a great sporting event.

But the main reason we're here is, on Veterans Day, we have an opportunity to say thank you. One of the greatest privileges of this job, and one of the greatest responsibilities of this job, is to serve as your Commander in Chief. And I can tell you that every day when I interact with our military, every day when I interact with the men and women in uniform, I could not be prouder to be an American.

And that gratitude that we have for our men and women of the Armed Forces does not stop when they take off the uniform. When they come home, part of the long line of those who defended our freedom, we have a sacred trust to make sure that they understand how much we appreciate what they do. And that's not just on Veterans Day. That is every day of every year where we salute them and we say thank you for making the sacrifices and for their families' sacrifices on our behalf.

This week, throughout the week, we've been celebrating our veterans, but we have to turn our words into action. So what we've done is make sure that Congress passed legislation that makes it a little bit easier for businesses to hire our veterans. We've put in place a series of reforms to help veterans, make sure they get the counseling and the job placement that they need.

The First Lady, along with Dr. Jill Biden, have put together something called Joining Forces that has now gotten commitments—100,000 jobs for veterans and military spouses all across the country. And we are grateful for them for that effort.

But every American citizen can make a solemn pledge today that they will find some opportunity to provide support to our troops, to those who are still Active Duty, to our National Guard, to our reservists, and to our veterans.

And it's especially appropriate that we do it here, because the USS *Carl Vinson* has been a messenger of diplomacy and a protector of our security for a long time. And the men and women who serve on this ship have done extraordinary service in the Pacific, in the Persian Gulf, in the Indian Ocean. It was from this aircraft carrier that some of the first assaults on Iraq were launched. This ship supports what's happening in Afghanistan.

I think some of you may know, because it's been reported, that the men and women on the *Carl Vinson* were part of that critical mission to bring Usama bin Laden to justice.

So to all our veterans, to all our men and women in uniform, we say thank you. And we want you to know that we are committed to making sure that we serve you as well as you have always served us.

Thank you. God bless you, and God bless the United States of America. Thank you.

NOTE: The President spoke at 4:10 p.m. aboard the USS *Carl Vinson*. In his remarks, he referred to Thomas Izzo, head coach, Michigan State University men's basketball team; Roy A. Williams, head coach, University of North Carolina men's basketball team; and Jill T. Biden, wife of Vice President Joe Biden.

The President's Weekly Address
November 12, 2011

I'm speaking to you from the primary flight control of the aircraft carrier USS *Carl Vinson* in San Diego. This is one of the biggest ships in the Navy, and on Friday it was home to one of the most unique college basketball games I have ever seen. It also gave members of our military and our veterans a chance to unwind a little bit, and on this Veterans Day, I want to take this opportunity to thank all our men and women in uniform for their service and their sacrifice.

But this day isn't just about thanking our veterans. It's about rededicating ourselves to serving our veterans as well as they've served us. And right now that's never been more important.

Last month, I announced that, as promised, we will end the war in Iraq by the end of the year. Many of our military families will be welcoming loved ones home for the holidays. At the same time, we've begun to wind down the war in Afghanistan. And in the next 5 years, over a million servicemembers will transition back into civilian life, joining the 3 million who have already done so over the last decade.

These are men and women who have served with distinction in some of the most dangerous places on the planet. But for many of them, the challenges don't end when they take off the uniform. Today, more than 850,000 veterans remain unemployed, and too many are struggling to find a job worthy of their talents and their experience.

That's not right. We ask these men and women to leave their families and their jobs and risk their lives to fight for our country. The last thing they should have to do is fight for a job when they get home.

To give our veterans the opportunity they've earned, I've directed the Federal Government to lead by example, and already we've hired 120,000 veterans. We've also challenged private companies to hire or train 100,000 post-9/11 veterans or their spouses by the end of 2013. So far, many patriotic companies have answered the call, hiring more than 16,000 Americans. And yesterday, thanks to the hard work of Michelle and Dr. Jill Biden, companies announced their commitment to train or hire 125,000 more over the next 2 years.

But we still need to do more. That's why, as part of the "American Jobs Act," I called on Congress to pass a returning heroes tax credit, which would give businesses a tax break for each unemployed veteran they hire and a wounded warriors tax credit, which would give businesses a tax break for hiring an unemployed veteran with a disability related to their service in uniform.

These proposals will go a long way towards putting our veterans back to work. And on Thursday, I was pleased to see the Senate put partisanship aside and came together to pass these tax credits. After all, standing up for our veterans isn't a Democratic responsibility or a Republican responsibility, it's an American responsibility. It's one that all of us have an obligation to meet. And the House should pass this bill as soon as possible so I can sign it into law.

As Commander in Chief, I want every veteran to know that America will always honor your service and your sacrifice, not just today, but every day. And just as you have fought for us, we're going to keep fighting for you, for more jobs, for more security, and for the opportunity to keep your families strong and America competitive in the 21st century.

So to all our veterans, thank you for your service. God bless you, and may God bless the United States of America.

NOTE: The address was recorded at approximately 5 p.m. on November 11 aboard the USS *Carl Vinson* in San Diego, CA, for broadcast on November 12. In the address, the President referred to Jill T. Biden, wife of Vice President Joe Biden. The transcript was made available by the Office of the Press Secretary on November 11, but was embargoed for release until 6 a.m. on November 12.

Remarks During a Meeting on the Trans-Pacific Partnership in Honolulu, Hawaii
November 12, 2011

I want to welcome, once again, all the leaders gathered around this table and their trade ministers to Hawaii. Here in Hawaii, the United States wants to send a clear message: We are a Pacific nation, and we are deeply committee to shaping the future security and prosperity of the transpacific region, the fastest growing region in the world.

I'm very pleased to be here with my partners with whom we're pursing a very ambitious new trade agreement, the Trans-Pacific Partnership. I want to thank my fellow leaders from Australia, New Zealand, Malaysia, Brunei, Singapore, Vietnam, Chile, and Peru.

We just had an excellent meeting, and I'm very pleased to announce that our nine nations have reached the broad outlines of an agreement. There are still plenty of details to work out, but we are confident that we can do so. So we've directed our teams to finalize this agreement in the coming year. It is an ambitious goal, but we are optimistic that we can get it done.

The TPP will boost our economies, lowering barriers to trade and investment, increasing exports, and creating more jobs for our people, which is my number-one priority. Along with our trade agreements with South Korea, Panama, and Colombia, the TPP will also help achieve my goal of doubling U.S. exports, which support millions of American jobs.

Taken together, these eight economies would be America's fifth largest trading partner. We already do more than $200 billion in trade with them every single year, and with nearly 500 million consumers between us, there's so much more that we can do together.

In a larger sense, the TPP has the potential to be a model not only for the Asia-Pacific, but for future trade agreements. It addresses a whole range of issues not covered by past agreements, including market regulations and how we can make them more compatible, creating opportunities for small and medium-sized businesses in the growing global marketplace. It will include high standards to protect workers' rights and the environment.

And I want to thank my U.S. Trade Representative, Ambassador Kirk, and all our teams for doing tireless work to achieve the progress that we've made so far. I want to thank all my fellow leaders for their partnership and their commitment to making the TPP a reality, which will be a win for all our countries.

So again, I am confident that we can get this done. Together, we can boost exports, create more goods available for our consumers, create good jobs, and compete and win in the markets of the future.

Ladies and gentlemen, thank you very much for your outstanding work. Thank you.

NOTE: The President spoke at 9:20 a.m. at the Hale Koa Hotel. A portion of these remarks could not be verified because the audio was incomplete.

Joint Statement by Trans-Pacific Partnership Leaders
November 12, 2011

We, the Leaders of Australia, Brunei Darussalam, Chile, Malaysia, New Zealand, Peru, Singapore, United States, and Vietnam, are pleased to announce today the broad outlines of a Trans-Pacific Partnership (TPP) agreement among our nine countries. We are delighted to have achieved this milestone in our common vision to establish a comprehensive, next-generation regional agreement that liberalizes trade and investment and addresses new and traditional trade issues and 21st-century challenges. We are confident that this agreement will be a model for ambition for other free trade agreements in the future, forging close linkages among our economies, enhancing our competitiveness, benefitting our consumers and supporting the creation and retention of jobs, higher living standards, and the reduction of poverty in our countries.

Building on this achievement and on the successful work done so far, we have committed here in Honolulu to dedicate the resources necessary to conclude this landmark agreement as rapidly as possible. At the same time, we recognize that there are sensitive issues that vary for each country yet to be negotiated, and have agreed that together, we must find appropriate ways to address those issues in the context of a comprehensive and balanced package, taking into account the diversity of our levels of development. Therefore, we have instructed our negotiating teams to meet in early

December of this year to continue their work and furthermore to schedule additional negotiating rounds for 2012.

We are gratified by the progress that we are now able to announce toward our ultimate goal of forging a pathway that will lead to free trade across the Pacific. We share a strong interest in expanding our current partnership of nine geographically and developmentally diverse countries to others across the region. As we move toward conclusion of an agreement, we have directed our negotiating teams to continue talks with other trans-Pacific partners that have expressed interest in joining the TPP in order to facilitate their future participation.

NOTE: An original was not available for verification of the content of this joint statement.

Remarks at an Asia-Pacific Economic Cooperation CEO Summit Question-and-Answer Session in Honolulu
November 12, 2011

U.S. Economy/Global Economic Stabilization Efforts

Announcer. Ladies and gentlemen, please welcome the President of the United States of America, Barack Obama. [*Applause*]

Boeing Company Chief Executive Officer W. James McNerney, Jr. You'd think you've been to Hawaii before. [*Laughter*] It's great to be here with you, thank you.

Mr. President, few forums are watched more closely by those of us in the business community than APEC, testimony to the extraordinary opportunity it represents for both sides of the Pacific rim.

As you know, APEC accounts for 55 percent of global GDP and is growing faster than the global average, significantly faster. It represents 2.7 billion consumers and purchases 58 percent of U.S. exports. So I'm honored, very honored, to represent many of the wide-ranging interests of the business community on stage with you today.

Unlocking the growth potential that exists within APEC is a huge opportunity for job creation here in the United States and for our economic

partners. Secretary Clinton spoke about that yesterday within the context of greater engagement of women and small businesses, for example.

Given that you represent—and I'm working my way up to a question here—given that you represent the largest economy in the group, your views on subjects pertinent to that growth potential are vital, and that's what I'd like to explore with you here this morning.

Just to start at 50,000 feet, you just participated in the G–20 meeting last week where global growth was a—and threats thereof—was a central topic of discussion. With the benefit of the viewpoints exchanged at the G–20 session, what now is your outlook for the global economy, and maybe with just an eye toward its impact on the APEC economies?

The President. Well, first of all, Jim, thank you for having me here. Thanks to all the business leaders who are participating. I understand that there have been some terrific conversations over the last couple of days.

I want to thank our Hawaiian hosts for the great hospitality. As many of you know, this is my birthplace. I know that was contested for a while—[*laughter*]—but I can actually show you the hospital if you want to go down there. [*Laughter*] And I also have to make mention, first of all, that in all my years of living in Hawaii and visiting Hawaii, this is the first time that I've ever worn a suit. [*Laughter*] So it feels a little odd.

Obviously, we have just gone through the worst financial crisis and the worst economic crisis since the 1930s. And one of the differences between now and the thirties is that the global economy is more integrated than ever, and so what happens in Asia has an impact here in the United States, what happens in Europe has an impact on Asia and the United States.

At the G–20 meeting, our most immediate task was looking at what's happening in the euro zone. And if you trace what's happened over the last 2 to 3 years, we were able to stabilize the world economy after the crisis with Lehman's and get the world financial system working again. We were able to get the economy growing again. But it has not been growing as robustly as it needs to in order to put people back to work. And my number-one priority has been to not only grow the economy, but also make sure that that translates into opportunities for ordinary people. And I think leaders from around the world are thinking the same way.

I was pleased to see that European leaders were taking seriously the need to not just solve the Greek crisis, but also to solve the broader euro zone crisis. There have been some positive developments over the last week: a new potential Government in Italy, a new Government in Greece, both committed to applying the sort internal structural reform that can give markets more confidence.

There is still work to be done in the broader European community to provide markets a strong assurance that countries like Italy will be able to finance their debt. These are economies that are large. They are economies that are strong. But they have some issues that the markets are concerned about. And that has to be addressed inside of Italy, but it's not going to be addressed overnight. So it's important that Europe as a whole stands behind its euro

zone members. And we have tried to be as supportive as we can, providing them some advice and technical assistance.

I think that we're not going to see massive growth out of Europe until the problem is resolved. And that will have a dampening effect on the overall global economy. But if we can at least contain the crisis, then one of the great opportunities we have is to see the Asia-Pacific region as an extraordinary engine for growth.

And part of the reason that we're here at APEC is to concentrate on what you just identified as about half of the world's trade, half of the world's GDP, and a growing share. And so the whole goal of APEC is to ensure that we are reducing barriers to trade and investment that can translate into concrete jobs here in the United States and all around the world.

If we're going to grow, it's going to be because of exports, it's going to be because of the great work that companies like Boeing is doing, it's going to be because we've got high standard trade agreements that are creating win-win situations for countries, the way we were able to do bilaterally with South Korea just recently. And if we can stay on that trajectory, letting this region of the world know that America is a Pacific power and we intend to be here, actively engaged in trying to boost the economy worldwide and for our respective countries, then I am cautiously optimistic that we'll get through this current crisis and will come out stronger over the next couple of years.

Asia-Pacific Region/U.S. Foreign Policy

Mr. McNerney. Fixing Europe obviously a priority, but the growth is here for now. Although as I've traveled around the Asia-Pacific region, I and others have detected a slight sense of unease and uncertainty among government and business leaders around whether the U.S. intends to maintain its role in helping to ensure the political, economic stability of this region, other forms of stability, including the free flow of communication and commerce. I do know that Secretary of State Clinton and Secretary Panetta recently delivered some very reassuring remarks, which I'm sure didn't happen by accident. But I think your view on that, on this subject, is of great interest not only to the business community, but to the community at large here in the region.

And so how does Asia fit as a priority for our country? And where is its place, in a multifaceted way, not just business, in the Asia-Pacific region?

The President. The United States is a Pacific power, and we are here to stay. And one of the messages that Secretary Clinton, Secretary Panetta have been delivering, but I am personally here to deliver over the next week, is that there's no region in the world that we consider more vital than the Asia-Pacific region, and we want, on a whole range of issues, to be working with our partner countries around the Pacific rim in order to enhance job growth, economic growth, prosperity, and security for all of us.

And let me just give you a couple of examples. The APEC conference that we're hosting here is going to have some very concrete deliverables around issues like regulatory convergence, which permits countries to all think about whether our regulations are as efficient, as effective as they can be, or where are they standing in the way of smart trade.

I'll be traveling to Australia to celebrate the 60th year of the American-Australian alliance, and that will signify the security infrastructure that allows for the free flow of trade and commerce throughout the region.

The TPP, the Trans-Pacific Partnership agreement that I just met with the countries who are involved, we're doing some outstanding work trying to create a high-level trade agreement that could potentially be a model not just for countries in the Pacific region, but for the world generally.

And so across the board, whether it's on security architecture, whether it's on trade, whether it's on commerce, we are going to continue to prioritize this region. And one of the gratifying things is that, as we talk to our partners in the region, they welcome U.S. reengagement. I think we spent a decade in which, understandably, after 9/11, we were very focused on security issues, particularly in the Middle East region. And those continue to be important. But we've turned our attention

back to the Asia-Pacific region, and I think that it's paying off immediately in a whole range of improved relations with countries, and businesses are starting to see more opportunities as a consequence.

Trade

Mr. McNerney. You know, I don't think the business community has fully understood the comprehensiveness of your approach out here, and I think—because it all does link together—security, business environment, bilateral trade facilitation, all these things really do link together. And I think Secretary Clinton has made a very comprehensive case for it. We've seen in some of her published work and some of her speeches. So this looks like—I wouldn't say a major new direction, but it is something that is a major priority for you over the next n number of years, is—am I capturing it right?

The President. There's no doubt. It is a reaffirmation of how important we consider this region. It has a range of components. Now, some of those are grounded in decade-long alliances. The alliance we have with Japan and South Korea, the alliance we have with Australia, the security architecture of the region is something that we pay a lot of attention to. And we're going to be going through some tough fiscal decisions back home——

Mr. McNerney. Yes.

The President. ——but nevertheless, what I've said when it comes to prioritizing our security posture here in this region, this has to continue to remain a top priority.

And on the business side, this is where the action is going to be. If we're going to not just double our exports, but make sure that good jobs are created here in the United States, then we're going to have to continue to expand our trade opportunities and economic integration with the fastest growing region in the world.

And that means, in some cases, some hard negotiations and some tough work, as we went through in South Korea. I think that was a great model of prioritizing trade with a key partner. It wasn't easy. I said at the outset that I wanted—I had no problem seeing Hyundais and Kias here in the United States, but I wanted to see some Chevrolets and Fords in Seoul. And after a lot of work and some dedicated attention from President Lee, we were able to get a deal that for the first time was endorsed not just by the business community, but also was endorsed by the United Auto Workers and a number of labor leaders. And that shows how we can build a bipartisan support for job creation in the United States and trade agreements that make sense.

Trans-Pacific Partnership/Japan

Mr. McNerney. You referenced Korea and Colombia, Panama: big, strong, protrade votes. I mean, it was a major legislative accomplishment. And the momentum that Ambassador Kirk talks about flowing into the Trans-Pacific Partnership, just let's spend a minute on that. You raised it earlier. Do you see other APEC countries joining—the obvious question is Japan? And how significant is the TPP for this region of the world and for the United States? Is there anything else you'd like to say about it?

The President. Well, keep in mind that almost two decades ago when APEC was formed, the notion was to create a transpacific free trade agreement. Obviously, the membership of APEC is extraordinarily diverse. It reflects countries with different levels of development. And so for many years that vision, that dream I think seemed very far off in the distance.

What happened was, is a group, a subset of APEC countries came together and said, let's see if we can create a high-standard agreement that is dealing with tariffs and nontariff barriers to trade, but let's also incorporate a whole range of new trade issues that are going to be coming up in the future: innovation, regulatory convergence, how are we thinking about the Internet and intellectual property.

And so what we've seen, and we just came from a meeting in which the TPP members affirmed a basic outline, and our goal is, by next year, to get the legal text for a full agreement. The idea here is to have a trade agreement that deals not just with past issues, but also future issues. And if we're successful, then I think it becomes the seed of a broader set of agree-

ments. And what's been really interesting is how, because of the success of these first few countries joining together, we're now seeing others like Japan expressing an interest in joining. And I'll have a meeting with Prime Minister Noda later this afternoon, and I'll get a sense from him about the degree to which Japan wants to go through the difficult process involved.

And I don't underestimate the difficulties of this because each member country has particular sensitivities, political barriers. It requires adjustments within these countries where certain industries or certain producers may push back. For Japan, for example, in the agricultural sector, that's going to be a tough issue for them.

But we're not going to delay. Our goal is to try to get something done by next year. And our hope is, is that if we can model this kind of outstanding trade agreement, then, potentially, you see a lot of others joining in.

Russia's Accession to the World Trade Organization/Trade

Mr. McNerney. Sounds like real momentum.

The President. Yes.

Mr. McNerney. Sounds like real momentum.

You know, another issue, just shifting gears slightly, same kind of subject—Russia, pending ascension——

The President. To the WTO.

Mr. McNerney. ——to the WTO. And as you know, Russia will host APEC in 2012. Assuming that the WTO process is successfully concluded, what kind of opportunities do you see as they try to integrate further into the global economy, become more Asia-facing themselves in the process? I mean, there is a clear agenda there for them as they've try to upgrade their economy. But there is a reason that you're making this happen, that you're going after WTO. And so maybe give us a few words on the benefits of it all.

The President. Well, first of all, we've had a excellent working relationship with President Medvedev. The United States and Russia obviously have a whole range of differences on a whole range of issues, but we also have some common interests. And I believe it is very much in the United States interest to see Russia in the WTO. Not only will it provide greater opportunities for U.S. businesses in Russia, but it also will create a even stronger incentive for Russia to proceed down a course of reforms that will be good for the Russian people, but will also integrate them with the world economy.

For the United States, I think a message that applies not only to the TPP, but also to Russia, is: The U.S. will do well if everybody is playing by the rules. I believe we've got some of the best entrepreneurs, businesses, universities. We have a system that has some flaws, but overall we have extraordinary transparency. We have a legal system that protects intellectual property. We are at the cutting edge of the information technology boom. And so if we can create a system in which everybody is playing by a common set of rules, everybody knows what those rules are, then I think U.S. workers and U.S. businesses are going to excel.

There's not reason why globalization should be something we fear. It's something that we should be able to excel at as long as everybody is in agreement about how we proceed. And so whether it's in the WTO, whether it's in the TPP, whether it's in forums like APEC, my message to all our trading partners, to other countries, is: If you are playing by the rules, then America is ready to do business. And we will remain open; we will fight against protectionist measures. But we are also going to be pushing hard to make sure that you are not engaging in gaming the system. And we want strong enforcement of these international norms and rules. We think that will be to everybody's benefit over the long term.

China-U.S. Relations

Mr. McNerney. Agree. And many of us have, I should say, benefited from the steadfastness that many in your Cabinet have shown in supporting this, the enforcement side of the WTO. We appreciate it.

China. You will be meeting here with China's senior leadership, and many of us in the business world face a common dilemma with China that perhaps you do at your level. We see a world where our interests lay in both competing with China, on one hand, in global markets and within their marketplace, and also engaging with China for access to its market, on the other. Yet challenges abound, and you alluded to a lot of them just a minute ago: intellectual property protections, adherence to the WTO, rules you mentioned, currency debate, drilling rights, et cetera. There's a long list.

But against the backdrop, will you be getting into specifics this week in your discussions? And how would you assess the U.S.-China relationship when voices now, on both the left and the right, are calling for a harder line from your administration? Tough to navigate.

The President. Well, first of all, I think that we have created a frank dialogue with the Chinese over the last 2 years that has benefited both countries. And my general view is that there can be a friendly and constructive competition between the United States and China and a whole range of areas where we share common interests and we should be able to cooperate.

We should be rooting for China to grow, because not only does that then present an enormous marketplace for American businesses and American exports, but to see so many millions of people, hundreds of millions of people, lifted out of poverty is a remarkable achievement. And so whether it's China, whether it's India, these emerging countries, what they're accomplishing in a few short decades—alleviating poverty, helping ordinary people all around the world get access to opportunity—that's a wonderful thing that we should be rooting for. And those are potential customers for us in the future.

But what I've said since I first came into office, and what we've exhibited in terms of our interactions with the Chinese, is we want you to play by the rules. And currency is probably a good example. There are very few economists who do not believe that the RMB is not undervalued. And that makes exports to China more expensive, and it makes exports from China cheaper. That disadvantages American business; it disadvantages American workers.

And we have said to them that this is something that has to change. And by the way, it would actually be good for China's economy if they refocused on their domestic market, that that kind of appreciation of their currency would help the overall balance of payments globally and it would increase growth in China and increase growth here in the United States.

Intellectual property. I don't think it's any secret—Jim, you talk to a lot of CEOs and probably a lot of folks in this room—for an economy like the United States, where our biggest competitive advantage is our knowledge, our innovation, our patents, our copyrights, for us not to get the kind of protection that we need in a large marketplace like China is not acceptable.

Government procurement. If we are allowing foreign countries to bid on projects in the United States of America, we want reciprocity. State-owned enterprises, how they work—all these issues I think have to be resolved. Some of them can be resolved in multilateral forums. Some of them will have to be resolved bilaterally. I am sympathetic to the fact that there are a lot of people in China who are still impoverished and there's a rapid pace of urbanization that's taking place there that Chinese leaders have to work through. But the bottom line is, is that the United States can't be expected to stand by if there's not the kind reciprocity in our trade relations and our economic relationships that we need.

So this is an issue that I've brought up with President Hu in the past. We will continue to bring it up. There is no reason why it inevitably leads to sharp conflict. I think there is a win-win opportunity there, but we've got to keep on working diligently to get there. And in the meantime, where we see rules being broken, we'll speak out, and in some cases, we will take action.

We've brought more enforcement actions against China over the last couple of years than had taken place in many of the preceding years, not because we're looking for conflict, but simply because we want to make sure that the interests of American workers and American businesses are protected.

Foreign Investment in the U.S.

Mr. McNerney. I think one related question, looking at the world from the Chinese side, is what they would characterize as impediments to investment in the United States. And so that discussion, I'm sure, will be part of whatever dialogue you have. And so how are you thinking about that?

The President. Well, this is an issue, generally. I think it's important to remember that the United States is still the largest recipient of foreign investment in the world. And there are a lot of things that make foreign investors see the U.S. as a great opportunity: our stability, our openness, our innovative free market culture.

But we've been a little bit lazy, I think, over the last couple of decades. We've kind of taken for granted—well, people will want to come here, and we aren't out there hungry, selling America and trying to attract new business into America. And so one of things that my administration has done is set up something called SelectUSA that organizes all the Government agencies to work with State and local governments where they're seeking assistance from us, to go out there and make it easier for foreign investors to build a plant in the United States and put outstanding U.S. workers back to work in the United States of America.

And we think that we can do much better than we're doing right now. Because of our federalist system, sometimes a foreign investor comes in and they've got to navigate not only Federal rules, but they've also got to navigate State and local governments that may have their own sets of interests. Being able to create, if not a one-stop shop, then at least no more than a couple of stops for people to be able to come into the United States and make investments, that's something that we want to encourage.

Exports/Promoting Small Businesses

Mr. McNerney. And I'm old enough to remember this process around Japanese automotive companies, 20 or 30 years ago. And the process moved slowly then, it had some of the similar dynamics, but some of those companies are very, very fine "American companies"—quote, unquote—and have contributed a lot to our economy.

The President. And look, these companies can put people back to work. They can have a terrific impact. And it's important for us to make sure that, since we want American companies to be able to invest in other countries, that we also show some openness to their investments here.

One thing I want to mention, Jim, that I think is important: I mentioned that we're on track to double our exports, a goal that I set when I first came into office. Part of the reason for that is because of some terrific work that's been done by our Export-Import Bank. We've substantially increased the amount of financing that we're providing to companies. I think Boeing appreciates the good work that——

Mr. McNerney. Upon occasion, we're at the teller window. [*Laughter*]

The President. On occasion, yes. But one of the things that I wanted to mention is we're starting to focus on how we can get small and medium-sized businesses plugged into the global economy as well.

Somebody mentioned earlier that I think Secretary Clinton had talked about women-owned businesses. Well, a lot of women-owned businesses are smaller businesses and medium-sized businesses. And they may have great products, but they may not have the infrastructure to be able to navigate a whole bunch of other countries' customs and regulatory impediments. And so for us to be a champion not only of financing, but also making it easier for them to enter into the global marketplace is something that we want to focus on.

Export Regulations

Mr. McNerney. That program is a big deal. And I see it from a Boeing perspective: a lot of our suppliers are tapping into it, and it's going to make a difference.

Speaking of exports, as Chairman of your Export Council, I've had the privilege of working with you and members of your Cabinet to pave the way to meet your goal of doubling exports. Priorities have been FTAs, intellectual property rights protection, export credit financing, technology release—which you haven't commented on, but you've made some progress on—and business and tourist visa processes, and you know the list.

What's your assessment of how we're doing?

The President. You guys are doing great. And I want to thank all the members of the Export Council. They've been giving us some terrific ideas. Some of them are modest, but they make a difference. Backstage before we came out, I just signed a piece of legislation that was voted on unanimously out of Congress that essentially sets up a APEC business gold card, a travel card that allows businesses to be able to—[*applause*]. Everybody here appreciates it because they're not going to have to wait in line as long at the airport. [*Laughter*] So that generated a lot of popularity.

But that's an idea that came out of the business council that we've been able to execute. And we're going to keep on trying to pursue every avenue that we have to see how we can ease and smooth the ability of doing business with the United States and U.S. businesses being able to operate overseas.

And some of that has to do with us changing our own internal operations. For the business leaders who are here, there's been a lot of commentary about regulations and my administration's approach to regulations. And frankly, there have been some misconceptions, particularly in the business press. And so let me just comment on this.

I make no apologies for wanting to make sure that we've got regulations that protect consumers from unfair practices or shoddy products, that protect the help of our kids here in the U.S., that make sure that our air and water is clean. But I think it's really important to know that over the first 2 years of the Obama administration, we've actually issued fewer new regulations than the previous two administrations; that we've applied, for the most part, a rigorous cost benefit, and we have seen a lot more benefit for every dollar that our regulations cost than previous administrations.

And this is where it's relevant to the export issue. One of the things we're also doing is engaging in what we call a regulatory look-back, where we've asked all the agencies that are under the executive branch control, but also independent agencies that voluntarily been willing to look at every regulation that's on the book, with a simple question: Is this helping to grow the economy, create jobs, and is it doing a good job in this 21st century of protecting the health and welfare of the public and consumers?

And if a rule isn't working anymore, we want to get rid of it. If a rule could be done cheaper and faster, then we want to hear about it. And our relationship with the business council is a great example of where you've given us some suggestions, where you said, you know what, this rule, we understand what you were trying to do, but it's actually creating a lot of unnecessary costs, and here's a way to do it that would meet your objective, but do it in a much more efficient, effective way. We are eager for that kind of input, and that's the kind of relationship with the business community we want to establish.

Mr. McNerney. And we will respond to that, and I appreciate those comments.

Another place is export controls, where your administration—at least as someone who deals in that world a lot, particularly in this region, where it becomes much more of a sticking point doing commerce than you'd imagine if you have any technology in your products—where I think your administration has made more of an effort than any administration in recent memory. And can you give us an update on that?

The President. Yes.

Mr. McNerney. Because there's been some progress recently.

The President. For those of you who may not be fully familiar with this issue—because we have such a terrific advantage in high-technology areas—in cutting-edge advance manufacturing or the work that we've been doing in information systems and so forth—traditionally, there has been a security element to U.S. export policy where we've said there are certain products that could be weaponized, could have

military applications, in which we are not going to permit an easy time of exporting those products.

And under the leadership of Bob Gates, my former Secretary of Defense, he actually recommended that we reexamine this whole issue of export controls to make sure that it was up to date and that we were not unnecessarily inhibiting U.S. companies from taking advantage of their biggest competitive advantage and going out there and selling high-value products made by high-wage workers that create a lot of opportunity for American workers and American businesses.

So we've gone through a very systematic process. We are, I think, starting to see that process bear fruit. We're going to need some cooperation from Congress, but there's some things we can do on the executive side. And essentially, the goal of the reform is to clear away impediments for export of those things that really at this point don't have a military application, or are first-generation stuff that everybody else has already caught up on, so that we can actually focus more on those very narrow sets of technologies where there really is a significant security component.

And we feel optimistic that over the next couple of years we're going to start being able to make progress. That will help contribute to American businesses being able to make sales, and American workers and American jobs being created here in the United States.

East Asia Summit/Association of Southeast Asian Nations Summit

Mr. McNerney. It will be a big deal for our customers out here, broadly speaking.

We have time for one more question, Mr. President. And as you mentioned earlier, following this meeting you're headed down to Australia—I just came from Australia, they can't wait—for a state visit and then to Indonesia for two regional meetings, the East Asia summit and the U.S.-ASEAN Summit. As you approach those, what are the issues? What do you hope to accomplish?

The President. In Australia, we're going to be focusing a lot on the security alliance between our two countries, but that obviously has broader implications for U.S. presence in the Pacific.

When we get to Bali for the ASEAN meeting and the East Asia summit, we're going to be speaking, again, about how can we, a great Pacific power, work with our partners to ensure stability, to ensure free flows of commerce, to ensure that maritime rules, drilling, a whole host of issues are managed in a open and fair way.

And one of the things that I'm very encouraged about is the eagerness of countries to see the U.S. reengaged in this region. I think back here in the United States, there are times where we question our influence around the world. And obviously, having gone through a couple of tough years, having been engaged in a decade of war, we recognize all the challenges that are out there for the United States and the reforms and changes that we're going to have to make to ensure that we are competitive in this 21st century global economy.

But the news I have to deliver for the American people is American leadership is still welcome. It's welcomed in this region. It's welcomed in the transatlantic region. And the reason it's welcomed I think is because we have shown that we are willing to not just look after our own interests, but try to set up a set of rules and norms in the international arena that everybody can follow and everybody can prosper from. And people appreciate that.

And so I am very proud of the leadership that America obviously has shown in the past. But I also don't want people to underestimate the leadership that we're showing now, whether it's on trade agreements like TPP or the security issues that face the Pacific. We are, I think, poised to work in a spirit of mutual interest and mutual respect with countries around the world, but we continue to be a country that people are looking to for active engagement.

Mr. McNerney. All very welcomed news. Mr. President, thank you very much. Your perspectives were very much appreciated.

The President. Thank you very much. Enjoy the good weather.

Mr. McNerney. Yes. *Mahalo.*

The President. Mahalo.

NOTE: The President spoke at 10:12 a.m. at the Sheraton Waikiki hotel. In his remarks, he referred to S. 1487, which was approved November 12 and assigned Public Law No. 112–54.

Remarks Prior to a Meeting With Prime Minister Yoshihiko Noda of Japan in Honolulu
November 12, 2011

President Obama. Well, I just want to welcome Prime Minister Noda to Hawaii, to the United States, for this APEC meeting. I had the opportunity to have my first extensive discussions with the Prime Minister recently, and I have been extremely impressed already with the boldness of his vision. And we confirmed, once again, the importance for both of our countries—the alliance between the United States and Japan has been a cornerstone of our relationship, but also for security in the Asia-Pacific region for a very long time. And I'm confident that working together we can continue to build on that relationship in the areas of commerce, in the areas of security, in not only the Asia-Pacific region, but around the world.

And, Prime Minister Noda, welcome to Honolulu. I'm sure that we'll have another round of productive discussions. And I want to thank you and the people of Japan for your friendship. We continue also, by the way, to be concerned about the rebuilding process in the wake of the terrible earthquake and tsunami. And I want to assure you that the American people continue to stand beside you and ready to help in any way they can.

Prime Minister Noda. Well, this is my first visit to Honolulu after 34 years. And this very morning I went to the Memorial Cemetery of the Pacific and laid a wreath there, and I got to see the panoramic view of Honolulu. And I renewed my recognition of how beautiful and great this city is. And I would like to express my deep appreciation for hosting us in—here in Honolulu as the chair of APEC.

I'm very much encouraged by the fact that America is increasing its presence in the Asia-Pacific region, and I do believe that Japan and the United States must work closely together to establish economic goals and also establish security order in this region. And I hope that in the meeting today I can discuss with you these issues.

President Obama. Thank you, everybody.

NOTE: The President spoke at 12:18 p.m. at the Hale Koa Hotel. Prime Minister Noda spoke in Japanese, and his remarks were translated by an interpreter.

Remarks Following a Meeting With President Dmitry A. Medvedev of Russia in Honolulu
November 12, 2011

President Obama. I want to welcome my friend Dmitry Medvedev to my birthplace, Honolulu, Hawaii. My understanding is that he's been spotted in a Hawaiian shirt walking and enjoying the good weather. And so I don't know if anybody got pictures of this, but I'm glad that he's enjoying himself so far.

President Medvedev and I have I think successfully established the reset of U.S.-Russia relationships—the U.S.-Russian relationship over the last several years. And it has borne concrete fruit in the form of a New START Treaty, a 123 Agreement, the work that we did together imposing sanctions on Iran, and most recently, the efforts that we've made on Russia's WTO accession.

Today we had a wide-ranging discussion. It focused on a number of security issues where the U.S. and Russia have a significant interest. We discussed Afghanistan and our plan to transition and the importance of all the regional parties assisting the Afghan Government in stabilizing the country for the benefit of the Afghan people.

We discussed Iran and reaffirmed our intention to work to shape a common response so that we can move Iran to follow its international obligations when it comes to its nuclear program.

We discussed a number of world trouble spots, including Syria. And we discussed the importance of APEC and our common interest in assuring global growth and increased opportunity, business investment, commercial ties, and most importantly, job creation in both our countries.

Although it's not official yet, the invitation has been extended to Russia to join the WTO, as a testament to the hard work of President Medvedev and his team. We believe this is going to be good for the United States, for the world, as well as for Russia, because it will provide increased opportunities for markets in which we can sell goods and products and services, as well as purchase good, products, and services, without some of the traditional barriers.

And so we very much appreciate the cooperation and partnership that we forged around this issue. We think it's an example of the importance that both countries place on economic reform and economic growth.

And on my part and on my administration's part, this is going to be a good time for us to consult closely with Congress about ending the application of Jackson-Vanik to Russia, so that the U.S. businesses can take advantage of Russia's membership in the WTO, and we can expand commerce and create jobs here in the United States. So those consultations will be taking place in the weeks and months to come.

So, President Medvedev, thank you again for a constructive conversation, but more importantly, thank you for several years of constructive engagement with the United States.

President Medvedev. Aloha. [*Laughter*]

Well, I would like to start by thanking Barack for this brilliant idea of hosting the

APEC summit here in his birthplace, in Honolulu, Hawaii. Not only is it a beautiful location, but it also offers a great opportunity to discuss all sorts of issues like we did today.

But today, my friend Barack and I discussed not only weather, but also issues he outlined just recently. But I would like to start by thanking President Obama and his team for his active support and engagement in our accession process to the WTO. Moreover, we've never received similar support from any previous U.S. administration, and this is probably the explanation of why we've been acceding to the Organization since 1993. As has been recognized just now, Russia's accession is good not only for Russia itself or for the U.S. or other countries, but for the entire system of trade relations in the world.

Our global economy, global finance is surviving not the best of times. So the more coordinated actions we take, the less there are trade barriers. The clearer instructions we give to our trade and economic ministries, the sooner we will be able to overcome recession, which unfortunately still continues globally, and the easier it will be to solve our unemployment, which remains our major problem.

That is why the summit of Asia-Pacific region countries is of great importance, so that we could coordinate and integrate our ideas. And I am sure that it will be very successful at the highest possible level.

Today, apart from Russian accession to the WTO and the need to repeal Jackson-Vanik amendment, we discussed with President Obama and his team a number of international issues. I'm referring to the discussions we had about the Middle East, Afghanistan, Syria. We also spoke about Iran nuclear program and discussed a number of other issues, including European missile defense. We agreed to continue search for possible solutions, though we understand that our positions remain far apart. But over the recent years, we achieved progress on matters where there was no progress for decades. Let us just recall the START Treaty. If we manage to emphasize similar efforts on European missile defense, just like other issues, I'm sure we'll succeed.

My turn, I would like to express a full satisfaction with the past and present relations with U.S. President. Our relations, and that's most important, have always been characterized by trust. And it is only when trust is present that we can resolve difficult tasks, and we did resolve some tasks, although, much remains to be done.

And I thank President Obama again for the invitation to take part in this summit.

President Obama. Thank you, everybody.

NOTE: The President spoke at 3:16 p.m. at the Hale Koa Hotel. In his remarks, he referred to the Jackson-Vanik amendment to the Trade Act of 1974, which places restrictions on normalized trade relations between the U.S. and Russia and other countries of the former Soviet Union based on their economic structure and emigration policies. President Medvedev spoke in Russian, and his remarks were translated by an interpreter.

Remarks Prior to a Meeting With President Hu Jintao of China in Honolulu
November 12, 2011

President Obama. Well, I want to extend a warm welcome to President Hu as he attends this APEC summit, and we are glad to be host him and the other world leaders who are attending.

This will be the first extensive discussions that we've had since our very successful state visit by President Hu to Washington.

As we emphasized at that state visit, as two of the world's largest countries and largest economies, cooperation between the United States and China is vital not only to the security and prosperity of our own people, but is also vital to the world.

Such cooperation is particularly important to the Asia-Pacific region, where both China and the United States are extraordinarily active. We are both Pacific powers. And I think many countries in the region look to a constructive relationship between the United

States and China as a basis for continued growth and prosperity.

As we did at the G–20 in Cannes, President Hu and I, I'm sure, will be discussing issues related to economic growth, how we can continue to rebalance growth around the world, emphasize the importance of putting people back to work, and making sure that the trade relationships and commercial relationships between our two countries end up being a win-win situation.

And I look forward to the opportunity to also discuss a range of both regional and global security issues, including nonproliferation and denuclearization of the Korean Peninsula, ways that we can work together on issues like climate change, and our efforts to jointly assure that countries like Iran are abiding by international rules and norms.

And although there are areas where we continue to have differences, I am confident that the U.S.-China relationship can continue to grow in a constructive way based on mutual respect and mutual interests. And I want to extend my appreciation to President Hu for the continuous engagement not only of him, but also of the entire Chinese Government in addressing a wide range of these issues.

So welcome, President Hu, and I look forward to not only a good discussion here, but also an outstanding APEC summit.

President Hu. I wish to thank you, Mr. President, for your warm invitation and welcome. I'm delighted to have this opportunity to come to the beautiful State of Hawaii to attend the APEC economic leaders meeting and to meet with you, Mr. President.

This is the ninth meeting between you and I, Mr. President, since you took office, and I look forward to a extensive and indepth discussion on China-U.S. relations, as well as major regional and international issues of shared interest.

As things stand, the international situation is undergoing complex and profound changes. There is growing instability and uncertainty in the world economic recovery and regional security threat has become more salient. Under these circumstances, it is all the more important for China and the United States to increase their communication and coordination.

China looks forward to maintaining and strengthening dialogue and cooperation with the United States, to respect each other's major concerns, appropriately manage sensitive issues, and ensure that the China-U.S. relationship will continue to grow on a sustainable and stable path.

This APEC meeting has drawn a lot of attention worldwide, and we appreciate the tremendous work the United States has done in preparing for this meeting. The Asia-Pacific region is the most dynamic region in today's world, with the biggest development potential. This region should become a region of active cooperation between China and the United States.

I sincerely wish this meeting a full success, and I hope that this meeting here will send out a positive message to the international community that economies in the Asia-Pacific region will reach out to each other like passengers on the same boat and work together to ensure the continued, steady growth of the economies.

Thank you once again, Mr. President.

President Obama. Thank you, everybody.

NOTE: The President spoke at 3:55 p.m. at the Hale Koa Hotel. President Hu spoke in Chinese, and his remarks were translated by an interpreter.

Statement on the Arab League's Actions Regarding Syria
November 12, 2011

I applaud the important decisions taken by the Arab League today, including the suspension of Syria's membership, consideration of economic sanctions, and downgrading of diplomatic relations. After the Asad regime flagrantly failed to keep its commitments, the Arab League has demonstrated leadership in its effort to end the crisis and hold the Syrian

Government accountable. These significant steps expose the increasing diplomatic isolation of a regime that has systematically violated human rights and repressed peaceful protests. The United States joins with the Arab League in its support for the Syrian people, who continue to demand their universal rights in the face of the regime's callous violence. We will continue to work with our friends and allies to pressure the Asad regime and support the Syrian people as they pursue the dignity and transition to democracy that they deserve.

Remarks at the Asia-Pacific Economic Cooperation Summit Dinner in Honolulu
November 12, 2011

Aloha. On behalf of Michelle and myself, welcome to Hawaii, and on behalf of the American people, welcome to the United States.

We have a busy day ahead of us tomorrow, and we have a luau tonight, including hula dancing, so I want to be brief. [*Laughter*]

We are 21 leaders from across the Asia-Pacific. We represent close to 3 billion people, from different continents and cultures, north, south, east, and west, men and women of every faith, color, and creed.

Yet whatever our differences, our citizens have sent us here with a common task: to bring our economies closer together, to cooperate, to create jobs and prosperity that our people deserve so that they can provide for their families, so that they can give their children a better future.

And so it was America's turn to host APEC, and I could not imagine a more fitting place than my home State of Hawaii. Here, we are literally in the center of the Pacific. Here, we're reminded of the progress that's possible when people of different backgrounds and beliefs come together. This is the most diverse State in our Nation, home to so many races and immigrants and Americans who trace their roots back to many of your countries.

Hawaii is not perfect, but I think Hawaii comes about as close as you'll come to a true melting pot of cultures, where people live and work together in mutual trust and mutual respect.

Here, we're a single *ohana*—one family. We remember that beneath the surface, behind all the different languages and some very long names, we all share the same hopes, the same struggles, and the same aspirations. And we've learned that we're more likely to realize our aspirations when we pursue them together.

That's the spirit of Hawaii. It's what made me who I am. It's what shapes my interactions with all of you. And it's the spirit that I hope guides us in our work this weekend.

And so I'd like to propose a toast with the words of a traditional Hawaiian proverb: 'A'ohe hana nui ke alu 'ia. And that means: No task is too big when done together by all.

Cheers. *Salud*. Everybody enjoy the evening.

NOTE: The President spoke at 7:43 p.m. at the Hale Koa Hotel.

Remarks at the Asia-Pacific Economic Cooperation Summit Reception and Cultural Performance in Honolulu
November 12, 2011

The President. Good evening, everybody. To all the leaders who are representing their countries here at APEC, I hope you've had a wonderful stay so far and hope you had a wonderful dinner. To members of the delegation, welcome.

Two years ago, when I was in Singapore and it was announced that we would be hosting the APEC summit here in Honolulu, I promised that you would all have to wear aloha shirts or grass skirts. [*Laughter*] But I was persuaded by our team to perhaps break tradition, and so we have not required you to wear your aloha shirts, although I understand that a few of you have tried them on for size, and we may yet see you in them in the next several days.

But one tradition that we did not want to break is the tradition of the luau. Here in Hawaii, there is a traditional gathering that we call luau, and it's basically an excuse for a good party, and it's used for every occasion. We have birthday luaus and graduation luaus. And now we have APEC luaus. And there is——

Audience member. Whoo!

The President. See? Somebody's ready to party already. [*Laughter*]

We have music. We have song. We have celebration. And we have hula dancing. And Michelle does not think I'm a very good dancer, so I will not be performing this evening.

[*Laughter*] But I think we will have some wonderful examples of traditional Polynesian dance and music and song. And it will capture, I think, the extraordinary spirit of these islands, but also capture, I think, the spirit in which I hope we proceed in our important work during the course of this APEC summit.

We are bound together by an ocean. We are bound together by a common belief and a common concern for our people, their aspirations, their hopes, their dreams. And so I hope that all of you feel the extraordinary spirit of Hawaii and very much look forward to a wonderful set of meetings tomorrow.

So with that, please enjoy.

NOTE: The President spoke at 9:30 p.m. at the Hale Koa Hotel.

Remarks at an Asia-Pacific Economic Cooperation Summit Working Session in Kapolei, Hawaii
November 13, 2011

Good morning, everybody. It is my great pleasure to welcome all of you, officially, to the APEC leaders meeting. This is the first time in nearly 20 years that the United States has hosted this forum, and it comes at a time when America is very focused on how we can work together in a cooperative, effective way in the transpacific region.

And obviously, I'm particularly pleased that we're meeting in my home State of Hawaii, which reflects the deep connections between the peoples of our region. And I hope everybody had a wonderful evening last night. I've heard that some of you wanted to join in the hula dancing. [*Laughter*] I'm sorry we did not give you that opportunity.

Now it's time to get down to work, and we have much to do. Our 21 economies, our nearly 3 billion citizens, are looking to us to bring our economies closer, to increase exports, to expand trade and opportunity that creates jobs and economic growth. That's why we're here.

I'm confident that we can make significant progress. We've done it before. Since APEC started, we've slashed tariffs and barriers to trade and investment. Commerce in the region has soared, creating new jobs, new markets, and raising living standards across the region.

And I want to emphasize that the Asia-Pacific region is absolutely critical to America's economic growth. We consider it a top priority. And we consider it a top priority because we're not going to be able to put our folks back to work and grow our economy and expand opportunity unless the Asia-Pacific region is also successful.

This region includes many of our top trading partners. This is where we do most of our trade and where we sell most of our exports. It's also the fastest growing region in the world. And as a consequence, the Asia-Pacific region is key to achieving my goal of doubling U.S. exports and creating new jobs.

Today we've got an opportunity to make progress towards our ultimate goal, which is a seamless regional economy. We're going to be focusing on three specific areas: increasing trade and investment, promoting green jobs, and streamlining and coordinating regulations so that we encourage trade and job creation.

And more broadly, we'll be discussing how we can work together to spur on quicker economic growth and more sturdy and sustainable economic growth. The economies of this region have a critical role to play in addressing the imbalances and making sure that growth is balanced and sustainable in the future.

So I want to thank my fellow leaders for being here. I'm confident that we can continue to make significant progress during the course of this day.

Before we begin discussing this morning's topic, I want to congratulate Japan on the superb job it did in hosting APEC in 2010. Prime Minister Noda of Japan set a high bar for us, so we are going to try to follow your footsteps.

I also want to recognize the outstanding work that's been done by our officials and ministers during the course of this year to move forward an ambitious set of initiatives.

The focus of our host year was to make progress towards a seamless regional economy, and we have made progress in the three themes that we set out: regional economic integration, green growth, and regulatory reform. We have agreed to address a set of next-generation trade issues, including removing frictions in the global supply chains, helping small and medium-size enterprises grow and better plug into the global trading system, and adopting smart, market-oriented innovation policies. Innovation is especially critical to all of us, and we all want to take appropriate steps to encourage it, because without it we can't grow, become more productive, or create enough jobs.

NOTE: The President spoke at 9:58 a.m. at the JW Marriott Ihilani Ko Olina Resort & Spa.

The President's News Conference in Kapolei
November 13, 2011

The President. Good afternoon, everybody. Aloha. I want to begin by thanking the people of Hawaii for their extraordinarily hospitality. Usually when Michelle and I and our daughters come back to visit, it's just one President, and this time, we brought 21. So thank you so much for the incredible graciousness of the people of Hawaii and their patience, because I know that traffic got tied up a little bit.

Now, the single greatest challenge for the United States right now, and my highest priority as President, is creating jobs and putting Americans back to work. And one of the best ways to do that is to increase our trade and exports with other nations. Ninety-five percent of the world's consumers are beyond our borders. I want them to be buying goods with three words stamped on them: Made in America. So I've been doing everything I can to make sure that the United States is competing aggressively for the jobs and the markets of the future.

No region will do more to shape our long-term economic future than the Asia-Pacific region. As I've said, the United States is and always will be a Pacific nation. Many of our top trading partners are in this region. This is where we sell most of our exports, supporting some 5 million American jobs. And since this is the world's fastest growing region, the Asia-Pacific is key to achieving my goal of doubling U.S. exports, a goal, by the way, which we are on track right now to meet.

And that's why I've been proud to host APEC this year. It's been a chance to help lead the way towards a more seamless regional economy with more trade, more exports, and more jobs for our people. And I'm pleased that we've made progress in three very important areas.

First, we agreed to a series of steps that will increase trade and bring our economies even closer. We agreed to a new set of principles on innovation to encourage the entrepreneurship that creates new businesses and new industries. With simplified customs and exemptions from certain tariffs, we'll encourage more businesses to engage in more trade. And that includes our small businesses, which account for the vast majority of the companies in our economies.

We agreed to a new initiative that will make it easier and faster for people to travel and conduct business across the region. And yesterday I was pleased to sign legislation, a new travel card that will help our American business men and women travel more easily and get deals done in this region.

I'd note that we also made a lot of progress increasing trade on the sidelines of APEC. As I announced yesterday, the United States and our eight partners reached the broad outlines of an agreement on the Trans-Pacific Partnership. And today I'm pleased that Japan, Canada, and Mexico have now expressed an interest in this effort.

This comes on the heels of our landmark trade agreements with South Korea, Panama, and Colombia, which will support tens of thousands of American jobs.

And in my meeting with President Medvedev, we discussed how to move ahead with Russia's accession to the WTO, which will also mean more exports for American manufacturers and American farmers and ranchers.

Second, APEC agreed on ways to promote the green growth we need for our energy security. We agreed to reduce tariffs on environmental goods and make it easier to export clean energy technologies that create green jobs. We raised the bar on ourselves, and we'll aim for even higher energy efficiencies. And we're moving ahead with the effort to phase out fossil fuel subsidies. This would be a huge step toward creating clean energy economies and fighting climate change, which is a threat to both the beauty and the prosperity of the region.

Third, we're redoubling our efforts to make sure that regulations are encouraging trade and job creation, not discouraging trade and job creation. And this builds on the work that we're doing in the United States to get rid of rules and regulations that are unjustified and that are overly burdensome. Our APEC partners are joining us in streamlining and coordinating regulations so that we're sparking innovation and growth even as we protect public health and our environment.

And finally, since many of the leaders here were also at the recent G–20 summit, we continued our efforts to get the global economy to grow faster. APEC makes up more than half the global economy, and it will continue to play a key role in achieving the strong and balanced growth that we need.

As I've said, as the world's largest economy, the best thing that the United States can do for the global economy is to grow our own economy faster. And so I will continue to fight for the "American Jobs Act" so that we can put our people back to work.

I was glad to see that Congress moved forward on one aspect of the jobs bill, tax credits for companies that are hiring veterans. But we've got to do a lot more than that.

So again, I want to thank the people of Hawaii for their extraordinary hospitality and for all that they've done to help make this summit such a success. I want to thank my fellow leaders for the seriousness and sense of common purpose that they brought to our work. And I believe that the progress we've made here will help create jobs and keep America competitive in a region that is absolutely vital not only for our economy, but also for our national security.

So with that, I'm going to take a few questions. I'll start with Ben Feller of AP [Associated Press].

Iran

Q. Thank you very much, Mr. President. I picked the side in the sun here, so—[*laughter*]. I'd like to ask you about Iran. Did you get any specific commitments from Russia or China on tightening sanctions? Did you move them at all? And do you fear the world is running out of options short of military intervention to keep Iran from getting nuclear weapons?

The President. One of the striking things over the last 3 years since I came into office is the degree of unity that we've been able to forge in the international community with respect to Iran. When I came into office, the world was divided and Iran was unified around its nuclear program. We now have a situation where the world is united and Iran is isolated. And because of our diplomacy and our efforts, we have, by far, the strongest sanctions on Iran that we've ever seen. And China and Russia were critical to making that happen. Had they not been willing to support those efforts in the United Nations, we would not be able to see the kind of progress that we've made.

And they're having an impact. All our intelligence indicates that Iran's economy is suffering as a consequence of this. And we're also seeing that Iran's influence in the region has ebbed, in part because their approach to repression inside of Iran is contrary to the Arab Spring that has been sweeping the Middle East.

So we are in a much stronger position now than we were 2 or 3 years ago with respect to Iran. Having said that, the recent IAEA report indicates what we already knew, which is, although Iran does not possess a nuclear weapon and is technically still allowing IAEA observers into their country, that they are engaging in a series of practices that are contrary to their international obligations and their IAEA obligations. And that's what the IAEA report indicated.

So what I did was to speak with President Medvedev, as well as President Hu, and all three of us entirely agree on the objective, which is making sure that Iran does not weaponize nuclear power and that we don't trigger a nuclear arms race in the region. That's in the interests of all of us.

In terms of how we move forward, we will be consulting with them carefully over the next several weeks to look at what other options we have available to us. The sanctions have enormous bite and enormous scope, and we're building off the platform that has already been established. The question is, are there additional measures that we can take. And we're going to explore every avenue to see if we can solve this issue diplomatically.

I have said repeatedly, and I will say today, we are not taking any options off the table, because it's my firm belief that an Iran with a nuclear weapon would pose a security threat not only to the region, but also to the United States. But our strong preference is to have Iran meet its international obligations, negotiate diplomatically, to allow them to have peaceful use of nuclear energy in accordance with international law, but at the same time, forswear the weaponization of nuclear power.

And so we're going to keep on pushing on that. And China and Russia have the same aims, the same objectives, and I believe that we'll continue to cooperate and collaborate closely on that issue.

Dan Lothian [CNN].

Interrogation Techniques

Q. Thank you, Mr. President. Last night at the Republican debate, some of the hopefuls—they hope to get your job—they defended the practice of waterboarding, which is a practice that you banned in 2009. Herman Cain said, quote, "I don't see that as torture." Michele Bachmann said that it's, quote, "very effective." So I'm wondering if you think that they're uninformed, out of touch, or irresponsible?

The President. That's a multiple-choice question, isn't it? [*Laughter*] Let me just say this: They're wrong. Waterboarding is torture. It's contrary to America's traditions. It's contrary to our ideals. That's not who we are. That's not how we operate. We don't need it in order to prosecute the war on terrorism. And we did the right thing by ending that practice.

If we want to lead around the world, part of our leadership is setting a good example. And anybody who has actually read about and understands the practice of waterboarding would say that that is torture. And that's not something we do, period.

Norah O'Donnell [CBS News].

Iran

Q. Thank you, Mr. President. If I could continue on that, the Republicans did have a debate on CBS last night. A lot of it was about foreign policy, and they were very critical of your record.

The President. That's shocking. [*Laughter*]

Q. So if I could get you to respond to something that Mitt Romney said. He said your biggest foreign policy failure is Iran. He said that if you are reelected, Iran will have a nuclear weapon. Is Mitt Romney wrong?

The President. I am going to make a practice of not commenting on whatever is said in Republican debates until they've got an actual nominee. But as I indicated to Ben in the earlier question, you take a look at what we've been able to accomplish in mobilizing the world community against Iran over the last 3 years, and it shows steady, determined, firm progress in isolating the Iranian regime and sending a clear message that the world believes it would be dangerous for them to have a nuclear weapon.

Now, is this an easy issue? No. Anybody who claims it is, is either politicking or doesn't know what they're talking about. But I think not only the world, but the Iranian regime understands very clearly how determined we are to prevent not only a nuclear Iran, but also a nuclear arms race in the region and a violation of nonproliferation norms that would have implications around the world, including in the Asia-Pacific region, where we have similar problems with North Korea.

David Nakamura [Washington Post].

China

Q. Thank you, Mr. President. Yesterday, in a speech before business leaders, you said that you want China to play by the rules. And then your staff later said that, in a bilateral meeting with President Hu, that you expressed that American business leaders are growing frustrated with the pace of change in China's economy. What rules is China not playing by? What specific steps do you need to see from China? And what punitive actions is your administration willing to take, as you said it would yesterday, if China does not play by the rules?

The President. Well, first of all, I also said yesterday that we welcome the peaceful rise of China. It is in America's interests to see China succeed in lifting hundreds of millions of people out of poverty. China can be a source of stability and help to underwrite international norms and codes of conduct.

And so what we've done over the last 2 years is to try to develop a frank, consistent, open relationship and dialogue with China, and it's yielded considerable benefits, for example, support for issues like Iran. But what I've also said to Chinese leadership since I came into office is that when it comes to their economic practices, there are a range of things that they have done that disadvantage not just the United States, but a whole host of their trading partners and countries in the region.

The most famous example is the issue of China's currency. Most economists estimate that the RMB is devalued by 20 to 25 percent. That means our exports to China are that much more expensive and their imports into the United States are that much cheaper. Now, there's been slight improvement over the last year, partly because of U.S. pressure, but it hasn't been enough. And it's time for them to go ahead and move towards a market-based system for their currency.

Now, we recognize they may not be able to do it overnight, but they can do it much more quickly than they've done it so far. And by the way, that would not necessarily be a bad thing for the Chinese economy, because they've been so focused on export-driven growth that they've neglected domestic consumption, building up domestic markets. It makes them much more vulnerable to shocks in the global economy. It throws the whole world economy out of balance because they're not buying as much as they could be from other countries.

And this is not something that's inconsistent with where Chinese leadership say they want to go. The problem is, is that you've got a bunch of export producers in China who like the system as it is and making changes are difficult for them politically. I get it. But the United States and other countries, I think understandably, feel that enough's enough.

That's not the only concern we have. Intellectual property rights and protections—companies that do business in China consistently report problems in terms of intellectual property not being protected. Now, that's particularly important for an advanced economy like ours, where that's one of our competitive advantages, is we've got great engineers, great entrepreneurs, we're designing extraordinary new products. And if they get no protection, and the next thing you know, China's operating as a low-cost producer and not paying any fees or revenues to folks who invented these products, that's a problem.

So those are two examples, but there are a number of others. These practices aren't secret. I think everybody understands that they've been going on for quite some time. Sometimes, American companies are wary about bringing them up because they don't want to be punished in terms of their ability to do business in China. But I don't have that same concern, so I bring it up.

And in terms of enforcement, the other thing that we've been doing is actually trying to enforce the trade laws that are in place. We've brought a number of cases. One that the U.S. press may be familiar with are the cases involving U.S. tires, where we brought very aggressive actions against China and won. And as a consequence, U.S. producers are in a better position, and that means more U.S. jobs.

So I think we can benefit from trade with China. And I want certainly to continue cultivating a constructive relationship with the Chinese Government, but we're going to continue to be firm in insisting that they operate by the same rules that everybody else operates under. We don't want them taking advantage of the United States or U.S. businesses.

Jake Tapper [ABC News].

Pennsylvania State University/Ensuring Institutions and Organizations Protect Vulnerable Segments of Society

Q. Thank you, Mr. President. The other day you told ESPN that the scandal at Penn State, which you said was heartbreaking, should prompt some soul-searching throughout the Nation. I'm wondering if you could elaborate on that, what exactly you meant and—I know you're a big fan of college sports—if this is something you think that is an indictment not just of what happened at Penn State, allegedly, but how athletics are revered in universities.

The President. Well, I think that's the kind of soul-searching that I was referring to, Jake. You're right, I'm a big college sports fan. I think that when it's kept in perspective, college athletics not only provides a great outlet for competition for our young people, but helps to build a sense of community and can help to brand a university in a way that is fun and important. But what happened at Penn State indicates that at a certain point, folks start thinking about systems and institutions and don't think about individuals. And when you think about how vulnerable kids are, for the alleged facts of that case to have taken place and for folks not to immediately say, nothing else matters except making sure those kids are protected, that's a problem.

It's not unique to a college sports environment. I mean, we've seen problems in other institutions that are equally heartbreaking. Not all of them involve children, by the way. I mean, there have been problems obviously with respect to sexual abuse or assault directed against women, where institutions sort of closed ranks instead of getting on top of it right away. And that's why I said I think all institutions, not just universities or sports programs, have to step back and take stock and make sure that we're doing everything we can to protect people who may be vulnerable in these circumstances, but also just keep in mind what's important: keeping in—making sure that our excitement about a college sports program doesn't get in the way of our basic human response when somebody's being hurt.

And it's been said that evil can thrive in the world just by good people standing by and doing nothing. And all of us, I think, have occasion where we see something that's wrong, we've got to make sure that we step up. That's true in college athletics. That's true in our Government. That's true everywhere.

Julianna Goldman [Bloomberg News].

China

Q. Thank you, Mr. President. In conversations that you've had over the past couple of days with the Asian-Pacific leaders, have any of them brought up the rhetoric that we're seeing from Republican Presidential candidates when it comes to China? And does that kind of rhetoric or posturing jeopardize the progress that your administration has made with China and the Asian-Pacific region as a whole?

The President. I think most leaders here understand that politics is not always measured or on the level, and so most of our discussions have to do with substance: How do we put our people back to work right now? How do we expand trade? How do we expand exports?

I've been very frank with Chinese leaders, though, in saying that the American people across the board—left, right, and center—believe in trade, believe in competition. We think we've got the best workers in the world. We think we've got the best universities, the best entrepreneurs, the best free market. We're ready to go out there and compete with anybody. But there is a concern across the political spectrum that the playing field is not level right now.

And so in conversations with President Hu and others, what I've tried to say is we have the opportunity to move in a direction in which this is a win-win: China is benefiting from trade with the United States; the United States is benefiting as well. Jobs are being created in the United States and not just in China. But right now things are out of kilter. And that is something that is shared across the board, as we saw with the recent vote on the Chinese currency issue in the Senate.

And I think leaders in the region understand that as China grows, as its economic influence expands, that the expectation is, is that they will be a responsible leader in the world economy, which is what the United States has tried to do. I mean, we try to set up rules that are universal, that everybody can follow, and then we play by those rules, and then we compete fiercely. But we don't try to game the system. That's part of what leadership's about.

China has the opportunity to be that same type of leader. And as the world's second largest economy, I think that's going to be important not just for this region, but for the world. But that requires them to take responsibility, to understand that their role is different now than it might have been 20 years ago or 30 years ago, where if they were breaking some rules, it didn't really matter, it did not have a significant impact. You weren't seeing huge trade imbalances that had consequences for the world financial system.

Now they've grown up, and so they're going to have to help manage this process in a responsible way.

Laura Meckler [Wall Street Journal].

Asia-Pacific Economic Cooperation Summit/Group of Twenty Summit/U.S. Economy

Q. Thank you, Mr. President. Why did you get rid of the aloha shirts and the grass skirts? [*Laughter*] Are you at all concerned that it not appear that you're having a party over here while so many people are living with such a tough economy? And I'm wondering if those perceptions were at all on your mind as you were making plans for this trip, which, by necessity, takes you to some pretty exotic and fun locations.

The President. Yes, I got rid of the Hawaiian shirts because I had looked at pictures of some of the previous APEC meetings and some of the garb that had appeared previously, and I thought this may be a tradition that we might want to break. I suggested to the leaders—we gave them a shirt, and if they wanted to wear the shirt, I promise you it would have been fine. But I didn't hear a lot of complaints about us breaking precedent on that one.

With respect to this trip, look, this is a pretty nice piece of scenery here, and I take enormous pride in having been raised in the State of Hawaii, but we're here for business. We're here to create jobs. We're here to promote exports. And we've got a set of tangible, concrete steps that have been taken that are going to make our economy stronger, and that's part of what our leadership has been about.

When I went to Europe last week, our job was to help shape a solution for the European crisis. And a lot of folks back home might have wondered, well, that's Europe's problem; why are we worrying about it? Well, if Europe has a major recession and the financial system in Europe starts spinning out of control, that will have a direct impact on U.S. growth and our ability to create jobs and people raising their living standards.

The same is true out here. If we're not playing out here in the world's largest regional economy and the world's fastest regional economy, if we've abandoned the field and we're not engaged, American businesses and—will lose out and those jobs won't be in the United States of America.

So part of my job is to make sure that the rules of the road are set up so that our folks can compete effectively. Part of my job is to sell America and our products and our services around the world, and I think we've done so very effectively.

And as I said, just to take the example of exports, we're on track to double our exports since I came into office. That was a goal I set, and we're on track to meet it. That's actually been one of the stronger parts of our economic growth over the last couple of years. And I want to make sure that we keep on driving that.

Chuck Todd [NBC News].

Joint Select Committee on Deficit Reduction/President Obama's Discussions With President Nicolas Sarkozy of France in Cannes, France/Middle East Peace Process

Q. Thank you, Mr. President. The Republican cochair of the supercommittee, Jeb Hensarling, went on TV today and said if the sequester happens—this idea of the automatic cuts in Medicare and defense—that there was plenty of motivation and plenty of votes to change the makeup of these automatic cuts.

I know you had a conversation with him about this and said that that was—changing it in any way was off the table. That means you're going to veto this bill, if that's the case, if it ends up they can't get a deal in the next 10 days.

And then, can you clarify your end of the "hot mike" conversation with French President Nicolas Sarkozy, as it involved Israeli Prime Minister Netanyahu?

The President. Could I just say that Chuck's the only guy who asked two questions so far. So just—when I cut off here, whoever was next in the queue—[*laughter*]—I'm messing with you, Chuck.

With respect to the supercommittee, in August we negotiated to initiate a trillion dollars in cuts over the next 10 years, primarily out of discretionary spending, but we also said that in order for us to move towards a more stable fiscal condition that we're going to have to get an additional 1.2, minimum. I actually argued that we needed more than that. And the whole idea of the sequester was to make sure that both sides felt obligated to move off rigid positions and do what was required to help the country.

And since that time, they've had a lot of conversations, but it feels as if people continue to try to stick with their rigid positions rather than solve the problem.

Now, I've put forward a very detailed approach that would achieve $3 trillion-plus in savings. And it's the sort of balanced approach that the American people prefer. It says everything's on the table. We've got to have discretionary spending cuts of the sort we've already put in place. We've got to have nondefense cuts. We've got to have defense cuts. We're going to have to look at entitlement programs. We've got to reduce our health care costs. And we're going to need additional revenue.

And when we're talking about revenue, if we've got to raise money, it makes sense for us to start by asking the wealthiest among us to pay a little bit more before we start asking seniors, for example, to pay a lot more for their Medicare.

Now, this is the same presentation that I made to Speaker Boehner back in August. It's the same kind of balanced approach that every single independent committee that's looked at this has said needs to be done. And it just feels as if people keep on wanting to jigger the math so that they get a different outcome.

Well, the equation, no matter how you do it, is going to be the same. If you want a balanced approach that doesn't gut Medicare and Medicaid, doesn't prevent us from making investments in education and basic science and research—all the things we've been talking about here at APEC, that every world leader understands is the key for long-term economic success—then prudent cuts have to be matched up with revenue.

My hope is that over the next several days, the congressional leadership on the supercommittee go ahead and bite the bullet and do what needs to be done, because the math won't change. There's no magic formula. There are no magic beans that you can toss on the ground, and suddenly, a bunch of money grows on trees. We got to just go ahead and do the responsible thing. And I'm prepared to sign legislation that is balanced, that solves this problem.

One other thing that I want to say about this: When I meet with world leaders, what's striking—whether it's in Europe or here in Asia—the kinds of fundamental reforms and changes both on the revenue side and the public pension side that other countries are having to make are so much more significant than what we need to do in order to get our books in order.

This doesn't require radical changes to America or its way of life. It just means that we spread out the sacrifice across every sector so that it's fair, so that people don't feel as if once again people who are well connected, people who have lobbyists, special interests get off easy, and the burden is placed on middle class families that are already struggling. So if other countries can do it, we can do it, and we can do it in a responsible way.

I'm not going to comment on whether I'd veto a particular bill until I actually see a bill, because I still hold out the prospect that there's going to be a light-bulb moment where everybody says: "Aha! Here's what we've got to do."

With respect to the "hot mike" in France, I'm not going to comment on conversations that I have with individual leaders, but what I will say is this: The primary conversation I had with President Sarkozy in that meeting revolved around my significant disappointment that France had voted in favor of the Palestinians joining UNESCO, knowing full well that under our laws, that would require the United States cutting off funding to UNESCO, and after I had consistently made the argument that the only way we're going to solve the Middle East situation is if Palestinians and Israelis sit down at the table and negotiate, that it is not going to work to try to do an end run through the United Nations.

So I had a very frank and firm conversation with President Sarkozy about that issue. And that is consistent with both private and public statements that I've been making to everybody over the last several months.

Ed Henry [FOX News].

Job Growth

Q. Mr. President, I have three questions—[*laughter*]—starting with Mitt Romney. Just one question, I promise. [*Laughter*]

You started with a $447 billion jobs bill. Two months later, many speeches later, you've got virtually nothing from that. You've got the veterans jobs bill, which is important, obviously, and a lot of Executive orders. Are you coming to the realization that you may just get nothing here and go to the American people in 2012 without another jobs bill, 9-percent unemployment, and them wondering about your leadership, sir?

The President. Well, I think, first of all, the American people at this point are wondering about congressional leadership in failing to pass the jobs bill, the components of which the majority of Americans, including many Republicans, think are a good idea.

And that's part of the reason why the American people right now aren't feeling real good about Congress. Normally, by the way, the way politics works is if the overwhelming majority of the American people aren't happy with what you're doing, you start doing something different. So far that hasn't happened in Congress, and the Republicans in Congress, in particular. They don't seem to have that same sense of urgency about needing to put people back to work.

I'm going to keep on pushing. My expectation is, is that we will get some of it done now, and I'll keep on pushing until we get all of it done. And that may take me all the way till November to get it all done. And it may take a new Congress to get it all done. But the component parts—cutting taxes for middle class families, cutting taxes for small businesses that are hiring our veterans, hiring the long-term unemployed, put teachers back in the classroom—here in the State of Hawaii, you have a bunch of kids who are going to school 4 days a week because of budget problems. How are we going to win the competition in the 21st century with our kids going to school basically half time?

The jobs bill would help alleviate those budget pressures at the State level.

Rebuilding our infrastructure. Every world leader that you talk to, they're saying to themselves, how can we make sure we've got a first-class infrastructure? And as you travel through the Asia-Pacific region, you see China having better airports than us, Singapore having superior ports to ours. Well, that's going to impact our capacity to do business here, our capacity to trade, our capacity to get U.S. products made by U.S. workers into the fastest growing market

in the world. And by the way, we could put a lot of people back to work at the same time.

So I'm going to keep on pushing. And my expectation is, is that we will just keep on chipping away at this. If you're asking me do I anticipate that the Republican leadership in the House or the Senate suddenly decide that I was right all along and they will adopt a hundred percent of my proposals, the answer is, no, I don't expect that. Do I anticipate that at some point they recognize that doing nothing is not an option? That's my hope. And that should be their hope too, because if they don't, I think we'll have a different set of leaders in Congress.

All right? Thank you very much, everybody. Thank you.

NOTE: The President's news conference began at 5:06 p.m. at the JW Marriott Ihilani Ko Olina Resort & Spa.

Remarks at an Obama Victory Fund 2012 Fundraiser in Kapolei
November 14, 2011

Thank you! Thank you so much. Aloha. Thank you very much. Thank you. Thank you. Please, everybody, have a seat. It is good to be home. It is wonderful to see somebody who actually knew my parents when they first met at the University of Hawaii—the Governor of the great State of Hawaii, Neil Abercrombie, and his wonderful wife Nancie Caraway. Give them a big round of applause.

Lieutenant Governor Brian Schatz is here; Congresswoman Mazie Hirono. Please give a big round of applause to outstanding singer John Cruz. I want to thank Jeff Stone and all of our host committee for helping to pull this together.

It is wonderful to be here, not just because the weather is perfect, but this has been a little trip down memory lane. I've got classmates who are here. I actually have Mr. Torrey, my—. was it seventh grade or eighth grade teacher? [*Laughter*] He looks great. Tenth grade—tenth grade—he looks exactly the same. [*Laughter*] I'm trying to figure out what he's eating. [*Laughter*]

Now, somebody said—they were passing on greetings from a guy who went to Kamehameha who said he blocked my shot into the bleachers. [*Laughter*] I didn't appreciate that. [*Laughter*] And then somebody else said, this guy who says he went to kindergarten with you says hi. [*Laughter*] And I got to admit, I don't remember my kindergarten class. [*Laughter*] But tell him I said hello as well.

It is great to be home, great to just feel that aloha spirit. And Michelle and the girls will be back shortly for Christmas vacation, as we do every year. We'll see if Washington gets its business done, so I can get here as well. But that's always a challenge.

But I'm here today not just because I need your help, it's also because the country needs your help. There was a reason why so many of you worked so hard, poured your hearts into our campaign in 2008. And obviously, there was a little bias here in Honolulu and here in Hawaii about the hometown kid. But it certainly wasn't because you thought it was going to be easy to elect me President. As Neil said, there was some skepticism about the prospects of my candidacy. I don't think that you would have, if you were looking for an easy campaign, you would have decided to support Barack Hussein Obama for President. [*Laughter*] The polls did not tell you that I was a sure thing.

And besides, the campaign wasn't about me. It was about a vision that we share for America. It wasn't a narrow, cramped vision of an America where everybody is left to fend for themselves. It was a vision of a big, generous, bold America, where we look out for one another. An America where everybody has a shot, that everybody, if they work hard, if they take care of their responsibilities, if they look after their family, that they can get their piece of the American Dream.

That was what the campaign was about: the belief that the more Americans succeed, the more America succeeds. And that's the vision we shared, and that was the change that we believed in. We knew it wouldn't come easy, we knew it wasn't going to come quickly, but 3 years later, because of what you did in 2008, we've already started to see what change looks like.

Let me give you some examples. Change is the first bill I signed into law, a law that says an equal day's work should mean an equal day's pay, because our daughters should deserve the same opportunities as our sons do. That's what change looks like.

Change is the decision we made—not a popular one at the time—to save the auto industry from collapse. There were a lot of folks who said, let Detroit go bankrupt. But we decided to not only save thousands of jobs, get hundreds of local businesses thriving again, but we are now seeing fuel-efficient cars rolling off the assembly lines, stamped with three proud words: Made in America. And those are going to be exported all around the world. That's because of you, because of the change that you brought.

Change is the decision we made to stop waiting for Congress to do something about our oil addiction and finally raise our fuel efficiency standards on our cars and on our trucks. And now, by the next decade, we'll be driving cars that get 56 miles per gallon. And that

means that we are not only saving consumers money, but we're also taking carbon out of the atmosphere, and it is going to make a huge difference in terms of our environment, and that's because of you and the campaign that you helped run in 2008.

Change is the fight that we won to stop sending $60 billion in taxpayer subsidies to the banks that were giving out student loans, and today that money is going directly to students. And as a consequence, there are millions of young people all across the country who have less of a debt burden and are better able to afford college. That's because of you, because of the work that you did.

Change is health care reform. After a century of trying, a reform that will finally make sure that nobody goes bankrupt in America just because they get sick. And by the way, change is the 1 million young Americans who are already receiving insurance that weren't getting it before, because they can now stay on their parent's health insurance until they're 26 years old. That's a change that you made. At the same time, it provides everybody protection, so that if you get sick, if you have a preexisting condition, you can still afford to get health insurance, you'll still have access to quality care. That's the kind of changes that you brought about because of the work you did in 2008.

Change is the fact that, for the first time in history, it doesn't matter who you love if you want to serve this country that we all love. We ended "don't ask, don't tell" because of the change that you made.

And change is keeping one of the first promises I made in my campaign in 2008. We are bringing the war in Iraq to a close. By the end of this year, all our troops will be home for the holidays.

And we've been working smarter and more effectively on national security, and that is why we have decimated Al Qaida. It's weaker than it's ever been before. And Usama bin Laden will never walk this Earth again.

But we've been able to do it while sticking to our values. I was asked yesterday at a press conference about waterboarding. We didn't need to resort to that in order to protect our homeland and protect the people we love.

Now, many of these changes weren't easy. Some of them were risky. Many of them came in the face of tough opposition and powerful lobbyists and special interests that were pouring millions of dollars into television ads to try to keep things just as they were. And it's no secret that the steps that we took weren't always politically popular. But this progress has been possible because of you, because you stood up and made your voices heard, because you knocked on doors and you made phone calls and you got in arguments with family members at Thanksgiving and—[*laughter*]. You kept up the fight for change long after the election was over, and that should make you proud. It should make you hopeful. But it can't make us satisfied. It can't make us complacent, because we've got so much more work to do.

Everything we fought for in the last election is now at stake in the next election. The very core of what this country stands for is on the line. The basic promise that no matter who you are or where you come from, what you look like, that you can make it in America if you try, that vision is on the line.

This financial and economic crisis that we've been through, it struck months before I took office, and it put more Americans out of work than at any time since the Great Depression. But it was also the culmination of a decade in which the middle class was falling further and further behind. More good jobs in manufacturing left our shores. More of our prosperity was built on risky financial deals instead of us actually making stuff. We racked up bigger and bigger piles of debt, even as incomes fell and wages flatlined and the cost of everything from college to health care kept on going up. All those things were taking place long before the 2008 financial crisis.

So these problems didn't happen overnight, and the truth is they won't be solved overnight. It's going to take a few more years to meet the challenges that have been a decade in the making, and I think the American people understand that.

What they don't understand is leaders who refuse to take action. They don't understand a Congress that can't seem to move with a sense of urgency about the problems that America is facing. What they're sick and tired of is watching the people who are supposed to represent them put party ahead of country and the next election before the next generation.

President Kennedy used to say that, after he took office, what surprised him most about Washington was finding out that things were just as bad as he'd been saying they were. [*Laughter*] I can relate. [*Laughter*] When you've got the top Republican in the Senate saying that his party's number-one priority isn't putting people back to work, isn't trying to fix the economy, but is to try to defeat me, you've got a sense that things in Washington aren't really on the level.

That's how you end up with Republicans in Congress voting against all kinds of jobs proposals that they actually supported in the past. Tax cuts for workers and small business, rebuilding our roads and our bridges, putting cops and teachers back to work, these aren't partisan issues. These are commonsense approaches to putting people back to work at a time when the unemployment rate is way too high. But politics seems to override everything in Washington these days. And people are tired of it, and they expect it to change.

They might think it's a smart political strategy, but it's not a strategy to make America stronger. It's not a strategy to relieve some of the pain and difficulty that families are feeling all across the country, including here in Hawaii. It's not a strategy to help middle class families who've been working two and three shifts just to put food on the table, if they can find a job. It's not a strategy for us winning the future.

So we've got a choice in 2012. The question is not whether people are still hurting. The question is whether—it not whether our economy is still on the mend. There's no doubt that things are tough right now. Of course, people are hurting. Of course, the economy is still struggling. The question is what do we do about it? The debate we need to have in this election is about where we go from here.

And the Republicans in Congress and the candidates running for President, they've got a very specific idea of where they want to take this country. To their credit, they're not hiding it. Watch these debates. [*Laughter*] They want to reduce the deficit by gutting our investment in education, in research and technology, our investment in rebuilding our roads and our bridges and our airports and our ports.

Now, I believe that since I already signed a trillion dollars' worth of spending cuts and have proposed to make even more, it's time to reduce the deficit not just by cutting, but also by asking the wealthiest among, the most fortunate among us, to do a little more to pay their fair share.

And by the way, most folks who can afford it, they're willing to do a little bit more to make this country stronger. They just want to make sure that if they're doing a little bit more, the Government is working a little bit better, that the money is being spent well, that it's going to things like education that are critical to our future.

The Republicans in Congress and on the campaign trail want to make Medicare a form of private insurance that seniors have to shop for with a voucher that probably will not cover all of the cost. I believe we can lower the cost of Medicare with reforms that still guarantee a dignified retirement that our seniors have earned.

And by the way, I speak as somebody who— it was only a couple of years ago when I was here watching my grandmother fade away. And she had had a successful career at Bank of Hawaii. She had the kind of retirement that a lot of people don't have these days, but knowing that Medicare was there for her made all the difference in the world. This is not an abstraction. Everybody here has a family member who knows how important that is.

The Republicans in Congress and these folks on the campaign trail, they think the best way for America to compete for new jobs and businesses is to follow other countries in a race to the bottom. Since places like China allow

companies to pay low wages, they want to roll back the minimum wage and the right to organize here at home.

Since other countries don't have the same antipollution measures that we have—dirtier air, dirtier water—their attitude is, let's go ahead and pollute. That's how we're going to compete.

Now, I don't think that we should have any more regulations than the health and the safety of the American people require. That's why I've already made reforms that will save businesses billions of dollars and why we put in place fewer regulations than the Bush administration did in its first 2 years.

Think about that. When you're watching television and everybody is talking about how the Obama administration is regulating businesses to death, we've actually put fewer regulations in place, smarter regulations in place, with much higher benefits at much lower cost. That's our track record.

But I don't believe, even as we're reforming our regulatory system, that we should have a race to the bottom. We're not going to the win the competition in Asia-Pacific region by seeing if we can have the lowest wages and the worst pollution. We can't win that race. We've got to have the highest skilled workers, the best infrastructure, the most dynamic innovation economy. That's the race that we can win. That should be our focus.

We should be competing to make our schools the envy of the world, to give our workers the best skills and training, to put college educations within the reach of anybody who is willing to work hard. We should be in a race to give our businesses the ability to move people and services quickly and effectively all around the world. We should be in a race to make those investments in NIH and the National Science Foundation and all the things that help to create to the Internet and GPS, those things that have created entire new industries.

We should be focused on clean energy. Folks here in Hawaii understand that we can't keep on doing business the way we're doing it. We've got to start changing. And it gives us enormous opportunities for jobs and growth.

That should be the race that we're trying to win.

We should make sure that the next generation of manufacturing takes route not in Asia, not in Europe, but right here in the United States of America. I don't want this nation just to be known for its consumption; I want us to be known for building and producing things and selling those goods all around the world. That's what this APEC conference has been about.

So this competition for new jobs and businesses and middle class security, that's the race I know we can win. But you don't win it by saying every American is in it on their own. We're not going to win it if we just hand out more tax cuts to people who don't need them, let companies play by their own rules without any restriction, and we just hope somehow that the success of the wealthiest few translates in the prosperity for everybody else.

We have tried that, by the way. We tried it for 10 years. It's part of what got into the mess that we're in. It doesn't work. It didn't work for Herbert Hoover, when it was called trickle-down economics during the Depression. It didn't work between 2000 and 2008, and it won't work today. And the reason it won't work is because we are not a country that is built on survival of the fittest. That's not who we are. We believe in the survival of the Nation. We believe that we all have a stake in each other's success, that if we can attract outstanding teachers to a profession by giving that teacher the pay that she deserves, that teacher goes on and educates the next Steve Jobs. And then suddenly, we've got a whole new business, whole new industry, and everybody can succeed.

We believe that if we provide faster Internet service to rural America or parts that have been left out of the Internet revolution so that a store owner can now sell goods around the world or if we build a new bridge that saves the shipping company time and money, then workers and customers all around the world are going to prosper. That is not a Democratic idea or a Republican idea. That is an American idea.

It was a Republican named Abraham Lincoln—you may have heard of him—who launched the transcontinental railroad, the National Academy of Sciences, the first land-grant colleges. He understood that we've got to make investments in our common future. It was a Republican, Teddy Roosevelt, who called for a progressive income tax, not a Democrat. It was a Republican named Dwight Eisenhower, who built the Interstate Highway System. It was with the help of Republicans in Congress that FDR gave millions of returning heroes, including my grandfather, the chance to go to college on the GI bill.

And that same spirit of common purpose I believe exists today; it just doesn't exist in Washington. But it exists among the American people. It exists here in Hawaii.

When I get out of the Capitol, I see it all the time—when you talk to people on Main Streets and in town halls. It's there when people get asked if they think you should build a new road or invest in clean energy or put teachers back in the classroom, they'll say absolutely—huge majorities—Democrats, Republicans, and Independents.

It's there when folks who are asked if the wealthiest Americans should pay their fair share. A majority—Democrats, Independents, Republicans—and the majority of wealthy folks, say, yes, that's a good idea for us to be able to lower our deficit and still invest in our future.

So our politics in Washington may be divided, but most Americans still understand that we can do more if we do it together, that no matter who we are or where we come from, we rise or fall as one Nation and one people. And that's what's at stake right now. That's what this election is about.

So I know it's been a tough 3 years, and I know that the change that we fought for in 2008 hasn't always been easy. There have been setbacks. There have been false starts. And sometimes, it may be tempting to believe that Washington, you just can't change. But remember what I always used to say during the campaign. Even on Inauguration night I said it. I said real change, big change is hard. It takes time. It takes more than a single term. It takes more than a single President. It takes all of you. It takes ordinary citizens who are committed to continuing to fight and to push to keep inching our country closer and closer to our ideals.

That's how a band of colonials were able to create this incredible country, just out of an idea, a revolutionary idea. That's how the greatest generation was able to overcome more than a decade of war and depression to build the greatest middle class on Earth. That's how we got the civil rights movement. That's how we got the women's rights movement. Inch by inch, step by step. Change is hard, and it takes time. But in America, it's always been possible.

And so I hope that all of you recommit yourselves and feel just as energized about 2012 as you did in 2008. And I'll remind you of something else that I said back then. I said, I am not a perfect man and I will not be a perfect President. Michelle can testify to that. [*Laughter*] But you know what I also promised in 2008? I said I would always tell you what I believe. I will always tell you where I stand. And I'll wake up every single day fighting for you and that vision of America that we share.

So if all of you still believe, if all of you still have hope—you may not have the old posters from 2008—[*laughter*]—but if you share that vision and determination to see it through, if you are willing to do just what you did in 2008 and maybe even a little more knocking on doors and making phone calls and getting people involved and getting people engaged, I guarantee you we will not just win an election, but more importantly, we will continue this country on a journey that makes sure that our children and our grandchildren have a better future. And we will remind the entire world just why it is that the United States of America is the greatest country on Earth.

Thank you very much, everybody. God bless you. God bless America. Thank you.

NOTE: The President spoke at 11:12 a.m. at the Aulani Disney Resort & Spa. In his remarks, he referred to Jeffrey R. Stone, founder, The Resort Group; and Robert Torrey, former teacher, Punahou School.

Message to the Senate Regarding the Agreement on Port State Measures To Prevent, Deter, and Eliminate Illegal, Unreported, and Unregulated Fishing
November 14, 2011

To the Senate of the United States:

I transmit herewith, for the advice and consent of the Senate to its ratification, the Agreement on Port State Measures to Prevent, Deter, and Eliminate Illegal, Unreported, and Unregulated Fishing, done at the Food and Agriculture Organization of the United Nations, in Rome, Italy, on November 22, 2009 (the "Agreement"). I also transmit, for the information of the Senate, the report of the Department of State with respect to the Agreement.

The Agreement established, for the first time at the global level, legally binding minimum standards for port states to control port access by foreign fishing vessels, as well as by foreign transport and supply ships that support fishing vessels. The Agreement also encourages Parties to apply similar measures to their own vessels. Involved Federal agencies and stake-

holders strongly support the Agreement. The Agreement establishes practical provisions to prevent fish from illegal, unreported, and unregulated fisheries from entering the stream of commerce. If widely ratified and properly implemented, the Agreement will thereby serve as a valuable tool in combating illegal, unreported, and unregulated fishing worldwide.

The legislation necessary to implement the Agreement will be submitted separately to the Congress. I recommend that the Senate give early and favorable consideration to this Agreement and give its advice and consent to ratification.

BARACK OBAMA

The White House,
November 14, 2011.

Statement on Congressional Passage of Legislation To Provide Tax Credits To Aid Businesses Hiring Veterans
November 16, 2011

I want to congratulate Republicans and Democrats in Congress for coming together to pass these tax credits that will encourage businesses to hire America's veterans. No veteran who fought for our country should have to fight for a job when they come home. That's why I proposed these tax credits back in August, and I look forward to signing them into law. This is a good first step, but it is only a step. Congress needs to pass the rest of my "American Jobs Act" so that we can create jobs and put money in the pockets of the middle class.

NOTE: The statement referred to H.R. 674.

The President's News Conference With Prime Minister Julia E. Gillard of Australia in Canberra, Australia
November 16, 2011

Prime Minister Gillard. Good evening, one and all. I take this opportunity to very warmly welcome President Obama to Australia for his first visit as President. President Obama is no stranger to our shores, having visited Australia before, but it is a special delight to have him here for his first visit as President. And it comes at an important time in our nation's history and in the history of our region.

We will be looking back during this visit. We'll be looking back at 60 years of the AN-ZUS alliance. We'll be looking back 10 years to the dreadful day of 9/11, a day we all remember with great sorrow. And we will be reflecting on those events. But we will be looking forward.

We live in the growing region of the world whose global—contribution to global growth is a profound one. We live in a region which is changing, changing in important ways. And as a result of those changes, President Obama and I have been discussing the best way of our militaries cooperating for the future.

So I'm very pleased to be able to announce with President Obama that we've agreed joint initiatives to enhance our alliance, 60 years old and being kept robust for tomorrow. It is a new agreement to expand the existing collaboration between the Australian Defence Force and the U.S. Marine Corps and the U.S. Air Force. What this means in very practical detail is from mid-2012, Australia will welcome deployments of a company-sized rotation of 200 to 250 marines in the Northern Territory for around 6 months at a time.

Over a number of years, we intend to build on this relationship in a staged way to a full force of around 2,500 personnel. That is a full Marine Air Ground Task Force.

A second component of these initiatives, which we have agreed, is greater access by U.S. military aircraft to the Royal Australian Air Force facilities in our country's north. This will involve more frequent movements of U.S. military aircraft into and out of northern Australia. Now, taken together, these two initiatives make our alliance stronger, they strengthen our cooperation in our region.

We are a region that is growing economically. But stability is important for economic growth too. And our alliance has been a bedrock of stability in our region. So building on our alliance through this new initiative is about stability. It will be good for our Australian Defence Force to increase their capabilities by joint training, combined training, with the U.S. Marines and personnel. It will mean that we are postured to better respond together, along with other partners in the Asia-Pacific, to any regional contingency, including the provision of humanitarian assistance and dealing with natural disasters.

In addition to discussing this global force posture review by the United States and these new initiatives in our alliance, the President of the United States and I have had an opportunity to reflect on a number of other issues: to reflect on circumstances in the global economy, to reflect on a clean energy future for our nations and for our planet, to reflect on the forthcoming East Asia Summit. President Obama will proceed from Australia to that summit in Indonesia, where he spent time growing up.

We've had a comprehensive discussion. I very much welcome President Obama to Australia. I think he's already seen that the welcome he's getting from Australians, including Australian schoolchildren, is a very warm one. And I know that that is going to be sustained during tonight's events and the events of tomorrow.

President Obama, over to you.

President Obama. Well, good day, everybody. And thank you, Madam Prime Minister, for your generous welcome, your friendship and your partnership. I am thrilled to be down under.

As you may know, this is not my first visit to Australia. In fact, I first visited Australia as a boy. And I've never forgotten the warmth and kindness that the Australian people extended to me when I was 6 and 8. And I can see that the Australian people have lost none of that warmth.

I very much wanted to take this trip last year, and although events back home prevented me from doing so, I was determined to come for a simple reason: The United States of America has no stronger ally than Australia. We are bound by common values, the rights and the freedoms that we cherish. And for nearly a century, we've stood together in defense of these freedoms. And I'm very happy to be here as we celebrate the 60th anniversary of our alliance and as we work together to strengthen it for the future.

We are two Pacific nations, and with my visit to the region I am making it clear that the United States is stepping up its commitment to the entire Asia-Pacific. In this work, we're deeply grateful for our alliance with Australia and the leadership role that it plays. As it has been for six decades, our alliance is going to be

indispensable to our shared future, the security we need and the prosperity that we seek not only in this region, but around the world.

I'm also very grateful for my partnership with Prime Minister Gillard. We've worked quite a bit together lately——

Prime Minister Gillard. You bet.

President Obama. ——spanning time zones: the G–20 in Cannes, APEC and TPP in Hawaii; now here in Australia; and next onto Bali for the East Asia Summit. And this speaks to how closely our countries work together on a wide range of issues. And in my friend Julia, I see the quality that we Americans admire most in our Australian friends: somebody who's down to earth, easy to talk to, and who says it like it is, straight up. And that's why we achieved so much today.

We agreed to push ahead with our efforts to create jobs for our people by bringing our economies and those of the region even closer together. Building on our progress at APEC, we're going to keep striving for a seamless regional economy. And as the two largest economies in the Trans-Pacific Partnership, Australia and the United States are helping to lead the way to a new model for trade across the region. And along with our G–20 partners, we agreed that we have to stay focused on the growth that creates jobs and that every nation needs to play by the same economic rules of the road.

As two global partners, we discussed the whole range of challenges where we stand shoulder to shoulder, including Afghanistan. Obviously, this has not been an easy mission for either of our countries, and our hearts go out to the families that were affected on October 29. But we both understand what's at stake, what happens when Al Qaida has safe havens. We've seen the awful loss of life, from 9/11 to Bali.

So I thanked the Prime Minister for Australia's strong commitment to this mission. I salute the extraordinary sacrifices of our forces who serve together, including your Australian troops who've shown that no job is too tough for your Diggers. Today the Prime Minister and I reaffirmed the way forward. The transition has begun. Afghans are stepping into the lead. As they do, our troops, American and Australian, will draw down responsibly together so that we preserve the progress that we've made, and by 2014, Afghans will take full responsibility for security in their country.

But our focus today, as the Prime Minister said, was on preparing our alliance for the future. And so I am very pleased that we are able to make these announcements here together on Australian soil. Because of these initiatives that are the result of our countries working very closely together as partners, we're going to be in a position to more effectively strengthen the security of both of our nations and this region.

As Julia described, we are increasing our cooperation, and I'd add, America's commitment to this region. Our U.S. Marines will begin rotating through Darwin for joint training and exercises. Our Air Force will rotate additional aircraft through more airfields in northern Australia. And these rotations, which are going to be taking place on Australian bases, will bring our militaries even closer and make them even more effective. We'll enhance our ability to train, exercise, and operate with allies and partners across the region, and that in turn will allow us to work with these nations to respond even faster to a wide range of challenges, including humanitarian crises and disaster relief, as well as promoting security cooperation across the region.

And this commitment builds upon the best traditions of our alliance. For decades, Australians have welcomed our servicemembers as they've come here to work, train, and exercise together. And I'm looking forward to joining the Prime Minister in Darwin tomorrow to thank our troops, Australians and Americans, for the incredible work that they are doing.

Finally, as I'll discuss more in my speech to Parliament tomorrow, this deepening of our alliance sends a clear message of our commitment to this region, a commitment that is enduring and unwavering. It's a commitment that I'll reaffirm in Bali as the United States joins the East Asia Summit. And I want to thank our Australian friends who supported our membership so strongly and have worked to make

sure that the EAS addresses regional challenges that affect all of us like proliferation and maritime security.

So again, I'm very pleased that we're able to make these important announcements during my visit. Madam Prime Minister, I thank you for being such a strong partner and a champion of our alliance.

And once again, I want to thank the Australian people for the kindness they showed me about 40 years ago and the kindness that they're showing me during my visit today. It's that friendship and that solidarity that makes and keeps our alliance one of the strongest in the world.

Prime Minister Gillard. Thank you.

We'll turn to taking some questions. I think we'll probably take one from the Australian media first. It's Phil Hudson.

U.S. Troop Deployment in Australia/China/U.S. Military Operations in Afghanistan

Q. Phillip Hudson from the Melbourne Herald Sun. Mr. President, welcome back to Australia.

President Obama. Thank you very much.

Q. You and Prime Minister Gillard have outlined what is for us a significant new U.S. troop buildup. How much of this is because you're worried about the rise of China? And as of today's deal, U.S. Marines will be for the first time conducting exercises by themselves on Australian soil. Why is that, and what will they be doing?

And, Mr. President, you also mentioned in your remarks that Afghanistan is not an easy mission. In the past few months, there have been three cases for Australia where our troops have been shot at by the Afghan soldiers who have been training, and sadly, four of our soldiers have died, and many others have been injured. Australian public opinion is strongly against our involvement continuing. You outlined the—just then, the drawdown. What can you say to the Australian people who don't want to wait, who want to leave immediately?

President Obama. Well, first, with respect to these new initiatives, this rotational deployment is significant because what it allows us to do is to not only build capacity and cooperation between our two countries, but it also allows us to meet the demands of a lot of partners in the region that want to feel that they're getting the training, they're getting the exercises, and that we have the presence that's necessary to maintain the security architecture in the region.

And so, as Julia mentioned, this is a region that's becoming increasingly important. The economy in this area is going to be the engine for world economic growth for some time to come. The lines of commerce and trade are constantly expanding. And it's appropriate then for us to make sure that not only our alliance, but the security architecture of the region is updated for the 21st century, and this initiative is going to allow us to do that.

It also allows us to respond to a whole host of challenges, like humanitarian or disaster relief, that frankly, given how large the Asia-Pacific region is, it can sometimes be difficult to do, and this will allow us to be able to respond in a more timely fashion and also equip a lot of countries, smaller countries who may not have the same capacity, it allows us to equip them so that they can respond more quickly as well.

And I guess the last part of your question, with respect to China, I've said repeatedly and I will say again today that we welcome a rising, peaceful China. What they've been able to achieve in terms of lifting hundreds of millions of people out of poverty over the last two decades has been nothing short of remarkable. And that is good not just for China, but it's potentially good for the region. And I know Australia's economy obviously has benefited by the increased demand that you're seeing in China.

The main message that I've said not only publicly, but also privately to the Chinese is that with their rise comes increased responsibilities. It's important for them to play by the rules of the road and in fact help underwrite the rules that have allowed so much remarkable economic progress to be made over the last several decades. And that's going to be true on a whole host of issues.

So where China is playing by those rules, recognizing its new role, I think this is a win-win situation. There are going to be times

where they're not, and we will send a clear message to them that we think that they need to be on track in terms of accepting the rules and responsibilities that come with being a world power.

With respect to Afghanistan, the impact of any loss of life among our troops is heartbreaking. And obviously, as President of the United States, there's no greater responsibility and nothing more difficult than putting our troops in harm's way. I think Prime Minister Gillard feels the same way that I do, which is we would not be sending our young men and women into harm's way unless we thought it was absolutely necessary for the security of our country.

What we have established is a transition process that allows Afghans to build up their capacity and take on a greater security role over the next 2 years. But it's important that we do it right. As some of you are aware, I just announced that all remaining troops in Iraq will be removed. It would have been tempting, given that I have been opposed to the Iraq war from the start, when I came into office, to say, we're going to get you all out right away. But what I recognized was that if we weren't thoughtful about how we proceed, then the enormous sacrifices that had been made by our men and women in the previous years might be for naught.

And what I'd say to the Australian people at this point is, given the enormous investment that's been made and the signs that we can, in fact, leave behind a country that's not perfect, but one that is more stable, more secure, and does not provide safe haven for terrorists, it's appropriate for us to finish the job and do it right.

Prime Minister Gillard. If I could just add to that and say, every time I have met President Obama and we've talked about our alliance, we've talked about our work in Afghanistan, and in our meetings, both formal and informal, the President has shown the greatest possible concern for our troops in the field. Now, the meetings we've had over the last few weeks at various international events have coincided with some of the most bitter and difficult news that we've had from Afghanistan, and every step of the way the President has gone out of his way to convey to me his condolences for the Australian people and particularly for the families that have suffered such a grievous loss.

President Obama. Laura MacInnis, Reuters.

Global Economic Stabilization Efforts/U.S. Economy

Q. Thank you, Mr. President. Chancellor Merkel said this week that Europe is in its toughest hour since World War II. Markets are now showing some anxiety about the possibility of instability spreading to France as well. Are you worried that the steps European leaders are taking are too incremental so far? Do you think something bolder or a more difficult set of decisions need to be taken to fully ring-fence that crisis?

I have a question for Prime Minister Gillard as well. Are you concerned that the fiscal pressures the United States is under at the moment may compromise its ability to sustain its plans for the region, including the initiatives announced today? Do you have to take those with something of a grain of salt until the supercommittee process is concluded?

President Obama. With respect to Europe, I'm deeply concerned, have been deeply concerned, I suspect we'll be deeply concerned tomorrow and next week and the week after that. Until we put in place a concrete plan and structure that sends a clear signal to the markets that Europe is standing behind the euro and will do what it takes, we're going to continue to see the kinds of turmoil that we saw in the markets today—or was it yesterday? I'm trying to figure out what—[*laughter*]—what time zone I'm in here.

Prime Minister Gillard. It's all of the time.

President Obama. All of the—right. [*Laughter*] We have consulted very closely with our European friends. I think that there is a genuine desire on the part of leaders like President Sarkozy and Chancellor Merkel to solve this crisis. But they've got a complicated political structure.

The problem right now is a problem of political will; it's not a technical problem. We saw some progress with Italy and Greece both put-

ting forward essentially unity governments that can implement some significant reforms that need to take place in those countries. But at this point, the larger European community has to stand behind the European project. And for those American readers or listeners, and those Australian readers or listeners, I think we all understand at this point, we've got an integrated world economy and what happens in Europe will have an impact on us.

So we are going to continue to advise European leaders on what options we think would meet the threshold where markets would settle down. It is going to require some tough decisions on their part. They have made some progress on some fronts, like their efforts to recapitalize the banks. But ultimately, what they're going to need is a firewall that sends a clear signal: "We stand behind the European project, and we stand behind the euro." And those members of the euro zone, they are going to have the liquidity they need to service their debt. So there's more work to do on that front.

And just—I don't want to steal your question, but I do want to just say, with respect to our budget, there's a reason why I'm spending this time out here in Asia and out here in the Pacific region. First and foremost, because this is the fastest growing economic region in the world, and I want to create jobs in the United States, which means we've got to sell products here and invest here and have a robust trading relationship here, and Australia happens to be one of our strongest trading partners.

But the second message I'm trying to send is that we are here to stay. This is a region of huge strategic importance to us. And I've been—I've made very clear, and I'll amplify in my speech to Parliament tomorrow, that even as we make a whole host of important fiscal decisions back home, this is right up there at the top of my priority list. And we're going to make sure that we are able to fulfill our leadership role in the Asia-Pacific region.

Prime Minister Gillard. And I was just going to make what I think is the commonsense point. I'm not going to issue words of advice about the fiscal position in the United States, but the commonsense point from the point of view of the leader is, ultimately, budgets are about choices and there are hard choices about the things you value. And I think, by President Obama being here, he is saying he values the role of the United States in this region and our alliance, and that's what the announcement we've made today is all about.

We've got a question from Mark Riley from the Australian media.

India/Australia-India Relations/Environment

Q. Thanks, Ma'am. This is Mark Riley from 7News, Australia. Mr. President, I wanted to ask you about the other rising giant of our region, India. And the Prime Minister might like to add some comments. How significant is it for the U.S. that Australia is now considering selling uranium to India? And could you clear up for us what influence or encouragement your administration gave Australia as it made that decision?

And also, the decision is so India can produce clean energy. In that regard, you're aware that our Parliament has passed a new bill pricing carbon, a carbon tax, if you like. But we're intrigued about where America is going on this issue. And countries like Australia don't see a carbon trading system in the world working unless America is a big part of it. Can you tell us, is it your wish that American will have an emissions trading scheme across the Nation within the next 5 years or so? How heavily do you want to see America involved in an emissions trading scheme globally? Or has this become too politically hard for you?

President Obama. Good. Well, first of all, with respect to India, we have not had any influence, I suspect, on Australia's decision to explore what its relationship in terms of the peaceful use of nuclear energy in India might be. I suspect that you've got some pretty smart Government officials here who figured out that India is a big player and that the Australia-India relationship is one that should be cultivated. So they—I don't think Julia or anybody else needs my advice in figuring that out. This is part of your neighborhood, and you are going

to make bilateral decisions about how to move forward.

I think, without wading into the details, the discussions that are currently taking place here in Australia around that relationship and the nuclear issue with India are ones that are compatible with international law, compatible with decisions that were made in the NPT. And I will watch with interest what's determined. But this is not something between the United States and Australia, this is something between India and Australia.

With respect to carbon emissions, I think I share the view of your Prime Minister and most scientists in the world that climate change is a real problem and that human activity is contributing to it and that we all have a responsibility to find ways to reduce our carbon emissions.

Each country is trying to figure out how to do that most effectively. Here in Australia, under the leadership of the Prime Minister, you've moved forward with a bold strategy. In the United States, although we haven't passed a what we call a cap-and-trade system, an exchange, what we have done is, for example, taken steps to double fuel efficiency standard on cars, which will have an enormous impact on removing carbon from the atmosphere.

We've invested heavily in clean energy research. We believe very strongly that with improved efficiencies and a whole step—a whole range of steps that we can meet and the commitments that we made in Copenhagen and Cancun. And as we move forward over the next several years, my hope is, is that the United States, as one of several countries with a big carbon footprint, can find further ways to reduce our carbon emissions. I think that's good for the world. I actually think, over the long term, it's good for our economies as well, because it's my strong belief that industries, utilities, individual consumers, we're all going to have to adapt how we use energy and how we think about carbon.

Now, another belief that I think the Prime Minister and I share is that the advanced economies can't do this alone. So part of our insistence when we are in multilateral fora—and I will continue to insist on this when we go to Durban—is that if we are taking a series of steps, then it's important that emerging economies like China and India are also part of the bargain. It doesn't mean that they have to do exactly what we do. We understand that in terms of per capita carbon emissions, they've got a long way to go before they catch up to us. But it does mean that they've got to take seriously their responsibilities as well.

And so ultimately, what we want is a mechanism whereby all countries are making an effort. And it's going to be a tough slog, particularly at a time when the economies are—a lot of economies are still struggling. But I think it's actually one that over the long term can be beneficial.

Jackie Calmes [New York Times].

China/Trade

Q. Thank you, Mr. President. Thank you, Prime Minister Gillard. I wanted to double back to the topic of China. It seems there's a bit of a schizophrenic aspect to this week of summitry in the Asian-Pacific, where China is participating from Hawaii to Indonesia, but then you have all the rest of you who are talking about, on the one hand, a trade bloc that excludes China, and now this—and an increased military presence for the United States, which is symbolized most by this agreement the two of you have made for a permanent U.S. presence in Australia.

What is it everyone fears so much from China? And isn't there some risk that you would increase tensions in a way that would take some of the—China might take some of the very actions you fear?

Prime Minister Gillard. I'm happy to start with that and then go to the President. I don't—I think there's actually a theme throughout the work we've been involved with at APEC, some of the discussion here and what we will take to the East Asia Summit. We may be on a journey from saying "aloha" to "good day" to *"bali hai"* or something like that. But I actually think in terms of strategic outlook, it remains the same, which is both of our nations are deeply engaged with China as it ris-

es and we want to see China rise into the global rules-based order.

That's our aspiration. I understand it to be the aspiration of the United States. It's something that we pursue bilaterally with China. It's something that we pursue multilaterally in the various forums that we work in.

This East Asia Summit will have a particular significance, coming for the first time with the President of the United States there and of course Russia represented around the table, so all of the players with the right mandate to discuss strategic, political, and economic questions for our region.

So I actually believe there's a continuity here: APEC fundamentally focused on trade and economic liberalization; here in Australia, longtime allies, talking about the future of their alliance and building for that future, as you would expect, but also preparing for a set of discussions in Bali, which will bring us together again with our friends across the region.

President Obama. Just to pick up on this theme, Jackie, I think the notion that we fear China is mistaken. The notion that we are looking to exclude China is mistaken. And I'll take TPP as a perfect example of this. We haven't excluded China from the TPP. What we have said is, the future of this region depends on robust trade and commerce and the only way we're going to grow that trade is if we have a high-standards trade agreement where everybody is playing by the same rules, where if one set of markets is open then there's reciprocity among the other trading partners, where there are certain rules that we abide by in terms of intellectual property rights protection or how we deal with government procurement, in addition to the traditional areas like tariffs.

And what we saw in Honolulu, in APEC, was that a number of countries that weren't part of the initial discussions—like Japan, Canada, Mexico—all expressed an interest in beginning the consultations to be part of this high-standard trade agreement that could potentially be a model for the entire region.

Now, if China says, we want to consult with you about being part of this as well, we welcome that. It will require China to rethink some of its approaches to trade, just as every other country that's been involved in the consultations for the TPP have had to think through, all right, what kinds of adjustments are we willing to make?

And so that's the consistent theme here. This is a growing region. It is a vital region. The United States is going to be a huge participant in both economic and security issues in the Asia-Pacific region, and our overriding desire is that we have a clear set of principles that all of us can abide by so that all of us can succeed. And I think it's going to be important for China to be a part of that. I think that's good for us.

But it's going to require China, just like all the rest of us, to align our existing policies and what we've done in the past with what's needed for a brighter future. All right?

Prime Minister Gillard. Thank you very much.

President Obama. Thank you very much, everybody.

Prime Minister Gillard. Thank you.

NOTE: The President's news conference began at 6:10 p.m. at Parliament House. In his remarks, he referred to President Nicolas Sarkozy of France; and Chancellor Angela Merkel of Germany.

Remarks Following a Dinner With Members of Parliament in Canberra
November 16, 2011

Well, Prime Minister Gillard and Leader Abbott, thank you both for your wonderfully warm words. And I thank you for showing that in Canberra, as in Washington, people may not always see eye to eye, but on this we are all united: There are no better friends than the United States and Australia.

Mr. Speaker, Mr. President, and distinguished guests, ladies and gentlemen, I am going to be brief, for we have had a busy day. I am not sure what day it is. [*Laughter*] And I'm going to subject you to a very long speech tomorrow.

But I do want to express my deep appreciation for the way you've welcomed me here today. I know that I am not the first guy from Chicago to come to these parts. A century ago, Walter Burley Griffin came here with a vision for this city. He said, "I have planned a city that is not like any other in the world." And tonight I want to thank all of you and the people of Australia for the hospitality that is unlike any other in the world.

Our toasts earlier tonight reminded me of a story. It's from our troops—this is true story—our troops serving together in Afghanistan. Our guys, the Americans, couldn't figure out why your guys were always talking about cheese, all day long, morning, noon, and night. Why are the Aussies always talking about

cheese? And then finally, they realized, it was their Australian friends just saying hello, just saying cheers. [*Laughter*]

So we Americans and Australians, we may not always speak the same way or use the same words, but I think it's pretty clear, especially from the spirit of this visit and our time together this evening, that we understand each other. And we see the world in the same way, even if we do have to disagree on the merits of vegemite. [*Laughter*]

As many of you know, I first came to Australia as a child. But despite my visits, I have to admit I never did learn to talk "Strine." I know there is some concern here that your Australian language is being Americanized. So perhaps it's time for us to reverse the trend. Tonight, with your permission, I'd like to give it a burl. [*Laughter*]

I want to thank the Prime Minister for a very productive meeting that we had today. I think she'll agree it was a real chinwag. [*Laughter*] When Julia and I meet, we listen to each other, we learn from each other. It's not just a lot of earbashing. [*Laughter*] That's a good one—earbashing. [*Laughter*] I can use that in Washington, because there's a lot of earbashing sometimes. [*Laughter*]

That's been the story of our two nations. Through a century of progress and struggle, we have stood together, in good times and in bad. We've faced our share of sticky wickets. [*Laughter*] In some of our darkest moments—when our countries have been threatened, when we needed a friend to count on—we've always been there for each other: at Darwin, at Midway, after 9/11, and after Bali.

It's that moment, in the midst of battle, when the bullets are flying and the outcome is uncertain, when Americans and Aussies look over at each other, knowing that we've got each other's backs, knowing in our hearts, "No worries, she'll be right." [*Laughter*]

And so tonight, as we mark 60 years of this remarkable alliance, through war and peace, hardship and prosperity, we gather together among so many friends who sustain the bonds between us, and we can say with confidence and with pride: The alliance between the United States and Australia is deeper and stronger than it has ever been, spot on—[*laughter*]—cracker jack—[*laughter*]—in top nick. [*Laughter*]

Thank you very much, everybody.

NOTE: The President spoke at 9:09 p.m. at Parliament House. In his remarks, he referred to Leader of the Opposition Anthony J. Abbott, Speaker of the House of Representatives Henry A. Jenkins, and President of the Senate John J. Hogg of Australia.

Remarks to the Parliament in Canberra
November 17, 2011

Prime Minister Gillard, Leader Abbott, thank you both for your very warm welcome. Mr. Speaker, Mr. President, Members of the House and Senate, ladies and gentlemen, I thank you for the honor of standing in this great chamber to reaffirm the bonds between the United States and the Commonwealth of Australia, two of the world's oldest democracies and two of the world's oldest friends.

To you and the people of Australia, thank you for your extraordinary hospitality. And here, in this city, this ancient meeting place, I want to acknowledge the original inhabitants of this land and one of the world's oldest continuous cultures, the first Australians.

I first came to Australia as a child, traveling between my birthplace of Hawaii and Indonesia, where I would live for 4 years. As an 8-year-old, I couldn't always understand your foreign language. [*Laughter*] Last night I did try to talk some "Strine." [*Laughter*] Today I don't want to subject you to any earbashing. I really do love that one, and I will be introducing that into the vernacular in Washington. [*Laughter*]

But to a young American boy, Australia and its people—your optimism, your easygoing ways, your irreverent sense of humor—all felt so familiar. It felt like home. I've always wanted to return. I tried last year twice. But this is a lucky country, and today I feel lucky to be here as we mark the 60th anniversary of our unbreakable alliance.

The bonds between us run deep. In each other's story we see so much of ourselves: ancestors who crossed vast oceans, some by choice, some in chains; settlers who pushed west across sweeping plains; dreamers who toiled with hearts and hands to lay railroads and to build cities; generations of immigrants who with each new arrival add a new thread to the brilliant tapestry of our nations; and we are citizens who live by a common creed—no matter who you are, no matter what you look like, everyone deserves a fair chance, everyone deserves a fair go.

Of course, progress in our society has not always come without tensions or struggles to overcome a painful past. But we are countries with a willingness to face our imperfections and to keep reaching for our ideals. That's the spirit we saw in this chamber 3 years ago, as this nation inspired the world with a historic gesture of reconciliation with Indigenous Australians. It's the spirit of progress, in America, which allows me to stand before you today as President of the United States. And it's the spirit I'll see later today when I become the first U.S. President to visit the Northern Territory, where I'll meet the traditional owners of the land.

Nor has our progress come without great sacrifice. This morning I was humbled and deeply moved by a visit to your war memorial to pay my respects to Australia's fallen sons and daughters. Later today, in Darwin, I'll join the Prime Minister in saluting our brave men and women in uniform. And it will be a reminder that from the trenches of the First World War to the mountains of Afghanistan, Aussies and Americans have stood together, we have fought together, we have given lives together in every single major conflict of the past hundred years—every single one.

This solidarity has sustained us through a difficult decade. We will never forget the attacks of 9/11 that took the lives not only of Americans, but people from many nations, including Australia. In the United States, we will never forget how Australia invoked the ANZUS Treaty for the first time ever, showing that our two nations stood as one. And none of us will ever forget those we've lost to Al Qaida's terror in the years since, including innocent Australians.

And that's why, as both the Prime Minister and the Opposition Leader indicated, we are determined to succeed in Afghanistan. It is why I salute Australia: outside of NATO, the largest contributor of troops to this vital mission. And it's why we honor all those who have served there for our security, including 32 Australian patriots who gave their lives, among them Captain Bryce Duffy, Corporal Ashley Birt, and Lance Corporal Luke Gavin. We will honor their sacrifice by making sure that Afghanistan is never again used as a source for attacks against our people—never again.

As two global partners, we stand up for the security and the dignity of people around the world. We see it when our rescue workers rush to help others in times of fire and drought and flooding rains. We see it when we partner to keep the peace, from East Timor to the Balkans, and when we pursue our shared vision: a world without nuclear weapons. We see it in the development that lifts up a child in Africa, the assistance that saves a family from famine, and when we extend our support to the people of the Middle East and North Africa, who deserve the same liberty that allows us to gather in this great hall of democracy.

This is the alliance we reaffirm today, rooted in our values, renewed by every generation. This is the partnership we worked to deepen over the past 3 years. And today I can stand before you and say with confidence that the alliance between the United States and Australia has never been stronger. It has been to our past—our alliance continues to be indispensable to our future. So here, among close friends, I'd like to address the larger purpose of my visit to this region: our efforts to advance security, prosperity, and human dignity across the Asia-Pacific.

For the United States, this reflects a broader shift. After a decade in which we fought two wars that cost us dearly in blood and treasure, the United States is turning our attention to the vast potential of the Asia-Pacific region. In just a few weeks, after nearly 9 years, the last American troops will leave Iraq, and our war there will be over. In Afghanistan, we've begun a transition, a responsible transition so Afghans can take responsibility for their future and so coalition forces can begin to draw down. And with partners like Australia, we've struck major blows against Al Qaida and put that terrorist organization on the path to defeat, including delivering justice to Usama bin Laden.

So make no mistake, the tide of war is receding, and America is looking ahead to the future that we must build. From Europe to the Americas, we've strengthened alliances and partnerships. At home, we're investing in the sources of our long-term economic strength: the education of our children, the training of our workers, the infrastructure that fuels commerce, the science and the research that leads to new breakthroughs. We've made hard decisions to cut our deficit and put our fiscal house in order. And we will continue to do more, because our economic strength at home is the foundation of our leadership in the world, including here in the Asia-Pacific.

Our new focus on this region reflects a fundamental truth: The United States has been, and always will be, a Pacific nation. Asian immigrants helped build America, and millions of American families, including my own, cherish our ties to this region. From the bombing of Darwin to the liberation of Pacific islands, from the rice paddies of Southeast Asia to a cold Korean Peninsula, generations of Americans have served here and died here so democracies could take root, so economic miracles could lift hundreds of millions to prosperity. Americans have bled with you for this progress, and we will not allow it—we will never allow it to be reversed.

Here, we see the future. As the world's fastest growing region, and home to more than half the global economy, the Asia-Pacific is critical to achieving my highest priority, and that's creating jobs and opportunity for the American people. With the world—with most of the world's nuclear power and some half of humanity, Asia will largely define whether the century ahead will be marked by conflict or cooperation, needless suffering or human progress.

As President, I have therefore made a deliberate and strategic decision: As a Pacific nation, the United States will play a larger and long-term role in shaping this region and its future by upholding core principles and in close partnership with our allies and friends.

Let me tell you what this means. First, we seek security, which is the foundation of peace and prosperity. We stand for an international order in which the rights and responsibilities of all nations and all people are upheld. Where international law and norms are enforced, where commerce and freedom of navigation are not impeded, where emerging powers contribute to regional security, and where disagreements are resolved peacefully. That's the future that we seek.

Now, I know that some in this region have wondered about America's commitment to upholding these principles. So let me address this directly. As the United States puts our fiscal house in order, we are reducing our spending. And yes, after a decade of extraordinary growth in our military budgets, and as we definitively end the war in Iraq and begin to wind down the war in Afghanistan, we will make some reductions in defense spending.

As we consider the future of our Armed Forces, we've begun a review that will identify our most important strategic interests and guide our defense priorities and spending over the coming decade. So here is what this region must know. As we end today's wars, I have directed my national security team to make our presence and mission in the Asia-Pacific a top priority. As a result, reductions in U.S. defense spending will not—I repeat, will not—come at the expense of the Asia-Pacific.

My guidance is clear. As we plan and budget for the future, we will allocate the resources necessary to maintain our strong military presence in this region. We will preserve our unique ability to project power and deter threats to peace. We will keep our commitments, including our treaty obligations to allies like Australia. And we will constantly strengthen our capabilities to meet the needs of the 21st century. Our enduring interests in the region demand our enduring presence in the region. The United States is a Pacific power, and we are here to stay.

Indeed, we are already modernizing America's defense posture across the Asia-Pacific. It will be more broadly distributed, maintaining our strong presence in Japan and the Korean Peninsula while enhancing our presence in Southeast Asia. Our posture will be more flexible, with new capabilities to ensure that our forces can operate freely. And our posture will be more sustainable by helping allies and partners build their capacity with more training and exercises.

We see our new posture here in Australia. The initiatives that the Prime Minister and I announced yesterday will bring our two militaries even closer together. We'll have new opportunities to train with other allies and partners, from the Pacific to the Indian Ocean. And it will allow us to respond faster to the full range of challenges, including humanitarian crises and disaster relief.

Since World War II, Australians have warmly welcomed American servicemembers who've passed through. On behalf of the American people, I thank you for welcoming those who will come next, as they ensure that our alliance stays strong and ready for the tests of our time.

We see America's enhanced presence in the alliance that we've strengthened: in Japan, where our alliance remains a cornerstone of regional security; in Thailand, where we're partnering for disaster relief; in the Philippines, where we're increasing ship visits and training; and in South Korea, where our commitment to the security of the Republic of Korea will never waver. Indeed, we also reiterate our resolve to act firmly against any proliferation activities by North Korea. The transfer of nuclear materials or material by North Korea to states or nonstate entities would be considered a grave threat to the United States and our allies, and we would hold North Korea fully accountable for the consequences of such action.

We see America's enhanced presence across Southeast Asia in our partnership with Indonesia against piracy and violent extremism and in our work with Malaysia to prevent proliferation, in the ships we'll deploy to Singapore and in our closer cooperation with Vietnam and Cambodia, and in our welcome of India as it looks east and plays a larger role as an Asian power.

At the same time, we'll reengage with our regional organizations. Our work in Bali this week will mark my third meeting with ASEAN leaders, and I'll be proud to be the first American President to attend the East Asia Summit. And together, I believe we can address shared challenges, such as proliferation and maritime security, including cooperation in the South China Sea.

Meanwhile, the United States will continue our effort to build a cooperative relationship with China. All of our nations—Australia, the United States—all of our nations have a profound interest in the rise of a peaceful and prosperous China. That's why the United States welcomes it. We've seen that China can be a partner, from reducing tensions on the Korean Peninsula to preventing proliferation. And we'll seek more opportunities for cooperation with Beijing, including greater communication between our militaries to promote understanding and avoid miscalculation. We will do this, even as we continue to speak candidly to Beijing about the importance of upholding international norms and respecting the universal human rights of the Chinese people.

A secure and peaceful Asia is the foundation for the second area in which America is leading again, and that's advancing our shared prosperity. History teaches us, the greatest force the world has ever known for creating wealth and opportunity is free markets. So we seek economies that are open and transparent. We seek trade that is free and fair. And we seek an open international economic system, where rules are clear and every nation plays by them.

In Australia and America, we understand these principles. We're among the most open economies on Earth. Six years into our landmark trade agreement, commerce between us has soared. Our workers are creating new partnerships and new products, like the advanced aircraft technologies we build together in Victoria. We're the leading investor in Australia, and you invest more in America than you do in any other nation, creating good jobs in both countries.

And we recognize that economic partnerships can't just be about one nation extracting another's resources. We understand that no long-term strategy for growth can be imposed from above. Real prosperity, prosperity that fosters innovation and prosperity that endures, comes from unleashing our greatest economic resource, and that's the entrepreneurial spirit, the talents of our people.

So even as America competes aggressively in Asian markets, we're forging the economic partnerships that create opportunity for all. Building on our historic trade agreement with South Korea, we're working with Australia and our other APEC partners to create a seamless regional economy. And with Australia and other partners, we're on track to achieve our most ambitious trade agreement yet and a potential model for the entire region, the Trans-Pacific Partnership.

The United States remains the world's largest and most dynamic economy. But in an interconnected world, we all rise and fall together. That's why I pushed so hard to put the G–20 at the front and center of global economic decisionmaking, to give more nations a leadership role in managing the international economy, including Australia. And together, we saved the world economy from a depression. And now our urgent challenge is to create the growth that puts people to work.

We need growth that is fair, where every nation plays by the rules, where workers rights are respected and our businesses can compete on a level playing field, where the intellectual property and new technologies that fuel innovation are protected, and where currencies are market driven so no nation has an unfair advantage.

We also need growth that is broad, not just for the few, but for the many, with reforms that protect consumers from abuse and a global commitment to end the corruption that stifles growth. We need growth that is balanced, because we will all prosper more when countries with large surpluses take action to boost demand at home.

And we need growth that is sustainable. This includes the clean energy that creates green jobs and combats climate change, which cannot be denied. We see it in the stronger fires, the devastating floods, and the Pacific islands confronting rising seas. And as countries with large carbon footprints, the United States and Australia have a special responsibility to lead.

Every nation will contribute to the solution in its own way, and I know this issue is not without controversy in both our countries. But what we can do, and what we are doing, is to work together to make unprecedented investments in clean energy, to increase energy efficiency, and to meet the commitments we made at Copenhagen and Cancun. We can do this, and we will.

As we grow our economies, we'll also remember the link between growth and good governance: the rule of law, transparent institutions, the equal administration of justice. Because history shows that over the long run democracy and economic growth go hand in hand. And prosperity without freedom is just another form of poverty.

And this brings me to the final area where we are leading: our support for the fundamental rights of every human being. Every nation will chart its own course. Yet it is also true that certain rights are universal, among them, freedom of speech, freedom of the press, freedom of assembly, freedom of religion, and the freedom of citizens to choose their own leaders.

These are not American rights or Australian rights or Western rights. These are human rights. They stir in every soul, as we've seen in the democracies that have succeeded here in Asia. Other models have been tried, and they have failed: fascism and communism, rule by one man and rule by committee. And they failed for the same simple reason: They ignore the ultimate source of power and legitimacy, the will of the people. Yes, democracy can be messy and rough. I understand you mix it up quite well during question time. [*Laughter*] But whatever our differences of party or of ideology, we know in our democracies we are blessed with the greatest form of government ever known to man.

So as two great democracies, we speak up for those freedoms when they are threatened. We partner with emerging democracies like Indonesia to help strengthen the institutions upon which good governance depends. We encourage open government because democracies depend on an informed and active citizenry. We help strengthen civil societies because they empower our citizens to hold their governments accountable. And we advance the rights of all people—women, minorities, and indigenous cultures—because when societies harness the potential of all their citizens, these societies are more successful, they are more prosperous and they are more just.

These principles have guided our approach to Burma, with a combination of sanctions and engagement. And today, Aung San Suu Kyi is free from house arrest, some political prisoners have been released, and the Government has begun a dialogue. Still, violations of human rights persist. So we will continue to speak clearly about the steps that must be taken for the Government of Burma to have a better relationship with the United States.

This is the future we seek in the Asia-Pacific: security, prosperity, and dignity for all. That's what we stand for. That's who we are. That's the future we will pursue in partnership with allies and friends and with every element of American power. So let there be no doubt: In the Asia-Pacific in the 21st century, the United States of America is all in.

Still, in times of great change and uncertainty, the future can seem unsettling. Across a vast ocean, it's impossible to know what lies beyond the horizon. But if this vast region and its people teach us anything, it's the yearning for liberty and progress will not be denied.

It's why women in this country demanded that their voices be heard, making Australia the first nation to let women vote and run for Parliament and one day become Prime Minister. It's why the people took to the streets, from Delhi to Seoul, from Manila to Jakarta, to throw off colonialism and dictatorship and build some of the world's largest democracies.

It's why a soldier in a watchtower along the DMZ defends a free people in the South and why a man from the North risks his life to escape across the border. Why soldiers in blue helmets keep the peace in a new nation. And why women of courage go into brothels to save young girls from modern-day slavery, which must come to an end.

It's why men of peace in saffron robes faced beatings and bullets and why every day, from some of the world's largest cities to dusty rural towns, in small acts of courage the world may never see, a student posts a blog, a citizen signs a charter, an activist remains unbowed, imprisoned in his home, just to have the same rights that we cherish here today.

Men and women like these know what the world must never forget. The currents of history may ebb and flow, but over time they move, decidedly, decisively, in a single direction. History is on the side of the free: free societies, free governments, free economies, free people. And the future belongs to those who stand firm for those ideals, in this region and around the world.

This is the story of the alliance we celebrate today. This is the essence of America's leadership; it is the essence of our partnership. This is the work we will carry on together, for the security and prosperity and dignity of all people.

So God bless Australia, God bless America, and God bless the friendship between our two peoples.

Thank you very much.

NOTE: The President spoke at 10:42 a.m. at Parliament House. In his remarks, he referred to Leader of the Opposition Anthony J. Abbott, Speaker of the House of Representatives Henry A. Jenkins, and President of the Senate John J. Hogg of Australia; and National League for Democracy in Burma Leader Aung San Suu Kyi.

Remarks and a Question-and-Answer Session at Campbell High School in Canberra
November 17, 2011

President Obama. So the—well, thank you for taking the time. Part of the reason we wanted to come by was when Julia came to Washington, DC, we had a visit with some high school students there. And I didn't want to miss out on the fun when I came to Australia. So I wanted to get a chance to find out what's going on and see if you guys had any questions.

I've had a wonderful time here. On the way here, your Prime Minister was telling me about all the deadly animals that could kill you if they bite you. [*Laughter*]

Prime Minister Julia E. Gillard of Australia. Just talking—[*inaudible*].

President Obama. There seems to be a surplus of those here in Australia.

But part of the reason that I love meeting with students is because so much of what we do together, your Prime Minister and I, is focused on your future: how we can make sure you've got good careers and have opportunity and the world is safe and we're taking care of our environment in a serious way. And I'm always inspired when I meet with young people because you're not stuck in some of the old stodgy ideas that the rest of us are sometimes.

So who wants to start first? Somebody have a question or a comment?

Yes, what's your name?

Education

Q. My name is Emily, and my question is directed to you, Mr. President. What directions will the American education system be taking for the future?

Prime Minister Gillard. Good question.

President Obama. Well, it's a great question. The United States historically became an economic superpower in part because we were ahead of the curve when it came to education: establishing compulsory public high schools, using the GI bill to help veterans coming home go to college. And we still have some outstanding schools in the United States. But we also have some schools that just aren't doing the job and a sizeable number of our young people who aren't getting the kind of preparation they need.

So one of my biggest priorities when I came in was, how do we reform the system overall? A lot of it starts with early childhood education. A lot of poor children don't get the support that they need when they're very young so, by the time they get to grammar school, they're already behind. They don't know their numbers, people haven't read to them, et cetera. So working with programs that are good for young people—or very young children when they're toddlers and infants—to give them a head start, that's very important. We're focusing a lot on math and science education, where I think we've fallen behind.

The most important thing for every grade level is the quality of teachers. So we're spending a lot of time thinking about how do we train teachers more effectively, how do we pay them

more so that they have fewer worries about supporting themselves and can really focus on the work that they do, and making sure that they are up to snuff when it comes to the subject matter that they teach. And then, we've seen studies that show that the biggest correlation, other than your parents, about how well the student does is the quality of their teachers.

So we're going to be spending a lot of time focusing on those issues over the next several years.

Secretary of Education Arne Duncan

Prime Minister Gillard. And Aussie influence.

President Obama. Absolutely.

Prime Minister Gillard. Secretary Duncan, who is the equivalent in the U.S. of the Federal Education Minister, played basketball in Australia.

President Obama. He was a professional basketball player here in Australia and is married to a Tasmanian wife. [*Laughter*] So he obviously was inspired when he was here by the excellent schools.

Who's next?

President's Influence

Q. Thank you, Mr. President. I'm Meg. Have you ever thought about teaming up with a high-profile celebrity such as Justin Bieber to appeal to more people? [*Laughter*]

President Obama. You know, that's an interesting question. The—we—I interact a lot with celebrities. They end up coming to the White House for a pet cause or some of them were very supportive of me during my campaign. But generally speaking, hopefully, if I'm going to be successful, it's going to be because of the ideas I put forward and not because I'm hanging out with Justin Bieber. [*Laughter*] Although he is a very nice young man, and I'll tell him you said hi.

NOTE: The President spoke at 11:53 a.m. In his remarks, he referred to Karen L. Duncan, wife of Secretary Duncan. Prime Minister Gillard referred to Minister of School Education, Early Childhood, and Youth Peter R. Garrett of Australia. A portion of these remarks could not be verified because the audio was incomplete.

Remarks to United States and Australian Military Personnel at Royal Australian Air Force Base Darwin, Australia
November 17, 2011

The President. Thank you! Hello, everybody!

Audience members. Hello!

The President. How are you going? Well, I know that you all have a great Australian cheer. I want to hear it. So let me say first, Aussie, Aussie, Aussie!

Audience members. Aussie, Aussie, Aussie!

The President. I enjoyed that. [*Laughter*] It is great to be here at RAAF Darwin—I mean, "Dah-win." [*Laughter*] I'm learning to speak "Strine." [*Laughter*] The Prime Minister said that she wanted to show me Australia at its best. And she's right, you all are all true blue. So thank you, Julia, for bringing us together today, for being such a great friend and champion of our alliance, and for this visit to Australia, which I will remember forever.

Now, it is good to be here in the Top End. I thank the people of Darwin for the incredibly warm welcome. And I'm proud to be the first U.S. President ever to visit the Northern Territory.

I want to begin by respectfully acknowledging the traditional owners of this land and their elders, past and present. You are one of the world's oldest continuous cultures, and I want you to know that your strength, your dignity is an inspiration to me and people all around the world.

I'm not going to give a big speech. It's a little hot. [*Laughter*] I already gave a big speech. What I really want to do is spend a little time shaking some hands.

Audience member. Yeah!

The President. I'm not sure I'm going to be able to reach all the way back there. [*Laughter*]

As the Prime Minister said, we're celebrating the 60th anniversary of our great alliance. And we couldn't think of a better group to do it with than you. All of you are the backbone of our alliance. It's an honor to be here with Australia's legendary Diggers. You are some of the toughest warriors in the world. And so are another group of folks here today, our extraordinary United States Marines.

Audience members. Hooah!

The President. Aussies and Americans like you have stood together since World War I, the war in which so much of your national character was born, your incredible ANZAC spirit.

But in a sense, it was here, in Darwin, where our alliance was born, during "Australia's Pearl Harbor." Against overwhelming odds, our forces fought back, with honor and with courage. The Prime Minister and I just paid our respects at the memorial to one of the ships lost that day, the USS *Peary*. And we looked out at those beautiful blue waters where so many Australians and Americans rest where they fell, together.

The days after Darwin were tough. Some thought Australia might fall. But we dusted ourselves off. We picked ourselves up. We rebuilt. And thanks to the extraordinary generation of troops, we went on to victory in the Coral Sea and at Midway and at Milne Bay.

And when that war was won, and as another raged in Korea, our countries forged a new alliance. We pledged our "collective defense for the preservation of peace and security." And that's a promise we've kept ever since.

As I said in Parliament earlier today, our alliance is rooted in the bonds between our people and the democratic values that we share and our commitment to stand with each other through thick and through thin, no matter what.

And that includes Afghanistan. I know many of you served there, including proud members of the 1st Brigade. Like generations before you, you've lived and served alongside your American colleagues, day in and day out. You work together so well, it's often said you can't tell where our guys end and you guys begin. Today I want to say thank you. Thank you for a job well done. Thank you for your incredible sacrifices. Thank you for your families' sacrifices. And welcome home.

Others among you served in Iraq and on dangerous missions around the globe. Among us today are families whose loved ones made the ultimate sacrifice in today's wars. This morning the Prime Minister and I paid our respects at the Australian War Memorial.

And in that magnificent space I saw the Roll of Honour, with the names of your fallen heroes, including those from Afghanistan. And to their families, I say, no words are sufficient for the depth of your sacrifice. But we will honor your loved ones by completing their mission, by making sure Afghanistan is never again used to attack our people. And I am confident that we are going to succeed.

Now here in Darwin and Northern Australia, we'll write the next proud chapter in our alliance. As the Prime Minister and I announced yesterday, some of our marines will begin rotating through these parts to train and exercise with you and to work as partners across the region for the security we all want.

Today, on behalf of the American people, I want to thank the people of this community for welcoming our men and women in uniform. We are grateful for your friendship, and we are grateful for your hospitality.

So we're deepening our alliance, and this is the perfect place to do it. I know the training conditions around here are tough, at least that's what I've heard: big, open spaces, harsh weather, mozzies—[*laughter*]—snakes, crocs. [*Laughter*] In fact, I was just presented with the most unique gift I've ever received as President, crocodile insurance. [*Laughter*] My wife Michelle will be relieved. [*Laughter*] I have to admit that when we reformed health care in

America, crocodile insurance is one thing we left out. [*Laughter*]

But there's another reason we're deepening our alliance here. This region has some of the busiest sea lanes in the world, which are critical to all our economies. And in times of crisis, from the Bali bombings to East Timor to relief after a tsunami, Darwin has been a hub, moving out aid, caring for victims, making sure that we do right by the people of this region. And that's what we're going to keep doing, together.

Going forward, our purpose is the same as it was 60 years ago: "the preservation of peace and security." And in a larger sense, you're answering the question once posed by the great Banjo Paterson. Of Australia, he wrote, "Hath she the strength for the burden laid upon her, hath she the power to protect and guard her own?"

Well, generations of Australians—and you, its men and women in uniform—have given your answer. And America has been honored to stand with you, as allies with an enduring commitment to human freedom.

On this 60th anniversary, we are saying together, proudly: Yes, we have the strength for the burden laid upon us, and we have the power to protect and guard our own, here in the Asia-Pacific and all around the world.

So thank you all for your extraordinary service. And thank you for representing the very best of our two countries. God bless Australia, God bless America, and God bless the great alliance between our two peoples. Thank you very much.

NOTE: The President spoke at 4:55 p.m. In his remarks, he referred to Prime Minister Julia E. Gillard of Australia.

Message to the Congress Extending the Period of Production of the Naval Petroleum Reserves
November 17, 2011

To the Congress of the United States:

Consistent with section 7422(c)(2) of title 10, United States Code, I am informing you of my decision to extend the period of production of the Naval Petroleum Reserves for a period of 3

years from April 5, 2012, the expiration date of the currently authorized period of production.

Attached is a copy of the report investigating continued production of the Reserves, consistent with section 7422(c)(2)(B) of title 10. In light of the findings contained in the report, I certify that continued production from the Naval Petroleum Reserves is in the national interest.

BARACK OBAMA

The White House,
November 17, 2011.

Remarks on Lion Air's Purchase Agreement With the Boeing Company in Bali, Indonesia
November 18, 2011

Well, I just want to make a brief statement. This is a remarkable example of the trade investment and commercial opportunities that exist in the Asia-Pacific region.

For the last several days, I've been talking about how we have to make sure that we've got a presence in this region, that it can result directly in jobs at home. And what we see here—a multibillion-dollar deal between Lion Air—one of the fastest growing airlines not just in the region, but in the world—and Boeing is going to result in over 100,000 jobs back in the United States of America over a long period of time.

This represents the largest deal, if I'm not mistaken, that Boeing has ever done. We are looking at over 200 planes that are going to be sold. And the U.S. administration and the Ex-Im Bank, in particular, were critical in facilitating this deal. And I want to thank all of the administration officials who were dogged in trying to get this completed. This is an example of how we are going to achieve the long-term goal that I set of doubling U.S. exports over the next several years.

And so I want to first of all congratulate Lion Air for their incredible success. I want to congratulate Boeing for making outstanding planes, including the one that I fly on. [*Laughter*] And this is an example of a win-win situation where the people of the region are going to be able to benefit from an outstanding airline. And our workers back home are going to be able to have job security and be able to produce an outstanding product made in America.

So congratulations, gentlemen. Thank you so much.

NOTE: The President spoke at 9:20 a.m. at the Grand Hyatt Bali hotel.

Remarks Prior to a Meeting With Prime Minister Manmohan Singh of India in Bali
November 18, 2011

President Obama. Well, it is a great pleasure, once again, to meet with my dear friend Prime Minister Singh and his delegation.

Last year around this time, I embarked on what was an extraordinary trip to India, in which we continued to strengthen the bonds, both commercial, on the security side, and strategic, between the world's two largest democracies. And since that time, we've continued to make progress on a wide range of issues. The bonds between our countries are not just at the leadership level, but they're obviously at the person-to-person level given the extraordinary contributions of Indian Americans to our culture, our politics, and our economy.

This would be a outstanding opportunity for us to continue to explore how we can work together not only on bilateral issues, but also in multilateral fora, like the East Asia Summit, which we believe can be the premier arena for us to be able to work together on a wide range of issues such as maritime security or nonproliferation, as well as expanding the kind of cooperation on disaster relief and humanitarian aid that's so important.

So, Mr. Prime Minister, it's wonderful to see you again. I look forward to a productive discussion, and I very much appreciate all our cooperation.

Prime Minister Singh. Mr. President, it's always a great pleasure and privilege to greet you. And I recall with immense pleasure your historic visit to our country by the same time last year. And in the last 1 year, we have made progress in every direction, strengthened by our bilateral cooperation in field of economy, investment, trade, in the field of higher education, in the field of clean energy, and strategy and defense relations.

And I am very happy to report to you that there are today no irritants whatsoever in our working together on a multiplicity of areas, both bilateral, regional, and global issues. It's a privilege for India to count you and your administration as deeply interested in ensuring that India makes a success of its historic journey to have the social and economic transformation carried out in the framework of an open society, a democratic polity, committed to the rule of law and respect for full human freedoms.

Mr. President, in the last 1 year, we have strengthened in many ways the path that you set up in your historic visit. And whether it is in civil nuclear cooperation, whether it is in humanitarian relief and disaster management, maritime security, all these are issues which unite us in our quest for a world free from the threat of war, want, and exploitation.

With these words, I once again thank you for giving me this opportunity to meet with you. And that is something which the people of India value a great deal. To find the goodwill that you have shown in your Presidency is something we deeply appreciate.

Thank you very much.

President Obama. Thank you, everyone.

NOTE: The President spoke at 9:37 a.m. at the Grand Hyatt Bali hotel.

Remarks Prior to a Meeting With President Benigno S. Aquino III of the Philippines in Bali
November 18, 2011

President Obama. Let me just say how much I appreciate the opportunity to meet again with President Aquino. He has been an outstanding partner in a whole range of multilateral issues. We just had an excellent meeting of APEC in Honolulu that I was happy to host.

Obviously, the bilateral relationship between the United States and the Philippines is one that goes back for decades. We have a 60-year alliance that assures that we are looking out for each other when it comes to security. But more importantly, we have incredible person-to-person relations between our two countries. Obviously, the contribution of Filipino Americans to the growth and prosperity of the United States has been incredibly important. And I think the Philippines obviously has benefited from their interactions with Americans on a whole range of issues.

This is an opportunity for us to discuss how we can further deepen that relationship; also, to discuss the topics of the East Asia Summit, issues like maritime security, nonproliferation, disaster and humanitarian relief.

And so I just want to commend President Aquino for his leadership, for his reform efforts. And I think that a relationship that's already very strong can only become stronger as a consequence of our continued interaction.

So it's wonderful to see you again, Mr. President.

President Aquino. Thank you, Mr. President. I am glad to have this opportunity to really share our viewpoints and our thoughts on a wide range of topics that you already covered.

It's true, we have one of the longest running relationships, strong based on our shared values and history. And we look forward, in these turbulent times of ours, to really further strengthen the relationships.

So thank you so much.

President Obama. Thank you.

Thank you, everybody.

NOTE: The President spoke at 11:13 a.m. at the Grand Hyatt Bali hotel.

Remarks Prior to a Meeting With Prime Minister Mohamed Najib bin Abdul Razak of Malaysia in Bali
November 18, 2011

President Obama. Well, I just want to say how much of a pleasure it is to be able to see once again Prime Minister Najib. We just had excellent conversations and consultations at the APEC conference that we hosted in Honolulu. This allows us to expand discussions not only on our bilateral relationship, which is strong, and the cooperation that we've seen on issues like the Trans-Pacific Partnership, but it also allows us to discuss how we can best use the East Asia Summit to assure shared prosperity and shared security across the region.

And so I appreciate the extraordinary cooperation that we've received on a whole range of issues. We want to be a strong partner with Malaysia, and Prime Minister Najib, I think, has shown great leadership not only in continuing to boost Malaysia's economy, but also in showing leadership on a wide range of multilateral fora.

So thank you very much, Prime Minister.

Prime Minister Najib. Thank you very much, Mr. President, for your very encouraging words. We believe we have a very, very productive relationship between our two countries. Before this, they've been very strong in the areas of trade and investment.

The United States is our fourth largest trading partner. On a cumulative basis, you're still the largest investor in Malaysia. We certainly look forward to expanding trade and investment linkages. And with the TPP, hopefully, we can meet the deadline next year. We see great prospects in terms of enhancing trade investment between our two countries. And certainly, we look forward to working in other areas as well.

We are very committed to ensuring peace and stability. We're working with you in the area of nuclear nonproliferation. We're doing our part to make sure that Malaysia is not a transit point for illicit goods that can be used for nuclear proliferation, working towards helping you in Afghanistan. And we're looking at new areas of cooperation, including receiving 50 English teachers from United States. They are coming in January.

So I'm excited about the prospects, and I look forward to deepening, strengthening, and enhancing our bilateral ties. And I thank you for your leadership in this.

President Obama. Thank you.

NOTE: The President spoke at 12:04 p.m. at the Grand Hyatt Bali hotel.

Remarks on Burma From Bali
November 18, 2011

Good afternoon, everybody. Throughout my administration and throughout this trip, I've underscored America's commitment to the Asia-Pacific region, but also I've underscored America's commitment to the future of human rights in the region. Today I'm announcing an important step forward in our efforts to move forward on both these fronts.

For decades, Americans have been deeply concerned about the denial of basic human rights for the Burmese people. The persecution of democratic reformers, the brutality shown towards ethnic minorities, and the concentration of power in the hands of a few military leaders has challenged our conscience and isolated Burma from the United States and much of the world.

However, we have always had a profound respect for the people of Burma and the promise of their country, a country with a rich history, at the crossroads of East and West; a people with a quiet dignity and extraordinary potential. For many years, both the promise and the persecution of the Burmese people has been symbolized by Aung San Suu Kyi. As the daughter of Burma's founding father and a fierce advocate for her fellow citizens, she's endured prison and house arrest, just as so many Burmese have endured repression.

Yet after years of darkness, we've seen flickers of progress in these last several weeks. President Thein Sein and the Burmese Parliament have taken important steps on the path toward reform. A dialogue between the Government and Aung San Suu Kyi has begun. The Government has released some political prisoners, media restrictions have been relaxed, and legislation has been approved that could open the political environment. So taken together, these are the most important steps toward reform in Burma that we've seen in years.

Of course, there's far more to be done. We remain concerned about Burma's closed political system, its treatment of minorities and holding of political prisoners, and its relationship with North Korea. But we want to seize what could be a historic opportunity for progress and make it clear that if Burma continues to travel down the road of democratic reform, it can forge a new relationship with the United States of America.

Last night I spoke to Aung San Suu Kyi directly and confirmed that she supports American engagement to move this process forward. So today I've asked Secretary Hillary Clinton to go to Burma. She will be the first American Secretary of State to travel to the country in over half a century, and she will explore whether the United States can empower a positive transition in Burma and begin a new chapter between our countries.

That possibility will depend upon the Burmese Government taking more concrete action. If Burma fails to move down the path of reform, it will continue to face sanctions and isolation. But if it seizes this moment, then reconciliation can prevail and millions of people may get the chance to live with a greater measure of freedom, prosperity, and dignity. And that possibility is too important to ignore.

Later today I'll reinforce these messages in America's meeting with ASEAN, including with President Thein Sein. Meanwhile, when she travels to Nay Pyi Taw and Rangoon, Hillary will have the chance to deliver that message to the Government, to civil society, and to democratic activists like Aung San Suu Kyi.

Again, there's more that needs to be done to pursue the future that the Burmese people deserve, a future of reconciliation and renewal. But today we've decided to take this step to respond to the positive developments in Burma and to clearly demonstrate America's commitment to the future of an extraordinary country, a courageous people, and universal values.

Thank you very much.

NOTE: The President spoke at 12:42 p.m. at the Grand Hyatt Bali hotel. In his remarks, he referred to National League for Democracy in Burma Leader Aung San Suu Kyi.

Remarks Following a Meeting With President Susilo Bambang Yudhoyono of Indonesia in Bali
November 18, 2011

President Obama. Selamat malam. Terima kasih, President Yudhoyono. Thank you so much for welcoming us here today. Thank you for your tremendous leadership and that of Indonesia as you host both ASEAN and the East Asia Summit. And this speaks to your commitment to the region, as well as Indonesia's role as an important leader.

Let me say the obvious: It is wonderful to be back in Bali. This is the first time I've been here in 18 years. I have to say, 18 years ago, this entire development did not exist. So it's a sign of the remarkable development that has taken place here. It is always a pleasure to be here and to have the opportunity to exchange views with my friend President Yudhoyono.

I'm pleased to be here as the first U.S. President to attend the East Asia Summit. This is another example of how the United States is refocusing on the Asia-Pacific and engaging more deeply in regional organizations so we can meet our common challenges together.

Our meeting just now focused on the growing relationship between our two nations. When I was here last year, we agreed to forge a comprehensive partnership across a whole range of areas, and today we reviewed the progress that we're making.

On the economic front, we welcome the completion of a deal that I witnessed this morning, the decision of Indonesia's Lion Air to purchase up to 230 Boeing aircraft, worth at least $20 billion and possibly much, much more. This is one of the largest commercial transactions ever between our two countries, and it's a sign of just how much potential our relationship has.

Today we're also signing, as President Yudhoyono mentioned, a Millennium Challenge Corporation compact that will provide $600 million to support environmentally sustainable economic development, public health, and improved public services in Indonesia.

With regard to security, we agreed to a number of steps that will expand our cooperation, including training and support to help the Indonesian military as it modernizes. And I'd note that this kind of defense cooperation not only helps build Indonesia's capacity to ensure its own security, it helps Indonesia play an active role in promoting security in the region.

Finally, I conveyed to President Yudhoyono our appreciation of Indonesia's regional leadership, which has helped us to achieve real progress on issues like disaster relief, maritime security, and nonproliferation. And I thanked him for Indonesia's efforts to promote democracy and human rights and advance security and peace.

So as I said, I wanted to thank President Yudhoyono for welcoming me back to Indonesia again. I know we're all very grateful for his leadership and for the hospitality of the Indonesian people and the people of Bali as they host these two important summits. And just as we deepen the partnership between our two nations, I am looking forward to the progress that we can make as a region towards greater security and prosperity for all of us.

So, President Yudhoyono, thank you very much.

President Yudhoyono. Terima kasih. Thank you.

President Obama. Terima kasih.

NOTE: The President spoke at 6:53 p.m. at the Bali Nusa Dua Convention Center.

Joint Statement by President Obama and President Susilo Bambang Yudhoyono of Indonesia
November 18, 2011

1. President Susilo Bambang Yudhoyono and President Barack Obama met in Bali on November 18, 2011. The two presidents reaffirmed the deepening engagement between the two countries on regional and global issues since establishing the U.S.-Indonesia Comprehensive Partnership in November 2010.

2. President Obama expressed the United States' admiration for Indonesia's democratic transformation, and the two presidents reaffirmed their commitment to strengthen democracy and human rights in their own societies. President Obama welcomed Indonesia's leadership of the Bali Democracy Forum as part of Indonesia's democracy promotion efforts. President Obama

also reiterated the United States' support for Indonesia's national unity and territorial integrity.

3. President Obama congratulated Indonesia on its chairmanship of ASEAN and the East Asia Summit (EAS); its efforts to promote regional security, nonproliferation, and disarmament; and commitment to making democracy and human rights platforms for ASEAN's development.

4. President Yudhoyono welcomed the United States' inclusion in the EAS, noting it was the first time a U.S. president participated in the Summit. The leaders affirmed the EAS as the region's premier forum for leaders to discuss strategic political and security issues.

5. The two presidents applauded the results of the second Comprehensive Partnership Joint Commission meeting that took place in Bali in July 2011 and emphasized the need to further deepen cooperation under the U.S.-Indonesia Comprehensive Partnership's Plan of Action. The two leaders looked forward to the next session of the Joint Commission meeting in 2012.

6. The two presidents announced a $600 million Millennium Challenge Corporation Compact to support environmentally-sustainable economic development through clean energy projects and sustainable landscapes projects, community-based nutrition programs, and procurement modernization.

7. The two presidents welcomed the outcome of the Indonesia-U.S. Security Dialogue (IUSSD) in Jakarta on September 22–23, 2011 and announced the planned transfer and upgrade of 24 Excess Defense Article F–16s to the Indonesian Air Force.

8. The two presidents celebrated the success of the U.S.-Indonesia Higher Education Summit, October 31, 2011 in Washington, D.C. The two presidents also reaffirmed their support for increased education opportunities that will benefit students from both nations and enhance people-to-people ties, and welcomed continued progress in the U.S.-Indonesia Higher Education Partnership. The two presidents welcomed the commemoration of the 60th anniversary of Fulbright in Indonesia and

the 20th anniversary of the American-Indonesian Exchange Foundation (AMINEF).

9. The two presidents noted their growing cooperation to address climate change and environmental challenges. The two presidents welcomed the signing of a second Tropical Forest Conservation Act debt-for-nature swap, as well as progress by the Indonesia Climate Change Center on science-based policy recommendations for peat lands, as milestones in bilateral efforts on conservation, biodiversity and climate change. They also agreed to work together, including through the Major Economies Forum on Energy and Climate and other international fora, to achieve a successful outcome at the upcoming climate change negotiations in Durban, South Africa.

10. The two presidents also noted the expanded cooperation on clean and renewable energy under the auspices of the U.S.-Indonesia Energy Policy Dialogue.

11. The two presidents reaffirmed the need for decisive action to achieve sustainable global food security. The two presidents set a goal of substantially increasing bilateral trade in food, fisheries, and sustainably managed forestry products, which will expand employment opportunities for both nations. The two presidents welcomed the development of the Advanced Science Center for Agriculture and Food Security and committed to bilateral efforts to increase agricultural productivity and sustainable fisheries.

12. President Yudhoyono appreciates President Obama's approval of the extension of the Generalized System of Preferences (GSP) facility to Indonesia on October 21, 2011. The two presidents reaffirmed their commitment to expanding commercial ties, noting that the newly-launched Commercial Dialogue will further expand trade opportunities and job creation. The two presidents welcomed the significant expansion of bilateral trade and investment, benefitting both countries' economies.

13. The two presidents welcomed the construction of Indonesia's Santi Dharma Peacekeeping Center, with U.S. support, as an important step forward in fulfilling Indonesia's

ambitious goals for increasing its peacekeeping contributions around the world.

14. The two presidents celebrated the ongoing success of Peace Corps in Indonesia and reaffirmed their support for the program's expansion on a gradual basis.

15. Under the framework of our bilateral Science and Technology Agreement, President Obama and President Yudhoyono decided to convene a new senior-level science and technology dialogue in the coming year and to strengthen joint research, education, and exchange opportunities.

16. The two presidents reaffirmed their commitment to work together in the area of public health to meet Millennium Development Goals to reduce deaths of young children and women in childbirth and to stem the spread of infectious diseases, especially tuberculosis, HIV/AIDS, and avian influenza.

17. The two presidents reaffirmed the importance of EAS and reaffirmed their commitment to working together—including through international fora—to promote peace and prosperity in both countries, the region, and the world. They expressed their commitment to work together with ASEAN and other regional partners to address key challenges in the region, including maritime security, disaster preparedness and relief, and nonproliferation.

18. President Yudhoyono congratulated President Obama on the success of the U.S.

Chairmanship of APEC 2011. President Obama expressed U.S. support for Indonesia's APEC Chairmanship in 2013.

19. President Yudhoyono welcomed President Obama's creation of the Open Government Partnership to improve government transparency, and the two leaders committed to rapidly implementing their national action plans. President Obama thanked Indonesia for its leadership on the steering committee of the Open Government Partnership.

20. The two presidents reaffirmed the importance of the G20 as the premier international economic forum, and discussed their efforts to promote economic recovery and create jobs by implementing the Cannes Summit commitments, and call on all G20 members to make progress on achieving G20 goals.

21. The two presidents reaffirmed their commitment to advancing the U.S.-Indonesia Comprehensive Partnership as a dynamic and enduring partnership that contributes to the security and prosperity of both countries. They also committed to work together to find solutions to strengthen international peace and cooperation in light of ongoing global economic conditions, political transitions, and other transnational challenges.

NOTE: An original was not available for verification of the content of this joint statement.

Remarks Prior to a Meeting With Prime Minister Yinglak Chinnawat of Thailand in Bali
November 19, 2011

President Obama. Well, the—I just want to extend my congratulations to Prime Minister Yinglak for her leadership. Obviously, she had an inspirational election. She's now been dealing with an extraordinary tragedy, the flooding that's been taking place in Thailand. I called her and extended our condolences, but also our assurances that we would provide any assistance that we can in dealing with this natural disaster.

The United States and Thailand are two of the oldest of allies. We have established a

great friendship over the years. We have a wide range of areas of common interest and cooperation. And I'm confident that under the Prime Minister's leadership we will continue to build on that relationship for many years to come.

So we look forward to speaking with her on a whole range of bilateral and multilateral issues. And, Madam Prime Minister, please extend our heartfelt condolences to those who have lost loved ones in the floods, and know that you have a strong friend in the United States.

Prime Minister Yinglak. Yes. First of all, I think, from—on behalf of Thai Government and Thai people, have to really appreciate for the condolence from U.S. and all the support from U.S. to give as a heartfelt to Thailand. And also, from the—our dialogue from Mr. President and the visiting of the Secretary Clinton to Thailand, that's really impact to Thailand to have the better relationship between Thailand and U.S.

And thank you again and—our congratulations for the success in APEC. But for me, very regret that I missed this great opportunity. Hopefully, I can go to U.S. in some days.

President Obama. Well, you definitely want to visit Hawaii whenever you get a chance. [*Laughter*]

Thank you so much. Thank you, everybody.

Prime Minister Yinglak. Thank you.

NOTE: The President spoke at 11:14 a.m. at the Grand Hyatt Bali hotel.

The President's Weekly Address
November 19, 2011

Today I'm speaking to you from Indonesia as I finish up my trip to the Asia-Pacific, the region where we do most of our trade and sell most of our exports. And over the past week, the progress we've made in opening markets and boosting exports here will help create more jobs and more growth in the United States.

Here in Indonesia, I was proud to join leaders from some of our Nation's top companies as they announced trade deals that will support nearly 130,000 American jobs and potentially increase U.S. exports by up to $39 billion. Boeing, for example, will sell more than 200 planes to Indonesia that are built with parts from suppliers in more than 40 States. And a deal to export GE engines will support jobs at plants in Ohio and North Carolina.

These agreements will help us reach my goal of doubling American exports by 2014, a goal we're on pace to meet. And they're powerful examples of how we can rebuild an economy that's focused on what our country has always done best, making and selling products all over the world that are stamped with three proud words: Made in America.

This is important, because over the last decade, we became a country that relied too much on what we bought and consumed. We racked up a lot of debt, but we didn't create many jobs at all.

If we want an economy that's built to last and built to compete, we have to change that.

We have to restore America's manufacturing might, which is what helped us build the largest middle class in history. That's why we chose to pull the auto industry back from the brink, saving hundreds of thousands of jobs in the process. And that's why we're investing in the next generation of high-tech, American manufacturing.

But building an economy that lasts isn't just about making things, it's about opening new markets for people to buy them. After all, 95 percent of the world's consumers live outside our borders. And as the fastest growing region in the world, no market is more important to our economic future than the Asia-Pacific, a region where our exports already support five million American jobs.

This is why we recently signed a landmark trade agreement with South Korea that will support tens of thousands of American jobs. And it's why I traveled here this week. In Hawaii, I hosted leaders from across the Asia-Pacific, and we agreed to make it easier for American companies to do business overseas. I also worked with President Medvedev of Russia to pursue trade that would increase exports and jobs for American manufacturers and farmers. And working with other leaders, we made progress towards our most ambitious trade agreement yet, a partnership with Pacific nations that holds the potential for more exports and more jobs in a region of nearly 3 billion consumers.

We may be going through tough times, but as I've said time and time again, the United States still has the world's most dynamic economy, the finest universities, the most innovative companies, and the hardest working people on Earth. We can compete against anybody, and we can win. As President, I intend to make sure that happens by doing everything I can to give American workers and businesses the chance to succeed.

NOTE: The address was recorded at approximately 2:55 p.m. on November 18 at the Grand Hyatt Bali hotel in Bali, Indonesia, for broadcast on November 19. The transcript was made available by the Office of the Press Secretary on November 18, but was embargoed for release until 6 a.m., EST, on November 19. Due to the 8-hour time difference, the address was broadcast after the President's remarks with Prime Minister Yinglak Chinnawat of Thailand in Bali.

Message to the Congress Reporting on the Executive Order Authorizing the Imposition of Certain Sanctions With Respect to the Provision of Goods, Services, Technology, or Support for Iran's Energy and Petrochemical Sectors
November 20, 2011

To the Congress of the United States:

Pursuant to the International Emergency Economic Powers Act (50 U.S.C. 1701 *et seq.*) (IEEPA), I hereby report that I have issued an Executive Order (the "order") that takes additional steps with respect to the national emergency declared in Executive Order 12957 of March 15, 1995.

In Executive Order 12957, the President found that the actions and policies of the Government of Iran threaten the national security, foreign policy, and economy of the United States. To deal with that threat, the President in Executive Order 12957 declared a national emergency and imposed prohibitions on certain transactions with respect to the development of Iranian petroleum resources. To further respond to that threat, Executive Order 12959 of May 6, 1995, imposed comprehensive trade and financial sanctions on Iran. Executive Order 13059 of August 19, 1997, consolidated and clarified the previous orders.

In the Comprehensive Iran Sanctions, Accountability, and Divestment Act of 2010 (Public Law 111–195) (22 U.S.C. 8501 *et seq.*) (CISADA), which I signed into law on July 1, 2010, the Congress found that the illicit nuclear activities of the Government of Iran, along with its development of unconventional weapons and ballistic missiles and its support for international terrorism, threaten the security of the United States. The Congress also found in

CISADA that economic sanctions imposed pursuant to the provisions of CISADA, the Iran Sanctions Act of 1996 (Public Law 104–172) (50 U.S.C. 1701 note) (ISA), and IEEPA, and other authorities available to the United States to prevent Iran from developing nuclear weapons, are necessary to protect the essential security interests of the United States. To take additional steps with respect to the national emergency declared in Executive Order 12957 and to implement section 105(a) of CISADA (22 U.S.C. 8514(a)), I issued Executive Order 13553 on September 28, 2010, to impose sanctions on officials of the Government of Iran and other persons acting on behalf of the Government of Iran determined to be responsible for or complicit in certain serious human rights abuses. To take additional steps with respect to the threat posed by Iran and to provide implementing authority for a number of the sanctions set forth in ISA, as amended by, *inter alia*, CISADA, I issued Executive Order 13574 on May 23, 2011, to authorize the Secretary of the Treasury to implement certain sanctions imposed pursuant to ISA by the Secretary of State.

This order expands upon actions taken pursuant to ISA, as amended by, *inter alia*, CISADA. The ISA requires that, absent a waiver, the President impose at least three of nine possible forms of sanctions on persons determined to have made certain investments in Iran's energy sector. The CISADA expanded ISA to, *inter alia*, require the same treatment of persons determined to have provided refined petroleum to Iran above specified monetary thresholds or have provided certain goods, services, technology, information, or support to Iran related to the importation or development of refined petroleum. This order authorizes the Secretary of State to impose similar sanctions on persons determined to have provided certain goods, services, technology, or support that contributes to either Iran's development of petroleum resources or to Iran's production of petrochemicals, two sectors that continue to fund Iran's illicit nuclear activities and that could serve as conduits for Iran to obtain proliferation sensitive technology. Because CISADA has impeded Iran's ability to develop its domestic refining capacity, Iran has tried to compensate by using its petrochemical facilities to refine petroleum. These new authorities will allow the United States to target directly Iran's attempts to subvert U.S. sanctions.

This order authorizes the Secretary of State, in consultation with the Secretary of the Treasury, the Secretary of Commerce, and the United States Trade Representative, and with the President of the Export-Import Bank, the Chairman of the Board of Governors of the Federal Reserve System, and other agencies and officials as appropriate, to impose sanctions on a person upon determining that the person:

- knowingly, on or after the effective date of the order, sells, leases, or provides to Iran goods, services, technology, or support that has a fair market value of $1,000,000 or more or that, during a 12-month period, has an aggregate fair market value of $5,000,000 or more, and that could directly and significantly contribute to the maintenance or enhancement of Iran's ability to develop petroleum resources located in Iran;

- knowingly, on or after the effective date of this order, sells, leases, or provides to Iran goods, services, technology, or support that has a fair market value of

$250,000 or more or that, during a 12-month period, has an aggregate fair market value of $1,000,000 or more, and that could directly and significantly contribute to the maintenance or expansion of Iran's domestic production of petrochemical products;

- is a successor entity to a person that engaged in a provision of goods, services, technology, or support for which sanctions may be imposed pursuant to this new order;

- owns or controls a person that engaged in provision of goods, services, technology, or support for which sanctions may be imposed pursuant to this new order and had actual knowledge or should have known that the person engaged in the activities; or

- is owned or controlled by, or under common ownership or control with, a person that engaged in the provision of goods, services, technology, or support for which sanctions may be imposed pursuant to this new order, and knowingly participated in the provision of such goods, services, technology, or support.

The following sanctions may be selected for imposition on a person that the Secretary of State determines to meet any of the above criteria:

- the Board of Directors of the Export-Import Bank shall deny approval of the issuance of any guarantee, insurance, extension of credit, or participation in an extension of credit in connection with the export of any goods or services to the sanctioned person;

- agencies shall not issue any specific license or grant any other specific permission or authority under any statute that requires the prior review and approval of the United States Government as a condition for the export or reexport of goods or technology to the sanctioned person;

- with respect to a sanctioned person that is a financial institution, the Chairman of the Board of Governors of the Federal Reserve System and the President of the Federal Reserve Bank of New York shall take such actions as they deem appropriate, including denying designation, or terminating the continuation of any prior designation of, the sanctioned person as a primary dealer in United States Government debt instruments; or agencies shall prevent the sanctioned person from serving as an agent of the United States Government or serving as a repository for United States Government funds;

- agencies shall not procure, or enter into a contract for the procurement of, any goods or services from the sanctioned person;

- the Secretary of the Treasury shall prohibit any United States financial institution from making loans or providing credits to the sanctioned person totaling more than $10,000,000 in any 12-month period unless such person is engaged in activities to relieve human suffering and the loans or credits are provided for such activities;

- the Secretary of the Treasury shall prohibit any transactions in foreign exchange that are subject to the jurisdiction of the United States and in which the sanctioned person has any interest;

- the Secretary of the Treasury shall prohibit any transfers of credit or payments between financial institutions or by, through, or to any financial institution, to the extent that such transfers or payments are subject to the jurisdiction of the United States and involve any interest of the sanctioned person;

- the Secretary of the Treasury shall block all property and interests in property that are in the United States, that come within the United States, or that are or come within the possession or control of any United States person, including any foreign branch, of the sanctioned person, and provide that such property and interests in property may not be transferred, paid, exported, withdrawn, or otherwise dealt in; or

- the Secretary of the Treasury shall restrict or prohibit imports of goods, technology, or services, directly or indirectly, into the United States from the sanctioned person.

I have delegated to the Secretary of the Treasury the authority, in consultation with the Secretary of State, to take such actions, including the promulgation of rules and regulations, and to employ all powers granted to the President by IEEPA as may be necessary to carry out the purposes of section 3 of the order. All agencies of the United States Government are directed to take all appropriate measures within their authority to carry out the provisions of the order.

I am enclosing a copy of the Executive Order I have issued.

BARACK OBAMA

The White House,
November 20, 2011.

NOTE: This message was released by the Office of the Press Secretary on November 21. The Executive order is listed in Appendix D at the end of this volume.

Remarks on Signing Legislation To Provide Incentives for Businesses To Hire Unemployed Veterans
November 21, 2011

Thank you. It is wonderful to see all of you. Thank you for being here. Thank you, Miche, who is a pretty good speaker, so I try not to follow her. But given the incredible work that she and Jill Biden have done in advocating for our veterans, I could not be more honored to be with them. And I know Joe shares my feeling; we could not be prouder of their efforts on this front.

Over the past 3 years, they have visited so many of our troops. They have thanked them for their service. They have comforted their spouses. They have given voice to their struggles. And they've challenged all of us at a National, State, and local level to do more for our veterans.

Joe Biden has been a champion for veterans for decades now. It is his birthday, so we speak in terms of decades. [*Laughter*] It was actually—[*laughter*]—actually, yesterday was his birthday. I won't say the number. You can ask Jill if you want. But for a man who cares as deeply about our troops as Joe does, this bill, I imagine, is a pretty good birthday gift.

Secretary Shinseki is here. Where's Ric? There he is. Ric's been doing an outstanding job leading our Department of Veterans Affairs. And I'm also proud to say that we are joined by some of the Nation's leading veterans' service organizations and Members of Congress who helped make this bill possible.

I have often said that the most humbling part of my job is serving as Commander in Chief to the world's finest military. Not a day goes by when I'm not awed by our troops, by the strength of their character, and by the depth of their commitment and the incredible sacrifices that they and their families make on behalf of our Nation's freedom and security. The men and women of our military don't just fight for each other; they don't just fight for their units or for their commanders; they fight for every single American, for the millions of fellow citizens who they have never met and who they will likely never know.

And just as they fight for us on the battlefield, it's up to us to fight for our troops and their families when they come home. And that's why today is such a wonderful day, because today a deeply grateful nation is doing right by our military and paying back just a little bit of what we owe to our veterans.

Today the message is simple: For businesses out there, if you are hiring, hire a veteran. It's the right thing to do for you, it's the right thing to do for them, and it's the right thing to do for our economy.

While we've added more than 350,000 private sector jobs over the last 3 months, we've got 850,000 veterans who can't find work. And even though the overall unemployment rate came down just a little bit last month, unemployment for veterans of Iraq and Afghanistan continue to rise. And that isn't right. These men and women are the best that America has to offer. They are some of the most highly trained, highly educated, highly skilled workers that we have. If they can save lives on the battlefield, then they can save a life in an ambulance. If they can manage convoys moving tons of equipment over dangerous terrain, they can manage a company's supply chain. If they can track millions of dollars of assets in Iraq, they can balance the books of any company here in the United States.

Our country has benefited enormously from our veterans' services overseas. And we will benefit just the same from their service here at home. And that's why, under my direction, the Federal Government has already hired more than 120,000 veterans. Thanks to the work that Jill and Michelle mentioned, some of our most patriotic businesses have pledged to hire 135,000 more veterans and military spouses. And today we're giving those businesses just one more reason to give veterans a job.

Back in September, I sent Congress a jobs bill. And in it, I proposed a tax credit for any business that hires a veteran who's been unemployed for at least 4 weeks. I proposed an even bigger tax break if a business hires a veteran who's been unemployed for at least 6 months. And if a business hires an unemployed veteran with a disability related to their service, I proposed doubling the tax break that we already have in place.

Today, because Democrats and Republicans came together, I'm proud to sign those proposals into law. And I urge every business owner out there who's hiring to hire a vet right away.

Now, over the past decade, nearly 3 million servicemembers have transitioned back to civilian life, joining millions who have served through the decades. And as we end the war in Iraq and we wind down the war in Afghanistan, over a million more will join them over the next 5 years. This bill is an important step towards helping those veterans transition into the workforce. And beyond the tax breaks that I mentioned, it also contains a number of other reforms, from education and training to career counseling, to job search assistance.

We're still going to need to do more. And that's why I've also announced a series of executive actions to help our veterans back to work. We've set up a Veteran Gold Card; this is a card that post-9/11 veterans can download today, and it gives you access to a suite of career services, including 6 months of personalized counseling at the roughly 3,000 one-stop career centers located across the country.

We've launched an easy-to-use online tool called My Next Move that allows veterans to enter information about the skills they've acquired during their service and then matches that information with the civilian careers that will best put that unique experience to use.

And we've created a new online service called Veterans Job Bank, a partnership with leading search engines that directly connects unemployed veterans to job openings. So all of these initiatives are up and running right now, and you can find them at whitehouse.gov/vets. That's whitehouse.gov/vets.

So to our veterans: Know that we will stand with you as long as it takes for you to find a job. And to our businesses, let me say again, if you are hiring, hire a veteran. Hire a veteran today. They will make you proud, just as they've made this Nation proud.

Now, I'm pleased that both parties came together to make this happen. So once again, I want to thank all Members of Congress who are involved. It is important to note that in addition to our veterans, there are millions of other Americans who are still looking for work right now. They deserve the same kind of bold, bipartisan action that we've seen here today. That's what people have sent us here to do. So my message to every Member of Congress is: Keep going, keep working, keep finding more ways to put partisanship aside and put more Americans back to work.

Tomorrow I'm heading to New Hampshire to talk about another proposal in the "American Jobs Act," and that's a tax cut for nearly every worker and small-business owner in America. Democrats and Republicans have traditionally supported these kinds of tax cuts. Independent economists from across the political spectrum have said this proposal is one of the best ways to boost our economy and spur hiring. It's going to be easier for us to hire our vets if the overall economy is going strong. So there's no reason not to vote for these tax cuts.

And if Congress doesn't act by the end of the year, then the typical family's taxes is going to go up by roughly $1,000. That's the last thing our middle class and our economy needs right now. It is the last thing that our veterans need right now.

So let's keep at it. No politics. No delays. No excuses. Let's keep doing everything we can to get America back to work. And on that note, it is my great pleasure to do my job and sign this bill into law. Thank you.

NOTE: The President spoke at 11:15 a.m. in the South Court Auditorium of the Dwight D. Eisenhower Executive Office Building. The transcript released by the Office of the Press Secretary also included the remarks of the First Lady, who introduced the President. H.R. 674, approved November 21, was assigned Public Law No. 112–56; the VOW to Hire Heroes Act of 2011 is title II of this law.

Remarks on the Joint Select Committee on Deficit Reduction
November 21, 2011

Good afternoon. As you all know, last summer I signed a law that will cut nearly $1 trillion of spending over the next 10 years. Part of that law also required Congress to reduce the deficit by an additional $1.2 trillion by the end of this year.

In September, I sent them a detailed plan that would have gone above and beyond that goal. It's a plan that would reduce the deficit by an additional $3 trillion by cutting spending, slowing the growth in Medicare and Medicaid, and asking the wealthiest Americans to pay their fair share.

In addition to my plan, there were a number of other bipartisan plans for them to consider from both Democrats and Republicans, all of which promoted a balanced approach. This kind of balanced approach to reducing our deficit—an approach where everybody gives a little bit and everyone does their fair share—is supported by an overwhelming majority of Americans: Democrats, Independents, and Republicans. It's supported by experts and economists from all across the political spectrum. And to their credit, many Democrats in Congress were willing to put politics aside and commit to reasonable adjustments that would have reduced the costs of Medicare, as long as they were part of a balanced approach.

But despite the broad agreement that exists for such an approach, there are still too many Republicans in Congress who have refused to listen to the voices of reason and compromise that are coming from outside of Washington. They continue to insist on protecting $100 billion worth of tax cuts for the wealthiest 2 percent of Americans at any cost, even if it means reducing the deficit with deep cuts to things like education and medical research, even if it means deep cuts in Medicare.

So, at this point at least, they simply will not budge from that negotiating position. And so far, that refusal continues to be the main stumbling block that has prevented Congress from reaching an agreement to further reduce our deficit.

Now, we are not in the same situation that we were in August. There is no imminent threat to us defaulting on the debt that we owe. There are already $1 trillion worth of spending cuts that are locked in. And part of the law that I signed this summer stated that if Congress could not reach an agreement on the deficit, there would be another $1.2 trillion of automatic cuts in 2013, divided equally between domestic spending and defense spending.

One way or another, we will be trimming the deficit by a total of at least $2.2 trillion over the next 10 years. That's going to happen, one way or another. We've got $1 trillion locked in, and either Congress comes up with $1.2 trillion, which so far they've failed to do, or the sequester kicks in, and these automatic spending cuts will occur that bring in an additional $1.2 trillion in deficit reduction.

Now, the question right now is whether we can reduce the deficit in a way that helps the economy grow—that operates with a scalpel, not with a hatchet—and if not, whether Congress is willing to stick to the painful deal that we made in August for the automatic cuts. Already, some in Congress are trying to undo these automatic spending cuts.

My message to them is simple: No. I will veto any effort to get rid of those automatic spending cuts to domestic and defense spending. There will be no easy off-ramps on this one.

We need to keep the pressure up to compromise, not turn off the pressure. The only way these spending cuts will not take place is if Congress gets back to work and agrees on a balanced plan to reduce the deficit by at least $1.2 trillion. That's exactly what they need to do. That's the job they promised to do. And they've still got a year to figure it out.

Although Congress has not come to an agreement yet, nothing prevents them from coming up with an agreement in the days ahead. They can still come together around a balanced plan. I believe Democrats are prepared to do so. My expectation is, is that there will be some Republicans who are still interested in preventing the automatic cuts from taking place. And as I have from the beginning, I stand ready and willing to work with anybody that's ready to engage in that effort to create a balanced plan for deficit reduction.

Now, in the meantime, we've got a lot of work left to do this year. Before Congress leaves next month, we have to work together to cut taxes for workers and small-business owners all across America. If we don't act, taxes will go up for every single American, starting next year. And I'm not about to let that happen. Middle class Americans can't afford to lose $1,000 next year because Congress won't act. And I can only hope that Members of Congress who've been fighting so hard to protect tax breaks for the wealthy will fight just as hard to protect tax breaks for small-business owners and middle class families.

We still need to put construction workers back on the job rebuilding our roads and our bridges. We still need to put our teachers back in the classroom educating our kids.

So when everybody gets back from Thanksgiving, it's time to get some work done for the American people. All around the country, Americans are working hard to live within their means and meet their responsibilities. And I know they expect Washington to do the same.

Thanks.

NOTE: The President spoke at 5:44 p.m. in the James S. Brady Press Briefing Room at the White House.

Statement on Iran
November 21, 2011

Today my administration has taken yet another step to further isolate and penalize Iran for its refusal to live up to its international obligations regarding its nuclear program. For years, the Iranian Government has failed to abide by its obligations under the Nuclear Non-Proliferation Treaty. It has violated repeated U.N. Security Council resolutions, as well as its commitments to the International Atomic Energy Agency. In the face of this intransigence, the world has spoken with one voice, at the IAEA, at the U.N., and in capitals, making it clear that Iranian actions jeopardize international peace and stability and will only further isolate the Iranian regime.

Today my administration has taken action to impose an additional cost on Iran for its actions. New sanctions target for the first time Iran's petrochemical sector, prohibiting the provision of goods, services, and technology to this sector and authorizing penalties against any person or entity that engages in such activity. They expand energy sanctions, making it more difficult for Iran to operate, maintain, and modernize its oil and gas sector. They also designate 11 individuals and entities for their role in assisting Iran's prohibited nuclear programs, including its enrichment and heavy water programs. And today we have taken the next significant step to escalate the pressure by acting under Section

311 of the USA PATRIOT Act, identifying for the first time the entire Iranian banking sector, including the Central Bank of Iran, as a threat to governments or financial institutions that do business with Iranian banks. We are joined in this action by the United Kingdom and Canada, who have also acted to cut off Iran from their financial systems today. I welcome these steps and encourage all of our partners to do the same.

As President, one of my highest national security priorities is to prevent the spread of nuclear weapons, including to the Iranian Government. Since taking office, I have made it clear that the United States is prepared to begin a new chapter with the Islamic Republic of Iran, offering the Iranian Government a clear choice: It can fulfill its international obligations and reap the benefits of greater economic and political integration with countries around the world or it can continue to defy its responsibilities and face even more pressure and isolation. Iran has chosen the path of international isolation. As long as Iran continues down this dangerous path, the United States will continue to find ways, both in concert with our partners and through our own actions, to isolate and increase the pressure upon the Iranian regime.

Remarks at PBS's "Country Music: In Performance at the White House"
November 21, 2011

Everybody, please have a seat. Thank you so much. Well, good evening, everybody. I have been on the road a lot lately; I know the entertainers who are here tonight can relate. Johnny Cash was really singing our song when he said, "I've been everywhere, man." [*Laughter*] So I appreciate you all coming out for the best welcome-home party that I've had in a long time. I even see some members of my Cabinet and Members of Congress in the house.

Michelle and I are delighted that all of you are here for the seventh in a series of evenings we've hosted here at the White House to celebrate the music that has helped to shape our Nation.

Now, over the past couple of years, some of the greatest artists from Motown, from jazz, classical, Broadway have honored us with their performances. We've celebrated Latin rhythms and the music that helped define the civil rights movement. And tonight we're transforming the East Room into a bona fide country music hall.

As Charley Pride, who played here 2 years ago, once said, "There is enough room in country music for everybody." And over the past 5 years, I've had the extraordinary opportunity to travel all across America. I've hopped on planes to big cities. I've ridden buses through small towns. And along the way, I've gained an appreciation for just how much country music means to so many Americans.

Tonight we're thrilled to welcome a couple of generations of music stars, some of whom have been singing stories of life in America since before our younger guests were born, before I was born. Artists like James Taylor, Lyle Lovett, and Kris Kristofferson are—[*applause*]—these are among the greats that helped carry country music from regional radio to national popularity. Today, artists like Mickey and Lauren Alaina, The Band Perry, and Dierks Bentley aren't just topping the charts, they're taking country worldwide. I am so pleased to welcome back to the White House one of the enduring voices of country music, Alison Krauss. I love her. And we have Hootie in the house—[*laughter*]—Darius Rucker is now one of the best loved country stars around.

I want also to thank Kris, Lyle, and Darius for joining Michelle this afternoon to lead a workshop on the history of country music for young musicians. It is a proud history that runs from barn stomping to the great honky-tonks to the big stage to the Grammys. It's a unique history that ties together many threads of our immigrant heritage—like the Irish fiddle, the German dulcimer, the Italian mandolin, the Spanish guitar, and the West African banjo—into music that is truly made in America. And at its most pure, that's what country music is all about: life in America. It's about storytelling, giving voice to the emotions of everyday life. Brad Paisley put it simply: "This is real, this is your life in a song. This is country music."

Country music can be about love. It can be about heartache. It can sing sad times, or it can yell out that I'm just here having a good time. And it can remind us, especially when lots of our friends and neighbors are going through tough times, of what we've got to fight for and who we have to be. It reminds us that this is America. This is a place where you can make it if you try. And there is a pretty good Brooks & Dunn song about that. I recommend it. [*Laughter*]

So as we look forward to celebrating this holiday season, let's take the time to appreciate the things that matter most in our lives: country, family, and community. And let's kick it off by giving thanks for a evening of down-home country music. Have fun, and enjoy the evening.

NOTE: The President spoke at 7:16 p.m. in the East Room at the White House. In his remarks, he referred to musician Mickey Guyton.

Remarks at Central High School in Manchester, New Hampshire
November 22, 2011

The President. Hello, New Hampshire! It is good to be back. Hello, Little Green! It is good to be back in New Hampshire, although I have to say that I feel a little winter coming on around here. [*Laughter*] This is what happens when you fly north.

It is wonderful to be here. I had a chance to see backstage Principal Mailhot, and he reminded me of what I said to him 4 years ago, almost to the day, that I was here. It was snowing that day. We were—surprising enough, there was a snowstorm in New Hampshire. [*Laughter*] And we ended up having to leave a little bit early. And we weren't able to do everything that we wanted, talking to some of the students. And we were worried that folks were going to be disappointed, and I promised him that I would be back. I just want to point out, we're keeping our promise—we are back. We are back.

In addition to Principal Mailhot, I want to acknowledge the superintendent, Tom Brennan, who is here with his lovely wife Wendy. Please give them a big round of applause.

Happy Thanksgiving a little bit early, everybody. To the—I understand we got the senior class here at Central High.

Audience members. Seniors! Seniors! Seniors!

The President. All right. You guys are pretty excited about being seniors, aren't you? I want to thank also somebody who is doing outstanding work each and every day, was doing it up here as a wonderful Governor, is now one of your most outstanding Senators in the country—Jeanne Shaheen is in the house.

So before I came to school today, I had coffee——

[*At this point, there was a disruption in the audience.*]

Audience member. Mike check!

Audience members. Mike check!

Audience member. Mr. President——

Audience members. Mr. President——

Audience member. Over 4,000 legal protestors——

Audience members. Over 4,000 legal protestors——

Audience member. Have been arrested——

Audience members. Have been arrested.

Audience members. Fired up and ready to go! Fired up and ready to go! Fired up and ready to go!

The President. All right. No, no, no, it's okay.

[*The disruption in the audience continued.*]

The President. That's okay. All right, okay, guys.

Audience members. Obama! Obama! Obama!

The President. Okay, it's okay. That's all right. Listen, the—I'm going to be talking about a whole range of things today, and I appreciate you guys making your point. Let me go ahead and make mine, all right? And I'll listen to you, you listen to me. All right?

Now, what I was saying was, I was having some coffee with some of your neighbors. And one of them was the Corkerys. You may know, as Mr. Corkery just said, that he's a math teacher here at Central High. And even though a visit from me tends to disrupt things a little bit—[*laughter*]—he did want me to remind all his students you still have homework to do. [*Laughter*]

But as Chris said, he's also a colonel, recently retired after 26 years in the military; tours of duty in Iraq, in Kuwait, in Haiti. And I couldn't thank him enough for his service, because obviously, we know our servicemembers, our veterans, they're the ones who keep us safe, they're the ones who are preserving our freedom at enormous sacrifice to themselves and their families. And in fact, this holiday season is going to be a season of homecomings for folks all across America, because by the end of next month, all of our troops will be out of Iraq.

Now, over coffee, we were joined by Chris's wife of 16 years, Kathy, who owns part of a local business. And they've got two sons; they're trying to save for their sons' college education. And like millions of families all across the country, they're doing the best that they can in some tough times.

And families like the Corkerys, families like yours, young people like the ones here today, including the ones who were just chanting at me, you're the reason I ran for office in the first place. Because it's folks like you who are why I spent so much time up here in the dead of winter 4 years ago. Because even then, we were going through a difficult decade for the middle class: more good jobs and manufacturing that was leaving our shores, more of our prosperity was built on risky financial deals and homes that weren't properly financed. And families watched their incomes fall and wages flatline, and the cost of everything from college to health care kept on going up. And then the financial crisis hit in the closing weeks of the campaign, and that made things even tougher.

Today, many Americans have spent months looking for work, and others are doing the best they can to get by. There are a lot of folks out there who are giving nights up—nights out, they just can't do that anymore because they've got to save on gas or make the mortgage. There are families who are putting off retirement to make sure their kids can go to college. And then there are young people who have gone to college, gotten a whole bunch of debt, and find themselves unable to find opportunity.

So a lot of the folks who have been down in New York and all across the country, in the Occupy movement, there is a profound sense of frustration about the fact that the essence of the American Dream—which is if you work hard, if you stick to it, that you can make it—feels like that's slipping away. And it's not the way things are supposed to be, not here, not in America.

This is a place where your hard work and your responsibility is supposed to pay off. It's supposed to be a big, compassionate country where everybody who works hard should have a chance to get ahead, not just the person who owns the factory, but the men and women who work on the factory floor.

This is a place that's always prospered most when we stay fundamental—we stay true to a fundamental idea, the idea that we're all in this together. That's what we're fighting for. That's what is at stake right now.

So we've been weathering some hard years. We've been taking some tough punches. But one thing I know about folks in Manchester and folks in New Hampshire and folks all across the country is we're tough. We're fighting back. We are moving forward. And we are going to get this right so that every single American has opportunity in this country. We are not going to let—[*applause*]—we are not going to have an America in which only a sliver of folks have opportunity. We're going to have an America where everybody has opportunity. And that's going to take some time, because our economic problems weren't caused overnight and they won't be solved overnight.

It's going to take time to rebuild an economy where hard work is valued and responsibility is rewarded. It's going to take time to rebuild an economy that restores security for the middle class and renews opportunity for folks trying to reach the middle class. It's going to take time to rebuild an economy that's not based on outsourcing or tax loopholes or risky financial deals, but one that is built to last, where we invest in education and small business and manufacturing and making things that the rest of the world is willing to buy.

And we're going to get it done. We're going to get there. And right now we've got to do everything we can to put our friends and neighbors back to work and help families like the Corkerys get ahead and give the economy the jolt that it needs.

And that's why 2 months ago I sent Congress the "American Jobs Act." It's a jobs bill that will put more Americans to work, put more money back into the pockets of working Americans. It's full of the kinds of ideas that in the past have been supported by Democrats and Republicans. And it's paid for by asking our wealthiest citizens to pay their fair share. Independent economists said it would create nearly 2 million jobs, grow the economy by an extra 2 percent. That's not my opinion, that's not my team's opinion, that's the opinion of folks who evaluate these things for a living. But you know what, some folks in Washington don't seem to get the message that people care right now about putting folks back to work and giving young people opportunity.

So when this bill came up for a vote, Republicans in the Senate got together and blocked it. They refused to even debate it. A hundred percent of Republicans opposed it, even though almost two-thirds of Americans supported the ideas in this bill: Democrats, Republicans, and Independents alike. Not one Republican in Washington was willing to say it was the right thing to do. Not one.

Now, what we've done is we've refused to quit. So I said I will do everything in my power to act on behalf of the American people, with or without Congress. So over the past several weeks, we've taken steps on our own to give working Americans a leg up in a tough economy.

We announced—on our own—a new policy that will help families refinance their mortgages and save thousands of dollars. A lot of the young people who are in New York and around the country, they're worrying about student loans. On our own, without Congress, we reformed the student loan process to make it easier for more young people to pay off their debt. By the way, that was building on top of legislation we passed a year ago that said instead of sending $60 billion to banks to manage the student loan program, let's give it directly to students so that millions more young people can afford a college education.

We enacted several new initiatives to help our returning veterans find new jobs and get trained for those jobs. The kind of outstanding young men and women that Chris was talking about, who come home—I was up in Minnesota, met a young man who had been an emergency medic in Iraq, saving lives under the most severe circumstances. He came home, and he was having to take nursing classes all over again, even though for the last 2 years he had been saving lives in the field, didn't get any credit for it. So we're starting to make changes to say if you're qualified to save a life on the battlefield, you can save a life in an ambulance.

And yesterday I signed into law two new tax breaks for businesses that hire America's vets, because nobody who fights for America overseas should have to fight for a job when they come home. Now, I proposed these tax breaks back in September as part of my jobs bill, and thanks to folks like Jeanne Shaheen—and some Republicans—we actually got this part of the bill passed. We finally got them to say yes to taking action that will create jobs and boost this economy.

But there is a lot more that we've got to do if we're going to get folks back to work and rebuild an economy that works for everybody. And next week, Congress is going to have another chance to do the right thing. Congress is going to have another chance to say yes to helping working families like the Corkerys.

You see, last year, both parties came together to cut payroll taxes for the typical household by $1,000 this year. That's been showing up in your paychecks each week. You may not know it, but it's been showing up because of the action that we took. Which reminds me, by the way, the next time you hear one of these folks from the other side coming in talking about raising your taxes, you just remind them that ever since I've gotten into office, I've lowered your taxes, haven't raised them. That's worth reminding them. But this payroll tax is set to expire at the end of next month. End of next month, end of the year, this tax cut ends. And if we allow that to happen—if Congress refuses to act—then middle class families are going to get hit with a tax increase at the worst possible time. For the average family, your taxes will go up $1,000 if Congress does not act by the end of the month.

Now, we can't let that happen, not right now. It would be bad for the economy. It would be bad for employment. That's why my jobs bill extends that tax cut. In fact, it does it one better: It expands the tax cut. Instead of a thousand-dollar-a-year tax cut next year, the average working family would get a tax cut of more than $1,500. And that's $1,500 that would have been taken out of your paycheck, would instead be going into your pocket. And that means you'd be spending in small businesses, and that would increase their business, which means they would potentially hire more people.

The "American Jobs Act" would also cut payroll taxes in half for small-business owners. Say you have 50 employees making $50,000 apiece. You'd get a tax cut of nearly $80,000. That is real money that you can use to hire new workers or buy new equipment.

Now, the Republicans in the Senate voted no on my jobs bill and those tax cuts. But in the spirit of Thanksgiving—[*laughter*]—we are going to give them another chance. [*Laughter*] Absolutely. Next week, they're going to get to take a simple vote.

If they vote no again, the typical family's taxes will go up $1,000 next year. If they vote yes, the typical working family will get a $1,500 tax cut. All right? So I just wanted to be clear for everybody: "no," your taxes go up; "yes," you get a tax cut. Which way do you think Congress should vote?

Audience members. Yes!

The President. Pretty simple. And we set up a straightforward tax calculator on whitehouse.gov—that's our website—so you can see what each vote would mean for your bottom line.

Now, I know Republicans like to talk about we're the party of tax cuts. A lot of them have sworn an oath—we're never going to raise taxes on anybody for as long as we live—even though they have already voted against these middle class tax cuts once. But the question they'll have to answer when they get back from Thanksgiving is this: Are they really willing to break their oath to never raise taxes and raise taxes on the middle class just to play politics?

I sure hope not. This isn't about who wins or loses in Washington. This is about delivering a win for the American people. Now, a $1,500 tax cut for middle class families, that isn't a bandaid. That is a big deal for people. How many business owners could stand to see their customers taking $1,000 less next year? That's $1,000 less that they can spend at a small business.

Now, how many of you could use an extra $1,000, an extra $1,500 in your pocket? It makes a big difference for families here in

New Hampshire and all across America. And keep in mind, we're going to do it responsibly, because unlike several tax cuts that were instituted over the past several years, we're going to make sure that it doesn't add to our deficit. We're asking the wealthiest Americans—the folks who got the biggest tax cuts over the past decade, the folks who made it through the recession better than most, folks who have seen their incomes go up much more quickly than anybody else over the last three decades, exponentially—we're asking them to contribute a little bit more to get our economy working for everybody. We're asking people like me to pay our fair share so middle class families can get a tax cut. And I believe that most Americans are willing to do their part.

The truth of the matter is, I can't tell you how many well-to-do Americans that I meet say to me, look, I want to do more because I know that the only reason I'm doing well is because somewhere along the line, somebody gave me a good education; somewhere along the line, somebody gave me a college scholarship; somewhere along the line, somebody gave me a chance. And I want to do the same thing for the young people who are coming up now. That is what America is all about.

So Congress has a very simple choice next week: Do you want to cut taxes for the middle class and those who are trying to get into the middle class, or do you want to protect massive tax breaks for millionaires and billionaires, many of whom want to actually help? Do you want to help working families get back on solid ground and grow this economy for all of us, or do you really want to vote to raise taxes on nearly 160 million Americans during the holidays? When push comes to shove, are you willing to fight as hard for working families as you are for the wealthiest Americans? What's that—what's it going to be? That's the choice.

As I look around this room and I see these young people, but I also see their parents, I'm thinking, folks in Manchester, you guys work hard. You play by the rules. You're meeting your responsibilities. And if you're working hard and you're meeting your responsibilities, at the very least, you should expect Congress to do the same. They should be doing everything in their power to make our economy stronger, not weaker. They should be doing everything they can to protect the middle class from tax hikes, not hike your taxes.

And this is where you can help. Now, your Members of Congress, they work for you. You've got an outstanding Senator here. She's already on the program. But to everyone who's here or watching at home or online, if your Members of Congress aren't delivering, you've got to send them a message. Make sure they're listening.

Tell them, "Don't be a grinch." [*Laughter*] Don't vote to raise taxes on working Americans during the holidays. Put the country before party. Put money back in the pockets of working families. Do your job. Pass our jobs bill.

Now, the American people are with us on this. And it's time for the folks who are running around spending all their time talking about what's wrong with America to spend some time rolling up their sleeves to help us rebuild America and rebuild our middle class and give young people opportunity. There is nothing wrong with this country that we can't fix.

I was just traveling in Asia over the last week, and let me tell you, this is the fastest growing region in the world. But what was amazing was how everybody still looked to America. They did a poll in Asia. They said, what do you think about America compared to China? Eight out of nine countries in Asia, they said, America is the country that we look to.

They understand that this experiment in democracy—this belief that everybody can make

it if they try; this belief in a broad middle class that lifts everybody up, not just some—they know that that idea of America is more powerful than anything else.

But we've got to have folks in Washington who have that same belief, that same sense that when this economy is going well, it's going well because it's going well for everybody, and when it goes well for everybody, it's good for folks at the top as well as folks at the bottom. And it's certainly good for folks in the middle.

So those values that built this country, those values that all of you represent, that's what we're fighting for. That's what the "American Jobs Act" is all about, that's what the debates in Washington are all about. And we've got to constantly remind ourselves of who we are and what we believe in.

We are Americans, and our story has never been about doing things easy. It's been about rising to the moment when the moment is hard. It's about doing what's right. It's about making sure that everybody has a chance, not just a few.

So let's do the right thing. Let's meet the moment. Let's prove once again that the best days of the United States of America are still ahead of us.

Thank you. God bless you. God bless the United States of America.

NOTE: The President spoke at 12:20 p.m. In his remarks, he referred to Andrew and Nicholas Corkery, sons of Bedford, NH, residents Christopher and Kathy Corkery.

Remarks at the Thanksgiving Turkey Presentation Ceremony
November 23, 2011

Hello, everybody! Well, it is wonderful to see all of you here today. Happy Thanksgiving, and welcome to the White House.

Tomorrow is one of the best days of the year to be an American. It's a day to count our blessings, spend time with the ones we love, and enjoy some good food and some great company. But it's also one of the worst days of the year to be a turkey. [*Laughter*] They don't have it so good.

The rare exception, of course, are the two birds who've joined me today. Now, is Peace here or just Liberty? Just Liberty is here, but Peace is back here somewhere. Some of you may know that recently I've been taking a series of executive actions that don't require congressional approval. [*Laughter*] Well, here's another one. We can't wait to pardon these turkeys. [*Laughter*] Literally. Otherwise they'd end up next to the mashed potatoes and stuffing.

I want to thank Richard Huisinga, the chairman of the National Turkey Federation, and his wonderful family for donating this year's turkey from his farm in Willmar, Minnesota. The turkey's name is Liberty—there he is—and along with his understudy named Peace, he has the distinction of being the luckiest bird on the face of the Earth. Right now he's also probably one of the most confused. [*Laughter*]

Liberty was chosen from a flock of about 30 other contestants for the honor of being here today. And for the first time in history, these two turkeys were raised by four students from nearby Willmar High School.

Now, I'm told that in order to prepare Liberty and Peace for their big day, the students exposed them to loud noises and flashbulbs so that they'd be ready to face the White House press corps. This is actually true. They also received the most important part of their media training, which involves learning how to gobble without really saying anything. [*Laughter*]

So Liberty is ready for his turn in the spotlight. And after he finishes a round of cable hits and a few Sunday shows, he's going to retire to a life of leisure at Mount Vernon, the same place where George Washington spent his golden years.

And later today Michelle, Malia, Sasha, and I will also be taking two unnamed turkeys, who weren't so lucky, to a local food bank here in DC that helps those in need. And I want to thank the folks at Jaindl's Turkey Farm in Orefield, Pennsylvania, for donating these dressed birds for the third year in a row.

A great writer once called Thanksgiving the "one day that is ours . . . the one day that is purely American."

When we gather around our tables tomorrow to share the fruits of our blessings, let's remember what that means. Let's be grateful for what we have. Let's be mindful of those who have less. Let's appreciate those who hold a special place in our lives and make sure that they know it. And let's think about those who can't spend the holiday with their loved ones, especially the members of our military serving overseas. I'd like to thank all our men and women in uniform and their families for their incredible service and devotion.

And that's what being an American is all about. Even when times are tough, we look out for each other. We lift each other up. And we remind ourselves just how lucky we are here, together, in the greatest country on Earth.

So from our family to yours, I want to wish everybody a wonderful and happy and healthy Thanksgiving.

And now, since Liberty and Peace have been so patient, it is my privilege to grant them the official pardon. And I'm going to—I've got to give them a little symbol. [*Laughter*]

[*At this point, the President made a hand gesture and pardoned the turkey.*]

You are hereby pardoned. [*Laughter*] Give him a round of applause.

NOTE: The President spoke at 10:40 a.m. on the North Portico at the White House. In his remarks, he referred to Brianna Hoover, Brenna Ahlquist, Val Brown, and Preston Asche, students, Willmar High School in Willmar, MN.

Statement on the Situation in Yemen
November 23, 2011

I welcome today's action by the Yemeni Government and the opposition to sign a political agreement brokered by the Gulf Cooperation Council to form a government of national unity within 14 days and hold early Presidential elections within 90 days. In particular, the United States welcomes President Ali Abdallah Salih's

decision to transfer executive powers immediately to the Vice President in accordance with the agreement. This represents an important step forward for the Yemeni people, who deserve the opportunity to determine their own future.

For 10 months, the Yemeni people have courageously and steadfastly voiced their demands for change in cities across Yemen in the face of violence and extreme hardship. Today's agreement brings them a significant step closer to realizing their aspirations for a new beginning in Yemen. The United States urges all parties to move immediately to implement the terms of the agreement, which will allow Yemen to begin addressing an array of formidable challenges and chart a more secure and prosperous path for the future. The United States will continue to stand by the Yemeni people as they embark on this historic transition. We also acknowledge the important work done by our GCC partners in supporting this step forward.

NOTE: The statement referred to Vice President Abd al-Rabuh Mansur Hadi of Yemen.

Message on Small Business Saturday
November 23, 2011

From the mom-and-pop storefront shops that anchor Main Street to the high-tech startups that keep America on the cutting edge, small businesses are the backbone of our economy and the cornerstones of our Nation's promise. These businesses create two out of every three new jobs in America, helping spur economic development in communities across our country and giving millions of families and individuals the opportunity to achieve the American dream. Through events such as Small Business Saturday, we keep our local economies strong and help maintain an American economy that can compete and win in the 21st century.

My Administration is committed to helping small businesses drive our economy toward recovery and long-term growth. I have signed into law 18 tax cuts for small businesses, including tax credits for hiring unemployed veterans as part of my American Jobs Act. The Small Business Administration had a record year, providing more than 60,000 small businesses with over $30 billion in lending support. And my Administration has helped provide 1,000 high-growth businesses with $2.6 billion more in capital, while also launching Startup America, an initiative to strengthen access to capital and mentoring while reducing barriers to growth for small businesses.

Through these and other initiatives, we are supporting the entrepreneurs and small businesses that are the engine of our prosperity and a proud reflection of our Nation's character. When small businesses do well, communities flourish and our economy grows.

America was built on the hard work and creativity of our people. On this occasion, we reaffirm our support for America's small business owners and their staff, and we celebrate the proud tradition of entrepreneurship they represent.

BARACK OBAMA

The President's Weekly Address
November 24, 2011

From my family to yours, I'd like to wish you a happy Thanksgiving. Like millions of Americans, Michelle, Malia, Sasha, and I will spend the day eating great food, watching a little football, and reflecting on how truly lucky we are.

As Americans, each of us has our own list of things and people to be thankful for. But there are some blessings we all share.

We're especially grateful for the men and women who defend our country overseas. To all the servicemembers eating Thanksgiving dinner far from your families: The American people are thinking of you today. And when you come home, we intend to make sure that we serve you as well as you're serving America.

We're also grateful for the Americans who are taking time out of their holiday to serve in soup kitchens and shelters, making sure their neighbors have a hot meal and a place to stay. This sense of mutual responsibility—the idea that I am my brother's keeper, that I am my sister's keeper—has always been part of what makes our country special. And it's one of the reasons the Thanksgiving tradition has endured.

The very first Thanksgiving was a celebration of community during a time of great hardship, and we have followed that example ever since. Even when the fate of our Union was far from certain—during a Civil War, two World Wars, a Great Depression—Americans drew strength from each other. They had faith that tomorrow would be better than today.

We're grateful that they did. As we gather around the table, we pause to remember the pilgrims, pioneers, and patriots who helped make this country what it is. They faced impossible odds, and yet somehow, they persevered. Today, it's our turn.

I know that for many of you, this Thanksgiving is more difficult than most. But no matter how tough things are right now, we still give thanks for that most American of blessings, the chance to determine our own destiny. The problems we face didn't develop overnight, and we won't solve them overnight. But we will solve them. All it takes is for each of us to do our part.

With all the partisanship and gridlock here in Washington, it's easy to wonder if such unity is really possible. But think about what's happening at this very moment: Americans from all walks of life are coming together as one people, grateful for the blessings of family, community, and country.

If we keep that spirit alive, if we support each other and look out for each other and remember that we're all in this together, then I know that we too will overcome the challenges of our time.

So today I'm thankful to serve as your President and Commander and Chief. I'm thankful that my daughters get to grow up in this great country of ours. And I'm thankful for the chance to do my part as, together, we make tomorrow better than today.

Thanks, and have a wonderful Thanksgiving.

NOTE: The address was recorded at approximately 12:45 p.m. on November 23 in the Diplomatic Reception Room at the White House for broadcast on November 24. The transcript was made available by the Office of the Press Secretary on November 23, but was embargoed for release until 6 a.m. on November 24.

Statement on the Death of Margaret C. Daley
November 25, 2011

Michelle and I were deeply saddened to learn of the passing of Maggie Daley. Maggie was an extraordinary woman who dedicated her life to public service. While she will be sorely missed, her initiatives on behalf of Chicago's youth live on as national models for how to create environments for children to learn and grow outside the classroom. Maggie's commitment to the children and people of Chicago was surpassed only by her devotion to her family. Tonight our thoughts and prayers are with Mayor Daley, Nora, Patrick, Lally, and the entire Daley family.

NOTE: The statement referred to former Mayor Richard M. Daley of Chicago, husband, and Nora Daley Conroy, Patrick Daley, and Elizabeth "Lally" Daley, children, of Mrs. Daley.

Statement on Representative Charles A. Gonzalez's Decision Not To Seek Reelection
November 26, 2011

For a combined 50 years, Charlie Gonzalez and his father have represented Texas's 20th congressional district in the United States House of Representatives. In Congress, Charlie has fought tirelessly for a cleaner environment, Wall Street reform, and more accessible health care for Texans. As chair of the Congressional Hispanic Caucus, he has worked nonstop to deliver much needed relief to deserving immigrant families and to protect the civil rights of Latinos and all Americans. Michelle and I wish him and his family the very best and join the people of Texas in thanking him for his many years of service.

Remarks Following a Meeting With President Herman Van Rompuy of the European Union and President Jose Manual Durao Barroso of the European Commission
November 28, 2011

President Obama. Good afternoon, everybody. I am very pleased to welcome Presidents Van Rompuy and Barroso to the White House. We have had several occasions to meet over the last year, but this is the first formal U.S.-EU summit that we've had an opportunity to have since the Lisbon summit last year.

Of course, much has changed over the last year. We've seen the incredible transformations that have been taking place throughout North Africa and the Middle East. What hasn't changed, though, is the fundamental bonds that exist between the European Union and the United States. Our common values, our common belief in the rule of law, in democracy, in freedom, in a free market system, all those things bind us together, as do the extraordinary economic and commercial relationships that we have and the people-to-people relationships that we have.

And so this is an extraordinarily important relationship. These aren't always the most dramatic meetings because we agree on so much that sometimes it's hard to make news. As the world's two largest economies and as each other's most important trading partners, we spent a lot of time focusing on how we can continue to grow our economies and create good jobs on both sides of the Atlantic. A large part of that conversation obviously revolved around the euro zone crisis, and Presidents Van Rompuy and Barroso have been very actively engaged with the heads of government and heads of state in Europe to try to resolve this crisis. I communicated to them that the United States stands ready to do our part to help them resolve this issue. This is of huge importance to our own economy. If Europe is contracting or if Europe is having difficulties, then it's much more difficult for us to create good jobs here at home because we send so many of our products and services to Europe; it is such an important trading partner for us.

And so we've got a stake in their success, and we will continue to work in a constructive way to try to resolve this issue in the near future. And I appreciate the leadership of both these gentlemen in trying to address this in a clear and forthright way.

With regard to security cooperation, we agreed to make sure that we continue to place pressure on the Iranian regime to stand down when it comes to the development of nuclear weapons, emphasizing that we continue to hope for a diplomatic resolution that allows them to use peaceful nuclear energy in a way that's consistent with their international obligations.

We have a shared stake in continued progress in Afghanistan, where the EU serves as a leading donor, and next week's Bonn conference will be an opportunity to make sure our security and development agenda is sustainable.

Meanwhile, with respect to aviation security, the EU has been extraordinarily cooperative, and in particular, thanks to the leadership of President Barroso and President Van Rompuy, we've been able to make progress in exchanging intelligence information that can keep our passengers safe and assure that we are preventing any kind of terrorist activity from taking place.

Finally, as global partners in support of universal values, we spent a lot of time discussing how we can be supportive of the best elements of what's taking place in North Africa and the Middle East, continuing to encourage democracy, continuing to encourage transparency, continuing to encourage economic development because we've both agreed that the aspirations that were expressed in Egypt and Tunisia and in Libya are not simply political issues, but they're also economic issues, and that we have to do everything we can to support increased opportunity for young people. These are very young populations, and if they have a sense of a future for themselves where they can work hard and use their skills and talents to develop themselves and support their families, then the likelihood of a successful political transition will exist as well.

Of course, these problems don't only exist in the Middle East and North Africa. We discussed, for example, the situation in Belarus, where we stand shoulder to soldier—shoulder in wanting to see a return to the rule of law and the flowering of democratic practices there; in the Ukraine, where we agree that we want Ukraine to continue down a reform path, and we want to do everything we can to encourage that.

And so both on security issues, as well as on economic issues, we could not have a closer partner than the European Union. There are many issues that don't get a lot of attention, for example, our cooperation on clean energy and green jobs, our continued exploration of ways where we can get increased regulatory cooperation that can facilitate increased commercial ties, a whole range of work that's done by both the European Council and the European Commission that benefits our peoples directly in a multitude of ways.

And so I'm very much appreciative of the partnership that I've formed with these two gentlemen. I hope they have a good visit. I understand they're going to be going to Capitol Hill, and I'm sure they'll receive a warm reception from the Senate majority leader. And I hope that they have a good, albeit brief, visit.

So thank you. Herman.

President Van Rompuy. Thank you. Let me first thank you, Mr. President, for your hospitality you have extended to us at this time of Thanksgiving. And I very much appreciated our discussions we had here in the White House today.

Let me make two points, one on the economy and one on the international issues. First, on the economy: We, the European Union and the United States, have the strongest trade and economic relationship in the world. And we therefore both need to take strong action to address the near-term growth concerns, as well as the fiscal and financial vulnerabilities, in order to strengthen the world economy. It is no secret the European Union is going through a difficult period. It is confronted with a confidence crisis, aggravated by the slowdown in global economic growth.

The Union has done a lot over the last 18 months, and we have taken decisions that were unthinkable just a year ago: in the fields of economic governance, on budgets and imbalances, financial support, and financial regulation. All member states of the Union are all engaged in policies of fiscal consolidation and strengthening competitiveness via comprehensive reforms. But we have to do more.

We are therefore working hard on three fronts: dealing with the immediate crisis, the medium term, while also establishing a sound perspective for the longer term. The 9th of December, I will present to the heads of state and government a roadmap on how to strengthen the economic union of the euro area commensurate with our monetary union. We are aiming for binding rules to ensure strong fiscal and economic discipline in all countries, to go hand in hand with fiscal and economic integration—not only discipline, but also integration in the euro area as a whole.

Improving fiscal sustainability is essential, but it's not enough. Promoting growth and employment is a challenge we share with the United States. The European Union is following a two-track approach on growth: We want to strengthen fiscal sustainability, while at the same time stimulating economic growth and employment by launching reforms, raising competitiveness, and deepening the Union's single market, the largest in the world.

But slower global growth is not only due to the problems in the euro zone. Others have to do their part of the job too, for instance, on exchange rates and on implementing the commitments made in Cannes, at the G–20, earlier this month.

My second point regards international challenges. Not since the end of the cold war has the world seen such a degree of transformation in global affairs. And I'm happy to say that during the last two decades, the world is going in our direction: towards market economy and democracy. In Europe, in Latin America, in Africa, in Asia, and now in the Arab world, sudden events and slow-moving trends bring us into a new world—in the Pacific and in the Mediterranean—and we welcome the new global governments in the G–20, reflecting the growing influence of emerging countries as well as their new responsibilities.

As the President said, Europe's relationship with the United States is built on shared fundamental values. These will continue to provide the basis for our cooperation and our alliance. Since the end of the cold war, there is no East anymore, but there is still a West. The EU's priority is its neighbors, to the south and to the east.

On the south: We worked together with the United States in supporting the economic and political transition process in the Arab world in the wake of the Arab Spring. In Libya, European action was given full support by NATO and by the United States. We both welcomed the democratic elections in Tunisia and in Morocco. In Egypt, we call for a peaceful, democratic

and successful transition to civilian rule. The unacceptable situation in Syria has prompted the European Union to call on the international community to join its efforts in imposing additional sanctions.

And on the east side: The EU and the U.S. worked hard to make Russia's accession to the WTO possible. I believe this will promote world trade and support Russia's modernization. And we also agree on the need to remain actively engaged with our Eastern partners in Europe, and to advance their political association and their economic integration with the European Union. We, however, share the strong concern about the latest signs of politicized justice in Ukraine. The democratic aspiration of Belarusian people also needs to be met.

A word on the Western Balkans: These countries belong in the European Union. We are making progress. And the EU will sign the accession treaty with Croatia next month.

On Iran, we need to step up pressure. The Union is prepared—preparing new restrictive measures, and in Afghanistan, we reaffirm that the Union is engaged in the long term, even after 2014.

Mr. President, let me conclude: Europe and the United States remain partners of first and last resort. Our entente cordiale was a mainstay in the past, and it will remain so in the future.

President Obama. Thank you.

Jose.

President Barroso. Thank you. Thank you very much. First of all, I'd like to thank President Obama for a very useful, substantive, and rewarding meeting. The European Union and the U.S. are longstanding partners and staunch allies. The transatlantic relationship. is indispensable to tackle the common challenges that we face. We have just reaffirmed our determination to work closely together for the stability of the global economy and for the benefit of our people.

I want to reassure President Obama, and also, I want to reassure the Americans: Europe is going through rough times, yes, but we are determined to overcome the current difficulties. I have full confidence in the determination of the European leaders, be it member states or European institutions, to tackle this crisis. We are absolutely serious about the magnitude of the challenge, we understand the challenge, but you have to understand that sometimes some decisions take time. But we are in that direction, and we are in fact taking strong measures for unprecedented situations.

Indeed, problems in Europe are, to some extent, part of a wider picture. The world economy has not yet been able to absorb and overcome all the effects of the 2008 financial crisis. We face the common challenge of bringing debt under control while relaunching growth and creating new jobs. We all know this is not an easy task.

In Europe, we have come a long way in addressing the causes and some symptoms of this crisis. We are now strengthening economic governance of the European Union and the euro area with more robust roles—rules to ensure sound budgetary policies and tackle imbalances. These new rules will enter into force in just a few weeks' time, but we want to go further. Just last week, I have put forward new proposals to further strengthen budgetary surveillance and fiscal discipline.

At the same time, we have an ambitious agenda for growth, based on far-reaching structural reforms. And today, the way forward in Europe is for more integration. This is a point I would like to underline to our American friends: No one in Europe is speaking about coming back. Everybody is speaking, how can we further deepen integration? In fact, I believe that we are now living one of those moments of the acceleration of history. We are seeing that in many parts of the world, in large measure because of the globalization.

And Europe also is feeling this acceleration of history. That's why we have to anticipate some steps in our integration, integration through discipline, of course, but also integration through more convergence, responsibility, and solidarity.

And if there is a silver lining to all of this, it is perhaps that it has shown just how interdependent our economies now are. As President Obama, it is—said, it is a fundamental interest of all of us in the world to solve these euro area problems. Therefore, we need to work ever more closely together. The European Union and the U.S. have the largest bilateral economic relationship in the world. Together, our economies account for around 50 percent of the world's GDP and one-third of total world trade.

European Union-U.S. trade and investment generates 15 million jobs on both sides of the Atlantic. In addition, Europe accounts for approximately 70 percent of foreign direct investment in the U.S., and U.S. investment is three times larger in Europe than in Asia.

So to help ensure that the transatlantic economy can be an engine for the recovery of the world economy, the European Union and the U.S. have today decided to gather a high-level working group for jobs and growth. On the European side, it will be chaired by Commissioner for Trade; on the American side, by U.S. Trade Representative. These groups will examine how to strengthen the European Union-U.S. trade and investment relationship and, in so doing, boost growth and job creation.

This is indeed the first priority: growth and jobs. We have to solve the other issues so that we can relaunch growth and jobs in Europe. I believe this will allow us to further benefit from the untapped potential of our existing strong economic ties. We know that today's world is not just about economy, it is also about values and standards. The European Union and the U.S. share a firm belief in freedom, democracy, human rights. They are the hallmarks of all societies and what binds us together. And the sweeping transformations that are now taking place in the Middle East and North Africa confirm that the values we share are, indeed, universal.

When given a choice, people everywhere choose freedom over oppression, democracy over tyranny. It is in the basis of these values that I believe our relationship will go forward. And today's meeting was a very important, substantive meeting in that direction. I thank you very much.

President Obama. Okay. Thank you very much, everybody.

NOTE: The President spoke at 2:01 p.m. in the Roosevelt Room at the White House. In his remarks, President Barroso referred to European Union Trade Commissioner Karel De Gucht; and U.S. Trade Representative Ronald Kirk.

Joint Statement by the United States and the European Union
November 28, 2011

1. We, the leaders of the United States and the European Union, met today at the White House to affirm our close partnership. Drawing upon our shared values and experience, and recognizing our deep interdependence, we are committed to ensuring that our partnership brings greater prosperity and security to our 800 million citizens, and to working together to address global challenges.

2. Since our meeting in Lisbon last November, the global economy has entered a new and difficult phase. We are committed to working together to reinvigorate economic growth, create jobs, and ensure financial stability. We will do so by taking actions that address near-term growth concerns, as well as fiscal and financial vulnerabilities, and that strengthen the foundations of long-lasting and balanced growth. In that regard, the United States welcomes the EU's actions and determination to take all necessary steps to ensure the euro area's financial stability and resolve the crisis. The EU looks forward to U.S. action on medium term fiscal consolidation. We agree on the importance of working together with emerging economies to foster policies supporting sustained and balanced global growth. We recall our commitment to implement fully the outcome of the G20 Cannes Summit.

3. We recall our G20 commitment to support the multilateral trading system and resist protectionism. We stand by the Doha Development Agenda mandate and recognize the progress achieved so far, but note that in order to contribute to confidence we must pursue fresh, credible approaches in 2012 to advance the negotiations and pursue new opportunities and challenges. We look forward to the upcoming Ministerial meeting in Geneva, which provides an important opportunity to work on such approaches.

4. We applaud the success of the Transatlantic Economic Council (TEC) on a wide range of issues and welcome the progress achieved in secure trade and supply chain security, electric vehicles and related infrastructure, regulatory practices, small and medium-sized enterprises, and in the Information Communications Technology (ICT) sector. We encourage the TEC's continued leadership in helping us avoid unnecessary divergence in regulations and standards that adversely affects trade. We urge the TEC, together with our regulators and standard-setters to step up cooperation in key sectors such as nanotechnology and raw materials to develop compatible approaches to emerging technologies. We also instruct the TEC to pursue its work on strategic economic questions, not least in the field of investment, innovation policy, and the protection of intellectual property rights to level the playing field for our companies in third countries, in particular emerging economies.

5. We must intensify our efforts to realize the untapped potential of transatlantic economic cooperation to generate new opportunities for jobs and growth, particularly in emerging sectors. We are committed to making the U.S.-EU trade and investment relationship—already the largest and most integrated in the world—stronger. To that end, we have directed the TEC to establish a joint High Level Working Group on Jobs and Growth, cochaired by the U.S. Trade Representative and the European Commissioner for Trade. We ask the Working Group to identify and assess options for strengthening the U.S.-EU economic relationship, especially those that have the highest potential to support jobs and growth. The Working Group is to report its recommendations and conclusions to Leaders by the end of 2012, with an interim report in June 2012 on the status of this work.

6. We recognize the vital role of the U.S.-EU Energy Council in fostering cooperation on energy security, renewables and other clean energy technologies, energy efficiency, and effective policies for facilitating trade and bringing clean energy technologies to market. We affirm the value of common approaches toward safe and sustainable development of energy resources and the diversification of supplies. We also call for reinforced bilateral and multilateral cooperation with a special focus on critical materials, smart grid technologies, hydrogen and fuel cell technologies, and nuclear fusion.

7. On climate change, we affirm our intent to work closely together to ensure a positive, balanced outcome in Durban, including mitigation, transparency and financing. We stand fully behind the commitments we made last year in Cancun. We affirm that Durban should deliver on operationalizing the Cancun agreements and helping the international community move a step further towards a comprehensive, global framework with the participation of all, including robust and transparent greenhouse gas emissions reduction commitments by all major economies, recalling the 2°C objective agreed upon in Cancun. With this in mind, we will cooperate closely in other relevant fora, notably the Major Economies Forum. We also intend to work together to address other global sources of emissions, including from the aviation and maritime sectors, in the appropriate multilateral forums and consistent with applicable agreements.

8. As the leading donors of development assistance, we reaffirm our commitment to aid effectiveness, recognizing that our joint efforts to advance division of labor, transparency, country ownership, and accountability will enhance the impact of our assistance. We are coordinating our preparations for the 4th High Level Forum on Aid Effectiveness, and will continue to work closely to strengthen partnerships among all development stakeholders, accelerate progress toward the Millennium Development Goals, and address the challenges encountered in fragile states. In 2012, we have committed to make information on foreign assistance programs more accessible and compatible with international standards, and will encourage the OECD DAC to become an international hub for aid transparency. We request the U.S.-EU Development Dialogue to pursue with vigor our joint efforts in areas such as food security, climate change, health and the MDGs. We agreed on the importance of close cooperation on security and development in the Sahel, the Horn of Africa and Afghanistan.

9. The events in Egypt, Tunisia, and Libya over the past year offer an historic opportunity for successful democratic reform in the Arab world, inclusive economic and social development, and regional integration. The unfolding democratic process in Tunisia is an encouraging example of the potential for democratic transition. Egypt today has just begun a complex election process as the Supreme Command of the Armed Forces begins to transfer authority over civilian functions to a new government. Still, considerable challenges lie ahead. As the two largest providers of foreign assistance to the region who share core principles and values that have helped our own societies and economies to integrate, we pledge to support the democratic transitions underway, as well as broader political and economic reform in the region, including the constitutional reforms in Jordan and Morocco. In Libya we are working together on short term assistance and needs assessments, and will continue to seek new opportunities for greater cooperation, in coordination with the Transitional National Council and the UN, to meet the needs of the Libyan people.

10. Jointly, and through the Deauville Partnership effort, we intend to promote democracy, peace, and prosperity, and to increase economic growth and integration in the Middle East and North Africa. We are committed to collaborate closely in areas such as support for democratic transitions, strengthening the positive role of civil society, and health and education programming. We also extend our support to making women's rights a legal and practical reality in the region. We share a strong interest in economic reform and will also jointly promote best practices that support trade, invest-

ment, and job creation and deepen intra-regional trade and integration. We are both eager to increase our trade and investment links with the region. We plan to work in partnership with international financial institutions to ensure robust donor coordination and in particular to ratify quickly necessary changes to the agreement establishing the European Bank for Reconstruction and Development to allow lending in the region.

11. We call on the Syrian government to end violence immediately, permit the immediate entry of human rights observers and international journalists, and allow for a peaceful and democratic transition. We also welcome the agreement for political transition in Yemen and call on all political actors to help implement it in good faith, and in accordance with UNSCR 2014.

12. We reaffirm the Quartet Statement adopted in New York on 23 September 2011 that provides a framework for direct negotiations between Israel and the Palestinians, and we call on the two parties to engage actively in this effort.

13. On Iran, we share deep concern about activities relating to the possible military dimensions of Iran's nuclear program, as highlighted in the latest International Atomic Energy Agency (IAEA) Director General's report and the November 18 Board of Governors' resolution. We stress our determination to ensure that Iran complies with its obligations, including abiding by United Nations Security Council resolutions, and to cooperate fully with the IAEA to address the international community's serious concerns over the nature of its nuclear program. We reaffirm our commitment to work toward a diplomatic solution, implement UN Security Council Resolution 1929 (2010) and other relevant Security Council Resolutions, and consider additional measures given Iran's continued failure to abide by its international obligations. We also note the recent plot to assassinate the Saudi Ambassador to the United States, the sanctions we have imposed thereafter on five individuals including the head of the Qods Force, and our determina-

tion to ensure the perpetrators and their accomplices are held to account.

14. With regard to the EU's Eastern neighbors, we are working together to support democracy, resolve protracted conflicts, foster economic modernisation, and advance their political association and economic integration with the EU, recognizing in this regard the importance of the EU's Eastern Partnership. We insist that the Government of Belarus immediately release and rehabilitate its political prisoners, and make progress towards respect for the principles of democracy, the rule of law, and human rights; and call on the Government of Ukraine to make good on commitments to uphold democratic values and the rule of law, notably to ensure a fair, transparent and impartial process in trials related to members of the former Government including any appeal in the case of Ms Tymoshenko. The right of appeal should not be compromised by imposing limitations on the defendants' ability to stand in future elections in Ukraine, including the parliamentary elections scheduled for next year.

15. We pledge to continue our close cooperation in the western Balkans and reaffirm our commitment to preserve stability and to support the reforms needed to move the region forward on its path to Euro-Atlantic integration.

16. The United States and the EU have a strategic interest in enhancing co-operation on political, economic, security, and human rights issues in the Asia-Pacific region to advance peace, stability and prosperity. We intend to increase our dialogue on Asia-Pacific issues and coordinate activities to demonstrate an enduring, high-level commitment to the region and encourage regional integration, including through the region's multilateral organizations.

17. We note our continued efforts in Afghanistan and Pakistan, with particular attention to plans for the December 5 Bonn Conference on Afghanistan and the international community's long-term commitment to support sustainable security and economic development in Afghanistan, based on effective and accountable institutions of governance and sustainable assistance levels, after the planned

drawdown of international military forces. We support economic development and wider reforms in Pakistan and note Pakistan's important role and ongoing commitment to combating terrorism and achieving peace and stability in Afghanistan and South Asia.

18. We note the considerable progress made since our last meeting in Lisbon on our commitments on a wide range of transnational security issues that affect our citizens. We welcome the successful completion of negotiations on a new Passenger Name Record agreement, and look forward to its early adoption and ratification. We are determined to finalize negotiations on a comprehensive U.S.-EU data privacy and protection agreement that provides a high level of privacy protection for all individuals and thereby facilitates the exchange of data needed to fight crime and terrorism. We reaffirm our desire to complete secure visa-free travel arrangements between the US and all Member States of the EU as soon as possible and consistent with applicable, domestic legislation. We look forward to a positive outcome for Administration-supported legislation that would refine the criteria for the Visa Waiver Program.

19. We encourage continued efforts to extend our partnership on counter-terrorism cooperation, both bilaterally and multilaterally, including through the UN. We applaud the establishment of the Global Counter-Terrorism Forum, and our cooperation to combat terrorist financing. We strongly support continuation of our joint efforts to empower diaspora communities to counter violent extremism.

20. To strengthen our collaboration on conflict prevention and crisis response, already ongoing in many theaters, the U.S. and EU signed a framework agreement in May 2011 that facilitates U.S. civilian participation in EU crisis management missions. As the trans-Atlantic community faces the challenges of crisis management in an era of fiscal austerity, we encourage further work to strengthen the EU-NATO strategic partnership in crisis management, including on capabilities development, ahead of the 2012 NATO Summit, in the spirit of mutual reinforcement, inclusiveness, and decision-making autonomy.

21. We reaffirm the commitments enshrined in the joint declaration on non-proliferation and disarmament we adopted in 2009 and the joint statement on UNSCR 1540 in 2011. We support the conclusions and recommendations of the May 2010 Non-Proliferation Treaty Review Conference, including the Action Plan and proposed 2012 Middle East conference. We are determined to promote the IAEA's safeguards, Additional Protocol, and the highest standards of safety and security for peaceful uses of nuclear energy, the Nuclear Security Summit objectives, a successful Biological Weapons Convention Review Conference, and the convening of a Diplomatic Conference on the Arms Trade Treaty in 2012.

22. We share a commitment to a single, global Internet, and will resist unilateral efforts to weaken the security, reliability, or independence of its operations—recognizing that respect for fundamental freedoms online, and joint efforts to strengthen security, are mutually reinforcing. We welcome the progress made by the U.S.-EU Working Group on Cybersecurity and Cybercrime, notably the successful Cyber Atlantic 2011 exercise. We endorse its ambitious goals for 2012, including combating online sexual abuse of children; enhancing the security of domain names and Internet Protocol addresses; promotion of international ratification, including by all EU Member States, of the Budapest Convention on Cybercrime ideally by year's end; establishing appropriate information exchange mechanisms to jointly engage with the private sector; and confronting the unfair market access barriers that U.S. and European technology companies face abroad.

23. Our meeting today is proof that a strong U.S.-EU partnership is crucial to building a more secure, democratic, and prosperous world. We know that our ability to respond to and overcome the global challenges we face is increased by the degree to which we can act in close coordination and cooperation. We will continue to seek every opportunity to increase our cooperation.

NOTE: An original was not available for verification of the content of this joint statement.

Statement on Representative Barney Frank's Decision Not To Seek Reelection
November 28, 2011

This country has never had a Congressman like Barney Frank, and the House of Representatives will not be the same without him. For over 30 years, Barney has been a fierce advocate for the people of Massachusetts and Americans everywhere who needed a voice. He has worked tirelessly on behalf of families and businesses and helped make housing more affordable. He has stood up for the rights of LGBT Americans and fought to end discrimi-nation against them. And it is only thanks to his leadership that we were able to pass the most sweeping financial reform in history designed to protect consumers and prevent the kind of excessive risk-taking that led to the financial crisis from ever happening again. Barney's passion and his quick wit will be missed in the halls of Congress, and Michelle and I join the people of the Bay State in thanking him for his years of service.

Remarks Prior to a Meeting With Prime Minister Mark Rutte of the Netherlands
November 29, 2011

President Obama. Hello, everybody. It is wonderful to welcome Prime Minister Rutte and his delegation to the White House.

Part of the reason we wanted to make this meeting happen is because we have no stronger ally than the Netherlands. They consistently punch above their weight on a whole range of issues related to global security. Prime Minister Rutte has been a strong supporter of NATO, as was his predecessor, and we've been able to work together on a whole host of issues. They've made an enormous contribution to Afghanistan; they made a very important contribution to Libya, on antipiracy. On a whole host of issues, the Netherlands consistently is supportive of efforts for our joint security, and we're very grateful for that.

In addition, despite the fact that the Netherlands doesn't have a huge population, they are one of our most important trading partners. The economic relationship between our two countries is deep; it is broad. We are one of the largest investors in the Netherlands. The Netherlands in turn is one of the largest investors in the United States. And so given both of our interests in promoting commerce, growth, and jobs, it is very important that we coordinate with the Netherlands.

On that score, obviously, we're both concerned about the situation in the euro zone, in which the Netherlands has a very significant voice. And I'm going to be interested in hearing from Mark his views in terms of how this issue gets resolved. Because, as I said yesterday during my meeting with Presidents Van Rompuy and Barroso, we have a very deep interest here in the United States in making sure that that process is resolved so that we can continue to grow our economy and put people back to work here at home.

In addition, we're going to be talking about a wide range of global issues, from the Middle East to the situation in Iran, where we both share a deep commitment to making sure that Iran abides by its international obligations, including in the nuclear area.

On that score, I think it's important for me to just note that all of us, I think, are deeply disturbed by the crashing of the English Embassy—the Embassy of the United Kingdom in Iran. That kind of behavior is not acceptable. And I strongly urge the Iranian Government to hold those who are responsible to task. They have a responsibility to protect diplomatic outposts. That is a basic international obligation that all countries need to observe. And for rioters, essentially, to be able to overrun the Embassy and set it on fire is an indication that the Iranian Government is not taking its international obligations seriously.

And so obviously, we're deeply concerned about that situation, and we expect to see some sort of definitive action sometime very quickly.

Overall, though, I'm pleased to say that the relationship between our two countries is extremely strong, as reflected not only in the relationship between our governments, but also the people-to-people contacts. And I'm hoping that I have an opportunity at some point during my Presidency to visit the Netherlands, because——

Prime Minister Rutte. Yes, yes. [*Laughter*]

President Obama. ——because all reports are that it is beautiful and the people are wonderful, and I look forward to enjoying some Dutch hospitality sometime soon.

So, Mr. Prime Minister.

Prime Minister Rutte. Yes. Well, thank you so much. I'm glad to be here and to meet once again with you, Barack Obama. And I hope very much to welcome you to the Netherlands. That would be a great honor and a great opportunity.

The relationship between our countries is very strong. It goes back a long time. And I came to the United States basically to discuss three issues: jobs, jobs, and jobs.

President Obama. Those are good issues to discuss.

Prime Minister Rutte. These are the main issues at the moment.

And first of all of course, our excellent economic ties—bilateral economic ties: 625,000 Americans are at work today because of our direct investment in the U.S. and also our trade relationship. And the total investment of the U.S. in the Netherlands is more than the U.S. investment in Brazil, Russia, India, and China combined. And I believe we can work very hard to have this job engine grow even more powerful.

Secondly, we'll discuss, no doubt, the euro zone. It's the intention of my government to keep the euro zone intact, to keep the euro intact, to fight the debt crisis, and at the same time, get growth and job growth going again in the European Union, which is vital for our own future.

And thirdly, we will discuss, I have no doubt, the upcoming NATO summit, in your hometown, in Chicago——

President Obama. It will be a wonderful visit.

Prime Minister Rutte. ——next year and our transatlantic alliance and international stability and, of course, the situation in the Arab region, where we pull on the same side, where we are working on progress and democracy in the Arab region and in the Middle East.

President Obama. Good.

Thank you very much, everybody.

NOTE: The President spoke at 2:33 p.m. in the Oval Office at the White House. In his remarks, he referred to former Prime Minister Jan Peter Balkenende of the Netherlands; President Herman Van Rompuy of the European Council; and President Jose Manuel Durao Barroso of the European Commission.

Remarks at Scranton High School in Scranton, Pennsylvania
November 30, 2011

The President. Hello, Scranton! Thank you. It is good to be back in Scranton. Go, Knights! The—[*applause*]—it is good to be here. Thank you, Principal Schaeffer, for letting us hold this little assembly here at the high school. [*Laughter*] The principal was bragging about both the basketball team and the football team. I understand they're—[*applause*]—this—right up there? All right.

Thank you, Donna, for the wonderful invitation. We had a chance to visit in the Festas' living room, and just a wonderful family, and their kids are doing great. So I'm really, really proud to be with all of you.

Audience member. Can you come to my house? [*Laughter*]

The President. What did she say? You want—next time, your house. [*Laughter*] All right?

Now, I will say, Donna put out some really good cookies. So—[*laughter*]—I'm just saying. [*Laughter*]

Audience member. [*Inaudible*]

The President. All right.

Now, I also want to bring greetings from somebody you guys know pretty well, a guy named Joe Biden. Joe is in Iraq as we speak, and he's visiting with our brave men and women in uniform, thanking them for their service. And part of the reason he's going now is because pretty soon, we'll all get a chance to say thank you. This holiday season is going to be a season of homecomings, because by the end of December, all of our troops are going to be out of Iraq. They're going to be back home.

Now, I mention Joe, first of all, because he loves Scranton. He was born here in Scranton. He spent his early years here in Scranton. This town helped make him who he is. This is a town where he and so many of you grew up with a faith in an America where hard work matters, where responsibility matters, where if you stay true to those things, you can get ahead. Where no matter who you are, no matter what you look like, whether you own a factory or you work on the factory floor, America is a place where you can make it if you try.

That's why Joe and I ran for this office. You are why we spent so much time in this State a few years ago. Because even then, those ideas—the idea that's at the very heart of the American Dream—felt like it was slipping away for a lot of people. I—it was wonderful visiting with Patrick and Donna, and we were talking about the fact that Patrick's been—Patrick Festa has been teaching in the school system for 25 years now; Donna has been a graphic artist. But they're still worried about if the washer-dryer goes out or if they have to do a car repair. Things are tight. And they're pretty lucky that they've got a good job, steady jobs. For a lot of folks, it's a lot tougher.

And we've gone through a difficult decade for middle class Americans. More good jobs in manufacturing left our shores over the last decade. More of our prosperity was built on risky financial deals and homes that a lot of folks couldn't afford. And a lot of you watched your incomes fall or your wages flatline. Meanwhile, the costs of everything from college to health care were all going up. And then, after all that, the financial crisis hit because of the irresponsibility of some on Wall Street. And that made things a whole lot tougher.

Today, we all know folks who've spent months looking for work. We all know families making deep sacrifices just to get by. We all know young people who've gone to college, they've taken on a bunch of debt, now they're finding that the opportunity that they worked so hard to find is getting harder and harder to come by. So there's a sense of deep frustration among people who've done the right thing, but don't see that hard work and that responsibility pay off. And that's not the way things are supposed to be, not here in America.

But here today with all of you, I'm thinking about something that is probably Joe's favorite expression. And some of you know Joe's story. He went through some tough times when he was a kid. And his father used to tell him, "Champ, when you get knocked down, you get up." You get up.

And Scranton, we've taken some punches these last few years. But there's one thing I know about people here in Scranton, people in Pennsylvania, and people all across America: We are tougher than the times. We are America. We get back up. We fight back. We move forward. We don't give up. We get back up.

And even though our economic problems weren't caused overnight and so they're not going to be solved overnight, even though it's going to take a few more years to meet all the challenges that were decades in the making, we're fighting to make things right again. We're fighting to make sure that if you are working hard and you are carrying out your responsibilities and you're looking out for your family, that you can live a good, solid, middle class life. That is what America is all about. And we are going to be fighting for that every day, every week, every month, and every year that we're in office.

We want an America where hard work is valued and responsibility is rewarded. We're fighting to rebuild an economy that restores security for the middle class and renews opportunity for folks that are trying to get into the middle class. We're fighting to build an economy that's not based on outsourcing and tax loopholes and risky financial schemes, but one that's built to last, one where we invest in things like education and small businesses, an economy that's built on manufacturing and building things again and selling them all around the world.

And we're going to keep fighting to make our economy stronger and put our friends and neighbors back to work, to give our young people opportunities greater than the opportunities that we had.

Now, that's what we've been doing for the last 3 years. But 2 months ago, I sent a particular piece of legislation to Congress called the "American Jobs Act." The—now, this is a jobs bill that will put more Americans to work, put more money back into the pockets of working families. It contains ideas that historically have been supported by Democrats and Republicans. It's paid for by asking our wealthiest citizens to pay their fair share. And independent economists said that it would create up to 2 million jobs and grow the economy by as much as 2 percent. And that's what we need right now.

Now, here's the problem—there is a problem. Folks in Washington don't seem to be getting the message. When this jobs bill came to a vote, Republicans in the Senate got together, and they blocked it. They refused to even debate it. Even though polls showed that two-thirds of Americans of all political stripes supported the ideas in this bill, not one single Republican stepped up to say this is the right thing to do. Not one. But here's the good news, Scranton. Just like you don't quit, I don't quit. So—[*applause*]—I don't quit. So I said, look, I'm going to do everything that I can do without Congress to get things done.

So let's just take a look over the past several weeks. We said, we can't wait. We just went ahead and started taking some steps on our own to give working Americans a leg up in a tough economy. For homeowners, I announced a new policy that will help families re-finance their mortgages and save thousands of dollars. For all the young people out here, we reformed our student loan process to make it easier for more students to pay off their debts earlier. For our veterans out here—and I see some veterans in the crowd—we ordered several new initiatives to help our returning heroes find new jobs and get trained for those jobs. Because you shouldn't have to fight for a job when you come home after fighting for America. You shouldn't have to do that.

And in fact, last week, I was able to sign into law two new tax breaks for businesses that hire veterans, because nobody out here who is a veteran should——

Audience member. [*Inaudible*]

The President. ——we have to make sure that they are getting the help that they need.

So—and by the way, I think we're starting to get, maybe, to the Republicans a little bit, because they actually voted for this veterans bill. I was glad to see that. I was glad that Democrats and Republicans got together with this bipartisan legislation.

Now, there's a lot more to do, though, if we're going to get every American back to work who wants to work and to rebuild an economy that works for every American, which is why we're going to give Congress another chance to do the right thing with the "American Jobs Act." We're going to give them another chance to help working families like yours.

Last year, both parties came together to cut payroll taxes for the typical household by a thousand dollars. Now, that's been showing up in your paychecks each week. You may not be aware of it, because times are tight. But you actually got a tax cut of a thousand dollars this year. Now, I know you hear a lot of folks on cable TV claiming that I'm this big tax-and-spend liberal. Next time you hear that, you just remind the people who are saying it that since I've taken office, I've cut your taxes.

Your taxes today—the average middle class family, your taxes today are lower than when I took office. Just remember that. We have cut taxes for small businesses not once, not twice, but 17 times. The average family's tax burden is among the lowest it's been in the last 60 years.

So the problem is not that we've been raising taxes. We've actually been trying to give families a break during these tough times. But here's the thing. That payroll tax cut that we passed in December of last year, it's set to expire at the end of this year, 1 month from now. If that happens, if Congress doesn't act to extend this tax cut, then most of you, the typical middle class family, is going to see your taxes go up by a thousand dollars at the worst possible time.

Audience member. I can't afford that.

The President. A young lady just said she can't afford that. It would be tough for you. It would also be a massive blow for the economy, because we're not fully out of the recession yet. Don't take my word for it; this is what every independent economist says. We can't let this tax cut lapse right now.

And that's why my jobs bill—part of the "American Jobs Act" was to extend this tax cut for another year. In fact, it does one better. It says, let's expand that tax cut. Instead of a thousand-dollar tax cut next year, the typical working family under my plan would get a tax cut of $1,500. Instead of it coming out of your paycheck, it would be going into your pocket. Now, that's money that you can spend on a small business right here in Scranton. If you're a small-business owner, my jobs bill will cut your payroll taxes in half. So if you've got 50 employees making $50,000 each, you'd get a tax cut of nearly $80,000. That's money that you can then use to hire some more workers and get this economy moving again. That's a good thing.

Now, this really should not be controversial. A lot of Republicans have agreed with this tax cut in the past. The Republican leader in the Senate said it would, quote—I'm quoting here—it would "put money back—a lot of money back in the hands of business and in the hands of individuals." That's what he said. Another Republican leader said it would help small-business owners create jobs and help their employees spend more money, creating even more jobs. One Republican even called it

a, quote, "conservative approach to help put our economy back on track." So what's the problem?

The bad news is some of those same Republicans voted no on my jobs bill and those tax cuts. I don't know whether it's just because I proposed it. I don't know. They said no to cutting taxes for small-business owners and working families. One of them said just 2 years ago that this kind of tax cut would boost job creation, and now that I'm proposing it, he said we should let it expire. I mean, what happened?

Republicans say they're the party of tax cuts. That's what they say. A lot of them have sworn an oath to never raise taxes on anybody as long as they live. That doesn't square with their vote against these tax cuts.

Audience member. [*Inaudible*]

The President. Are they—[*laughter*]—I mean, how is it that they can break their oath when it comes to raising your taxes, but not break their oath when it comes to raising taxes for wealthy people? That doesn't make any sense. I mean, I hope that they don't want to just score political points. I hope that they want to help the economy.

This cannot be about who wins and loses in Washington. This is about delivering a win for the American people. That's what this is about. You know, a 1,500-dollar—$1,500, that's not a bandaid for middle class families, that's a big deal. How many people here could use an extra $1,500? Yes, I thought so.

So I'll tell you what, Scranton. They may have voted no on these tax cuts once. But I'm already filled with the Christmas spirit. There's kind of some chill in the air. [*Laughter*] I saw some Christmas decorations at the Festas'. So I'm in a Christmas spirit. I want to give them another chance. I want to give them a chance to redeem themselves. We're going to give them another chance.

So as early as Friday, this Friday, in a couple of days, we're going to give them a chance to take a simple vote on these tax cuts. If they vote no, then the typical family's taxes will go up by a thousand dollars next year. If they vote yes, then the typical family will have an extra

$1,500 in their pocket. So let's just be clear: If they vote no, your taxes go up; vote yes, you get a tax cut. Which way do you think Congress should vote?

Audience members. Yes!

The President. They should vote yes. It's pretty simple.

Now, if you want to see what this vote will mean for your bottom line, we have this spiffy new tax calculator on our Internet site, whitehouse.gov. So you can go on there, and you can punch in your numbers and figure out what it would mean to your family. But this is real money that would go into the economy at a time it needs it.

Now, I really do think your voices are already getting through, because some of the folks in Congress are starting to say, well, maybe we're open to this thing. Maybe we'll be open to these tax cuts. And that's good news. But I want to make sure that we do this responsibly. So what I've said is, to pay for this tax cut, we need to ask wealthy Americans to pay their fair share. Right?

We're asking—[*applause*]—what we've said is, let's ask the folks who've seen their incomes rise fastest, who've gotten bigger tax breaks under Bush, let's ask them to help out a little bit, because they made it better through the recession than most of us. Let's ask them to contribute a little bit more to get the economy going again.

And I just want to point out, I've done pretty well over these last few years. So I've said, let me pay a little bit more. I promise you, I can afford it. [*Laughter*] I really can. We're asking people like me to sacrifice just a little bit so that you guys have a little bit of a leg up.

And by the way, let me say this. When you talk to most folks who are making a million dollars a year, they are willing to do more if they're asked. Warren Buffett's a good example. They're willing to do more if they're asked.

I—now, I mean, I don't want to exaggerate. It's not like they're volunteering, you know. [*Laughter*] But if they're asked, if they feel like it's going to help middle class families, help grow the economy, help to reduce the deficit, they're willing to help. I can't tell you

how many well-to-do folks I meet who say, look, America gave me a chance to succeed. Somewhere along the line, somebody gave me a good education. Somewhere along the line, somebody gave me a college scholarship. Somewhere along the line, somebody built the information and transportation networks that have helped my business grow. Somewhere along the line, somebody gave me a shot. And so now it's my turn to do the next generation that same good thing. I've got to give something back to them as well.

Because, Scranton, I—this is something everybody in this audience understands. When you think about the history of Scranton and the immigrants who came here and worked hard, each successive generation doing a little bit better, you guys know that what America is about is that we're all in this together, that each of us has to do our own individual part, but we also have to be looking out for one another.

And that's the very simple choice that's facing Congress right now: Are you going to cut taxes for the middle class and those who are trying to get into the middle class, or are you going to protect massive tax breaks for millionaires and billionaires, many of whom don't even want those tax breaks? Are you going to ask a few hundred thousand people who have done very, very well to do their fair share, or are you going to raise taxes for hundreds of millions of people across the country—160 million Americans? Are you willing to fight as hard for middle class families as you do for those who are most fortunate? What's it going to be?

That's the choice in front of Congress. And I hope Members of Congress think hard about this, because their actions lately don't reflect who we are as a people. What does it say about our priorities when we'd rather protect a few really well-to-do people than fight for the jobs of teachers and firefighters? What does it say when we—about our values when we'd rather fight for corporate tax breaks than put construction workers back on the job rebuilding our roads and our bridges and our schools? What does it say about us if we're willing to cut taxes for the people who don't need them and raise them on folks who do need a tax break?

We are better than that. America is better than that. We celebrate individual achievement, we expect everybody to work hard, but we don't believe in every person for themselves; we believe that out of many, we come together as one. We're a people who reach for our own success, but we also reach back for the people—to bring somebody up, reach back to help others earn their own success as well. And we believe that if the folks at the bottom and the folks in the middle succeed, then American succeeds, and the folks at the top succeed as well.

The decisions we make today are going to determine whether or not our kids grow up in a country where those values still thrive. And, Scranton, I don't know about you, but I want our kids to grow up—I want Malia and Sasha and all your kids, I want them to come into a country that is built on those big, generous values, those—an America that reflects the values that we inherited from our parents and our grandparents.

So if you agree with me, I need you to tell Congress where your priorities lie. Members of Congress, they work for you. Scranton, you've got a great Senator in Senator Casey. I love Senator Casey.

So I want you to know, Casey's already on the program. But to everybody who is here, everybody who is watching, send your Senate a message—send your Senators a message. Tell them, "Don't be a grinch." [*Laughter*] Don't be a grin-

ch. Don't vote to raise taxes on working Americans during the holidays. Make sure to renew unemployment insurance during the holidays. Stop saying no to steps that would make our economy stronger. Put our country before party. Put money back into the pockets of working Americans. Do your job. Pass this bill.

Scranton, the American people are with us on this. It is time for folks to stop running around spending all their time talking about what's wrong with America. Spend some time, roll up your sleeves, and help us rebuild America. That's what we need to do.

There is nothing wrong with this country that we can't fix. We're Americans, and our story has never been about things coming easy to us. That's not what Scranton's been about. That's not what Pennsylvania, that's not what America is about. It's been about rising to the moment and meeting the moment when things are hard. It's about doing what's right. So let's do what's right. Let's prove that the best days of America are still ahead of us.

God bless you, and God bless the United States of America.

NOTE: The President spoke at 2:37 p.m. In his remarks, he referred to Eric Schaeffer, principal, Scranton High School; Bridget Festa, daughter, and Patrick Festa, son, of Scranton, PA, residents Donna and Patrick Festa; Sen. Orrin G. Hatch; and Warren E. Buffett, chief executive officer and chairman, Berkshire Hathaway Inc.

Joint Statement by the United States and the Republic of Iraq Higher Coordinating Committee
November 30, 2011

The United States of America and the Republic of Iraq are committed to forging a strong partnership based on mutual interests that will continue to grow for years to come. Our two nations are entering a new phase in our relationship. We have a historic opportunity to strengthen our ties beyond security and build a multi-faceted relationship through

trade, education, culture, law enforcement, environment, energy, and other important areas.

Three years ago, our nations signed the Strategic Framework Agreement (SFA), affirming both sides' desire to establish long-term bonds of cooperation and friendship. The SFA is a lasting agreement, and one that serves as the foundation on which we are building a durable and mutually beneficial relationship. Today, we gather again in Baghdad to reaffirm our commitment to this important partnership and to the principles of cooperation, sovereignty, and mutual respect articulated in the SFA.

Vice President Joe Biden and Prime Minister Nuri al-Maliki convened the SFA's Higher Coordinating Committee on November 30. Together, they affirmed the significant accomplishments under the SFA thus far and charted a course for further joint efforts.

Cultural and Education Cooperation

The Republic of Iraq seeks the cooperation of the United States in its efforts to build a stronger higher education system, expanding English language programs, and preserving Iraq's rich cultural heritage, especially through assistance in conserving archeological sites such as the Babylon historical site, which the United States has helped preserve, and through support to the Iraqi Institute for Conservation of Antiquities and Heritage.

Energy Cooperation

The United States is committed to supporting the Republic of Iraq in its efforts to develop the energy sector. Together, we are exploring ways to help boost Iraq's oil production, including through better protection for critical infrastructure. The U.S. also supports Iraq through training in operations and maintenance, the provision of spare parts, and the development of the Government of Iraq's Electricity Master Plan, which will guide Iraq's electricity sector development over the next 30 years.

Law Enforcement and Judicial Cooperation

The United States and the Iraq believe that an independent judicial system is an essential component of a stable, democratic Iraq. The United States has provided assistance and professional support to develop and professionalize the Iraqi corrections system through judicial training programs for Iraqis through the Judicial Development Institute. Under the Police Development Program, the United States will continue providing advisory and technical assistance to the Iraqi police, including an ex-

change program that will bring groups of Iraqi police to the United States for leadership development over the next three years.

Political and Diplomatic Cooperation

The United States will continue to cooperate closely with Iraq in international fora in pursuit of shared interests. The United States also reaffirms its support for efforts aimed at resolving all remaining Chapter VII issues. In December 2010, the U.S. chaired a special session of the United Nations Security Council to bring closure to several Chapter VII issues dating to the time of the former regime in Iraq.

Services, Technology, Environment, and Transportation Cooperation

The United States is committed to supporting the Iraqi government's plans to improve services, develop its system of roads and bridges, and bring its airports up to international standards. We will improve agriculture and irrigation, support trade, and generate export opportunities through exchange programs between U.S. and Iraqi businessmen. The United States is providing Iraq the expertise it needs to design and implement an advanced banking system that will meet Iraq's current and future needs. The United States pledges to support Iraq in developing its health care services, improving public health, and health awareness campaigns.

Trade and Finance Cooperation

The United States and Iraq will continue their efforts to reinforce their financial and trade cooperation and to strengthen ties between our nations' business communities. For the first time since 1988, the U.S. participated in the recent Baghdad International Trade Fair, showcasing 85 American businesses and organizations and building on the success of the Business and Investment Conference held in Washington, D.C. in 2009. The United States is supporting the Government of Iraq's efforts in the financial sector by providing the technical expertise needed to develop private banks and microfinance institutions. In this context, the United States is developing new lending products for small and medium enterprises, in addition to the roughly $50 million set aside for such loans. Our governments are looking forward to the next meeting and recommendations of the U.S.-Iraq Business Dialogue, a forum of Iraqi and U.S. companies that promises to strengthen commercial ties between our countries.

Security and Defense Cooperation

The United States and Iraq recognize the importance of working closely together in the area of security and defense to strengthen our two countries' security and stability. Through the Strategic Framework Agreement, we have committed ourselves to continuing and strengthening our cooperation, guided by our common interests and shared goals. At the dawn of a new chapter in our relationship, the United States and Iraq stand shoulder to shoulder in increasing our efforts to build a better future for our two nations

NOTE: An original was not available for verification of the content of this joint statement.

Remarks at an Obama Victory Fund 2012 Fundraiser in New York City
November 30, 2011

Well, let me begin by just thanking Jack and Phyllis and their adorable grandchildren. [*Laughter*] And their children—I don't want to skip over a generation. [*Laughter*] But the grandchildren are really my buddies. This guy says he's going to be a future President. [*Laughter*] So I'm just kind of warming up the seat for him. [*Laughter*]

But in addition to the Rosens, I want to make sure that everybody had a chance to say hello to somebody who has been a dear friend and is an outstanding DNC chair, Debbie Wasserman Schultz.

I'm going to keep my remarks very brief at the top, because what I want to do is spend as much time in dialogue and answering questions as possible.

When I came into office, we knew that this was going to be an extraordinary time in the life of the country and in the world. I don't think any of us realized what an extraordinary transformation would be taking place over these last several years. They've been tough years. They've been tough years for the American people, they've been tough for the world, and we're not out of the woods yet. But I begin any meeting like this by saying that we should remind ourselves how much we've accomplished over the last 3 years.

When we came into office, the economy was contracting at 9 percent. It has grown over the last 3 years, not as fast as we'd like, but we have been able to sustain a fairly steady pace of growth. When I came into office, we had lost 4 million jobs before I was sworn in and 4 million jobs in the 3 months after I was sworn in. About 6 months later, we were creating jobs, and we've had private sector job growth for 20 consecutive months.

Along the way, in addition to preventing a financial meltdown and preventing a second Great Depression, we were able to pass a historic health care bill that's going to make sure that 30 million people have coverage. We were able to pass a Wall Street reform package that, although some folks in New York are still grousing about it—[*laughter*]—is going to ensure that we do not have the same kinds of crisis that we had in the past. We were able to make sure that we ended the war in Iraq as promised, and by the end of this year, we're going to have all of our troops out, which is going to be an extraordinary homecoming for families all across America. Thanks to the great work of folks like Debbie, we were able to end practices like "don't ask, don't tell," make sure that we expanded college loans for millions of students all across the country.

So a huge amount of progress has been made, but what we also know is we've still got a lot more work to do. On the domestic front—Jack and I were just downstairs talking—the housing market and the real estate market is still way too weak, and we've got to do more. We're doing some stuff administratively. We're hoping that we can get a little more cooperation from Congress to be more aggressive in tackling the housing market and the real estate market.

We still have to put people back to work. And I was just in Pennsylvania talking about why it's so important to make sure that we pass a—continue, essentially, a payroll tax cut that helps small businesses and individual families so that there's more money in circulation and businesses can really latch on to this recovery and start expanding their payrolls.

Internationally, we've been managing, I think, an extraordinary period not just of two wars, which we're now winding down, but as Jack alluded to, enormous tumult in the Middle East. And so far at least, what we've been able to do is manage it in a way that positions America to stand on the side of democracy, but also be very firm with respect to the security of our allies. And obviously, no ally is more important than the State of Israel.

And as Jack alluded to, this administration—I try not to pat myself too much on the back, but this administration has done more in terms of the security of the State of Israel than any previous administration. And that's not just our opinion, that's the opinion of the Israeli Government. Whether it's making sure that our intelligence cooperation is effective, to making sure that we're able to construct something like an Iron Dome so that we don't have missiles raining down on Tel Aviv, we have been consistent in insisting that we don't compromise when it comes to Israel's security. And that's not just something I say privately, that's something that I said in the U.N. General Assembly. And that will continue.

We do have enormous challenges in making sure that the changes that are taking place in Egypt, the changes that are taking place throughout the region do not end up manifesting themselves in anti-Western or anti-Israel policies. And that's something that we're going to have to pay close attention to and work diligently on in the months to come.

In the meantime, there are other regions in the world in which we're making enormous progress. I mean, we've been able to not only reset relations with Russia, manage relations with China, but we've also been able to mobilize world opinion around U.S. leadership in a way that many people had thought had been lost when I came into office back in 2008.

So the bottom line is this: Over the last 3 years, we have made enormous progress. People aren't feeling all that progress yet because we had fallen so far and some of the problems that we faced, whether it was on health care or energy or employment, those are problems that had been building up over decades. And we never anticipated that we would solve them over night because these problems weren't created overnight. But the trajectory of the country at this point is sound.

The question is, in 2012, does it continue? And frankly, we've got another party that—how will I say this charitably—[*laughter*]—in the past, I think, has been willing, at times, to put country ahead of party, but I'd say over the last couple of years, has not. Everything has become politicized, from the most modest appointment to getting judges on the bench, to trying to make sure the economy grows. Everything has been looked at through a political lens. And that is what people are tired of. And frankly, that's the reason that Congress right now is polling at 9 percent.

People want Washington to work on behalf of the American people, not on behalf of folks in Washington and special interests. And that has been a great challenge. This election in 2012 is going to pose a decision for the American people in terms of what direction we want to go in. There's fundamental differences in terms of direction.

Their view is that less regulation, a shriveled government that is not doing much for people in terms of giving them a ladder up into the middle class, that that's their best vision; that we don't invest in science, that we don't invest in education, that we don't invest in infrastructure and transportation—all the things that made us a great power, they seem willing to abandon for ideological reasons.

And I was so moved listening to Jack's story, because Jack is exactly right: His story is our story. It's my story; it's your story. At some point our parents, grandparents, great-grandparents came to this country seeking opportunity. And they had to work hard, they had to hold themselves personally responsible, they had to take risks. But they also knew that there was a country here where if you did try hard, then somebody might give you a little bit of help; that we were in it together, there were ladders of opportunity that existed.

And that's what we have to rebuild for the 21st century. And that requires us to make some decisions about, are we going to have the best schools in this country, are we going to have the best infrastructure, are we going to do what it takes so these guys end up being part of an America where everybody can still make it if they try, regardless of whether they came from Russia or they came from Poland or they came from Mexico or they came from Kenya, that they're going to have a chance to succeed and live out the same kind of dreams that the Rosen family has been able to live out.

Our kids are going to be fine. And I always tell Malia and Sasha, look, you guys, I don't worry about you—I mean, I worry the way parents worry—but they're on a path that is going to be successful, even if the country as a whole is not successful. But that's not our vision of America. I don't want an America where my kids are living behind walls and gates and can't feel a part of a country that is giving everybody a shot.

And that's what we're fighting for. That's what 2012 is going to be all about. And I'm going to need your help to do it.

So thank you very much.

NOTE: The President spoke at 6:17 p.m. at the residence of Jack and Phyllis Rosen. Audio was not available for verification of the content of these remarks.

Remarks at an Obama Victory Fund 2012 Fundraiser in New York City
November 30, 2011

Thank you very much. You're making me blush. [*Laughter*]

Well, because I see so many good friends around this room, I am not going to give a long speech. What I like to do when I see you guys is just have a good conversation.

We are going through a very interesting time in Washington. We have spent the last 2 or 3 months insisting that Congress needs to act, but that we are not going to wait for them to act, because the American people expect that we're going to be doing some things to make sure that we're putting people back to work and we're getting the economy growing again.

And we're starting to see just a hint of a response out of Congress. Last week, part of our "American Jobs Act," which provided tax benefits for companies that hire veterans, was actually passed and signed into law. Over the last couple of days, Mr. Boehner and Mr. McConnell have both indicated that it probably does make sense not to have taxes go up for middle class families, particularly since they've all taken an oath not to raise taxes.

And so it's possible that we see some additional progress over the next couple of weeks that can continue to help strengthen the economy and get us through what has been a very difficult period not just for the United States, but obviously for the world economy.

We still have a lot of headwinds ahead of us. Europe is probably the biggest one. And I'm spending an awful lot of time making transatlantic calls, because when you look at what's happening in Europe, both to the banks and for countries like Italy that need to refinance their debt, that can have a profound impact on what happens here. But I am cautiously hopeful that they end up recognizing that they need to do the right thing, and we're providing them as much assistance as we can to make sure that the situation is stabilized, because it will have an impact all around the world.

In the meantime, even if we get through this budget cycle, even if we get the payroll tax cut passed, the challenges that led me to run in 2008, many of them are still there. We still have a health care system that has to get more efficient and that has to improve its quality.

And so we're going to have to implement the Affordable Care Act in 2014, and that means I've got to win in 2012.

We still have to implement Dodd-Frank in an effective way that assures that banks are properly capitalized and that folks are not socializing the risks that they take on Wall Street. And we've made enormous progress on implementation, but in order to finish the job, I'm going to have to have a second term.

We still don't have all the energy policies in place that we need to free ourselves from dependence on foreign oil and adequately deal with climate change, despite the fact that we've doubled fuel economy standards on cars and made enormous progress on clean energy, and that means that I'm going to need another term to finish the job.

We have made enormous progress in education and broken through a lot of the traditional left-right arguments about accountability and charter schools and teacher training. But in order for us to implement what is necessarily a decade-long project to get our education system back to where it needs to be, I'm going to need a few more years to finish the job.

On foreign policy, I just came back from an extraordinary trip to Asia. And it's fascinating, here in the United States, it's fashionable to talk about America's diminished role in the world. But you wouldn't know it if you were traveling around Asia, the fastest growing part of the world, where folks are incredibly hungry for American leadership and where we were organizing a trade partnership with most of the major economies there that everybody was eager to join because they recognize that America is willing to play by the rules and those rules can benefit everybody and not just some.

We were able to solidify security arrangements that assure freedom of passage and navigation and help to underwrite the mutual security of the Asia-Pacific region. And what was fascinating was how much people still look to America as a power that is not simply self-interested, but it also interested in the well-being of people outside our borders, and a power—a superpower that not only projects military might, but also projects values.

In the Middle East, obviously, it's an enormous time of transition, and there are going to be some bumpy moments along the way. But we have positioned ourselves squarely on the side of freedom and democracy. And we are, I think, in a position—particularly as we end the war in Iraq and have all our troops home in time for the holidays this year and as we begin to transition in Afghanistan—we're in a position to help shape what, over the long term, could be a transformation in that region that benefits millions of people. And we can do it even as we are foursquare insisting on Israel's security.

And so this is a moment of enormous promise. But I need a couple more years to finish the job. And that's why it's going to be so important that, having worked through all the angst of the last year or two, where people are trying to figure out, why didn't we get everything done in the first 3 years, it's time for us to refocus and make sure that we understand that change that we can believe in was never change overnight, but rather, it was going to be a slow, steady progression in which this aircraft carrier we call the United States of America slowly shifts in a direction that promises more opportunity, more caring for those who need help, more tolerance of our differences, the kind of America we want our kids and our grandkids to grow up in.

We're well on our way, but we've got to finish the job. And for that I'm going to need your help. And that's why, as I look around the room, I could not be more grateful for friends who have stood with me through thick and through thin.

So thank you very much, everybody. Appreciate it.

NOTE: The President spoke at 7:30 p.m. at Gotham Bar and Grill. Audio was not available for verification of the content of these remarks.

Remarks at an Obama Victory Fund 2012 Fundraiser in New York City
November 30, 2011

Hello, New York! It is good to be in New York in the holiday season. Everybody is out and about, there's a little nip in the air, Christmas tree at Rockefeller Center up and lit. Something about this time of year makes this city feel like anything is possible. It is great to be here. And I see some familiar faces in the crowd, so thank you for being here.

We have some special guests. All of you are special, but I want to make sure that you acknowledge them. First of all, the head of the DNC, Congresswoman Debbie Wasserman Schultz, is here. She's doing an outstanding job. One of the finest public servants we have up and coming, New York Attorney General Eric Schneiderman is in the house. The New York City public advocate, Bill de Blasio, is here. And give it up for the folks who performed for you; Ali Wentworth and Regina Spektor, thank you.

Now, I am here today because I need your help. But I'm also here because the country needs your help. There was a reason why so many of you worked so hard on our 2008 campaign, and it wasn't because you thought that it was going to be a cakewalk to elect Barack Hussein Obama. [*Laughter*] If you were going for easy, that was not the route to take. You did not take a poll that told you that this was going to be a sure thing. And besides, our campaign was not about me, it was about a vision that we shared for America. It wasn't a narrow, cramped vision of an America where everybody is fending for themselves. It was a vision of a big and a compassionate America, where everybody who works hard has a chance to get ahead, not just those at the very top, not just those born into wealth or privilege, a vision that says the more Americans who succeed, the more America succeeds.

That's the vision that we share. That's the change that we believed in. And we knew it wasn't going to come easy, and we knew it wasn't going to come quickly. But 3 years later, because of what you did in 2008, we have already started to see what change looks like.

Think about it. Change is the first bill I signed into law, a law that says you get an equal day's work—somebody who puts in an equal day's work should get equal day's pay, because our daughters should be treated just like our sons and have the same opportunities. That's change.

Change is the decision we made to rescue the auto company from collapse, even when some politicians were saying we should let Detroit go bankrupt. Change is the more than 1 million jobs that we saved and the local businesses that are picking up again and the fuel-efficient cars that are now rolling off the assembly lines with that word "Made in America" stamped on them.

Change is the decision we made to stop waiting for Congress to do something about our addiction to oil and finally raise fuel efficiency standards for the first time in 30 years. And because of that, by the next decade, we'll be driving cars that get 55 miles a gallon at least. That's what change is.

Change is the fight we won to stop handing out $60 billion worth of tax subsidies to banks and put that $60 billion into student loans. And today, millions of students are getting more help going to college at a time when they need it most. That's because of your work in 2008.

Change is health care reform that we passed after a century of trying, reform that will finally ensure that in the United States of America, nobody is going to go bankrupt because they get sick. And you've got a million young people who are already with health insurance today, on their parent's plan because of the laws that we passed. Change is the millions of Americans who can no longer be denied or dropped from their health insurance at a time when they need the care the most. That's what change is.

Change is the fact that for the first time in history, you don't have to hide who you love in order to serve the country that you love—ending "don't ask, don't tell." Change is keeping one of the first promises I made in 2008: By the end of December, the war in Iraq will be officially over, our troops are coming home. They will be rejoining their families for the holidays.

And it hasn't made us weaker, it's made us stronger. We've refocused our efforts on the terrorists who actually carried out 9/11. And thanks to our brave men and women in uniform, Al Qaida is weaker than it has ever been and Usama bin Laden will never walk this Earth again. That's because of what you did in 2008.

A lot of this wasn't easy. Some of it was risky. It came in the face of tough opposition and powerful lobbyists and special interests who spent millions of dollars to keep things the way they were. It's no secret that the steps we took haven't always been politically popular with the crowd in Washington. But all this progress was made because of you, because you stood up and made your voices heard, because you knocked on doors and you made phone calls and sent out e-mails. And you kept up the fight for change long after the election was over.

You should be proud of what got done. It should make you hopeful. But it can't make us complacent, because everything that we fought for during the last election and everything that we still have to do to make sure this country gives a fair shot to everybody is at stake in 2012. Every single thing that we care about is at stake in this next election. The very core of what this country stands for is on the line. The basic promise that no matter who you are, no matter where you come from, this is a place where you can make it if we try.

You know, I just came from another fundraising event at the home of somebody now extraordinarily successful. His parents were Holocaust survivors, and he described, in introducing me, how they were able to come over here with almost nothing and yet still provide a good public education for their kids and still give them a leg up and allow them to succeed. And the question is, 20 years from now, 30 years from now, are we going to be able to say the same thing about the next generation coming up?

The crisis that struck in the months before I took office put more Americans out of work than at any time since the Great Depression. And if you actually look at a chart, 3 months before I was sworn in we lost 4 million jobs; 3 months after I was sworn in we lost another 4 million. A few months later, because of our economic policies, the economy started to grow again and people started going to work again. And we've had private sector job growth for 21 consecutive months.

But that 8 million that lost their jobs, it has been brutal. And it was the culmination of a decade in which the middle class fell further and further behind. More good jobs in manufacturing left our shores. More of our prosperity was built on risky financial deals or on a housing bubble, and we racked up greater piles of debt, even as our incomes fell and our wages flatlined and the cost of everything from college to health care kept on going up.

These problems didn't happen overnight, and they weren't going to be solved overnight. And it's going to take more than a few years to meet the challenges that had been decades in the making. The American people understand that. But what the American people don't understand are leaders who refuse to take action at such a critical time in this Nation's history. They're sick and tired of watching people who are supposed to represent America put party ahead of country or the next election ahead of the next generation.

President Kennedy used to say, after he took office, what surprised him most about Washington was finding out that things were just as bad as he'd been saying they were. [*Laughter*] And I can relate to that. [*Laughter*] When you've got the top Republican in the Senate saying almost from the get-go that his number-one concern, his party's number-one priority, wasn't to fix the economy, wasn't to put people back to work, but was to beat the President, then you get a sense that things really aren't on the level.

That's how you end up with Republicans in Congress voting against all kinds of jobs proposals that they supported in the past: tax cuts for workers, tax cuts for small businesses, rebuilding roads and bridges, putting cops and teachers back to work. And they're at it again right now.

Last year, right around this time, both parties came together to cut payroll taxes for the typical household by a thousand dollars this year. And that helped boost the economy at a time when it was weak. And it is still weak, so we should be doing the same thing. Except the tax cut is set to expire by the end of this month, and if that happens, a typical middle class family will see a thousand-dollar tax increase at the worst possible time for the economy and for these families.

So what I've said is, let's not just extend that tax cut another year to help folks get back on solid footing, let's expand it. Let's give the typical working family a $1,500 tax cut. And while we're at it, let's cut taxes for small businesses who are creating jobs in America. Some Republicans used to love these tax cuts, until I proposed them. [*Laughter*] Suddenly, they've started lining up against them. A lot of them have sworn—they've taken an oath: "We're never going to raise taxes as long as we live"—religion.

But now they're voting against this tax cut, and as a consequence, you could potentially see working folks see an extra thousand dollars coming out of their paycheck this year. They'll fight with everything they have to protect the tax cuts of the wealthiest Americans, but they've got no problem breaking the oath when it comes to raising taxes on middle class families, just to score some political points.

And they may think that's a smart political strategy, although I'm noticing that over the last couple of days they've been realizing this may not work out so well for them. [*Laughter*] It's not a strategy to create jobs. It's not a strategy to help middle class families who have been working two to three shifts just to put food on the table. And it's not a strategy to help America succeed, and we've all got a stake in that.

If you were able to come to this fundraiser, you've probably got a job, and you're doing pretty well, relatively speaking. But you know what, our success depends on everybody's suc-

cess. If you've got a business, you need customers. If you're a law firm, you need clients. If you've got a restaurant, you need somebody who can afford to buy dinner at your restaurant. If you are a parent, then it's not good enough that you can get a good education for your child, because your child's success is going to depend on how well educated every child is in this country.

We have a choice in 2012. The question is not whether people are still hurting or whether the economy is growing as fast as it should be—it is not. A lot of folks are still hurting out there. Of course, the economy is still struggling. The question is, what are we going to do about it; what vision do we have for where we want to take this country? And it is not a technical question, it is a values question. It's about who we are, what we believe in. And that's the debate that we're going to have to have over the next year. It's about where we're going to go.

The Republicans in Congress and the candidates who are running for President—I hope all of you are watching these Republican debates. [*Laughter*] You need to see what's going on to get a sense of what's at stake. [*Laughter*] They've got a very specific idea about where they want to take this country. They want to reduce the deficit, which we need to do, not in a balanced way, but by gutting our investments in education, by slashing spending in research and technology, by letting our infrastructure, our roads and our bridges and our airports, crumble.

Now, I believe that since I already signed a law that reduced our deficit by a trillion dollars and I proposed to do another $2.5 million in deficit reduction, I've got some credibility in saying that I'm prepared to make some tough decisions to close that gap. But we've got to do it in a way that is fair for everybody. And that means asking the wealthiest among us to do our fair share. That we don't just ask for sacrifices from seniors, we don't just ask for sacrifices from union members, we don't just ask for sacrifices from teachers, we ask for sacrifices from the people who are in the best position to sacrifice. That's a fundamental difference in—

[*applause*]—it's a fundamental difference in our vision about where we want to take this country.

The Republicans in Congress and on the campaign trail want to make Medicare a form of private insurance that seniors have to shop for with a voucher that most independent analysts say won't cover the full cost of their health care. Now, I believe we can lower the cost of Medicare—and we need to—with reforms that still guarantee a dignified retirement that our seniors have earned. That's what I believe. That is a values question. It is not just a technical question.

They think the best way for America to compete for new jobs and businesses is to follow other countries in a race to the bottom. So their attitude is, well, since places like China allow companies to pay much lower wages, let's roll back our minimum wage. Let's eliminate our right to organize here at home. Since other countries allow corporations to pollute as much as they want, we need to get rid of our regulations that protect us from dirty air and dirty water.

I don't think we should have any more regulations than the health and safety of the American people require. And I've already made reforms that will save businesses billions of dollars. We've put in place fewer regulations than the Bush administration, although the benefits have been a lot higher.

But I don't believe that a race to the bottom is a race that America should try to win. We should be in a race to the top. And that is a race we can win. We shouldn't be competing to see if we can pay the lowest wages, we should be competing to see if our schools are the envy of the world. If we're giving our workers the best skills and the best training and we're putting a college education within the reach of every young person who wants to go, that should be the race that we're trying to win.

We should be in a race to give our businesses the best access to the newest airports and the newest roads and the newest bridges, the most Internet access. We should be in a race to support the scientists and researchers who are trying to make the next breakthrough in clean energy or medicine and make it happen right here in the United States of America. That's the race we should be in.

We should be in a race to make sure that the next generation of manufacturing takes root not in Asia, not in Europe, but in Detroit and Cleveland and Pittsburgh and here in New York. I don't want this country to just be known for buying and consuming. I want us to be known for building and selling products all around the world. That's what we should be focused on. And this competition for new jobs and new businesses, middle class security, that's a race we can win. That's a race we can win.

You know, I took a trip to Asia, and here, sometimes the pundits and the newspapers and the TV commentators love to talk about how America is slipping and America is in decline, and you know what, that's not what you feel when you're in Asia. They're looking to us for leadership. They know that America is great not just because we're powerful, but also because we have a set of values that the world admires, that we don't just think about what's good for us, but we're also thinking about what's good for the world. That's what makes us special. That's what makes us exceptional.

But we can't win this race and we can't continue American leadership with an attitude that says, it's every American for themselves. We're not going to win it if our whole philosophy is built on handing out more tax cuts to people who don't need them and weren't even asking for them and telling companies, don't worry, you can play by your own set of rules regardless of the consequences, and hope that the success of the wealthiest few translates somehow into prosperity for everybody else. That is not how America was built. That theory does not work. It didn't work when Herbert Hoover called it "trickle-down economics" before the Depression. It didn't work when we tried it in the last decade. It won't work today.

It won't work because we aren't a country that practices survival of the fittest. We believe in the survival of the Nation, and we believe that we all have a stake in each other's success. We believe that if we can attract outstanding teachers to the profession by giving him or her the pay that they deserve and that teacher goes on to educate some real smart kid, the next Steve Jobs, we all benefit. That's good for all of us. If we provide faster Internet service to rural America and that store owner out in some small town is now selling his goods all around the world, that's good for all of us. If we build a new bridge that saves a shipping company time and money, workers and customers all over the country will do better. If we have rules in place that protect consumers from unscrupulous financial practices, that will be good for the consumer, and by the way, that will be good for the financial system.

This idea has not been, historically, a Democratic or a Republican idea, this is an American idea. The first Republican President—pretty good President, guy named Abraham Lincoln—[*laughter*]—launched the transcontinental railroad, the National Academy of Sciences, the first land-grant colleges, Government programs in the middle of a Civil War. It was a Republican—Teddy Roosevelt—who called for a progressive income tax, saying, you know what, I want each generation to have opportunity, and we don't want just a small segment of our society that is able to amass more and more political power. It was a Republican—Dwight Eisenhower—who built the Interstate Highway System. Republicans participated with FDR in giving millions of returning heroes, including my grandfather, the chance to go to college on the GI bill. This is an American idea.

And that same spirit of common purpose, it still exists. I see it every single day, maybe not always in Washington, but out in America, it's there. Here in New York, it's there. It's in small towns, it's in big cities. You talk to folks on Main Streets, you talk to folks in town halls, you go to a diner, our politics may be divided, but most Americans still understand we will stand or fall together. And no matter who we are, no matter where we come from, we're one Nation, and we're one people. And that's what's at stake in this election. That's what this election is all about.

Now, I know it has been 3 wrenching years for this country. And when you look back at 2008, I think a lot of folks thought, boy, this is so exciting, and it's going to just—we're going to snap our fingers, and as soon as we get in there everything will be solved. And after all that's happened in Washington, it may be tempting to believe that, you know what, change isn't as possible as we thought. But I've got to remind people of what I said not just during the campaign, but even on the night we won. I said real change, big change, is hard. It takes time. It takes more than a single term. It may take more than a single President. It requires ordinary citizens who are committed to keep—continuing the fight, to keep pushing, to keep inching this country closer to its highest ideals.

It's how this Nation was created: a band of colonists deciding, you know what, we're going to try this new idea, a government of and by and for the people. It's how the greatest generation was able to overcome more than a decade of war and a depression to build the largest middle class in history.

It's how young people fought against billy clubs and fire hoses and dogs to ensure that their kids and their grandkids could grow up in a country where there was no barrier to who you can become.

Change has always been hard, but it's possible. I've seen it, and I have lived it, and so have many of you. So you know, I've been saying at some of these fundraisers and events around the country, you know, I know I'm a little grayer than I was. [*Laughter*] And I know that the cynicism has risen again since the last election. And I know that folks are frustrated with Washington. But the only way to end the game-playing and the point-scoring that passes for politics this day is to send a message in this election that we are not backing down, we are not giving up, that we are going to keep pushing and we continue to fight and we still hope and we are still going after change that we believe in.

And I'm going to need you to do it. I've often—I've said—I said this all the time during the campaign: I am not a perfect man; I will not be a perfect President. But there are some things I can promise you: I will always tell you what I believe in, I will always tell you where I stand, and every single day I am thinking about you, your families, our kids, and how we can make America work for everybody. That's always been my promise. And I've kept that promise.

So if you're willing to keep pushing through all the frustrations that we may see and if you keep reminding yourselves of all that we've accomplished so far and if you keep your eyes on that prize, all the things that we can accomplish over the next 5 years, change will come.

If you are willing to work harder in this election than you did in the last election, change will come. If you are willing to get on the phone again and knock on doors again, change will come. If you stick with me on this, change will come. Press on, everybody. Change will come.

God bless you. God bless the United States of America.

NOTE: The President spoke at 9:09 p.m. at the Sheraton New York Hotel & Towers. In his remarks, he referred to Jack Rosen, chair, American Jewish Congress.

Remarks at George Washington University
December 1, 2011

Well, thank you, Sanjay. It is an honor to be with you today and to follow President Kikwete and President Bush. To Bono and Alicia, to the ONE campaign, thank you for bringing us together. Because of your work, all across Africa there are children who are no longer starving, mothers who are no longer dying of treatable diseases, fathers who are again providing for their families. And because of all of you, so many people are now blessed with hope.

We've got Members of Congress who have done so much for this cause who are here today, and we want to thank them. Let me also thank President Bush for joining us from Tanzania and for his bold leadership on this issue. I believe that history will record the President's Emergency Plan for AIDS Relief as one of his greatest legacies. And that program, more ambitious than even the leading advocates thought was possible at the time, has saved thousands and thousands and thousands of lives and spurred international action and laid the foundation for a comprehensive global plan that will impact the lives of millions. And we are proud that we have the opportunity to carry that work forward.

Today is a remarkable day. Today we come together as a global community, across continents, across faiths and cultures, to renew our commitment to ending the AIDS pandemic once and for all.

Now, if you go back and you look at the themes of past World AIDS Days, if you read them one after another, you'll see the story of how the human race has confronted one of the most devastating pandemics in our history. You'll see that in those early years, when we started losing good men and women to a disease that no one truly understood, it was about ringing the alarm, calling for global action, proving that this deadly disease was not isolated to one area or one group of people.

And that's part of what makes today so remarkable, because back in those early years, few could have imagined this day, that we would be looking ahead to the beginning of the end, marking a World AIDS Day that has gone from that early beginning, when people were still uncertain, to now a theme: "Getting to Zero." Few could have imagined that we'd be talking about the real possibility of an AIDS-free generation. But that's what we're talking about. That's why we're here. And we arrived here because of all of you and your unwavering belief that we can, and we will, beat this disease.

Because we invested in antiretroviral treatment, people who would have died, some of whom are here today, are living full and vibrant lives. Because we developed new tools, more and more mothers are giving birth to children free from this disease. And because of a persistent focus on awareness, the global rate of new infections and deaths is declining.

So make no mistake, we are going to win this fight. But the fight is not over, not by a long shot. The rate of new infections may be going down elsewhere, but it's not going down here in America. The infection rate here has been holding steady for over a decade. There are communities in this country being devastated still by this disease.

When new infections among young Black gay men increase by nearly 50 percent in 3 years, we need to do more to show them that their lives matter. When Latinos are dying sooner than other groups and when Black women feel forgotten, even though they account for most of the new cases among women, then we've got to do more.

So this fight is not over. Not for the 1.2 million Americans who are living with HIV right now. Not for the Americans who are infected every day. This fight is not over for them, it's not over for their families, and as a consequence, it can't be over for anybody in this room, and it certainly isn't over for your President.

Since I took office, we've had a robust national dialogue on HIV/AIDS. Members of my administration have fanned out across the country to meet people living with HIV, to meet researchers, faith leaders, medical providers, and private sector partners. We've spoken to over 4,000 people. And out of all those conversations, we drafted a new plan to combat this disease. Last year, we released that plan, our first-ever national HIV/AIDS strategy.

We went back to basics: prevention, treatment, and focusing our efforts where the need is greatest. And we laid out a vision where every American, regardless of age, gender, race, ethnicity, sexual orientation, gender identity, or socioeconomic status, can get access to life-extending care.

And I want to be clear about something else: Since taking office, we've increased overall funding to combat HIV/AIDS to record levels. With bipartisan support, we reauthorized the Ryan White Care Act. And as I signed that bill,

I was so proud to also announce that my administration was ending the ban that prohibited people with HIV from entering America. Because of that step, next year, for the first time in two decades, we will host the International AIDS Conference.

So we've done a lot over the past 3 years, but we can do so much more. Today I'm announcing some new commitments. We're committing an additional $15 million for the Ryan White Program that supports care provided by HIV medical clinics across the country. We want to keep those doors open so they can keep saving lives. We're committing an additional $35 million for State AIDS-drug assistance programs.

The Federal Government can't do this alone, so I'm also calling on State governments and pharmaceutical companies and private foundations to do their part to help Americans get access to all the lifesaving treatments.

This is a global fight, and it's one that America must continue to lead. In looking back at the history of HIV/AIDS, you'll see that no other country has done more than this country, and that's testament to our leadership as a country. But we can't be complacent.

I think this is an area where we can also look back and take pride that both Republicans and Democrats in Congress have consistently come together to fund this fight, not just here, but around the world. And that's a testament to the values that we share as Americans, a commitment that extends across party lines, that's demonstrated by the fact that President Bush, President Clinton, and I are joining you all today.

Since I took office, we've increased support for the Global Fund To Fight AIDS, Tuberculosis, and Malaria. We've launched a Global Health Initiative that has improved access to health care, helping bring down the cost of vaccines, and over the next 5 years, will help save the lives of 4 million more children. And all along, we kept focusing on expanding our impact.

Today I'm proud to announce that as of September, the United States now supports antiretroviral treatment for nearly 4 million people worldwide—4 million people. And in just the past year, we've provided 600,000 HIV-positive mothers with access to drugs so that 200,000 babies could be born HIV-free. And nearly 13 million people have received care and treatment, including more than 4 million children. So we've got some stuff to be proud of.

But we've got to do more. We're achieving these results not by acting alone, but by partnering with developing countries like Tanzania and with leaders like President Kikwete.

Now as we go forward, we've got to keep refining our strategy so that we're saving as many lives as possible. We need to listen when the scientific community focuses on prevention. That's why, as a matter of policy, we're now investing in what works, from medical procedures to promoting healthy behavior.

And that's why we're setting a goal of providing antiretroviral drugs to more than 1½ million HIV-positive pregnant women over the next 2 years so that they have the chance to give birth to HIV-free babies.

We're not going to stop there. We know that treatment is also prevention. And today we're setting a new target of helping 6 million people get treatment by the end of 2013. So that's 2 million more people than our original goal.

And on this World AIDS Day, here's my message to everybody who is out there: To the global community, we ask you to join us. Countries that have committed to the Global Fund need to give the money that they promised. Countries that haven't made a pledge, they need to do so. That includes countries that in the past might have been recipients, but now are in a position to step up as major donors. China and other major economies are in a position now to transition in a way that can help more people.

To Congress, keep working together and keep the commitments you've made intact. At a time when so much in Washington divides us, the fight against this disease has united us across parties and across Presidents. And it shows that we can do big things when Republicans and Democrats put their common humanity before politics. So we need to carry that spirit forward.

And to all Americans, we've got to keep fighting. Fight for every person who needs our help today, but also fight for every person who didn't live to see this moment, for the Rock Hudsons and the Arthur Ashes and every person who woke us up to the reality of HIV/AIDS. We've got to fight for Ryan White and his mother Jeanne and the Ray brothers and every person who forced us to confront our destructive prejudices and our misguided fears. Fight for Magic Johnson and Mary Fisher and every man, woman, and child, who, when told they were going to die from this disease, they said: "No, we're not. We're going to live."

Keep fighting for all of them because we can end this pandemic. We can beat this disease. We can win this fight. We just have to keep at it, steady, persistent: today, tomorrow, every day until we get to zero. And as long as I have the honor of being your President, that's what this administration is going to keep doing. That's my pledge. That's my commitment to all of you. And that's got to be our promise to each other, because we've come so far and we've saved so many lives, we might as well finish the fight.

Thank you for all you've done. God bless you. God bless America. Thank you.

NOTE: The President spoke at 10:27 a.m. In his remarks, he referred to Sanjay Gupta, chief medical correspondent, CNN, who introduced the President; former President George W. Bush; musicians Paul D. "Bono" Hewson and Alicia Keys; Jeanne White-Ginder, mother of Ryan White, who died of AIDS in 1990; Randy Ray, whose brothers Ricky and Robert Ray died of AIDS in 1992 and 2000, respectively; Earvin "Magic" Johnson, Jr., former guard, National Basketball Association's Los Angeles Lakers; and HIV/AIDS activist Mary Fisher.

Remarks on Lighting the National Christmas Tree
December 1, 2011

The President. It's nice having your own band. Please have a seat, everyone. Merry Christmas! Merry Christmas!

Thank you, Secretary Salazar, for that introduction and for your hard work to preserve and protect our land and our water and our wildlife. I also want to thank Minister Rogers for the beautiful invocation, as well as Neil Mulholland and everyone at the National Park Foundation and the National Park Service who helped put this outstanding event together. I'd like to thank Carson Daly and Big Time Rush and all of tonight's performers for joining us to kick off the holiday season here at the White House.

For 89 years, Presidents and Americans have come together to light the National Christmas Tree. And this year is a special one. This year, we have a brand new tree. The last one stood here for more than 30 years, until we lost it in a storm earlier this year. But we all know that this tradition is much larger than any single tree. And tonight, once again, we gather here not simply to light some decorations, but to honor a story that lights the world.

More than 2,000 years ago, a child was born to two faithful travelers who could find rest only in a stable, among the cattle and the sheep. But this was not just any child. Christ's birth made the angels rejoice and attracted shepherds and kings from afar. He was a manifestation of God's love for us. And He grew up to become a leader with a servant's heart who taught us a message as simple as it is powerful: that we should love God and love our neighbor as ourselves.

That teaching has come to encircle the globe. It has endured for generations. And today, it lies at the heart of my Christian faith and that of millions of Americans. No matter who we are or where we come from or how we worship, it's a message that can unite all of us on this holiday season.

So long as the gifts and the parties are happening, it's important for us to keep in mind the central message of this season and keep Christ's words not only in our thoughts, but also in our deeds. In this season of hope, let's help those who need it most: the homeless, the hungry, the sick and shut in. In this season of plenty, let's reach out to those who struggle to find work or provide for their families. In this season of generosity, let's give thanks and honor to our troops and our veterans, and their families who've sacrificed so much for us. And let's welcome all those who are happily coming home.

And this holiday season, let us reaffirm our commitment to each other, as family members, as neighbors, as Americans, regardless of our color or creed or faith. Let us remember that we are one and we are a family.

So on behalf of Malia and Sasha and Michelle and our grandmother in chief, Marian—[*laughter*]—I wish you all the happiest holiday season, the merriest of Christmases. God bless you all, and may God bless the United States of America.

And with that, I'm going to invite the entire Obama clan up here to light the Christmas tree. I need some help, and there's a lot of technical aspects to this. [*Laughter*] Come on, guys. All right.

Okay, we're going to start counting down here. We've got the switch right here.

The First Lady. All right, come on.

The President. Everybody ready? And this is the new tree. I know it's not quite as big as the old tree, but it's going to take time to grow. But we're going to fill it up with some spirit and start a new tradition right now.

All right, everybody ready? We're going to start counting down. Five, four, three, two, one—[*applause*]—whoa! There you go. That's a good-looking tree. Thank you, everyone.

NOTE: The President spoke at 5:31 p.m. on the Ellipse at the White House. In his remarks, he referred to Perrin Rogers, elder, Triumphant Church, Hyattsville, MD; Neil J. Mulholland, president and chief executive officer, National Park Foundation; and talk show host Carson Daly. He also referred to his mother-in-law Marian Robinson.

Statement on Senate Action on Tax Cut Legislation
December 1, 2011

Tonight Senate Republicans chose to raise taxes on nearly 160 million hard-working Americans because they refused to ask a few hundred thousand millionaires and billionaires to pay their fair share. They voted against a bill that would have not only extended the $1,000 tax cut for a typical family, but expanded that tax cut to put an extra $1,500 in their pockets next year and given nearly 6 million small-business owners new incentives to expand and hire. That is unacceptable. It makes absolutely no sense to raise taxes on the middle class at a time when so many are still trying to get back on their feet.

Now is not the time to put the economy and the security of the middle class at risk. Now is the time to rebuild an economy where hard work and responsibility pay off and everybody has a chance to succeed. Now is the time to put country before party and work together on behalf of the American people. And I will continue to urge Congress to stop playing politics with the security of millions of American families and small-business owners and get this done.

Remarks on the Better Buildings Initiative With Former President William J. Clinton and an Exchange With Reporters
December 2, 2011

Former President Clinton. Well, I never got to open for the Rolling Stones, so I'll try to do my best for the President.

Thank you all for being here, and I want to thank the—all the people involved in the tour that we just received for their commitment to energy efficiency and all the people they put to work.

[At this point, former President Clinton made brief remarks, concluding as follows.]

You know that I haven't been in that job for a long time, and I'm getting older, but I have some memory left. And a thousand people ask you to do a thousand things. And one of the tests of whether things work out or not, since you can't do all thousand, is whether you can actually set up a process to do things and follow up. And I am full of gratitude and praise, Mr. President, for you and your whole team, not just for your commitment to green energy, but for your commitment to energy efficiency, which gives you, on buildings like this, averages 7,000 jobs for every billion dollars invested, by far the greatest bang for the buck of any available investment I know.

So thank you, Tom. Thank you, Ricki—Randi. And, Mr. President, thanks for giving me a chance to work on this.

Thank you.

President Obama. Well, good morning, everybody. I want to first of all thank Randi and Tom for their participation. And I am thrilled that President Clinton has been willing to take this on. As he pointed out, partly thanks to me, he's home alone too often. And this has been a passion for him for quite some time. So I am very grateful for his involvement.

I thank everybody at Transwestern and all the folks who are participating here for giving us this remarkable tour.

There are the equivalent of 250 full-time workers as a consequence of the project that's taking place here. It is a win for the business owners. It is a win for the tenants of this building. It is a win for the construction workers who are participating and for the property manager that's doing such a great job. So this is a great example of what's possible.

As President, my most pressing challenge is doing everything I can every single day to get this economy growing faster and create more jobs. This morning we learned that our economy added another 140,000 private sector jobs in November. The unemployment rate went down. And despite some strong headwinds this year, the American economy has now created, in the private sector, jobs for the past 21 months in a row. That's nearly 3 million new jobs in all and more than half a million over the last 4 months.

So we need to keep that growth going. Right now that means Congress needs to extend the payroll tax cut for working Americans for another year. Congress needs to renew unemployment insurance for Americans who are still out there pounding the pavement and looking for work. Failure to take either of these steps would be a significant blow to our economy. It would take money out of the pocket of Americans who are most likely to spend it, and it would harm small businesses that depend on the spending. It would be a bad idea.

I think it's worth noting, by the way, I noticed that some folks on the other side have been quoting President Clinton about it's a bad idea to raise taxes during tough economic times. That's precisely why I've sought to extend the payroll tax this year and next year. It doesn't mean that we lock in tax cuts for the wealthiest Americans—I don't think President Clinton's been on board for that—for perpetuity. But just thought it—that might be worth mentioning.

That's why it's so disappointing last night, by the way, that Senate Republicans voted to block that payroll tax cut. That effectively would raise taxes on nearly 160 million hard-working Americans because they didn't want to ask a few hundred thousand of the wealthiest Americans to pay their fair share and get the economy growing faster than everybody. And I think that's unacceptable.

We're going to keep pushing Congress to make this happen. Now is not the time to slam the brakes on the recovery. Right now it's time to step on the gas. We need to get this done. And I expect that it's going to get done before Congress leaves. Otherwise, Congress may not be leaving, and we can all spend Christmas here together.

Now, our longer term challenge is rebuilding an economy where hard work is valued and responsibility is rewarded and the middle class and folks who are trying to get into the middle class regain some security; an economy that's built to compete with the rest of the world and an economy that's built to last.

And that's why we are here today, in a place where, clearly, there is some building going on. President Clinton, leaders of business, leaders of labor, we're all here to announce some new steps that are going to create good jobs rebuilding America.

This building is in the middle of a retrofitting project to make it more energy efficient. Already, this retrofit is saving this building $200,000 a year on its energy bills. And as I mentioned earlier, by the time it's finished, it will have created more than 250 full-time jobs in construction here in this building. Consider—you know, President Clinton's coming down from New York—the fact that the owners of the Empire State Building did the same thing. They are retrofitting that iconic landmark from top to bottom. It's a big investment, but it will pay for itself by saving them $4.4 million a year in energy costs. And it's estimated that all the retrofitting that they're doing will pay for itself in about 4½ years.

Making our buildings more energy efficient is one of the fastest, easiest, and cheapest ways for us to create jobs, save money, and cut down on harmful pollution. It is a trifecta, which is why you've got labor and business behind it. It could save our businesses up to $40 billion a year on their energy bills, money better spent growing and hiring new workers. It would boost manufacturing of energy-efficient materials. And when millions of construction workers have found themselves out of work since the housing bubble burst, it will put them back to work doing the work that America needs done. So this is an idea whose time has come.

And that's why in February I announced the Better Buildings Initiative. It's an ambitious plan to improve the energy efficiency of America's commercial buildings 20 percent by the year 2020. And I asked President Clinton and my jobs council to challenge the private sector, as part of the initiative, to step up, make these cost-saving investments, and prove that it works, so that other companies follow their lead.

Now, I believe that if you're willing to put people to work making your buildings more efficient, America should provide you some incentives to do so. That's something that would require congressional action. And we have asked Congress to work with us to move on providing more effective incentives for commercial building owners all across the country to move forward on these energy-efficient steps. But we can't wait for Congress to act. And if they won't act, I will.

Which is why today I'm directing all Federal agencies—all Federal agencies—to make at least $2 billion worth of energy efficiency upgrades over the next 2 years. None of these upgrades will require taxpayer money to get them going. We're going to use performance-based contracts that use savings on energy and utility bills to pay the contractors that do the work. And it should keep construction workers pretty busy. In fact, this is something that the Chamber of Commerce has said is critical to private sector job creation.

The private sector and community leaders are also stepping up to the plate alongside the Federal Government. President Clinton and the Global—Clinton Global Initiative have been tremendous partners in rallying them to join this effort. So in June, at CGI America, we announced initial commitments of $500 million to upgrade 300 million square feet of building space. Some of these projects are already underway.

The good news is, today we can announce that we're going even bigger. We've received larger commitments. We now have 60 major companies, universities, labor unions, hospitals, cities, and States, and they are stepping up with nearly $2 billion in financing to upgrade an additional 1.6 billion square feet of commercial industrial space by our target year of 2020. That's more than 500 Empire State Buildings.

I just had the chance, along with President Clinton, to meet with representatives of these 60 institutions that are involved and hear firsthand how they can put Americans back to work, but also improve their bottom lines.

So you've got companies like Best Buy and Walgreens that are going to upgrade store lighting, which is going to save them money. You've got manufacturers like Alcoa that are going to make their manufacturing plants more efficient, dramatically reducing their operating costs, which means they can compete more effectively all around the world.

You've got property management companies that are upgrading their buildings to make their real estate portfolios more attractive to businesses, and one is already upgrading 4—40,000 units of military housing all across the country, which will give our military families lower utility bills and a higher quality of life. And all of this will create jobs.

So over the past decade we've seen what happens if we don't make investments like these. We've seen what happens when we don't come together for a common purpose: wages flatline, incomes fall, employment stalls, and we lose our competitive edge. But we've also seen what happens when we do what's right. When Bill Clinton was President, we didn't shortchange investment. We didn't say we're going to cut back on the things that we know are going to help us grow in the future. We didn't make decisions that put the burden on the middle class or the poor. We lived within our means. We invested in our future. We asked everybody to pay their fair share. And you know what happened? The private sector thrived, jobs were created, the middle class grew, its income grew, millions rose out of poverty, we ran a surplus. We were actually on track to be able to pay off all of our debt. We were firing on all cylinders.

We can be that Nation again. That's our goal. We will be that Nation again. But we're going to have to fight for it. So there's work to be done. There are workers, like these guys, who are ready to do it. There are businesses that are ready to step up. We've just got to get organized, get mobilized, and move.

And so I just want to thank everybody who's participating here for stepping up to the plate and showing extraordinary leadership. I am confident that this is going to be one important piece of the puzzle to get the economy moving again.

Thank you very much, everybody. Thank you, guys.

Former President Clinton's Advice for the President/National Economy

Q. President Clinton, any advice to your friend, President Clinton? Do you have any advice to President Obama about the economy?

President Obama. Oh, he gives me advice all the time. [*Laughter*]

Former President Clinton. No, I just want to—I'll say again, this announcement today—the reason you should be encouraged by this, you can run the numbers and see how many jobs he announced. But this meeting we just came from, as Dick Parsons said, represented trillions of dollars in potential investment. And if the President, by doing this, can trigger pools of investment so that you have more buildings like this, keep in mind it can also change what goes on in every rural place and small town in America.

Upstate New York, which is in trouble, every little county has got one bonded contractor. That bonded contractor can guarantee to every public school, every State, county, and local building, every little office building in Chappaqua, New York, where Hillary and I live, what the savings are going to be. They've got software. We have to have breakthroughs

on financing. That's really the long-term potential significance of what the President announced today. And the fact that he did something that only a President can do: He got all these people together, and then to have the AFL–CIO and the AFT and others sort of lead the way in saying we will put our members' pensions into this because we can get a good return, it's a stable return, we'll put our current members to work and other working people to work, and get a return on the pension.

This is a big deal. That's the significance to this. This announcement the President made today is the jobs that you can multiply 7,000 times a billion, but it's potentially literally 50, 70, 80 times that because of who's involved.

President Obama. Thanks, guys.

NOTE: The President spoke at 11:28 a.m. at 815 Connecticut Avenue NW, a Transwestern-managed property. In his remarks, he referred to Randi Weingarten, president, American Federation of Teachers; and Thomas J. Donahue, president and chief executive officer, U.S. Chamber of Commerce. Former President Clinton referred to Richard D. Parsons, chairman of the board of directors of Citigroup Inc., in his capacity as a member of the President's Council on Jobs and Competitiveness. Former President Clinton also referred to his wife, Secretary of State Hillary Rodham Clinton.

Remarks at the White House Tribal Nations Conference
December 2, 2011

Thank you so much. Thank you. Everybody, please have a seat. It is wonderful to see all of you. Thank you, Phyliss, for the wonderful introduction.

I want to thank all the tribal leaders who are here for making this year's conference the most successful yet. I want to acknowledge outstanding members of my team that have helped pull this together, but more importantly, day in and day out are thinking about what we can do to make sure that all the tribes that are represented have a voice here in Washington.

First of all, my outstanding Secretary of the Interior, Ken Salazar, we are so proud of him; Assistant Secretary for Indian Affairs, Larry Echo Hawk—[*applause*]—hey—and our outstanding Solicitor for the Department of Interior, Hilary Tompkins.

Now, today, I'm here not only as President. As I've mentioned before, I am also here as an adopted member of the Crow Nation. So I'd like to recognize my adoptive mom and dad, Sonny and Mary Black Eagle, who are backstage. They're going to be coming out here in a little bit. I'm so grateful they took me into their family. I bet they're grateful that I never went through the "terrible twos"—[*laughter*]—or "terrible teens." They got me after I was a little more polished. [*Laughter*]

Ken Salazar, he works so hard on the issues that matter to all of you. And we also have Members of Congress here as well who are great partners in this effort. And finally—I want to give a shout-out to the young people who are here as part of the White House program called Champions for Change. Really remarkable young people. I had a chance to meet them backstage. There's Teressa Baldwin, who's working to prevent teen suicide among Alaska Natives; LeVon Thomas, who's bringing green jobs to the Navajo Nation; Dallas Duplessis, who started a gardening club to promote healthy eating in Tulalip, Washington. She wrote, "Our goal is not to be couch potatoes, but to grow some potatoes." [*Laughter*] I think Michelle would like that one.

Standing in this room with leaders of all ages, it's impossible not to be optimistic about the future of Indian Country. Obviously, we face tough times. But you still believe that tomorrow can be better than today. You're out there making your communities better places to live. What you expect, and what you deserve, is a Federal Government that helps, not hinders, your efforts. You deserve leaders in Washington who fight for you every single day.

That's one of the reasons I ran for this office. When I visited the Crow Nation during the campaign, I said my job was not just to win an election, it was to make sure that Washington starts focusing on you. I promised a true government-to-government relationship, a relationship that recognizes our sometimes painful history, a relationship that respects the unique heritage of Native Americans and that includes you in the dream that we all share.

And together, we're building that relationship. I told you I would bring tribal leaders to Washington to reflect—to develop an agenda that reflects your hopes and your concerns. And now, for a third year in a row, we have kept that promise. I told you that when I was President, we wouldn't just pay lip service to the idea of consultation. And today, we're holding every Cabinet agency responsible for working together with Indian tribes.

I told you I'd appoint Native Americans to senior positions in the White House. And I know that many of you have worked with Kim Teehee of Cherokee Nation, my Senior Policy Adviser for Native American issues, and Charlie Galbraith of the Navajo Nation, in our Office of Intergovernmental Affairs.

We're working to make our government-to-government relationship even stronger. We asked Congress to recognize the power of tribes to prosecute perpetrators of domestic violence, whether they're Indian or non-Indian. And in the wake of the Carcieri decision, we've asked Congress to restore the Secretary of the Interior's authority to take land into trust for federally recognized Indian tribes.

So this new relationship represents a major step forward. It is change. But I promised even more than that. I told you that as President, I would work with you to tackle the most difficult problems facing Native American families. And that's exactly what we've done. We passed the Tribal Law and Order Act and began making Indian Country a safer place to live. We permanently authorized the Indian Health Care Improvement Act and made quality health care accessible to more Native Americans.

Just this week, we streamlined leasing regulations, which will lead to more homes, more businesses, more renewable energy on the reservation. That's what change is.

And finally, we said that even as we include Indian tribes in the broader promise of America, we're going to keep native traditions alive. So when Michelle launched "Let's Move!" in Indian Country, she brought lacrosse players to the White House and invited Native American children to plant the "three sisters" crops in the White House vegetable garden.

While our work together is far from over, today we can see what change looks like. It's the Native American-owned small business that's opening its doors or a worker helping a school renovate. It's new roads and houses. It's wind turbines going up on tribal lands and crime going down in tribal communities. That's what change looks like.

So we should be proud of what we've done together. But of course, that should sharpen our resolve to do even more. Because as long as Native Americans face unemployment and poverty rates that are far higher than the national average, we're going to have more work to do. And I wake up every day focused on how to get this economy growing and create jobs for every American faster. We're working to rebuild an economy where no matter who you are, no matter what you look like—Black, White, Latino, Asian, Native American—you can make it if you try.

And that's why I proposed the "American Jobs Act," to help all Americans, including first Americans, make it through these tough times. It's why my administration has addressed the obstacles that are unique to Indian Country by guaranteeing loans for homeowners and small-business owners and tribes. It's why we're working to equip your communities with high-speed Internet access.

And even as we meet at this moment, we have to prepare the next generation for the future, which is why earlier today I signed an Executive order to launch the White House Initiative on American Indian and Alaska Native Education.

Secretary Duncan, who is here, Secretary Salazar, they're going to work together on this effort to prepare Native American youth to compete for the high-skilled, good jobs of tomorrow. We're going to find ways to reduce the dropout rate. We're going to help students who've already dropped out reenter the education system. And we're going to strengthen our tribal colleges and universities. They are cornerstones of their community, and they deserve our support.

So we've made progress together. And a lot of that progress is possible because of all of you, because the ideas that you've shared at the last two conferences and that you're sharing at this conference. And that's why I'm looking forward to hearing the results of the discussion that you have today. I want to know what we can do to keep tackling the tough issues, from education to jobs to health care to public safety.

It would be nice to say that the work was done, but we know the truth. We haven't solved all our problems. We've got a long road ahead. But I believe that one day, we're going to be able to look back on these years and say that this was a turning point. This was the moment when we began to build a strong middle class in Indian Country, the moment when businesses, large and small, began opening up in reservations, the moment when we stopped repeating the mistakes of the past and began building a better future together, one that honors old traditions and welcomes every Native American into the American Dream.

We've got to finish what we started. So today I want to thank all of you for everything that you do. I want to ask you to keep going. And when you go back home, making your communities better places to live, I want you all to know that you've got a partner in Washington. You have an administration that understands the challenges that you face, and most importantly, you've got a President who's got your back.

So thank you. God bless you. God bless the United States of America.

NOTE: The President spoke at 2:20 p.m. at the Department of the Interior. In his remarks, he referred to Phyliss J. Anderson, tribal chief, Mississippi Band of Choctaw Indians.

Memorandum on the Implementation of Energy Savings Projects and Performance-Based Contracting for Energy Savings
December 2, 2011

Memorandum for the Heads of Executive Departments and Agencies

Subject: Implementation of Energy Savings Projects and Performance-Based Contracting for Energy Savings

The Federal Government owns and operates nearly 3 billion square feet of Federal building space. Upgrading the energy performance of buildings is one of the fastest and most effective ways to reduce energy costs, cut pollution, and create jobs in the construction and energy sectors. We have a responsibility to lead by example, reduce our energy use, and operate our buildings efficiently.

Meeting that responsibility requires executive departments and agencies (agencies) to evaluate their facilities, identify potential savings, and appropriately leverage both private and public sector funding to invest in comprehensive energy conservation projects that cut energy costs. The Federal Government can do so by increasing the pace of the implementation of energy conservation measures, and improving the results from its energy efficiency investments.

In Executive Order 13514 of October 5, 2009 (Federal Leadership in Environmental, Energy, and Economic Performance), my Administration reaffirmed a commitment to reduce energy intensity in agency buildings. In addition, through my memorandum of June 10, 2010 (Disposing of Unneeded Federal Real Estate—Increasing Sales Proceeds, Cutting Operating Costs, and Improving Energy Efficiency), and through the Campaign to Cut Waste, my Administration has directed agencies to cut energy costs in agency facilities as part of a broader effort to reduce spending and shrink the Federal Government's real estate footprint. In order to ensure agencies fully meet these goals and maximize the cost reduction and job creation potential of making Fed-

eral buildings more energy efficient, I hereby direct the following:

Section 1. Implement and Prioritize Energy Conservation Measures. (a) Agencies shall fully implement energy conservation measures (ECMs) in Federal buildings with a payback time of less than 10 years, consistent with real property and capital improvement plans. Agencies shall prioritize ECMs with the greatest return on investment, leveraging both direct appropriations and performance contracting, consistent with guidance by the Office of Management and Budget (OMB).

(b) The Federal Government shall enter into a minimum of $2 billion in performance-based contracts in Federal building energy efficiency within 24 months from the date of this memorandum. Each agency shall include its anticipated total performance-based contract volume in its plan submitted pursuant to subsection (d) of this section.

(c) In order to maximize efficiency and return on investment to the American taxpayer, agencies are encouraged to enter into installation-wide and portfolio-wide performance contracts and undertake comprehensive projects that include short-term and long-term ECMs, consistent with Government-wide small business contracting policies.

(d) Agencies shall prioritize new projects under this section based on return on investment, develop a planned implementation schedule, and reconcile all investments with actions undertaken pursuant to Executive Order 13576 of June 13, 2011 (Delivering an Efficient, Effective, and Accountable Government). Agencies shall ensure that any performance-based contracts are consistent with, and do not duplicate or conflict with, real property plans or planned capital improvements.

(e) No later than January 31, 2012, agencies shall report their planned implementation schedule described in subsection (d) of this section to the Department of Energy's Federal Energy Management Program (FEMP),

OMB, and the Council on Environmental Quality (CEQ).

(f) Beginning in 2012, agencies shall incorporate the planned implementation schedule into their annual Strategic Sustainability Performance Plans in furtherance of Executive Order 13514.

Sec. 2. Complete Required Energy and Water Evaluations. (a) Agencies shall identify in the Department of Energy's Compliance Tracking System (CTS) any ECMs that have been implemented, and ensure that the CTS is regularly updated.

(b) Consistent with section 432 of the Energy Independence and Security Act of 2007 (42 U.S.C. 8253(f)(2)), agencies shall complete all energy and water evaluations and report the ECMs and associated cost saving opportunities identified through these evaluations to the CTS.

Sec. 3. Transparency and Accountability. (a) Agencies shall, where technically feasible, continue efforts to connect meters and advanced metering devices to enterprise energy management systems to streamline and optimize measurement, management, and reporting of facility energy use.

(b) The FEMP shall assist agencies with timely implementation of subsection (a) of this section. Consistent with its mission and responsibilities, FEMP shall also track Government-wide implementation progress. Subject to the protection of critical infrastructure information and avoidance of disclosure of sensitive information relating to national security, FEMP shall annually publish these results, as well as facility energy usage data, in machine readable formats on agency websites, consistent with applicable OMB guidance.

(c) The OMB shall continue to track agency implementation and progress towards goal achievement on its Energy and Sustainability Scorecard, and publicly report on agency progress, pursuant to the requirements of Executive Order 13514.

Sec. 4. Applicability. This memorandum shall apply to agency activities, personnel, resources, and facilities located within the United States. The head of an agency may apply this memorandum to activities, personnel, re-

sources, and facilities of the agency that are not located within the United States, to the extent the head of the agency determines that doing so is in the interest of the United States.

Sec. 5. Exemption Authority. (a) The Director of National Intelligence may exempt an intelligence activity of the United States, and related personnel, resources, and facilities, from the provisions of this memorandum, to the extent the Director determines necessary to protect intelligence sources and methods from unauthorized disclosure.

(b) The head of an agency may exempt particular facilities from the provisions of this memorandum where doing so is in the interest of national security. If the head of an agency issues an exemption under this subsection, the agency must notify the Chair of CEQ in writing within 30 days of issuance of the exemption. To the maximum extent practicable, and without compromising national security, each agency shall strive to comply with the purposes, goals, and implementation steps in this memorandum.

Sec. 6. Definitions. For the purposes of this memorandum:

(a) "energy conservation measure" (ECM) has the same meaning as in 42 U.S.C. 8259(d).

(b) "energy savings performance contract" (ESPC), as authorized by 42 U.S.C. 8287, means a contract (or task order) awarded to an energy service company (ESCO) for up to 25 years that provides for the design, acquisition, financing, installation, testing, operation, and maintenance and repair of identified ECMs at one or more locations. Under an ESPC, the ESCO incurs the costs of project implementation, including audits, acquiring and installing equipment, and training personnel, in exchange for a predetermined price. Payment to the ESCO is contingent upon realizing a guaranteed stream of future savings, with excess savings accruing to the Federal Government.

(c) "performance-based contract" means a contract that identifies expected deliverables, performance measures, or outcomes, and makes payment contingent on their successful achievement. Performance-based contracts also use appropriate techniques, which may include consequences or incentives to ensure that the agreed-upon value to the agency is received. Performance-based contracts, which include ESPCs, can be performed by any qualified contractor, including utilities.

(d) "agency" has the same meaning as in Executive Order 13514.

(e) "United States" means the fifty States, the District of Columbia, the Commonwealth of Puerto Rico, Guam, American Samoa, the United States Virgin Islands, the Northern Mariana Islands, and associated territorial waters and airspace.

Sec. 7. General Provisions. (a) This memorandum shall be implemented consistent with applicable law, including international trade obligations, and subject to the availability of appropriations.

(b) Nothing in this memorandum shall be construed to impair or otherwise affect:

(i) authority granted by law to a department, agency, or the head thereof; or

(ii) functions of the Director of OMB relating to budgetary, administrative, or legislative proposals.

(c) This memorandum is not intended to, and does not, create any right or benefit, substantive or procedural, enforceable at law or in equity by any party against the United States, its departments, agencies, or entities, its officers, employees, or agents, or any other person.

BARACK OBAMA

The President's Weekly Address
December 3, 2011

This week, we learned that our economy added another 140,000 private sector jobs in November. Despite some strong headwinds this year, America's economy has now created private sector jobs for the past 21 months in a row, almost 3 million new jobs in all, more than half a million of them in the past 4 months alone.

We need to keep this growth going and strengthen it. And that's why we've been fighting to pass a series of jobs bills through Congress, bills that independent economists say will create more jobs and grow the economy even faster. Because now is the time to step on the gas, not slam on the brakes.

Unfortunately, too many Republicans in Congress don't seem to share that same sense of urgency. Over the last few months, they've said no to most of these jobs bills: no to putting teachers and firefighters back to work, no to putting construction workers back on the job. And this week, they actually said no to cutting taxes for middle class families.

You see, last year, both parties came together to cut payroll taxes for the typical middle class family by about a thousand dollars. But that tax cut is set to expire at the end of this month. If that happens, that same family will see its taxes go up by a thousand dollars. We can't let that happen. In fact, I think we should cut taxes on working families and small-business owners even more.

And we're going to keep pushing Congress to make this happen. They shouldn't go home for the holidays until they get this done. And if you agree with me, I could use your help.

We've set up a simple tax cut calculator on whitehouse.gov so that you can see exactly what the stakes are for your family. Try it out. Then let your Members of Congress know where you stand.

Tell them not to vote to raise taxes on working Americans during the holidays. Tell them to put country before party, put money back in the pockets of working Americans, pass these tax cuts.

And we're all in this together. The more Americans succeed, the more America succeeds. And if we remember that and do what it takes to keep this economy growing and opportunity rising, then I'm confident that we'll come out of this stronger than before.

NOTE: The address was recorded at approximately 1:35 p.m. on December 2 in the Map

Room at the White House for broadcast on December 3. The transcript was made available by the Office of the Press Secretary on December 2, but was embargoed for release until 6 a.m. on December 3.

Remarks at a Kennedy Center Honors Reception
December 4, 2011

The President. Well, good evening, everybody. Welcome to the White House. What a spectacular-looking crowd here. [*Laughter*] I want to start by thanking David Rubenstein, Michael Kaiser, and the Kennedy Center Trustees, and everyone who has made the Kennedy Center such a wonderful place for so many people for so many years. I also want to acknowledge my good friend Caroline Kennedy for continuing her family's legacy of supporting the arts. And finally, I want to thank the creator of the Kennedy Center Honors and the Cochair of the President's Committee on the Arts and the Humanities, George Stevens. George and his son Michael are still bringing this show to life after 34 years, and we are grateful to both of them. So—[*applause*].

Tonight we honor five giants from the world of the arts, not just for a single role or a certain performance, but for a lifetime of greatness. And just to be clear, this doesn't mean that they're over the hill. [*Laughter*] It just means they've come a long way.

Now, at first glance, the men and women on this stage could not be more different. They come from different generations, different walks of life. They have different talents, and they've traveled different paths. And yet they belong here together because each of tonight's honorees has felt the need to express themselves and share that expression with the world.

It's a feeling that all of us have at some point in our lives. That's why we sing, even if it's just in the shower. [*Laughter*] It's why we act, even if we never get past the school auditorium. That's why we dance, even if, as Michelle says, I look silly doing it. [*Laughter*] It's one of the downsides of being President: Your dance moves end up on YouTube. [*Laughter*]

But tonight's honorees take it a step further. By expressing themselves, they help us learn something about ourselves. They make us laugh, they move us to tears, they bring us together, and they push the boundaries of what we think is possible. And each of them has been blessed with an extraordinary gift. Tonight we thank them for sharing that gift with us.

Barbara Cook has been said to have the most magnificent voice in popular music, but she was born into a family that didn't know the first thing about singing. Growing up, while the other kids in her neighborhood were out playing hide and seek, Barbara would be inside listening to opera on the radio. By the time she was 23, Barbara was starring in her first Broadway show, and she went on to win a Tony for her performance as the original "Marian the Librarian" in "The Music Man."

But success didn't come without pain, and she faced more than her share of challenges, before a show-stopping concert at Carnegie Hall in 1975 catapulted her back into the spotlight. Barbara's greatest strength has always been her ability to put her own feelings and experiences into her songs. As she says, "If I sing about emotion, and you say, yes, I've felt that too, then it brings us together, even if it's just for a little while."

These days, Barbara has been through enough to sing just about anything, so now she teaches up-and-coming singers to do the same. The lesson always starts with "be yourself," a piece of advice that she has always taken to heart. Maybe that's what has kept her so young. And Barbara says that some days she feels like she is 30, and tonight you look like you're 30. [*Laughter*] Some days she feels like she's 12, although her knee apparently does not agree. [*Laughter*] All we know is that we've never heard a voice like hers, so tonight we Barbara—honor Barbara Cook.

1511

Now, Neil Diamond's songwriting career began like so many others: He was trying to impress a girl. [*Laughter*] The difference was that it worked, and he went on to marry the girl. As Neil says, "I should have realized then the potential power of songs and been a little more wary." [*Laughter*]

Even after such a promising start, music wasn't Neil's first choice. He wanted to go to medical school and find a cure for cancer. But then he met reality, which for him came in the form of organic chemistry. [*Laughter*] Neil ended up dropping out of college to take a 50-dollar-a-week songwriting job, and the "Solitary Man" was born. With a voice he describes as being full of gravel, potholes, left turns, and right turns, he went on to sell more than 125 million records. Elvis and Frank Sinatra asked to record versions of his songs, and today, Neil is the rare musician whose work can be heard everywhere from kids' movies to Red Sox games. [*Laughter*]

When someone asked him why "Sweet Caroline" remains so popular, Neil said, "It's because anybody can sing, no matter how many drinks you've had." [*Laughter*]

Now, his shirts aren't as flashy as they used to be; I noticed you're buttoned up all the way to the top there. [*Laughter*] Neil can still—some good laughs here. [*Laughter*] Neil can still put a generation of fans in their seats. And so tonight we honor one of the great American songwriters for making us all want to sing along. Thank you, Neil Diamond.

When Sonny Rollins was growing up, he and his friends would sneak into jazz clubs by drawing mustaches on themselves—[*laughter*]—with an eyebrow pencil—[*laughter*]—to try to look older. Did that work, Sonny? [*Laughter*] We don't know if it fooled anybody, but they did get into the clubs.

Harlem in the 1930s was a hotbed of jazz, and for a young musician with a big horn and bigger dreams, it was heaven. Duke Ellington and Coleman Hawkins lived around the corner. Sonny learned melody and harmony from Thelonious Monk, and Miles Davis was a regular playing partner.

It wasn't long before Sonny earned the nickname the "Saxophone Colossus" and became known as one of the greatest improvisers in the history of jazz. Today, he often plays hour-long solos without any repetition, leaving audiences speechless. People sometimes wonder how he can play for so long, but in Sonny's words, "It just means there's something out there, and I know I have to find it."

Sonny also loves to roam the crowd during a performance. One story goes that he was halfway through a solo one night when he jumped off the stage and disappeared. [*Laughter*] Just when the band was about to go looking for him, the solo started back up. Sonny had broken his foot and was lying on the floor, but he finished the set with so much energy and passion, the audience didn't notice.

To hear Sonny tell it, he's just keeping things pure. "The worst thing in the world to me is to play by rote," he says. "You have to play from the inside; that's real jazz." So tonight we honor a real jazz master, Mr. Sonny Rollins.

Meryl Streep was once described as a cross between a den mother and a class cutup. [*Laughter*] I don't know who that was, but— [*laughter*].

When a reporter asked Clint Eastwood why he chose Meryl to star opposite him in "The Bridges of Madison County," he shrugged and replied, "She's the greatest actor in the world." At 15, Meryl won the role of "Marian the Librarian"—there's a theme here—[*laughter*]—in her high school's production of "The Music Man," following the footsteps of her idol Barbara Cook. [*Laughter*] That led to Yale drama school and then to Hollywood, where Meryl won two Oscars in 4 years. And then she turned 38—[*laughter*]—which, in Washington at least, according to Meryl, is the sell-by date for Hollywood actresses. And she remembers turning to her husband Don and saying, "Well, it's over."

Luckily, it was not over. Since then, Meryl has tackled incredibly complex roles, ranging from Julia Child to, most recently, Margaret Thatcher. Today, she's the most nominated actress in the history of the Academy Awards.

She's tossed aside more than a few stereotypes along the way. Each of her roles is different, and different from what we expect Meryl Streep to be. As she says, "I've picked the weirdest little group of personalities, but I think they've all deserved to have a life." For giving life to those characters and joy to so many of us, let's give Meryl Streep a round of applause.

One final honoree is something of a regular here at the White House. I was telling him we need to give him a room—[*laughter*]—the Blue Room, the Red Room, and the Yo-Yo Ma room. [*Laughter*] We keep inviting him, and for some reason, he keeps on coming back. [*Laughter*]

When Yo-Yo Ma took his first cello lesson, there wasn't a chair short enough for him, so he sat on three phone books instead. By the age of 4, he was learning the Bach suites. At age 7, he was performing for President Kennedy in this room. Today, he has 16 Grammys and is considered one of the greatest classical musicians alive.

But maybe the most amazing thing about Yo-Yo Ma is that everybody likes him. [*Laughter*] You've got to give me some tips. [*Laughter*] It's remarkable.

In a profession known for, let's face it, some temperament among its stars, Yo-Yo is a little different. He named one of his 300-year-old cellos "Petunia." He's a big hugger. [*Laughter*] For every question you ask him, he asks you two in return. He's been named one of People magazine's sexiest men alive. [*Laughter*] He's appeared on "Sesame Street." I thought about asking him to go talk to Congress. [*Laughter*]

And yet somehow, he's also found the time to become one of the most innovative and versatile musicians in the world. Yo-Yo likes to say that his goal is to take listeners on a trip with him and make a lasting connection. His sense of curiosity has driven him to experiment from everything from the Argentine tango to Chinese folk music, and he has brought musicians from around the world together with the sheer force of his personality. As he says, "If I know what music you love, and you know what music

I love, we start out having a better conversation."

The great Pablo Casals once described himself as a human being first, a musician second, and a cellist third. There is no doubt that Yo-Yo Ma is a great musician and a great cellist, but tonight we also honor him because he is a great human being. Thank you, Yo-Yo Ma.

Barbara Cook, Neil Diamond, Sonny Rollins, Meryl Streep, Yo-Yo Ma: At a time of year when Americans everywhere are counting their blessings, we want to give thanks to their extraordinary contributions. They have been blessings to all of us. We are grateful that they've chosen to share their gifts, to enrich our lives, and to inspire us to new heights.

And I think, for all of us, each of us can probably remember some personal moment. Michelle, during the rope line, was talking about how her dad loved jazz and could hear Sonny Rollins blasting through their little house on South Side. And it's true: Everybody sings Neil Diamond songs no matter how many drinks they've had. [*Laughter*]

Yo-Yo Ma, unfortunately, my association with him is studying at law school, listening to Bach and his—no, it soothed my mind. [*Laughter*]

Meryl Streep, anybody who saw "The French Lieutenant's Woman" had a crush on her. I assume they—everybody remembers that. [*Laughter*]

Audience member. [*Inaudible*]

The President. I'm ad libbing here a little bit. [*Laughter*]

So each of them have made these extraordinary contributions, and it's worthwhile then for us to commit ourselves to making this a place where the arts can continue to thrive. Because right now, somewhere in America, there is a future Kennedy Center honoree practicing on some phone books or writing songs to impress a girl or wondering if she can cut it on the big stage. Let's make sure our young people can dream big dreams and follow them as far as they can go. And let's make sure the arts continue to be an important—no, a critical—part of who we are in the kind of world that we want to live in.

Tonight we congratulate all our extraordinary honorees. Thank you very much.

NOTE: The President spoke at 5:29 p.m. in the East Room at the White House. In his remarks, he referred to David M. Rubenstein, Chairman, and Michael M. Kaiser, President, John F. Kennedy Center for the Performing Arts; Caroline B. Kennedy, daughter of former President John F. Kennedy; Jaye "Posey" Posner, former wife of Neil L. Diamond; Don Gummer, husband of Meryl Streep; and former Prime Minister Margaret Thatcher of the United Kingdom.

Remarks on Payroll Tax Cuts and Unemployment Insurance
December 5, 2011

Good afternoon, everybody. My number-one priority right now is doing everything that I can, every single day, to create jobs faster and to provide more security for middle class families and those trying to get into the middle class. And at this moment, that means making sure that nearly 160 million hard-working Americans don't see an increase in their taxes on January 1.

A year ago at this time, both parties came together to cut payroll taxes for the typical American family by about $1,000. But as soon as this year ends, so does that tax cut. If Congress fails to renew this tax cut before then, that same family will see a tax hike of about $1,000 a year. There aren't many folks either in the middle class or those trying to get into the middle class who can afford to give up $1,000, not right now. And that's why Congress must act.

Although the unemployment rate went down last month, our recovery is still fragile, and the situation in Europe has added to that uncertainty. And that's why the majority of economists believe it's important to extend the payroll tax cut. And those same economists would lower their growth estimates for our economy if it doesn't happen.

Not only is extending the payroll tax cut important for the economy as a whole, it's obviously important for individual families. It's important insurance for them against the unexpected. It will help families pay their bills, it will spur spending, it will spur hiring, and it's the right thing to do.

And that's why in my jobs bill I proposed not only extending the tax cut, but expanding it to give a typical working family a tax cut of $1,500 next year. And it was paid for by asking a little more from millionaires and billionaires, a few hundred thousand people paying a little bit more could have not only extended the existing payroll tax cut, but expanded it.

Last week, virtually every Senate Republican voted against that tax cut. Now, I know many Republicans have sworn an oath never to raise taxes as long as they live. How could it be that the only time there's a catch is when it comes to raising taxes on middle class families? How can you fight tooth and nail to protect high-end tax breaks for the wealthiest Americans and yet barely lift a finger to prevent taxes going up for 160 million Americans who really need the help? It doesn't make sense.

Now, the good news is, I think the American people's voices are starting to get through in this town. I know that last week Speaker Boehner said this tax cut helps the economy because it allows every working American to keep more of their money. I know that over the weekend Senate Republican leaders said we shouldn't raise taxes on working people going into next year.

I couldn't agree more. And I hope that the rest of their Republican colleagues come around and join Democrats to pass these tax cuts and put money back into the pockets of working Americans.

Now, some Republicans who have pushed back against the idea of extending this payroll tax cut have said that we've got to pay for these tax cuts. And I'd just point out that they haven't always felt that way. Over the last decade, they didn't feel the need to pay for massive tax cuts for the wealthiest Americans, which is one of the reasons that we face such large deficits. Indeed, when the Republicans took over the

House at the beginning of this year, they explicitly changed the rules to say that tax cuts don't have to be paid for. So forgive me a little bit of a confusion when I hear folks insisting on tax cuts being paid for.

Having said that, we all recognize that we've got to make progress on the deficit, and I'm willing to work with Republicans to extend the payroll tax cut in a responsible way. What I'm not willing to do is to pay for the extension in a way that actually hurts the economy.

As Americans are well aware, this summer I signed into law nearly $1 trillion in spending cuts with another trillion dollars in cuts in the pipeline. And it would be irresponsible to now make additional deep cuts in areas like education or innovation or our basic safety net that are critical to the economy in order to pay for an extension of the payroll tax cut. We're not going to do that. Nor are we going to undo the budget agreement that I signed just a few short months ago.

Finally, with millions of Americans still looking for work, it would be a terrible mistake for Congress to go home for the holidays without extending unemployment insurance. If that happens, then in January they'll be leaving 1.3 million Americans out in the cold. For a lot of families, this emergency insurance is the last line of defense between hardship and catastrophe. Taking that money out of the economy now would do extraordinary harm to the economy.

And if you believe that Government shouldn't take money out of people's pockets, I hope Members of Congress realize that it's even worse when you take it out of the pockets of people who are unemployed and out there pounding the pavement looking for work.

We are going through what is still an extraordinary time in this country and in this economy. And I get letters every single day, and I talk to people who say to me: This unemployment insurance is what allowed me to keep my house before I was able to find another job; this is what allowed me to still put gas in the tank to take my kids to school.

We cannot play games with unemployment insurance when we still have an unemployment rate that is way too high. I've put forward a whole range of ideas for reform of the unemployment insurance system, and I'm happy to work with Republicans on those issues. But right now the most important thing is making sure that that gets extended as well.

This isn't just something that I want. This isn't just a political fight. Independent economists, some of whom have in the past worked for Republicans, agree that if we don't extend the payroll tax cut and we don't extend unemployment insurance, it will hurt our economy. The economy won't grow as fast, and we won't see hiring improve as quickly. It will take money out of the pockets of Americans just at a time when they need it. It will harm businesses that depend on the spending just at the time when the economy is trying to get some traction in this recovery. It will hurt all of us. And it will be a self-inflicted wound.

So my message to Congress is this: Keep your word to the American people, and don't raise taxes on them right now. Now is not the time to slam on the brakes, now is the time to step on the gas. Now is the time to keep growing the economy, to keep creating jobs, to keep giving working Americans the boost that they need. Now is the time to make a real difference in the lives of the people who sent us here. So let's get to work.

Thank you very much.

NOTE: The President spoke at 2:10 p.m. in the James S. Brady Press Briefing Room at the White House.

Remarks at Osawatomie High School in Osawatomie, Kansas
December 6, 2011

The President. Hello! Thank you, everybody. Please, please have a seat. Thank you so much. Thank you. Good afternoon, everybody.

Audience members. Good afternoon.

The President. Well, I want to start by thanking a few folks who've joined us today.

We've got the mayor of Osawatomie, Phil Dudley is here. We have your superintendent Gary French in the house. And we have the principal of Osawatomie High, Doug Chisam. Yay! And I have brought your former Governor, who is doing now an outstanding job as Secretary of Health and Human Services, Kathleen Sebelius is in the house. We love Kathleen.

Well, it is great to be back in the State of Tex—[*laughter*]—State of Kansas. I was giving Bill Self a hard time; he was here a while back. As many of you know, I have roots here. I'm sure you're all familiar with the Obamas of Osawatomie. [*Laughter*] Actually, I like to say that I got my name from my father, but I got my accent and my values from my mother. She was born in Wichita. Her mother grew up in Augusta. Her father was from El Dorado. So my Kansas roots run deep.

My grandparents served during World War II. He was a soldier in Patton's army; she was a worker on a bomber assembly line. And together, they shared the optimism of a nation that triumphed over the Great Depression and over fascism. They believed in an America where hard work paid off and responsibility was rewarded and anyone could make it if they tried, no matter who you were, no matter where you came from, no matter how you started out.

And these values gave rise to the largest middle class and the strongest economy that the world has ever known. It was here in America that the most productive workers, the most innovative companies turned out the best products on Earth. And you know what? Every American shared in that pride and in that success, from those in the executive suites to those in middle management to those on the factory floor. So you could have some confidence that if you gave it your all, you'd take enough home to raise your family and send your kids to school and have your health care covered, put a little away for retirement.

Today, we're still home to the world's most productive workers. We're still home to the world's most innovative companies. But for most Americans, the basic bargain that made this country great has eroded. Long before the recession hit, hard work stopped paying off for too many people. Fewer and fewer of the folks who contributed to the success of our economy actually benefited from that success. Those at the very top grew wealthier from their incomes and their investments, wealthier than ever before. But everybody else struggled with costs that were growing and paychecks that weren't, and too many families found themselves racking up more and more debt just to keep up.

Now, for many years, credit cards and home equity loans papered over this harsh reality. But in 2008, the house of cards collapsed. We all know the story by now: mortgages sold to people who couldn't afford them or even sometimes understand them; banks and investors allowed to keep packaging the risk and selling it off; huge bets and huge bonuses made with other people's money on the line; regulators who were supposed to warn us about the dangers of all this, but looked the other way or didn't have the authority to look at all.

It was wrong. It combined the breathtaking greed of a few with irresponsibility all across the system. And it plunged our economy and the world into a crisis from which we're still fighting to recover. It claimed the jobs and the homes and the basic security of millions of people, innocent, hard-working Americans who had met their responsibilities, but were still left holding the bag.

And ever since, there's been a raging debate over the best way to restore growth and prosperity, restore balance, restore fairness. Throughout the country, it's sparked protests and political movements, from the Tea Party to the people who've been occupying the streets of New York and other cities. It's left Washington in a near-constant state of gridlock. It's been the topic of heated and sometimes colorful discussion among the men and women running for President. [*Laughter*]

But, Osawatomie, this is not just another political debate. This is the defining issue of our time. This is a make-or-break moment for the middle class and for all those who are fighting to get into the middle class. Because what's at stake is whether this will be a country where working people can earn enough to raise a family, build a modest savings, own a home, secure their retirement.

Now, in the midst of this debate, there are some who seem to be suffering from a kind of collective amnesia. After all that's happened, after the worst economic crisis, the worst financial crisis since the Great Depression, they want to return to the same practices that got us into this mess. In fact, they want to go back to the same policies that stacked the deck against middle class Americans for way too many years. And their philosophy is simple: We are better off when everybody is left to fend for themselves and play by their own rules.

I am here to say they are wrong. I'm here in Kansas to reaffirm my deep conviction that we're greater together than we are on our own. I believe that this country succeeds when everyone gets a fair shot, when everyone does their fair share, when everyone plays by the same rules. These aren't Democratic values or Republican values. These aren't 1 percent values or 99 percent values. They're American values. And we have to reclaim them.

You see, this isn't the first time America has faced this choice. At the turn of the last century, when a nation of farmers was transitioning to become the world's industrial giant, we had to decide: Would we settle for a country where most of the new railroads and factories were being controlled by a few giant monopolies that kept prices high and wages low? Would we allow our citizens and even our children to work ungodly hours in conditions that were unsafe and unsanitary? Would we restrict education to the privileged few? Because there were people who thought massive inequality and exploitation of people was just the price you paid for progress.

Theodore Roosevelt disagreed. He was the Republican son of a wealthy family. He praised what the titans of industry had done to create jobs and grow the economy. He believed then what we know is true today, that the free market is the greatest force for economic progress in human history. It's led to a prosperity and a standard of living unmatched by the rest of the world.

But Roosevelt also knew that the free market has never been a free license to take whatever you can from whomever you can. He understood the free market only works when there are rules of the road that ensure competition is fair and open and honest. And so he busted up monopolies, forcing those companies to compete for consumers with better services and better prices. And today, they still must. He fought to make sure businesses couldn't profit by exploiting children or selling food or medicine that wasn't safe. And today, they still can't.

And in 1910, Teddy Roosevelt came here to Osawatomie, and he laid out his vision for what he called a New Nationalism. "Our country," he said, ". . . means nothing unless it means the triumph of a real democracy . . . of an economic system under which each man shall be guaranteed the opportunity to show the best that there is in him."

Now, for this, Roosevelt was called a radical. He was called a Socialist—[*laughter*]—even a Communist. But today, we are a richer nation and a stronger democracy because of what he fought for in his last campaign: an 8-hour work day and a minimum wage for women, insurance for the unemployed and for the elderly and those with disabilities, political reform and a progressive income tax.

Today, over 100 years later, our economy has gone through another transformation. Over the last few decades, huge advances in technology have allowed businesses to do more with less, and it's made it easier for them to set up shop and hire workers anywhere they want in the world. And many of you know firsthand the painful disruptions this has caused for a lot of Americans.

Factories where people thought they would retire suddenly picked up and went overseas, where workers were cheaper. Steel mills that needed a hundred—or a thousand employees are now able to do the same work with a hundred employees, so layoffs too often became permanent, not just a temporary part of the business cycle. And these changes didn't just affect blue-collar workers. If you were a bank teller or a phone operator or a travel agent, you saw many in your profession replaced by ATMs and the Internet.

Today, even higher skilled jobs like accountants and middle management can be outsourced to countries like China or India. And if you're somebody whose job can be done cheaper by a computer or someone in another country, you don't have a lot of leverage with your employer when it comes to asking for better wages or better benefits, especially since fewer Americans today are part of a union.

Now, just as there was in Teddy Roosevelt's time, there is a certain crowd in Washington who, for the last few decades, have said, let's respond to this economic challenge with the same old tune. The market will take care of everything, they tell us. If we just cut more regulations and cut more taxes, especially for the wealthy, our economy will grow stronger. Sure, they say, there will be winners and losers. But if the winners do really well, then jobs and prosperity will eventually trickle down to everybody else. And, they argue, even if prosperity doesn't trickle down, well, that's the price of liberty.

Now, it's a simple theory. And we have to admit, it's one that speaks to our rugged individualism and our healthy skepticism of too much government. That's in America's DNA. And that theory fits well on a bumper sticker. [*Laughter*] But here's the problem: It doesn't work. It has never worked. It didn't work when it was tried in the decade before the Great Depression. It's not what led to the incredible postwar booms of the fifties and sixties. And it didn't work when we tried it during the last decade. I mean, understand, it's not as if we haven't tried this theory.

Remember in those years, in 2001 and 2003, Congress passed two of the most expensive tax cuts for the wealthy in history. And what did it get us? The slowest job growth in half a century, massive deficits that have made it much harder to pay for the investments that built this country and provided the basic security that helped millions of Americans reach and stay in the middle class, things like education and infrastructure, science and technology, Medicare and Social Security.

Remember that in those same years, thanks to some of the same folks who are now running Congress, we had weak regulation, we had little oversight, and what did it get us? Insurance companies that jacked up people's premiums with impunity and denied care to patients who were sick, mortgage lenders that tricked families into buying homes they couldn't afford, a financial sector where irresponsibility and lack of basic oversight nearly destroyed our entire economy.

We simply cannot return to this brand of "you're on your own" economics if we're serious about rebuilding the middle class in this country. We know that it doesn't result in a strong economy. It results in an economy that invests too little in its people and in its future. We know it doesn't result in a prosperity that trickles down. It results in a prosperity that's enjoyed by fewer and fewer of our citizens.

Look at the statistics. In the last few decades, the average income of the top 1 percent has gone up by more than 250 percent to $1.2 million per year. I'm not talking about millionaires, people who have a million dollars. I'm saying people who make a million dollars every single year. For the top one-hundredth of 1 percent, the average income is now $27 million per year. The typical CEO who used to earn about 30 times more than his or her worker now earns a hundred and ten times more. And yet over the last decade, the incomes of most Americans have actually fallen by about 6 percent.

Now, this kind of inequality—a level that we haven't seen since the Great Depression—hurts us all. When middle class families can no longer afford to buy the goods and services that businesses are selling, when people are slipping out of the middle class, it drags down the entire economy from top to bottom. America was built on the idea of broad-based prosperity, of strong consumers all across the country. That's why a CEO like Henry Ford made it his mission to pay his workers enough so that they could buy the cars he made. It's also why a recent study showed that countries with less inequality tend to have stronger and steadier economic growth over the long run.

Inequality also distorts our democracy. It gives an outsized voice to the few who can afford high-priced lobbyists and unlimited campaign contributions, and it runs the risk of selling out our democracy to the highest bidder. It leaves everyone else rightly suspicious that the system in Washington is rigged against them, that our elected representatives aren't looking out for the interests of most Americans.

But there's an even more fundamental issue at stake. This kind of gaping inequality gives lie to the promise that's at the very heart of America: that this is a place where you can make it if you try. We tell people—we tell our kids—that in this country, even if you're born with nothing, work hard and you can get into the middle class. We tell them that your children will have a chance to do even better than you do. That's why immigrants from around the world historically have flocked to our shores.

And yet over the last few decades, the rungs on the ladder of opportunity have grown farther and farther apart, and the middle class has shrunk. You know, a few years after World War II, a child who was born into poverty had a slightly better than 50–50 chance of becoming middle class as an adult. By 1980, that chance had fallen to around 40 percent. And if the trend of rising inequality over the last few decades continues, it's estimated that a child born today will only have a one-in-three chance of making it to the middle class—33 percent.

It's heartbreaking enough that there are millions of working families in this country who are now forced to take their children to food banks for a decent meal. But the idea that those children might not have a chance to climb out of that situation and back into the middle class, no matter how hard they work? That's inexcusable. It is wrong. It flies in the face of everything that we stand for.

Now, fortunately, that's not a future that we have to accept, because there's another view about how we build a strong middle class in this country, a view that's truer to our history, a vision that's been embraced in the past by people of both parties for more than 200 years.

It's not a view that we should somehow turn back technology or put up walls around America. It's not a view that says we should punish profit or success or pretend that government knows how to fix all of society's problems. It is a view that says in America we are greater together, when everyone engages in fair play and everybody gets a fair shot and everybody does their fair share.

So what does that mean for restoring middle class security in today's economy? Well, it starts by making sure that everyone in America gets a fair shot at success. The truth is we'll never be able to compete with other countries when it comes to who's best at letting their businesses pay the lowest wages, who's best at busting unions, who's best at letting companies pollute as much as they want. That's a race to the bottom that we can't win, and we shouldn't want to win that race. Those countries don't have a strong middle class. They don't have our standard of living.

The race we want to win, the race we can win is a race to the top, the race for good jobs that pay well and offer middle class security. Businesses will create those jobs in countries with the highest skilled, highest educated workers, the most advanced transportation and communication, the strongest commitment to research and technology.

The world is shifting to an innovation economy, and nobody does innovation better than America. Nobody does it better. No one has better colleges. Nobody has better universities. Nobody has a greater diversity of talent and ingenuity. No one's workers or entrepreneurs are more driven or more daring. The things that have always been our strengths match up perfectly with the demands of the moment.

But we need to meet the moment. We've got to up our game. We need to remember that we can only do that together. It starts by making education a national mission—a national mission—government and businesses, parents and citizens. In this economy, a higher education is the surest route to the middle class. The unemployment rate for Americans with a college degree or more is about half the national average. And their incomes are twice as high as those who don't have a high school diploma. Which means we shouldn't be laying off good teachers right now, we should be hiring them. We shouldn't be expecting less of our schools, we should be demanding more. We shouldn't be making it harder to afford college, we should be a country where everyone has a chance to go and doesn't rack up $100,000 of debt just because they went.

In today's innovation economy, we also need a world-class commitment to science and research, the next generation of high-tech manufacturing. Our factories and our workers shouldn't be idle. We should be giving people the chance to get new skills and training at community colleges so they can learn how to make wind turbines and semiconductors and high-powered batteries. And by the way, if we don't have an economy that's built on bubbles and financial speculation, our best and brightest won't all gravitate towards careers in banking and finance. Because if we want an economy that's built to last, we need more of those young people in science and engineering. This country should not be known for bad debt and phony profits. We should be known for creating and selling products all around the world that are stamped with three proud words: Made in America.

Today, manufacturers and other companies are setting up shop in the places with the best infrastructure to ship their products, move their workers, communicate with the rest of the world. And that's why the over 1 million construction workers who lost their jobs when the housing market collapsed, they shouldn't be sitting at home with nothing to do. They should be rebuilding our roads and our bridges, laying down faster railroads and broadband, modernizing our schools, all the things other countries are already doing to attract good jobs and businesses to their shores.

Yes, business, and not government, will always be the primary generator of good jobs with incomes that lift people into the middle class and keep them there. But as a nation, we've always come together, through our Government, to help create the conditions where both workers and businesses can succeed. And historically, that hasn't been a partisan idea. Franklin Roosevelt worked with Democrats

and Republicans to give veterans of World War II, including my grandfather Stanley Dunham, the chance to go to college on the GI bill. It was a Republican President, Dwight Eisenhower, a proud son of Kansas, who started the Interstate Highway System and doubled down on science and research to stay ahead of the Soviets.

Of course, those productive investments cost money. They're not free. And so we've also paid for these investments by asking everybody to do their fair share. Look, if we had unlimited resources, no one would ever have to pay any taxes and we would never have to cut any spending. But we don't have unlimited resources. And so we have to set priorities. If we want a strong middle class, then our Tax Code must reflect our values. We have to make choices.

Today that choice is very clear. To reduce our deficit, I've already signed nearly $1 trillion of spending cuts into law, and I've proposed trillions more, including reforms that would lower the cost of Medicare and Medicaid.

But in order to structurally close the deficit, get our fiscal house in order, we have to decide what our priorities are. Now, most immediately, short term, we need to extend a payroll tax cut that's set to expire at the end of this month. If we don't do that, 160 million Americans, including most of the people here, will see their taxes go up by an average of a thousand dollars starting in January, and it would badly weaken our recovery. That's the short term.

In the long term, we have to rethink our tax system more fundamentally. We have to ask ourselves: Do we want to make the investments we need in things like education and research and high-tech manufacturing, all those things that helped make us an economic superpower? Or do we want to keep in place the tax breaks for the wealthiest Americans in our country? Because we can't afford to do both. That is not politics. That's just math. [*Laughter*]

Now, so far, most of my Republican friends in Washington have refused under any circumstance to ask the wealthiest Americans to go to the same tax rate they were paying when Bill

Clinton was President. So let's just do a trip down memory lane here.

Keep in mind, when President Clinton first proposed these tax increases, folks in Congress predicted they would kill jobs and lead to another recession. Instead, our economy created nearly 23 million jobs, and we eliminated the deficit. Today, the wealthiest Americans are paying the lowest taxes in over half a century. This isn't like in the early fifties, when the top tax rate was over 90 percent. This isn't even like the early eighties, when the top tax rate was about 70 percent. Under President Clinton, the top rate was only about 39 percent. Today, thanks to loopholes and shelters, a quarter of all millionaires now pay lower tax rates than millions of you, millions of middle class families. Some billionaires have a tax rate as low as 1 percent—1 percent.

That is the height of unfairness. It is wrong. It's wrong that in the United States of America, a teacher or a nurse or a construction worker, maybe earns $50,000 a year, should pay a higher tax rate than somebody raking in $50 million. It's wrong for Warren Buffett's secretary to pay a higher tax rate than Warren Buffett. And by the way, Warren Buffett agrees with me. [*Laughter*] So do most Americans: Democrats, Independents, and Republicans. And I know that many of our wealthiest citizens would agree to contribute a little more if it meant reducing the deficit and strengthening the economy that made their success possible.

This isn't about class warfare. This is about the Nation's welfare. It's about making choices that benefit not just the people who've done fantastically well over the last few decades, but that benefits the middle class and those fighting to get into the middle class and the economy as a whole.

Finally, a strong middle class can only exist in an economy where everyone plays by the same rules, from Wall Street to Main Street. As infuriating as it was for all of us, we rescued our major banks from collapse, not only because a full-blown financial meltdown would have sent us into a second depression, but because we need a strong, healthy financial sector in this country.

But part of the deal was that we wouldn't go back to business as usual. And that's why last year we put in place new rules of the road that refocus the financial sector on what should be their core purpose: getting capital to the entrepreneurs with the best ideas and financing millions of families who want to buy a home or send their kids to college.

Now, we're not all the way there yet, and the banks are fighting us every inch of the way. But already, some of these reforms are being implemented.

If you're a big bank or a risky financial institution, you now have to write out a living will that details exactly how you'll pay the bills if you fail, so that taxpayers are never again on the hook for Wall Street's mistakes. There are also limits on the size of banks and new abilities for regulators to dismantle a firm that is going under. The new law bans banks from making risky bets with their customers' deposits, and it takes away big bonuses and paydays from failed CEOs, while giving shareholders a say on executive salaries.

This is the law that we passed. We are in the process of implementing it now. All of this is being put in place as we speak. Now, unless you're a financial institution whose business model is built on breaking the law, cheating customers, and making risky bets that could damage the entire economy, you should have nothing to fear from these new rules.

Some of you may know, my grandmother worked as a banker for most of her life, worked her way up, started as a secretary, ended up being a vice president of a bank. And I know from her, and I know from all the people I— that I've come in contact with, that the vast majority of bankers and financial service professionals, they want to do right by their customers. They want to have rules in place that don't put them at a disadvantage for doing the right thing. And yet Republicans in Congress are fighting as hard as they can to make sure that these rules aren't enforced.

I'll give you a specific example. For the first time in history, the reforms that we passed put in place a consumer watchdog who is charged with protecting everyday Americans from being taken advantage of by mortgage lenders or payday lenders or debt collectors. And the man we nominated for the post, Richard Cordray, is a former attorney general of Ohio who has the support of most attorney generals, both Democrat and Republican, throughout the country. Nobody claims he's not qualified.

But the Republicans in the Senate refuse to confirm him for the job; they refuse to let him do his job. Why? Does anybody here think that the problem that led to our financial crisis was too much oversight of mortgage lenders or debt collectors?

Audience members. No!

The President. Of course not. Every day we go without a consumer watchdog is another day when a student or a senior citizen or a member of our Armed Forces—because they are very vulnerable to some of this stuff—could be tricked into a loan that they can't afford, something that happens all the time. And the fact is that financial institutions have plenty of lobbyists looking out for their interests. Consumers deserve to have someone whose job it is to look out for them. And I intend to make sure they do. And I want to hear—I want you to hear me, Kansas: I will veto any effort to delay or defund or dismantle the new rules that we put in place.

We shouldn't be weakening oversight and accountability. We should be strengthening oversight and accountability. Give you another example: Too often, we've seen Wall Street firms violating major antifraud laws because the penalties are too weak, and there's no price for being a repeat offender. No more. I'll be calling for legislation that makes those penalties count so that firms don't see punishment for breaking the law as just the price of doing business.

The fact is this crisis has left a huge deficit of trust between Main Street and Wall Street. And major banks that were rescued by the taxpayers have an obligation to go the extra mile in helping to close that deficit of trust. At minimum, they should be remedying past mortgage abuses that led to the financial crisis. They should be working to keep responsible homeowners in their home. We're going to keep pushing them to provide more time for unemployed homeowners to look for work without having to worry about immediately losing their house.

The big banks should increase access to refinancing opportunities to borrowers who haven't yet benefited from historically low interest rates. And the big banks should recognize that precisely because these steps are in the interest of middle class families and the broader economy, it will also be in the banks' own long-term financial interest. What will be good for consumers over the long term will be good for the banks.

Investing in things like education that give everybody a chance to succeed. A Tax Code that makes sure everybody pays their fair share. And laws that make sure everybody follows the rules. That's what will transform our economy. That's what will grow our middle class again. In the end, rebuilding this economy based on fair play, a fair shot, and a fair share will require all of us to see that we have a stake in each other's success. And it will require all of us to take some responsibility.

It will require parents to get more involved in their children's education. It will require students to study harder. It will require some workers to start studying all over again. It will require greater responsibility from homeowners not to take out mortgages they can't afford. They need to remember that if something seems too good to be true, it probably is.

It will require those of us in public service to make Government more efficient and more effective, more consumer friendly, more responsive to people's needs. That's why we're cutting programs that we don't need to pay for those we do. That's why we've made hundreds of regulatory reforms that will save businesses billions of dollars. That's why we're not just throwing money at education, we're challenging schools to come up with the most innovative reforms and the best results.

And it will require American business leaders to understand that their obligations don't just end with their shareholders. Andy Grove, the legendary former CEO of Intel, put it best. He said, "There is another obligation I feel personally, given that everything I've achieved in my career, and a lot of what Intel has achieved . . . were made possible by a climate of democracy, an economic climate and investment climate provided by the United States."

This broader obligation can take many forms. At a time when the cost of hiring workers in China is rising rapidly, it should mean more CEOs deciding that it's time to bring jobs back to the United States, not just because it's good for business, but because it's good for the country that made their business and their personal success possible.

I think about the Big Three auto companies who, during recent negotiations, agreed to create more jobs and cars here in America, and then decided to give bonuses not just to their executives, but to all their employees, so that everyone was invested in the company's success.

I think about a company based in Warroad, Minnesota. It's called Marvin Windows and Doors. During the recession, Marvin's competitors closed dozens of plants, let hundreds of workers go. But Marvin's did not lay off a single one of their 4,000 or so employees—not one. In fact, they've only laid off workers once in over a hundred years. Mr. Marvin's grandfather even kept his eight employees during the Great Depression.

Now, at Marvin's, when times get tough, the workers agree to give up some perks and some pay, and so do the owners. As one owner said, "You can't grow if you're cutting your lifeblood, and that's the skills and experience your workforce delivers." For the CEO of Marvin's, it's about the community. He said: "These are people we went to school with. We go to church with them. We see them in the same restaurants. Indeed, a lot of us have married local girls and boys. We could be anywhere, but we are in Warroad."

That's how America was built. That's why we're the greatest nation on Earth. That's what our greatest companies understand. Our success has never just been about survival of the fittest. It's about building a nation where we're all better off. We pull together. We pitch in. We do our part. We believe that hard work will pay off, that responsibility will be rewarded, and that our children will inherit a nation where those values live on.

And it is that belief that rallied thousands of Americans to Osawatomie—maybe even some of your ancestors—on a rain-soaked day more than a century ago. By train, by wagon, on buggy, bicycle, on foot, they came to hear the vision of a man who loved this country and was determined to perfect it.

"We are all Americans," Teddy Roosevelt told them that day. "Our common interests are as broad as the continent." In the final years of his life, Roosevelt took that same message all across this country, from tiny Osawatomie to the heart of New York City, believing that no matter where he went, no matter who he was talking to, everybody would benefit from a country in which everyone gets a fair chance.

And well into our third century as a nation, we have grown, and we've changed in many ways since Roosevelt's time. The world is faster, and the playing field is larger, and the challenges are more complex. But what hasn't changed, what can never change, are the values that got us this far. We still have a stake in each other's success. We still believe that this should be a place where you can make it if you try. And we still believe in the words of the man who called for a New Nationalism all those years ago. "The fundamental rule of our national life," he said, "the rule which underlies all others—is that, on the whole, and in the long run, we shall go up or down together." And I believe America is on the way up.

Thank you. God bless you. God bless the United States of America.

NOTE: The President spoke at 12:59 p.m. In his remarks, he referred to Bill Self, head coach, University of Kansas men's basketball team; Warren E. Buffett, chief executive officer and chairman, Berkshire Hathaway Inc.; Richard A. Cordray, Director-designate, Consumer Financial Protection Bureau; Susan Marvin, president, Marvin Windows and Doors; and John W. "Jake" Marvin, chairman and chief executive officer, Marvin Lumber and Cedar Co.

Statement on Indonesia's Ratification of the Comprehensive Test Ban Treaty
December 6, 2011

The United States welcomes Indonesia's ratification of the Comprehensive Test Ban Treaty (CTBT), which provides a strong example of the positive leadership role Indonesia can play in the global effort to prevent the spread of nuclear weapons. The Comprehensive Test Ban Treaty is a critical element of the international effort to prevent the proliferation of nuclear weapons, and I urge all states to sign and ratify the agreement so that it can be brought into force at the earliest possible date. The United States remains fully committed to pursuing ratification of the Test Ban Treaty and will continue to engage Members of the Senate on the importance of this treaty to U.S. security. America must lead the global effort to prevent proliferation, and adoption and early entry into force of the CTBT is a vital part of that effort.

Statement on Senate Action To Block the Nomination of Caitlin J. Halligan To Be a Judge on the United States Court of Appeals for the District of Columbia Circuit
December 6, 2011

I am deeply disappointed that a minority of the United States Senate has blocked the nomination of Caitlin Halligan to serve on the U.S. Court of Appeals for the District of Columbia Circuit. Ms. Halligan has the experience, integrity, and judgment to serve with distinction on this court, and she has broad bipartisan support from the legal and law enforcement communities. But today her nomination fell victim to the Republican pattern of obstructionism that puts party ahead of country. Today's vote dramatically lowers the bar used to justify a filibuster, which had required extraordinary circumstances. The only extraordinary things about Ms. Halligan are her qualifications and her intellect.

Currently, Senate Republicans are blocking 20 other highly qualified judicial nominees, half of whom I have nominated to fill vacancies deemed judicial emergencies by the Administrative Office of the Courts. These are distinguished nominees who historically would be confirmed without delay. All of them have already been approved by the Senate Judiciary Committee, most of them unanimously, only to run into partisan roadblocks on the Senate floor. The American people deserve a fair and functioning judiciary. So I urge Senate Republicans to end this pattern of partisan obstructionism and confirm Ms. Halligan and the other judges they have blocked for purely partisan reasons.

Memorandum on International Initiatives To Advance the Human Rights of Lesbian, Gay, Bisexual, and Transgender Persons
December 6, 2011

Memorandum for the Heads of Executive Departments and Agencies

Subject: International Initiatives to Advance the Human Rights of Lesbian, Gay, Bisexual, and Transgender Persons

The struggle to end discrimination against lesbian, gay, bisexual, and transgender (LGBT) persons is a global challenge, and one that is central to the United States commitment to promoting human rights. I am deeply concerned by the violence and discrimination targeting LGBT persons around the world—whether it is passing laws that criminalize LGBT status, beating citizens simply for joining peaceful LGBT pride celebrations, or killing men, women, and children for their perceived sexual orientation. That is why I declared before heads of state gathered at the United Nations, "no country should deny people their rights because of who they love, which is why we must stand up for the rights of gays and lesbians everywhere." Under my Administration, agencies engaged abroad have already begun taking action to promote the fundamental human rights of LGBT persons everywhere. Our deep commitment to advancing the human rights of all people is strengthened when we as the United States bring our tools to bear to vigorously advance this goal.

By this memorandum I am directing all agencies engaged abroad to ensure that U.S. diplomacy and foreign assistance promote and protect the human rights of LGBT persons. Specifically, I direct the following actions, consistent with applicable law:

Section 1. Combating Criminalization of LGBT Status or Conduct Abroad. Agencies engaged abroad are directed to strengthen existing efforts to effectively combat the criminalization by foreign governments of LGBT status or conduct and to expand efforts to combat discrimination, homophobia, and intolerance on the basis of LGBT status or conduct.

Sec. 2. Protecting Vulnerable LGBT Refugees and Asylum Seekers. Those LGBT persons who seek refuge from violence and persecution face daunting challenges. In order to improve protection for LGBT refugees and asylum seekers at all stages of displacement, the Departments of State and Homeland Security shall enhance their ongoing efforts to ensure that LGBT refugees and asylum seekers have equal access to protection and assistance, particularly in countries of first asylum. In addition, the Departments of State, Justice, and Homeland Security shall ensure appropriate training is in place so that relevant Federal Government personnel and key partners can effectively address the protection of LGBT refugees and asylum seekers, including by providing to them adequate assistance and ensuring that the Federal Government has the ability to identify and expedite resettlement of highly vulnerable persons with urgent protection needs.

Sec. 3. Foreign Assistance to Protect Human Rights and Advance Nondiscrimination. Agencies involved with foreign aid, assistance, and development shall enhance their ongoing efforts to ensure regular Federal Government engagement with governments, citizens, civil society, and the private sector in order to build respect for the human rights of LGBT persons.

Sec. 4. Swift and Meaningful U.S. Responses to Human Rights Abuses of LGBT Persons Abroad. The Department of State shall lead a standing group, with appropriate interagency representation, to help ensure the Federal Government's swift and meaningful response to serious incidents that threaten the human rights of LGBT persons abroad.

Sec. 5. Engaging International Organizations in the Fight Against LGBT Discrimination. Multilateral fora and international organizations are key vehicles to promote respect for the human rights of LGBT persons and to bring global attention to LGBT issues. Building on the State Department's leadership in this area, agencies engaged abroad should strengthen the work they have begun and initiate additional efforts in these multilateral fora and organizations to: counter discrimination on the basis of LGBT status; broaden the number of countries willing to support and defend LGBT issues in the multilateral arena; strengthen the role of civil society advocates on behalf of LGBT issues within and through multilateral fora; and strengthen the policies and programming of multilateral institutions on LGBT issues.

Sec. 6. Reporting on Progress. All agencies engaged abroad shall prepare a report within 180 days of the date of this memorandum, and annually thereafter, on their progress toward advancing these initiatives. All such agencies shall submit their reports to the Department of State, which will compile a report on the Federal Government's progress in advancing these initiatives for transmittal to the President.

Sec. 7. Definitions. (a) For the purposes of this memorandum, agencies engaged abroad include the Departments of State, the Treasury,

Defense, Justice, Agriculture, Commerce, Health and Human Services, and Homeland Security, the United States Agency for International Development (USAID), the Millennium Challenge Corporation, the Export-Import Bank, the United States Trade Representative, and such other agencies as the President may designate.

(b) For the purposes of this memorandum, agencies involved with foreign aid, assistance, and development include the Departments of State, the Treasury, Defense, Justice, Health and Human Services, and Homeland Security, the USAID, the Millennium Challenge Corporation, the Export-Import Bank, the United States Trade Representative, and such

other agencies as the President may designate.

This memorandum is not intended to, and does not, create any right or benefit, substantive or procedural, enforceable at law or in equity by any party against the United States, its departments, agencies, or entities, its officers, employees, or agents, or any other person.

The Secretary of State is hereby authorized and directed to publish this memorandum in the *Federal Register*.

BARACK OBAMA

NOTE: This memorandum was not received for publication in the *Federal Register*.

The President's News Conference With Prime Minister Stephen J. Harper of Canada
December 7, 2011

President Obama. Good afternoon, everybody. Please be seated.

I am very pleased to welcome my friend and partner, Prime Minister Harper, back to the White House. Whenever we get together, it's a chance to reaffirm the enduring alliance between our nations, the extraordinary bonds between our peoples, the excellent cooperation between our governments, and my close personal friendship to the Prime Minister.

Stephen, I believe this is the 11th time that we've sat down and worked together, not including our many summits around the world. And on occasions like this, unfortunately, I only speak one language; Stephen moves effortlessly between two. But no matter what language we speak, we always understand each other. In Stephen, I've got a trusted partner, and I think he'll agree that perhaps no two nations match up more closely together or are woven together more deeply, economically, culturally, than the United States and Canada.

And that deep sense of interconnection, our shared values, our shared interests, infused the work that we have done today, from supporting a resolution to the euro zone crisis to moving ahead with the transition in Afghanistan, from

deepening security cooperation here in the Americas to supporting reform and democratic transitions in the Middle East and North Africa.

Our focus today, however, is on our highest priority and my top priority as President, and that's creating jobs faster and growing the economy faster. And in this mission, Canada has a special role to play. As most of you know, Canada is our single largest trading partner, our top export market, and those exports—from cars to food—support some 1.7 million good-paying American jobs. Canada, in turn, is one of the top foreign investors in the United States, and that creates even more jobs and prosperity.

And the Prime Minister and I are determined not just to sustain this trade, but to expand it, to grow it even faster, so we're creating even more jobs and more opportunity for our people. Canada is key to achieving my goal of doubling American exports and putting folks back to work. And the two important initiatives that we agreed to today will help us do just that.

First, we're agreeing to a series of concrete steps to bring our economies even closer and to improve the security of our citizens, not just along our shared border, but beyond the border. And put simply, we're going to make it easier to conduct the trade and travel that creates jobs, and we're going to make it harder for those who would do us harm and threaten our security.

For example, some 90 percent of all our trade—more than a billion dollars in trade every single day—passes through our roads, our bridges, and our ports. But because of old systems and heavy congestion, it still takes too many products too long to cross our borders. And for every business, either Canadian or American, time is money.

So we're going to improve our infrastructure, we're going to introduce new technologies, we're going to improve cargo security and screening, all designed to make it easier for our companies to do business and create jobs. And that, by the way, includes our small businesses, which create most of the new jobs here in America. And when they look to export, typically, Canada is one of the most likely places they are to start getting a foothold in the global economy. So it's hugely important for our small and medium-sized businesses.

Last year, more than 100 million people crossed our shared border, including lots of Canadians who, I'd note, spend more money in the United States than any other visitors. So I want to make a pitch: We want even more Canadians visiting the United States. And please spend more money here. We want to make it easier for frequent travelers and our business-people to travel, and we're going to create a simplified entry-exit system.

I'd add that along with better screening and sharing more information, this will help us be even smarter about our joint security, concentrating our resources where they're needed most: identifying real threats to our security before they reach our shores.

The second thing we're doing is we're ramping up our effort to get rid of outdated, unjustified regulations that stifle trade and job creation. This is especially important in sectors like the auto industry, where so many cars and products are built on both sides of the border.

But sometimes that's slowed down by regulations and paperwork that frankly just doesn't make sense.

So we're going to strike a better balance with sensible regulations that unleash trade and job creation, while still protecting public health and safety. And this builds on the efforts that we have here in the United States, led by Cass Sunstein at OIRA, where we're eliminating billions of dollars in costs from regulations.

Now, our two nations are going to be going further, streamlining, eliminating and coordinating regulations, slashing redtape, and we're going to focus on several key sectors, including autos, agriculture, and health care. So this can be a win-win situation, where not only are we making our regulatory systems more efficient in our respective countries, but we're also seeing greater convergence between our two countries.

Even as we pursue these two new initiatives, the Prime Minister and I discussed our broader economic relationship. I'm pleased that Canada has expressed an interest in the Trans-Pacific Partnership. Many of you accompanied me to the APEC meeting where you know that this has generated a great deal of interest. So we look forward to consulting with Canada, as well as our TPP partners and others, about how all of us can meet the high standards demanded by this trade agreement. And it can be, I think, a real model, not only for the region, but for the world.

We did discuss the proposed Keystone XL Pipeline, which is very important to Canada. And I think the Prime Minister and our Canadian friends understand that it's important for us to make sure that all the questions regarding the project are properly understood, especially its impact on our environment and the health and safety of the American people. And I assured him that we will have a very rigorous process to work through that issue.

So we're going to continue to work as partners and as friends. And, Stephen, on this day and in all the discussions that we have, I want to thank you again for your candor, your sense of common purpose, what you bring and your team brings to this partnership. It's been extraordinary. And I want to personally thank you for the progress that our teams made in these two very important announcements that we made today.

I'm confident, by the way, that we are going to implement them diligently. We have folks like Secretary Napolitano from Department of Homeland Security and Cass Sunstein, who are going to be heading up our team and making sure that these things go into effect in a way that benefits both the Canadian people and the American people.

And so, Stephen, to all the people of Canada, thank you. To you, thank you. And I wish everybody a wonderful holiday season.

Prime Minister Harper. Well, thank you, Barack. Thank you for, first of all, our candid conversation today, as always. We always appreciate that. We appreciate all the work that's been done on this. I did mention Bob Hamilton, Simon Kennedy working on our side. But I do want to thank all the officials on both sides who've been working hard over very many months to do what is a very important initiative.

And of course, I do want to thank you for your friendship, not just personally, Barack, but I know the friendship you feel for the entire nation of Canada, and we all do appreciate it.

[*At this point, Prime Minister Harper spoke in French and translated his remarks into English. The English translation is as follows.*]

Today we are pleased to announce ambitious agreements on perimeter security and economic competitiveness, as well as on regulatory cooperation. These agreements create a new, modern order for a new century. Together, they represent the most significant steps forward in Canada-U.S. cooperation since the North American Free Trade Agreement.

The first agreement merges U.S. and Canadian security concerns with our mutual interest in keeping our border as open as possible to legitimate commerce and travel.

As I said in February, Canada has no friend among America's enemies. What threatens the security and well-being of the United States threatens the security and well-being of Canada. Nevertheless, measures to deal with crimi-

nal and terrorist threats can thicken the border, hindering our efforts to create jobs and growth.

Today our two governments are taking practical steps to reverse that direction. We are agreed, for example, that the best place to deal with trouble is at the continental perimeter; that smarter systems can reduce the needless inconvenience posed to manufacturers and travelers by multiple inspections of freight and baggage.

We also believe that just as threats should be stopped at the perimeter, trusted travelers should cross the border more quickly. Indeed, these priorities are complementary. The key that locks the door against terrorists also opens a wider gate to cross-border trade and travel.

The second joint initiative will reduce regulatory barriers to trade by streamlining and aligning standards where it makes sense to do so. Naturally, in this area, as in all others, no loss of sovereignty is contemplated by either of our governments. However, every rule needs a reason. Where no adequate reason exists for a rule or standard and that rule hinders us from doing business on both sides of the border, then that rule needs to be reexamined.

Ladies and gentlemen, today's agreements will yield lasting benefits to travelers, traders, manufacturers, in fact everybody whose legitimate business or pleasure takes them across the border. And we take these steps, both of us, to protect jobs, to grow our economies, and to keep our citizens safe. And I say "we" because we are each other's largest export customers. The benefits of cooperation will therefore be enjoyed on both sides of the border.

Let me also take this opportunity, Barack, to recognize your leadership in this work. This does reflect the vision—the large vision—that you have for continental trade and security and your commitment to the creation of jobs and growth. And it is, I believe—these agreements today—it's always necessary to say it, the next chapter in a marvelous relationship, and a relationship that really is a shining example to the world.

We talked today about other parts of the world that are more troubled, and believe me, if we could replicate our relationship anywhere in the world, the world would be a better place. We're always delighted to be here, always thankful of having the United States as our great friend and neighbor, and once again, delighted to be here today.

President Obama. Thank you so much.

We've got one question each. David Jackson [USA Today].

Payroll Tax Cut/Keystone XL Pipeline Project/Domestic Energy Sources

Q. Thank you, Mr. President. I have Keystone questions for both of you. Mr. President, we've got some House Republicans who are saying they won't approve any extension of the payroll tax cut unless you move up this oil pipeline project. Is that a deal you would consider? And also, how do you respond to their criticism that you punted this issue past the election for political reasons?

And, Prime Minister Harper, you seemed to suggest the other day that politics is behind the way the Keystone issue has been handled. Do you really feel that way?

President Obama. First of all, any effort to try to try—tie Keystone to the payroll tax cut I will reject. So everybody should be on notice. And the reason is because the payroll tax cut is something that House Republicans, as well as Senate Republicans, should want to do regardless of any other issues. The question is going to be, are they willing to vote against a proposal that ensures that Americans, at a time when the recovery is still fragile, don't see their taxes go up by a thousand dollars? So it shouldn't be held hostage for any other issues that they may be concerned about.

And so my warning is not just specific to Keystone. Efforts to tie a whole bunch of other issues to what is something that they should be doing anyway will be rejected by me.

With respect to the politics, look, this is a big project with big consequences. We've seen Democrats and Republicans express concerns about it. And it is my job as President of the United States to make sure that a process is followed that examines all the options, looks at all the consequences before a decision is made.

Now, that process is moving forward. The State Department is making sure that it crosses all its t's and dots all its i's before making a final determination. And I think it's worth noting, for those who want to try to politicize this issue, that when it comes to domestic energy production, we have gone all in, because our belief is, is that we're going to have to do a whole range of things to make sure that U.S. energy independence exists for a long time to come, U.S. energy security exists for a long time to come.

So we have boosted oil production. We are boosting natural gas production. We're looking at a lot of traditional energy sources, even as we insist on transitioning to clean energy. And I think this shouldn't be a Democratic or a Republican issue, this should be an American issue: How do we make sure that we've got the best possible energy mix to benefit our businesses, benefit our workers, but also benefit our families to make sure that the public health and safety of the American people are looked after? And that's what this process is designed to do.

[*Prime Minister Harper spoke in English.*]

Prime Minister Harper. I think my position, the position of the Government of Canada, on this issue is very well known, and of course, Barack and I have discussed that on many occasions. He's indicated to me, as he's indicated to you today, that he's following a proper project to eventually take that decision here in the United States and that he has an open mind in regards to what the final decision may or may not be.

And that's—I take that as his answer. And you can appreciate that I would not comment on the domestic politics of this issue or any other issue here in the United States.

Q. Excuse me, Mr. President. By rejecting a veto—would you veto any payroll tax cuts if it had something else on it?

President Obama. I think it's fair to say that if the payroll tax cut is attached to a whole bunch of extraneous issues not related to making sure that the American people's taxes don't go up on January 1, then it's not something that

I'm going to accept. And I don't expect to have to veto it because I expect they're going to have enough sense over on Capitol Hill to do the people's business and not try to load it up with a bunch of politics.

Prime Minister Harper. I have Lee-Anne Goodman, Canadian Press.

Border Security

Q. Hi, there. Prime Minister, will Canada warn Americans about visitors to Canada from suspect countries like Pakistan, even if they have no intention of coming to the U.S. under this new agreement?

And, Mr. President, do you want to be warned? Do you want that kind of information? And *en francais, s'il vous plait aussi,* Mr. Harper.

[*Prime Minister Harper responded in English as follows and then translated his remarks into French.*]

Prime Minister Harper. We do—I think, as you know, our two countries cooperate on international security issues very closely and very regularly. That cooperation, at the same time, is governed by agreements and defined protocols, and those will remain in effect.

President Obama. I don't think I can expand any more on that. [*Laughter*] Far more eloquent than I could ever express it. Okay?

Thank you so much, everybody.

Prime Minister Harper. Thanks, everybody.

NOTE: The President's news conference began at 3:16 p.m. in the South Court Auditorium of the Dwight D. Eisenhower Executive Office Building. In his remarks, Prime Minister Harper referred to Associate Deputy Minister of Environment Bob Hamilton and Deputy Secretary to the Cabinet for Plans and Consultations Simon Kennedy of Canada.

Statement on National Pearl Harbor Remembrance Day
December 7, 2011

Seventy years ago today, a bright Sunday morning was darkened by the unprovoked attack on Pearl Harbor. Today Michelle and I join the American people in honoring the memory of the more than 2,400 American patriots—military and civilian; men, women, and children—who gave their lives in our first battle of the Second World War. Our thoughts and prayers are with the families for whom this day is deeply personal—the spouses, brothers and sisters, and sons and daughters—who have known seven decades without a loved one, but who have kept their legacy alive for future generations.

We salute the veterans and survivors of Pearl Harbor who inspire us still. Despite overwhelming odds, they fought back heroically, inspiring our Nation and putting us on the path to victory. They are members of that greatest generation who overcame the Depression, crossed oceans and stormed the beaches to defeat fascism, and turned adversaries into our closest allies. When the guns fell silent, they came home, went to school on the GI bill, and built the largest middle class in history and the strongest economy in the world. They remind us that no challenge is too great when Americans stand as one. All of us owe these men and women a profound debt of gratitude for the freedoms and standard of living we enjoy today.

On this National Pearl Harbor Remembrance Day, we also reaffirm our commitment to carrying on their work, to keeping the country we love strong, free, and prosperous. And as today's wars in Iraq and Afghanistan come to an end and we welcome home our 9/11 generation, we resolve to always take care of our troops, veterans, and military families as well as they've taken care of us. On this solemn anniversary, there can be no higher tribute to the Americans who served and sacrificed 70 years ago today.

Remarks on Senate Action To Block the Nomination of Richard A. Cordray To Be Director of the Consumer Financial Protection Bureau and an Exchange With Reporters
December 8, 2011

The President. Good morning, everybody. A couple of days ago I said that we are in a make-or-break moment when it comes to America's middle class. We either have a country where everybody fends for themselves, or we create a country where everybody does their fair share, everybody has got a fair chance, and we ensure that there's fair play out there.

Now, to ensure fair play, one of the things that I talked about was the importance of making sure we implement financial reform, Wall Street reform that was passed last year. And a key component of that was making sure that we have a consumer watchdog in place who can police what mortgage brokers and payday lenders and other nonbank financial entities are able to do when it comes to consumers.

This is a big deal. About one in five people use these kinds of mechanisms to finance everything from buying a house to cashing their checks. And we passed a law last year that said we need this consumer watchdog in place to make sure that people aren't taken advantage of.

Now, we have nominated somebody—Richard Cordray, former attorney general and treasurer of Ohio—who everybody says is highly qualified. The majority of attorney generals, Republican and Democrat, from across the country have said this is somebody who can do the job with integrity, who has a tradition of being a bipartisan individual who looks out for the public interest, and is ready to go. And he actually helped set up the consumer finance protection board.

This morning Senate Republicans blocked his nomination, refusing to let the Senate even go forward with an up-or-down vote on Mr. Cordray. This makes absolutely no sense.

Consumers across the country understand that part of the reason we got into the financial mess that we did was because regulators were not doing their jobs. People were not paying attention to what was happening in the housing market; people weren't paying attention to who was being taken advantage of. There were folks who were making a lot of money taking advantage of American consumers.

This individual's job is to make sure that individual consumers are protected, everybody from seniors to young people who are looking for student loans to members of our Armed Services, who are probably more vulnerable than just about anybody when it comes to unscrupulous financial practices.

There is no reason why Mr. Cordray should not be nominated and should not be confirmed by the Senate and should not be doing his job right away in order to carry out his mandate and his mission.

So I just want to send a message to the Senate: We are not giving up on this. We are going to keep on going at it. We are not going to allow politics as usual on Capitol Hill to stand in the way of American consumers being protected by unscrupulous financial operators. And we're going to keep on pushing on this issue.

Payroll Tax Cut/Unemployment Insruance Benefits

Now, the second thing I want to make clear about is that, with respect to the payroll tax—you guys have all seen our countdown clock behind us. This is about doing—making sure that everybody is doing their fair share and that the middle class does not see their taxes go up by a thousand dollars in 23 days.

And we've heard recently some intimations from the Senate majority leader and from the Speaker of the House—or the Senate minority leader and the Speaker of the House—that they think we should do a payroll tax, but the question is what price will they extract from the President in order to get it done.

And I just want to make clear: This is not about me. They shouldn't extend the payroll tax cut for me. They shouldn't extend unemployment insurance for me. This is for 160 million people who, in 23 days, are going to see their taxes go up if Congress doesn't act. This is for 5 million individuals who are out there looking for a job and can't find a job right now in a tough economy who could end up not being able to pay their bills or keep their house if Congress doesn't act.

So rather than trying to figure out what can they extract politically from me in order to get this thing done, what they need to do is be focused on what's good for the economy, what's good for jobs, and what's good for the American people.

And I made very clear I do not expect Congress to go home unless the payroll tax cut is extended and unless unemployment insurance is extended. It would be wrong for families, but it would also be wrong for the economy as a whole.

All right, with that, I'm going to take a couple questions. Ben [Ben Feller, Associated Press].

President's Foreign Policy Agenda/Department of Health and Human Services Ruling on Over-the-Counter Availability of Emergency Contraceptives

Q. Thank you, Mr. President. It's a very busy time. If I may, I'd like to ask you about two other important issues in the news. Republican candidates have taken aim at your approach to foreign policy, particularly the Middle East and Israel, and accused you of appeasement. I wanted to get your reaction to that. And also, I'm wondering if you personally intervened in any way in halting the sale of the morning-after pill to those under 17 and whether you think politics trumps science in this case.

The President. Ask Usama bin Laden and the 22 out of 30 top Al Qaida leaders who've been taken off the field whether I engage in appeasement. Or whoever's left out there, ask them about that.

With respect to the Plan B, I did not get involved in the process. This was a decision that was made by Kathleen Sebelius, the Secretary of HHS.

I will say this, as the father of two daughters. I think it is important for us to make sure that

we apply some common sense to various rules when it comes to over-the-counter medicine. And as I understand it, the reason Kathleen made this decision was she could not be confident that a 10-year-old or an 11-year-old going to a drugstore should be able—alongside bubble gum or batteries—be able to buy a medication that potentially, if not used properly, could end up having an adverse effect. And I think most parents would probably feel the same way.

So the expectation here is—I think it's very important to understand that for women, for those over 17, this continues to be something that you can go in and purchase from a drugstore. It has been deemed safe by the FDA. Nobody is challenging that. When it comes to 12-year-olds or 13-year-olds, the question is, can we have confidence that they would potentially use Plan B properly? And her judgment was that there was not enough evidence, that this potentially could be used improperly in a way that had adverse health effects on those young people.

Q. Do you fully support the decision?
The President. I do.

Director-Designate Cordray's Nomination/Financial Regulatory Reform/Federal Nomination Process

Q. Mr. President, is a recess appointment for Richard Cordray on the table, number one? And number two, the Italian Prime Minister, the new Prime Minister indicated today he may be coming to the White House next month. Do you think he and other European leaders are stepping up in the way you've urged them to, to sort of clear up the debt crisis?

The President. I will not take any options off the table when it comes to getting Richard Cordray in as Director of the consumer finance protection board. And I want to repeat what I said earlier: This is a law that was passed by Congress that I signed into law that is designed solely to protect American consumers.

I don't think there's any consumer out there—I don't think there's any American out there—who thinks that the reason we got into the big financial mess that we did was because of too much regulation of Wall Street or the financial services industry. I take it back. I'm sure there are some folks in the financial service industry who make that argument, although I'm not sure that they make it with a straight face.

So let's just take a very specific example: All the families out there who have now lost their home, after having paid their mortgage over and over again because they were told that they could afford this home, they didn't understand all the documentation that was involved. This was peddled deliberately to them, even though a mortgage broker might have known that there was no way that they could keep up with these payments, and now they're out on the street because nobody was making sure that there's fair play and fair dealing in the mortgage industry on it. Now, why wouldn't we want to have somebody just to make sure that people are being treated fairly? Especially when not only is that family affected, but our whole economy is affected.

This is part of what I was talking about a couple of days ago. We have a Congress right now, Republicans in Congress right now, who seem to have entirely forgotten how we got into this mess. And part of the reason was because we did not empower our regulators to make sure that they were ensuring fair play. That's what the consumer finance protection board is designed to do.

We had Holly Petraeus, wife of General Petraeus, who's been working to make sure that our Armed Services personnel aren't taken advantage of. They get transferred to a base, and next thing they know they're taking out loans that they think are a good deal, but it turns out that they're paying 100-, 150-, 200-percent interest rates. Why wouldn't we want somebody in place to make sure that doesn't happen? It doesn't make any sense.

So the bottom line is—you asked about the recess appointment—we're going to look at all our options. My hope and expectation is, is that the Republicans who blocked this nomination come to their senses. And I know that some of them have made an argument, well, we just

want to sort of make some modifications in the law. Well, they're free to introduce a bill and get that passed.

But part of what's happened over on Capitol Hill—not just on this issue, but on every issue—is they will hold up nominations, well-qualified judges aren't getting a vote, I've got Assistant Secretaries to the Treasury who get held up for no reason, just because they're trying to see if they can use that to reverse some sort of law that's already been passed. And that's part of what gets the American people so frustrated, because they don't feel like this thing is on the level.

Europe's Economic Stabilization Efforts

Q. The European crisis, do you have any sense——

The President. Oh, on the European debt crisis, I am obviously very concerned about what's happening in Europe. I've expressed those concerns repeatedly to President Sarkozy, Chancellor Merkel, all the key leaders involved. I think they now recognize the urgency of doing something serious and bold. The question is whether they can muster the political will to get it done.

Look, Europe is wealthy enough that there's no reason why they can't solve this problem. It's not as if we're talking about some impoverished country that doesn't have any resources and is being buffeted by the world markets and they need to come hat in hand and get help. This is Europe, with some of the wealthiest countries on Earth, collectively one of the largest markets on Earth, if not the largest. And so if they muster the political will, they have the capacity to settle markets down, make sure that they are acting responsibly, and that governments like Italy are able to finance their debt.

And I think that Chancellor Merkel has made some progress with other European leaders in trying to move towards a fiscal compact where everybody's playing by the same rules and nobody's acting irresponsibly. I think that's all for the good, but there's a short-term crisis that has to be resolved to make sure that markets have confidence that Europe stands behind the euro.

And we're going to do everything we can to push them in a good direction on this, because it has a huge impact on what happens here in the United States. They are our largest trading partner, and we're seeing some positive signs in our economy, but if we see Europe tank, that obviously could have a big impact on our ability to generate the jobs that we need here in the United States.

I'm going to answer one last question. Kristen—Kristen Welker [NBC News].

Iran/Payroll Tax Cut/Unemployment Insurance Benefits/Keystone XL Pipeline Project

Q. Mr. President, thank you. You just called on Congress not to leave until they resolve this issue over the payroll tax cuts and unemployment insurance benefits. Can you say definitively that you will postpone your own vacation until these two matters are resolved?

And also, on Iran, we've heard some sharper language from members of your administration about Iran recently. Are you intentionally trying to ramp up the pressure on Iran? And given that you've stated that no options are off the table, should we take that to mean that you are considering some other options?

The President. No options off the table means I'm considering all options.

Q. Can you tell us specifically what those options might be?

The President. No. But what I can say with respect to Iran, and I think it's very important to remember, particularly given some of the political noise out there, that this administration has systematically imposed the toughest sanctions on Iraq—on Iran ever.

When we came into office, the world was divided, Iran was unified and moving aggressively on its own agenda. Today, Iran is isolated, and the world is unified in applying the toughest sanctions that Iran has ever experienced. And it's having an impact inside of Iran. And that's as a consequence of the extraordinary work that's been done by our national security team.

Now, Iran understands that they have a choice: They can break that isolation by acting responsibly and foreswearing the development of nuclear weapons, which would still allow them to pursue peaceful nuclear power, like every other country that's a member of the Non-Proliferation Treaty, or they can continue to operate in a fashion that isolates them from the entire world. And if they are pursuing nuclear weapons, then I have said very clearly, that is contrary to the national security interests of the United States, it's contrary to the national security interests of our allies, including Israel, and we are going to work with the world community to prevent that.

With respect to my vacation, I would not ask anybody to do something I'm not willing to do myself. So I know some of you might have been looking forward to a little sun and sand—[*laughter*]—but the bottom line is, is that we are going to stay here as long as it takes to make sure that the American people's taxes don't go up on January 1 and to make sure that folks who desperately need unemployment insurance get that help. And there's absolutely no excuse for us not getting it done.

Keep in mind, on the payroll tax cut, this is something that Democrats and Republicans agreed to last year with little fanfare, and it was good for the economy. And independent economists estimate that for us to not extend it right now—to not extend payroll tax cut, not extend unemployment insurance—would have a significant, adverse impact on our economy, right at a time when we're supposed to be growing the economy.

So when I hear the Speaker or the Senate Republican leader wanting to dicker, wanting to see what can they extract from us in order to get this done, my response to them is, just do the right thing. Focus on the American people, focus on the economy right now.

I know the suggestion right now is, is that somehow, well, this Keystone issue will create jobs. That's being determined by the State Department right now, and there is a process. But here's what I know: However many jobs might be generated by a Keystone pipeline, they're going to be a lot fewer than the jobs that are created by extending the payroll tax cut and extending unemployment insurance.

Get it done. And if not, maybe we'll have a white Christmas here in Washington. And I look forward to spending a lot of time with you guys—[*laughter*]—between now and the new year.

All right? Thank you, guys.

Remarks at a Hanukkah Reception
December 8, 2011

The President. Well, good evening, everybody. Welcome to the White House. Thank you all for joining us tonight to celebrate Hanukkah, even if we're doing it a little bit early. [*Laughter*]

I want to start by recognizing a few folks who are here. The Ambassador to the United States from Israel, Michael Oren, is in the house.

We are honored to be joined by one of the Justices of the Supreme Court, Ruth—Justice Ruth Bader Ginsburg is here. We are thrilled to see her. She's one of my favorites. I got to—[*laughter*]—so I've got a soft spot for Justice Ginsburg.

And we've got more than a few Members of Congress here and members of my administration in the house, including our new Director of Jewish Outreach, Jarrod Bernstein is here. Where's Jarrod? Hey, Jarrod.

I also want to thank the West Point Jewish Chapel Cadet Choir, the Voice of Tradition, for their wonderful performance, but more importantly, for their extraordinary service to our country.

And I want to thank all the rabbis and lay leaders who have come far and wide to be here with us today.

Now, as I said, we're jumping the gun just a little bit. The way I see it, we're just extending the holiday spirit. We're stretching it out. [*Laughter*] But we do have to be careful that your kids don't start thinking Hanukkah lasts 20 nights instead of 8. [*Laughter*] That will cause some problems.

This Hanukkah season we remember a story so powerful that we all know it by heart, even us gentiles. It's a story of right over might, of faith over doubt, of a band of believers who rose up and freed their people and discovered

NOTE: The President spoke at 11:40 a.m. in the James S. Brady Press Briefing Room at the White House. In his remarks, he referred to Gen. David H. Petraeus, USA (Ret.), Director, Central Intelligence Agency; President Nicolas Sarkozy of France; and Chancellor Angela Merkel of Germany. A reporter referred to Prime Minister Mario Monti of Italy.

that the oil left in their desecrated temple, which should have lasted only 1 night, ended up lasting 8.

It's a timeless story. And for 2,000 years, it has given hope to Jews everywhere who are struggling. And today, it reminds us that miracles come in all shapes and sizes. Because to most people, the miracle of Hanukkah would have looked like nothing more than a simple flame, but the believers in the temple knew it was something else. They knew it was something special.

This year, we have to recognize the miracles in our own lives. Let's honor the sacrifices our ancestors made so that we might be here today. Let's think about those who are spending this holiday far away from home, including members of our military who guard our freedom around the world. Let's extend a hand to those who are in need and allow the value of *tikkun olam* to guide our work this holiday season.

This is also a time to be grateful for our friendships, both with each other and between our nations. And that includes, of course, our unshakeable support and commitment to the security of the nation of Israel.

So while it is not yet Hanukkah, let's give thanks for our blessings, for being together to celebrate this wonderful holiday season. And we never need an excuse for a good party. [*Laughter*] So we are going to see all of you in a second downstairs——

The First Lady. No. Aren't we in the Blue Room?

The President. Or wherever we are. [*Laughter*] I think we're downstairs. We are downstairs in the Map Room. So as I look around, I see a whole bunch of good friends. We can't wait to give you a hug and a kiss and wish you a happy holiday. The guys with whiskers, I won't give you a kiss. [*Laughter*]

Thank you very much, everybody.

NOTE: The President spoke at 6:10 p.m. in the Grand Foyer at the White House.

The President's Weekly Address
December 10, 2011

Today, America faces a make-or-break moment for the middle class.

After the worst economic crisis of our lifetimes, some still want to return to the same policies that got us into this mess. They're the same policies that have stacked the deck against working Americans for way too long. They're part of a philosophy that says we're better off when everyone is left to fend for themselves and play by their own rules.

But I have a different vision. I believe that we are greater together than we are on our own. I believe that this country succeeds when everyone gets a fair shot, everyone does their fair share, and everyone engages in fair play.

To ensure fair play, last year, we passed the toughest financial reform in generations.

See, for too long, the rules weren't the same on Wall Street as they were on Main Street. Risky bets were made with other people's money. Some folks made a lot of money taking advantage of consumers. It was wrong. And this irresponsible behavior on the part of some contributed to the worst financial crisis since the Great Depression.

So this financial reform refocuses the financial sector on what's really important: getting capital to entrepreneurs who want to grow their businesses and financing to millions of families who want to buy a house or send their kids to college.

A key part of that was putting in place the first-ever consumer watchdog, someone whose job it is to protect American families from being taken advantage of by mortgage lenders, payday lenders, and debt collectors.

Tens of millions of Americans use these services. Protecting them from unscrupulous practices is an important job. And that's why I nominated Richard Cordray to serve as the head of this consumer watchdog agency.

As the former attorney general of Ohio, Richard helped recover billions of dollars on behalf of retirees and stood up to dishonest lending practices. He has the support of most attorney generals across the country, both Democrats and Republicans. Members of Congress from both parties say he's more than qualified for the job. And yet on Thursday, Republicans blocked his nomination. They refused to even allow it to come up for a vote.

That doesn't make any sense. Do Republicans in Congress think our financial crisis was caused by too much oversight of mortgage lenders or debt collectors? Of course not. And every day America has to wait for a new consumer protection watchdog is another day that dishonest businesses can target and take advantage of students, seniors, and servicemembers.

So I refuse to take no for an answer. Financial institutions have plenty of high-powered lawyers and lobbyists looking out for them. It's time consumers had someone on their side.

And while they're at it, Republicans in Congress should stop the games and extend the payroll tax cut for working Americans. Because if they don't, nearly 160 million Americans will see their taxes go up at the end of this month.

Congress cannot end the year by taking money out of the pockets of working Americans. Now's not the time for playing politics. Now's the time to do what's right for the American people.

No one should go home for the holidays until we get this done. So tell your Members of Congress, "Don't be a grinch." Tell them to do the right thing for you and for our economy. Thanks.

NOTE: The address was recorded at approximately 4:35 p.m. on December 9 in the Roosevelt Room at the White House for broadcast on December 10. In the address, the President referred to Richard A. Cordray, Director-designate, Consumer Financial Protection Bureau. The transcript was made available by the Office of the Press Secretary on December 9, but was embargoed for release until 6 a.m. on December 10.

Remarks at "Christmas in Washington"
December 11, 2011

Good evening, everybody. I just want to start by thanking all the folks who have joined us at the National Building Museum. Let's give it up for our host, who also happens to be the host of the best late night show on TBS, Conan O'Brien. [*Laughter*] And I want to thank all the spectacular artists and choirs and glee clubs who've made this such a spectacular evening. Please give them a big round of applause.

I want to congratulate 30 years of "Christmas in Washington." It's always an extraordinary honor to be a part of this event because it benefits such a special place, the Children's National Medical Center. For so many children and their parents, the work that they do to save lives and improve care is nothing short of a miracle. And that's fitting, because this is the season to celebrate miracles.

This is the season to celebrate the story of how, more than 2,000 ago, a child was born to two faithful travelers who could find rest only in a stable, among cattle and sheep. He was no ordinary child. He was the manifestation of God's love. And every year we celebrate His birth because the story of Jesus Christ changed the world. For me and for millions of Americans, His story has filled our hearts and inspired our lives. It moves us to love one another, to help and serve those less fortunate, to forgive, to draw close to our families, to be grateful for all that has been given to us, to keep faith, and to hold on to an enduring hope in humanity.

Service to others, compassion to all, treating others as we wish ourselves to be treated, those values aren't just at the center of Christianity, those are values that are shared by all faiths. So tonight let us all rededicate ourselves to each other. And in that spirit, from my family to yours, happy holidays. Merry Christmas.

God bless you all, and God bless the United States of America.

NOTE: The President spoke at 7:31 p.m. at the National Building Museum.

The President's News Conference With Prime Minister Nuri al-Maliki of Iraq
December 12, 2011

President Obama. Please have a seat. Good afternoon, everyone.

When I took office, nearly 150,000 American troops were deployed in Iraq, and I pledged to end this war responsibly. Today, only several thousand troops remain there, and more are coming home every day.

This is a season of homecomings, and military families across America are being reunited for the holidays. In the coming days, the last American soldiers will cross the border out of Iraq with honor and with their heads held high. After nearly 9 years, our war in Iraq ends this month.

Today I'm proud to welcome Prime Minister Maliki, the elected leader of a sovereign, self-reliant, and democratic Iraq. We're here to mark the end of this war, to honor the sacrifices of all those who made this day possible, and to turn the page, begin a new chapter in the history between our countries, a normal relationship between sovereign nations, an equal partnership based on mutual interests and mutual respect.

Iraq faces great challenges, but today reflects the impressive progress that Iraqis have made. Millions have cast their ballots—some risking or giving their lives—to vote in free elections. The Prime Minister leads Iraq's most inclusive government yet. Iraqis are working to build institutions that are efficient and independent and transparent.

Economically, Iraqis continue to invest in their infrastructure and development. And I think it's worth considering some remarkable statistics. In the coming years, it's estimated that Iraq's economy will grow even faster than China's or India's. With oil production rising, Iraq is on track to once again be one of the region's leading oil producers.

With respect to security, Iraqi forces have been in the lead for the better part of 3 years, patrolling the streets, dismantling militias, conducting counterterrorism operations. Today, despite continued attacks by those who seek to derail Iraq's progress, violence remains at record lows.

And, Mr. Prime Minister, that's a tribute to your leadership and to the skill and the sacrifices of Iraqi forces.

Across the region, Iraq is forging new ties of trade and commerce with its neighbors, and Iraq is assuming its rightful place among the community of nations. For the first time in two decades, Iraq is scheduled to host the next Arab League Summit, and what a powerful message that will send throughout the Arab world. People throughout the region will see a new Iraq that's determining its own destiny, a country in which people from different religious sects and ethnicities can resolve their differences peacefully through the democratic process.

Mr. Prime Minister, as we end this war and as Iraq faces its future, the Iraqi people must know that you will not stand alone. You have a strong and enduring partner in the United States of America.

And so today the Prime Minister and I are reaffirming our common vision of a long-term partnership between our nations. This is in keeping with our strategic framework agreement, and it will be like the close relationships we have with other sovereign nations. Simply

put, we are building a comprehensive partnership.

Mr. Prime Minister, you've said that Iraqis seek democracy, "a state of citizens and not sects." So we're partnering to strengthen the institutions upon which Iraq's democracy depends: free elections, a vibrant press, a strong civil society, professional police and law enforcement that uphold the rule of law, an independent judiciary that delivers justice fairly, and transparent institutions that serve all Iraqis.

We're partnering to expand our trade and commerce. We'll make it easier for our businesses to export and innovate together. We'll share our experiences in agriculture and in health care. We'll work together to develop Iraq's energy sector even as the Iraqi economy diversifies, and we'll deepen Iraq's integration into the global economy.

We're partnering to expand the ties between our citizens, especially our young people. Through efforts like the Fulbright Program, we're welcoming more Iraqi students and future leaders to America to study and form friendships that will bind our nations together for generations to come. And we'll forge more collaborations in areas like science and technology.

We'll partner for our shared security. Mr. Prime Minister, we discussed how the United States could help Iraq train and equip its forces, not by stationing American troops there or with U.S. bases in Iraq—those days are over—but rather, the kind of training and assistance we offer to other countries. Given the challenges we face together in a rapidly changing region, we also agreed to establish a new, formal channel of communication between our national security advisers.

And finally, we're partnering for regional security. For just as Iraq has pledged not to interfere in other nations, other nations must not interfere in Iraq. Iraq's sovereignty must be respected. And meanwhile, there should be no doubt, the drawdown in Iraq has allowed us to refocus our resources, achieve progress in Afghanistan, put Al Qaida on the path to defeat, and to better prepare for the full range of challenges that lie ahead.

So make no mistake, our strong presence in the Middle East endures, and the United States will never waver in defense of our allies, our partners, or our interests.

This is the shared vision that Prime Minister Maliki and I reaffirm today: an equal partnership, a broad relationship that advances the security, the prosperity, and the aspirations of both our people.

Mr. Prime Minister, you've said it yourself: Building a strong and durable relationship between our two countries is vital. And I could not agree more.

So this is a historic moment. A war is ending. A new day is upon us. And let us never forget those who gave us this chance, the untold number of Iraqis who've given their lives; more than 1 million Americans, military and civilian, who have served in Iraq; nearly 4,500 fallen Americans who gave their last full measure of devotion; tens of thousands of wounded warriors; and so many inspiring military families. They are the reason that we can stand here today. And we owe it to every single one of them—we have a moral obligation to all of them—to build a future worthy of their sacrifice.

Mr. Prime Minister.

[At this point, Prime Minister Maliki spoke in Arabic, and his remarks were translated by an interpreter and joined in progress.]

Prime Minister Maliki. ——positive atmosphere that prevailed among us, and for the obligations, the common obligations, of ending the war, and the commitment to which the American forces will withdraw from Iraq, which is a withdrawal that affects—that indicates success, and not like others have said, that it was negative, but the goals that we established were achieved.

Iraq had a political process established, a democratic process, and adoption of the principles of elections and the transfer—peaceful transfer of authority. Iraq is following a policy, a foreign policy, which does not intervene in the affairs of others and does not allow the others to intervene in its own affairs. Iraq is looking for common grounds with the others and

establishes its interest at the forefront and the interest of the others, which it is concerned about, like from any confusion.

Your Excellency, today we meet in Washington after we have completed the first page of a constructive cooperation in which we also thank you and appreciate you for your commitment to everything that you have committed yourself to. And anyone who observes the nature of the relationship between the two countries will say that the relationship will not end with the departure of the last American soldier. It only started when we signed in 2008, in addition to the withdrawal treaty, the strategic framework agreement for the relationship between our two countries.

And because we have proven success in the first mission, a very unique success—nobody imagined that we would succeed in defeating terrorism and the Al Qaida—we must also establish the necessary steps in order to succeed in our second stage, which is the dual relationship under the strategic framework agreement, in the economic sphere, as well as in educational and commercial and cultural and judicial and security cooperation fields.

Iraq now has become reliant completely on its own security apparatus and internal security as a result of the expertise that it gained during the confrontations and the training and the equipping. But it remains in need of cooperation with the United States of America in security issues and information and combating terrorism and in the area of training and the area of equipping, which is needed by the Iraqi Army. And we have started that. And we want to complete the process of equipping the Iraqi Army in order to protect our sovereignty and does not violate the rights of anybody—or do not take any missions that violate the sovereignty of others.

Today, the joint mission is to establish the mechanisms and the commitments that will expedite our—we have reached an agreement, and we have held a meeting for the higher joint committee under the chairmanship of Mr. Biden, the Vice President, and myself in Baghdad, and we spoke about all the details that would put the framework agreement into implementation.

And here we talked about it and its activation. And there will be other discussions and other meetings with the higher committee here in Washington in order to put the final touches regarding the necessary mechanisms for cooperation and achieving the common vision that we followed, which was based on our common wills and political independent decision and the desire to respect the sovereignty of each other.

And we feel that we need political cooperation as well, in addition to cooperating in the security and economic and commercial fields. We need a political cooperation, particularly with regard to the matters that are common and are of concern for us as two parties that want to cooperate.

The common vision that we used as a point of departure we have confirmed today. And I am very happy. Every time we meet with the American side, I find determination and a strong will to activate the strategic framework agreement. And I will say frankly, this is necessary, and it serves the interests of Iraq, as it is necessary and serves the interests of the United States of America.

This makes us feel that we will succeed with the same commitment, common commitment that we had in combating terrorism and accomplishing the missions, the basis of which Iraq was independent. Iraq today has a lot of wealth, and it needs experience and expertise, and American and foreign expertise, to help Iraq exploiting its own wealth in an ideal way. Iraq is still suffering from a shortage of resources, and we have established a strategy to increase the Iraqi wealth. And we hope that the American companies will have the largest role in increasing our wealth in the area of oil and other aspects as well.

Iraq wants to rebuild all these sectors that were harmed because of the war and because of the adventurous policies that were used by the former regime, and we need a wide range of reform in the area of education.

We have succeeded in signing several agreements through the educational initiative, which put hundreds of our college graduates to continue their graduate studies and specialized subject in American universities. And I am putting it before everyone who is watching the relationship between the U.S. and Iraq. It is a very—it has very high aspirations.

And I would like to renew my thanks for His Excellency the President for giving me this opportunity, and I wish him more success, God willing. Thank you very much.

President Obama. We have time for a few questions. I'm going to start with Ben Feller of AP [Associated Press].

Syria/Iraq/Iran

Q. Thank you, Mr. President and Mr. Prime Minister. Mr. President, I have two questions for you on the region. In Syria, you have called for President Asad to step down over the killing of his people, but Prime Minister Maliki has warned that Asad's removal could lead to a civil war that could destabilize the whole region. I'm wondering if you're worried that Iraq could be succumbing to Iran's influence on this matter and perhaps helping to protect Asad.

And speaking of Iran, are you concerned that it will be able to weaken America's national security by discovering intelligence from the fallen drone that it captured?

Prime Minister Maliki, I'd like to ask you the question about Syria. Why haven't you demanded that Asad step down, given the slaughter of his people?

President Obama. First of all, the Prime Minister and I discussed Syria, and we share the view that when the Syrian people are being killed or are unable to express themselves, that's a problem. There's no disagreement there.

I have expressed my outrage in how the Syrian regime has been operating. I do believe that President Asad missed an opportunity to reform his Government, chose the path of repression, and has continued to engage in repressive tactics so that his credibility, his capacity to regain legitimacy inside Syria, I think, is deeply eroded.

It's not an easy situation. And I expressed to Prime Minister Maliki my recognition that given Syria is on Iraq's borders, Iraq is in a tough neighborhood, that we will consult closely with them as we move forward.

But we believe that international pressure, the approach we've taken along with partners around the world to impose tough sanctions and to call on Asad to step down, a position that is increasingly mirrored by the Arab League states, is the right position to take.

Even if there are tactical disagreements between Iraq and the United States at this point in how to deal with Syria, I have absolutely no doubt that these decisions are being made based on what Prime Minister Maliki believes is best for Iraq, not based on considerations of what Iran would like to see.

Prime Minister Maliki has been explicit here in the United States; he's been explicit back in Iraq in his writings, in his commentary, that his interest is maintaining Iraqi sovereignty and preventing meddling by anybody inside of Iraq. And I believe him. And he has shown himself to be willing to make very tough decisions in the interest of Iraqi nationalism even if they cause problems with his neighbor.

And so we may have some different tactical views in terms of how best to transition to an inclusive, representative government inside of Syria, but every decision that, I believe, Prime Minister Maliki is making he is making on the basis of what he thinks is best for the Iraqi people. And everything that we've seen in our interactions with Prime Minister Maliki and his Government over the last several years would confirm that.

With respect to the drone inside of Iran, I'm not going to comment on intelligence matters that are classified. As has already been indicated, we have asked for it back. We'll see how the Iranians respond.

[*Prime Minister Maliki spoke in Arabic, and his remarks were translated by an interpreter and joined in progress.*]

Prime Minister Maliki. ——difficult in Syria, and perhaps in other states as well. But I know that peoples must get their freedom and

their will and democracy and equal citizenship. We are with these rights, the rights of people and with their wills, because we have achieved that ourselves. And if we could compare Iraq today with the past, we find that there is a great difference in democracy and elections and freedom.

Therefore, we honor the aspirations of the Syrian people. But I cannot have—I do not have the right to ask a President to abdicate. We must play this role, and we cannot give ourselves this right.

Iraq is a country that is bordering on Syria, and I am concerned about the interest of Iraq and the interest of the security of the region. And I wish that what is required by the Syrian people would be achieved without having— without affecting the security of Iraq. And I know the two countries are related to each other, and we must be very prudent in dealing with this matter.

We were with the initiative by the Arab League. But frankly speaking, because we suffered from the blockade and the military interventions, we do not encourage a blockade because it exhausts the people and the government. But we stood with the Arab League, and we were very frank with ourselves when they visited us in Baghdad, and we agreed on an initiative. Perhaps it will be the last initiative that we'll see in this situation and will achieve the required change in Syria without any violent operations that could affect the area in general.

I believe that the parties, all the parties realize the dangers of a sectarian war in Iraq, in Syria, and in the region, because it will be like a snowball that it will expand and it will be difficult to control it.

We will try to reach a solution, and I discussed the matter with His Excellency, the President, President Obama, and the Secretary General of the Arab League. And there is agreement even from the Syrian opposition, who are leading the opposition in Syria, to search for a solution. If we can reach a solution, it will avoid all the evils and the dangers. And if we don't, there must be another way to reach a solution that will calm the situation in Syria and in the area in general.

[*A reporter spoke in Arabic, and the question was translated by an interpreter and joined in progress.*]

Iraq-U.S. Relations

Q. ——establish a new relationship—to establish the characteristics of a new relationship with the United States after the withdrawal of the U.S. forces from Iraq? Relying on the strategic framework agreement, have you reached a specific mechanism for the implementation of the framework agreement?

Your Excellency, President Obama, you said that there will be long-range relationships with Iraq. Can you tell us exactly, will Iraq be an ally of the United States or just a friend, or will have a different type of relationship?

Thank you very much.

Prime Minister Maliki. Definitely, without mechanisms, we will not be able to achieve anything we have. These mechanisms will control our continuous movement. Therefore, the framework agreement has a higher committee, or a joint committee from the two countries that meets regularly, and it has representatives from all the sectors that we want to develop relationship in: commerce, industry, agriculture, economy, security.

So the joint higher committee is the mechanism in which the ideas will be reached in relationship between the ministries that will implement what is agreed upon. We believe through these two mechanisms, the mechanism of the joint committee and the mechanism of contact between each minister and his counterpart, we will achieve success, and this will expedite achieving our goal.

President Obama. As the Prime Minister described, I think our goal is to have a comprehensive relationship with Iraq. And what that means is, is that on everything from expanding trade and commerce to scientific exchanges, to providing assistance as Iraq is trying to make sure that electricity and power generation is consistent for its people, to joint exercises militarily, to a whole range of issues, we want to make sure that there is a constant communication between our governments, that there are deep and rich exchanges between our two governments and between our peoples, because what's happened over the last several years has linked the United States and Iraq in a way that is potentially powerful and could end up benefiting not only America and Iraq, but also the entire region and the entire world.

It will evolve over time. What may be discovered is, is that there are certain issues that Prime Minister Maliki and his Government think are especially important right now, for example, making sure that oil production is ramped up, and we are helping to encourage global investment in that sector.

I know that the Prime Minister has certain concerns right now, militarily, that 5 years from now or 10 years from now, when the Iraqi Air Force is fully developed or the Iraqi Navy is fully developed, he has less concern about.

Our goal is simply to make sure that Iraq succeeds, because we think a successful, democratic Iraq can be a model for the entire region. We think an Iraq that is inclusive and brings together all people—Sunni, Shia, Kurd—together to build a country, to build a nation, can be a model for others that are aspiring to create democracy in the region.

And so we've got an enormous investment of blood and treasure in Iraq, and we want to make sure that, even as we bring the last troops out, that it's well understood both in Iraq and here in the United States that our commitment to Iraq's success is going to be enduring.

Christi Parsons [Chicago Tribune].

U.S. Military Operations in Iraq/Iraq-U.S. Relations

Q. Thank you. You were a little delayed coming out today. I was wondering if you could talk about any agreements that you may have reached that you haven't detailed already. For instance, can you talk a little bit more about who will be left behind after the U.S. leaves, how big their footprint will be, and what their role will be?

And, Mr. President, could you also address how convinced you are that the Maliki Government is ready to govern the country and protect the gains that have been made there in recent years? I also wonder if, on this occasion, you still think of this as "a dumb war."

President Obama. I'll take the last question first. I think history will judge the original decision to go into Iraq. But what's absolutely clear is, as a consequence of the enormous sacrifices that have been made by American soldiers and civilians—American troops and civilians—as well as the courage of the Iraqi people, that what we have now achieved is an Iraq that is self-governing, that is inclusive, and that has enormous potential.

There are still going to be challenges. And I think the Prime Minister is the first one to acknowledge those challenges. Many of them, by the way, are economic. After many years of war and, before that, a brutal regime, it's going to take time to further develop civil society, further develop the institutions of trade and commerce and the free market so that the extraordinary capacity of the Iraqi people is fully realized. But I have no doubt that Iraq can succeed.

With respect to security issues, look, when I came into office, I said we're going to do this in a deliberate fashion. We're going to make sure that we leave Iraq responsibly, and that's exactly what we've done. We did it in phases. And because we did it in phases, it—we were continually able to build up Iraqi forces to a point where when we left the cities, violence didn't go up in the cities; when we further reduced our footprint, violence didn't go up. And I have no doubt that that will continue.

First question you had had to do with what footprint is left. We're taking all of our troops out of Iraq. We will not have any bases inside of Iraq. We will have a strong diplomatic presence inside of Iraq. We've got an Embassy there that is going to be carrying out a lot of the functions of this ongoing partnership and executing on the strategic framework agreement.

We will be working to set up effective military-to-military ties that are no different from the ties that we have with countries throughout the region and around the world. The Iraqi

Government has already purchased F–16s from us. We've got to train their pilots and make sure that they're up and running and that we have an effective Iraqi Air Force.

We both have interests in making sure that the sea lanes remain open in and around Iraq and throughout the region, and so there may be occasion for joint exercises. We both have interests in counterterrorism operations that might undermine Iraqi sovereignty, but also could affect U.S. interests, and we'll be working together on those issues.

But what we are doing here today, and what we'll be executing over the next several months, is a normalization of the relationship. We will have a strong friend and partner in Iraq; they will have a strong friend and partner in us, but as one based on Iraqi sovereignty and one based on equal partnerships of mutual interest and mutual respect. And I'm absolutely confident that we're going to be able to execute that over the long term.

While I'm at it, since this may be the last question I receive, I just want to acknowledge: None of this would have been successful obviously without our extraordinary men and women in uniform. And I'm very grateful for the Prime Minister asking to travel to Arlington to recognize those sacrifices.

There are also some individuals here who've been doing a bang-up job over the last year to help bring us to this day. And I just want to acknowledge General Lloyd Austin, who was a warrior and, turns out, is also a pretty good diplomat, as well as Ambassador Jim Jeffreys [Jeffrey].* Both of them have done extraordinary work on the ground, partnering with their Iraqi counterparts.

And I'm going to give a special shout-out to my friend and partner Joe Biden, who, I think, ever since I came in, has helped to establish high-level, strong links and dialogue between the United States and Iraq through some difficult times. And I think Prime Minister Maliki would agree that the Vice President's investment in making this successful has been hugely important.

° White House correction.

Prime Minister Maliki. Thank you very much. I believe the remaining of the question that was given was answered by His Excellency the President. And I also—I said at the beginning, the dialogues that were to confirm the confidence and to move into the implementation of the framework agreement and to find the companies and to train our soldiers on the weapons that were bought from America and the need for expertise in other civil fields and the protection of their movement in Iraq.

We talked also about the political issues, which is a common interest for us. And we spoke also about the question of armament. As the President said, Iraq has bought some weapons and now is applying for buying other weapons to develop its capabilities in the protection of Iraq.

These are all titles of what we discussed, but it was done in an atmosphere of harmony.

Iraq-U.S. Security Cooperation/Iraq-U.S. Relations

Q. Mr. Prime Minister, you stated that there is cooperation in the area of armament. Can you tell us the amount of military cooperation between the United States and Baghdad in this area? Specifically, have you received any promises from President Obama in this regard, specifically—of the U.S. Embassy in Baghdad? There is argument going on inside Iraqi politician now regarding the size; it's 15,000. And I wonder if you discussed with Prime Minister to reduce the number of the diplomats. Thank you.

Prime Minister Maliki. Definitely, we have raised the issue of Iraqi need for weapons, for aerial protection and naval and ground protection. We have a lot of weapons, American weapons, and it requires trainers. And we received promises for cooperation from His Excellency the President for some weapons that Iraq is asking for, especially those related to its protection of its airspace. And we hope that the Congress will approve another group of F–16 airplanes to Iraq because our air force was destroyed completely during the war that Iraq entered into.

And this is not all. We also need technical equipment related to the security field. These are issues that are being discussed by the concerned people in both countries, between the ministers of defense and interior, with their counterparts in the United States, and we received promises and facilitations. And we agreed on how to make this relationship continuous in the security field, because both of us need each other and need cooperation, especially in chasing Al Qaida, which we started and was not defeated anywhere except in Iraq. And we hope to cooperate with all those who feel the dangers of this organization—to cooperate with us as well.

President Obama. Our view is a sovereign Iraq that can protect its borders, protect its airspace, protect its people. And our security cooperation with other countries I think is a model for our security cooperation with Iraq. We don't want to create big footprints inside of Iraq—and that's, I think, demonstrated by what will happen at the end of this month, which is we're getting our troops out. But we will have a very active relationship, military-to-military, that will, hopefully, enhance Iraqi capabilities and will assure that we've got a strong partner in the region that is going to be effective.

With respect to the Embassy, the actual size of our Embassy with respect to diplomats is going to be comparable to other countries that we think are important around the world. There are still some special security needs inside of Iraq that make the overall number larger. And we understand some questions have been raised inside of Iraq about that.

Look, we're only a few years removed from an active war inside of Iraq. I think it's fair to say that there are still some groups, although they are greatly weakened, that might be tempted to target U.S. diplomats or civilians who are working there to improve the performance of the power sector inside of Iraq or are working to help train agricultural specialists inside of Iraq. And as President of the United States, I want to make sure that anybody who is out in Iraq trying to help the Iraqi people is protected.

Now, as this transition proceeds, it may turn out that the security needs for our diplomats and for our civilians gradually reduces itself, partly because Iraq continues to make additional progress. But I think the Iraqi people can understand that, as President of the United States, if I'm putting civilians in the field in order to help the Iraqi people build their economy and improve their productivity, I want to make sure that they come home, because they are not soldiers.

So that makes the numbers larger than they otherwise would be, but the overall mission that they're carrying out is comparable to the missions that are taking place in other countries that are big, that are important, and that are friends of ours. Okay?

Thank you very much, everybody.

NOTE: The President's news conference began at 12:24 p.m. in the South Court Auditorium of the Dwight D. Eisenhower Executive Office Building. In his remarks, the President referred to Gen. Lloyd J. Austin III, USA, commanding general, U.S. Forces—Iraq. Prime Minister Maliki referred to Secretary General Nabil Elaraby of the League of Arab States; Acting Minister of Defense Sadun al-Dulaymi of Iraq; and Secretary of Defense Leon E. Panetta. Prime Minister Maliki and two reporters spoke in Arabic, and their remarks were translated by an interpreter.

Remarks at an Obama Victory Fund 2012 Fundraiser
December 13, 2011

Hello, everybody! Hello, hello, hello! Thank you. Love you guys. Thank you so much. All right, everybody have a seat. I don't want to milk this too much here. [*Laughter*]

To Matthew, thank you for your extraordinary leadership. We could not be prouder of you. And for you to have made all the life-changing sacrifices to take on this job, it's something that I couldn't be prouder of. So please give Matthew a big round of applause. He's working hard.

Jane Stetson, Andy Tobias, they are doing remarkable work for the DNC. And our outstanding chairwoman of the DNC, Debbie Wasserman Schultz, is in the house. Give her a big round of applause as well.

I don't want to give a long speech. I want to save most of my time for questions and discussion with all of you. I've got two simple messages. Number one, thank you. I look around the room: Everybody here has gone above and beyond the call of duty, not just for the last few months, but for several years now. I'm reminded of what my friend Ab Mikva said about being friends with a politician: It's like having a perpetual child in college. [*Laughter*] It just never stops. [*Laughter*] But all of you have just done incredible work with great cheer and great determination. And I'm thankful for it.

Which brings me to the second point. The reason you do it, I'd like to think, is a little bit because you like me and you think I'm a pretty good guy. [*Laughter*] I definitely know that part of it is because you love Michelle and think she's one of the best First Ladies we've ever had. But the main reason you do it is because you know what's at stake.

Back in 2008, we used to talk about this being a historic moment for America, that we were at a crossroads in our history. Well, we haven't fully crossed the road, and in some ways, 2012 is even more important than it was 4 years ago. The choices could not be starker. The vision about where we want to take the country could not be more different.

I gave a speech in Kansas last week where I talked about where we need to go as a country, a country that's based on everybody having a fair shot, a country that depends on everybody doing their fair share, a country where fair play applies across the board. And I talked about how, for decades now, people have felt that the basic compact that if you worked hard, you acted responsibly, you looked after your family, that you would be able to be in the middle class, stay in the middle class, get into the middle class, that your kids would have a better life than you did, that you'd have some semblance of security, that that compact had eroded.

1545

And it hadn't happened overnight, it wasn't going to be solved overnight, but there were going to be some critical things that we had to do to make sure that compact was restored: making investments in education so our kids are better prepared than anybody in the world, making sure that we've got the best infrastructure to move products and services and our businesses can thrive, making sure that we're investing in science and basic research, making sure that the rules of the road apply to everybody. So we're not building a bubble economy, but we're building an economy based on making stuff and exporting it around the world stamped with the words "Made in America." And most fundamentally, understanding that we're all in this together, it's not a few of us doing well and then the rest of us hoping that we get lucky, but rather, everybody as a team moving this country forward.

And that vision, in contrast to a vision that basically says you are on your own, is what this election was about in 2008. It's what this election is going to be about in 2012. I am confident that the vision that we believe in so deeply and that we've worked so hard for is the vision that is truest to our history and most representative of the core decency of the American people.

But we're going to have to fight for it. It's not a slam dunk. We're going to have to deliver this message effectively all across the country. And at a time when people have been battered by the worst financial crisis since the Great Depression and the worst economic crisis since the 1930s, it's understandable if people aren't feeling as chipper as they were back in 2008.

There's going to be some skepticism. There's going to be some pushback.

All of the things that we've done over the last 3 years—to rescue the economy and rescue the auto industry and end the war in Iraq and end "don't ask, don't tell" and make sure that health care is in place and financial reform brings back some integrity to the financial sector—all those things don't mean that much to somebody if they're still out of work right now or if their house is still underwater by $100,000.

So yes, this is going to be tough. But I just want to remind all of you that you didn't decide to support Barack Hussein Obama because it was going to be easy. There were always easier choices to make, just as there would have been easier political choices for me to make. We took a flyer on this thing because we believe passionately in an America in which everybody is getting ahead.

That's worth fighting for. And here's my message to you. If you guys stick with this, if you don't falter, if you stay steady, we are going to win this thing. We are going to win this thing, and America is going to win as a consequence.

All right? Thank you, everybody. Thank you.

NOTE: The President spoke at 12:05 p.m. at the Hyatt Regency Washington on Capitol Hill. In his remarks, he referred to Matthew W. Barzun, national finance chair of the President's 2012 election campaign; Jane Stetson, national finance chair, and Andrew Tobias, treasurer, Democratic National Committee; and former White House Counsel Abner J. Mikva.

Remarks at Fort Bragg, North Carolina
December 14, 2011

The President. Hello, everybody! Hello, Fort Bragg! All the way!

Audience members. Airborne!

The President. Now, I'm sure you realize why I don't like following Michelle Obama. [*Laughter*] She's pretty good. And it is true, I am a little biased, but let me just say it: Michelle, you are a remarkable First Lady. You are a great advocate for military families. And you're cute. [*Laughter*] I'm just saying—gentlemen, that's your goal: to marry up. Punch above your weight.

Fort Bragg, we're here to mark a historic moment in the life of our country and our military. For nearly 9 years, our Nation has been at war in Iraq. And you, the incredible men and women of Fort Bragg, have been there every step of the way, serving with honor, sacrificing greatly, from the first waves of the invasion to some of the last troops to come home. So as your Commander in Chief, and on behalf of a grateful nation, I'm proud to finally say these two words, and I know your families agree: Welcome home! Welcome home. Welcome home. [*Applause*] Welcome home.

It is great to be here at Fort Bragg, home of the Airborne and Special Operations Forces. I want to thank General Anderson and all your outstanding leaders for welcoming us here today, including General Dave Rodriguez, General John Mulholland. And I want to give a shout-out to your outstanding senior enlisted leaders, including Command Sergeant Major Roger Howard, Darrin Bohn, Parry Baer. And give a big round of applause to the Ground Forces Band.

We've got a lot of folks in the house today. We've got the XVIII Airborne Corps, the Sky Dragons.

Audience members. Hooah!

The President. We've got the legendary, All-American 82d Airborne Division.

Audience members. Hooah!

The President. We've got America's quiet professionals, our Special Operations Forces.

Audience members. Hooah!

The President. From Pope Field, we've got Air Force.

Audience members. Whoo!

The President. And I do believe we've got some Navy and Marine Corps here too.

Audience member. Yes! [*Laughter*]

The President. And though they're not here with us today, we send our thoughts and prayers to General Helmick, Sergeant Major Rice, and all the folks from the XVIII Airborne and Bragg who are bringing our troops back from Iraq. We honor everyone from the 82d Airborne and Bragg serving and succeeding in Afghanistan and General Votel and those serving around the world.

And let me just say, one of the most humbling moments I've had as President was when

I presented our Nation's highest military decoration, the Medal of Honor, to the parents of one of those patriots from Fort Bragg who gave his life in Afghanistan, Staff Sergeant Robert Miller.

I want to salute Ginny Rodriguez, Miriam Mulholland, Linda Anderson, Melissa Helmick, Michelle Votel, and all the inspiring military families here today. We honor your service as well.

And finally, I want to acknowledge your neighbors and friends who help keep your—this outstanding operation going, all who help to keep you "Army Strong," and that includes Representatives Mike McIntyre and Dave Price and Heath Shuler and Governor Bev Perdue. I know Bev is so proud to have done so much for our military families. So give them a big round of applause.

Today I've come to speak to you about the end of the war in Iraq. Over the last few months, the final work of leaving Iraq has been done. Dozens of bases with American names that housed thousands of American troops have been closed down or turned over to the Iraqis. Thousands of tons of equipment have been packed up and shipped out. Tomorrow the colors of United States Forces—Iraq, the colors you fought under, will be formally cased in a ceremony in Baghdad. Then, they'll begin their journey across an ocean, back home.

Over the last 3 years, nearly 150,000 U.S. troops have left Iraq. And over the next few days, a small group of American soldiers will begin the final march out of that country. Some of them are on their way back to Fort Bragg. As General Helmick said, "They know that the last tactical road march out of Iraq will be a symbol, and they're going to be a part of history."

As your Commander in Chief, I can tell you that it will indeed be a part of history. Those last American troops will move south on desert sands and then they will cross the border out of Iraq with their heads held high. One of the most extraordinary chapters in the history of the American military will come to an end. Iraq's future will be in the hands of its people. America's war in Iraq will be over.

Now, we knew this day would come. We've known it for some time. But still, there is something profound about the end of a war that has lasted so long.

Now, 9 years ago, American troops were preparing to deploy to the Persian Gulf and the possibility that they would be sent to war. Many of you were in grade school. I was a State senator. Many of the leaders now governing Iraq, including the Prime Minister, were living in exile. And since then, our efforts in Iraq have taken many twists and turns. It was a source of great controversy here at home with patriots on both sides of the debate. But there was one constant: your patriotism, your commitment to fulfill your mission, your abiding commitment to one another. That was constant. That did not change. That did not waiver.

It's harder to end a war than begin one. Indeed, everything that American troops have done in Iraq—all the fighting and all the dying, the bleeding and the building, and the training and the partnering—all of it has led to this moment of success. Now, Iraq is not a perfect place. It has many challenges ahead. But we're leaving behind a sovereign, stable, and self-reliant Iraq with a representative government that was elected by its people. We're building a new partnership between our nations. And we are ending a war not with a final battle, but with a final march toward home.

This is an extraordinary achievement nearly 9 years in the making. And today we remember everything that you did to make it possible.

We remember the early days, the American units that streaked across the sands and skies of Iraq, the battles from Karbala to Baghdad, American troops breaking the back of a brutal dictator in less than a month.

We remember the grind of the insurgency, the roadside bombs, the sniper fire, the suicide attacks. From the "Triangle of Death" to the fight for Ramadi, from Mosul in the north to Basra in the south, your will proved stronger than the terror of those who tried to break it.

We remember the specter of sectarian violence, Al Qaida's attacks on mosques and pilgrims, militias that carried out campaigns of intimidation and campaigns of assassination. And in the face of ancient divisions, you stood firm to help those Iraqis who put their faith in the future.

We remember the surge, and we remember the "Awakening," when the abyss of chaos turned toward the promise of reconciliation. By battling and building block by block in Baghdad, by bringing tribes into the fold and partnering with the Iraqi Army and police, you helped turn the tide toward peace.

And we remember the end of our combat mission and the emergence of a new dawn, the precision of our efforts against Al Qaida in Iraq, the professionalism of the training of Iraqi security forces, and the steady drawdown of our forces. In handing over responsibility to the Iraqis, you preserved the gains of the last 4 years and made this day possible.

Just last month, some of you—members of the Falcon Brigade—turned over the Anbar Operations Center to the Iraqis in the type of ceremony that has become commonplace over these last several months. In an area that was once the heart of the insurgency, a combination of fighting and training, politics and partnership brought the promise of peace. And here's what the local Iraqi deputy governor said: "This is all because of the U.S. forces' hard work and sacrifice."

That's in the words of an Iraqi: hard work and sacrifice. Those words only begin to describe the costs of this war and the courage of the men and women who fought it.

We know too well the heavy cost of this war. More than 1.5 million Americans have served in Iraq—1.5 million. Over 30,000 Americans have been wounded, and those are only the wounds that show. Nearly 4,500 Americans made the ultimate sacrifice, including 202 fallen heroes from here at Fort Bragg—202. So today we pause to say a prayer for all those families who have lost their loved ones, for they are part of our broader American family. We grieve with them.

We also know that these numbers don't tell the full story of the Iraq war, not even close. Our civilians have represented our country with skill and bravery. Our troops have served tour after tour of duty with precious little dwell time in between. Our Guard and Reserve units stepped up with unprecedented service. You've endured dangerous foot patrols, and you've endured the pain of seeing your friends and comrades fall. You've had to be more than soldiers, sailors, airmen, marines, and coast-guardsmen; you've also had to be diplomats and development workers and trainers and peacemakers. Through all this, you have shown why the United States military is the finest fighting force in the history of the world.

As Michelle mentioned, we also know that the burden of war is borne by your families. In countless base communities like Bragg, folks have come together in the absence of a loved one. As the mayor of Fayetteville put it: "War is not a political word here. War is where our friends and neighbors go." So there have been missed birthday parties and graduations. There are bills to pay and jobs that have to be juggled while picking up the kids. For every soldier that goes on patrol, there are the husbands and the wives, the mothers, the fathers, the sons, the daughters praying that they come back.

So today, as we mark the end of the war, let us acknowledge, let us give a heartfelt round of applause for every military family that has carried that load over the last 9 years. You too have the thanks of a grateful nation.

Part of ending a war responsibly is standing by those who fought it. It's not enough to honor you with words. Words are cheap. We must do it with deeds. You stood up for America; America needs to stand up for you.

That's why, as your Commander in Chief, I am committed to making sure that you get the care and the benefits and the opportunities that you've earned. For those of you who remain in uniform, we will do whatever it takes to ensure the health of our force, including your families. We will keep faith with you.

We will help our wounded warriors heal, and we will stand by those who've suffered the unseen wounds of war. And make no mistake: As we go forward as a nation, we are going to keep America's Armed Forces the strongest fighting force the world has ever seen. That will not stop.

That will not stop. But our commitment doesn't end when you take off the uniform. You're the finest that our Nation has to offer. And after years of rebuilding Iraq, we want to enlist our veterans in the work of rebuilding America. That's why we're committed to doing everything we can to extend more opportunities to those who have served.

That includes the post-9/11 GI bill, so that you and your families can get the education that allows you to live out your dreams. That includes a national effort to put our veterans to work. We've worked with Congress to pass a tax credit so that companies have the incentive to hire vets. And Michelle has worked with the private sector to get commitments to create 100,000 jobs for those who've served.

And by the way, we're doing this not just because it's the right thing to do by you, we're doing it because it's the right thing to do for America. Folks like my grandfather came back from World War II to form the backbone of this country's middle class. For our post-9/11 veterans, with your skill, with your discipline, with your leadership, I am confident that the story of your service to America is just beginning.

But there's something else that we owe you. As Americans, we have a responsibility to learn from your service. I'm thinking of an example, Lieutenant Alvin Shell, who was based here at Fort Bragg. A few years ago, on a supply route outside Baghdad, he and his team were engulfed by flames from an RPG attack. Covered with gasoline, he ran into the fire to help his fellow soldiers and then led them 2 miles back to Camp Victory where he finally collapsed, covered with burns. When they told him he was a hero, Alvin disagreed. "I'm not a hero," he said. "A hero is a sandwich." [*Laughter*] "I'm a paratrooper."

We could do well to learn from Alvin. This country needs to learn from you. Folks in Washington need to learn from you.

Policymakers and historians will continue to analyze the strategic lessons of Iraq. That's important to do. Our commanders will incorporate the hard-won lessons into future military campaigns. That's important to do. But the most important lesson that we can take from you is not about military strategy, it's a lesson about our national character.

For all of the challenges that our Nation faces, you remind us that there's nothing we Americans can't do when we stick together.

For all the disagreements that we face, you remind us there's something bigger than our differences, something that makes us one Nation and one people regardless of color, regardless of creed, regardless of what part of the country we come from, regardless of what backgrounds we come out of. You remind us we're one Nation.

And that's why the United States military is the most respected institution in our land because you never forget that. You can't afford to forget it. If you forget it, somebody dies. If you forget it, a mission fails. So you don't forget it. You have each other's backs. That's why you, the 9/11 generation, has earned your place in history.

Because of you, because you sacrificed so much for a people that you had never met, Iraqis have a chance to forge their own destiny. That's part of what makes us special as Americans. Unlike the old empires, we don't make these sacrifices for territory or for resources. We do it because it's right. There can be no fuller expression of America's support for self-determination than our leaving Iraq to its people. That says something about who we are.

Because of you, in Afghanistan we've broken the momentum of the Taliban. Because of you, we've begun a transition to the Afghans that will allow us to bring our troops home from there. And around the globe, as we draw down in Iraq, we have gone after Al Qaida so that terrorists who threaten America will have no safe haven and Usama bin Laden will never again walk the face of this Earth.

So here's what I want you to know and here's what I want all our men and women in uniform to know: Because of you, we are ending these wars in a way that will make America stronger and the world more secure. Because of you.

That success was never guaranteed. And let us never forget the source of American leadership: our commitment to the values that are written into our founding documents and a unique willingness among nations to pay a great price for the progress of human freedom and dignity. This is who we are. That's what we do as Americans, together.

The war in Iraq will soon belong to history. Your service belongs to the ages. Never forget that you are part of an unbroken line of heroes spanning two centuries, from the colonists who overthrew an empire to your grandparents and parents who faced down fascism and communism to you, men and women who fought for the same principles in Fallujah and Kandahar and delivered justice to those who attacked us on 9/11.

Looking back on the war that saved our Union, a great American, Oliver Wendell Holmes, once paid tribute to those who served. "In our youth," he said, "our hearts were touched with fire. It was given to us to learn at the outset that life is a profound and passionate thing."

All of you here today have lived through the fires of war. You will be remembered for it. You will be honored for it, always. You have done something profound with your lives. When this Nation went to war, you signed up to serve. When times were tough, you kept fighting. When there was no end in sight, you found light in the darkness.

And years from now, your legacy will endure in the names of your fallen comrades etched on headstones at Arlington and the quiet memorials across our country, in the whispered words of admiration as you march in parades, and in the freedom of our children and our grandchildren. And in the quiet of night, you will recall that your heart was once touched by fire. You will know that you answered when your country called, you served a cause greater than yourselves, you helped forge a just and lasting peace with Iraq and among all nations.

I could not be prouder of you, and America could not be prouder of you.

God bless you all, God bless your families, and God bless the United States of America.

NOTE: The President spoke at 11:52 a.m. In his remarks, he referred to Lt. Gen. Frank G. Helmick, USA, commanding general, Maj. Gen. Rodney O. Anderson, USA, deputy commanding general, and CSM Earl L. Rice, USA, command sergeant major, XVIII Airborne Corps; Melissa Helmick, wife of Lt. Gen. Helmick; Linda Anderson, wife of Maj. Gen. Anderson; Gen. David M. Rodriguez, USA, commanding general, CSM Darrin J. Bohn, USA, command sergeant major, and CSM Roger Howard, USA, acting command sergeant major, U.S. Army Forces Command; Ginny Rodriguez, wife of Gen. Rodriguez; Gen. John F. Mulholland, Jr., USA, commanding general, and CSM Parry L. Baer, USA, command sergeant major, U.S. Army Special Operations Command; Miriam Mulholland, wife of Gen. Mulholland; Lt. Gen. Joseph L. Votel, USA, commanding general, Joint Special Operations Command, and his wife Michelle; Philip and Maureen Miller, parents of posthumous Medal of Honor recipient S. Sgt. Robert J. Miller, USA; Prime Minister Nuri al-Maliki of Iraq; Deputy Governor Hikmat Jassim Zaidon of Anbar Province, Iraq; and Mayor Anthony G. Chavonne of Fayetteville, NC.

Statement on the Legacy of Laura Pollan
December 14, 2011

Today, as the National Endowment for Democracy awards the Democracy Service Medal posthumously to Laura Pollan, the founder of las Damas de Blanco, we honor and celebrate her life by recognizing her significant contributions to the struggle to defend human rights in Cuba.

Laura Pollan and the quiet dignity of the Ladies in White have courageously voiced the core desire of the Cuban people and of people everywhere to live in liberty. Taking to the streets in peaceful protest to draw attention to the plight of those unjustly held in Cuba's prisons, Laura Pollan and the Ladies in White have stood bravely against Cuban authorities who unleash mobs and resort to house arrest and temporary detention in a failed attempt to silence them. Through Laura Pollan's and the Damas' brave actions, the world bore witness to the repressive actions of Cuban authorities, eventually leading to the release of political prisoners wrongly jailed in the spring of 2003.

Though Laura is not with us today, her bravery in the face of repression and her selfless commitment to democracy and human rights in Cuba offer a living legacy that inspires us to keep moving forward. To las Damas de Blanco who will watch or listen to today's ceremony, you have our utmost respect for your efforts to stand up for the rights of the Cuban people, even in the face of this weekend's crackdown directed at you, and we honor each of you as well.

The United States is steadfast in supporting the simple desire of the Cuban people to freely determine their future and to enjoy the rights and freedoms that define the Americas and that should be universal to all human beings. I remain committed to supporting civil society in Cuba, including by protecting the ability of Cuban Americans to support their families in Cuba through unrestricted family visits and remittances.

Remarks on Ensuring Fair Pay for Homecare Workers
December 15, 2011

Hello, everybody. As I said in Kansas last week, the defining issue of our time is whether we can build an economy where hard work pays off and responsibility is rewarded. It's whether this is going to be a country where working people can earn enough to raise a family and build a modest savings and own a home, secure their own retirement, look after their kids. That's the test of our time.

In some cases, building this kind of economy is going to require some action from Congress. And right now Congress needs to make sure that 160 million working Americans don't see their taxes go up on January 1. None of the workers who joined us here today can afford a thousand-dollar tax increase next year. And it wouldn't be good for the economy. Every economist indicates that it's important for us to extend the payroll tax cut and make sure that unemployment insurance is extended. So this Congress cannot and should not leave for vacation until that—until they have made sure that that tax increase doesn't happen. Let me repeat that: Congress should not and cannot go on vacation before they have made sure that working families aren't seeing their taxes go up by a thousand dollars and those who are out there looking for work don't see their unemployment insurance expire.

There's no reason why we shouldn't be able to extend these items—the payroll tax cut, UI—before the holidays. There's no reason the Government should shut down over this. And I expect all of us to do what's necessary in order to do the people's business and make sure that it's done before the end of the year.

Now, only Congress can prevent the payroll tax from going up next year. But there are also some things that we can do without Congress to help make sure that hard work pays off. And that's why we're here today.

Right behind me here is my friend Pauline Beck. One day back in 2007, Pauline was my boss. I was in California to take part in an event called Walk a Day in My Shoes, where you'd spend the day working the job of someone who was in the service industry. And I was lucky enough to be paired up with Pauline, and I have tell you, it ended up being one of my favorite days of the entire campaign.

Pauline is a home health care worker. When we met, she was getting up every day at 5 a.m. to go to work taking care of an 86-year-old amputee named Mr. John. And each day, she'd dress Mr. John and help him into his wheelchair. She'd make him breakfast. She'd scrub his floors. She'd clean his bathroom. She was his connection to the outside world. And when the workday was done, she would go home to take care of a grandnephew and two foster children who didn't have families of their own. Heroic work and hard work, that's what Pauline was all about.

And one of the things I remember about Pauline was her patience. She was patient with me even when I didn't wring out the mop properly or I didn't shake out the sheets before putting them in the laundry bin. But I also remember listening to her talk about the hardships in her life, and she did so without any self-pity. She was glad to be working hard, and she was glad to be helping someone. All she wanted in return for a hard day's work was enough to take care of those kids she was going home to, enough to save a little bit for retirement, maybe take a day off once in a while to rest her aching back.

Now, each of the folks who are here today has a story like Pauline's. They represent nearly 1.8 million homecare workers across the country, hard-working professionals, mostly women, who work around the clock so that folks who need help, including many of our family members, can live independently in their own home. Right now home care is one of the fastest growing industries in America, partly because we're getting older as a society. And as the baby boom generation heads into retirement, more and more Americans are going to need the services of these outstanding workers.

But here's the thing: As the homecare business has changed over the years, the law hasn't changed to keep up. So even though workers like Pauline do everything from bathing to cooking, they're still lumped in the same category as teenage babysitters when it comes to how much they make. That means employers are allowed to pay these workers less than minimum wage with no overtime. That's right, you can wake up at 5 in the morning, care for somebody every minute of the day, take the late bus home at night, and still make less than the minimum wage. And this means that many homecare workers are forced to rely on things like food stamps just to make ends meet.

And that's just wrong. In this country, it's unexcusable. I can tell you firsthand that these men and women, they work their tails off, and they don't complain. And they deserve to be treated fairly. They deserve to be paid fairly for a service that many older Americans couldn't live without. And companies who do pay fair wages to these women shouldn't be put at a disadvantage.

Now, 4 years ago, a homecare worker named Evelyn Coke took her case all the way up to the Supreme Court. And Evelyn was working up to 70 hours a week with no overtime pay. But the Court ruled against her, saying that to change the law would require action from Congress or the Department of Labor. I'm sure many of you won't be surprised to know that Congress hasn't acted on this issue so far.

Today I will. Today we're guaranteeing homecare workers minimum wage and overtime pay protection. And that's thanks to the hard work of my Secretary of Labor, Hilda Solis. We are going to make sure that over a million men and women in one of the fastest growing professions in the country don't slip through the cracks. We're going to make sure that companies who do right by their workers aren't undercut by companies who don't. We're going to do what's fair, and we're going to do what's right.

Now, Evelyn Coke didn't live to see this day. But the truth is, Americans like Evelyn and Pauline and the rest of the workers who are here today, they're one of the reasons that I ran for President. They work hard. They play by the rules. In exchange, they just want to see that their hard work and their responsibility is rewarded. It's that simple. Americans all deserve a fair shake and a fair shot. And as long as I have the honor of serving as President, I'm going to do everything in my power to make sure that those very modest expectations are fulfilled. I'm going to make sure that they are treated right. I'm going to make sure that every American is treated fairly.

Thanks very much, everybody. Thank you.

NOTE: The President spoke at 12:13 p.m. in the Dwight D. Eisenhower Executive Office Building. In his remarks, he referred to Damian Beck, grandnephew of homecare worker Pauline Beck of Oakland, CA.

Letter to Congressional Leaders on the Deployment of United States Combat-Equipped Armed Forces
December 15, 2011

Dear Mr. Speaker: (Dear Mr. President:)

I am providing this supplemental consolidated report, prepared by my Administration and consistent with the War Powers Resolution (Public Law 93–148), as part of my efforts to keep the Congress informed about deployments of U.S. Armed Forces equipped for combat.

MILITARY OPERATIONS AGAINST AL-QA'IDA, THE TALIBAN, AND ASSOCIATED FORCES AND IN SUPPORT OF RELATED U.S. COUNTERTERRORISM OBJECTIVES

Since October 7, 2001, the United States has conducted combat operations in Afghanistan against al-Qa'ida terrorists and their Taliban supporters. In support of these and other overseas operations, the United States has deployed combat-equipped forces to a number of locations in the U.S. Central, Pacific, European, Southern, and Africa Command areas of operation. Previously such operations and deployments have been reported, consistent with Public Law 107–40 and the War Powers Resolution, and operations and deployments remain ongoing. These operations, which the United States has carried out with the assistance of numerous international partners, have been successful in seriously degrading al-Qa'ida's capabilities and brought an end to the Taliban's leadership of Afghanistan.

United States Armed Forces are also actively pursuing and engaging remaining al-Qa'ida and Taliban fighters in Afghanistan. The total number of U.S. forces in Afghanistan is approximately 93,000, of which more than 78,000 are assigned to the North Atlantic Treaty Organization (NATO)-led International Security Assistance Force (ISAF) in Afghanistan. The U.N. Security Council most recently reaffirmed its authorization of ISAF for a 12-month period until October 13, 2012, in U.N. Security Council Resolution 2011 (October 12, 2011). The mission of ISAF, under NATO command and in partnership with the Government of the Islamic Republic of Afghanistan, is to conduct population centric counterinsurgency operations, enable expanded and effective capabilities of the Afghan National Security Forces, support improved governance and development in order to protect the Afghan people, and promote sustainable security. Forty-nine nations, including the United States and all 28 NATO Allies, contribute troops to ISAF. These combat operations are gradually pushing insurgents to the edges of secured population areas in a number of important regions, largely resulting from the increase in U.S. forces over the past 2 years.

United States and other coalition forces will continue to execute the strategy of clear-hold-build, and transition, until full responsibility for security rests with the Afghan National Security Forces.

The United States continues to detain approximately 2,500 al-Qa'ida, Taliban, and associated force fighters who are believed to pose a continuing threat to the United States and its interests.

The combat equipped forces, deployed since January 2002 to Naval Base, Guantanamo Bay, Cuba, continue to conduct secure detention operations for the approximately 170 detainees at Guantanamo Bay under Public Law 107–40 and consistent with principles of the law of war.

In furtherance of U.S. efforts against members of al-Qa'ida, the Taliban, and associated forces, the United States continues to work with partners around the globe, with a particular focus on countries within the U.S. Central Command's area of responsibility. In this con-

text, the United States has deployed U.S. combat-equipped forces to assist in enhancing the counterterrorism capabilities of our friends and allies, including special operations and other forces for sensitive operations in various locations around the world. The United States is committed to thwarting the efforts of al-Qa'ida and its associated forces to carry out future acts of international terrorism, and we have continued to work with our counterterrorism partners to disrupt and degrade the capabilities of al-Qa'ida and its associated forces. As necessary, in response to the terrorist threat, I will direct additional measures against al-Qa'ida, the Taliban, and associated forces to protect U.S. citizens and interests. It is not possible to know at this time the precise scope or the duration of the deployments of U.S. Armed Forces necessary to counter this terrorist threat to the United States. A classified annex to this report provides further information.

MILITARY OPERATIONS IN IRAQ

Since the expiration of the authorization and mandate for the Multinational Force in Iraq in U.N. Security Council Resolution 1790 on December 31, 2008, U.S. forces have continued operations to support Iraq in its efforts to maintain security and stability in Iraq, pursuant to the bilateral Agreement Between the United States of America and the Republic of Iraq on the Withdrawal of United States Forces from Iraq and the Organization of Their Activities during Their Temporary Presence in Iraq (Security Agreement), which entered into force on January 1, 2009. These contributions have included, but have not been limited to, assisting in building the capability of the Iraqi security forces, supporting the development of Iraq's political institutions, enhancing the capacity of the Ministries of Defense and Interior, providing critical humanitarian and reconstruction assistance to the Iraqis, and supporting the U.S. diplomatic mission. The United States continues its responsible drawdown, in accordance with commitments in the Security Agreement, to withdraw U.S. forces from Iraq by December 31, 2011. The number of U.S.

forces in Iraq as of October 28, 2011, was 36,011.

MILITARY OPERATIONS IN LIBYA

As I reported on March 21 and June 15, and at my direction, consistent with a request from the Arab League, and as authorized by the U.N. Security Council under the provisions of U.N. Security Council Resolution 1973, U.S. military forces commenced operations on March 19, 2011, to prevent a humanitarian catastrophe and address the threat posed to international and regional peace and security by the crisis in Libya and to protect the people of Libya from the Qadhafi regime, which had made a lawless challenge to the authority of the Security Council. The initial phase of U.S. military involvement in Libya was conducted under the U.S. Africa Command. By April 4, however, the United States had transferred responsibility for the military operations in Libya to NATO and the U.S. involvement assumed a supporting role in the coalition's efforts. From April 4 through October 31, U.S. participation consisted of: (1) non-kinetic support to the NATO-led operation, including intelligence, logistical support, and search and rescue assistance; (2) aircraft that have assisted in the suppression and destruction of air defenses in support of the no-fly zone; and (3) since April 23, precision strikes by unmanned aerial vehicles against a limited set of clearly defined targets in support of the NATO-led coalition's efforts. Although the United States was no longer in the lead, U.S. support for the NATO based coalition remained crucial to ensuring the success of international efforts to protect civilians and civilian populated areas from the actions of the Qadhafi regime, and to address the threat to international and regional peace and security posed by the crisis in Libya. With the exception of operations to rescue the crew of a U.S. aircraft on March 21, 2011, and approximately 16 U.S. military personnel deployed under Chief of Mission authority to assist with re-establishment of U.S. Embassy Tripoli in September, the United States deployed no ground forces to Libya. The U.N. Security Council adopted Resolution 2016 on October 27, 2011,

which terminated the no-fly zone and civilian protection mandates effective October 31. NATO terminated its mission at the same time.

MILITARY OPERATIONS IN SUPPORT OF U.S. EMBASSY CAIRO SECURITY

On January 31, 2011, a security force of approximately 40 U.S. military personnel from the U.S. Central Command deployed to bolster the security of the U.S. Embassy in Cairo and its personnel. The force ended its deployment on July 4, 2011. This security force was separate from, and in addition to, the U.S. contingent of the Multinational Force and Observers, which have been present in Egypt since 1981.

MILITARY OPERATIONS IN CENTRAL AFRICA

On October 13, an initial team of U.S. military personnel with appropriate combat equipment deployed to Uganda to advise regional forces that are working to protect civilians, apprehend or remove Joseph Kony and other senior Lord's Resistance Army (LRA) commanders from the battlefield, and disarm and demobilize the remaining LRA fighters. During the next month, additional U.S. military personnel deployed to the region, including a second combat-equipped team and associated headquarters, communications, and logistics personnel. The total number of U.S. military personnel deployed for this mission, including those providing logistical and support functions, is approximately 100. United States forces are providing information, advice, and assistance to select partner nation forces. Subject to the approval of each respective host nation, elements of these U.S. forces have begun to deploy to forward locations in the LRA-affected areas of the Central African Republic to enhance regional efforts against the LRA, and similar movements are planned for the Republic of South Sudan and the Democratic Republic of the Congo. However, these forces will not engage LRA forces except in self-defense. The deployment of these U.S. Armed Forces furthers U.S. national security interests and foreign policy efforts and is contributing to advancing peace and respect for human rights in central Africa.

MARITIME INTERCEPTION OPERATIONS

As noted in previous reports, the United States remains prepared to conduct maritime interception operations on the high seas in the areas of responsibility of each of the geographic combatant commands. These maritime operations are aimed at stopping the movement, arming, and financing of certain international terrorist groups, and also include operations aimed at stopping proliferation by sea of weapons of mass destruction and related materials.

U.S.-NATO OPERATIONS IN KOSOVO

The U.N. Security Council authorized Member States to establish a NATO-led Kosovo Force (KFOR) in Resolution 1244 on June 10, 1999. The original mission of KFOR was to monitor, verify, and, when necessary, enforce compliance with the Military Technical Agreement between NATO and the then-Federal Republic of Yugoslavia (now Serbia), while maintaining a safe and secure environment. Today, KFOR deters renewed hostilities in cooperation with local authorities and international institutions. The principal military tasks of KFOR forces are to help maintain a safe and secure environment and to ensure freedom of movement throughout Kosovo.

Currently, 22 NATO Allies contribute to KFOR. Eight non-NATO countries also participate. The United States contribution to KFOR is approximately 800 U.S. military personnel out of the total strength of approximately 6,240 personnel, plus a temporarily deployed Operational Reserve Force.

I have directed the participation of U.S. Armed Forces in all of these operations pursuant to my constitutional and statutory authority as Commander in Chief (including the authority to carry out Public Law 107–40 and other statutes) and as Chief Executive, as well as my constitutional and statutory authority to conduct the foreign relations of the United States. Officials of my Administration and I communicate regularly with the leadership and other Members of Congress with regard to these deployments, and we will continue to do so.

Sincerely,

BARACK OBAMA

NOTE: Identical letters were sent to John A. Boehner, Speaker of the House of Representatives, and Daniel K. Inouye, President pro tempore of the Senate.

Remarks to the General Assembly of the Union for Reform Judaism at National Harbor, Maryland
December 16, 2011

Thank you. Please, please have a seat. You're making me blush. [*Laughter*] Thank you, Eric, for that extraordinary introduction and for your many years of leadership in the Reform movement. And even though it is a few hours early, I'd like to wish all of you *shabbat shalom*.

Now, there are a lot of familiar faces in the house: David Saperstein, Alan Solow, Rick Jacobs, Howard Kohr.

I want to welcome Israel's Deputy Prime Minister and Defense Minister Ehud Barak. The cooperation between our militaries has never been stronger, and I want to thank Ehud for his leadership and his lifelong commitment to Israel's security and the quest for a just and lasting peace. I also want to recognize Israeli Ambassador Michael Oren, who's with us here today.

And finally, I want to give a shout-out to NFTY, I understand is in the house. Young people are going to lead the way, and they're leading the way. There you go. I'm fired up just listening to them. [*Laughter*]

I am honored to be here because of the proud history and tradition of the Union for Reform Judaism, representing more than 900 congregations, around 1.5 million American Jews.

I want to congratulate all of you on the golden anniversary of the Religious Action Center.

As Eric mentioned, when President Kennedy spoke to leaders from the RAC in 1961, I was 3 months old, so my memory is a bit hazy. [*Laughter*] But I am very familiar with the work that you've done ever since, and so is the rest of America.

And that's because you helped draft the Civil Rights Act and the Voting Rights Act. You helped to liberate Soviet Jews. You have made a difference on so many of the defining issues of the last half-century. And without these efforts, I probably wouldn't be standing here today. So thank you. Thank you. You have brought to life your faith and your values, and the world's a better place for it.

Now, since my daughter Malia has reached the age where it seems like there's always a bar or bat mitzvah—[*laughter*]—every weekend, and there is quite a bit of negotiations around the skirts that she wears at these bat mitzvahs. [*Laughter*] Do you guys have these conversations as well? [*Applause*] All right. I just wanted to be clear it wasn't just me. [*Laughter*] What time you get home.

As a consequence, she's become the family expert on Jewish tradition. [*Laughter*] And if there's one thing I've learned from her, it's that it never hurts to begin a speech by discussing the Torah portion. [*Laughter*] It doesn't hurt.

So this week—[*laughter*]—congregations around the world will retell the story of Joseph. As any fan of Broadway musicals will tell you—[*laughter*]—there is a lot going on in this reading. [*Laughter*] But many scholars have focused on a single word that Joseph uses when he replies to his father Jacob.

In Hebrew, that word is *hineni*. It translates, "I"—[*applause*]—it translates to "Here I am." *Hineni*. It's the same word Abraham uses to reply to God before the binding of Isaac. It's the same word Moses uses when God summons him from the burning bush: *Hineni*. The text is telling us that while Joseph does not know what lies ahead, he is ready to answer the call.

In this case, *hineni* leads Joseph to Egypt. It sets in motion a story of enslavement and exodus that would come to inspire leaders like Martin Luther King as they sought freedom. It's a story of persecution and perseverance that has repeated itself from Inquisition-era Spain to czarist Russia to Hitler's Germany.

And in that often tragic history, this place, America, stands out. Now, we can't whitewash the past. Like so many ethnic groups, Jews faced prejudice, and sometimes violence, as they sought their piece of the American Dream. But here, Jews finally found a place where their faith was protected, where hard work and responsibility paid off, where no matter who you were or where you came from, you could make it if you tried. Here in America, you really could build a better life for your children.

I know how much that story means to many of you, because I know how much that story means to me. My father was from Kenya, my mother was from Kansas—not places with a large Jewish community. [*Laughter*] But when my Jewish friends tell me about their ancestors, I feel a connection. I know what it's like to think, "Only in America is my story even possible."

Now—I have to interrupt. My friend Debbie Wasserman Schultz just got in the house. She was—[*applause*].

Now, the Jewish community has always understood that the dream we share is about more than just doing well for yourself. From the moment our country was founded, American Jews have helped make our Union more perfect. Your parents, your grandparents, your great-grandparents, they remembered what it was like to be a stranger, and as a result treated strangers with compassion. They pursued *tikkun olam*, the hard work of repairing the world.

They fought bigotry because they had experienced bigotry. They fought for freedom of religion because they understood what it meant to be persecuted for your religious beliefs. Our country is a better place because they did. The same values that bring you here today led Justice Brandeis to fight for an America that protects the least of these. Those same values led Jewish leaders to found RAC 50 years ago. They led Abraham Joshua Heschel to pray with his feet and march with Dr. King. And over the last 3 years, they have brought us together on the most important issues of our time.

When we began this journey, we knew we would have to take on powerful special interests. We would have to take on a Washington culture where doing what's politically convenient is often valued above doing what's right, where the focus is too often on the next election instead of the next generation.

And so time and time again, we've been reminded that change is never easy. And a number of the rabbis who are here today, when I see them, they've been saying a prayer. They notice my hair is grayer. [*Laughter*] But we didn't quit. You didn't quit. And today, we're beginning to see what change looks like.

And Eric mentioned what change looks like. Change is the very first bill I signed, the Lilly Ledbetter Fair Pay Act, which says in this country an equal day's work gets an equal day's pay. That's change.

Change is finally doing something about our addiction to oil and raising fuel efficiency standards for the first time in 30 years. That's good for our economy, it's good for our national security, and it's good for our environment.

Change is confirming two Supreme Court Justices who will defend our rights, including our First Amendment rights surrounding religion—happen to be two women, by the way. That's also a good thing.

Change is repealing "don't ask, don't tell," so that in the first time in history, you don't have to hide who you love to serve the country that you love. That's change.

Change is working with the Reform movement and other faith-based groups to reform the Federal faith-based initiatives, improving the way we partner with organizations that serve people in need.

Change is health care reform that we passed after a century of trying, reform that will finally ensure that in the United States of America, nobody goes bankrupt just because they get sick. That's change.

Change is the 2.5 million young people—maybe some of those NFTY folks—who have already—[*applause*]—who have health insur-

ance on their parents' plans because of the Affordable Care Act. That's change.

It's making family planning more accessible to millions of Americans. It's insurance companies not being able to charge you more just because you're a woman or deny you coverage if you have breast cancer.

Change is committing to real, persistent education reform, because every child in America deserves access to a good school and to higher education—every child.

And change is keeping one of the first promises I made in 2008: After nearly 9 years, our war in Iraq is ending this month and our troops are coming home.

That's what change is. And none of this would have happened without you. That's the kind of change we'll keep fighting for in the months and years ahead.

And just last night you took another step towards the change we need and voted for a set of principles of economic justice in a time of fiscal crisis. And I want to thank you for your courage. That statement could not have come at a more important time, for as you put it, we're at a crossroads in American history. Last Tuesday I gave a speech in Osawatomie, Kansas, where I described that crossroads. And I laid out a vision of our country where everybody gets a fair shot, and everybody does their fair share, and everyone plays by the same rules. And these are not Democratic values or Republican values; they're not Christian values or Jewish values or Hindu or Muslim values. They're shared values, and we have to reclaim them. We have to restore them to a central place in America's political life.

I said it last week, I'll say it again: This is not just a political debate; this is a moral debate, this is an ethical debate, it's a values debate. It's the defining issue of our time. It is a make-or-break moment for the middle class and for all those who are fighting to get into the middle class and for those of us who remember parents or grandparents or great-grandparents who had to fight to get in the middle class, but they understood that the American Dream was available to them because we were all in it together. That's what this is about. And last night you reaffirmed the moral dimension of this debate.

We have to decide who we are as a country. Is this a place where everyone is left to fend for themselves, the most powerful can play by their own rules? Or do we come together to make sure that working people can earn enough to raise a family, send their kids to college, buy their own home, have a secure health care and a secure retirement? That is the story that almost all of us here share, in one way or another. This is a room full of folks who come from immigrants and remember what it was like to scratch and claw and work. You haven't forgotten. You know what it's like to see those in your own family struggle.

Well, we have to apply those same values to the American family. We're not a country that says, you're on your own. When we see neighbors who can't find work or pay for college or get the health care they need, we answer the call. We say, "Here I am," and, "We will do our part."

That's what you affirmed last night. But more importantly, it's what you affirm every day with your words and your actions. And I promise you that as you pray with your feet, I will be right there with you every step of the way. I'll be fighting to create jobs and give small businesses a chance to succeed. I'll be fighting to invest in education and technology. I will fight to strengthen programs like Medicare and Social Security. I will fight to put more money in the pockets of working families. I won't be afraid to ask the most well off among us—Americans like me—to pay our fair share, to make sure that everybody's got a shot. I will fight alongside you every inch of the way.

And as all of you know, standing up for our values at home is only part of our work. Around the world, we stand up for values that are universal, including the right of all people to live in peace and security and dignity. That's why we've worked on the international stage to promote the rights of women, to promote strategies to alleviate poverty, to promote the dignity of all people, including gays and lesbians and people with disabilities, to promote human rights and democracy. And that's why,

as President, I have never wavered in pursuit of a just and lasting peace: two states for two peoples, an independent Palestine alongside a secure Jewish State of Israel. I have not wavered and will not waver. That is our shared vision.

Now, I know that many of you share my frustration sometimes, in terms of the state of the peace process. There's so much work to do. But here's what I know. There's no question about how lasting peace will be achieved. Peace can't be imposed from the outside. Ultimately, it is the Israelis and the Palestinians who must reach agreement on the issues that divide them.

And the fact that peace is hard can't deter us from trying. Because now more than ever, it's clear that a just and lasting peace is in the long-term interests of Israel. It is in the long-term interests of the Palestinian people. It is in the interest of the region. It is the interest of the United States, and it is in the interest of the world. And I am not going to stop in pursuit of that vision. It is the right thing to do.

Now, that vision begins with a strong and secure State of Israel. And the special bonds between our nations are ones that all Americans hold dear because they're bonds forged by common interests and shared values. They're bonds that transcend partisan politics—or at least they should.

We stand with Israel as a Jewish democratic state because we know that Israel is born of firmly held values that we, as Americans, share: a culture committed to justice, a land that welcomes the weary, a people devoted to *tikkun olam*.

So America's commitment and my commitment to Israel and Israel's security is unshakeable. It is unshakeable.

I said it in September at the United Nations. I said it when I stood amid the homes in Sderot that had been struck by missiles: No nation can tolerate terror. And no nation can accept rockets targeting innocent men, women, and children. No nation can yield to suicide bombers.

And as Ehud has said, it is hard to remember a time when the United States has given stronger support to Israel on its security. In fact, I am proud to say that no U.S. administration has done more in support of Israel's security than ours—none. Don't let anybody else tell you otherwise. It is a fact.

I'm proud that even in these difficult times we've fought for and secured the most funding for Israel in history. I'm proud that we've helped Israel develop a missile defense system that's already protecting civilians from rocket attacks.

Another grave concern—and a threat to the security of Israel, the United States, and the world—is Iran's nuclear program. And that's why our policy has been absolutely clear: We are determined to prevent Iran from acquiring nuclear weapons. And that's why we've worked painstakingly from the moment I took office with allies and partners, and we have imposed the most comprehensive, the hardest hitting sanctions that the Iranian regime has ever faced. We haven't just talked about it, we have done it. And we're going to keep up the pressure. And that's why, rest assured, we will take no options off the table. We have been clear.

We're going to keep standing with our Israeli friends and allies, just as we've been doing when they've needed us most. In September, when a mob threatened the Israeli Embassy in Cairo, we worked to ensure that the men and women working there were able to get out safely. Last year, when raging fires threatened Haifa, we dispatched fire-fighting planes to help put out the blaze.

On my watch, the United States of America has led the way, from Durban to the United Nations, against attempts to use international forums to delegitimize Israel. And we will continue to do so. That's what friends and allies do for each other. So don't let anybody else tell a different story. We have been there, and we will continue to be there. Those are the facts.

And when I look back on the last few years, I'm proud of the decisions I've made, and I'm proud of what we've done together. But today isn't about resting on our laurels. As your tradition teaches, we're not obligated to finish the work, but neither are we free to desist from it.

We've got to keep going. So today we look forward to the world not just as it is, but as it could be. And when we do, the truth is clear: Our Union is not yet perfect. Our world is still in desperate need of repair. And each of us still hears that call.

And the question is, how will we respond? In this moment, every American, of every faith, every background has the opportunity to stand up and say: Here I am—*Hineni*. Here I am. I am ready to keep alive our country's promise. I am ready to speak up for our values at home and abroad. I am ready to do what needs to be done. The work may not be finished in a day, in a year, in a term, in a lifetime, but I'm ready to do my part.

And I believe that with tradition as our guide, we will seize that opportunity. And in the face of daunting odds, we will make the choices that are hard, but are right. That's how we've overcome tougher times before. That's how we will overcome the challenges that we face today. And together, we will rewrite the next chapter in America's story and prove that our best days are still to come.

Thank you. God bless you. God bless the United States of America.

NOTE: The President spoke at 2:37 p.m. at the Gaylord National Hotel & Convention Center. In his remarks, he referred to Eric H. Yoffie, president, and Richard Jacobs, president-elect, Union for Reform Judaism; David Saperstein, director and counsel, Religious Action Center of Reform Judaism; Alan P. Solow, former chairman, Conference of Presidents of Major American Jewish Organizations; and Howard Kohr, executive director, American Israel Public Affairs Committee. He also referred to the North American Federation of Temple Youth (NFTY).

The President's Weekly Address
December 17, 2011

This week marked a historic moment in the life of our country and our military. For nearly 9 years, our Nation has been at war in Iraq. More than 1.5 million Americans have served there with honor, skill, and bravery. Tens of thousands have been wounded. Military families have sacrificed greatly, none more so than the families of those nearly 4,500 Americans who made the ultimate sacrifice. All of them—our troops, veterans, and their families—will always have the thanks of a grateful nation.

On Thursday, the colors our Armed Forces fought under in Iraq were formally cased in a ceremony in Baghdad before beginning their journey back home. Our troops are now preparing to make their final march across the border and out of the country. Iraq's future will be in the hands of its own people. Our war there will be over. All of our troops will be out of Iraq. And this holiday season, all of us can finally say: Welcome home.

This is an extraordinary achievement, one made possible by the hard work and sacrifice of the men and women who had the courage to serve. And there's a lesson to learn from that, a lesson about our character as a nation.

See, there's a reason our military is the most respected institution in America. They don't see themselves or each other as Democrats first or Republicans first. They see themselves as Americans first.

For all of our differences, all of our disagreements, they remind us that we are all a part of something bigger, that we are one Nation and one people. And for all our challenges, they remind us that there is nothing we can't do when we stick together.

They're the finest our Nation has to offer. Many will remain in the military and go on to the next mission. Others will take off the uniform and become veterans. But their commitment to service doesn't end when they take off the uniform. In fact, I'm confident the story of their service to America is just beginning.

After years of rebuilding Iraq, it is time to enlist our veterans and all our people in the work of rebuilding America.

Folks like my grandfather came back from World War II to form the backbone of the largest middle class in history. And today's generation of veterans—the 9/11 generation of veterans—is armed with the skills, discipline, and leadership to attack the defining challenge of our time: rebuilding an economy where hard work pays off, where responsibility is rewarded and anyone can make it if they try.

Now it is up to us to serve these brave men and women as well as they serve us. Every day, they meet their responsibilities to their families and their country. Now it's time to meet ours, especially those of us who you sent to serve in Washington. This cannot be a country where division and discord stand in the way of our progress. This is a moment where we must come together to ensure that every American has the chance to work for a decent living, own their own home, send their kids to college, and secure a decent retirement.

This is a moment for us to build a country that lives up to the ideals that so many of our bravest Americans have fought and even died for. That is our highest obligation as citizens. That is the welcome home that our troops deserve.

Thanks.

NOTE: The address was recorded at approximately 4:25 p.m. on December 16 in the Roosevelt Room at the White House for broadcast on December 17. The transcript was made available by the Office of the Press Secretary on December 16, but was embargoed for release until 6 a.m. on December 17.

Remarks on Congressional Action on Tax Cut Legislation
December 17, 2011

Hello, everybody. In the last few weeks, I set out a simple principle: Congress should not go home for vacation until it finds a way to avoid hitting 160 million Americans with a tax hike on January 1. Extending the payroll tax cut that shows up in people's paychecks every week is an idea that I proposed in September as part of the "American Jobs Act."

At a time when so many Americans are working harder and harder just to keep up, the extra $1,000 or so that the average family would get from this tax cut makes a real difference when you're trying to buy groceries or pay the bills, make a mortgage or make a repair. And all kinds of independent economists agree: The number-one challenge facing businesses right now is a lack of demand from consumers, which is why more people spending money means companies that are more successful and more able to hire more workers.

Today Congress has finally agreed to extend this middle class tax cut into next year. And they've also agreed to another part of my jobs plan, extending unemployment insurance for millions of Americans who are out there trying as hard as they can to find a job. This is spending money that also benefits families and businesses and the entire economy. And it's a lifeline that would have been lost for more than 2½ million people in the first 2 months of next year if Congress had not acted.

So I'm very pleased to see the work that the Senate has done. While this agreement is for 2 months, it is my expectation—in fact, it would be inexcusable for Congress not to further extend this middle class tax cut for the rest of the year. It should be a formality. And hopefully, it's done with as little drama as possible when they get back in January.

This really isn't hard. There are plenty of ways to pay for these proposals. This is a way to boost the economy that has been supported by these very same Democrats and Republicans in the past. It is something that economists believe will assure that the economy and the recovery is on a more stable footing than it otherwise would be. And my preference, and the preference of most Americans, is that we ask the wealthiest few Americans to pay their fair share and corporations to do without special taxpayer subsidies to cover some of the costs. But I think that it's important for us to get it done.

We've got a lot more work to do for the people who sent us here. But today I'm glad that both parties in Congress came together, and I want to thank them for ensuring that as we head into the holidays, folks at home don't have to worry about their taxes going up.

So I had a chance to talk to Senator Reid and Senator McConnell. I thanked them for their cooperation on this issue. I'm looking forward to the House moving forward and getting this done when they get back on Monday. And hopefully, we're going to be able to make sure that when everybody gets back next year, we extend this further all the way to the end of the year.

Thank you very much, everybody.

NOTE: The President spoke at 12:30 p.m. in the James S. Brady Press Briefing Room at the White House.

Statement on the Death of Former President Vaclav Havel of the Czech Republic
December 18, 2011

I was deeply saddened to learn of the passing today of Vaclav Havel, a playwright and prisoner of conscience who became President of Czechoslovakia and of the Czech Republic. Having encountered many setbacks, Havel lived with a spirit of hope, which he defined as "the ability to work for something because it is good, not just because it stands a chance to succeed." His peaceful resistance shook the foundations of an empire, exposed the emptiness of a repressive ideology, and proved that moral leadership is more powerful than any weapon. He played a seminal role in the Velvet Revolution that won his people their freedom and inspired generations to reach for self-determination and dignity in all parts of the world. He also embodied the aspirations of half a continent that had been cut off by the Iron Curtain and helped unleash tides of history that led to a united and democratic Europe.

Like millions around the world, I was inspired by his words and leadership and was humbled to stand with the Czech people in a free and vibrant Hradcany Square as President. We extend our condolences to President Havel's family and all those in the Czech Republic and around the world who remain inspired by his example. Vaclav Havel was a friend to America and to all who strive for freedom and dignity, and his words will echo through the ages.

Statement on Storm and Flood Damage in the Philippines
December 19, 2011

On behalf of the American people, I wish to express my deep condolences for the tremendous loss of life and devastation caused by recent flooding in the Philippines. In the spirit of our long history of friendship and cooperation with the Philippines, the United States stands ready to assist the Philippine people and Government should humanitarian assistance and recovery efforts be needed.

Remarks During White House Press Secretary James F. "Jay" Carney's Briefing
December 20, 2011

The President. Hello, everybody. Sorry to interrupt.

Press Secretary Carney. It's all yours, sir.

The President. Thank you. Well, good afternoon, everybody. It is no secret that there hasn't been an abundance of partisanship in Washington this year. And that's why what happened on Saturday was such a big deal.

Nearly the entire Senate, including almost all of the Republicans, voted to prevent 160 million working Americans from receiving a tax increase on January 1. Nearly the entire Senate voted to make sure that nearly 2.5 million Americans who are out there looking for a job don't lose their unemployment insurance in the first 2 months of next year. And just about everybody, Democrats and Republicans, committed to making sure that early next year we find a way to extend the payroll tax cut and unemployment insurance through the end of 2012.

But now, even though Republicans and Democrats in the Senate were willing to compromise for the good of the country, a faction of Republicans in the House are refusing to even vote on the Senate bill, a bill that cuts taxes for 160 million Americans. And because of their refusal to cooperate, all those Americans could face a tax hike in just 11 days, and millions of Americans who are out there looking for work could find their unemployment insurance expired.

Now, let's be clear: Right now the bipartisan compromise that was reached on Saturday is the only viable way to prevent a tax hike on January 1. It's the only one. All of the leaders in Congress, Democrats and Republicans, say they are committed to making sure we extend the payroll tax cut and unemployment insurance for the entire year. And by the way, this is something I called for months ago.

The issue is, is that the Republican and Democratic leaders of the Senate worked on a

1-year deal, made good progress, but determined that they needed more time to reach an agreement. And that's why they passed an insurance policy, to make sure that taxes don't go up on January 1.

In fact, the House Republicans say they don't dispute the need for a payroll tax cut. What they're really trying to do, what they're holding out for, is to wring concessions from Democrats on issues that have nothing to do with the payroll tax cut, issues where the parties fundamentally disagree. So a 1-year deal is not the issue; we can and we will come to that agreement, as long as it's focused on the payroll tax cut and unemployment insurance and not focused on extraneous issues.

The issue right now is this: The clock is ticking; time is running out. And if the House Republicans refuse to vote for the Senate bill, or even allow it to come up for a vote, taxes will go up in 11 days. I saw today that one of the House Republicans referred to what they're doing as "high-stakes poker." He's right about the stakes, but this is not poker, this is not a game. This shouldn't be politics as usual. Right now the recovery is fragile, but it is moving in the right direction. Our failure to do this could have effects not just on families, but on the economy as a whole. It's not a game for the average family, who doesn't have an extra thousand bucks to lose. It's not a game for somebody who's out there looking for work right now and might lose his house if unemployment insurance doesn't come through. It's not a game for the millions of Americans who will take a hit when the entire economy grows more slowly because these proposals aren't extended.

I just got back from a ceremony at Andrews Air Force Base, where we received the flag and the colors that our troops fought under in Iraq, and I met with some of the last men and women to return home from that war. And these Americans, and all Americans who serve, are the embodiment of courage and selflessness and patriotism, and when they fight together, and sometimes die together, they don't know and they certainly don't care who's a Democrat and who's a Republican and how somebody is doing in the polls and how this might play in the spin room. They work as a team, and they do their job. And they do it for something bigger than themselves.

The people in this town need to learn something from them. We have more important things to worry about than politics right now. We have more important things to worry about than saving face or figuring out internal caucus politics. We have people who are counting on us to make their lives just a little bit easier, to build an .economy where hard work pays off and responsibility is rewarded. And we owe it to them to come together right now and do the right thing. That's what the Senate did. Democrats and Republicans in the Senate said, we're going to put our fights on other issues aside and go ahead and do what's right on something we all agree to. Let's go ahead and do it. We'll have time later for the politics; we'll have time later to have fights around a whole bunch of other issues. Right now, though, we know this is good for the economy, and they went ahead and did the right thing.

I need the Speaker and House Republicans to do the same: Put politics aside, put aside issues where there are fundamental disagreements, and come together on something we agree on. And let's not play brinksmanship. The American people are weary of it; they're tired of it. They expect better. I'm calling on the Speaker and the House Republican leadership to bring up the Senate bill for a vote. Give the American people the assurance they need in this holiday season.

Thank you.

NOTE: The President spoke at 1:59 p.m. in the James S. Brady Press Briefing Room at the White House. In his remarks, he referred to Rep. Thomas J. Rooney.

Statement on the Observance of Hanukkah
December 20, 2011

Michelle and I send our warmest wishes to all those celebrating Hanukkah around the world.

This Hanukkah season we remember the powerful story of a band of believers who rose up and freed their people, only to discover that the oil left in their desecrated temple, which should have been enough for only one night, ended up lasting for eight.

It's a timeless story of right over might and faith over doubt, one that has given hope to Jewish people everywhere for over 2,000 years. And tonight, as families and friends come together to light the menorah, it is a story that reminds us to count our blessings, to honor the sacrifices of our ancestors, and to believe that through faith and determination we can work together to build a brighter, better world for generations to come.

From our family to the Jewish community around the world, *chag sameach.*

Remarks on Payroll Tax Cut and Unemployment Insurance Legislation
December 22, 2011

Thank you, everybody. Please have a seat. Good afternoon to all of you. Merry Christmas. Happy holidays.

We've been doing everything we can over the last few weeks to make sure that 160 million working Americans aren't hit with a holiday tax increase on January 1. We've also been doing everything we can to make sure that millions of people who are out there looking for work in a very tough environment don't start losing their unemployment insurance on January 1.

Now, on Saturday, we reached a bipartisan compromise that would do just that: make sure that people aren't seeing a tax cut the first of the year; make sure that they still have unemployment insurance the first of the year. Nearly every Democrat in the Senate voted for that compromise; nearly every Republican in the Senate voted for that compromise. Democrats and even some Republicans in the House voted for that compromise. I am ready to sign that compromise into law the second it lands on my desk.

So far, the only reason it hasn't landed on my desk—the only reason—is because a faction of House Republicans have refused to support this compromise.

Now, if you're a family making about $50,000 a year, this is a tax cut that amounts to about $1,000 a year. That's about 40 bucks out of every paycheck. It may be that there's some folks in the House who refuse to vote for this compromise because they don't think that 40 bucks is a lot of money. But anyone who knows what it's like to stretch a budget knows that at the end of the week, or the end of the month, $40 can make all the difference in the world.

And that's why we thought we'd bring your voices into this debate. So many of these debates in Washington end up being portrayed as which party is winning, which party is losing. But what we have to remind ourselves of is this is about people. This is about the American people and whether they win. It's not about a contest between politicians.

So on Tuesday, we asked folks to tell us what would it be like to lose $40 out of your paycheck every week. And I have to tell you that the response has been overwhelming. We haven't seen anything like this before. Over 30,000 people have written in so far, as many as 2,000 every hour. We're still hearing from folks. And I want to encourage everybody who's been paying attention to this to keep sending your stories to whitehouse.gov and share them on Twitter and share them on Facebook.

The responses we've gotten so far have come from Americans of all ages and Americans of all backgrounds, from every corner of the country. Some of the folks who responded are on stage with me here today, and they should remind every single Member of Congress what's at stake in this debate. Let me just give you a few samples.

Joseph from New Jersey talked about how he would have to sacrifice the occasional pizza night with his daughters. He said, and I'm quoting: "My 16-year-old twins will be out of the house soon. I'll miss this."

Richard from Rhode Island wrote to tell us that having an extra $40 in his check buys enough heating oil to keep his family warm for three nights. In his words—I'm quoting—"If someone doesn't think that 12 gallons of heating oil is important, I invite them to spend three nights in an unheated home. Or you can believe me when I say that it makes a difference."

Pete from Wisconsin told us about driving more than 200 miles each week to keep his father-in-law company in a nursing home. Forty dollars out of his paycheck would mean he'd only be able to make three trips instead of four.

We heard from a teacher named Claire from here in DC who goes to the thrift store every week and uses her own money to buy pencils and books for her fourth grade class. Once in a while she splurges on science or art supplies. Losing $40, she says, would mean she couldn't do that anymore.

For others, $40 means dinner out with a child who's home for Christmas, a new pair of shoes, a tank of gas, a charitable donation. These are the things at stake for millions of Americans. They matter to people. A lot.

And keep in mind that those are just the individual stories. That doesn't account for the overall impact that a failure to extend the payroll tax cut and a failure to extend unemployment insurance would have on the economy as a whole. We've seen the economy do better over the last couple of months, but there's still a lot of sources of uncertainty out there: what's going on in Europe, what's going on around the world. And so this is insurance to make sure that our recovery continues.

So it's time for the House to listen to the voices who are up here, the voices all across the country, and reconsider. What's happening right now is exactly why people just get so frustrated with Washington. This is it; this is exactly why people get so frustrated with Washington. This isn't a typical Democratic versus Republican issue. This is an issue where an overwhelming number of people in both parties agree. How can we not get that done? I mean, has this place become so dysfunctional that even when people agree to things we can't do it? It doesn't make any sense.

So enough is enough. The people standing with me today can't afford any more games. They can't afford to lose $1,000 because of some ridiculous Washington standoff. The House needs to pass a short-term version of this compromise, and then we should negotiate an agreement as quickly as possible to extend the payroll tax cut and unemployment insurance for the rest of 2012. It's the right thing to do for the economy, and it's, most importantly, the right thing to do for American families all across the country.

This is not just my view. Just a few hours ago, this is exactly what the Republican leader of the Senate said we should do. Democrats agree with the Republican leader of the Senate. We should go ahead and get this done. This should not be hard. We all agree it should happen. I believe it's going to happen sooner or later. Why not make it sooner, rather than later? Let's give the American people—the people who sent us here—the kind of leadership they deserve.

Thank you, everybody.

NOTE: The President spoke at 1 p.m. in the South Court Auditorium of the Dwight D. Eisenhower Executive Office Building.

Statement on Humanitarian Assistance to East Africa
December 22, 2011

As we enter the season of giving and renewal, more than 13.3 million people in Ethiopia, Kenya, and Somalia remain in urgent need of humanitarian assistance amid the worst drought the region has seen in 60 years. The heartbreaking accounts of lives lost and of those struggling to survive remind us of our common humanity and the need to reach out to people in need. I want to thank the many Americans who have reached out in support and made donations over the last several months to support people in need in the Horn of Africa.

Today, on behalf of the U.S. Government and the American people, I am announcing an additional $113 million in emergency relief assistance for the Horn of Africa. This funding will support urgently needed food, health,

shelter, water, and assistance needs. To date, the U.S. has provided approximately $870 million for relief purposes. Importantly, and even as we help to meet the emergency needs of the people of this region, we are also investing in their long-term food security: www.feedthefuture.gov.

For more information, please visit the FWD Campaign, run by the U.S. Agency for International Development, and to learn more about how you can get involved, please visit action.usaid.gov.

Statement on Congressional Action on Payroll Tax Cut and Unemployment Insurance Legislation
December 22, 2011

For the past several weeks, I've stated consistently that it was critical that Congress not go home without preventing a tax increase on 160 million working Americans. Today I congratulate Members of Congress for ending the partisan stalemate by reaching an agreement that meets that test.

Because of this agreement, every working American will keep his or her tax cut, about $1,000 for the average family. That's about $40 in every paycheck. Vital unemployment insurance will continue for millions of Americans who are looking for work. And when Congress

returns, I urge them to keep working to reach an agreement that will extend this tax cut and unemployment insurance for all of 2012 without drama or delay.

This is good news, just in time for the holidays. This is the right thing to do to strengthen our families, grow our economy, and create new jobs. This is real money that will make a real difference in people's lives. And I want to thank every American who raised your voice to remind folks in this town what this debate was all about. It was about you. And today your voices made all the difference.

Remarks on Congressional Action on Payroll Tax Cut and Unemployment Insurance Legislation
December 23, 2011

Good afternoon, everybody. I know you're all looking forward to spending time with your their families over the holidays, but we did have one last piece of business to finish up. I said it was critical for Congress not to go home without preventing a tax increase on 160 million working Americans, and I'm pleased to say that they've got it done. So I want to thank all the Members of Congress for ending the stalemate and making this happen.

Because of this agreement, every working American will keep their tax cut, about $1,000

for a typical family. And that's—translates into an extra $40 or so in every paycheck. Vital unemployment insurance will continue for millions of Americans who are looking for work. And when Congress returns, I urge them to keep working, without drama, without delay, to reach an agreement that extends this tax cut as well as unemployment insurance through all of 2012.

Last week, I said that this should be a formality, and that's still the case. So let's make sure that we extend this tax break and unemployment insurance for a full year for our families, but also for our economy. It's the right thing to do because more money spent by more Americans means more businesses hiring more workers. And that's a boost for everybody, and it's a boost that we very much need right now.

Finally, I want to take a moment to thank my fellow Americans for bringing their voices to this debate. I met with several here at the White House yesterday. I really think it takes courage to believe that your voice can make a difference. And I promise you, the American people, your voices made a difference on this debate. Whether you tweeted or called or wrote, you reminded people in this town what this debate and what all of our debates should be about. It's about you. It's about your lives. It's about your families. You didn't send us to this town to play partisan games and to see who's up and who's down. You sent us here to serve and make your lives a little bit better, to do what's right. And fortunately, that's how this week ended.

So this is some good news, just in the nick of time for the holidays. I do want to be clear though: We have a lot more work to do. This continues to be a make-or-break moment for the middle class in this country, and we're going to have to roll up our sleeves together—Democrats and Republicans—to make sure that the economy is growing and to make sure that more jobs are created.

We've got an economy that is showing some positive signs. We've seen many consecutive months of private sector job growth. But it's not happening as fast as it needs to. And that means that we've got to redouble our efforts,

working together. It also means that we've got to make sure we're rebuilding an economy where if you work hard, that work will be rewarded, the kind of economy where everyone is doing their fair share and everybody plays by the same set of rules, everybody has a fair chance and everybody is acting responsibly, including those of us here in Washington.

So there are going to be some important debates next year, some tough fights, I'm sure, in the years to come. But that's the kind of country that I'm fighting for, one where everybody has a fair chance and everybody is doing their fair share. That's the kind of country that I think the American people deserve and the kind of country that American people want.

So I want to wish everybody a merry Christmas, happy holidays, a happy New Year to you and your families, and that includes everybody here in the press corps. I know you guys have been working hard, and your families will be happy to spend a little more time with you over the next few days.

I also want to make sure to send the warmest holiday wishes to all the men and women in uniform who are serving overseas right now and may not have a chance to see their families during this holiday season. We are grateful for everything that you do.

All right? Thank you, guys. Aloha.

NOTE: The President spoke at 1:25 p.m. in the James S. Brady Press Briefing Room at the White House.

Statement on Signing the Consolidated Appropriations Act, 2012
December 23, 2011

Today I have signed into law H.R. 2055, the "Consolidated Appropriations Act, 2012." This bill provides the funding necessary for the smooth operation of our Nation's Government.

I have previously announced that it is the policy of my Administration, and in the interests of promoting transparency in Government, to indicate when a bill presented for Presidential signature includes provisions that are subject to well-founded constitutional ob-

jections. The Department of Justice has advised that a small number of provisions of H.R. 2055 raise constitutional concerns.

In this bill, the Congress has once again included provisions that would bar the use of appropriated funds for transfers of Guantanamo detainees into the United States (section 8119 of Division A), as well as transfers to the custody or effective control of foreign countries unless specified conditions are met (section 8120 of Division A). These provisions are similar to others found in the National Defense Authorization Act for Fiscal Year 2012. My Administration has repeatedly communicated my objections to these provisions, including my view that they could, under certain circumstances, violate constitutional separation of powers principles. In approving this bill, I reiterate the objections my Administration has raised regarding these provisions, my intent to interpret and apply them in a manner that avoids constitutional conflicts, and the promise that my Administration will continue to work towards their repeal.

The Congress has also included certain provisions in this bill that could interfere with my constitutional authorities in the areas of foreign relations and national security. Section 113 of Division H requires the Secretary of Defense to notify the Appropriations Committees of both Houses of Congress 30 days in advance of "any proposed military exercise involving United States personnel" that is anticipated to involve expenditures of more than $100,000 on construction. Language in Division I, title I, under the headings International Organizations, Contributions for International Peacekeeping Activities, disallows the expenditure of funds "for any United Nations peacekeeping mission that will involve United States Armed Forces under the command or operational control of a foreign national," unless my military advisers have advised that such an involvement is in the national interest, and unless I have made the same recommendation to the Congress. In approving this bill, I reiterate the understanding, which I have communicated to the Congress, that I will apply these provisions in a manner consistent with my constitutional authority as Commander in Chief.

Certain provisions in Division I, including sections 7013, 7025, 7029, 7033, 7043, 7046, 7049, 7059, 7062, and 7071, restrict or require particular diplomatic communications, negotiations, or interactions with foreign governments or international organizations. Others, including sections 7031, 7037, and 7086, hinder my ability to receive diplomatic representatives of foreign governments. Finally, section 7041 requires the disclosure to the Congress of information regarding ongoing diplomatic negotiations. I have advised the Congress that I will not treat these provisions as limiting my constitutional authorities in the area of foreign relations.

Moreover, several provisions in this bill, including section 627 of Division C and section 512 of Division D, could prevent me from fulfilling my constitutional responsibilities, by denying me the assistance of senior advisers and by obstructing my supervision of executive branch officials in the execution of their statutory responsibilities. I have informed the Congress that I will interpret these provisions consistently with my constitutional duty to take care that the laws be faithfully executed.

Additional provisions in this bill, including section 8013 of Division A and section 218 of Division F, purport to restrict the use of funds to advance certain legislative positions. I have advised the Congress that I will not construe these provisions as preventing me from fulfilling my constitutional responsibility to recommend to the Congress's consideration such measures as I shall judge necessary and expedient.

Numerous provisions of this bill purport to condition the authority of executive branch officials to spend or reallocate funds on the approval of congressional committees. These are constitutionally impermissible forms of congressional aggrandizement in the execution of the laws. Although my Administration will notify the relevant committees before taking the specified actions, and will accord the recommendations of such committees appropriate and serious consideration, our spending decisions shall not be treated as dependent on the approval of congressional committees. In particular, section 1302 of Division G conditions the authority of the Librarian of the Congress to transfer funds between sections of the Library upon the approval of the Committees on Appropriations of the House of Representatives and the Senate. I have advised the Congress of my understanding that this provision does not apply to funds for the Copyright Office, which performs an executive function in administering the copyright laws.

BARACK OBAMA

The White House,
December 23, 2011.

NOTE: H.R. 2055, approved December 23, was assigned Public Law No. 112–74.

Letter to Congressional Leaders Designating Funds for Overseas Contingency Operations/Global War on Terrorism
December 23, 2011

Dear Mr. Speaker: (Dear Mr. President:)

In accordance with section 5 of the Consolidated Appropriations Act, 2012, I hereby designate for Overseas Contingency Operations/Global War on Terrorism all funding (including the rescission of funds) so designated by the Congress in the Act pursuant to section 251(b)(2)(A) of the Balanced Budget and Emergency Deficit Control Act of 1985, as amended, as outlined in the enclosed list of accounts.

The details of this action are set forth in the enclosed letter from the Director of the Office of Management and Budget.

Sincerely,

BARACK OBAMA

NOTE: Identical letters were sent to John A. Boehner, Speaker of the House of Representatives, and Joseph R. Biden, Jr., President of the Senate.

The President's Weekly Address
December 24, 2011

The President. Hi, everyone. As you gather with family and friends this weekend, Michelle, Malia, Sasha, and I, and of course Bo, want to wish you all merry Christmas and happy holidays.

The First Lady. This is such a wonderful time of year. It's a time to honor the story of love and redemption that began 2,000 years ago, a time to see the world through a child's eyes and rediscover the magic all around us, and a time to give thanks for the gifts that bless us every single day.

This holiday season at the White House, we wanted to show our thanks with a very special holiday tribute to some of the strongest, bravest, and most resilient members of our American family, the men and women who wear our country's uniform and the families who support them.

The President. For many military families, the best gift this year is a simple one: welcoming a loved one back for the holidays. You see, after nearly 9 years, our war in Iraq is over.

Our troops are coming home, and across America, military families are being reunited.

So let's take a moment to give thanks for their service, for their families' service, for our veterans' service. And let's say a prayer for all our troops standing post all over the world, especially our brave men and women who are in Afghanistan and serving, even as we speak, in harm's way to protect the freedoms and security we hold so dear.

The First Lady. Our veterans, troops, and military families sacrifice so much for us. So this holiday season, let's make sure that all of them know just how much we appreciate everything they do.

Let's ask ourselves: "How can I give back? How can my family serve them as well as they've served us?" And one way you can get started is to visit joiningforces.gov to find out how you can get involved right in your own community.

The President. Giving of ourselves, service to others, that's what this season is all about.

For my family and millions of Americans, that's what Christmas is all about. It reminds us that part of what it means to love God is to love one another, to be our brother's keeper and our sister's keeper. But that belief is not just at the center of our Christian faith, it's shared by Americans of all faiths and backgrounds. It's why so many of us, every year, volunteer our time to help those most in need, especially our hungry and our homeless.

So whatever you believe, wherever you're from, let's remember the spirit of service that connects us all to this season as Americans. Each of us can do our part to serve our communities and our country, not just today, but every day.

The First Lady. So from our family to yours, merry Christmas.

The President. Merry Christmas, happy holidays, happy New Year, everybody.

NOTE: The address was recorded at approximately 4:30 p.m. on December 16 in the Roosevelt Room at the White House for broadcast on December 24. The transcript was made available by the Office of the Press Secretary on December 23, but was embargoed for release until 6 a.m. on December 24.

Statement on the Terrorist Attacks in Nigeria
December 25, 2011

We condemn this senseless violence and tragic loss of life on Christmas Day. We offer our sincere condolences to the Nigerian people and especially those who lost family and loved ones. We have been in contact with Nigerian officials about what initially appear to be terrorist acts and pledge to assist them in bringing those responsible to justice.

Statement on the Observance of Kwanzaa
December 26, 2011

Michelle and I send our warmest wishes to all those celebrating Kwanzaa this holiday season. Today marks the beginning of the weeklong celebration honoring African American heritage and culture through the seven principles of Kwanzaa: unity, self-determination, collective work and responsibility, cooperative economics, purpose, creativity, and faith.

We celebrate Kwanzaa at a time when many African Americans and all Americans reflect on our many blessings and memories over the past year and our aspirations for the year to come. And even as there is much to be thankful for, we know that there are still too many Americans going through enormous challenges and trying to make ends meet. But we also know that in the spirit of unity, or *umoja*, we can overcome those challenges together.

As families across America and around the world light the red, black, and green candles of the kinara this week, our family sends our well wishes and blessings for a happy and healthy new year.

NOTE: The statement was released by the Office of the Press Secretary as a statement by the President and the First Lady.

Statement on Senator E. Benjamin Nelson's Decision Not To Seek Reelection
December 27, 2011

I want to thank Senator Nelson for his years of service representing the people of Nebraska, first as Governor, and then for more than a decade in the United States Senate. Over the course of his career, Ben's commitment to working with both Democrats and Republicans across a broad range of issues is a trait far too often overlooked in today's politics. Michelle and I commend Ben for his service and wish him and his family well in the future.

The President's Weekly Address
December 31, 2011

Hello, everybody. As 2011 comes to an end and we look ahead to 2012, I want to wish everyone a happy and healthy New Year.

The last year has been a time of great challenge and great progress for our country. We ended one war and began to wind down another. We dealt a crippling blow to Al Qaida and made America more secure. We stood by our friends and allies around the world through natural disasters and revolutions. And we began to see signs of economic recovery here at home, even as too many Americans are still struggling to get ahead.

There's no doubt that 2012 will bring even more change. And as we head into the new year, I'm hopeful that we have what it takes to face that change and come out even stronger: to grow our economy, create more jobs, and strengthen the middle class.

I'm hopeful because of what we saw right before Christmas, when Members of Congress came together to prevent a tax hike for 160 million Americans, saving a typical family about $40 in every paycheck. They also made sure Americans looking for work won't see their unemployment insurance cut off. And I expect Congress to finish the job by extending these provisions through the end of 2012.

It was good to see Members of Congress do the right thing for millions of working Americans. But it was only possible because you added your voices to the debate. Through e-mail and Twitter and over the phone, you let your representatives know what was at stake: your lives, your families, your well-being. You had the courage to believe that your voices could make a difference. And at the end of the day, they made all the difference.

More than anything else, you are the ones who make me hopeful about 2012. Because we've got some difficult debates and some tough fights to come. As I've said before, we are at a make-or-break moment for the middle class. And in many ways, the actions we take in the months ahead will help determine what kind of country we want to be and what kind of world we want our children and grandchildren to grow up in.

As President, I promise to do everything I can to make America a place where hard work and responsibility are rewarded, one where everyone has a fair shot and everyone does their fair share. That's the America I believe in. That's the America we've always known. And I'm confident that if we work together, and if you keep reminding folks in Washington what's at stake, then we will move this country forward and guarantee every American the opportunities they deserve.

Thanks for watching, and from Michelle, Malia, Sasha, and Bo, as well as myself, happy New Year.

NOTE: The address was recorded at approximately 3 p.m. on December 29 at a private residence in Kailua, HI, for broadcast on December 31. The transcript was made available by the Office of the Press Secretary on December 30, but was embargoed for release until 6 a.m. on December 31.

Statement on Signing the National Defense Authorization Act for Fiscal Year 2012
December 31, 2011

Today I have signed into law H.R. 1540, the "National Defense Authorization Act for Fiscal Year 2012." I have signed the Act chiefly because it authorizes funding for the defense of the United States and its interests abroad, crucial services for service members and their families, and vital national security programs that must be renewed. In hundreds of separate sections totaling over 500 pages, the Act also contains critical Administration initiatives to control the spiraling health care costs of the Department of Defense (DoD), to develop counterterrorism initiatives abroad, to build the security capacity of key partners, to modernize the force, and to boost the efficiency and effectiveness of military operations worldwide.

The fact that I support this bill as a whole does not mean I agree with everything in it. In particular, I have signed this bill despite having serious reservations with certain provisions that regulate the detention, interrogation, and prosecution of suspected terrorists. Over the last several years, my Administration has developed an effective, sustainable framework for the detention, interrogation and trial of suspected terrorists that allows us to maximize both our ability to collect intelligence and to incapacitate dangerous individuals in rapidly developing situations, and the results we have achieved are undeniable. Our success against al-Qa'ida and its affiliates and adherents has derived in significant measure from providing our counterterrorism professionals with the clarity and flexibility they need to adapt to changing circumstances and to utilize whichever authorities best protect the American people, and our accomplishments have respected the values that make our country an example for the world.

Against that record of success, some in Congress continue to insist upon restricting the options available to our counterterrorism professionals and interfering with the very operations that have kept us safe. My Administration has consistently opposed such measures. Ultimately, I decided to sign this bill not only because of the critically important services it provides for our forces and their families and the national security programs it authorizes, but also because the Congress revised provisions that otherwise would have jeopardized the safety, security, and liberty of the American people. Moving forward, my Administration will interpret and implement the provisions described below in a manner that best preserves the flexibility on which our safety depends and upholds the values on which this country was founded.

Section 1021 affirms the executive branch's authority to detain persons covered by the 2001 Authorization for Use of Military Force (AUMF) (Public Law 107–40; 50 U.S.C. 1541 note). This section breaks no new ground and is unnecessary. The authority it describes was included in the 2001 AUMF, as recognized by the Supreme Court and confirmed through lower court decisions since then. Two critical limitations in section 1021 confirm that it solely codifies established authorities. First, under section 1021(d), the bill does not "limit or expand the authority of the President or the scope of the Authorization for Use of Military Force." Second, under section 1021(e), the bill may not be construed to affect any "existing law or authorities relating to the detention of United States citizens, lawful resident aliens of the United States, or any other persons who are captured or arrested in the United States." My Administration strongly supported the inclusion of these limitations in order to make clear beyond doubt that the legislation does nothing more than confirm authorities that the Federal courts have recognized as lawful under the 2001 AUMF. Moreover, I want to clarify that my Administration will not authorize the indefinite military detention without trial of American citizens. Indeed, I believe that doing so would break with our most important traditions and values as a Nation. My Administration will interpret section 1021 in a manner that ensures that any detention it authorizes complies with the Constitution, the laws of war, and all other applicable law.

Section 1022 seeks to require military custody for a narrow category of non-citizen detainees who are "captured in the course of hostilities authorized by the Authorization for Use of Military Force." This section is ill-conceived and will do nothing to improve the security of the United States. The executive branch already has the authority to detain in military custody those members of al-Qa'ida who are captured in the course of hostilities authorized by the AUMF, and as Commander in Chief I have directed the military to do so where appropriate. I reject any approach that would mandate military custody where law enforcement provides the best method of incapacitating a terrorist threat. While section 1022 is unnecessary and has the potential to create uncertainty, I have signed the bill because I believe that this section can be interpreted and applied in a manner that avoids undue harm to our current operations.

I have concluded that section 1022 provides the minimally acceptable amount of flexibility to protect national security. Specifically, I have signed this bill on the understanding that section 1022 provides the executive branch with broad authority to determine how best to implement it, and with the full and unencumbered ability to waive any military custody requirement, including the option of waiving appropriate categories of cases when doing so is in the national security interests of the United States. As my Administration has made clear, the only responsible way to combat the threat al-Qa'ida poses is to remain relentlessly practical, guided by the factual and legal complexities of each case and the relative strengths and weaknesses of each system. Otherwise, investigations could be compromised, our authorities to hold dangerous individuals could be jeopardized, and intelligence could be lost. I will not tolerate that result, and under no circumstances will my Administration accept or adhere to a rigid across-the-board requirement for military detention. I will therefore interpret

and implement section 1022 in the manner that best preserves the same flexible approach that has served us so well for the past 3 years and that protects the ability of law enforcement professionals to obtain the evidence and cooperation they need to protect the Nation.

My Administration will design the implementation procedures authorized by section 1022(c) to provide the maximum measure of flexibility and clarity to our counterterrorism professionals permissible under law. And I will exercise all of my constitutional authorities as Chief Executive and Commander in Chief if those procedures fall short, including but not limited to seeking the revision or repeal of provisions should they prove to be unworkable.

Sections 1023–1025 needlessly interfere with the executive branch's processes for reviewing the status of detainees. Going forward, consistent with congressional intent as detailed in the Conference Report, my Administration will interpret section 1024 as granting the Secretary of Defense broad discretion to determine what detainee status determinations in Afghanistan are subject to the requirements of this section.

Sections 1026–1028 continue unwise funding restrictions that curtail options available to the executive branch. Section 1027 renews the bar against using appropriated funds for fiscal year 2012 to transfer Guantanamo detainees into the United States for any purpose. I continue to oppose this provision, which intrudes upon critical executive branch authority to determine when and where to prosecute Guantanamo detainees, based on the facts and the circumstances of each case and our national security interests. For decades, Republican and Democratic administrations have successfully prosecuted hundreds of terrorists in Federal court. Those prosecutions are a legitimate, effective, and powerful tool in our efforts to protect the Nation. Removing that tool from the executive branch does not serve our national security. Moreover, this intrusion would, under certain circumstances, violate constitutional separation of powers principles.

Section 1028 modifies but fundamentally maintains unwarranted restrictions on the executive branch's authority to transfer detainees to a foreign country. This hinders the executive's ability to carry out its military, national security, and foreign relations activities and like section 1027, would, under certain circumstances, violate constitutional separation of powers principles. The executive branch must have the flexibility to act swiftly in conducting negotiations with foreign countries regarding the circumstances of detainee transfers. In the event that the statutory restrictions in sections 1027 and 1028 operate in a manner that violates constitutional separation of powers principles, my Administration will interpret them to avoid the constitutional conflict.

Section 1029 requires that the Attorney General consult with the Director of National Intelligence and Secretary of Defense prior to filing criminal charges against or seeking an indictment of certain individuals. I sign this based on the understanding that apart from detainees held by the military outside of the United States under the 2001 Authorization for Use of Military Force, the provision applies only to those individuals who have been determined to be covered persons under section 1022 before the Justice Department files charges or seeks an indictment. Notwithstanding that limitation, this provision represents an intrusion into the functions and prerogatives of the Department of Justice and offends the longstanding legal tradition that decisions regarding criminal prosecutions should be vested with the Attorney General free from outside interference. Moreover, section 1029 could impede flexibility and hinder exigent operational judgments in a manner that damages our security. My Administration will interpret and implement section 1029 in a manner that preserves the operational flexibility of our counterterrorism and law enforcement professionals, limits delays in the investigative process, ensures that critical executive branch functions are not inhibited, and preserves the integrity and independence of the Department of Justice.

Other provisions in this bill above could interfere with my constitutional foreign affairs powers. Section 1244 requires the President to submit a report to the Congress 60 days prior to sharing any U.S. classified ballistic missile defense information with Russia. Section 1244 further specifies that this report include a detailed description of the classified information to be provided. While my Administration intends to keep the Congress fully informed of the status of U.S. efforts to cooperate with the Russian Federation on ballistic missile defense, my Administration will also interpret and implement section 1244 in a manner that does not interfere with the President's constitutional authority to conduct foreign affairs and avoids the undue disclosure of sensitive diplomatic communications. Other sections pose similar problems. Sections 1231, 1240, 1241, and 1242 could be read to require the disclosure of sensitive diplomatic communications and national security secrets; and sections 1235, 1242, and 1245 would interfere with my constitutional authority to conduct foreign relations by directing the Executive to take certain positions in negotiations or discussions with foreign governments. Like section 1244, should any application of these provisions conflict with my constitutional authorities, I will treat the provisions as non-binding.

My Administration has worked tirelessly to reform or remove the provisions described above in order to facilitate the enactment of this vital legislation, but certain provisions remain concerning. My Administration will aggressively seek to mitigate those concerns through the design of implementation procedures and other authorities available to me as Chief Executive and Commander in Chief, will oppose any attempt to extend or expand them in the future, and will seek the repeal of any provisions that undermine the policies and values that have guided my Administration throughout my time in office.

BARACK OBAMA

The White House,
December 31, 2011.

NOTE: H.R. 1540, approved December 31, was assigned Public Law No. 112–81.

Appendix A—Digest of Other White House Announcements

The following list includes the President's public schedule and other items of general interest announced by the Office of the Press Secretary and not included elsewhere in this book.

July 1

In the morning, in the Oval Office, the President had an intelligence briefing followed by a meeting with senior advisers.

In the afternoon, the President traveled to Camp David, MD.

The President announced his intention to nominate Thomas J. Curry to be Comptroller of the Currency at the Department of Treasury.

The President announced his intention to nominate Mary John Miller to be Under Secretary for Domestic Finance at the Department of the Treasury.

The President announced his intention to nominate Wendy R. Sherman to be Under Secretary for Political Affairs at the Department of State.

The President announced his intention to nominate Matthew G. Olsen to be Director of the National Counterterrorism Center.

The President announced his intention to appoint Rafael Anchia to be a member of the Advisory Committee for Trade Policy and Negotiations.

The President announced his intention to appoint Carmen Lucca Nazario to be U.S. Representative on the Executive Board of the United Nations Children's Fund.

The President declared a major disaster in Texas and ordered Federal aid to supplement State and local recovery efforts in the area struck by wildfires from April 6 through May 3.

July 3

In the afternoon, the President returned to Washington, DC.

In the evening, the President met with Speaker of the House of Representatives John A. Boehner to discuss the deficit reduction and debt limit negotiations.

July 4

In the evening, on the South Lawn, the President and Mrs. Obama hosted a barbecue and concert for military personnel and their families. Later, they watched the Independence Day fireworks display on the National Mall from the White House.

July 5

In the morning, in the Oval Office, the President had an intelligence briefing followed by a meeting with his senior advisers. Then, also in the Oval Office, he and Vice President Joe Biden met with U.S. Ambassador to Afghanistan Ryan C. Crocker and Lt. Gen. John R. Allen, USMC, commander-designate, NATO International Security Assistance Force, Afghanistan.

In the afternoon, in the Oval Office, the President and Vice President Biden met with Secretary of Defense Leon E. Panetta.

The President announced his intention to nominate Matan A. Koch and Stephanie Orlando to be members of the National Council on Disability.

The President announced his intention to appoint the following individuals as members of the President's Advisory Commission on Educational Excellence for Hispanics:

Denis J. Cruz;
Millie Garcia;
Monica R. Martinez; and
Veronica E. Melvin.

The President announced his intention to appoint B. Sue Fulton as a member of the Board of Visitors to the U.S. Military Academy.

The President announced his intention to appoint Tom Healy as a member of the J. William Fulbright Foreign Scholarship Board.

The President announced his intention to appoint Warren G. Hioki as a member of the Board of Trustees of the Christopher Columbus Fellowship Foundation.

The President announced his intention to appoint Marc P. Lefar as a member of the President's National Security Telecommunications Advisory Committee.

July 6

In the morning, in the Oval Office, the President and Vice President Joe Biden had an intelligence briefing. Then, he met with his senior advisers. Later, also in the Oval Office, the President and Vice President Biden met with Secretary of the Treasury Timothy F. Geithner.

In the afternoon, in the Private Dining Room, the President and Vice President Biden had lunch. Later, in the Oval Office, they met with Secretary of State Hillary Rodham Clinton.

During the day, in the Roosevelt Room, the President stopped by a meeting between National Security Adviser Thomas E. Donilon and President-elect Ollanta Moises Humala Tasso of Peru.

The President announced the designation of the following individuals as members of a Presidential delegation to South Sudan to attend a ceremony marking the declaration of the independence of South Sudan on July 9:

Susan E. Rice (head of delegation);
Donald M. Payne;
Colin L. Powell;
Johnnie Carson;
Princeton N. Lyman;
Brooke D. Anderson;
Donald K. Steinberg;
Carter F. Ham;
R. Barrie Walkley; and
Kenneth F. Hackett.

July 7

In the morning, in the Oval Office, the President and Vice President Joe Biden had an intelligence briefing. Then, also in the Oval Office, he met with his senior advisers. Later, in the Cabinet Room, he and Vice President Biden met with congressional leaders to discuss the deficit reduction and debt limit negotiations.

In the afternoon, in the Oval Office, the President participated in a credentialing ceremony for newly appointed Ambassadors to the U.S.

The White House announced that the President will welcome Prime Minister John P. Key of New Zealand to the White House on July 22.

July 8

In the morning, in the Oval Office, the President and Vice President Joe Biden met with House Democratic Leader Nancy Pelosi. Later, in the outer Oval Office, he watched the launch of Space Shuttle *Atlantis*. Then, in the Map Room, he participated in separate television interviews with Kent Wainscott of WISN in Milwaukee, WI, Mike Clark of WTAE in Pittsburgh, PA, Jean Enersen of KING in Seattle, WA, and Larry Stogner of WTVD in Raleigh-Durham, NC, to discuss the national economy and deficit reduction and debt limit negotiations.

The President announced his intention to nominate Michael A. Hammer to be Assistant Secretary for Public Affairs at the Department of State.

The President announced his intention to nominate Charles D. McConnell to be Assistant Secretary for Fossil Energy at the Department of Energy.

The President announced his intention to nominate Joseph H. Gale to be a judge on the U.S. Tax Court.

The President announced his intention to appoint Terry Guen and Dorothy T. Lippert as members of the Advisory Council on Historic Preservation.

The President announced his intention to appoint Rosemary A. Joyce as a member of the Cultural Property Advisory Committee.

The President declared a major disaster in Arkansas and ordered Federal aid to supplement State and local recovery efforts in the area struck by severe storms, tornadoes, and flooding from May 24 through 26.

The President declared a major disaster in Vermont and ordered Federal aid to supplement State and local recovery efforts in the area struck by severe storms and flooding on May 26 and 27.

July 9

In the morning, the President traveled to Camp David, MD.

July 10

In the afternoon, the President returned to Washington, DC.

In the evening, in the Cabinet Room, the President and Vice President Joe Biden met with congressional leaders to discuss the deficit reduction and debt limit negotiations.

July 11

In the afternoon, in the Oval Office, the President and Vice President Joe Biden had an intelligence briefing. Then, in the Cabinet Room, they met with congressional leaders to discuss the deficit reduction and debt limit negotiations. Later, in the South Court Auditorium, he made remarks at the closing session of the Hispanic Policy Conference.

During the day, the President had a telephone conversation with President Dmitry A. Medvedev of Russia to discuss the situations in Libya, Sudan, and Afghanistan and to express his condolences for the loss of life due to the sinking of the MS *Bulgaria.*

The President announced his intention to nominate Mary B. DeRosa, Frank E. Loy, and Kendrick B. Meek to be U.S. Representatives to the 66th Session of the United Nations General Assembly.

The President announced his intention to appoint the following individuals as members of the National Infrastructure Advisory Council:

Jack Baylis;
David J. Grain;
Donald R. Knauss;
Constance H. Lau; and
Beverly A. Scott.

The President announced that he has nominated Danya A. Dayson, Peter A. Krauthamer, and John F. McCabe, Jr., to be associate judges on the Superior Court for the District of Columbia.

July 12

In the morning, in the Oval Office, the President and Vice President Joe Biden had an intelligence briefing. Then, also in the Oval Office, he met with his senior advisers.

In the afternoon, in the Cabinet Room, the President and Vice President Biden met with congressional leaders to discuss the deficit reduction and debt limit negotiations.

July 13

In the morning, in the Oval Office, the President and Vice President Joe Biden had an intelligence briefing. Later, also in the Oval Office, he met with Foreign Minister Sergey V. Lavrov of Russia. Then, in the Roosevelt Room, he met with members of the President's Intelligence Advisory Board.

In the afternoon, in the Oval Office, the President met with his senior advisers. Then, in the Private Dining Room, he and Vice President Biden had lunch. Later, in the Cabinet Room, they met with congressional leaders to discuss the deficit reduction and debt limit negotiations.

The President declared a major disaster in Ohio and ordered Federal aid to supplement State and local recovery efforts in the area struck by a severe storms from April 4 through May 15.

The President declared a major disaster in Pennsylvania and ordered Federal aid to supplement Commonwealth and local recovery efforts in the area struck by a severe storms from April 25 through 28.

July 14

In the morning, in the Oval Office, the President and Vice President Joe Biden had an intelligence briefing. Then, also in the Oval Office, he met with his senior advisers.

In the afternoon, in the Map Room, the President participated in separate television interviews with Natalie Pasquarella of WSOC in

Charlotte, NC, Jim Vance of WRC in Washington, DC, and Scott Pelley of KYW in Philadelphia, PA. Later, in the Oval Office, the President and Vice President Biden met with Secretary of the Treasury Timothy F. Geithner. Then, in the Cabinet Room, they met with congressional leaders to discuss the deficit reduction and debt limit negotiations.

The President announced his intention to nominate David A. Montoya to be Inspector General of the Department of Housing and Urban Development.

The President announced his intention to nominate Chester J. Culver and Bruce J. Sherrick to be a members of the Board of Directors of the Federal Agricultural Mortgage Corporation.

The President announced his intention to appoint Roland Garcia to be a member of the Board of Visitors to the U.S. Naval Academy.

The President announced his intention to appoint Timothy Johns to be a Commissioner of the Commission for the Conservation and Management of Highly Migratory Fish Stocks in the Western and Central Pacific Ocean.

The President declared a major disaster in Puerto Rico and ordered Federal aid to supplement Commonwealth and local recovery efforts in the area struck by a severe storms, flooding, mudslides, and landslides from May 20 through June 8.

July 15

In the morning, in the Oval Office, the President had an intelligence briefing.

In the afternoon, in the Oval Office, the President had a telephone conversation with crewmembers of the Space Shuttle *Atlantis* and the International Space Station. Later, also in the Oval Office, he met with Ruby Bridges Hall and representatives of the Norman Rockwell Museum in Stockbridge, MA, to view and discuss Rockwell's painting, "The Problem We All Live With," which will be displayed in the White House through October 31.

The President announced the designation of the following individuals as members of a Presidential delegation to attend the final game of the Women's World Cup in Germany on July 17: Jill T. Biden (head of delegation); Philip D. Murphy; and Chelsea Clinton.

July 16

In the morning, in the Map Room, the President met with Tenzin Gyatso, the 14th Dalai Lama.

July 17

In the morning, the President, Mrs. Obama, and their daughters Sasha and Malia attended a church service at St. John's Episcopal Church.

In the afternoon, in the Treaty Room, the President, Mrs. Obama, and their daughters Sasha and Malia watched the U.S. versus Japan Women's World Cup soccer game.

During the day, the President met with Speaker of the House of Representatives John A. Boehner and Rep. Eric I. Cantor to discuss the deficit reduction and debt limit negotiations.

July 18

In the morning, in the Oval Office, the President had an intelligence briefing followed by a meeting with his senior advisers. Later, in the State Dining Room, the President met with members of the philanthropic project, "The Giving Pledge," including cofounders Warren E. Buffett, Melinda F. Gates, and William H. Gates III.

In the afternoon, at the Dwight D. Eisenhower Executive Office Building, the President hosted a roundtable discussion on education with business leaders, Secretary of Education Arne Duncan, White House Senior Adviser Valerie B. Jarrett, White House Domestic Policy Council Director Melody C. Barnes, America's Promise Alliance Chair Alma J. Powell, and former Secretary of State Colin L. Powell.

Later in the afternoon, in the Roosevelt Room, the President held a roundtable discussion on financial reform, including the implementation of the Dodd-Frank Wall Street Reform and Consumer Protection Act.

July 19

In the morning, in the Oval Office, the President and Vice President Joe Biden had an intelligence briefing. Then, he met with his senior advisers. Later, also in the Oval Office, he had a telephone conversation with Chancellor Angela Merkel of Germany to discuss economic stabilization efforts in Europe, the global financial markets, and Germany's successful hosting of the Women's World Cup soccer games.

Later in the morning, in the Oval Office, the President had a telephone conversation with Gen. John R. Allen, USMC, to congratulate him on his promotion to the rank of four-star general and his assumption of command of the NATO International Security Assistance Force, Afghanistan.

In the evening, the President had a telephone conversation with Senate Majority Leader Harry M. Reid, Senate Minority Leader A. Mitchell McConnell, Speaker of the House of Representatives John A. Boehner, and House Democratic Leader Nancy Pelosi to discuss the deficit reduction and debt limit negotiations.

The White House announced that the President will travel to College Park, MD, on July 22.

The President announced his intention to nominate Maureen K. Ohlhausen to be a Commissioner of the Federal Trade Commission.

The President announced his intention to nominate Roslyn A. Mazer to be Inspector General at the Department of Homeland Security.

The President announced his intention to appoint Gabriel Guerra-Mondragon as a member of the J. William Fulbright Foreign Scholarship Board.

The President announced his intention to appoint Dallin Jensen as a member of the Utah Reclamation Mitigation and Conservation Commission.

July 20

In the morning, in the Oval Office, the President and Vice President Joe Biden had an intelligence briefing. Then, also in the Oval Office, he met with his senior advisers.

Later in the morning, in the Diplomatic Reception Room, the President participated in separate television interviews with Lara Moritz of KMBC in Kansas City, MO, David Ono of KABC in Los Angeles, CA, and Jerry Revish of WBNS in Columbus, OH, to discuss the national economy and deficit reduction and debt limit negotiations.

In the afternoon, in the Oval Office, the President and Vice President Biden met with Secretary of Defense Leon E. Panetta. Later, he met with Senate Majority Leader Harry M. Reid, Sen. Richard J. Durbin, House Democratic Leader Nancy Pelosi, and Rep. Steny H. Hoyer to discuss the deficit reduction and debt limit negotiations.

In the evening, the President met with Speaker of the House of Representatives John A. Boehner and Rep. Eric I. Cantor to discuss the deficit reduction and debt limit negotiations.

The President announced that he has nominated Michael W. Fitzgerald to be a judge on the U.S. District Court for the Central District of California.

The President declared a major disaster in Tennessee and ordered Federal aid to supplement State and local recovery efforts in the area struck by severe storms, straight-line winds, tornadoes, and flooding from June 18 through 24.

July 21

In the morning, in the Oval Office, the President and Vice President Joe Biden had an intelligence briefing. Then, he met with his senior advisers.

Later in the morning, in the Oval Office, the President participated in separate telephone interviews for the radio shows of Ricardo Brown, Isabel Gomez-Bassols, Steve Harvey, and Michel Martin.

In the afternoon, in the Private Dining Room, the President and Vice President Biden had lunch.

Later in the afternoon, in the Oval Office, the President met with Gen. James E. "Hoss"

Cartwright, USMC, Vice Chairman, Joint Chiefs of Staff. Then, he met with Marc H. Morial, president, National Urban League, and Benjamin T. Jealous, president, National Association for the Advancement of Colored People. Later, also in the Oval Office, he and Vice President Biden met with Secretary of the Treasury Timothy F. Geithner.

In the evening, the President met with Senate Majority Leader Harry M. Reid, Sen. Richard J. Durbin, House Democratic Leader Nancy Pelosi, and Rep. Steny H. Hoyer.

The President announced his intention to nominate Larry W. Walther to be a member of the Board of Directors of the U.S. Export-Import Bank.

The President announced his intention to nominate James T. Ryan to be a member of the Board of Directors of the National Institute of Building Sciences.

The President announced his intention to appoint Abbey Johnston as a member of the Medal of Valor Review Board.

The President announced his intention to appoint Sharon Long as a member of the President's Committee on the National Medal of Science.

The President announced his intention to appoint Alapaki Nahale-a and Jeanne Unemori Skog as members of the Commission on Presidential Scholars.

The President announced his intention to appoint Errol R. Schwartz as a member of the Board of Visitors to the U.S. Military Academy.

July 22

In the morning, in the Oval Office, the President and Vice President Joe Biden had an intelligence briefing. Then, he traveled to College Park, MD.

In the afternoon, the President returned to Washington, DC. Later, in the Oval Office, he met with Secretary of Defense Leon E. Panetta and Adm. Michael G. Mullen, USN, Chairman, Joint Chiefs of Staff. Later, also in the Oval Office, he met with former U.S. Ambassador to Afghanistan Karl W. Eikenberry and his wife Ching.

The President announced his intention to appoint Sue B. Clark, Rodney C. Ewing, and Linda K. Nozick as members of the Nuclear Waste Technical Review Board.

The President declared a major disaster in New Hampshire and ordered Federal aid to supplement State and local recovery efforts in the area struck by severe storms and flooding from May 26 through 30.

The President declared a major disaster in Wyoming and ordered Federal aid to supplement State and local recovery efforts in the area struck by severe storms, flooding, and landslides from May 18 through July 8.

July 23

In the morning, in the Cabinet Room, the President and Vice President Joe Biden met with Congressional leaders, including Senate Majority Leader Harry M. Reid, Senate Minority Leader A. Mitchell McConnell, Speaker of the House of Representatives John A. Boehner, and House Democratic Leader Nancy Pelosi, to discuss the deficit reduction and debt limit negotiations.

In the afternoon, in the Oval Office, the President had a telephone conversation with Prime Minister Jens Stoltenberg of Norway to express his condolences for the terrorist attacks in Oslo and Utoya on July 22. Then, also in the Oval Office, he had a telephone conversation with President Nicolas Sarkozy of France to discuss France-U.S. strategic priorities.

July 24

In the evening, in the Oval Office, the President and Vice President Joe Biden met with Senate Majority Leader Harry M. Reid and House Democratic Leader Nancy Pelosi to discuss the deficit reduction and debt limit negotiations.

July 25

In the morning, in the Oval Office, the President had an intelligence briefing followed by a meeting with his senior advisers.

In the afternoon, in the Blue Room, the President met with Willie H. Mays, Jr., assistant to the president and former center fielder, and Bruce Bochy, manager, Major League Baseball's San Francisco Giants.

The President declared a major disaster in Kentucky and ordered Federal aid to supplement Commonwealth and local recovery efforts in the area struck by severe storms, tornadoes, and flooding from June 19 through 23.

July 26

In the morning, in the Oval Office, the President and Vice President Joe Biden had an intelligence briefing followed by a meeting with his senior advisers.

In the afternoon, at the official residence of Norway's Ambassador to the U.S. Wegger Christian Strommen, the President and Vice President Biden extended their condolences for the terrorist attacks in Oslo and Utoya on July 22 and signed the Norwegian Embassy's book of condolences.

Later in the afternoon, in the East Room, the President participated in a photo opportunity with participants in the American Legion Auxiliary's Girls Nation event. Later, in the Oval Office, he and Vice President Biden met with Secretary of Defense Leon E. Panetta.

July 27

In the morning, in the Oval Office, the President and Vice President Joe Biden had an intelligence briefing followed by a meeting with his senior advisers.

The White House announced that the President will hold an event announcing the next round of a national program to improve fuel efficiency for cars and light-duty trucks at the Walter E. Washington Convention Center on July 29.

The President announced the designation of the following individuals as members of a Presidential delegation to attend the Inauguration of Ollanta Moises Humala Tasso as President of Peru in Lima, Peru, on July 28: Daniel A. Restrepo (head of delegation); and Rose M. Likins.

The President announced his intention to nominate David T. Danielson to be Assistant Secretary for Energy Efficiency and Renewable Energy at the Department of Energy.

The President announced his intention to nominate LaDoris Guess Harris to be Director of the Office of Minority Economic Impact at the Department of Energy.

July 28

In the morning, in the Oval Office, the President and Vice President Joe Biden had an intelligence briefing.

In the afternoon, in the Oval Office, the President met with the Domestic Policy Council. Later, also in the Oval Office, he had separate meetings with Secretary of the Treasury Timothy F. Geithner and Secretary of State Hillary Rodham Clinton.

The President announced that he has nominated Evan J. Wallach to be a judge on the U.S. Court of Appeals for the Federal Circuit.

The President announced that he has nominated Ronnie Abrams to be a judge on the U.S. District Court for the Southern District of New York.

The President announced that he has nominated Rudolph Contreras to be a judge on the U.S. District Court for the District of Columbia.

The President announced that he has appointed the following individuals as members of the Government Accountability and Transparency Board:

Earl E. Devaney;
Ashton B. Carter;
W. Scott Gould;
Allison C. Lerner;
Daniel R. Levinson;
Ellen Murray;
Calvin L. Scovel III;
Kathleen S. Tighe;
Daniel I. Werfel;
David C. Williams; and
Neal S. Wolin.

July 29

In the morning, in the Oval Office, the President had an intelligence briefing.

The President announced his intention to nominate Michael E. Horowitz to be Inspector General at the Department of Justice.

The President announced his intention to nominate Anneila I. Sargent to be a member of the National Science Board of the National Science Foundation.

The President announced his intention to appoint Elizabeth B. Castor and Susan Ness as members of the J. William Fulbright Foreign Scholarship Board.

The President announced his intention to appoint Clement A. Price as Vice Chairman of the Advisory Council on Historic Preservation.

The President declared a major disaster in Kansas and ordered Federal aid to supplement State and local recovery efforts in the area struck by severe storms, straight-line winds, tornadoes, and flooding from May 19 through June 4.

July 30

In the afternoon, in the Oval Office, the President and Vice President Joe Biden met with Senate Majority Leader Harry M. Reid and House Democratic Leader Nancy Pelosi to discuss the deficit reduction and debt limit negotiations.

July 31

During the day, in the office of White House Chief of Staff William M. Daley, the President had a telephone conversation with Senate Majority Leader Harry M. Reid and House Democratic Leader Nancy Pelosi to discuss the deficit reduction and debt limit negotiations. Also present during the meeting were Chief of Staff Daley, National Economic Council Eugene B. Sperling, and Secretary of the Treasury Timothy F. Geithner.

August 1

In the morning, in the Oval Office, the President had an intelligence briefing followed by a meeting with Secretary of Commerce Gary F. Locke. Later, also in the Oval Office, he had a meeting with his senior advisers.

During the day, in the Oval Office, the President met with U.S. Ambassador to Syria Robert S. Ford to discuss the situation in Syria and Syria-U.S. relations.

The White House announced that the President will travel to Chicago, IL, on August 3.

August 2

In the morning, in the East Room, the President met with the AFL–CIO Executive Council to discuss job creation and the economy. Then, in the Oval Office, he had an intelligence briefing followed by a meeting with his senior advisers.

In the afternoon, in the Oval Office, the President met with the crew of the Space Shuttle *Endeavour* and U.S. Commander Scott J. Kelly of the International Space Station. Later, also in the Oval Office, he met with Secretary of Defense Leon E. Panetta.

The White House announced that the President will hold an event to discuss work to prepare veterans for the workforce at the Washington Navy Yard on August 5.

The President announced his intention to nominate Ashton B. Carter to be Deputy Secretary of Defense.

The President announced his intention to nominate I. Charles McCullough III to be Inspector General of the Intelligence Community at the Office of the Director of National Intelligence.

The President announced his intention to nominate Ernest Mitchell, Jr., to be Administrator of the U.S. Fire Administration at the Federal Emergency Management Agency.

The President announced his intention to nominate Nancy M. Ware to be Director of the Court Services and Offender Supervision Agency for the District of Columbia.

The President announced his intention to nominate Gregory H. Woods to be General Counsel at the Department of Energy.

The President announced his intention to appoint Carol Pensky and Robert M. Saltzman as members of the Commission on Presidential Scholars.

The President announced that he has nominated Miranda Du to be a judge on the U.S. District Court for the District of Nevada.

The President announced that he has nominated Adalberto J. Jordan to be a judge on the U.S. Court of Appeals for the Eleventh Circuit.

The President announced that he has nominated Catharine F. Easterly to be a judge on the U.S. Court of Appeals for the District of Columbia.

The President announced that he has nominated David B. Barlow to be U.S. attorney for the District of Utah.

August 3

In the morning, in the Oval Office, the President had a telephone conversation with President Dmitry A. Medvedev of Russia to discuss World Trade Organization negotiations. Then, also in the Oval Office, he had an intelligence briefing.

In the afternoon, at Good Stuff Eatery, the President had lunch with senior White House officials. Then, in the Oval Office, he had separate meetings with Secretary of State Hillary Rodham Clinton and Attorney General Eric H. Holder, Jr.

Later in the afternoon, the President traveled to Chicago, IL, where he participated in a Democratic National Committee video teleconference at the Aragon Entertainment Center.

In the evening, the President returned to Washington, DC.

The White House released further details on an event the President will hold to discuss work to prepare veterans for the workforce at the Washington Navy Yard on August 5.

The White House announced that the President will welcome the 2011 Super Bowl Champion Green Bay Packers to the White House on August 12.

August 4

In the morning, in the Oval Office, the President had an intelligence briefing.

During the day, in the Oval Office, the President met with Secretary of the Treasury Timothy F. Geithner.

The White House announced that the President will travel to Springfield, VA, on August 9.

The White House announced that the President will travel to Holland, MI, on August 11.

The White House announced that the President will deliver remarks at the Martin Luther King, Jr. Memorial dedication on the National Mall on August 28.

The President announced his intention to appoint Maria Lombardo as Chairman of the Board of Trustees of the Christopher Columbus Fellowship Foundation.

The President announced his intention to appoint William Sisk as a member of the Committee for Purchase From People Who Are Blind or Severely Disabled.

The President announced his intention to appoint Steven L. VanRoekel as U.S. Chief Information Officer and Administrator of the Office of Electronic Government at the Office of Management and Budget.

The President made additional disaster assistance available to the Sovereign Tribal Nation of the Havasupai Tribe in Arizona by authorizing an increase in the level of Federal funding for recovery efforts in the area struck by severe storms and flooding from October 3 through 6.

August 5

In the morning, in the Oval Office, the President had an intelligence briefing.

In the afternoon, the President had separate telephone conversations with President Nikolas Sarkozy of France and Chancellor Angela Merkel of Germany to discuss the European economy and the situation in Syria. Later, he traveled to Camp David, MD.

The White House released further details on the President's visit to Springfield, VA, on August 9.

The White House announced that the President will travel to Peosta, IA, on August 16.

August 6

During the day, the President had a teleconference briefing with Secretary of Defense Leon E. Panetta; Adm. Michael G. Mullen, USN, Chairman, Joint Chiefs of Staff; National Security Adviser Thomas E. Donilon; White House Chief of Staff William M. Daley; and members of his national security staff to discuss U.S. and Afghan military personnel killed during a mission earlier in the day.

August 7

In the afternoon, the President returned to Washington, DC.

During the day, the President had separate telephone conversations with Gen. John R. Allen, USMC, commander, NATO International Security Assistance Force, Afghanistan; Lt.

Gen. Joseph L. Votel, USA, commander, Joint Special Operations Command; Gen. James N. Mattis, USMC, commander, U.S. Central Command; and Adm. Eric T. Olson, USN, commander, U.S. Special Operations Command, to express his condolences for U.S. military personnel killed during a mission in Afghanistan on August 6. He also had a telephone conversation with President Hamid Karzai of Afghanistan to express his condolences for the Afghan military personnel killed during the same mission.

August 8

In the morning, in the Oval Office, the President had an intelligence briefing.

In the afternoon, in the Oval Office, the President had separate telephone conversations with Prime Minister Jose Luis Rodriguez Zapatero of Spain and Prime Minister Silvio Berlusconi of Italy to discuss the economic situation in Europe and the global economy, the situation in Syria, and U.S. and Afghan military personnel killed during a mission in Afghanistan on August 6.

The White House announced that the President will travel to Holland, MI, on August 11.

The White House announced that the President will travel to New York City on August 11.

The President made additional disaster assistance available to North Dakota by authorizing an increase in the level of Federal funding for recovery efforts in the area struck by flooding from February 14 through July 20.

The President declared a major disaster in Utah and ordered Federal aid to supplement State, tribal, and local recovery efforts in the area struck by flooding from April 18 through July 16.

August 9

In the morning, in the Oval Office, the President had an intelligence briefing. Later, in the Roosevelt Room, he met with industry leaders to discuss fuel efficiency standards for work trucks, buses, and heavy-duty vehicles.

Later in the morning, the President traveled to Dover Air Force Base, DE, where, upon arrival in the afternoon, he witnessed the dignified transfer of the remains of U.S. military

personnel killed during a mission in Afghanistan on August 6. Then, he met with the families of the deceased. Later, he returned to Washington, DC, arriving in the evening.

The White House announced that the President will travel to southern Minnesota, northeastern Iowa, and western Illinois on a 3-day bus tour from August 15 through 17.

August 10

In the morning, in the Oval Office, the President had an intelligence briefing. Then, also in the Oval Office, the President had separate telephone conversations with Prime Minister David Cameron of the United Kingdom to discuss the global economy and Prime Minister Benjamin Netanyahu of Israel to discuss the Middle East peace process.

In the afternoon, in the Oval Office, the President participated in an interview with Galina Espinoza of Latina magazine. Then he had an economic briefing with Federal Reserve Chairman Ben S. Bernanke. Later, also in the Oval Office, he had separate meetings with Secretary of State Hillary Rodham Clinton and Secretary of the Treasury Timothy F. Geithner.

August 11

In the morning, in the Oval Office, the President had a telephone conversation with Prime Minister Recep Tayyip Erdogan of Turkey to discuss the situation in Syria and the famine and humanitarian crisis affecting East Africa. Then, in the Situation Room, he had a video teleconference with U.S. Ambassador to Afghanistan Ryan C. Crocker and Lt. Gen. John R. Allen, USMC, commander, NATO International Security Assistance Force, Afghanistan.

Later in the morning, the President traveled to Holland, MI, arriving in the afternoon.

In the afternoon, the President traveled to Johnson Controls, Inc., where he toured an advanced battery facility with Vice President of Operations Elizabeth Rolinski. Later, he traveled to New York City.

In the evening, the President attended a Democratic National Committee fundraiser at the Ritz-Carlton New York, Battery Park hotel. Later, he returned to Washington, DC.

The White House released further details on the President's visit to Minnesota to begin a 3-day bus tour on August 15.

August 12

In the morning, in the Situation Room, the President had a video teleconference with President Hamid Karzai of Afghanistan to discuss progress in Afghanistan.

In the afternoon, in the Roosevelt Room, the President met with business leaders to discuss the economy.

The White House released further details on the President's visit to Iowa on August 15 and 16.

The White House released further details on the President's visit to Illinois on August 17.

The White House announced that the President will award the Medal of Honor to Sgt. Dakota L. Meyer, USMC, on September 15.

The President declared a major disaster in Missouri and ordered Federal aid to supplement State and local recovery efforts in the area struck by flooding from June 1 through August 1.

The President declared a major disaster in Nebraska and ordered Federal aid to supplement State and local recovery efforts in the area struck by flooding from May 24 through August 1.

The President declared a major disaster in Nebraska and ordered Federal aid to supplement State and local recovery efforts in the area struck by severe storms, tornadoes, straight-line winds, and flooding from June 19 through 21.

August 13

In the morning, the President had separate telephone conversations with King Abdallah bin Abd al-Aziz Al Saud of Saudi Arabia to discuss the situation in Syria; Prime Minister-elect Yinglak Chinnawat of Thailand to congratulate her on her election victory and to discuss Thailand-U.S. relations; and Prime Minister David Cameron of the United Kingdom to discuss United Kingdom-U.S. relations, the situation in Syria, and other issues.

August 15

In the morning, the President traveled to St. Paul, MN, where he began a 3-day bus tour.

In the afternoon, the President traveled to Cannon Falls, MN. Later, at the Old Market Deli in Cannon Falls, he had lunch with Henry B. Mathia, Scott J. Peer, Timothy K. Loney, Thomas B. Newman, and Joseph D. Kidd, veterans of military operations in Iraq and Afghanistan. Then, he traveled to Decorah, IA. While en route, he stopped at the Coffee Mill restaurant in Zumbrota, MN, where he visited with patrons, and at Chatfield High School in Chatfield, MN, where he met with campers and staff of the Valleyland Kids summer camp.

In the evening, the President traveled to Hotel Winneshiek in Decorah, IA.

August 16

In the morning, the President traveled to Guttenberg, IA, where, at Rausch's Cafe, he had breakfast with small-business owners Michael Sexton, Joel Althoff, Kenneth Hach, and Eric and Fern Unruh. Then, he traveled to Peosta, IA.

In the afternoon, at Northeast Iowa Community College, the President participated in five breakout sessions at the White House Rural Exconomic Forum. Later, also at Northeast Iowa Community College, he participated in separate television interviews with Wolf Blitzer of CNN's "The Situation Room With Wolf Blitzer" program, Mike Bush of KSDK in St. Louis, MO, and Phil Witt of WDAF in Kansas City, MO.

Later in the afternoon, the President traveled to Davenport, IA. While en route, he stopped in Maquoketa, IA, where, at Maquoketa High School, he met with student athletes and coaches, and in DeWitt, IA, where, at DeWitt Dairy Treats, he visited with patrons. Later, in LeClaire, IA, he stopped at Grasshoppers gift shop and then Kernel Cody's Popcorn Shoppe, where he also visited with patrons.

In the evening, the President traveled to Hotel Blackhawk in Davenport, IA.

The White House announced that the President will travel to Cape Cod, MA, on August 18.

August 17

In the morning, the President traveled to Atkinson, IL. While en route, he stopped in Morrison, IL, where, at the Whiteside County Fair, he visited with patrons.

In the afternoon, at the Wyffels Hybrids, Inc., production facility in Atkinson, IL, the President participated in an interview with Anthony Mason of CBS's "Sunday Morning" program. Later, he traveled to Alpha, IL. While en route, he stopped at Galesburg High School in Galesburg, IL, where he met with student athletes and coaches.

Later in the afternoon, at Country Corner Farm Market in Alpha, IL, the President participated in separate interviews with Tom Steever, president-elect, National Association of Farm Broadcasting, and Douglas Burns of the Daily Times Herald of Carroll, IA.

In the evening, the President returned to Washington, DC.

August 18

In the morning, in the Oval Office, the President met with his economic advisers. Later, in the Situation Room, he had an intelligence briefing.

In the afternoon, the President traveled to Martha's Vineyard, MA.

The President announced his intention to nominate Susan D. Page to be Ambassador to South Sudan.

The President announced his intention to appoint Modesto E. Abety-Gutierrez and Lily Eskelsen as members of the President's Advisory Commission on Educational Excellence for Hispanics.

The President announced his intention to appoint Christopher S. Hart as a member of the Architectural and Transportation Barriers Compliance Board.

The President announced his intention to appoint Choco G. Meza and E. Faye Williams as members of the Commission on Presidential Scholars.

The President declared a major disaster in Louisiana and ordered Federal aid to supplement State and local recovery efforts in the area struck by flooding from April 25 through July 7.

August 19

In the morning, the President had an economic briefing. Also in the morning, he had an intelligence briefing with Homeland Security and Counterterrorism Adviser John O. Brennan.

August 21

During the day, the President received regular updates from Homeland Security and Counterterrorism Adviser John O. Brennan on the situation in Libya.

In the evening, the President had a conference call with senior members of his national security team to discuss the situation in Libya.

August 22

In the morning, the President received a briefing from Homeland Security and Counterterrorism Adviser John O. Brennan on the situation in Libya. Then, he received an economic briefing from National Economic Council Deputy Director Brian C. Deese. He also received a briefing on Hurricane Irene.

Later in the morning, the President had separate telephone conversations with Warren E. Buffett, chief executive officer and chairman, Berkshire Hathaway Inc., and Alan Mulally, president and chief executive officer, Ford Motor Company, to discuss the economy.

In the afternoon, the President had a conference call with the National Security Council, Homeland Security and Counterterrorism Adviser Brennan, and other members of his national security team to discuss the situation in Libya.

During the day, the President had a telephone conversation with Prime Minister David Cameron of the United Kingdom to discuss the situation in Libya.

The White House announced that the President will travel to Detroit, MI, on September 5.

The President declared an emergency in Puerto Rico and ordered Federal aid to supplement Commonwealth and local recovery efforts in the area struck by Hurricane Irene beginning on August 21 and continuing.

August 23

In the morning, the President received a briefing from Homeland Security and Counterterrorism Adviser John O. Brennan on the situation in Libya and Hurricane Irene. Then, he received an economic briefing from National Economic Council Deputy Director Brian C. Deese.

In the afternoon, the President had a conference call with members of his national security team and other senior advisers to discuss the earthquake that struck the East Coast of the United States and the Federal Government's preparations for Hurricane Irene.

During the day, the President had a telephone conversation with President Nicolas Sarkozy of France to discuss the situation in Libya and the global economy.

August 24

In the morning, the President received an intelligence briefing from Homeland Security and Counterterrorism Adviser John O. Brennan on the situation in Libya and the Federal Government's preparations for Hurricane Irene. Then, he received an economic briefing from National Economic Council Deputy Director Brian C. Deese.

Also in the morning, the President had a conference call with Jeffrey R. Immelt, Chair, and Kenneth I. Chenault, member, President's Council on Jobs and Competitiveness, to discuss job creation and the economy.

The President declared a major disaster in Iowa and ordered Federal aid to supplement State and local recovery efforts in the area struck by severe storms, straight-line winds, and flooding from July 9 through 14. .

August 25

In the morning, the President received an intelligence briefing from Homeland Security and Counterterrorism Adviser John O. Brennan, which included an update on the situation in Libya. Later, he had a conference call with Secretary of Homeland Security Janet A. Napolitano, Federal Emergency Management Agency Administrator W. Craig Fugate, White House Chief of Staff William M. Daley, and other senior advisers to discuss the Federal Government's preparations for Hurricane Irene.

Also in the morning, the President had a conference call with Secretary of the Treasury Timothy F. Geithner, Office of Management and Budget Director Jacob J. "Jack" Lew, National Economic Council Director Eugene B. Sperling, and White House Chief of Staff Daley to discuss the economy, job creation, and deficit reduction.

The President declared an emergency in North Carolina and ordered Federal aid to supplement State and local recovery efforts in the area struck by Hurricane Irene beginning on August 25 and continuing.

August 26

In the morning, the President had a conference call with Homeland Security and Counterterrorism Adviser John O. Brennan, Secretary of Homeland Security Janet A. Napolitano, Federal Emergency Management Agency Administrator W. Craig Fugate, and White House Chief of Staff William M. Daley to discuss the Federal Government's preparations for Hurricane Irene.

Later in the morning, the President and Homeland Security and Counterterrorism Adviser John O. Brennan had a conference call with Govs. Christopher J. Christie of New Jersey, Andrew M. Cuomo of New York, Jack A. Markell of Delaware, Robert F. McDonnell of Virginia, Martin J. O'Malley of Maryland, Deval L. Patrick of Massachusetts, and Beverly E. Perdue of North Carolina; and Mayors Michael R. Bloomberg of New York City; Paul D. Fraim of Norfolk, VA; Vincent C. Gray of Washington, DC; Michael A. Nutter of Philadelphia, PA; Stephanie C. Rawlings-Blake of Baltimore, MD; and William D. Sessoms, Jr., of Virginia Beach, VA, to discuss Federal, State, and local government preparations for Hurricane Irene.

Also in the morning, the President received an economic briefing from National Economic Council Deputy Director Brian C. Deese. He also had a telephone conversation with International Monetary Fund Managing Director Christine Lagarde to discuss the global economy.

In the evening, the President, Mrs. Obama, and their daughters Sasha and Malia returned to Washington, DC.

The White House announced that the President will travel to Minneapolis, MN, on August 30.

The President declared an emergency in New York and ordered Federal aid to supplement State and local recovery efforts in the area struck by Hurricane Irene beginning on August 25 and continuing.

August 27

In the morning, in the Oval Office, the President had a conference call with Secretary of Homeland Security Janet A. Napolitano, Federal Emergency Management Agency Administrator W. Craig Fugate, and other senior members of his emergency management team to discuss the Federal Government's preparations for Hurricane Irene. Later, also in the Oval Office, he had a telephone conversation with Chancellor Angela Merkel of Germany to discuss economic stabilization efforts in Europe and the Middle East peace process.

During the day, the President visited the Federal Emergency Management Agency's National Response Coordination Center, where he participated in a video teleconference with Governors and emergency managers in areas impacted by Hurricane Irene.

In the evening, the President and Vice President Joe Biden had a conference call with Secretary of Homeland Security Janet A. Napolitano, Secretary of Energy Steven Chu, Federal Emergency Management Agency Administrator W. Craig Fugate, and Homeland Security and Counterterrorism Adviser John O. Brennan to discuss the Federal Government's preparations for Hurricane Irene.

The President declared an emergency in Virginia and ordered Federal aid to supplement Commonwealth and local response efforts in the area struck by Hurricane Irene beginning on August 26 and continuing.

The President declared an emergency in Massachusetts and ordered Federal aid to supplement Commonwealth and local response

efforts in the area struck by Hurricane Irene beginning on August 26 and continuing.

The President declared an emergency in Connecticut and ordered Federal aid to supplement State and local response efforts in the area struck by Hurricane Irene beginning on August 26 and continuing.

The President declared an emergency in New Jersey and ordered Federal aid to supplement State and local response efforts in the area struck by Hurricane Irene beginning on August 26 and continuing.

The President declared an emergency in New Hampshire and ordered Federal aid to supplement State and local response efforts in the area struck by Hurricane Irene beginning on August 26 and continuing.

The President declared an emergency in Rhode Island and ordered Federal aid to supplement State and local response efforts in the area struck by Hurricane Irene beginning on August 26 and continuing.

The President declared an emergency in Maryland and ordered Federal aid to supplement State and local response efforts in the area struck by Hurricane Irene beginning on August 26 and continuing.

The President declared a major disaster in Puerto Rico and ordered Federal aid to supplement Commonwealth and local recovery efforts in the area struck by Hurricane Irene beginning on August 21 and continuing.

August 28

In the morning, in the Situation Room, the President and Vice President Joe Biden had a video teleconference with White House Chief of Staff William M. Daley, Secretary of Homeland Security Janet A. Napolitano, Secretary of the Treasury Timothy F. Geithner, Secretary of Transportation Raymond H. LaHood, Secretary of Energy Steven Chu, Federal Emergency Management Agency Administrator W. Craig Fugate, and Homeland Security and Counterterrorism Adviser John O. Brennan to discuss ongoing response and recovery efforts in the areas struck by Hurricane Irene.

The President declared an emergency in Delaware and ordered Federal aid to supplement State and local response efforts in the area struck by Hurricane Irene beginning on August 26 and continuing.

The President declared an emergency in the District of Columbia and ordered Federal aid to supplement District and local response efforts in the area struck by Hurricane Irene beginning on August 26 and continuing.

August 29

In the morning, in the Oval Office, the President had an intelligence briefing. Then, also in the Oval Office, he participated in separate telephone interviews for the radio shows of Tom Joyner and Matt McGill.

In the afternoon, in the Oval Office, the President met with his senior advisers. Later, in the Private Dining Room, he and Vice President Joe Biden had lunch.

The President announced his intention to nominate Alan B. Krueger to be Chairman of the Council of Economic Advisers.

The President declared an emergency in Vermont and ordered Federal aid to supplement State and local response efforts in the area struck by Hurricane Irene beginning on August 26 and continuing.

The President declared an emergency in Pennsylvania and ordered Federal aid to supplement Commonwealth and local response efforts in the area struck by Hurricane Irene beginning on August 26 and continuing.

August 30

In the morning, the President traveled to Minneapolis, MN.

In the afternoon, the President returned to Washington, DC.

The President announced his intention to appoint Nina M. Archabal and Barbara Bluhm-Kaul as members of the Cultural Property Advisory Committee.

The President announced his intention to appoint Regina Blye as a member of the Architectural and Transportation Barriers Compliance Board.

The President announced his intention to appoint Cindy Campbell as a member of the American Battle Monuments Commission.

The President declared a major disaster in Iowa and ordered Federal aid to supplement State and local recovery efforts in the area struck by severe storms and flooding from July 27 through 29.

August 31

In the morning, in the Oval Office, the President had an intelligence briefing followed by a meeting with his senior advisers.

In the afternoon, in the Roosevelt Room, the President and Vice President Joe Biden had a meeting with Secretary of the Treasury Timothy F. Geithner, White House Chief of Staff William M. Daley, White House Senior Adviser David Plouffe, and other senior advisers.

During the day, the President called Gen. David H. Petraeus, USA, commander, NATO International Security Assistance Force, Afghanistan, to congratulate him on his retirement from the U.S. military, thank him for his contributions to U.S. national security in Iraq and Afghanistan, and discuss his new role as Director of the Central Intelligence Agency.

The White House announced that the President will travel to Paterson, NJ, on September 4.

The President declared an emergency in North Carolina and ordered Federal aid to supplement State and local response efforts in the area struck by Hurricane Irene beginning on August 25 and continuing.

The President declared an emergency in New York and ordered Federal aid to supplement State and local response efforts in the area struck by Hurricane Irene beginning on August 26 and continuing.

The President declared an emergency in New Jersey and ordered Federal aid to supplement State and local response efforts in the area struck by Hurricane Irene beginning on August 27 and continuing.

September 1

In the morning, in the Oval Office, the President called Prime Minister-elect Yoshihiko Noda of Japan to congratulate him on his election, discuss global economic stabilization efforts, and reaffirm Japan-U.S. relations. Then, also in the Oval Office, he and Vice President Joe Biden had an intelligence briefing.

In the afternoon, in the Oval Office, the President met with Secretary of the Treasury Timothy F. Geithner. Later, also in the Oval Office, he met with his senior advisers.

During the day, in the Oval Office, the President met with White House Chief of Staff William M. Daley, White House Senior Adviser David A. Plouffe, and National Economic Council Director Eugene B. Sperling.

The White House announced that the President will travel to Detroit, MI, on September 5.

The White House announced that the President will travel to New York City from September 19 through 21.

The White House announced that the President will welcome 2010 NASCAR Sprint Cup Series champion Jimmie Johnson and other NASCAR drivers to the White House on September 7.

The President declared a major disaster in Vermont and ordered Federal aid to supplement State and local recovery efforts in the area struck by Tropical Storm Irene beginning on August 29 and continuing.

September 2

In the afternoon, the President traveled to Camp David, MD.

The President declared a major disaster in Connecticut and ordered Federal aid to supplement State and local recovery efforts in the area struck by Tropical Storm Irene beginning on August 27 and continuing.

The White House released further details on the President's visit to Paterson, NJ, on September 4.

September 3

The President declared a major disaster in New Hampshire and ordered Federal aid to supplement State and local recovery efforts in the area struck by Tropical Storm Irene on August 26 and continuing.

The President declared a major disaster in Virginia and ordered Federal aid to supplement Commonwealth and local recovery efforts in the area struck by Hurricane Irene from August 26 through 28.

The President declared a major disaster in Pennsylvania and ordered Federal aid to supplement Commonwealth and local recovery efforts in the area struck by Hurricane Irene from August 26 through 30.

The President declared a major disaster in Rhode Island and ordered Federal aid to supplement State and local recovery efforts in the area struck by Tropical Storm Irene from August 27 through 29.

The President declared a major disaster in Massachusetts and ordered Federal aid to supplement Commonwealth and local recovery efforts in the area struck by Tropical Storm Irene from August 27 through 29.

September 4

In the morning, the President traveled to Newark, NJ, arriving in the afternoon.

In the afternoon, the President toured areas affected by affected by Hurricane Irene, accompanied by Administrator W. Craig Fugate and Federal Coordinating Officer William L. Vogel of the Federal Emergency Management Agency; Environmental Protection Agency Administrator Lisa P. Jackson; American Red Cross Chief Executive Officer and President Gail J. McGovern; Gov. Christopher J. Christie of New Jersey; Sens. Frank R. Lautenberg and Robert Menendez; Reps. William J. Pascrell, Jr., and Steven R. Rothman; Mayor Jeffery Jones of Patterson, NJ; and Mayor Christopher Vergano of Wayne, NJ.

Later in the afternoon, the President returned to Camp David, MD.

September 5

In the morning, the President traveled to Detroit, MI, arriving in the afternoon.

In the afternoon, the President returned to Washington, DC.

September 6

In the morning, in the Oval Office, the President and Vice President Joe Biden had an intelligence briefing. Then, he met with his senior advisers.

In the afternoon, in the Private Dining Room, the President and Vice President Biden had lunch. Later, in the Situation Room, he met with Homeland Security and Counterterrorism Adviser John O. Brennan, Secretary of Homeland Security Janet A. Napolitano, and members of his homeland security team to discuss security measures in advance of the upcoming 10th anniversary of the September 11, 2011, terrorist attacks.

The President announced his intention to nominate Catherine Allgor and Drew R. McCoy to be members of the Board of Trustees of the James Madison Memorial Fellowship Foundation.

The President announced his intention to nominate Eduardo Arriola and J. Kelly Ryan to be members of the Board of Directors of the Inter-American Foundation.

The President announced his intention to nominate Sara M. Aviel to be U.S. Alternate Executive Director of the International Bank for Reconstruction and Development.

The President announced his intention to nominate Daniel J. Becker and James R. Hannah to be members of the Board of Directors of the State Justice Institute.

The President announced his intention to nominate Dana K. Bilyeu and David A. Jones to be members of the Federal Retirement Thrift Investment Board.

The President announced his intention to nominate Steven H. Cohen to be a member of the Board of Trustees of the Harry S. Truman Scholarship Foundation.

The President announced his intention to nominate Albert DiClemente to be Director of the Amtrak Board of Directors.

The President announced his intention to nominate Michael A. Khouri to be a Commissioner of the Federal Maritime Commission.

The President announced his intention to nominate David J. McMillan and Wenona Singel to be members of the Advisory Board of the Saint Lawrence Seaway Development Corporation.

The President announced his intention to nominate Adam E. Namm to be Ambassador to Ecuador.

The President announced his intention to nominate Mary B. Verner to be a member of the Board of Directors of the National Institute of Building Sciences.

The President announced his intention to appoint the following individuals as members of the Advisory Committee on the Arts for the John F. Kennedy Center for the Performing Arts:

Jean Bailey;
Susan M. DiMarco Johnson;
Sonya M. Halpern;
Mattie McFadden-Lawson;
Melissa Moss;
Deborah Dozier Potter;
Kristin Gatchel Replogle;
Jennifer Scully-Lerner;
Ellen Schapps Richman;
Mary Rouse-Terlevich; and
Ellen Susman.

The President announced his intention to appoint Mona K. Sutphen and Philip D. Zelikow as members of the President's Intelligence Advisory Board.

The President announced his intention to appoint Harry J. Wilson as a member of the Advisory Committee to the Pension Benefit Guaranty Corporation.

September 7

In the morning, in the Oval Office, the President and Vice President Joe Biden had an intelligence briefing.

In the afternoon, in the Oval Office, the President and Vice President Biden had separate meetings with Secretary of State Hillary Rodham Clinton and Secretary of Defense Leon E. Panetta.

During the day, the President had a telephone conversation with Gov. J. Richard Perry of Texas to express his condolences for the loss of life resulting from wildfires and to discuss Federal assistance for recovery efforts and combating ongoing fires.

The White House announced that the President will travel to Richmond, VA, on September 9.

The White House announced that the President will travel to Shanksville, PA, on September 11.

The White House announced that the President will award the Medal of Honor to Sgt. Dakota L. Meyer, USMC, on September 15.

The President announced his intention to nominate Cyrus Amir-Mokri to be Assistant Secretary for Financial Institutions at the Department of the Treasury.

The President announced his intention to nominate Cyrus Amir-Mokri to be a member of the Board of Directors of the National Consumer Cooperative Bank.

The President announced his intention to nominate Kathryn Keneally to be Assistant Attorney General of the Tax Division at the Department of Justice.

The President announced his intention to nominate Michael J. Warren to be a member of the Overseas Private Investment Corporation.

September 8

In the morning, in the Oval Office, the President and Vice President Joe Biden had an intelligence briefing.

The White House announced that the President and Mrs. Obama will travel to New York City on September 11.

The White House announced that the President will travel to Columbus, OH, on September 13.

The President announced that he has nominated Stephanie D. Thacker to be a judge on the U.S. Court of Appeals for the Fourth Circuit.

The President announced that he has nominated Gregg J. Costa to be a judge on the U.S. District Court for the Southern District of Texas.

The President declared an emergency in New York and ordered Federal aid to supplement State and local recovery efforts in the areas struck by Tropical Storm Lee on September 7 and continuing.

The President declared an emergency in Pennsylvania and ordered Federal aid to supplement Commonwealth and local recovery efforts in the areas struck by Tropical Storm Lee on September 3 and continuing.

September 9

In the morning, in the Oval Office, the President met with Homeland Security and Counterterrorism Adviser John O. Brennan, Secretary of Homeland Security Janet A. Napolitano, and members of his homeland security team to discuss security measures in advance of the upcoming 10th anniversary of the September 11, 2011, terrorist attacks. Then, he traveled to Richmond, VA.

In the afternoon, the President returned to Washington, DC. Later, in the Oval Office, he participated in a credentialing ceremony for newly appointed Ambassadors to the U.S.

During the day, the President had a telephone conversation with Prime Minister Benjamin Netanyahu of Israel to discuss the situation at the Israeli Embassy in Cairo, Egypt.

The White House announced that the President will travel to Raleigh-Durham, NC, on September 14.

The President announced his intention to appoint Glenn S. Gerstell as a member of the National Infrastructure Advisory Council.

The President announced his intention to appoint Charles "Chip" Lyons as U.S. Alternate Representative on the Executive Board of the United Nations Children's Fund.

The President declared a major disaster in Texas and ordered Federal aid to supplement State and local recovery efforts in the area struck by wildfires on August 30 and continuing.

September 10

In the morning, in the Oval Office, the President met with his national security team to review ongoing counterterrorism efforts. Later, he and Mrs. Obama traveled to Arlington, VA, where, at Arlington National Cemetery, they paid their respects to U.S. servicemembers killed in Iraq and Afghanistan.

In the afternoon, the President and Mrs. Obama returned to Washington, DC. Then, they and their daughters Sasha and Malia visited the DC Central Kitchen, where they participated in a service project to commemorate the

September 11 National Day of Service and Remembrance.

September 11

In the morning, the President and Mrs. Obama traveled to New York City, where, at the National September 11 Memorial, they met with former President George W. Bush, Mrs. Bush, families of victims of the September 11, 2001, terrorist attacks, and local elected officials; toured the site; and participated in a ceremony to commemorate the 10th anniversary of the September 11, 2001, terrorist attacks. Later, he and Mrs. Obama traveled to Shanksville, PA.

In the afternoon, the President and Mrs. Obama visited the site of the September 11, 2001, crash of United Airlines Flight 93, participated in a wreath-laying ceremony for victims of the crash, and met with victims' families. Then, they traveled to Arlington, VA, where, at the Pentagon, they attended a wreath-laying ceremony to commemorate the September 11, 2001, terrorist attacks. Later, they returned to Washington, DC.

September 12

In the morning, in the Oval Office, the President and Vice President Joe Biden had an intelligence briefing.

In the afternoon, in the South Court Auditorium of the Dwight D. Eisenhower Executive Office Building, the President dropped by a question-and-answer session between senior administration officials and journalists.

The White House announced that the President will travel to Raleigh-Durham, NC, on September 14.

The White House announced that the President will travel to Australia from November 16 through 17.

September 13

In the morning, in the Oval Office, the President and Vice President Joe Biden had an intelligence briefing. Then, he met with his senior advisers. Later, in the Roosevelt Room, he dropped by a meeting between Vice President Biden and President Traian Basescu of Romania. Then, in the Oval Office, he and

Vice President Biden met with Secretary of State Hillary Rodham Clinton.

In the afternoon, the President traveled to Columbus, OH, where he toured a newly modernized graphic design classroom at the Fort Hayes Metropolitan Education Center. Later, he returned to Washington, DC. Then, in the Oval Office, he and Vice President Biden met with Secretary of Defense Leon E. Pannetta.

The White House announced that the President will welcome President Lee Myung-bak of South Korea to the White House on October 13.

The President announced his intention to appoint Manuel Gomez and Sara Lundquist as members of the President's Advisory Commission on Educational Excellence for Hispanics.

The President announced his intention to appoint Katrina L. Peebles as a member of the President's Advisory Committee on the Arts for the John F. Kennedy Center for the Performing Arts.

The President declared a major disaster in Maine and ordered Federal aid to supplement State and local recovery efforts in the area struck by Tropical Storm Irene from August 27 through 29.

The President declared a major disaster in Pennsylvania and ordered Federal aid to supplement Commonwealth and local recovery efforts in the area struck by Tropical Storm Lee beginning on September 3 and continuing.

The President declared a major disaster in New York and ordered Federal aid to supplement State and local recovery efforts in the area affected by the remnants of Tropical Storm Lee beginning on September 7 and continuing.

September 14

In the morning, in the Oval Office, the President and Vice President Joe Biden had an intelligence briefing. Later, he traveled to Apex, NC, where he toured the WestStar Precision manufacturing facility.

In the afternoon the President traveled to Raleigh, NC. Later, he returned to Washington, DC. Then, in the Oval Office, he met with Vice President Biden. Later, on the patio outside the Oval Office, he had a beer with Medal of Honor recipient Sgt. Dakota L. Meyer, USMC.

The White House announced that the President will travel to Alexandria, VA, on September 16.

The President announced his intention to nominate Brad Carson to be General Counsel of the Department of the Army.

The President announced his intention to nominate Alastair M. Fitzpayne to be Assistant Secretary for Legislative Affairs at the Department of the Treasury.

The President announced his intention to nominate Michael A. McFaul to be Ambassador to Russia.

The President announced his intention to nominate Kevin A. Ohlson to be a judge on the U.S. Court of Appeals for the Armed Forces.

The President announced his intention to nominate Ronald Buch to be a judge on the U.S. Tax Court.

The President announced his intention to appoint H. Fisk Johnson as a member of the Advisory Committee for Trade Policy and Negotiations.

The President announced his intention to appoint Thomas L. McKiernan as a member of the Board of Visitors to the U.S. Air Force Academy.

The President announced that he has nominated David C. Guaderrama to be a judge on the U.S. District Court for the Western District of Texas.

September 15

In the morning, in the Oval Office, the President met with Secretary of the Treasury Timothy F. Geithner.

The White House announced that the President will travel to New York City from September 19 through 21.

The White House announced that the President will travel to Cincinnati, OH, on September 22.

The President declared a major disaster in New Jersey and ordered Federal aid to supplement State and local recovery efforts in the area struck by severe storms and flooding from August 13 through 15.

September 16

In the morning, in the Oval Office, the President had an intelligence briefing. Later, he traveled to Alexandria, VA, where he visited a classroom and viewed student science and technology projects at Thomas Jefferson High School for Science and Technology.

In the afternoon, the President returned to Washington, DC.

The White House announced that the President will visit Benjamin Banneker Academic High School in Washington, DC, on September 28.

The President announced his intention to nominate Ann Marie Buerkle and Russ Carnahan to be U.S. Representatives to the 66th Session of the United Nations General Assembly.

The President announced his intention to appoint Teresita Fernandez as a member of the Commission of Fine Arts.

The President announced his intention to appoint John M. Spratt, Jr., as Chairman of the U.S. section of the Permanent Joint Board on Defense, U.S. and Canada.

The President declared a major disaster in Maryland and ordered Federal aid to supplement State and local recovery efforts in the area struck by Hurricane Irene from August 24 through September 5.

September 19

In the morning, in the Oval Office, the President had an intelligence briefing. Later, also in the Oval Office, he had a telephone conversation with Chancellor Angela Merkel of Germany to discuss the global economy and Middle East peace efforts.

In the afternoon, the President and Mrs. Obama traveled to New York City. Later, at the Ronald H. Brown U.S. Mission to the United Nations Building, he met with U.S. Mission staff and their families.

The White House announced that the President will deliver remarks on education at the White House on September 23.

September 20

In the morning, at U.N. Headquarters, the President met with Chairman Mustafa Mohammed Abdul Jalil of the Transitional National Council of Libya.

In the afternoon, at the Waldorf-Astoria Hotel, the President met with President Dilma Rousseff of Brazil. Later, also at the Waldorf-Astoria Hotel, he participated in a photographic opportunity with leaders attending an Open Government Partnership event.

The White House announced that the President will travel to Cincinnati, OH, on September 22.

The White House announced that the President will travel to Mountain View, CA, on September 26.

The President announced his intention to appoint Kimberly A. Owens and Sima F. Sarrafan as members of the Christopher Columbus Fellowship Foundation.

The President announced his intention to appoint Jan R. Frye and Carol E. Lowman as members of the Committee for Purchase From People Who Are Blind or Severely Disabled.

September 21

In the morning, the President and Mrs. Obama traveled to the U.N. Headquarters.

In the afternoon, at U.N. Headquarters, the President met with U.N. General Assembly President Nassir Abdulaziz Al-Nasser. Then, he met with U.N. Secretary-General Ban Ki-moon. Later, he traveled to the Sheraton New York Hotel and Towers.

Later in the afternoon, the President traveled to the Waldorf-Astoria Hotel, where he met separately with President Salva Kiir Mayardit of South Sudan and President Mahmoud Abbas of the Palestinian Authority.

In the evening, at the New York Public Library, the President and Mrs. Obama attended a reception for the U.N. General Assembly. Later, they returned to Washington, DC.

The White House announced further details on the President's remarks on education at the White House on September 23.

The White House announced further details on the President's visit to Mountain View, CA, on September 25.

The President announced his intention to appoint Laurie R. Garduque as a member of the Coordinating Council on Juvenile Justice and Delinquency Prevention.

The President announced his intention to appoint Tyler Jacks as a member of the National Cancer Advisory Board.

The President announced his intention to appoint Karen J. McCulloh and Lisa M. Wilusz as members of the Committee for Purchase From People Who Are Blind or Severely Disabled.

The President announced his intention to appoint Joan E. Silber as a member of the Commission for the Preservation of America's Heritage Abroad.

September 22

In the morning, in the Oval Office, the President and Vice President Joe Biden had an intelligence briefing. Then, also in the Oval Office, he met with his senior advisers.

In the afternoon, the President traveled to Cincinnati, OH. Later, he returned to Washington, DC.

The White House announced further details on the President's visit to Seattle, WA, on September 25.

The White House announced further details on the President's visit to San Diego and Los Angeles, CA, on September 26.

The President announced that he has nominated Jacqueline H. Nguyen to be a judge on the U.S. Court of Appeals for the Ninth Circuit.

The President announced that he has nominated Michael A. Hughes to be a U.S. marshal for the Superior Court for the District of Columbia.

The President announced that he has nominated Brian C. Wimes to be a judge on the U.S. District Court for the Eastern and Western Districts of Missouri.

September 23

In the morning, in the Oval Office, the President had an intelligence briefing. Later, in the Cabinet Room, he met with members of the Congressional Asian Pacific American Caucus.

In the afternoon, the President had a telephone conversation with Sultan Qaboos bin Said Al Said of Oman to thank him for his role in the release of Shane Bauer and Joshua Fattal, U.S. citizens detained by the Iranian Government.

The White House announced that the President will welcome President Porfirio Lobo Sosa of Honduras to the White House on October 5.

The White House announced further details on the President's visit to Denver, CO, on September 27.

The White House announced further details on the President's visit to Benjamin Banneker Academic High School on September 28.

The President announced his intention to nominate Gary Blumenthal to be a member of the National Council on Disability.

The President announced his intention to nominate Maurice A. Jones to be Deputy Secretary at the Department of Housing and Urban Development.

The President announced his intention to nominate Susan A. Maxman to be a member of the Board of Directors of the National Institute of Building Sciences.

The President announced his intention to nominate Matthew S. Rutherford to be Assistant Secretary for Financial Markets at the Department of the Treasury.

The President announced his intention to appoint Rachel F. Moran as a member of the Permanent Committee for the Oliver Wendell Holmes Devise.

The President declared a major disaster in Kansas and ordered Federal aid to supplement State and local recovery efforts in the area affected by flooding from June 1 through August 1.

September 24

In the afternoon, the President traveled to Joint Base Andrews, MD, where he played a round of golf with former President William J. Clinton, White House Chief of Staff William M. Daley, and Douglas J. Band, counselor to former President Clinton.

In the evening, the President returned to Washington, DC.

September 25

In the morning, the President traveled to Medina, WA, arriving in the afternoon.

In the afternoon, the President traveled to Seattle, WA. Later, he traveled to Woodside, CA. Then, he traveled to Atherton, CA.

In the evening, the President traveled to the Fairmont San Jose hotel in San Jose, CA.

September 26

In the morning, the President traveled to Mountain View, CA.

In the afternoon, the President traveled to La Jolla, CA. Later, he traveled to West Hollywood, CA.

In the evening, the President traveled to the Beverly Wilshire hotel in Beverly Hills, CA.

September 27

In the morning, the President traveled to Denver, CO, arriving in the afternoon.

In the afternoon, the President returned to Washington, DC, arriving in the evening.

The White House announced that the President will welcome Prime Minister Beji Caid Essebsi of Tunisia to the White House on October 7.

The President announced his intention to nominate Earl W. Gast to be Assistant Administrator for Africa at the U.S. Agency for International Development.

The President announced his intention to nominate Roberta S. Jacobson to be Assistant Secretary for Western Hemisphere Affairs at the Department of State.

The President announced his intention to nominate Glen F. Post III to be a member of the President's National Security Telecommunications Advisory Committee.

The President announced his intention to nominate Michael T. Scuse to be Under Secretary for Farm and Foreign Agricultural Services at the Department of Agriculture.

September 28

In the morning, the President had a telephone conversation with President Islom Karimov of Uzbekistan to congratulate him on the 20th anniversary of Uzbekistan's independence and to discuss Uzbekistan-U.S. relations and the situation in Afghanistan.

In the afternoon, in the Private Dining Room, the President and Vice President Joe Biden had lunch. Later, in the Oval Office, they met with Secretary of Defense Leon E. Panetta.

The President declared a major disaster in the District of Columbia and ordered Federal aid to supplement District and local recovery efforts in the area struck by Hurricane Irene from August 26 through September 1.

September 29

In the morning, in the Oval Office, the President had an intelligence briefing followed by a meeting with his senior advisers. Then, also in the Oval Office, he met with Secretary of the Treasury Timothy F. Geithner. Later, in the Diplomatic Room, the President participated in separate television interviews with Vicki Yates of WTVF in Nashville, TN, Cameron Kent of WXII in Greensboro-Winston-Salem, NC, and Jim Payne of WESH in Orlando, FL, to discuss the "American Jobs Act."

In the afternoon, in the Oval Office, the President met with Secretary of State Hillary Rodham Clinton. Later, in the Situation Room, he met with the National Security Council.

The White House announced that the President will travel to St. Louis, MO, on October 4.

The White House announced that the President will travel to Mesquite, TX, on October 4.

September 30

In the morning, the President was briefed by Homeland Security and Counterterrorism Adviser John O. Brennan on the Central Intelligence Agency counterterrorism operation in Yemen that resulted in the death of Al Qaida in the Arabian Peninsula senior member Anwar al-Awlaki. Later, in the Oval Office, he and Vice President Joe Biden had an intelligence briefing. Then, they traveled to Joint Base Myer-Henderson Hall, VA.

In the afternoon, the President and Vice President Biden returned to Washington, DC. Later, in the Oval Office, he participated in an interview with radio host Michael Smerconish.

The White House announced that the President will welcome Prime Minister Jens Stoltenberg of Norway to the White House on October 20.

The White House announced that the President will welcome the Super Bowl XX champion Chicago Bears to the White House on August 12 to celebrate the 25th anniversary of their Super Bowl victory.

The White House released further details on the President's visit to Mesquite, TX, on October 4.

The President declared a major disaster in Delaware and ordered Federal aid to supplement State and local recovery efforts in the area struck by Hurricane Irene from August 25 through 31.

October 1

The White House announced that the President will welcome the 2011 NCAA champion Texas A&M University women's basketball team to the White House on October 6.

October 3

In the morning, in the Oval Office, the President had an intelligence briefing followed by a meeting with senior advisers.

In the afternoon, in the Blue Room, the President participated in an interview with George Stephanopoulos of ABC News. Later, in the Oval Office, he met with Shree Bose, Lauren Hodge, and Naomi Shah, winners of the 2011 Google Science Fair. Then, also in the Oval Office, he met with U.S. Ambassador to the Netherlands Fay Hartog Levin.

October 4

In the morning, the President traveled to Dallas, TX.

In the afternoon, the President traveled to Mesquite, TX, where he visited Eastfield College, toured the campus's Children's Laboratory School, and met with students and teachers. Later, he traveled to St. Louis, MO.

In the evening, the President returned to Washington, DC.

The President announced his intention to nominate Adam Gamoran and Judith D. Singer to be members of the Board of Directors of the National Board for Education Sciences.

The President announced his intention to nominate James Timberlake to be a member of the Board of Directors of the National Institute of Building Sciences.

October 5

In the morning, in the Oval Office, the President signed H.R. 2608, the Continuing Appropriations Act, 2012. Later, also in the Oval Office, he and Vice President Joe Biden had an intelligence briefing.

In the afternoon, in the Oval Office, the President met with his senior advisers. Then, in the Private Dining Room, he and Vice President Biden had lunch. Later, in the Oval Office, he met with the 2011 Boys & Girls Clubs of America Youth of the Year winner and regional finalists.

The White House announced that the President will deliver remarks at the White House American Latino Heritage Forum on October 12.

The President announced his intention to appoint the following individuals to be members of the President's Advisory Commission on Educational Excellence for Hispanics:

Shakira Isabel Mebarak Ripoll;
Nancy Navarro;
Adrian A. Pedroza; and
Kent P. Scribner.

The President announced that he has nominated Patty Shwartz to be a judge on the U.S. Court of Appeals for the Third Circuit.

The President declared a major disaster in Maryland and ordered Federal aid to supplement State and local recovery efforts in the area affected by the remnants of Tropical Storm Lee from September 6 through 9.

October 6

In the morning, in the Oval Office, the President had an intelligence briefing.

In the afternoon, in the Oval Office, the President and Vice President Joe Biden met with Secretary of State Hillary Rodham Clinton.

The White House announced that the President will travel to Pittsburgh, PA, on October 11.

The White House announced that the President will travel to Orlando, FL, on October 11.

The President announced his intention to appoint the following individuals as members of Presidential Emergency Board No. 243:

Ira F. Jaffe;
Roberta Golick;
Joshua M. Javits;
Gil Vernon; and
Arnold M. Zack.

October 7

In the morning, in the Oval Office, the President had an intelligence briefing. Then, he and Vice President Joe Biden met with Senate Majority Leader Harry M. Reid and Sens. Richard J. Durbin and Charles E. Schumer to discuss job growth legislation.

Later in the morning, in the Oval Office, the President met with Secretary of the Treasury Timothy F. Geithner.

In the afternoon, in the Oval Office, the President met with his senior advisers.

The White House announced that the President will welcome Prime Minister Petr Necas of the Czech Republic to the White House on October 27.

The President announced his intention to nominate Elizabeth M. Cousens to be U.S. Representative to the U.N. Economic and Social Council.

The President announced his intention to nominate Paul W. Hodes to be a member of the National Council on the Arts.

The President announced his intention to nominate Robert L. Sumwalt III to be a member of the National Transportation Safety Board.

The President announced his intention to appoint May Y. Chen, Tung Thanh Nguyen, and Apolo Anton Ohno as members of the President's Advisory Commission on Asian Americans and Pacific Islanders.

The President announced his intention to appoint Marta Araoz de la Torre and Jane A.

Levine as members of the Cultural Property Advisory Committee.

The President announced his intention to appoint Janet R. Kahn as a member of the Advisory Group on Prevention, Health Promotion, and Integrative and Public Health.

October 8

In the afternoon, the President and Mrs. Obama traveled to Camp David, MD.

October 9

In the afternoon, the President and Mrs. Obama returned to Washington, DC.

October 10

In the morning, the President had separate telephone conversations with Prime Minister David Cameron of the United Kingdom and President Nicolas Sarkozy of France to discuss the economic situation in Europe. He also congratulated Prime Minister Cameron on the occasion of his 45th birthday and spoke with President Sarkozy about the Middle East peace process.

In the afternoon, the President traveled to Bethesda, MD, where, at the Walter Reed National Military Medical Center, he met with wounded U.S. military personnel and their families and presented Purple Hearts to four servicemembers. Later, he returned to Washington, DC.

The White House announced that the President will travel with President Lee Myung-bak of South Korea to Lake Orion, MI, on October 14.

October 11

In the morning, in the Situation Room, the President met with members of his national security team to thank them for their work in disrupting an alleged Iranian-backed plot to assassinate Saudi Arabia's Ambassador to the U.S. Then, he traveled to Pittsburgh, PA, where he toured the International Brotherhood of Electrical Workers Local No. 5 Apprenticeship Training Center.

In the afternoon, the President traveled to Orlando, FL.

During the day, the President had a telephone conversation with Saudi Arabia's Ambassdor to the U.S. Adil al-Ahmad al-Jubayr to discuss the disruption of an alleged Iranian-backed plot to assassinate him and express U.S. solidarity with Saudi Arabia.

In the evening, at the Harp and Celt Restaurant and Irish Pub, the President met with Mayor John H. "Buddy" Dyer, Jr., of Orlando, FL, and unemployed construction workers Michael Whidden of Gotha, FL, Patricia Mooney-Hildebrand of Titusville, FL, Mark Mckim of Sanford, FL, and Jesse Morgan of Auburndale, FL, to discuss job creation and the economy. Later, he returned to Washington, DC.

October 12

In the afternoon, in the Roosevelt Room, the President met with the National Association of Evangelicals Executive Committee. Then, in the Oval Office, he presented the Defense Superior Service Medal to Military Aide to the President Lt. Col. Barrett Bernard, USA, during a departure ceremony. Later, also in the Oval Office, he met with Secretary of Defense Leon E. Panetta.

Later in the afternoon, in the Oval Office, the President had a telephone conversation with King Abdallah bin Abd al-Aziz Al Saud of Saudi Arabia to discuss the disruption of an alleged Iranian-backed plot to assassinate Saudi Arabia's Ambassador to the U.S.

In the evening, the President and President Lee Myung-bak of South Korea traveled to Tysons Corner, VA, where, at the Woo Lae Oak Korean restaurant, they had dinner. Later, they returned to Washington, DC.

The White House announced that the President will travel to North Carolina and Virginia on a 3-day bus tour from October 17 through 19.

The President announced the designation of the following individuals as members of a Presidential delegation to attend the opening ceremony of the XVI Pan American Games in Guadalajara, Mexico, on October 14: Earl A. Wayne (head of delegation); Julie S. Ertel; and Allyson M. Felix.

October 13

In the morning, in the Oval Office, the President and Vice President Joe Biden had a bilateral meeting with President Lee Myung-bak of South Korea. Later, in the Cabinet Room, they had an expanded bilateral meeting with U.S. and South Korean officials.

In the afternoon the President had a telephone conversation with boxer Dewey Rader Bozella to wish him luck on his upcoming match.

During the day, the President had a telephone conversation with Speaker of the House of Representatives John A. Boehner to thank him for his assistance in winning congressional approval for trade agreements with Colombia, Panama, and South Korea and the renewal of the Trade Adjustment Assistance program.

In the evening, on the North Portico, the President and Mrs. Obama greeted President Lee and his wife Kim Yoon-ok upon their arrival for a state dinner and reception. Then, on the Grand Staircase, they participated in a photo opportunity.

The White House released further details on the President's 3-day bus tour through North Carolina and Virginia from October 17 through 19.

The President announced his intention to nominate Grande Lum to be Director of the Community Relations Service at the Department of Justice.

The President announced his intention to nominate Kamilah Oni Martin-Proctor to be a member of the National Council on Disability.

The President announced his intention to nominate Sharon Villarosa to be Ambassador to Mauritius and Seychelles.

October 14

In the morning, the President and President Lee Myung-bak of South Korea traveled to Lake Orion, MI, arriving in the afternoon.

In the afternoon, the President and President Lee toured the facilities of the General Motors Orion Assembly Plant. Later, President Obama returned to Washington, DC.

Also in the afternoon, the President had a telephone conversation with Chancellor Angela Merkel of Germany to discuss the economic situation in Europe and preparations for the upcoming G–20 summit in Cannes, France.

The White House released further details on the President's 3-day bus tour through North Carolina and Virginia from October 17 through 19.

The President declared a major disaster in New Jersey and ordered Federal aid to supplement State and local recovery efforts in the area struck by the remnants of Tropical Storm Lee from September 6 through 11.

October 16

In the afternoon, in the Blue Room, the President and Mrs. Obama hosted a reception with members of the civil rights community in honor of Martin Luther King, Jr., and his family.

The White House released further details on the President's 3-day bus tour through North Carolina and Virginia from October 17 through 19.

October 17

In the morning, the President traveled to Fletcher, NC, where he began a 3-day bus tour.

In the afternoon, the President traveled to Millers Creek, NC. While en route, he stopped in Marion, NC, where, at the Countryside Barbecue restaurant, he had lunch and visited with patrons. Then, in Boone, NC, he stopped at the Mast General Store and Our Daily Bread bakery, where he also visited with patrons.

Later in the afternoon, at West Wilkes High School, the President participated in separate telephone interviews for the radio shows of Jodi Berry of WFXC/WFXK in Durham, NC, and Larry "No Limit Larry" Mims of WPEG in Charlotte, NC, both of which were taped for later broadcast. Later, he participated in a television interview with Dave Wagner of WCNC in Charlotte, NC, which was also taped for later broadcast.

In the evening the President traveled to Greensboro, NC.

The President announced his intention to nominate Gina Abercrombie-Winstanley to be Ambassador to Malta.

The President announced his intention to nominate Julissa Reynoso to be Ambassador to Uruguay.

The President announced his intention to nominate Wendy Spencer to be Chief Executive Officer of the Corporation for National and Community Service.

The President announced his intention to nominate Robert E. Whitehead to be Ambassador to Togo.

The President announced his intention to appoint Robert L. Blazs as U.S. Commissioner of the Canadian River Commission.

The President announced his intention to appoint Jayne D. Greenberg as a member of the President's Council on Fitness, Sports, and Nutrition.

The President announced that he has nominated Paul J. Watford to be a judge on the U.S. Court of Appeals for the Ninth Circuit.

October 18

In the morning, the President traveled to Jamestown, NC. Later, in the Children's Center at Guilford Technical Community College, he participated in an interview with Jake Tapper for ABC's "Nightline" program.

In the afternoon, the President traveled to Skipwith, VA. While en route, he stopped at Reid's House Restaurant in Reidsville, NC, where he had lunch and visited with patrons. Upon arrival in Skipwith, VA, he toured a computer lab and viewed a robotics demonstration at Bluestone High School.

Later in the afternoon, the President traveled to Emporia, VA. While en route, he stopped at Patricia's Child Care Center, in Brodnax, VA, where he greeted children and visited with staff, and at Brodnax Post Office, where he greeted patrons.

In the evening, the President traveled to Hampton, VA.

The White House announced that the President will award the 2010 National Medals of Science and the National Medals of Technology and Innovation on October 21.

The President announced his intention to nominate Freddy Balsera to be a member of the U.S. Advisory Commission on Public Diplomacy.

The President announced his intention to appoint Albert Gonzales as a member of the National Selective Service Appeal Board.

The President declared a major disaster in Puerto Rico and ordered Federal aid to supplement Commonwealth and local recovery efforts in the area struck by severe storms from September 8 through 14.

October 19

In the morning, the President traveled to Joint Base Langley-Eustis, VA, where he was joined by Mrs. Obama. Later, he and Mrs. Obama visited Wood's Orchards Farm Market in Hampton, VA, where they visited with patrons.

In the afternoon, at Anna's Pizza and Italian Kitchen in Hampton, the President and Mrs. Obama had lunch with veterans Amanda Leigh, Brian Sullivan, Jill A. Lynch, and Patrick L. Burrows. Then, they traveled to North Chesterfield, VA. While en route, the President participated separate telephone interviews for the radio shows of Baye "DJ Bee" Reel of WOWI in Norfolk, VA, and Charles Black of WVKL in Norfolk, VA, both of which were taped for later broadcast.

Later in the afternoon, the President and Mrs. Obama returned to Washington, DC.

The President announced his intention to nominate Carol J. Galante to be Assistant Secretary for Housing and Federal Housing Commissioner at the Department of Housing and Urban Development.

The President announced his intention to nominate David J. Chard, Larry V. Hedges, and Hirokazu Yoshikawa to be members of the Board of Directors of the National Board for Education Sciences.

October 20

In the morning, in the Oval Office, the President had an intelligence briefing.

During the day, the President participated in a videoconference with Prime Minister David Cameron of the United Kingdom, Chancellor Angela Merkel of Germany, and President Nicolas Sarkozy of France to discuss developments in Libya and the economic situation in Europe.

The White House announced that the President will travel to Los Angeles, CA, on October 24.

The President announced his intention to nominate Bonnie L. Bassler to be a member of the National Science Board of the National Science Foundation.

The President announced his intention to nominate Carla M. Leon-Decker to be a member of the National Credit Union Administration Board.

The President announced his intention to nominate Mark W. Lippert to be Assistant Secretary for Asian and Pacific Security Affairs at the Department of Defense.

The President announced his intention to nominate Thomas M. Hoenig to be Vice Chairman of the Board of Directors of the Federal Deposit Insurance Corporation.

October 21

In the morning, in the Situation Room, the President had a teleconference call with Prime Minister Nuri al-Maliki of Iraq. Later, in the Oval Office, he signed H.R. 2832, legislation to renew the Trade Adjustment Assistance program; H.R. 3080, the U.S.-Korea Free Trade Agreement Implementation Act; H.R. 3078, the U.S.-Colombia Trade Promotion Agreement Implementation Act; and H.R. 3079, the U.S.-Panama Trade Promotion Agreement Implementation Act. Then, in the Rose Garden, he dropped by a reception with business and labor leaders and individuals who would benefit from the bills.

In the afternoon, the President had separate telephone conversations with President Juan Manuel Santos Calderon of Colombia and President Ricardo Martinelli Berrocal of Panama to discuss the signing of trade promotion legislation for their respective countries.

The White House announced that the President will travel to Las Vegas, NV, on October 24.

The White House announced that the President will travel to San Francisco, CA, on October 25.

The White House announced that the President will travel to Denver, CO, on October 25.

October 23

During the day, the President had a telephone conversation with King Abdallah bin Abd al-Aziz Al Saud of Saudi Arabia to express his condolences for the death of Crown Prince Sultan bin Abd al-Aziz Al Saud.

October 24

In the morning, the President had a telephone conversation with Defense Minister Field Marshal Mohamed Hussein Tantawi of Egypt to discuss the upcoming Egyptian elections, the economic situation in Egypt, and Egypt-U.S. counterterrorism and security cooperation. Later, he traveled to Las Vegas, NV.

In the afternoon, the President traveled to Los Angeles, CA. Later, he visited Roscoe's House of Chicken 'n Waffles.

In the evening, the President traveled to Beverly Hills, CA.

The White House announced that the President will host the White House Tribal Nations Conference at the Department of the Interior on December 2.

October 25

In the morning, at the Beverly Wilshire hotel, the President met with a group of entertainment industry executives. Then, he traveled to Burbank, CA, where, at NBC Studios, he participated in an interview with Jay Leno of "The Tonight Show." Later, he traveled to San Francisco, CA, arriving in the afternoon.

In the afternoon, the President traveled to Denver, CO, arriving in the evening.

The President announced the designation of the following individuals as members of a Presidential delegation to Saudi Arabia to offer condolences for the death of Crown Prince Sultan bin Abd al-Aziz Al Saud:

Joseph R. Biden, Jr. (head of delegation);
James B. Smith;
John S. McCain III;
William S. Cohen;
Raymond E. Mabus, Jr.;
David H. Petraeus; and
James N. Mattis.

October 26

In the morning, the President returned to Washington, DC, arriving in the afternoon.

October 27

In the morning, in the Oval Office, the President had an intelligence briefing. Later, also in the Oval Office, he met with Secretary of the Treasury Timothy F. Geithner, and then with his senior advisers.

In the afternoon, the President called Cheryl Reeve, head coach of the Women's National Basketball Association's Minnesota Lynx, to congratulate her and her team on winning the WNBA Finals. Later, in the East Room, he hosted a reception for municipal leaders from across the country.

In the evening, the President traveled to Arlington, VA, where, at the Liberty Tavern, he had dinner with Casey Helbling of Minneapolis, MN, Ken Knight of Chandler, AZ, Juanita Martinez of Brighton, CO, and Wendi Smith of Corydon, IN, winners of a contest held by his reelection campaign. Later, he returned to Washington, DC.

The White House released further details on the President's visit to Australia from November 16 through 17.

October 28

In the morning, in the Oval Office, the President had an intelligence briefing followed by a meeting with senior advisers.

In the afternoon, in the Oval Office, the President met with Secretary of State Hillary Rodham Clinton. Later, at the Dwight D. Eisenhower Executive Office Building, he attended a Diwali reception.

The President announced his intention to appoint the following individuals as members of the U.S. Holocaust Memorial Council:

Joseph D. Gutman;
Roman R. Kent;
Howard D. Unger;
Clemantine Wamariya; and
Elie Wiesel.

The President declared a major disaster in Louisiana and ordered Federal aid to supplement State and local recovery efforts in the area affected by Tropical Storm Lee from September 1 through 5.

October 29

In the evening, on the North Portico, the President and Mrs. Obama greeted trick-or-treaters. Later, they hosted a Halloween reception for military families and local students.

October 31

In the morning, in the Oval Office, the President and Vice President Joe Biden had an intelligence briefing. Later, also in the Oval Office, he met with Quartet Representative in the Middle East Tony Blair.

The White House announced that the President will visit Georgetown Waterfront Park in Washington, DC, on November 2.

The President declared an emergency in Connecticut and ordered Federal aid to supplement State and local recovery efforts due to the emergency conditions resulting from a severe storm from October 29 through 30.

The President announced his intention to nominate Ajit V. Pai and Jessica Rosenworcel to be Commissioners at the Federal Communications Commission.

The President announced his intention to nominate Rebecca M. Blank to be Deputy Secretary of Commerce.

The President announced his intention to nominate Larry L. Palmer to be Ambassador to Barbados, St. Kitts and Nevis, St. Lucia, Antigua and Barbuda, Dominica, Grenada, and St. Vincent and the Grenadines.

The President announced his intention to nominate Coral W. Pietsch to be a judge on the U.S. Court of Appeals for Veterans Claims.

The President announced his intention to nominate Michael A. Sheehan to be Assistant Secretary of Defense for Special Operations and Low Intensity Conflict at the Department of Defense.

November 1

In the morning, in the Oval Office, the President and Vice President Joe Biden had an intelligence briefing. Later, in the Cabinet Room, he participated in separate interviews with Nikole Killion of Hearst Television news bureau in Washington, DC, Tom Schaad of WAVY in Portsmouth, VA, Mark Wilson of WTVT in Tampa, FL, Dave Ward of KTRK in Houston, TX, Rob McCartney of KETV in Omaha, NE, Amelia Santaniello of WCCO in Minneapolis, MN, Brian Taff of WPVI in Philadelphia, PA, Adele Arakawa of KUSA in Denver, CO, John Hook of KSAZ in Phoenix, AZ, and Tracy Barry of KGW in Portland, OR.

In the afternoon, in the Oval Office, the President greeted Janet L. Kavandi, Director, NASA's Flight Crew Operations Directorate, and Christopher J. Ferguson, commander, Douglas G. Hurley, pilot, and Rex J. Walheim and Sandra H. Magnus, mission specialists, Space Shuttle *Atlantis*.

In the afternoon, in the Oval Office, the President and Vice President Biden met with House of Representatives Democratic leadership.

The White House announced that the President will participate in a ceremony honoring the France-U.S. alliance in Cannes, France, on November 4.

The President declared an emergency in Massachusetts and ordered Federal aid to supplement Commonwealth and local recovery efforts due to the emergency conditions resulting from a severe storm from October 29 through 30.

The President declared an emergency in New Hampshire and ordered Federal aid to supplement State and local recovery efforts due to the emergency conditions resulting from a severe storm from October 29 through 30.

November 2

In the morning, in the Oval Office, the President and Vice President Joe Biden had an intelligence briefing. Then, also in the Oval Office, he met with his senior advisers.

In the afternoon, in the Private Dining Room, the President and Vice President Biden had lunch. Later, in the Oval Office, they met with Senate Democratic leadership.

During the day, in the Cabinet Room, the President met with his national security team.

In the evening, the President traveled to Cannes, France, arriving the following morning.

The President announced his intention to appoint the following individuals as members of the Advisory Group on Prevention, Health Promotion, and Integrative and Public Health:

Jerry L. Johnson;
Jacob Lozada;
Dean Ornish; and
Herminia Palacio.

The President announced his intention to appoint Kent A. Salazar as a member of the Board of Directors of the Valles Caldera Trust.

The President announced that he has nominated Andrew D. Hurwitz to be a judge on the U.S. Court of Appeals for the Ninth Circuit.

The President announced that he has nominated Kristine G. Baker to be a judge on the U.S. District Court for the Eastern District of Arkansas.

November 3

In the morning, the President traveled to the Palais de Festivals et des Congres in Cannes, France, where, in the Espace Riviera, he was greeted by President Nicolas Sarkozy of France.

In the afternoon, at the InterContinental Carlton Cannes Hotel, the President met with international labor leaders at the Labor 20 summit. Later, at the Espace Riviera, he participated in a working lunch with Group of Twenty (G–20) leaders, followed by a G–20 working session. Then, he participated in a G–20 group photo opportunity, followed by another G–20 working session.

In the evening, at the Espace Riviera, the President participated in a working dinner with G–20 leaders. Later, he returned to the Inter-Continental Carlton Cannes Hotel.

The President announced his intention to appoint Sondra Myers and Jackie Norris as members of the Commission on Presidential Scholars.

November 4

In the morning, at the Espace Riviera, the President participated in G–20 working sessions.

In the afternoon, at the Espace Riviera, the President participated in a working lunch with G–20 leaders. Later, in Cannes's Town Hall, he and President Nicolas Sarkozy of France participated in a television interview with Laurence Ferrari of TF1 and David Pujadas of France 2.

In the evening, the President returned to Washington, DC.

The White House announced that the President will welcome Prime Minister Nuri al-Maliki of Iraq to the White House on December 12.

The President announced his intention to nominate Anne C. Richard to be Assistant Secretary for Population, Refugees, and Migration at the Department of State.

The President announced his intention to nominate Tara D. Sonenshine to be Under Secretary for Public Diplomacy at the Department of State.

The President announced his intention to nominate Meredith M. Broadbent to be a member of the U.S. International Trade Commission.

The President announced his intention to appoint Julie A. Petty and Lauren E. Potter as members of the President's Committee for People with Intellectual Disabilities.

The President declared a major disaster in Virginia and ordered Federal aid to supplement Commonwealth and local recovery efforts in the area affected by an earthquake from August 23 through October 25.

November 5

The White House announced that the President will welcome President Anibal Antonio Cavaco Silva of Portugal to the White House on November 9.

November 6

The White House announced that the President will travel to Philadelphia, PA, on November 8.

November 7

In the morning, in the Oval Office, the President had an intelligence briefing followed by a meeting with his senior advisers. Later, also in the Oval Office, he greeted representatives from veterans' service organizations.

In the afternoon, in the Oval Office, the President had a meeting with Secretary General Anders Fogh Rasmussen of the North Atlantic Treaty Organization. Then, he met with Secretary of State Hillary Rodham Clinton.

Later in the afternoon, in the Oval Office, the President had a telephone conversation with St. Louis Cardinals Manager Anthony La Russa, Jr., to congratulate him on his team's victory over the Texas Rangers in the 2011 World Series.

November 8

In the morning, the President traveled to Yeadon, PA, where he toured classrooms at the Yeadon Regional Head Start Center and met with students and teachers.

In the afternoon, the President returned to Washington, DC.

The White House announced that the President and Mrs. Obama will travel to Arlington, VA, and San Diego, CA, on November 11.

The White House announced that the President and Mrs. Obama will travel to Honolulu, HI, on November 11 for the Asia-Pacific Economic Cooperation summit.

The President declared a major disaster in Vermont and ordered Federal aid to supplement State and local recovery efforts in the area struck by severe storms and flooding on May 20.

The President declared a major disaster in the District of Columbia and ordered Federal aid to supplement District recovery efforts in the area affected by an earthquake from August 23 through 28.

November 9

In the morning, in the Oval Office, the President and Vice President Joe Biden had an intelligence briefing. Then, in the Roosevelt Room, he met with Vice President Biden, White House Chief of Staff William M. Daley, White House Domestic Policy Council Director Melody C.

Barnes, and other senior advisers to discuss the economy.

In the afternoon, in the Oval Office, the President met with his senior advisers. Then, in the Private Dining Room, he had lunch with Vice President Biden. Later, in the Oval Office, he met with President Anibal Antonio Cavaco Silva of Portugal.

November 10

In the afternoon, in the Oval Office, the President met with his senior advisers.

During the day, the President had separate telephone conversations with President Giorgio Napolitano of Italy, Chancellor Angela Merkel of Germany, and President Nicolas Sarkozy of France to discuss economic stabilization efforts in Europe.

During the day, in the Oval Office, the President met with White House Chief of Staff William M. Daley, White House Communications Director H. Daniel Pfeiffer, White House Press Secretary James F. "Jay" Carney, White House Senior Advisers Valerie B. Jarrett and David A. Plouffe, and Counselor to the President Peter M. Rouse.

The President announced that he has nominated Richard G. Taranto to be a judge on the U.S. Court of Appeals for the Federal Circuit.

The President announced that he has nominated Gonzalo P. Curiel to be a judge on the U.S. District Court for the Southern District of California.

The President announced that he has nominated John Z. Lee and John J. Tharp, Jr., to be judges on the U.S. District Court for the Northern District of Illinois.

The President announced that he has nominated George L. Russell III to be a judge on the U.S. District Court for the District of Maryland.

The President announced that he has nominated Scott L. Silliman and William B. Pollard III to be judges on the U.S. Court of Military Commission Review.

November 11

In the morning, in the East Room, the President and Mrs. Obama hosted a breakfast for veterans. Later, they traveled to Arlington, VA, where they participated in a Veterans Day wreath-laying ceremony at Arlington National Cemetery.

In the afternoon, the President and Mrs. Obama traveled to San Diego, CA. While en route aboard Air Force One, he had a telephone conversation with President Felipe de Jesus Calderon Hinojosa of Mexico to express his condolences for the helicopter crash near Mexico City that killed eight Mexican Government officials, including Secretary of Government Jose Francisco Blake Mora.

Later in the afternoon, on the deck of the USS *Carl Vinson* at North Island Naval Station, the President participated in a radio interview with Jim Gray of Westwood One Sports.

During the day, the President had separate telephone conversations with Sen. Patricia L. Murray and Rep. T. Jeb Hensarling, cochairs of the bipartisan Joint Select Committee on Deficit Reduction, to urge them to reach an agreement before the November 23 deadline.

In the evening, the President participated in a television interview with Andy Katz of ESPN. Later, the President and Mrs. Obama traveled to Honolulu, HI.

November 12

In the evening, at the Hale Koa Hotel, the President and Mrs. Obama participated in an arrival ceremony for Asia-Pacific Economic Cooperation leaders and their spouses. Later, they traveled to the Hilton Hawaiian Village Waikiki Beach Resort.

November 13

In the morning, the President traveled to the JW Marriott Ihilani Ko Olina Resort & Spa, where he participated in a meeting with the Asia-Pacific Economic Cooperation (APEC) Business Advisory Council.

In the afternoon, at the JW Marriott Ihilani Ko Olina Resort & Spa, the President met with Prime Minister Stephen J. Harper of Canada to discuss Canada-U.S. relations, the Trans-Pacific Partnership, and Canada's participation in military operations in Libya and Afghanistan. Then, he had a working lunch with APEC leaders. Later, he participated in a photo opportunity and working session with APEC leaders.

During the day, the President met with President Ollanta Moises Humala Tasso of Peru to discuss Peru-U.S. relations and the upcoming Summit of the Americas.

November 14

The President announced his intention to nominate Deborah J. Jeffrey to be Inspector General of the Corporation for National and Community Service.

The President announced his intention to nominate Mark J. Mazur to be Assistant Secretary for Tax Policy at the Department of the Treasury.

The President announced his intention to appoint Janie Barrera and Sherry S. Black as members of the President's Advisory Council on Financial Capability.

November 15

In the morning, the President traveled to Canberra, Australia, crossing the international dateline and arriving the following afternoon.

During the day, the President had a telephone conversation with former Prime Minister Georgios Andreas Papandreou of Greece to thank him for his contributions to Greece and discuss Greece-U.S. relations.

The White House announced that the President will travel to Manchester, NH, on November 22.

November 16

In the afternoon, upon arrival in Canberra, Australia, the President traveled to Parliament House, where he participated in an arrival ceremony with Prime Minister Julia E. Gillard of Australia. Then, he met with Prime Minister Gillard.

In the evening, the President traveled to the Hyatt Hotel Canberra.

November 17

In the morning, the President traveled to the Australian War Memorial, where he participated in a wreath-laying ceremony in the Hall of Memory. Later, he traveled to Parliament

House, where he met with Leader of the Opposition Anthony J. Abbott.

In the afternoon, the President traveled to the Chancery, the U.S. Ambassador's residence, where he greeted U.S. Embassy personnel. Then, on the grounds, he participated in a tree dedication ceremony with U.S. Ambassador to Australia Jeffrey L. Bleich. Later, he traveled to Darwin, Australia, where he visited the USS *Peary* Memorial and participated in a wreath-laying ceremony with Prime Minister Julia E. Gillard of Australia.

In the evening, the President traveled to the Grand Hyatt Bali hotel in Bali, Indonesia. While en route, aboard Air Force One, he had a telephone conversation with Aung San Suu Kyi, leader of the National League for Democracy in Burma, to discuss the situation in Burma and Secretary of State Hillary Rodham Clinton's upcoming visit.

The President announced his intention to nominate Sara A. Gelser to be a member of the National Council on Disability.

The President announced his intention to nominate Margaret A. Sherry to be Chief Financial Officer at the Department of Homeland Security.

The President announced that he has nominated Gershwin A. Drain to be a judge on the U.S. District Court for the Eastern District of Michigan.

The President announced that he has nominated Roy W. McLeese III to be a judge on the U.S. Court of Appeals for the District of Columbia.

The President declared a major disaster in Virginia and ordered Federal aid to supplement Commonwealth and local recovery efforts in the area affected by the remnants of Tropical Storm Lee on September 8 and 9.

The President declared a major disaster in Connecticut and ordered Federal aid to supplement State and local recovery efforts in the area affected by a severe storm on October 29 and 30.

November 18

In the afternoon, the President traveled to the Bali International Convention Centre, where he participated in a meeting with Association of Southeast Asian Nations (ASEAN) leaders.

In the evening, the President traveled to the Grand Hyatt Bali hotel. Later, he returned to the Bali International Convention Centre, where he participated in a photo opportunity and dinner with East Asia Summit leaders. Later, he returned to the Grand Hyatt Bali hotel.

The White House announced further details on the President's visit to Manchester, NH, on November 22.

The White House announced that the President will hold the Thanksgiving turkey pardoning at the White House on November 23.

November 19

In the morning, at the Grand Hyatt Bali hotel, the President met with U.S. Embassy personnel. Later, he had a meeting with Premier Wen Jiabao of China to discuss the global economic situation and the territorial dispute in the South China Sea. Later, he traveled to the Bali International Convention Centre, where he attended an East Asia Summit plenary session.

In the afternoon, the President participated in a social lunch for the East Asia Summit with other Asia-Pacific leaders. Then, he participated in the East Asia Summit group photograph and attended the East Asian Summit retreat. Later, he traveled to Anderson Air Force Base, Guam.

In the evening, the President traveled to Honolulu, HI, crossing the International Date Line and arriving in the afternoon. Later, he returned to Washington, DC, arriving the following morning.

November 21

In the morning, in the Oval Office, the President and Vice President Joe Biden had an intelligence briefing. Later, also in the Oval Office, he had a telephone conversation with Prime Minister Mario Monti of Italy to congratulate him on his appointment as Prime Minister and discuss the economic situation in Europe.

In the afternoon, in the Oval Office, the President had a telephone conversation with

Prime Minister Lukas Papademos of Greece to congratulate him on his appointment as Prime Minister and to discuss the economic situation in Europe. Then, he had a telephone conversation with President-elect Otto Perez Molina of Guatemala to congratulate him on his election and commend the Guatemalan people on their commitment to democracy. Later, also in the Oval Office, he had a meeting with Secretary of the Treasury Timothy F. Geithner.

Later in the afternoon, in the Oval Office, the President held a signing ceremony for S. 1280, the Kate Puzey Peace Corps Volunteer Protection Act of 2011, and greeted Peace Corps staff, former Peace Corps volunteers, and David Puzey, brother, and other relatives of Catherine "Kate" Puzey, a Peace Corps volunteer who was murdered in Benin in 2009. Later, also in the Oval Office, he participated in separate interviews for the syndicated radio shows of Michael Baisden and Alfred C. Sharpton, Jr.

The White House announced that the President will welcome Prime Minister Mark Rutte of the Netherlands to the White House of November 29.

November 22

In the morning, the President traveled to Manchester, NH. Later, at Julien's Corner Kitchen restaurant, he met with Bedford, NH, residents Christopher and Kathy Corkery and their sons Andrew and Nicholas.

In the afternoon, the President returned to Washington, DC.

The White House announced that the President will travel to Scranton, PA, on November 30.

November 23

In the morning, in the South Court Auditorium of the Dwight D. Eisenhower Executive Office Building, the President participated in a 50th anniversary celebration for the Peace Corps and the U.S. Agency for International Development.

In the afternoon, at the Capital Area Food Bank, the President, Mrs. Obama, and their daughters Sasha and Malia handed out Thanksgiving groceries to families.

The President announced his intention to nominate Marilyn B. Tavenner to be Administrator of the Center for Medicare and Medicaid Services at the Department of Health and Human Services.

The President announced his intention to appoint Mark L. Alderman as a member of the Advisory Board of the National Air and Space Museum.

The President announced his intention to appoint Keith M. Harper as a member of the President's Commission on White House Fellowships.

The President announced his intention to appoint Fletcher "Flash" Wiley as a member of the Board of Visitors to the United States Air Force Academy.

The President declared a major disaster in New Mexico and ordered Federal aid to supplement State, tribal, and local recovery efforts in the area struck by flooding from August 19 through 24.

November 24

In the morning, the President had separate telephone conversations with 10 members of the Armed Forces to thank them for their service.

During the day, the President celebrated Thanksgiving at the White House with his family, friends, and members of his staff.

November 26

In the afternoon, the President, Mrs. Obama, and their daughters Sasha and Malia traveled to Towson University in Towson, MD, to attend a men's basketball game. Later, they returned to Washington, DC.

November 27

The White House announced that the President will travel to Scranton, PA, on November 30.

November 28

In the morning, in the Oval Office, the President had an intelligence briefing. Later, in the Roosevelt Room, he met with European Union leaders to discuss global economic stabilization efforts, international humanitarian assistance,

nonproliferation negotiations with Iran, and counterterrorism cooperation.

In the afternoon, in the Cabinet Room, the President had lunch with European Union leaders.

The White House announced that the President will travel to New York City on November 30.

The White House announced that the President will deliver remarks at George Washington University on December 1.

November 29

In the morning, in the Oval Office, the President had an intelligence briefing.

In the afternoon, in the Oval Office, the President met with his senior advisers.

The President announced the designation of the following individuals as members of a Presidential delegation to attend the Inauguration of Almazbek Atambayev as Prime Minister of Kyrgyzstan in Bishkek, Kyrgyzstan, on December 1: Pamela L. Spratlen (head of delegation); and Robert O. Blake, Jr.

The President announced his intention to nominate Fredrick Barton to be Assistant Secretary for Conflict and Stabilization Operations and Coordinator for Reconstruction and Stabilization at the Department of State.

The President announced his intention to nominate Arun Majumdar to be Under Secretary for Energy at the Department of Energy.

The President announced his intention to nominate Marie F. Smith to be a member of the Social Security Advisory Board.

The President announced his intention to appoint Barbara K. Rimer as Chairman of the President's Cancer Panel.

The President announced his intention to appoint Owen N. Witte as a member of the President's Cancer Panel.

November 30

In the morning, in the Oval Office, the President had an intelligence briefing.

In the afternoon, the President traveled to Scranton, PA. Upon arrival in Scranton, he traveled to the residence of Patrick and Donna Festa. Then, he traveled to New York City.

In the evening, the President returned to Washington, DC.

During the day, the President had a telephone conversation with 2011 NASCAR Sprint Cup Series champion Tony Stewart to congratulate him and his team on winning the series. He also had a telephone conversation with Major League Soccer's Los Angeles Galaxy head coach Bruce Arena to congratulate him and the team on winning the 2011 MLS Cup.

The President announced that he has nominated Timothy S. Hillman to be a judge on the U.S. District Court for the District of Massachusetts.

The President announced that he has nominated Robin S. Rosenbaum to be a judge on the U.S. District Court for the Southern District of Florida.

The President announced that he has nominated Robert J. Shelby to be a judge on the U.S. District Court for the District of Utah.

The President declared a major disaster in New Jersey and ordered Federal aid to supplement State and local recovery efforts in the area affected by a severe storm on October 29.

December 1

In the morning, in the Oval Office, the President had an intelligence briefing.

During the day, the President met with military officials and took them on a tour of the East Wing Christmas decorations.

The President announced his intention to nominate Jonathan D. Farrar to be Ambassador to Panama.

The President announced his intention to nominate Joseph E. Macmanus to be U.S. Representative to the Vienna Office of the U.N. and U.S. Representative to the International Atomic Energy Agency.

The President announced his intention to nominate Phyllis M. Powers to be Ambassador to Nicaragua.

The President announced his intention to nominate William E. Todd to be Ambassador to Cambodia.

The President announced his intention to appoint Philip G. Freelon as a member of the Commission of Fine Arts.

December 2

In the morning, in the Oval Office, the President had an intelligence briefing. Later, he and former President William J. Clinton toured the Chanin Building at 815 Connecticut Ave., NW, an office building undergoing an efficiency upgrade.

In the afternoon, in the Oval Office, the President met with his senior advisers.

The President announced his intention to nominate Mark A. Robbins to be a member of the Merit Systems Protection Board.

The President announced his intention to nominate Tony Hammond to be a Commissioner on the Postal Regulatory Commission.

The President announced his intention to nominate Pauline R. Maier to be a member of the Board of Trustees of the James Madison Memorial Fellowship Foundation.

The President announced his intention to appoint Joan W. Harris as a member of the Library of Congress Trust Fund Board.

The President announced his intention to appoint Dallas L. Salisbury as a member of the Advisory Committee to the Pension Benefit Guaranty Corporation.

December 3

The White House announced that the President will travel to Osawatomie, KS, on December 6.

December 4

In the morning, the President had a telephone conversation with President Asif Ali Zardari of Pakistan to discuss Pakistan-U.S. relations and to express his condolences for the recent loss of Pakistani soldiers along the Pakistan-Afghanistan border.

In the evening, at the John F. Kennedy Center for the Performing Arts, the President and Mrs. Obama attended the Kennedy Center Honors Gala. Later, they returned to the White House.

December 5

In the morning, in the Oval Office, the President had an intelligence briefing followed by a meeting with Secretary of the Treasury Timothy F. Geithner. Then, also in the Oval Office, he met with his senior advisers. Later, in the Roosevelt Room, he and Secretary of Education Arne Duncan met with the heads of several postsecondary education institutions and organizations to discuss education affordability.

The President declared a major disaster in New Hampshire and ordered Federal aid to supplement State and local recovery efforts in the area affected by a severe storm and snowstorm on October 29 and 30.

December 6

In the morning, the President traveled to Osawatomie, KS, arriving in the afternoon.

In the afternoon, the President traveled to Osawatomie High School, where he participated in the first part of an interview with Steve Kroft of CBS's "60 Minutes" program for later broadcast.

Later in the afternoon, the President traveled to Paola, KS, where, at the We B Smokin' restaurant, he met with employees and patrons. Then, he returned to Washington, DC, arriving in the evening.

December 7

In the morning, in the Oval Office, the President and Vice President Joe Biden met with the Senate Democratic leadership. Later, he had a telephone conversation with James P. Hoffa of the International Brotherhood of Teamsters to congratulate him on his election as president.

In the afternoon, the President had a telephone conversation with Chancellor Angela Merkel of Germany to discuss Europe's economic stabilization efforts. Then, in the Oval Office, he met with Prime Minister Stephen J. Harper of Canada. Later, at the Jefferson hotel, he attended an Obama Victory Fund 2012 fundraiser.

The President announced his intention to appoint Preeta D. Bansal and Boris Bershteyn as members of the Advisory Council of the Administrative Conference of the U.S.

December 8

In the morning, in the Oval Office, the President had an intelligence briefing followed by a meeting with House Democratic leadership.

In the afternoon, in the Diplomatic Reception Room, the President participated in separate television interviews with Debby Knox of WISH in Indianapolis, IN, Jim Snyder of KSNV in Las Vegas, NV, Richard Ransom of WREG in Memphis, TN, and Pat Callaghan of WCSH in Portland, ME.

The White House announced that the President will attend the Army-Navy football game on December 10 and that he and Mrs. Obama will travel to Fort Bragg, NC, on December 14.

The President announced the designation of the following individuals as members of a Presidential delegation to Buenos Aires, Argentina, to attend the Inauguration of Cristina Fernandez de Kirchner as President of Argentina in Buenos Aires, Argentina, on December 10: Hilda L. Solis (head of delegation); Vilma S. Martinez; and Daniel A. Restrepo.

December 9

In the morning, in the Oval Office, the President had an intelligence briefing. Later, also in the Oval Office, he participated in the second part of an interview with Steve Kroft of CBS's "60 Minutes" program for later broadcast.

In the afternoon, at the Blair House, the President attended a holiday reception.

December 10

In the afternoon, the President traveled to Landover, MD, where, at FedEx Field, he attended the Army-Navy football game with Vice President Joe Biden and his wife Jill, Secretary of Defense Leon E. Panetta, and Chairman of the Joint Chiefs of Staff Martin E. Dempsey. Later, he returned to Washington, DC.

The White House released further details on the President and Mrs. Obama's visit to Fort Bragg, NC, on December 14 to commemorate the withdrawal of U.S. troops from Iraq and recognize the service and dedication of military personnel and families.

December 12

In the morning, in the Oval Office, the President and Vice President Joe Biden met with Prime Minister Nuri al-Maliki of Iraq. Later, also in the Oval Office, the President met separately with Prime Minister Maliki.

In the afternoon, the President, Vice President Biden, and Prime Minister Maliki traveled to Arlington, VA, where, at Arlington National Cemetery, they participated in a wreath-laying ceremony. Then, they returned to Washington, DC. Later, in the Oval Office, he met with Secretary of State Hillary Rodham Clinton.

December 13

In the morning, the President participated in separate television interviews with David Alan of WVEC in Norfolk, VA, Bob Solarski of WEAR in Pensacola, FL, Rob Quirk of KOAA in Colorado Springs, CO, and Angela Russell of KIRO in Seattle, WA, to discuss the withdrawal of U.S. troops from Iraq and extension of the payroll tax cut.

December 14

In the morning, in the Oval Office, the President and Vice President Joe Biden had an intelligence briefing. Later, he and Mrs. Obama traveled to Fort Bragg, NC, where they met with military personnel and families.

In the afternoon, the President and Mrs. Obama returned to Washington, DC.

During the day, the President met with his national security team to discuss enhanced security preparations for the upcoming holiday season.

The President announced his intention to nominate Sharon Block and Richard F. Griffin, Jr., to be members of the National Labor Relations Board.

The President announced his intention to nominate Michael A. Raynor to be Ambassador to Benin.

The President announced his intention to nominate Jacob Walles to be Ambassador to Tunisia.

December 15

In the morning, in the Oval Office, the President and Vice President Joe Biden had an intelligence briefing.

In the afternoon, in the Private Dining Room, the President and Vice President Biden had lunch.

The President announced his intention to nominate David Medine to be Chairman of the Privacy and Civil Liberties Oversight Board.

The President announced his intention to nominate Rachel L. Brand and Patricia M. Wald to be members of the Privacy and Civil Liberties Oversight Board.

December 16

In the morning, in the Oval Office, the President had a telephone conversation with President Dmitry A. Medvedev of Russia to discuss the World Trade Organization's formal invitation to Russia for membership, recent elections and political demonstrations in Russia, and Russia-U.S. relations. Then, also in the Oval Office, he had an intelligence briefing.

In the afternoon, in the Oval Office, the President had a meeting with his senior advisers.

The President announced his intention to nominate Richard B. Berner to be Director of the Office of Financial Research at the Department of the Treasury.

The President announced his intention to nominate Nancy J. Powell to be Ambassador to India.

The President announced that he has nominated John T. Fowlkes, Jr., to be a judge on the U.S. District Court for the Western District of Tennessee.

The President announced that he has nominated Kevin McNulty to be a judge on the U.S. District Court for the District of New Jersey.

December 18

In the evening, the President was briefed by White House Chief of Staff William M. Daley on the death of Chairman Kim Jong Il of North Korea.

December 19

In the morning, in the Oval Office, the President had a telephone conversation with President Lee Myung-bak of South Korea to discuss the situation on the Korean Peninsula following the death of Chairman Kim Jong Il of

North Korea and reaffirm the U.S. commitment to South Korea's security.

Later in the morning, in the Oval Office, the President and Vice President Joe Biden had an intelligence briefing. Then, also in the Oval Office, he met with his senior advisers.

During the day, the President had a telephone conversation with Prime Minister Hamadi Jebali of Tunisia to congratulate him on his appointment and discuss Tunisia's democratic transition.

In the evening, the President had a telephone conversation with Prime Minister Yoshihiko Noda of Japan to discuss the situation on the Korean Peninsula following the death of Chairman Kim Jong Il of North Korea and reaffirm the U.S. commitment to Japan's security.

December 20

In the morning, in the Oval Office, the President had a telephone conversation with Prime Minister-elect Mariano Rajoy Brey of Spain to congratulate him on his election victory and discuss Spain-U.S. relations. Then, also in the Oval Office, he and Vice President Joe Biden had an intelligence briefing. Later, they traveled to Joint Base Andrews, MD, where, in the afternoon, they participated in a ceremony marking the return of the Colors of U.S. Forces—Iraq and the end of military operations in Iraq.

Later in the afternoon, the President and Vice President Biden returned to Washington, DC.

December 21

In the morning, in the Oval Office, the President had an intelligence briefing followed by a meeting with his senior advisers.

In the afternoon, the President had separate telephone conversations with Speaker of the House of Representatives John A. Boehner and Senate Majority Leader Harry M. Reid to discuss the ongoing negotiations over legislation to extend the payroll tax cut.

Later in the afternoon, the President traveled to Alexandria, VA, where he shopped for Christmas gifts. Then, he returned to Washington, DC.

The President announced the designation of the following individuals as members of a Presidential delegation to attend the funeral of former President Vaclav Havel of the Czech Republic in Prague, Czech Republic, on December 23:

Hillary Rodham Clinton (head of delegation);
William J. Clinton;
Norman L. Eisen; and
Madeleine K. Albright.

The President announced his intention to appoint Margaret M. Murnane as Chairman of the President's Committee on the National Medal of Science.

The President announced his intention to appoint Judith Kimble and Henry T. Yang as members of the President's Committee on the National Medal of Science.

The President announced his intention to appoint Beth White as a member of the National Capital Planning Commission.

The President announced his intention to appoint Susan York as a member of the Commission for the Preservation of America's Heritage Abroad.

December 22

In the morning, in the Oval Office, the President had an intelligence briefing. Later, he had a telephone conversation with Speaker of the House of Representatives John A. Boehner to discuss the ongoing negotiations over legislation to extend the payroll tax cut.

In the afternoon, in the Oval Office, the President met with his senior advisers. Later, also in the Oval Office, he was briefed by Assistant to the President for Legislative Affairs Robert L. Nabors II on the congressional agreement to extend the payroll tax cut.

The President declared a major disaster in Alaska and ordered Federal aid to supplement State and local recovery efforts in the area struck by severe winter storms and flooding from November 8 through 10.

December 23

In the morning, in the Oval Office, the President had an intelligence briefing followed by a meeting with his senior advisers.

In the afternoon, the President traveled to Honolulu, HI, arriving in the evening.

In the evening, upon arrival at Joint Base Pearl Harbor-Hickam, HI, the President traveled to his vacation residence in Kailua, HI.

December 24

In the morning, the President had an intelligence briefing.

In the evening, the President had separate telephone conversations with 10 members of the Armed Forces to thank them for their service.

December 25

In the morning, the President had an intelligence briefing. Later, he, Mrs. Obama, and their daughters Sasha and Malia attended a Christmas service at the chapel on Marine Corps Base Hawaii, Kaneohe Bay. Then, they returned to Kailua, HI.

In the afternoon, the President and Mrs. Obama returned to Marine Corps Base Hawaii, where, in Anderson Hall, they visited with members of the U.S. military and their families. Later, they returned to Kailua, HI.

December 26

In the morning, the President had an intelligence briefing.

December 27

In the morning, the President had an intelligence briefing.

In the afternoon, the President, Mrs. Obama, and their daughters Sasha and Malia visited Hanauma Bay Nature Preserve, where they released four green sea turtles born in captivity into the wild. Later, they traveled to Waimanalo, HI, where they toured Sea Life Park Hawaii. Then, they returned to Kailua, HI.

The President announced his intention to nominate Jerome H. Powell and Jeremy C. Stein to be Governors of the Board of Governors of the Federal Reserve System.

December 28

In the morning, the President had an intelligence briefing.

December 29

In the morning, the President had an intelligence briefing.

In the afternoon, the President and Mrs. Obama traveled to the World War II Valor of the Pacific National Monument at Pearl Harbor, HI, where they toured the USS *Arizona* Memorial and participated in a wreath-laying ceremony. Later, they returned to Kailua, HI.

December 30

In the morning, the President had an intelligence briefing.

December 31

In the morning, the President had an intelligence briefing.

Appendix B—Nominations Submitted to the Senate

The following list does not include promotions of members of the Uniformed Services, nominations to the Service Academies, or nominations of Foreign Service officers.

Submitted July 5

Thomas J. Curry,
of Massachusetts, to be Comptroller of the Currency for a term of 5 years, vice John C. Dugan, resigned.

Mary John Miller,
of Maryland, to be an Under Secretary of the Treasury, vice Jeffrey Alan Goldstein.

Matthew G. Olsen,
of Maryland, to be Director of the National Counterterrorism Center, Office of the Director of National Intelligence, vice Michael E. Leiter, resigned.

Wendy Ruth Sherman,
of Maryland, to be an Under Secretary of State (Political Affairs), vice William J. Burns, resigned.

Submitted July 11

Danya Ariel Dayson,
of the District of Columbia, to be an Associate Judge of the Superior Court of the District of Columbia for the term of 15 years, vice Stephanie Duncan-Peters, retired.

Joseph H. Gale,
of Virginia, to be a Judge of the U.S. Tax Court for a term of 15 years (reappointment).

Michael A. Hammer,
of the District of Columbia, a career member of the Senior Foreign Service, class of Counselor, to be an Assistant Secretary of State (Public Affairs), vice Philip J. Crowley, resigned.

Peter Arno Krauthamer,
of the District of Columbia, to be an Associate Judge of the Superior Court of the District of Columbia for the term of 15 years, vice John Henry Bayly, Jr., retired.

John Francis McCabe,
of the District of Columbia, to be an Associate Judge of the Superior Court of the District of Columbia for the term of 15 years, vice James E. Boasberg, resigned.

Charles DeWitt McConnell,
of Ohio, to be an Assistant Secretary of Energy (Fossil Energy), vice James J. Markowsky, resigned.

Submitted July 12

Matan Aryeh Koch,
of New York, to be a member of the National Council on Disability for a term expiring September 17, 2013, vice Carol Jean Reynolds, term expired.

Stephanie Orlando,
of New York, to be a member of the National Council on Disability for the remainder of the term expiring September 17, 2011, vice Heather McCallum, resigned.

Stephanie Orlando,
of New York, to be a member of the National Council on Disability for a term expiring September 17, 2014 (reappointment).

Submitted July 18

Richard Cordray,
of Ohio, to be Director, Bureau of Consumer Financial Protection for a term of 5 years (new position).

Chester John Culver,
of Iowa, to be a member of the Board of Directors of the Federal Agricultural Mortgage Corporation, vice Julia Bartling.

David A. Montoya,
of Texas, to be Inspector General, Department of Housing and Urban Development, vice Kenneth M. Donohue, Sr., resigned.

Bruce J. Sherrick,
of Illinois, to be a member of the Board of Directors of the Federal Agricultural Mortgage Corporation, vice Glen Klippenstein.

Submitted July 20

Michael Walter Fitzgerald,
of California, to be U.S. District Judge for the Central District of California, vice A. Howard Matz, retired.

Submitted July 21

Roslyn Ann Mazer,
of Maryland, to be Inspector General, Department of Homeland Security, vice Richard L. Skinner, resigned.

Maureen K. Ohlhausen,
of Virginia, to be a Federal Trade Commissioner for a term of 7 years from September 26, 2011, vice William E. Kovacic, term expiring.

Submitted July 22

Mary B. DeRosa,
of the District of Columbia, to be an Alternate Representative of the United States of America to the Sixty-sixth Session of the General Assembly of the United Nations.

Frank E. Loy,
of the District of Columbia, to be an Alternate Representative of the United States of America to the Sixty-sixth Session of the General Assembly of the United Nations.

Kendrick B. Meek,
of Florida, to be a Representative of the United States of America to the Sixty-sixth Session of the General Assembly of the United Nations.

James T. Ryan,
of Utah, to be a member of the Board of Directors of the National Institute of Building Sciences for a term expiring September 7, 2013, vice James Broaddus, resigned.

Larry W. Walther,
of Arkansas, to be a member of the Board of Directors of the Export-Import Bank of the United States for a term expiring January 20, 2013, vice J. Joseph Grandmaison, term expired.

Submitted July 26

Robert S. Mueller III,
of California, to be Director of the Federal Bureau of Investigation for a term expiring September 4, 2013 (reappointment).

Submitted July 28

Ronnie Abrams,
of New York, to be U.S. District Judge for the Southern District of New York, vice Lewis A. Kaplan, retired.

Rudolph Contreras,
of Virginia, to be U.S. District Judge for the District of Columbia, vice Ricardo M. Urbina, retired.

David T. Danielson,
of California, to be an Assistant Secretary of Energy (Energy Efficiency and Renewable Energy), vice Catherine Radford Zoi, resigned.

LaDoris Guess Harris,
of Georgia, to be Director of the Office of Minority Economic Impact, Department of Energy, vice Jose Antonio Garcia, resigned.

Evan Jonathan Wallach,
of New York, to be U.S. Circuit Judge for the Federal Circuit, vice Arthur Gajarsa, retiring.

Submitted July 29

Michael E. Horowitz,
of Maryland, to be Inspector General, Department of Justice, vice Glenn A. Fine, resigned.

Anneila I. Sargent,
of California, to be a member of the National Science Board, National Science Foundation, for a term expiring May 10, 2016, vice Gerald Wayne Clough, term expired.

Withdrawn July 29

Goodwin Liu,
of California, to be U.S. Circuit Judge for the Ninth Circuit, vice a new position created by Public Law 110–177, approved January 7, 2008, which was sent to the Senate on January 5, 2011.

Barbara K. McQuiston,
of California, to be an Assistant Secretary of Defense (new position), which was sent to the Senate on May 9, 2011.

Michael F. Mundaca,
of New York, to be an Assistant Secretary of the Treasury, vice Eric Solomon, resigned, which was sent to the Senate on January 26, 2011.

Submitted August 2

David B. Barlow,
of Utah, to be U.S. Attorney for the District of Utah for the term of 4 years, vice Brett L. Tolman, term expired.

Ashton B. Carter,
of Massachusetts, to be Deputy Secretary of Defense, vice William J. Lynn III.

Miranda Du,
of Nevada, to be U.S. District Judge for the District of Nevada, vice Roger L. Hunt, retired.

Catharine Friend Easterly,
of the District of Columbia, to be an Associate Judge of the District of Columbia Court of Appeals for the term of 15 years, vice A. Noel Anketell Kramer, retired.

Adalberto Jose Jordan,
of Florida, to be U.S. Circuit Judge for the Eleventh Circuit, vice Susan H. Black, retired.

Irvin Charles McCullough III,
of Maryland, to be Inspector General of the Intelligence Community, Office of the Director of National Intelligence (new position).

Ernest Mitchell, Jr.,
of California, to be Administrator of the U.S. Fire Administration, Federal Emergency Management Agency, Department of Homeland Security, vice Kelvin James Cochran, resigned.

Nancy Maria Ware,
of the District of Columbia, to be Director of the Court Services and Offender Supervision Agency for the District of Columbia for a term of 6 years, vice Paul A. Quander, Jr., term expired.

Gregory Howard Woods,
of New York, to be General Counsel of the Department of Energy, vice Scott Blake Harris, resigned.

Withdrawn August 2

Leon Rodriguez,
of Maryland, to be Administrator of the Wage and Hour Division, Department of Labor, vice Paul DeCamp, which was sent to the Senate on January 5, 2011.

Submitted September 6

Catherine Allgor,
of California, to be a member of the Board of Trustees of the James Madison Memorial Fellowship Foundation for a term expiring September 27, 2014, vice John Richard Petrocik, term expired.

Eduardo Arriola,
of Florida, to be a member of the Board of Directors of the Inter-American Foundation for a term expiring October 6, 2016, vice Kay Kelley Arnold, term expired.

Sara Margalit Aviel,
of California, to be U.S. Alternate Executive Director of the International Bank for Reconstruction and Development for a term of 2 years, vice Ana M. Guevara.

Daniel J. Becker,
of Utah, to be a member of the Board of Directors of the State Justice Institute for a term expiring September 17, 2013 (reappointment).

Dana Katherine Bilyeu,
of Nevada, to be a member of the Federal Retirement Thrift Investment Board for a term expiring October 11, 2015 (reappointment).

Mark Francis Brzezinski,
of Virginia, to be Ambassador Extraordinary and Plenipotentiary of the United States of America to Sweden.

Steven H. Cohen,
of Illinois, to be a member of the Board of Trustees of the Harry S. Truman Scholarship Foundation for a term expiring December 10, 2013, vice Luis D. Rovira, term expired.

Albert DiClemente,
of Delaware, to be a Director of the Amtrak Board of Directors for a term of 5 years (reappointment).

James R. Hannah,
of Arkansas, to be a member of the Board of Directors of the State Justice Institute for a term expiring September 17, 2013 (reappointment).

David Avren Jones,
of Connecticut, to be a member of the Federal Retirement Thrift Investment Board for a term expiring October 11, 2014, vice Alejandro Modesto Sanchez, resigned.

Michael A. Khouri,
of Kentucky, to be a Federal Maritime Commissioner for a term expiring June 30, 2016 (reappointment).

Alan B. Krueger,
of New Jersey, to be a member of the Council of Economic Advisers, vice Austan Dean Goolsbee, resigned.

Drew R. McCoy,
of Massachusetts, to be a member of the Board of Trustees of the James Madison Memorial Fellowship Foundation for a term expiring January 27, 2016 (reappointment).

David J. McMillan,
of Minnesota, to be a member of the Advisory Board of the Saint Lawrence Seaway Development Corporation, vice Scott Kevin Walker.

Adam E. Namm,
of New York, a career member of the Senior Foreign Service, class of Minister-Counselor, to be Ambassador Extraordinary and Plenipotentiary of the United States of America to the Republic of Ecuador.

Susan Denise Page,
of Illinois, to be Ambassador Extraordinary and Plenipotentiary of the United States of America to the Republic of South Sudan.

J. Kelly Ryan,
of Maryland, to be a member of the Board of Directors of the Inter-American Foundation for the remainder of the term expiring September 20, 2012, vice Thomas A. Shannon, Jr., resigned.

Wenona Singel,
of Michigan, to be a member of the Advisory Board of the Saint Lawrence Seaway Development Corporation, vice Jack Edwin McGregor.

Mary B. Verner,
of Washington, to be a member of the Board of Directors of the National Institute of Building Sciences for a term expiring September 7, 2012, vice Steve M. Hays, term expired.

Mary B. Verner,
of Washington, to be a member of the Board of Directors of the National Institute of Building Sciences for a term expiring September 7, 2015 (reappointment).

Michael James Warren,
of the District of Columbia, to be a member of the Board of Directors of the Overseas Private Investment Corporation for a term expiring December 17, 2014 (reappointment).

Submitted September 8

Cyrus Amir-Mokri,
of New York, to be an Assistant Secretary of
the Treasury, vice Michael S. Barr, resigned.

Cyrus Amir-Mokri,
of New York, to be a member of the Board of
Directors of the National Consumer Cooperative Bank for a term of 3 years, vice David
George Nason, term expired.

Kathryn Keneally,
of New York, to be an Assistant Attorney General, vice Nathan J. Hochman, resigned.

Gregg Jeffrey Costa,
of Texas, to be U.S. District Judge for the
Southern District of Texas, vice John D. Rain-
ey, retired.

Stephanie Dawn Thacker,
of West Virginia, to be U.S. Circuit Judge for
the Fourth Circuit, vice M. Blane Michael, deceased.

Submitted September 14

Michael Anthony McFaul,
of California, to be Ambassador Extraordinary
and Plenipotentiary of the United States of
America to the Russian Federation.

David Campos Guaderrama,
of Texas, to be U.S. District Judge for the
Western District of Texas, vice David Briones,
retired.

Submitted September 15

Ronald Lee Buch,
of Virginia, to be a Judge of the U.S. Tax Court
for a term of 15 years, vice David Laro, term
expired.

Brad Carson,
of Oklahoma, to be General Counsel of the
Department of the Army, vice Benedict S. Cohen, resigned.

Alastair M. Fitzpayne,
of Maryland, to be a Deputy Under Secretary
of the Treasury, vice Kim N. Wallace.

Kevin A. Ohlson,
of Virginia, to be a Judge of the U.S. Court of
Appeals for the Armed Forces or the term of
15 years to expire on the date prescribed by
law, vice Andrew S. Effron, term expiring.

Submitted September 19

Ann Marie Buerkle,
of New York, to be a Representative of the
United States of America to the Sixty-sixth Session of the General Assembly of the United
Nations.

Russ Carnahan,
of Missouri, to be a Representative of the United States of America to the Sixty-sixth Session
of the General Assembly of the United Nations.

Submitted September 22

Michael A. Hughes,
of the District of Columbia, to be U.S. Marshal
for the Superior Court of the District of Columbia for the term of 4 years, vice Stephen
Thomas Conboy, resigned.

Jacqueline H. Nguyen,
of California, to be U.S. Circuit Judge for the
Ninth Circuit, vice a new position created by
Public Law 110–177, approved January 7,
2008.

Brian C. Wimes,
of Missouri, to be U.S. District Judge for the
Eastern and Western Districts of Missouri,
vice Nanette K. Laughrey, retired.

Submitted September 23

Maurice A. Jones,
of Virginia, to be Deputy Secretary of Housing
and Urban Development, vice Ronald C. Sims,
retired.

Matthew S. Rutherford,
of Illinois, to be an Assistant Secretary of the Treasury, vice Mary John Miller.

Submitted September 26

Gary Blumenthal,
of Massachusetts, to be a member of the National Council on Disability for a term expiring September 17, 2013 (reappointment).

Susan A. Maxman,
of Pennsylvania, to be a member of the Board of Directors of the National Institute of Building Sciences for a term expiring September 7, 2012, vice William Hardiman, term expired.

Susan A. Maxman,
of Pennsylvania, to be a member of the Board of Directors of the National Institute of Building Sciences for a term expiring September 7, 2015 (reappointment).

Submitted October 3

Earl W. Gast,
of California, to be an Assistant Administrator of the U.S. Agency for International Development, vice Katherine Almquist, resigned.

Roberta S. Jacobson,
of Maryland, a career member of the Senior Executive Service, to be an Assistant Secretary of State (Western Hemisphere Affairs), vice Arturo A. Valenzuela, resigned.

James T. Ryan,
of Utah, to be a member of the Board of Directors of the National Institute of Building Sciences for a term expiring September 7, 2013, vice James Broaddus, resigned.

Michael T. Scuse,
of Delaware, to be Under Secretary of Agriculture for Farm and Foreign Agricultural Services, vice James W. Miller, resigned.

Michael T. Scuse,
of Delaware, to be a member of the Board of Directors of the Commodity Credit Corporation, vice James W. Miller, resigned.

Withdrawn October 3

Terry D. Garcia,
of Florida, to be Deputy Secretary of Commerce, vice Dennis F. Hightower, resigned, which was sent to the Senate on May 16, 2011.

James T. Ryan,
of Utah, to be a member of the Board of Directors of the National Institute of Building Sciences for a term expiring September 7, 2013, vice James Broaddus, resigned, which was sent to the Senate on July 22, 2011.

Submitted October 5

Patty Shwartz,
of New Jersey, to be U.S. Circuit Judge for the Third Circuit, vice Maryanne Trump Barry, retired.

Submitted October 11

Adam Gamoran,
of Wisconsin, to be a member of the Board of Directors of the National Board for Education Sciences for a term expiring November 28, 2015 (reappointment).

Judith D. Singer,
of Massachusetts, to be a member of the Board of Directors of the National Board for Education Sciences for a term expiring November 28, 2014, vice Carol D'Amico, term expired.

James Timberlake,
of Pennsylvania, to be a member of the Board of Directors of the National Institute of Building Sciences for a term expiring September 7, 2014, vice Jose Teran, term expired.

Submitted October 12

Elizabeth M. Cousens,
of Washington, to be Representative of the United States of America on the Economic and Social Council of the United Nations, with the rank of Ambassador.

Elizabeth M. Cousens,
of Washington, to be an Alternate Representative of the United States of America to the Sessions of the General Assembly of the United Nations, during her tenure of service as Representative of the United States of America on the Economic and Social Council of the United Nations.

Paul W. Hodes,
of New Hampshire, to be a member of the National Council on the Arts for a term expiring September 3, 2016 (new position).

Robert L. Sumwalt III,
of South Carolina, to be a member of the National Transportation Safety Board for a term expiring December 31, 2016 (reappointment).

Submitted October 20

Bonnie L. Bassler,
of New Jersey, to be a member of the National Science Board, National Science Foundation for a term expiring May 10, 2016, vice Steven C. Beering, term expired.

David James Chard,
of Texas, to be a member of the Board of Directors of the National Board for Education Sciences for a term expiring November 28, 2015, vice Jonathan Baron, term expiring.

Carol J. Galante,
of Virginia, to be an Assistant Secretary of Housing and Urban Development, vice David H. Stevens, resigned.

Larry V. Hedges,
of Illinois, to be a member of the Board of Directors of the National Board for Education Sciences for a term expiring November 28, 2015, vice Frank Philip Handy, term expiring.

Thomas Hoenig,
of Missouri, to be Vice Chairperson of the Board of Directors of the Federal Deposit Insurance Corporation, vice Martin J. Gruenberg.

Thomas Hoenig,
of Missouri, to be a member of the Board of Directors of the Federal Deposit Insurance Corporation for a term expiring December 12, 2015, vice Thomas J. Curry, term expired.

Carla M. Leon-Decker,
of Virginia, to be a member of the National Credit Union Administration Board for a term expiring August 2, 2017, vice Gigi Hyland, term expired.

Mark William Lippert,
of Ohio, to be an Assistant Secretary of Defense, vice Wallace C. Gregson, resigned.

Hirokazu Yoshikawa,
of Massachusetts, to be a member of the Board of Directors of the National Board for Education Sciences for a term expiring November 28, 2015, vice Sally Epstein Shaywitz, term expiring.

Withdrawn October 31

Charles Bernard Day,
of Maryland, to be U.S. District Judge for the District of Maryland, vice Peter J. Messitte, retired, which was sent to the Senate on January 5, 2011.

Submitted November 1

Rebecca M. Blank,
of Maryland, to be Deputy Secretary of Commerce, vice Dennis F. Hightower, resigned.

Thomas Hoenig,
of Missouri, to be a member of the Board of Directors of the Federal Deposit Insurance Corporation for a term of 6 years, vice Thomas J. Curry, term expired.

Ajit Varadaraj Pai,
of Kansas, to be a member of the Federal Communications Commission for a term of 5

years from July 1, 2011, vice Meredith Attwell Baker, term expired.

Larry Leon Palmer,
of Georgia, a career member of the Senior Foreign Service, class of Minister-Counselor, to be Ambassador Extraordinary and Plenipotentiary of the United States of America to Barbados, and to serve concurrently and without additional compensation as Ambassador Extraordinary and Plenipotentiary of the United States of America to St. Kitts and Nevis, Saint Lucia, Antigua and Barbuda, the Commonwealth of Dominica, Grenada, and Saint Vincent and the Grenadines.

Coral Wong Pietsch,
of Hawaii, to be a Judge of the U.S. Court of Appeals for Veterans Claims for the term of 15 years, vice William P. Greene, Jr., retired.

Jessica Rosenworcel,
of Connecticut, to be a member of the Federal Communications Commission for a term of 5 years from July 1, 2010, vice Michael Joseph Copps, term expired.

Michael A. Sheehan,
of New Jersey, to be an Assistant Secretary of Defense, vice Michael G. Vickers.

Withdrawn November 1

Thomas Hoenig,
of Missouri, to be a member of the Board of Directors of the Federal Deposit Insurance Corporation for a term expiring December 12, 2015, vice Thomas J. Curry, term expired, which was sent to the Senate on October 20, 2011.

Submitted November 2

Kristine Gerhard Baker,
of Arkansas, to be U.S. District Judge for the Eastern District of Arkansas, vice James M. Moody, retired.

Andrew David Hurwitz,
of Arizona, to be U.S. Circuit Judge for the Ninth Circuit, vice Mary M. Schroeder, retiring.

Submitted November 8

Meredith M. Broadbent,
of Virginia, to be a member of the U.S. International Trade Commission for a term expiring June 16, 2017, vice Deanna Tanner Okun, term expired.

Anne Claire Richard,
of New York, to be an Assistant Secretary of State (Population, Refugees, and Migration), vice Eric P. Schwartz, resigned.

Tara D. Sonenshine,
of Maryland, to be Under Secretary of State for Public Diplomacy, vice Judith A. McHale.

Submitted November 10

Gonzalo P. Curiel,
of California, to be U.S. District Judge for the Southern District of California, vice Thomas J. Whelan, retired.

John Z. Lee,
of Illinois, to be U.S. District Judge for the Northern District of Illinois, vice David H. Coar, retired.

William B. Pollard III,
of New York, to be a Judge of the U.S. Court of Military Commission Review (new position).

George Levi Russell III,
of Maryland, to be U.S. District Judge for the District of Maryland, vice Peter J. Messitte, retired.

Scott L. Silliman,
of North Carolina, to be a Judge of the U.S. Court of Military Commission Review (new position).

Richard Gary Taranto,
of Maryland, to be U.S. Circuit Judge for the Federal Circuit, vice Paul R. Michel, retired.

John J. Tharp, Jr.,
of Illinois, to be U.S. District Judge for the Northern District of Illinois, vice Blanche M. Manning, retired.

Withdrawn November 10

Edward Carroll DuMont,
of the District of Columbia, to be U.S. Circuit Judge for the Federal Circuit, vice Paul R. Michel, retired, which was sent to the Senate on January 5, 2011.

Submitted November 15

Deborah J. Jeffrey,
of the District of Columbia, to be Inspector General, Corporation for National and Community Service, vice Gerald Walpin.

Mark J. Mazur,
of New Jersey, to be an Assistant Secretary of the Treasury, vice Michael F. Mundaca, resigned.

Submitted November 17

Gershwin A. Drain,
of Michigan, to be U.S. District Judge for the Eastern District of Michigan, vice Bernard A. Friedman, retired.

Roy Wallace McLeese III,
of the District of Columbia, to be an Associate Judge of the District of Columbia Court of Appeals for the term of 15 years, vice Vanessa Ruiz, retired.

Submitted November 18

Sara A. Gelser,
of Oregon, to be a member of the National Council on Disability for a term expiring September 17, 2014 (reappointment).

Margaret Ann Sherry,
of Virginia, to be Chief Financial Officer, Department of Homeland Security, vice David L. Norquist, resigned.

Submitted December 1

Marilyn B. Tavenner,
of Virginia, to be Administrator of the Centers for Medicare and Medicaid Services, vice Donald M. Berwick, resigned.

Withdrawn December 1

Donald M. Berwick,
of Massachusetts, to be Administrator of the Centers for Medicare and Medicaid Services, vice Mark B. McClellan, which was sent to the Senate on January 26, 2011.

Submitted December 5

Jonathan Don Farrar,
of California, a career member of the Senior Foreign Service, class of Minister-Counselor, to be Ambassador Extraordinary and Plenipotentiary of the United States of America to the Republic of Panama.

Tony Hammond,
of Missouri, to be a Commissioner of the Postal Regulatory Commission for the remainder of the term expiring October 14, 2012, vice Dan Gregory Blair, resigned.

Joseph E. Macmanus,
of New York, a career member of the Senior Foreign Service, class of Minister-Counselor, to be Representative of the United States of America to the Vienna Office of the United Nations, with the rank of Ambassador.

Joseph E. Macmanus,
of New York, a career member of the Senior Foreign Service, class of Minister-Counselor, to be Representative of the United States of America to the International Atomic Energy Agency, with the rank of Ambassador.

Pauline R. Maier,
of Massachusetts, to be a member of the Board of Trustees of the James Madison Memorial Fellowship Foundation for a term expiring November 17, 2017, vice J. C. A. Stagg, term expired.

Phyllis Marie Powers,
of Virginia, a career member of the Senior Foreign Service, class of Minister-Counselor, to be Ambassador Extraordinary and Plenipotentiary of the United States of America to the Republic of Nicaragua.

Mark A. Robbins,
of California, to be a member of the Merit Systems Protection Board for the term of 7 years expiring March 1, 2018, vice Mary M. Rose, term expired.

William E. Todd,
of Virginia, a career member of the Senior Executive Service, to be Ambassador Extraordinary and Plenipotentiary of the United States of America to the Kingdom of Cambodia.

Withdrawn December 5

Jonathan Don Farrar,
of California, a career member of the Senior Foreign Service, class of Minister-Counselor, to be Ambassador Extraordinary and Plenipotentiary of the United States of America to the Republic of Nicaragua, which was sent to the Senate on April 14, 2011.

Submitted December 15

Sharon Block,
of the District of Columbia, to be a member of the National Labor Relations Board for the term of 5 years expiring December 16, 2014, vice Craig Becker.

Rachel L. Brand,
of Iowa, to be a member of the Privacy and Civil Liberties Oversight Board for a term expiring January 29, 2017 (new position).

Richard F. Griffin, Jr.,
of the District of Columbia, to be a member of the National Labor Relations Board for the term of 5 years expiring August 27, 2016, vice Wilma B. Liebman, term expired.

David Medine,
of Maryland, to be Chairman and member of the Privacy and Civil Liberties Oversight Board for a term expiring January 29, 2012 (new position).

David Medine,
of Maryland, to be Chairman and member of the Privacy and Civil Liberties Oversight

Board for a term expiring January 29, 2018 (reappointment).

Michael A. Raynor,
of Maryland, a career member of the Senior Foreign Service, class of Counselor, to be Ambassador Extraordinary and Plenipotentiary of the United States of America to the Republic of Benin.

Patricia M. Wald,
of the District of Columbia, to be a member of the Privacy and Civil Liberties Oversight Board for a term expiring January 29, 2013 (new position).

Jacob Walles,
of Delaware, a career member of the Senior Foreign Service, class of Minister-Counselor, to be Ambassador Extraordinary and Plenipotentiary of the United States of America to the Tunisian Republic.

Withdrawn December 15

Craig Becker,
of Illinois, to be a member of the National Labor Relations Board for the term of 5 years expiring December 16, 2014, vice Dennis P. Walsh, which was sent to the Senate on January 26, 2011.

Submitted December 16

Richard B. Berner,
of Massachusetts, to be Director, Office of Financial Research, Department of the Treasury, for a term of 6 years (new position).

John Thomas Fowlkes, Jr.,
of Tennessee, to be U.S. District Judge for the Western District of Tennessee, vice Bernice B. Donald, elevated.

Kevin McNulty,
of New Jersey, to be U.S. District Judge for the District of New Jersey, vice Garrett E. Brown, Jr., retiring.

Nancy J. Powell,
of Iowa, a career member of the Senior Foreign Service, personal rank of Career Ambassador, to be Ambassador Extraordinary and Plenipotentiary of the United States of America to India.

Withdrawn December 16

Richard Sorian,
of New York, to be an Assistant Secretary of Health and Human Services, vice Christina H. Pearson, resigned, which was sent to the Senate on January 26, 2011.

Appendix C—Checklist of White House Press Releases

The following list contains releases of the Office of the Press Secretary that are neither printed items nor covered by entries in the Digest of Other White House Announcements.

Released July 1

Statement by the Press Secretary: Council of Economic Advisers Releases Seventh Quarterly Report on the Economic Impact of the Recovery Act

Released July 2

Statement by the Press Secretary on the situation in Bahrain

Released July 5

Transcript of a press briefing by Press Secretary James F. "Jay" Carney

Released July 7

Transcript of a press briefing by Press Secretary James F. "Jay" Carney

Released July 8

Transcript of a press briefing by Press Secretary James F. "Jay" Carney

Text: Statement by Council of Economic Advisers Chairman Austan D. Goolsbee on the employment situation in June

Released July 9

Text: Statement by White House Communications Director H. Daniel Pfeiffer on Federal budget negotiations

Released July 10

Statement by the Press Secretary on Assistant to the President for Homeland Security and Counterterrorism John O. Brennan's meeting with President Ali Abdallah Salih of Yemen

Released July 11

Statement by the Press Secretary: Obama Administration Launches *Strong Cities, Strong Communities* To Support Local Development

Text: Statement by Office of Management and Budget Office of Information and Regulatory Affairs Administrator Cass R. Sunstein: The President's Executive Order on Improving and Streamlining Regulation by Independent Regulatory Agencies

Released July 12

Transcript of a press briefing by Press Secretary James F. "Jay" Carney

Released July 13

Transcript of a press briefing by Press Secretary James F. "Jay" Carney

Released July 14

Transcript of a press briefing by Press Secretary James F. "Jay" Carney

Released July 18

Transcript of a press briefing by Press Secretary James F. "Jay" Carney

Released July 19

Transcript of a press briefing by Press Secretary James F. "Jay" Carney

Statement by the Press Secretary: White House Chief of Staff Daley Highlights Priority for the President's Export Control Reform Initiative

Released July 20

Transcript of a press briefing by Press Secretary James F. "Jay" Carney

Statement by the Press Secretary: White House Announces Plans To Shut Down Hundreds of Duplicative Data Centers as Part of Campaign To Cut Waste

Statement by the Press Secretary on the arrest of Goran Hadzic by the International Criminal Tribunal for the former Yugoslavia (ICTY)

Released July 21

Transcript of a press briefing by Press Secretary James F. "Jay" Carney

Released July 22

Text: Certification and transmittal letters concerning the repeal of the Department of Defense's "don't ask, don't tell" policy

Released July 23

Statement by the Press Secretary on Federal budget negotiations

Released July 25

Statement by the Press Secretary on Federal budget negotiations

Fact sheet: Strategy To Combat Transnational Organized Crime

Text: Strategy To Combat Transnational Organized Crime: Addressing Converging Threats to National Security

Text: Statement by White House Communications Director H. Daniel Pfeiffer: Some Republicans in Congress Once Argued Against Short-Term Solutions—They Were Right

Advance text of the President's remarks on the Federal budget

Transcript of remarks by senior administration officials on the strategy to combat transnational organized crime

Released July 26

Transcript of a press briefing by Press Secretary James F. "Jay" Carney

Statement by the Press Secretary: On Anniversary of the Americans with Disabilities Act, Obama Administration Recommits To Enforcing and Protecting the Civil Rights of All

Statement by the Press Secretary announcing that the President signed S. 1103

Released July 27

Transcript of a press briefing by Press Secretary James F. "Jay" Carney

Statement by the Press Secretary announcing that the President will hold an event on the na-

tional program to improve fuel efficiency on cars and light-duty trucks for model years 2017–2025

Released July 28

Transcript of a press briefing by Press Secretary James F. "Jay" Carney and Secretary of Transportation Raymond H. LaHood

Statement by the Press Secretary: White House Launches Government Accountability and Transparency Board To Cut Waste and Boost Accountability

Released July 29

Transcript of a press briefing by Press Secretary James F. "Jay" Carney

Statement by the Press Secretary: President Obama Announces Historic 54.5 mpg Fuel Efficiency Standard

Statement by the Press Secretary on Federal budget negotiations

Text: Statement by Council of Economic Advisers Chairman Austan D. Goolsbee on the advance estimate of GDP for the second quarter of 2011 and annual revision

Released July 31

Fact sheet: Bipartisan Debt Deal: A Win for the Economy and Budget Discipline

Released August 1

Transcript of a press briefing by Press Secretary James F. "Jay" Carney

Released August 2

Transcript of a press briefing by Press Secretary James F. "Jay" Carney

Statement by the Press Secretary announcing that the President signed S. 365

Released August 3

Transcript of a press briefing by Press Secretary James F. "Jay" Carney and Secretary of Transportation Raymond H. LaHood

Statement by the Press Secretary announcing that the President signed H.R. 1383

Text: Empowering Local Partners To Prevent Violent Extremism in the United States

Released August 4

Transcript of a press briefing by Press Secretary James F. "Jay" Carney

Fact sheet: President Obama Directs New Steps To Prevent Mass Atrocities and Impose Consequences on Serious Human Rights Violators

Released August 5

Statement by the Press Secretary: President Obama To Participate in White House Rural Economic Forum at Northeast Iowa Community College in Peosta, Iowa

Statement by the Press Secretary announcing that the President signed H.R. 2553

Text: Statement by Council of Economic Advisers Chairman Austan D. Goolsbee on the employment situation in July

Text: Statement by National Security Council Spokesman Thomas F. Vietor on Cuba's detention of Alan Gross

Fact sheet: President Obama's Commitment to Employing America's Veterans

Released August 6

Statement by the Press Secretary on bipartisan efforts to strengthen the national economy

Released August 8

Transcript of a press briefing by Press Secretary James F. "Jay" Carney, White House Domestic Policy Council Director Melody C. Barnes, and Secretary of Education Arne Duncan

Statement by the Press Secretary on additional funding for famine and humanitarian assistance to Africa

Released August 9

Statement by the Press Secretary: White House Announces First Ever Oil Savings Standards for Heavy Duty Trucks, Buses

Statement by the Press Secretary: White House Announces Ron Bloom To Step Down From His Position as Assistant to the President for Manufacturing Policy

Released August 10

Transcript of a press briefing by Press Secretary James F. "Jay" Carney

Released August 11

Transcript of a press gaggle by Press Secretary James F. "Jay" Carney

Fact sheet: Fueling American Innovation (dated August 10)

Released August 12

Transcript of a press gaggle by Principal Deputy Press Secretary Joshua R. Earnest

Statement by the Press Secretary: White House Rural Council Delivers Report on Rural America

Statement by the Press Secretary announcing that the President signed H.R. 2715

Text: Statement by National Security Council Spokesman Thomas F. Vietor on U.S.-Brazil Strategic Energy Dialogue Launch

Released August 15

Transcript of a press gaggle by Press Secretary James F. "Jay" Carney

Released August 16

Transcript of a press gaggle by Press Secretary James F. "Jay" Carney

Statement by the Press Secretary: President Announces New Jobs Initiatives for Rural America (dated August 15; embargoed until August 16)

Text: Statement by the Office of Communications: President Obama Announces Major Initiative To Spur Biofuels Industry and Enhance America's Energy Security

Released August 18

Transcript of a press gaggle by Principal Deputy Press Secretary Joshua R. Earnest

Transcript of a press briefing by senior administration officials on the situation in Syria

Statement by the Press Secretary on the terrorist attack in southern Israel

Fact sheet: Administration Steps To Pressure Syrian Regime and Support Universal Rights of the Syrian People

Released August 19

Statement by the Press Secretary on World Humanitarian Day

Released August 22

Transcript of a press gaggle by Principal Deputy Press Secretary Joshua R. Earnest

Released August 24

Transcript of a press briefing by Principal Deputy Press Secretary Joshua R. Earnest

Released August 26

Transcript of a press gaggle by Principal Deputy Press Secretary Joshua R. Earnest

Released August 29

Transcript of a press briefing by Press Secretary James F. "Jay" Carney and Federal Emergency Management Agency Administrator W. Craig Fugate

Released August 30

Transcript of a press gaggle by Press Secretary James F. "Jay" Carney

Advance text of the President's remarks at the American Legion National Convention in Minneapolis, MN

Released August 31

Transcript of a press briefing by Press Secretary James F. "Jay" Carney

Statement by the Press Secretary: President's Council on Jobs and Competitiveness Announces Industry Leaders' Commitment To Double Engineering Internships in 2012

Statement by the Press Secretary: White House Announces Steps To Expedite High Impact Infrastructure Projects To Create Jobs

Statement by the Press Secretary on the President's address to a joint session of the Congress

Text: Letter from the U.S. Conference of Mayors on the surface transportation bill and the Federal Aviation Administration reauthorization

Released September 1

Transcript of a press briefing by Press Secretary James F. "Jay" Carney

Statement by the Press Secretary: White House Announces *We the People*

Statement by the Press Secretary on the President's acceptance of an invitation to address a joint session of the Congress on September 8

Released September 2

Text: Statement by Council of Economic Advisers member Katherine G. Abraham regarding the August employment situation

Text: Statement by Deputy Assistant to the President for Energy and Climate Change Heather Zichal regarding the steps the Obama administration has taken to reduce harmful air pollution while promoting the Nation's economic growth and well-being

Text: Letter from White House Office of Information and Regulatory Affairs Administrator Cass Sunstein to Environmental Protection Agency Administrator Lisa P. Jackson regarding the ozone national ambient air quality standards

Released September 4

Transcript of a press gaggle by Press Secretary James F. "Jay" Carney

Released September 5

Transcript of a press gaggle by Principal Deputy Press Secretary Joshua R. Earnest

Released September 6

Transcript of a press briefing by Press Secretary James F. "Jay" Carney

Released September 7

Transcript of a press briefing by Press Secretary James F. "Jay" Carney

Text: Op-ed piece by the President for USA Today: Let's Reclaim the Post-9/11 Unity

Released September 8

Text: Statements by members of the President's Council on Jobs and Competitiveness in support of the "American Jobs Act"

Fact sheet: The American Jobs Act

Excerpts of the President's address to a joint session of the Congress on the "American Jobs Act"

Advance text of the President's address to a joint session of the Congress

Text: Guest list for the First Lady's Box at the address to a joint session of the Congress

Released September 9

Transcript of a press gaggle by Press Secretary James F. "Jay" Carney

Text: Statement by National Security Council Spokesman Thomas F. Vietor on the credentialing of Libya's Ambassador to the U.S.

Released September 11

Transcript of a press gaggle by Principal Deputy Press Secretary Joshua R. Earnest

Advance text of the President's remarks at "A Concert for Hope" commemorating the 10th anniversary of the September 11 terrorist attacks

Released September 12

Transcript of a press briefing by Press Secretary James F. "Jay" Carney and Office of Management and Budget Director Jacob J. "Jack" Lew

Text: Section-by-section analysis and explanation of the "American Jobs Act of 2011"

Text: Full text of the "American Jobs Act of 2011"

Fact sheet: Repairing and Modernizing America's Schools (embargoed until September 13)

Released September 13

Transcript of a press gaggle by Press Secretary James F. "Jay" Carney

Fact sheet: The American Jobs Act: Impact for Montana

Released September 14

Transcript of a press gaggle by Press Secretary James F. "Jay" Carney

Released September 15

Transcript of a press briefing by Press Secretary James F. "Jay" Carney

Statement by the Press Secretary on the "American Jobs Act"

Text: Remarks by the First Lady at a "Let's Move!" initiative restaurant announcement in Hyattsville, MD

Fact sheet: Implementing Missile Defense in Europe

Released September 16

Transcript of a press gaggle by Press Secretary James F. "Jay" Carney and Deputy National Security Adviser for Strategic Communications Benjamin J. Rhodes on the 66th Session of the United Nations General Assembly

Statement by the Press Secretary: White House To Launch "Digital Promise" Initiative

Statement by the Press Secretary: President Obama Signs America Invents Act, Overhauling the Patent System To Stimulate Economic Growth, and Announces New Steps To Help Entrepreneurs Create Jobs

Statement by the Press Secretary announcing that the President signed H.R. 2887

Text: Remarks by Assistant to the President for Homeland Security and Counterterrorism John O. Brennan at Harvard Law School's "Law, Security & Liberty After 9/11: Looking to the Future" conference in Cambridge, MA

Released September 19

Transcript of a press briefing by Press Secretary James F. "Jay" Carney, Secretary of the Treasury Timothy F. Geithner, and Office of Management and Budget Director Jacob J. "Jack" Lew

Transcript of a press gaggle by Press Secretary James F. "Jay" Carney and Deputy National Security Adviser for Strategic Communications Benjamin J. Rhodes

Text: Living Within Our Means and Investing in the Future: The President's Plan for Economic Growth and Deficit Reduction

Fact sheet: Living Within Our Means and Investing in the Future—The President's Plan for Economic Growth and Deficit Reduction

Released September 20

Fact sheet: Advancing U.S. Interests at the United Nations

Fact sheet: The Open Government Partnership

Advance text of the President's remarks at a U.N. meeting on Libya in New York City

Advance text of the President's remarks at an Open Government Partnership event in New York City

Released September 21

Fact sheet: The United States Commitment to Breaking Down Barriers to Women's Economic and Political Participation

Advance text of the President's remarks to the U.N. General Assembly in New York City

Released September 22

Transcript of a press briefing by Press Secretary James F. "Jay" Carney and Deputy National Security Adviser for Strategic Communications Benjamin J. Rhodes

Transcript of a press gaggle by Press Secretary James F. "Jay" Carney

Statement by the Press Secretary: Obama Administration Sets High Bar for Flexibility for No Child Behind in Order To Advance Equity and Support Reform (embargoed until September 23)

Statement by the Press Secretary on the 10th anniversary of the World Conference Against Racism in Durban, South Africa

Fact sheet: Global Health Security

Advance text of the President's remarks at Hilltop Resources, Inc., in Cincinnati, OH

Released September 23

Statement by the Press Secretary announcing that the President signed S. 846

Released September 26

Transcript of a press gaggle by Press Secretary James F. "Jay" Carney

Statement by the Press Secretary: The White House and National Science Foundation Announce New Workplace Flexibility Policies To Support America's Scientists and Their Families

Statement by the Press Secretary: President Obama Honors Outstanding Early-Career Scientists

Released September 27

Transcript of a press gaggle by Press Secretary James F. "Jay" Carney

Statement by the Press Secretary: President Obama Honors Nation's Top Scientists and Innovators

Fact sheet: Repairing and Modernizing America's Schools

Advance text of the President's remarks at Abraham Lincoln High School in Denver, CO

Advance text of the President's remarks at Benjamin Banneker Academic High School

Released September 28

Transcript of a press briefing by Press Secretary James F. "Jay" Carney

Released September 29

Transcript of a press briefing by Press Secretary James F. "Jay" Carney

Statement by the Press Secretary on the conviction of Pastor Youcef Nadarkhani in Iran

Released September 30

Transcript of a press briefing by Press Secretary James F. "Jay" Carney

Statement by the Press Secretary announcing that the President signed H.R. 2005, H.R. 2017, H.R. 2883, and H.R. 2943

Released October 3

Transcript of a press briefing by Press Secretary James F. "Jay" Carney

Released October 4

Transcripts of press gaggles by Press Secretary James F. "Jay" Carney

Statement by the Press Secretary on the terrorist attack in Mogadishu, Somalia

Fact sheet: American Jobs Act Supports Nearly 400,000 Education Jobs

Excerpts of the President's remarks at Eastfield College in Mesquite, TX

Released October 5

Transcript of a press briefing by Press Secretary James F. "Jay" Carney

Statement by the Press Secretary announcing that the President signed H.R. 2608

Statement by the Press Secretary announcing that the President signed H.R. 2646

Released October 6

Statement by the Press Secretary: President Obama Announces the Creation of a Presidential Emergency Board, Names Members

Released October 7

Transcript of a press briefing by Press Secretary James F. "Jay" Carney

Statement by the Press Secretary on the situation in Syria

Text: Statement by Council of Economic Advisers member Katherine G. Abraham regarding the September employment situation

Fact sheet: Safeguarding the U.S. Government's Classified Information and Networks

Fact sheet: The President's Framework for Investing in Tunisia

Released October 10

Statement by the Press Secretary on the situation in Egypt

Released October 11

Transcript of a press gaggle by Principal Deputy Press Secretary Joshua R. Earnest

Statement by the Press Secretary: Obama Administration Announces Selection of 14 Infrastructure Projects To Be Expedited Through Permitting and Environmental Review Process

Statement by the Press Secretary on the conviction in Ukraine of former Prime Minister Yuliya Tymoshenko of Ukraine

Text: Letter From Democratic Governors to Congressional Leadership on the American Jobs Act

Text: Letter From Florida Mayors Urging Congress To Pass American Jobs Act

Released October 12

Transcript of a press briefing by Press Secretary James F. "Jay" Carney

Statement by the Press Secretary: President Obama Honors Recipients of the 2011 Citizens Medal

Released October 13

Statement by the Press Secretary announcing that the President signed H.R. 771 and H.R. 1632

Released October 14

Transcript of a press gaggle by Press Secretary James F. "Jay" Carney

Text: "Creating Pathways to Opportunity" report highlighting efforts to help underserved communities and strengthen the middle class

Text: Op-ed by United Auto Workers President Bob King for the Detroit Free Press: UAW Backs Korea Trade Agreement

Fact sheet: Creating Pathways to Opportunity

Released October 15

Statement by the Press Secretary on the death of Laura Pollan

Released October 17

Transcript of a press gaggle by Press Secretary James F. "Jay" Carney

Released October 18

Transcript of a press gaggle by Press Secretary James F. "Jay" Carney

Text: Statement by National Security Council Spokesman Thomas F. Vietor on the United Kingdom's announcement of sanctions against individuals presumed to have connections to the assassination attempt on Saudi Arabia's Ambassador to the U.S.

Released October 19

Transcript of a press gaggle by Press Secretary James F. "Jay" Carney

Statement by the Press Secretary: First Lady Michelle Obama Announces Major Private Sector Commitment To Hire 25,000 Veterans and Military Spouses in Support of Joining Forces

Released October 20

Transcript of a press briefing by Press Secretary James F. "Jay" Carney

Statement by the Press Secretary: White House To Eliminate $3.5 Billion in Wasteful Federal Real Estate Costs

Fact sheet: The United States and Norway—NATO Allies and Global Partners

Released October 21

Transcript of a press briefing by Press Secretary James F. "Jay" Carney, Deputy National Security Adviser Denis R. McDonough, and National Security Adviser to the Vice President Antony J. Blinken

Statement by the Press Secretary: President Obama Presents the National Medals of Science & National Medals of Technology and Innovation, and Announces Additional Steps To Help Bring More Cutting-Edge Ideas to Market

Statement by the Press Secretary on the passage of U.N. Security Council Resolution 2014

Statements by the Press Secretary announcing that the President signed H.R. 2832, H.R. 2944, H.R. 3080, H.R. 3078, and H.R. 3079

Text: Op-ed piece by National Economic Council Director Eugene B. Sperling for the

Wall Street Journal: The Case for the President's Jobs Act

Text: Statement by National Security Council Spokesman Thomas F. Vietor on the ETA terrorist organization's announcement renouncing the use of violence in Spain

Released October 24

Transcript of a press gaggle by Press Secretary James F. "Jay" Carney

Advance text of the President's remarks in Las Vegas, NV

Released October 25

Transcript of a press gaggle by Press Secretary James F. "Jay" Carney

Statement by the Press Secretary: White House Announces Secretary Ken Salazar as Administration's Senior Official Responsible for Oversight of Implementation of Extractive Industries Transparency Initiative

Fact sheet: We Can't Wait: Obama Administration's New Initiatives To Help Create Jobs for Veterans

Fact sheet: We Can't Wait: Obama Administration To Lower Student Loan Payments for Millions of Borrowers

Fact sheet: Help Americans Manage Student Loan Debt

Released October 26

Transcript of a press gaggle by Press Secretary James F. "Jay" Carney

Released October 27

Transcript of a press briefing by Press Secretary James F. "Jay" Carney

Text: Statement by Council of Economic Advisers member Katharine Abraham on the GDP for the third quarter of 2011

Fact sheet: The United States and the Czech Republic—NATO Allies and Partners in Prosperity and Democracy

Fact sheet: The United States and Czech Republic: Civil Nuclear Cooperation

Released October 28

Transcript of a press briefing by Press Secretary James F. "Jay" Carney

Statement by the Press Secretary on the North American Leaders' Summit

Text: Op-ed piece by the President for the Financial Times: A Firewall To Stop Europe's Crisis Spreading

Fact sheet: We Can't Wait: Obama Administration Announces Two Steps To Help Businesses Create Jobs, Strengthen Competitiveness

Released October 29

Statement by the Press Secretary on the meeting between Iraqi National Security Adviser Falah al-Fayyadh and National Security Adviser Thomas E. Donilon

Released October 31

Transcript of a press gaggle by Press Secretary James F. "Jay" Carney, Deputy National Security Adviser for International Economic Affairs Michael B. Froman, Deputy National Security Adviser for Strategic Communications Benjamin J. Rhodes, and Treasury Undersecretary for International Affairs Lael Brainard on the President's visit to Cannes, France, for the G–20 summit

Statement by the Press Secretary on the U.S.-EU summit

Fact sheet: We Can't Wait: Obama Administration Takes Action To Reduce Prescription Drug Shortages, Fight Price Gouging

Text: Release of the President's Medical Exam

Released November 1

Transcript of a press briefing by Press Secretary James F. "Jay" Carney

Statement by the Press Secretary: President Obama To Sign Proclamation Designating Fort Monroe a National Monument

Released November 2

Transcript of a press briefing by Press Secretary James F. "Jay" Carney

Statement by the Press Secretary: President Obama Urges Congress To Put Construction Workers Back on the Job

Statement by the Press Secretary: White House Launches 2011 Campus "Champions of Change" Challenge

Released November 3

Transcript of a press briefing by Press Secretary James F. "Jay" Carney, Deputy National Security Adviser for Strategic Communications Benjamin J. Rhodes, and Deputy National Security Adviser for International Economic Affairs Michael B. Froman

Transcript of a press briefing by Press Secretary James F. "Jay" Carney, Treasury Undersecretary for International Affairs Lael Brainard, and Deputy National Security Adviser for Strategic Communications Benjamin J. Rhodes on the G–20 meetings

Released November 4

Text: The Cannes Action Plan for Growth and Jobs

Text: Cannes Summit Final Declaration

Text: Cannes G–20 Communique

Text: Statement by Council of Economic Advisers Chairman Alan B. Krueger regarding the October employment situation

Fact sheet: G–20: Common Global Challenges

Fact sheet: G–20: Cannes Action Plan for Growth and Jobs

Fact sheet: G–20: U.S. Financial Reform and the G–20 Leaders' Agenda

Released November 5

Transcript of a weekly address by Vice President Joe Biden (dated November 4; embargoed until November 5)

Released November 7

Transcript of a press briefing by Press Secretary James F. "Jay" Carney

Statement by the Press Secretary: We Can't Wait: Leading Veterans Organizations Back Returning Heroes, Wounded Warrior Tax

Credits; President Obama Announces Initiatives To Get Veterans Back to Work

Statement by the Press Secretary announcing that the President signed H.R. 489, H.R. 765, H.R. 1843, H.R. 1975, H.R. 2062, and H.R. 2149

Released November 8

Transcript of a press gaggle by Press Secretary James F. "Jay" Carney

Statement by the Press Secretary: We Can't Wait: President Obama Takes Action To Improve and Promote Accountability in Head Start Programs

Released November 9

Transcript of a press briefing by Press Secretary James F. "Jay" Carney, Deputy National Security Adviser for Strategic Communications Benjamin J. Rhodes, and National Security Council Senior Director for Asian Affairs Daniel R. Russel on the President's visit to Hawaii, Australia, and Indonesia

Statement by the Press Secretary: We Can't Wait: President Obama To Sign Executive Order To Cut Waste and Promote Efficient Spending and White House To Announce 2011 SAVE Award Finalists

Statement by the Press Secretary announcing that the President signed H.R. 368, H.R. 818, and S. 894

Fact sheet: The President's Agenda and the African American Community

Advance text of the President's remarks at the National Women's Law Center annual awards dinner

Released November 10

Transcript of a press briefing by James F. "Jay" Carney

Statement by the Press Secretary on the bombings in South Sudan

Released November 11

Transcript of a press gaggle by Press Secretary James F. "Jay" Carney and Deputy National Security Adviser for Strategic Communications Benjamin J. Rhodes

Transcript of a press gaggle by Deputy National Security Adviser for Strategic Communications Benjamin J. Rhodes on the President's meeting with President Felipe de Jesus Calderon Hinojosa of Mexico

Released November 12

Transcript of a press briefing by Press Secretary James F. "Jay" Carney, Deputy National Security Adviser for Strategic Communications Benjamin J. Rhodes, Deputy National Security Adviser for International Economic Affairs Michael B. Froman, and National Security Council Senior Director for Asia Daniel R. Russel

Transcript of a press briefing by Principal Deputy Press Secretary Joshua R. Earnest, William C. Weldon, chief executive officer, Johnson & Johnson, Inc., Richard P. Lavin, group president, Caterpillar, Inc., and Eric E. Schmidt, executive chairman, Google, Inc.

Transcript of a press gaggle by Deputy National Security Adviser for International Economic Affairs Michael B. Froman

Statement by the Press Secretary announcing that the President has signed S. 1487

Fact sheet: The United States in the Trans-Pacific Partnership

Fact sheet: APEC on Travel Facilitation

Released November 13

Transcript of a press briefing by Deputy National Security Adviser for Strategic Communications Benjamin J. Rhodes and Adm. Robert F. Willard, USN, commander, U.S. Pacific Command

Fact sheet: 19th Annual APEC Leaders Meeting Outcomes: Creating Jobs, Growth, and Economic Opportunity with AELM Declaration & Annexes

Text of remarks by the First Lady at the Asia-Pacific Economic Cooperation summit spouses luncheon in Ka'a'awa, HI

Text of remarks by the First Lady during a roundtable with members of MA'O Organic Farms in Wai'anae, HI

Released November 14

Transcript of a press briefing by Principal Deputy Press Secretary Joshua R. Earnest

Statement by the Press Secretary: White House Forum on Nonprofit Leadership

Text: Statement by White House Communications Director H. Daniel Pfeiffer on the Supreme Court and the Patient Protection and Affordable Care Act

Text of remarks by the First Lady at a jobs fair at Joint Base Pearl Harbor-Hickman, HI

Released November 15

Transcript of a press gaggle by Press Secretary James F. "Jay" Carney and Deputy National Security Adviser for Strategic Communications Benjamin J. Rhodes

Statement by the Press Secretary: We Can't Wait: Agencies Cut Nearly $18 Billion in Improper Payments, Announce New Steps for Stopping Government Waste

Statement by the Press Secretary: President Obama Honors Outstanding Science, Math, and Engineering Mentors

Released November 16

Transcript of a press briefing by James F. "Jay" Carney, Deputy National Security Adviser for Strategic Communications Benjamin J. Rhodes, and National Security Council Senior Director for Asia Daniel R. Russel

Statement by the Press Secretary: We Can't Wait: Obama Administration Proposes Historic Fuel Economy Standards To Reduce Dependence on Oil, Save Consumers Money at the Pump

Text: Statement by Assistant Press Secretary for National Security and Defense Tanya Bradsher: Prime Minister Gillard and President Obama Announce Force Posture Initiative

Text: Memorandum of Understanding between the Government of the United States of America and the Government of Australia on Enhancing Cooperation in Preventing and Combating Crime

Text: Statement on Memorandum of Understanding on Combating Crime

Text: Statement on Clean Energy Cooperation

Text: Statement on Education Cooperation

Text: Statement on Development Cooperation

Fact sheet: New Australia-United States Cooperation

Released November 17

Fact sheet: U.S. Exports Promotion and the Asia-Pacific

Excepts of the President's address to Parliament in Canberra, Australia

Released November 18

Transcript of a press briefing by senior administration officials on Burma

Statement by the Press Secretary on the International Atomic Energy Agency Board of Governors' passage of a resolution against Iran

Statement by the Press Secretary on the United Nations General Assembly's resolution condemning the Iranian-backed plot to assassinate Saudi Arabia's Ambassador to the U.S. Adil al-Ahmad al-Jubayr

Statement by the Press Secretary announcing that the President has signed H.R. 2112

Fact sheet: Expansion of the Peace Corps Indonesia Program

Fact sheet: United States-Indonesia Comprehensive Partnership

Fact sheet: U.S.-Indonesia Education Partnership

Fact sheet: Excess Defense Article (EDA) F-16 Refurbishment

Released November 19

Transcript of a press briefing by Press Secretary James F. "Jay" Carney, National Security Adviser Thomas E. Donilon, and Deputy National Security Adviser for Strategic Communications Benjamin J. Rhodes

Transcript a briefing by a senior administration official on the President's meetings at the ASEAN Summit and East Asia Summit

Statement by the Press Secretary: President Obama To Sign Legislation Providing Tax Credits To Help Put Veterans Back to Work

Statement by the Press Secretary on Ukrainian Holodomor Remembrance Day

Fact sheet: East Asia Summit

Released November 20

Fact sheet: ASEAN-United States Leaders Meeting

Released November 21

Transcript of a press briefing by Press Secretary James F. "Jay" Carney

Statement by the Press Secretary: President Obama Grants Pardons and Commutation

Statement by the Press Secretary announcing that the President signed S. 1280

Fact sheet: U.S. Pressure and Sanctions Against Iran

Fact sheet: Returning Heroes and Wounded Warrior Tax Credits

Text of remarks by the First Lady at a country music student workshop

Released November 22

Transcript of a press gaggle by Press Secretary James F. "Jay" Carney

Advance text of remarks by National Security Adviser Thomas E. Donilon at the Brookings Institution

Released November 23

Statement by the Press Secretary on Bahrain

Statement by the Press Secretary announcing that the President signed H.R. 398, H.R. 2447, and S. 1412

Released November 25

Statement by the Press Secretary on the situation in Egypt

Released November 28

Transcript of a press briefing by Press Secretary James F. "Jay" Carney

Statement by the Press Secretary: We Can't Wait: President Signs Memorandum To Modernize Management of Government Records

Fact sheet: High-Level Working Group on Jobs and Growth

Released November 29

Transcript of a press briefing by Press Secretary James F. "Jay" Carney and Council of Economic Advisers Chairman Alan B. Krueger

Statement by the Press Secretary on the storming of the United Kingdom's Embassy in Tehran, Iran

Statement by the Press Secretary announcing that the President signed H.R. 3321 and S. 1637

Released November 30

Transcript of a press gaggle by Principal Deputy Press Secretary Joshua R. Earnest

Statement by the Press Secretary: Transatlantic Economic Council

Text: Statement by National Security Council Spokesman Thomas F. Vietor on Turkey's actions targeting Syria

Text: Transatlantic Economic Council: Joint Statement

Released December 1

Transcript of a press briefing by Press Secretary James F. "Jay" Carney

Statement by the Press Secretary on European Union actions targeting Iran and Syria

Statement by the Press Secretary: We Can't Wait: President Obama Announces Nearly $4 Billion Investment in Energy Upgrades to Public and Private Buildings (embargoed until December 2)

Fact sheet: The Beginning of the End of AIDS

Fact sheet: The United States' Relationship With the European Union: An Enduring Partnership

Advance text of the President's remarks at George Washington University

Released December 2

Transcript of a press briefing by Press Secretary James F. "Jay" Carney

Statement by the Press Secretary: President Obama Hosts 2011 White House Tribal Nations Conference

Text: 2011 White House Tribal Nations Conference Progress Report: Achieving a Brighter Future for Tribal Nations

Text: Statement by Council of Economic Advisers Chairman Alan B. Krueger regarding the November employment situation

Text: Statement by National Security Council Spokesman Thomas F. Vietor on actions by Russia's Government against the independent election monitoring organization Golos

Released December 4

Statement by the Press Secretary: White House Releases New Report on the Importance of a Consumer Financial Protection Bureau Director

Text: National Economic Council report: Improving Americans' Financial Security: The Importance of a CFPB Director

Released December 5

Transcript of a press briefing by Press Secretary James F. "Jay" Carney

Text: Statements on the departure of Assistant to the President and Special Adviser Philip M. Schiliro

Fact sheet: Seventh Review Conference of the Biological and Toxin Weapons Convention

Released December 6

Transcript of a press gaggle by Press Secretary James F. "Jay" Carney

Statement by the Press Secretary on U.S. Ambassador to Syria Robert S. Ford returning to Syria

Fact sheet: Working To Advance the Human Rights of Lesbian, Gay, Bisexual, and Transgender (LGBT) Persons Globally

Advance text of the President's remarks at Osawatomie High School in Osawatomie, KS

Released December 7

Transcript of a press gaggle by Press Secretary James F. "Jay" Carney and Deputy Secretary of the Treasury Neal S. Wolin

Statement by the Press Secretary on the Iranian Government's blockage of the web-based, virtual U.S. Embassy in Tehran

Statement by the Press Secretary announcing that the President signed H.R. 394

Fact sheet: U.S.-Canada Beyond the Border and Regulatory Cooperation Council Initiatives

Released December 8

Transcript of a press briefing by Press Secretary James F. "Jay" Carney

Statement by the Press Secretary: We Can't Wait: Obama Administration Announces $2 Billion in Resources To Support Job-Creating Startups

Text: Strategic Implementation Plan for Empowering Local Partners To Prevent Violent Extremism in the United States

Released December 9

Transcript of a press briefing by Press Secretary James F. "Jay" Carney

Released December 12

Transcript of a press gaggle by Press Secretary James F. "Jay" Carney

Statement by the Press Secretary: President Obama Names Commerce Secretary John E. Bryson and NEC Chair Eugene B. Sperling as Co-chairs of White House Office of Manufacturing Policy

Statement by the Press Secretary on the filibuster in the Senate of the nomination for the Ambassador to El Salvador

Released December 13

Transcript of a press briefing by Press Secretary James F. "Jay" Carney

Statement by the Press Secretary: Campaign To Cut Waste: Vice President Biden Announces U.S. Will Halt Production of Excess Dollar

Coins and Department of Justice Recovered a Record $5.6 Billion in Fraud in 2011

Statement by the Press Secretary: Obama Administration Holds Major Gulf of Mexico Oil and Gas Lease Sale

Statement by the Press Secretary on House of Representatives action on payroll tax cut legislation

Statement by the Press Secretary announcing that the President signed H.R. 2192, S. 1541, and S. 1639

Released December 14

Transcript of a press gaggle by Press Secretary James F. "Jay" Carney

Text: Statement by National Security Council Spokesman Thomas F. Vietor on the International Engagement Conference for South Sudan

Text: Statement by White House Communications Director H. Daniel Pfeiffer on congressional action on Federal budget legislation

Released December 15

Transcript of a press briefing by Press Secretary James F. "Jay" Carney

Statement by the Press Secretary: We Can't Wait: President Obama Will Announce Administrative Action To Provide Minimum Wage and Overtime Protection for Nearly 2 Million In-Home Care Workers

Statement by the Press Secretary: Obama Administration Releases Report and Interactive Maps Highlighting Critical American Jobs Act Investments in Education

Text: Education & The American Jobs Act: Creating Jobs Through Investments In Our Nation's Schools report

Text: Joint Statement by the United States and the Republic of South Sudan at the International Engagement Conference for South Sudan

Fact sheet: Supporting South Sudan's Vision for the Future

Released December 16

Transcript of a press briefing by Press Secretary James F. "Jay" Carney

Statement by the Press Secretary: We Can't Wait: Nine States Awarded Race to the Top Early Learning Challenge Grants

Statement by the Press Secretary on the lifting of sanctions in Libya

Statement by the Press Secretary announcing that the President signed H.J. Res. 94

Text: Statement by White House Communications Director H. Daniel Pfeiffer on payroll tax cut legislation

Released December 17

Statement by the Press Secretary announcing that the President signed H.J. Res. 95

Released December 18

Statement by the Press Secretary on the death of Chairman Kim Jong Il of North Korea

Text: Statement by Communications Director H. Daniel Pfeiffer on Senate action on payroll tax cut legislation

Released December 19

Transcript of a press briefing by Press Secretary James F. "Jay" Carney

Statement by the Press Secretary announcing that the President signed S. 535, S. 683, and S.J. Res. 22

Text: The United States National Action Plan on Women, Peace, and Security

Fact sheet: The United States National Action Plan on Women, Peace, and Security

Released December 20

Transcript of a press briefing by Press Secretary James F. "Jay" Carney

Statement by the Press Secretary announcing that the President signed H.R. 470 and H.R. 2061

Released December 21

Transcript of a press briefing by Press Secretary James F. "Jay" Carney

Statement by the Press Secretary on Syria

Released December 22

Statement by the Press Secretary on the terrorist attacks in Iraq

Released December 23

Statements by the Press Secretary announcing that the President signed H.R. 2055, H.R. 2867, H.R. 3421, H.R. 3672, H.R. 3765, S. 278, and S. 384

Fact sheet: Successful Conclusion of the Seventh Review Conference of the Biological and Toxin Weapons Convention

Released December 29

Statement by Principal Deputy Press Secretary Joshua R. Earnest on the U.S. sale of defense equipment to Saudi Arabia

Released December 31

Statement by the Press Secretary announcing that the President signed H.R. 1540

Appendix D—Presidential Documents Published in the *Federal Register*

This appendix lists Presidential documents released by the Office of the Press Secretary and published in the Federal Register. *The texts of the documents are printed in the* Federal Register (F.R.) *at the citations listed below. The documents are also printed in title 3 of the* Code of Federal Regulations *and in the Compilation of Presidential Documents.*

PROCLAMATIONS

Proc. No.	Date 2011	Subject	76 F.R. Page
8691	July 1	40th Anniversary of the 26th Amendment	40215
8692	July 15	Captive Nations Week, 2011	43109
8693	July 24	Suspension of Entry of Aliens Subject to United Nations Security Council Travel Bans and International Emergency Economic Powers Act Sanctions	44751
8694	July 25	Anniversary of the Americans With Disabilities Act, 2011	
8695	July 26	National Korean War Veterans Armistice Day, 2011	45395
8696	July 27	World Hepatitis Day, 2011	46183
8697	Aug. 4	Suspension of Entry as Immigrants and Nonimmigrants of Persons Who Participate in Serious Human Rights and Humanitarian Law Violations and Other Abuses	49277
8698	Aug. 5	National Health Center Week, 2011	49647
8699	Aug. 25	Women's Equality Day, 2011	53809
8700	Aug. 31	National Preparedness Month, 2011	54919
8701	Aug. 31	National Alcohol and Drug Addiction Recovery Month, 2011	54921
8702	Aug. 31	National Childhood Obesity Awareness Month, 2011	55207
8703	Sept. 1	National Ovarian Cancer Awareness Month, 2011	55209
8704	Sept. 1	National Wilderness Month, 2011	55211
8705	Sept. 1	National Childhood Cancer Awareness Month, 2011	55549
8706	Sept. 1	National Prostate Cancer Awareness Month, 2011	55551
8707	Sept. 2	Labor Day, 2011	55779
8708	Sept. 9	National Days of Prayer and Remembrance, 2011	56939
8709	Sept. 9	National Grandparents Day, 2011	56941
8710	Sept. 9	Patriot Day and National Day of Service and Remembrance, 2011	56943
8711	Sept. 12	National Health Information Technology Week, 2011	57617
8712	Sept. 12	National Hispanic Heritage Month, 2011	58375
8713	Sept. 15	National POW/MIA Recognition Day, 2011	58377
8714	Sept. 16	Constitution Day and Citizenship Day, Constitution Week, 2011	58707

PROCLAMATIONS (Continued)

Proc. No.	Date 2011	Subject	76 F.R. Page
8715	Sept. 16	National Employer Support of the Guard and Reserve Week, 2011	58709
8716	Sept. 16	National Farm Safety and Health Week, 2011	58711
8717	Sept. 16	National Historically Black Colleges and Universities Week, 2011	58713
8718	Sept. 21	National Hispanic-Serving Institutions Week, 2011	59499
8719	Sept. 22	National Public Lands Day, 2011	59881
8720	Sept. 23	National Hunting and Fishing Day, 2011	59883
8721	Sept. 23	Minority Enterprise Development Week, 2011	60353
8722	Sept. 23	Gold Star Mother's and Family's Day, 2011	60355
8723	Oct. 3	National Arts and Humanities Month, 2011	62283
8724	Oct. 3	National Breast Cancer Awareness Month, 2011	62285
8725	Oct. 3	National Cybersecurity Awareness Month, 2011	62287
8726	Oct. 3	National Disability Employment Awareness Month, 2011	62289
8727	Oct. 3	National Domestic Violence Awareness Month, 2011	62291
8728	Oct. 3	National Substance Abuse Prevention Month, 2011	62293
8729	Oct. 3	Child Health Day, 2011	62295
8730	Oct. 6	National Energy Action Month, 2011	63529
8731	Oct. 6	German-American Day, 2011	63531
8732	Oct. 7	Fire Prevention Week, 2011	63803
8733	Oct. 7	National School Lunch Week, 2011	63805
8734	Oct. 7	Leif Erikson Day, 2011	63807
8735	Oct. 7	Columbus Day, 2011	63809
8736	Oct. 11	General Pulaski Memorial Day, 2011	63999
8737	Oct. 14	National Character Counts Week, 2011	65095
8738	Oct. 14	National Forest Products Week, 2011	65097
8739	Oct. 14	Blind Americans Equality Day, 2011	65099
8740	Oct. 24	United Nations Day, 2011	66847
8741	Oct. 25	To Take Certain Actions Under the African Growth and Opportunity Act	67035
8742	Oct. 31	To Modify the Harmonized Tariff Schedule of the United States	68273
8743	Nov. 1	Military Family Month, 2011	68611
8744	Nov. 1	National Adoption Month, 2011	68613
8745	Nov. 1	National Alzheimer's Disease Awareness Month, 2011	68615
8746	Nov. 1	National Diabetes Month, 2011	68617
8747	Nov. 1	National Entrepreneurship Month, 2011	68619
8748	Nov. 1	National Family Caregivers Month, 2011	68621
8749	Nov. 1	National Native American Heritage Month, 2011	68623
8750	Nov. 1	Establishment of the Fort Monroe National Monument	68625
8751	Nov. 3	Veterans Day, 2011	69081

PROCLAMATIONS (Continued)

Proc. No.	Date 2011	Subject	76 F.R. Page
8752	Nov. 8	World Freedom Day, 2011	70633
8753	Nov. 14	American Education Week, 2011	71447
8754	Nov. 15	America Recycles Day, 2011	71863
8755	Nov. 16	Thanksgiving Day, 2011	72079
8756	Nov. 18	National Family Week, 2011	72603
8757	Nov. 18	National Farm-City Week, 2011	72605
8758	Nov. 18	National Child's Day, 2011	72607
8759	Nov. 21	50th Anniversary of the United States Agency for International Development	72821
8760	Nov. 30	Critical Infrastructure Protection Month, 2011	76021
8761	Nov. 30	National Impaired Driving Prevention Month, 2011	76023
8762	Nov. 30	World AIDS Day, 2011	76025
8763	Dec. 2	International Day of Persons With Disabilities, 2011	76601
8764	Dec. 6	National Pearl Harbor Remembrance Day, 2011	76871
8765	Dec. 8	Human Rights Day and Human Rights Week, 2011	77363
8766	Dec. 8	Bill of Rights Day, 2011	77365
8767	Dec. 15	Wright Brothers Day, 2011	79021

Proc. No.	Date 2011	Subject	77 F.R. Page
8768	Dec. 28	National Mentoring Month, 2012	209
8769	Dec. 28	National Stalking Awareness Month, 2012	211
8770	Dec. 29	To Modify Duty-Free Treatment Under the Generalized System of Preferences and for Other Purposes	407
8771	Dec. 29	To Modify the Harmonized Tariff Schedule of the United States and for Other Purposes	413
8772	Dec. 30	National Slavery and Human Trafficking Prevention Month, 2012	1007

EXECUTIVE ORDERS

E.O. No.	Date 2011	Subject	76 F.R. Page
13578	July 6	Coordinating Policies on Automotive Communities and Workers	40591
13579	July 11	Regulation and Independent Regulatory Agencies	41587
13580	July 12	Interagency Working Group on Coordination of Domestic Energy Development and Permitting in Alaska	41989
13581	July 24	Blocking Property of Transnational Criminal Organizations	44757
13582	Aug. 17	Blocking Property of the Government of Syria and Prohibiting Certain Transactions With Respect to Syria	52209
13583	Aug. 18	Establishing a Coordinated Government-Wide Initiative to Promote Diversity and Inclusion in the Federal Workforce	52847
13584	Sept. 9	Developing an Integrated Strategic Counterterrorism Communication Initiative and Establishing a Temporary Organization To Support Certain Government-Wide Communications Activities Directed Abroad	56945
13585	Sept. 30	Continuance of Certain Federal Advisory Committees	62281
13586	Oct. 6	Establishing an Emergency Board To Investigate Disputes Between Certain Railroads Represented by the National Carriers' Conference Committee of the National Railway Labor Conference and Their Employees Represented by Certain Labor Organizations	63533
13587	Oct. 7	Structural Reforms To Improve the Security of Classified Networks and the Responsible Sharing and Safeguarding of Classified Information	63811
13588	Oct. 31	Reducing Prescription Drug Shortages	68295
13589	Nov. 9	Promoting Efficient Spending	70863
13590	Nov. 20	Authorizing the Imposition of Certain Sanctions With Respect to the Provision of Goods, Services, Technology, or Support for Iran's Energy and Petrochemical Sectors	72609
13591	Nov. 23	Continuance of Certain Federal Advisory Committees	74623
13592	Dec. 2	Improving American Indian and Alaska Native Educational Opportunities and Strengthening Tribal Colleges and Universities	76603
13593	Dec. 13	2011 Amendments to the Manual for Courts-Martial, United States	78451
13594	Dec. 19	Adjustments of Certain Rates of Pay	80191
13595	Dec. 19	Instituting a National Action Plan on Women, Peace, and Security	80205
13596	Dec. 19	Amendments to Executive Orders 12131 and 13539	80725

OTHER PRESIDENTIAL DOCUMENTS

Doc No.	Date 2011	Subject	76 F.R. Page
	July 19	Memorandum: Delegation of Certain Function and Authority Conferred Upon the President by Section 1535(c)(1) of the Ike Skelton National Defense Authorization Act for Fiscal Year 2011	76869
	July 20	Notice: Continuation of the National Emergency With Respect to the Former Liberian Regime of Charles Taylor	43801
	July 28	Notice: Continuation of the National Emergency With Respect to Actions of Certain Persons To Undermine the Sovereignty of Lebanon or Its Democratic Processes and Institutions...	45653
11–12	Aug. 8	Presidential Determination: Unexpected Urgent Refugee and Migration Needs Related to the Horn of Africa	53297
11–13	Aug. 10	Presidential Determination: Continuation of U.S. Drug Interdiction Assistance to the Government of Colombia	53299
	Aug. 12	Notice: Continuation of Emergency Regarding Export Control Regulations	50661
11–14	Aug. 30	Presidential Determination: Waiver of Restriction on Providing Funds to the Palestinian Authority................	59493
	Sept. 9	Notice: Continuation of the National Emergency With Respect to Certain Terrorist Attacks	56633
	Sept. 12	Memorandum: Delegation Under Section 2(a) of the Special Agent Samuel Hicks Families of Fallen Heroes Act..........	57621
11–15	Sept. 13	Presidential Determination: Continuation of the Exercise of Certain Authorities Under the Trading With the Enemy Act	57623
11–16	Sept. 15	Presidential Determination: Presidential Determination on Major Illicit Drug Transit or Major Illicit Drug Producing Countries for Fiscal Year 2012	59495
	Sept. 21	Notice: Continuation of the National Emergency With Respect to Persons Who Commit, Threaten To Commit, or Support Terrorism......................................	59001
	Sept. 28	Memorandum: Provision of Aviation Insurance Coverage for Commercial Air Carrier Service in Domestic and International Operations	61247

OTHER PRESIDENTIAL DOCUMENTS (Continued)

Doc No.	Date 2011	Subject	76 F.R. Page
11–17	Sept. 30	Presidential Determination: Fiscal Year 2012 Refugee Administrations Numbers and Authorizations of In-Country Refugee Status Pursuant to Sections 207 and 101(a)(42), Respectively, of the Immigration and Nationality Act, and Determination Pursuant to Section 2(b)(2) of the Migration and Refugee Assistance Act, as Amended	62597
11–18	Sept. 30	Presidential Determination: Presidential Determination With Respect to Foreign Governments' Efforts Regarding Trafficking in Persons	62599
12–01	Oct. 4	Presidential Determination: Certification and Determination With Respect to the Child Soldiers Prevention Act of 2008	65927
12–02	Oct. 14	Presidential Determination: Provision of U.S. Drug Interdiction Assistance to the Government of Brazil	70635
	Oct. 19	Notice: Continuation of the National Emergency With Respect to Significant Narcotics Traffickers Centered in Colombia	65355
	Oct. 25	Notice: Continuation of the National Emergency With Respect to the Situation in or in Relation to the Democratic Republic of the Congo......	66599
	Oct. 28	Memorandum: Making It Easier for America's Small Businesses and America's Exporters To Access Government Services To Help Them Grow and Hire...	68049
	Nov. 1	Notice: Continuation of the National Emergency With Respect to Sudan......	68055
	Nov. 7	Notice: Continuation of the National Emergency With Respect to Iran	70035
	Nov. 9	Notice: Continuation of the National Emergency With Respect to Weapons of Mass Destruction	70319
	Nov. 28	Memorandum: Managing Government Records......	75423
12–03	Dec. 2	Presidential Determination: Suspension of Limitations Under the Jerusalem Embassy Act......	82073
	Dec. 15	Memorandum: Determinations Under Section 1106(a) of the Omnibus Trade and Competitiveness Act of 1988—Russian Federation......	79023
	Dec. 21	Memorandum: Flexible Implementation of the Mercury and Air Toxics Standards Rule......	80727

Subject Index

ABC
  ABC News—1599
  "Nightline" program—1603
Accountability and Transparency Board, Government—1583
Administrative Conference of the U.S., Advisory Council of the—1613
Advancement of Colored People, National Association for the—1582
Aeronautics and Space Administration, National. *See* Space program
Afghanistan
  Afghan military and security forces—838, 856, 920, 932, 934, 936, 1020, 1067, 1088, 1098, 1185, 1238, 1265, 1313, 1317, 1354–1355, 1379, 1399, 1413, 1433, 1435, 1550, 1554, 1587
  Civilian casualties—1089
  Democracy efforts—1230
  Economic growth and development—1088–1089
  Former regime—856, 1019, 1186, 1238, 1399, 1550, 1553–1554
  Insurgency and terrorist attacks—855, 1067, 1089, 1433
  International diplomatic efforts—1479, 1599
  NATO
    International Security Assistance Force, commander—1577, 1581, 1585, 1591
    Role—1112, 1238, 1313, 1481, 1526
  President—934, 1088, 1586–1587
  Reconciliation efforts—1089, 1587
  Reconstruction and infrastructure development—1088
  Relations with U.S.—1098
  U.S. Ambassador—1577, 1582, 1586
  U.S. military forces
    Casualties—855–857, 932, 934–935, 1051, 1067–1068, 1238, 1435, 1586
    Deployment—833, 838, 855–857, 862–863, 901, 920, 931–932, 936, 941, 944, 950, 953, 957, 959, 968, 978, 990, 997, 1014, 1019–1020, 1048–1050, 1066–1067, 1079–1080, 1084, 1092, 1098, 1135, 1137, 1156, 1185, 1200, 1230, 1238, 1253, 1281, 1310, 1317, 1320, 1324, 1342, 1380, 1384, 1399, 1401–1402, 1434–1435, 1441, 1460, 1490, 1492, 1538, 1547, 1550, 1553, 1570, 1572, 1579, 1586, 1594
Africa
  See also Developing countries; *specific country*
  African Union, role in Sudan—845
  Central Africa
    Human rights issues—1278
    U.S. military forces, deployment—1278–1279

Africa—Continued
  Democracy efforts—909–910
  East Africa
    Famine and humanitarian crisis—910, 913, 941, 1023, 1103, 1374, 1379, 1566, 1586
    U.S. assistance—1566–1567
  Economic Community of West African States (ECOWAS)—910, 1382
  Economic growth and development—909–910
  Food security, strengthening efforts—1567
  International assistance—913
  ONE humanitarian campaign—1498
  Relations with U.S.—910, 913
  Security cooperation with U.S.—910
  Trade with U.S.—910
  West African leaders, meeting with President—909–910
Agricultural Mortgage Corporation, Federal—1580
Agriculture
  Farm subsidies, elimination—837
  Food markets and prices—837, 861, 978, 980, 1005
  Food safety—902, 1146
  Government and private sector, coordination efforts—965, 1000
  Strengthening efforts—987
Agriculture, Department of
  Farm and Foreign Agricultural Services, Under Secretary for—1598
  Pigford class-action lawsuit on discrimination, settlement—1124, 1356
  Secretary—951, 955, 957, 963–964, 971, 977, 980–983, 986, 991, 993, 996, 1000, 1356
AIDS. *See* HIV/AIDS; *specific country or region*
Air Force, Department of the
  Air Force Academy, U.S.—1596, 1611
  Secretary—1302
Alaska, disaster assistance—1615
Al Qaida. *See* Terrorism
American. *See other part of subject*
American Indians and Alaska Natives
  Carcieri lawsuit on Indian land trust management—1506
  Cobell class-action lawsuit on Indian trust management, settlement—1291
  Education
    Performance and completion rates, improvement efforts—1507
    Tribal Colleges and Universities—1507
  Indian Health Care Improvement Act—1506
  Job creation and growth—1507

American Indians and Alaska Natives—Continued
Poverty—1507
Public health issues—1506
Reservations, violent crime rate—910, 1506
Tribal Law and Order Act of 2010—910, 1506
Tribal nations
Consultation with Federal Government—1604
Law enforcement agencies, Federal Government assistance—910
Relations with Federal Government—910, 1505–1507
White House Tribal Nations Conference—1505
Unemployment rate—1507
American Latino Heritage, White House Forum on—1259
Antigua and Barbuda, U.S. Ambassador—1605
Appropriations. *See* Budget, Federal
Arab States, League of—1087, 1099, 1415, 1538, 1541
Arab States of the Gulf, Cooperation Council for the (GCC)—1470–1471
Architectural and Transportation Barriers Compliance Board—1588, 1591
Argentina
President—1371, 1613
Relations with U.S.—1371
Arizona
Disaster assistance—1585
Illegal immigration enforcement legislation—1172
KSAZ in Phoenix—1606
Arkansas, disaster assistance—1578
Armed Forces, U.S.
See also Defense and national security; Defense, Department of; *specific military branch*
"Don't ask, don't tell" policy, repeal—833, 886, 919, 921, 1092–1094, 1131, 1136, 1140, 1154, 1159, 1163, 1184, 1187, 1190, 1198, 1211, 1214, 1253, 1324, 1329, 1332, 1336, 1342, 1347, 1427, 1489, 1493, 1558
Female servicemembers—1394
Funding—838, 1573
GI bill legislation—929–930, 1022, 1303
Military families—824–825, 840, 856, 1017, 1019, 1021, 1037, 1048, 1302–1304, 1316–1317, 1380–1382, 1385, 1399, 1401, 1460, 1501, 1530, 1546–1549, 1561, 1570, 1586
Military family benefits, expansion—825, 1549, 1573
Military officials, meeting with President—1612
Military technologies, development and funding—825, 1048
National Guard—1015, 1549
Servicemembers
Casualties—824, 840, 941, 1259, 1316, 1549, 1601
Deployment—838, 1012, 1050, 1112, 1183, 1316, 1471, 1501, 1547, 1550, 1553
Hispanic servicemembers—1259

Armed Forces, U.S.—Continued
Servicemembers—Continued
Meeting with President—1616
Muslim American servicemembers—940
Posttraumatic stress disorder (PTSD), treatment efforts—840, 1021, 1549
Service and dedication—824–825, 840, 855–857, 886, 929, 934–935, 941, 1019, 1048–1050, 1067–1068, 1093, 1115, 1190, 1238, 1262, 1297, 1302–1304, 1310, 1316, 1319–1320, 1361, 1401–1402, 1433–1434, 1460, 1465, 1470–1471, 1530, 1535, 1547–1550, 1561, 1564, 1568, 1570, 1611, 1613, 1616
Traumatic brain injuries, treatment efforts—840, 1021, 1549
Arms and munitions
See also specific country
Nuclear weapons and material
Comprehensive Test Ban Treaty—1524
Global Nuclear Security Summit—1265
Nonproliferation efforts—1102, 1264, 1421, 1463, 1480, 1524, 1611
Security—1102, 1107, 1480
Strategic Arms Reduction Treaty (START) with Russia, expansion—833, 1102, 1184, 1368, 1413
Treaty on the Non-Proliferation of Nuclear Weapons—1437, 1463, 1534
Weapons of mass destruction—1392
Army, Department of the
Chief of Staff—855, 1361
General Counsel—1596
Military Academy, U.S.—1577, 1582
Secretary—855
Walter Reed Army Medical Center—1037
Arts
See also Smithsonian Institution
"Country Music: In Performance at the White House"—1464
Arts, National Council on the—1600
Arts and Humanities, President's Committee on the—1511
Asia
Association of Southeast Asian Nations (ASEAN)—1412, 1443, 1452, 1454–1455, 1610
Defense relationship with U.S.—1442–1443
East Asia Summit—885, 1433–1434, 1443, 1449–1455, 1610
Economic growth and development—1436, 1439
International diplomatic efforts—1479
President Obama's visit—1456
Relations with U.S.—1441–1443, 1445
Security cooperation with U.S.—1412, 1442, 1449
South China Sea, territorial dispute—1610
Trade with U.S.—1195, 1433, 1435, 1449, 1456, 1492

Asian Americans and Pacific Islanders, President's Advisory Commission on—1600

Asia-Pacific Economic Cooperation (APEC)—884–885, 1265, 1404–1408, 1410, 1412–1419, 1423–1424, 1430, 1433, 1438, 1450–1451, 1455, 1607–1608

Atomic Energy Agency, International (IAEA)—1369, 1420, 1463, 1479, 1612

Atrocities Prevention Board, Interagency—926–927

Attorney General. *See* Justice, Department of

Australia

Afghanistan, Australian military forces, deployment—1433, 1435, 1441, 1447

Campbell High School in Canberra—1445

Counterterrorism efforts, cooperation with U.S.—1441

Defense relationship with U.S.—1411, 1434–1435, 1441–1442, 1447–1448, 1492

Energy, alternative and renewable sources and technologies—1437

Nuclear energy, cooperation with India—1437

President Obama's visit—1432–1434, 1439–1440, 1445, 1447, 1595, 1605, 1609

Prime Minister—1432, 1439–1442, 1445–1448, 1609

Relations with China—1435

Relations with India—1437

Relations with U.S.—1406, 1433–1434, 1439–1441, 1447

Trade with U.S.—1436, 1443

U.S. Ambassador—1609

U.S. Embassy personnel, meeting with President Obama—1609

Aviation

Airport improvement projects—1059

Air traffic control system, modernization—882, 1215

Air travel security measures, expansion—1048, 1474

Awards. *See* Decorations, medals, and awards

Azerbaijan

Independence Day—1315

Relations with U.S.—1315

Bahrain

Democracy efforts—1100

Relations with U.S.—1100

Balkans, Western. *See* Europe

Banks. *See* Business and industry; Development banks and funds

Barbados, U.S. Ambassador—1605

Battle Monuments Commission, American—1591

Belarus

Democracy efforts—1474, 1479

Human rights issues—1479

Benin

Peace Corps volunteer Catherine "Kate" Puzey, 2009 murder—1610

President—909

U.S. Ambassador-designate—1614

Better Buildings Initiative—1502–1503

Blind or Severely Disabled, Committee for Purchase From People Who Are—1585, 1597

Boeing Company—1449, 1453

Boys & Girls Clubs of America—1600

Brazil

Energy, alternative and renewable sources and technologies—839, 993

President—1089, 1091, 1597

Budget, Federal

See also specific Federal agency or organization

Accountability and transparency—825, 844

Appropriations

Continuation—1568

Defense, Department of—1569

Homeland Security, Department of—1047

Transportation, Department of—1029

Budget Control Act of 2011—914, 916, 937–938, 945, 989, 1083, 1461–1462

Congressional spending restraint—827, 834, 844, 846, 852, 861, 863, 866, 875, 896, 903, 906, 912, 933, 937, 939, 944, 953, 958, 965, 1057, 1060, 1066, 1078, 1095, 1129, 1135, 1137, 1191, 1248

Deficit and national debt—823, 825, 827, 829, 833–834, 837–839, 841–844, 846–849, 851–853, 858–868, 870–871, 873–875, 877, 883, 886–893, 896–897, 899, 901–906, 908, 911–916, 921, 924–925, 928–929, 931, 933–934, 936–939, 942, 944–945, 951–954, 956–959, 964–968, 970, 978, 984–985, 988–989, 991, 994–995, 997–998, 1000, 1002–1003, 1018, 1020, 1039–1040, 1045, 1052, 1054, 1057, 1060, 1064, 1073, 1076, 1078–1085, 1095–1096, 1102, 1110, 1116–1117, 1126, 1128, 1132–1133, 1138, 1142, 1153, 1155, 1160, 1167–1168, 1191, 1199–1201, 1203, 1206–1207, 1212, 1215, 1219–1222, 1228–1229, 1232, 1240–1241, 1248, 1254, 1258, 1261, 1296–1298, 1306, 1324–1325, 1341–1342, 1345, 1377, 1386, 1388–1389, 1425, 1429–1430, 1436, 1442, 1456, 1461–1462, 1468, 1486, 1495, 1514, 1518, 1520–1521, 1562, 1577–1582, 1584, 1589, 1608

Entitlement spending, reform—825, 834, 844, 846, 849, 859–860, 867, 871, 886–888, 891–893, 903, 906, 911–912, 936, 939, 947, 958–959, 989, 998, 1079, 1084, 1137

Fiscal Responsibility and Reform, National Commission on—825, 852, 859, 862, 933, 988–989

Fiscal year 2012 budget—847, 849, 853, 901, 903, 1047, 1206

Government programs, spending reductions—823, 825, 834–835, 837, 846, 850–852, 854, 858, 861–863, 867, 871, 874, 881, 886, 888, 890–893, 896, 902–905, 911–912, 914, 916, 925, 933, 944, 953–954, 958, 965, 985, 988–989, 994, 997–998, 1039, 1041, 1045, 1052, 1057, 1064, 1079–1080, 1083, 1095, 1116, 1128–1129, 1132, 1137, 1142, 1153,

Budget, Federal—Continued
Government programs, spending reductions—Continued
1155, 1160, 1164, 1200, 1206, 1212, 1215, 1248, 1254, 1258, 1261, 1296, 1346, 1388–1389, 1424, 1429, 1461–1462, 1495, 1515, 1520, 1522
Revenue
Decrease—916
Increase—936, 938, 969, 989, 1219, 1221–1222, 1285–1286, 1424
Building Sciences, National Institute of—1600
Burma
Democracy efforts—1451–1452, 1609
Human rights issues—1445, 1451–1452
President—1452
Relations with North Korea—1452
Relations with U.S.—1444, 1452
Business and industry
See also Commerce, international; Employment and unemployment; *specific State or company*
Automobile industry
Decline—908, 955, 1131, 1158, 1276
Improvement—827, 836, 908, 918, 937, 943, 955, 1032, 1094, 1131, 1198, 1214, 1252, 1276, 1279
Strengthening efforts—827, 830, 833, 836, 907–908, 918, 921, 965, 979, 996, 1032, 1041, 1071, 1094, 1135, 1154, 1158, 1162, 1198, 1203, 1210, 1252, 1264, 1276, 1279, 1336, 1342, 1427, 1456, 1493, 1523, 1527, 1602
Bank loans to small businesses, increase—908, 915, 957, 978, 981–982, 1223
Business Roundtable—1270
Construction industry, decline—1025, 1044, 1114, 1125, 1131, 1142, 1154, 1159, 1164, 1248, 1253, 1327, 1365–1366, 1520
Corporate executives, compensation packages—1521
Credit cards, regulations and consumer protections—869, 897, 1146, 1226, 1228
Credit freeze situation—832, 980, 1052, 1223–1224
Domestic investment, tax breaks—988, 1040
Entrepreneurship, promotion efforts—828–830, 832, 842, 844, 874, 896, 915, 931, 944, 950, 953, 980, 985, 1054, 1081, 1171, 1187, 1247, 1357–1358, 1418
Facility and equipment purchases, tax incentives—832, 853, 997, 1038, 1052, 1145
Foreign investment in U.S., promotion efforts—903, 1409
Global competitiveness—830, 835, 842, 851, 854, 920, 930, 935, 938, 942, 944, 946, 991, 1022, 1034, 1041, 1046, 1052, 1057, 1060, 1075–1077, 1081, 1096, 1110, 1120, 1122, 1139, 1142, 1187, 1219, 1221–1222, 1225, 1227, 1230, 1232, 1262–1263, 1282, 1284, 1298, 1305, 1318, 1336–1337, 1341, 1357, 1380, 1384, 1395, 1412, 1418, 1430, 1496, 1519

Business and industry—Continued
Home loan industry—870, 1146, 1522, 1533
Intellectual property law, strengthening efforts—1409, 1421
Internet commerce—956, 1076, 1349
Manufacturing industry
Advanced manufacturing, promotion efforts—828, 950, 1041, 1077, 1225, 1456, 1496
Decline—898
Government and private sector, coordination efforts—828, 937, 1025
Improvement—898
Strengthening efforts—828, 1032, 1187, 1214, 1279, 1384, 1430, 1456
Minority-owned businesses—897, 1391
Sarbanes-Oxley Act of 2002—1242–1243
Small businesses
Economic impact—902, 980, 1058, 1085, 1116, 1206, 1471
Federal assistance for international marketing and development—957
Hiring incentives—1016, 1038, 1044–1045, 1052, 1054, 1056, 1059, 1063, 1076, 1078, 1095, 1109, 1116, 1132, 1142, 1145, 1160, 1167, 1171, 1200, 1206, 1212, 1218, 1225, 1232, 1240, 1247, 1254, 1261, 1285, 1289, 1306–1307, 1333, 1345, 1495, 1502
Promotion efforts—832, 853, 954, 964, 978, 1052, 1056–1057, 1059, 1075, 1118, 1143, 1145, 1167–1168, 1192, 1212, 1224, 1242, 1270, 1285, 1289, 1294, 1299, 1329, 1337, 1350, 1395, 1471, 1484–1485, 1527
Unemployed workers, incentives to hire—850, 896, 930, 1016, 1039, 1045, 1052, 1056, 1059, 1063, 1083, 1155, 1166, 1280, 1307
Wage discrimination—904, 1393–1394

Cabinet
See also specific Federal department or executive branch agency
Members, meetings with President—916, 1192
California
Democratic Party events—1134, 1139, 1153, 1157, 1162, 1328, 1330, 1338
Governor—1162, 1164
KABC in Los Angeles—1581
President's visits—1134, 1139–1141, 1153, 1157, 1162, 1328, 1330, 1338, 1401, 1597–1598, 1604, 1607–1608
Roscoe's House of Chicken 'n Waffles in Los Angeles—1604
U.S. Representative, election—858
Cambodia, U.S. Ambassador—1612

Canada
　Afghanistan, Canadian military forces, deployment—1608
　Border with U.S., infrastructure and security—1527, 1530
　Investment and business ventures in U.S.—1526
　Keystone XL Pipeline project with U.S.—1527, 1529
　Prime Minister—1526, 1608, 1613
　Relations with U.S.—1526–1527, 1608
　Security cooperation with U.S.—1526–1527
　Trade with U.S.—1526–1527
　Trans-Pacific Partnership, membership bid—1419, 1527
Canadian River Commission—1603
Cancer Advisory Board, National—1597
Cancer Panel, President's—1611
Capital Planning Commission, National—1615
CBS
　"60 Minutes" program—1613
　"Sunday Morning" program—1588
Central African Republic, U.S. military detachment—1279
Central America
　See also Commerce, international; *specific country*
　Security cooperation with U.S.—1216
Central Intelligence Agency—1591
Chamber of Commerce, U.S.—1030, 1116, 1241, 1270, 1367, 1504
Children and youth
　See also Education
　Abuse, prevention efforts—1422
　Girls Nation—1583
China
　Economic growth and development—907, 1408, 1421, 1423, 1435
　Energy, alternative and renewable sources and technologies—830, 1225, 1227, 1438
　Monetary policy—1374
　Poverty, reduction efforts—1229, 1435
　Premier—1610
　President—1409, 1414, 1420, 1423
　Relations with Australia—1435
　Relations with U.S.—1408, 1414–1415, 1421, 1435, 1443, 1490
　Security cooperation with U.S.—1415
　Trade and economic policies—1229–1230, 1408–1409, 1421–1423, 1439
　Trade with U.S.—1143, 1415, 1422–1423
Christopher Columbus Fellowship Foundation—1578, 1585, 1597
Civil rights
　Civil Rights Act of 1964—1282
　Civil rights movement—1189, 1217, 1280–1283, 1393–1394, 1557, 1602

Civil rights—Continued
　Disabled persons, assistance and accommodation efforts—881
　Freedom of religion—876, 941, 1558
　Freedom of speech—975
　Lesbian, gay, bisexual, and transgender persons, equality—886, 919, 1092, 1139, 1189–1191, 1481, 1524
　Lilly Ledbetter Fair Pay Act of 2009—918, 924, 1034, 1131, 1140, 1154, 1159, 1187, 1198, 1342, 1394–1395, 1427, 1558
　Matthew Shepard and James Byrd, Jr. Hate Crimes Prevention Act—1189
　Minorities
　　Anti-Semitism—1557
　　Minority rights and ethnic tolerance—1139, 1173
　　Racial equality—1139, 1189, 1281–1282, 1356
　　Same-sex domestic partnerships—1174, 1189
　　Suffrage—973
　　Voting Rights Act of 1965—1282
　　Wage equality—1136, 1163, 1211, 1253, 1493
　　Women's rights and gender equality—843, 1103, 1159, 1239, 1392–1395
Claims Resolution Act of 2010—1291
Climate change. *See* Environment
Clinton Global Initiative—1108, 1110–1111, 1504
CNN, "The Situation Room With Wolf Blitzer" program—1587
Colombia
　Economic growth and development—1193
　Free trade agreement with U.S.—865, 931, 1041, 1193–1194, 1262, 1277, 1403, 1419, 1602, 1604
　Narcotics traffickers, continuation of national emergency—1309
　President—1604
　Relations with U.S.—1193–1194
　Trade with U.S.—1376
Colorado
　Colorado College in Colorado Springs—1343
　Democratic Party events—1335, 1343
　Denver
　　Abraham Lincoln High School—1165
　　KUSA—1606
　　University of Colorado Denver—1348
　Governor—1165–1166, 1335, 1344, 1348
　KOAA in Colorado Springs—1614
　Lieutenant Governor—1335, 1348
　President's visits—1165, 1335, 1343–1344, 1348, 1598, 1604
Commerce, Department of
　Deputy Secretary—1605
　Secretary—1069–1070, 1315, 1584

Commerce, international
See also specific country or region
Asia-Pacific, regional trade promotion efforts—884, 1417–1418, 1433, 1443, 1449, 1456
Environmental protection standards—885, 1244
Export controls, U.S. national emergency—950
Financial regulations, modernization efforts—853, 1299
Fishing regulations, strengthening efforts—1431
Free and fair trade—944, 953, 978, 1009, 1128, 1143, 1229–1230, 1313, 1403–1408, 1417–1418, 1435, 1438, 1444, 1477
Generalized System of Preferences (GSP)—1454
Global financial markets
Stabilization efforts—1102, 1119, 1154, 1231–1232, 1241, 1354, 1356, 1360, 1369–1370, 1373–1375, 1397, 1405, 1415–1416, 1437–1438, 1444, 1473, 1477, 1491, 1581, 1586, 1591, 1596, 1611
Unrest—848, 933, 935, 952, 964, 980, 1102, 1108, 1111–1112, 1128, 1139, 1169, 1171, 1173, 1215, 1231, 1239, 1241, 1245, 1355, 1371, 1373, 1392, 1405, 1477, 1566, 1585, 1610
Group of Twenty (G–20) nations—1231–1232, 1264–1265, 1360, 1369–1371, 1373–1375, 1405, 1415, 1419, 1433, 1455, 1602, 1606–1607
Intellectual property law, strengthening efforts—1143, 1262, 1438
Piracy—1264
U.S. exports
Expansion—842, 851, 874, 896, 915, 919, 931, 941, 943–944, 950, 953, 957, 965, 978–979, 985, 987, 998, 1009, 1033, 1041, 1061, 1128, 1172, 1193–1195, 1208, 1214, 1221, 1228, 1232, 1262, 1265, 1276–1277, 1279, 1286, 1289, 1295, 1300, 1315, 1374, 1397, 1403, 1406, 1410, 1417–1419, 1424, 1436, 1449, 1456, 1526, 1602, 1604
Export control reforms—1411
National security issues—1411
Commission. *See other part of subject*
Communications
See also specific news organization, State, or country
Broadband technology—897, 956, 958, 978, 982, 1142, 1155, 1166, 1430, 1497, 1520
Infrastructure, national, improvement efforts—832, 971, 1026, 1110, 1203, 1215, 1249, 1341
News media
Journalists, meeting with President—1595
Presidential interviews—1578, 1581, 1586–1588, 1591, 1599, 1602–1605, 1607, 1610, 1613–1614
Social networking and new media—1142, 1565
Communications Commission, Federal—1605

Community Service, Corporation for National and—1312, 1603, 1609
Congo, Democratic Republic of the
U.S. military forces, deployment—1279
U.S. national emergency, continuation—1334
Congress
Bipartisanship—823, 825–826, 829, 832, 837, 841–844, 846–852, 859, 867, 870–872, 874, 881, 886, 888–890, 892–893, 896, 898, 901–906, 909, 911, 913–915, 926, 928, 931, 937, 939, 945–946, 950–951, 954, 956, 964–965, 972, 978–979, 982, 989, 1016, 1025–1026, 1029–1030, 1033, 1042, 1044, 1046, 1051, 1057, 1061, 1063, 1065, 1075–1079, 1081, 1083, 1085, 1093, 1095, 1119–1120, 1165, 1173, 1189, 1191, 1204, 1208, 1220–1222, 1225, 1227, 1241–1242, 1250–1251, 1270, 1277, 1279–1280, 1282, 1285–1286, 1289, 1294, 1300, 1339, 1344–1345, 1347, 1350, 1359–1360, 1362, 1367, 1402, 1460–1462, 1484, 1499–1500, 1510, 1514, 1562–1567, 1572, 1608
Congressional Asian Pacific American Caucus—1597
Congressional Black Caucus—1123–1124, 1127
Congressional Hispanic Caucus—1062, 1065, 1473
Deficit Reduction, Joint Select Committee on—1083–1084, 1461
Earmark reform—1025, 1039, 1116
Ethics reforms—1025
House of Representatives
Majority leader—1208
Minority leader—843, 852, 871, 887–888, 899, 909, 1062, 1065, 1192, 1338, 1578, 1581–1582, 1584
Republican caucus—870
Speaker—832, 846, 848–850, 852, 862, 864–865, 870–871, 886–889, 892, 902–903, 933, 953, 965, 989, 1023, 1037, 1047, 1079–1080, 1116, 1192, 1205, 1229, 1270, 1367, 1424, 1514, 1531, 1534, 1564, 1577, 1580–1582, 1602, 1615
Lobbyist gift ban and campaign finance regulations—1536
Members, meetings with President—846, 858, 862, 865, 1578–1580, 1600, 1606, 1613
Presidential nominations, confirmation process—1524, 1531, 1533
Senate
Majority leader—852, 871, 887–888, 905, 1192, 1326, 1474, 1562, 1581–1582, 1584, 1600, 1615
Minority leader—848, 862, 864, 887–888, 905, 1066, 1116–1117, 1192, 1205, 1229, 1270, 1323, 1339, 1346, 1367, 1428, 1485, 1494, 1531, 1534, 1562, 1566, 1581–1582
Republican caucus—1536
Congressional Hispanic Caucus Institute—1062
Connecticut, disaster assistance—1590, 1592, 1605, 1609
Consumer Cooperative Bank, National—1594
Corporation. *See other part of subject*

Cote d'Ivoire
  Democracy efforts—1107, 1112
  Political unrest and violence—909, 1099
  President—909, 1099, 1112
  United Nations, role—1099
Credit Union Administration Board, National—1604
Crime. *See* Law enforcement and crime
Cuba
  Cuban Liberty and Democratic Solidarity (LIBERTAD) Act of 1996—866
  Democracy efforts—866, 1175–1176, 1551
  Economic growth and development—1175
  Guantanamo Bay, U.S. Naval Base, detention of alleged terrorists—1568
  Human rights issues—1175, 1551
  Ladies in White opposition movement—1551
  Relations with U.S.—1175–1176, 1551
  Travel restrictions—1175
  U.S. policy changes, remittances and communications regulations—1175
  U.S. sanctions—1175
Cultural Property Advisory Committee—1578, 1591, 1601
Czech Republic
  Afghanistan, Czech military forces, deployment—1354–1355
  Democracy efforts—1563
  Energy cooperation with U.S.—1354–1355
  Former President—1615
  Prime Minister—1353, 1355, 1600
  Relations with U.S.—1354–1355
  Security cooperation with U.S.—1355
  Trade with U.S.—1354

Deaths
  Awlaki, Anwar al- —1183, 1599
  Chavez, Richard E.—904
  Crown Prince Sultan bin Abd al-Aziz Al Saud—1604
  Daley, Margaret C.—1472
  Ford, Elizabeth A.—843
  Havel, Vaclav—1562, 1615
  Jobs, Steven P.—1218
  Kim Jong Il—1614–1615
  Maathai, Wangari Muta—1156
  Qadhafi, Muammar Abu Minyar al- —1309, 1319
  Rabbani, Burhanuddin—1089
  Shalikashvili, John M.—893
  Shuttlesworth, Fred L.—1217
  Sultan bin Abd al-Aziz Al Saud, Crown Prince of Saudi Arabia—1320, 1604
Decorations, medals, and awards
  Defense Superior Service Medal—1601
  Democracy Service Medal—1551

Decorations, medals, and awards—Continued
  Medal of Honor—855, 857, 1066, 1068, 1259, 1361, 1547, 1587, 1594–1595
  Nobel Prize—1156, 1238–1239, 1281
  Presidential Citizens Medal—1311–1312
  Presidential Medal of Freedom—1370, 1513
  Purple Heart—1601
  Science, National Medal of—1317, 1319, 1603
  Technology and Innovation, National Medal of—1317, 1319, 1603
Defense, Department of
  See also Armed Forces, U.S.; Defense and national security; *specific military branch*
  Assistant Secretaries
    Asian and Pacific Security Affairs—1604
    Special Operations and Low Intensity Conflict—1605
  Defense contracts, contracting policies, reform—837
  Deputy Secretary—855, 1584
  Funding—825, 834, 838–840, 844, 846, 858, 861–862, 867, 871, 874, 886, 902, 958, 1442
  Joint Chiefs of Staff—855, 886, 928, 1036, 1183–1185, 1398, 1582, 1585, 1613
  Secretary—840, 886, 899, 1183, 1185, 1360, 1398, 1406, 1569, 1574–1575, 1577, 1581–1585, 1593, 1595, 1599, 1601, 1613
  Unified Command Plan—1053
Defense and national security
  See also Armed Forces, U.S.; Defense, Department of; Terrorism
  Border security—1048, 1169–1170, 1172
  Cybersecurity, strengthening efforts—1480
  Missile defense—1092, 1575
  Piracy, efforts to combat—1481
  Potential terrorist attacks, preparedness efforts—1048, 1573
Defense of Marriage Act—1174, 1190
Delaware
  Disaster assistance—1590, 1599
  Governor—1589
  President's visit—1586
Democracy, National Endowment for—1551
Democratic Party
  See also specific State
  Democratic National Committee—917, 921, 924, 935, 938, 945, 1071, 1073, 1084, 1093, 1128, 1130, 1134, 1139, 1153, 1157, 1162, 1186, 1197, 1202, 1209, 1214, 1251, 1256, 1321, 1328, 1330, 1335, 1338, 1343, 1489, 1493, 1585–1586
Deposit Insurance Corporation, Federal—1604
Developing countries
  See also Development banks and funds; *specific country or region*
  Economic growth and development—1263, 1408
  Food aid, U.S. programs—920

Developing countries—Continued
Health and medical care, promotion efforts—1103, 1110, 1313, 1499
Poverty—1103, 1265
Water, access and availability—1110
Development, U.S. Agency for International—1567, 1598, 1610
Development banks and funds
See also Developing countries
International Bank for Reconstruction and Development—1593
Disability, National Council on—1577, 1598, 1602, 1609
Disaster assistance
See also Natural disasters; *specific State, country, or executive branch agency*
Alaska—1615
Arizona—1585
Arkansas—1578
Connecticut—1590, 1592, 1605, 1609
Delaware—1590, 1599
District of Columbia—1591, 1599, 1607
Hurricane Irene—1015, 1030–1031, 1047, 1595–1596, 1599
Iowa—1589, 1591
Kansas—1584, 1598
Kentucky—1583
Louisiana—1588, 1605
Maine—1595
Maryland—1590, 1596, 1600
Massachusetts—1590, 1592, 1606
Missouri—1587
Nebraska—1587
New Hampshire—1582, 1590, 1592, 1606, 1613
New Jersey—1590–1591, 1596, 1602, 1612
New Mexico—1611
New York—1590–1591, 1594–1595
North Carolina—1589, 1591
North Dakota—1586
Ohio—1579
Pennsylvania—1579, 1591–1592, 1594–1595
Puerto Rico—1580, 1588, 1590, 1603
Rhode Island—1590, 1592
Tennessee—1581
Texas—1577, 1594
Utah—1586
Vermont—1579, 1591–1592, 1607
Virginia—1590, 1592, 1607, 1609
Wyoming—1582
Diseases
See also HIV/AIDS
AIDS, Tuberculosis and Malaria, Global Fund to Fight—1499–1500

District of Columbia
Air and Space Museum, National—1611
Benjamin Banneker Academic High School—1179, 1596, 1598
Building Museum, National—1537
Capital Area Food Bank—1610
Children's National Medical Center—1537
Court Services and Offender Supervision Agency—1584
DC Central Kitchen—1594
DC Prep Public Charter School—1120
Democratic Party events—935, 938, 1071, 1073, 1186, 1383, 1545, 1613
Disaster assistance—1591, 1599, 1607
Fiscal year 2012 budget request—1196
Georgetown Waterfront Park—1605
George Washington University—1498, 1611
Good Stuff Eatery—1585
Martin Luther King, Jr. Memorial—947, 1280–1281, 1283, 1311, 1391, 1585
St. John's Episcopal Church—1580
Washington Navy Yard—928
WRC in Washington—1580
Dominican Republic, U.S. Ambassador—895
Dominica, Commonwealth of, U.S. Ambassador—1605
Drug abuse and trafficking
See also specific country or region
Addiction treatment and reduction efforts—837, 843, 879, 1176
Education and prevention efforts—837, 843, 879, 910, 1176
Foreign narcotics traffickers—1013, 1216, 1224
Interdiction efforts—837, 879, 1176, 1225

Economy, international. *See* Commerce, international
Economy, national
See also Budget, Federal; Employment and unemployment; *specific State*
American Recovery and Reinvestment Act of 2009—827, 830, 834, 850, 853, 863, 874, 960, 971, 985, 1143, 1243
Consumer Financial Protection Bureau—868–870, 976, 1032, 1223, 1226, 1228, 1324, 1521–1522, 1531, 1536
Credit markets, stabilization efforts—892, 903, 1135, 1162, 1223, 1257, 1332, 1521, 1536
Dodd-Frank Wall Street Reform and Consumer Protection Act—869–870, 897, 919, 976, 1131, 1158, 1198, 1223–1224, 1336, 1492, 1521, 1531–1532, 1536, 1580
Economic concerns—841–842, 846, 848, 858, 871, 887, 895, 901, 903, 906, 911–914, 918, 925, 928, 931, 933, 935–936, 938, 941–944, 946, 950–952, 954, 957, 964, 966, 968, 973, 975, 977–979, 981, 984, 987–988, 995, 1016, 1018, 1029, 1032, 1043,

Economy, national—Continued

Economic concerns—Continued

1046, 1051, 1053–1055, 1066, 1072–1077, 1079, 1085, 1094, 1097, 1119, 1128, 1130, 1134, 1139–1141, 1151–1152, 1157–1158, 1162, 1171, 1173, 1180, 1187, 1198, 1204, 1206, 1218–1219, 1221, 1228, 1232, 1241, 1258, 1278, 1281, 1283, 1286–1287, 1291, 1296–1298, 1302, 1306, 1323, 1337, 1344, 1347–1349, 1359, 1371, 1373–1374, 1377, 1383, 1388, 1390–1391, 1394, 1428, 1466, 1483, 1491, 1494, 1502, 1516–1518, 1531, 1536, 1545–1546, 1561–1562, 1566, 1572, 1584, 1601

Economic recovery, oversight and transparency—1223, 1243

Financial regulations, modernization efforts—869–870, 920, 936, 1006, 1032, 1041, 1085, 1094, 1124, 1131, 1136, 1146, 1154, 1158, 1198, 1203, 1211, 1223–1224, 1226, 1228, 1252, 1257, 1289, 1307, 1332, 1342, 1346, 1373–1374, 1489, 1497, 1521–1522, 1531, 1533, 1536, 1580

Government bonds, creditworthiness—877, 906, 911, 933, 942, 946–947, 954, 958, 964, 968, 985

Household incomes, decline—834, 836, 852, 867, 873, 895, 897, 914, 916, 928, 935, 942, 977, 991, 999, 1072–1073, 1094, 1124, 1126, 1128, 1130, 1158, 1202, 1207, 1220, 1248, 1257, 1281, 1284, 1293, 1298, 1323, 1329, 1331, 1336, 1340, 1344, 1483

Improvement—832, 844, 847, 851, 853, 873, 924, 928, 935, 942–943, 952, 958, 979, 984–985, 988, 996, 1214, 1344, 1510, 1534, 1566, 1572

Income inequality, increase—965, 1016, 1207, 1210, 1260, 1281, 1359, 1518–1519

Market volatility—877, 891, 928, 935, 938, 942, 945–946, 954, 958, 967, 1228, 1375

Poverty

Efforts to combat—839, 904, 1124, 1259

Rate, increase—1124

Recession, effects—823, 827, 831–832, 838, 841–842, 844, 846, 850, 853, 863, 868–870, 873, 878, 889, 893, 895, 901, 906, 908, 914, 916, 918, 921, 928, 931, 933–936, 941–942, 950–951, 953, 957, 963–966, 976–977, 984, 989, 996–997, 1008, 1014, 1016, 1034, 1037, 1045, 1052, 1054, 1061–1062, 1073, 1076, 1078–1079, 1083, 1085, 1094, 1108–1110, 1114, 1117, 1124, 1128, 1135, 1138–1139, 1143, 1152, 1154, 1156–1158, 1162–1163, 1171, 1179, 1188, 1197–1198, 1204, 1210, 1213–1215, 1220–1221, 1223–1224, 1231–1232, 1239–1240, 1245, 1251–1252, 1256–1257, 1260–1261, 1284, 1288, 1290, 1293, 1297, 1303–1305, 1322, 1329, 1332, 1336, 1338, 1341, 1344, 1365–1366, 1384, 1388, 1390, 1483, 1489, 1494, 1503, 1516, 1522

Economy, national—Continued

Strengthening efforts—823, 825–827, 832, 834, 841–842, 844, 846, 849–851, 853–854, 867–868, 871, 873, 883, 889, 892–893, 896–898, 901, 906–909, 912–916, 918–919, 921, 928, 930–931, 934–938, 942–943, 945–946, 950, 952, 954–955, 957–958, 960, 963–965, 968, 970, 973, 977–979, 982, 984, 990, 992, 994, 1016, 1018, 1021–1022, 1025, 1029–1033, 1035, 1038, 1040–1041, 1043–1047, 1051–1052, 1054–1055, 1057–1058, 1061–1064, 1071–1073, 1075–1079, 1082–1085, 1096, 1108–1110, 1117–1119, 1122, 1126, 1128–1129, 1133, 1135–1136, 1141–1143, 1149, 1152, 1154–1156, 1168, 1171, 1187–1188, 1190–1191, 1193–1195, 1200, 1203–1204, 1206–1207, 1213, 1218–1222, 1225, 1228, 1231, 1239–1241, 1245–1249, 1252, 1254, 1259–1261, 1269, 1276, 1279–1280, 1282, 1285–1289, 1291, 1293–1295, 1298–1299, 1305–1307, 1315, 1320, 1324–1326, 1328–1329, 1336–1337, 1339–1342, 1345, 1349–1350, 1355, 1359–1360, 1364, 1366, 1368, 1371, 1373, 1376–1377, 1381, 1383, 1390, 1395, 1411, 1417, 1419, 1424, 1430, 1441, 1456, 1460–1462, 1466–1467, 1471, 1481, 1483–1484, 1486–1487, 1489, 1491, 1494, 1502–1505, 1507, 1510, 1515–1516, 1519–1522, 1526, 1536, 1546, 1558–1559, 1561–1562, 1564, 1568, 1578, 1581, 1587–1589

Travel and tourism, promotion efforts—1001, 1004, 1321, 1323

Ecuador, U.S. Ambassador—1593

Education

See also specific State

American Graduation Initiative—1259

Bullying, reduction efforts—1173, 1190

Early childhood education programs—1292, 1446

Foreign exchange programs—1265, 1316

Global competitiveness—836, 892, 897, 908, 919, 925, 935, 938, 946, 970, 974, 991–992, 1039, 1044, 1046, 1054–1055, 1060, 1064, 1073, 1075, 1095, 1110, 1115, 1118, 1121–1122, 1132, 1139, 1142–1143, 1149–1150, 1152, 1164, 1166, 1181, 1187, 1199, 1205, 1211–1212, 1222, 1232, 1248, 1257, 1263, 1282, 1290, 1292, 1295, 1300, 1318, 1325, 1337, 1341, 1345, 1386, 1395, 1429, 1446, 1496, 1580

Government and private sector, coordination efforts—1076, 1120, 1150, 1580

High school dropout rate—1119, 1122, 1150

Hispanic students

Dropout rates—1172, 1177

Performance and completion, improvement efforts—897, 1064, 1172, 1177

Low-income students—946

Minority students—1150, 1171–1172

No Child Left Behind Act—960, 1118, 1120, 1122–1123, 1151, 1326, 1350, 1386–1387, 1596–1597

Education—Continued
  Parental involvement—1119, 1151, 1522
  Postsecondary education
    Affordability—823, 828, 837, 840, 844, 850, 893,
      902, 908, 985, 1032, 1060, 1085, 1094, 1124,
      1139, 1147, 1155, 1182, 1187, 1257, 1318, 1337,
      1347, 1350–1352, 1483, 1489, 1520, 1536, 1613
    Career training and continuing education—828–
      829, 897, 930, 944, 990, 1046, 1077, 1141,
      1145, 1147, 1172, 1177, 1181, 1242, 1318, 1522
    College dropout rate—1181
    Community colleges—829, 866, 897, 980, 1032,
      1041, 1064, 1077, 1124, 1145, 1520
    Higher education institution leaders and advo-
      cates, meeting with President—1613
    Historically Black Colleges and Universities—1124
    Pell grants—828, 878, 897, 937, 1060, 1064,
      1077, 1124, 1128, 1147, 1154, 1386
    Sexual assault, prevention efforts—1422
    Student loans, elimination of subsidies to private
      providers—828, 849–850, 878, 1032, 1094,
      1124, 1131, 1147, 1154, 1158, 1172, 1198,
      1211, 1253, 1257, 1324, 1332, 1336, 1342,
      1347, 1351, 1427, 1467
    Student loans, refinancing and repayment op-
      tions—828, 1351–1352, 1360, 1377, 1386, 1467,
      1484
  Reform legislation—835, 1119–1120, 1122, 1336, 1345
  School improvement and renovation—836, 985,
    1017, 1038, 1044, 1052, 1054–1057, 1059–1060,
    1063, 1076, 1078, 1083, 1095, 1109, 1115, 1122,
    1125, 1136, 1142, 1155, 1164–1166, 1168, 1187–
    1188, 1191, 1199, 1211, 1219, 1221, 1240, 1248,
    1253, 1261, 1270, 1292, 1295, 1299, 1304, 1333,
    1337, 1339, 1520
  School lunch programs, improvement efforts—1002
  Science and math programs—828, 897, 1046, 1074–
    1075, 1077, 1120, 1122–1123, 1150, 1318, 1520
  Standards and school accountability—823, 827,
    834, 836, 890, 897, 935, 938, 960, 1032, 1034,
    1073, 1079, 1082, 1119–1122, 1140, 1150–1151,
    1161, 1163, 1171, 1177, 1182, 1198–1199, 1202–
    1203, 1215, 1326, 1342–1343, 1386–1387, 1390,
    1492, 1519, 1522, 1558
  Teachers—836, 897, 959–960, 970, 974, 1032,
    1034, 1039, 1044, 1051, 1054, 1060, 1063, 1076,
    1095, 1109–1110, 1115, 1117–1118, 1120, 1122,
    1132, 1136, 1142, 1150, 1155, 1168, 1171, 1182,
    1199, 1204, 1207, 1212, 1219, 1248, 1254, 1260,
    1270, 1289–1292, 1294–1295, 1297, 1299–1300,
    1304, 1318, 1329, 1333, 1337, 1339, 1345, 1386–
    1387, 1395, 1446, 1497
  Technology and innovation, expansion efforts—836,
    992, 1120, 1139
  Vocational and technical education programs—1151

Education, Department of
  Funding—839, 902, 1119
  Race to the Top Fund—835, 897, 936, 960, 1064,
    1119–1120, 1122, 1149, 1177, 1318
  Secretary—1055, 1118–1119, 1179, 1182, 1242,
    1446, 1507, 1580, 1613
Education Sciences, National Board for—1600, 1603
Educational Excellence for Hispanics, President's
  Advisory Commission on—1577, 1588, 1595, 1600
Egypt
  Counterterrorism efforts, cooperation with U.S.—1604
  Democracy efforts—1010, 1099, 1271, 1474, 1478,
    1490, 1604
  Minister of Defense—1604
  Parliamentary elections—1478
  Relations with Israel—1594
  Security cooperation with U.S.—1604
Elections
  See also specific State or country
  2012 Presidential and congressional elections—850,
    865, 887, 898, 921, 923–925, 937–939, 942, 947, 950,
    953–954, 956, 966, 968, 972, 976, 979, 1042, 1047,
    1053, 1057, 1061, 1065, 1072–1074, 1077, 1085,
    1093–1095, 1097, 1118, 1129, 1131, 1133, 1137–
    1140, 1142, 1155–1156, 1158, 1161–1162, 1164,
    1168, 1187, 1198, 1201–1204, 1208, 1213, 1215–
    1216, 1223–1224, 1228–1229, 1232, 1250, 1256–
    1257, 1259, 1280, 1286, 1291, 1321, 1330, 1338,
    1340–1341, 1344, 1346–1348, 1374, 1377, 1428,
    1430, 1490–1492, 1494–1495, 1497–1498, 1546
  Campaign finance laws—837, 976
  Voter participation—1177
Emergency Board No. 243, Presidential—1600
Emergency Management Agency, Federal. *See*
  Homeland Security, Department of
Employment and unemployment
  See also Economy, national; *specific State*
  College graduates, employment outlook—1119
  Employment opportunities for ex-felons, strength-
    ening efforts—973
  Equal employment opportunity—876
  Job creation and growth—823, 827–830, 832–833,
    838, 841–842, 844, 850–851, 853–854, 865–866,
    868, 874, 883, 887, 895–897, 907–908, 913–916,
    919, 921–922, 926, 928–931, 933, 935–936, 942–
    946, 950–955, 957–958, 963–964, 968, 970–971,
    978, 980, 982, 984–985, 990–992, 994–997,
    1009, 1016, 1018, 1022, 1024–1026, 1029–1031,
    1033, 1037–1040, 1042, 1044–1047, 1051, 1053–
    1061, 1063–1065, 1071–1076, 1078–1079, 1081–
    1085, 1090, 1095–1096, 1102, 1108–1110, 1115–
    1119, 1122, 1125–1126, 1129, 1131–1132, 1136–
    1137, 1142–1143, 1145, 1147–1148, 1154–1155,
    1159, 1164–1167, 1171–1172, 1186, 1188–1190,
    1192–1196, 1199–1201, 1204–1208, 1211–1215,

Employment and unemployment—Continued
  Job creation and growth—Continued
    1218–1222, 1225, 1228, 1232, 1239–1243, 1245–
    1251, 1253–1254, 1256–1257, 1260–1263, 1269–
    1270, 1277–1280, 1284–1290, 1292–1301, 1304–
    1308, 1315, 1317, 1320, 1322, 1326–1329, 1332–
    1333, 1337, 1339, 1344–1345, 1349–1350, 1359–
    1360, 1364–1371, 1373–1374, 1377, 1380–1381,
    1386, 1390, 1395, 1397–1398, 1401, 1406, 1410–
    1411, 1413, 1415, 1417–1419, 1423, 1425, 1428,
    1432–1433, 1436, 1442, 1444, 1449, 1456, 1460–
    1461, 1463, 1466–1469, 1471, 1473, 1477, 1481–
    1482, 1484–1485, 1491, 1494, 1496, 1502–1504,
    1507–1508, 1510, 1514–1515, 1520, 1526–1527,
    1534, 1561–1562, 1568, 1584, 1589, 1600–1601
  Job losses—823, 827, 832, 841–842, 850, 853, 896–
    897, 901, 915, 918, 928, 931, 942, 950, 957, 960,
    970, 977, 985, 996, 1009, 1024–1025, 1029–
    1030, 1032–1033, 1044, 1051, 1076, 1095, 1125,
    1139, 1143, 1159–1160, 1164, 1205, 1218, 1220,
    1223, 1228, 1240–1241, 1279, 1284, 1286, 1290,
    1295, 1307, 1345, 1394, 1461, 1489, 1494, 1546
  Job training assistance—839, 897, 995, 1039, 1056,
    1059, 1063, 1078, 1109, 1125, 1194–1195, 1277,
    1286, 1290, 1296
  Job training programs—853, 1032, 1041, 1054,
    1166, 1246
  Outsourcing to foreign countries—851, 1257, 1518
  Undocumented workers, reduction and prevention
    efforts—1170, 1335
  Unemployment insurance—833, 850, 861, 865,
    883, 901, 915, 929, 931, 934, 957, 967, 984, 989,
    995, 997, 1039, 1045, 1052, 1054, 1056, 1059,
    1063, 1124–1125, 1152, 1166, 1171, 1220, 1296,
    1487, 1503, 1514–1515, 1531–1532, 1534–1535,
    1552, 1562–1567, 1572
  Unemployment rate—841, 853, 861, 865, 895, 928,
    952, 1072–1073, 1085, 1124, 1129, 1136, 1171,
    1241, 1260, 1270, 1281, 1298, 1328, 1345, 1377,
    1380, 1390, 1428, 1502, 1514–1515, 1519
  Young adults, employment opportunities—1039,
    1044, 1052, 1056, 1059, 1063, 1078, 1109, 1125,
    1171, 1280, 1390
Energy
  See also Environment; *specific State or country*
  Alternative and renewable sources and technolo-
    gies
    Federal Government use—955
    Promotion efforts—830, 834, 836, 893, 896, 902,
      907–908, 919, 938–939, 943, 950, 955, 978, 980,
      982, 993, 996, 1032, 1128, 1164, 1227, 1265,
      1374, 1384, 1398, 1419, 1429, 1437, 1444, 1492
    U.S. production—828, 919, 981, 1225
  Biofuels and ethanol—836, 839, 862, 908, 955,
    971, 978, 980, 982, 993

Energy—Continued
  Carbon dioxide emissions, reduction—836, 946,
    1103, 1437
  Developing countries, energy sources—1227
  Domestic sources—830, 836, 907, 943, 955, 978,
    980, 982, 1398, 1529
  Energy efficiency and weatherization
    Homes and buildings—919, 1110, 1502–1504, 1508
    Tax incentives—1504
  Foreign sources—836, 896, 907–909, 919, 937,
    946, 970, 980, 1128, 1155, 1163, 1313, 1492
  Fuel efficiency standards, strengthening efforts—836,
    906–907, 943, 946, 955, 968, 1029, 1136, 1140,
    1155, 1210, 1336, 1342, 1347, 1384, 1398, 1427,
    1437, 1492–1493, 1558, 1583, 1586
  Gasoline, oil, and natural gas costs—837, 861, 896,
    907, 914, 916, 919, 942, 952, 955, 964, 985, 994, 997,
    1005, 1151, 1154, 1171, 1219, 1227, 1241, 1298
  Greenhouse gas emissions, regulation—1029
  Hybrid and alternative fuel automobiles
    Battery technology, U.S. production—830, 908,
      941–942, 946, 955, 1032, 1225, 1347, 1586
    Promotion efforts—836, 907, 919, 936, 955, 1207
  Infrastructure and grid improvements—832, 936,
    970–971, 1026
  National energy policy—836, 907–908, 924–925,
    1073, 1135, 1140, 1154, 1161, 1202, 1214, 1227,
    1232, 1257, 1298, 1324, 1332–1333, 1342, 1384
  Naval Petroleum and Oil Shale Reserve—1448
  Oil and gas industry
    Federal regulations and oversight—1397, 1527, 1534
    Keystone XL Pipeline project—1527, 1529, 1534
    Safety and environmental issues—1398
    Subsidies, elimination—834, 837, 859, 861, 867, 893,
      907, 914, 944, 969, 1000, 1060, 1084, 1168, 1419
  Solar and wind energy—828, 830, 836, 919, 955,
    970–971, 980–982, 1225
Energy, Department of
  Assistant Secretaries
    Energy Efficiency and Renewable Energy—1583
    Fossil Energy—1578
  Energy, Under Secretary for—1611
  General Counsel—1584
  Minority Economic Impact, Office of—1583
  Secretary—1590
England. *See* United Kingdom
Environment
  See also Energy
  Air quality, improvement efforts—853, 908, 955,
    1029, 1187, 1228, 1244, 1346
  Carbon emissions—908, 919, 939, 1163, 1336
  Climate change—908, 936, 1103, 1107, 1109–
    1110, 1137, 1313, 1374, 1419, 1437, 1444, 1454,
    1478, 1492
  Deforestation, prevention efforts—1156, 1454

Environment—Continued
  Quality, improvement efforts—827, 908, 946, 1001, 1306
  United Nations Climate Change Conference—1103
  Water quality, improvement efforts—853, 908, 1187, 1244, 1346
  Whaling—1069–1070
Environmental Protection Agency—1029, 1346, 1592
ESPN—1608
Europe
  See also specific country
  Afghanistan, role—1473
  Counterterrorism efforts, cooperation with U.S.—1611
  Economic growth and development—1474, 1491
  European Union
    Common foreign and security policy—1473
    Counterterrorism efforts, cooperation with U.S.—1480
    Energy cooperation with U.S.—1478
    European Commission President—1473–1474, 1481
    European Commission Trade Minister—1477
    European Council President—1473–1474, 1481
    International assistance—1478
    Leaders, meeting with President Obama—1611
    Relations with U.S.—1473–1474, 1477, 1480
    Security cooperation with U.S.—1480
  Financial markets
    Stabilization efforts—1313, 1354–1356, 1369–1370, 1373, 1375–1376, 1405, 1436, 1481, 1533, 1581, 1586, 1590, 1601–1603, 1608, 1610, 1613
    Unrest—842, 914, 916, 931, 942, 952, 964, 985, 997, 1151, 1154, 1171, 1218, 1231, 1353, 1356, 1369–1370, 1405, 1423, 1436, 1473, 1481, 1514, 1526, 1533, 1566
  Trade with U.S.—1373, 1473, 1534
  Western Balkans, NATO presence and peacekeeping efforts—1479
Evangelicals, National Association of—1601
Export-Import Bank, U.S.—1449, 1582

Faith-based and community organizations, programs and services—1558
Farm Broadcasting, National Association of—1588
FDIC. *See* Deposit Insurance Corporation, Federal
Federal. *See other part of subject*
FEMA. *See* Homeland Security, Department of
Fine Arts, Commission of—1596, 1612
Fish Stocks in the Western and Central Pacific Ocean, Commission for the Conservation and Management of Highly Migratory—1580
Fitness, Sports, and Nutrition, President's Council on—1603

Florida
  Democratic Party events—1251, 1256
  Harp and Celt Restaurant and Irish Pub in Orlando—1601
  President's visits—935, 1251, 1256, 1600–1601
  WEAR in Pensacola—1614
  WTVT in Tampa—1606
Foreign policy, U.S.
  See also specific country or region
  Civil and human rights, promotion efforts—920, 926–927, 1008, 1090, 1100, 1103, 1239, 1262, 1271, 1441, 1444, 1451, 1524, 1551, 1559
  Democratization—920, 1008, 1089–1092, 1100, 1164, 1230–1231, 1271, 1347, 1442, 1444, 1474, 1490
  Diplomatic efforts, expansion—912, 1101, 1135, 1156, 1163, 1215, 1259, 1316, 1406, 1412, 1441, 1480, 1490
  Foreign aid funding—838
  Foreign Ambassadors, credentialing ceremony—1578, 1594
  Humanitarian assistance programs—920, 1478, 1611
  Human rights violations, prevention efforts—926–927
  Open government and transparency, promotion efforts—1089–1091, 1103, 1455, 1474
  Peace efforts, expansion—838, 1111, 1169, 1230
  Poverty, efforts to combat—1103
France
  Afghanistan, French military forces, deployment—1112, 1379
  France 2 television—1607
  Libya, role—1378
  President—1112, 1231, 1369, 1373–1379, 1425, 1436, 1533, 1582, 1585, 1589, 1601, 1603, 1606–1608
  President Obama's visit—1369–1371, 1373, 1377, 1606
  Relations with U.S.—1112, 1369, 1377–1379, 1606
  Security cooperation with U.S.—1582
  TF1 television—1607

Germany
  Chancellor—1231, 1370, 1375–1376, 1436, 1533, 1581, 1585, 1590, 1596, 1602–1603, 1608, 1613
  Defense cooperation with U.S.—1370
  Energy, alternative and renewable sources and technologies—830
  Relations with U.S.—1370
  U.S. Ambassador—1580
Government organization and employees
  See also Budget, Federal; *specific agency or organization*
  Accountability and transparency, strengthening efforts—966, 1090–1091
  Federal buildings, operating cost inefficiencies, elimination efforts—1388

Government organization and employees—Continued
Federal employee pay freeze—831
Federal Government contracting policies, reform—1041, 1059, 1326, 1391
Federal programs, improvement efforts—839, 975, 1006, 1341, 1388–1389, 1522
Federal regulations, review—854, 987, 990, 1023–1024, 1026, 1029, 1041, 1145–1146, 1242, 1244–1245, 1323, 1326, 1339, 1341, 1410–1411, 1419, 1429, 1496, 1527
Veterans, Federal employment opportunities—1148, 1303, 1380, 1399, 1402
Great Britain. *See* United Kingdom
Greece
Financial markets
Stabilization efforts—1405
Unrest—842, 1152, 1369, 1405
Former Prime Minister—1609
Prime Minister—1375, 1610
Relations with U.S.—1609
Grenada, U.S. Ambassador—1605
Guam, President's visit—1610
Guantanamo Bay, U.S. Naval Base. *See* Cuba
Guatemala
Democracy efforts—1610
President-elect—1610
Guinea, President—909

Haiti, earthquake, damage and recovery efforts—824
Harry S. Truman Scholarship Foundation—1593
Hawaii
Democratic Party event—1426
Governor—1426
Hanauma Bay Nature Preserve—1616
Lieutenant Governor—1426
President's visit—1403–1404, 1412–1414, 1416–1419, 1426, 1607–1608, 1610, 1616
Sea Life Park Hawaii in Waimanalo—1616
World War II Valor of the Pacific National Monument at Pearl Harbor—1616
Health and Human Services, Department of
Food and Drug Administration—1362–1363
Funding—846
Head Start programs—834, 849, 1386–1387
Low Income Home Energy Assistance Program (LIHEAP)—994
Medicare and Medicaid Services, Center for—1611
Secretary—1363, 1385, 1516, 1532
Health and medical care
See also Diseases; HIV/AIDS; Science and technology
Affordability and costs—837, 840, 938, 961–962, 1032, 1073, 1140, 1144, 1163, 1202, 1257, 1282, 1483, 1573
Contraception and family planning—1532

Health and medical care—Continued
Cost control reforms—849, 858, 871, 875, 896, 919, 953, 958, 993, 1003, 1080, 1140, 1143, 1187, 1362, 1394, 1491
Employer-based health insurance coverage—830, 1032
Generic drug production, approval process, improvement efforts—1080
Health insurance exchange—962, 968–969, 1178
Health insurance mandates, constitutionality—962
Health insurance reforms—897, 935, 938, 946, 961–962, 967–969, 972, 1032, 1072, 1080, 1085, 1094, 1125, 1128, 1131, 1135, 1144, 1154–1155, 1159, 1163, 1187, 1198–1199, 1203, 1211, 1253, 1257, 1289, 1294, 1299, 1306, 1324, 1329, 1332, 1336, 1350, 1390, 1393, 1395, 1427, 1489, 1492–1493, 1558
Healthy, Hunger-Free Kids Act of 2010—1002
Home health care—1551–1553
Information technology—1021
Insurance coverage and access to providers—924, 962, 968, 978, 1178, 1346
Medical fraud and negligence, efforts to combat and prevent—902, 1363
Medicare and Medicaid—834, 844, 846, 849, 858, 860–861, 863, 867, 871, 874, 886, 888, 890–893, 896, 901–902, 912, 914, 933, 936–939, 947, 958, 961, 969, 985, 989, 991, 993, 1000, 1003–1004, 1032, 1040, 1064, 1079–1080, 1082, 1084, 1129, 1144–1145, 1153, 1155, 1189, 1191, 1215, 1258, 1424, 1429, 1462, 1496, 1520
Patient Protection and Affordable Care Act—860, 878, 897, 921, 924, 961–962, 967, 975, 1073, 1080, 1138, 1159, 1178, 1198–1199, 1211, 1253, 1342, 1346–1347, 1558
Prescription drugs, shortages—1362–1363
Preventive care and public health programs—1178
Research and development—849–850, 893, 919, 1076, 1082
Seniors, prescription drug benefits—860, 863, 957, 961, 969, 989, 997, 1137, 1200, 1211
Small businesses, tax credits to purchase insurance coverage—969
Young adults, insurance coverage as dependents, age limit extension—961, 969, 1032, 1159, 1178, 1199, 1211, 1253, 1324, 1346
Hearst Television—1606
Hispanic Policy Conference—1579
Historic Preservation, Advisory Council on—1578, 1584
HIV/AIDS
See also specific country or region
Domestic prevention and treatment strategy—1190, 1499–1500
Emergency Plan for AIDS Relief, President's—1498

HIV/AIDS—Continued
    HIV-positive immigrants, elimination of ban on
        entry—1499
    International AIDS Conference—1499
    International prevention and treatment efforts—1498–
        1500
    Minorities—1499
    Ryan White HIV/AIDS Treatment Extension Act
        of 2009—1499
Holidays and special observances—1140
    Armenian National Day—1113
    Cesar Chavez Day—904
    Christmas—1501, 1537, 1571, 1616
    Diwali—1353, 1605
    Eid al-Adha—1379
    Eid al-Fitr—1023
    Hajj—1379
    Halloween—1360, 1605
    Hanukkah—1535–1536, 1565
    Hispanic Heritage Month—1062
    Independence Day—823–825
    Italian American Heritage Month, National—1360
    Kwanzaa—1571
    Labor Day—1031
    Nelson Mandela International Day—868
    Pearl Harbor Remembrance Day, National—1530
    Ramadan—913, 940, 1100
    Rosh Hashanah—1168–1169
    September 11th National Day of Service and Re-
        membrance—1595
    Sikhism, anniversary of founder's birth—1396
    Small Business Saturday—1471
    Thanksgiving—1469–1472, 1610–1611
    Veterans Day—1380, 1398, 1400–1402, 1608
    World AIDS Day—1498, 1500
    Yom Kippur—1168
Holocaust Memorial Council, U.S.—1605
Homeland Security, Department of
    See also Defense and national security; Terrorism
    Chief Financial Officer—1609
    Emergency Management Agency, Federal—959,
        1012, 1014–1015, 1017, 1030–1031, 1129, 1584,
        1589–1590, 1592
    Inspector General, Office of the—1581
    Secretary—1014–1015, 1360, 1528, 1589–1590,
        1593–1594
Honduras
    Democracy efforts—1216
    Economic growth and development—1216
    Human rights issues—1216
    President—1216, 1598
    Relations with U.S.—1216
    Trade with U.S.—1216

Housing
    Fannie Mae and Freddie Mac corporations
        Mortgage refinancing program—831
        Reform—1079
    Foreclosure
        Avoidance efforts—831, 835, 987–988
        Rate—827, 1335
    Housing market
        Decline—827, 831–832, 842, 865, 931, 953, 964,
            970, 985, 987–988, 1041, 1136, 1143, 1241,
            1326–1328, 1335, 1365, 1489, 1503, 1520
        Improvement—831
        Stabilization efforts—827, 835, 987–988, 1054,
            1192, 1327–1328, 1335–1336, 1390, 1536
    Hurricane-displaced households, Federal assis-
        tance—1017
    Mortgage refinancing regulations—1041, 1143,
        1327, 1330–1331, 1335–1337, 1350, 1359, 1467,
        1484, 1522
    Urban and metropolitan policy—882, 1035
Housing and Urban Development, Department of
    Deputy Secretary—1598
    Housing Commissioner, Federal—1603
    Housing, Assistant Secretary for—1603
    Inspector General—1580
    Neighborhood Stabilization Program—1326–1328,
        1335
    Secretary—977
    Strong Cities, Strong Communities initiative—1035
Housing Finance Agency, Federal—1327
Human Rights Campaign—1189–1191
Hurricanes. *See* Disaster assistance; Natural disas-
    ters; *specific Federal agency or State*

Iceland, whaling—1069–1070
Illinois
    Aragon Entertainment Center in Chicago—1585
    Democratic Party events—917, 921, 924, 1585
    Galesburg High School in Galesburg—1588
    Governor—917, 996–997, 1004
    President's visits—917, 921, 924, 936, 983, 996,
        1008, 1584–1588
    U.S. Representative, retirement—1209
    Whiteside County Fair in Morrison—1588
    Wyffels Hybrids, Inc., in Atkinson—1588
Immigration and naturalization
    See also Defense and national security; *specific
        country or region*
    American "melting pot"—830, 897, 899, 919, 937,
        1050, 1065, 1259
    Citizenship—1170
    Deportation rates—898
    HIV-positive immigrants, elimination of ban on
        entry—1190, 1499
    Illegal immigration—1170, 1214

Immigration and naturalization—Continued
> Reform—829–830, 897–898, 919, 1064–1065, 1156, 1161, 1164, 1169–1170, 1172–1174, 1242, 1259, 1324, 1333, 1335, 1342, 1384
> Visa policy, U.S.—1242, 1323

India
> Counterterrorism efforts, cooperation with U.S.—857
> Economic growth and development—907
> Energy, alternative and renewable sources and technologies—1438
> President Obama's visit—857, 1353
> Prime Minister—1449
> Relations with Australia—1437
> Relations with Pakistan—1230
> Relations with U.S.—857, 1449–1450
> Terrorist attacks in Mumbai—857
> U.S. Ambassador-designate—1614

Indiana, WISH in Indianapolis—1613

Indonesia
> Comprehensive Test Ban Treaty, ratification—1524
> Economic growth and development—1453
> Energy cooperation with U.S.—1454
> Governmental accountability and transparency, strengthening efforts—1444
> Lion Air—1449, 1453
> President—1452–1453
> President Obama's visit—1449–1453, 1455–1456, 1609
> Relations with U.S.—1453–1455
> Science and technology—1455
> Security cooperation with U.S.—1453–1454
> Student exchanges with U.S.—1454–1455
> Trade with U.S.—1449, 1453–1454, 1456
> U.S. Embassy personnel, meeting with President Obama—1610

Infrastructure Advisory Council, National—1579, 1594

Institute of Building Sciences, National—1582, 1593, 1598

Intellectual Disabilities, President's Committee for People with—1607

Intelligence. *See* Defense and national security; *specific Federal agency*

Intelligence, Office of the Director of National—1584

Intelligence Advisory Board, President's—1579, 1593

Inter-American Foundation—1593

Interior, Department of the
> Indian Affairs, Bureau of—1505
> Park Service, National—1501
> Public lands, conservation and management—1364
> Secretary—977, 1165, 1259, 1364, 1501, 1505–1507
> Solicitor—1505

International. *See other part of subject*

International Trade Commission, U.S.—1607

Iowa
> Daily Times Herald of Carroll—1588
> DeWitt Dairy Treats in DeWitt—1587
> Disaster assistance—1589, 1591
> Guttenberg
>> Rausch's Cafe—1587
>> Small-business owners, meeting with President—1587
> LeClaire
>> Grasshoppers gift shop—1587
>> Kernel Cody's Popcorn Shoppe—1587
> Maquoketa High School in Maquoketa—1587
> Northeast Iowa Community College in Peosta—1587
> President's visit—963, 977, 979–981, 984, 1585–1587

Iran
> Detained U.S. citizens, release—1112–1113, 1598
> Human rights issues—1100
> International and U.S. sanctions—1267–1268, 1413, 1419–1421, 1457, 1463, 1534, 1560
> International diplomatic efforts—1268, 1369, 1420, 1463, 1473, 1481
> Nuclear energy, civilian usage—1463
> Nuclear weapons development—1102, 1268, 1369, 1413, 1415, 1419–1421, 1463, 1473, 1479, 1481, 1534, 1560, 1611
> Oil supply and refining—1463
> Political unrest and violence—1481
> Relations with Syria—1268
> Terrorism, sponsorship—1267–1269
> U.S. national emergency, continuation—1383
> U.S. surveillance drone crash—1541

Iraq
> Civilian casualties—1539
> Democracy efforts—1538, 1542–1543
> Economic growth and development—1538, 1543
> Educational system, development—1488
> Energy cooperation with U.S.—1488
> Governmental accountability and transparency, strengthening efforts—1488
> Infrastructure and economic development—1488
> Insurgency and terrorist attacks—1548
> Iraqi military and security forces—1316, 1319, 1538, 1542–1544, 1548
> Oil supply and refining—1538, 1542
> President—1113
> Prime Minister—1488, 1537, 1548, 1604, 1607, 1613
> Reconciliation efforts—1542
> Relations with Arab States—1316
> Relations with U.S.—1098, 1316, 1487–1488, 1537–1539, 1542–1543, 1548
> Security cooperation with U.S.—1316, 1489, 1538, 1543–1544
> Strategic framework agreement with U.S.—1316, 1487, 1538, 1543
> Student exchanges with U.S.—1538

Iraq—Continued
  Trade with U.S.—1316, 1488, 1538
  U.S. Ambassador—1543
  U.S. military forces
    Casualties—941, 1051, 1539, 1543, 1548
    Deployment—824, 833, 838, 855, 862–863, 901, 920, 922, 931, 936, 941, 944, 950, 953, 957, 959, 968, 978, 990, 997, 1014, 1019–1020, 1048–1050, 1066, 1079–1080, 1084, 1098, 1135, 1137, 1140, 1154, 1163, 1185, 1200, 1214, 1238, 1253, 1257, 1281, 1310, 1316–1317, 1319–1320, 1324, 1329, 1332, 1336, 1342, 1347, 1379–1380, 1384, 1399, 1401–1402, 1427, 1435, 1441, 1460, 1465, 1483, 1489–1490, 1492, 1494, 1537–1539, 1542–1544, 1547–1550, 1554, 1558, 1561, 1564, 1570, 1572, 1594, 1613–1615
Ireland, U.S. Ambassador—1246
Israel
  See also Middle East
  Ambassador to U.S.—1535, 1556
  Minister of Defense—1556, 1559
  Prime Minister—1104, 1586
  Relations with Egypt—1594
  Relations with U.S.—1101, 1104, 1169, 1490, 1534–1535, 1559–1560
  Security cooperation with U.S.—1104, 1490, 1492, 1535, 1560
  Terrorist attacks—1559
  U.S. assistance—1560
Italian American Foundation, National—1360
Italy
  Ambassador to U.S.—1360
  Financial markets
    Stabilization efforts—1405
    Unrest—1533
  President—1608
  Prime Minister—1376, 1586, 1610
  Relations with U.S.—1360
  U.S. Ambassador—1360

James Madison Memorial Fellowship Foundation—1593, 1612
Japan
  Defense relationship with U.S.—1105, 1615
  Earthquake and tsunami, damage and recovery efforts—885, 914, 916, 931, 942, 952, 964, 985, 997, 1105, 1241, 1412
  Economic growth and development—1105
  Prime Minister—1023, 1105, 1407, 1412, 1418, 1591, 1615
  Relations with U.S.—1023, 1105, 1406, 1412, 1591
  Trans-Pacific Partnership, membership bid—1407, 1419
Jordan, political reform efforts—1478

Judiciary
  Federal court nominations and confirmations—1524, 1533, 1578–1579, 1581, 1583–1585, 1594, 1596–1597, 1600, 1603, 1605–1606, 1608–1609, 1612, 1614
  Supreme Court, Associate Justices—895, 899, 1062, 1159, 1198, 1253, 1257, 1259, 1535, 1558
Justice, Department of
  Attorney General—1224–1226, 1267, 1269, 1356, 1575, 1585
  Community Relations Service—1602
  Inspector General—1583
  Inspector General, Acting—1225
  Tax Division, Assistant Attorney General—1594
Juvenile Justice and Delinquency Prevention, Coordinating Council on—1597
J. William Fulbright Foreign Scholarship Board—1577, 1581, 1584

Kansas
  Disaster assistance—1584, 1598
  Osawatomie High School in Osawatomie—1515, 1613
  President's visit—1515, 1612–1613
  We B Smokin' restaurant in Paola—1613
Kennedy Center. *See* Smithsonian Institution
Kentucky, disaster assistance—1583
Kenya, U.S. Embassy bombing, 13th anniversary—932
Kosovo, KFOR international security force—1556
Kyoto Protocol. *See* Environment
Kyrgyzstan
  Democracy efforts—1363
  President—1363
  Presidential elections—1363
  Prime Minister—1611
  Relations with U.S.—1363

Labor, Department of
  Secretary—895, 899, 1031, 1242, 1259, 1330, 1332, 1553
  Trade Adjustment Assistance program—1194–1195, 1277, 1279, 1602, 1604
Labor issues
  Homecare workers—1551–1553
  Labor 20 (L–20) summit—1606
  Minimum wage—830, 904, 1032, 1551–1553
  Unions
    America Federation of Labor and Congress of Industrial Organizations (AFL–CIO)—1025, 1030–1031, 1116, 1241, 1246, 1367, 1584
    Labor movement and organized labor—830, 973–974, 1031–1035, 1041
    Public employees, unionization and collective bargaining—830–831, 974, 1034
    Service Employees International Union (SEIU)—1031
  Workplace safety, improvement efforts—1034

Labor Relations Board, National—1614
La Raza, National Council of—895–898
Law enforcement and crime
　Crime rate, decline—1005
　Gun control—1005
　Illegal arms trade, reduction efforts—1224
　Illegal immigration, deportation of criminals—1065, 1170
　State and community law enforcement agencies, Federal support—1005
　Transnational criminal organizations—894, 1013, 1224
Lebanon, U.S. national emergency, continuation—905
Legislation, enacted
　Asia-Pacific Economic Cooperation Business Travel Cards Act of 2011—1410
　Consolidated Appropriations Act, 2012—1568
　Continuing Appropriations Act, 2012—1600
　Kate Puzey Peace Corps Volunteer Protection Act of 2011—1610
　Leahy-Smith America Invents Act—1074–1076
　National Defense Authorization Act for Fiscal Year 2012—1573–1574
　Temporary Payroll Tax Cut Continuation Act of 2011—1567
　VOW to Hire Heroes Act of 2011—1459
Legislation, proposed
　"Airport and Airway Extension Act of 2011, Part IV"—915–917, 926, 930
　"American Jobs Act of 2011"—1054–1055
　"FAA Air Transportation Modernization and Safety Improvement Act"—1024–1026
　"Middle Class Tax Cut of 2011"—1502
　"Surface Transportation Extension Act of 2011"—1024–1026, 1029–1030
　"VOW to Hire Heroes Act of 2011"—1398, 1432
Liberia
　Civil war and ethnic conflict—1382
　Democracy efforts—1239, 1382
　Former President—872
　Liberian refugees in the U.S., status—982
　Political reform efforts—1382
　President—1239
　Presidential election—1382
　Relations with U.S.—1382
　U.S. national emergency, continuation—872
Library of Congress—1569, 1612
Libya
　Arms embargo and naval blockade—1010, 1086
　Democracy efforts—1009–1011, 1020, 1086–1088, 1099, 1107, 1111–1112, 1237, 1265, 1271, 1309–1310, 1313–1314, 1319–1320, 1378, 1474, 1478, 1588–1589, 1603
　Economic growth and development—1088
　Former leader—1086, 1088, 1099, 1309, 1319

Libya—Continued
　Human rights issues—1010–1011, 1086, 1088, 1099, 1309–1310, 1320
　International and U.S. assistance—1011, 1087, 1321
　International and U.S. sanctions—1010–1011, 1086, 1088
　International diplomatic efforts—1010–1011
　Leader—1009–1011, 1020
　NATO, role—1010–1011, 1087, 1099, 1310, 1313, 1320, 1481
　No-fly zone
　　International military forces—1010–1011, 1087, 1092, 1112, 1310, 1314, 1317, 1378, 1555, 1608
　　U.S. military forces—1010–1011, 1087, 1310, 1314, 1319, 1378, 1399, 1555
　Oil supply and refining—1088
　Political unrest and violence—1009–1010, 1086, 1237, 1310, 1320, 1555, 1579
　Relations with U.S.—1011, 1087–1088, 1099, 1310, 1321
　Terrorism, sponsorship—1011, 1310
　Transitional National Council—1009–1011, 1086–1087, 1099, 1596
　United Nations, role—1086–1087, 1099
　U.S. Ambassador—1087
　Women, status—1088
LinkedIn—1140, 1142, 1148, 1152
Louisiana
　Disaster assistance—1017, 1588, 1605
　Hurricane Katrina, damage and recovery efforts—1016

Maine
　Disaster assistance—1595
　WCSH in Portland—1613
Malaria. *See* Diseases
Malaysia
　Prime Minister—1451
　Relations with U.S.—1451
Malta, U.S. Ambassador—1602
Management and Budget, Office of—1585, 1589
Marine Corps, U.S. *See* Navy, Department of the
Maritime Commission, Federal—1593
Marshals Service, U.S.—1597
Maryland
　Disaster assistance—1590, 1596, 1600
　Governor—873, 1589
　President's visits—872, 1556, 1577, 1579, 1581–1582, 1585, 1592, 1598, 1601, 1611, 1613, 1615
　Towson University in Towson—1611
　University of Maryland in College Park—873
Massachusetts
　Disaster assistance—1590, 1592, 1606
　Governor—1589
　Norman Rockwell Museum in Stockbridge—1580

Massachusetts—Continued
  President's visit—1010, 1012, 1587–1588
  University Park Campus School in Worcester—1120
  U.S. Representative, retirement—1353, 1481
Mauritius, U.S. Ambassador—1602
Medal of Valor Review Board—1582
Medals. *See* Decorations, medals, and awards
Medicare and Medicaid. *See* Health and medical care
Merit Systems Protection Board—1612
Mexico
  Counternarcotics and drug interdiction efforts—879
  Counternarcotics efforts, cooperation with U.S.—879, 1013, 1176, 1224
  Economic growth and development—1173–1174
  Helicopter crash outside Mexico City—1608
  President—879, 1173, 1176, 1608
  Relations with U.S.—1173
  Royale San Jeronimo Casino firebombing in Monterrey—1012
  Secretary of Government—1608
  Trade with U.S.—1174
  Trans-Pacific Partnership, membership bid—1419
Michigan
  General Motors Orion Assembly Plant in Lake Orion—1274
  Johnson Controls, Inc., in Holland—941–944, 946, 1586
  Michigan State University in East Lansing—1401
  President's visits—941, 946, 950, 954, 1031, 1274, 1279, 1585–1586, 1588, 1592, 1601–1602
  U.S. Representative, retirement—866
Middle East
  See also Palestinian Authority and Palestinians; *specific country*
  Arab-Israeli conflict, peace process—1101–1102, 1104, 1111–1112, 1313, 1356, 1425, 1479, 1559, 1586, 1590, 1596, 1601
  Democracy efforts—836, 916, 931, 941, 952, 963, 985, 997, 1023, 1049, 1090, 1151, 1154, 1241, 1265, 1268, 1310, 1315, 1320, 1356, 1420, 1473–1474, 1478, 1490, 1492, 1526
  Political unrest and violence—942
  Quartet Representative for the Middle East—1605
Military Academy, U.S. *See* Army, Department of the
Millennium Challenge Corporation—1453–1454
Minnesota
  Governor—951
  Old Market Deli in Cannon Falls—1587
  President's visits—951, 963, 1017, 1586–1587, 1590–1591
  The Coffee Mill restaurant in Zumbrota—1587
  Valleyland Kids summer camp in Chatfield—1587
  WCCO in Minneapolis—1606

Mississippi, Hurricane Katrina, damage and recovery efforts—1017
Missouri
  Democratic Party events—1209, 1214
  Disaster assistance—1587
  Governor—1209
  KMBC in Kansas City—1581
  KSDK in St. Louis—1587
  President's visit—1209, 1214, 1599
  WDAF in Kansas City—1587
Monetary Fund, International—1373, 1375–1376, 1392, 1589
Morocco, political reform efforts—1478

National. *See other part of subject*
National security. *See* Defense and national security
NATO. *See* North Atlantic Treaty Organization
Natural disasters
  See also Disaster assistance; *specific State or country*
  East Coast earthquake—1589, 1607
  Hurricane Irene—1012, 1014–1018, 1030, 1047, 1058, 1588–1592, 1595–1596, 1599
  Hurricane Katrina, 6th anniversary—1016
  Japan, earthquake and tsunami—885
  New Zealand, earthquake—884
  Philippines, floods—1563
  Preparedness efforts—884, 1012, 1015–1017, 1030–1031, 1047, 1434–1435, 1590
  Response and recovery efforts, international cooperation—885
  Turkey, earthquake—1321
Navy, Department of the
  Marine Corps, U.S.—1066, 1068
  Naval Academy, U.S.—1580
  Secretary—1066
NBC, "The Tonight Show"—1604
Nebraska
  Disaster assistance—1587
  KETV in Omaha—1606
  U.S. Senator, retirement—1571
Netherlands
  Prime Minister—1481–1482, 1610
  Relations with U.S.—1481–1482
  U.S. Ambassador—1599
Nevada
  Democratic Party event—1321
  Housing market, decline—1326–1328, 1331, 1335
  KSNV in Las Vegas—1613
  President's visit—1321, 1325, 1335, 1604
  Unemployment rate—1331
New Hampshire
  Disaster assistance—1582, 1590, 1592, 1606, 1613
  Governor—1069

New Hampshire—Continued
  Manchester
    Central High School—1465
    Julien's Corner Kitchen—1610
  President's visit—1465, 1609–1610
New Jersey
  Disaster assistance—1590–1591, 1596, 1602, 1612
  Governor—1030, 1589, 1592
  Hurricane Irene, damage and recovery efforts—1030
  President's visit—1030, 1591–1592
New Mexico, disaster assistance—1611
New York
  Democratic Party events—945, 1084, 1093, 1489, 1491, 1493, 1586
  Disaster assistance—1590–1591, 1594–1595
  Governor—945, 947, 1589
  Hurricane Irene, damage and recovery efforts—1030–1031
  National September 11 Memorial in New York City—1049, 1595
  President's visits—945, 1049, 1084, 1086, 1088–1089, 1091, 1093, 1098, 1104–1106, 1108, 1111–1112, 1489, 1491, 1493, 1586, 1592, 1594–1596, 1611
New Zealand
  2011 Rugby World Cup—885
  Earthquake, damage and recovery efforts—884
  Prime Minister—884, 1578
  Regulatory cooperation and harmonization with U.S.—885
  Relations with U.S.—884
  Trade with U.S.—885
Nicaragua, U.S. Ambassador—1612
Niger, President—909–910
Nigeria
  Counterterrorism efforts, cooperation with U.S.—1571
  Relations with U.S.—1013
  Terrorist attacks—1571
  United Nations
    Role—1013
    Terrorist attack on headquarters in Abuja—1013
North Africa, democracy efforts—941, 1023, 1049, 1090, 1265, 1310, 1314, 1356, 1473–1474, 1478, 1526
North Atlantic Treaty Organization—1010–1011, 1087, 1091, 1099, 1184, 1310, 1313, 1317, 1320, 1354–1355, 1360, 1378, 1392, 1481–1482, 1554, 1607
North Carolina
  Asheville Regional Airport in Fletcher—1284
  Bluestone High School in Skipwith—1603
  Boone
    Mast General Store—1602
    Our Daily Bread bakery—1602
  Countryside Barbecue restaurant in Marion—1602
  Disaster assistance—1589, 1591
  Governor—1058–1059, 1290, 1547, 1589

North Carolina—Continued
  Hurricane Irene
    Damage and recovery efforts—1015, 1058
    Preparedness efforts—1012
  Jamestown
    Guilford Technical Community College—1292, 1603
    Mary Perry Ragsdale Family YMCA—1292
  Lieutenant Governor—1288
  North Carolina State University in Raleigh—1058
  President's visits—1058, 1072, 1284, 1287–1288, 1291–1295, 1297, 1299, 1546, 1594–1595, 1601–1603, 1613–1614
  Reid's House Restaurant in Reidsville—1603
  University of North Carolina in Chapel Hill—1401
  WCNC in Charlotte—1602
  WestStar Precision manufacturing facility in Apex—1595
  West Wilkes High School in Millers Creek—1287
  WFXC in Durham—1602
  WFXK in Durham—1602
  WPEG in Charlotte—1602
  WSOC in Charlotte—1579
  WTVD in Raleigh-Durham—1578
North Dakota, disaster assistance—1586
North Korea
  Chairman—1614–1615
  Human rights issues—1271
  International diplomatic efforts—1265
  Nuclear weapons development—1102, 1265, 1415, 1421, 1443
  Relations with Burma—1452
  Relations with South Korea—1102
  U.S. sanctions—1268
Norway
  Ambassador to U.S.—1583
  Prime Minister—1313, 1582, 1599
  Relations with U.S.—1313–1314
  Security cooperation with U.S.—1481
  Terrorist attacks in Oslo and Utoya—885, 1313, 1582–1583
  Trade with U.S.—1481
Nuclear energy. *See specific country*
Nuclear Waste Technical Review Board—1582
Nuclear weapons. *See* Arms and munitions; *specific country*

Office. *See other part of subject*
Ohio
  Disaster assistance—1579
  Fort Hayes Metropolitan Education Center in Columbus—1055, 1595
  Governor—1061

Ohio—Continued
  Hilltop Basic Resources, Inc., River Terminal in
    Cincinnati—1114
  President's visits—1055, 1072, 1114, 1205, 1594–1597
  WBNS in Columbus—1581
Oliver Wendell Holmes Devise, Permanent Com-
  mittee for the—1598
Oman, Sultan—1113, 1598
Open Government Partnership—1089–1091, 1103,
  1355, 1455, 1597
Oregon, KGW in Portland—1606
Overseas Private Investment Corporation—1594

Pakistan
  International diplomatic efforts—1479
  Pakistani military forces, casualties—1612
  Political reform efforts—1231
  Political unrest and violence—1231
  Poverty and economic instability—1230
  President—1612
  Relations with India—1230
  Relations with U.S.—1231, 1612
  Security cooperation with U.S.—1230
  Terrorism—1185
  U.S. assistance—838
Palestinian Authority and Palestinians
  See also Middle East
  President—1597
  UNESCO, membership bid—1425
Panama
  Economic growth and development—1194
  Free trade agreement with U.S.—865, 931, 1041,
    1193–1195, 1262, 1277, 1403, 1419, 1602, 1604
  President—1604
  Relations with U.S.—1194–1195
  Trade with U.S.—1376
  U.S. Ambassador—1612
Park Service, National. *See* Interior, Department of the
PBS, "Country Music: In Performance at the White
  House"—1464
Peace Corps, U.S.—1455, 1610
Pennsylvania
  Disaster assistance—1579, 1591–1592, 1594–1595
  Infrastructure, improvement efforts—1248
  International Brotherhood of Electrical Workers
    Local Union No. 5 in Pittsburgh—1246, 1601
  Job creation and growth—1248
  KYW in Philadelphia—1580
  Pennsylvania State University in State College—1422
  President's visits—1240, 1246, 1385, 1389, 1482,
    1594–1595, 1600–1601, 1607, 1610–1611
  Scranton High School in Scranton—1482
  WPVI in Philadelphia—1606

Pennsylvania—Continued
  WTAE in Pittsburgh—1578
  Yeadon Regional Head Start Center in Yeadon—1385,
    1607
Pension Benefit Guaranty Corporation—1593, 1612
Permanent Joint Board on Defense, Canada-U.S.—1596
Peru
  President—1578, 1583, 1609
  Relations with U.S.—1609
Philippines
  Floods, damage and recovery efforts—1563
  President—1450
  Relations with U.S.—1450, 1563
  Security cooperation with U.S.—1450
Portugal
  Afghanistan, Portuguese military forces, deploy-
    ment—1392
  President—1391, 1607–1608
  Relations with U.S.—1391–1392
  Security cooperation with U.S.—1392
  U.S.-Portugal Bilateral Commission—1391
Postal Regulatory Commission—1612
Preservation of America's Heritage Abroad, Com-
  mission for the—1597, 1615
Presidency, U.S.
  Constitutional role and powers—877, 898, 1568–1569
  Joint session of Congress, address—1037
President. *See other part of subject*
Presidential Scholars, Commission on—1582, 1584,
  1588, 1606
Prevention, Health Promotion, and Integrative and
  Public Health, Advisory Group on—1601, 1606
Privacy and Civil Liberties Oversight Board—1614
Public Diplomacy, U.S. Advisory Commission on—1603
Puerto Rico
  Disaster assistance—1580, 1588, 1590, 1603
  Political status—1178

Railroad Passenger Corporation, National (Amtrak)—1593
Red Cross, American—1030
Reserve System, Federal—1586, 1616
Retirement Thrift Investment Board, Federal—1593
Rhode Island
  Disaster assistance—1590, 1592
  Governor—1118
Romania, President—1595
Russia
  Energy cooperation with U.S.—1397
  Governmental accountability and transparency,
    strengthening efforts—1397
  Military equipment transit into Afghanistan, agree-
    ment with U.S.—1397
  MS *Bulgaria*, sinking—1579
  President—1397, 1407, 1413, 1419–1420, 1456,
    1579, 1585, 1614

Russia—Continued
    Relations with U.S.—1397, 1407, 1413, 1490
    Security cooperation with U.S.—1397, 1413
    Strategic Arms Reduction Treaty (START) with U.S., expansion—833, 1102, 1397, 1413
    Trade and economic policies—1397
    Trade with U.S.—1413, 1456
    U.S. Ambassador—1596
    World Trade Organization, membership bid—1397, 1408, 1413, 1419

Saint Lawrence Seaway Development Corporation—1593
Saudi Arabia
    Ambassador to U.S.—1267–1268, 1479, 1601
    Counterterrorism efforts—1356
    Crown Prince—1320, 1356
    Deputy Prime Minister—1356
    King—1320, 1356, 1587, 1601, 1604
    Relations with U.S.—1320, 1356, 1601
Science, President's Committee on the National Medal of—1582, 1615
Science and technology
    See also Health and medical care
    2011 Google Science Fair—1318, 1599
    Global competiveness—1396
    Patent approval process, improvement efforts—842, 915, 944, 950, 953, 964, 985, 998, 1041, 1075–1077, 1221, 1228, 1318, 1358, 1376
    Research and development—823, 828, 834, 837, 839, 844, 849, 854, 866, 890, 902, 907–908, 925, 937–938, 943–944, 985, 993, 1075–1076, 1079, 1110, 1128, 1136, 1140, 1142–1143, 1153, 1156, 1164, 1172, 1191, 1207, 1215, 1222, 1232, 1249, 1254, 1258, 1317–1318, 1341, 1357–1358, 1392, 1424, 1429, 1437, 1496, 1520
Science Board, National—1583, 1604
Science Foundation, National—1583, 1604
Securities and Exchange Commission, U.S.—1243
Selective Service Appeal Board, National—1603
Seychelles, U.S. Ambassador—1602
Small Business Administration
    Administrator—977, 979–980
    Loan fees, reduction—833
    Loan guarantee facility—833, 981, 1225, 1227, 1471
Smithsonian Institution
    Air and Space Museum, National—1611
    John F. Kennedy Center for the Performing Arts—1511, 1513, 1593, 1595, 1612
Social Security Advisory Board—1611
Social Security and retirement
    IRA, 401(k), and 403(b) accounts—974
    Social Security program—834, 846, 849, 851, 860–861, 863, 886, 888–891, 897, 959, 969, 989, 993–994, 1005, 1032, 1144, 1153, 1179, 1191, 1215, 1258

Social Security and retirement—Continued
    Social Security reform—849, 851, 860, 867, 871, 959, 1002–1004, 1045, 1080, 1144
    Social Security trust fund—849, 851, 993–994
Somalia, famine and humanitarian crisis—910, 913
South Korea
    Afghanistan, role—1264–1265
    Civil and human rights, promotion efforts—1262
    Defense relationship with U.S.—1263, 1265, 1615
    Free trade agreement with U.S.—865, 931, 1041, 1193, 1195–1196, 1262–1265, 1270–1271, 1274, 1276–1277, 1279, 1286, 1289, 1295, 1300, 1403, 1405–1406, 1419, 1443, 1456, 1602, 1604
    Iraq, role—1264
    Minister of Foreign Affairs and Trade—1276
    President—1109, 1115, 1132, 1136, 1199, 1205, 1249, 1253, 1262, 1264, 1271, 1274–1278, 1295, 1407, 1595, 1601–1602, 1614
    President Obama's visit—1018, 1205
    Relations with North Korea—1102
    Relations with U.S.—1018, 1262–1265, 1271–1272, 1406
    Student exchanges with U.S.—1265
    Trade with U.S.—1229, 1264, 1376
    U.S. Ambassador—1271
South Sudan
    Democracy efforts—1099, 1101, 1107
    Independence—845, 1099, 1313, 1578
    President—1597
    Relations with Sudan—845, 1313
    Relations with U.S.—845
    United Nations, role—1099
    U.S. Ambassador—1588
    U.S. assistance—845
    U.S. military detachment—1279
Space program
    Aeronautics and Space Administration, National—837, 843, 1318, 1606
    Shuttle—837, 843, 1578, 1580, 1584, 1606
Space Station, International—837, 843, 1580, 1584
Spain
    Prime Minister—1586, 1615
    Princess—1062
    Relations with U.S.—1615
Sports
    Auto racing—1036–1037
    Baseball—899–900, 1197, 1583, 1607
    Basketball—1130, 1251, 1256, 1338, 1401, 1605, 1611
    Boxing—1602
    Football—948, 1114, 1130, 1197, 1234–1236, 1585, 1599, 1613
    Golf—1598
    NASCAR—1592, 1612
    NCAA championship teams—1233, 1599
    Pan American Games—1601

Sports—Continued
  Rugby—885
  Soccer—1580–1581, 1612
State, Department of
  Ambassadors. *See specific country*
  Assistant Secretaries
    Conflict and Stabilization Operations—1611
    Population, Refugees, and Migration—1607
    Public Affairs—1578
    Western Hemisphere Affairs—1598
  Reconstruction and Stabilization Coordinator—1611
  Secretary—885, 1011, 1091, 1108, 1242, 1364, 1393, 1406, 1410, 1452, 1578, 1583, 1585–1586, 1593, 1595, 1599–1600, 1605, 1607, 1609, 1614
  Under Secretaries
    Political Affairs—1577
    Public Diplomacy—1607
State Justice Institute—1593
St. Kitts and Nevis, U.S. Ambassador—1605
St. Lucia, U.S. Ambassador—1605
St. Vincent and the Grenadines, U.S. Ambassador—1605
Sudan
  International diplomatic efforts—845
  Political unrest and violence—1579
  Relations with South Sudan—845, 1313
  Relations with U.S.—845
  U.S. national emergency, continuation—1365
Summit of the Americas—1609
Supreme Court. *See* Judiciary
Syria
  Democracy efforts—912, 1007–1008, 1100, 1415, 1479, 1541
  Human rights issues—912, 1007, 1100, 1416, 1479
  International and U.S. sanctions—1006, 1008, 1100, 1541
  Political unrest and violence—912, 1006–1008, 1268, 1413, 1540–1541, 1584–1587
  President—912, 1007–1008, 1415, 1540–1541
  Relations with Iran—1008, 1268
  Relations with U.S.—1008, 1584
  Trade with U.S.—1008
  U.S. Ambassador—1584
  U.S. national emergency, continuation—1006

Tanzania
  President—1498, 1500
  U.S. Embassy bombing, 13th anniversary—932
Taxation
  Capital gains tax—853, 954, 991, 1145
  Child and dependent care expenses, tax credit—1394
  Child tax credit—1124, 1394
  Corporate tax rates—835, 847, 859, 867, 875, 893, 896, 902, 914, 944, 985, 989, 991, 1040, 1081, 1201, 1206–1207, 1228, 1346, 1502
  Earned-income tax credit—1124

Taxation—Continued
  Itemized deductions, limits—902–903
  Payroll tax cut—832–834, 847, 850, 853, 861, 865, 869, 883, 902, 921–922, 929, 934, 943, 950, 952, 964, 967, 978, 982, 984, 988, 997, 1009, 1033, 1038, 1044, 1052, 1054, 1056, 1083, 1124, 1206, 1220–1221, 1270, 1296, 1301, 1308, 1461, 1467, 1484–1487, 1490–1491, 1495, 1503, 1510, 1514–1515, 1520, 1529, 1531–1532, 1534–1536, 1552, 1562–1567, 1572, 1614–1615
  Tax Code, reform—823, 825, 834, 837, 844, 846–850, 852, 858–859, 861, 863, 867, 875, 887, 893, 896, 902–903, 906, 911–912, 914, 922, 933, 938, 947, 953, 965, 969, 985, 989, 991, 997–1000, 1040, 1045, 1052, 1054, 1057, 1060, 1064, 1080–1082, 1084, 1095–1096, 1116–1117, 1126, 1129, 1132, 1137, 1142, 1145, 1148–1149, 1153, 1155, 1160, 1164, 1167, 1191, 1200–1201, 1203, 1206–1207, 1212, 1221, 1228, 1240, 1247–1249, 1254–1255, 1261, 1287, 1290, 1293, 1296, 1301, 1306, 1308, 1322, 1339, 1345–1346, 1359, 1424, 1429–1430, 1462, 1466, 1468, 1484, 1486, 1495, 1502, 1514, 1520–1522, 1562
  Tax cuts, budgetary effects—823, 825, 834, 838, 844, 847, 850, 852, 863, 867, 875, 887–889, 891, 893, 896, 901–902, 911, 914, 944, 953–954, 956–958, 965, 997, 1040, 1079–1080, 1082, 1132, 1137, 1160, 1191, 1200, 1337, 1462, 1514, 1520
  Tax relief—827, 832–834, 836, 838, 842, 846–847, 853, 862, 873, 896–897, 915, 931, 943, 950, 964, 967, 970, 997, 1032, 1039, 1044–1045, 1047, 1052, 1054, 1056–1057, 1059–1061, 1063–1064, 1076, 1078, 1081, 1094–1095, 1109, 1116–1118, 1125, 1131–1132, 1136, 1143, 1145, 1155, 1160, 1167, 1188, 1191, 1198, 1200, 1206–1207, 1211, 1218–1221, 1240, 1247, 1250–1251, 1253–1254, 1260–1261, 1280, 1285–1286, 1289–1290, 1294, 1296, 1298–1299, 1301, 1304, 1306–1308, 1322, 1337, 1339, 1345, 1359, 1377, 1395, 1428, 1462, 1466, 1468, 1484–1485, 1565–1566
Tennessee
  Disaster assistance—1581
  Governor—1118
  WREG in Memphis—1613
Terrorism
  See also Defense and national security; *specific country or region*
  Al Qaida terrorist group—855–856, 920, 932, 1014, 1019–1020, 1048, 1098, 1135, 1183, 1185, 1230, 1238, 1253, 1310, 1316, 1320, 1324, 1342, 1379, 1399, 1427, 1433, 1494, 1538, 1548, 1550, 1553–1554, 1572–1574, 1599
  Christmas Day 2009 airline bombing attempt—1183

Terrorism—Continued
Counterterrorism efforts—857, 885, 932, 1014, 1019, 1048, 1183–1184, 1230, 1269, 1309, 1313, 1316, 1406, 1427, 1474, 1494, 1532, 1550, 1554, 1570–1571, 1573, 1593–1594, 1599
Explosive devices on U.S.-bound flights—1183
Global threat—885, 932, 1114, 1433, 1554
Guantanamo Bay detainees
Review and disposition—1574
Transfer—1568, 1575
National Counterterrorism Center—1577
Persons who commit, threaten to commit, or support terrorism, U.S. national emergency—1114
Saudi Arabia's Ambassador to U.S., assassination plot—1267–1269, 1479, 1601
September 11, 2001, attacks—855–857, 940–941, 1013–1014, 1018–1019, 1037, 1048–1051, 1067, 1098, 1112, 1114, 1238, 1342, 1399, 1406, 1494, 1550, 1593–1595
Terrorist attacks, U.S. national emergency—1047
Terrorists
Detention policies and standards, reform—1573–1574
Prosecution—1573–1574
Torture of terrorism suspects, prohibition—1420, 1427
Texas
Democratic Party events—1197, 1202
Disaster assistance—1577, 1594
Eastfield College in Mesquite—1204, 1599
Governor—1137, 1593
KTRK in Houston—1606
President's visit—1197, 1202, 1204–1206, 1208, 1599
Texas A&M University in College Station—1233
U.S. Representative, retirement—1473
Wildfires, damage and recovery efforts—1137, 1593–1594
Thailand
Elections—1587
Flooding, damage and recovery efforts—1455
Prime Minister—1455, 1587
Relations with U.S.—1455, 1587
Tibet, Dalai Lama—1580
Togo, U.S. Ambassador—1603
Trade. *See* Business and industry; Commerce, international
Trade agreements or negotiations. *See* Commerce, international; *specific country or region*
Trade Commission, Federal—1581
Trade Policy and Negotiations, Advisory Committee for—1577, 1596
Trade Representative, Office of the U.S.—1197, 1202, 1276, 1403, 1477
Transatlantic Economic Council (TEC)—1477

Trans-Pacific Partnership (TPP)—884, 1403–1404, 1406–1408, 1412, 1419, 1433, 1438–1439, 1444, 1451, 1456, 1527, 1608
Transportation
High-speed rail lines, development and expansion—1026
Highway system, modernization efforts—902, 990, 1029, 1055, 1076, 1078–1079, 1115, 1191, 1270
Infrastructure, national, improvement efforts—827–828, 832, 842, 844, 849, 851, 853, 865–866, 874, 890, 896, 915, 919, 922, 929–931, 934, 936, 943, 950, 953, 964, 970, 978, 982, 985, 990, 996, 998, 1009, 1016, 1024–1026, 1029, 1033, 1038–1039, 1044, 1052, 1054, 1056, 1059–1060, 1063, 1083, 1085, 1095, 1108–1110, 1115–1116, 1118, 1125, 1131, 1136, 1140, 1142–1143, 1152, 1154, 1159, 1163–1166, 1168, 1171–1172, 1187–1188, 1199–1200, 1203, 1205, 1207, 1211, 1215, 1219–1220, 1222, 1232, 1240–1244, 1246, 1248–1249, 1253, 1259, 1261, 1270, 1280, 1284–1287, 1289–1290, 1294–1296, 1300–1301, 1307–1308, 1322, 1329, 1333, 1337, 1339, 1341, 1345, 1365–1367, 1371, 1374, 1377, 1390, 1426, 1428–1429, 1496–1497, 1520
Mass transit and rail infrastructure, improvement efforts—1026, 1029, 1115
Transportation, Department of
Federal Aviation Administration—915–916, 926, 930, 974
Funding—1024–1025, 1029
Infrastructure innovation and finance fund—865, 1025
Secretary—916, 977, 983, 991, 996, 1025, 1114, 1367, 1590
Transportation Safety Board, National—1600
Treasury, Department of the
Assistant Secretaries
Financial Institutions—1594
Financial Markets—1598
Legislative Affairs—1596
Tax Policy—1609
Comptroller of the Currency—1577
Consumer Financial Protection Bureau, Special Adviser to the Secretary—869–870
Domestic Finance, Under Secretary for—1577
Financial Capability, President's Advisory Council on—1609
Financial institutions, assessment and regulation—1243
Financial Research, Office of—1614
Secretary—848, 870, 889, 1230, 1578, 1580, 1582–1586, 1589–1592, 1596, 1599–1600, 1605, 1610, 1612
Tunisia
Democracy efforts—1010, 1099, 1236–1237, 1271, 1321, 1474, 1478, 1615
Economic growth and development—1237
Elections—1321

Tunisia—Continued
  Human rights issues—1236
  Libyan refugees, status—1237
  Prime Minister—1236, 1598, 1615
  Relations with U.S.—1237
  Trade with U.S.—1237
  U.S. Ambassador-designate—1614
  U.S. assistance—1237
Turkey
  Afghanistan, Turkish military forces, deployment—1092
  Ankara, terrorist attack—1092
  Counterterrorism efforts, cooperation with U.S.—1092
  Cukurca, terrorist attack—1309
  Defense relationship with U.S.—1092
  Earthquake, damage and recovery efforts—1321, 1379
  Kurdistan Workers' Party (PKK)—1309
  Prime Minister—1091, 1586
  Relations with U.S.—1091, 1309, 1321
  U.S. assistance—1321
Twitter—826, 828–829, 834, 840

Uganda
  Lord's Resistance Army insurgent group—1278–1279, 1555
  U.S. military detachment—1279
Ukraine
  Democracy efforts—1474, 1479
  Former Prime Minister—1479
  Human rights issues—1479
UNESCO. *See* United Nations
Union for Reform Judaism—1556
United Farm Workers of America—904
United Kingdom
  Libya, role—1111
  Prime Minister—1010, 1111, 1586–1588, 1601, 1603
  Relations with U.S.—1111, 1587
United Nations
  Children's Fund—1577, 1594
  Economic and Social Council—1600
  Food and Agriculture Organization—1431
  Framework Convention on Climate Change—1437, 1454
  General Assembly—1011, 1086, 1089, 1098–1100, 1104, 1107, 1579, 1596–1597
  Liberia, U.N. Mission in (UNMIL)—1382
  Libya, U.N. Support Mission in—1010–1011, 1087
  Millennium Development Goals—1453–1455, 1478
  Peacekeeping operations—1107, 1392, 1569
  Secretary-General—1011, 1086, 1098, 1106, 1271, 1597
  Security Council—1010, 1099–1100, 1392, 1554
  U.N. Educational, Scientific and Cultural Organization (UNESCO)—1425
  U.S. Mission staff, meeting with President—1596

United Nations—Continued
  U.S. Representatives
    Economic and Social Council—1600
    Permanent Representative—1011
  World Health Organization—1103
Urban League, National—1582
Uruguay, U.S. Ambassador—1602
U.S. *See other part of subject*
USAID. *See* Development, U.S. Agency for International
Utah, disaster assistance—1586
Utah Reclamation Mitigation and Conservation Commission—1581
Uzbekistan
  President—1598
  Relations with U.S.—1599

Valles Caldera Trust—1606
Vermont
  Disaster assistance—1579, 1591–1592, 1607
  Hurricane Irene, damage and recovery efforts—1030–1031
Veterans
  Access to health and medical care—825, 838, 1017, 1020–1021, 1238, 1394, 1399
  American Legion—1017, 1380
  Disabled American Veterans organization—1380
  Disabled veterans—1381
  Education and job training assistance—930, 953, 978, 1022, 1147–1148, 1303, 1401, 1461, 1549, 1584–1585
  Employment and job training assistance—1461
  Hiring incentives—930–931, 1009, 1017, 1022, 1039, 1044, 1052, 1056, 1058–1059, 1063, 1076, 1078, 1083, 1095, 1108, 1115, 1118, 1125, 1132, 1145, 1148, 1155, 1160, 1166, 1191, 1200, 1206, 1212, 1218, 1240, 1247, 1254, 1261, 1270, 1280, 1285, 1289, 1294, 1299, 1301, 1303–1304, 1306–1307, 1317, 1322, 1329, 1333, 1339, 1345, 1350, 1359, 1380–1382, 1385, 1398, 1401–1402, 1419, 1432, 1459–1460, 1467, 1471, 1484, 1491, 1549
  Homelessness—1017, 1021
  Iraq and Afghanistan Veterans of America—1380
  Meeting with President in Cannon Falls, MN—1587
  Service and dedication—833, 929, 1018–1019, 1302, 1380, 1382, 1398, 1460, 1530, 1561
  Service organizations—1607
  Unemployment and underemployment—929–930, 944, 953, 990, 1017, 1022, 1147, 1304, 1380–1382, 1385, 1402, 1460–1461
  Veterans of Foreign Wars—1380
  VOW to Hire Heroes Act of 2011—1467, 1484
  Women veterans—1020

Veterans Affairs, Department of
  Agent orange exposure, disability benefits—1020–1021
  Funding—840, 902, 1020
  Health and medical care system
    Electronic recordkeeping—1021
    Funding—861–862, 1017, 1020
  Homelessness, assistance and mitigation efforts—1021
  Persian Gulf and Iraq operations-related illnesses, study and assessment—1020
  Posttraumatic stress disorder (PTSD), disability benefits—1021
  Secretary—1020–1021, 1066, 1398, 1460
Vice President. *See* White House Office
Virginia
  Arlington
    Arlington National Cemetery—941, 1398, 1594, 1608, 1614
    Liberty Tavern—1605
  College of William & Mary in Williamsburg—1035
  Disaster assistance—1590, 1592, 1607, 1609
  Fire Station 9 in North Chesterfield—1305
  Fort Monroe National Monument—1363–1364
  Governor—1302, 1589
  Greensville County High School in Emporia—1297
  Hampton
    Anna's Pizza and Italian Kitchen—1603
    Wood's Orchards Farm Market—1603
  Hurricane Irene, damage and recovery efforts—1015
  Joint Base Langley-Eustis—1302, 1603
  Patricia's Child Care Center in Brodnax—1603
  President's visits—1043, 1072, 1074, 1183, 1284, 1297, 1299, 1302, 1305, 1398, 1585, 1593–1596, 1599, 1601–1603, 1605, 1607–1608, 1614–1615
  Thomas Jefferson High School for Science and Technology in Alexandria—1074, 1077, 1596
  University of Richmond in Richmond—1043
  WAVY in Portsmouth—1606
  Woo Lae Oak Korean restaurant in Tysons Corner—1601
  WOWI in Norfolk—1603
  WVEC in Norfolk—1614
  WVKL in Norfolk—1603
Voluntarism—1013, 1400, 1471, 1535, 1571, 1594

Washington
  Democratic Party events—1128, 1130
  Governor—1130
  KING in Seattle—1578
  KIRO in Seattle—1614
  President's visit—1128, 1130, 1597–1598
Washington, DC. *See* District of Columbia
Weapons of mass destruction. *See* Arms and munitions

Western Hemisphere
  See also Central America; Commerce, international; Developing countries
  Americas, Summit of the—1371
  Energy and climate, regional cooperation—1415
  Organization of American States—1216
Westwood One Sports—1608
Whaling Commission, International—1069–1070
White House Office
  African American Policy in Action Leadership Conference—1389
  American Indian and Alaska Native Education, White House Initiative on—1507
  American Latino Heritage Forum, White House—1600
  Assistants to the President
    Chief of Staff—1584–1585, 1589–1592, 1598, 1607–1608, 1614
    Communications Director—1608
    Consumer Financial Protection Bureau adviser—869–870
    Counselor to the President—1608
    Domestic Policy—1583, 1607
    Homeland Security and Counterterrorism—1588–1590, 1593–1594, 1599
    Jewish Outreach Director, Public Engagement Office—1535
    Legislative Affairs—1615
    National Security Adviser—927, 1578, 1585
    Native American Affairs, Senior Policy Adviser for—1506
    Press Secretary—825, 841, 870, 1563, 1608
    Senior Adviser—1591, 1608
  Drug Control Policy, Office of National—1176
  Economic Advisers, Council of—1015–1016, 1591
  Economic Council, National—1241, 1243, 1391, 1584, 1588–1589, 1592
  Export Council, President's—1410–1411
  Hispanic Policy, White House Conference on—895
  Information and Regulatory Affairs, Office of—1245, 1527–1528
  Intergovernmental Affairs, Office of—1506
  Jobs and Competitiveness, President's Council on—1025, 1041, 1110, 1192, 1240, 1246–1248, 1250, 1270, 1503, 1589
  Joining Forces initiative—930
  Pay freeze, senior White House staff—831
  Rural Council, White House—957, 978
  Rural Economic Forum, White House—977, 979–981, 1587
  Security Council, National—1010, 1588, 1599
  Telecommunications Advisory Committee, President's National Security—1578, 1598

White House Office—Continued
  Vice President—823, 855, 1037, 1053, 1183, 1389, 1483, 1488, 1543, 1577–1579, 1581–1584, 1590–1595, 1597, 1599–1601, 1605–1608, 1610, 1613–1615
  White House Fellowships, President's Commission on—1611
  Women and Girls, White House Council on—1394
Wisconsin
  Orion Energy Systems, Inc., in Manitowoc—948
  President's visit—948
  WISN in Milwaukee—1578
Women's Law Center, National, award dinner—1392
World Trade Organization—1230, 1397, 1408, 1413, 1419, 1585
Wyoming, disaster assistance—1582

Yemen
  Democracy efforts—1100, 1239, 1470–1471
  Human rights issues—1183
  Political unrest and violence—1100
  President—1100, 1470
  Security cooperation with U.S.—1183–1184
  Vice President—1470

Zambia
  Democracy efforts—1121
  Economic growth and development—1121
  Elections—1121
  President—1121
  Relations with U.S.—1121

Name Index

Abbas, Mahmoud—1597
Abbott, Anthony J.—1439, 1440–1441, 1609
Abdallah bin Abd al-Aziz Al Saud, King—1320, 1587, 1601, 1604
Abdul Jalil, Mustafa Mohammed—1086–1087, 1597
Abercrombie, Neil—1426
Abercrombie-Winstanley, Gina—1602
Abety-Gutierrez, Modesto E.—1588
Abrams, Ronnie—1583, 1618
Adams, Danielle—1233
Adams, Samuel W., III—1297
Adkins, Heather—824
Ahlquist, Brenna—1470
Akerson, Daniel F.—1276
Alan, David—1614
Albright, Madeleine K.—927, 1615
Alderman, Elizabeth—1311
Alderman, Mark L.—1611
Alderman, Stephen—1311
Allen, John R.—1577, 1581, 1585–1586
Allgor, Catherine—1593, 1619
Al-Nasser, Nassir Abdulaziz—1098, 1597
Althoff, Joel—1587
Amir-Mokri, Cyrus—1594, 1621
Amos, James F.—1066
Anchia, Rafael—1577
Anderson, Austin—1025
Anderson, Brooke D.—1578
Anderson, Linda—1547
Anderson, Phyliss J.—1505
Anderson, Rodney O.—1547
Aquino, Benigno S., III—1450
Arbarian, Mansoor—1267
Archabal, Nina M.—1591
Arena, Bruce—1612
Arendt, Donald P.—963
Arpaio, Joseph M.—1172
Arriola, Eduardo—1593, 1619
Asad, Bashar al- —912, 1007–1008, 1415, 1540–1541
Asche, Preston—1470
Ashworth, Carlene—1017
Atambaev, Almazbek—1611
Auch, Korvin D.—1302
Auch, Kristen—1302
Aung San Suu Kyi—1444, 1452, 1609
Austin, Lloyd J., III—1543
Austin, Reggie L.—1302
Avalon, Frankie—1360
Avenarius, Richard—977
Aviel, Sara M.—1593, 1619

Awlaki, Anwar al- —1183, 1599
Ayers, Edward L.—1043

Baer, Laurence M.—899
Baer, Parry L.—1547
Bagley, Conor R.—1073
Bagley, Elizabeth F.—1073–1074
Bagley, Vaughan E.—1073
Bailey, Jean—1593
Bailey, Megan Dempsey—1185
Baisden, Michael—1610
Baker, Kristine G.—1606, 1624
Baldwin, Teressa—1506
Bales, Susan Ford—843
Baliga, B. Jayant—1318
Balkenende, Jan Peter—1481
Balsera, Freddy—1603
Band, Douglas J.—1598
Banda, Rupiah—1121
Banderas, Antonio—1330
Ban Ki-moon—1011, 1086, 1098, 1106, 1271, 1597
Bansal, Preeta D.—1613
Barak, Ehud—1556, 1559
Barlow, David B.—1585, 1619
Barnes, Melody C.—1580, 1608
Baroz, Robert—1219
Barrera, Janie—1609
Barroso, Jose Manuel Durao—1376, 1473–1474, 1481
Barry, Tracy—1606
Barton, Fredrick—1611
Barton, Jacqueline K.—1318
Barton, Joe L.—1233
Barzun, Matthew W.—938, 1545
Basescu, Traian—1595
Bassler, Bonnie L.—1604, 1623
Bauer, Shane—1112–1113, 1598
Baylis, Jack—1579
Beck, Damian—1552
Beck, Pauline—1552–1553
Becker, Craig—1626
Becker, Daniel J.—1593, 1620
Becker, John—1120, 1123
Bellamy, Terry M.—1284
Ben Ali, Zine el Abidine—1099–1100
Bennet, Michael F.—1165, 1167, 1335, 1343–1346, 1348–1350
Bentley, Dierks—1464
Berger, Anita M.—1179, 1181
Berlusconi, Silvio—1376, 1586
Bernanke, Ben S.—1586

Bernard, Barrett—1601
Berner, Richard B.—1614, 1626
Bernstein, Jake—1182
Bernstein, Jarrod—1535
Bernstein, Simone—1182
Berry, Jodi—1602
Bershteyn, Boris—1613
Berwick, Donald M.—1625
Biden, Jill T.—825, 930, 1022, 1037, 1304, 1360, 1381, 1400–1402, 1459–1460, 1580, 1613
Biden, Joseph R., Jr.—823, 855, 1037, 1053, 1138, 1183, 1389, 1460, 1483, 1488, 1543, 1577–1579, 1581–1584, 1590–1595, 1597, 1599–1601, 1604–1608, 1610, 1613–1615
Bieber, Justin—1446
Bilyeu, Dana K.—1593, 1620
Bird, Jeremy—922–923
Black, Charles—1603
Black, Sherry S.—1609
Black Eagle, Hartford "Sonny"—1505
Black Eagle, Mary—1505
Blair, Gary—1233–1234
Blair, Tony—1363, 1605
Blake Mora, Jose Francisco—1608
Blake, Robert O., Jr.—1611
Blank, Rebecca M.—1074, 1605, 1623
Blazs, Robert L.—1603
Bleich, Jeffrey, L.—1609
Blitzer, Wolf—1587
Block, Sharon—1614, 1626
Bloomberg, Michael R.—1589
Bloomquist, Camilla "Milly"—1311–1312
Bluhm-Kaul, Barbara—1591
Blumenthal, Gary—1598, 1622
Blye, Regina—1591
Bochy, Bruce—900, 1583
Boehner, John A.—832, 846, 848–850, 852, 862, 864–865, 870–871, 886–889, 892, 902–903, 933, 953, 965, 989, 1023, 1037, 1079–1080, 1116, 1155, 1192, 1205, 1229, 1270, 1367, 1424, 1491, 1514, 1531, 1534, 1564, 1577, 1580, 1581–1582, 1602, 1615
Bohn, Darrin J.—1547
Bolden, Charles F., Jr.—1318
Bonilla, Franco—1325, 1331, 1335–1336
Bonilla, Jose—1325, 1327–1328, 1331, 1333, 1335
Bonilla, Lissette—1325, 1327–1328, 1331, 1333, 1335
Bonilla, Margarita—1325, 1331, 1335–1336
Bonilla, Mario—1325, 1331, 1335–1336
Booker, Cory A.—1093
Bose, Shree—1318–1319, 1396, 1599
Bowles, Erskine B.—852, 862, 988
Bowman, Denny—1114
Bozella, Dewey R.—1602
Brady, Robert A.—1385
Brand, Rachel L.—1614, 1626

Brants, Lisa L.—983
Brennan, John O.—1588–1590, 1593–1594, 1599
Brennan, Thomas J.—1465
Brennan, Wendy—1465
Broadbent, Meredith M.—1607, 1624
Brochand, Bernard—1377
Brooks, Leon E. "Kix," III—1464
Brown, Corrine—1251, 1256
Brown, Edmund G. "Jerry," Jr.—1162, 1164
Brown, James L.—1235
Brown, Jay—1328
Brown, Kawanna—1328
Brown, Ricardo—1581
Brown, Sherrod—1055
Brown, Val—1470
Bruni-Sarkozy, Carla—1369
Bruska, Lisa—1204
Bryan, J. Shelby—945
Bryson, John E.—1315
Brzezinski, Mark F.—1620
Buch, Ronald L.—1596, 1621
Buerkle, Ann Marie—1596, 1621
Buffett, Warren E.—852, 875, 933, 954, 965, 967, 969, 985, 991, 999, 1040, 1081, 1095, 1117, 1126, 1132, 1137, 1142, 1155, 1160, 1164, 1167, 1200, 1206, 1212, 1221, 1254, 1296, 1486, 1521, 1580, 1588
Burns, Douglas—1588
Burrows, Patrick L.—1603
Bush, Antoinette—1383
Bush, Dwight—1383
Bush, George H.W.—834, 903, 956
Bush, George W.—834, 903, 911, 1050, 1120, 1151, 1173, 1429, 1498–1499, 1595
Bush, Laura—1595
Bush, Mike—1587
Butler, Cathy—1236
Butler, Kevin—1236

Caid Essebsi, Beji—1236, 1598
Cain, Matt—901
Calderon Hinojosa, Felipe de Jesus—879, 1173, 1176, 1608
Callaghan, Pat—1613
Cambell, Nancy Duff—1392
Cameron, David—1010–1111, 1586–1588, 1601, 1603
Campbell, Cindy—1591
Canales, Maria—929
Cantor, Eric I.—1046, 1208, 1580–1581
Caraway, Nancie—1426
Cardin, Benjamin L.—873
Carnahan, J. Russell—1209, 1215, 1596, 1621
Carnahan, Lisa—1214
Carnahan, Thomas S.—1214
Carney, James F. "Jay"—825, 841, 870, 1563, 1608
Carr, Jeremy—1400

Carr, Teresa—1400
Carson, Andre—940
Carson, Brad—1596, 1621
Carson, Johnnie—1578
Carter, Ashton B.—1185, 1583–1584, 1619
Carter, Rebecca—1328
Carter, Sydney—1233
Carter, Troy—1328
Cartwright, James E. "Hoss"—855, 1582
Case, Stephen M.—1243
Casey, Robert P., Jr.—1249, 1487
Castor, Elizabeth B.—1584
Castro, Julian—1330
Cavaco Silva, Anibal Antonio—1391, 1607–1608
Chafee, Lincoln D.—1118
Chambliss, Saxby—870–871, 886, 989
Chapman, Georgina—945
Chard, David J.—1603, 1623
Chavern, David C.—1025, 1029
Chavez, Richard E.—904
Chavonne, Anthony G.—1549
Chen, May Y.—1600
Chenault, Kenneth I.—1589
Chisam, Doug—1516
Christie, Christopher J.—1030, 1589, 1592
Chu, Steven—1590
Chuong, Jason—1056
Chyao, Amy—1182
Clark, Mike—1578
Clark, Robert G.—1214
Clark, Sue B.—1582
Clarke, Hansen H.—1031
Clay, William L., Jr.—1209
Cleaver, Emanuel, II—1123
Clements, Jami—1297
Clinton, Chelsea—1580
Clinton, Hillary Rodham—885, 1011, 1091, 1108, 1242,
    1364, 1393, 1406, 1410, 1452, 1578, 1583, 1585, 1593,
    1595, 1599–1600, 1605, 1607, 1609, 1614–1615
Clinton, William J.—834, 852, 867, 874–875, 883, 893,
    903, 936, 939, 956, 965, 988, 1000, 1108–1111, 1126,
    1248, 1499, 1502, 1520–1521, 1598, 1612, 1615
Cloobeck, Stephen J.—1321
Cobell, Elouise P.—1291
Coburn, Thomas A.—870–871, 886, 893, 989, 1388
Cohen, Steven H.—1593, 1620
Cohen, William S.—927, 1604
Colangelo, Jerry—1360
Coleman, Michael B.—1055
Colgin, Nicholas—929, 1380
Colson, Sydney—1233
Conde, Alpha—909
Conrad, Kent—870–871, 886, 989
Conroy, Nora Daley—1472
Contreras, Rudolph—1583, 1618

Conyers, John, Jr.—1031
Cook, Barbara—1511, 1513
Cordray, Danny—869
Cordray, Holly—869
Cordray, Margaret "Peggy"—869
Cordray, Richard A.—868, 976, 1223, 1522, 1531,
    1536, 1617
Corkery, Andrew—1465, 1610
Corkery, Christopher—1465–1467, 1610
Corkery, Kathy—1465–1467, 1610
Corkery, Nicholas—1465, 1610
Cornell, Chris—1135
Corner, Greg—917
Costa, Gregg J.—1594, 1621
Costello, Jerry F.—1209
Cousens, Elizabeth M.—1600, 1623
Crapo, Michael D.—870–871, 886, 989
Cray, Robert—1130
Cretz, Gene A.—1087
Cristina, Princess—1062
Crocker, Ryan C.—1577, 1586
Crumb-Gesme, Beverly—973
Cruz, Denis J.—1577
Cruz, John—1426
Cuetara, Jay—1362, 1363
Culver, Chester J.—1580, 1617
Cuomo, Andrew M.—945, 947, 1589
Cuomo, Mario M.—968
Curiel, Gonzalo P.—1608, 1624
Curry, Bruce—996
Curry, Charles—996
Curry, Thomas J.—1577, 1617

Dalai Lama Tenzin Gyatso—1580
Daley, Elizabeth "Lally"—1472
Daley, Margaret C.—1472
Daley, Patrick—1472
Daley, Richard M.—1472
Daley, William M.—1584–1585, 1589–1592, 1598,
    1607–1608, 1614
Dalton, Walter—1288
Daly, Carson—1501
Daly, Jennifer—856
Danielson, David T.—1583, 1618
Davis, Danny K.—996, 1002, 1004–1005
Davis, Sylvia D.—1071
Day, Charles B.—1623
Dayson, Danya A.—1579, 1617
Dayton, Mark B.—951, 1017
de Blasio, Warren "Bill"—1093, 1493
Decerega, Reynaldo—1062
Deese, Brian C.—1588–1589
DeGette, Diana L.—1165, 1349
De Gucht, Karel—1477
de la Torre, Marta Araoz—1600

Del Raso, Joseph V.—1360
Dempsey, Caitlin—1185
Dempsey, Christopher—1185
Dempsey, Deanie—1185, 1398
Dempsey, Martin E.—855, 1183–1185, 1398, 1613
Dent, Richard—1235
DeRosa, Mary B.—1579, 1618
Dervan, Peter P.—1318
Devaney, Earl E.—1583
Diamond, Neil L.—1512–1513
DiClemente, Albert—1593, 1620
DiMarco Johnson, Susan M.—1593
Dingell, John D., Jr.—1031
Dinkins, David N.—1093
Ditka, Michael K.—948, 1235–1236
Dixon, Cathleen—1188–1189
Doerr, John—1243
Dole, Robert J.—852
Donilon, Thomas E.—927, 1578, 1585
Donley, Michael B.—1302
Donohue, Thomas J.—1502
Donovan, Shaun L.S.—977
Dooley, Charlie A.—1209
Dorsey, Jack—826–840
D'Orta, James—1186–1187
Dougherty, Tim—997
Drain, Gershwin A.—1609, 1625
Driver, Donald—948
Du, Miranda—1584, 1619
Dudley, Philip A.—1516
Duerson, Alicia—1235
DuMont, Edward C.—1625
Duncan, Arne—1055–1056, 1118–1119, 1179, 1182, 1242, 1446, 1507, 1580, 1613
Duncan, Karen L.—1446
Dunn, Ronnie G.—1464
Duplessis, Dallas—1506
Durbin, Richard J.—870–871, 886, 917, 925, 989, 1581–1582, 1600
Dyer, John H. "Buddy," Jr.—1251, 1256, 1601

Earnhardt, Dale—1036
Easterly, Catharine F.—1584, 1619
Eastwood, Clint—1512
Echo Hawk, Larry—1505
Edwards, Donna F.—1389
Eikenberry, Ching—1582
Eikenberry, Karl W.—1582
Eisen, Norman L.—1615
Ellison, Keith M.—940, 951, 960, 1017
Emanuel, Rahm I.—925
Enersen, Jean—1578
Erdogan, Recep Tayyip—1091, 1586
Ertel, Julie S.—1601

Eshoo, Anna G.—1135
Eskelsen, Lily—1588
Espinoza, Galina—1586
Estrate, Francois—1377
Estrop, David C.—1121, 1123
Evans, Donald L.—1070
Ewing, Rodney C.—1582

Faber, Kim P.—1188–1189
Faber, Steven G.—1188
Farrar, Jonathan D.—1612, 1625–1626
Fattah, Chaka—1385
Fattal, Joshua—1112–1113, 1598
Feinstein, Dianne—899
Felix, Allyson M.—1601
Fellows, Andrew M.—873
Fencik, J. Gary—1235
Ferguson, Christopher J.—843, 1606
Ferguson, Jesse T.—1157
Ferguson, Roger W., Jr.—1245
Fernandez, Giselle—1330, 1333
Fernandez, Teresita—1596
Fernandez de Kirchner, Cristina—1371, 1613
Ferrari, Laurence—1607
Festa, Bridget—1482
Festa, Donna—1482–1483, 1485, 1611
Festa, Patrick—1482–1483
Festa, Patrick, Sr.—1482, 1485, 1611
Filner, Bob—1154
Fisher, Mary—1500
Fitzgerald, Michael W.—1581, 1618
Fitzpayne, Alastair M.—1596, 1621
Flanagan, Susannah—1022
Ford, Elizabeth A.—843
Ford, John G.—843
Ford, Michael G.—843
Ford, Robert S.—1584
Ford, Steven M.—843
Foreman, Louis—1074
Forester, Christine—1153–1154
Foster, Heather J.—1389
Foster, Jimmie L.—1017
Foster, Rehta—1017
Fowlkes, John T., Jr.—1614, 1626
Fraim, Paul D.—1589
France, Amy—1036
France, Brian—1036
Frank, Barney—1481
Franken, Al—951, 957, 960, 1017
Franzen, John—970
Frawley, Bonnie C.—1362–1363
Freelon, Philip G.—1612
Freitas, Curlta—1068
French, Gary—1516
Frye, Jan R.—1597

Fugate, W. Craig—1012, 1014–1015, 1589–1590, 1592
Fulton, B. Sue—1577

Gaffney, Mark T.—1031
Galante, Carol J.—1603, 1623
Galbraith, Charles—1506
Gale, Joseph H.—1578, 1617
Gallogly, Mark T.—1244
Gamoran, Adam—1599, 1622
Gang, Justin—824
Garcia, Joseph A.—1335, 1348
Garcia, Millie—1577
Garcia, Roland—1580
Garcia, Terry D.—1622
Garduque, Laurie R.—1597
Gast, Earl W.—1598, 1622
Gates, Melinda F.—1580
Gates, Robert M.—1035, 1234, 1411
Gates, William H., III—1207, 1580
Gathercole, Edward F.—856
Gault, Willie J.—1235
Gaytan, Peter S.—1017
Gbagbo, Laurent—1099–1100
Gbowee, Leymah—1238–1239
Geithner, Timothy F.—848, 870, 889, 1230, 1578,
    1580, 1582–1586, 1589–1592, 1596, 1599–1600,
    1605, 1610, 1612
Gelser, Sara A.—1609, 1625
Germanotta, Stefani J.A. "Lady Gaga"—1189
Gerstell, Glenn S.—1594
Gillard, Julia E.—1432, 1439, 1440–1442, 1445–
    1448, 1609
Gingrich, Newton L.—852, 867
Ginsberg, Alan H.—1251
Ginsburg, Ruth Bader—1535
Giunta, Salvatore A.—855, 1361
Glazer, Evan M.—1074
Goldberg, David B.—1139
Golick, Roberta—1600
Gomez, Manuel—1595
Gomez-Bassols, Isabel—1581
Gonzales, Albert—1603
Gonzalez, Charles A.—1062, 1473
Goodlatte, Robert W.—1074
Goodwin-Dye, Ghana—1031
Goolsbee, Austan D.—1016
Gould, W. Scott—1583
Grain, David J.—1579
Gray, Jim—1608
Gray, Vincent C.—1179, 1366–1367, 1589
Greenberg, Jayne D.—1603
Greenberger, Marcia D.—1392
Greer, Mahala—1348
Gregoire, Christine O.—1130
Griffin, Michael A., Jr.—1626

Griffin, Richard F., Jr.—1614
Griffith, Melanie—1330
Grommer, Don—1512
Grove, Andrew S.—1522
Guaderrama, David C.—1596, 1621
Guen, Terry—1578
Guerra-Mondragon, Gabriel—1581
Gupta, Sanjay—1498
Gutierrez, Carlos M.—1070
Gutman, Joseph D.—1605
Guyton, Mickey—1464

Hach, Kenneth—1587
Hackett, Kenneth F.—1578
Hadi, Abd al-Rabuh Mansur—1470
Hagan, Carrie C.—1284
Hagan, Kay R.—1284, 1286
Hahn, Janice K.—858
Haines, Maryann—856
Hall, Ricci W.—1120, 1122
Hall, Ruby Bridges—1580
Halligan, Caitlin J.—1524
Halpern, Sonya M.—1593
Ham, Carter F.—1578
Hamburg, Margaret A.—1363
Hammer, Michael A.—1578, 1617
Hammond, Tony—1612, 1625
Hampton, Daniel—1235
Hancock, Herbie—917
Hancock, Michael B.—1165, 1335, 1343, 1348
Hannah, James R.—1593, 1620
Harkin, Thomas R.—1118, 1120
Harper, Keith M.—1611
Harper, Stephen J.—1526, 1608, 1613
Harris, Dot—1583
Harris, Gene T.—1055
Harris, Joan W.—1612
Harris, LaDoris G.—1618
Harrison, Robert S.—1108
Hart, Christopher S.—1588
Hartley, Jane D.—1084
Harvey, Steve—1581
Haslam, Annie—1118
Haslam, William E.—1118
Hatch, Orrin G.—1485
Havel, Vaclav—1562, 1615
Haysbert, Dennis D.—1157
Healy, Tom—1577
Hearty, Eileen M.—1388
Hedges, Larry V.—1603, 1623
Heister, Janda K.—981
Helbling, Casey—1605
Helmick, Frank G.—1547
Helmick, Melissa—1547
Hendrick, Rick—1036

Henry, Mary Kay—1031
Hensarling, Jeb T.—1608
Hewson, Paul D. "Bono"—1498
Hickenlooper, John W.—1165–1166, 1335, 1344, 1348
Higgins, Daniel—855–856
Hillman, Timothy S.—1612
Hioki, Warren G.—1578
Hirono, Mazie K.—1426
Hodes, Paul W.—1600, 1623
Hodge, Lauren—1318, 1396, 1599
Hoenig, Thomas M.—1604, 1623–1624
Hoffa, James P.—1031, 1613
Hogg, John J.—1439, 1440
Holder, Eric H., Jr.—1224–1226, 1267, 1269, 1356, 1585
Holton, Anne—1043
Honda, Michael M.—1134
Hook, John—1606
Hoover, Brianna—1470
Hornsby, Bruce—1135
Horowitz, Michael E.—1583, 1618
Hostage, G. Michael, III—1302
Hostage, Kathy—1302
Howard, Dwight D., Jr.—1251
Howard, Roger—1547
Howell, Kevin J.—1302
Hoyer, Steny H.—1581–1582
Hudson, Jennifer—917
Huerta, Dolores C.—904, 1330
Hughes, Ed—1108
Hughes, Michael A.—1597, 1621
Huisinga, Richard—1470
Hu Jintao—1409, 1414, 1420, 1423
Humala Tasso, Ollanta Moises—1578, 1583, 1609
Hunt, James B., Jr.—1058
Hurley, Douglas G.—843, 1606
Hurwitz, Andrew D.—1606, 1624
Hutchison, Kathryn A. "Kay" Bailey—1039, 1116, 1367
Hyndman, Rebecca—1074
Immelt, Jeffrey R.—1240, 1242, 1245, 1589

Issoufou Mahamadou—909–910
Izzo, Thomas—1401

Jacks, Tyler—1597
Jackson, Lisa P.—1029, 1592
Jacobs, Richard—1556
Jacobson, Roberta S.—1598, 1622
Jaffe, Ira F.—1600
Jarrett, Valerie B.—1242, 1383, 1391, 1580, 1608
Javits, Joshua M.—1600
Jealous, Benjamin T.—1582
Jebali, Hamadi—1615
Jeffrey, Deborah J.—1609, 1625
Jeffrey, James F.—1543
Jenkins, Henry A. "Harry"—1439–1440

Jensen, Dallin—1581
Jibril, Mahmoud—1086
Jobs, Laurene Powell—1218
Jobs, Steven P.—1075, 1207, 1218
Jodice, Ralph J., III—1378
Johns, Timothy—1580
Johnson, Alice—1188–1189
Johnson, Cathy—1036
Johnson, Chandra—1036
Johnson, Earvin "Magic," Jr.—1330, 1500
Johnson, Gary—1036
Johnson, Genevieve M.—1036
Johnson, H. Fisk—1596
Johnson, Jack—1338
Johnson, Jerry L.—1606
Johnson, Jimmie—1036–1037, 1592
Johnson, Kevin—1338
Johnson, Kona—1338
Johnson, Robert L.—1288
Johnson Sirleaf, Ellen—1238–1239
Johnston, Abbey—1582
Jones, David A.—1593, 1620
Jones, Dwight C.—1043
Jones, Emil, Jr.—917
Jones, Jeffery—1030, 1592
Jones, Maurice A.—1598, 1621
Jones-Butler, Dolores—1385
Jordan, Adalberto J.—1584, 1619
Joyce, Rosemary A.—1578
Joyner, Tom—1591
Jubayr, Adil al-Ahmad al- —1267–1268, 1479, 1601
Junior, August "Gus"—983

Kagan, Elena—1159, 1198, 1211, 1253, 1257–1558
Kahn, Janet R.—1601
Kaine, Timothy M.—1043
Kaiser, Michael M.—1511
Kappos, David J.—1074
Karimov, Islom—1598
Karman, Tawakkul—1238–1239
Karzai, Hamid—934, 1088, 1586–1587
Kasich, John R.—1061
Katz, Andy—1608
Katzenberg, Jeffrey—1162–1164
Kavandi, Janet L.—1606
Kelly, Gary C.—882, 1109
Kelly, Scott J.—1584
Kemp, Brian—1307
Kemp, Roger—1311
Keneally, Kathryn—1594, 1621
Kennedy, Caroline B.—1511
Kent, Cameron—1599
Kent, Roman R.—1605
Kerlikowske, R. Gil—1176
Kerry, John F.—1039, 1116, 1367

Kesterson, R. Keith—824
Key, John P.—884, 1578
Keys, Alicia—1093, 1498
Khan, Elsheba—941
Khouri, Michael A.—1593, 1620
Kibben, Margaret G.—1066
Kidd, Joseph D.—1020, 1587
Kiir Mayardit, Salva—1597
Kikwete, Jakaya Mrisho—1498, 1500
Kildee, Dale E.—866
Killion, Nikole—1606
Kim, Sung Y.—1271
Kim, Will—1182
Kimble, Judith—1615
Kim Jong Il—1614–1615
Kim Sung-hwan—1276
Kim Yoon-ok—1262–1264, 1272, 1602
King, Robert—1031, 1276
King, Ron—1114
Kinsler-Johnson, Pleasantte—1386
Kirk, Ronald—1197, 1202–1204, 1276, 1403, 1477
Klobuchar, Amy J.—951, 957, 960, 1017, 1366
Klukas, Martin S.—1302
Knaus, Chad—1036
Knauss, Donald R.—1579
Knight, Ken—1605
Knox, Debby—1613
Koch, Matan A.—1577, 1617
Koehler, David—996
Kohr, Howard—1556
Kony, Joseph—1278–1279
Korzeniewski, Kevin—1388
Koster, Chris—1209
Kratovil, Frank M.—873, 878
Krauss, Alison—1464
Krauthamer, Peter A.—1579, 1617
Kristof, Nicholas D.—833
Kristofferson, Kris—1464
Kroft, Steve—1613
Krueger, Alan B.—1015, 1591, 1620
Kullman, Ellen J.—1074

Lagarde, Christine—1589
LaHood, Raymond H.—916, 977, 983, 991, 996–998, 1025, 1114, 1367, 1590
Landeau, Jon—1162
Langbehn, Janice—1189, 1311
Langford, Michael D.—1031
Larimer, Brent A.—824
Larson, John B.—1366, 1368
La Russa, Anthony, Jr.—1361, 1607
Lassiter, James—1328
Lassiter, Mai—1328
Lau, Constance H.—1579

Lauper, Cyndi—1189
Lautenberg, Frank R.—1592
Lavrov, Sergey V.—1579
Laws, Stephen C.—1287
Leahy, Patrick J.—1074–1075
Lechleiter, John C.—1074
Lee, Edwin, M.—899
Lee, John Z.—1608, 1624
Lee, Melissa Renie—1302
Lee Myung-bak—1109, 1115, 1132, 1136, 1199, 1205, 1249, 1253, 1262, 1264, 1271, 1274–1279, 1295, 1407, 1595, 1601–1602, 1614
Lefar, Marc P.—1578
Leigh, Amanda—1603
Leno, Jay—1604
Leon-Decker, Carla M.—1604, 1623
Lerner, Allison C.—1583
Lerner, Gabriel—1170, 1172–175, 1177, 1179
Levin, Carl M.—941, 943, 1031, 1033
Levin, Fay Hartog—1599
Levin, Sander M.—1031
Levine, Jane A.—1601
Levinson, Daniel R.—1583
Lewis, John R.—1127
Lew, Jacob L. "Jack"—1589
Likins, Rose M.—1583
Lincecum, Timothy L.—900
Lippert, Dorothy T.—1578
Lippert, Mark W.—1604, 1623
Liu, Goodwin—1619
Lobo Sosa, Porfirio—1216, 1598
Locke, Gary F.—1069–1070, 1584
Locklear, Samuel J., III—1011, 1378
Loh, Wallace D.—873
Lombardo, Maria—1585
Loney, Timothy K.—1587
Long, Sharon—1582
Longoria, Enrique, Jr.—1332
Longoria, Eva—1162, 1330, 1332
Lopez, Oralia—899
Loren, Sophia—1361
Love, Reginald L.—882
Lovett, Lyle P.—1464
Lowery, Joseph E.—1123
Lowman, Carol E.—1597
Loy, Frank E.—1579, 1618
Lozada, Jacob—1606
Lum, Grande—1602
Lundquist, Sara—1595
Lyman, Princeton N.—1578
Lynch, Jill A.—1603
Lynch, John H.—1069
Lynn, William J., III—855, 1185
Lyons, Charles "Chip"—1594

Ma, Yo-Yo—1513
Maathai, Wangari Muta—1156
Mabus, Raymond E., Jr.—1066, 1604
Macmanus, Joseph E.—1612, 1625
Magnus, Sandra H.—843, 1606
Maier, Pauline R.—1612, 1625
Mailhot, Robert—1465
Majumdar, Arun—1611
Maliki, Nuri al- —1316, 1488, 1537, 1548, 1604, 1607, 1613
Mallory, Mark—1114, 1389
Mandela, Nelson R.—868
Markell, Jack A.—1589
Marshall, Wilber—1235
Martin, Ida—1311
Martin, Michel—1581
Martin-Proctor, Kamilah Oni—1602
Martinelli Berrocal, Ricardo—1604
Martinez, Juanita—1605
Martinez, Monica R.—1577
Martinez, Vilma S.—1613
Marvin, John W. "Jake"—1523
Marvin, Susan—1523
Mason, Anthony—1588
Mathia, Henry B.—1587
Matthews, Clay—948
Matthews, Jessica O.—1074
Mattis, James N.—1586, 1604
Maude, Francis—1091
Maxman, Susan A.—1598, 1622
Mays, Willie H., Jr.—899–900, 1582
Mazer, Roslyn A.—1581, 1618
Mazur, Mark J.—1609, 1625
McCabe, John F., Jr.—1579, 1617
McCain, John S., III—1604
McCarthy, Michael J.—948–949
McCartney, Rob—1606
McCaskill, Claire—1209, 1388
McConnell, A. Mitchell—848, 862, 864, 871, 887–888, 905, 1066, 1116–1117, 1192, 1205, 1221, 1229, 1270, 1323, 1339, 1346, 1367, 1428, 1485, 1491, 1494, 1531, 1534, 1562, 1566, 1581–1582
McConnell, Charles D.—1578, 1617
McCovey, Willie L.—900
McCoy, Drew R.—1593, 1620
McCulloh, Karen J.—1597
McCullough, I. Charles, III—1584, 1619
McCully, Murray S.—885
McDonnell, Maureen—1302
McDonnell, Robert F.—1302, 1589
McFadden-Lawson, Mattie—1593
McFaul, Michael A.—1596, 1621
McGill, Matt—1591
McGinn, Michael P.—1131
McGovern, Gail J.—1592

McHugh, John M.—855
McIntyre, Douglas C. "Mike"—1547
McKiernan, Thomas L.—1596
Mckim, Mark—1601
McLeese, Roy W., III—1609, 1625
McMahon, James R., Jr.—1235–1236
McMichael, Steven—1235
McMillan, David J.—1593, 1620
McMillen, C. Thomas—882–883
McNerney, W. James, Jr.—1404–1412
McNulty, Kevin—1614, 1626
McQuiston, Barbara K.—1619
Mebarak Ripoll, Shakira Isabel—1600
Medina, Karine—1171, 1173, 1175–1176, 1178
Medine, David—1614, 1626
Medvedev, Dmitry A.—1397, 1407, 1413, 1419–1420, 1456, 1579, 1585, 1614
Meek, Kendrick B.—1579, 1618
Melvin, Veronica E.—1577
Menendez, Robert—1062, 1330, 1332, 1592
Merkel, Angela—1231, 1370, 1375–1376, 1436, 1533, 1581, 1585, 1590, 1596, 1602–1603, 1608, 1613
Meyer, Dakota L.—1066, 1587, 1594, 1596
Meyer, Dwight—1066
Meyer, Jean—1066
Meyer, Mike—1066
Meza, Choco G.—1588
Mikva, Abner J.—1545
Miller, Darlene—1245
Miller, George—1118, 1120
Miller, Mary J.—1577, 1617
Miller, Maureen—1547
Miller, Philip—1547
Miller, Thomas J.—963
Mills, Karen Gordon—977, 979–980
Mims, Larry "No Limit Larry"—1602
Mireles, Ella E.—1332
Mitchell, Ernest, Jr.—1584, 1619
Monaco, John—1204, 1207
Monti, Mario—1610
Montoya, David A.—1580, 1618
Mooney-Hildebrand, Patricia—1601
Moran, James P.—1074
Moran, Rachel F.—1598
Morgan, Jesse—1601
Morgan, John—1256
Morgan, Ultima—1256
Morial, Marc H.—1582
Moritz, Lara—1581
Moss, Melissa—1593
Mubarak, Mohamed Hosni—1099–1100
Mueller, Robert S., III—1618
Mulally, Alan—1588
Mulholland, John F., Jr.—1547
Mulholland, Miriam—1547

Mulholland, Neil J.—1501
Mullen, Deborah—1183, 1185
Mullen, John—1183
Mullen, Michael G.—886, 928, 1183–1185, 1582, 1585
Mundaca, Michael F.—1619
Murguia, Janet—895
Murnane, Margaret M.—1615
Murphy, Mark—948
Murphy, Patrick J.—1385, 1386
Murphy, Philip D.—1580
Murray, Ellen—1583
Murray, Patricia L.—1608
Myers, Sondra—1606

Nabors, Robert L., II—1615
Nahale-a, Alapaki—1582
Najib bin Abdul Razak, Mohamed—1451
Namm, Adam E.—1593, 1620
Napolitano, Giorgio—1608
Napolitano, Janet A.—1014–1015, 1360, 1528, 1589–
  1590, 1593–1594
Navarro, Nancy—1600
Nayif bin Abd al-Aziz Al Saud, Prince—1356
Nazario, Carmen L.—1577
Neal, Emily—966–967
Neal, Kaia—967
Necas, Petr—1353, 1355, 1600
Negley, Chris—1024
NeJame, Mark E.—1251
Nelson, E. Benjamin—1571
Nelson, Phillip—1000
Ness, Susan—1584
Netanyahu, Benjamin—1104, 1586, 1594
Neukom, William H.—899, 901
Newman, Thomas B.—1020, 1587
Newsom, Gavin C.—899, 1157
Nguyen, Jacqueline H.—1597, 1621
Nguyen, Tung Thanh—1600
Nixon, Jeremiah W. "Jay"—1209
Noda, Yoshihiko—1023, 1105, 1407, 1412, 1418,
  1591, 1615
Norris, Jackie—1606
Nozick, Linda K.—1582
Nutter, Michael A.—1385, 1389, 1589
Nwagwu, Obi—824

Obama, Malia—824, 868, 877, 907, 919, 925, 954,
  1001, 1005, 1093–1094, 1119, 1127, 1129, 1157,
  1159, 1181, 1211, 1233, 1258, 1261, 1283, 1324,
  1348, 1351–1352, 1360, 1364, 1369, 1393, 1418,
  1426, 1470–1472, 1487, 1491, 1501, 1532, 1557,
  1565, 1570, 1572, 1580, 1590, 1594, 1610–1611, 1616

Obama, Michelle—824–825, 828, 843, 866, 868, 873,
  881, 894, 900, 904, 913, 930, 954, 963, 972, 986,
  1001–1002, 1013, 1022–1023, 1037, 1066, 1069,
  1093–1094, 1096, 1108, 1119, 1126, 1149, 1154,
  1156–1157, 1169, 1190, 1201, 1207, 1209, 1212, 1214,
  1217–1218, 1238, 1255, 1258, 1261, 1263–1264,
  1272, 1291, 1293, 1297, 1302–1304, 1313, 1325, 1343,
  1347–1348, 1351–1353, 1360, 1364, 1379, 1381,
  1385, 1393, 1395, 1399–1402, 1416–1418, 1426,
  1431, 1448, 1459–1460, 1464, 1470–1473, 1481,
  1501, 1506, 1511, 1513, 1530, 1535, 1545–1546, 1549,
  1565, 1570–1572, 1577, 1580, 1590, 1594, 1596–
  1597, 1601–1603, 1605, 1607–1608, 1610–1614, 1616
Obama, Natasha "Sasha"—824, 868, 877, 919, 925,
  954, 1001, 1093–1094, 1119, 1127, 1129, 1157, 1159,
  1181, 1211, 1233, 1258, 1261, 1283, 1324, 1348,
  1351–1352, 1360, 1364, 1369, 1393, 1418, 1426,
  1470, 1471–1472, 1487, 1491, 1501, 1532, 1565,
  1570, 1572, 1580, 1590, 1594, 1610–1611, 1616
Odierno, Raymond T.—1036, 1361
Ohlhausen, Maureen K.—1581, 1618
Ohlson, Kevin A.—1596, 1621
Ohno, Apolo Anton—1600
Olsen, Matthew G.—1577, 1617
Olson, Eric T.—1586
Olver, John W.—1353
Olver, Martha J.—1353
Olver, Rose, R.—1353
Ono, David—1581
Onorato, Dan—1246
Oren, Michael—1535, 1556
Orlando, Stephanie—1577, 1617
Ornish, Dean—1606
Otunbaeva, Roza—1363
Ouattara, Alassane Dramane—909, 1099, 1112
Owens, Donae—1179, 1181, 1183
Owens, Kimberly A.—1597
O'Brien, Conan—1537
O'Malley, Martin J.—873, 881, 1589
O'Shea, Lawrence J.—1386

Page, Susan D.—1588, 1620
Pagett, Riley—981
Pai, Ajit V.—1605, 1623
Paisley, Brad D.—1464
Palacio, Herminia—1606
Palmer, Larry L.—1605, 1624
Panetta, Leon E.—886, 899, 1183, 1185, 1360, 1398,
  1406, 1577, 1581–1585, 1593, 1595, 1599, 1601, 1613
Papademos, Lukas—1610
Papandreou, Georgios Andreas—1375, 1609
Pascrell, William J., Jr.—1592
Pasquarella, Natalie—1579
Patrick, Deval L.—1589
Paul, Randal H.—1114

Payne, Donald M.—1123, 1578
Payne, Jim—1599
Payton, Connie—1235
Pedroza, Adrian A.—1600
Peebles, Katrina L.—935, 1595
Peebles, R. Donahue—935
Peer, Scott J.—1587
Pelley, Scott—1580
Pelosi, Nancy—843, 852, 871, 887–899, 909, 1062, 1065, 1192, 1338, 1360–1361, 1393, 1578, 1581–1582, 1584
Pena, Federico F.—1165
Pensky, Carol—1584
Perdue, Beverly E.—1058–1059, 1290, 1547, 1589
Perez Molina, Otto—1610
Perlmutter, Edwin G.—1165
Perry, J. Richard—1137, 1593
Perry, Kimberly—1464
Perry, Neil—1464
Perry, Reid—1464
Peters, Gary C.—1031
Petit Higa, Josefina—1166
Petraeus, David H.—1533, 1591, 1604
Petraeus, Holly—1533
Petry, Ashley—855–856
Petry, Landon—855–856
Petry, Larry—855
Petry, Larry A.—855
Petry, Leroy A.—855, 1066, 1259, 1261
Petry, Lincoln—855
Petry, Lloyd—855
Petry, Lyndon—855
Petty, Julie A.—1607
Petty, Richard—1036
Pfeiffer, H. Daniel—1608
Phelps, Elizabeth—1153–1154
Phelps, Mason—1153–1154
Phillips, Linda—1292, 1295
Piazza, Michael J.—1361
Pietsch, Coral W.—1605, 1624
Plouffe, David A.—1591–1592, 1608
Polis, Jared—1154
Pollan, Laura—1551
Pollard, William B., III—1608, 1624
Popli, Karishma—1074
Portman, Ervin F.—1058–1060
Posner, Jaye "Posey"—1512
Post, Glen F., III—1598
Potter, Deborah D.—1593
Potter, Lauren E.—1607
Powell, Alma J.—1580
Powell, Colin L.—1578, 1580
Powell, Jerome H.—1616
Powell, Nancy J.—1614, 1627
Powers, Phyllis M.—1612, 1625
Price, Clement A.—1584

Price, David E.—1547
Pride, Charley F.—1464
Puga, Benoit—1377
Pujadas, David—1607
Puzey, David—1610

Qaboos bin Said Al Said—1113, 1598
Qadhafi, Muammar Abu Minyar al- —1009–1011, 1020, 1086, 1088, 1099–1100, 1309, 1317, 1319
Quan, Jean—1135
Quinn, Patrick J., III—917, 996–997, 1004

Rabbani, Burhanuddin—1089
Rajahni, Rakesh—1091
Rajoy Brey, Mariano—1615
Ransom, Richard—1613
Rasmussen, Anders Fogh—1607
Ravenstahl, Luke R.—1246–1247
Rawlings, Michael S.—1197, 1203–1204, 1207
Rawlings-Blake, Stephanie C.—1589
Ray, Randy—1500
Raynor, Michael A.—1614, 1626
Reel, Baye "DJ Bee"—1603
Reeve, Cheryl—1605
Reid, Harry M.—852, 871, 887–888, 905, 1192, 1251, 1326, 1474, 1562, 1581–1582, 1584, 1600, 1615
Replogle, Kristin G.—1593
Restrepo, Daniel A.—1583, 1613
Revish, Jerry—1581
Reynoso, Julissa—1602
Rhoads, Roger—1388
Rice, Earl L.—1547
Rice, Susan E.—1011, 1578
Richard, Anne C.—1607, 1624
Richardson, Nigel—1043–1044
Richie, Boyd—1197
Richman, Ellen S.—1593
Riklon, Marlene—824
Rimer, Barbara K.—1611
Ritsko, Matthew W.—1388
Robbins, Kevin J.—1302
Robbins, Mark A.—1612, 1626
Robinson, Craig M.—881
Robinson, Lucas—855–856
Robinson, Marian—1126, 1144, 1351, 1501
Robinson, Robby—951
Rodgers, Aaron—948–949
Rodham, Dorothy H.—1364
Rodriguez, Leon—1619
Rodriquez, David M.—1547
Rodriquez, Ginny—1547
Rodriguez-Chavez, Juan J.—1067–1068
Roell, Stephen A.—941–942
Rogers, Marie Lopez—899
Rogers, Perrin—1501

Rolinski, Elizabeth—941, 1586
Rollins, Theodore "Sonny"—1512–1513
Romney, W. Mitt—962, 972, 1267
Rooney, Daniel M.—1246
Rooney, Thomas J.—1564
Rose, Matthew—1244
Rosen, Jack—1489–1490, 1494
Rosen, Phyllis—1489
Rosenbaum, Robin S.—1612
Rosenworcel, Jessica—1605, 1624
Ross, Thomas W.—1058
Rothman, Steven R.—1592
Rouse, Peter M.—1608
Rouse-Terlevich, Mary—1593
Rousseff, Dilma—1089, 1091, 1597
Rubenstein, David M.—1511
Rucker, Darius—1464
Ruffin, Milton V.—1055
Russell, Angela—1614
Russell, George L., III—1608, 1624
Russell, Kimberly—1204, 1207–1208
Russell, William F.—1130
Rutherford, Donald L.—855
Rutherford, Matthew S.—1598, 1622
Rutte, Mark—1481, 1610
Ryan, James D. "Buddy"—1235
Ryan, James T.—1582, 1618, 1622
Ryan, J. Kelly—1593, 1620
Ryan, Paul D.—861, 1116, 1346, 1367
Ryan, Rex—1235
Ryan, Rob—1235
Rybak, Raymond T.—1017

Sabean, Brian R.—900–901
Salazar, Kenneth L.—977, 1062, 1165, 1259, 1364,
    1501, 1505–1507
Salazar, Kent A.—1606
Salih, Ali Abdallah—1100, 1470
Salisbury, Dallas L.—1612
Saltzman, Robert M.—1584
Sanchez, Amelia—1165
Sandberg, Sheryl K.—1139–1140, 1243
Santaniello, Amelia—1606
Santos Calderon, Juan Manuel—1604
Saperstein, David—1556
Sargent, Anneila I.—1583, 1619
Sarkozy, Giulia—1369
Sarkozy, Nicolas—1112, 1231, 1369, 1373–1379, 1425,
    1436, 1533, 1582, 1585, 1589, 1601, 1603, 1606–1608
Sarrafan, Sima F.—1597
Sata, Michael—1121
Schaad, Tom—1606
Schaeffer, Eric—1482
Schakowsky, Janice D.—917
Schatz, Brian—1426

Schilling, Robert T.—984
Schlosstein, Ralph L.—1084
Schmidt, Kendall—1501
Schmitt, James J.—948
Schnedar, Cynthia A.—1225
Schneiderman, Eric T.—1493
Schumer, Charles E.—1230, 1600
Schwartz, Errol R.—1582
Scott, Beverly A.—1579
Scott, Elsie L.—1123
Scott, Robert C.—1302
Scott, Wayne—1297
Scovel, Calvin L., III—1583
Scribner, Kent P.—1600
Scully-Lerner, Jennifer—1593
Scuse, Michael T.—1598, 1622
Sealey, Hector—1025
Sebelius, Kathleen—1363, 1385, 1516, 1532
Self, Bill—1516
Senter, Edward Loy, Jr.—1305
Sessoms, William D., Jr.—1589
Sexton, Michael—1587
Shah, Naomi—1318, 1396, 1599
Shaheen, C. Jeanne—1465, 1467, 1469
Shalikashvili, Brant—894
Shalikashvili, Joan E.—894
Shalikashvili, John M.—893
Sharpton, Alfred C., Jr.—1610
Sheehan, Michael A.—1605, 1624
Shelby, Robert J.—1612
Shell, Alvin E., Jr.—1549
Shepard, Judy—1189
Shepherd, J. Wayne—1288
Sherman, Wendy R.—1577, 1617
Sherrick, Bruce J.—1580, 1618
Sherry, Margaret A.—1609, 1625
Shinseki, Eric K.—1020–1021, 1066, 1398, 1460
Shirley, Jon A.—1128
Shirley, Mary—1128
Shuler, Heath—1547
Shuttlesworth, Fred L.—1217
Shuttlesworth, Sephira B.—1217
Shwartz, Patty—1600, 1622
Siade, Jose—1169, 1173, 1176, 1178–1179
Silber, Joan E.—1597
Silliman, Scott L.—1608, 1624
Simpson, Alan K.—852, 862, 988
Singel, Wenona—1593, 1620
Singer, Judith D.—1599, 1622
Singh, Manmohan—1449
Singletary, Michael—1235
Sisk, William—1585
Sisterhen, Tom—1055–1056
Slay, Francis G.—1209
Smerconish, Michael—1599

Smith, Dexter—829
Smith, Emmitt J.—1197, 1199, 1203
Smith, Jada Pinkett—1328
Smith, James B.—1604
Smith, Kelly—911
Smith, Lamar S.—1074, 1075
Smith, Marie F.—1611
Smith, Wendi—1605
Smith, Will—1328, 1330
Snyder, Jim—1613
Solarski, Bob—1614
Solis, Hilda L.—895, 899, 1031, 1062, 1242, 1259, 1330, 1332, 1553, 1613
Solmonese, Joe—1189
Solow, Alan P.—1556
Sonenshine, Tara D.—1607, 1624
Sorian, Richard—1627
Sotomayor, Sonia M.—895, 899, 1062, 1159, 1198, 1211, 1253, 1257, 1259, 1558
Spektor, Regina—1493
Spencer, Wendy—1603
Sperling, Eugene B.—1241–1244, 1391, 1584, 1589, 1592
Spratlen, Pamela L.—1611
Spratt, John M., Jr.—1596
Springsteen, Bruce—1129
Stabenow, Deborah A.—1031
Stanfield, Faith—1388
Stang, Peter J.—1318
Stavridis, James G.—1378
Stearns, Clifford B.—1225
Steele, Celeste—1388
Steever, Tom—1588
Stein, Jeremy C. "Jay"—1616
Steinberg, Donald K.—1578
Stephanopoulos, George—1599
Stetson, Jane—1545
Stevens, George, Jr.—1511
Stevens, Michael—1511
Stewart, Tony—1612
Stogner, Larry—1578
Stoltenberg, Jens—1313, 1582, 1599
Stone, Jeffrey R.—1426
Streep, Meryl—1512–1513
Strommen, Wegger Christian—1583
Suddeth, Lauren Alaina K.—1464
Sullivan, Brian—1603
Sullivan, John M.—996
Sultan bin Abd al-Aziz Al Saud, Crown Prince—1320, 1604
Sumwalt, Robert L., III—1600, 1623
Sunstein, Cass R.—1527–1528
Susman, Ellen—1593
Sutphen, Mona K.—1593
Swaine, Emily—1050
Swaine, Hannah—1050

Swaine, Sarah—1050
Swaine, Suzanne—1050

Taff, Brian—1606
Talabani, Jalal—1113
Tantawi, Mohamed Hussein—1604
Tapia, Lorella—855
Tapia, Richard A.—1318
Tapper, Jake—1603
Taranto, Richard G.—1608, 1624
Tavenner, Marilyn B.—1611
Taylor, Charles—872, 1239
Taylor, James V.—1464
Teehee, Kimberly K.—1506
Teneal, CeCe—1251
Terzi di Sant' Agata, Giulio—1360
Thacker, Stephanie D.—1594, 1621
Tharp, John J., Jr.—1608, 1624
Thatcher, Margaret H.—1512
Thein Sein—1452
Thomas, LeVon—1506
Thompson, John W.—1134
Thompson, Sandra—1134–1135
Thompson, Ted—948
Thorne, David H.—1360
Tighe, Kathleen S.—1583
Timberlake, James—1600, 1622
Tobias, Andrew—1093, 1545
Todd, William E.—1612, 1626
Tompkins, Hilary—1505
Toomey, Patrick J.—1249
Torrey, Robert—1426
Trumka, Richard L.—1025, 1030–1031, 1246
Tymoshenko, Yuliya V.—1479

Udall, Mark E.—1165, 1167, 1335, 1349
Unemori, Jeanne—1582
Unger, Howard D.—1605
Unruh, Eric—1587
Unruh, Fern—1587
Urquhart, Vincent A.—1305

Vance, Jim—1580
VanRoekel, Steven L.—1585
Van Rompuy, Herman—1473–1474, 1481
Velotta, Brittany—855–856
Vencill, Adam—1024
Vergano, Christopher—1592
Verner, Mary B.—1593, 1620
Vernon, Gil—1600
Villaraigosa, Antonio R.—1330
Villarosa, Sharon—1602
Vilsack, Thomas J.—955, 957, 963–964, 971–972, 977, 980–983, 986, 991, 993, 996, 1000, 1356
Vinolcavak, Jordan—1005–1006

Vogel, William L.—1592
Volz, Keith L.—1292, 1294
Votel, Joseph L.—1547, 1586
Votel, Michelle—1547

Wagner, Dave—1289, 1602
Wainscott, Kent—1578
Wald, Patricia M.—1614, 1626
Walheim, Rex J.—843, 1606
Walker, Scott K.—948
Walkley, R. Barrie—1578
Wallach, Evan J.—1583, 1618
Walles, Jacob—1614, 1626
Walther, Larry W.—1582, 1618
Walz, Timothy J.—951, 960
Wamariya, Clemantine—1605
Ward, Dave—1606
Ware, Nancy M.—1584, 1619
Warner, Mark R.—870–871, 886, 989
Warren, Elizabeth—869–870
Warren, Michael J.—1594, 1620
Wasserman Schultz, Deborah—1489, 1493, 1545, 1557
Watford, Paul J.—1603
Watt, Melvin L.—1074, 1292, 1296
Watters, Marvin—996
Wayne, Earl A.—1601
Wee, Liang C.—977
Weiner, Jeff—1140–1143, 1145–1148, 1150–1153
Weingarten, Randi—1502
Weinstein, Harvey—945–947
Wen Jiabao—1610
Wentworth, Alexandra—1493
Werfel, Daniel I.—1583
West, Austin—855–856
West, Reagan—855–856
Whealy, Diane O.—963
Wheeler, Daniel S.—1017
Wheeler, Destiny—1188–1189
Whidden, Michael—1601
White, Beth—1615
White, Jesse—917
White, Tyra—1233
White-Ginder, Jeanne—1500
Whitehead, Robert E.—1603
Whitehouse, Sheldon—1366
Wiesel, Elie—1605

Wilder, L. Douglas—1043
Wiley, Fletcher "Flash"—1611
Wilkens, Leonard R.—1130
Williams, David C.—1583
Williams, E. Faye—1588
Williams, Roy A.—1401
Williams, Saundra L.—1031
Wilson, Brian—900
Wilson, Harry J.—1593
Wilson, Mark—1606
Wilson, Otis—1235
Wilusz, Lisa M.—1597
Wimes, Brian C.—1597, 1621
Winfrey, Oprah—1140
Winnefeld, James A. "Sandy," Jr.—1185
Wintour, Anna—945
Witt, Phil—1587
Witte, Owen N.—1611
Wolf, Robert—1243–1244
Wolin, Neal S.—1583
Woods, Gregory H.—1584, 1619
Woodson, Charles—948–949
Woodson, W. Randolph—1058
Worrell, Philip L.—1297
Wyffels, Robert—983–984
Wyffels, William, Jr.—983–984

Yang, Henry T.—1615
Yarmuth, John A.—1114
Yates, Vicki—1599
Yayi, Thomas Boni—909
Yinglak Chinnawat—1455, 1587
Yoffie, Eric H.—1556–1558
York, Susan—1615
Yoshikawa, Hirokazu—1603, 1623
Yudhoyono, Susilo Bambang—1452–1453
Yzaguirre, Raul H.—895

Zack, Arnold M.—1600
Zaidon, Hikmat Jassim—1548
Zandi, Mark—1322, 1339
Zapatero, Jose Luis Rodriguez—1586
Zardari, Asif Ali—1612
Zelikow, Philip D.—1593
Zuckerberg, Mark E.—1139

Document Categories List

Addresses to the Nation
  Federal budget—901
  Joint session of Congress—1037

Addresses and Remarks
  See also Addresses to the Nation; Appointments
    and Nominations; Bill Signings and Vetoes; In-
    terviews With the News Media; Meetings With
    Foreign Leaders and International Officials
  1986 Super Bowl champion Chicago Bears—1234
  Abraham Lincoln High School in Denver, CO—1165
  "A Concert for Hope" commemorating the 10th
    anniversary of the September 11 terrorist at-
    tacks—1049
  African American Policy in Action Leadership
    Conference—1389
  Alpha, IL, town hall meeting and question-and-an-
    swer session—996
  American Legion, national convention in Minne-
    apolis, MN—1017
  Asia-Pacific Economic Cooperation summit
    CEO question-and-answer session in Honolulu,
      HI—1404
    Dinner in Honolulu, HI—1416
    Reception and cultural performance in Honolu-
      lu, HI—1416
    Working session in Kapolei, HI—1417
  Atkinson, IL, town hall meeting and question-and-
    answer session—983
  Australia
    Campbell High School, question-and-answer
      session in Canberra—1445
    Dinner with Parliament Members in Canberra—1439
    Parliament in Canberra—1440
    Royal Australian Air Force Base Darwin, remarks
      to U.S. and Australian military personnel—1447
  Benjamin Banneker Academic High School—1179
  Better Buildings Initiative, remarks with former
    President William J. Clinton—1502
  Burma, remarks from Bali, Indonesia—1451
  Cabinet meetings—916, 1192
  Cannon Falls, MN, town hall meeting and ques-
    tion-and-answer session—951
  Central High School in Manchester, NH—1465
  Christmas
    "Christmas in Washington"—1537
    National Christmas tree lighting ceremony—1501
  Clinton Global Initiative, annual meeting in New
    York City—1108

Addresses and Remarks—Continued
  College Park, MD, town hall meeting and ques-
    tion-and-answer session—872
  Congressional Black Caucus Foundation, Phoenix
    Awards dinner—1123
  Congressional Hispanic Caucus Institute annual
    awards gala—1062
  "Country Music: In Performance at the White
    House"—1464
  Decorah, IA, town hall meeting and question-and-
    answer session—963
  Deficit Reduction, Joint Select Committee on—1461
  Democratic National Committee fundraisers
    Chicago, IL—917, 924
    Dallas, TX—1197, 1202
    Denver, CO—1335, 1343
    La Jolla, CA—1153
    Las Vegas, NV—1321
    Los Angeles, CA—1328, 1330
    Medina, WA—1128
    New York City—945, 1084, 1093
    Orlando, FL—1251, 1256
    San Francisco, CA—1338
    San Jose, CA—1134, 1139
    Seattle, WA—1130
    St. Louis, MO—1209, 1214
    Washington, DC—935, 938, 1071, 1073, 1186
    West Hollywood, CA—1157, 1162
  Democratic National Committee video teleconfer-
    ence and question-and-answer session in Chica-
    go, IL—921
  Eastfield College in Mesquite, TX—1204
  Economy, national—841, 933
  Federal budget—886, 905, 912, 914
  Federal budget and job growth legislation—1078
  Federal Government, cutting waste and promoting ef-
    ficient spending, signing an Executive order—1388
  Fire Station 9 in North Chesterfield, VA—1305
  Fort Bragg, NC—1546
  Fort Hayes Arts and Academic High School in Co-
    lumbus, OH—1055
  Fort Monroe National Monument, signing the
    proclamation establishing—1363
  France, Cannes City Hall in Cannes—1377
  Fuel efficiency standards—906
  General Motors Orion Assembly Plant in Lake Ori-
    on, MI—1274
  George Washington University—1498
  Greensville County High School in Emporia, VA—1297

Addresses and Remarks—Continued
  Guilford Technical Community College in James-
    town, NC—1292
  Hanukkah reception—1535
  Hilltop Basic Resources, Inc., River Terminal in
    Cincinnati, OH—1114
  Homecare workers, ensuring fair pay—1551
  Human Rights Campaign, annual national din-
    ner—1189
  Hurricane Irene
    Relief efforts—1014
    Remarks from Martha's Vineyard, MA—1012
    Tour of damage in Paterson, NJ—1030
  Iftar dinner—940
  Independence Day celebration—824
  International Brotherhood of Electrical Workers
    Local Union No. 5 in Pittsburgh, PA—1246
  Iraq, withdrawal of U.S. military personnel—1316
  Italian American Foundation, National, gala—1360
  Jamestown, NC, roundtable discussion with educa-
    tors—1291
  Job growth legislation—1051
  John F. Kennedy Center for the Performing Arts,
    honors reception—1511
  Johnson Controls, Inc., in Holland, MI—941
  Joint Base Langley-Eustis, VA—1302
  Joint Chiefs of Staff, change of command ceremo-
    ny at Fort Myer, VA—1183
  Labor Day in Detroit, MI—1031
  La Raza, National Council of—895
  Las Vegas, NV—1325
  Libya situation from Martha's Vineyard, MA—1010
  LinkedIn participants, question-and-answer ses-
    sion in Mountain View, CA—1140
  Lion Air, purchase agreement with the Boeing
    Company, remarks in Bali, Indonesia—1449
  Martin Luther King, Jr. Memorial, dedication cer-
    emony—1280
  Medal of Honor
    Meyer, Sgt. Dakota L., presentation—1066
    Petry, Sfc. Leroy A., presentation—855
  NASCAR Sprint Cup Series champion, 2010—1036
  National Medal of Science and National Medal of
    Technology and Innovation, presentation—1317
  National Women's Law Center awards dinner—1392
  NCAA women's basketball champion Texas A&M
    University Aggies—1233
  New York City
    Libya, United Nations meeting—1086
    Open Government Partnership, closing event—1091
    Open Government Partnership, opening
      event—1089
  No Child Left Behind Act—1118
  North Carolina State University in Raleigh, NC—1058

Addresses and Remarks—Continued
  Obama Victory Fund 2012 fundraisers
    Kapolei, HI—1426
    New York City—1489, 1491, 1493
    Washington, DC—1383, 1545
  "Open for Questions" Hispanic Roundtable, ques-
    tion-and-answer session—1169
  Osawatomie High School in Osawatomie, KS—1515
  Payroll tax cut and unemployment insurance legis-
    lation
    Congressional action—1562, 1567
    Remarks—1514, 1565
  Prescription drug shortages, signing an Executive
    order reducing—1362
  Presidential Citizens Medal, presentation—1311
  President's Council on Jobs and Competitiveness,
    meeting—1240
  Qadhafi, Muammar Abu Minyar al-, death of for-
    mer leader of Libya—1309
  Quicken Loans Carrier Classic in San Diego, CA—1401
  Rosh Hashanah, videotaped remarks—1168
  Scranton High School in Scranton, PA—1482
  September 11 Memorial, National, in New York
    City, reading—1049
  Super Bowl champion Green Bay Packers—948
  Surface Transportation and Federal Aviation Ad-
    ministration, reauthorization legislation—1024
  Thanksgiving turkey presentation ceremony—1469
  Trans-Pacific Partnership, meeting in Honolulu,
    HI—1403
  Transportation infrastructure improvement and
    job growth legislation—1365
  Twitter question-and-answer session—826
  Union for Reform Judaism, general assembly at
    National Harbor, MD—1556
  United Nations General Assembly in New York
    City—1098
  University of Colorado Denver in Denver, CO—1348
  University of Richmond in Richmond, VA—1043
  Veterans Day ceremony in Arlington, VA—1398
  Veterans, employment programs—1380
  Washington Navy Yard—928
  Weekly addresses—823, 844, 867, 892, 911, 931,
    950, 1008, 1013, 1029, 1048, 1078, 1122, 1188,
    1239, 1279, 1319, 1359, 1401, 1456, 1471,
    1510, 1536, 1561, 1570, 1572
  West Wilkes High School in Millers Creek, NC—1287
  White House Forum on American Latino Heri-
    tage—1259
  White House Press Secretary James F. "Jay" Car-
    ney briefing
    Remarks during—1563
    Remarks prior—825, 841, 870
  White House Rural Economic Forum in Peosta,
    IA—977, 979–981

Addresses and Remarks—Continued
  White House Tribal Nations Conference—1505
  World Series champion San Francisco Giants—899
  Yeadon Regional Head Start Center in Yeadon, PA—1385

Appointments and Nominations
  See also Digest, Nominations Submitted, and Checklist at the end of this volume
  Consumer Financial Protection Bureau, Director, remarks—868, 1531
  Council of Economic Advisers, Chairman, remarks—1015
  U.S. Court of Appeals judge, District of Columbia, statement—1524

Bill Signings and Vetoes
  Consolidated Appropriations Act, 2012, statement—1568
  Leahy-Smith America Invents Act, remarks—1074
  National Defense Authorization Act for Fiscal Year 2012, statement—1573
  VOW to Hire Heroes Act of 2011, remarks—1459

Communications to Congress
  Afghanistan and Pakistan, letter transmitting report—1185
  Central Africa, deployment of U.S. military forces, letter reporting—1278
  Colombia
    Colombia-U.S. trade promotion agreement, message transmitting legislation—1193
    Significant narcotics traffickers, U.S. national emergency, message on continuation—1309
  Combat-equipped Armed Forces, U.S., deployment, letter—1553
  Congo, Democratic Republic of the, U.S. national emergency, message on continuation—1334
  Cuban Liberty and Democratic Solidarity (LIBERTAD) Act of 1996, review of title III, letter—866
  Disaster relief funding request, letter—1047
  District of Columbia, fiscal year 2012 budget request, message transmitting—1196
  Economic growth and deficit reduction plan, message transmitting—1083
  Export control regulations, U.S. national emergency, message on continuation—950
  Fishing, port state measures to prevent, deter, and eliminate illegal, unreported, and unregulated practices, message—1431
  Iceland, whaling, Pelly certification, message reporting—1070

Communications to Congress—Continued
  Iran
    Executive order authorizing certain sanctions, message reporting—1457
    U.S. national emergency, message on continuation—1383
  Job creation and growth, message transmitting proposed legislation—1054
  Lebanon, U.S. national emergency, message on continuation—905
  Liberia, U.S. national emergency, message on continuation—872
  Minimization of regulatory burdens, letter transmitting—1023
  Naval Petroleum Reserves, message extending production period—1448
  Overseas contingency operations and global war on terrorism, letter designating funds—1570
  Panama-U.S. trade promotion agreement, message transmitting legislation—1194
  Public debt limit increase, message certifying—916
  South Korea-U.S. trade promotion agreement, messages transmitting legislation—1195–1196
  Sudan, U.S. national emergency, message on continuation—1365
  Syria, blocking property of the Government and prohibiting certain transactions, message reporting—1006
  Terrorism, persons who commit, threaten to commit, or support, U.S. national emergency, message on continuation—1114
  Terrorist attacks, U.S. national emergency, message on continuation—1047
  Transnational criminal organizations, Executive order blocking property, message reporting—894
  Weapons of mass destruction, U.S. national emergency, message on continuation—1392

Communications to Federal Agencies
  Atrocities Prevention Board, Interagency, creation, and corresponding review, directive—926
  Energy savings projects and performance-based contracting, memorandum—1508
  Human Rights of Lesbian, Gay, Bisexual, and Transgender Persons, memorandum—1524
  Iceland, whaling, Pelly certification, memorandum—1069
  Infrastructure development, memorandum on expediting permitting and review process—1026
  Liberia, refugees in the U.S., memorandum on deferred enforced departure—982
  Regulation and independent regulatory agencies, memorandum—854
  Russia, Strategic Arms Reduction Treaty (START), delegation of authority, memorandum—1368

Communications to Federal Agencies—Continued
  Technology transfer and commercialization, Federal research in support of high-growth businesses, memorandum on acceleration efforts—1357
  Unified Command Plan, memorandum on revisions—1053

Interviews With the News Media
  Exchanges with reporters
    New York City—1091, 1111
    Paterson, NJ—1030
    White House—841, 868, 886, 916, 1192, 1236, 1313, 1353, 1362–1363, 1502, 1531
  Interviews
    ABC, "Nightline" program—1603
    ABC News—1599
    Alfred C. Sharpton, Jr.—1610
    CBS, "60 Minutes" program—1613
    CBS, "Sunday Morning" program—1588
    CNN, "The Situation Room With Wolf Blitzer" program—1587
    Daily Times Herald in Carroll, IA—1588
    ESPN—1608
    Farm Broadcasting, National Association of—1588
    France 2—1607
    Hearst Television—1606
    Isabel Gomez-Bassols—1581
    KABC in Los Angeles, CA—1581
    KETV in Omaha, NE—1606
    KGW in Portland, OR—1606
    KING in Seattle, WA—1578
    KIRO in Seattle, WA—1614
    KMBC in Kansas City, MO—1581
    KOAA in Colorado Springs, CO—1614
    KSAZ in Phoenix, AZ—1606
    KSDK in St. Louis, MO—1587
    KSNV in Las Vegas, NV—1613
    KTRK in Houston, TX—1606
    KUSA in Denver, CO—1606
    KYW in Philadelphia, PA—1580
    Latina magazine—1586
    Matt McGill—1591
    Michael Baisden—1610
    Michael Smerconish—1599
    Michel Martin—1581
    NBC, "The Tonight Show"—1604
    Ricardo Brown—1581
    Steve Harvey—1581
    TF1—1607
    Tom Joyner—1591
    WAVY in Portsmouth, VA—1606
    WBNS in Columbus, OH—1581
    WCCO in Minneapolis, MN—1606
    WCNC in Charlotte, NC—1602
    WCSH in Portland, ME—1613

Interviews With the News Media—Continued
  Interviews—Continued
    WDAF in Kansas City, MO—1587
    WEAR in Pensacola, FL—1614
    WESH in Orlando, FL—1599
    Westwood One Sports—1608
    WFXC/WFXK in Durham, NC—1602
    WISH in Indianapolis, IN—1613
    WISN in Milwaukee, WI—1578
    WOWI in Norfolk, VA—1603
    WPEG in Charlotte, NC—1602
    WPVI in Philadelphia, PA—1606
    WRC in Washington, DC—1580
    WREG in Memphis, TN—1613
    WSOC in Charlotte, NC—1580
    WTAE in Pittsburgh, PA—1578
    WTVD in Raleigh-Durham, NC—1578
    WTVF in Nashville, TN—1599
    WTVT in Tampa, FL—1606
    WVEC in Norfolk, VA—1614
    WVKL in Norfolk, VA—1603
    WXII in Greensboro-Winston-Salem, NC—1599
  Joint news conferences
    Australia, Prime Minister Gillard—1432
    Canada, Prime Minister Harper—1526
    Iraq, Prime Minister Maliki—1537
    South Korea, President Lee—1264
  News conferences
    July 11—846
    July 15—858
    October 6—1218
    November 4—1373
    November 13—1418

Joint Statements
  Czech Republic, Prime Minister Necas—1355
  European Union leaders—1477
  Indonesia, President Yudhoyono—1453
  Iraq, Higher Coordinating Committee—1487
  Portugal, President Silva—1391
  Trans-Pacific Partnership leaders—1403

Letters and Messages
  See also Communications to Congress
  Small Business Saturday—1471

Meetings With Foreign Leaders and International Officials
  See also Interviews With the News Media; Joint Statements
  Afghanistan, President Karzai—1088, 1586–1587
  Argentina, President Fernandez de Kirchner—1371
  Asia-Pacific Economic Cooperation, leaders—1608–1609
  Association of Southeast Asian Nations, leaders—1610

Meetings With Foreign Leaders and International Officials—Continued

Australia, Prime Minister Gillard—1609
Brazil, President Rousseff—1597
Canada, Prime Minister Harper—1608, 1613
China
   Premier Wen—1610
   President Hu—1414
Colombia, President Santos—1604
Czech Republic, Prime Minister Necas—1353
East Asia Summit leaders—1610
European Commission, President Barroso—1473
European Council, President Van Rompuy—1473
France, President Sarkozy—1112, 1369, 1582, 1585, 1589, 1601, 1603, 1606, 1608
Germany, Chancellor Merkel—1370, 1581, 1585, 1590, 1596, 1602–1603, 1608
Greece
   Prime Minister Papademos—1610
   Prime Minister Papandreou—1609
Group of Twenty (G–20) nations, leaders—1606–1607
Guatemala, President-elect Perez Molina—1610
Honduras, President Lobo—1216
India, Prime Minister Singh—1449
Indonesia, President Yudhoyono—1452
Iraq, Prime Minister Maliki—1604, 1613
Israel, Prime Minister Netanyahu—1104, 1586, 1594
Italy
   President Napolitano—1608
   Prime Minister Berlusconi—1586
   Prime Minister Monti—1610
Japan, Prime Minister Noda—1105, 1412, 1591, 1615
Libya, Transitional National Council Chairman Jalil—1597
Malaysia, Prime Minister Najib—1451
Mexico, President Calderon—1608
Netherlands, Prime Minister Rutte—1481
New Zealand, Prime Minister Key—884
North Atlantic Treaty Organization, Secretary General Rasmussen—1607
Norway
   Ambassador to the U.S. Christian Strommen—1583
   Prime Minister Stoltenberg—1313, 1582, 1599
Oman, Sultan Qaboos—1598
Pakistan, President Zardari—1612
Palestinian Authority, President Abbas—1597
Peru, President Humala—1609
Philippines, President Aquino—1450
Portugal, President Cavaco Silva—1608
Romania, President Basescu—1595
Russia, President Medvedev—1413, 1614
Saudi Arabia, King Abdallah—1587, 1601, 1604
South Korea, President Lee—1262, 1271, 1601–1602, 1614

Meetings With Foreign Leaders and International Officials—Continued

South Sudan, President Kiir—1597
Spain
   Prime Minister-elect Rajoy—1615
   Prime Minister Zapatero—1586
Thailand, Prime Minister Yinglak—1455, 1587
Tunisia
   Prime Minister Caid Essebsi—1236, 1598
   Prime Minister Jebali—1615
Turkey, Prime Minister Erdogan—1091, 1586
United Kingdom, Prime Minister Cameron—1111, 1586–1588, 1601, 1603
United Nations
   President Al-Nasser—1597
   Secretary-General Ban—1106, 1597
Uzbekistan, President Karimov—1598
West African leaders—909

Statements by the President
See also Appointments and Nominations; Bill Signings and Vetoes; Joint Statements
Afghanistan
   10th anniversary of U.S. military operations—1238
   U.S. military casualties—932
Arab States, League of, actions regarding Syria—1415
Armenian National Day—1113
Azerbaijan, Independence Day—1315
Bryson, John E., Senate confirmation as Secretary of Commerce—1315
Colombia-U.S. Free Trade Agreement
   Congressional passage—1262
   Submission—1193
Costello, Rep. Jerry F., decision not to seek reelection—1209
Deaths
   Chavez, Richard E.—904
   Cobell, Elouise P.—1291
   Daley, Margaret C.—1472
   Ford, Elizabeth A.—843
   Havel, Vaclav—1562
   Jobs, Steven P.—1218
   Maathai, Wangari Muta—1156
   Shalikashvili, John M.—893
   Shuttlesworth, Fred L.—1217
   Sultan bin Abd al-Aziz Al Saud, Crown Prince of Saudi Arabia—1320
Diwali—1353
"Don't ask, don't tell" policy
   Certification of repeal—886
   Repeal—1092
East Africa, humanitarian assistance—1566
Eid al-Fitr—1023
Europe, economic stabilization efforts—1356

Statements by the President—Continued

Federal Aviation Administration reauthorization legislation
  Congressional passage—928
  Promotion efforts—926
Frank, Rep. Barney, decision not to seek reelection—1481
Gates, Robert M., former Secretary of Defense—1035
Gonzalez, Rep. Charles A., decision not to seek re-election—1473
Hahn, Janice K., election to U.S. House of Representatives—858
Hajj and Eid al-Adha—1379
Hanukkah—1565
Hurricane Katrina, 6th anniversary—1016
India, terrorist attacks in Mumbai—857
Indonesia, Comprehensive Test Ban Treaty, ratification—1524
Iran
  Detained U.S. citizens, release—1113
  U.S. sanctions—1463
Japan, Prime Minister, selection—1023
Job growth legislation, Senate action—1251, 1315, 1371
Keystone XL Pipeline, Department of State announcement—1397
Kildee, Rep. Dale E., decision not to seek reelection—866
Kwanzaa—1571
Kyrgyzstan, Presidential election—1363
Liberia, elections—1382
Libya
  Declaration of liberation—1320
  Situation—1009
Lynch, Gov. John H., decision not to seek reelection—1069
Mexico, Royale San Jeronimo Casino firebombing in Monterrey—1012
Nelson Mandela International Day—868
Nelson, Sen. E. Benjamin, decision not to seek re-election—1571
Nigeria
  Terrorist attacks—1571
  United Nations headquarters in Abuja, terrorist attack—1013

Statements by the President—Continued

Nobel Peace Prize, congratulating 2011 recipients—1239
Olver, Rep. John W., decision not to seek reelection—1353'
Ozone national ambient air quality standards—1029
Panama-U.S. Free Trade Agreement
  Congressional passage—1262
  Submission—1193
Payroll tax cut and unemployment insurance legislation, Congressional action—1567
Pearl Harbor Remembrance Day, National—1530
Philippines, storm and flood damage—1563
Pigford II class-action lawsuit on discrimination by the Department of Agriculture, settlement—1356
Pollan, Laura, legacy—1551
Presidential condolence letters, policy change—840
Ramadan—913
Russia, World Trade Organization accession, progress—1397
Saudi Arabia, Crown Prince and Deputy Prime Minister, selection—1356
Sikhism, birth of founder, anniversary—1396
South Korea-U.S. Free Trade Agreement
  Congressional passage—1262
  Submission—1193
South Sudan, U.S. recognition as an independent and sovereign state—845
Space Shuttle Atlantis launch—843
Syria situation—912, 1007
Tax cut legislation, Senate action—1502
Tribal Law and Order Act of 2010, first anniversary—910
Tunisia, elections—1321
Turkey
  Earthquake—1321
  Terrorist attack in Cukurca—1309
U.S. Embassies in Africa, 13th anniversary of terrorist attacks—932
Veterans, hiring incentives legislation
  Congressional passage—1432
  Senate passage—1398
Yemen situation—1470
Zambia, elections—1121